Introduction

'What Is Soul?' screamed Ben E. King in 1967, or more to the point, 'What Is R&B' I scream in 1998. Well one thing it sure ain't is Peter Andre and All Saints. R&B is currently the most abused term of all music genres and soul is not far behind. Time and time again in publications such as *Music Week*, and with biogs from record companies I read 'exciting new R&B singer' and I immediately bite my tongue. R&B and Soul music is essentially music sung by black artists. There are a very few exceptions with artists such as Dusty 'the white negress' Springfield. But these artists have earned their stripes over many years. In the USA the R&B chart now contains rap acts, yet another anomaly. Yet if you look through the excellent book by Joel Whitburn *Top R&B Singles 1942-1995*, you will get a better picture of what I am attempting to say. We have stuck to the path of old R&B and 60s soul, together with the new talent who are closely aligned to that spirit. So, in addition to Ruth Brown and Aretha Franklin there are Mary J Blige and Dionne Farris, and in addition to Fats Domino and Otis Redding there are Keith Sweat and Tony Rich. Similarly, pop acts singing in a soulful style such as the Lighthouse Family are also included, but other pop acts will be placed in another of our books. To me the essence of R&B is music that rock 'n' roll was stolen from; Wynonie Harris, Jackie Wilson and Johnny Ace. Soul is Stax, Atlantic Records, Memphis, Motown and Philadelphia followed by the Will Downings and Melba Moores. To me the division is clear but send your complaints to me politely if you don't agree. *The Virgin Encyclopedia Of R&B And Soul* is one in the major series of books taken from the *Encyclopedia Of Popular Music*. Other titles already available are:

The Virgin Encyclopedia Of Sixties Music
The Virgin Encyclopedia Of Seventies Music
The Virgin Encyclopedia Of Eighties Music
The Virgin Encyclopedia Of Popular Music
The Virgin Encyclopedia Of Indie & New Wave
The Virgin Encyclopedia Of The Blues
The Virgin Encyclopedia Of Country Music
in preparation
The Virgin Encyclopedia Of Reggae
The Virgin Encyclopedia Of Fifties Music

Entry Style

Albums, EPs (extended play 45s), newspapers, magazines, television programmes, films and stage musicals are referred to in italics. All song titles appear in single quotes. We spell rock 'n' roll like this. There are two main reasons for spelling rock 'n' roll with 'n' as opposed to 'n'. First, historical precedent: when the term was first coined in the 50s, the popular spelling was 'n'. Second, the 'n' is not simply an abbreviation of 'and' (in which case 'n' would apply) but a phonetic representation of n as a sound. The ' ', therefore, serve as inverted commas rather than as apostrophes. The further reading section at the end of each entry has been expanded to give the reader a much wider choice of available books. These are not necessarily recommended titles but we have attempted to leave out any publication that has little or no merit.

We have also started to add videos at the ends of the entries. Again, this is an area that is expanding faster than we can easily cope with, but there are many items in the videography and further items in the filmography, which is another new section we have decided to include. Release dates in keeping with albums attempt to show the release date in the country of origin. We have also tried to include both US and UK titles where applicable.

Album Rating

Due to many requests from our readers we have now decided to rate all albums. All new releases are reviewed either by myself or by our team of contributors. We also take into consideration the review ratings of the leading music journals and critics' opinions.

Our system is slightly different to most 5 Star ratings in that we rate according to the artist in question's work. Therefore, a 4 Star album from James Brown may have the overall edge over a 4 Star album by Keith Washington. Sorry Keith.

Our ratings are carefully made, and consequently you will find we are very sparing with 5 Star and 1 Star albums.

★★★★★

Outstanding in every way. A classic and therefore strongly recommended. No comprehensive record collection should be without this album.

★★★★

Excellent. A high standard album from this artist and therefore highly recommended.

★★★

Good. By the artist's usual standards and therefore recommended.

★★

Disappointing. Flawed or lacking in some way.

Poor. An album to avoid unless you are a completist.

PLAGIARISM

In maintaining the largest text database of popular music in the world we are naturally protective of its content. We license to approved licensees only. It is both flattering and irritating to see our work reproduced without credit. Time and time again over the past few years I have read an obituary, when suddenly: hang on, I wrote that line. Secondly, it has come to our notice that other companies attempting to produce their own rock or pop encyclopedias use our material as a core. Flattering this might also be, but highly illegal. We have therefore dropped a few more textual 'depth charges' in addition to the original ones. Be warned.

ACKNOWLEDGEMENTS

Our in-house editorial team is lean and efficient. Our Database is now a fully grown child and needs only regular food, attention and love. Thanks to the MUZE UK team and their efficiency while the cat's away: Susan Pipe, Nic Oliver and Sarah Lavelle and the jump jivin' Roger Kohn's parrot. Our outside contributors are further reduced in number, as we now write and amend all our existing text. Nic Oliver has risen to this task brilliantly. However, we could not function without the continuing efforts and dedication of Big John Martland, Alex Ogg and Brian Hogg. America's premier authority Robert Pruter continues to supply his specialist knowledge and experience.

Other past contributors' work may appear in this volume and I acknowledge once again; Simon Adams, David Ades, Mike Atherton, Gavin Badderley, Alan Balfour, Michael Barnett, Steve Barrow, John Bauldie, Lol Bell-Brown, Johnny Black, Chris Blackford, Pamela Boniface, Keith Briggs, Michael Ian Burgess, Paul M. Brown, Tony Burke, John Child, Linton Chiswick, Rick Christian, Alan Clayson, Tom Collier, Paul Cross, Bill Dahl, Norman Darwen, Roy Davenport, Peter Doggett, Kevin Eden, John Eley, Lars Fahlin, John Fordham, Per Gardin, Ian Garlinge, Mike Gavin, Andy Hamilton, Harry Hawk, Mark Hodkinson, Mike Hughes, Arthur Jackson, Mark Jones, Max Jones, Simon Jones, Ian Kenyon, Dave Laing, Steve Lake, Paul Lewis, Graham Lock, John Masouri, Bernd Matheja, Chris May, Dave McAleer, Ian McCann, David McDonald, York Membery, Toru Mitsui, Greg Moffitt, Nick Morgan, Michael Newman, Pete Nickols, Lyndon Noon, Zbigniew Nowara, James Nye, Ken Orton, Ian Peel, Dave Penny, Alan Plater, Barry Ralph, John Reed, Emma Rees, Lionel Robinson, Johnny Rogan, Alan Rowett, Jean Scrivener, Roy Sheridan, Dave Sissons, Neil Slaven, Chris Smith, Steve Smith, Mitch Solomons, Christopher Spencer, Jon Staines, Mike Stephenson, Sam Sutherland, Jeff Tamarkin, Ray Templeton, Liz Thompson, Gerard Tierney, John Tobler, Adrian T'Vell, Pete Wadeson, Frank Warren, Ben Watson, Pete Watson, Simon Williams, Val Wilmer, Dave Wilson and Barry Witherden.

Record company press offices are often bombarded with my requests for biogs and review copies. Theirs is a thankless task, but thanks anyway, especially to Alan Robinson of Demon, Sue and Dave Williams at Frontier, Mal Smith at Delta, Richard Wooton and his colleagues at the Manor House and Pat Naylor and Nicola Powell at Ryko/Hannibal.

Thanks for the enthusiasm and co-operation of all our new colleagues at Virgin Publishing under the guidance of the meteorological Rob Shreeve, in particular to the slinky smooth Roz Scott who is so efficient.

To our owners at Muze Inc., who feed the smooth running of the UK operation and are the business partners I always knew I wanted but never knew where to find. To all colleagues at the office on 304 Hudson Street in New York. In particular to the thorough Tony Patterson, the neatly dappered Paul Zullo, Steve 'Numbers' Figard, Marc 'Who?' Miller, Mike Nevins, America's Sex Pistol Gary Geller, all other Klugettes and the gigantic pussycat Trev Huxley. And lastly to my listening tin lids, who are beginning to understand why old R&B and doo-wop is the best music for our Saturday night cooking sessions.

Colin Larkin, March 1998

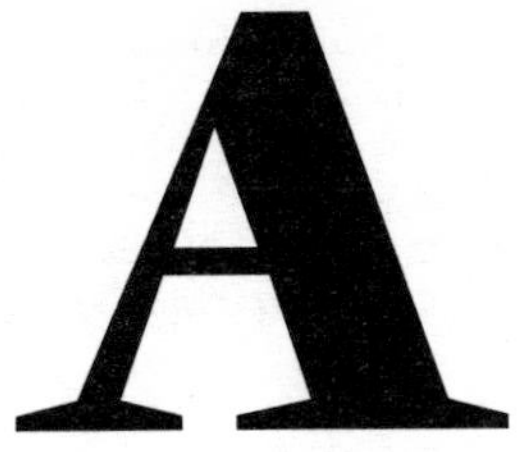

Aaliyah

b. Detroit, Michigan, USA. Pronounced Ah-Lee-Yah, this female artist is another of the growing New Jill Swing movement. Her early career was fostered by R. Kelly and her debut album, *Age Ain't Nothing But A Number* (although it was important enough for her to conceal her own date of birth), included the debut single 'Back And Forth', which made a strong showing in the national and R&B charts. She travelled to Kelly's home in Chicago for the sessions while she was still a student at the Detroit High School of the Performing Arts. She remained a 'straight A's' student throughout the first stage of her recording career, persevering with her education despite commercial success.

● ALBUMS: *Age Ain't Nothing But A Number* (Jive 1994)★★★, *One In A Million* (Atlantic 1996)★★★.

Abbott, Gregory

b. Harlem, New York City, New York, USA. Abbott exploded onto the R&B scene in 1986 with the huge dance hit 'Shake You Down' (number 1 R&B, number 1 pop). In the UK, the song went to number 6 on the chart. Abbott began pursuing a music career while working for his doctorate at the University of California at Berkeley. He soon moved to Los Angeles and married famed songstress Freda Payne, and she recorded four of his songs. He returned to his home in New York and began working as a researcher in a stockbroking firm. Associates at the firm took an interest in Abbott's music career and financed a studio and label, Gramercy Park Records. Abbott recorded a few acts for the label before trying to record himself. In 1986 he signed with Columbia Records, and achieved a giant hit with 'Shake You Down'. Abbott continued his success in the R&B field with 'I Got The Feelin' (It's Over)' (number 5 R&B) in 1987, and 'I'll Prove It To You' (number 5 R&B) in 1988.

● ALBUMS: *Shake You Down* (Columbia 1986)★★★, *I'll Prove It To You* (Columbia 1988)★★★.

Abner, Ewert

b. 11 May 1923, Chicago, Illinois, USA, d. 1997. Abner was one of the most notable African-American record executives of the post-World War II era, heading at different times two of the biggest black-owned labels of all time, Vee Jay and Motown. He attended Howard University and DePaul University, graduating with an accounting degree in 1949. He was hired by Chicago record entrepreneur Art Sheridan to handle the books at his distributorship and his pressing plant, and soon graduated to running the pressing plant. In 1950 he joined Sheridan in operating his Chance label, which nurtured the early careers of the Moonglows and the Flamingos. Chance Records closed its doors in 1954, and Abner joined Vee Jay Records as the company's general manager in 1955, running the company for owners Vivian Carter And James Bracken (Abner eventually became a co-owner). In 1961 he became president. Under his stewardship the company became a major independent by not only enjoying hits with such R&B acts as Jerry Butler, Gene Chandler, Dee Clark, Betty Everett, but also for signing major pop acts, notably the Beatles and the Four Seasons. In 1963 Abner was fired from Vee Jay and formed Constellation. The label folded in 1966 after a successful run of hits by Gene Chandler. Abner, meanwhile, returned to Vee Jay in 1965 to try to save the faltering company, but could not prevent its bankruptcy in 1966. In 1967 Berry Gordy brought Abner into Motown to handle the company's artist management, and from 1973 to 1975 he served as the company's president. Abner continued an indirect association with Motown by handling business affairs for Stevie Wonder. After Gordy sold Motown in 1988, he brought in Abner as an executive at his newly formed Gordy Company.

Abramson, Herb

b. *c.*1920, Brooklyn, New York, USA. A record collector from his teens, Abramson staged jazz concerts with Ahmet Ertegun and his brother Nesuhi in New York and Washington in the early 40s, while training as a dentist. He was also a part-time producer for National from 1944-47, working with Billy Eckstine and the Ravens. Abramson briefly ran the Jubilee and Quality labels with Jerry Blaine before he and Ahmet Ertegun set up Atlantic in 1947. Over the next five years, he and Ertegun worked as producers, promoters and distributors in building up the company into a leading R&B label. From 1953-55, Abramson did military service and on his return launched the Atco subsidiary, working with the Coasters, Clyde McPhatter, Bobby Darin and Wynonie Harris. However, tensions between the Atlantic team, which by then included his wife Miriam, caused Abramson to sell his interest in Atlantic in 1957 for $300,000. He then set up labels such as Triumph, Festival and Blaze, which provided his only big pop hit, 'Tennessee Waltz' by Bobby Comstock (1959). After those companies failed, Abramson continued as an independent producer, supervising tracks by Gene Pitney, Don Covay and others. In the R&B field, he recorded sessions by Elmore James, Tommy Tucker ('Hi Heel Sneekers' 1964), Titus Turner and Louisiana Red (Atco 1971).

Ace, Johnny

b. John Marshall Alexander Jnr., 9 June 1929, Memphis, Tennessee, USA, d. 24 December 1954. Ace began his professional career as an R&B singer in 1949, playing piano in a band that eventually evolved into the Beale Streeters, which included at various times B.B. King, Bobby Bland, Roscoe Gordon and Earl Forest. The Beale Streeters established a considerable reputation and toured Tennessee and the surrounding states, giving Ace the experience to develop into an outstanding blues ballad singer. In 1952, he was signed by Duke Records and secured a number 1 R&B hit with his debut, 'My Song' (a hit for Aretha Franklin in 1968). The languid song, sung with Ace's distinctive blues-flavoured smoothness and a touch of sadness in his voice, determined his direction for seven subsequent hits in the USA, notably 'Saving My Love' (number 2 R&B 1953), 'Please Forgive Me' (number 2 R&B 1954), 'Cross My Heart' (number 3 R&B 1953), 'The Clock' (number 1 R&B 1953) and 'Never Let Me Go' (number 9 R&B 1954). Ace, by committing suicide playing Russian Roulette backstage at a concert on Christmas Eve 1954, made his death his claim to fame, unfairly obscuring the fine music of his legacy. He had two posthumous hits, 'Pledging My Love' (number 1 R&B 1955) and 'Anymore' (number 7 R&B 1955); the former was Ace's only mainstream success, reaching number 17 on *Billboard*'s national pop chart. Duke Records released a 10-inch and 12-inch album, and both became perennial sellers.

● ALBUMS: *The Johnny Ace Memorial Album* 10-inch album (Duke 1955)★★★, *The Johnny Ace Memorial Album* 12-inch album (Duke 1957)★★★.

Acklin, Barbara

b. 28 February 1944, Chicago, Illinois, USA. A vocalist in the style of Dionne Warwick and Brenda Holloway, Acklin first recorded under the name Barbara Allen. In 1966, following a spell as a backing singer, she worked as a receptionist at the Brunswick Records offices, and submitted some of her own compositions to producer Carl Davis. One of these, 'Whispers', co-written with David Scott (of the Five Dutones), was a major hit for Jackie Wilson, who returned the favour by helping Acklin to secure a recording contract with Brunswick. 'Love Makes A Woman', her US Top 20 pop hit from the summer of 1968, was followed by 'Just Ain't No Love' and 'Am I The Same Girl' (a UK hit in 1992 for Swing Out Sister), while a duet with Gene Chandler, 'From The Teacher To The Preacher', also charted. Meanwhile, Acklin began writing with Eugene Record from the Chi-Lites, a partnership that resulted in several of that group's finest moments, including 'Have You Seen Her' and 'Stoned Out Of My Mind'. The relationship continued despite Acklin's departure for Capitol Records, but in spite of her early promise with 'Raindrops' (1974), she was dropped from the label in 1975 and has barely recorded since. *Groovy Ideas* collects the cream of her Brunswick recordings.

● ALBUMS: *Love Makes A Woman* (Brunswick 1968)★★, *Seven Days Of Night* (Brunswick 1969)★★, *Someone Else's Arms* (Brunswick 1970)★★, *I Did It* (Brunswick 1971)★★, *I Call It Trouble* (Brunswick 1971)★★, *A Place In The Sun* (Capitol 1975)★★.

● COMPILATIONS: *Groovy Ideas* (Kent 1987)★★★.

Adams, Faye

b. Fayle Tuell, *c.*1925, New Jersey, USA. Adams exploded onto the R&B scene in the early 50s with a series of gospel-infused hits that foreshadowed soul music years before its time. She began her career in gospel at the age of five when she and her siblings formed a group called the Tuell Sisters. She joined the Joe Morris Orchestra in 1952, and as part of that organization recorded the three songs that established her name in the R&B world, 'Shake A Hand' (number 1 R&B, number 22 pop), 'I'll Be True' (number 1 R&B), and 'Hurts Me To My Heart' (number 1 R&B). Her last chart record was 'Keeper Of My Heart' in 1957. Adams later returned to the church, abandoning her R&B career.

● COMPILATIONS: *Softly He Speaks* (Savoy 1976)★★★, *I'm Goin' To Leave You* (Mr. R&B 1990)★★★.

Adams, Johnny

b. Lathan John Adams, 5 January 1932, New Orleans, Mississippi, USA. A former member of several gospel groups, Adams' first recordings appeared in 1959 on Ric Records. Three years later he secured a minor R&B success with 'A Losing Battle', a slow ballad co-written by Dr. John. In 1968 he joined Shelby Singleton's SSS International outlet and enjoyed a hit the following year with 'Reconsider Me', an inspired piece of country soul. Although subsequent releases failed to match this performance, the strong *Heart And Soul* followed. Johnny signed with Atlantic Records in the early 70s, but his work there was disappointing. A later move to Ariola Records resulted in a remake of Conway Twitty's two-year-old country hit 'After All The Good Is Gone', giving Adams a 1978 US R&B chart entry. He has since recorded for various labels, including, notably, Rounder Records. From 1989 to the present Adams has had something of an artistic revival, recording a number of fine albums, including tributes to Percy Mayfield and Doc Pomus, songwriters to whom Adams' excellent voice is particularly suited.

● ALBUMS: *Heart And Soul* (SSS International 1969)★★★, *Stand By Me* (Atlantic 1976)★★, *After All The Good Is Gone* (Ariola 1978)★★, *From The Heart* (Rounder 1984)★★★, *After Dark* (Rounder 1986)★★★, *Christmas In New Orleans With Johnny Adams* (Maison Du Soul 1988)★★, *Walking On A Tightrope: The Songs Of Percy Mayfield* (Rounder 1989)★★★★, *Johnny Adams Sings Doc Pomus: The Real Me* (Rounder 1991)★★★★, *Good Morning Heartache* (Rounder 1993)★★★, *The Verdict* (Rounder 1995)★★, *One Foot In The Blues* (Rounder 1997)★★★★.

● COMPILATIONS: *Heart And Soul '78* (1978)★★, *The Tan Nightingale* (Charly 1984)★★★, *Reconsider Me* (Charly 1987)★★★, *Room With A View Of The Blues* (Rounder 1988)★★★★.

Adams, Marie

b. Ollie Marie Givens, 19 October 1925, Linden, Texas, USA. Known affectionately as 'TV Mama' (the one with the big wide screen), by her colleagues in the Johnny Otis band, singer Marie Adams began her recording career in Houston, Texas, for the local Peacock label in 1952, accompanied by the bands of Bill Harvey, Chuck Dillon and Pluma Davis, finding success with her first release, 'I'm Gonna Play The Honky Tonks'. Covering Johnny Ace's 'My Song' in 1953 at a Peacock session in New York City with the Cherokee Conyers Orchestra (a cut-down Buddy Johnson unit), she joined Johnny Otis's band, staying until the late 50s and appearing on Otis recordings for Peacock and, as lead singer with the Three Tons Of Joy, for Capitol Records on such pop rock 'n' roll classics as 'Ma, He's Making Eyes At Me', 'In The Dark', and 'What Do You Want To Make Those Eyes At Me For'. In the early 60s she made records in Los Angeles for Sure Play and Encore Artists. She was back performing with the Three Tons Of Joy and was on a world tour with Otis in 1972, but she is believed to have died shortly afterwards.

ADAMS, OLETA

This fine soul singer had a typical gospel upbringing in Yakima, Washington, USA. Adams formed her own trio in the 80s and recorded two self-funded albums for a Kansas label that sold poorly. She was singing cabaret in a hotel bar in Kansas when she was discovered by Roland Orzabel and Curt Smith of Tears For Fears in 1985. In 1987, they invited her to sing on two tracks, 'Woman In Chains' and 'Badman's Song', on their much vaunted *The Seeds Of Love*. She went on to join the band as a semi-permanent third member, both live and in the studio. This led to her own contract with Tears For Fears' Phonogram label, and Orzabel was on hand to produce her solo *Circle Of One*, which topped the UK chart and reached the US Top 20. Her first single from it, 'Rhythm Of Life', was originally written by Orzabel for *The Seeds Of Love*, but was eventually omitted. Her biggest hit to date came with the Brenda Russell song 'Get Here' in 1991. Her second album was less successful and her third album, *Movin' On*, reversed the trend of smooth balladry to funky uptempo dance-orientated numbers, including a powerful cover version of Elton John's 'Don't Let The Sun Go Down On Me'. She moved into the Gospel market with *Come Walk With Me*, but whatever style of music she attempts, her voice is consistently outstanding.

● ALBUMS: *Circle Of One* (Fontana 1990)★★★, *Evolution* (Fontana 1993)★★, *Movin' On* (Fontana 1995)★★★, *Come Walk With Me* (Harmony 1997)★★★.

ADC BAND

This funk band from Detroit, Michigan, USA, comprised Artwell Matthews (drums), Audrey Matthews (lead vocals), Mark Patterson (bass), Mike Judkins (keyboards), Curtin Hobson (lead guitar), James Maddox (vocals and percussion), and Sam Burns (trombone). The core members of the group were Artwell and Audrey Matthews, son and daughter of the veteran Detroit record entrepreneur Johnnie Mae Matthews. They, along with Mark Patterson, formed a group called Black Nazty, which in 1971 signed with Enterprise, a subsidiary of Stax Records. In their several years with the company the only single that made any impact was 'Talking To The People' (1974). Shortening their name to Nazty, they signed with the Mankind label in 1976, achieved their first chart single, 'It's Summertime' (number 100 R&B), and recorded an album called *Nazty's Got The Move*. By this time the group consisted of the two Matthews, Patterson, Mike Judkins, Jackie Casper, Larry Thomas, and Alice Myers. In 1977 the group became General Assistance and the ADC Band and recorded an album for Johnnie Mae Matthews' Northern label. Wisely shortening their name, the group signed with Cotillion in 1978 and finally made the charts with the funk hit 'Long Stroke' (number 6 R&B), which was very much in the George Clinton vein. Subsequent success for ADC was less notable, and of their five subsequent chart records during 1979-82 the most successful was 'Roll With The Punches' (number 46 R&B).

● ALBUMS: *Looking For My Roots* (Northern 1978)★★★, *Long Stroke* (Cotillion 1978)★★★, *Talk That Stiff* (Cotillion 1979)★★★, *Renaissance* (Cotillion 1980)★★★, *Brother Luck* (Cotillion 1981)★★★, *Roll With The Punches* (Cotillion 1982)★★★.

ADEVA

b. Patricia Daniels, 1960, Paterson, New Jersey, USA. The youngest of six children, Adeva joined the church choir at the age of 12 where she remained for 10 years, eventually becoming its director and vocal coach. Her mother was a missionary and her father a deacon, and her parents had once instructed, 'You sing gospel or nothing at all.' Between stints of teaching (for slow and emotionally disturbed children), she found time to take part regularly in talent contests. She was eventually banned from entering several competitions for winning so often, and turned professional by starting out on the local club scene in the mid-80s. She teamed up with Mike Cameron of the Smack Productions team to record 'In And Out Of My Life' for New York label Easy Street before signing to Cooltempo in 1988. Her success in the singles chart, initially more so in the UK than the USA (where, strangely, her first three solo releases all went to number 17), included a cover version of Aretha Franklin's 'Respect', 'Treat Me Right', 'Warning', 'Beautiful Love', and the collaboration with New York producer and recording artist Paul Simpson, 'Musical Freedom (Moving On Up)'. However, Adeva never made quite the commercial transition that was expected, and she was dropped by Cooltempo in 1992.

● ALBUMS: *Adeva* (Cooltempo 1989)★★★, *Love Or Lust* (Cooltempo 1991)★★.

● COMPILATIONS: *Hits* (Cooltempo 1992)★★★.

● VIDEOS: *Live At The Town And Country Club* (Chrysalis Music Video 1991).

ADMIRATIONS

This vocal quintet was formed in Brooklyn, New York, USA, in 1958 by 15-year-olds Joe 'Cookie' Lorello (lead), Fred Mastanduno (first tenor), Ralph Minichino (baritone), Lou Moshella (bass) and John Mahlan (second tenor). 'The Bells Of Rosa Rita' was released on Mercury in November 1959 but did not sell well and the group disbanded. However, they soon re-formed when Joe Mertens and Diane Salemme replaced John Mahlan and Ralph Minichino. 'In The Aisle'/'Hey Senorita' was released in 1961, but by that point the band was again breaking up. The Admirations played a series of reunion gigs in 1974 in New York, but this was not a permanent return.

AFTER 7

After 7, which comprises brothers Kevon and Melvin Edmonds (both b. Indianapolis, Indiana, USA) alongside long-time friend Keith Mitchell, have become one of the most successful urban R&B/soul acts in the USA in the 90s. The brothers met Mitchell at Indiana University where he and Kevon were pursuing business studies degrees, and were also members of the Indiana University Soul Review. Melvin joined them after touring with the group Deele and working in the studio with Shalamar. After 7's self-titled debut album was released in 1989 and documented what was already a potent live repertoire, based on 50s doo-wop harmonies combined with 90s hip-hop rhythms. It produced four Top 10 US singles, including 'Ready Or Not', 'Can't Stop' and 'In The Heat Of The Moment', and accrued a host of awards (including a Grammy nomination for Best Soul Group). The trio waited three years and toured with artists including Hammer, Gladys Knight and Whitney Houston before releasing the follow-up collection, *Takin' My Time*, which achieved gold status. Further exposure came through soundtrack commissions for the films *Sugar Hill* ('Gonna Love You Right') and *The Five Heartbeats* ('Nights Like This') and for the television programme *Beverly Hills 90210* ('Not Enough Hours In The Night'). After contributing to the group's debut, third brother Kenny 'Babyface' Edmonds returned to provide production assistance on *Reflections*, also writing three of the songs and singing on 'Honey (Oh How I Need You)'.

● ALBUMS: *After 7* (Virgin 1989)★★★★, *Taking' My Time* (Virgin 1992)★★★, *Reflections* (Virgin 1995)★★.
● COMPILATIONS: *The Very Best Of After 7* (Virgin 1997)★★★.

Aladdin Records

Founded in 1945 by brothers Edward and Leo Mesner, Aladdin Records, always distinguished by its prominent 'magic lamp' label insignia, went on to enshrine the rise of blues and R&B in post-war America. The label confronted and overcame opposition to black musicians and also navigated censorship of some of their artists' favoured lyrical topics (loose women and drugs) by the clever manipulation of language and song titles. The original choice of name was Philo Records, and the Mesner brothers soon enjoyed success with songs by Helen Humes (a veteran of work with bands led by the likes of Count Basie), Three Blazers and other artists drawn from the jazz and blues spectrum. The change of name was engendered by potential legal problems with the similarly titled Philco Company. By this time Philo had already enjoyed hits with Humes' 'Be Baba Leba', which became a *Billboard* number 3 hit, and the Three Blazers' 'Drifting Blues'. Drawn from the latter group, pianist and singer Charles Brown would go on to enjoy 11 Top 10 R&B hits with Aladdin. Another artist who had first recorded with Philo but who would find more enduring fame on Aladdin was Amos Milburn. His tally of 18 Top 10 R&B appearances included such minor classics as 'One Scotch, One Bourbon, One Beer' and 'Rooming House Boogie'. Floyd Dixon, who had also worked with the Three Blazers' Eddie Williams, proved another chart mainstay, enjoying significant success with 1951's 'Telephone Blues' and the related 'Call Operator 210', which emerged in 1952. Another bluesman who recorded widely with the label was Lightnin' Hopkins. Indeed, 'Shotgun Blues', for Aladdin, was the artist's biggest seller over a prolific career. Hopkins also introduced his protégé, Peppermint Harris, to the label, who in turn found huge sales with 'I Got Loaded', one of the most powerful performances of the early 50s. Another blues legend, Clarence 'Gatemouth' Brown, also began his career with Aladdin, while the already established Louis Jordan was another to join the label, though he failed to repeat his immediate post-war success. The ultimate accolade for any jazz, blues or R&B label would surely be the employment of Billie Holiday, and this honour was conferred on Aladdin over a short spate of 1951 recordings. Jesse Belvin also recorded briefly for the label with 'Goodnight My Love', as did P.F. Sloan, as Flip Sloan. The Sweethearts Of The Blues, Shirley And Lee (to give them their full title), were the most popular of several duo acts, a New Orleans pairing who broke with hits such as 'Let The Good Times Roll' and 'Feel So Good'. Others included Gene And Eunice and Bip And Bop, both backed by Johnny's Combo, under the tutelage of Johnny Otis. The Lovers, namely Alden Bunn and Anna Sandford, produced a pop hit with 'Darling It's Wonderful', on the Lamp subsidiary label, before going on to further success as Tarheel Slim and Little Ann. Another fruit of the Lamp catalogue was female trio the Cookies, who had 'Don't Let Go' (aka 'Hold Me, Hold Me, Hold Me') written for them by Charles Calhoun, who wrote 'Shake Rattle And Roll' for Joe Turner. Aladdin had, in fact, several spin-off labels, the first of which was Score Records. This pursued two avenues, gospel and pop-orientated R&B, the first explored most successfully by the Trumpeteers, aka the Four Rockets, and the second by vocal group the Robins (from whose ashes would rise the Coasters). Other outlets included 7-11 and Ultra. The main label's good fortunes, meanwhile, were continued with the arrival of the Five Keys, one of the finest vocal groups of the period. However, by the late 50s Aladdin was trying less successfully to ape the rise of rock 'n' roll. Though they did find a degree of reward for Thurston Harris And The Sharps' 1957 treatment of 'Little Bitty Pretty One', in competition with a version by the song's author, Bobby Day, the writing was on the wall. The label was purchased by Imperial Records in 1961, who were in turn bought out by Liberty Records, who discontinued the catalogue when they joined with United Artists to become EMI Records. A spectacular compilation package was issued in 1994.

● COMPILATIONS: *The Aladdin Records Story* (EMI 1994)★★★★.
● FURTHER READING: *The Aladdin/Imperial Labels: A Discography*, Michael Ruppli.

Alaimo, Steve

b. 6 December 1939, Rochester, New York, USA. Alaimo was a skilled songwriter and producer, whose most well-known recording was the soulful 'Everyday I Have To Cry'. Very much a 'white Negro', Alaimo formed the Redcoats at the University of Miami and made his earliest recordings at the local Criteria Studios. These included the local hit 'I Want You To Love Me'. In 1962 he signed to Checker, a subsidiary of the Chicago-based Chess group, recording an unsuccessful version of the dance song

'Mashed Potatoes', before taking the Arthur Alexander composition 'Everyday I Have To Cry' into the Top 50. The song became a soul standard with later recordings by the McCoys, Ike And Tina Turner and Dusty Springfield. From 1965 to 1966 he was the star of the US television music series *Where The Action Is*. Alaimo made later records for ABC Paramount (a cover version of Vince Guaraldi's instrumental hit 'Cast Your Fate To The Wind'), Atco ('After The Smoke Is Gone', a duet with Betty Wright) and Entrance ('When My Little Girl Is Smiling', 1971). However, from the mid-60s he was more active in production, working for Henry Stone, owner of the Miami-based TK Records with such artists as Sam And Dave, Harold Melvin And The Blue Notes, Ral Donner, Latimore and Betty Wright, for whom he wrote the hit 'Clean Up Woman'.

● ALBUMS: *Twist With Steve Alaimo* (Checker 1961)★★★, *Mashed Potatoes* (Checker 1962)★★★, *Every Day I Have To Cry* (Checker 1963)★★★★, *Steve Alaimo* (Crown 1963)★★★, *Starring Steve Alaimo* (ABC Paramount 1963)★★★, *Where The Action Is* (ABC Paramount 1965)★★★, *Steve Alaimo Sings And Swings* (ABC Paramount 1966)★★★.

Alexander, Arthur

b. 10 May 1940, Florence, Alabama, USA, d. 9 June 1993. Despite his own interpretations, Alexander's recordings are often better recalled for their inspirational quality. 'Anna (Go To Him)', a US R&B Top 10 hit, and 'You Better Move On' were covered, respectively, by the Beatles and the Rolling Stones, while 'A Shot Of Rhythm And Blues' became an essential British beat staple (notably by Johnny Kidd). Although 'You Better Move On' was recorded at the rudimentary Fame studios, Alexander's subsequent work was produced in Nashville, where his poppier perceptions undermined the edge of his earlier work. Later singles included 'Go Home Girl' and the haunting 'Soldier Of Love', but his fragile personality was particularly susceptible to pressure. This problem bedevilled his move to another label, Sound Stage 7, and although a 1972 album for Warner Brothers Records was promising, the singer's potential once again seemed to wither. A pop hit was secured on Buddah Records with 'Every Day I Have To Cry Some' (1975), but the success remained short-lived. For many years Alexander was forced to work outside of the music business; he was a bus driver for much of this time. Alexander began to perform again in 1993 as renewed interest arose in his small but important catalogue. *Lonely Just Like Me* was his first album in 21 years and showed a revitalized performer. He signed a new recording and publishing contract in May 1993, suffering the cruellest fate when he collapsed and died the following month, three days after performing in Nashville with his new band.

● ALBUMS: *You Better Move On* (Dot 1962)★★★, *Alexander The Great* (Dot 1964)★★★, *Arthur Alexander i* (Dot 1965)★★★, *Arthur Alexander ii* (Warners 1972)★★, *Arthur Alexander iii* (Buddah 1975)★★, *Lonely Just Like Me* (Elektra 1993)★★★.

● COMPILATIONS: *A Shot Of Rhythm And Soul* (Ace 1985)★★★, *Soldier Of Love* (Ace 1987)★★★, *The Greatest* (Ace 1989)★★★, *The Ultimate Arthur Alexander* (Razor & Tie 1993)★★★, *You Better Move On* (1994)★★★, *Rainbow Road - The Warner Bros. Recordings* (Warner Archives 1994)★★★.

Alive And Kicking

Brooklyn, New York, USA vocal group Alive And Kicking were formed in 1968 around singers Bruce Sudano, Woody Wilson, John Parisio, Vito Albano, Peppie Cordova and Sandy Todar. The group then made contact with singer Tommy James, who began to write material for the group and took them to his old label, Roulette Records, in 1970. Their debut release was James's track 'Tighter, Tighter', which reached number 7 in the USA. However, 'Just Let It Come' and 'Good Old Lovin' Back Home' performed much less spectacularly and they broke up immediately afterwards. They briefly re-formed in 1976 with a revised line-up (newcomers Richie Incorvaia and Steve Spagis with Wilson, Cordova and Albano). The group has continued to perform sporadically ever since, though without Bruce Sudano, who moved on to a new group, Brooklyn Dreams, and later married Donna Summer.

● ALBUMS: *Alive 'N Kickin'* (Roulette 1970)★★★.

● VIDEOS: *And The Music Speaks* (WarnerVision 1995).

Allen, Annisteen

b. Ernestine Letitia Allen, 11 November 1920, Champaign, Illinois, USA, d. 10 August 1992, New York, USA. Raised by her grandmother in Toledo, Ohio, Allen was an exceptionally soulful big-band vocalist who excelled at both ballads and blues. She was influenced by Ella Fitzgerald and discovered by Louis Jordan. He recommended her to fellow bandleader Lucky Millinder, with whom she toured from 1945 and recorded for Queen/King, Decca and RCA Victor, scoring R&B chart hits such as 'More, More, More', 'Let It Roll', 'Moanin' The Blues' and 'I'll Never Be Free'. In 1951 she went solo and continued her recording career on King/Federal (1951-53), Capitol Records (1954-55) and Decca (1956-57). She finished the decade recording singles for small concerns such as Todd, Warwick and Wig Records, before cutting a much acclaimed debut album in 1961 with King Curtis's band on Tru-Sound and retiring from the music business.

● ALBUMS: *Let It Roll* (Tru-Sound 1961)★★★, *Love For Sale* (1961)★★★, *Fujiyama Mama* (1986)★★.

● COMPILATIONS: *Give It Up 1945-1953* (Official 1989)★★.

Allen, Donna

b. Key West, and raised in Tampa, Florida, USA. Allen first made it into the public eye as a cheerleader for the Tampa Bay Buccaneers football team. Signed to 21 Records in 1986 she immediately hit the charts with 'Serious' (number 5 R&B, number 21 pop). 'Serious' was also a big hit in the UK, reaching number 8 on the chart. Her subsequent chart entries, 'Satisfied' (number 14 R&B) and 'Sweet Somebody' (number 55 R&B), both in 1987, ended her chart success in the USA. In 1988, on the Oceana label, she recorded an album, *Heaven On Earth*, from which was taken her biggest single, 'Joy & Pain' (number 3 R&B), in 1989. In the UK, 'Joy & Pain' reached number 10 on the chart. She charted again in 1989 with 'Can We Talk' (number 43 R&B), but all her big hits were behind her. In 1994 Allen had a flurry of success with a dance single called 'Real', for Epic Records.

● ALBUMS: *Perfect Timing* (21 Records/Atco 1986)★★★, *Heaven On Earth* (Oceana 1988)★★★.

Allen, Lee

b. 2 July 1926, Pittsburg, Kansas, USA, d. 18 October 1994, Los Angeles, California, USA. One of the great tenor saxophonist sessionmen of the classic R&B era, Allen played with a verve and excitement equalled by few musicians. He is best known for his notable instrumental hit from 1958, 'Walkin' With Mr. Lee' (number 54 pop). Allen began his professional career in 1947 playing in the Paul Gayten band in New Orleans. By the 50s he was a key member of the famed Dave Bartholomew session band that played behind just about every R&B artist who recorded in New Orleans. Behind such artists as Fats Domino, Smiley Lewis, Amos Milburn, Lloyd Price and Little Richard, Allen played exciting solos as well as great riffs in tandem with baritone saxophonist Alvin 'Red' Tyler. Allen recorded his first solo record in 1956 for the Aladdin label, 'Rockin' At Cosimo's'. Following his 'Walkin' With Mr. Lee' hit, he charted once more in 1958 with 'Tic Toc' (number 92 pop). During much of the remainder of his career he worked in Fats Domino's touring band. During the late 60s, however, he left the music world for a time to work in an aircraft factory in Los Angeles. In the 80s, he recorded with the Los Angeles band the Blasters.

● ALBUMS: *Walking With Mr. Lee* (Ember 1958)★★★.

Allen, Rance, Group

Family vocal and instrumental soul ensemble from Monroe, Michigan, USA. The group consisted of brothers Rance (lead vocals, piano, guitar), Tom (vocals, drums) and Steve (vocals, electric guitar). In the early years of the group, brother Esau (congas) also participated. The Rance Allen Group, featuring Rance's soaring falsetto lead, epitomized the secularized gospel sound of soul music. The group first recorded in 1969 for the tiny Reflect label in their home-town of Monroe. In 1971 they were discovered by Memphis-based Stax, which began recording them on its Gospel Truth (later Truth) label. The group's first releases were in the gospel vein, notably 'Just My Salvation' (a spiritual version of the Temptations' 'Just My Imagination'). The Rance Allen Group's first chart record, 'I Got To Be Myself' (number 31 R&B), in 1973, established their name in soul music. The group next recorded for Capitol, but the label produced only one single to make the charts, 'Truth Is Marching On' (number 100 R&B) in 1977. After Fantasy picked up the catalogue of Stax in 1976, it revived the label for several years in the late 70s. The Rance Allen Group were signed in 1978, having their biggest hits with 'I Belong To You' (number 24 R&B) and 'Smile' (number 41 R&B), both in 1979. After recording their third album for the revived Stax in 1980, the group joined a gospel company, Word, and recorded for several years on Word's subsidiary label, Myrrh. In 1991 the Rance Allen Group returned to secular music when they recorded for Al Bell's Bellmark.

● ALBUMS: *Truth Is Where It's At* (Gospel Truth 1972)★★★, *A Soulful Experience* (Truth 1975)★★, *The Way It Is* (Capitol 1979)★★, *Straight From The Heart* (Stax 1978)★★, *Smile* (Stax 1979)★★, *I Feel Like Going On* (Myrrh 1980)★★★, *Hear My Voice* (Myrrh 1983)★★★, *I Give Myself To You* (Myrrh 1984)★★★, *Phenomenon* (Bellmark 1991)★★.

● COMPILATIONS: *The Best Of The Rance Allen Group* (Stax 1991)★★★★, *Up Above My Head* (Stax 1995)★★★.

Allen, Ricky

b. 6 January 1935, Nashville, Tennessee, USA. R&B singer Allen is a perfect example of an artist who recorded in the amalgam style called soul-blues, but he did so in the early 60s, long before anybody gave that genre a name. It was a style that was an inevitable product of his background in both the black church and in the blues milieu. Allen started his singing in church choirs in his native Nashville, but after he moved to Chicago in 1958, he immersed himself in the West Side blues scene. He began recording for Mel London's Age label in 1961, and had a local hit with 'You Better Be Sure', a fast blues with a rock 'n' roll feel. Allen made a name for himself nationally in 1963 with 'Cut You A-Loose' (number 20 R&B), a compelling song in which Allen's riveting soul-blues vocals were propelled by a magnificent organ-driven throbbing rhythm. Before he retired from the scene in the early 70s, Allen had other local hits with 'It's A Mess I Tell You' (1966) and 'I Can't Stand No Signifying' (1967).

Alley Cats

This R&B vocal group from Los Angeles, California, USA, comprised Billy Storm (lead), Chester Pipkin, Ed Wallis, and Bryce Caulfield. A classic one-hit-wonder, the Alley Cats had just one chart record, 'Puddin N' Tain (Ask Me Again, I'll Tell You The Same)' (number 21 R&B, number 43 pop) in 1963, and nobody ever heard of them again. The record was produced by legendary producer Phil Spector and was released on his Philles label, but apparently Spector was not interested in continuing the association, and he never again worked with the group. The unit first recorded on Keen in 1957, and recorded as the Untouchables for Madison in 1960, on both occasions without success.

Allison, Gene

b. 29 August 1934, Nashville, Tennessee, USA. Allison worked for several years in the famed Nashville gospel groups the Fairfield Four and Skylarks, before he hit the R&B and pop charts in 1957 with 'You Can Make It If You Try'. In 1956 producer/songwriter Ted Jarrett plucked Allison out of the Skylarks and launched him on a solo secular career on Jarrett's Calvert label. The following year, Chicago-based Vee Jay picked up his 'You Can Make It If You Try', penned by Jarrett, and made the record a number 3 R&B hit and a Top 40 record on the pop chart. The song was a slow ballad sung with smouldering gospel fervour, which made it a soul record before the word 'soul' was coined. Allison followed that record in 1958 with two more gospel-flavoured hits, 'Have Faith' (number 11 R&B) and 'Everything Will Be All Right' (number 19 R&B), but failed to find success on the national charts afterwards.

● ALBUMS: *Gene Allison* (Vee Jay 1959)★★.

Alomar, Carlos

This guitarist became known principally as a rhythm player after an apprenticeship in James Brown's employ qualified him for the house band at the trend-setting Sigma Sound complex, from which emanated Philadelphia's feathery soul style in the 70s. Nevertheless, as well as backing the likes of the Stylistics and the Three Degrees, he served David Bowie, an irregular Sigma client, who was sufficiently impressed by Alomar's urgent precision and inventiveness on 1975's *Young Americans* to retain him as a full-time accompanist and sometime bandleader on tour and on disc. During one *Young Americans* session, Alomar, Bowie and John Lennon composed its infectious hit single ('Fame'), but more typical of Alomar's years with Bowie (and later, Iggy Pop) was his terse chord and ostinato picking beneath the soloing of Earl Slick, Robert Fripp and Stevie Ray Vaughan. This had become something of a trademark when Alomar returned to lucrative studio work in the mid-80s.

Altairs

This vocal quintet was formed in 1958 in Pittsburgh, USA, by Timothy Johnson (lead), Richard Harris (baritone), William Herndon (first tenor), Nathaniel Benson (second tenor) and Ralph Terry (bass). After their early shows at local schools, Johnson was replaced as lead by Nathaniel's cousin, George Benson. For their first recording they backed Annie Keith on 'Lover's Prayer' and performed with her throughout the area. Several singles were released by the New York label Amy Records, including 'If You Love Me' and 'Groovie Time'. By 1960 George Benson had left to join the Four Counts. The songwriter Otis Blackwell used the Altairs to demo songs for other artists, including the original version of 'Return To Sender' recorded by Elvis Presley. They later toured extensively with Dinah Washington, Chubby Checker, the Shirelles and many others. The Altairs then metamorphosed into Dinah's Gentlemen - which featured Herndon, Benson and Harris from the Altairs, plus new members Johnny Carter, Cornell Gunter and Chuck Barksdale. When Washington died in December 1963, Dinah's Gentlemen folded too.

Ama, Shola

b. March 1979, London, England. A rising star of the British R&B scene, Shola Ama grew up listening to her mother's Aretha Franklin and Gladys Knight records while still at school. She was first spotted by Kwame of the UK jazz-funk group D-Influence when she was just 15 years old. Kwame overheard her humming a tune on the westbound Piccadilly line platform at Hammersmith, while waiting for a train to Heathrow with her mother, and invited her to audition for him right there and then. Two songs, one by Mariah Carey and one by Mary J. Blige, convinced him of her potential. He signed her to his London independent label FreakStreet, who released Ama's debut single, 'Celebrate', in 1995. Although there were encouraging reviews, particularly for her mature, strident voice, the single faltered through lack of distribution. Kwame addressed this impasse by securing an agreement with WEA Records that would ensure much more widespread distribution and name-recognition. 'You're The One I Love', released in November 1996, was custom-written and produced by Shaun Labelle, and featured a confident, streetwise urban R&B performance from Ama. It was followed by 'You Might Need Somebody' in March 1997. She also took a hand in writing the songs for her debut, in collaboration with members of D-Influence, songwriter Paul Waller, and some of America's top-flight producers. In February 1998 she was voted Best Female Artist at the BRIT Awards.

● ALBUMS: *Much Love* (FreakStreet 1997)★★★.

Ambersunshower

b. New York, USA. Ambersunshower - which is her real name - made a big impact in 1996 with the release of her debut album for Gee Street Records. Marketed by her label as 'alternative soul', the record's judicious combination of R&B, swing, pop and hip-hop endeared her to a wide-ranging audience. The title *Walter T. Smith* came from the artist's grandfather, who was also a musician. 'Walter T.' was also the first single to be taken from the album, which was produced by PM Dawn and Tikk Takk, among others. Her first performance experiences had come when combining soul music with poetry and spoken-word work, ensuring that when she toured with a full band to promote her debut, she was well versed with stage etiquette and had the confidence to animate her eclectic songwriting.

● ALBUMS: *Walter T. Smith* (Gee Street 1996)★★★.

Anderson, Kip

A high-quality soul singer whose limited output is legendary, particularly among lovers of the 'deep' style. Anderson's first records came in the pre-soul era of 1959 with 'The Home Fires Are Brighter After All' for Derrick (leased to Vee Jay), and 'Till Your Love Is Mine' for Sharp. A year later the dramatic early soul of 'I Will Cry' was released on Everlast. In the mid-60s, 'That's When The Crying Begins' was Anderson's sole ABC single, while 'Here Am I' appeared on Tomorrow. His marginally better-known material was issued on Checker in the second half of the decade. The first release was the southern country-soul 'Woman How Do You Make Me Love You', leased from True Spot. Anderson's next Checker release, 'Without A Woman', a Quin Ivy/Dan Penn song recorded at Rick Hall's legendary 'Fame' studio, and the follow-up, 'A Knife And A Fork', were as good as any of the deep soul ever recorded there. Lack of promotion by the Checker label caused Anderson to move to the Nashville-based Excello label where he cut three more fine singles, 'You'll Lose A Good Thing', 'Letter From My Darling', and 'I Went Off And Cried', all still in the emotional southern-soul mould. There followed an alleged flirtation with Lelan Rogers' House Of Fox Label and a rare cut in 1973 for Ala, before Anderson faded from view until the 90s, when he re-emerged on Ichiban, recording two credible albums, the latter named after one of his old Checker sides.

● ALBUMS: *A Dog Don't Wear No Shoes* (Ichiban 1992)★★★, *A Knife And A Fork* (Ichiban 1993)★★★.
● COMPILATIONS: *Southern Soul Stock Volume 2* 9 tracks (1985)★★★★.

Andrews, Lee, And The Hearts

Formed originally as the Dreams in 1953, the group's best-known line-up was Lee Andrews (b. 1938, Lee Andrew Thompson, North Carolina, USA; lead), Roy Calhoun (first tenor), Wendell 'Breeze' Calhoun (bass), Butch Curry (second tenor) and Ted Weems (baritone). The Philadelphia-based vocal group, who, like many others of the time, started by singing on street corners, made their first recording, 'Maybe You'll Be There', in early 1954 on Rainbow. They recorded three singles and in 1957 they released one of Andrews' compositions, 'Long Lonely Nights', on the local Mainline label (co-owned by top disc jockey Jocko Henderson) and it succeeded nationally after being leased to Chess Records, despite being covered by top R&B stars Clyde McPhatter and the Ravens (under the name 'the Kings'). Their follow-up, 'Tear Drops', another of their compositions, made the US Top 20. They then moved to the newly formed United Artists label but they only managed one more memorable single, 'Try The Impossible', in 1958. In 1965 pop balladeer Bobby Vinton had a US Top 20 hit with a revival of their 'Long Lonely Nights'. The group, whose leader had a lighter, more MOR voice than most doo-wop groups, later recorded without chart success on various record labels. Andrews is backed onstage by two female Hearts and claims he works more shows as an 'oldies' attraction than he did in the late 50s. This supplements his income as a boutique owner. He is also involved with an artist association that helps acts from the 50s and 60s.

Andrews, Ruby

b. Ruby Stackhouse, 12 March 1947, Hollandale, Mississippi, USA. This Chicago R&B singer made her reputation in 1967 with her one crossover hit, 'Casanova (Your Playing Days Are Over)', which went to number 9 in the R&B charts and number 51 in the pop charts. The song, co-written and produced by Joshie Jo Armstead, featured a typical Chicago-style mid-tempo lope, but was recorded and arranged by Mike Terry in Detroit. Most of Andrews' releases on the Chicago-based Zodiac label, however, were produced and written by the team of Fred Bridges, Robert Eaton and Richard Knight, who previously were moderately successful as the vocal group Brothers Of Soul (of 'I Guess That Don't Make Me A Loser' fame). Andrews evolved into a powerful vocalist on such aggressive stand-outs as 'You Made A Believer (Out Of Me)' (number 18 in the R&B charts and number 96 in the pop charts in 1969), 'Everybody Saw You' (number 34 in the R&B charts in 1970), and 'You Ole Boo You' (number 47 in the R&B charts in 1971). Most of her records were recorded in Detroit and Memphis. A period with ABC Records during 1976-77 produced no hits. The song that established Andrews' career, 'Casanova', saw second life in 1980, when a female trio from Chicago, Coffee, released a disco version that went to number 13 in the UK but proved unsuccessful in the USA. In 1991, Jerry (Swamp Dogg) Williams produced an appealing album with Andrews in California, called *Kiss This*.

● ALBUMS: *Everybody Saw You* (1970)★★★, *Black Ruby* (1972)★★★, *Genuine Ruby* (ABC 1977)★★, *Kiss This* (Ichiban 1991)★★★.
● COMPILATIONS: *Casanova (Your Playing Days Are Over)* (1989)★★★.

Annointed

A mixed-gender gospel trio, Annointed's sound blends traditional church-singing with pop and R&B nuances. Their broad appeal was confirmed in 1996 when singles from their third album were serviced by Myrrh Records not just to Gospel, but also Contemporary Christian and R&B stations. The group originally comprised four singer-songwriters, all born in Ohio. Steve Crawford, his sister Da'dra Crawford-Greathouse, Mary Tiller and Denise 'Nee-C' Wallis began performing together in their hometown of Columbus in the early 90s. They had soon secured a contract with the local independent label Brainstorm, at that time distributed by Word Records. Crawford-Greathouse, reflecting on the group's debut, noted that '[it was] really heavy R&B gospel, because that was pretty much our surroundings growing up.' The group then switched to the Nashville-based gospel label, Myrrh. *The Call*, with an accent on pop melodies to ensnare the Contemporary Christian audience, proved their breakthrough album. It collected three Gospel Music Association Dove Awards, a Stellar Award for Best Performance By A Group Or Duo, Contemporary, and a Grammy nomination for Best Contemporary Soul Gospel Album. The attendant single, 'In God's Hands Now', also received significant mainstream exposure, as the group supported Groove Theory on a national promotional tour. Tiller departed in January 1996 prior to the release of *Under The Influence*, though this did not seem to impede their commercial ascendancy. In November the group embarked on the multi-artist Christian music Christmas tour dubbed 'Emmanuel'.

● ALBUMS: *Spiritual Love Affair* (Brainstorm 1993)★★, *The Call* (Myrrh 1995)★★★, *Under The Influence* (Myrrh 1996)★★★.

Apollas

An R&B female vocal group from Los Angeles, California, USA, the Apollas were one of myriad acts from the soul era to have created one enduring hit that developed cult status years later. Their record was 'All Sold Out' (1967), one of the classic soul sounds of the 60s. Members of the group were Leola Jiles (b. 2 April 1942, Louisiana, USA), Ella Jamerson (b. Rome, Georgia, USA), and Dorothy Ramsey (b. Birmingham, Alabama, USA). The Apollas signed with Warner Brothers' Loma subsidiary in 1966, and their first release, 'Sorry Mama' (1966), sold well in the Los Angeles area, but it was not until 'All Sold Out' came out that they became nationally known. Other singles followed, but none caught on and the group soon faded from the recording scene.

Aquarian Dream

This US eight-piece group featured two female lead vocalists, Pat Shannon and Connie Harvey, backed by six musicians, Claude Bartee Jr (soprano, alto and tenor saxophone), David Worthy (percussion), Pete Bartee (lead guitar), Ernie Adams (bass), Jim Morrison (drums) and Winston Daley (keyboards). Discovered and groomed by Norman Connors, the latter secured the group a contract with Buddah Records and produced their debut in 1976, from which 'Phoenix' and 'East 6th Street' attracted considerable club play, if little chart action (both were re-released in 1979 following their success with Elektra). After switching to that label in 1977, they had a UK hit with 'You're A Star', and the song was re-recorded in 1978 (featuring future solo artist Sylvia Striplin on vocals). After one further release the group disappeared from the scene, although 'You're A Star' has enjoyed a renaissance.

● ALBUMS: *Norman Connors Presents Aquarian Dream* (Buddah 1976)★★★★, *Fantasy* (Elektra 1977)★★, *Chance To Dance* (Elektra 1979)★★.

Armstead, 'Joshie' Jo

b. Josephine Armstead, 8 October 1944, Yazoo City, Mississippi, USA. A former member of the Ikettes, she sang on the 1962 US Top 20 pop hit 'I'm Blue (The Gong Gong Song)'. Armstead began her solo career under the name Dina Johnson and she subsequently formed a songwriting partnership with Ashford And Simpson, with whom she penned 'Let's Go Get Stoned' (Ray Charles) and 'Never Had It So Good' (Ronnie Milsap). Armstead also produced several acts, including Garland Green and Ruby Andrews, as well as founding her own Giant label on which she had two 1968 R&B hits, 'A Stone Good Lover' and 'I've Been Turned On'. Her final chart entry came in 1974 with the emotional 'Stumblin' Blocks, Steppin' Stones' which was issued on the Stax subsidiary Truth. Her work, both as a writer and performer, is vastly underrated.

Artistics

An R&B vocal group from Chicago, Illinois, USA. The Artistics, who combined sweet soul singing with horn-driven arrangements, represent the full flowering of the Chicago brand of uptown soul music during the 60s. The group came together in 1958 with original members Robert Dobyne, Larry Johnson, Jessie Bolian, and Aaron Floyd. They were signed to OKeh Records in 1963 by producer Carl Davis, who first recorded them as an imitation Motown act, using Detroit composer Barrett Strong. The Artistics' debut record, 'I Need Your Love' (1963), featured Dobyne as lead, but he was replaced by Marvin Smith, and the group then had minor hits with 'Got To Get My Hands On Some Lovin'' (a 1964 cover version of a Marvin Gaye album track) and 'This Heart Of Mine' (1965). Their one album for OKeh, *Got To Get My Hands On Some Lovin'*, is a classic. After moving to Brunswick Records in 1966, the Artistics had their biggest hits with two records firmly in the Chicago mode, 'I'm Gonna Miss You' (number 9 R&B, number 55 pop), with Smith as lead vocalist, and 'Girl I Need You' (number 26 R&B, number 69 pop), with Tommy Green as lead. Their first Brunswick album, *I'm Gonna Miss You*, collects both of these first hits and a selection of other solid cuts, and ranks as one of their best album collections. The group's last chart record was 'Make My Life Over' (1971) with Fred Pettis as lead. The Artistics made their last recordings in 1973 and disbanded shortly thereafter.

● ALBUMS: *Get My Hands On Some Lovin'* (OKeh 1966)★★★★, *I'm Gonna Miss You* (Brunswick 1967)★★★★, *The Articulate Artistics* (Brunswick 1968)★★★, *What Happened* (Brunswick 1969)★★★, *Make My Life Over* (Brunswick 1970)★★, *Look Out* (Brunswick 1973)★★.

Ashford And Simpson

Nickolas 'Nick' Ashford (b. 4 May 1942, Fairfield, South Carolina, USA) and Valerie Simpson (b. 26 August 1946, The Bronx, New York, USA). This performing and songwriting team met in the choir of Harlem's White Rock Baptist Church. Having recorded, unsuccessfully, as a duo, they joined another aspirant, Jo 'Joshie' Armstead, at the Scepter/Wand label where their compositions were recorded by Ronnie Milsap ('Never Had It So Good'), Maxine Brown ('One Step At A Time'), the Shirelles and Chuck Jackson. Another of the trio's songs, 'Let's Go Get Stoned', gave Ray Charles a number 1 US R&B hit in 1966. Ashford and Simpson then joined Holland / Dozier / Holland at Motown Records where their best-known songs included 'Ain't No Mountain High Enough', 'You're All I Need To Get By', 'Reach Out And Touch Somebody's Hand' and 'Remember Me'. Simpson also began 'ghosting' for Tammi Terrell when the latter became too ill to continue her partnership with Marvin Gaye, and she sang on part of the duo's *Easy* album. In 1971 Simpson embarked on a solo career, but two years later she and Ashford were recording together for Warner Brothers Records. A series of critically welcomed, if sentimental, releases followed, but despite appearing on the soul chart, few crossed over into pop. However, by the end of the decade, the couple achieved their commercial reward with the success of 'It Seems To Hang On' (1978) and 'Found A Cure' (1979). At the same time their production work for Diana Ross (*The Boss*) and Gladys Knight (*The Touch*) enhanced their reputation. Their status as imaginative performers and songwriters was further assured in 1984 when 'Solid' became an international hit single. Ashford and Simpson, who were married in 1974, remain one of soul's quintessential partnerships.

● ALBUMS: *Gimme Something Real* (Warners 1973)★★, *I Wanna Be Selfish* (Warners 1974)★★, *Come As You Are* (Warners 1976)★★, *So, So Satisfied* (Warners 1977)★★★, *Send It* (Warners 1977)★★★, *Is It Still Good To Ya?* (Warners 1978)★★★, *Stay Free* (Warners 1979)★★★, *A Musical Affair* (Warners 1980)★★★, *Performance* (Warners 1981)★★★, *Street Opera* (Capitol 1982)★★★, *High-Rise* (Capitol 1983)★★★, *Solid* (Capitol 1984)★★★, *Real Love* (Capitol 1986)★★★, *Love Or Physical* (Capitol 1989)★★.

● COMPILATIONS: *The Best Of* (1993)★★★★.

● VIDEOS: *The Ashford And Simpson Video* (EMI 1982).

● FILMS: *Body Rock* (1984).

Atlantic Starr

Soul/dance act comprising Sharon Bryant (vocals), David Lewis (vocals, keyboards, guitar), Jonathan Lewis (keyboards, trombone), Wayne Lewis (vocals, keyboards), Koran Daniels (saxophone), William Suddeeth III (trumpet), Clifford Archer (bass), Joseph Phillips (percussion) and Porter Caroll Jnr. (drums). The Lewis component of the group is made up of three brothers who had previously led their own bands - Newban, Exact Change and Unchained Youth - on the east coast of America. Atlantic Starr were formed in 1976 when they moved to Los Angeles. Later in the 70s they enlisted the services of New York-born Bryant as lead singer, and signed to A&M Records. Under the auspices of Philadelphia producer Bobby Eli (whose other work includes Major Harris, Brenda and the Tabulations, Booker Newbury III and Ronnie Dyson), they recorded their first two albums. 'Gimme Your Lovin', from the first of these, became a hit in the UK charts, before they switched to the production tutelage of James Anthony Carmichael (Commodores, Lionel Ritchie) for a series of three albums. Bryant departed after *Yours Forever* to marry Rick Gallway from Change. She then worked as a session singer before re-emerging in 1989 with the solo *Here I Am* and the single 'Foolish Heart'. Her replacement in Atlantic Starr was Barbara Weathers, although Daniels, Suddeeth, Archer and Carroll also parted company around the same time. The nucleus of the Lewis brothers and Weathers continued, and they took to producing themselves, starting with *As The Band Turns*, which spawned hits in 'Silver Shadow', 'One Love', 'Secret Lovers' and 'If Your Heart Isn't In It' during 1985 and 1986 - their first singles chart success since 1978. In 1987 they signed to Warner Brothers Records, an association that produced a US number 1 (UK number 3) in the ballad 'Always'. Weathers left in 1989 for a solo career (aided by Wayne Lewis, and Maurice White from Earth, Wind And Fire), to be replaced by Porscha Martin, who was in turn replaced by Rachel Oliver in 1991. Aisha Tanner became the band's next vocalist, replacing Oliver in 1994.

● ALBUMS: *Atlantic Starr* (A&M 1978)★★★★, *Straight To The Point* (A&M 1979)★★★, *Radiant* (A&M 1980)★★★, *Brilliance* (A&M 1982)★★★, *Yours Forever* (A&M 1983)★★★, *As The Band Turns* (A&M 1985)★★★, *All In The Name Of Love* (Warners 1987)★★★, *We're Movin' Up* (Warners 1989)★★★, *Love Crazy* (Reprise 1992)★★★.

Solo: Sharon Bryant *Here I Am* (Reprise 1989)★★.

Atmosfear

Adrzej (Andy) Sojka, from London, England, formed Atmosfear in late 1977 to record the type of danceable jazz/funk that he knew would sell in UK specialist soul shops, including his own, All Ears. This influential group's nucleus included Sojka (guitar), Lester Batchelor (bass), Anthony Antoniou (rhythm guitar) and Stewart Cawthorne (saxophone). Various drummers and other session people were involved, often including Light Of The World's Peter Hinds. Atmosfear claims to be the first UK group to record jazz-funk and the first to start its own label, Elite. Whenever it looked as though they had a hit on their hands, they would lease the master to a major label. This happened with their debut single on MCA in 1979, 'Dancing in Outer Space', which entered the UK Top 50. The group continued to record throughout the 80s but never revisited the pop chart. A businessman, musician, producer and prolific writer, Sojka has also produced several other acts on Elite and later Jam Today labels, including Level 42, whom he signed to Polydor Records in 1980.

● ALBUMS: *En Trance* (Elite 1981)★★★, *First/Foremost* (Elite 1984)★★.

August, Joe 'Mr. Google Eyes'

b. Joseph Augustus, 13 September 1931, New Orleans, Louisiana, USA, d. 9 October 1992. A soulful R&B singer in the Roy Brown tradition, August began performing as a novelty act - The Nation's Youngest Blues Singer - in his early teens, performing with the likes of Paul Gayten and Annie Laurie. In 1949 he was signed to Coleman Records who brought him north to record with Billy Ford And His Musical V-8s, and although none of the tracks charted, the mighty Columbia Records were interested enough to buy his contract and re-record the Coleman tracks with Billy Ford's band. August stayed in the New York area for the next few years, making one-off recordings for various record labels including Domino, Lee and Regal. In the early 50s he settled for a short time in Los Angeles, recording for Duke (with Johnny Otis) and Flip. In the late 50s he returned to New Orleans and made his last recordings for Dot and Instant. He continued to perform into the early 90s and was active in management and politics until his death from a heart attack in October 1992.

● ALBUMS: *Rock My Soul* (Route 66 1986)★★★.

Austin, Patti

b. 10 August 1948, California, USA. Austin first sang on stage at the age of three at the famous Apollo Theatre in New York City during Dinah Washington's set. As a child performer, she appeared on television, including Sammy Davis Jnr.'s programme, and in the theatre. Her stage work included *Lost In The Stars* and *Finian's Rainbow*. At the age of nine she travelled to Europe with the bandleader/arranger Quincy Jones. As a 16-year-old, she toured with Harry Belafonte and began recording at the age of 17. Austin's first recordings were for Coral in 1965 and in 1969, 'Family Tree' (United Artists) was an R&B hit. Austin's immaculate vocals brought work on television jingles and during the 70s she was one of the busiest session singers in New York. Her session work includes credits for Paul Simon, Billy Joel, Frankie Valli, Joe Cocker, George Benson and Roberta Flack. Her solo albums included material she had written herself, and showed some jazz influences. Further session work during 1980 saw Austin working with Marshall Tucker, Steely Dan and the Blues Brothers. Her long-standing association with father-figure Quincy Jones continued and his composition 'The Dude' featured her lead vocal, winning a Grammy in 1982. Austin had another hit with the title track of *Every Home Should Have One* on Jones's Qwest label. Although it only just made the UK Top 100,

'Razzamatazz' (with Quincy Jones) was a UK Top 20 hit in 1981. Her duet with James Ingram, 'Baby Come To Me', became the theme music for the television soap opera *General Hospital* and was a US number 1 and a UK number 11 in 1983. Another Austin/Ingram duet, 'How Do You Keep The Music Playing?', from the film *Best Friends*, was nominated for an Oscar. She also sang themes for the films *Two Of A Kind* (1984) and *Shirley Valentine* (1988), and had an R&B hit with 'Gimme Gimme'. *The Real Me* was a collection of standards ranging from Duke Ellington's 'Mood Indigo' to 'How Long' by the UK group Ace. Her 1990 album was produced by Dave Grusin for GRP Records, while Austin was a guest vocalist on an album of George Gershwin songs released in 1992 by the Hollywood Bowl Orchestra. Already successful, Austin has yet to receive the critical acclaim her achievements merit.

● ALBUMS: *End Of A Rainbow* (CTI 1976)★★★, *Havana Candy* (CTI 1977)★★★, *Live At The Bottom Line* (CTI 1979)★★★, *Body Language* (CTI 1980)★★★, *Every Home Should Have One* (Qwest 1981)★★★★, *Patti Austin* (Qwest 1984)★★★, *Gettin' Away With Murder* (Qwest 1985)★★, *The Real Me* (Qwest 1988)★★★, *Love's Gonna Get You* (GRP 1990)★★, *Carry On* (GRP 1991)★★★, *Live* (1992)★★★.

● FILMS: *Tucker* (1988).

AVERAGE WHITE BAND

This sextet was the natural culmination of several soul-influenced Scottish beat groups. The line-up featured Alan Gorrie (b. 19 July 1946, Perth, Scotland; bass, vocals), Mike Rosen (trumpet, guitar, ex-Eclection), replaced by Hamish Stuart (b. 8 October 1949, Glasgow, Scotland; guitar, vocals), Owen 'Onnie' McIntyre (b. 25 September 1945, Lennoxtown, Scotland; guitar), Malcolm 'Mollie' Duncan (b. 24 August 1945, Montrose, Scotland; saxophone), Roger Ball (b. 4 June 1944, Broughty Ferry, Scotland; saxophone, keyboards) and Robbie McIntosh (b. 6 May 1950, Dundee, Scotland, d. 23 September 1974, Hollywood, USA; drums). Although their 1973 debut album, *Show Your Hand*, showed promise, it was not until the band was signed to Atlantic Records that its true potential blossomed. *AWB*, also known as the 'White Album' in deference to its cover art, was a superb collection and paired the group's dynamism with Arif Mardin's complementary production. The highlights included a spellbinding version of the Isley Brothers' 'Work To Do', and the rhythmic original instrumental 'Pick Up The Pieces', a worthy US number 1/UK Top 10 single. *AWB* also topped the US album charts but this euphoric period was abruptly halted in 1974 by the tragic death of Robbie McIntosh following a fatal ingestion of heroin at a Hollywood party. He was replaced by Steve Ferrone (b. 25 April 1950, Brighton, England), a former member of Bloodstone. The group secured further success with 'Cut The Cake', the title song to a third album, but subsequent releases, despite an obvious quality, betrayed a creeping reliance on a proven formula. However, a pairing with singer Ben E. King (*Benny And Us*) seemed to galvanize a new-found confidence and two later recordings, 'Walk On By' and 'Let's Go Round Again', reclaimed the group's erstwhile inventiveness. The Average White Band retired during much of the 80s as the members pursued individual projects, the most surprising of which was Ferrone's work with Duran Duran. Hamish Stuart later surfaced in Paul McCartney's *Flowers In The Dirt* touring group, and was sadly unavailable when the band reformed in 1989. The resultant album, *After Shock*, featured original members Gorrie, Ball and McIntyre alongside Alex Ligertwood, a fellow-Scot and former vocalist with Santana. Gorrie continues to write songs; in 1997 he wrote for and performed with Hall And Oates.

● ALBUMS: *Show Your Hand* reissued as *Put It Where You Want It* (MCA 1973)★★★, *AWB* (Atlantic 1974)★★★★, *Cut The Cake* (Atlantic 1975)★★★, *Soul Searching* (Atlantic 1976)★★, *Person To Person* (Atlantic 1977)★★★, with Ben E. King *Benny And Us* (Atlantic 1977)★★★, *Warmer Communications* (RCA 1978)★★, *Feel No Fret* (RCA 1979)★★★, *Shine* (RCA 1980)★★, *Volume VIII* (RCA 1980)★★, *Cupid's In Fashion* (RCA 1982)★★, *After Shock* (Polydor 1989)★★★, *Soul Tattoo* (Artful 1997)★★★.

Solo: Alan Gorrie *Sleepless Nights* (1985)★★.

● COMPILATIONS: *Best Of The Average White Band* (RCA 1984)★★★★.

AYERS, ROY

b. 10 September 1940, Los Angeles, California, USA. A popular jazz vibraphonist and vocalist, Ayers reached the peak of his commercial popularity during the mid-70s and early 80s. He played piano as a child and took an interest in the vibes after meeting Lionel Hampton. In high school Ayers formed his first group, the Latin Lyrics, and in the early 60s began working professionally with flautist/saxophonist Curtis Edward Amy. Ayers' first album under his own name was *West Coast Vibes* on United Artists Records in 1964, which featured Amy. He also worked with Chico Hamilton, Hampton Hawes and Herbie Mann, with whom he first gained prominence between 1966 and 1970. He recorded three albums for Atlantic Records in the late 60s. In 1971 Ayers formed Roy Ayers Ubiquity, incorporating funk and R&B styles into his jazz. The group was signed to Polydor Records. Using a number of prominent sidemen such as Herbie Hancock, Ron Carter, Sonny Fortune, George Benson and Billy Cobham, Ubiquity's albums helped popularize the jazz/funk crossover style. The group charted with five albums and three R&B singles between 1974 and 1977, including the Top 20 disco-influenced R&B hit 'Running Away'. Ayers dropped the Ubiquity group name in 1978 and continued to have chart success with both his solo albums and singles through the late 80s. The 1978 single 'Heat Of The Beat' was billed as a duet with Wayne Henderson of the Crusaders. After touring Africa, Ayers recorded *Africa, Center Of The World* with Fela Kuti in 1979. He switched to Columbia Records in 1984 but released records less frequently as the 80s came to a close. During the early 90s he was under contract with Ronnie Scott's Jazz House label, but in 1995 he had secured a contract with RCA and the Groovetown label. The resulting album was well received.

● ALBUMS: *West Coast Vibes* (United Artists 1964)★★★,

Virgo Vibes (Atlantic 1967)★★★, *Stoned Soul Picnic* (Atlantic 1968)★★★, *Daddy's Back* (Atlantic 1969)★★★, *Ubiquity* (Polydor 1970)★★★, *He's Coming* (Polydor 1971)★★★, *Live At Montreux* (Polydor 1972)★★★, *Red, Black And Green* (Polydor 1973)★★★, *Virgo Red* (Polydor 1974)★★★, *Change Up The Groove* (Polydor 1974)★★★, *A Tear To A Smile* (Polydor 1975)★★, *Mystic Voyage* (Polydor 1976)★★, *Everybody Loves The Sunshine* (Polydor 1976)★★, *Vibrations* (Polydor 1976)★★, *Lifeline* (Polydor 1977)★★, *Starbooty* (Polydor 1978)★★, *Let's Do It* (Polydor 1978)★★, *You Send Me* (Polydor 1978)★★, *Step Into Our Life* (Polydor 1978)★★, *Fever* (Polydor 1979)★★, *No Stranger To Love* (Polydor 1979)★★, *Love Fantasy* (Polydor 1980)★★, *Prime Time* (Polydor 1980)★★, *Africa, Center Of The World* (Polydor 1981)★★★, *Feeling Good* (Polydor 1982)★★★, *In The Dark* (Columbia 1984)★★★, *You Might Be Surprised* (Columbia 1985)★★★, *I'm The One (For Your Love Tonight)* (Columbia 1987)★★★, *Drive* (Ichiban 1988)★★★, *Wake Up* (Ichiban 1989)★★★, *Easy Money: Live At Ronnie Scott's* (Essential 1990)★★★, *Rare* (Polydor 1990)★★★, *Rare Vol II* (Polydor 1990)★★★, *Searchin'* (Ronnie Scott's Jazz House 1993)★★★, *Hot* (Ronnie Scott's Jazz House 1993)★★★, *Naste* (Groovetown 1995)★★★.

● COMPILATIONS: *Best Of Roy Ayers* (Polydor 1979)★★★★, *Get On Up, Get On Down: Best Of Vol. 2* (Polydor 1993)★★★, *A Shining Symbol: The Ultimate Collection* (Polydor 1993)★★★★, *Vibrant - The Very Best Of* (Connoisseur 1993)★★★.

● VIDEOS: *At Ronnie Scott's 1988* (Hendring Video 1989).

B.T. Express

Originally formed as the King Davis House Rockers in 1972, this Brooklyn-based septet underwent several name changes, including the Madison Street Express and the Brothers Trucking, before finally settling on the above. Bill Risbrook (saxophone, vocals), his brother Louis (bass, organ), Carlos Ward (saxophone, woodwind), Richard Thompson (lead guitar, vocals), Dennis Rowe (congas), Terrell Woods (drums) and Barbara Joyce Lomas (vocals) had two gold discs with their first hits, 'Do It ('Til You're Satisfied)' (1974) and 'Express' (1975). Although the group continued to enjoy consistent chart success, they suffered from the facelessness that bedevilled many funk and disco outfits. Despite personnel changes, their later releases achieved little musically.

● ALBUMS: *Do It ('Til You're Satisfied)* (Roadshow 1974)★★, *Non-Stop* (Roadshow 1975)★★, *Energy To Burn* (Columbia 1976)★★, *Function At The Junction* (Columbia 1977)★★, *Shout!* (Columbia 1978)★★, *B.T. Express 1980* (Columbia 1980)★★.

● COMPILATIONS: *Old Gold Future Gold* (Excaliber 1981)★★.

Babyface

b. Kenneth Edmonds, 10 April 1959, Indianapolis, Indiana, USA. Babyface's achievements as a songwriter and producer throughout the late 80s and 90s, especially with L.A. Reid, sometimes overshadowed his own efforts as a performer, which go back to the mid-70s with the funk outfit Manchild. His early solo efforts showed a sophisticated, adult-orientated strain of urban soul, going against the current grain of rap-influenced explicitness and raunchy swingbeat; wisely, perhaps, as his light, pleasant voice could not really compare to earthier singers such as R. Kelly. It was not until 1995, when the single 'When Can I See You' won a Grammy, that he could claim the commercial success that had been heaped on his own protégés such as Boyz II Men, Bobby Brown and Toni Braxton. In fact, since the split with Reid, Babyface's main success has been as a producer and writer of film soundtracks, with *The Bodyguard* and *Waiting To Exhale* both going multi-platinum. Expectations were high for his 1996 solo album, which should have sealed his claim to be taken seriously as a contemporary soul performer. Unfortunately, *The Day* turned out to be something of a back-slappers' showcase; guest spots by the likes of Stevie Wonder, Eric Clapton, LL Cool J, Mariah Carey and even Shalamar could not obscure the fact that the songs Babyface kept for himself simply were not as strong as those he provided for other members of the R&B royalty.

● ALBUMS: *Lovers* (Solar 1987)★★, *Tender Lover* (Solar 1989)★★, *It's No Crime* (1989)★★, *A Closer Look* (Solar 1991)★★, *For The Cool In You* (Epic 1993)★★★, *The Day* (Epic 1996)★★, *MTV Unplugged NYC 1997* (Epic 1998)★★.

Badu, Erykah

b. 1971, Memphis, Tennessee, USA. Based in Dallas, Texas, Erykah Badu is an uncompromising R&B performer who has made rapid progress in her brief career to date. Signed to Kedar Entertainment, Badu seems to be well on the way to repeating the label's blueprint for success that propelled D'Angelo to international stardom. Her debut album was largely self-written, and was co-produced with the Roots, D'Angelo collaborator Bob Power and several old friends and colleagues from her days on the Memphis music scene. Among them were her cousin, Free. Before electing to turn solo, Badu had performed alongside Free in the group Erykah Free. The album's contents, which fluctuated between warm jazz textures and hip-hop and soul rhythms, won almost universal critical praise, Badu finding herself on the cover of the UK's *Blues & Soul* magazine. She also attracted features in magazines as diverse as *Vibe*, *Spin*, *Time*, *The Source* and *Rolling Stone*. Her profile was raised by a promotional video clip for 'On & On' that was scripted by Badu, and based on the film *The Color Purple*.

● ALBUMS: *Baduizm* (Kedar/Universal 1997)★★★★.

Bailey, Philip

b. 8 May 1951, Denver, Colorado, USA. Bailey is a talented soul singer who originally joined Earth, Wind And Fire in 1972 as a co-vocalist and percussionist. By 1983 he had released his first solo effort, *Continuation*, produced by George Duke. However, more influential was Phil Collins' production of his second album. Collins provided percussion throughout, and also co-wrote the sparkling duet 'Easy Lover', which topped the UK charts in March 1985 and reached number 2 in the USA. Unfortunately his only other UK hit to date has been the follow-up, 'Walking On The Chinese Wall', while his second album made number 11 in the USA. Bailey also released several pop-gospel albums during the 80s.

● ALBUMS: *Continuation* (Columbia 1983)★★, *The Chinese Wall* (Columbia 1984)★★★, *The Wonders Of His Love* (Myrrh 1984)★★★, *Inside Out* (Columbia 1986)★★★★, *Triumph* (Myrrh 1986)★★★, *Family Affair* (Myrrh 1989)★★★, *Philip Bailey* (Zoo Entertainment 1995)★★★.

● COMPILATIONS: *The Best Of Philip Bailey: A Gospel Collection* (Word 1991)★★★★.

Baker, Anita

b. 20 December 1957, Detroit, Michigan, USA. Soul singer Anita Baker was being hailed as the voice of the 90s after working her way up the ladder during the late 70s and early 80s. The granddaughter of a minister, she had a religious upbringing which included church music and gospel singing. After vocal duties with local bands she joined the semi-professional Chapter 8 in 1979 and was the vocalist on their minor US chart hit, 'I Just Wanna Be Your Girl', the following year. Several years later she left the band and was working in an office when she persuaded the Beverly Glen label to record and release her debut album in 1983. *The Songstress* brought her to wider notice and after disagreements with Beverly Glen she chose to sign with Elektra Records. Her second album was partly funded by Baker herself, who also acted as executive producer, with former Chapter 8 colleague Michael Powell assisting with writing and production. *Rapture*, a wonderfully mature and emotional album, saw Baker hailed as 'a female Luther Vandross' and she began to win R&B awards with 'Sweet Love', 'Caught Up In The Rapture' and 'Giving You The Best That I Got'. In 1987 she appeared on the Winans' 'Ain't No Need To Worry' and in 1990 duetted with former Shalamar singer Howard Hewlett. *Compositions* was self-penned bar two tracks and featured former Wonderlove musician Greg Phillinganes on keyboards, ex-Average White Band Steve Ferrone on drums, along with top Los Angeles session drummer Ricky Lawson, and Nathan East on bass. The album was recorded live in the studio with few overdubs. The birth of her first child delayed the release of her fourth Elektra album, the disappointing *Rhythm Of Love*.

● ALBUMS: *The Songstress* (Beverly Glen 1983)★★★, *Rapture* (Elektra 1986)★★★★, *Giving You The Best That I've Got* (Elektra 1988)★★★, *Compositions* (Elektra 1990)★★★, *Rhythm Of Love* (Elektra 1994)★★.

● VIDEOS: *Sweet Love* (WEA Music Video 1989), *One Night Of Rapture* (WEA Music Video 1989).

Baker, LaVern

b. Delores Williams, 11 November 1929, Chicago, Illinois, USA, d. 10 March 1997, New York, USA. Baker was a pioneering voice in the fusion of R&B and rock 'n' roll in the 50s. In 1947 she was discovered in a Chicago nightclub by bandleader Fletcher Henderson. Although still in her teens, the singer won a recording contract with the influential OKeh Records, where she was nicknamed 'Little Miss Sharecropper' and 'Bea Baker'. Having toured extensively with the Todd Rhodes Orchestra, Baker secured a prestigious contract with Atlantic Records, with whom she enjoyed a fruitful relationship. 'Tweedle Dee' reached both the US R&B and pop charts in 1955, selling in excess of one million copies, and the artist was awarded a second gold disc two years later for 'Jim Dandy'. In 1959, she enjoyed a number 6 pop hit with 'I Cried A Tear' and throughout the decade Baker remained one of black music's leading performers. Although eclipsed by newer acts during the 60s, the singer enjoyed further success with 'Saved', written and produced by Leiber And Stoller, and 'See See Rider', both of which inspired subsequent versions, notably by the Band and the Animals. Baker's final chart entry came with 'Think Twice', a 1966 duet with Jackie Wilson, as her 'classic' R&B intonation grew increasingly out of step with the prevalent soul/Motown boom. After leaving Atlantic, Baker is probably best known for 'One Monkey Don't Stop The Show'. In the late 60s, while entertaining US troops in Vietnam, she became ill, and went to the Philippines to recuperate. She stayed there in self-imposed exile for 22 years, reviving her career at New York's Village Gate club in 1991. During the following year she undertook a short UK tour, but audience numbers were disappointing for the only female, along with Aretha Franklin, who had, at that time, been elected to the US Rock And Roll Hall Of Fame. She replaced Ruth Brown in the Broadway musical *Black And Blue* in the early 90s but suffered ill health from diabetes and had both her legs amputated. Baker had a stunning voice that with little effort could crack walls, and yet her ballad singing was wonderfully sensitive.

● ALBUMS: *LaVern* (Atlantic 1956)★★★, *LaVern Baker* (Atlantic 1957)★★★★, *Rock And Roll With LaVern* (Atlantic 1957)★★★★, *LaVern Baker Sings Bessie Smith* (Atlantic 1958)★★★, *Blues Ballads* (Atlantic 1959)★★★★, *Precious Memories* (Atlantic 1959)★★★, *Saved* (Atlantic 1961)★★★, *See See Rider* (Atlantic 1963)★★★, *I'm Gonna Get You* (1966)★★.

● COMPILATIONS: *The Best Of LaVern Baker* (Atlantic 1963)★★★★, *Real Gone Gal* (Charly 1984)★★★, *Soul On Fire - The Best Of* (Atlantic 1993)★★★★, *Blues Ballads* with 6 extra tracks (Sequel 1997)★★★★, *Rock & Roll* (Sequel 1997)★★★★.

Ballard, Florence

b. 30 June 1943, Detroit, Michigan, USA, d. 22 February 1976. In her teens, Ballard formed the vocal group the Primettes with schoolfriends Mary Wilson and Betty Travis. Diana Ross completed the line-up in 1960. The following year, the Primettes were signed by Motown, who renamed them the Supremes. As the group's acknowledged leader, Ballard was the featured vocalist on their early Motown singles, but label boss Berry Gordy insisted that Diana Ross become the lead singer in 1963. Thereafter, Ballard was allowed few opportunities to take the limelight, either on record or in concert. Unhappy with her diminishing role in the Supremes, she repeatedly complained to Gordy and his executives, and the resulting friction led to her being ousted from the group in 1967. Throughout the drama, Motown maintained that she was retiring because of the strain of constant touring. The label annulled Ballard's contract, and she signed with ABC, for whom she made two singles under the direction of ex-Satintone Robert Bateman. Ballard was legally barred from capitalizing on her glorious past with the Supremes, and while her former group went from strength to strength, her solo releases flopped. Her contract with ABC was terminated. Other labels were wary of offending Gordy by signing her up, and Ballard became an increasingly embittered figure, ignored by the Detroit music scene in which she had played such a pivotal role. By the early 70s, Ballard was living in extreme poverty on a Detroit housing project. Her reliance on a lethal cocktail of alcohol and diet pills had weakened her health, and in February 1976 her tragic career ended when she suffered a cardiac arrest. Ironically, her contribution to the success of the Supremes has now been recognized, and her fate has been described as a telling verdict on the way in which Motown handled its more uncompromising artists.

Ballard, Hank, And The Midnighters

b. Henry Ballard, 18 November 1936, Detroit, Michigan, USA. His truck-driving father died when Ballard was seven years old and he was sent to Bessemer, Alabama, to live with relations. The strict religious and gospel upbringing caused him to run away, and by the age of 15, Ballard was working on an assembly line at Ford Motors in Detroit. His cousin, Florence Ballard, became a member of the Detroit girl group the Supremes. Hank Ballard's singing voice was heard by Sonny Woods of the Royals, who was amused by his mixture of Jimmy Rushing and Gene Autry. He was asked to replace frontman Lawson Smith during the latter's army service. The Royals had been recommended to King Records by Johnny Otis and had previously recorded 'Every Beat Of My Heart', later an R&B hit for Gladys Knight And The Pips. In 1953, Ballard's first session with the Royals led to their first US R&B Top 10 entry, 'Get It', which he also wrote. Ballard composed their 1954 R&B chart-topper, 'Work With Me, Annie', although its sexual innuendoes were too strong for some radio stations to broadcast. Its popularity spawned sequels ('Annie's Aunt Fanny', 'Annie Had A Baby') as well as answer records (the Platters' 'Annie Doesn't Work Here Anymore'). Etta James's 'Roll With Me, Henry' was modified by Georgia Gibbs to 'Dance With Me, Henry', while Hank himself responded with 'Henry's Got Flat Feet'! The group also had success with 'Sexy Ways', 'Don't Change Your Pretty Ways', 'Open Up Your Back Door' and 'Tore Up Over You'. In 1955, the Drifters had converted a gospel song into 'What'cha Gonna Do?' and, in 1957, Hank Ballard And The Midnighters used the same melody for 'Is Your Love For Real?'. They then modified the arrangement and changed the lyrics to 'The Twist'. Not realizing the song's potential, it was released as the b-side of 'Teardrops On Your Letter', a number 4 US R&B hit. Shortly afterwards, 'The Twist' was covered by Chubby Checker, who added dance steps and thus created a new craze. As a result of 'The Twist', Hank Ballard And The Midnighters received exposure on pop radio stations and made the US pop charts with such dance hits as 'Finger Poppin' Time' (number 7), 'Let's Go, Let's Go, Let's Go' (number 6), 'The Hoochi Coochi Coo' (number 23), 'Let's Go Again (Where We Went Last Night)' (number 39), 'The Continental' (number 33) and 'The Switch-A-Roo' (number 26). On the strength of Chubby Checker's success, their original version of 'The Twist' made number 28 on the US pop charts. In 1963, Hank Ballard split with the Midnighters, but he retained the group's name, which has enabled him to work with numerous musicians using that name. For some years he worked with James Brown, who has paid tribute to him on record. He recorded a double album at the Hammersmith Palais in London and he also recorded 'Two Bad Boys (Just Out Makin' Noise)', with Tim Hauser of Manhattan Transfer.

● ALBUMS: *Their Greatest Hits* (1954)★★, *The Midnighters, Volume 2* (1957)★★, *Greatest Juke Box Hits* (1958)★★★, *Singin' And Swingin''* (King 1959)★★★, *The One And Only Hank Ballard* (King 1960)★★★, *Mr. Rhythm And Blues* (King 1960)★★★, *Finger Poppin' Time* (King 1960)★★★★, *Spotlight On Hank Ballard* (King 1961)★★★★, *Sing Along* (King 1961)★★★, *Let's Go Again* (King 1961)★★★★, *Jumpin' Hank Ballard* (King 1962)★★★, *The Twistin' Fools* (King 1962)★★★, *The 1963 Sound* (King 1963)★★★, *A Star In Your Eyes* (King 1964)★★, *Those Lazy Lazy Days* (King 1965)★★, *Glad Songs, Sad Songs* (King 1966)★★, *24 Hit Tunes* (King 1966)★★★, *24 Great Songs* (King 1968)★★★, *You Can't Keep A Good Man Down* (King 1969)★★, *Hank Ballard Live At The Palais* (Charly 1987)★★, *Naked In The Rain* (1993)★★.

● COMPILATIONS: *Biggest Hits* (King 1963)★★★, *What You Get When The Gettin' Gets Good* (Charly 1985)★★★.

Banashak, Joe

b. 15 February 1923, Baltimore, Maryland, USA, d. 1985. A jazz fan as a teenager, Banashak entered record distribution after serving in World War II. After marrying a Texan, he moved to Houston and in the mid-50s took charge of a distribution network based in New Orleans. There he founded Minit Records with local disc jockey Larry McKinley in 1959. With Allen Toussaint as house producer and songwriter, Minit and its sister label Instant were responsible for many hits of the early 60s from New Orleans artists such as Ernie K-Doe ('Mother-In-Law'), Chris Kenner ('I Like It Like That'), Jessie Hill ('Oo Poo Pah Doo') and the Showmen ('It Will Stand'). National distribution was handled by Imperial and when Toussaint left for army service in 1963, the creative dynamic was gone and Banashak sold the Minit catalogue to Lew Chudd of Imperial. Banashak persevered with Instant Records and a new partner, Irving Smith. The label's most successful artist was Kenner who continued to record for Instant until 1969, while Toussaint's studio band backed other local artists such as Art Neville, Eskew Reeder (aka Esquerita) and Lee Dorsey. On the subsidiary label Alon, Toussaint's group the Stokes recorded 'Whipped Cream', later a big hit for Herb Alpert's Tijuana Brass. Shortly afterwards, Toussaint left the company. Banashak continued with new A&R men Sax Kari and Eddie Bo who produced blues and soul tracks for Instant until the late 60s. The company became inactive in the 70s.

BANKS, DARRELL

b. Darrell Eubanks, 1938, Mansfield, Ohio, USA, d. March 1970, Detroit, Michigan, USA. Banks sprang to fame in 1966 with his magnificent debut single, 'Open The Door To Your Heart', one of the finest non-Motown releases to emerge from Detroit. A second hit, 'Somebody (Somewhere) Needs You', followed that same year, but the singer's progress was undermined by an inability to remain with one label for any length of time. By 1967, he had signed to Atlantic (Atco) and in 1969 to Stax (Volt). Banks' later work included superb performances in 'I'm The One Who Loves You' and 'No One Blinder (Than A Man Who Won't See)', but tragically he was shot dead in March 1970 during a gun duel with a policeman who had been having an affair with his girlfriend.

● ALBUMS: *Darrell Banks Is Here* (Atco 1967)★★★, *Here To Stay* (Volt 1969)★★.

● COMPILATIONS: *Don Davis Presents The Sound Of Detroit* (1993)★★★, *The Lost Soul* (Goldmine Soul Supply 1997)★★★.

BANKS, HOMER

b. 2 August 1941, Memphis, Tennessee, USA. A former member of the Soul Consolidators gospel group, in the late 50s Banks worked as a clerk in the offices of the Satellite Studio in Memphis, hoping that the emergent label, later to become Stax Records, would recognize his talent as a singer and songwriter. At first his talents went largely unnoticed at Stax, although Isaac Hayes and David Porter were instrumental in setting up Banks' own solo recording debut for the Genie label in 1964, and in 1966 they wrote one of his early songs for the recently reactivated Minit label, '60 Minutes Of Your Love'. Banks recorded five singles for Minit between 1966 and 1968, including the self co-penned 'A Lot Of Love', the strident riff of which would later be borrowed by the Spencer Davis Group for their hit 'Gimme Some Lovin''. Meanwhile, Banks, still a Memphis resident, had maintained his connections with Stax Records and, by the 70s, was writing many hits with regular collaborators such as Raymond Jackson, Carl Hampton and Bettye Crutcher, including 'Who's Making Love' for Johnnie Taylor, 'Be What You Are' and 'If You're Ready (Come Go With Me)' for the Staple Singers, and 'If Loving You Is Wrong (I Don't Want To Be Right)' for the Koko Records artist Luther Ingram, a 1972 million-seller, later covered by Millie Jackson, Isaac Hayes and Rod Stewart. Banks also co-wrote Shirley Brown's 1974 hit on the Truth label, 'Woman To Woman'. After the demise of Stax, Banks went on to write for and/or produce artists on various labels. He also formed Two's Company with Lester Snell, which has released albums on the Platinum Blue label, including 1993 sets from J. Blackfoot and Ann Hines.

BANKS, ROSE

b. Rosemary Stewart, 21 March 1945, Dallas, Texas, USA. The younger sister of Sylvester Stewart. When he formed Sly And the Family Stone in 1966, Sly invited Rose to join as keyboard player and vocalist. She then followed her brother in changing her surname to 'Stone'. She remained with the group until 1975, playing and singing on hits such as 'Dance To The Music' and 'Family Affair', and handling lead vocals on the 1972 single 'Running Away'. When Sly disbanded the group in 1975, she recorded a demo tape with her husband Bubba Banks, who took it to Motown. They signed Rose up under her married name, sent her out as support to Marvin Gaye on a European tour, and issued an album called *Rose*, which produced a minor R&B hit, 'Whole New Thing', in 1976. Motown chose not to renew her contract, however, and Rose Banks subsequently retired from the music business.

● ALBUMS: *Rose* (Motown 1976)★★.

BAR-KAYS

Jimmy King (b. 1949; guitar), Ronnie Caldwell (b. 1948; organ), Phalin Jones (b. 1949; saxophone), Ben Cauley (b. 1947; trumpet), James Alexander (bass) and Carl Cunningham (b. 1949; drums) were originally known as the River Arrows. Signed to Stax, the Bar-Kays were groomed as that label's second-string house band by Al Jackson, drummer in Booker T. And The MGs. The Bar-Kays were employed as Otis Redding's backing group on tour, and the tragic plane crash in 1967 that took his life also claimed King, Caldwell, Jones and Cunningham. Alexander, who missed the flight, put together a new line-up with Ben Cauley, the sole survivor of the accident. The latter musician soon dropped out, leaving the bassist at the helm of a frequently changing line-up. Primarily a session group, the Bar-Kays provided the backing on many releases, including Isaac Hayes' *Shaft* and several of Albert King's 70s recordings. The group pursued a funk-based direction on their own releases with the addition of vocalist Larry Dodson, but while 'Son Of Shaft' reached the US R&B Top 10 in 1972, consistent success was only secured on their move to Mercury Records. Later singles, including 'Shake Your Rump To The Funk' (1976), 'Move Your Boogie Body' (1979) and 'Freakshow On The Dancefloor' (1984), were aimed squarely at the disco market. Since 1987 the group has featured Dodson, Harvey Henderson (tenor saxophone) and Winston Stewart (keyboards).

● ALBUMS: *Soul Finger* (Stax 1967)★★★★, *Gotta Groove*

(Stax 1969)★★★, *Black Rock* (Volt 1971)★★, *Do You See What I See* (Polydor 1972)★★★, *Cold Blooded* (Stax 1974)★★, *Too Hot To Stop* (Mercury 1976)★★, *Flying High On Your Love* (Mercury 1977)★★★, *Money Talks* (Stax 1978)★★, *Light Of Life* (Mercury 1978)★★, *Injoy* (Mercury 1979)★★, *As One* (Mercury 1980)★★★, *Night Cruisin'* (Mercury 1981)★★, *Propositions* (Mercury 1982)★★, *Dangerous* (Mercury 1984)★★, *Banging The Wall* (Mercury 1985)★★, *Contagious* (Mercury 1987)★★★, *Animal* (Mercury 1988)★★★.
● COMPILATIONS: *The Best Of The Bar-Kays* (Stax 1988)★★★★, *The Best Of The Bar-Kays* (Mercury 1993)★★★, *The Best Of The Bar-Kays Vol. 2* (Mercury 1996)★★.
● FILMS: *Breakdance - The Movie* (1984).

Barbara And The Uniques

An R&B vocal trio from Chicago, Illinois, USA, consisting of sisters Barbara and Gwen Livsey, and Doris Lindsey. Barbara And The Uniques were a minor group who came out of Chicago during the latter part of the soul era in the early 70s. The mainspring of the group was Barbara Livsey, who had earlier been a part of a duo with Mary-Francis Hayes called the Duettes, which recorded some regional hits with the Chicago-based One-derful label in the mid-60s. By the late 60s she had teamed up with her sister, Gwen, and made some singles, one of which, 'Right On', received some local play in 1970. The duo added Doris Lindsey to become Barbara And The Uniques. The addition of a third voice boosted their sound, and their 'There It Goes Again', written by Eugene Record of the Chi-lites, became a national hit (number 8 R&B) in early 1971. In 1974 the group began recording for Chicago producer Jimmy Vanleer, but the singles and one album that were issued for LA-based 20th Century Records all failed. The group broke up in 1975.
● ALBUMS: *Barbara Blake And The Uniques* (20th Century 1974)★★.

Barnes, J.J.

b. James Jay Barnes, 30 November 1943, Detroit, Michigan, USA. Barnes built his reputation with a classic series of hard-driving Detroit soul records in the 60s, and is better known in the British 'northern soul' scene than he is in his native America. A former member of the Halo Gospel Singers, Barnes' first single was 'Won't You Let Me Know' (1960) for Kable, and later singles followed on Mickays and Ring with no success. He signed with Ric Tic in 1965 and three remarkable releases followed: 'Please Let Me In' (1965), 'Real Humdinger' (1966, US R&B Top 20 and pop number 60) and 'Day Tripper' (1966), the latter a George Clinton production of the Beatles classic. In 1966, Barnes, as part of Holidays, an *ad hoc* group that also included Edwin Starr and Steve Mancha, had a big hit with 'I'll Love You Forever' (US R&B Top 10). Barnes' contract and masters were acquired by Motown in 1966 but the company never released any of his recordings. In 1967, he moved to Don Davis's Groovesville, where he achieved two hits, 'Baby Please Come Back Home' (US R&B Top 10) and 'Now That I Got You Back' (US R&B Top 50), sounding uncannily like Marvin Gaye. In 1968, Barnes switched to a companion label, Revilot, which yielded a northern soul favourite, 'Our Love (Is In The Pocket)'. Recognition in northern soul circles resulted in an album and a batch of singles recorded in the UK in the late 70s and early 80s that were of much lesser merit than his Detroit output. In 1991 he released two singles and *Try It One More Time* for Ian Levine's Motor City label.
● ALBUMS: *Born Again* (1974)★★, *Sara Smile* (Contempo 1978)★★, *Try It One More Time* (Motor City 1991)★★★, *King Of Nothern Soul* (Motor City 1996)★★.
● COMPILATIONS: *Ric Tic Relics* 5 tracks (1968)★★★, *Rare Stamps* one side by Steve Mancha (Stax 1969)★★★, *The Groovesville Masters* (Contempo 1975)★★★, *Free To Be Me* (1982)★★, *Don Davis Presents The Sound Of Detroit* 6 tracks (1993)★★.

Barrow, Keith

b. 1956, Chicago, Illinois, USA, d. 22 October 1983. Barrow's warm, naturally delicate falsetto was put to remarkable use during the late 70s and early 80s in a small but solid body of music. His only real hit was 'You Know You Wanna Be Loved' (number 26 R&B) in 1978, a sweet soul-style mid-tempo number with a disco instrumentation. 'Turn Me Up', a disco raver, also reached the charts the following year. Barrow's first singing experience was in gospel music, as befitting the son of a famous Chicago minister, Willie T. Barrow (she served as national executive director of Operation Push, an African-American civil rights organization). Barrow was an early victim of AIDS.
● ALBUMS: *Keith Barrow* (Columbia 1977)★★★, *Physical Attraction* (Columbia 1978)★★, *Just As I Am* (Capitol 1980)★★.

Barry, Len

b. Leonard Borrisoff, 6 December 1942, Philadelphia, Pennsylvania, USA. Barry began his career as the anonymous vocalist on the Bosstones' 1958 single 'Mope-Itty Mope' before joining the Dovells between 1961 and 1963. As a solo artist, his white soul vocals were best exemplified on the scintillating chart-topper '1-2-3' and the similarly paced 'Like A Baby'. With his sharp suits and clean-cut image, Barry seemed a Philadelphia teen-idol chronologically cut adrift in 1965, and his contention that long-haired groups were on the way out caused a few ripples in the pop press. Although he enjoyed another minor hit in the USA with the *West Side Story* anthem 'Somewhere', the song had already charted in the UK courtesy of P.J. Proby. During the psychedelic boom of the late 60s, Barry went out of fashion and gradually toned down his lively stage act for cabaret purposes. By the end of the decade and through the 70s, he moved into production work.
● ALBUMS: with the Dovells *Len Barry Sings With The Dovells* (Cameo 1964)★★★, *1-2-3* (Decca 1965)★★, *My Kind Of Soul* (RCA Victor 1967)★★.
● COMPILATIONS: *The Very Best Of ...* (Taragon 1995)★★.

Bartholomew, Dave

b. 24 December 1920, Edgard, Louisiana, USA. Dave Bartholomew was one of the most important shapers of

New Orleans R&B and rock 'n' roll during the 50s. A producer, arranger, songwriter, bandleader and artist, Bartholomew produced and co-wrote most of Fats Domino's major hits for Imperial Records. Bartholomew started playing the trumpet as a child, encouraged by his father, a Dixieland jazz tuba player. He performed in marching bands throughout the 30s and then on a Mississippi riverboat band led by Fats Pichon beginning in 1939, and learned songwriting basics during a stint in the US Army. Upon his return to New Orleans in the late 40s he formed his first band, which became one of the city's most popular. He also backed Little Richard on some early recordings. Bartholomew worked for several labels, including Specialty, Aladdin and De Luxe, for whom he had a big hit in 1949 with 'Country Boy'. In the same year he started a long-term association with Imperial as a producer and arranger. The previous year Bartholomew had discovered Domino in New Orleans' Hideaway Club and he introduced him to Imperial. They collaborated on 'The Fat Man', which, in 1950, became the first of over a dozen hits co-authored by the pair and produced by Bartholomew. Others included 'Blue Monday', 'Walking To New Orleans', 'Let The Four Winds Blow', 'I'm In Love Again', 'Whole Lotta Loving', 'My Girl Josephine' and 'I'm Walkin'', the latter also becoming a hit for Ricky Nelson. Bartholomew's other credits included Smiley Lewis's 'I Hear You Knocking' (later a hit for Dave Edmunds) and 'One Night' (later a hit for Elvis Presley, with its lyrics tamed), Lloyd Price's 'Lawdy Miss Clawdy', and records for Shirley And Lee, Earl King, Roy Brown, Huey 'Piano' Smith, Bobby Mitchell, Chris Kenner, Robert Parker, Frankie Ford and Snooks Eaglin. In 1963, Imperial was sold to Liberty Records, and Bartholomew declined an invitation to move to their Hollywood base, preferring to stay in New Orleans. In 1972, Chuck Berry reworked 'My Ding-A-Ling', a song Bartholomew had penned in 1952, and achieved his only US number 1 single. Although Bartholomew, who claims to have written over 4,000 songs, recorded under his own name, his contribution was primarily as a backstage figure. He recorded a Dixieland album in 1981 and in the early 90s was still leading a big band at occasional special events such as the New Orleans Jazz & Heritage Festival.

● ALBUMS: *Fats Domino Presents Dave Bartholomew* (Imperial 1961)★★★, *New Orleans House Party* (Imperial 1963)★★★, *Jump Children* (Pathe Marconi 1984)★★, *The Monkey* (Pathe Marconi 1985)★★, *Heritage* (1986)★★, *Graciously* (1987)★★, *The Spirit Of New Orleans* (1993)★★★.

● COMPILATIONS: *The Best Of Dave Bartholomew: The Classic New Orleans R&B Band Sound* (Stateside 1989)★★★★.

BARTLEY, CHRIS

b. 17 April 1947, Harlem, New York, USA. Inspired by local groups such as the Teenagers, high-voiced tenor Bartley formed the Soulful Inspirations in 1959 with Willam Graham, Henry Powell, Ronald Marshall and Sam Nesbitt. With various personnel and name changes, the group stayed together until the mid-60s. Bartley and Marshall then formed a soul duo that came to the attention of top producer/writer Van McCoy, who subsequently signed Bartley to his new Vando label. His first release, 'The Sweetest Thing This Side Of Heaven', shot into the US Top 40 and the R&B Top 10 in 1967. Unfortunately, neither the follow-up, 'Baby It's Wonderful', nor any of his other records on Vando, and later Buddah, managed to dent the US charts. His time in the spotlight was short, but he did have the chance to perform outside New York and even made a trip to the UK on the strength of that one hit single.

● ALBUMS: *The Sweetest Thing This Side Of Heaven* (Vando 1967)★★.

BASIN STREET BOYS

This four-piece vocal group was formed in 1945 in Los Angeles, California, USA, by Ormand Wilson. Wilson had originally been taught the guitar by Steve Gibson, whose band was called the Basin Street Boys, and so when Wilson formed his own band he named it after Gibson's as a mark of respect. The other three singers in Wilson's band were Gene Price, Reuben Saunders and Arthur Rainwater (aka Artie Waters), and they performed in a style in keeping with the nascent R&B boom. They signed with the local Exclusive Records label and their debut release was backing Judy Carroll on 'I Want To Love And Be Loved'. Their first effort under their own name, 'Jumpin' At The Jubilee', earned them a local following, but it was the ballad 'I Sold My Heart To The Junkman' that established their name (Patti Labelle And The Blue Belles later took the song into the charts). With a great deal of radio support for the single, the Basin Street Boys toured the USA during 1947, including a date at the Apollo Theatre in New York. In the meantime, singles such as 'This Is The End Of A Dream', 'I'm Gonna Write A letter To My Baby', 'I'll Get Along Somehow' and 'Summertime Gal' also failed to chart, but the group maintained a strong local following. In 1948 the group was renamed Ormand Wilson And The Basin Street Boys and moved to Mercury Records, but, starved of any commercial success, the Basin Street Boys broke up in 1951.

BASS, FONTELLA

b. 3 July 1940, St. Louis, Missouri, USA. The daughter of gospel luminary Martha Bass, Fontella toured as keyboard player and singer with the Little Milton band during the early 60s. Simultaneously, she made several solo records, including one for Ike Turner's Prann label. When Milton's bandleader, Oliver Sain, left to form his own group, he took Fontella with him, and teamed her with another featured vocalist, Bobby McClure. The duo was subsequently signed to Checker, on which 'Don't Mess Up A Good Thing' and 'You'll Miss Me (When I'm Gone)' were hits in 1965. 'Rescue Me', a driving song, gave Fontella success in her own right that same year with an R&B number 1 and a UK/US Top 20 hit. Other solo hits, including 'Recovery', followed, but by the end of the decade she had moved to Paris with her husband, jazz trumpeter Lester Bowie. When they later returned to America, Fontella recorded a series of fine records for the Shreveport-based Ronn/Jewel/Paula complex. She has also worked with Bowie's *avant garde* group, the Art

Ensemble Of Chicago. In Milan in 1980 Bass recorded a real 'back to basics' gospel album in the company of her mother Martha, her brother and fellow soul artist David Peaston, and Amina Myers. In 1985 she had resumed working for Oliver Sain in St. Louis.

● ALBUMS: *The New Look* (Checker/Chess 1966)★★★, *Les Stances A Sophie* film soundtrack (1970)★★, *Free* (Paula/Mojo 1972)★★★, with Martha Bass, David Peaston *From The Root To The Source* (1980)★★, *No Ways Tired* (Nonesuch 1995)★★.

● COMPILATIONS: *Sisters Of Soul* 14 tracks Fontella Bass/12 tracks Sugar Pie DeSanto (Roots 1990)★★★, *The Best Of* (1992)★★★.

BASS, RALPH

b. 1 May 1911, New York City, New York, USA. A pivotal figure in the history of R&B, Bass began his career during the 40s, promoting live jazz shows in Los Angeles. He subsequently worked for Black And White Records, producing 'Open The Door, Richard' for Jack McVea, but later left to found several small-scale outlets with releases by Errol Garner and Dexter Gordon. Bass also recorded (Little) Esther Phillips, the Robins and Johnny Otis for the Savoy label, and in 1951 became one of the era's first independent producers through the aegis of the Cincinnati-based King company. Armed with his own outlet, Federal, and its Armo publishing wing, he built an impressive roster of acts around Hank Ballard And The Midnighters, the Dominoes and James Brown, whom Bass signed in 1955 on hearing a demo disc at an Atlanta radio station. Although initially unimpressed by the singer's untutored delivery, King managing director Syd Nathan changed his mind when 'Please Please Please' became a bestseller. Brown remained a Federal artist until 1960 but was switched to the parent outlet when Bass departed for Chess Records. The producer brought Etta James and Pigmeat Markham to his new employers, and in turn, worked with several established acts, including Muddy Waters, Howlin' Wolf and Ramsey Lewis. Bass remained with the label until the mid-70s when its Chicago office was closed. He continued to record R&B acts, the masters from which were latterly compiled on a series of albums under the generic title *I Didn't Give A Damn If Whites Bought It*.

BATTISTE, HAROLD

b. New Orleans, Louisiana, USA. A former jazz pianist, Battiste turned to production on joining the staff at Specialty Records. Initially based in Los Angeles, he returned to his home-town in 1956 to administer a newly founded wing, but the venture floundered upon head-office intransigence. In 1960 Battiste switched to Ric, where he produced Joe Jones's US Top 3 hit 'You Talk Too Much', and arranged several sessions for Lee Dorsey, including the singer's debut hit 'Ya Ya'. Battiste also established the ambitious musicians' collective AFO (All For One). The house band included pianist Allen Toussaint, but although the label enjoyed chart entries with Prince La La and Barbara George, recurring arguments with distributors brought about its downfall. Having returned to Los Angeles, Battiste secured work as an arranger with Phil Spector, and became reacquainted with Sonny Bono. A former colleague at Specialty, Bono later formed a singing duo with his wife and invited Battiste to assist with production. Initial releases by Sonny And Cher, as well as attendant solo singles, proved highly popular, but a rift developed when Battiste's contributions were largely uncredited. However, a new partnership with fellow New Orleans exile Mac Rebennack resulted in the creation of the moniker Dr. John. Battiste matched the singer's husky inflections with a skillful blend of voodoo incantations and classic 'Crescent City' rhythms, exemplified on the highly popular *Gris Gris* (1968).

BAY BOPS

This vocal quartet was formed in Brooklyn, New York, USA, in 1957 by Barney Zarzana, Danny Zipfel, Bobby Serrao and George Taylor Jnr. 'Joannie', arranged by a young Neil Sedaka, was their debut Coral single in March 1958 and it went on to sell over a quarter of a million copies. Appearances on Dick Clark's television show and the *Dean Martin Telethon*, plus tours with the Drifters and Flamingos, helped to make the Bay Bops perhaps the most well-known white doo-wop group of the time. After their second single, 'My Darling, My Sweet'/'To The Party', in May 1958, the group broke up when Zipfel started another vocal group. The three remaining Bay Bops used the Ravens' Lou Frazier as lead for a brief time. In the mid-60s Zipfel recorded for MGM Records without a great deal of success. In 1958 a new version of the Bay Bops was formed by Barney Zarzana and his brothers Michael, Vinnie and Sal, but they did not record.

BEAVERS

This four-piece vocal group was formed in 1949 in New York, USA, when a music school voice teacher, Joe Thomas, encouraged four of his most talented students, Fred Hamilton (tenor), John Wilson (baritone), Raymond Johnson (bass) and Dick Palmer (tenor), to form a group, and secured them a recording contract with Coral Records. The group released two beautiful singles for Coral, 'If You See Tears In My Eyes' and 'I'd Rather Be Wrong Than Blue', neither of which were hits. The Beavers' success did not come under their own name but as the Hamptones, with Lionel Hampton And His Orchestra, featuring Wes Montgomery on guitar, when they reached number 4 in the R&B charts in 1950 with a cover version of the Ames Brothers' 'Ragmop'. The Beavers also backed Herb Lance on 'That Lucky Old Son' (number 6 R&B, 1949). The Beavers broke up in 1950 when Johnson and Palmer left to join the Blenders. Johnson joined the Marshall Brothers in 1951.

BEL BIV DEVOE

On their arrival on the music scene in 1989, this trio of former New Edition members, Ricky Bell (b. 18 September 1967, Boston, Massachusetts, USA), Michael Bivins (b. 10 August 1968, Boston, Massachusetts, USA) and Ronnie DeVoe (b. 17 November 1967, Boston, Massachusetts, USA), heralded a new development in US rap, infusing their rhymes with a more stylish and less brutal timbre. The hybrid became known as Ghetto

Swing, a mix of rap and swingbeat (eventually New Jack Swing). Their debut single, 'Poison', produced by Dr Freeze, made US number 3, and the album that followed was similarly successful, earning three million sales. In 1991, at the initiation of Motown Records president Joe Busby, Bivins was asked to become A&R executive for his own record company - Biv Entertainment - to be licensed through Motown. Signings included Another Bad Creation and Boyz II Men, both of whom found almost immediate success. Bell and DeVoe would oversee a similar set-up through PolyGram Records, established in 1992. The second Bel Biv DeVoe album included a New Edition reunion on 'Word To The Mutha!'. More recent work has followed an R&B-orientated path. Bivins has produced for MC Brains in addition to the aforementioned Another Bad Creation and Boyz II Men, and put together the East Coast Family hip-hop project. After the release of *Hootie Mack*, and the attendant 'Gangsta' single, the trio launched their own range of clothes through Starter merchandising.

● ALBUMS: *Poison* (MCA 1990)★★★★, *WBBD-Bootcity!* (MCA 1991)★★★, *Hootie Mack* (MCA 1993)★★★.

BELL, ARCHIE, AND THE DRELLS

This vocal soul group was formed by Archie Bell (b. 1 September 1944, Henderson, Texas, USA), with friends James Wise (b. 1 May 1948, Houston, Texas, USA), Willie Parnell (b. 12 April 1945, Houston, Texas, USA), L.C. Watts and Cornelius Fuller, all students at the Leo Smith Junior High School, in Houston, Texas. By the time their first record was made for the Ovid label in 1967, the group consisted of Bell, Wise, Huey 'Billy' Butler and Joe Cross. The single, produced by their manager Skippy Lee Frazier, was released by Atlantic Records. Although initially a poor seller, it found real success after the b-side was given airplay. 'Tighten Up' sold in excess of three million copies and reached number 1 in both the US R&B and pop charts. By this time, Bell, who had been drafted into the army, was recuperating from a wound received in Vietnam. The Drells continued recording, now with the production team of Gamble And Huff. For live performances, fake 'Archie Bells' were enlisted and whenever possible, the real Bell would join them in the studio. These sessions produced three more hits in 'I Can't Stop Dancing', 'Doin' The Choo-Choo' (both 1968) and '(There's Gonna Be A) Showdown' (1969). Paradoxically, the singles were less successful once Bell left the forces. 'Here I Go Again', an early Atlantic master, became a belated UK chart hit in 1972. Reunited with Gamble and Huff in 1975, they enjoyed several R&B successes on their TSOP/Philadelphia International label, including 'Let's Groove (Part 1)' (1976) and 'Soul City Walk' (1975) which entered the UK Top 20 in 1976. Archie Bell recorded a solo album for the Becket label in 1981 and charted with the single 'Any Time Is Right'. He still actively pursues a singing career within the US east coast 'beach music' scene.

● ALBUMS: *Tighten Up* (Atlantic 1968)★★★★, *I Can't Stop Dancing* (Atlantic 1968)★★★, *There's Gonna Be A Showdown* (Atlantic 1969)★★★, *Dance Your Troubles Away* (TSOP 1976)★★★, *Where Will You Go, When The Party's Over* (TSOP 1976)★★, *Hard Not To Like It* (TSOP 1977)★★★.

Solo: Archie Bell *I Never Had It So Good* (Becket 1981)★★.

● COMPILATIONS: *Artists Showcase: Archie Bell* (DM Streetsounds 1986)★★★.

BELL, MADELINE

b. 23 July 1942, Newark, New Jersey, USA. Bell arrived in the UK in 1962 with the cast of *Black Nativity*, a gospel show, but remained to embark on a solo career. Although early releases veered towards MOR, the singer's mid-60s recordings, including 'I Really Got Carried Away' and 'Doin' Things Together With You', were among Britain's strongest home-grown soul singles. A respected session vocalist, her powerful tones were also heard on numerous pop releases alongside Doris Troy, Lesley Duncan and Rosetta Hightower. Bell later secured consistent success as a member of Blue Mink, and more recently forged a lucrative career singing jingles for television advertisements, during which time she has released two singles, in 1982 duetting with Dave Martin on 'East Side West Side' and 'I'm Not Really Me Without You'. In 1991, she appeared in a UK stage production of *The Cotton Club*.

● ALBUMS: *Bell's A'Poppin'* (Philips 1967)★★★, *Doin' Things* (Philips 1969)★★★, *Madeline Bell* (1971)★★, *16 Star Tracks By Madeline Bell* (1971)★★★, *Comin' Atcha'* (Victor 1974)★★★, *This Is One Girl* (Pye 1976)★★, with John Telfer *Rubadub-Pop Goes The Nursery Rhymes* (Rubberband 1984)★.

BELL, THOM

b. 1941, Philadelphia, Pennslyvania, USA. Born into a middle-class family, Bell studied classical piano as a child. In 1959 he teamed up with schoolfriend Kenny Gamble in a vocal duo and soon afterwards joined the latter's harmony group, the Romeos. By the time he was 19 years old, Bell was working with Chubby Checker and for three years conducted and arranged the singer's material. Bell accompanied him on live dates, contributed original songs and later joined Checker's production company. The office shared a building with Cameo Records and when the former venture folded, Bell worked for the label as a session pianist. It was here he met the Delfonics, and when their manager, Stan Watson, formed his Philly Groove outlet in 1968, Bell's shimmering production work for the group resulted in some of sweet soul's finest moments, including 'La La Means I Love You' (1968) and 'Didn't I Blow Your Mind This Time' (1970). Bell then resumed his relationship with Kenny Gamble, who with Leon Huff, was forging the classic Philadelphia sound. Bell's brilliant arrangements for the O'Jays and Jerry Butler were particularly innovative, but his definitive work was saved for the Stylistics. Between 1971 and 1974 Bell fashioned the group's finest releases - 'You Are Everything' (1971), 'Betcha By Golly Wow' and 'I'm Stone In Love With You' (both 1972) - without descending into the bathos that lesser artists provided for the hapless quintet on his departure. Elsewhere, Bell enjoyed success with a revitalized (Detroit) Spinners, the Bee Gees and

Johnny Mathis, and continued his remarkable career as a producer, arranger and songwriter. Despite the soft, almost luxurious, sound he fashioned for his acts, this craftsman skilfully avoided MOR trappings.

BELL, WILLIAM

b. William Yarborough, 16 July 1939, Memphis, Tennessee, USA. Having recorded in 1957 as part of the Del Rios, Bell emerged on the fledgling Stax label with 'You Don't Miss Your Water' (1961), a cornerstone in the development of country R&B. Military service sadly undermined his musical career, and on its resumption he found the label bursting with competition. His original songs, often composed with either Steve Cropper or Booker T. Jones, included 'Share What You've Got' (1966), 'Everyday Will Be Like A Holiday' (1967) and 'Eloise' (1967), while his effective homage to Otis Redding, 'A Tribute To A King', was genuinely moving. 'Private Number', a sumptuous duet with Judy Clay, provided one of his best-remembered releases, but a further US hit followed with 'I Forgot To Be Your Lover' (1968), which was remade into a US Top 10 pop hit by Billy Idol in 1986 as 'To Be A Lover'. Bell moved to Atlanta, Georgia, in 1969 where he set up his Peach Tree label. His biggest hit came on signing to Mercury when 'Tryin' To Love Two' (1976) was a US Top 10 single. During the 80s he enjoyed R&B successes on Kat Family and Wilbe, still endeavouring to develop southern soul styles.

● ALBUMS: *The Soul Of A Bell* (Stax 1967)★★★★, *Tribute To A King* (Stax 1968)★★★★, *Bound To Happen* (Stax 1969)★★★, *Wow ... William Bell* (Stax 1971)★★★, *Phases Of Reality* (Stax 1973)★★★, *Relating* (Stax 1974)★★★, *Coming Back For More* (Mercury 1977)★★★, *It's Time You Took Another Listen* (Mercury 1977)★★★, *Survivor* (Kat 1983)★★, *Passion* (Tout Ensemble 1985)★★★, *On A Roll* (Wilbe 1989)★★★, *Bedtime Stories* (1992)★★★.

● COMPILATIONS: *Do Right Man* (Charly 1984)★★★, *The Best Of William Bell* (Warners 1988)★★★★, *A Little Something Extra* (Stax 1991)★★★, with Judy Clay, Mavis Staples, Carla Thomas *Duets* (1994)★★★.

BELLE, REGINA

b. *c.*1963, Englewood, New Jersey, USA. Belle first considered a career in the music business in her teenage years, after being inspired to sing by the gospel music greats Shirley Caesar and Inez Andrews. Both her mother and father were gospel singers and encouraged her to follow the same path - they were initially resistant to the idea that she should become involved in secular music. Further exposure to shows such as *American Bandstand* and *Soul Train* encouraged her to take up an instrument, and while at high school she learned trombone, tuba and steel drums, playing along to R&B and jazz standards as part of the school band. Her performance of the Emotions' 'Don't Ask My Neighbours' at a high school concert won her $25, encouraging her to take up semi-professional employment singing at fashion shows and weddings (often with the band Private Property). She secured a scholarship to the prestigious Manhattan School Of Music to study voice and opera, and then Rutgers University. There she became the first vocalist to sing with the music department's jazz ensemble - a jazz influence has remained detectable in much of her subsequent output. At the same time she began to perform in the Greenwich Village folk circuit, attracting the attention of New York disc jockey Vaughn Harper. Through his recommendation and a subsequent viewing of Belle singing the black national anthem 'Lift Every Voice And Sing', she joined the Manhattans, an opening act to Dionne Warwick, Gladys Knight and Patti Labelle. Spending two years touring with the Manhattans, she appeared on the Bobby Womack-produced single, 'Where Did We Go Wrong' (a duet with Gerald Alston of the band). She also contributed to their 1986 Columbia Records album, *Back To Basics*. A year later she was signed to the label as a solo artist. *All By Myself* received immediate acclaim, particularly for the hit singles 'Show Me The Way' and 'So Many Tears'. It was promoted by tours with Guy, the O'Jays and the Whispers. *Stay With Me* included the R&B hits 'Baby, Come To Me' and 'Make It Like It Was' (written by a member of the Winans). It earned Belle her first RIAA gold award, and also included a duet with J.T. Taylor of Kool And The Gang, 'All I Want Is Forever'. The early 90s were spent on more domestic concerns. She married sportsman John Battle III of the Cleveland Cavaliers and started a family. It was 1993 before she returned to the mainstream music scene. *Passion* included the major international hit 'A Whole New World ('Aladdin's Theme')', from the film *Aladdin*, a duet with Peabo Bryson that won four Grammy awards including Song Of The Year, Record Of The Year, Best Pop Performance By A Duo Or Group and Best Song Written Specifically For A Motion Picture Or For Television. It was also a US number 1 hit. *Reachin' Back*, released in 1995, featured assistance from Gerald LeVert, Keith Thomas, and En Vogue producers Thomas McElroy and Denzil Foster. On this record, Belle attempted to recreate the atmosphere of vintage Philly soul. Material chosen included the Delfonics' 'Didn't I (Blow Your Mind This Time)', Teddy Pendergrass's 'Love TKO' and the Spinners' 'Could It Be I'm Falling In Love'. As she told the press, 'I wanted to make an album that would remind folks of the blue light that hung in their basements or slow dancing with one's first love.'

● ALBUMS: *All By Myself* (Columbia 1987)★★, *Stay With Me* (Columbia 1989)★★★, *Passion* (Columbia 1993)★★★★, *Reachin' Back* (Columbia 1995)★★★.

BELVIN, JESSE

b. 15 December 1932, San Antonio, Texas, USA, d. 6 February 1960. Raised in Los Angeles, Belvin became a part of the city's flourishing R&B scene while in his teens. He was featured on 'All The Wine Is Gone', a 1950 single by Big Jay McNeely, but his career was then interrupted by a spell in the US Army. 'Earth Angel', a collaboration with two fellow conscripts, was recorded successfully by the Penguins, while Belvin enjoyed a major hit in his own right with 'Goodnight My Love', a haunting, romantic ballad adopted by disc jockey Alan Freed as the closing theme to his highly influential radio show. He also recorded with fellow songwriter Marvin Phillips as Jesse

& Marvin, achieving a Top 10 R&B hit in 1953 with 'Dream Girl'. In 1958 Belvin formed a vocal quintet, the Shields, to record for Dot Records the national Top 20 hit 'You Cheated'. That same year the singer was signed to RCA Records, who harboured plans to shape him in the mould of Nat 'King' Cole and Billy Eckstine. Further hits, including 'Funny' and 'Guess Who' - the latter of which was written by his wife and manager Jo Ann - offered a cool, accomplished vocal style suggestive of a lengthy career, but Belvin died, along with his wife, following a car crash in February 1960.

● ALBUMS: *The Casual Jesse Belvin* (Crown 1959)★★★★, *The Unforgettable Jesse Belvin* (Crown 1959)★★★★, *Just Jesse Belvin* (RCA Victor 1959)★★★, *Mr. Easy* (RCA Victor 1960)★★★, *True To Myself* (Warners 1996)★★★.

● COMPILATIONS: *Yesterdays* (RCA 1975)★★★, *Memorial Album* (Ace 1984)★★★★, *Hang Your Tears Out To Dry* (Earth Angel 1987)★★★, *Jesse Belvin: The Blues Balladeer* (Specialty 1990)★★★★.

BENÉT, ERIC

b. Milwaukee, Wisconsin, USA. Along with Rahsaan Patterson, D'Angelo and Tony Rich, Benét is representative of the current revival of the singer-songwriter tradition in modern urban soul. After gaining valuable experience as a featured singer with touring bands, Benét formed his own self-titled trio with his sister and his cousin George Nash Jnr. Having developed his own songwriting, he signed with Warner Brothers Records as a solo artist, writing and co-producing his acclaimed 1997 debut *True To Myself*. Heavily influenced by Stevie Wonder, Al Green and Sly Stone, the album's highlights varied from the slow-burning, confessional title track and the romantic balladry of 'I'll Be There', to the funky groove of 'Spiritual Thang' and the cover version of Stone's 'If You Want Me To Stay'. Following an acclaimed US support slot for Erykah Badu, Benét visited the UK to join Shola Ama and D-Influence on the Rhythm Nation Tour.

● ALBUMS: *True To Myself* (Warners 1997)★★★★.

BENSON, GEORGE

b. 22 March 1943, Pittsburgh, Pennsylvania, USA. This guitarist and singer successfully planted his feet in both the modern jazz and easy-listening pop camps in the mid-70s when jazz-pop as well as jazz-rock became a most lucrative proposition. Before a move to New York in 1963, he had played in various R&B outfits local to Pittsburgh, and recorded a single, 'It Should Have Been Me', in 1954. By 1965, Benson was an established jazz guitarist, having worked with Brother Jack McDuff, Herbie Hancock - and, crucially, Wes Montgomery, whose repertoire was drawn largely from pop, light classical and other non-jazz sources. When Montgomery died in 1969, critics predicted that Benson - contracted to Columbia Records in 1966 - would be his stylistic successor. Further testament to Benson's prestige was the presence of Hancock, Earl Klugh, Miles Davis, Joe Farrell and other jazz musicians on his early albums. Four of these were produced by Creed Taylor, who signed Benson to his own CTI label in 1971. Benson was impressing audiences in concert with extrapolations of songs such as 'California Dreamin'', 'Come Together' and, digging deeper into mainstream pop, 'Cry Me A River' and 'Unchained Melody'. From *Beyond The Blue Horizon*, an arrangement of Jefferson Airplane's 'White Rabbit' was a turntable hit, and chart success seemed inevitable - especially as he was now recording a majority of vocal items. After *Bad Benson* reached the US album lists and, via disco floors, the title song of *Supership* cracked European charts, he was well placed to negotiate a favourable contract with Warner Brothers Records, who immediately reaped a Grammy-winning harvest with 1976's *Breezin'* (and its memorable 'This Masquerade'). As a result, companies with rights to the prolific Benson's earlier product cashed in, with reissues such as *The Other Side Of Abbey Road*, a track-for-track interpretation of the entire Beatles album. Profit from film themes such as 'The Greatest Love Of All' (from the Muhammed Ali biopic *The Greatest*), the million-selling *Give Me The Night* and the television-advertised *The Love Songs* have allowed him to indulge artistic whims, including a nod to his jazz roots via 1987's excellent *Collaboration* with Earl Klugh, and a more commercial merger with Aretha Franklin on 'Love All The Hurt Away'. Moreover, a fondness for pop standards has also proved marketable, epitomized by revivals of 'On Broadway' - a US Top 10 single from 1978's *Weekend In LA* - and Bobby Darin's 'Beyond The Sea (La Mer)'. Like Darin, Benson also found success with Nat 'King' Cole's 'Nature Boy' (a single from *In Flight*) - and a lesser hit with Cole's 'Tenderly' in 1989, another balance of sophistication, hard-bought professionalism and intelligent response to chart climate. In 1990 he staged a full-length collaboration with the Count Basie Orchestra, accompanied by a sell-out UK tour. Benson is one of a handful of artists who have achieved major critical and commercial success in different genres - soul, jazz and pop, and this pedigree makes him one of the most respected performers of the past 30 years.

● ALBUMS: with the Brother Jack McDuff Quartet *The New Boss Guitar Of George Benson* (Prestige 1964)★★★★, *It's Uptown* (Columbia 1966)★★★★, *Most Exciting* (Columbia 1966)★★★, *Benson Burner* (Columbia 1966)★★★★, *The George Benson Cook Book* (Columbia 1967)★★★, *Giblet Gravy* (Verve 1968)★★★, *Goodies* (Verve 1969)★★★, *Shape Of Things To Come* (A&M 1969)★★, *Tell It Like It Is* (A&M 1969)★★, *The Other Side Of Abbey Road* (A&M 1970)★★★, *Beyond The Blue Horizon* (CTI 1970)★★★, *White Rabbit* (CTI 1973)★★, *Body Talk* (CTI 1974)★★★, *Bad Benson* (CTI 1974)★★, *Supership* (CTI 1975)★★★, *Breezin'* (Warners 1976)★★★★, *Good King Bad* (CTI 1976)★★★, with Joe Farrell *Benson And Farrell* (CTI 1976)★★★, *George Benson In Concert: Carnegie Hall* (CTI 1977)★★, *In Flight* (Warners 1977)★★★★, with Jack McDuff *George Benson And Jack McDuff* (Prestige 1977)★★★, *Weekend In LA* (Warners 1978)★★, *Living Inside Your Love* (Warners 1979)★★, *Give Me The Night* (Warners 1980)★★★★, *Blue Benson* (Polydor 1983)★★★, *In Your Eyes* (Warners 1983)★★★, *Stormy Weather* (Columbia 1984)★★, *20/20* (Warners 1985)★★, *The Electrifying George Benson* (Affinity 1985)★★★, *In Concert* (Premier 1985)★★, *Love*

Walked In (Platinum 1985)★★, *While The City Sleeps* (Warners 1986)★★, with Earl Klugh *Collaboration* (Warners 1987)★★★★, *Love For Sale* (Masters 1988)★★★, *Twice The Love* (Warners 1988)★★, *Detroit's George Benson* (Parkwood 1988)★★★, *Tenderly* (Warners 1989)★★, with the Count Basie Orchestra *Big Boss Band* (Warners 1990)★★★, *Lil' Darlin'* (Thunderbolt 1990)★★★, *Live At The Casa Caribe Vols 1-3* (Jazz View 1992)★★★, *Love Remembers* (Warners 1993)★★, *That's Right* (MCA 1996)★★★.

● COMPILATIONS: *The George Benson Collection* (Warners 1981)★★★★, *Early Years* (CTI 1982)★★★, *Best Of George Benson* (A&M 1982)★★★, *The Wonderful Years* (Proton 1984)★★★, *The Love Songs* (K-Tel 1985)★★★★, *The Silver Collection* (Verve 1985)★★★, *Compact Jazz* (Verve 1988)★★★, *Best Of* (Epic 1992)★★, *Guitar Giants* (Pickwick 1992)★★★, *The Best Of George Benson* (Warners 1995)★★★.

BENTON, BROOK

b. Benjamin Franklin Peay, 19 September 1931, Camden, South Carolina, USA, d. 9 April 1988. A stylish, mellifluent singer, Benton's most ascendant period was the late 50s/early 60s. Although he began recording in 1953, Benton's first major hit came in 1959 on forging a songwriting partnership with Clyde Otis and Belford Hendricks. 'It's Just A Matter Of Time' reached the US Top 3 and introduced a remarkable string of successes, including 'So Many Ways' (1959), 'The Boll Weevil Song' (1961) and 'Hotel Happiness' (1962). Duets with Dinah Washington, 'Baby (You've Got What It Takes)', a million-seller, and 'A Rockin' Good Way (To Mess Around And Fall In Love)', topped the R&B listings in 1960. Benton's warm, resonant delivery continued to prove popular into the early 60s. A versatile vocalist, his releases encompassed standards, blues and spirituals, while his compositions were recorded by Nat 'King' Cole, Clyde McPhatter and Roy Hamilton. Brook remained signed to the Mercury label until 1964 before moving to RCA Records, then Reprise Records. Releases on these labels failed to recapture the artist's previous success, but by the end of the decade, Benton rose to the challenge of younger acts with a series of excellent recordings for Atlantic Records' Cotillion subsidiary. His languid, atmospheric version of 'Rainy Night In Georgia' (1970) was an international hit and the most memorable product of an artistically fruitful period. Benton continued to record for a myriad of outlets during the 70s, including Brut (owned by the perfume company), Stax and MGM. Although his later work was less incisive, the artist remained one of music's top live attractions. He died in April 1988, aged 56, succumbing to pneumonia while weakened by spinal meningitis.

● ALBUMS: *Brook Benton At His Best* (Epic 1959)★★, *It's Just A Matter Of Time* (Mercury 1959)★★★, *Brook Benton* (Mercury 1959)★★★, *Endlessly* (1959)★★★, *So Many Ways I Love You* (Mercury 1960)★★★, with Dinah Washington *The Two Of Us - With Dinah Washington* (Mercury 1960)★★★★, *Songs I Love To Sing* (Mercury 1960)★★★, *The Boll Weevil Song (& Eleven Other Great Hits)* (Mercury 1961)★★★, *Sepia* (1961)★★, *If You Believe* (Mercury 1961)★★★, *Singing The Blues - Lie To Me* (Mercury 1962)★★★, *There Goes That Song Again* (Mercury 1962)★★★, *Best Ballads Of Broadway* (Mercury 1963)★★, *Born To Sing The Blues* (Mercury 1964)★★★, *Laura (What's He Got That I Ain't Got)* (Reprise 1967)★★, *Do Your Own Thing* (Cotillion 1969)★★, *Brook Benton Today* (Cotillion 1970)★★, *Home Style* (Cotillion 1970)★★★, *The Gospel Truth* (Cotillion 1971)★★, *Something For Everyone* (1973)★★, *Sings A Love Story* (RCA 1975)★★, *Mr. Bartender* (All Platinum 1976)★★, *This Is Brook Benton* (All Platinum 1976)★★★, *Makin' Love Is Good For You* (1977)★★, *Ebony* (1978)★★, *Brook Benton Sings The Standards* (RCA 1984)★★★.

● COMPILATIONS: *Brook Benton's Golden Hits* (Mercury 1961)★★★, *Golden Hits Volume Two* (Mercury 1963)★★★, *Spotlight On Brook Benton* (Philips 1977)★★★, *The Incomparable Brook Benton* (Audio Fidelity 1982)★★★, *Sixteen Golden Classics* (Unforgettable/Castle 1986)★★★, *The Brook Benton Anthology* (Rhino 1986)★★★★, *His Greatest Hits* (Mercury 1987)★★★, *40 Greatest Hits* (Mercury 1990)★★★★, *A Rainy Night In Georgia* (Mainline 1990)★★★, *Greatest Hits* (Curb 1991)★★★.

BERNS, BERT

b. 1929, New York, USA, d. 30 December 1967, New York, USA. This exceptional songwriter and producer was responsible for some of urban, 'uptown' soul's most treasured moments. He began his career as a record salesman, before being drawn into a new role as a copywriter and session pianist. Berns then began composing, often under such pseudonyms as 'Bert Russell' and 'Russell Byrd', and in 1960 formed a partnership with Phil Medley, the first of several similar working relationships. Their first major success came with 'Twist And Shout', originally recorded by the Top Notes but later transformed into an anthem by the Isley Brothers and regularly performed as a show-stopper by the Beatles. Berns' work then appeared on several New York-based outlets, but his next important step came when he replaced the team of Leiber And Stoller as the Drifters' writer/producer. Now firmly in place at the Atlantic label, he was involved with several other artists including Ben E. King and Barbara Lewis, although his finest work was saved for Solomon Burke and such definitive releases as 'Goodbye Baby', 'Everybody Needs Somebody To Love' and 'The Price'. Berns also forged an exceptional partnership with Jerry Ragovoy which included stellar work for Garnet Mimms and Lorraine Ellison, plus 'Piece Of My Heart' which was recorded by Erma Franklin and later by Janis Joplin. A spell in Britain resulted in sessions with Them and Lulu, Berns returned home to inaugurate the Bang and Shout labels. The former, pop-oriented company boasted a roster including the McCoys, the Strangeloves and former Them lead singer Van Morrison, while Shout was responsible for several excellent soul releases by Roy C, Bobby Harris, Erma Franklin and Freddy Scott. An astute individual, Berns once proffered a photograph of the Beatles to writer Nik Cohn: 'These boys have genius. They may be the ruin of us all.' He was referring to an endangered generation of hustling backroom talent, responsible for gathering songs, musicians and arrangements. He did not survive to see his prophecy fulfilled - Berns died of a heart attack in a New York hotel room on 30 December 1967.

Berry, Richard

b. 11 April 1935, Extension, Louisiana, USA, d. 23 January 1997. Berry was brought to Los Angeles as an infant, where he learned piano, playing along with the records of Joe Liggins and his Honeydrippers. In high school he formed a vocal group and began recording in 1953 under various names (the Hollywood Blue Jays, the Flairs, the Crowns, the Dreamers, the Pharaohs) as well as doing solo sessions for Modern's Flair subsidiary. His most famous moments on record are his bass vocal contributions to the Robins' 'Riot In Cell Block No. 9' and as 'Henry', Etta James's boyfriend, on her early classic 'Roll With Me Henry (The Wallflower)'. His main claim to fame is composing rock 'n' roll's famous standard 'Louie Louie', which he recorded in 1956 on Flip Records, but he had to wait seven years for its success with the Kingsmen's hit. The song spawned over 300 cover versions, including those by the Kinks, the Beach Boys and Paul Revere And The Raiders, none of which approached the Kingsmen's definitive recording. The sensual rhythm and theme of the song led to Berry's being accused of writing pornographic lyrics, but as they were virtually unintelligible, Berry took their secret to the grave with him. During the 60s and 70s, Berry, inspired by Bobby Bland and his wife Dorothy (herself a recording artist), became a soul singer. He recorded for myriad west coast labels (including his debut album for Johnny Otis's Blues Spectrum label) and continued performing into the 90s until his death.

● ALBUMS: *Richard Berry And The Dreamers* (Crown 1963)★★★, with the Soul Searchers *Live At The Century Club* (Pam 1968)★★, with the Soul Searchers *Wild Berry* (Pam 1968)★★, *Great Rhythm & Blues Oldies* (1977)★★★, *Layin' In The Alley* (Black Top 1994)★★.

● COMPILATIONS: *Get Out Of The Car* (Ace 1982)★★★★, *Louie, Louie* (Earth Angel 1986)★★.

Big Maybelle

b. Mabel Louise Smith, 1 May 1924, Jackson, Tennessee, USA, d. 23 January 1972, Cleveland, Ohio, USA. Maybelle was discovered singing in church by Memphis bandleader Dave Clark in 1935. When Clark disbanded his orchestra to concentrate on record promotion, Smith moved to Christine Chatman's orchestra with whom she first recorded for Decca in 1944. Three years later, Smith made solo records for King and in 1952 she recorded as Big Maybelle when producer Fred Mendelsohn signed her to OKeh, a subsidiary of CBS Records. Her blues shouting style (a female counterpart to Big Joe Turner) brought an R&B hit the next year with 'Gabbin' Blues' (a cleaned-up version of the 'dirty dozens' on which she was partnered by songwriter Rose Marie McCoy). 'Way Back Home' and 'My Country Man' were also bestsellers. In 1955, she made the first recording of 'Whole Lotta Shakin' Goin' On', which later became a major hit for Jerry Lee Lewis. Big Maybelle was also a star attraction on the chitlin' circuit of black clubs, with an act that included risqué comedy as well as emotive ballads and brisk boogies. Leaving OKeh for Savoy, her 'Candy' (1956) brought more success and in 1958, she appeared in *Jazz On A Summer's Day*, the film of that year's Newport Jazz Festival. Despite her acknowledged influence on the soul styles of the 60s, later records for Brunswick, Scepter and Chess made little impact until she signed to the Rojac label in 1966. There she was persuaded to record some recent pop hits by the Beatles and Donovan and had some minor chart success of her own with versions of 'Don't Pass Me By' and '96 Tears'. The latter was composed by Rudy Martinez who also recorded it with his band ? And The Mysterians. Maybelle's career was marred by frequent drug problems which contributed to her early death from a diabetic coma.

● ALBUMS: *Big Maybelle Sings* (Savoy 1958)★★★★, *Blues, Candy And Big Maybelle* (Savoy 1958)★★★★, *Saga Of The Good Life And Hard Times* (Rojac 60s)★★★, *What More Can A Woman Do?* (Brunswick 1962)★★★, *The Gospel Soul Of Big Maybelle* (Brunswick 1964)★★★★,*The Great Soul Hits Of Big Maybelle* (Brunswick 1964)★★★★, *Gabbin' Blues* (Scepter 1965)★★★, *Got A Brand New Bag* (Rojac 1967)★★★, *The Gospel Soul Of Big Maybelle* (Brunswick 1968)★★★, *The Last Of Big Maybelle* (Paramount 1973)★★★.

● COMPILATIONS: *The OKeh Sessions* (Charly 1983)★★★★, *Roots Of R&B And Early Soul* (Savoy Jazz 1985)★★★★, *Candy* (Savoy 1995)★★★, *The Last Of Big Maybelle* (Muse 1996)★★.

Big Twist And The Mellow Fellow

Big Twist (b. Larry Nolan, 23 September 1937, Terra Haute, Indiana, USA, d. 14 March 1990, Broadview, Illinois, USA) was the lead singer and leader of this R&B big band. He began singing in church in southern Illinois when he was six years old, and in the 50s was drummer and vocalist with the Mellow Fellows, an R&B group. In the early 70s he teamed with guitarist Pete Special and tenor saxophonist Terry Ogolini, and the group had albums released by Flying Fish and Alligator. Their work revealed an approach and breadth of repertoire (including blues, R&B and soul) that was ahead of its time. Big Twist died of a heart attack in March 1990, but the group continued, fronted by singer Martin Allbritton from Carbondale, Illinois, and with saxophonist-producer Gene Barge on vocals.

● ALBUMS: *Big Twist And The Mellow Fellows* (1980)★★★, with Big Twist *Playing For Keeps* (Alligator 1983)★★★, *One Track Mind* (Red Lightnin' 1982)★★★, *Live From Chicago - Bigger Than Life* (Alligator 1987)★★★, with Martin Allbritton *Street Party* (1990)★★★.

Bihari Brothers

The Bihari family moved in 1941 from Oklahoma to Los Angeles where eldest brother Jules went into business as a supplier and operator of juke-boxes for the black community. The next step was to ensure the supply of suitable blues and R&B recordings to feed the juke-boxes and with Joe and Saul, he founded the Modern Music Company in 1945. As well as recording west coast artists such as Jimmy Witherspoon and Johnny Moore's Three Blazers, the brothers worked with local producers in Houston, Detroit and Memphis who supplied Modern with more rough-hewn blues material by such artists as Lightnin' Hopkins, John Lee Hooker and B.B. King. In 1951, the fourth Bihari brother, Lester, set up the Meteor label in Memphis. Meteor was responsible for some of Elmore James's earliest records as well as rockabilly by Charlie Feathers. Other Modern group labels included RPM (for which Ike Turner produced Howlin' Wolf), Blues & Rhythm and Flair. During the early 50s, the Bihari brothers released a wide range of material, even aiming at the pop charts by covering R&B titles from other labels. Among its successes were Etta James's 'Wallflower', 'Stranded In The Jungle' by the Cadets, 'Eddie My Love' by the Teen Queens and Jessie Belvin's 'Goodnight My Love'. The arranger/producer of many Modern tracks was Maxwell Davis. However, by the late 50s, the Modern group turned its attention towards reissuing material on the Crown budget-price label, which also included a series of big-band tribute albums masterminded by Davis. When the company found itself in financial difficulties, the Biharis released recordings by Z.Z. Hill, Lowell Fulson and B.B. King on the Kent label, but the death of Saul Bihari in 1975 and Joe's departure from the company led to a virtual cessation of recording, and the remaining brothers concentrated on custom pressing at their vinyl record plant. In 1984, the year of Jules Bihari's death, the family sold the catalogues of Modern, Flair, Kent, Crown and RPM. Seven years later, the labels passed into the hands of a consortium of Virgin Records (USA), Ace (Europe) and Blues Interactions (Japan). These companies continued an extensive reissue programme that the Ace label had initiated as licensee of the Modern group in the early 80s.

Black, Bill

b. William Patton Black, 17 September 1926, Memphis, Tennessee, USA, d. 21 October 1965, Memphis, Tennessee, USA. Black was the bass-playing half of the Scotty And Bill team that backed Elvis Presley on his earliest live performances. After leaving Presley, Black launched a successful career of his own as leader of the Bill Black Combo. Initially playing an acoustic stand-up bass, Black was hired as a session musician by Sun Records, where he met Presley in 1954. He played on the earliest Sun tracks, including 'That's All Right'. Black toured with Presley alongside guitarist Scotty Moore; later, drummer D.J. Fontana was added to the group. Black and Moore left Presley's employment in 1957 owing to what they felt was unfair payment. The Bill Black Combo was formed in 1959, with Black (electric bass guitar), Reggie Young (guitar), Martin Wills (saxophone), Carl McAvoy (piano) and Jerry Arnold (drums). Signed to Hi Records in Memphis, the group favoured an instrumental R&B-based sound tempered with jazz. Their first chart success was 'Smokie Part 2' in late 1959, but it was the follow-up, 'White Silver Sands' in the spring of 1960, that gave the group its biggest US hit, reaching number 9. Black retired from touring in 1962, and the group continued performing under the same name without him, with Bob Tucker playing bass. The group also backed other artists, including Gene Simmons on the 1964 number 11 hit 'Haunted House'. Saxophonist Ace Cannon was a member of the group for some time. The group continued playing even after Black died of a brain tumour in October 1965. The Bill Black Combo achieved a total of 19 US chart singles and was still working under the leadership of Tucker in the late 80s.

● ALBUMS: *Smokie* (Hi 1960)★★★, *Saxy Jazz* (Hi 1960)★★★, *Solid And Raunchy* (Hi 1960)★★★★, *That Wonderful Feeling* (Hi 1961)★★★, *Movin'* (Hi 1961)★★★, *Bill Black's Record Hop* (Hi 1962)★★★, *Let's Twist Her* (Hi 1962)★★★★, *Untouchable Sound Of Bill Black* (Hi 1963)★★★, *Bill Black Plays The Blues* (Hi 1964)★★★, *Bill Black Plays Tunes By Chuck Berry* (Hi 1964)★★, *Bill Black's Combo Goes Big Band* (Hi 1964)★★, *More Solid And Raunchy* (Hi 1965)★★, *All Timers* (Hi 1966)★★, *Black Lace* (Hi 1967)★★, *King Of The Road* (Hi 1967)★★, *The Beat Goes On* (Hi 1968)★★, *Turn On Your Lovelight* (London 1969)★★, *Solid And Raunchy The 3rd* (Hi 1969)★★, *Soulin' The Blues* (London 1969)★★.

● COMPILATIONS: *Greatest Hits* (Hi/London 1963)★★★.

Blackbyrds

The original Blackbyrds were formed in 1973 by jazz trumpeter Donald Byrd. A doctor of ethnomusicology, Byrd lectured at Washington DC's Howard University and the group, named after *Black Byrd*, the artist's million-seller, was drawn from his students. The Blackbyrds' debut album charted in the soul, jazz and pop listings, while the follow-up, *Flying Start*, featured their 1975 US Top 10 single, 'Walking In Rhythm'. This infectious performance became the group's first major success, by which point founder-members Kevin Toney (keyboards) and Keith Killgo (vocals, drums) had been joined by Joe Hall (bass), Orville Saunders (guitar) and Jay Jones (flute, saxophone). The following year the group hit the US charts again with 'Happy Music' reaching the Top 20. Sadly, the unit's adventurousness gave way to a less spirited direction. The compulsive rhythmic pulse became increasingly predictable as the group, once so imaginative, pursued a style reliant on a safe and tested formula, the repetitiveness of which brought about their demise.

● ALBUMS: *The Blackbyrds* (Fantasy 1974)★★★, *Flying Start* (Fantasy 1974)★★★★, *Cornbread, Earl And Me* (Fantasy 1975)★★, *City Life* (Fantasy 1975)★★, *Unfinished Business* (Fantasy 1976)★★, *Action* (Fantasy 1977)★★, *Better Days* (Fantasy 1980)★★.

● COMPILATIONS: *Night Grooves - The Blackbyrds Greatest Hits* (Fantasy 1978)★★★, *The Best Of The Blackbyrds Volume 1* (Fantasy 1988)★★★★, *The Best Of The Blackbyrds Volume 2* (Fantasy 1988)★★★.

BLACKstreet

Among the most highly rated of the new generation of urban R&B groups, BLACKstreet is the brainchild of gifted musician and producer Teddy Riley. The group, formed in Los Angeles, California, USA, originally comprised songwriters Riley and Chauncey Hannibal, with Levi Little and David Hollister as additional vocalists.

The quartet made their self-titled debut for Interscope Records in 1994. This well-received collection, dominated by hip-hop rhythms, provided a compulsive rhythmic soundtrack to the summer of 1994, selling close to one million copies and featuring the hit single 'Before I Let You Go'. For the follow-up, Hollister and Little were replaced by Mark Middleton and Eric Williams, and the musical accent changed from hip-hop to pure R&B. The only exception was the promotional single, 'No Diggity', which featured a guest rap from Dr. Dre. More arresting was 'The Lord Is Real', a vocal track which borrowed heavily from the gospel tradition, and a completely restyled version of the Beatles' 'Can't Buy Me Love'.

● ALBUMS: *BLACKstreet* (Interscope 1994)★★★, *Another Level* (Interscope 1996)★★★.

BLACKWELL, OTIS

b. 1931, Brooklyn, New York, USA. The author of 'Great Balls Of Fire', 'Fever' and 'All Shook Up', Blackwell was one of the greatest songwriters of the rock 'n' roll era. He learned piano as a child and grew up listening to both R&B and country music. Victory in a talent contest at Harlem's Apollo Theatre led to a recording contract with the Joe Davis label. His first release was his own composition 'Daddy Rolling Stone', which became a favourite in Jamaica where it was recorded by Derek Martin. The song later became part of the Who's 'Mod' repertoire. During the mid-50s, Blackwell also recorded in a rock 'n' roll vein for RCA Records and Groove before turning to writing songs for other artists. His first successes came in 1956 when Little Willie John's R&B hit with the sultry 'Fever' was an even bigger pop success for Peggy Lee. Subsequently, 'All Shook Up' (first recorded by David Hill on Aladdin Records) began a highly profitable association with Elvis Presley, who was credited as co-writer. The rhythmic tension of the song perfectly fitted Elvis's stage persona and it became his first UK number 1. It was followed by 'Don't Be Cruel' (1956), 'Paralysed' (1957), and the more mellow 'Return To Sender' (1962) and 'One Broken Heart For Sale'. There was a distinct similarity between Blackwell's vocal style and Presley's, which has led to speculation that Elvis adopted some of his songwriter's mannerisms. The prolific Blackwell (who wrote hundreds of songs) also provided hits for Jerry Lee Lewis ('Breathless' and his most famous recording, 'Great Balls Of Fire', 1958), Dee Clark ('Hey Little Girl' and 'Just Keep It Up', 1959), Jimmy Jones ('Handy Man', 1960) and Cliff Richard ('Nine Times Out Of Ten', 1960). As the tide of rock 'n' roll receded, Blackwell reorded R&B material for numerous labels including Atlantic, MGM and Epic. In later years, he was in semi-retirement, making only occasional live appearances.

● ALBUMS: *Singin' The Blues* (Davis 1956)★★, *These Are My Songs* (Inner City 1978)★★.

BLACKWELL, ROBERT 'BUMPS'

b. Robert A. Blackwell, 23 May 1918, Seattle, Washington, USA (of mixed French, Negro and Indian descent), d. 9 March 1985. An arranger and studio bandleader with Specialty Records, Blackwell had led a band in Seattle. After arriving in California in 1949, he studied classical composition at the University of California, Los Angeles, and within a few years was arranging and producing gospel and R&B singles for the likes of Lloyd Price and Guitar Slim. Previously, he had written a series of stage revues - *Blackwell Portraits* - very much in the same vein as the *Ziegfeld Follies*. His Bumps Blackwell Jnr. Orchestra featured, at various times, Ray Charles and Quincy Jones. He also worked with Lou Adler and Herb Alpert before taking over the A&R department at Specialty Records, where he first came into contact with Little Richard. His boss, Art Rupe, sent him to New Orleans in 1955 where he recorded 'Tutti Frutti' and established a new base for rock 'n' roll. Blackwell was a key producer and songwriter in the early days of rock 'n' roll, particularly with Little Richard. He was responsible for tracking down the latter and buying his recording contract from Peacock in 1955. Blackwell helped to rewrite 'Tutti Frutti' in a cleaned-up version more appropriate to white audiences, which he recorded at Richard's first Specialty session in New Orleans. As well as being involved with the writing of some of Richard's hits, he also produced some of his early work, and became his personal manager. Along with John Marascalco he wrote 'Ready Teddy', 'Rip It Up', and, with Enotris Johnson and Richard Penniman (Little Richard), 'Long Tall Sally'. He also helped launch the secular careers of former gospel singers Sam Cooke and Wynona Carr. After leaving Specialty, he was involved in setting up Keen Records, which furthered the careers of Sam Cooke and Johnny 'Guitar' Watson, among others. In 1981 he co-produced the title track of Bob Dylan's *Shot Of Love*, before his death from pneumonia in 1985.

BLAND, BILLY

b. 5 April 1932, Wilmington, North Carolina, USA. Billy Bland was an R&B singer whose best-known recording was the 1960 US Top 10 hit 'Let The Little Girl Dance'. Bland, the youngest of 19 children, began his career in 1947 in New York City, where he performed in the bands of Lionel Hampton and Buddy Johnson before starting his own group, the Four Bees. He was brought to New Orleans by producer Dave Bartholomew in 1954 and sang on a single for Imperial Records, 'Toy Bell'. Bland signed to Old Town Records in 1955 and recorded singles that were hits regionally, such as 'Chicken In The Basket' and 'Chicken Hop'. He recorded the bouncy 'Let The Little Girl Dance' in late 1959, also for Old Town, and it reached the charts in early 1960, eventually climbing to number 7. Bland had three further singles in the pop charts, but recorded no albums. He retired in the 70s.

BLAND, BOBBY

b. Robert Calvin Bland, 27 January 1930, Rosemark, Tennessee, USA. Having moved to Memphis with his mother, Bobby 'Blue' Bland started singing with local gospel groups, including the Miniatures. Eager to expand his interests, he began frequenting the city's infamous Beale Street, where he became associated with an *ad hoc* circle of aspiring musicians, named, not unnaturally, the Beale Streeters. Bland's recordings from the early 50s show him striving for individuality, but his progress was halted by a stint in the US Army. When the singer returned to Memphis in 1954 he found several of his former associates, including Johnny Ace, enjoying considerable success, while Bland's recording label, Duke, had been sold to Houston entrepreneur Don Robey. In 1956 Bland began touring with 'Little' Junior Parker. Initially, he doubled as valet and driver, a role he reportedly performed for B.B. King, but simultaneously began asserting his characteristic vocal style. Melodic big-band blues singles, including 'Farther Up The Road' (1957) and 'Little Boy Blue' (1958), reached the US R&B Top 10, but Bland's vocal talent was most clearly heard on a series of superb early 60s releases, including 'Cry Cry Cry', 'I Pity The Fool' and the sparkling 'Turn On Your Lovelight', which was destined to become a much-covered standard. Despite credits to the contrary, many such classic works were written by Joe Scott, the artist's bandleader and arranger. Bland continued to enjoy a consistent run of R&B chart entries throughout the mid-60s, but his recorded work was nonetheless eclipsed by a younger generation of performers. Financial pressures forced the break-up of the group in 1968, and his relationship with Scott, who died in 1979, was irrevocably severed. Nonetheless, depressed and increasingly dependent on alcohol, Bland weathered this unhappy period. In 1971, his record company, Duke, was sold to the larger ABC Records group, resulting in several contemporary blues/soul albums including *His California Album* and *Dreamer*. Subsequent attempts at pushing the artist towards the disco market were unsuccessful, but a 1983 release, *Here We Go Again*, provided a commercial lifeline. Two years later Bland was signed by Malaco Records, specialists in traditional southern black music, who offered a sympathetic environment. One of the finest singers in post-war blues, Bobby Bland has failed to win the popular acclaim his influence and talent perhaps deserve.

● ALBUMS: with 'Little' Junior Parker *Blues Consolidated* (Duke 1958)★★★, with Parker *Barefoot Rock And You Got Me* (Duke 1960)★★★, *Two Steps From The Blues* (Duke 1961)★★★★, *Here's The Man!!!* (Duke 1962)★★★★, *Call On Me* (Duke 1963)★★★, *Ain't Nothin' You Can Do* (Duke 1964)★★★, *The Soul Of The Man* (Duke 1966)★★★, *Touch Of The Blues* (Duke 1967)★★, *Spotlighting The Man* (Duke 1968)★★, *His California Album* (Dunhill 1973)★★, *Dreamer* (Dunhill 1974)★★, with B.B. King *Together For The First Time - Live* (Dunhill 1974)★★★★, *Get On Down With Bobby Bland* (ABC 1975)★★, with King *Together Again - Live* (ABC 1976)★★★, *Reflections In Blue* (ABC 1977)★★, *Come Fly With Me* (ABC 1978)★★, *I Feel Good I Feel Fine* (MCA 1979)★★, *Sweet Vibrations* (MCA 1980)★★, *You Got Me Loving You* (MCA 1981)★★, *Try Me, I'm Real* (MCA 1981)★★, *Here We Go Again* (MCA 1982)★★, *Tell Mr. Bland* (MCA 1983)★★, *Members Only* (Malaco 1985)★★, *After All* (Malaco 1986)★★, *Blues You Can Use* (Malaco 1987)★★, *Midnight Run* (Malaco 1989)★★★, *Portrait Of The Blues* (Malaco 1991)★★★, *Sad Street* (Malaco 1995)★★★.

● COMPILATIONS: *The Best Of Bobby Bland* (Duke 1967)★★★★, *The Best Of Bobby Bland Vol. 2* (Duke 1968)★★★★, *Introspective Of The Early Years* (MCA 1974)★★★, *Woke Up Screaming* (Ace 1981)★★★, *The Best Of Bobby Bland* (ABC 1982)★★★, *Foolin' With The Blues* (Charly 1983)★★★, *Blues In The Night* (Ace 1985)★★★, *The Soulful Side Of Bobby Bland* (Kent 1986)★★, *First Class Blues* (Malaco 1987)★★★, *Soul With A Flavour 1959-1984* (Charly 1988)★★★, *The '3B' Blues Boy: The Blues Years 1952-59* (Ace 1991)★★★★, *The Voice: Duke Recordings 1959-1969* (Ace 1992)★★★★, *I Pity The Fool: The Duke Recordings Vol. 1* (1993)★★★, *That Did It! The Duke Recordings Vol. 3* (MCA 1996)★★★.

BLESSID UNION OF SOULS

Formed in Cincinnati, Ohio, USA, modern soul/rock quintet Blessid Union Of Souls broke through in 1995 with the hit singles 'I Believe' and 'Let Me Be The One'. As a consequence, the group's debut album of that year, *Home*, became an international bestseller. Led by songwriters Elliot Sloan (b. USA; vocals) and Jeff Pence (b. USA; guitar), the group also includes Eddie Hedges (percussion), C.P. Roth (keyboards), Tony Clark (bass) and production collaborator Emosia. After intensive touring following their debut, the group enrolled the expertise of writers Tommy Sims and Shelley Peiken to help with new compositions for their self-titled follow-up set. Peiken's contribution, 'Peace And Love', and Sims' 'Light In Your Eyes', were among the strongest tracks on *Blessid Union Of Souls*, which the group conceptualized as a canon of 'rural soul' songs. As Sloan told the press: 'We're not just straightforward pop, but country-flavoured, rock, and spiritual - all that pretty much meshes into one.' However, the critical reaction that greeted the first single lifted from the album, 'I Wanna Be There', was less encouraging than expected.

● ALBUMS: *Home* (EMI 1995)★★★★, *Blessid Union Of Souls* (EMI 1997)★★★.

BLIGE, MARY J.

b. Mary Jane Blige, 11 January 1971, Atlanta, Georgia, USA. After being promoted by her record company as 'The original queen of hip-hop and soul', Mary J. Blige's debut album sold over two million copies (many of the best songs being written for her by POV). The hip-hop quotient was represented by bass-driven rhythms, the soul stylings including her affecting voice. Guest appearances from rappers Grand Puba and Busta Rhymes were merely a bonus on this accomplished piece of work. When she journeyed to England for live shows in 1993 she was widely criticized for overpricing a set that was merely six songs long, but quality rather than quantity remains the keynote to Blige's career. According to her publicity handout, *Share My World* marked 'her personal and musical rebirth'; rebirth or not, it was certainly another excellent album.

● ALBUMS: *What's The 411?* (Uptown 1992)★★★, *What's The 411? - Remix Album* (Uptown 1993)★★★, *My Life* (Uptown 1994)★★★, *Share My World* (MCA 1997)★★★★.

BLINKY

b. Sandra Williams, California, USA. Blinky began her singing career in gospel, before signing to Vee Jay

Records in 1964 as a member of the Logics (alongside future Motown writer Gloria Jones). She enjoyed brief solo contracts with Atlantic and Gospel, before signing to Motown in 1968. There she teamed up with Edwin Starr, and the duo registered a soul hit with 'Oh How Happy' prior to recording an album of duets. When Starr was groomed by Motown as a soloist, Blinky's own career took second place. She issued sporadic singles, but all three of her Motown albums were cancelled before release. Later singles on Reprise also proved unsuccessful.

● ALBUMS: with Edwin Starr *Just We Two* (Gordy 1969)★★★.

BLOODSTONE

An R&B self-contained band from Kansas City, Missouri, USA. Sweet soul stand-up vocal groups were highly fashionable in the early 70s and Bloodstone, although a self-contained band, with their falsetto-led and vocally harmonized hits, were a part of the phenomenon along with the Moments, Chi-lites, and Stylistics, among others. Original members were Charles McCormick (lead vocal, bass guitar), Charles Love (lead vocal, guitar), Willis Draffen (vocal, guitar), Henry Williams (vocal, percussion), Eddie Summers (drummer) and Roger Lee Durham (d. 1973). Bloodstone became hitmakers in the USA via the unusual route of being discovered by an English producer, Mike Vernon, who recorded them in the UK. Their biggest hits, on the London label in the USA, came early in their career from 1973-74, namely 'Natural High' (number 4 R&B, number 10 pop), 'Never Let You Go' (number 7 R&B, number 43 pop), 'Outside Woman' (number 2 R&B, number 34 pop), and 'My Little Lady' (number 4 R&B, number 57 pop). In the UK charts, 'Natural High' was the only entry, peaking at number 40. The group moved to the Isley Brothers' T-Neck label in 1982, and immediately had a Top 5 R&B hit with 'We Go A Long Way Back'. Their pop success remained behind them, however, but Bloodstone continued to appear on the R&B charts until 1984, when they disbanded.

● ALBUMS: *Bloodstone* (London 1972)★★, *Natural High* (London 1973)★★★, *Never Let You Go* (London 1973)★★★, *Unreal* (London 1973)★★★, *I Need Time* (London 1974)★★★, *Riddle Of The Sphinx* (London 1974)★★★, *Train Ride To Hollywood* (London 1975)★★★, *Do You Wanna Do A Thing* (London 1976)★★★, *Don't Stop* (Motown 1978)★★★, *We Go A Long Way Back* (T-Neck 1982)★★, *Party* (T-Neck 1984)★★.

● COMPILATIONS: *Greatest Hits* (Columbia 1985)★★★.

BLOSSOMS

The Blossoms began their career in Los Angeles, USA, in 1954 under the name of the Dreamers, with a line-up comprising Fanita Barrett (later James), Gloria Jones, Nanette Williams (later Jackson) and Annette Williams. The following year they recorded as Richard Berry's backing group. Darlene Wright (later Love) then replaced Nanette Williams and by 1957 the quartet were renamed the Blossoms. Releases on Capitol (1957-58) and Challenge (1961-62) were interspersed with session work for Duane Eddy and several one-off singles under such pseudonyms as the Coeds And The Playgirls. Love and James were also members of Bob B. Soxx And The Blue Jeans, a trio that worked with Phil Spector. The famed producer used Love on several Crystals sessions and the singer also released several singles under her own name. The Blossoms became a permanent fixture on the *Shindig* US television show. By 1965 the group had been reduced to a trio of Love, James and Jean King. They recorded for Challenge, and 'Son-In Law', a response to Ernie K-Doe's 'Mother-In-Law', was their only single to chart. They had a minor R&B hit in 1967 with 'Good Good Lovin''. The line-up underwent several further changes; Edna Wright (Darlene's sister) and Grazia Nitzsche were also members as the Blossoms progressed through several outlets including Ode (1967), Bell (1969-70) and Lion (1972). Love then left to pursue an intermittent solo career. Of the other ex-members, Jones and Jackson formed the Girlfriends with Carolyn Willis. Jones later recorded the original version of 'Tainted Love', which later became a UK number 1 hit in 1981 for Soft Cell, and achieved a certain notoriety for her marriage to Marc Bolan. Willis subsequently joined Edna Wright in the Honey Cone. Fanita James, meanwhile, continued to lead the Blossoms during the 80s.

● ALBUMS: *Shockwave* (1972)★★★.

BLUE JAYS

An R&B vocal group from Los Angeles, California, USA, the Blue Jays perfectly embody the transitional era between 50s R&B and 60s soul in their renditions of doo-wop-styled songs with a gospel-style lead vocal. Comprising lead singer Leon Peels (b. 1936, Newport, Arkansas, USA), Alex Manigo, Van Earl Richardson, and Leonard Davidson, the group came together in 1961, and the same year were signed by country singer Werly Fairburn to his Milestone label. The Blue Jays' first record, 'Lovers Island' (number 31 in the US pop chart) in 1961, was at the time considered to be one of the last gasps of doo-wop, yet in retrospect, one can hear the first glimmerings of soul in Peels' gospel-edged vocals. Peculiarly, the song only made the local R&B charts. The group followed the hit with some excellent numbers, notably 'Tears Are Falling' (1961) and 'The Right To Love' (1962), but achieved little success; they disbanded in early 1962.

● ALBUMS: *The Blue Jays Meet Little Caesar* (Milestone 1962)★★★.

● COMPILATIONS: *Lovers Island* (Relic 1987)★★★.

BLUE MAGIC

This Philadelphia-based vocal quintet of the 70s consisted of Theodore 'Ted' Mills (lead), Vernon Sawyer (tenor, baritone), Wendell Sawyer (baritone), Keith Beaton (tenor) and Richard Pratt (bass). Produced by Norman Harris, a Philly sweet soul veteran, the group's textured harmonies were ably supported by the classic MFSB house band, resulting in some of the genre's finest moments. Although early releases were confined to the R&B chart, Blue Magic broke through in 1974 with the million-selling US Top 10 hit 'Sideshow', and the equally evocative 'Three Ring Circus'. Subsequent singles fared less well on the pop chart, but for the next two years, the group remained a consistent fixture on the black music listings. They then left the Atco label, since which time their success has been more intermittent. Their later US hits have included 'Magic' (1983) and, owing to renewed popularity in the late 80s, 'It's Like Magic' and 'Romeo And Juliet'.

● ALBUMS: *Blue Magic* (Atco 1974)★★★, *Magic Of The Blue* (Atco 1974)★★★, *Thirteen Blue Magic Lane* (Atco 1975)★★, *Mystic Dragons* (Atco 1976)★★, *Message From The Magic* (Atco 1978)★★★, *From Out Of The Blue* (OBR 1989)★★.

● COMPILATIONS: *Greatest Hits* (Omni/Atlantic 1986)★★★.

BLUE STARS

This 70s vocal group quintet featured Louis De Carlo (lead and first tenor), Tony Millone (lead and second tenor), Jack Scandura (lead and second tenor), Bobby Thomas (lead and baritone) and Ken Mewes (lead and bass). Formed in Queens, New York, USA, in 1974, they drew membership from several previous local groups, including Ricky And The Hallmarks (Scandura), the Devotions, Mr. Bassman and Symbols (De Carlo), Jordan And The Fascinations and Boulevards (Thomas) and Fulton Fish Market (Millone). Soon after they started rehearsing their a cappella and doo-wop harmonies, Millone departed to be replaced by Larry Galvin (himself formerly of the Velvet Five). Their first year together produced three singles for the local Arcade Records outlet, cover versions of the Channels' 'My Love Will Never Die', the Flamingos' 'I Only Have Eyes For You' and the Heartbeats' 'Your Way'. They retired soon afterwards, however, with three of the band going on to the Blendairs. Backing Johnny 'Ace' Acuino in this more R&B-orientated vehicle, Galvin, Scandura and Mewes added Eddie Conway to the line-up. By 1976 Mewes had been replaced by Sam Wood (the former Sparrows Quartette bass singer), and the Blendairs readied themselves for recording sessions. Just as they did so, Acuino received the call to rejoin his old working partner Elvin Bishop, but it was too late to stop the release of their 'Sweet Sue' single (this time, a Crows cover version). Conway left the group in 1977, but by the following year the members elected to press ahead with a sound that retreated back to their original love of doo-wop and vocal records. Beverly Warren, another former member of Ricky And The Hallmarks, joined at the same time as Al Vieco, who had previously worked with Galvin in side-project Oasis. The first recording with the reshuffled line-up was 'He's Gone' for Story Untold Records in 1978. Two further singles followed, 'Gee Whizz' and 'Don't Leave Me', before Wood retired and the Blendairs ground to a halt. However, by 1983 they had been reactivated, but this time they returned to their original title, the Blue Stars. The new members were Jay Ortsman (bass) and Bix Boyle (second tenor), joining Anthony Millone (returning on first tenor), Bobby Thomas (now just baritone) and Jack Scandura (lead). They continued to play concerts in the New York area but with the passing of the years the line-up soon evolved to feature Rick Wakeman (not the UK keyboard player) and Don Raphael with Scandura, Galvin and Millone. They did little recording work, but managed to pay the bills by supporting artists such as Little Caesar and the Medallions on the oldies circuit. However, they broke up once more in 1990, just before the release of their acclaimed *Blue Velvet A Cappella* collection. Most of the former members continue to be involved in low-key live bands of various kinds, and so further reunions can hardly be ruled out.

● ALBUMS: *Reunion* (Clifton 1989)★★★, *Blue Velvet A Cappella* (Clifton 1991)★★★★.

BLUE-BELLES

(see LaBelle)

BLUES BROTHERS

Formed in 1978, this US group was centred on comedians John Belushi (b. 24 January 1949, Chicago, Illinois, USA, d. 5 March 1982, Los Angeles, California, USA) and Dan Aykroyd (1 July 1952, Ottawa, Ontario, Canada). Renowned for contributions to the satirical *National Lampoon* team and television's *Saturday Night Live*, the duo formed this 60s-soul-styled revue as a riposte to disco. Assuming the epithets Joliet 'Jake' Blues (Belushi) and Elwood Blues (Aykroyd), they embarked on live appearances with the assistance of a crack backing group, which included Steve Cropper (guitar), Donald 'Duck' Dunn (bass) and Tom Scott (saxophone). *Briefcase Full Of Blues* topped the US charts, a success that in turn inspired the film *The Blues Brothers* (1980). Although reviled by several music critics, there was no denying the refreshing enthusiasm the participants brought to R&B and the venture has since acquired a cult status. An affectionate, if anarchic, tribute to soul and R&B, it featured cameo appearances by Aretha Franklin, Ray Charles, John Lee Hooker and James Brown. Belushi's death from a drug overdose in 1982 brought the original concept to a premature end, since which time Aykroyd has continued a successful acting career, notably in *Ghostbusters*. However, several of the musicians, including Cropper and Dunn, later toured and recorded as the Blues Brothers Band. The original Blues Brothers have also inspired numerous copy-cat/tribute groups who still attract sizeable audiences, over 15 years after the film's release. In August 1991, interest in the concept was again boosted with a revival theatre production in London's West End. A new film was planned for release in 1998, with the Belushi role taken by ex-*Roseanne* star John Goodman.

● ALBUMS: *Briefcase Full Of Blues* (Atlantic 1978)★★, *The Blues Brothers* film soundtrack (Atlantic 1980)★★★, *Made In America* (Atlantic 1980)★★, as the Blues Brothers Band *The Blues Brothers Band Live* (Warners 1990)★, *Red, White & Blues* (1992)★.

● COMPILATIONS: *The Best Of The Blues Brothers* (Atlantic 1981)★★.

● VIDEOS: *Live At Montreux* (WEA Music Video 1990), *Things We Did Last Summer* (Brave World 1991).

● FILMS: *The Blues Brothers* (1980).

BO, EDDIE

b. Edwin J. Bocage, 20 September 1930, New Orleans, Louisiana, USA. After serving in the army, Bocage enrolled at the Grunewald School of Music to study piano and music theory. His penchant for playing jazz and the more remunerative R&B led to him leading the house band at the Tijuana Club as 'Spider' Bocage. Later, with the Spider Bocage Orchestra, he toured with Guitar Slim, Smiley Lewis and Earl King. He first recorded for Johnny Vincent's Ace label in 1955, before signing with Apollo in New York. His hit, 'I'm Wise', one of five Apollo singles, became the basis of Little Richard's 'Slippin' And Slidin''. Further singles for Checker, Chess and Ace made little impression, although Etta James later had a hit with 'My Dearest Darling'. He signed with Ric, a local independent label, in 1959, and enjoyed local success with his third release, 'Tell It Like It Is'. Five records later, he started a dance craze with 'Check Mr Popeye', but failed to have a nationwide hit because of competition from Huey Smith and Chubby Checker. During the 60s, he recorded prolifically for a host of New Orleans labels, including Rip, At Last, Cinderella, Arrow, Blue Jay, Seven-B and Nola. His biggest success came in 1969 with 'Hook And Sling' for Scram. Two years later, he had a local hit with 'Check Your Bucket' on his own Bo-Sound label, before leaving the music business temporarily. In the late 80s, he toured Europe as part of a New Orleans package that included Dr John and Mink Deville.

● ALBUMS: *Check Mr Popeye* (Rounder/Edsel 1988)★★★, *Vippin' & Voppin'* (Charly 1988)★★★.

BOB AND EARL

Formed in Los Angeles, California, USA, in 1960, this duo comprised Bobby Day (b. Bobby Byrd, 1 July 1932, Fort Worth, Texas, USA) and Earl Lee Nelson. Day had previously formed the Hollywood Flames, a group best recalled for the rock 'n' roll hit 'Buzz-Buzz-Buzz' (1957), which featured Nelson on lead vocal. Day then secured a solo hit with 'Rockin' Robin' before briefly joining Nelson in the original Bob And Earl. Bob Relf replaced Day when the latter resumed his own career. The Barry White-produced 'Harlem Shuffle', the pairing's best-known song, was originally released in 1963. A minor hit in the USA, the single proved more durable in Britain. Although it failed to chart when first released, a reissue reached number 7 in 1969. Bob And Earl had meanwhile continued to record excellent singles, although the prophetically titled 'Baby It's Over' (1966) was their only further hit. Nelson recorded under the name of Jay Dee for Warner Brothers Records in 1973, and also as Jackie Lee, charting in the USA with 'The Duck' (1965), 'African Boo-Ga-Loo' (1968) and 'The Chicken' (1970). Relf wrote Love Unlimited's 1974 hit 'Walking In The Rain' and was latterly replaced by Bobby Garrett. The new duo continued to record together, and individually, during the 70s.

● ALBUMS: *Harlem Shuffle* (Tip/Sue 1966)★★★, *Bob And Earl* (Crestview/B&C 1969)★★, *Together* (Joy 1969)★★.

BOB B. SOXX AND THE BLUE JEANS

One of several groups created by producer Phil Spector, this short-lived trio consisted of two members of the Blossoms (Darlene Love and Fanita James), and soul singer Bobby Sheen. The Blue Jeans scored a US Top 10 hit in 1962 with a radical reading of 'Zip-A-Dee-Do-Dah', wherein the euphoric original was slowed to a snail-like pace. Its success spawned an album which mixed restructured standards ('The White Cliffs Of Dover', 'This Land Is Your Land') with original songs, of which 'Why Do Lovers Break Each Other's Heart?' and 'Not Too Young To Get Married' were also issued as singles. The group made a contribution to Spector's legendary *Christmas Album*.

● ALBUMS: *Zip-A-Dee-Doo-Dah* (Philles 1963)★★★.

BOBBETTES

The first all-female R&B group to have a major pop hit record was not the Chantels, as is popularly believed, but the Bobbettes. Their 'Mr. Lee' beat the Chantels' 'He's Gone' to the charts by one month and outranked it in the US pop charts. The Bobbettes formed in 1955 in Harlem, New York City, USA, at PS 109, where they attended school. Consisting of Emma Pought (b. 1944), her sister Jannie (b. 1945), Laura Webb (b. 1943), Helen Gathers (b. 1944) and Reather Dixon (b. 1945), the group was originally called the Harlem Queens. The girls were aged between 11 and 13 years at the time of the group's formation. In 1957 they appeared on a local television programme, which led to an audition for Atlantic Records. 'Mr. Lee' was a song the girls had written in honour of their fifth-grade teacher, although the lyrics were not as kind in their original version (in fact, their second chart single was titled 'I Shot Mr. Lee'). The infectious 'Mr. Lee' was released in the summer of 1957 and ascended to number 6 in the US chart. Follow-up singles on Atlantic did not chart; the Bobbettes' subsequent singles were issued on the Triple-X, Gone, Jubilee, Diamond and RCA Records labels. Although their last chart success was in 1961, four of the original members were still performing together in the late 80s.

● COMPILATIONS: *Mr Lee & Other Big Hits* (Revival 1989)★★★.

BOFILL, ANGELA

b. 1954, West Bronx, New York City, USA, Bofill began writing songs at the age of 12. She formed her first group while still at high school, the Puerto Rican Supremes, which performed in church and local school dances. Her father, another Latin music singer, had once sung with Cuban bandleader Machito. After graduating from the Manhattan School of Music she toured with Ricardo Morrero and recorded her first single, 'My Friend', which earned her a nomination as best Latin female vocalist from *Latin New York* magazine. Encouraged by this success, she embarked on a solo career, writing and performing the jazz suite 'Under The Moon And Over The Sky', in conjunction with the Brooklyn Academy of Music. She then became lead vocalist with the Dance Theater of Harlem Chorus, and performed alongside Stan Getz and Benny Goodman at Madison Square Garden.

Following an introduction by Dave Valentin, she was signed as a soloist with Dave Grusin's GRP record label. The debut *Angie* included a reworking of 'Under The Moon', as well as 'Baby, I Need Your Love' and 'The Only Thing I Would Wish For'. Straying from jazz, Bofill worked in more conventional soul and R&B territory on her albums for Arista, where she teamed with producer Narada Michael Waldren before the System production team helmed her final three efforts for the label. She moved to Capitol later in the decade, where producers including Norman Connors were invited to assist. Bofill continued to tour widely between recording sessions, often with the New York Jazz Explosion, and also guested on Stanley Clarke's 'Where Do We Go' cut (from his *Hideaway* album). Although she has yet to chart a hit single outside the *Billboard* R&B lists, she has recorded impressive albums in the 90s within the jazz-soul style, and has established herself as an accomplished vocalist.

● ALBUMS: *Angie* (GRP 1978)★★★, *Angel Of The Night* (GRP 1979)★★, *Something About You* (Arista 1981)★★★, *Too Tough* (Arista 1983)★★★, *Teaser* (Arista 1983)★★, *Let Me Be The One* (Arista 1984)★★★, *Tell Me Tomorrow* (Arista 1985)★★, *Intuition* (Capitol 1988)★★★, *I Wanna Love Somebody* (Jive 1993)★★★, *Love In Slow Motion* (Cachet/Shanachie 1996)★★★.

● COMPILATIONS: *Best Of Angela Bofill* (Arista 1986)★★★, *Best Of Angie (Next Time I'll Be Sweeter)* (Arista 1991)★★★.

Bohannon, Hamilton

b. 7 March 1942, Newnam, Georgia, USA, Bohannon graduated from Clark College with a BA in musical education and went into teaching before accepting an invitation to join a band that also included Jimi Hendrix, as drummer. He came to the attention of Stevie Wonder, who appointed him drummer in his touring band in 1965. Over the next two years Bohannon's style impressed the hierarchy at Motown to such an extent that they made him top bandleader, responsible for live arrangements for all Motown's top acts. When Motown relocated to Los Angeles, Bohannon stayed in Detroit, assembling his own band. Having signed with Brunswick, he went on to have huge success in the UK with 'South African Man', 'Disco Stomp' (a Top 10 hit) and 'Foot Stompin' Music'. Ironically quiet during the disco boom, he resurfaced with Mercury Records in 1978, returning to the charts with 'Let's Start The Dance', featuring Carolyn Crawford. Despite one further hit (in 1982 with 'Let's Start To Dance Again'), Bohannon's sound and appeal had been overtaken by countless others.

● ALBUMS: *South African Man* (Brunswick 1975)★★★★, *Insides Out* (Brunswick 1975)★★★, *Dance Your Ass Off* (Brunswick 1976)★★★, *Phase II* (Mercury 1977)★★, *Summertime Groove* (Mercury 1978)★★★, *Cut Loose* (Mercury 1979)★★, *One Step Ahead* (Phase II 1980)★★★, *Bohannon's Drive* (Compleat 1983)★★, *Make Your Body Move* (Compleat 1983)★★, *Motions* (MCA 1984)★★, *Here Comes Bohannon* (MCA 1989)★★★, *It's Time To Jam* (South Bound 1990)★★.

● COMPILATIONS: *Bohannon's Best* (Brunswick 1975)★★★★.

Bonds, Gary 'U.S.'

b. Gary Anderson, 6 June 1939, Jacksonville, Florida, USA. Having initially sung in various gospel groups, Bonds embraced secular music upon moving to Norfolk, Virginia. A successful spell in the region's R&B clubs resulted in a recording contract with local entrepreneur Frank Guida, whose cavernous production techniques gave Bonds' releases their distinctive sound. The ebullient 'New Orleans' set the pattern for the artist's subsequent recordings and its exciting, 'party' atmosphere reached an apogee on 'Quarter To Three', a US chart-topper and the singer's sole million-seller. Between 1961 and 1962 Bonds enjoyed further similar-sounding hits with 'School Is Out', 'School Is In', 'Dear Lady Twist' and 'Twist Twist Senora', but his career then went into sharp decline. He toured the revival circuit until 1978 when long-time devotee Bruce Springsteen joined the singer onstage during a live engagement. Their friendship resulted in *Dedication*, produced by Springsteen and E Street Band associate Miami Steve Van Zandt. The former contributed three original songs to the set, one of which, 'This Little Girl', reached the US Top 10 in 1981. Their collaboration was maintained with *On The Line*, which included Bonds' version of the Box Tops' 'Soul Deep', but he later asserted his independence with the self-produced *Standing In The Line Of Fire*. Little has been heard of him in the 90s.

● ALBUMS: *Dance 'Til Quarter To Three* (Legrand/Top Rank 1961)★★★, *Twist Up Calypso* (Legrand/Stateside 1962)★★★, *Dedication* (EMI America 1981)★★★, *On The Line* (EMI America 1982)★★, *Gary 'U.S.' Bonds Meets Chubby Checker* (EMI 1983)★★, *Standing In The Line Of Fire* (Phoenix 1984)★★.

● COMPILATIONS: *Greatest Hits Of Gary 'U.S.' Bonds* (Legrand/Stateside 1962)★★★★, *Certified Soul* (Rhino 1982)★★, *The School Of Rock 'n' Roll: The Best Of Gary 'U.S' Bonds* (Rhino 1990)★★★★, *Take Me Back To New Orleans* (Ace 1995)★★★, *The Best Of Gary U.S. Bonds* (EMI 1996)★★★★.

● FILMS: *It's Trad, Dad* aka *Ring-A-Ding Rhythm* (1962).

Booker T. And The MGs

Formed in Memphis, Tennessee, USA, in 1962 as a spin-off from the Mar-Keys, the group comprised Booker T. Jones (b. 12 November 1944, Memphis, Tennessee, USA; organ), Steve Cropper (b. 21 October 1941, Willow Spring, Missouri, USA; guitar), Lewis Steinberg (bass) and Al Jackson Jr. (b. 27 November 1934, Memphis, Tennessee, USA, d. 1 October 1975, Memphis, Tennessee, USA; drums). 'Green Onions', the MGs' renowned first hit, evolved out of a blues riff they had improvised while waiting to record a jingle. Its simple, smoky atmosphere, punctuated by Cropper's cutting guitar, provided the blueprint for a series of excellent records, including 'Jellybread', 'Chinese Checkers', 'Soul Dressing', 'Mo' Onions' and 'Hip Hug-Her'. Pared to the bone, this sparseness accentuated the rhythm, particularly when Steinberg was replaced on bass by Donald 'Duck' Dunn (b. 24 November 1941, Memphis, Tennessee, USA). Their intuitive interplay became the bedrock of classic Stax, the foundation on which the label and studio sound was built. The quartet appeared on all of the company's notable releases, including 'In The Midnight Hour' (Wilson Pickett), 'Hold On I'm Comin'' (Sam And Dave) and 'Walkin' The Dog' (Rufus Thomas), on which Jones also played saxophone. Although Jones divided his time between recording and studying at Indiana University (he subsequently earned a BA in music), the MGs (Memphis Group) continued to chart consistently in their own right. 'Hang 'Em High' (1968) and 'Time Is Tight' (1969) were both US Top 10 singles, while as late as 1971 'Melting Pot' climbed into the same Top 50. The group split that year; Jones moved to California in semi-retirement, recording with his wife, Priscilla, while his three ex-colleagues remained in Memphis. In 1973 Jackson and Dunn put together a reconstituted group. Bobby Manuel and Carson Whitsett filled out the line-up, but the resultant album, *The MGs*, was a disappointment. Jackson, meanwhile, maintained his peerless reputation, particularly with work for Al Green and Syl Johnson, but tragically in 1975, he was shot dead in his Memphis home after disturbing intruders. Cropper, who had released a solo album in 1971, *With A Little Help From My Friends*, set up his TMI studio/label and temporarily seemed content with a low-key profile. He latterly rejoined Dunn, ex-Bar-Kay drummer Willie Hall and the returning Jones for *Universal Language*. Cropper and Dunn also played musicians' roles in the film *The Blues Brothers* in 1980. During the late 70s UK R&B revival, 'Green Onions' was reissued and became a Top 10 hit in 1979. Jones's 1981 album, *I Want You*, reached the R&B charts. The group did, however, complete some British concert dates in 1990, and backed Neil Young in 1993. They were inducted into the Rock And Roll Hall Of Fame in 1992.

● ALBUMS: *Green Onions* (Stax 1962)★★★★, *Mo' Onions* (1963)★★★★, *Soul Dressing* (Stax 1965)★★★★, *My Sweet Potato* (1965)★★★, *And Now!* (Stax 1966)★★★, *In The Christmas Spirit* (Stax 1966)★★, *Hip Hug-Her* (Stax 1967)★★★, with the Mar-Keys *Back To Back* (Stax 1967)★★★, *Doin' Our Thing* (Stax 1968)★★★, *Soul Limbo* (Stax 1968)★★★, *Uptight* (Stax 1969)★★, *The Booker T. Set* (Stax 1969)★★★, *McLemore Avenue* (Stax 1970)★★, *Melting Pot* (Stax 1971)★★, as the MG's *The MGs* (Stax 1973)★★, *Memphis Sound* (Warners 1975)★★, *Union Extended* (Warners 1976)★★, *Time Is Tight* (Warners 1976)★★, *Universal Language* (Asylum 1977)★.
Solo: Booker T. Jones *Try And Love Again* (A&M 1978)★★, *The Best Of You* (A&M 1980)★★, *I Want You* (A&M 1981)★★, *The Runaway* (MCA 1989)★★, *That's The Way It Should Be* (Columbia 1994)★★.

● COMPILATIONS: *The Best Of Booker T. And The MGs* (Atlantic 1968)★★★★★, *Booker T. And The MG's Greatest Hits* (Stax 1970)★★★★, *The Best Of Booker T And The MG's (Very Best Of)* (Rhino 1993)★★★★★, *Play The Hip Hits* (Stax/Ace 1995)★★★★.

Booker, James

b. 17 December 1939, New Orleans, Louisiana, USA, d. 8 November 1983, New Orleans, Louisiana, USA. As an exceptionally talented child, Booker studied classical piano, but balanced his virtuosity with blues and boogie learned from Isidore 'Tuts' Washington and Edward Frank. In his early teens he appeared on radio WMRY and formed a band he called Booker Boy And The Rhythmaires. He made his first record for Imperial in 1954, 'Doin' The Hambone', and 'Thinkin' 'Bout My Baby', produced by Dave Bartholomew, led to sessions for Fats Domino, Smiley Lewis and Lloyd Price, among others. Booker made just two more singles during the 50s, 'Heavenly Angel' for Chess and 'Open The Door' for Ace. In 1959 he enrolled at Southern University to study music. A year later, he signed to Peacock and had the only hit of his career, an organ instrumental called 'Gonzo', which reached number 3 in the R&B charts. Further singles such as 'Tubby' and 'Big Nick' failed to achieve similar success. By this point, however, drugs had added to his psychological problems and his work became erratic. In 1970 he served time in Angola State Penitentiary for drug possession. His appearance at the 1975 Jazz Fest led to a recording contract for Island Records. Other records appeared sporadically but his deteriorating mental state and an inability to control his drug problem led to a fatal heart attack. His highly individual style can sometimes be heard in the work of Harry Connick Jnr., who was a student and friend of Booker's.

● ALBUMS: *Junco Partner* (Island/Hannibal 1975/1993)★★★, *New Orleans Piano Wizard Live!* (Rounder 1981)★★★, *Classified* (Rounder 1982)★★★, *Mr Mystery* (Sundown 1985)★★★.

● COMPILATIONS: *Spirit Of New Orleans: The Genius Of Dave Bartholomew* (EMI America 1992)★★★★, *Resurrection Of The Bayou Maharajah* (Rounder 1993)★★★, *Spiders On The Keys* (Rounder 1993)★★★.

Bostic, Earl

b. Eugene Earl Bostic, 25 April 1913, Tulsa, Oklahoma, USA, d. 28 October 1965. The romantic and smooth sound of Bostic's band, usually featuring the vibes of Gene Redd, piano of Fletcher Smith, bass of Margo Gibson, drums of Charles Walton, guitar of Alan Seltzer, and the marvellous alto saxophone of Bostic, was one of the great and distinctive sounds of both R&B and pop music, and his records became perennials on the juke-boxes during the 50s. Bostic was best known for his alto saxophone sound but he also played tenor saxophone, flute and clarinet on his records. Bostic was formally trained in music, having received a degree in music theory from Xavier University. He moved to New York City and formed a jazz combo in 1938. In the early 40s he was playing in the Lionel Hampton band. He left Hampton in 1945 to form a combo, recording tracks for Majestic, but did not make much of an impression until he signed with New York-based Gotham in 1948. He had immediate success with 'Temptation' (US R&B number 10). During the 50s he recorded prolifically for Cincinnati-based King Records, and had two big singles, 'Sleep' (US R&B number 6) and 'Flamingo' (US R&B number 1), in 1951. The smooth but perky performance on the latter became his signature tune and made him something of a Beach Music artist in the Carolinas.

● ALBUMS: *The Best of Earl Bostic* (King 1956)★★★★, *Bostic For You* (King 1956)★★★, *Alto-Tude* (King

1956)★★★, *Dancetime* (King 1957)★★★★, *Let's Dance With Earl Bostic* (King 1957)★★★, *Invitation To Dance* (King 1957)★★★, *C'mon & Dance With Earl Bostic* (King 1958)★★★, *Bostic Rocks-Hits From The Swing Age* (King 1958)★★★, *Bostic Showcase Of Swinging Dance Hits* (King 1958)★★★, *Alto Magic In Hi-Fi* (King 1958)★★, *Sweet Tunes Of The Fantastic 50's* (King 1959)★★★, *Workshop* (King 1959)★★★, *Sweet Tunes Of The Roaring 20's* (King 1959)★★, *Sweet Tunes Of the Swinging 30's* (King 1959)★★★, *Sweet Tunes Of The Sentimental 40's* (King 1959)★★, *Musical Pearls* (King 1959)★★★, *Hit Tunes Of The Big Broadway Shows* (King 1960)★★, *25 Years Of Rhythm And Blues Hits* (King 1960)★★★, *By Popular Demand* (King 1962)★★★, *Earl Bostic Plays Bossa Nova* (King 1963)★★★, *Jazz As I Feel It* (King 1963)★★, *The Best Of Earl Bostic* (King 1964)★★★, *New Sound* (King 1964)★★★, *The Great Hits Of 1964* (King 1964)★★★, *The Song Is Not Ended* (Philips 1967)★★★, *Harlem Nocturne* (King 1969)★★, *Sax'O Boogie* (Oldie Blues 1984)★★, *Blows A Fuse* (Charly 1985)★★★, *That's Earl, Brother* (Spotlite 1985)★★★, *Bostic Rocks* (Swingtime 1987)★★★, *Dance Time* (Sing 1988)★★★, *Bostic For You* (Sing 1988)★★★, *Dance Music From The Bostic Workshop* (Charly 1988)★★★, *Flamingo* (Charly 1995)★★★.

Boys

The Los Angeles, California, USA family pop group the Boys comprised Tajh Ustadi Abdulsamad (b. 12 August 1976, Northridge, California, USA), Khiry Hasan Abdulsamad (b. 10 November 1973, Northridge, California, USA), Bilal Dinari Abdulsamad (b. 17 April 1979, Northridge, California, USA) and Hakeem Saheed Abdulsamad (b. 3 June 1975, Northridge, California, USA). An obvious attempt to follow in the footsteps of the Jackson Five, the Boys enjoyed fleeting fame as an accomplished vocal R&B act, though their naïvety shone through in interviews. Bilal once informed *Smash Hits* that he would like to 'get rid of all wars and I would tell the Russians to disable those big bombs, what do you call them? Nuclear bombs, that's it.' Signed to Motown Records, they enjoyed minor UK chart hits in 1988 with 'Dial My Heart' and in 1990 with 'Crazy'. Their debut album, *Message From The Boys*, charted at number 33 in the US *Billboard* charts in April 1989, but in common with many Motown acts of the period they failed to use their initial success as a launching pad to a stable career.

● ALBUMS: *Message From The Boys* (Motown 1989)★★★, *The Boys* (Motown 1990)★★, *The Saga Continues* (Motown 1992)★★.

Boyz II Men

This versatile close-harmony teenage soul group were a major success in the USA during the early 90s, beginning with their Top 3 debut single 'Motownphilly'. They comprise Wanya 'Squirt' Morris (b. 29 July 1973, Philadelphia, USA), Michael 'Bass' McCary (b. 16 December 1972, Philadelphia, USA), Shawn 'Slim' Stockman (b. 26 September 1972) and Nathan 'Alex-Vanderpool' Morris (b. 18 June 1971). They met at the Philadelphia High School Of Creative And Performing Arts, forming the band in 1988. Michael Bivins of Bell Biv Devoe took the group under his wing and brought them, fittingly, to Motown Records. Their debut album was one side dance, one side ballad, and was a huge seller in the USA. By the middle of 1993 the album was still high on the US chart with sales of over seven million copies. The formula was repeated with uncanny accuracy in 1994, their follow-up (imaginatively titled *II*) becoming a huge hit, and less than a year later it had sold eight million copies in the USA. It spawned three massive-selling number 1 singles in 'I'll Make Love To You', 'On Bended Knee' and 'One Sweet Day' (with Mariah Carey).

● ALBUMS: *Cooleyhighharmony* (Motown 1991)★★★, *II* (Motown 1994)★★★★, *Remix, Remake, Remember* (Motown 1996)★★★★, *Evolution* (Motown 1997)★★★.

● VIDEOS: *Then II Now* (Motown Video 1994).

Boze, Calvin

Remembered as being a senior - and the school bandleader - by Charles Brown at Prairie View College in Texas, trumpeter Boze (or Boaz, as his name appears earlier) first came to the public's attention on recordings with the west coast band's of Russell Jacquet (Globe) and Marvin Johnson (G&G). In 1949, he began recording as a vocalist in a strong Louis Jordan vein for Aladdin Records with Maxwell Davis and his band. Although he never made a huge impression on the R&B charts, his recordings were all solid, earthy R&B jive advocating 'Working With My Baby' (who made his lolly pop, and his peanut brittle), and 'Waiting And Drinking'. He is best known for the classic 'Safronia B' and the b-side 'Angel City Blues', as well as a couple of songs he wrote for old homeboy Charles Brown - 'Texas Blues' and 'Hot Lips And Seven Kisses' - also recorded for Aladdin.

● COMPILATIONS: *Havin' A Ball* (Moonshine 1988)★★★, *Choo Choo's Bringing My Baby Home* (Route 66 1989)★★★.

Bradford, Geoff

b. *c*.1934. Bradford (aka Jeff), an accomplished guitarist, served an apprenticeship in several early British R&B bands, including Blues By Six and Alexis Korner's Blues Incorporated. He was also a part of the embryonic Rolling Stones, but left the line-up following the inclusion of what he considered to be 'commercial' material. Bradford then joined Cyril Davies' R&B All-Stars, the breakaway group from Alexis Korner's Blues Incorporated, which mutated into Long John Baldry's Hoochie Coochie Men upon Davies' death from leukaemia in 1964. Baldry subsequently dissolved this band, leaving Bradford free to reform the Original All-Stars with bassist Cliff Barton. From then on, Bradford worked as a backing musician for several visiting blues performers. Despite a low public profile, Bradford enjoys the respect of his peers and has continued to forge a career in the London club circuit.

● ALBUMS: *Magnolia* (Christabel 1986)★★★, *Rockin' The Blues* (Black Lion 1988)★★.

Bradley, Jan

b. Addie Bradley, 6 July 1943, Byhalia, Mississippi, USA. Bradley is best known for the 1963 pop/R&B hit 'Mama

Didn't Lie'. She took singing lessons as a child and was discovered in 1961 by Don Talty, then manager of guitarist Phil Upchurch. Talty signed her to Chess Records and enlisted the songwriting talents of a young Curtis Mayfield, himself riding high at the time with the Impressions. Mayfield penned 'We Girls', a local hit in the Chicago area. In 1963 he returned with 'Mama Didn't Lie', an R&B dance track that reached number 14 on the pop charts. Bradley was unable to follow her one national hit with any others, and by the end of the 60s had left showbusiness. She was employed as a social worker in the late 80s, while her single contribution to pop music was still popular on US radio stations that played vintage rock 'n' roll.

Bradshaw, Tiny

b. Myron Bradshaw, 23 September 1905, Youngstown, Ohio, USA, d. 26 November 1958. While studying psychology at Wilberforce University, Ohio, Bradshaw became involved in the campus's flourishing musical subculture. He joined Horace Henderson's Collegians as the band's singer. In 1932 he went to New York where he played drums with several bands, including the Savoy Bearcats and the Mills Blue Rhythm Band. In the same year he sang with Luis Russell and then formed his own band which toured extensively, playing several long engagements at hotels and dancehalls. During this period, Bradshaw modelled his style on that of Cab Calloway, both men having spent time in Marion Hardy's Alabamians. He had some success on record in the 30s, notably with 'Shout, Sister, Shout' and 'The Darktown Strutters' Ball'. During World War II Bradshaw led a US Army big band. After the war he kept a band together by adapting to the popularity of R&B, attracting the attention of several young white performers, among whom was Buddy Holly. In the mid-50s poor health forced Bradshaw to fold his band and he died in November 1958. A lively entertainer, Bradshaw never quite made the big time. Indeed, at one time he suffered the mild indignity of being billed as the 'super Cab Calloway'. Bradshaw often hired first-rate musicians and arrangers for his bands, among them Shad Collins, Russell Procope, Happy Caldwell, Charlie Shavers, Billy Kyle, Charlie Fowlkes, Bobby Plater, Shadow Wilson, Fred Radcliffe, Sonny Stitt, Gil Fuller, Big Nick Nicholas, Gigi Gryce and Red Prysock.

● COMPILATIONS: *Tiny Bradshaw 1934* (Harlequin 1987)★★★, *The Great Composer (1950-58)* (King 1988)★★★★, *Stomping Room Only* (Krazy Kat 1984)★★, *Breaking Up The House (50s)* (Charly 1985)★★★, *A Tribute To The Late Tiny Bradshaw* (Sing 1987)★★, *I'm A High Ballin' Daddy* (Juxebox Lil 1988)★★★, *Bird Nest On The Ground* (Antone's 1994)★★★.

Brand New Heavies

Simon Bartholomew and Andy Levy are the central duo behind Ealing, London band the Brand New Heavies, alongside drummer Jan Kincaid and (initially) keyboardist Ceri Evans. They had already suffered one failed contract with Acid Jazz, who tried to launch them as a 'rare groove' outfit, before they joined with US label Delicious Vinyl. The latter's management put them in touch with N'Dea Davenport (b. Georgia, USA), who had previously provided backing vocals for George Clinton, Bruce Willis and appeared in videos for Young MC and Madonna's former band the Breakfast Club. Word spread throughout the USA of their liaison, and soon hip-hop teams picked up on the group. They were sampled heavily on a number of early 90s rap records, before inviting members of that community to provide guest raps on their second album, *Heavy Rhyme Experience: Vol. 1*. These included Black Sheep, Gang Starr, Grand Puba, Main Source, Kool G. Rap, Ed.Og, Master Ace, Tiger and Pharcyde. Ceri Evans left the group in January 1992 to undertake production work for Alison Limerick and Galliano, recording solo as Sunship ('Muthafuckin''/'The 13th Key', for Dorado). Their huge success in the USA was soon mirrored in the UK, with the singles 'Dream On Dreamer' and 'Midnight At The Oasis' reaching the Top 20 in 1994. Soul singer Siedah Garrett became the new front-person in 1997 after Davenport's departure the previous year, the group enjoying further chart success with their version of James Taylor's 'You've Got A Friend'.

● ALBUMS: *Brand New Heavies* (Acid Jazz 1990)★★★, *Heavy Rhyme Experience: Vol. 1* (ffrr 1992)★★★, *Brother Sister* (ffrr 1994)★★★, *Original Flava* (Acid Jazz 1995)★★, *Excursions: Remixes & Rare Grooves* (Delicious Vinyl 1996)★★, *Shelter* (London 1997)★★★.

Brandy

b. Brandy Norwood, 11 February 1979, McComb, Mississippi, USA. Among the best of the 90s crop of R&B's 'new jill swingers', Brandy is actually much less sex and violence-obsessed than most of her peers. Her career in entertainment began early - at the age of 15 she was nominated for a Youth In Film Award for her portrayal of schoolgirl Denesha in the ABC television situation comedy *Thea*. Her breakthrough in music followed quickly. Her self-titled debut album, produced by Keith Crouch and the Somethin' For The People collective, reached number 6 in the R&B album charts, selling over 1.3 million copies. It included the successful crossover single, 'I Wanna Be Down'. That song was then transformed in an alternative version marketed specifically at rap fans. The 'Hyman Rhythm Hip Hop Remix' featured guest rhymes from Queen Latifah, MC Lyte and Yo Yo. Released on the b-side of the follow-up single, 'Baby', it helped the a-side become one of the fastest-selling R&B number 1s in recent US chart history. Both single and album won awards at the inaugural Soul Train Lady of Soul Awards in Los Angeles in 1995. Regarded as a comparatively wholesome performer, she was also named spokeswoman for the 1996 Sears/Seventeen Peak Performance Scholarship Program and tour, which supports the efforts of young women to achieve specific goals. In 1996 her brother, Ray-J, made his recording debut for Elektra Records.

● ALBUMS: *Brandy* (Atlantic 1994)★★★.

Brass Construction

Led by keyboards player and singer Randy Muller (b. Guyana), Brass Construction was a leading group in the disco movement of the 70s. Muller originally formed the band in Brooklyn, New York, as Dynamic Soul, mixing funk, salsa and reggae rhythms with a more orthodox jazz line-up to create a highly danceable sound. Renamed Brass Construction, the nine-piece group was signed by United Artists in 1975. The members included Michael Grudge (b. Jamaica) and Jesse Ward Jnr. (saxophones), Wayne Parris (b. Jamaica) and Morris Price (trumpets), Joseph Arthur Wong (b. Trinidad; guitar), Wade Williamson (bass), Larry Payton (drums) and percussionist Sandy Billups. With infectious polyrhythms and minimal, chanted vocals, the group's first release, 'Movin'', topped the R&B charts and was a pop Top 20 hit. It was followed by 'Changin'', 'Ha Cha Cha' and 'L-O-V-E-U', which were all bestsellers. Later singles were less successful, although successive Brass Construction albums rode the disco boom. Muller also wrote for and produced New York disco group Skyy and B.T. Express. The group's popularity dwindled in the 80s, although the remix craze brought numerous versions of their early hits into the clubs in 1988, including 'Ha Cha Cha (Acieed Mix)'.

● ALBUMS: *Brass Construction* (United Artists 1976)★★★, *Brass Construction II* (United Artists 1976)★★, *Brass Construction III* (United Artists 1977)★★, *Brass Construction IV* (United Artists 1978)★★, *Brass Construction 5* (United Artists 1979)★★, *Brass Construction 6* (United Artists 1980)★★, *Attitudes* (Liberty 1982)★★, *Conversations* (Capitol 1983)★★, *Renegades* (Capitol 1984)★★, *Conquest* (Capitol 1985)★★.

● COMPILATIONS: *Movin' - The Best Of Brass Construction* (Syncopate 1988)★★★.

Braxton, Toni

b. 7 October 1968, Severn, Maryland, USA. Braxton, with her four sisters, was signed to Arista Records in 1990 as the Braxtons. It was their 'The Good Life' single which brought them to the attention of producers L.A. And Babyface, who provided her with solo successes such as 'Another Sad Love Song' and 'You Mean The World To Me'. Though she has been widely described as the 'new Whitney Houston' (a fate that befalls many female vocalists), her vocal talent has found an audience in garage and house circles, causing her debut album to sell more than two million copies. She won a Grammy for Best New Artist in 1993. *Secrets* repeated the success of her debut, particularly in her homeland (eight million sales) where she threatens to make Whitney Houston appear to be 'the old Toni Braxton'.

● ALBUMS: *Toni Braxton* (Arista 1994)★★★, *Secrets* (Arista 1996)★★★.

● VIDEOS: *The Home Video* (1994).

Braxtons

Comprising Towanda, Trina and Tamar Braxton, the younger sisters of LaFace Records' Toni Braxton, the Braxtons launched their own career in the mid-90s as a hip-hop and soul-inspired vocal trio. The idea for the group developed when the sisters joined Toni on her concert and television appearances. Indeed, when the group was first launched in 1990 it had featured Toni, as well as a fifth sister, Traci. However, the group in this formation recorded only one single for Arista Records; 'Good Life' reached number 79 on *Billboard*'s Hot R&B chart, but was never followed up. The present trio would doubtless have remained members of the LaFace roster, but when Bryant Reid moved to a new A&R position at Atlantic Records, he persuaded the group to follow him. The group's Atlantic debut featured 11 original tracks with two cover versions, Diana Ross's 'The Boss' and Klymaxx's 'I'd Still Say Yes'. Production was supplied by R&B luminaries Jermaine Dupri, Darryl Simmons and Louie Vega, among others.

● ALBUMS: *So Many Ways* (Atlantic 1996)★★.

Brecker Brothers

Randy (b. 27 November 1945, Philadelphia, Pennsylvania, USA) and Michael Brecker (b. 29 March 1949, Philadelphia, Pennsylvania, USA) are two of the most in-demand musicians around, having supplied the horn licks to untold major records over the last 25 years. Randy originally attended Indiana University to study under David Baker, and undertook a lengthy State Department tour with the university's band, directed by Jerry Coker. He relocated to New York in 1966 and joined Blood, Sweat And Tears, staying for a year before joining up with Horace Silver's quintet. Michael, another Indiana University student, turned professional at the age of 19 with Edwin Birdsong's band, before teaming up with his older brother, Billy Cobham, Chuck Rainey and Will Lee in the pop-jazz co-operative Dreams. Both became in demand for session work (notably on Cobham's three Atlantic albums of the mid-70s), but by 1974, the brothers were ready to branch out on their own. They signed with Arista early the following year, releasing their debut, 'Sneakin' Up Behind You', in a style reminiscent of the Average White Band. It received heavy club rotation, although it was 'East River' from their second album that broke onto the singles charts in 1978. The group split in 1982, with both brothers recording solo albums in addition to session work (Michael with Ashford And Simpson and Spyro Gyra, Randy with Breakwater, among others). The success of the *Collection* issues reunited the brothers in 1992.

● ALBUMS: *The Brecker Brothers* (Arista 1975)★★★, *Back To Back* (Arista 1976)★★★, *Don't Stop The Music* (Arista 1977)★★★, *Heavy Metal Be-Bop* (Arista 1978)★★★, *Detente* (Arista 1980)★★★, *Straphangin'* (Arista 1981)★★, *Return Of The Brecker Brothers* (GRP 1992)★★★, *Out Of The Loop* (GRP 1994)★★.

● COMPILATIONS: *The Brecker Bros. Collection Volume One* (RCA 1989)★★★, *The Brecker Bros. Collection Volume Two* (RCA 1992)★★.

● VIDEOS: *Return Of The Brecker Brothers: Live In Barcelona* (1993).

Brenda And The Tabulations

This R&B vocal group from Philadelphia, Pennsylvania, USA, consisting of Brenda Payton, Jerry Jones, Eddie Jackson, and Maurice Coates, was recognizable for the fetchingly innocent-sounding vocals of Payton on a series of intensely sung ballads. Their biggest hit was their 1967 debut single on the Dionn label, 'Dry My Eyes' (number 8 US R&B chart, number 29 pop chart). Their most successful records were a remake of the Miracles' 'Who's

Lovin' You' (number 19 R&B) and 'When You're Gone' (number 27 R&B). Bernard Murphy joined the line-up in 1969, and, reorganized in 1970 around Brenda Payton, Pat Mercer, and Deborah Martin, the group achieved their biggest hit the following year with 'Right On The Tip Of My Tongue' (number 10 R&B, number 23 pop) on the Top & Bottom label. A stint at Epic produced no major hits, but in 1973 their excellent 'One Girl Too Late' (number 43 R&B) deserved far greater recognition and success. The group's last chart success was in 1977.

● ALBUMS: *Dry Your Eyes* (Dionn 1967)★★, *Brenda And The Tabulations* (Top & Bottom 1970)★★, *I Keep Coming Back For More* (Chocolate City 1977)★★.

BRISTOL, JOHNNY

b. 3 February 1939, Morgantown, North Carolina, USA. Bristol's career began within the nascent Tamla/Motown circle. He first recorded in 1960 as part of the duo of Johnny And Jackie (Jackie Beavers, whom Bristol met while in the US Air Force). On Gwen Gordy and Harvey Fuqua's Tri-Phi label, they recorded the original version of 'Someday We'll Be Together' (1961), which was a runaway success for the Supremes in 1969. Bristol remained with the company, and over the next 10 years, in a partnership with Harvey Fuqua, forged a successful career as a producer and songwriter with Edwin Starr, David Ruffin, Detroit Spinners, Stevie Wonder and Junior Walker. Bristol left Motown in 1973, and joined CBS Records as house producer, but despite that, was still unable to persuade them to release his solo album. He eventually achieved this by negotiating an outside contract with MGM Records, and relaunched his performing career with an international smash, 'Hang On In There Baby' (1974). Subsequent releases reinforced its machismo-based approach but lacked the depth and variety that the artist was able to produce for other performers. Despite a prolific work-rate, he was unable to repeat that early hit, except for a UK Top 40 hit in 1980, duetting with Ami Stewart on 'My Guy - My Girl'. After making singles for Ariola and Handshake Records in the 80s he briefly recorded for Ian Levine's Motor City label in 1989, issuing two UK singles.

● ALBUMS: *Hang On In There Baby* (MGM 1974)★★★, *Bristol's Creme* (Atlantic 1976)★★, *Free To Be Me* (Ariola Hansa 1981)★.

● COMPILATIONS: *The Best Of Johnny Bristol* (Polydor 1988)★★.

BROOKLYN BRIDGE

Johnny Maestro (b. John Mastrangelo, 7 May 1939, Brooklyn, New York, USA) had been the lead singer of the Crests in the 50s, and his voice was behind one of the most memorable doo-wop songs ever, '16 Candles', in 1958. He was also the featured vocalist on follow-up hits such as 'The Angels Listened In', 'Step By Step' and 'Trouble In Paradise'. When Maestro left the group to go solo in 1961, his career took a downturn. In 1968 he formed a new group, Brooklyn Bridge, with singers Les Cauchi, Fred Ferrara, both formerly of the Del-Satins (once the backing group for Dion), and an eight-member backing band, formerly known as the Rhythm Method. The new group fashioned an orchestral, more modernized style of doo-wop, and with the dramatic vocals of Maestro, were signed to Buddah Records. Their first single was a Jimmy Webb song, 'The Worst That Could Happen', which became a number 3 US hit at the beginning of 1969. The group achieved a total of seven chart singles and two albums by the end of 1970. They became a mainstay at revival concerts featuring old rock 'n' roll. Maestro continued to front the band through many personnel changes, and Brooklyn Bridge were still a top concert and club attraction on the east coast in the early 90s.

● ALBUMS: *Brooklyn Bridge* (Buddah 1969)★★★, *The Second Brooklyn Bridge* (Buddah 1969)★★, with the Isley Brothers and Edwin Hawkins *Live At Yankee Stadium* (T-Neck 1969)★★, *Brooklyn Bridge* (1970)★★, *Bridge In Blue* (1972)★★.

BROTHERS JOHNSON

This duo featured George Johnson (b. 17 May 1953, Los Angeles, California, USA; guitar, vocals) and Louis Johnson (b. 13 April 1955, Los Angeles, California, USA; bass). Having previously worked with Billy Preston and appeared on Quincy Jones's 1975 US Top 20 album *Mellow Madness*, the duo signed to A&M Records. This hard-funk duo had three notable disco and US Top 10 hits with 'I'll Be Good To You' (1976), 'Strawberry Letter 23' (1977) and 'Stomp!' (1980). A brief hiatus, involving the duo in studio production and session work, came to an end with the recording of the not altogether successful *Kickin'*.

● ALBUMS: *Look Out For Number One* (A&M 1976)★★★, *Right On Time* (A&M 1977)★★★, *Blam!!* (A&M 1978)★★, *Light Up The Night* (A&M 1980)★★, *Winners* (A&M 1981)★★★, *Out Of Control* (A&M 1984)★★, *Kickin'* (A&M 1988)★★.

● COMPILATIONS: *Blast! (The Latest And The Greatest)* (A&M 1983)★★★.

BROTHERS OF SOUL

An R&B vocal group from Detroit, Michigan, USA, comprising Fred Bridges, Richard Knight, and Robert Eaton. Knight, who possessed a sweet, smooth voice, and Bridges, who had a rougher-hewn voice, tended to share the leads equally, and the group became known for their sweet vocal harmonies and romantic sound. The trio was originally a writing and producing act working with a Detroit label. In 1967, Chicago producer Ric Williams came to Detroit looking for songwriting talent for his recording artists, namely Ruby Andrews, Candace Love and Chuck Bernard. Williams immediately recruited Bridges, Knight and Eaton, who subsequently wrote, arranged, and produced many of Ruby Andrews' best hits, notably 'You Made A Believer Out Of Me'. The Brothers Of Soul first recorded on their own in 1967 as the Creations, but after changing their name the following year, they made their first impact with the Bridges-led 'Hurry Don't Linger' on Williams' Boo label. It was followed by their only national hit, the Knight-led 'I Guess That Don't Make Me A Loser' (number 32 R&B), which reached the charts in the spring of 1968. They had their second successful single with the Bridges-led 'You

Better Believe It' in 1970. Subsequent releases failed to find an audience and the group made their final records in 1971. The Brothers Of Soul continued together for several more years, working as one of Detroit's most in-demand vocal session groups; they were used on many of Holland/Dozier/Holland's Invictus/Hot Wax productions, notably with Freda Payne.

● COMPILATIONS: *I Guess That Don't Make Me A Loser* (Collectables 1995)★★★.

Brown Dots

A vocal group formed in 1944 by Ivory 'Deek' Watson (tenor singer for the Ink Spots, who left because of personality clashes), the Brown Dots' style, modelled on the Ink Spots, featured a high tenor lead and a talking deep bass. In contrast to the Ink Spots, however, the emphasis was more on the jive jump numbers - reflecting the interests of Watson - rather than the ballads. Original members, besides Watson, were Joe King (tenor), Pat Best (baritone and guitar), and Jimmy Gordon (bass), but within a few months King was replaced by Jimmie Nabbie. At first the group went by the name 'Ink Spots', but the courts, at the behest of the original group, prevented Watson from using the name, so he adopted the simple variation 'Brown Dots'. Recording for the New Jersey-based Manor Records, the Brown Dots produced some outstanding tracks, notably 'Let's Give Love Another Chance' and 'Just In Case You Change Your Mind', both led by Best, and 'For Sentimental Reasons', led by Nabbie. In 1948 Best, Gordon, and Nabbie left Watson and formed another group, the Sentimentalists. Watson recruited a new Brown Dots group, but was never able to sustain the group at its previous level of artistry and commercial appeal. Meanwhile, the Sentimentalists changed their name to the Four Tunes, and became one of the more popular vocal ensembles of the early 50s.

Brown, Bobby

b. Robert Beresford Brown, 5 February 1969, Roxbury, Massachusetts, USA. A former member of New Edition, Brown emerged in the late 80s as the king of New Jack Swing. Like many of the genre's stars, Brown is not gifted with either huge ability or personality, yet he has stamped his authority on the dance scene via a series of immaculately presented crossover singles. On his debut album he was joined by Larry Blackmon and John Luongo, but it was the follow-up set, and the seamless production technique of Teddy Riley and L.A. And Babyface, that pushed him high in the charts. Cuts such as the US number 1 'My Prerogative' were infectious, irresistible dance workouts, confirming Brown's presence as a commercial hot potato. He married Whitney Houston in July 1992, and has appeared in film roles, including a cameo in *Ghostbusters II*. He had a Top 10 UK hit with 'Two Can Play That Game' in 1995, the same year he was arrested on a felony charge. In 1996 he was arrested on a drink-driving charge and made an out-of-court settlement over an assualt charge, following which he began working again with the members of New Edition. A new album appeared at the end of 1997 amid further stories of marital strife and bad behaviour.

● ALBUMS: *King Of Stage* (MCA 1986)★★, *Don't Be Cruel* (MCA 1988)★★★★, *Dance! ... Ya Know It!* (MCA 1989)★★★★, *Bobby* (MCA 1992)★★★, *Forever* (MCA 1997)★★★.

● VIDEOS: *His Prerogative* (MCA 1989).

Brown, Buster

b. Wayman Glasco, 15 August 1911, Cordele, Georgia, USA, d. 31 January 1976, Brooklyn, New York, USA. Brown played harmonica at local clubs and made a few recordings, including 'I'm Gonna Make You Happy' in 1943. Brown moved to New York in 1956 where he was discovered by Fire Records owner Bobby Robinson while working in a chicken and barbecue joint. In 1959, he recorded the archaic-sounding blues, 'Fannie Mae', whose tough harmonica riffs took it into the US Top 40. His similar-sounding 'Sugar Babe' (1961) was covered in the UK by Jimmy Powell. In later years he recorded for Checker and for numerous small labels including Serock, Gwenn and Astroscope.

● ALBUMS: *New King Of The Blues* (Fire 1959)★★★, *Get Down With Buster Brown* (Fire 1962)★★★, *Raise A Ruckus Tonite* (1976)★★★, *Good News* (Charly 1988)★★★.

Brown, Chuck, And The Soul Searchers

Formed in Washington, DC, USA, the group comprised Chuck Brown, John Buchanan (trombone, vocals), Donald Tillery (trumpet, vocals), Leroy Fleming (saxophone, flute, timbales), Le Ron Young (guitar), Chris Johnson (organ), Skip Fennell (keyboards), 'Jerry Wildman' Wilder (bass), Ricardo 'Tricky Sugar' Wellman (drums) and Gregory 'Bright Moments' Gerran (congas, percussion). This expansive soul group topped the R&B chart for four weeks in 1979 with the powerful 'Bustin' Loose, Part 1'. The dance-orientated single also reached the pop chart, but follow-up releases, 'Game Seven' and 'Sticks And Stones', failed to emulate its success. Brown subsequently switched record labels, and in 1984 enjoyed another US soul Top 30 hit with 'We Need Some Money (Bout Money)'. This was the group's last chart entry to date. During the mid-80s the Future label released four excellent Chuck Brown And The Soul Searchers EPs.

● ALBUMS: *Bustin' Loose* (Source 1979)★★★, *This Is A Journey Into Time* (1993)★★.

Brown, Horace

b. Charlotte, North Carolina, USA. The first signing to Motown Records under the 90s stewardship of Andre Harrell, southern soul singer Horace Brown had first been contracted to Harrell's Uptown Records. The son of a Baptist minister, he came to their attention in 1991 when DeVante Swing of Jodeci received a copy of Brown's demo tape from a friend. Significantly, Brown sang, played all the instruments and wrote the music on the cassette. The following year he was flown to Los Angeles to co-write and sing backing vocals for Christopher Williams' 'All I See' single. Thereafter, Harrell, who was at the session, signed him to Uptown. He recorded an album for the label, but it was never

released. In fact, the only product that emerged from his three years at the label was his 1994 debut single, 'Taste Your Love'. This peaked at number 56 in the *Billboard* R&B charts, but failed to secure any mainstream acclaim. Brown was frustrated at the label's concentration on platinum-selling artists such as Mary J. Blige and Jodeci, but was more than happy to move with Harrell to Motown in 1996. 'I can't believe I've been given the chance to be a part of that history', he told *Billboard* magazine. His first recordings for the label were two singles, 'One For The Money' and 'Enjoy Yourself', which accompanied his self-titled debut album in 1996. The album included a duet with Faith Evans on 'Doing Wrong', and 'Tell Me', a collaboration with Sean 'Puffy' Combs.
● ALBUMS: *Horace Brown* (Motown 1996)★★★.

BROWN, JAMES

b. 3 May 1928, Barnwell, South Carolina, USA. Brown claims he was born in 1933 in Macon, Georgia. 'The Hardest Working Man In Show-Business', 'The Godfather Of Soul', 'The Minister Of The New New Super Heavy Funk' – such sobriquets only hint at the protracted James Brown legend. Convicted of theft at the age of 16, he was imprisoned at the Alto Reform School, but secured an early release on the approbation of local singer Bobby Byrd. Brown later joined his group, the Gospel Starlighters, who evolved into the Flames after embracing R&B. In 1955 they recorded a demo of 'Please Please Please' at WIBB, a Macon, Georgia radio station. Local airplay was such that talent scout Ralph Bass signed the group to the King/Federal company. A re-recorded version of the song was issued in March 1956. Credited to 'James Brown And The Famous Flames', it eventually climbed to number 5 in the US R&B list. Further releases fared poorly until 1958, when 'Try Me' rose to number 1 in the same chart. Once again Brown found it difficult to maintain this level of success, but 'I'll Go Crazy' and 'Think' (both 1960) put his progress on a surer footing. From thereon, until 1977, almost every 'official' single charted. However, it was an album, *Live At The Apollo* (1962), that assuredly established the singer. Raw, alive and uninhibited, this shattering collection confirmed Brown as the voice of black America - every track on the album is a breathtaking event. More than 30 years on, with all the advances in recording technology, this album stands as one of the greatest live productions of all time. His singles continued to enthrall: energetic songs such as 'Night Train' and 'Shout And Shimmy' contrasted with such slower sermons as 'I Don't Mind' and 'Bewildered', but it was the orchestrated weepie, 'Prisoner Of Love' (1963), that gave Brown his first US Top 20 pop single. Such eminence allowed Brown a new manoeuvrability. Dissatisfied with his record label King, he ignored contractual niceties and signed with Smash Records. By the time his former outlet had secured an injunction, 'Out Of Sight' had become another national hit. More importantly, however, the single marked the beginning of a leaner, tighter sound that would ultimately discard accepted western notions of harmony and structure. This innovative mid-60s period is captured on film in his electrifying performance on the *TAMI Show*.

Throughout the 60s, Brown proclaimed an artistic freedom with increasingly unconventional songs, including 'Papa's Got A Brand New Bag', 'I Got You (I Feel Good)', 'It's A Man's Man's Man's World' (with a beautifully orchestrated string section) and 'Money Won't Change You'. In 1967 Alfred Ellis replaced Nat Jones as Brown's musical director and 'Cold Sweat' introduced further radical refinements to the group's presentation. With Clyde Stubblefield on drums, 'Say It Loud – I'm Black And I'm Proud' (1968), 'Mother Popcorn' (1969), and 'Get Up (I Feel Like Being A) Sex Machine' (1970) were each stripped down to a nagging, rhythmic riff, over which the singer soared, sometimes screaming, sometimes pleading, but always with an assertive urgency. In 1971 Brown moved to Polydor Records and unveiled a new backing band, the JBs. Led by Fred Wesley, it featured such seasoned players as Maceo Parker and St. Clair Pinckney, as well as a new generation of musicians. Elsewhere, former bassist Bootsy Collins defected with other ex-members to George Clinton's Funkadelic. Such changes, coupled with Sly Stone's challenge, simply reinforced Brown's determination. He continued to enjoy substantial hits; in 1974 he had three successive number 1 R&B singles in 'The Payback', 'My Thang' and 'Papa Don't Take No Mess (Part 1)', and Brown also scored two film soundtracks, *Black Caesar* and *Slaughter's Big Rip Off*. However, as the decade progressed, his work became less compulsive, suffering a drop in popularity with the advent of disco. A cameo role in the movie *The Blues Brothers* marked time, and in 1980 Brown left the Polydor label. Subsequent releases on such smaller labels as TK, Augusta Sound and Backstreet were only marginally successful. However, Brown returned with a vengeance in 1986 (the year he was inducted into the Rock And Roll Hall Of Fame) with 'Livin' In America', the theme song from the *Rocky IV* film soundtrack. An international hit single, it was followed by two R&B Top 10 entries, 'How Do You Stop' (1987) and 'I'm Real' (1988), the latter of which inspired a compulsive album of the same name. The Brown resurrection was abruptly curtailed that same year when the singer was arrested after a high-speed car chase. Charged with numerous offences, including illegal possession of drugs and firearms, aggravated assault and failure to stop for the police, he was sentenced to six and a half years' imprisonment at the State Park Correctional Centre. He was released in 1991, having reportedly written new material while incarcerated.

Brown's considerable influence has increased with the advent of hip-hop. New urban-based styles are indebted to the raw funk espoused by 'The Godfather of Soul', while Stubblefield's rhythmic patterns, particularly those on 1970's 'Funky Drummer', have been heavily sampled, as have Brown's notorious whoops, screams, interjections and vocal improvisations. Artists as disparate as Public Enemy, George Michael, Sinead O'Connor and Candy Flip have featured beats taken from Brown's impressive catalogue. During the 90s he has continued to have further problems with the law and a continuing battle to quit drugs; in 1995 he was forced to cope with a tragic medical accident when his ex-wife Adrienne died during surgery for 'liposuction'. In January 1998 there were new fears for his own health, and he was treated in hospital for addiction to painkillers. Shortly afterwards he was arrested and charged for possession of marijuana and unlawful use of a firearm. Through all this he is still seen as one of the most dynamic performers of the century and a massive influence on most forms of black music - soul, hip-hop, funk, R&B and disco.

● ALBUMS: *Please Please Please* (King 1959)★★★, *Try Me* (King 1959)★★, *Think* (King 1960)★★★, *The Amazing James Brown* (King 1961)★★★, *James Brown Presents His Band/Night Train* (King 1961)★★★, *Shout And Shimmy* (King 1962)★★★, *James Brown And His Famous Flames Tour The USA* (King 1962)★★, *Excitement Mr Dynamite* (King 1962)★★★, *Live At The Apollo* (King 1963)★★★★★, *Prisoner Of Love* (King 1963)★★★, *Pure Dynamite! Live At The Royal* (King 1964)★★★, *Showtime* (Smash 1964)★★, *The Unbeatable James Brown* (King 1964)★★★, *Grits And Soul* (Smash 1964)★★, *Out Of Sight* (Smash 1964)★★★, *Papa's Got A Brand New Bag* (King 1965)★★★, *James Brown Plays James Brown Today And Yesterday* (Smash 1965)★★, *I Got You (I Feel Good)* (King 1966)★★★, *Mighty Instrumentals* (King 1966)★★, *James Brown Plays New Breed (The Boo-Ga-Loo)* (Smash 1966)★★, *Soul Brother No. 1: It's A Man's Man's Man's World* (King 1966)★★★, *James Brown Sings Christmas Songs* (King 1966)★★, *Handful Of Soul* (Smash 1966)★★, *The James Brown Show* (Smash 1967)★★, *Sings Raw Soul* (King 1967)★★★, *James Brown Plays The Real Thing* (Smash 1967)★★★, *Live At The Garden* (King 1967)★★, *Cold Sweat* (King 1967)★★★, *James Brown Presents His Show Of Tomorrow* (King 1968)★★★, *I Can't Stand Myself (When You Touch Me)* (King 1968)★★, *I Got The Feelin'* (King 1968)★★★, *Live At The Apollo, Volume 2* (King 1968)★★★★, *James Brown Sings Out Of Sight* (King 1968)★★★, *Thinking About Little Willie John And A Few Nice Things* (King 1968)★★★, *A Soulful Christmas* (King 1968)★★, *Say It Loud, I'm Black And I'm Proud* (King 1969)★★★★, *Gettin' Down To It* (King 1969)★★★, *The Popcorn* (King 1969)★★★, *It's A Mother* (King 1969)★★★, *Ain't It Funky* (King 1970)★★★, *Soul On Top* (King 1970)★★★, *It's A New Day - Let A Man Come In* (King 1970)★★★, *Sex Machine* (King 1970)★★★, *Hey America* (King 1970)★★★, *Super Bad* (King 1971)★★, *Sho' Is Funky Down Here* (King 1971)★★, *Hot Pants* (Polydor 1971)★★, *Revolution Of The Mind/Live At The Apollo, Volume 3* (Polydor 1971)★★★, *There It Is* (Polydor 1972)★★★, *Get On The Good Foot* (Polydor 1972)★★★, *Black Caesar* (Polydor 1973)★★★, *Slaughter's Big Rip-Off* (Polydor 1973)★, *The Payback* (Polydor 1974)★★★, *Hell* (Polydor 1974)★★★, *Reality* (Polydor 1975)★★★, *Sex Machine Today* (Polydor 1975)★★★, *Everybody's Doin' The Hustle And Dead On The Double Bump* (Polydor 1975)★★, *Hot* (Polydor 1976)★★★, *Get Up Offa That Thing* (Polydor 1976)★★, *Bodyheat* (Polydor 1976)★★, *Mutha's Nature* (Polydor 1977)★★★, *Jam/1980's* (Polydor 1978)★★★, *Take A Look At Those Cakes* (Polydor 1979)★★★, *The Original Disco Man* (Polydor 1979)★★★, *People* (Polydor 1980)★★★, *James Brown . . . Live/Hot On The One* (Polydor 1980)★★, *Soul Syndrome* (TK 1980)★★★★, *Nonstop!* (Polydor 1981)★★★, *Live In New York* (Audio Fidelity 1981)★★★, *Bring It On* (Churchill 1983)★★★, *Gravity* (Scotti Brothers 1986)★★★, *James Brown And Friends* (Polydor 1988)★★★, *I'm Real* (Scotti Brothers 1988)★★★, *Soul Session Live* (Scotti Brothers 1989)★★★★, *Love Over-Due* (Scotti Brothers 1991)★★★, *Universal James* (1993)★★, *Funky President* (1993)★★★, *Live At The Apollo 1995* (Scotti Brothers 1995)★★★.

● COMPILATIONS: *James Brown Soul Classics* (Polydor 1972)★★★, *Soul Classics, Volume 2* (Polydor 1973)★★★, *Solid Gold* (Polydor 1977)★★★, *The Fabulous James Brown* (HRB 1977)★★★, *Can Your Heart Stand It?* (Solid Smoke 1981)★★★, *The Best Of James Brown* (Polydor 1981)★★★★, *The Federal Years, Part 1* (Solid Smoke 1984)★★★★, *The Federal Years, Part 2* (Solid Smoke 1984)★★★, *Roots Of A Revolution* (1984)★★★, *Ain't That A Groove - The James Brown Story 1966-1969* (Polydor 1984)★★★, *Doing It To Death - The James Brown Story 1970-1973* (Polydor 1984)★★★, *Dead On The Heavy Funk 1974-1976* (Polydor 1985)★★★, *The CD Of JB: Sex Machine And Other Soul Classics* (Polydor 1985)★★★★, *James Brown's Funky People* (Polydor 1986)★★★★, *In The Jungle Groove* (Polydor 1986)★★★, *The CD Of JB (Cold Sweat And Other Soul Classics)* (Polydor 1987)★★★★, *James Brown's Funky People (Part 2)* (Polydor 1988)★★★, *Motherlode* (Polydor 1988)★★★, *Messin' With The Blues* (Polydor 1990)★★★, *20 All-Time Greatest Hits!* (Polydor 1991)★★★★, *Star Time* 4-CD box set (Polydor 1991)★★★★★, *The Greatest Hits Of The Fourth Decade* (Scotti Brothers 1992)★★★, *Chronicles - Soul Pride* (1993)★★★, *JB40: 40th Anniversary Collection* (Polydor 1996)★★★★, *On Stage* (Charly 1997)★★★.

● VIDEOS: *Video Biography* (Virgin Vision 1988), *Live In London: James Brown* (Virgin Vision 1988), *James Brown And Friends* (Video Collection 1988), *Live In Berlin* (Channel 5 1989), *Soul Jubilee* (MMG Video 1990), *Live On Stage (With Special Guest B.B. King)* (Old Gold 1990), *Sex Machine (The Very Best Of James Brown)* (Polygram Music Video 1991), *The Lost Years (Live In Santa Cruz)* (BMG Video 1991), *Live In New York* (Enteleky 1991), *James Brown Live* (MIA 1995).

● FURTHER READING: *James Brown: The Godfather Of Soul*, James Brown with Bruce Tucker. *Living In America: The Soul Saga Of James Brown*, Cynthia Rose. *James Brown: A Biography*, Geoff Brown.

● FILMS: *The Blues Brothers* (1980).

Brown, Maxine

b. Kingstree, South Carolina, USA. Having sung in two New York gospel groups, Brown made her recording debut on Nomar with 'All In My Mind'. A US hit in 1961, this uptown soul ballad was followed by 'Funny'. A period at ABC-Paramount then passed before Brown signed to Wand Records and proceeded to make a series of excellent singles. She is best recalled for 'Oh No Not My Baby' (1964), a beautifully written David Goffin and Carole King song that was later covered by Manfred Mann, Rod Stewart and Aretha Franklin. Brown also recorded with Chuck Jackson - their version of 'Something You Got' made the US R&B Top 10 - but her position at Wand was undermined by the company's preoccupation with Dionne Warwick. Releases on a new outlet,

Commonwealth United, resulted in two R&B chart entries, including the acclaimed 'We'll Cry Together' (1969). Maxine signed with Avco in 1971, but her work there failed to re-establish her former profile.

● ALBUMS: *The Fabulous Sound Of Maxine Brown* (Wand 1962)★★★, *Spotlight On Maxine Brown* (Wand 1964)★★★, *We'll Cry Together* (Common 1969)★★★.

● COMPILATIONS: *Maxine Brown's Greatest Hits* (Wand 1964)★★★, *One In A Million* (Kent/Ace 1984)★★★, *Like Never Before* Wand recordings(Kent/Ace 1985)★★★, *Oh No Not My Baby - The Best Of ...* (Kent/Ace 1990)★★★, *Maxine Brown's Greatest Hits* (Tomato 1995)★★★.

Brown, Nappy

b. Napoleon Brown Culp, 12 October 1929, Charlotte, North Carolina, USA. Brown began his career as a gospel singer, but moved to R&B when an appearance in Newark, New Jersey, led to a recording contract with Savoy in 1954. A deep-voiced, highly individual R&B singer, he had a number of hits during the 50s, including 'Don't Be Angry' (1955), the Rose Marie McCoy/Charlie Singleton song 'Pitter Patter' (a pop hit in Patti Page's cover version), 'It Don't Hurt No More' (1958) and 'I Cried Like A Baby' (1959). He also made the original version of 'The Night Time Is The Right Time', a 1958 hit for Ray Charles. A prison term kept Brown inactive for much of the 60s. He returned to music with an album for Elephant V in 1969 and recorded gospel music in the 70s with the Bell Jubilee Singers for Jewel and as Brother Napoleon Brown for Savoy. In the 80s, Brown was rediscovered by a later generation of blues enthusiasts. He performed at festivals and recorded for Black Top and Alligator, with guitarist Tinsley Ellis accompanying him on *Tore Up*. Brown also appeared on a live album recorded at Tipitina's in New Orleans in 1988. He has continued recording in the 90s, although his most recent albums have not managed to recapture the power of his work of the 50s.

● ALBUMS: *Nappy Brown Sings* (London 1955)★★★★, *The Right Time* (London 1958)★★★★, *Thanks For Nothing* (Elephant V 1969)★★★,*Tore Up* (Alligator 1984)★★★, *Something Gonna Jump Out The Bushes* (Black Top 1988)★★★, *Apples & Lemons* (Ichiban 1990)★★, *Aw, Shucks* (Ichiban 1991)★★, *I'm A Wild Man* (New Moon 1994)★★, *Don't Be Angry* (Savoy 1995)★★, *Who's Been Foolin' You* (New Moon 1997)★★★.

Brown, Oscar, Jnr.

b. 10 October 1926, Chicago, Illinois, USA. Brown is a witty songwriter operating on the borders of soul and jazz. The son of a lawyer, Brown acted in a radio soap opera as a child and did a variety of jobs (copywriter, publicist, real estate agent) before serving in the US Army in 1954-56. Afterwards, he turned to professional songwriting and performing. The first of his compositions to be recorded was 'Brown Baby' by Mahalia Jackson. In 1961, his stage musical, *Kicks And Company*, was performed in Chicago, containing numerous songs which he later used in his stage act. Brown made his first album for CBS Records in 1960. It included some of his most well-known pieces, such as 'Signifyin' Monkey', and versions of Bobby Timmons' soul jazz tune 'Dat Dere' and Herbie Hancock's 'Watermelon Man', to which Brown set lyrics. Later records contained such originals as 'Forbidden Fruit' (also recorded by Nina Simone) and 'The Snake', two hipster's versions of the biblical story of Adam and Eve. Brown's most popular setting of lyrics to a jazz instrumental was 'Work Song', composed by Nat Adderley and covered by Georgie Fame in Britain, where Brown's slick lyrics had a minor vogue among the more jazz-inspired R&B groups, and both the Mark Leeman 5 and the Nashville Teens issued 'Forbidden Fruit' as a single in 1966. *Movin' On* was made for Atlantic Records and included Bernard 'Pretty' Purdie, Richard Tee and Cissie Houston among the backing musicians. In the late 80s, Brown appeared at nightspots with his son, Oscar Brown III (d. 12 August 1996), and daughter Maggie.

● ALBUMS: *Sin And Soul* (Columbia 1960)★★★, *Between Heaven And Hell* (Columbia 1961)★★★, *Tells It Like It Is* (Columbia 1962)★★★, *Live At The Cellar Door* (Columbia 1964)★★★, *Movin' On* (Atlantic 1965)★★★.

Brown, Randy

Born and raised in Memphis, this vocalist (and brother of William Brown of Mad Lads' fame) signed with Stax Records shortly before its demise, recording one album that finally saw the light of day once he had established a name for himself. He resurfaced on Parachute in 1978, with *Welcome To My Room*, written and produced by former Stax stalwarts Homer Banks and Carl Hampton. The album was aimed fairly and squarely at the late-night seductive soul market then in vogue. Despite critical acclaim and the enforced absence of competition such as Marvin Gaye and Isaac Hayes, two further albums failed to penetrate the market and Brown slipped back into obscurity. He was last sighted in 1988 with an EP, *Are You Lonely*, for Three Way Records.

● ALBUMS: *Welcome To My Room* (Parachute 1978)★★, *Check It Out* 1975 recording (Stax 1979)★★★, *Midnight Desire* (Parachute 1979)★★★, *Intimately* (Chocolate City 1980)★★.

Brown, Roy

b. Roy James Brown 10 September 1925, New Orleans, Louisiana, USA, d. 25 May 1981, Los Angeles, California, USA. Brown formed his own gospel quartet, the Rookie Four, and frequently sang in the local church before moving to California in 1942. After two years as a professional boxer, he began entering and winning amateur talent contests with his renditions of the pop songs of his idol, Bing Crosby. He returned to Louisiana in 1945 and formed his first jump band, the Mellodeers, for a long-term residency at the Club Granada in Galveston, Texas. There he worked for some time with Clarence Samuels as a double act, the Blues Twins, and was illicitly recorded by the local Gold Star label. By this time, Brown had eschewed Tin Pan Alley pop for jump blues, and was singing in a highly original style for the time, utilizing his gospel background and his extremely soulful voice. Returning to New Orleans penniless in 1947, Brown tried in vain to sell a song he had written to the great blues shouter Wynonie Harris. When Harris turned the song down, Brown sang the number with Harris's band and, legend has it, tore up the house. The song, 'Good Rockin' Tonight', was soon recorded by Brown for DeLuxe and sold so well throughout the south that, ironically, Wynonie Harris covered it for King Records. A popular phrase from the song persuaded Brown to rename his combo the Mighty Mighty Men, and he recorded extensively for DeLuxe and, later, King Records between 1947-55, during which time he had further success with such songs as 'Boogie At Midnight', 'Hard Luck Blues', 'Love Don't Love Nobody', 'Long About Sundown' and 'Trouble At Midnight'. During this phase of his career, the gospel-soul singer wailed about earthy secular subjects (some of them too ribald to be released for 30 years or more) and inspired devotees including B.B. King, Bobby Bland, Jackie Wilson, Little Richard and James Brown. In 1956, Dave Bartholomew signed Brown to Imperial Records, where he spent his time split successfully between making mediocre Fats Domino-styled records and covering pop-rockabilly hits. He moved further towards pop during 1959 at King Records. In the soul era, Brown made a handful of good Willie Mitchell-arranged singles in Memphis for Home Of The Blues. A decade of label-hopping followed, with Brown frequently working with Johnny Otis's band, until 1977 when a great deal of interest was generated with the release of *Laughing But Crying*, a collection of vintage tracks issued on Jonas Bernholm's Route 66 label. The following year, Brown toured Europe to packed houses and rave reviews and returned to the USA to a similar reception. A string of successful nationwide appearances culminated in Brown's storming return to the New Orleans Jazz & Heritage Festival in April 1981. He died peacefully the following month.

● ALBUMS: *Roy Brown Sings 24 Hits* (King 1966)★★★★, *The Blues Are Brown* (Bluesway 1968)★★★★, *Hard Times* (Bluesway 1968)★★★★, *Hard Luck Blues* (King 1971)★★★★, *Live At Monterey* (Epic 1971)★★★, *Great Rhythm & Blues Oldies* (1977)★★★★, *Good Rocking Tonight* (Quicksilver 1978)★★★★, *Cheapest Price In Town* (Faith 1979)★★★★.

● COMPILATIONS: *Laughing But Crying* (Route 66 1977)★★★★, *Saturday Nite* (Mr R&B 1982)★★★, *Good Rockin' Tonight* (Route 66 1984)★★★, *I Feel That Young Man's Rhythm* (1985)★★★, *Boogie At Midnight* (Charly 1985)★★★, *The Bluesway Sessions* (Charly 1988)★★★★, *Blues DeLuxe* (1992)★★★★, *The Complete Imperial Recordings* (Capitol 1995)★★★.

BROWN, RUTH

b. 30 January 1928, Portsmouth, Virginia, USA. Brown started her musical career singing gospel at an early age in the church choir led by her father. In 1948 she was singing with a band led by her husband Jimmy in Washington, DC, when Willis Conover (from the radio show *Voice Of America*) recommended her to Ahmet Ertegun of the newly formed Atlantic Records. Ertegun signed her, despite competition from Capitol, but on the way up to New York for an appearance at the Apollo Theatre, she was involved in a car crash. Hospitalized for nine months, her medical bills were paid by Atlantic and she rewarded them handsomely with her first big hit, 'Teardrops From My Eyes', in 1950. More hits followed with '5-10-15 Hours' (1952) and 'Mama, He Treats Your Daughter Mean' (1953). Atlantic's first real star, Brown became a major figure in 50s R&B, forming a strong link between that music and early rock 'n' roll. Her records were characterized by her rich and expressive singing voice (not unlike that of Dinah Washington) and accompaniment by breathy saxophone solos (initially by Budd Johnson, later by Willie Jackson). Between 1949 and 1955 her songs were on the charts for 129 weeks, including five number 1s. Brown's concentration upon R&B has not kept her from associations with the jazz world; very early in her career she sang briefly with the Lucky Millinder band, and has recorded with Jerome Richardson and the Thad Jones-Mel Lewis big band. She also brought a distinctively soulful treatment to varied material such as 'Yes, Sir, That's My Baby', 'Sonny Boy', 'Black Coffee' and 'I Can Dream, Can't I?'. In 1989 she won a Tony Award for her performance in the Broadway show *Black And Blue*, and was receiving enthusiastic reviews for her nightclub act in New York, at Michael's Pub and the Blue Note, into the 90s. In 1993 Brown was to be heard broadcasting on a New York radio station, and was inducted into the Rock And Roll Hall Of Fame. In 1994 she undertook a European tour, much to the delight of her small but loyal group of fans. On that tour she was recorded live at Ronnie Scott's club for an album that appeared on their own Jazzhouse label.

● ALBUMS: *Ruth Brown Sings Favorites* (Atlantic 1952)★★★, *Ruth Brown* (Atlantic 1957)★★★★, *Late Date With Ruth Brown* (Atlantic 1959)★★★★, *Miss Rhythm* (Atlantic 1959)★★★★, *Along Comes Ruth* (Atlantic 1962)★★★★, *Gospel Time* (Atlantic 1962)★★★, *Ruth Brown '65* (Mainstream 1965)★★★, *Black Is Brown And Brown Is Beautiful* (Rhapsody 1969)★★★, *The Real Ruth Brown* (70s)★★★, *You Don't Know Me* (70s)★★, *Touch Me In The Morning* (70s)★★, *Sugar Babe* (President 1977)★★★, *Takin' Care Of Business* (1980)★★★, *The Soul Survives* (1982)★★, *Brown Sugar* (Topline 1986)★★★, *Sweet Baby Of Mine* (Route 66 1987)★★, *I'll Wait For You* (Official 1988)★★, *Blues On Broadway* (Fantasy 1989)★★★, with Linda Hopkins, Carrie Smith *Black And Blue* (1989)★★★, *Fine And Mellow* (1992)★★★, *The Songs Of My Life* (Fantasy 1993)★★★, *Live In London* (Jazzhouse 1995)★★★.

● COMPILATIONS: *The Best Of Ruth Brown* (Atlantic 1963)★★★★, *Rockin' With Ruth* 1950-60 recordings (Charly 1984)★★★★, *Brown Black And Beautiful* (SDEG 1990)★★★, *Miss Rhythm, Greatest Hits And More* (Atlantic 1993)★★★★, *Blues On Broadway* (Ace 1994)★★★★, *You Don't Know Me* (Indigo 1997)★★★★, *R + B = Ruth Brown* (Bullseye 1997)★★★★.

● FURTHER READING: *Miss Rhythm*, Ruth Brown with Andrew Yule.

BROWN, SHIRLEY

b. 6 January 1947, West Memphis, Arkansas, USA. Brown was discovered and managed by bluesman Albert King, and spent several years working on the St. Louis night-club circuit prior to recording 'Woman To Woman' in

1974. Written by the songwriting team of Homer Banks and Henderson Thigpen, this dramatic tale of infidelity, complete with its renowned spoken introduction, encapsulated the 'cheating' genre and not only became a massive hit in its own right, but inspired several 'answer' songs in the process, among which Millie Jackson's 'Still Caught Up' is a good example. Brown had further, if lesser, R&B hits with 'It Ain't No Fun' (1975) and 'Blessed Is The Woman (With A Man Like That)' (1977), and continued her recording career into the 90s recording with the Malaco subsidiary Dome. She is most comfortable with aching soul ballads and her voice deserves a much wider audience.

● ALBUMS: *Woman To Woman* (Truth 1974)★★★★, *Shirley Brown* (Arista 1977)★★★, *For The Real Feeling* (Stax 1979)★★★, *Intimate Storm* (4th & Broadway 1985)★★★, *Fire And Ice* (Malaco 1989)★★★, *Joy And Pain* (1993)★★★, *Diva Of Soul* (Malaco 1995)★★★.

Brown, Tommy

Discovered by the Griffin Brothers while touring in Atlanta, Georgia, in 1950, Brown recorded for Savoy Records in Atlanta under his own name - with the Griffins' band in support - before moving north to Washington, DC, to join the brothers in their touring and recording unit. His first Dot recording with the Griffin Brothers was a cover version of Dave Bartholomew's 'Tra-La-La', and it was a huge success, peaking at number 7 in the R&B charts in August 1951. This was followed by an even bigger hit in December when Brown's emotional 'Weepin' & Cryin'' reached number 3, and heralded a succession of such histrionic records. Leaving the Griffin Brothers in 1952, Brown returned to Savoy for one session billed as 'Tommy 'Weepin' & Cryin'' Brown'. He then recorded in a variety of blues and R&B styles for various labels - King Records (including a vocal version of 'Honky Tonk' with Bill Doggett), United (with Walter Horton), Groove, Imperial and ABC. He remained a nightclub singer and comedian in Atlanta throughout the 60s and 70s and was last reported to be working in a nursing home.

● COMPILATIONS: with the Griffin Brothers *Riffin' With The Griffin Brothers Orchestra* (Ace 1985)★★★, with Walter Horton and Alfred Harris *Harmonica Blues Kings* (1986)★★★.

Brownstone

Vocal R&B/hip-hop trio Brownstone were formed in Los Angeles by Nicci (b. Nicole Gilbert, Detroit, Michigan, USA), Maxee (b. Charmayne Maxwell, Guyana) and Mimi (b. Monica Doby, New Orleans, Louisiana, USA). Signed after performing a cappella at their audition, the group became the first act on the Epic-distributed MJJ Music label. Their debut album featured the Grammy-nominated Top 10 single 'If You Love Me', and led to a prestigious support slot on Boyz II Men's 1995 US tour. Despite a personnel change when Kina (b. Kina Cosper, Detroit, Michigan, USA) replaced Mimi in June 1995, their growing reputation led to further tours with Anita Baker, BLACKstreet and Patti Labelle. Recorded over the course of a busy year, *Still Climbing* featured the same successful blend of hip-hop grooves and vocal harmonies that characterized their platinum-selling debut.

● ALBUMS: *From The Bottom Up* (Epic 1995)★★★, *Still Climbing* (Epic 1997)★★★.

Brownsville Station

This Detroit-based quartet - Cub Koda (b. Michael Koda, 1 August 1948, Detroit, Michigan, USA; guitar, harmonica), Michael Lutz (guitar, vocals), Bruce Nazarian (guitar, synthesiser) and Henry Week (drums, vocals) - forged its early reputation as a superior 'oldies' group. Their attention to 'roots' music was later fused to an understanding of pop's dynamics, exemplified in 'Smokin' In The Boys' Room' (1973), which reached number 3 in the US charts and made the UK Top 30 the following year. Subsequent releases lacked the quartet's early sense of purpose and the band was latterly dissolved. Koda later fronted several 'revival'-styled units while proclaiming his love of R&B and blues through columns in US collectors' magazines.

● ALBUMS: *Brownsville Station* (Palladium 1970)★★★, *No B.S.* (1970)★★★, *A Night On The Town* (Big Tree 1972)★★, *Yeah!* (Big Tree 1973)★★, *School Punks* aka *Smokin' In The Boys' Room* (Big Tree 1974)★★★, *Motor City Connection* (Big Tree 1975)★★, *Brownsville Station* (Private Stock 1977)★★, *Air Special* (1980)★★.

Bryant, Don

b. 1942, Memphis, Tennessee, USA. A significant songwriter for Joe Cuoghi's (and then Willie Mitchell's) Hi label, especially for (and sometimes with) his wife, Ann Peebles, Bryant was also a superb soul stylist, although most of his own recordings for Hi were cut long before Al Green, in particular, gave the label the commercial soul base it needed for continued survival. One of 10 children, Bryant's father (Donald Snr.) featured in the gospel quartet the Four Stars Of Harmony, and in 1955, Don Jnr. and four of his brothers formed their own gospel group, the Five Bryant Brothers, which soon became 'secularized' as the doo-wopping Quails. At Booker T. Washington High School, Bryant joined a group variously called the Canes and The Four Canes, named after their 'manager', local Radio WLOK DJ, D. Cane Cole. For their live gigs the Canes dressed in striped jackets and straw hats and carried walking canes. Don's brother James was also in the group, along with Lee Jones and William Walker, reputed to be the later Goldwax, Checker and Pawn soulman, (Wee) Willie Walker. A group called the Canes were taken to Stax Records by D. Cane Cole in early 1962 where they cut 'Why Should I Suffer With The Blues', but they have since been identified as probably being the Largoes, led by Lorece Thompson. Eventually, Bryant split from Cole and changed the group's name to the Four Kings. The new quartet became Willie Mitchell's singing group at the bandleader's live gigs at Memphis clubs. Bryant himself was still underage, and, to enable him to work, Mitchell became his legal guardian. Mitchell was also producer for the Home of The Blues label, whose featured artists included the ex-King group the Five Royales. They recorded Bryant's first commercial composition, 'Is There Someone Else On Your Mind'. Meanwhile, the Four Kings cut 'Crawl Parts 1 & 2' with the Willie Mitchell Band for Hi, before the group dissolved. Bryant went solo in 1964, making his debut with a storming version of Chris Kenner's 'I Like It Like That'. Between 1964 and 1969 Bryant often recorded cover versions of other artists' hits, and several were included on his only Hi album, *Precious Soul*. He proved that he could also sing both up-tempo and particularly 'deep' original soul, on tracks such as 'Don't Turn Your Back On Me', 'The Call of Distress', 'Is That Asking Too Much', 'Clear Days And Stormy Nights', and 'It Ain't Easy'. In the mid-60s, he also paired with Marion Brittnam (ex-Marianne Brittenum of the Drapels, who recorded for Volt), the results appearing on the Hi subsidiary MOC, some credited simply to 1 + 1. However, Bryant was mostly in demand as a songwriter once Ann Peebles had joined the label. He wrote much of the material recorded by most of Hi's major 70s soul acts, including Al Green, O.V. Wright, Syl Johnson and Otis Clay, as well as for Peebles. After the demise of Hi in the early 80s (and a final 1981 duet with his wife on 'Mon Belle Amour'), Bryant and Peebles returned to gospel music, with Bryant recording *What Do You Think About Jesus* for his By Faith label in 1986. Peebles returned to secular music for Willie Mitchell's short-lived Waylo venture, and again, more recently, for Rounder/Bullseye. Bryant has once more involved himself with her career, but has yet to make a secular vocal comeback of his own. His finest recordings for Hi (including many previously unissued items) have been released in the 90s by UK Hi, one of the Demon group of labels.

● ALBUMS: *Precious Soul* (Hi 1969)★★★, *What Do You Think About Jesus* (By Faith 1986)★★.

● COMPILATIONS: *Doin' The Mustang* (Hi/Demon 1991)★★★, *Comin' On Strong* (Hi/Demon 1992)★★★.

Bryson, Peabo

b. Robert Peabo Bryson, 13 April 1951, Greenville, South Carolina, USA. This talented soul singer and producer is a former member of Moses Dillard and the Tex-Town Display and Michael Zager's Moon Band. Between 1976 and 1978, Bryson had hits with this latter group, with 'Reaching For The Sky' and 'I'm So Into You'. His numerous appearances in *Billboard*'s R&B chart include 'Underground Music', 'Feel The Fire', 'Crosswinds', 'She's A Woman' and 'Minute By Minute'. 'Gimme Some Time', a 1979 duet with Natalie Cole, was the first of several successful partnerships. However, despite hits with Melissa Manchester and Regina Belle, the singer is best known for his work with Roberta Flack, and in particular the dewy-eyed ballad 'Tonight, I Celebrate My Love', which reached number 5 on the US R&B chart and number 2 in the UK pop chart in 1983. Such releases have obscured Bryson's own career, which included, notably, the US Top 10 hit 'If Ever You're In My Arms Again' from 1984, but he remains an able and confident performer blessed with an effortless voice. Soundtrack duets with Celine Dion ('Beauty And The Beast') and Regina Belle ('A Whole New World (Aladdin's Theme)') in 1992 provided Bryson with further chart success.

● ALBUMS: *Reaching For The Sky* (Capitol 1978)★★★, *Crosswinds* (Capitol 1978)★★★, with Natalie Cole *We're The Best Of Friends* (Capitol 1979)★★★, *Paradise* (Capitol 1980)★★★, with Roberta Flack *Live And More* (Atlantic 1980)★★★, *Turn The Hands Of Time* (Capitol 1981)★★★, *I Am Love* (Capitol 1981)★★★, *Don't Play With Fire* (Capitol 1982)★★★, with Flack *Born To Love* (Capitol 1983)★★★, *Straight From The Heart* (Elektra 1984)★★★, *Take No Prisoners* (Elektra 1985)★★★, *Quiet Storm* (Elektra 1986)★★★, *Positive* (Elektra 1988)★★★, *Can You Stop The Rain* (Columbia 1991)★★★.

● COMPILATIONS: *The Peabo Bryson Collection* (Capitol 1984)★★★★.

Buccaneers

This vocal quartet was formed in 1952 in Philadelphia, USA, by Ernest Smith (lead), Richard Gregory (tenor), Julius Robinson (tenor) and Donald Marshall (bass). They were spotted playing in their home-town in November 1952 by Ed Kresnel and Jerry Halperin, two white teenagers who saw in them the potential for great things. Krensel and Halperin persuaded the Buccaneers that they had music business connections, which was not, in fact, true. They did, however, finance a recording session at Reco-Art Studios in Philadelphia, where the group recorded 'Dear Ruth' (written by Halperin for his girlfriend) and 'Fine Brown Fame'. Placing the single proved difficult, so Krensel and Halperin started their own label, Southern Records, in January 1953, and soon 'Dear Ruth' began to sell well. Rainbow Records then distributed it nationally, but it failed to repeat its local success. Halperin moved the group to Rama Records, who released 'In The Mission Of St. Augustine' backed by 'You Did Me Wrong'. However, the simultaneous release of the same song by the Orioles killed any chance the Buccaneers' version might have had. After the similarly unsuccessful release of 'The Stars Will Remember'/'Come Back My Love' in 1954, the Buccaneers broke up.

Burke, Solomon

b. 1936, Philadelphia, Pennsylvania, USA. The former 'Wonder Boy Preacher', Burke's first recordings appeared on the New York-based Apollo label. From 1955-59 he attempted various styles until a brisk rocker, 'Be Bop Grandma', attracted the attention of Atlantic Records. An eclectic performer, his reading of a sentimental country song, 'Just Out Of Reach' (1961), was a US Top 30 hit, but the following year, the 'King of Soul' began asserting a defined soul direction with 'Cry To Me'. Burke's sonorous voice was then heard on a succession of inspired singles, including 'If You Need Me' (1963), 'Goodbye Baby (Baby Goodbye)' and the declamatory 'Everybody Needs Somebody To Love' (both 1964). This exceptional period culminated with 'The Price', an impassioned release that marked the end of Burke's relationship with producer Bert Berns. Although further strong records appeared (indeed, in 1965, 'Got To Get You Off My Mind' became his biggest hit), they lacked the drama of the earlier era. Still based in New York, Burke was now overshadowed by Otis Redding, Sam And Dave and other acts who recorded at Stax and Fame Records. A belated Memphis session did provide a US Top 50 entry in 'Take Me (Just As I Am)', but

Burke left Atlantic for Bell Records in 1968. The ensuing album, *Proud Mary*, was a southern soul classic, while the title track, written by John Fogerty, charted as a single in the USA. The 70s saw a move to MGM Records, but his work there was marred by inconsistency. The same was true of his spells at Dunhill and Chess Records, although his collaborations with Swamp Dogg collected on *From The Heart* recalled his old power. Following several strong gospel albums for Savoy, Burke's rebirth continued on *Soul Alive*, where, recorded in concert, he sounded inspired, infusing his 'greatest hits' with a new-found passion. A strong studio collection, *A Change Is Gonna Come*, followed 1987's European tour and displayed Burke's enduring talent. Two albums, *The Best Of Solomon Burke* (1965) and *Cry To Me* (1984), compile his Atlantic singles, while *The Bishop Rides South* (1988) adds four extra tracks to the original *Proud Mary* album. Burke has carried on recording into the 90s, releasing several worthy albums.

● ALBUMS: *Solomon Burke* (Apollo 1962)★★★, *If You Need Me* (Atlantic 1963)★★★, *Rock 'N' Soul* (Atlantic 1964)★★★, *I Wish I Knew* (Atlantic 1968)★★★, *King Solomon* (Atlantic 1968)★★★, *Proud Mary* (Bell 1969)★★★★, *Electronic Magnetism* (Polydor 1972)★★, *King Heavy* (1972)★★, *We're Almost Home* (Polydor 1972)★★, *I Have A Dream* (Dunhill 1974)★★, *Midnight And You* (Dunhill 1975)★★, *Music To Make Love By* (Chess 1975)★★, *Back To My Roots* (Chess 1977)★★, *Please Don't You Say Goodbye To Me* (Amherst 1978)★★★, *Sidewalks Fences & Walls* (Infinity 1979)★★, *Lord I Need A Miracle Right Now* (Savoy 1981)★★, *Into My Life You Came* (Savoy 1982)★★, *Take Me, Shake Me* (Savoy 1983)★★, *This Is His Song* (Savoy 1984)★★, *Soul Alive* (Rounder 1984)★★, *A Change Is Gonna Come* (Rounder 1986)★★★, *Love Trap* (Polygram 1987)★★★, *The Bishop Rides South* (Charly 1988)★★★★, *Home Land* (Bizarre 1991)★★★, *Soul Of The Blues* (Black Top 1993)★★★, *Live At The House Of Blues* (Black Top 1994)★★, *Definition Of Soul* (Pointblank/Virgin 1997)★★★.

● COMPILATIONS: *Solomon Burke's Greatest Hits* (Atlantic 1962)★★★, *I Almost Lost My Mind* (1964)★★★, *The Best Of Solomon Burke* (Atlantic 1965)★★★★, *King Of Rock 'N' Soul/From The Heart* (Charly 1981)★★★, *Cry To Me* (Charly 1984)★★★★, *You Can Run But You Can't Hide* (Mr R&B 1987)★★★, *Hold On I'm Coming* (1991)★★★, *Home In Your Heart: The Best Of Solomon Burke* (Rhino 1992)★★★★, *The King Of Soul* (1993)★★★, *Greatest Hits: If You Need Me* (Sequel 1997)★★★.

BURRAGE, HAROLD

b. 30 March 1931, Chicago, Illinois, USA, d. 26 November 1966, Chicago, Illinois, USA. A great singer and pianist in the city blues tradition, Burrage was a well-known face on Chicago's west side R&B scene by his late teens. In 1950 he made his first recordings for Decca backed by Horace Henderson's septet, resulting in Claude Trenier's suggestive 'Hi Yo Silver', which spawned several cover versions. He completed one-off sessions for Aladdin (1951) and States (1954) before hitting his stride between 1956 and 1958 with Cobra Records, with whom he recorded in his own right in a soul-blues vein, as well as backing artists such as Magic Sam, Otis Rush and Ike Turner. He continued in the same style in his brief associations for Vee Jay Records, Paso and Foxy, but in 1962 he joined One-Derful's M-Pac subsidiary and over the following four years produced his prime work, including his only real hit, 'Got To Find A Way', which reached number 31 in the August 1965 R&B charts. He died of a heart attack at the age of 35, at the home of his friend Tyrone Davis.

● COMPILATIONS: *Harrold Burrage: The Pioneer Of Chicago Soul* (P-Vine 1979)★★★, *She Knocks Me Out* (Flyright 1981)★★★.

BUTLER, BILLY, AND THE (EN)CHANTERS

Formed in Chicago, the band members were Billy Butler (b. 7 June 1945, Chicago, Illinois, USA), Jesse Tillman, Erroll Batts, Alton Howel and John Jordan. As students at Wells High School, the Enchanters were introduced to OKeh Records by Butler's elder brother, Jerry Butler, and Curtis Mayfield. The group's debut single, 'Found True Love' (1963), was a regional R&B hit, but despite the quality of several subsequent singles, notably 'Can't Live Without Her' (1964), it was 1965 before they reached the R&B chart with 'I Can't Work No Longer'. In the meantime, Howel and Jordan had left and the group's name was cut to the Chanters. 'Right Track', from 1966, marked the end of Butler's OKeh contract. It was 1969 before he secured another hit, by which time the singer had formed Infinity with Erroll Banks, Larry Wade and Phyllis Knotts. 'Get On The Case' peaked at number 41 in the R&B charts, while two years later, 'I Don't Want To Lose You' reached number 38 (R&B). Further releases made little impression and Billy subsequently worked with his brother, Jerry, in the Butler Writers Workshop in Chicago, making demos and producing other artists. Butler was an accomplished composer - Major Lance, Gene Chandler and Otis Leavill all recorded his songs - and 'I Stand Accused', his composition recorded by brother Jerry in 1964, has since become a soul standard. A brief interlude on Curtom notwithstanding, Billy Butler entered the 80s a talented, but backroom, figure.

● ALBUMS: *Right Track* (OKeh 1966)★★★, as Infinity *Hung Up On You* (Pride 1972)★★★, *Sugar Candy Lady* (Curtom 1977)★★★.

● COMPILATIONS: *Right Track* (Edsel 1985)★★★.

BUTLER, JERRY

b. 8 December 1939, Sunflower, Mississippi, USA. Jerry, older brother of Billy Butler, moved to Chicago as a child and was later part of the city's burgeoning gospel circuit. He subsequently joined several secular groups, including the Roosters, an aspiring trio of Sam Gooden and Richard and Arthur Brooks. Butler then suggested they add his friend, Curtis Mayfield, on guitar. Now called the Impressions, the quintet secured a Top 3 US R&B hit with the haunting 'For Your Precious Love' (1958). However, the label credit, 'Jerry Butler And The Impressions', caused friction within the group. A second single, 'Come Back My Love', was less successful and Butler left for a solo career. His early releases were minor hits until 'He Will Break Your Heart' reached number 1 in the US R&B

and number 7 in the pop charts in 1960. The song was written by Mayfield who added guitar and sang backing vocals. Their differences clearly resolved, two subsequent hits, 'Find Another Girl' and 'I'm A Telling You' (both 1961), featured the same partnership. Mayfield's involvement lessened as the Impressions' own career developed, but Butler's chart run continued. 'Make It Easy On Yourself' (1962) and 'I Stand Accused' (1964) were among his finest singles. Butler switched to Mercury in 1966 where he honed the style that won him his 'Ice Man' epithet. 'Hey Western Union Man' and 'Only The Strong Survive' topped the soul chart in 1968 and 1969, while duets with Gene Chandler and Brenda Lee Eager punctuated his early 70s recordings. With his brother, Billy Butler, he formed the Butler Writers Workshop, which encouraged aspiring songwriters and musicians, among whom were Marvin Yancey and Chuck Jackson of the Independents and Natalie Cole. Butler's Motown releases preceded a more successful spell with Philadelphia International, while the 80s saw his work appear on Fountain and CTI. *Up On Love* (1980) mixes the best of Butler's Vee Jay singles with that first Impressions hit. Butler is now an elected official in Chicago.

● ALBUMS: *Jerry Butler Esquire* (Abner 1959)★★★, *He Will Break Your Heart* (Vee Jay 1960)★★★, *Love Me* (Vee Jay 1961)★★, *Aware Of Love* (Vee Jay 1961)★★★, *Moon River* (Vee Jay 1962)★★, *Folk Songs* (Vee Jay 1963)★★, *Need To Belong* (Vee Jay 1964)★★★, with Betty Everett *Delicious Together* (Vee Jay 1964)★★★, *Soul Artistry* (Mercury 1967)★★★, *Mr. Dream Merchant* (Mercury 1967)★★★, *Jerry Butler's Golden Hits Live* (Mercury 1968)★★, *Just Beautiful* (Mercury 1968)★★★, *The Soul Goes On* (Mercury 1968)★★★, *The Ice Man Cometh* (Mercury 1968)★★★★, *Ice On Ice* (Mercury 1969)★★★★, *You & Me* (Mercury 1970)★★★, *Special Memory* (Mercury 1970)★★★, *Jerry Butler Sings Assorted Sounds By Assorted Friends And Relatives* (Mercury 1971)★★★, with Gene Chandler *Gene & Jerry - One & One* (Mercury 1971)★★★, *The Sagittarius Movement* (Mercury 1971)★★★, *The Spice Of Life* (Mercury 1972)★★★, *Melinda* (Mercury 1972)★★★, *Introducing The Ice Man Band* (Mercury 1972)★★★, with Brenda Lee Eager *The Love We Have, The Love We Had* (Mercury 1973)★★★, *The Power Of Love* (Mercury 1973)★★★, *Sweet Sixteen* (Mercury 1974)★★★, *Love's On The Menu* (Motown 1976)★★, *Make It Easy On Yourself* (Motown 1976), *Suite For The Single Girl* (Motown 1977)★★, with Thelma Houston *Thelma And Jerry* (Motown 1977)★★, with Houston *Two To One* (Motown 1978)★★, *It All Comes Out In My Song* (Motown 1978)★★, *Nothing Says I Love You Like I Love You* (Philadelphia International 1978)★★★, *Best Love I Ever Had* (Philadelphia International 1981)★★★, *Ice 'N Hot* (Fountain 1982)★★, *Time & Faith* (1993)★★★, *Simply Beautiful* (Valley Vue 1994)★★★.

● COMPILATIONS: *The Best Of Jerry Butler* (1962)★★★, *More Of The Best Of Jerry Butler* (1965)★★★, *Best Of Jerry Butler* (Mercury 1970)★★★★, *The Vintage Years* double album shared with the Impressions (Sire 1977)★★★, *Up On Love* (1980)★★★, *Only The Strong Survive (The Legendary Philadelphia Hits)* (Mercury 1984)★★★★, *Whatever You Want* (Charly 1986)★★★★, *Soul Workshop* (Charly 1986)★★★★, *The Legendary Philadelphia Hits* (Mercury 1987)★★★★, *The Best Of Jerry Butler* (Rhino 1987)★★★, *Iceman: The Mercury Years* (Mercury 1992)★★★★.

Byrd, Bobby

b. Toccoa, Georgia, USA. Beginning his musical career in church choirs, Byrd formed the Gospel Starlighters in the late 50s, until he chanced upon the talents of a young James Brown. Brown was subsequently enlisted into Byrd's next group, the R&B-orientated Furious Flames. Like Brown, Byrd gravitated through gospel to blues, soul, and finally funk in his own solo career, enjoying most of his success in the mid-60s. His first hit came for Smash Records, a duet with Anna King entitled 'Baby Baby Baby', which made number 52 in *Billboard*'s soul chart in 1964. The following year 'We Are In Love' reached number 14 in the same chart. Afterwards, he moved towards funk, spurred on by Brown's success in that medium. However, he achieved only one further Top 20 hit, 'I Need Help (I Can't Do It Alone)', for King Records. Reaching number 14 on the soul listings, it featured vocals from Gig Kinard and Roberta Dubois. The 70s proved a lean period artistically, and it was only in the 80s that his name re-emerged with any frequency. This was primarily the result of sampling by hip-hop artists, who used his funk breaks and vocals as they had done with Brown. The most famous example was Eric B And Rakim's 1987 single 'I Know You Got Soul', which sampled Byrd's 1971 track of the same title. The title of his 1990 compilation for Rhythm Attack Records, *Finally Getting Paid*, neatly expressed his feelings at this revival. His first studio album since 1970 was released in 1994, *On The Move*, as Byrd embarked on concert tours with his wife, Vicki Anderson, and children.

● ALBUMS: including *On The Move* (Polydor 1994)★★★.

● COMPILATIONS: *Finally Getting Paid* (Rhythm Attack 1990)★★★, *Bobby Byrd Got Soul: The Best Of Bobby Byrd* 1963-72 recordings (Polydor Chronicles 1995)★★★★.

Byrd, Gary

b. 1954, Buffalo, New York, USA. Byrd became at 15 the state's youngest radio disc jockey. His exuberant personality dictated that he venture into what was later recognized as nascent rapping - or, as he named it, 'disc journalism'. Entering Stevie Wonder's social circle, he wrote lyrics to two pieces on 1976's *Songs In The Key Of Life*, and it was through Wonder than Byrd came a decade later to record 'The Crown', a lengthy single that, with multi-tracked accompaniment by his sponsor (as the GB Experience), related black racial history from ancient Egypt to Malcolm X. Issued via Tamla Motown on Wonder's Wonderdisc label, it climbed charts in both the UK and Europe. With no further chart success, Byrd was heard commercially mostly on US airwaves as a chat-show host and inquisitor (on the nationally syndicated *Star Quiz*). A born-again Christian, he also presented *Sweet Inspiration*, a BBC series featuring gospel music, in 1985.

C & THE SHELLS

(see Sandpebbles)

C., ROY

b. Roy Charles Hammond, 1943, New York City, New York, USA. A member of the Genies, with whom he recorded for several labels, Roy C's most enduring moment came with 'Shotgun Wedding' (1965). A US R&B Top 20 hit, it proved even more popular in the UK, reaching number 6 the following year, and made the Top 10 again in 1972. The singer later recorded, without success, for Black Hawk and Shout, but 'Got To Get Enough (Of Your Sweet Love Stuff)' was a soul hit in 1971. Released on C's own Alaga label, he subsequently secured further success on Mercury Records. He also wrote 'Honey I Still Love You', a 1972 bestseller for the Mark IV.

● ALBUMS: *Sex And Soul* (1973)★★★, *More Sex And Soul* (1977)★★.

CADETS/JACKS

An R&B vocal group from Los Angeles, California, USA. This unit, who recorded for Modern as the Cadets and for RPM as the Jacks, is an example of a house group, used by a record company to record cover hits or songs in styles of other groups. As the Cadets, the group had a hit with the novelty jump 'Stranded In The Jungle' (number 4 R&B, number 15 pop), in 1956, and as the Jacks with the ballad 'Why Don't You Write Me' (number 4 R&B, number 82 pop) in 1955. 'Stranded' was a cover of a record by the original Jayhawks and 'Why Don't You Write Me' was a cover of a record by the Feathers. The unit came together as a gospel group in 1947, and by the time they were signed to Modern in 1955 the members were Willie Davis (first tenor), Ted Taylor (first tenor), Aaron Collins (second tenor), Lloyd McGraw (baritone), and Will 'Dub' Jones (bass). When the group left Modern in 1957, Ted Taylor dropped out of the group and established a successful solo career as a hard soul singer during the 60s. Davis and Collins kept the group together under the name Cadets, recording several singles for minor labels without success. In 1961 Collins and Davis, with several new members, recorded as the Flares and had a hit with 'Foot Stompin''.

● ALBUMS: as the Cadets *Rockin 'N' Rollin With The Cadets* (Crown 1957)★★★, *The Cadets* (Crown 1963)★★★; as the Jacks *Jumpin' With The Jacks* (RPM 1956)★★★, *Jumpin' With The Jacks* (Crown 1960)★★★, *The Jacks* (1963)★★★.

● COMPILATIONS: *The Best Of The Jacks* (Relic 1975)★★★, *The Best Of The Cadets* (Relic 1975)★★★, *The Cadets Meet The Jacks* (Ace 1987)★★★.

CADILLACS

This vocal quintet, initially called the Carnations, was formed in 1953 in New York, USA, and consisted of Earl Carroll (b. 2 November 1937, New York, USA), LaVerne Drake, Bobby Phillips, Johnny Willingham and James Clark, who also sang with the Five Crowns. The Cadillacs' debut single, 'Gloria', was released by Josie Records in July 1954, and although it did not chart at the time, it was later considered a doo-wop classic. Clark and Willingham were then replaced by Earl Wade (ex-Crystals) and Charles Brooks. Their next two singles, 'No Chance'/'Sympathy' and 'Down The Road', failed to chart, but 'Speedoo', released in October 1955, did reach number 17 in the *Billboard* R&B charts. Meanwhile, the group's dance steps were being choreographed by Charles Atkinson (aka Cholly Atkins), who later worked with a number of Motown Records' acts. Following lucrative tours with Ray Charles, Fats Domino and others, in May 1956 Drake was replaced by James Bailey (ex-Crickets), and after two more unsuccessful singles the Cadillacs returned to the charts (number 11) with 'Rudolph The Red Nosed Reindeer'. They returned to their roots with the wonderful 'Sugar Sugar' (not the song later made famous by the Archies) but by this time their original audience was confused about their direction. The group split in two early in 1957, with both parties continuing to use the name Cadillacs and remaining on Josie Records. Caroll, Phillips, Wade and Brooks became known as the Original Cadillacs, while Bailey hired Bobby Spencer (Harptones), Bill Lindsey (Starlings) and Champ Rollow to join his version of the group. After Bailey's group flopped with 'My Girlfriend' and the Original Cadillacs flopped with 'Lucy', Bailey rejoined Caroll, Phillips Wade and new member Caddy Spencer, and together they recorded 'Speedo Is Back'. Their next single, 'Peek-A-Boo', reached number 28 in the *Billboard* R&B chart in October 1958, but the next year Caroll left the group (later recording as Speedo And The Pearls) and was replaced by a string of ex-members of the Solitaires. The Cadillacs then signed to Mercury Records, and in the next decade Curtis Williams, Ray Brewster and Irving Lee Gails all sang with the group, as did Earl Caroll and Roland Martinez. They could not, however, match their former achievements. Reunions of the various formations of the Cadillacs have occurred from time to time.

● COMPILATIONS: *The Best Of The Cadillacs* (Rhino 1990)★★★★.

● FILMS: *Go Johnny Go* (1958).

CALLIER, TERRY

b. 24 May 1945, Chicago, Illinois, USA. A childhood friend of Curtis Mayfield's, Callier grew up singing on the streets as a member of several rival doo-wop groups. He was first recorded by Chess Records in 1963, releasing a one-off single 'Look At Me Now'. Recorded in 1965, his debut album for Prestige was delayed for almost four years when the errant producer disappeared into the Mexican desert with the master tapes. When it was eventually released in 1968, the carefully crafted blend of soul, folk and jazz styles marked the arrival of a gifted musician and songwriter. Callier never received the wider acclaim that seemed his due, however, and despite a series of strong albums for Cadet and Elektra in the 70s, he retired from music in 1983 to become a computer programmer at the University Of Chicago. In the early 90s, English acid jazz DJs Gilles Peterson and Russ Dewbury revived dancefloor interest in Callier's music, echoing his earlier popularity on the 70s' Northern Soul scene. Drawn back to performing in Europe, Callier recorded his first album of new material in over 20 years for the London-based Talkin' Loud label. The resulting *Time Peace* gained strong reviews and support from celebrity fans such as Paul Weller and Beth Orton. Callier had collaborated with Orton the previous year on her *Best Bits* EP.

● ALBUMS: *The New Folk Sound Of Terry Callier* (Prestige 1968)★★★★, *Occasional Rain* (Cadet 1972)★★★★, *What Colour Is Love* (Cadet 1973)★★★, *I Just Can't Help Myself* (Cadet 1975)★★★, *Fire On Ice* (Elektra 1977)★★★, *Turn You To Love* (Elektra 1978)★★★, *I Don't Want To See Myself (Without You)* mini-album (Acid Jazz 1991)★★★, *T.C. In D.C.* (Premonition 1997)★★★, *Time Peace* (Talkin' Loud 1998)★★★★.

CAMEO

This US soul/funk group, originally called the New York City Players, was formed in 1974 by the core members Larry 'Mr. B' Blackmon (b. New York City, New York, USA; drums, vocals) and vocalists Thomas Jenkins and Nathan Leftenant. Building up a strong following by undergoing rigorous touring schedules, with their backing group at times numbering almost a dozen members, they signed with the Casablanca subsidiary label Chocolate City, where they recorded their debut, *Cardiac Arrest*, produced by Blackmon. Touring alongside Parliament and Funkadelic enhanced their reputation and subsequent album releases gained modest positions in the US pop chart. In Britain, they enjoyed a loyal cult following, but it was not until Cameo's seventh album release, *Knights Of The Sound Table*, that they were afforded a UK release. However, in 1984, the single 'She's Strange' crossed over from soul/funk into the pop market and Cameo found themselves with their first UK Top 40 single. After the success of the following year's 'Single Life' (UK Top 20), 'She's Strange' was remixed and peaked at number 22. Three sell-out shows at London's Hammersmith Odeon followed. Having won over the UK pop market, it was not until 1986 that they finally broke into the US Top 40 chart; 'Word Up' had reached number 3 in the UK, and subsequently reached number 1 in the US R&B chart and number 6 in the *Billboard* pop chart. Having trimmed down the group to the core trio of Blackmon, Jenkins and Leftenant, and only using additional session players when necessary, Blackmon attracted most of the media attention. His image was helped by the expansive, bright red codpiece he wore on stage. Blackmon's own studio Atlanta Artists allowed him almost total control over Cameo's sound and helped him to promote and nurture local musical talent. By the 90s, however, their commercial success had dramatically waned, and founder member Jenkins left in 1992.

● ALBUMS: *Cardiac Arrest* (Chocolate City 1977)★★, *We All Know Who We Are* (Chocolate City 1978)★★, *Ugly Ego* (Chocolate City 1978)★★, *Secret Omen* (Chocolate City 1979)★★, *Cameosis* (Chocolate City 1980)★★★, *Feel Me* (Chocolate City 1980)★★★, *Knights Of The Sound Table* (Chocolate City 1981)★★★, *Alligator Woman* (Chocolate City 1982)★★, *Style* (Atlanta Artists 1983)★★★, *She's Strange* (Atlanta Artists 1984)★★★, *Single Life* (Atlanta Artists 1985)★★★★, *Word Up!* (Atlanta Artists 1986)★★★★, *Machismo* (Atlanta Artists 1988)★★★, *Real Men Wear Black* (Atlanta Artists 1990)★★★, *Emotional Violence* (Reprise 1992)★★★.

● COMPILATIONS: *Best Of Cameo* (Phonogram 1993)★★★★.

● VIDEOS: *Cameo: The Video Singles* (Channel 5 1987), *Back And Forth* (Club 1987).

CAMERON, G.C.

b. Jackson, Mississippi, USA. He joined the Detroit group the Spinners in 1967, having completed a tour of duty in Vietnam as a US Marine. Cameron remained their lead singer until 1972, when the group left Motown for Atlantic Records. During this period, he provided the gutsy lead vocals on two major hits produced by Stevie Wonder, 'It's A Shame' and 'We'll Have It Made'. He began a solo career with Motown in 1971, and enjoyed occasional soul hits until 1977 - the last was a duet with Syreeta, a pairing that Motown hoped would rival the success of the Marvin Gaye/Tammi Terrell partnership. When this combination failed to register, Cameron left Motown for a series of short-lived contracts with small labels, the most profitable of which was with soul specialists Malaco Records in 1988. In 1989 he moved to Ian Levine's Motor City label and duetted with Martha Reeves on a remake of 'You're All I Need To Get By', and issued *Right Or Wrong* in 1991.

● ALBUMS: *Love Songs And Other Tragedies* (Motown 1974)★★★, *G.C. Cameron* (Motown 1976)★★, *You're What's Missing In My Life* (Motown 1977)★★, with Syreeta *Rich Love, Poor Love* (Motown 1977)★★, *Give Me Your Love* (Malaco 1988)★★★, *Right Or Wrong* (Motor City 1991)★★★.

CAMPBELL, CHOKER

b. 21 March 1916, Shelby, Mississippi, USA, d. 20 July 1993, Detroit, Michigan, USA. Tenor saxophonist Campbell led the first of Tamla/Motown's road bands that accompanied the fledgling label's acts on tour. When his position was taken by Earl Van Dyke, Campbell instead led the resident band at Detroit's Graystone Ballroom. Several live sessions were recorded at this Motown-owned venue, including Campbell's unreleased *Shades Of Time*. His eventual contribution to the label's catalogue was *Hits Of The Sixties*, but Campbell left the company soon after its release. In 1969 he established the Tri-City Recording Company, an ambitious enterprise responsible for several musically contrasting outlets, including Tri-City, Moonville USA, Ultra City and Gospel Train.

● ALBUMS: *Hits Of The Sixties* (Motown 1965)★★★.

Campbell, Tevin

b. 12 November 1978, Waxahachie, Texas, USA. Discovered by Quincy Jones (or the flautist Bobbi Humphrey, according to some accounts), the singer Tevin Campbell first appeared in 1988 on the US television show *Wally & The Valentines*, which was followed by a part in Prince's film *Graffiti Bridge*. He was still only 14 years old when he appeared on Quincy Jones's *Back On The Block* album, masterfully handling lead vocals on the track 'Tomorrow'. This earned him a contract with QWest Records, primarily through Jones's recommendation. His excellent 1991 debut collection, *T.E.V.I.N.*, included two major pop hits, 'Round And Round', written by Prince and featured on the *Graffiti Bridge* soundtrack, and 'Tell Me What You Want Me To Do'. As well as up-tempo dance numbers, it also included a series of ballads handled with maturity. The reaction to *I'm Ready* was slightly frostier, with several critics mentioning the limitations its urban R&B put on Campbell's expressive singing.

● ALBUMS: *T.E.V.I.N.* (QWest/Reprise 1991)★★★★, *I'm Ready* (QWest/Reprise 1993)★★★, *Back To The World* (QWest 1996)★★★.

Cap-Tans

A vocal group from Washington, DC, USA, the original members were Harmon Bethea (lead), Sherman Buckner (lead), Floyd Bennett (first tenor), Alfred Slaughter (second tenor, bass) and Lester Fountain (guitar, baritone). The Cap-Tans, with their polished harmonies, represented the 40s pop tradition of African-American vocal harmony, exemplified by such groups as the Ink Spots, Charioteers, and Deep River Boys. The Cap-Tans came together when, in 1950, record label entrepreneur Lillian Clairborne pulled Bethea out of a veteran gospel group, the Progressive Four, and teamed up the fledling Cap-Tans with a group called the Buddies. Their first hit, 'I'm So Crazy For Love' (1950), became a local sensation on Claiborne's DC label, but after Dot Records picked it up, it enjoyed sales across the country. The next release, on Dot, paired a prototype rock 'n' roll song, 'Chief Turn The Hose On Me', with another smooth pop styling, 'With All My Love', and both sides received good airplay in early 1951. Of all these songs, most looked back to the past in their smooth pop style; only 'Chief, Turn The Hose On Me' exhibited a hard R&B style. The original group started to dissolve in 1951, when Fountain was drafted and replaced by Ray Reader. A few more releases on the Gotham and Coral labels appeared without success, and the group disbanded in 1953. Harmon Bethea resurrected the Cap-Tans in 1958, but the magic of the original group was gone, and this outfit folded in the early 60s. Around 1967 Bethea formed Mask Man And The Agents.

● ALBUMS: *I Always Remember* contains five Cap-Tans' Gotham recordings (Flyright 1992)★★★.

● COMPILATIONS: *Gotham Recording Stars: The Capris* (Collectables 1990)★★★.

Capitols

An R&B trio from Detroit, Michigan, USA, originally known as the Three Caps, the Capitols were best known for their 1966 hit 'Cool Jerk'. Originally formed around 1962 as a quintet, the two principal members were Donald Storball (guitar, vocals) and Samuel George (d. 17 March 1982; drums, lead vocals). Discovered by record producer Ollie McLaughlin and signed to his Karen label, their first single was 'Dog And Cat', which failed to have any impact. Four years later, after splitting from the other members, Storball and George added pianist/vocalist Richard McDougall to the line-up and they recorded the soulful dance number 'Cool Jerk', which became their only hit, reaching the US Top 10. The group was unable to produce a successful follow-up and disbanded in 1969. Storball enrolled in the Detroit police force, while George was fatally stabbed in March 1982.

● ALBUMS: *Dance The Cool Jerk* (Atco 1966)★★, *We Got A Thing That's In The Groove* (Atco 1966)★★.

● COMPILATIONS: *Their Greatest Recordings* (Solid Smoke 1984)★★, *Golden Classics* (Collectables 1991)★★.

Capris (50s)

This R&B vocal group from Philadelphia, Pennsylvania, USA, comprised Rena Hinton, Bobby Smart, Eddie Warner, Harrison Scott, and Reuben White. Their one claim to fame was 'God Only Knows' (not the Beach Boys' hit) in 1954, which featured the quivering and fetching lead of Hinton. His vocals typified the delicate high-pitched lead work of Philadelphia doo-wop groups. The Capris originally formed in the early 50s in west Philadelphia, and in 1953 established their recording configuration when original member Charlie Stroud left the group to be replaced by Hinton. The Capris signed with Gotham in June 1954. 'God Only Knows' attracted considerable east coast play and they made radio and television appearances. The follow-ups, 'It's A Miracle' and 'It Was Moonglow', both ballads featuring the same vocal approach, were fine examples of the Philadelphia sound, but they did not sustain the group's commercial success. When some of the members entered the Air Force in early 1955, the Capris were forced to disband. The group re-formed in 1958, with Fred Hale replacing Harrison Scott. They recorded 'My Weakness', but its lack of success served to break up the group for good. Some members of the Capris later formed the Moniques.

● COMPILATIONS: *Gotham Recording Stars: The Capris* (Collectables 1990)★★★.

Capris (60s)

Formed in Queens, New York, USA, in 1958, this vocal quintet consisted of Nick Santamaria (lead vocals), Mike Mincelli (first tenor), Vinny Nacardo (second tenor), Frank Reins (baritone) and John Apostol (bass). They were best known for the doo-wop ballad 'There's A Moon Out Tonight', a US number 3 single in early 1961. The song was recorded by the Capris in 1958 and released on the small Planet Records label; however, it was not a hit and the group disbanded. Late in 1960, the owners of Lost Nite Records, one of the first labels to specialize in reissuing earlier rock 'n' roll recordings, purchased the master of the recording and re-released it. It was then leased to the larger, more established Old Town Records, and, owing to the revived interest in group harmony singing, the record nearly reached the top of the chart. The group re-formed and recorded further singles for Old Town and the Mr. Peeke label, but although three reached the charts, they never had another hit. The group has stayed together since the early 60s, however, and in 1982 recorded an album for Ambient Sound Records that included an update of their hit.

● ALBUMS: *There's A Moon Out Again* (Ambient Sound 1982) re-released as *Morse Code Of Love* (Collectables 1992)★★.

CARDINALS

An R&B vocal group from Baltimore, Maryland, USA, the Cardinals were part of the first wave of R&B vocal groups that emerged in the early 50s, making a series of records featuring deep vocal harmony with a high tenor lead. The outfit formed some time around 1947, and sang in the style of the Ink Spots and other black pop groups of the era. Signing with Atlantic Records in 1951, the group drastically altered their style for the R&B market. The group at that time were Ernie Warren (tenor lead), Meredith Brothers (tenor), Donald Johnson (baritone), Leon Hardy (bass), and Jack Aydelotte (tenor, guitarist). Their biggest hits were 'Shouldn't I Know' (number 7 R&B) from 1951, 'The Wheel Of Fortune' (number 6 R&B) from 1952, and 'The Door Is Still Open' (number 4 R&B) from 1955. The Cardinals broke up in 1956; during the late 50s and early 60s Warren kept a re-formed Cardinals together, but never recorded.

CARNATIONS

R&B vocal group the Carnations were formed in 1954 in Bridgeport, Connecticut, USA, by leads Matthew Morales and Carl Hatton, with Harvey Arrington, Alan Mason and Arthur Blackwell. Based in the Yellow Mill River ghetto school Watersville Junior High, they started singing together aged 13 and initially took the name Startones. Under this name they recorded two singles, 'Betty', from 1954, and 'I Love You So Dearly', in 1956. The following year their career was interrupted when two members, Hatton and Arrington, joined and Blackwell's younger brother, Tommy, took his place. In 1959 Edward Kennedy stepped in for Mason, who had joined another group. At this stage a further name change was required, and the Startones became the Teardrops. As such they made the acquaintance of Bo Diddley, who took them on tour and in 1959 asked them to back him on the recording of his R&B hit I'm Sorry'. Also recorded at the same sessions was 'Crackin' Up', which became Diddley's first record to reach the *Billboard* Top 100, though on neither of the releases were the Teardrops properly credited. By 1960 the group had moved on to a near-residency at the Apollo Theatre in New York, winning its famed talent contests for six weeks in a row. They still remained without a contract, however, despite their treks through New York's music industry corridors. After one particularly frustrating day, the group retired to a toilet in one record company building to revive their spirits by practising harmony. Joe René, A&R director of Beltone Records, was in the vicinity, and a contract was arranged with subsidiary label Lescay Records. However, Beltone insisted on a change of name from the generic Teardrops, and the quartet became the Carnations. Their October 1961 debut single, 'Long Tall Girl', sold well locally (and has become a major doo-wop favourite for later generations), but not enough to establish them as serious chart contenders. Lescay pulled the plug quickly, leaving two proposed singles, 'Arlene' and 'Crying Shame', unreleased.

CARNE, JEAN

Jean Carne was born in Columbus, Georgia, USA, but was raised in Atlanta, where her parents encouraged her at the age of four to sing in the church choir and to take piano lessons. Indeed, to this day, Carne is an accomplished performer on piano, clarinet and bassoon. She first revealed her formidable musical talents as a teenager on a morning radio talk show, *Today In Georgia*, when she sang 'Misty' to the accompaniment of Errol Garner's piano. After winning a music scholarship to Morris Brown College, Carne learned to play almost every instrument in the orchestra. Her recording career began in 1971 with her husband Doug, and together they made three albums for Ovation Records that brought widespread recognition, built upon by touring engagements across the USA. At this stage Carne was often praised for being one of the first Afro-American women to define her own voice and image, rather than being moulded by the industry. Afterwards, she performed with Duke Ellington, the last vocalist to do so before his death. She then teamed up with Norman Connors for four acclaimed albums, contributed 'Reach For It' to George Duke's *Gold* album and sang lead vocals on the first two albums by Earth, Wind And Fire. The four albums she recorded for Philadelphia International are probably her best and introduced Carne to pop and R&B audiences for the first time. She then moved to Motown Records for *Trust Me*, which provided her first major singles success with 'If You Don't Know Me By Now', which was recorded with the Temptations. Carne later found time to contribute to records by Kenny Gamble ('Love Is Beautiful When It's Right') and Stanley Turrentine ('Night Breeze'), and recorded for Omni/Atlantic Records. She continues to tour for six months every year, spending the rest of her time at home in Atlanta with her three children.

● ALBUMS: With Doug Carne: *Infant Eyes* (Ovation 1971)★★★, *Spirit Of The New Land* (Ovation 1972)★★★, *Revelation* (Ovation 1973)★★★. With Norman Connors: *Slewfoot* (Buddah 1974)★★★, *Saturday Night Special* (Buddah 1975)★★★, *This Is Your Life* (Buddah 1978)★★★, *Invitation* (Buddah 1979)★★★. With Earth, Wind And Fire: *Earth, Wind And Fire* (Warners 1971)★★, *The Need Of Love* (Warners 1972)★★. Solo: *Jean Carne* (Philadelphia International 1977)★★★★, *Happy To Be With You* (Philadelphia International 1979)★★★, *Sweet And Wonderful* (Philadelphia International 1981)★★★, *When I Find Your Love* (Philadelphia International 1982)★★★★, *Trust Me* (Motown 1983)★★★, *Closer Than Close* (Omni 1986)★★★, *You're A Part Of Me* (Omni 1988)★★★, *Love Lessons* (Moja 1996)★★★.

Carollons

The Carollons were formed in New York, USA, in the mid-50s. Originally called the Emeralds, the quintet featured Robert Dunson, Irving Brodsky, Artie Levy, Jimmy Laffey and Tyler Volks. Volks and Dunson were shortly replaced by Richard Jackson and Eric Nathonson. Inspired by the Moonglows and the Dells, they wrote much of their own material. 'Chapel Of Tears' was their debut release on Mohawk in 1958 and was a considerable local success. They toured the north-east throughout the year and appeared on Clay Cole's television show. The more pop-orientated 'Hold Me Close' followed but failed to build on their initial breakthrough. When 'You Say' was also ignored the group disappeared with it.

Carols

Originally formed as a gospel group called United Baptist Five, in Detroit, Michigan, USA, in 1949, the Carols consisted of Tommy Evans (bass lead), Wilbert Tindle (baritone), James Worthy (piano), Richard Coleman (first tenor) and William Davis (second tenor). They met while working in a car factory, before discovering a shared love of harmony singing and spirituals. However, as the Carols, they sang secular songs and started to make an impression performing live in Harlem, New York. Columbia Records released their debut single, 'Please Believe In Me', in June 1950. Neither this nor the follow-up 'If I Could Steal You From Somebody Else' was a success on the charts and the Carols moved to Savoy Records. By this time, Kenneth Duncan had replaced Coleman, but their only Savoy issue, 'Fifty Million Women' flopped and the Carols broke up when Evans joined the Ravens.

Carr, James

b. 13 June 1942, Coahoma, Mississippi, USA. One of soul music's greatest and most underrated voices, Carr sang gospel in the Sunset Travellers and the Harmony Echoes and was discovered by Memphis gospel-group mentor Roosevelt Jamison. This budding manager and songwriter brought Carr to the Goldwax label. It took four singles to define the singer's style, but the deep, magnificent 'You've Got My Mind Messed Up' burned with an intensity few contemporaries could match. A US Top 10 R&B hit in 1966, 'Love Attack' and 'Pouring Water On A Drowning Man' also followed that year. In 1967 Carr released 'Dark End Of The Street', southern soul's definitive guilt-laced 'cheating' song, which inspired several cover versions. His later work included 'Let It Happen' and 'A Man Needs A Woman', but his fragile personality was increasingly disturbed by drug abuse. 'To Love Somebody' (1969) was Carr's final hit. Goldwax Records collapsed the following year and Carr moved to Atlantic Records for 'Hold On' (1971), which was recorded at Malaco Studios in Jackson, Mississippi. His problems worsened until 1977, when a now-impoverished Carr was reunited with Jamison. One single, the rather average 'Let Me Be Right', appeared on the River City label and the singer temporarily disappeared from the scene. Carr resurfaced in 1979 on a tour of Japan, the first concert of which was a disaster when he 'froze' on stage, having taken too much medication before his performance. In 1991 he had an album of new material entitled *Take Me To The Limit* released by Goldwax Records in the USA (Ace Records in the UK), with Quinton Claunch and Roosevelt Jamison back among the production credits. The following year, Carr appeared at the Sweet Soul Music annual festival in northern Italy, and three of his songs were included on a 'live' album of the festival on the Italian '103' label. By 1993, Claunch had left Goldwax and set up his own Soultrax Records, for which Carr recorded his *Soul Survivor* album (again also on UK Ace), the title track of which had a single release in the USA. Meanwhile, having lost Carr to Claunch, Goldwax's new President, E.W. Clark, exhumed some prime late 60s Carr material for inclusion on *Volume 1* of the projected (and perhaps optimistically titled) *Complete James Carr* (a US-only release).

● ALBUMS: *You Got My Mind Messed Up* (Goldwax 1966)★★★★, *A Man Needs A Woman* (Goldwax 1968)★★★, *Freedom Train* (Goldwax 1968)★★★, *Take Me To The Limit* (Goldwax 1991)★★★, *Soul Survivor* (Soultrax 1993)★★★.

● COMPILATIONS: *At The Dark End Of The Street* (1987)★★★, *The Complete James Carr, Volume 1* (Goldwax 1993)★★★★, with the Jubilee Hummingbirds *Guilty Of Serving God* (Ace 1996)★★.

Carroll, Dina

b. Newmarket, Suffolk, England. Dina Carroll's place of birth could actually be a contentious issue bearing in mind that it took place in the back of a taxi speeding towards Newmarket Hospital. The daughter of a US serviceman and British mother, Carroll spent a few years in Philadelphia, but was largely brought up in the UK. Her soulful voice (sounding somewhat like Evelyn King) brought her to the attention of Streetsounds, where she auditioned and was rewarded with session work. She released 'People All Around The World' on Jive in 1989 as Deana Carroll before reverting to Dina for a cover of 'Walk On By'. In 1990 she provided vocals for Quartz's 'It's Too Late'. Following their split, Carroll nearly abandoned the music business, but A&M signed her as a solo act, and released the hit singles 'It's Too Late' and 'Ain't No Man', followed by her debut album. After a three year break she returned in 1996 with further chart success in the UK, and a follow-up album *Only Human*.

● ALBUMS: *So Close* (A&M 1993)★★★, *Only Human* (Mercury 1996)★★★.

● VIDEOS: *So Close - The Videos* (1994).

Carter, Clarence

b. 14 January 1936, Montgomery, Alabama, USA. Carter's earliest releases were as half of the duo Clarence And Calvin. Also known as the C And C Boys, the blind duo made seven singles, the last of which was recorded at Fame's Muscle Shoals studio. When his partner, Calvin Thomas (aka Scott), suffered serious injuries in a car accident in 1966, Carter became a solo act (Calvin Scott himself later reappeared as a solo act to record two Dave Crawford-produced Atco singles in 1969/70 and a

Clarence Paul-produced 1971 album for Stax, *I'm Not Blind ... I Just Can't See*, from which two singles were also culled). 'Tell Daddy', released in January 1967, began a fruitful spell of Fame-produced hits by Carter, released on the Atlantic label. Noteworthy were 'Thread The Needle', 'Looking For A Fox' and 'Slip Away', where the singer combined his outstanding voice with his skill as an arranger and musician. 'Patches', first recorded by Chairmen Of The Board, was a UK number 2 and a US number 4 in 1970, but despite further strong offerings, Clarence was unable to sustain the momentum. He remained with Fame until 1973, where he also helped guide Candi Staton, who was now his wife, before moving to ABC Records the subsequent year. Further recordings on Venture and Big C took Carter's career into the 80s and of late the artist has found a sympathetic outlet with the Ichiban label. Despite being blinded as a child, he developed a distinctive guitar style that complemented his earthy delivery, and was just as comfortable on keyboards, writing songs or arranging sessions. The first two albums, *This Is Clarence Carter* and *The Dynamic Clarence Carter* show off his versatile talent to good effect.

● ALBUMS: *This Is Clarence Carter* (Atlantic 1968)★★★, *The Dynamic Clarence Carter* (Atlantic 1969)★★★, *Testifyin'* (Atlantic 1969)★★★, *Patches* (Atlantic 1970)★★★, *Sixty Minutes With Clarence Carter* (1973)★★, *Real* (1974)★★, *Loneliness And Temptation* (ABC 1975)★★★, *A Heart Full Of Song* (ABC 1976)★★★, *I Got Caught* (ABC 1977)★★★, *Let's Burn* (Venture 1981)★★★, *Messin' With My Mind* (Ichiban 1985)★★★, *Dr. CC* (Ichiban 1986)★★★, *Hooked On Love* (Ichiban 1987)★★★, *Touch Of Blues* (Ichiban 1989)★★★, *Between A Rock And A Hard Place* (Ichiban 1990)★★★, *Have You Met Clarence Carter ... Yet?* (1992)★★★, *I Couldn't Refuse* (Ron 1995)★★★.

● COMPILATIONS: *The Best Of Clarence Carter* (Atlantic 1971)★★★, *Soul Deep* (Edsel 1984)★★★, *The Dr.'s Greatest Prescriptions* (Ichiban 1991)★★, *Snatching It Back: The Best Of Clarence Carter* (Rhino/Atlantic 1992)★★★.

CARTER, MEL

b. 22 April 1943, Cincinnati, Ohio, USA. Although an African-American who began his career in an R&B milieu, Carter possessed a warm and smooth tenor that lent itself best to middle-of-the-road pop music. His mid-60s hits were essentially in that style, and although they possessed enough rock 'n' roll edge to make the Top 40 radio play, there was not quite enough for them to be heard on R&B stations. He first sang on local radio at the age of four, and performed with Lionel Hampton at the age of nine. His first hit, for Sam Cooke's Derby Records, was 'When A Boy Falls In Love' (1963), which made both the R&B and pop charts. After joining Imperial in 1964, all his records were on the pop charts, recording hits such as 'Hold Me, Thrill Me, Kiss Me' (number 8 pop) in 1965, '(All Of A Sudden) My Heart Sings' (number 38 pop) in 1965, and 'Band Of Gold' (number 32 pop) in 1966. 'Hold Me, Thrill Me, Kiss Me' was an earlier hit by the Orioles in 1953 and 'Band Of Gold' for Don Cherry in 1955. Chart success eluded Carter after 1966, but in later decades he had built a career on American television, parlaying his handsome looks on shows such as *Quincy*, *Sanford And Son*, *Marcus Welby, MD*, and *Magnum P.I.*

● ALBUMS: *When A Boy Falls In Love* (Derby 1963)★★★, *Hold Me, Thrill Me, Kiss Me* (Imperial 1965)★★★, *My Heart Sings* (Imperial 1965)★★, *Easy Listening* (Imperial 1966)★★, *Be My Love* (Liberty 1967)★★.

● VIDEOS: *Live In Hollywood* (CSP 1996).

CARTER, VIVIAN, AND JAMES BRACKEN

(see Vee Jay Records)

CASE

b. New York City, New York, USA. This rising star of swingbeat performed cameo roles on records by Al B. Sure, Christopher Williams and Jodeci, among others, before launching his solo career proper in 1996. His self-titled debut album was composed of romantic R&B with hip-hop grooves, though the high sexual quotient normally associated with swingbeat was largely absent. Having grown up listening to Marvin Gaye, Donny Hathaway and Stevie Wonder, he confirmed to *Billboard* magazine that he focuses 'heavily on the melody of a song'. The album's attendant single, 'Touch Me, Tease Me', was written in collaboration with Mary J. Blige, and featured Foxy Brown on backing vocals. It was included on the soundtrack to *The Nutty Professor*, the multi-million-dollar-grossing Eddie Murphy film. In a tribute to Case's hip-hop roots, the single featured a sample of Schoolly D's 'PSK', one of the first gangsta rap narratives. Blige, said to be romantically linked with Case, also collaborated on the second single release, 'I Gotcha'.

● ALBUMS: *Case* (Spoiled Rotten/Def Jam 1996)★★★.

CASTELLES

An R&B vocal group from Philadelphia, Pennsylvania, USA, comprising lead George Grant, Octavious Anthony, William Taylor, Frank Vance, and Ronald Everett. The Castelles, featuring the delicate and quivering falsetto tenor of Grant, perfectly exemplified the Philadelphia vocal group sound of the 50s. The group joined Herb Slotkin's Grand Records in 1954, and under the production aegis of an up-and-coming producer, Jerry Ragovoy, achieved a hit with their very first effort, 'My Girl Awaits Me' (1954), which sold well in Philadelphia, New York, and Washington, DC. The follow-up, 'This Silver Ring', composed by Ragovoy, was a commercial disappointment, but artistically it was as evocative and pristine as their debut The third release, 'Do You Remember', had little impact, but the b-side, a version of the old standard 'If You Were The Only Girl', sold well in Philadelphia. Other notable songs followed, 'Heavenly Father' (a remake of the Edna McGriff hit from 1952), and 'Over A Cup Of Coffee' (1955). The group moved to Atlantic Records, and had one Coasters-styled release before breaking up in 1956. Members of the Atco-based group were Grant, Anthony, Taylor, and new member, lead Clarence Scott.

● COMPILATIONS: *The Sweet Sound Of The Castelles* (Collectables 1990)★★★.

Castor, Jimmy

b. 2 June 1943, New York City, New York, USA. Jimmy Castor was a contemporary of Frankie Lymon and the Teenagers during the mid-50s. His group, Jimmy Castor And The Juniors, recorded a song for Wing Records that Castor had penned, 'I Promise To Remember', which Lymon and his group then covered and turned into a hit in 1956. Due to the similarity of their singing styles, Castor often sang with the Teenagers in Lymon's place. After that brief flirtation with music, Castor finished school, but he returned to the music business in the mid-60s, forming the Jimmy Castor Bunch. The group had a US soul hit in 1967 with 'Hey Leroy', on Smash Records, and then disappeared for six years. In 1972, now signed to RCA Records, Castor and his current Bunch - Gerry Thomas (keyboards), Doug Gibson (bass), Harry Jensen (guitar), Lenny Fridie Jnr. (percussion) and Robert Manigault (drums) - came back with their biggest hit, 'Troglodyte (Cave Man)', which reached number 6 in the US singles chart. Castor had two final charting dance singles, 'The Bertha Butt Boogie (Part 1)' and 'King Kong (Part 1), on Atlantic Records in 1975. The Jimmy Castor Bunch went on to record several albums for various labels, four of which charted in the USA during the 70s.

● ALBUMS: *Hey Leroy!* (Smash 1967)★★★, *It's Just Begun* (RCA 1972)★★★, *Phase Two* (RCA 1972)★★★, *Dimension III* (RCA 1973)★★, *Everything Man* (Atlantic 1973)★★, *Butt Of Course* (Atlantic 1975)★★★, *Supersound* (Atlantic 1975)★★, *E-Man Groovin'* (Atlantic 1976)★★★, *Maximum Stimulation* (Atlantic 1977)★★, *Let It Out* (1978)★★, *Jimmy Castor Bunch* (1979)★★, *'C'* (1980)★★, *E-Man Boogie 82* (Salsoul 1982)★★, *The Return Of Leroy* (1983)★★, *Don't Waste The Time* (Dream 1984)★★.

Cats 'N' Jammers

A vocal/instrumental R&B trio from Chicago, Illinois, USA, the Cats 'N' Jammers are one of the best representatives of the 40s jive/vocal harmony groups who created a fusion sound of jazz, pop, and blues in the immediate post-war years. Members were Adam Lambert (guitar), Sylvester Hickman (bass), and Bill Samuels (piano, lead vocals), and each had experience in other groups before coming together in 1945. The trio was soon featured on Dave Garroway's radio show, which brought them to the attention of the newly formed Mercury Records. They had immediate success with their very first release, 'I Cover The Waterfront' (number 3 R&B), and also had considerable success with 'Port Wine' (number 5 R&B) in 1946. The Cats 'N' Jammers left Mercury in 1949 and then recorded for Miracle Records as the Bill Samuels Trio. The group broke up shortly afterwards, when Samuels moved to Minnesota.

Cats And The Fiddle

This African-American vocal/instrumental group from Chicago, Illinois, USA, featured original members Austin Powell (lead vocals, guitar), Jimmy Henderson (first tenor, tipple), Ernie Price (second tenor, tipple) and Chuck Barksdale (bass vocals, bass). The Cats And The Fiddle were one of the finest representatives of the string band/vocal harmony ensembles that were common in black nightclubs during the 40s. The group came together in 1937 as a vocal harmony group patterned after the Mills Brothers, and first appeared on local radio and in local clubs, particularly the Pioneer Lounge, which for the next 15 years they used as their home base between tours. The unit also appeared in motion pictures, including *Too Hot To Handle* (1938), *Going Places* (1939), and many short features. Signed in 1939 to RCA-Victor, recording on its Bluebird subsidiary, the following year they achieved success with a excellent Henderson-composed ballad, 'I Miss You So' (the song would become a hit for Little Anthony And The Imperials in 1965). The song represented only one aspect of Cats And The Fiddle's music; they also played blues-based numbers such as 'I'm Gonna Pull My Hair' and frenetic scat-jazz numbers such as 'Gang Busters'. The group switched to the Regis/Manor label complex in 1944, but their best recordings lay behind them. After recording a few tracks for the Philadelphia-based Gotham label in 1950, they made their last recordings for Decca in 1951. Cats And The Fiddle experienced a bewildering series of personnel changes. Henderson died in 1940 and was replaced by Herbie Miles, who in turn in 1941 was replaced by Lloyd 'Tiny' Grimes, who a year later was replaced by Mifflin Branford. Barksdale died in 1941 and was replaced by George Steinbeck. While Powell was in the army during 1943-46, he was replaced by Hank Haslett, who in turn in 1945 was replaced by Herbie Miles. More changes followed in the late 40s when tenor and congo drum player Johnny Davis replaced Branford and vocalist Shirley Moore was added. After Powell disbanded the group in 1951, Ernie Price re-formed the group and they played in Chicago clubs for the next two years before disbanding again. Price died in 1960.

● COMPILATIONS: *I Miss You So* (RCA 1976)★★★.

Central Line

Of all the bands involved in the early 80s 'Brit Funk' revival, Central Line came closest to exporting the movement across the Atlantic. Comprising Lipson Francis, Henry Defoe, C. Beckles (lead vocals) and Camelle G. Hinds, Central Line formed in London in April 1978. The membership was drawn largely from the defunct East London group TFB, whose line-up also included future Light Of The World trumpeter Kenny Wellington and future Imagination drummer Errol Kennedy. Central Line's first single was 'What We Got (It's Hot)', a lively exposition of their R&B-based dance material. It led to tours with Roy Ayers, the Real Thing and Grover Washington Jnr. However, the follow-up single flopped and caused the rethink that produced February 1981's '(You Know) You Can Do It', a UK Top 40 chart hit. Re-energized, Central Line embarked on sessions with producer Roy Carter (ex-Heatwave) to produce 'Walking Into Sunshine' - which fared well in both the US and UK dance charts. It was followed by 'Don't Tell Me' (UK number 55) and 'You've Said Enough' (UK number 58). Their biggest hit came in January 1983 when 'Nature Boy' peaked at number 21 in the UK charts. However, by now the Brit

Funk movement was in decline and the group achieved only one further chart hit, June 1983's 'Surprise Surprise', before disbanding.

● ALBUMS: *Breaking Point* (Mercury 1982)★★★.

Chairmen Of The Board

Briefly known as the Gentlemen, this Detroit-based quartet was instigated by General Norman Johnson (b. 23 May 1944, Norfolk, Virginia, USA). A former member of the Showmen, he left that group in 1968 intent on a solo path, but instead joined Danny Woods (b. 10 April 1944, Atlanta, Georgia, USA), Harrison Kennedy (b. Canada) and Eddie Curtis (b. Philadelphia, Pennsylvania, USA) in this budding venture. Signed to the newly formed Invictus label, the group secured an international hit with their debut single, 'Give Me Just A Little More Time'. His elated performance established the General's emphatic delivery, which combined the emotional fire of the Four Tops' Levi Stubbs with the idiomatic 'trilling' of Billy Stewart. Its follow-up, the vibrant '(You've Got Me) Dangling On A String', was a more substantial hit in the UK than America, the first of several releases following this pattern. Such commercial contradictions did not detract from the excellence of 'Everything's Tuesday', 'Pay To The Piper' (both 1971) and 'I'm On My Way To A Better Place' (1972) as the group furthered its impressive repertoire. Although Johnson provided the most recognizable voice, Woods and Kennedy also shared the lead spotlight, while the overall sound varied from assertive R&B to the melancholia of 'Patches', later a hit for Clarence Carter. The group ceased recording in 1971, but singles continued to appear until 1976, while a final album, *Skin I'm In* (1974), was also compiled from old masters. Curtis left Invictus altogether but the remaining trio each issued solo albums. Johnson also worked with stablemates the Honey Cone and 100 Proof, while he and Woods kept the Chairmen name afloat with live performances. The General subsequently signed with Arista, where he enjoyed a series of late 70s R&B hits before reuniting with Woods. 'Loverboy' (1984) reflected their enduring popularity on the American 'beach'/vintage soul music scene, and was a minor hit in the UK three years later.

● ALBUMS: as the Chairmen Of The Board *Chairmen Of The Board* (Invictus 1969)★★★, *In Session* (Invictus 1970)★★, *Men Are Getting Scarce (Bittersweet)* (Invictus 1972)★★, *Skin I'm In* (Invictus 1974)★★★, as General Johnson And The Chairmen *Success* (1981)★★, *A Gift Of Beach Music* (1982)★★, *The Music* (Surfside 1987)★★. Solo: General Johnson *Generally Speaking* (Invictus 1972)★★, *General Johnson* (Arista 1976)★★★. Harrison Kennedy *Hypnotic Music* (Invictus 1972)★★. Danny Woods *Aries* (Invictus 1972)★★.

● COMPILATIONS: *Salute The General* (HDH/Demon 1983)★★★, *A.G.M.* (HDH/Demon 1985)★★★, *Soul Agenda* (HDH 1989)★★, *Greatest Hits* (HDH/Fantasy 1991)★★★★, *The Best Of* (Castle 1997)★★★★.

Champaign

Based in Champaign, Illinois, USA, this self-contained pop-funk band came together in 1981 and took their name from their home city. A white instrumental unit fronted by two black vocalists, Champaign was a merger of veterans of previous bands and consisted of Michael Day (guitar, keyboards), Rocky Maffit (drums), Leon Reeder (guitar), Dana Walden (keyboards), Michael Reed (bass), Pauli Carman (vocals) and Rena Jones (vocals). In the UK the group was known only for 'How 'Bout Us', a delightful ballad that hit number 5 in 1981, while in the USA the song reached number 4 in the R&B chart and the national Top 30. The group had follow-ups in the USA, hitting the charts with another strong ballad, 'Try Again' (number 2 R&B, 1983), and a strong dance groove, 'On And Off Love' (number 10 R&B, 1984). Although the group issued three albums before their break-up in 1985, Champaign's success remained only with singles. Following the group's break-up, Carman had a moderately successful solo career. A reunion of Champaign in 1990 proved short-lived, but their fourth album briefly made the charts in 1991.

● ALBUMS: *How 'Bout Us* (Columbia 1981)★★★, *Modern Heart* (Columbia 1983)★★, *Woman In Flames* (Columbia 1984)★★, *Champaign IV* (1991)★★★.
Solo: Pauli Carman *Dial My Number* (Columbia 1986)★★.

Chandler, Gene

b. Eugene Dixon, 6 July 1937, Chicago, Illinois, USA. Recalled for the gauche but irresistible 1962 US number 1, 'Duke Of Earl', Chandler's million-selling single in fact featured the Dukays, a doo-wop quintet he fronted (Eugene Dixon, Shirley Jones, James Lowe, Earl Edwards and Ben Broyles). His record company preferred to promote a solo artist and thus one of soul's most enduring careers was launched. Temporarily bedevilled by his 'dandy' image, the singer was rescued by a series of excellent Curtis Mayfield-penned songs, including 'Rainbow' and 'Man's Temptation'. These were hits in 1963, but the relationship blossomed with 'Just Be True' (1964) and the sublime 'Nothing Can Stop Me' (1965), both US Top 20 singles. Chandler later recorded under the aegis of producer Carl Davis, including '(The) Girl Don't Care', 'There Goes The Lover' and 'From The Teacher To The Preacher', a duet with Barbara Acklin. Switching to Mercury Records in 1970, 'Groovy Situation' became another major hit, while an inspired teaming with Jerry Butler was an artistic triumph. Chandler's career was revitalized during the disco boom when 'Get Down' was an international hit on Chi-Sound (Chandler was also a vice-president for the label). Further releases, 'When You're Number 1' and 'Does She Have A Friend', consolidated such success, while recordings for Salsoul, with Jaime Lynn and Fastfire, continued his career into the 80s.

● ALBUMS: *The Duke Of Earl* (Vee Jay 1962)★★★★, *Just Be True* (1964)★★★, *Gene Chandler Live On Stage In '65* (Constellation 1965, reissued as *Live At The Regal*)★★, *The Girl Don't Care* (Brunswick 1967)★★★, *The Duke Of Soul* (Checker 1967)★★★, *There Was A Time* (Brunswick 1968)★★, *The Two Sides Of Gene Chandler* (Brunswick 1969)★★, *The Gene Chandler Situation* (Mercury 1970)★★★, with Jerry Butler *Gene And Jerry - One & One* (Mercury 1971)★★★, *Get Down*

(Chi-Sound 1978)★★★, *When You're Number One* (20th Century 1979), *Gene Chandler '80* (20th Century 1980)★★★, *Your Love Looks Good On Me* (Fastfire 1985)★★★.
● COMPILATIONS: *Greatest Hits By Gene Chandler* (Constellation 1964)★★★, *Just Be True* (1980)★★★, *Stroll On With The Duke* (Solid Smoke 1984)★★★, *60s Soul Brother* (Kent/Ace 1986)★★★, *Get Down* (Charly 1992)★★★, *Nothing Can Stop Me: Gene Chandler's Greatest Hits* (Varese Sarabande 1994)★★★.
● FILMS: *Don't Knock The Twist* (1962).

CHANGE

Although the group was led by Paolo Granolio (guitar) and David Romani (bass), this was ostensibly a studio creation by producers Jacques Fred Petrus and Mauro Malavasi, who first linked to form Goody Music in 1975. With material recorded in Bologna (where the producers' own 24-track studio was based) and New York, *The Glow Of Love* launched the group on a high note, with success on the UK charts arriving with 'Searching' and its Luther Vandross-led vocal. With touring engagements forthcoming, a permanent aggregation of personnel was vaunted, with James Robinson taking over from Vandross on vocals. Following *Miracles* and *Sharing Your Love*, he would embark on a solo career, to be replaced at the front of the group by Debra Cooper and Rick Brenna, backed by Timmy Allen (bass), Vince Henry (saxophone) and Michael Campbell (guitar). The emerging production team of Jam and Lewis took over for *Change Of Heart*, which brought two further UK hits (the title track and 'You Are My Melody'). That success proved difficult to emulate on later recordings, although *Turn On The Radio* did give rise to three minor UK hits ('Let's Go Together', 'Oh What A Feeling' and 'Mutual Attraction').
● ALBUMS: *The Glow Of Love* (RFC/Atlantic 1980)★★★, *Miracles* (Atlantic 1981)★★★, *Sharing Your Love* (Atlantic 1982)★★★, *This Is Your Time* (Atlantic 1983)★★, *Change Of Heart* (Atlantic 1984)★★, *Turn On The Radio* (Atlantic 1985)★★★.

CHANGING FACES

This female R&B duo, comprising Charisse Rose (b. USA) and Cassandra Lucas (b. USA), first established itself in 1994 with the minor US hits 'Stroke You Up' and 'Foolin' Around'. Both singles were included on the New York, USA-based group's self-titled debut of that year. *Changing Faces* eventually sold half a million copies, and reached number 1 on *Billboard*'s Top R&B Albums chart. The carefully crafted follow-up, *All Day All Night*, was eventually released in 1997. This time there was a higher quota of ballad material, as opposed to the silky R&B dance rhythms of the debut. The new style was exemplified by songs such as 'G.H.E.T.T.O.U.T', the first single released from the album, which dealt with male infidelity from a female perspective. A cover version of Cyndi Lauper's 'Time After Time' was also included. On the subject of this new polemic, Rose commented to the press: 'We wanted to show people, especially young women, that they can stay true to themselves and still be real.' *All Day All Night* featured the production expertise of R. Kelly and Bryce Wilson, ensuring a strong reception in the international R&B markets.
● ALBUMS: *Changing Faces* (Big Beat/Atlantic 1994)★★★★, *All Day All Night* (Big Beat/Atlantic 1997)★★★.

CHANNELS

Formed in Harlem, New York City, New York, USA, the Channels were one of the best practitioners of the 'greasy' sound of doo-wop that was being recorded in New York during the late 50s, with exaggerated parts - exotic-sounding lead, high falsetto tenor - weaving in and out of the mix, with a burbling bass throughout. Members were lead Earl Lewis, first tenor Larry Hampden, second tenor Billy Morris, baritone Edward Dolphin, and bass Clifton Wright. They were signed to Bobby Robinson's Whirlin' Disc label in 1956 and recorded their most renowned numbers, 'The Closer You Are' (1956), 'The Gleam In Your Eye' (1956) and 'I Really Love You' (1957), all of which sold heavily on the east coast. A stay at George Goldner's Gone label in 1958 produced 'That's My Desire' and the below-standard 'Altar Of Love'. The group returned to Bobby Robinson in 1959 and produced one of their finest songs, 'My Love Will Never Die'. During the 70s Earl Lewis, with varying ensembles of Channels, regularly worked the east coast revival circuit.
● COMPILATIONS: *The Channels Greatest Hits* (Relic 1990)★★★★, *Earl Lewis And The Channels* (Collectables 1990)★★★.

CHANTERS

An R&B vocal group from the Queens Borough of New York City, New York, USA, the Chanters, formed in 1957, were one of the best of the many groups who patterned their pre-teen lead sound after Frankie Lymon And The Teenagers. The members were Larry Pendergrass (lead), Fred Paige (tenor), Bud Johnson, Jnr. (tenor), Elliot Green (baritone) and Bobby Thompson (bass). Johnson's father, saxophonist and long-time bandleader Budd Johnson, used his ensemble to back the Chanters and he wrote the arrangements for all the sessions. The group, with little success, recorded an excellent body of tunes, notably 'My My Darling' and 'Five Little Kisses', before achieving their one hit, 'No, No, No'. However, even 'No, No, No' (recorded in 1958) did not reach the charts until it was re-released in 1961 (number 9 R&B, number 41 pop) - a re-release stimulated by the neo-doo-wop resurgence on the east coast in the early 60s. However, by that time, the group had disbanded.

CHARIOTEERS

The members of this classic vocal group, formed at Wilberforce College, Ohio, USA, were tenor lead Wilfred 'Billy' Williams (b. 28 December 1910, Waco, Texas, USA, d. 17 October 1972), second tenor Edward Jackson, baritone Ira Williams, and vocal arranger and bass Howard Daniels. The Charioteers, in common with many black vocal ensembles of the 40s, were a pop music act in the manner of the Ink Spots rather than an R&B ensemble. The Charioteers came together in 1930 and after winning an all-Ohio quartet contest in 1934, were rewarded with a two-record recording contract with Decca and a short radio show on WLW-Cincinnati. The original group included Williams, Daniels, Peter Leubers, and John Harewood, but in 1936 when the group moved to New York, Leubers and Harewood were replaced with Jackson and Ira Williams, respectively. The group appeared on the Mutual radio network and in 1937 signed with Vocalion Records, finally launching their extensive recording career in earnest. Most of their 30s recordings were in the vein of jubilees, spirituals, and Negro folk tunes, such as 'Wade In The Water' and 'Ezekiel Saw De Wheel'. When the group moved to Columbia Records in 1940, the label recorded the Charioteers as a pop group, and national success for the group was immediate with one of their biggest chart hits, 'So Long' (number 23 pop). The group appeared regularly on network radio, most notably Bing Crosby's show, and made appearances in motion pictures, while also touring in the musical revue 'Hellzapoppin''. Despite recording an enormous amount of material during the war years, the Charioteers only returned to the national charts in 1946 with 'On The Boardwalk In Atlanta City' (number 12 pop). The Charioteers secured their biggest hit with their 1947 sensation, a humorous novelty called 'Open The Door, Richard' (number 6 pop), in which they competed on the charts with six other versions. The group received more national exposure with the double-sided hit 'What Did He Say? (number 21 pop) backed with 'Ooh! Look-A There, Ain't She Pretty' (number 20 pop) in 1948, and 'A Kiss And A Rose' (number 8 R&B, number 19 pop). In 1950 Williams left the Charioteers to form his own quartet and prospered immensely during the 50s. The Charioteers persevered with new lead Herbert Dickerson for a time, but disbanded in 1957.

● ALBUMS: *Sweet And Low* 10-inch album (Columbia 1950)★★★.

● COMPILATIONS: *Jesus Is A Rock In A Weary Land* (Gospel Jubilee 1991)★★★, *On The Sunny Side Of The Street* (Dr. Horse 1991)★★★.

CHARLES AND EDDIE

This soul duo consisting of Charles Pettigrew and Eddie Chacon met on a New York subway train. Apparently, Chacon was clutching a copy of Marvin Gaye's 'Trouble Man', and so the two of them struck up a conversation and later started performing together. Chacon had grown up in Oakland, California, where he was in a soul band, and later moved to Miami, Florida, where his recording career continued on projects with the Dust Brothers and Daddy-O. Daddy-O produced Chacon's two solo albums, both of which left him feeling frustrated and determined to return to the soul music he had known in his youth. Pettigrew, meanwhile, was raised in Philadelphia, and went on to study jazz vocals at the Berklee School of Music in Boston, while also singing with the pop band Down Avenue. Charles and Eddie debuted with the worldwide hit 'Would I Lie To You?', which was followed in early 1993 with 'NYC (Can You Believe This City)', based on the story of their meeting. Both tracks were on their debut *Duophonic*, which was produced by Josh Deutsch and consisted mainly of original material, notably Chacon's 'December 2', a tribute to his brother's death on that date. A second album was belatedly released three years later, but proved to be a disappointingly bland collection.

● ALBUMS: *Duophonic* (Stateside/Capitol 1992)★★★, *Chocolate Milk* (Capitol 1995)★★.

CHARLES, BOBBY

b. Robert Charles Guidry, 1938, Abbeville, Louisiana, USA. Charles became well known in the 50s when three of his songs - 'See You Later Alligator', 'Walkin' To New Orleans' and 'But I Do' - were successfully covered by Bill Haley, Fats Domino and Clarence 'Frogman' Henry. The composer also recorded in his own right for Chicago's Chess label, but returned to the south the following decade for a series of low-key, largely unsuccessful, releases. The singer's career was relaunched in 1972 upon signing with Albert Grossman's Bearsville label. *Bobby Charles* featured support from several members of the Band, and this excellent album combined the artist's R&B and Cajun roots to create a warm, mature collection. The set offered several excellent compositions, the highlight of which was the much-covered 'Small Town Talk'. Charles then guested on both of the albums by Paul Butterfield's Better Days, but he has since maintained a relatively low profile. However, a new recording, *Clean Water*, was released in Europe in 1987.

● ALBUMS: *Bobby Charles* reissued as *Small Town Talk* (Bearsville 1972)★★★★, *Clean Water* (Zensor 1987)★★★, *Wish You Were Here Right Now* (Stony Plain 1995)★★★.

● COMPILATIONS: *Bobby Charles* (Chess 1983)★★★, *Chess Masters* (Chess 1986)★★★★.

CHARLES, RAY

b. Ray Charles Robinson, 23 September 1930, Albany, Georgia, USA. Few epithets sit less comfortably than that of genius; Ray Charles has borne this title for over 30 years. As a singer, composer, arranger and pianist, his prolific work deserves no other praise. Born in extreme poverty, Charles was slowly blinded by glaucoma until, by the age of seven, he had lost his sight completely. Earlier, he had been forced to cope with the tragic death of his brother, whom he had seen drown in a water tub. He learned to read and write music in braille and was proficient on several instruments by the time he left school. His mother Aretha died when Charles was 15, and he continued to have a shared upbringing with Mary Jane (the first wife of Charles's absent father). Charles drifted around the Florida circuit, picking up work where he could, before moving across the country to Seattle. Here he continued his itinerant career, playing piano at several nightclubs in a style reminiscent of Nat 'King' Cole. Charles began recording in 1949 and this early, imitative approach was captured on several sessions. Three years later, Atlantic Records acquired his contract, but initially the singer continued his 'cool' direction, revealing only an occasional hint of the passions later unleashed. 'It Should've Been Me', 'Mess Around' and 'Losing Hand' best represent this early R&B era, but Charles's individual style emerged as a result of his work with Guitar

Slim. This impassioned, almost crude blues performer sang with a gospel-based fervour that greatly influenced Charles's thinking. He arranged Slim's million-selling single, 'Things That I Used To Do', on which the riffing horns and unrestrained voice set the tone for Charles's own subsequent direction. This effect was fully realized in 'I Got A Woman' (1954), a song soaked in the fervour of the Baptist Church, but rendered salacious by the singer's abandoned, unrefined delivery. Its extraordinary success, commercially and artistically, inspired similarly compulsive recordings, including 'This Little Girl Of Mine' (1955), 'Talkin' 'Bout You' (1957) and the lush and evocative 'Don't Let The Sun Catch You Crying' (1959), a style culminating in the thrilling call and response of 'What'd I Say' (1959). This acknowledged classic is one of the all-time great encore numbers performed by countless singers and bands in stadiums, clubs and bars all over the world. However, Charles was equally adept at slow ballads, as his heartbreaking interpretations of 'Drown In My Own Tears' and 'I Believe To My Soul' (both 1959) clearly show. Proficient in numerous styles, Charles's recordings embraced blues, jazz, standards and even country, as his muscular reading of 'I'm Movin' On' attested.

In November 1959 Charles left the Atlantic label for ABC Records, where he secured both musical and financial freedom. Commentators often cite this as the point at which the singer lost his fire, but early releases for this new outlet simply continued his groundbreaking style. 'Georgia On My Mind' (1960) and 'Hit The Road Jack' (1961) were, respectively, poignant and ebullient, and established the artist as an international name. This stature was enhanced further in 1962 with the release of the massive-selling album *Modern Sounds In Country And Western*, a landmark collection that produced the million-selling single 'I Can't Stop Loving You'. Its success defined the pattern for Charles's later career; the edges were blunted, the vibrancy was stilled as Charles's repertoire grew increasingly inoffensive. There were still moments of inspiration: 'Let's Go Get Stoned' and 'I Don't Need No Doctor' brought glimpses of a passion now too often muted, while *Crying Time*, Charles's first album since kicking his heroin habit, compared favourably with any Atlantic release. This respite was, however, temporary and as the 60s progressed so the singer's work became less compulsive and increasingly MOR. Like most artists, he attempted cover versions of Beatles songs and had substantial hits with versions of 'Yesterday' and 'Eleanor Rigby'. Two 70s releases, *A Message From The People* and *Renaissance*, did include contemporary material in Stevie Wonder's 'Living In The City' and Randy Newman's 'Sail Away', but subsequent releases reneged on this promise. Charles's 80s work included more country-flavoured collections and a cameo appearance in the film *The Blues Brothers*, but the period is better marked by the singer's powerful appearance on the USA For Africa release, 'We Are The World' (1985). It brought to mind a talent too often dormant, a performer whose marriage of gospel and R&B laid the foundations for soul music. His influence is inestimable, and his talent widely acknowledged and imitated by formidable white artists such as Steve Winwood, Joe Cocker, Van Morrison and Eric Burdon. Charles has been honoured with countless awards during his career including the Lifetime Achievement Award. He has performed rock, jazz, blues and country with spectacular ease, but it is 'father of soul music' that remains his greatest title; it was fitting that, in 1992, an acclaimed documentary, *Ray Charles: The Genius Of Soul*, was broadcast by PBS television. *My World* was a sparkling return to form, and was one of his finest albums in many years, being particularly noteworthy for his version of Leon Russell's 'A Song For You', a song that sounds as if it has always been a Charles song, such is the power of his outstanding voice. *Strong Love Affair* continued in the same vein with a balance of ballads matching the up-tempo tracks; however, it was clear that low-register, slow songs such as 'Say No More', 'Angelina' and 'Out Of My Life' should be the focus of Charles's concentration.

● ALBUMS: *Hallelujah, I Love Her So* aka *Ray Charles* (Atlantic 1957)★★★, *The Great Ray Charles* (Atlantic 1957)★★★★, with Milt Jackson *Soul Brothers* (Atlantic 1958)★★★, *Ray Charles At Newport* (Atlantic 1958)★★★, *Yes Indeed* (Atlantic 1959)★★★, *Ray Charles* (Hollywood 1959)★★★★, *The Fabulous Ray Charles* (Hollywood 1959)★★★, *What'd I Say* (Atlantic 1959)★★★, *The Genius Of Ray Charles* (Atlantic 1959)★★★★★, *Ray Charles In Person* (Atlantic 1960)★★★, *The Genius Hits The Road* (ABC 1960)★★★, *Dedicated To You* (ABC 1961)★★★, *Genius + Soul = Jazz* (Impulse! 1961)★★★★★, *The Genius After Hours* (Atlantic 1961)★★★★, with Betty Carter *Ray Charles And Betty Carter* (ABC 1961)★★★★, *The Genius Sings The Blues* (Atlantic 1961)★★★★, with Jackson *Soul Meeting* (Atlantic 1961)★★★, *Do The Twist With Ray Charles* (Atlantic 1961)★★★, *Modern Sounds In Country And Western* (ABC 1962)★★★★★, *Modern Sounds In Country And Western Volume 2* (ABC 1962)★★★★, *Ingredients In A Recipe For Soul* (ABC 1963)★★★★, *Sweet And Sour Tears* (ABC 1964)★★★, *Have A Smile With Me* (ABC 1964)★★★, *Ray Charles Live In Concert* (ABC 1965)★★★, *Country And Western Meets Rhythm And Blues* aka *Together Again* (ABC 1965)★★★, *Crying Time* (ABC 1966)★★★, *Ray's Moods* (ABC 1966)★★★, *Ray Charles Invites You To Listen* (ABC 1967)★★★, *A Portrait Of Ray* (ABC 1968)★★, *I'm All Yours, Baby!* (ABC 1969)★★, *Doing His Thing* (ABC 1969)★★★, *My Kind Of Jazz* (Tangerine 1970)★★★, *Love Country Style* (ABC 1970)★★, *Volcanic Action Of My Soul* (ABC 1971)★★, *A Message From The People* (ABC 1972)★★, *Through The Eyes Of Love* (ABC 1972), *Jazz Number II* (Tangerine 1972)★★★, *Ray Charles Live* (Atlantic 1973)★★★, *Come Live With Me* (Crossover 1974)★★, *Renaissance* (Crossover 1975)★★, *My Kind Of Jazz III* (Crossover 1975)★★, *Live In Japan* (1975)★★★, with Cleo Laine *Porgy And Bess* (RCA 1976)★★★, *True To Life* (Atlantic 1977)★★, *Love And Peace* (Atlantic 1978)★★, *Ain't It So* (Atlantic 1979)★★, *Brother Ray Is At It Again* (Atlantic 1980)★★, *Wish You Were Here Tonight* (Columbia 1983)★★, *Do I Ever Cross Your Mind* (Columbia 1984)★★, *Friendship* (Columbia 1985)★★, *The Spirit Of Christmas* (Columbia 1985)★★, *From The Pages Of My Mind* (Columbia 1986)★★, *Just Between Us* (Columbia

1988)★★, *Seven Spanish Angels And Other Hits* (Columbia 1989)★★, *Would You Believe* (Warners 1990)★★, *My World* (Warners 1993)★★★★, *Strong Love Affair* (Qwest 1996)★★, *Berlin, 1962* (Pablo 1996)★★★★.
● COMPILATIONS: *The Ray Charles Story* (Atlantic 1962)★★★, *Ray Charles' Greatest Hits* (ABC 1962)★★★★, *A Man And His Soul* (ABC 1967)★★★, *The Best Of Ray Charles 1956-58* (Atlantic 1970)★★★★, *A 25th Anniversary In Show Business Salute To Ray Charles* (ABC 1971)★★★★, *The Right Time* (Atlantic 1987)★★★, *A Life In Music 1956-59* (Atlantic 1982)★★★★, *Greatest Hits Vol. 1 1960-67* (Rhino 1988)★★★★, *Greatest Hits Vol. 2 1960-72* (Rhino 1988)★★★★, *Anthology* (Rhino 1989)★★★★, *The Collection* ABC recordings (Castle 1990)★★★, *Blues Is My Middle Name* 1949-52 recordings (Double Play 1991)★★★, *The Birth Of Soul 1952-59* (Atlantic 1991)★★★★★, *The Complete Atlantic Rhythm And Blues Recordings* 4-CD box set (Atlantic 1992)★★★★★, *The Living Legend* (1993)★★★, *The Best Of The Atlantic Years* (Rhino/Atlantic 1994)★★★, *Classics* (Rhino 1995)★★★, *Genius & Soul* 5-CD box set (Rhino 1997)★★★.
● FURTHER READING: *Ray Charles*, Sharon Bell Mathis. *Brother Ray, Ray Charles' Own Story*, Ray Charles and David Ritz.
● FILMS: *Blues For Lovers* aka *Ballad In Blue* (1964), *The Blues Brothers* (1980).

CHARMS

A popular R&B group of the mid-50s, the Charms were formed in Cincinnati, USA, by Otis Williams (lead), Richard Parker (bass), Joseph Penn (baritone), Donald Peak (tenor) and Rolland Bradley (tenor). 'Heaven Only Knows' was released by Deluxe Records, followed by 'Happy Are We', 'Bye-Bye Baby', 'Quiet Please' and 'My Baby Dearest Darling', all of which failed to secure significant success. However, their September 1954 cover version of the Jewels' 'Hearts Of Stone' took them into the US charts and by January of the following year the song had peaked at number 15 (number 1 in the R&B charts), despite competing versions by both the Jewels and the Fontane Sisters. December 1954 produced two follow-ups: 'Mambo Sha-Mambo' and another cover version, this time the Five Keys' 'Ling, Ting, Tong', were released concurrently, the latter keeping stride with the Five Keys' original version and reaching number 26 on the *Billboard* charts. The policy of outgunning the opposition over 'hot new songs' soon became a Charms trait, but it was not always so successful. An attempt to hijack Gene And Eunice's 'Ko Ko Mo' in February 1955 failed, and saw the group return to writing originals. 'Two Hearts' was written by Otis Williams and King Records' A&R head Henry Glover, but was in turn covered within a week by Pat Boone, who took it to US number 16. The Charms then toured as part of the Top Ten R&B Show package with the Moonglows, Clovers and others. After asking for a pay rise from Deluxe the entire band, with the exception of Otis Williams, was sacked. Williams was joined by Rollie Willis, Chuck Barksdale (ex-Dells) and Larry Graves. This version of the Charms was imaginatively renamed 'Otis Williams And His New Group'. Some things, though, did not change. The success of 'Gum Drop' was usurped by a *Billboard* Top 10 version by the Crewcuts. Meanwhile, the remaining four-fifths of the original Charms had left for Miami, where they filed suit against Deluxe over their continued use of the brand name. Deluxe countered by issuing two singles under the name Otis Williams And His Charms, while Parker, Penn, Peak and Bradley released 'Love's Our Inspiration' for their new label, Chart Records. Without Otis Williams there was little residual interest, especially as Williams' incarnation of the Charms went on to score two significant hits in 'That's Your Mistake' and 'Ivory Tower'. However, both Barksdale (back to the Dells) and Graves quit, with Winfred Gerald, Matt Williams (no relation) and Lonnie Carter taking their places. A poor chart run was then ended with the release of another cover version, this time of the Lovenotes' 'United', in June 1957. It was their last significant success, despite a continuing and prolific relationship with Deluxe, and then King Records, until 1963. Only 'Little Turtle Dove' and 'Panic', both from 1961, scraped the lower reaches of the charts. Ironically, by this time Lonnie Carter had joined the original Charms, who had now become the Escos. Williams then transferred to Okeh Records but without success, before signing to Stop Records as a solo country artist. The Charms' complicated but fascinating history ended with the move.

CHARTS

An R&B vocal group from Harlem, New York City, New York, USA, the Charts were one of the finest examples of the 'greasy' style of doo-wop for which New York was famed in the late 50s, in which harsh leads, piercing tenors, deep basses, and exotic changes produced a rather unwholesome sound and a predominant image of greasy-haired young hoodlums. The members were lead Joe Grier, first tenor Steve Brown, second tenor Glenmore Jackson, baritone Leroy Binns and bass Ross Buford, who had formed the group in 1957 on a street corner on 115th Street. They were a classic one-hit-wonder group; their 'Deserie', recorded for Danny Robinson's Everlast label, became a perennial as an oldies standard after becoming a hit in 1957. 'Deserie' was distinctive in that it featured no bridge between the second and third verse. Grier, as the principal songwriter of the group, came up with equally appealing songs for the group, notably 'Dance Girl' and 'My Diane', both from 1957, but like so many vocal groups of the day, could not repeat their initial success. By 1958 the Charts had broken up. Grier took up saxophone and was the featured player on Les Cooper's 1962 hit, 'Wiggle Wobble'. A re-formed Charts, with Brown and Binns, and new members Frankie Harris and Tony Pierce, appeared with an updated version of 'Deserie' in 1967, but their career was short-lived. During the 70s and 80s several members of the group worked the doo-wop east coast revival circuit. Grier played saxophone behind many such groups, and Brown and Binns formed a revival Charts as well as working in groups such as the Coasters, Cadillacs, and Del-Vikings.
● COMPILATIONS: *The Charts Greatest Hits* (Collectables 1990)★★★.

CHECKMATES, LTD.

Formed in Fort Wayne, Indiana, in 1957, this self-contained band was one of the first racially mixed ensembles. The members were lead singer and keyboardist Sonny Charles (b. Charles Hemphill, 4 September 1940, Fort Wayne, Indiana, USA), bassist Bill Van Buskirk (b. 7 February 1941, Fort Wayne, Indiana, USA), drummer Marvin Smith (b. 25 September 1940, Fort Wayne, Indiana, USA), vocalist Bobby Stevens (b. 6 September 1939, Fort Wayne, Indiana, USA), and lead guitarist Harvey Trees (b. 14 June 1940, Aitkin, Minnesota, USA). The group, which began recording in 1963 when they made a single for the Chicago-based I.R.P. label, is inexorably linked with the legendary producer Phil Spector, who gave them their one national hit, 'Black Pearl', for A&M Records in 1969. The soul-styled song was one of Spector's few successes after he re-emerged in the business following a hiatus in the late 60s. Two other Spector-produced singles that sandwiched 'Black Pearl', 'Love Is All I Have To Give' and 'Proud Mary' (a remake of the Creedence Clearwater Revival song), failed to dent the charts. The Checkmates were inactive between 1970 and 1974, but a re-formed ensemble led by Charles and Smith returned to the charts with a minor hit, 'All Alone By The Telephone' for Polydor in 1976. In the early 80s Charles pursued a solo career and hit with 'Put It In A Magazine' and *The Sun Still Shines* in 1982, but afterwards continued his career as a member of the Checkmates, Ltd. The group's album output reflects their years playing the Las Vegas lounges.

● ALBUMS: *Live At Harvey's* (Ikon 1965)★★★, *Live At Caesar's Palace* (Capitol 1966)★★★, *Love Is All We Have To Give* (A&M 1969)★★★, *Bobby Stevens & The Checkmates, Ltd.* (Rustic 1971)★★, *F/S/O* (Rustic 1974)★★★, *We Got The Moves* (Fantasy 1978)★★.
Solo: Sonny Charles The Sun Still Shines (Highrise 1982)★★.

CHEEKS, JUDY

b. Florida, Miami, USA. Of mixed black American and Cherokee ancestry, Cheeks is the daughter of gospel singer Rev. Julius Cheeks, cited by James Brown, Otis Redding and others as a pivotal influence in the development of black music. She grew up in Miami where her godfather was Sam Cooke, who once plucked her from the front row of a 6,000 audience and sang the rest of the set to her while cradling her in his arms. Before her solo career began in earnest her voice had been employed by Tina Turner, Jon Bulter, Betty Wright, Leon Ware, Georgio Moroder and Harold Faltermayer, and she has long been a close friend of Stevie Wonder. Indeed, her recording career stretches back to the mid-70s, when she recorded a debut album with Ike and Tina Turner. She subsequently moved to Europe and Ariola records, her first record for whom, 'Mellow Lovin', was an international success. After she had traversed the language barrier, she became a major German star, appearing in several movies and hosting a television game show with a hamster called Willie. She came to England in 1987, though an album for Polydor was never released outside of mainland Europe. Her career lapsed until she finally began recording demos again in the 90s. There was interest from the PWL stable, but she eventually settled on Positiva, a contract cemented by the release of 'So In Love', written by China Burton. Remixes from Frankie Foncett and Sasha added greatly to the cult status of this minor garage classic. The follow-up, 'Reach', capitalized on this and her tours of select dance venues, and this time employed the Brothers In Rhythm production team. She subsequently worked with Nigel Lowis (producer of Eternal and Dina Carroll) on tracks for her first Positiva album.

● ALBUMS: *No Outsiders* (Polydor 1988)★★★.

CHENIER, C.J.

b. 28 September 1957, Port Arthur,Texas, USA. C.J. is the son of the 'king of zydeco', Clifton Chenier. He began playing saxophone while at school, but grew up knowing little about Louisiana zydeco music, and he spoke English at home. However, he learned quickly when he became a member of his father's band, replacing saxophonist John Hart. He recorded with his father and around 1984 he began to play accordion, graduating to opening shows as his father's health deteriorated. When his father died, he left his accordion to C.J., who has since recorded under his own name and rapidly established himself as a force to be reckoned with in the blues and zydeco market.

● ALBUMS: with the Red Hot Louisiana Band *Let Me In Your Heart* (Arhoolie 1988)★★★, *Hot Rod* (London 1991)★★★, *Too Much Fun* (Alligator 1995)★★★, *The Big Squeeze* (Alligator 1996)★★★.

CHENIER, CLIFTON

b. 25 June 1925, Opelousas, Louisiana, USA, d. 12 December 1987. This singer, guitarist, and harmonica and accordion player is regarded by many as the 'king of zydeco music'. Chenier was given lessons on the accordion by his father, and started performing at dances. He also had the advantage of being able to sing in French patois, English and Creole. In 1945, Chenier was working as a cane cutter in New Iberia. In 1946, he followed his older brother, Cleveland, to Lake Charles. He absorbed a wealth of tunes from musicians such as Zozo Reynolds, Izeb Laza, and Sidney Babineaux, who, despite their talents, had not recorded. The following year, Chenier travelled to Port Arthur, along with his wife Margaret, where he worked for the Gulf and Texaco oil refineries until 1954. Still playing music at weekends, Chenier was discovered by J.R. Fulbright, who recorded him at radio station KAOK, and issued records of these and subsequent sessions. In 1955, 'Ay Tee Tee' became Chenier's best-selling record, and he became established as an R&B guitarist. By 1956, having toured with R&B bands, he had turned to music full-time. In 1958, Chenier moved to Houston, Texas, and from this base played all over the south. Although ostensibly a Cajun musician, he had also absorbed zydeco and R&B styles influenced by Lowell Fulson. During the 60s, Chenier played one concert in San Francisco, backed by Blue Cheer, and recorded for a number of notable labels, including Argo and Arhoolie, in a bid to reach a wider audience. 'Squeeze Box Boogie' became a hit in Jamaica in the 50s, but generally his style of music was not widely heard before the 60s. In later life, in addition to suffering from diabetes, he had part of his right foot removed due to a kidney infection in 1979. Although he no longer toured as frequently, his influence was already established. *Sings The Blues* was compiled from material previously released on the Prophecy and Home Cooking labels. His son C.J. Chenier carries on the tradition into a third generation of the family.

● ALBUMS: *Louisiana Blues And Zydeco* (Arhoolie 1965)★★★★, *Black Snake Blues* (Arhoolie 1966)★★★★, with Lightnin' Hopkins, Mance Lipscomb *Blues Festival* (1966)★★★, *Bon Ton Roulet* (Arhoolie 1967)★★★, *Sings The Blues* (Arhoolie 1969)★★★★, *King Of The Bayous* (Arhoolie 1970)★★★, *Bayou Blues* (Specialty/Sonet 1970)★★★★, *Live At St. Marks* (Arhoolie 1971)★★★, *Live At A French Creole Dance* (Arhoolie 1972)★★★, *Out West* (Arhoolie 1974)★★★, *Bad Luck And Trouble* (1975)★★★, *Bogalusa Boogie* (Arhoolie 1975)★★★★, *Red Hot Louisiana Band* (Arhoolie 1978)★★★★, with Rob Bernard *Boogie In Black And White* (Jin 1979)★★★, *In New Orleans* (GNP Crescendo 1979)★★★, *Frenchin' The Boogie* (Barclay 1979)★★★, *King Of Zydeco* (Home Cooking 1980)★★★, *Boogie 'N' Zydeco* (Sonet 1980)★★★, *Live At The 1982 San Francisco Blues Festival* (Arhoolie 1982)★★★, *I'm Here* (Alligator 1982)★★★★, *Live At Montreux* (Charly 1984)★★★, *The King Of Zydeco, Live At Montreux* (Arhoolie 1988)★★★, *Playboy* (1992)★★★.

● COMPILATIONS: *Clifton Chenier's Very Best* (Harvest 1970)★★★★, *Classic Clifton* (Arhoolie 1980)★★★★, *Sixty Minutes With The King Of Zydeco* (Arhoolie 1987)★★★★.

● VIDEOS: *King Of Zydeco* (Arhoolie 1988), *Hot Pepper* (Kay Jazz 1988).

CHERRELLE

b. Cheryl Norton, Los Angeles, California, USA. This cousin of soul singer Pebbles is an accomplished drummer as well as a vocalist. She was discovered by her neighbour Michael Henderson, with whom she toured widely and appeared on his *In The Night-Time* (1978). Five years later she made her solo debut with *Fragile* for Tabu, featuring the production team of Jimmy Jam and Terry Lewis. The album included two lynchpin cuts, 'I Didn't Mean To Turn You On' (later a hit for Robert Palmer) and 'When I Look In Your Eyes'. In 1985 she achieved her first hit, with 'Saturday Love', a duet with labelmate Alexander O'Neal, hitting the UK Top 10, eventually provoking interest in her homeland the following year. However, she has continued to enjoy considerably greater success in the UK, with another O'Neal duet, 'Never Knew Love Like This', reaching the Top 30. The 90s saw her move to a new contract with A&M.

● ALBUMS: *Fragile* (Tabu 1984)★★★, *High Priority* (Tabu 1985)★★★, *Affair* (Tabu 1988)★★★, *The Woman I Am* (A&M 1991)★★★.

CHESS RECORDS

Polish-born brothers Leonard and Philip Chess were already proprietors of several Chicago nightclubs when they bought into the Aristocrat label in 1947. Its early repertoire consisted of jazz and jump-blues combos, but these acts were eclipsed by the arrival of Muddy Waters. This seminal R&B performer made his debut with 'I Can't Be Satisfied', the first of many superb releases that helped to establish the fledgling company. Having then secured the services of Sunnyland Slim and Robert Nighthawk, the brothers confidently bought out a third partner, Evelyn Aron, renaming their enterprise Chess in 1950. Initial releases consisted of material from former Aristocrat artists, but the new venture quickly expanded its roster with local signings Jimmy Rogers and Eddie Boyd, as well as others drawn from the southern states, including Howlin' Wolf. Their recordings established Chess as a leading outlet for urban blues, a position emphasized by the founding of the Checker subsidiary and attendant releases by Little Walter, Sonny Boy Williamson (Rice Miller) and Elmore James. Other outlets, including Argo and Specialist were also established, and during the mid-50s the Chess empire successfully embraced rock 'n' roll with Chuck Berry and Bo Diddley. White acts, including Bobby Charles and Dale Hawkins, also provided hits, while the label's peerless reputation was sufficient to attract a new generation of virtuoso blues performers, led by Otis Rush and Buddy Guy. The R&B boom of the 60s, spearheaded by the Rolling Stones and later emphasized by John Mayall and Fleetwood Mac, brought renewed interest in the company's catalogue, but the rise of soul, in turn, deemed it anachronistic. Although recordings at the Fame studio by Etta James, Irma Thomas and Laura Lee matched the artistic achievements of Motown and Atlantic, ill-advised attempts at aiming Waters and Wolf at the contemporary market with *Electric Mud* and *The New Howlin' Wolf Album*, marked the nadir of their respective careers. The death of Leonard Chess on 16 October 1969 signalled the end of an era and Chess was then purchased by the GRT corporation. Phil left the company to run the WVON radio station, while Leonard's son, Marshall, became managing director of Rolling Stones Records. Producer Ralph Bass remained in Chicago, cataloguing master tapes and supervising a studio reduced to recording backing tracks, but he too vacated the now moribund empire. Chess was later acquired by the All Platinum/Sugarhill companies, then MCA, who, in tandem with European licensees Charly, have undertaken a major reissue programme.

● COMPILATIONS: *Chess: The Rhythm And The Blues* (1988)★★★★, *The Chess Story: Chess Records 1954-1969* (1989)★★★★, *First Time I Met The Blues* (1989)★★★, *Second Time I Met The Blues* (1989)★★★, *Chess Blues* 4-CD box set (1993)★★★★, *Chess Rhythm & Roll* 4-CD box set (MCA 1995)★★★★.

● FURTHER READING: *The Chess Labels*, Michel Ruppli. *Chess Blues Discography*, L. Fancourt.

CHI-LITES

Formed in Chicago in 1960 and originally called the Hi-Lites, the group featured Eugene Record (b. 23 December 1940, Chicago, Illinois, USA), Robert Lester (b. 1942, McComb, Mississippi, USA), Creadel Jones (b. 1939, St. Louis, Missouri, USA) and Marshall Thompson (b. April 1941, Chicago, Illinois, USA). Imbued with the tradition of doo-wop and street corner harmony, Record and Lester came together with Clarence Johnson in the Chanteurs, who issued a single on Renee Records in 1959. The trio then teamed with Marshall Thompson and Creadel 'Red' Jones, refugees from another local group, the Desideros. The resultant combination was dubbed the Hi-Lites and a series of releases followed. 'I'm So Jealous' from late 1964 introduced the group's new name, Marshall And The Chi-Lites, the amended prefix celebrating their 'Windy City' origins. Johnson left the group later that year and with the release of 'You Did That To Me', the quartet became simply the Chi-Lites. Further singles confirmed a growing reputation while their arrival at Brunswick Records in 1968 pitched them alongside the cream of Chicago's soul hierarchy. Record formed a songwriting partnership with Barbara Acklin, a combination responsible for many of his group's finest moments. 'Give It Away' (1969) became the Chi-Lites' first US national hit, and introduced a string of often contrasting releases. Although equally self-assured on up-tempo songs, the group became noted for its slower, often sentimental performances. The wistful 'Have You Seen Her' (1971), which reached number 3 on both sides of the Atlantic, highlighted Record's emotive falsetto, and later singles, including the US number 1 'Oh Girl' (1972) and 'Homely Girl' (1974), continued this style. Although American pop success eluded the Chi-Lites' later work, in the UK they hit the Top 5 with 'It's Time For Love' (1975) and 'You Don't Have To Go' (1976). Their continuity was maintained despite several line-up changes. Creadel Jones left the group in 1973, but his successor, Stanley Anderson, was latterly replaced by Willie Kensey. Doc Roberson subsequently took the place of Kensey. The crucial change came in 1976 when Eugene Record left for a short-lived solo career. David Scott and Danny Johnson replaced him but the original quartet of Record, Jones, Lester and Thompson re-formed in 1980. Record set up the Chi-Sound label at the same time, bringing in Gene Chandler as a vice-president. The title track of *Bottoms Up* (1983) became a Top 10 soul single but further releases failed to sustain that success. The group continued as a trio on Creadel Jones' retirement, but by the end of the decade Record once again left the group (replaced by Anthony Watson), leaving Thompson with the Chi-Lites' name. They moved to Ichiban for *Just Say You Love Me*, and continued touring into the 90s.

● ALBUMS: *Give It Away* (Brunswick 1969)★★★, *(For God's Sake) Give More Power To The People* (Brunswick 1971)★★★★, *A Lonely Man* (Brunswick 1972)★★★, *A Letter To Myself* (Brunswick 1973)★★★, *The Chi-Lites* (Brunswick 1973)★★★, *Toby* (Brunswick 1974)★★★, *Half A Love* (Brunswick 1975)★★, *Happy Being Lonely* (Mercury 1976)★★★, *The Fantastic Chi-Lites* (Mercury 1977)★★★, *Heavenly Body* (Chi-Sound 1980)★★, *Me And You* (Chi-Sound 1982)★★, *Bottoms Up* (Larc 1983)★★★, *Steppin' Out* (Private I 1984)★★, *Just Say You Love Me* (Ichiban 1990)★★★.

Solo: Eugene Record *Welcome To My Fantasy* (Warners 1979)★★.

● COMPILATIONS: *The Chi-Lites Greatest Hits* (Brunswick 1972)★★★★, *The Chi-Lites Greatest Hits Volume Two* (Brunswick 1975)★★★, *The Best Of The Chi-Lites* (Kent 1987)★★★, *Greatest Hits* (Street Life 1988)★★★, *Very Best Of The Chi-Lites* (BR Music 1988)★★★, *The Chi-Lites Greatest Hits* (Rhino 1992)★★★★, *Have You Seen Her? The Very Best Of ...* (Pickwick 1995)★★★.

CHIC

Arguably *the* band of the disco generation, Chic was built around Nile Rodgers (b. 19 September 1952, New York, USA; guitar) and Bernard Edwards (b. 31 October 1952, Greenville, Carolina, USA, d. 18 April 1996, Tokyo, Japan; bass). During the 60s Rodgers had played in a rock group, New World Rising, before joining the Apollo Theatre house band. Edwards had played with several struggling musicians prior to meeting his future partner through a mutual friend. They both joined the Big Apple Band in 1971, which subsequently toured, backing hit group New York City. Chic evolved out of a collection of demos that Edwards and Rodgers had recorded. Two female singers, Norma Jean Wright and Luci Martin, were added to the line-up, along with Tony Thompson, a former drummer with LaBelle. Wright later left for a solo career and was replaced by Alfa Anderson. The quintet scored an immediate hit with 'Dance Dance Dance (Yowsah, Yowsah, Yowsah)' (1977), which introduced wit and sparkling instrumentation to the maligned disco genre. In 1978 'Le Freak' became the biggest-selling single in Atlantic/WEA's history, with a total of over four million copies moved. Chic's grasp of melody was clearly apparent on 'I Want Your Love' (1979), while US number 1 'Good Times', with its ferocious bass riff, was not only a gold disc in itself, but became the sampled backbone to several 80s scratch and rap releases. Edwards' and Rodgers' skills were also in demand for outside projects and their handiwork was evident on 'Upside Down' (Diana Ross), 'We Are Family' (Sister Sledge) and 'Spacer' (Sheila B. Devotion). However, their distinctive sound grew too defined to adapt to changing fashions and Chic's later work was treated with indifference. Edwards' solo album, *Glad To Be Here*, was a disappointment, and Rodgers' effort, *Adventures In The Land Of Groove*, fared little better. However, Rodgers' unique work on David Bowie's 'Let's Dance' provided much of the track's propulsive bite. Rodgers later produced Madonna's first major hit, 'Like A Virgin', while Edwards took control of recording the Power Station, the Duran Duran offshoot that also featured Tony Thompson. Edwards also provided the backbone to Robert Palmer's 1986 hit, 'Addicted To Love'. In 1992 the duo re-formed Chic as a rebuff to the rap and techno-dance styles, releasing, 'Chic Mystique', and an album. Chic's revival looks to have ended with the death of Bernard Edwards in 1996, but their influence on dance music ensures a place in pop history.

● ALBUMS: *Chic* (Atlantic 1977)★★★, *C'Est Chic* (Atlantic 1978)★★★, *Risqué* (Atlantic 1979)★★★★, *Real People* (Atlantic 1980)★★★★, *Take It Off* (Atlantic 1981)★★★★, *Tongue In Chic* (Atlantic 1982)★★★, *Believer* (Atlantic 1983)★★★, *Chic-Ism* (Warners 1992)★★★.

● COMPILATIONS: *Les Plus Grands Succès De Chic -*

Chic's Greatest Hits (Atlantic 1979)★★★★, *Megachic - The Best Of Chic* (Warners 1990)★★★★, *Dance Dance Dance: The Best Of Chic* (Atlantic 1991)★★★★, *Everybody Dance* (Rhino 1995)★★★★.

CHIFFONS

Formed in the Bronx, New York, USA, where all the members were born, erstwhile backing singers Judy Craig (b. 1946), Barbara Lee Jones (b. 16 May 1947, d. 15 May 1992), Patricia Bennett (b. 7 April 1947) and Sylvia Peterson (b. 30 September 1946), are best recalled for 'He's So Fine', a superb girl-group release and an international hit in 1963. The song later acquired a dubious infamy when its melody appeared on George Harrison's million-selling single, 'My Sweet Lord'. Taken to court by the original publishers, the ex-Beatle was found guilty of plagiarism and obliged to pay substantial damages. This battle made little difference to the Chiffons, who despite enjoying hits with 'One Fine Day' (1963) and 'Sweet Talkin' Guy' (1966), were all too soon reduced to the world of cabaret and 'oldies' nights. They did, however, record their own version of 'My Sweet Lord'.

● ALBUMS: *He's So Fine* (Laurie 1963)★★, *One Fine Day* (Laurie 1963)★★, *Sweet Talkin' Guy* (Laurie 1966)★★.

● COMPILATIONS: *Everything You Ever Wanted To Hear ... But Couldn't Get* (Laurie 1981)★★★, *Doo-Lang Doo-Lang Doo-Lang* (Impact/Ace 1985)★★★, *Flips, Flops And Rarities* (Impact/Ace 1986)★★, *Greatest Recordings* (Ace 1990)★★★★, *The Fabulous Chiffons* (Ace 1991)★★★.

CHIMES (UK)

UK soul/dance trio originating in Edinburgh, Scotland, in 1981, when they were initially put together by Mike Pedan (keyboards and bass) and the much-travelled James Locke (keyboards and drums, ex-Heartbeat; Rhythm Of Life; Bathers; Hipsway; Indian Givers). The pair had met when they were backing former Parliament keyboard player Bernie Worrell at a local club. Deciding to form their own group, they set about writing material and auditioning female singers, eventually settling on Pauline Henry in 1987. With the duo's desperation mounting, her successful audition was held over the telephone, after which she was flown up from London for sessions. After signing to CBS in 1988 they finally released their debut single a year later. '1-2-3' was produced by Jazzie B (from Soul II Soul), a group to whom the Chimes were frequently compared. Their biggest UK breakthrough came in 1990 when they covered U2's 'I Still Haven't Found What I'm Looking For'. Apparently approved by Bono, the cover version was chosen when the band heard Henry singing it in the studio. Aided by an appearance on the mainstream television show *Wogan*, it eventually went Top 5 in both the UK and USA. The boys also contributed to old friend Paul Haig's solo LP during 1990, and produced several other artists. Subsequent minor hits included 'True Love' and 'Love Comes To Mind', before Henry left for a solo career midway through sessions for a second album.

● ALBUMS: *The Chimes* (Columbia 1990)★★★.

CHIMES (USA)

Formed in Brooklyn, New York, in 1959, this vocal quintet consisted of Lenny Cocco (lead), Joe Croce (baritone), Pat DePrisco (first tenor), Rich Mercado (second tenor) and Pat McGuire (bass). Signed to the small Tag label, the group reached the US Top 20 in 1961 with 'Once In Awhile'. A cover version of 'I'm In The Mood For Love' managed a US Top 40 placing the following year but the Chimes had no subsequent hits, disbanding in 1965. They re-formed in 1970 and performed at oldies shows until 1973. Cocco assembled a new Chimes group in 1981, which was still performing in the New York area in the early 90s. 'Once In Awhile' has grown in stature, and routinely features among the 10 all-time favourite hits of listeners to New York's 'oldies' radio station. A re-recording was made in the 80s that did not have the lustre of the original.

● ALBUMS: *Once In Awhile* (Ambient Sound 1987)★★.

● COMPILATIONS: *Best Of Chimes And Classics* (Rare Bird 1974)★★★.

CHINA BLACK

China Black is the collective title given to Simon Fung (b. Hong Kong, China) and Errol Reid (b. Montego Bay, Jamaica). Reid emigrated to the UK with his parents, settling in Birmingham. He began singing at an early age, heavily influenced by artists such as Luther Vandross, Freddie Jackson and Teddy Pendergrass. He entered and won numerous talent competitions and recorded a number of solo outings, subsequently relocating to London. Fung was also living in London at the time and had graduated into production work with artists such as the Fredericks, Cornell McKoy and jazz guitarist Ronny Jordan. It was Jordan who introduced Fung and Reid in 1990, which led to the formation of China Black. The duo's first recordings were heavily soul-influenced, and in 1992, 'Searching' was released. The single topped the reggae chart, maintaining a high profile for three months. In 1994 the ballad was licensed to Wildcard, which led to a crossover hit in the UK Top 10 when remixed by ex-Steel Pulse and Reggae Philharmonic Orchestra performer Mykaell S. Riley. The group followed the hit with 'Stars' and in 1995, 'Almost See You (Somewhere)', neither of which were able to repeat the success of their debut. Their fourth release, 'Don't Throw It All Away', became a club anthem with remixes by Rokstone and the Beatmasters.

● ALBUMS: *Born* (Wildcard 1994)★★.

CHIPS

Formed in the Bedford-Stuyvesant district of Brooklyn, New York, USA, in 1956, the Chips drew their membership from teenage friends Charles Johnson (lead), Nathaniel Epps (baritone), Paul Fulton (bass), Sammy Strain (first tenor) and Shedwick Lincoln (second tenor). The group's first recording would be their most enduring; 'Rubber Biscuit' started life as Johnson's answer to the marching rhythms of the Warwick School For Delinquent Teenagers while he was an intern there. When Josie Records heard the tune, which he had perfected with the rest of the Chips, they signed the band and issued the record in September 1956. Although it did not chart, 'Rubber Biscuit' became an instant east coast R&B radio favourite, and saw its authors joining touring bills alongside the Dells, Cadillacs and Bo Diddley. Appearances at the Apollo and Empire Theaters followed, but the momentum gained by their debut single was waning rapidly. The group broke up at the end of 1957, with Fulton joining the Velours and the Poets, and Strain working with the Fantastics, Little Anthony And The Imperials and O'Jays. Johnson joined the Platters while Lincoln became part of the Invitations. This might well have signalled the end of the Chips story, had it not been for the Dan Aykroyd and John Belushi (aka the Blues Brothers) cover version of 'Rubber Biscuit' in 1979, which made the US Top 40. The resultant interest saw the Chips (minus Strain, replaced by Dave Eason) reunite in the same year. One record was released, which coupled two cover versions, 'Everyone's Laughing' (Spaniels) and 'When I'm With You' (Moonglows).

CHORDS

The original members were brothers Carl (d. 23 January 1981; lead tenor) and Claude Feaster (baritone), Jimmy Keyes (d. 22 July 1995; tenor), Floyd McRae (tenor), William Edwards (bass) and pianist Rupert Branker, all schoolfriends from the Bronx, New York, USA. The Chords, who evolved out of three other groups, the Tunetoppers, the Keynotes and the Four Notes, were one of the first acts signed to the Atlantic subsidiary label Cat. Their debut disc was a doo-wop version of the then current Patti Page hit 'Cross Over The Bridge'. On the b-side of this 1954 release, Cat grudgingly issued one of the group's own songs, 'Sh-Boom', which became a milestone in rock 'n' roll music. This fun piece of nonsense took the USA by storm and featured the joyous but contentious lyric, 'Ah, life could be a dream, sh-boom, sh-boom!'. Some claim that this was rock 'n' roll's first 'drug song'! It shot into the US Top 10, a unique occurrence in those days for an R&B record, while a watered-down cover version by Canada's Crew-Cuts had the honour of being America's first number 1 rock 'n' roll hit. The song created such a furore that even ace satirist Stan Freberg's cruel take-off of the Chords' record also made the Top 20. Since a group on Gem Records was already using the same name, the group quickly became the Chordcats. They tried to follow the monster novelty hit with other similar tracks, such as the follow-up 'Zippety-Zum', but with no success. Some personnel changes and another new name, the inevitable Sh-Booms, also failed to return them to the charts. The Chords, who were probably the first R&B group to appear on USA television nationwide, also recorded on Vik, Roulette (under the name Lionel Thorpe), Atlantic and Baron, among others. They occasionally reunited to play 'oldies' shows until lead singer Carl died on 23 January 1981.

CHRISTIANS

This UK group was formed in Liverpool in 1984 and comprised former Yachts and It's Immaterial keyboard player Henry Priestman (b. 21 June 1955, Hull, Humberside, England) and the Christian brothers Roger (b. 13 February 1950, Merseyside, England), Garry (b. Garrison Christian, 27 February 1955, Merseyside, England) and Russell (b. 8 July 1956, Merseyside, England). Up until then, the brothers, who came from a family of 11, with a Jamaican immigrant father and Liverpudlian mother, had performed as a soul a cappella trio and had previously worked under a variety of names, most notably as Natural High when they made an appearance on UK Television's *Opportunity Knocks* talent show in 1974. The Christian brothers met Priestman, who became the group's main songwriter, at Pete Wylie's Liverpool studios, where Priestman convinced the trio to try recording his compositions. The resulting demo session tapes eventually led to the Christians signing to Island Records. The group's combination of pop and soul earned them a string of UK hits including, in 1987, 'Forgotten Town', 'Hooverville (They Promised Us The World)', 'When The Fingers Point' and 'Ideal World'. The media usually focused their attention on the striking appearance of the tall, shaven-headed Garry. This, and a reluctance to tour, led to Roger quitting the group in 1987. The Christians' self-titled album, meanwhile, would become Island's best-selling debut. With the exception of the Top 30 hit 'Born Again' in the spring, 1988 was much quieter, with the group touring and recording. The year was brought to a climax, however, with the Top 10 cover version of the Isley Brothers hit, 'Harvest For The World'. The Hillsborough football crowd disaster in April 1989 prompted a charity record, 'Ferry Across The Mersey', on which they were given joint credit alongside Paul McCartney, Gerry Marsden, Holly Johnson and Stock, Aitken And Waterman. In 1989, Roger Christian released a solo single, 'Take It From Me', achieving a minor UK hit (number 63), plus a well-received album, *Roger Christian*, which did not chart. The Christians' only hit that year came with the the Top 20 'Words'. The labours over recording the second album, *Colours*, paid off when it hit the UK number 1 spot on its first week in the chart. Subsequent singles failed to break into the Top 50, and 1992's *Happy In Hell* proved to be a commercial failure. Island recouped their losses with a compilation album the following year (including two new songs). The band have since pursued solo projects, with Garry Christian releasing an acclaimed album in 1997.

● ALBUMS: *The Christians* (Island 1987)★★★★, *Colours* (Island 1990)★★★, *Happy In Hell* (Island 1992)★★★. Solo: Roger Christian *Checkmate* (Island 1989)★★★, Garry Christian *Your Cool Mystery* (Coalition 1997)★★★.

● COMPILATIONS: *The Best Of The Christians* (Island 1993)★★★★.

● VIDEOS: *The Best Of The Christians* (Island 1993)★★★★.

CHUDD, LEW

Chudd was a US radio producer during the 30s, creating the *Let's Dance* show which featured Benny Goodman and Xavier Cugat. He later became the head of the Los Angeles bureau of the NBC network. During the early 40s Chudd worked for the Office of War Information and set up Crown Records to record jazz. After selling Crown, he founded Imperial Records in 1946 to cater for the growing black and Hispanic populations of southern California. Chudd maintained a roster of Mexican artists such as Los Madrugadores and Herman Padilla until 1953. In the R&B field, Imperial initially recorded west coast jump blues by artists including Charlie Davis, King Porter and Poison Gardner. However, after meeting New Orleans bandleader Dave Bartholomew in Houston in 1949, Chudd moved into the newer R&B style. He came to New Orleans in December of the same year and almost immediately he and Bartholomew discovered Fats Domino. Domino's 'The Fat Man' and '3 x 7 = 21' by Jewel King were the label's first hits, in 1950. Leaving Bartholomew to record further R&B artists, Chudd signed performers in the gospel, blues (Smokey Hogg) and country fields, although, of these, only Slim Whitman was commercially successful. Consequently, Imperial focused exclusively on R&B for the next few years. In New Orleans, Bartholomew provided hits by Chris Kenner and Roy Brown in addition to Domino, while Los Angeles bandleader Ernie Freeman had a pop hit with 'Raunchy'. By 1957, Chudd was ready to plunge into the white teenage market, signing boyish television star Ricky Nelson, who had over a dozen Top 20 hits in the following five years. Imperial also released rock material by Sandy Nelson and Frankie Ford. In 1961, Chudd purchased New Orleans label Minit from Joe Banashak, but two years later Imperial was itself bought out by Al Bennett's Liberty/United Artists company, based in Los Angeles. Chudd himself retired from the music business.

CHURCH, EUGENE

b. 23 January 1938, Los Angeles, California, USA, d. 16 April 1993. Church first recorded with Jesse Belvin in a duo called the Cliques; their 1956 song 'Girl Of My Dreams' was classic Los Angeles-styled R&B, featuring a dreamy, smooth sound. His debut solo record, 'Open Up Your Heart', was in essence a group record, since on it he was backed by the Turks. This was followed by 'Rock & Roll Show', on which Church sang as a member of the Saxons. Church had his biggest hit in 1958 with 'Pretty Girls Everywhere' (number 6 R&B, number 36 pop), which featured backing from Jesse Belvin and members of the Turks. Subsequent chart successes were 'Miami' (number 24 R&B, number 67 pop) in 1959 and 'Mind Your Own Business' (number 19 R&B) in 1961. With the exception of a one-off record in 1986, his recording career was essentially over by 1963. Church died from AIDS in 1993.

CHURCHILL, SAVANNAH

b. Savannah Valentine, 21 August 1920, Colfax, Louisiana, USA, and raised in Brooklyn, New York City, d. 20 April 1974. Churchill typified the urbane R&B style of the 40s that could be characterized as jazz, blues, or pop depending on the song and the arrangement. She began her professional career in music in 1941, and a year later made her recording debut with Joe Davis's Beacon label, producing the notable jump hits 'Fat Meat Is Good Meat' and 'Two-Faced Man'. After recording a single with the Benny Carter big band for Capitol in 1943, she signed with New York-based Manor in 1945. Her recordings for the label brought her national renown, notably 'Daddy Daddy' (number 3 R&B) from 1945, 'I Want To Be Loved (But Only By You)' (number 1 R&B) from 1947, and 'Time Out For Tears' (number 10 R&B) from 1948. She had no more hits, although during 1951-52 she made some of the finest recordings of her career, largely sad and mellow ballads, for RCA-Victor. On both Manor and RCA she generally recorded with a vocal harmony group, at first the Four Tunes and later with her own touring group, the Striders. In 1953 she joined Decca, and recorded in more of an R&B vein, covering Faye Adams's 'Shake A Hand' and the Harptones' 'Life Is But A Dream', but the company could not return her to the charts. In 1956 her career was virtually ended when she suffered long-term debilitating injuries after a drunk fell on top of her from a club balcony. She was still able to record, and in 1961 managed a session for Jamie, for which she recorded her debut album, *Time Out For Tears*, which featured remakes of her 40s hits. However, by this time Churchill's sophisticated mellow style was out of vogue with musical trends and she did not record again.

● ALBUMS: *Time Out For Tears* (Jamie 1961)★★★.
● COMPILATIONS: *Time Out For Tears* (Jukebox Lil 1985)★★★.

CLANTON, JIMMY

b. 2 September 1940, Baton Rouge, Louisiana, USA. Pop vocalist Clanton celebrated his 18th birthday with his co-written debut hit, the R&B ballad 'Just A Dream', at number 4 in the US Hot 100. His smooth singing style appealed to the teen market and his subsequent releases were aimed in that direction. These included 'My Own True Love', which used the melody of 'Tara's Theme' from *Gone With The Wind.* The title track of the film *Go, Jimmy, Go*, in which he starred, gave him another US Top 5 smash and the ballad 'Another Sleepless Night' reached the UK Top 50 in July 1960. His most famous record, 'Venus In Blue Jeans', co-written by Neil Sedaka, gave him his last US Top 10 hit, in late 1962. The song became a bigger hit in the UK, when Mark Wynter took his version into the Top 5. Clanton went on to become a DJ in Pennsylvania.

● ALBUMS: *Just A Dream* (Ace 1959)★★★, *Jimmy's Happy* (Ace 1960)★★★, *Jimmy's Blue* (Ace 1960)★★★, *My Best To You* (Ace 1961)★★★, *Teenage Millionaire* (Ace 1961)★★★, *Venus In Bluejeans* (Ace 1962)★★★.
● COMPILATIONS: *The Best Of Jimmy Clanton* (Philips 1964)★★★.
● FILMS: *Go Johnny Go* (1958).

CLARK, CHRIS

Christine Clark joined Motown Records as a receptionist in 1964 and followed a familiar career structure within the company by graduating from office work to a recording contract. Her strident, bluesy vocals led her to be nicknamed 'The White Negress' by British fans, but this style excluded her from Motown's musical mainstream. After having an R&B hit with 'Love Gone Bad' in 1966 on the VIP subsidiary label, she graduated to Tamla in 1967, where she found some success with 'From Head To Toe'. In 1969 she became the Vice-President of

Motown's film division, co-writing the screenplay for *Lady Sings The Blues* in 1971. In 1981 she was appointed Vice-President of Motown Productions, with jurisdiction over the company's creative affairs. Clark left the organization in 1989 and re-recorded 'From Head To Toe' with producer Ian Levine for Motor City Records in 1991.

● ALBUMS: *Soul Sounds* (Tamla 1967)★★★, *CC Rides Again* (Weed 1969)★★★.

CLARK, DEE

b. Delecta Clark, 7 November 1938, Blytheville, Arkansas, USA, d. 7 December 1990. Clark had a wonderfully impassioned tenor voice and enjoyed a spate of rock 'n' roll hits in the late 50s and a lesser body of soul work in the 60s. Clark's entertainment career began in 1952 as a member of the Hambone Kids, who, with band leader Red Saunders, recorded a novelty number in which Clark's group patted a rhythm known as the Hambone. Clark later joined a vocal group, the Goldentones, who won first prize in a talent show at Chicago's Roberts Show Lounge. Noted disc jockey Herb 'Kool Gent' Kent then took the group to Vee Jay Records, where they recorded as the Kool Gents. Clark's distinctive stylings soon engendered a solo contract and in 1958 he had a US hit with 'Nobody But You' (R&B number 3 and pop Top 30). 'Just Keep It Up' (R&B number 9 and pop Top 20) and 'Hey Little Girl' (R&B number 2 and pop Top 20) proved equally popular the following year. The artist's major success came in 1962 with 'Raindrops' (R&B number 3 and pop number 2). This plaintive offering, co-written by Clark and Phil Upchurch, eventually sold in excess of one million copies. Sadly, Clark was unable to repeat this feat, but continued on Chicago-based Constellation with a spate of moderate R&B hits, namely, 'Crossfire Time' (1963), 'Heartbreak' (1964), and 'TCB' (1965). His career faded after Constellation went out of business in 1966. In the UK he had a sizable hit in 1975 with 'Ride A Wild Horse'; in the USA the record failed to chart. Clark died of a heart attack in 1990.

● ALBUMS: *Dee Clark* (Abner 1959)★★★, *How About That* (Abner 1960)★★★, *You're Looking Good* (Vee Jay 1960)★★★, *Hold On, It's Dee Clark* (Vee Jay 1961)★★★, *Hey Little Girl* (Vee Jay 1982)★★★.

● COMPILATIONS: *The Best Of Dee Clark* (Vee Jay 1964)★★★★, *Keep It Up* (Charly 1980)★★★, *The Delectable Sound Of Dee Clark* (Charly 1986)★★★★, *Raindrops* (Charly 1987)★★★★, *Ultimate Collection* (Marginal 1997)★★★★.

CLARKE, TONY

b. New York City, New York, USA, and raised in Detroit, Michigan, USA, d. 1970. Clarke was a songwriter who managed to step briefly to the forefront to record a couple of classic records that developed cult status. His first success in the recording business was writing 'Pushover' and 'Two Sides To Every Story' for Etta James. His only hit was 'The Entertainer' (number 10 R&B, number 31 pop), from 1965, recorded for Chess Records. This delightful mid-tempo song, and its b-side 'This Heart Of Mine', became something of a perennial favourite on the Beach Music circuit. In the UK, among northern soul fans, an intense devotion was given to an obscure Chess single, 'Landslide' (1966), and a song recorded later in Detroit on MS called '(They Call Me) A Wrong Man'. Clarke had a minor role in the film *They Call Me Mr. TIBBS* (1970).

CLASSICS

Formed as the Perennials in 1958 in Brooklyn, New York, USA. The Classics were a one-hit vocal group who made the Top 20 in 1963 with a doo-wop version of the Mills Brothers' hit 'Till Then'. The group, all from Brooklyn, consisted of Emil Stucchio (b. 9 April 1944; lead vocals), Tony Victor (b. 11 April 1943; first tenor), Johnny Gambale (b. 4 February 1942; second tenor) and Jamie Troy (b. 22 November 1942; bass singer). The quartet all lived in the same street, attended the same high school and by 1958 had developed an act to perform at local events. They changed their name to the Classics at the suggestion of a local club performer. They were introduced to the owner of the small Dart label and recorded three singles for that company, none of which saw significant sales. Switching to the Musicnote label in 1963 they covered the 1944 Mills Brothers ballad and it became a local favourite, eventually peaking at number 20 in the USA. Further singles for Musicnote and other small companies failed and the group disbanded in the mid-60s, without releasing any albums.

● COMPILATIONS: *Best Of Chimes And Classics* (Rare Bird 1974)★★★.

CLAY, JUDY

b. Judy Guions, St. Paul, North Carolina, USA. Guions began singing in church in St. Paul at a very early age, before moving to Fayetteville, North Carolina, to be raised by her grandmother. A move to Brooklyn in the early 50s saw her join a church choir that also sang on Sunday night radio broadcasts. After her grandmother took Guions back to North Carolina, the young teenager asked to return to New York, where she first stayed with a girlfriend and had a church minister as temporary guardian. Soon, however, Lee Warrick Drinkard of the Drinkard Singers 'adopted' her and, from the age of 14, she became a regular performer with the 'family' gospel group, originally formed in Savannah, Georgia, around 1938, when Emily Drinkard (today better known as Cissy Houston, and Lee's cousin) was only five. The family group had moved to East Orange, New Jersey, and Guions joined them around 1953, at which point the family comprised her adopted mother, Lee, and sometimes (though never on record) Lee's two daughters, Marie Dionne (later just Dionne) Warrick (later Warwick) and Delia, also known as Dee Dee Warrick (Warwick), plus regulars Emily/Cissy Drinkard (whose married name at the time was Garland), Emily's married sisters Marie Epps and Ann Moss, and their brothers Larry and Nick Drinkard, who often helped out on piano. This invaluable experience honed the young Guions' forceful and interpretive contralto, and she regularly shared lead-vocal duties with the other girls, even on three 50s Drinkard albums (a 1954 Newport Spiritual Stars set on Savoy, a 1957 live set from the Newport Jazz Festival on Verve and a 1958 studio set for RCA-Victor). After marrying John Houston, Cissy Drinkard went on to form the backing group the Sweet Inspirations and, in the early 60s, Guions began her own secular recording career singing with Cissy and other girls in various backing groups that predated the first incarnation of 'The Sweets'. Her first solo recordings (now as Judy Clay, though her record company had wanted to call her Amanda Knight) comprised two singles for the New York-based Ember label in 1961/2, followed by three 1963 sides (one duet and two solo) for Lavette. Next, she moved across town in early 1964 to Scepter Records, where fellow ex-Drinkard Singer Dionne Warwick had by then already successfully started her own secular career. Four singles appeared in 1964/5, with a later one seeing release after she had moved on. The next port of call was Atlantic Records, where Clay had already done much back-up work, but Jerry Wexler decided to send her south to Stax in Memphis, where she recorded 'You Can't Run Away From Your Heart' in mid-1967. A return to New York saw her achieve her first hits via two duets on Atlantic with blue-eyed soulman Billy Vera, 'Storybook Children' (a promo of which Vera had first cut with Nona Hendryx and Patti LaBelle's Bluebelles) and 'Country Girl - City Man', with the Sweet Inspirations on back-ups. Later in 1968, Clay returned to Stax to record her best-remembered track, the fine duet with William Bell, 'Private Number', which had been originally intended as a vehicle for Otis Redding and Carla Thomas. A solo outing by Clay, 'Bed Of Roses', failed to register, and she returned to duets, this time with Bell again on 'My Baby Specialises', which at least made the R&B chart. Again a solo follow-up, 'It Ain't Long Enough', coupled with the exquisite 'Give Love To Save Love', failed to chart, and Clay's association with Stax ended with a song on Booker T.'s soundtrack for the film *Uptight* and a lone track on Stax's spring 1969 compilation, *Soul Explosion*. Next, it was back to Atlantic for another, this time non-charting duet with Billy Vera, 'Reaching For The Moon', recorded in Muscle Shoals, where solo sessions were also intended to produce a Judy Clay album. In fact, only two solo singles were released, 'Sister Pitiful' and her one and only solo R&B hit, 'Greatest Love'. She continued working through most of the 70s as a back-up singer but had to have major brain surgery later in the decade, before returning briefly to the scene with one unsuccessful single, a live version of the Bee Gees' 'Stayin' Alive', recorded by Dave Crawford in a Newark club and intended as part of a never-issued album. Since then, Clay has satisfied herself with being a wife and mother, although she quite regularly travels up to New Jersey from her North Carolina home for gospel work, including appearances with Cissy Houston's choir at The New Hope Baptist Church in Newark.

● ALBUMS: with Billy Vera *Storybook Children* (Atlantic 1967)★★★.

● COMPILATIONS: with Velda Brown *Private Numbers* (1993)★★★.

CLAY, OTIS

b. 11 February 1942, Waxhaw, Mississippi, USA. Clay was introduced to music as a member of his family's gospel quintet, the Morning Glories. From there he joined the Voices Of Hope and the Christian Travellers. Upon moving to Chicago's West Side in 1957 he sang with several groups including the Golden Jubilaires, the Blue Jays and the Pilgrim Harmonizers. However, it was with the Gospel Songbirds that he first recorded in 1964 with 'Jesus I Love To Call His Name'. Soon after its release, Clay accepted an offer to join the renowned Sensational Nightingales, with whom he toured until mid-1965. Clay then decided to cross into the R&B field and signed with the One-derful label. 'That's How It Is (When You're In Love)' took the singer into the R&B chart in 1967. The follow-up, 'Lasting Love', was also a hit, but Clay's contract was latterly sold to Cotillion Records as One-derful faced bankruptcy. His releases there included 'She's About A Mover' and 'Do Right Woman - Do Right Man' (both of which were recorded at Muscle Shoals), as well as a searing version of 'Pouring Water On A Drowning Man'. The marriage between southern soul and Chicago grit was never so inspired. 'Is It Over' (1971) was the artist's first session with Willie Mitchell and anticipated his subsequent move to Hi Records. Clay's most productive period then followed, the highlights of which included the emotive 'Trying To Live My Life Without You' (1972), 'Home Is Where The Heart Is' (1971) and 'If I Could Reach Out' (1973). Although fiercely popular in the southern states, such releases failed to kindle a national interest, and Otis was dropped from Hi's roster in 1974. He returned north and set up his own label, Echo, before recording a version of the Tyrone Davis hit 'Turn Back The Hands Of Time' for the equally short-lived Elka. Clay also re-formed the Gospel Songbirds for one release and made further singles for the labels Glades and Kayvette. Like several soul singers, he remained highly popular in Japan and *Live Otis Clay* documents his 1978 tour there. Throughout the 80s, Clay continued to flit between secular and gospel performances/recordings, cutting for his own Echo label or simply making demos and hawking them around. In 1989 he linked up with Willie Mitchell's fairly short-lived Waylo venture, where he provided Mitchell with reissues of earlier material, recorded a new solo album and also appeared on a live album featuring various Waylo stars, recorded in Berlin in October 1989 as part of that city's 'wall-removing' celebrations. By 1991 Clay had moved to the Rounder/Bullseye labels. He continues to perform live and to record when the mood takes him.

● ALBUMS: *Trying To Live My Life Without You* (Hi 1972)★★★★, *I Can't Take It* (Hi 1977)★★★★, *Live Otis Clay* (Victor 1978)★★★, *The Only Way Is Up* (Victor 1982)★★, *Live Again* (Rooster Blues 1985)★★★, *Watch Me Now* (Waylo 1989)★★★, *I'll Treat You Right* (Bullseye Blues 1992)★★, *The Gospel Truth* (Blind Pig 1993)★★.

● COMPILATIONS: *The Beginning: Got To Find A Way* (P-Vine 1979)★★★★, *Trying To Live My Life Without You* (Hi UK 1987)★★★★, *That's How It Is* (Demon 1991)★★★, *Otis Clay - The 45s* (1993)★★★★, *On My Way Home - The Gospel Collection* (1993)★★★.

CLAYTON, MERRY

b. Mary Clayton. This powerful American vocalist made her debut in 1963 with 'The Doorbell Rings', before recording a version of 'The Shoop Shoop Song (It's In His Kiss)', a song later popularized by Betty Everett and Cher. Clayton went on to record further singles before beginning a successful career as a session singer. She appeared on several Joe Cocker releases, but is best known for her impassioned appearance on the Rolling Stones' 'Gimmie Shelter'. A member of Ray Charles' Raelettes during the late 60s, Clayton then resumed her solo work and enjoyed several R&B hits including 'After All This Time' (1971) and 'Oh No Not My Baby' (1973). She subsequently enjoyed sporadic success. 'Yes', from the film *Dirty Dancing*, reached the US Top 50 in 1988, but latterly Clayton has also pursued an acting career with roles in *Maid To Order* and television's *Cagney And Lacey*. She performed cabaret-style with Marianne Faithfull and Darlene Love as '20th Century Pop' in 1996.

● ALBUMS: *Gimme Shelter* (Ode 1970)★★, *Merry Clayton* (Ode 1971)★★, *Celebration* (Ode 1973)★★, *Keep Your Eye On The Sparrow* (Ode 1975)★★.

Clayton, Willie

b. 29 March 1955, Indianola, Mississippi, USA. Raised in Chicago, Clayton has a full-throated, flavourful voice, characteristic of many artists from that city during the soul era, and one that has won the hearts of both soul and blues fans. He first recorded for an obscure label in Dallas in 1969, but in 1974 burst onto the scene with 'I Must Be Losing You' on Hi Records' Pawn subsidiary. Since that release, he has produced a consistent body of work - now called soul-blues, first out of Memphis and later out of Chicago - that has magnificently kept the down-home soul sound alive in contemporary African-American music. His output has rarely made the national charts, but his regional successes have been many. Two Clayton releases on the Nashville-based Compleat label, 'Tell Me' and 'What A Way To Put It', both produced by General Crook in Chicago, made the lower reaches of the charts in 1984. After an ill-advised swing to a contemporary sound on a Polydor album, Clayton returned to a down-home sound with his self-produced *Feels Like Love* in 1992, and *Let's Get Together* a year later.

● ALBUMS: *Forever* (P-Vine 1988)★★★, *Never Too Late* (Polydor 1989)★★, *Feels Like Love* (Kirstee/Ichiban 1992)★★★, *Let's Get Together* (Ace 1993)★★★, *Simply Beautiful* (Valley Vue 1995)★★★, *No Getting Over Me* (Ichiban 1995)★★★, *Ace In The Hole* (Ace 1997)★★★.

● COMPILATIONS: *At His Best* (Ichiban 1996)★★★★.

Clefs

Formed at high school in Arlington, Virginia, USA, in 1951 by Scotty Mansfield (lead), Fred Council (baritone), Gerald Bullock (bass), Pavel Bess (tenor) and Frank Newman (second tenor), this R&B vocal group's early performances were limited to fraternity parties and school hops. For the recording of their first demo a year later, Leroy Flack (brother of Roberta Flack) had replaced Bullock on bass, with James Sheppard adding further tenor support. Through manager Lillian Claiborne they were brought to the attention of Chess Records, who subsequently released their cover version of the Ink Spots' 'We Three'. Afterwards they returned to the local club circuit, losing one member (Flack) in 1955, at which time Bess took over bass duties. One further single emerged before they were offered a contract with Peacock Records in Houston, Texas. However, the Clefs declined, opting to pursue their fortunes with the more musically sympathetic Vee Jay Records. However, 1955's 'I'll Be Waiting' failed to provide any degree of success. Their name was then changed to Scotty Mann And The Masters, but 'Just A Little Bit Of Loving' also failed to work the miracle for them, in light of which they returned solely to live performances and, finally, more secure day jobs. This turn of events had become inevitable when Vee Jay failed to release them from contract, despite not wishing to release any new material by the band in either incarnation.

Cleftones

This R&B vocal group from Queens, New York, USA, consisted of Herb Cox (b. 6 May 1939, Cincinnati, Ohio, USA; lead), Charlie James (b. 1940; first tenor), Berman Patterson (b. 1938; second tenor), William McClain (b. 1938; baritone), and Warren Corbin (b. 1939; bass). The group came together at Jamaica High School in 1955. After joining George Goldner's Gee label, the group launched their recording career with 'You Baby You', a regional hit in late 1955. The record, with Cox's dry lead, Warren Corbin's effective bassfills, and session musician Jimmy Wright's frantic saxophone blowing, set the tenor of the group's subsequent records. With their second record, 'Little Girl Of Mine', another peppy number, the group became nationally known as the record went to number 8 R&B and number 57 pop in 1956. Two excellent follow-ups the same year, 'Can't We Be Sweethearts' and 'String Around My Heart', were superbly representative of the Cleftones' exuberant style, but both remained regional hits. A move to a ballad in 1957, the outstanding 'See You Next Year', did not restore the Cleftones to national prominence. In 1959 Gene Pearson (from the Rivileers) replaced McClain, and the following year Patricia Spann was added to the group. The addition of the female to the group also signalled a slight change in style; the leads began to take greater prominence over the ensemble sound as doo-wop was beginning to fade. 'Heart And Soul', a rock 'n' roll remake of an evergreen, typified the new approach and proved to be the group's biggest hit, going to number 10 R&B and number 18 pop in 1961. Other important tracks from this era included the album cut 'Please Say You Want Me' (featuring Pat Spann in a beautiful remake of the Schoolboys' hit) and another evergreen remake, 'For Sentimental Reasons'. The Cleftones' recording career came to an end in 1964.

● ALBUMS: *Heart And Soul* (Gee 1961)★★★, *For Sentimental Reasons* (Gee 1962)★★★.

● COMPILATIONS: *The Best Of The Cleftones* (Rhino 1990)★★★, *For Collectors Only* (Collectables 1992)★★★.

Clifford, Buzz

b. Reese Francis Clifford III, 8 October 1942, Berwyn, Illinois, USA. Buzz Clifford is best known for his one US Top 10 single, 'Baby Sittin' Boogie', in 1961. Clifford learned to play guitar as a child and, enamoured of television westerns, created his own cowboy songs. After winning a talent contest in New Jersey as a teenager, he was signed to Columbia Records. His first single, 'Hello Mr. Moonlight', did not chart but 'Baby Sittin' Boogie', a novelty rock 'n' roll number, charted on the pop, country and R&B charts. Clifford went on to record further singles for Columbia and became a producer for ABC-Paramount in the late 60s. He attempted a comeback, first as a folk rock singer for RCA Records and later as a long-haired country rock artist, in 1969. In the same year, he released a final album on Dot Records that did not reach the charts.

● ALBUMS: *Baby Sittin' With Buzz* (Columbia 1961)★★★, *See Your Way Clear* (Dot 1969)★★.

Clifford, Linda

b. *c.*1944, Brooklyn, New York, USA. Clifford was singing professionally at the age of seven and appeared on television variety programmes in 1950-51. At the age of 17 she had won the Miss New York State beauty pageant and by the mid-60s was singing in nightclubs, performing show music, jazz, standards and R&B material. In 1974 Clifford recorded a single, 'A Long, Long Winter', for Paramount Records, which made the R&B charts. That was followed by another the next year for the small Gemigo label, a division of Curtis Mayfield's Curtom label. She switched to Curtom itself in 1977 and recorded in the disco genre. An album, *Linda*, and the single 'From Now On' were critically favoured but not commercially successful. However, 'Runaway Love' (1978) reached number 3 in the US R&B charts. Her album, *If My Friends Could See Me Now*, was also a success that year and the title song reached the Top 50 in the UK. Clifford transferred to the Robert Stigwood-owned RSO Records in 1979 and continued to have moderate R&B hits, including a disco-styled remake of Simon And Garfunkel's 'Bridge Over Troubled Water' (a UK Top 30 hit) and two duets with Mayfield. Clifford continued to appear in the US R&B charts with Capitol Records and the small Red label, but by the mid-80s was no longer a factor on the charts.

● ALBUMS: *Linda* (Curtom 1977)★★★, *If My Friends Could See Me Now* (Curtom 1978)★★★, *Here's My Love* (RSO 1979)★★, with Curtis Mayfield *The Right Combination* (RSO 1980)★★, *I'm Yours* (RSO 1980)★★★.

● FILMS: *Fame* (1980).

Clinton, George

b. 22 July 1940, Kannapolis, North Carolina, USA. The mastermind behind the highly successful Parliament(s) and Funkadelic, George 'Dr Funkenstein' Clinton's seemingly impregnable empire crumbled at the beginning of the 80s. Restrained from recording by a damaging breach-of-contract lawsuit and unable to meet the running expenses of his considerable organization, he found himself personally and professionally destitute. Clinton, nonetheless, tackled his problems. He settled most of his outstanding debts, overcame an addiction to freebase cocaine and resumed recording. An *ad hoc* group, the P-Funk All Stars, secured two minor hits with 'Hydrolic Pump' and 'One Of Those Summers' (both 1982), before the singer introduced a solo career with the magnificent 'Loopzilla', a rhythmic *tour de force* abounding with references to black music past (the Supremes and the Four Tops) and present (Afrika Baambaataa's 'Planet Rock'). The ensuing album, *Computer Games*, featured several ex-Funkadelic/Parliament cohorts, including Bernie Worrell and Bootsy Collins, while a further track, 'Atomic Dog', was a US R&B number 1 single in 1983. Clinton then continued to work both as a soloist and with the P-Funk All Stars, pursuing his eclectic, eccentric vision on such innovatory albums as *Some Of My Best Jokes Are Friends* and *The Cinderella Theory*. The latter was the first of a succession of recordings released on Prince's Paisley Park label. His *Hey Man ... Smell My Finger* set featured a cameo by ex-NWA artist Dr. Dre, who in turn invited Clinton to guest rap on 'You Don't Wanna See Me' from Dre's collaboration with Ice Cube, *Helter Skelter*. As Dre and many other recent American rappers confess, they owe a great debt to Clinton, not least for their liberal use of his music. Clinton was not one to complain, however, as the young guns' heavy use of Parliament and Funkadelic samples had helped him overcome a crippling tax debt in the early 80s. Ironically enough, Clinton too makes use of samples in his recent recordings, returning to his past ventures for beats, breaks and riffs as so many of his legion of admirers have done before him. Clinton's 1996 album *The Awesome Power Of A Fully Operational Mothership* was a superb blend of the Funkadelic and Parliament sounds.

● ALBUMS: *Computer Games* (Capitol 1982)★★★, *You Shouldn't-Nuf Bit Fish* (Capitol 1984)★★★★, with the P-Funk All Stars *Urban Dance Floor Guerillas* (1984)★★★, *Some Of My Best Jokes Are Friends* (Capitol 1985)★★★★, *R&B Skeletons In The Closet* (Capitol 1986)★★★, *The Cinderella Theory* (Paisley Park 1989)★★★, *Sample A Bit Of Disc And A Bit Of Dat* (AEM 1993)★★★, *Hey Man ... Smell My Finger* (Paisley Park 1993)★★★, *A Fifth Of Funk* (Castle Communications 1995)★★★, *The Music Of Red Shoe Diaries* (Wenerworld 1995)★★★, *Mortal Kombat* (London 1996)★★★, with the P-Funk All Stars *Tapoafom* (Epic 1996)★★★, *The Awesome Power Of A Fully Operational Mothership* (Epic 1996)★★★, *P-Funk All Stars Live At The Beverly Theatre* (Westbound 1996)★★★, with the P-Funk All Stars *Live And Kickin'* (Intersound 1997)★★★.

● COMPILATIONS: *The Best Of George Clinton* (Capitol 1986)★★★★, *Family Series: Testing Positive 4 The Funk* (Essential 1994)★★★, *Greatest Funkin' Hits* (Capitol 1996)★★★★.

● VIDEOS: *Mothership Connection* (Virgin Vision 1987).

Clovers

This US R&B vocal ensemble formed in Washington, DC, in 1946, and built a career recording smooth ballads and bluesy jumps for New York independent Atlantic Records, in the process becoming one of the most popular vocal groups of the 50s. By the time the group first recorded for Rainbow Records in early 1950, the Clovers consisted of John 'Buddy' Bailey (b. 1930, Washington, DC, USA; lead), Matthew McQuater (tenor), Harold Lucas (baritone) and Harold Winley (bass), with instrumental accompaniment from Bill Harris (b. 14 April 1925,

Nashville, North Carolina, USA, d. 5 December 1988; guitar). Later in the year the Clovers joined the fledgling Atlantic label. In 1952 Charles White (b. 1930, Washington, DC, USA), who had earlier experience in the Dominoes and the Checkers, became the Clovers' new lead, replacing Buddy Bailey who was drafted into the US Army. In late 1953 Billy Mitchell took over from White. Bailey rejoined the group in 1954 but Mitchell remained and the two alternated the leads. Whoever was the lead, from 1951-56 the Clovers achieved a consistent sound and remarkably consistent success. They had three US number 1 R&B hits with 'Don't You Know I Love You', 'Fool, Fool, Fool' (both 1951) and 'Ting-A-Ling' (1952), plus four number 2 R&B hits with 'One Mint Julep', 'Hey, Miss Fannie' (both 1952), 'Good Lovin' (1953) and 'Lovey Dovey' (1954). The best-known of the remaining 11 other Top 10 hits for Atlantic was 'Devil Or Angel', a song frequently covered, most notably by Bobby Vee. The Clovers only made the US pop charts with 'Love Love Love' (number 30, 1956) and 'Love Potion No. 9' (number 23, 1959). The latter, one of Leiber And Stoller's best songs, was recorded for United Artists, the only label other than Atlantic that saw the Clovers reach the charts. In 1961 the Clovers split into rival groups led, respectively, by Buddy Bailey and Harold Lucas, and the hits dried up. Various permutations of the Clovers continued to record and perform for years afterwards, particularly in the Carolinas where their brand of music was popular as 'beach music'.

● ALBUMS: *The Clovers* (Atlantic 1956)★★★★, *Dance Party* (Atlantic 1959)★★★★, *In Clover* (Poplar 1959)★★, *Love Potion Number Nine* (United Artists 1959)★★★, *Clovers Live At CT's* (1989)★★.

● COMPILATIONS: *The Original Love Potion Number Nine* (Grand Prix 1964)★★★★, *Their Greatest Recordings - The Early Years* (Atco 1975)★★★★, *The Best Of The Clovers: Love Potion Number Nine* (EMI 1991)★★★★, *Down In The Alley* (Atlantic 1991)★★★, *Dance Party* (Sequel 1997)★★★★.

COASTERS

This R&B vocal group hailed from Los Angeles, USA. The illustrious career of the Coasters, the pre-eminent vocal group of the early rock 'n' roll era, was built on a remarkable body of cleverly comic R&B songs by their producers, Leiber And Stoller. Under their direction, the Coasters exchanged the crooning of ballads favoured by most groups of the era for robust and full-throated R&B shouting. The group came together in 1955 from remnants of the Robins, who had a dispute with their producers/songwriters, Leiber and Stoller. The original Coasters consisted of two ex-Robins, Carl Gardner (b. 29 April 1928, Tyler, Texas, USA; lead) and Bobby Nunn (b. 1925, Birmingham, Alabama, USA, d. 5 November 1986; bass), plus Leon Hughes (b. 1938; tenor), Billy Guy (b. 20 June 1936, Itasca, Texas, USA; lead and baritone) and Adolph Jacobs (b. Oakland, California, USA; guitar). Hughes was replaced in 1956 by Young Jessie, who in turn was replaced by ex-Flairs Cornell Gunther (b. 14 November 1936, Los Angeles, California, USA, d. 26 February 1990). In 1958 Nunn was replaced by ex-Cadets Will 'Dub' Jones (b. 1939, Los Angeles, California, USA). Ex-Cadillacs Earl Carroll (b. Gregory Carroll, 2 November 1937, New York, New York, USA) replaced Gunther in 1961. The Coasters first charted with 'Down In Mexico' (US R&B Top 10) in 1956, but the double-sided hit from 1957, 'Searchin'' (US R&B number 1 and pop number 3) and 'Young Blood' (US R&B number 2 and pop Top 10) established the group as major rock 'n' roll stars (in the UK, 'Searchin'' reached number 30). Three more giant hits sustained the Coasters' career, namely 'Yakety Yak' (US R&B and pop number 1 in 1958), 'Charlie Brown' (US R&B and pop number 2 in 1959), and 'Poison Ivy' (US R&B number 1 and pop Top 10 in 1959). In the UK, 'Yakety Yak' went to number 12, 'Charlie Brown' to number 6, and 'Poison Ivy' to number 15, the group's last chart record in the UK. By this time, they were generally regarded as one of the wittiest exponents of teenage growing problems to emerge from the rock 'n' roll era. By the early 60s the lustre had worn off, as the hits increasingly emphasized the comic lyrics to the detriment of the music. The group continued for decades as an oldies act, and fractured into two different groups playing the oldies circuit. Bobby Nunn died on 5 November 1986; Cornell Gunther on 26 February 1990. The group was inducted into the Rock And Roll Hall Of Fame in 1987.

● ALBUMS: *The Coasters* (Atco 1958)★★★★, *One By One* (Atco 1960)★★★★, *Coast Along With The Coasters* (Atco 1962)★★★, *That's Rock And Roll* (Clarion 1964)★★, *On Broadway* (King 1973)★★.

● COMPILATIONS: *The Coasters' Greatest Hits* (Atco 1959)★★★★, *Their Greatest Recordings: The Early Years* (Atco 1971)★★★, *20 Great Originals* (Atlantic 1978)★★★, *What Is The Secret Of Your Success?* (Mr R&B 1980)★★★, *Thumbin' A Ride* (Edsel 1985)★★★, *The Ultimate Coasters* (Warners 1986)★★★, *Let's Go To The Dance* (Harmony 1988)★★★, *Poison Ivy* (1991)★★★★, *50 Coastin' Classics: The Coasters Anthology* (Rhino/Atlantic 1992)★★★★, *Yakety Yak* (Pickwick 1995)★★★★.

● FURTHER READING: *The Coasters*, Bill Millar.

COCHRAN, WAYNE

b. *c.*1939, Thomaston, Georgia, USA. Wayne Cochran was a white R&B singer whose dynamic stage show was often compared to those of his influences James Brown and Otis Redding. Cochran started singing in the 50s while attending high school and grew his hair long, piling it on his head in the style worn by many blacks at the time. This behaviour inspired his school to invite him to cut it or leave, and he chose the latter option, after which he dyed his hair blond and had it set a foot high, after seeing two albino blues singers, Johnny Winter and his brother Edgar Winter. He released his first single in 1959 and fronted a soul band with horns in the early 60s, winning his first break when a song he wrote, 'Last Kiss', was covered by J. Frank Wilson And The Cavaliers, and went to number 2 in the US pop charts. The following year comedian Jackie Gleason saw Cochran's act and hired him to appear on his television show; Gleason wrote the liner notes for Cochran's self-titled debut album on Chess Records in 1967. That album contained cover versions of popular blues and R&B songs. 1970 was a busy year for Cochran. He released *Livin' In A Bitch Of A World* on King

Records, followed by two albums, both titled *High And Ridin*, one with vocals and one all-instrumental. In 1973 he recorded *Cochran* for Epic Records. Cochran also released numerous singles in the 60s and early 70s, none of which charted. In the 80s he became a television evangelist, following in the footsteps of his fashion idol Little Richard.

● ALBUMS: *Wayne Cochran!* (Chess 1967)★★★, *Alive And Well* (1969)★★, *Livin' In A Bitch Of A World* (King 1970)★★★, *High And Ridin'* (1970)★★, *High And Ridin'* (1970)★★, *Cochran* (Epic 1973)★★.

Coday, Bill

b. 10 May 1942, Coldwater, Mississippi, USA. Coday is one of those revered soulmen about whom little is known but whose limited number of recordings are of an extremely high standard. Although born in Mississippi, he was raised near Blytheville, Arkansas, and, while still in high school, sang with a band that included future blues-man Son Seals. In 1963, Coday moved to Chicago, and in 1969 was 'discovered' by the blues/soul singer, and then Crajon label-owner, Denise LaSalle, while performing at the Black Orchid club under the name of Chicago Willie. At that time, LaSalle was recording for the Westbound label at the Royal Recording Studios in Memphis, under Willie Mitchell's production, with the same musicians and arrangers who regularly worked there for the Hi label, and it was there that Coday cut most of the material for his four Crajon singles. 'Sixty Minute Teaser', a fine bluesy number, was followed by the ballad 'You're Gonna Want Me'; however, 'Get Your Lie Straight' was a superb mid-pacer, with Coday's potent delivery backed by the formidable Hi rhythm section. The latter track was later picked up by Galaxy, and led to two more good Coday singles for that label, notably, 'When You Find A Fool, Bump His Head' (1971). In 1972, Coday's final release for Crajon, 'I'm Back To Collect', was coupled with a fine reworking of O.V. Wright's deep 'Jury Of Love (8 Men, 4 Women)', which was also recorded at the Royal Studios. Four other previously unissued Coday sides appeared in the 80s on a now very rare Japanese Vivid Sound album, which also included the best of his released material. After Galaxy, Coday recorded a good single, 'I Don't Want To Play This Game', for Epic in 1975, which later featured on that label's *Lost Soul* compilation album. Bill Coday still performs occasionally and appeared with Denise LaSalle at an Utrecht Blues Festival in late 1992. *Sneakin' Back* and *Can't Get Enough* were albums of brand new recordings.

As Coday's earlier recorded work has traditionally been very hard to come by, collectors might like to note that 'You're Gonna Want Me' appeared on the 1992 UK Ace CD compilation of Galaxy masters, *All Night Long They Played The Blues*, four other of his Crajon/Galaxy tracks are on the 1993 UK Ace compilation *Bad, Bad Whiskey*, and his 1975 Epic *Lost Soul* set is repeated on a 1994 part reissue of that collection under the same title from US Sony/Legacy.

● ALBUMS: *Sneakin' Back* (Ecko 1995)★★★, *Can't Get Enough* (Ecko 1997)★★★.

● COMPILATIONS: *Bill Coday* (1978)★★★.

CODs

An R&B vocal group formed in Chicago, Illinois, USA, the CODs comprised Larry Brownlee (d. 1978), Robert Lewis and Carl Washington. They were successful disseminators, albeit minor, of the mid-tempo soul sound that Chicago produced during the 60s. The CODs were discovered while singing in a park by a representative of Kellmac Records, one of the myriad of little labels the city generated during its golden era of soul. Their first record, 'Michael (The Lover)' (number 5 R&B, number 41 pop), from 1965, with its delightful upbeat loping tempo, was a surprise hit on the pop charts. Unfortunately, the group could not sustain their success with a hit follow-up, and soon broke up. The CODs were much more talented than their limited success indicated. Brownlee, the principal songwriter, later became a member of the Lost Generation, who had a spate of hits for the Brunswick label, and later a member of Mystique on Curtom Records.

Coffee

An R&B female vocal group from Chicago, Illinois, USA, the members were Betty Caldwell (lead), Gwen Hester, Elaine Sims and Dee Dee Bryant. Coffee, who appeared at the tail-end of the soul era, a group that managed to produced some memorable work before being caught up in the disco wave. After recording a local hit for producer Clarence Johnson, 'Your Love Ain't As Good As Mine', in 1977, Caldwell left, and lead vocals were taken over by Hester. The group thereafter adapted to the demands of the growing disco movement and opted to record in a disco style. Their first album, *Slippin' And Dippin'*, featured a version of the Lovelites' 'How Can I Tell My Mom And Dad', and the record enjoyed good airplay. A second album, recorded in New Jersey by producer Tony Valor, failed to find a market and Coffee soon disappeared.

● ALBUMS: *Slippin' And Dippin'* (De-Lite 1980)★★★.

Cold Blood

A popular live attraction in their native San Francisco, Cold Blood featured the bluesy voice of Lydia Pense and echoed the brassy sound of Tower Of Power. Formed in 1968, the group - Larry Field (guitar), Paul Matute (keyboards), Danny Hull (saxophone), Jerry Jonutz (saxophone), David Padron (trumpet), Larry Jonutz (trumpet), Paul Ellicot (bass), Frank J. David (drums), plus Pense - was signed to impresario Bill Graham's San Francisco label Fillmore the following year. Two albums resulted from this relationship before the group moved to Reprise Records. Later releases failed to recapture the gritty quality of those early records, although their final album was produced by guitarist Steve Cropper. Most of the group then dropped out from active performing, but a late-period drummer, Gaylord Birch, later worked with Santana, the Pointer Sisters and Graham Central Station.

● ALBUMS: *Cold Blood* (San Francisco 1969)★★★, *Sisyphus* (San Francisco 1971)★★★, *First Taste Of Sin* (Reprise 1972)★★, *Thriller!* (Reprise 1973)★★, *Lydia* (Warners 1974)★★, *Lydia Pense And Cold Blood* (ABC 1976)★★.

Cole, Natalie

b. 6 February 1950, Los Angeles, California, USA. The daughter of celebrated singer/pianist Nat 'King' Cole, Natalie survived early pressures to emulate her father's laid-back style. Signed to Capitol Records in 1975, her debut release, 'This Will Be', was a US Top 10 hit and the first of three consecutive number 1 soul singles. This early success was continued with 'I've Got Love On My Mind' and 'Our Love' (both 1977), which continued the astute, sculpted R&B style forged by producers Chuck Jackson and Marvin Yancey, who, like herself, attended Jerry Butler's Writers Workshop. Yancey and Cole later married. Cole's work continued to enjoy plaudits, and although it lacked the intensity of several contemporaries, there was no denying its quality and craft. She maintained her popularity into the 80s but an increasing drug dependency took a professional and personal toll. Her marriage ended in divorce, but in May 1984, the singer emerged from a rehabilitation centre. Now cured, Natalie picked up the pieces of her career, and a 1987 album, *Everlasting*, provided three hit singles, 'Jump Start', 'I Live For Your Love' and 'Pink Cadillac', the latter reaching number 5 in the UK and US pop charts. This Bruce Springsteen song was uncovered from the b-side of 'Dancing In The Dark'. In 1991, she recorded a unique tribute to her late father - a 'duet' with him on his original recording of the song 'Unforgettable'. The song took on a moving significance, with the daughter perfectly accompanying her deceased father's voice. The single's promotional video featured vintage black-and-white footage of Nat 'King' Cole at his peak on his US television show, interspersed with colour clips of Natalie. The accompanying album on Elektra Records later won seven Grammy awards, including best album and song the following year. Two years later she released *Take A Look*, which included a superb cover version of the standard 'Cry Me A River'.

● ALBUMS: *Inseparable* (Capitol 1975)★★★★, *Natalie* (Capitol 1976)★★★, *Unpredictable* (Capitol 1977)★★★, *Thankful* (Capitol 1977)★★★, *Natalie ... Live!* (Capitol 1978)★★★★, *I Love You So* (Capitol 1979)★★★, with Peabo Bryson *We're The Best Of Friends* (Capitol 1979)★★★, *Don't Look Back* (Capitol 1980)★★, *Happy Love* (Capitol 1981)★★, with Johnny Mathis *Unforgettable: A Musical Tribute To Nat 'King' Cole* (Columbia 1983)★★★, *I'm Ready* (Epic 1983)★★, *Dangerous* (Modern 1985)★★, *Everlasting* (Manhattan 1987)★★, *Good To Be Back* (EMI 1989)★★, *Unforgettable ... With Love* (Elektra 1991)★★★★, *Take A Look* (Elektra 1993)★★★, *Star Dust* (Elektra 1996)★★★.

● COMPILATIONS: *The Natalie Cole Collection* (Capitol 1988)★★★, *The Soul Of Natalie Cole (1974-80)* (Capitol 1991)★★★★.

● VIDEOS: *Video Hits* (PMI 1989), *Holly & Ivy* (Warner Music Vision 1995).

Coleman Brothers

This spiritual/jubilee vocal group from Newark, New Jersey, USA, consisted of brothers Lander (lead, first tenor), Russell (first tenor), Wallace (baritone), Melvin (bass) and Everitte Coleman (guitar), plus Danny Owens (tenor). The Coleman Brothers were one of the most renowned groups in the 40s performing in the light spiritual or jubilee style. They came from a musical family and prior to the formation of the group in 1925, there had been an earlier Coleman Brothers line-up from 1918-26 that played in churches and meeting halls throughout New Jersey. The membership of the new Coleman Brothers group was, in its early days, constantly in flux and did not crystallize until the mid-30s. The group toured the south and made many appearances on radio before signing their first recording contract, with Decca, in 1944. Their first record, 'Low Down Chariot', launched a series of successful singles - notably 'His Eye Is On The Sparrow', 'New Milky White Way' and 'Sending Up My Timber' - in the marketplace for Decca as well as for Manor and for their own Coleman label. The group continued to make its presence felt in radio, performing as a staff vocal group for CBS in 1945 and from 1946-48 working at WLW in Cincinnati. In 1945, Melvin left the group and was replaced with A.J. Eldridge, but by 1951 the Coleman Brothers had disbanded. Lander Coleman re-formed the Coleman Brothers in 1964 with second tenor John Bryant, baritone Fred Perry and bass A.J. Eldridge. They made an album for Savoy, *Milky White Way*, and continued as a group until disbanding in 1977. Lander Coleman pursued a solo career and recorded a number of albums for his own label, Golden Records.

● ALBUMS: *Milky White Way* (Savoy 1964)★★★.

Coleman, Margi

b. USA. With her 1995 debut album, *Margi*, Los Angeles singer Coleman became the first urban R&B/soul performer to sign with rap label Priority Records. The album, a joint production project between Coleman and Courtney Branch and Tracy Kendrick of Total Trak Productions, featured several songs written by the artist herself. With a strong spiritual perspective as well as emotive songwriting addressing relationships, it followed her debut 1994 single, 'Winnin' Ova You'. The video that accompanied the single featured the artist in African-American clothing and Afro haircut, communing with nature in a forest. The single released to accompany the album, 'Let Me Down Gently', included a horse-riding sequence along a beach in an effort to reiterate Coleman's association with green causes.

● ALBUMS: *Margi* (Priority 1995)★★★.

Collier, Mitty

b. 21 June 1941, Birmingham, Alabama, USA. As a member of the travelling gospel group the Hayes Ensemble, Collier toured throughout Alabama and Georgia. Switching to secular music, she was discovered singing in a talent show by Chess Records scout Ralph Bass. Her early releases lacked direction until 'I'm Your Part Time Love', an 'answer' to Little Johnny Taylor's 'Part Time Love', reached the US R&B Top 20 in 1963. 'I Had A Talk With My Man' (1964), remains her definitive single. Adapted from a Rev. James Cleveland song, 'I Had A Talk With God Last Night', Collier's deep contralto soared against producer Billy Davis's sumptuous backing.

Another Cleveland composition, 'No Cross, No Crown', then inspired the follow-up, 'No Faith, No Love' (1965). Although the quality of her subsequent recordings remained high, 'Sharing You' (1966) was her final hit. Her spell with Chess ended in 1968 with 'Everybody Makes A Mistake Sometimes', a southern soul-styled offering recorded at Muscle Shoals. Following five singles for William Bell's Peachtree label and one release for Entrance, Mitty Collier returned to gospel music. *The Warning*, her first of several albums in this field, featured 'I Had A Talk With God Last Night'.

● ALBUMS: *Shades Of A Genius* (Chess 1965)★★★, *The Warning* (1972)★★★, *Hold The Light* (1977)★★★, *I Am Love* (1987)★★★.

Collins, Bootsy

b. William Collins, 26 October 1951, Cincinnati, Ohio, USA. This exceptional showman was an integral part of the JBs, the backing group fashioned by James Brown to replace the Famous Flames. Between 1969 and 1971, the distinctive Collins basswork propelled some of the era's definitive funk anthems. Collins was later part of the large-scale defection in which several of Brown's most valued musicians switched to George Clinton's Parliament/Funkadelic organization. The bassist's popularity inspired the formation of Bootsy's Rubber Band, a spin-off group featuring such Brown/Clinton associates as Fred Wesley, Maceo Parker and Bernie Worrell. Collins's outrageous image - part space cadet, part psychedelic warlord - emphasized a mix of funk and fun exemplified by 'Psychoticbumpschool' (1976), 'The Pinocchio Theory' (1977) and 'Bootzilla' (1978), a US R&B chart-topper. The internal problems plaguing the Clinton camp during the early 80s temporarily hampered Collins's career, although the subsequent comeback album, *What's Bootsy Doin'?*, revealed some of his erstwhile charm. Collins and the Bootzilla Orchestra were employed for the production of Malcolm McLaren's 1989 album *Waltz Darling* and by the early 90s the Rubber Band had started touring again. Although he has found plenty of work on various hip-hop/rap projects during the 90s, Collins' own releases have tended to be competent rather than inspired. However, a return to a major label for 1997's *Fresh Outta "P" University* produced his best work since his 70s' peak.

● ALBUMS: *Stretchin' Out In Bootsy's Rubber Band* (Warners 1976)★★★, *Ahh...The Name Is Bootsy, Baby!* (Warners 1977)★★★, *Bootsy? Player Of The Year* (Warners 1978)★★★, *This Boot Is Made For Fonk-n* (Warners 1979)★★, *Ultra Wave* (Warners 1980)★★★, *The One Giveth, The Count Taketh Away* (Warners 1982)★★★, *What's Bootsy Doin'?* (Columbia 1988)★★★, *Jungle Bass* (4th & Broadway 1990)★★★, *Blasters Of The Universe* (Rykodisc 1994)★★★, *Fresh Outta "P" University* (Warners 1997)★★★.

● COMPILATIONS: *Back In The Day: The Best Of ...* (Warners 1995)★★★★.

Color Me Badd

This US harmony and a cappella group triumphed on both sides of the Atlantic in 1991 with the dubious sexual slant of 'I Wanna Sex You Up'. The group comprises four Oklahoma college kids, Bryan Abrams (b. 16 November 1969, USA), Mark Calderon (b. 27 September 1970, USA), Sam Watters (b. 23 July 1970, USA) and Kevin Thornton (b. 17 June 1969, USA). It was while they were performing as a support band in Oklahoma that they were spotted by Robert Bell (of Kool And The Gang), who swept them off to New York. Originally arranged by Dr. Freeze, 'I Wanna Sex You Up' was featured in the soundtrack to the film *New Jack City*. Their poppy R&B harmony shared similarities with the Pasadenas, though their unshaven, adolescent hoodlum image was doubtless more contrived. The follow-ups, 'I Adore Mi Amore' and 'Heartbreaker', were typical radio-friendly pop workouts, though the vocal harmonics were rendered with aplomb. For their second album Whitney Houston/Barbra Streisand producer David Foster was recruited, alongside the barely complementary skills of DJ Pooh, more familiar from his work with Ice Cube. The gangsta rapper himself stopped by to direct the video for the title track, which was also the first single to be lifted from the album. They returned to the charts in 1996 with 'The Earth, The Sun, The Rain'.

● ALBUMS: *Color Me Badd* (Giant 1991)★★★, *Time & Chance* (Giant 1993)★★★.

Colts

R&B vocal group the Colts honed their act in front of truck drivers at a drive-in eatery in Bakersfield, California, USA. At the core of the group were brothers Ruben (lead) and Joe Grundy, plus Carl Moland, accompanied by several part-time contributors. It was not until the trio started attending Los Angeles City College that the line-up was finalized with the addition of former New Jersey boxer Leroy Smith. They then secured the management and writing services of Buck Ram, a veteran of work with the Platters and Penguins. Through Ram they signed to Vita Records in Pasadena and recorded one of Ram's compositions, 'Adorable', in August 1955, backed by 'Lips Like Red Wine'. It became a staple of clubs and radio stations throughout California, leading to the Drifters recording a version that went to number 1 in *Billboard*'s R&B chart (the Colts' own take on 'Adorable' stalled at number 11). Touring slots with the Platters, Penguins and Dinah Washington ensued, as well as an appearance at New York's Apollo Theatre. If the Drifters' hijacking of their tune had put the Colts in the shade, then Ram's decision to spend more time with the Platters (after they had enjoyed a US number 1 with his song 'The Great Pretender') eclipsed them completely. 'Sweet Sixteen' and 'Never No More' were their final two releases before Ram switched them to his new Antler Records label. However, neither 'Sheik Of Araby' (1957) nor 'I Never Knew' (for Delco Records in 1959) returned them to the limelight.

Commodores

The Commodores were formed at Tuskagee Institute, Alabama, USA, in 1967, when two groups of students merged to form a six-piece band. Lionel Richie (b. 20 June 1949, Tuskegee, Alabama, USA; keyboards, saxophone, vocals), Thomas McClary (b. 6 October 1950; guitar) and William King (b. 30 January 1949, Alabama, USA; trumpet) had been members of the Mystics; Andre Callahan (drums), Michael Gilbert (bass) and Milan Williams (b. 28 March 1949, Mississippi, USA; keyboards) previously played with the Jays. Callahan and Gilbert were replaced, respectively, by Walter 'Clyde' Orange (b. 10 December 1947, Florida, USA) and Ronald LaPread (b. 1950, Florida, USA), before the Commodores moved to New York in 1969, where they became established as a club band specializing in funk instrumentals. A year later, they recorded an album for Atlantic Records, left unissued at the time but subsequently released as *Rise Up*, which included instrumental cover versions of recent R&B hits, plus some original material. In 1972, the group's manager, Bernie Ashburn, secured them a support slot on an American tour with the Jackson Five, and the Commodores were duly signed to Motown Records. They continued to tour with the Jackson Five for three years, after which they supported the Rolling Stones on their 1975 US tour. By this time, their mix of hard-edged funk songs and romantic ballads, the latter mostly penned and sung by Richie, had won them a national following. The instrumental 'Machine Gun' gave them their first US hit, followed by 'Slippery When Wet'. The Commodores soon found consistent success with Richie's smooth ballads; 'Sweet Love', 'Just To Be Close To You' and 'Easy' all enjoyed huge sales between 1975 and 1977. Although Clyde Orange's aggressive 'Too Hot To Trot' broke the sequence of ballads in 1977, the Commodores were increasingly regarded as a soft-soul outfit. This perception was underlined when Richie's sensitive love song to his wife, 'Three Times A Lady', became a number 1 record in the USA and UK, where it was Motown's biggest-selling record to date. The follow-up, 'Sail On', introduced a country flavour to Richie's work, and he began to receive commissions to write material for artists such as Kenny Rogers. After 'Still' gave them another US pop and soul number 1 in 1979, confirming the Commodores as Motown's best-selling act of the 70s, the group attempted to move into a more experimental blend of funk and rock on *Heroes* in 1980. The commercial failure of this venture, and the success of Lionel Richie's duet with Diana Ross on 'Endless Love', persuaded him to leave the group for a solo career. The remaining Commodores were initially overshadowed by the move, with the replacement Kevin Smith unable to emulate Richie's role in live performances.

In 1984, Thomas McClary also launched a solo career with an album for Motown. He was replaced by Englishman J.D. Nicholas (b. 12 April 1952, Watford, Hertfordshire, England), formerly vocalist with Heatwave, and this combination was featured on the group's enormous 1985 hit 'Nightshift', an affecting tribute to Marvin Gaye and Jackie Wilson that successfully captured Gaye's shifting, rhythmic brand of soul. Later that year, the Commodores left Motown for Polydor, prompting Ronald LaPread to leave the band. Their new contract began promisingly with a major US soul chart hit, 'Goin' To The Bank' (1986), but subsequent releases proved less successful. The group made an unexpected return to the UK chart in 1988 when 'Easy' was used for a television commercial for the Halifax Building Society, and reached number 15. With an ever-declining audience, the Commodores have lost much of their status as one of America's most popular soul bands.

● ALBUMS: *Machine Gun* (Motown 1974)★★★★, *Caught In The Act* (Motown 1975)★★★, *Movin' On* (Motown 1975)★★★, *Hot On The Tracks* (Motown 1976)★★★, *Commodores* aka *Zoom* (Motown 1977)★★★, *Commodores Live!* (Motown 1977)★★★, *Natural High* (Motown 1978)★★★, *Midnight Magic* (Motown 1979)★★★, *Heroes* (Motown 1980)★★★, *In The Pocket* (Motown 1981)★★★, *Commodores 13* (Motown 1983)★★★, *Nightshift* (Motown 1985)★★★, *United* (Polydor 1986)★★, *Rise Up* (Blue Moon 1987)★★, *Rock Solid* (Polydor 1988)★★.

● COMPILATIONS: *Commodores' Greatest Hits* (Motown 1978)★★★★, *All The Great Hits* (Motown 1981)★★★, *Love Songs* (K-Tel 1982)★★, *Anthology* (Motown 1983)★★★, *The Best Of The Commodores* (Telstar 1985)★★★, *14 Greatest Hits* (1993)★★★, *The Very Best Of the Commodores* (Motown 1995)★★★★.

● VIDEOS: *Cover Story* (Stylus Video 1990).

Con Funk Shun

Formed initially in 1968 as Project Soul by Mike Cooper (guitar, sitar, timbales, percussion, vocals) and Louis McCall (drums, vocals), the group's rise began when they accepted an offer to back the Soul Children, necessitating a move from California to Memphis. Upon arrival in 1972, Project Soul became Con Funk Shun, having been augmented by group members Karl Fuller (trumpet, flugelhorn, vocals), Paul Harrell (saxophone, flute, vocals), Cedric Martin (bass and vocals), Felton Pilate (trombone, bass trumpet, piano, synthesizer, acoustic guitar, vocals) and Danny Thomas (clavinet, piano, synthesizer, organ, vocals). To make ends meet they initially worked as a Stax Records studio band. After recording a couple of singles with small local label Fretone they signed with Mercury, releasing their debut album in 1976. The following year they achieved a gold disc with *Secrets*, aided by the success of 'Ffun', which would go Top 30 in early 1978. Further albums consolidated their success, but the lack of a focal point within the group (as opposed to contemporaries such as Lionel Richie and the Commodores) meant they were never likely to attain superstar status. In the mid-80s they split, with Felton Pilate becoming an in-demand producer.

● ALBUMS: *Con Funk Shun* (Mercury 1976)★★★, *Secrets* (Mercury 1977)★★, *Loveshine* (Mercury 1978)★★, *Candy* (Mercury 1979)★★, *Spirit Of Love* (Mercury 1980)★★★, *Touch* (Mercury 1980)★★, *Con Funk Shun 7* (Mercury 1981)★★, *To The Max* (Mercury 1982)★★, *Fever* (Mercury 1983)★★, *Electric Lady* (Mercury 1985)★★, *Burnin' Love* (Mercury 1986)★★.

● COMPILATIONS: *The Best Of Con Funk Shun* (Mercury 1993)★★★.

Concords

Formed in 1959 in the Brighton Beach enclave of Brooklyn, New York, USA, the Concords' membership originally teamed Mike Lewis (lead and tenor), Dickie

Goldman (lead and tenor), Murray Moshe (baritone), Charles 'Chippy' Presti (second tenor) and Steve Seider (bass). Signed by RCA Records, the Concords made their debut with a vocal group standard, 'Again'. Songwriter Stu Wiener then took them to his father's Gramercy Records label, where they released two singles, 'Cross My Heart' and 'My Dreams'. After losing Goldman and deciding to continue as a quartet, they chose to re-release 'Again' on Rust Records in 1962, before finding a more permanent home at Herald Records. Their most successful single, 'Marlene', followed, which became a major regional hit in the north-west, and led to them performing in Detroit with the Supremes. However, it was not enough to dampen disquiet in the ranks and the Concords broke up in 1963. Lewis briefly formed the Planets but returned to a reshuffled Concords in 1964, wherein he and Seider were joined by Teddy Graybill (ex-Stardrifts), Sal Tepedino (ex-Travelers) and Bobby Ganz. A new contract with Epic Records led to the release of 'Should I Cry', although Lewis and Wiener enjoyed more success with their production of Roddie Joy's 'Come Back Baby'. A remake of the Quintones' 'Down The Aisle Of Love' was the final Concords single in 1966, with only Lewis remaining in the music industry thereafter (principally as a writer and producer).

● ALBUMS: *The Concords* (Crystal Ball 1991)★★.

CONLEY, ARTHUR

b. 4 January 1946, Atlanta, Georgia, USA. Recalled as something of a one-hit-wonder, this Otis Redding protégé remains underrated. Conley first recorded for the NRC label as Arthur And The Corvets. After signing to his mentor Otis Redding's Jotis label, further singles were leased to Volt and Stax Records before 'Sweet Soul Music' (1967) hit both the US R&B and pop charts. A thin reworking of Sam Cooke's 'Yeah Man' saw the song's original lyrics amended to pay homage to several contemporary soul singers. Although 'Funky Street' was a US Top 20 hit, Redding's tragic death forestalled Conley's progress. Minor successes followed throughout 1968 and 1969 before the singer switched to the Capricorn label in 1971. His debut album, *Sweet Soul Music*, is a strong collection, highlighted by each of his first five singles and two Redding originals. Later, Conley had a set of recordings for Swamp Dogg released, and then, having relocated to Europe, a live album recorded in Amsterdam in 1980 under his pseudonym of Lee Roberts finally emerged some eight years later.

● ALBUMS: *Sweet Soul Music* (Atco 1967)★★★★, *Shake, Rattle And Roll* (Atco 1967)★★★, *Soul Directions* (Atco 1968)★★★, *More Sweet Soul* (Atco 1969)★★★, *One More Sweet Soul Music* (Warners 1988)★★, as Lee Roberts And The Sweater *Soulin'* (Blue Shadow 1988)★★★.

● COMPILATIONS: *Arthur Conley* (Atlantic 1988)★★★.

● FURTHER READING: *Sweet Soul Music*, Peter Guralnick.

CONTOURS

The Contours formed as an R&B vocal group in Detroit in 1959, featuring lead vocalist Billy Gordon, Billy Hoggs, Joe Billingslea and Sylvester Potts. Hubert Johnson (d. 11 July 1981) joined the line-up in 1960, and it was his cousin Jackie Wilson who secured the group an audition and then a contract with Motown Records in 1961. Initial singles proved unsuccessful, but in 1962 the dance-orientated number 'Do You Love Me' became one of the label's biggest hits to date, topping the R&B charts and reaching number 3 in the US pop listing. The same frantic blend of R&B and the twist dance craze powered the follow-up, 'Shake Sherry', in 1963. Both songs heavily influenced the British beat group scene, with 'Do You Love Me' being covered by Brian Poole And The Tremeloes, Faron's Flamingos and the Dave Clark Five. Unfortunately, the Contours were unable to capitalize on their early success, and their exciting, slightly chaotic sound lost favour at Motown, usurped by the choreographed routines and tight harmonies of acts such as the Temptations and the Four Tops. As the Contours' line-up went through a rapid series of changes, they had occasional R&B successes with 'Can You Jerk Like Me', Smokey Robinson's witty 'First I Look At The Purse', and the dance number 'Just A Little Misunderstanding'. Although 'It's So Hard Being A Loser' (1967) was the Contours' last official single, posthumous releases, particularly in Britain, kept their name alive. Former lead vocalist Dennis Edwards later enjoyed consistent success with the Temptations, and as a soloist. Versions of the Contours appeared on the revival circuit from 1972 onwards, and while Johnson committed suicide in 1981, a trio consisting of Billingslea, Potts and Jerry Green were still performing into the 80s. In 1988, 'Do You Love Me' returned to the US Top 20 after its inclusion in the film *Dirty Dancing*. The current line-up of Billingslea, Potts, Arthur Hinson, Charles Davis and Darrel Nunlee issued *Running In Circles* on Ian Levine's Motor City label in 1990. The former lead vocalist Joe Stubbs also recorded *Round And Round* for the same label.

● ALBUMS: *Do You Love Me* (Gordy 1962)★★★, *Running In Circles* (Motor City 1990)★★.

● COMPILATIONS: *Baby Hit And Run* (1974)★★★, *The Very Best* (Essential Gold 1996)★★★.

CONTROLLERS

Formed by four schoolfriends from Fairfield, near Birmingham, Alabama, USA, in the late 60s, the Soul Controllers comprised Reginald MacArthur, Leonard Brown, Ricky Lewis and Larry MacArthur. They recorded two singles for local labels while still at school, 'Right On, Right On' and 'Hate Is The Thing, Rap Is The Peace'. Some time later they were spotted by producer Frederick Knight (who had a hit with 'I've Been Lonely For So Long') and signed to his Juana label as the Controllers. They had immediate success with 'Somebody's Gotta Win, Somebody's Gotta Lose', an R&B hit in 1977 and the title track of their first Juana album, while another hit arrived with 'I Can't Turn The Boogie Loose' from *Next In Line*. After three albums for Juana they set up their own label, CMP, recording one single ('Distant Lovers', 1982) before signing with MCA. They recorded three albums for that label, coming closest to success with their debut single, 'Crushed'. In 1988 they signed with Capitol, releasing *Just In Time* the following year.

● ALBUMS: *Somebody's Gotta Win, Somebody's Gotta Lose*

(Juana 1977)★★★, *My Love Is Real* (Juana 1978)★★★, *Next In Line* (Juana 1979)★★, *The Controllers* (MCA 1984)★★★, *Stay* (MCA 1986)★★★, *For the Love Of My Woman* (MCA 1987)★★, *Just In Time* (Capitol 1989)★★.

Cooke, Sam

b. Sam Cook, 22 January 1931, Clarksdale, Mississippi, USA, d. 11 December 1964, Los Angeles, California, USA. Cooke first performed publicly with his brother and two sisters in their Baptist quartet, the Soul Children. As a teenager he joined the Highway QCs, before replacing Robert 'R.H.' Harris in the Soul Stirrers. Between 1951 and 1956 Cooke sang lead with this innovative gospel group. His distinctive florid vocal style was soon obvious on 'Touch The Hem Of His Garment' and 'Nearer To Thee'. The Soul Stirrers recorded for the Specialty label, where the singer's popularity encouraged producer 'Bumps' Blackwell to provide Sam with pop material. 'Loveable'/'Forever' was issued as a single, disguised under the pseudonym 'Dale Cook' to avoid offending the gospel audience. Initially content, the label's owner, Art Rupe, then objected to the sweetening choir on a follow-up recording, 'You Send Me', and offered Cooke a release from his contract in return for outstanding royalties. The song was then passed to the Keen label, where it sold in excess of two million copies. Further hits, including 'Only Sixteen' and 'Wonderful World', followed. The latter was used extensively in a television jeans commercial and in 1986 the reissue reached number 2 in the UK charts. Cooke left the label for RCA Records where 'Chain Gang' (1960), 'Cupid' (1961) and 'Twistin' The Night Away' (1962), displayed a pop craft later offset by such grittier offerings as 'Bring It On Home To Me' and 'Little Red Rooster'. Cooke also founded the Sar and Derby labels on which the Simms Twins' 'Soothe Me' and the Valentinos' 'It's All Over Now' were issued. Cooke's own career remained in the ascendant with '(Ain't That) Good News' and 'Good Times', but the purity of such music made his tawdry fate all the more perplexing. On 11 December 1964, following an altercation with a girl he had picked up, the singer was fatally shot by the manageress of a Los Angeles motel. The ebullient 'Shake' became a posthumous hit, but its serene coupling, 'A Change Is Gonna Come', was a more melancholic epitaph. Arguably his finest composition, its title suggested a metaphor for the concurrent Civil Rights movement. Cooke's legacy continued through his various disciples - Johnnie Taylor, who had replaced Cooke in the Soul Stirrers, bore an obvious debt, as did Bobby Womack of the Valentinos. Cooke's songs were interpreted by acts as diverse as Rod Stewart, the Animals and Cat Stevens, while the Rolling Stones' version of 'Little Red Rooster' echoed Cooke's reading rather than that of Howlin' Wolf. Otis Redding, Aretha Franklin, Smokey Robinson - the list of those acknowledging Cooke's skill is a testimony in itself. A seminal influence on soul music and R&B, his effortless and smooth delivery has rarely been surpassed. *Sam Cooke: A Man And His Music* provides an excellent overview of the singer's career.

● ALBUMS: *Sam Cooke* i (Keen 1958)★★★, *Sam Cooke Encore* (Keen 1959)★★★, *Tribute To The Lady* (Keen 1959)★★★, *Hit Kit* (Keen 1960)★★★, *I Thank God* (Keen 1960)★★★, *Wonderful World Of Sam Cooke* (Keen 1960)★★★, *Cooke's Tour* (RCA 1960)★★★, *Hits Of The 50s* (RCA 1960)★★★, *Swing Low* (1961)★★★, *My Kind Of Blues* (RCA 1961)★★★★, *Twisting The Night Away* (RCA 1962)★★★★, *Mr. Soul* (RCA 1963)★★★★, *Night Beat* (RCA 1963)★★★, *Ain't That Good News* (RCA 1964)★★★, *Sam Cooke At The Copa* (RCA 1964)★★★★, *Shake* (RCA 1965)★★★, *Try A Little Love* (RCA 1965)★★★, *Sam Cooke Sings Billie Holiday* (RCA 1976)★★★, *Sam Cooke Live At The Harlem Square Club, 1963* (RCA 1985)★★★.

● COMPILATIONS: *The Best Of Sam Cooke, Volume 1* (RCA 1962)★★★★, *The Best Of Sam Cooke, Volume 2* (RCA 1965)★★★★, *The Late And Great* (1969)★★★, *The Gospel Soul Of Sam Cooke With The Soul Stirrers, Volume 1* (Specialty 1969)★★★★, *The Gospel Soul Of Sam Cooke With The Soul Stirrers, Volume 2* (Specialty 1970)★★★★,*The Two Sides Of Sam Cooke* (Specialty 1970)★★★, *This Is Sam Cooke* (RCA 1971)★★★, *That's Heaven To Me: Sam Cooke With The Soul Stirrers* (Specialty 1972)★★★★, *The Golden Age Of Sam Cooke* (RCA 1976)★★★, *The Man And His Music* (RCA 1986)★★★★★, *Forever* (Specialty 1986)★★★, *Sam Cooke* ii (Deja Vu 1987)★★★, *You Send Me* (Topline/Charly 1987)★★★, *20 Greatest Hits* (Compact Collection 1987)★★★★, *Wonderful World* (Fame 1988)★★★★, *The World Of Sam Cooke* (Instant 1989)★★★★, *Legend* (EMS 1990)★★★, *The Magic Of Sam Cooke* (Music Club 1991)★★★, *Sam Cooke With The Soul Stirrers* (Specialty 1991)★★★★, *Sam Cooke's Sar Records Story* (1994)★★★.

● FURTHER READING: *Sam Cooke: The Man Who Invented Soul: A Biography In Words & Pictures*, Joe McEwen. *You Send Me: The Life And Times*, S.R. Crain, Clifton White and G. David Tenenbaum.

Cookies

This US vocal group trio was formed in the early 50s by Doretta (Dorothy) Jones (b. South Carolina, USA). Early members included Pat Lyles, Ethel 'Dolly' McCrae and Margorie Hendrickse. They were signed by Atlantic Records in 1956 where they recorded four singles, of which 'In Paradise' reached the R&B Top 10. However, the group was better known for session work, and can be heard on successful releases by Joe Turner ('Lipstick, Powder And Paint') and Chuck Willis ('It's Too Late'). The Cookies also backed Ray Charles on several occasions and Hendrickse, now known as Margie Hendrix, left to form Charles's own singing ensemble, the Raelettes. Her erstwhile colleagues continued their career as contract singers with newcomer Margaret Ross. Work with Neil Sedaka resulted in their meeting songwriter Carole King, who in turn brought the trio to the Dimension label. Here they enjoyed two US Top 20 hits with the effervescent 'Chains' (later covered by the Beatles) and 'Don't Say Nothin' Bad (About My Baby)', while their voices also appeared on various releases by Little Eva, herself an auxiliary member of the group. The Cookies later moved to Warner Brothers following Dimension's collapse. Altogether the trio recorded seven singles, all of which are excellent examples of the girl-group genre. Jones and

McCrae also recorded in their own right, the latter under the name Earl-Jean.

● COMPILATIONS: *The Complete Cookies* (Sequel 1994)★★★.

COOPER, TRENTON

b. 1923, Hope, Arkansas, USA. This talented blues pianist played in his college orchestra before joining an R&B band led by Jay Franks. The band also featured Nelson Carson on guitar, and Cooper co-wrote Franks's 'Fish Tail'. After 1950 Cooper played in the Drops Of Joy, the popular R&B combo led by Jimmy Liggins. When he was traced by blues historian Jim O'Neal in 1976, he was the director of the Co-operative Education office at the University of Arkansas in Pine Bluff.

● COMPILATIONS: with various artists *Keep It To Yourself - Arkansas Blues, Volume 1* (1983).

CORNELIUS BROTHERS AND SISTER ROSE

An R&B family group from Dania, Florida, USA, their highly infectious mid-tempo soft soul was heavily orchestrated, and was more typical of northern US cities than the south. This broke the mode of Miami-based music, which tended to be of the 'deep soul' variety. The original group, consisting of Edward (who wrote most of the songs), Carter and Rose Cornelius, first recorded in 1971. They had immediate success with a million-seller, 'Treat Her Like A Lady', a US R&B Top 20 and pop number 3 hit. The next year they added a second sister, Billie Jo, and achieved their biggest hit, another million-seller, 'Too Late To Turn Back Now' (US R&B number 5 and pop number 2). Thereafter, each succeeding record did less well. Their last chart record was the minor-placed R&B hit 'Since I Found My Baby' in 1974. The group broke up in 1976 when Carter joined a black Hebrew sect in Miami and adopted the name Prince Gideon Israel. He wrote, recorded and mixed the sect's music and videos for the next 15 years. He was working on a comeback song to return to the pop field when he died on 7 November 1991.

● ALBUMS: *Cornelius Brothers And Sister Rose* (United Artists 1972)★★★, *Big Time Lover* (United Artists 1973)★★, *Got To Testify* (United Artists 1974)★★.

CORSAIRS

A family group from LaGrange, North Carolina, USA, this vocal quartet consists of three brothers - lead Jay 'Bird' Uzzell (b. 13 July 1942), James Uzzell (b. 1 December 1940), and Moses Uzzell (b. 13 September 1939) - and a cousin, George Wooten (b. 16 January 1940). Their songs have a standard mid-tempo pop feel, yet have an edge provided by Jay Uzzell's wailing lead, burbling bass and strong chorusing. The Corsairs found their opportunity by moving from their native North Carolina to New Jersey in 1961 to be nearer to the New York recording business. They were discovered in a Jersey club by independent producer Abner Spector, who released their records on his Tuff Record label. In 1962 they reached the charts twice, with 'Smokey Places' (number 10 R&B, number 12 pop) and 'I'll Take You Home' (number 26 R&B, number 68 pop). One unrecognized classic in their repertoire is 'Stormy' (their 1963 remake of a 1956 hit by Illinois group the Prophets). The Corsairs ideally evoke that fuzzy, intermediate era when the shuffle beats and the doo-wop harmonies of the 50s were fast fading and had yet to be superseded by gospelized soul stylings. By 1965 Abner's well had run dry and the Corsairs' recording career was finished.

CORTEZ, DAVE 'BABY'

b. David Cortez Clowney, 13 August 1938, Detroit, Michigan, USA. Cortez played piano in church as a boy and progressed from there to Hammond organ, performing on the chittlin' circuit through the Midwest and California in the late 50s. From 1955-57 he performed with vocal group the Pearls and in 1956-57 also worked with the Valentines. In 1956 he made his first recording (under the name of Dave Clooney) for the Ember label. He recorded for RCA Victor in September 1959 and had a hit with Clock Records ('Happy Organ') in the same year. In 1962 he hit again with 'Rinky Dink', a crude 'Louie Louie'-type instrumental that could define 60s teen rock naïvety. He recorded an album for Chess Records in 1963 called, predictably, *Rinky Dink* and then signed with Roulette Records, who issued 'Shindig', 'Tweetie Pie' and 'In Orbit'. In February 1966 *The Fabulous Dave 'Baby' Cortez* appeared on Metro. In 1972 All Platinum released *Soul Vibration* with Frank Prescod (bass) and Bunky Smith (drums). Producer Joe Richardson gave the bass a funk depth comparable to reggae dub experiments. The hilarious dialogue of 'Tongue Kissing', plus liner notes by the organist's mum, make the album a gem. Signed to the T-Neck label - a Buddha subsidiary - he worked with the Isley Brothers to produce *The Isley Brothers Go All The Way*.

● ALBUMS: *Dave 'Baby' Cortez And His Happy Organ* (RCA Victor 1959)★★★★, *Dave 'Baby' Cortez* (Clock 1960)★★★, *Rinky Dink* (Chess 1962)★★★, *Organ Shindig* (Roulette 1965)★★★, *Tweety Pie* (Roulette 1966)★★★, *In Orbit With Dave 'Baby' Cortez* (Roulette 1966)★★★, *The Fabulous Dave 'Baby' Cortez* (Metro 1966)★★★, *Soul Vibration* (All Platinum 1972)★★★.

● COMPILATIONS: *Happy Organs, Wild Guitars And Piano Shuffles* (Ace 1993)★★★★.

COURTNEY, LOU

b. 1944, Buffalo, New York, USA. Courtney had a minor impact on the soul music scene in the 60s with a series of dance hits that could be considered a proto-funk style. He made his first record for Imperial Records in 1962, but much of his work over the next few years was behind the scenes, writing with producer Dennis Lambert; he wrote songs for artists such as Mary Wells and Chubby Checker. In 1966 Courtney signed with Riverside and began recording a series of dance hits that made him a national star, notably 'Skate Now' (number 13 R&B, number 70 pop) from 1967, and 'Do The Thing' (number 17 R&B, number 80 pop). He went to Buddah in 1968 and recorded 'Tryin' To Find My Woman', which did not chart at the time of its release but later became a cult favourite among UK northern soul fans. Courtney spent a period as lead vocalist with the Packers (who recorded 'Go Ahead'). In 1973 he began working with producer Jerry Ragovoy, and had a hit single with 'What Do You Want Me To Do' (number 48 R&B) on Epic. A second single on the label, 'I Don't Need Nobody Else' (number 67 R&B) from 1974, was his last chart record.

● ALBUMS: *Skate Now, Shing-A-Ling* (Riverside 1967)★★, *I'm In Need Of Love* (Epic 1974)★★★, *Buffalo Smoke* (RCA 1976)★★.

Covay, Don

b. March 1938, Orangeburg, South Carolina, USA. Covay resettled in Washington during the early 50s and initially sang in the Cherry Keys, his family's gospel quartet. He crossed over to secular music with the Rainbows, a formative group that also included Marvin Gaye and Billy Stewart. Covay's solo career began in 1957 as part of the Little Richard revue. The most tangible result of this liaison was a single, 'Bip Bop Bip', on which Covay was billed as 'Pretty Boy'. Released on Atlantic, it was produced by Richard and featured the weight of his backing band, the Upsetters. Over the next few years Covay drifted from label to label. His original version of 'Pony Time' (credited to the Goodtimers) lost out to Chubby Checker's cover version, but a further dance-oriented offering, 'Popeye Waddle', was a hit in 1962. Covay, meanwhile, honed his songwriting skills and formed partnerships with several associates including Horace Ott and Ronnie Miller. Such work provided Solomon Burke with 'I'm Hanging Up My Heart For You' while Gladys Knight And The Pips reached the US Top 20 with 'Letter Full Of Tears'. Covay's singing career continued to falter until 1964 when he signed with New York's Rosemart label. Still accompanied by the Goodtimers (Ace Hall, Harry Tiffen and George Clane), his debut single there, the vibrant 'Mercy Mercy', established his effortless, bluesy style. Atlantic subsequently bought his contract but while several R&B hits followed, it was a year before Covay returned to the pop chart. 'See-Saw', co-written with Steve Cropper and recorded at Stax Records, paved the way for other exceptional singles, including 'Sookie Sookie' and 'Iron Out The Rough Spots' (both 1966). Covay's late 60s output proved less fertile, while the ill-founded Soul Clan (with Solomon Burke, Wilson Pickett, Joe Tex and Ben E. King) ended after one single. Covay's songs still remained successful, Aretha Franklin won a Grammy for her performance of his composition 'Chain Of Fools'. Covay switched to Janus in 1971; from there he moved to Mercury Records where he combined recording with A&R duties. *Superdude 1* (1973), a critics' favourite, reunited the singer with Horace Ott. Further releases appeared on the Philadelphia International (1976), U-Von (1977) and Newman (1980) labels, but while Randy Crawford and Bonnie Raitt resurrected his songs, Covay's own career continued to slide downhill. In 1993 the Rhythm & Blues Foundation honoured the singer-songwriter with one of its prestigious Pioneer Awards. Covay, unfortunately, was by then suffering the after-effects of a stroke. A tribute album, *Back To The Streets: Celebrating The Music Of Don Covay*, recorded by many first-rate artists including Chuck Jackson, Ben E. King, Bobby Womack, Robert Cray and Todd Rundgren, was released by Shanachie in 1994. The same year the Razor & Tie label released a fine 23-track retrospective of his best work, compiled and annotated by soulman and producer Billy Vera.

● ALBUMS: *Mercy* (Atlantic 1964)★★★, *See Saw* (Atlantic 1966)★★★★, with the Lemon Jefferson Blues Band *House Of Blue Lights* (Atlantic 1969)★★★, *Different Strokes* (Atlantic 1970)★★, *Superdude 1* (Mercury 1973)★★★, *Hot Blood* (Mercury 1975)★★, *Travellin' In Heavy Traffic* (Philadelphia International 1976)★★.

● COMPILATIONS: *Sweet Thang* (Topline 1987)★★★, *Checkin' In With Don Covay* (1989)★★★, *Mercy Mercy - The Definitive Don Covay* (Razor & Tie 1994)★★★★.

Cox, Deborah

b. *c.*1974, Canada. R&B singer Cox was signed by Arista Records' famed president Clive Davis, previously responsible for discovering names such as Bruce Springsteen, Whitney Houston, Janis Joplin and TLC. Davis's reputation in the industry is such that he was able to unite Cox with some of American R&B's finest producers. Her debut album was recorded with the aid of Vince Herbert (Toni Braxton), Keith Thomas (Vanessa Williams, Amy Grant), Keith Crouch, Darryl Simmons and Dallas Austin. Cox had begun singing in her childhood and turned professional at the age of 12, playing small Toronto clubs before attending a performing arts school. She first met her songwriting partner Lascelles Stephens when she was 18, forging a creative relationship that is still at the core of her work. A demo recorded together served to alert Davis to Cox's presence, and within months she had moved to Los Angeles and signed with Arista. Before the recording of her debut album was complete she had toured Canada with Celine Dion and performed at showcases in Europe and Asia. Her first single, 'Sentimental', was released in October 1995.

● ALBUMS: *Deborah Cox* (Vaz/Arista 1995)★★★.

Crawford, Carolyn

US-born soul singer Carolyn Crawford won a 1963 talent contest staged by radio station WCHB in Detroit, the prize being a contract with the city's biggest label, Motown Records. Her debut single, 'Forget About Me', proved unsuccessful, but she had a minor US hit in 1964 with Smokey Robinson's 'My Smile Is Just A Frown (Turned Upside Down)'. Her third release, 'When Someone's Good To You', flopped in the USA, but became a cult record among British soul fans. Crawford left Motown shortly afterwards, working as a backing vocalist and session singer until joining the Detroit soul group Chapter 8 in 1975. She left that group a year later, to be replaced by Anita Baker, and after a spell with the vocal trio Hodges, James & Smith, she relaunched her solo career in 1979, registering another minor hit with 'Coming On Strong' on Mercury. After several years with Chapter 8 she recorded for Ian Levine's Motor City label, releasing *Heartaches*.

● ALBUMS: *Heartaches* (Motor City 1990)★★.

Crawford, Randy

b. Veronica Crawford, 18 February 1952, Macon, Georgia, USA. Raised in Cincinnati, from the age of 15 Randy Crawford was a regular performer at the city's nightclubs.

She later moved to New York and began singing with several jazz musicians including George Benson and Cannonball Adderley. Crawford was subsequently signed to Warner Brothers Records as a solo act, but achieved fame as the (uncredited) voice on 'Street Life', a major hit single for the Crusaders. Crawford toured extensively with the group, whose pianist, Joe Sample, provided her with 'Now We May Begin', a beautiful ballad that established the singer's independent career. Crawford enjoyed further successes with 'One Day I'll Fly Away' (UK number 2), 'You Might Need Somebody', 'Rainy Night in Georgia' (both UK Top 20 hits) and her 1981 album *Secret Combination*, considered by many to be her finest, reached number 2 in the UK. After a five-year respite, she made a return to the top flight of the chart in 1986 with 'Almaz' which reached the Top 5. Curiously, this soulful, passionate singer has found greater success in the UK than in her homeland and the album *Rich And Poor* was recorded in London.

● ALBUMS: *Miss Randy Crawford* (Warners 1977)★★★, *Raw Silk* (Warners 1979)★★★, *Now We May Begin* (Warners 1980)★★★, *Everything Must Change* (Warners 1980)★★★, *Secret Combination* (Warners 1981)★★★★, *Windsong* (Warners 1982)★★★, *Nightline* (Warners 1983)★★★, *Abstract Emotions* (Warners 1986)★★★, *Rich And Poor* (Warners 1989)★★★, *Naked And True* (Bluemoon 1995)★★★.

● COMPILATIONS: *Miss Randy Crawford - Greatest Hits* (K-Tel 1984)★★★, *Love Songs* (Telstar 1987)★★★, *The Very Best Of* (Dino 1992)★★★, *The Best Of* (Warners 1996)★★★★.

CRESTS

Formed in New York City, USA, in 1956, the Crests soon became one of the most successful of the 'integrated' doo-wop groups of the period, after being discovered by Al Browne. Headed by the lead tenor of Johnny Mastro (b. Johnny Mastrangelo, 7 May 1930, USA), the rest of the band comprised Harold Torres, Talmadge Gough, J.T. Carter and Patricia Van Dross. By 1957 they were recording for Joyce Records and achieved their first minor pop hit with 'Sweetest One'. Moving to the new Coed label, the Crests (without Van Dross) recorded their signature tune and one of doo-wop's enduring classics, '16 Candles', a heartfelt and beautifully orchestrated ballad. It became a national pop hit at number 2 in the *Billboard* charts, paving the way for further R&B and pop successes such as 'Six Nights A Week', 'The Angels Listened In' and 'Step By Step'. At this time the band were almost permanently on the road. Following 'Trouble In Paradise' in 1960, the band's final two chart singles would be credited to The Crests featuring Johnny Mastro. However, this was evidently not enough to satisfy their label, Coed, whose priority now was to launch the singer as a solo artist. Mastro's decision to go solo in 1960 (subsequently calling himself Johnny Maestro) weakened the band, although they did continue with James Ancrum in his stead. Their former vocalist made the charts with 'Model Girl', still for Coed, in the following year, before re-emerging as leader of Brooklyn Bridge, an 11-piece doo-wop group who are best remembered for their 1968 single 'Worst That Could Happen'. After 'Little Miracles' failed to break the *Billboard* Top 100 (the first such failure for the Crests in 10 singles), Gough moved to Detroit and a job with General Motors. He was replaced by Gary Lewis. However, the Crests were now entangled in legal disputes with Coed over the ownership of their name. They eventually moved to Selma, although the songs made available to the group were now of significantly inferior quality, including 'You Blew Out The Candles', a blatant attempt to revisit the success of '16 Candles'. The band continued to tour throughout the 60s, though Torres had left to become a jeweller, leaving a core of Carter, Lewis and Ancrum. Later line-ups were organized by Carter for lounge sessions (although there are no recordings from this period), and in June 1987 the original line-up (minus Van Dross) was re-formed for a show in Peepskill, New York.

● COMPILATIONS: *The Best Of The Crests* (Coed 1960)★★★★, *Crests Sing All Biggies* (Coed 1985)★★★, *16 Fabulous Hits* (Coed 1988)★★★, *Best Of The Crests* (Rhino 1990)★★★★, *Best Of The Rest* (Coed 1991)★★★.

CREW-CUTS

Formed in Toronto, Ontario, Canada, in 1952, the Crew-Cuts were a white vocal quartet that had success in the early 50s by covering black R&B songs. Their version of 'Sh-Boom', originally a number 2 R&B hit for the Chords in 1954, became a number 1 pop hit for the Crew-Cuts, staying in that position for nine weeks and helping to usher in the rock 'n' roll era. The group was comprised of Rudi Maugeri (b. 21 January 1931; baritone), Pat Barrett (b. 15 September 1931; tenor), John Perkins (b. 28 August 1931; lead) and his brother Ray Perkins (b. 28 November 1932; bass), all born in Toronto. The group met at Toronto's Cathedral School, where they all sang in the choir, and decided to form a barber shop-style group. Initially called the Canadaires, the group received its first break in Cleveland, Ohio, USA, where they appeared on Gene Carroll's television programme. After that show they were introduced to the influential local disc jockey Bill Randle, who suggested the name change (after a popular short-cropped hairstyle). Randle introduced the group to Mercury Records, who signed them. Their first recording, an original composition called 'Crazy 'Bout Ya Baby', made the Top 10 in the US charts. Mercury suggested covering 'Sh-Boom' and its massive success led to further cover versions of R&B records by the group, including the Penguins' 'Earth Angel', Nappy Brown's 'Don't Be Angry' and the Nutmegs' 'A Story Untold'. The success of the Crew-Cuts and other white cover artists helped pave the way for recognition and acceptance of the black originators. In addition to 'Sh-Boom', other Top 10 placings were 'Earth Angel' (1955), 'Ko Ko Mo (I Love You So)' (1955) and 'Gum Drop' (1955). The Crew-Cuts placed 14 singles in the charts throughout 1957, moving to RCA Records in 1958; they disbanded in 1963.

● ALBUMS: *The Crew-Cuts On The Campus* (Mercury 1954)★★★, *The Crew-Cuts Go Longhair* (Mercury 1956)★★★, *Crew-Cut Capers* (Mercury 1957)★★★, *Music Ala Carte* (Mercury 1957)★★★, *Rock And Roll Bash* (Mercury 1957)★★★, *Surprise Package* (RCA Victor

1958)★★★, *The Crew-Cuts Sing!* (RCA Victor 1959)★★★, *You Must Have Been A Beautiful Baby* (RCA Victor 1960)★★★, *The Crew Cuts Sing Out!* (RCA Victor 1960)★★★, *The Crew Cuts Have A Ball And Bowling Tips* (RCA Victor 1960)★★★, *The Crew Cuts* (RCA Victor 1962)★★★, *High School Favorites* (RCA Victor 1962)★★★, *Sing The Masters* (RCA Victor 1962)★★★, *The Crew-Cuts Sing Folk* (RCA Victor 1963)★★.

Crickets

An R&B vocal group from the Bronx section of New York City, New York, USA, the members were Grover 'Dean' Barlow (lead), Harold Johnson (tenor, guitar), Eugene Stapleton (tenor), Leon Carter (baritone) and Rodney Jackson (bass). The Crickets' only hit was with 'You're Mine' (number 10 R&B) on the MGM label in 1953. Their lack of success probably stemmed from their pop sound, a sound that was typical for black groups during the 40s when the Ink Spots, Deep River Boys, and Charioteers held sway. However, during 1953-55, when the Crickets were recording, the more bluesy Clovers, Dominoes, and Five Royales were storming up the charts, so to both listeners and radio programmers the Crickets, with their pretty singing and tasteful but thin arrangements, may have sounded dated. Veteran record man Joe Davis produced their sessions both for the MGM label and for his own Davis label. It is fortunate for posterity that Davis was there, because what may not have been commercial in 1953 sounded fabulous decades later to record collectors, making Crickets records prized collector items. The ballads, such as 'Be Faithful', 'You're Mine' and the jump 'My Little Baby's Shoes', were the most desired and the most rewarding.

● COMPILATIONS: *Dreams & Wishes* (Relic 1992)★★★.

Crook, General

b. 28 February 1945, Mound Bayou, Mississippi, USA. Crook was raised in nearby Greenville, and moved to Chicago in 1963. He was one of many soul artists of the late 60s and early 70s who, in the footsteps of James Brown, began forging the new funk style of soul music. He first recorded for Capitol Records in 1969, but first hit the R&B charts on the tiny Down To Earth label, notably with 'Gimme Some' (number 22 R&B), from 1970, and 'What Time It Is' (number 31 R&B), from 1971. He made an album and two singles, 'Tell Me What'Cha Gonna Do' (1974) and 'There's A Fever In The Funkhouse' (1974), for Wand Records. Since then he has mainly confined his career to producing, including hits for Syl Johnson and Willie Clayton.

● ALBUMS: *General Crook* (Wand 1974)★★★.

Cropper, Steve

b. 21 October 1942, Willow Spring, Missouri, USA. This economical but effective guitarist was a founder-member of the Mar-Keys, a high school band whose instrumental single, 'Last Night', provided a cornerstone for the emerging Stax label in 1961. Cropper worked with several groups constructed around the company's house musicians, the most successful of which was Booker T. And The MGs. The latter group not only had several hits under its own identity, but over the next few years was the muscle behind almost every performance released via the Stax studio. However, Cropper's prowess was not only confined to playing. His songwriting and arranging skills were prevalent on many of these performances, including 'Knock On Wood' (Eddie Floyd), 'Sookie Sookie' (Don Covay), 'In The Midnight Hour' (Wilson Pickett) and 'Mr. Pitiful' and '(Sittin' On) The Dock Of The Bay' (Otis Redding). The MGs continued to record until the end of the decade, but they broke up when organist Booker T. Jones moved to California. Cropper preferred to maintain a low-key profile and although he recorded a pleasant solo album, *With A Little Help From My Friends*, he chose to concentrate on running his Memphis-based studio, TMI, rather than embrace the public acclaim he richly deserved. TMI subsequently folded and Cropper resettled in Los Angeles, returning to session work and production. He featured prominently on the Rod Stewart 1975 UK number 1, *Atlantic Crossing*. The surviving MGs were reunited following the death of drummer Al Jackson, and the group has since pursued this erratic existence.

The guitarist was also a member of the Blues Brothers, a band formed by comedians John Belushi and Dan Aykroyd that led to the successful film of the same name. The group recorded three albums, following which Cropper released his second solo collection, *Playing My Thang*. Cropper has continued a low-key approach to his art during the 80s although he made several live appearances in the UK in the early 90s, particularly in the wake of a revived interest in the Blues Brothers. His distinctive sparse, clipped, high treble sound with his Fender Telecaster has been heard on literally hundreds of singles and albums. His reluctance to hog the limelight cannot disguise the fact that he is one of the major figures in soul music, remarkable in that he is an 'all-American white boy'.

● ALBUMS: with Albert King, 'Pops' Staples *Jammed Together* (Stax 1969)★★★, *With A Little Help From My Friends* (Stax 1971)★★, *Playing My Thang* (1980)★★.

● FILMS: *The Blues Brothers* (1980).

Crouch, Andrae

b. Andrae Edward Crouch, 1 July 1942, Los Angeles, California, USA. Crouch's 70s legacy is one of the richest in the gospel genre, yet he has never appealed to the music's purists. The conservative elements in gospel music have seen his incorporation of rock 'n' roll showmanship and riffs as inappropriate at best, and blasphemy at worst. A gifted singer, songwriter and keyboardist, Crouch undertook a traditional apprenticeship by playing piano and singing in church. Later he formed COGICS (Church Of God In Christ Singers) in the early 60s with twin sister Sandra, Blinky Williams, Gloria Jones, Frankie Spring, Edna Wright and Billy Preston. Together they recorded one album for Vee Jay Records and won numerous awards and competitions throughout California. While members of that group moved on to successful solo careers, Crouch concentrated on launching the Disciples in 1965. Although only one album emerged, the group toured widely and was the first to play gospel rock, the music with which Crouch's name would become synonymous. When Sandra returned from back-up singing duties with Diana Ross in 1970 she reunited with her brother (they are cousins to poet, actor and drummer Stanley Crouch). They made a series of recordings together throughout the 70s that were highlighted by guest slots from the Crusaders and Stevie Wonder. Crouch was awarded several Grammy awards for his songs, some of which were recorded by Elvis Presley, the Imperials and Pat Boone. He also published an autobiography.

● ALBUMS: *Andrae Crouch & The Disciples - Live In London* (Light 1978)★★★.

● COMPILATIONS: *Volume 1 - The Classics* (Royal 1991)★★★, *Volume 2 - We Sing The Praises* (Royal 1992)★★★, *Volume 3 - Contemporary Man* (Royal 1991)★★★, *Mercy* (Quest 1994)★★★.

● FURTHER READING: *Through It All*, Andrae Crouch.

Crown Heights Affair

An eight-piece band formed in New York in the early 70s, comprising Philip Thomas (lead vocals), Bert Reid (saxophone), Raymond Reid (guitar), William Anderson (guitar, vocals), James 'Ajax' Baynard (trumpet), Raymond Rock (vocals, drums, percussion), Howie Young (keyboards) and Muki Wilson (bass, vocals). They were initially signed by RCA, for whom they recorded one album and enjoyed a regional hit single with 'Super Rod', before switching to De-Lite Records. Under the guidance of producers, writers and arrangers Freda Nerangis and Britt Britton, Crown Heights Affair leapt to the forefront of commercial funk, recording four hit singles from their first two albums - 'Dreaming A Dream', 'Every Beat Of My Heart', 'Foxy Lady' and 'Dancin''. De-Lite's subsequent worldwide pact with Polygram saw the group break internationally, with 'Galaxy Of Love' hitting the UK Top 30. Further chart success and the emerging songwriting abilities within the group consolidated their position; 'I'm Gonna Love You Forever' (UK Top 50 in 1978), 'Dance Lady Dance' (UK Top 50 in 1979) and the double-sided smash, 'You Gave Me Love'/'Use Your Body And Soul' (a Top 10 success in 1980). While this represented the peak of their chart success, Crown Heights Affair continued to churn out competent singles and albums for much of the next decade, although the Reid brothers and William Anderson left the group in 1986 to pursue outside production interests.

● ALBUMS: *Crown Heights Affair* (RCA 1974)★★★, *Dreaming A Dream* (De-Lite 1975)★★★, *Do It Your Way* (De-Lite 1976)★★, *Dancin'* (De-Lite 1977)★★, *Dream World* (De-Lite 1978)★★, *Dance Lady Dance* (De-Lite 1979)★★, *Sure Shot* (De-Lite 1980)★★, *Think Positive* (De-Lite 1982)★★.

● COMPILATIONS: *Essential Dance Floor Artists Volume 1: Crown Heights Affair* (Deep Beats 1994)★★★.

Crows

This R&B vocal group from Harlem, New York City, New York, USA, comprised members Daniel 'Sonny' Norton (lead), Bill Davis (baritone-tenor), Harold Major (tenor), Gerald Hamilton (bass) and Mark Jackson (tenor, guitar). The Crows have gained a place in history as makers of one of the first rock 'n' roll hits, 'Gee', by virtue of the fact that as an R&B record it crossed over onto the pop charts. Because of its early date, early 1954, many historians of popular music consider it to be the first rock 'n' roll record. The group formed in 1952 as the Four Notes, and recorded for Jubilee without success. In 1953 they signed with George Goldner to record for his Rama label. Their debut, 'Seven Lonely Days', did nothing. The second release, destined to make history, paired 'Gee' with a ballad, 'I Love You So', and that too failed, initially (Goldner's faith in 'I Love You So' was justified in 1958 when the Chantels made it a big hit). The group's third release featured a good, deep, street-corner sound, pairing two remakes, 'Heartbreaker' (a ballad originally recorded by the Heartbreakers) and 'Call A Doctor' (a jump originally done by the Cap-Tans as 'Chief, Turn The Hose On Me'). In early 1954, 'Gee' (number 2 R&B, number 14 pop) started climbing the charts and the Crows had their first, and last, hit. After subsequent records failed, such as the marvellous 'Untrue' (1954), the Crows broke up.

● COMPILATIONS: *Echoes Of A Rock Era* 12 tracks by the Crows, 12 by the Harptones (Roulette 1972)★★★, *Gee It's The Crows* (Murray Hill 1988)★★★, *Echoes Of A Rock Era* (Collectables 1991)★★★.

Crystals

This highly influential 60s US female vocal group were the product of Phil Spector, for his pioneering Philles record label. They, along with the Ronettes, were one of the definitive 'wall of sound' groups of the 60s. They came together after meeting in the legendary Brill Building where the group were preparing demos for the Aberbach's famous publishing company Hill and Range. The line-up comprised Dee Dee Kennibrew (b. Dolores Henry, 1945, Brooklyn, New York, USA), La La Brooks (b. 1946, Brooklyn, New York, USA), Pat Wright (b. 1945, Brooklyn, New York, USA), Mary Thomas (b. 1946, Brooklyn, New York, USA) and Barbara Alston, who was their manager's niece. Spector was impressed and produced the debut 'There's No Other (Like My Baby)' in 1961. At this time Spector was developing his unique sound by mixing numerous layers of vocals and instruments onto one mono track. The blurred result was demonstrated on 'Uptown' but it was taken to its glorious extreme on Gene Pitney's song 'He's A Rebel'. The latter featured the lead vocals of Darlene Wright (Love), and, as Spector owned the name, he could use whoever he wanted as the Crystals. It became a number 1 single in the USA (UK number 19). La la Brooks returned to the lead vocal on two further hits that have since become timeless classics, 'Da Doo Ron Ron (When He Walked Me Home)' and 'Then He Kissed Me', both major hits in 1963. The Beach Boys attempted a Spector-like production with their own version, 'Then I Kissed Her', in 1967. The Crystals were soon overtaken when their mentor devoted more time to the Ronettes, and consequently their career faltered. New members passed through, including Frances Collins, and the band were prematurely banished to the nostalgia circuit.

● ALBUMS: *Twist Uptown* (Philles 1962)★★, *He's A Rebel* (Philles 1963)★★★.
● COMPILATIONS: *The Crystals Sing Their Greatest Hits* (Philles 1963)★★★, *Uptown* (Spectrum 1988)★★★, *The Best Of* (ABKCO 1992)★★★.

Cues

The Cues' marvellous harmonizing underpinned many of the great records of the 50s. The group was in effect an in-house vocal harmony group created by Atlantic Records' arranger Jesse Stone to accompany a variety of his artists in the studio. They were built around vocalist and songwriter Ollie Jones (ex-Blenders), with Robie Kirk (baritone), Abel DeCosta (tenor; also ex-Blenders), Jimmy Breedlove (second tenor) and Eddie Barnes (bass). As well as backing other artists the Cues were to have a second function: demoing potential songs for name acts to choose from. Soon their work in this vein also came from outside the label, with various writers and publishers learning of the Cues' abilities to animate new material. Their first backing engagement came on Ruth Brown's 'Oh What A Dream' in July 1954, a number 1 *Billboard* R&B success, which stayed at the top for eight weeks. Their first own-name recording (they were given a variety of names on record labels, including the title Rhythm Makers in the case of Ruth Brown) came when Stone moved to Aladdin Records. October 1954 saw 'Scoochie Scoochie' released on Aladdin's Lamp subsidiary to little fanfare. In the wake of its lack of success the Cues returned to their former employment, backing artists including Ivory Joe Hunter, Joe Turner, Carmen Taylor, LaVern Baker, Ray Charles, Nat King Cole and Bobby Darin. They became so busy, in fact, that a 'second team' of Cues was started by Stone, which included members of the Ravens, Four Buddies and Shirelles. Eventually the Cues were offered a contract in their own right by Capitol Records. Their debut release was 'Burn That Candle', which charted but lost sales due to a competing version from Bill Haley. Neither 'Charlie Brown' nor 'Destination 2100 And 65' did particularly well. Their final brace of releases for Capitol, 'The Girl I Love' (later recorded by the Cadillacs) and 'Why', flopped. They switched to subsidiary label Prep for May 1957's 'I Pretend', but continued to find more success as backing singers. After a final single, 'Old Man River', in 1960, the group dispersed to concentrate on separate projects. Ollie Jones joined the Billy Williams Quartet and Breedlove joined the Ink Spots.

Culley, Frank 'Floorshow'

b. 7 August 1918, Salisbury, Maryland, USA, and raised in Norfolk, Virginia. Culley was a pioneer of the R&B tenor saxophone in the post-World War II period, who demonstrated how the instrument could be an exciting component in the emerging R&B sound. Culley began learning the tenor saxophone at the age of 10 and made his first professional mark playing with Johnson's Happy Pals around Richmond, Virginia. He formed his own R&B group in the mid-40s, recording for Lenox and Continental and backing Wynonie Harris on King. In 1948, he was signed by the fledgling Atlantic label and led its first house band, backing the early stars of R&B as well as recording around 30 tracks under his own name - including the hit 'Coleslaw' - mainly with his band's superb pianist, Van Walls. Other fine Atlantic recordings include a wild version of the Lionel Hampton number 'Central Avenue Breakdown' and 'Floorshow', a minor hit for Culley. After leaving Atlantic in 1950, he recorded for RCA Victor, Parrot, Chess and Baton without success. Known for being a histrionic showman (hence the nickname 'Floorshow') as well as a good musician, he retired from music in 1975 and today lives in Newark, New Jersey.

● ALBUMS: *Rock 'N' Roll* five tracks by Frank 'Floorshow' Culley and five by Buddy Tate (Baton 1955)★★★.
● COMPILATIONS: *Rock 'N' Roll* five tracks by Frank 'Floorshow' Culley and seven by Buddy Tate (Krazy Kat 1985)★★★.

Curry, Clifford

b. Knoxville, Tennessee, USA. This singer's long career began in high school as a member of the Echoes, after which he joined the Five Pennies, for whom he wrote a 1956 release, 'Mr. Moon'. Curry was later a member of several groups, including the Hollyhocks (1957) and the Bubba Suggs Band (1957-1964). As Sweet Clifford he recorded for the Nashville-based Excello label, before beginning work with the Fabulous Six and the Contenders. He resumed his solo status in 1967 with the pulsating 'She Shot A Hole In My Soul'. An R&B hit that year, the song is better known in Britain for Geno Washington's tame cover version. Curry was unable to repeat this success, although he continues to record and perform on the thriving vintage soul-based 'beach' music scene.

● ALBUMS: *The Provider* (Appaloosa 1993)★★★, *Clifford's Blues* (Appaloosa 1995)★★.
● COMPILATIONS: *Clifford Curry's Greatest Hits* (1981)★★★, *She Shot A Hole In My Soul* (Collectables 1995)★★★.

Curtom Records

A label owned by Curtis Mayfield in Chicago from 1968-80. Curtom, which stands for Curtis and Tom (the 'Tom' being Eddie Thomas), was the most successful label owned by Mayfield and one of the most successful independent labels operating in Chicago during the late 60s and 70s. Like most such independents Curtom developed distribution and manufacturing alliances with larger labels, first with Buddah, then with Warner Brothers, and finally with RSO. The label's core of talent was at first the Curtis Mayfield-led Impressions, but in 1970 that core became Curtis Mayfield after he split from the group. Other recording acts that had early success on the label were the Five Stairsteps, Leroy Hutson, and Natural Four. The label declined rapidly in the late 70s as Curtom seemed unable to adapt to the rise of disco and funk. Their most notable disco act was Linda Clifford, who sustained the label until its demise in 1980. Mayfield moved to Atlanta and took the Curtom studio with him.

D'Angelo

b. Michael Archer, *c.*1974, Richmond Virginia, USA. R&B singer-songwriter and multi-instrumentalist D'Angelo was signed by EMI Records at the age of 18, whereupon he relocated to New York to develop his musical career. He quickly repaid EMI's investment, co-writing and co-producing the major US hit single 'U Will Know', sung by an all-star cast (including Jodeci, R. Kelly and Tevin Campbell), and credited to Black Men United. Influenced by Marvin Gaye and Curtis Mayfield, with a vernacular lifted from modern urban R&B, D'Angelo won the Harlem Apollo talent contest three times in succession before embarking on sessions for his debut album. This utilized antiquated equipment including a Wurlitzer and old effects boxes as well as modern technology in the form of drum machines and computers. Alongside Ben Harper, it saw D'Angelo celebrated as representing a return to the singer-songwriter tradition in black music following the dominance of hip-hop. Ironically, it emerged on dance/rap label Cooltempo Records in the UK. His concert appearances in support of the record, with strictly live instrumentation, also drew strong reviews and further mainstream press.

● ALBUMS: *Brown Sugar* (EMI 1995)★★★.

D'Arby, Terence Trent

b. 15 March 1962, New York, USA. A soulful pop singer, D'Arby first became involved with the music business while posted as a soldier in Germany where he joined a local funk band, Touch, in 1983 (*Early Works*, a collection of his contributions to Touch, was released in 1989). Following his move to London he recorded a demo tape which was impressive enough for CBS Records to sign him. His first single, 'If You Let Me Stay', reached the UK Top 10 and *Introducing The Hardline According To Terence Trent D'Arby* was one of the most successful debut albums of recent years. In addition to reaching number 1, it spent over a year in the top half of the UK charts as well as selling several million copies worldwide. D'Arby's self-publicity was less well received, and his clumsy criticism of his homeland and his posing naked on a cross both backfired. This was followed by the commercial and artistic failure of 1989's *Neither Fish Nor Flesh* which spent barely a month in the UK charts (a commercial decline repeated in the USA). Although *Symphony Or Damn* was well received, its more rock-orientated styles were still suspiciously viewed. *Vibrator* finally arrived after a two-year wait, and continued the transition from smooth soul to a harder-edged sound. It was preceded by the Sam Cooke-influenced single 'Holding On To You', and 'Supermodel Sandwich', which achieved strong airplay because of its inclusion on the soundtrack of the much-publicized Robert Altman film *Pret-A-Porter*. The album featured a new recording line-up of Luke Goss (drums, ex Bros), Branford Marsalis (saxophone), Patrice Rushen (piano) and Charlie Sepulveda (trumpet).

● ALBUMS: *Introducing The Hardline According To Terence Trent D'Arby* (Columbia 1987)★★★★, *Neither Fish Nor Flesh* (Columbia 1989)★★, *Symphony Or Damn* (Columbia 1993)★★★, *Vibrator* (Columbia 1995)★★★.

● VIDEOS: *Introducing The Hardline: Live* (CBS-Fox 1988).

● FURTHER READING: *Neither Fish Nor Flesh: Inspiration For An Album*, Paolo Hewitt.

D-Influence

A jazz funk quartet from London, England, D-Influence made an immediate impact with their debut white label release in 1990. 'I'm The One'/'The Classic' combined a hip-hop beat, programmed by the band's guitarist, Ned B (aka Ed Baden Powell), with the distinctive vocals of the then 18-year-old jazz singer Sarah Ann Webb. Steve Marston (multi-instrumentalist) and Kwame Kwaten (keyboards) are the other long-standing members. Previously the band had worked with artists such as Neneh Cherry, and came together through a mutual interest in club music and nightlife. By the advent of their debut album they had signed to East West Records, but the record saw them suffer numerous comparisons to Soul II Soul and De La Soul. However, its sales of only 30,000 attested more to a lack of adequate promotion and radio play than talent, and it did earn the group the admiration of artists such as Prince, Michael Jackson and Mick Jagger, each of whom they would support later in their career. They also collaborated with Björk (on her *Later With Jools Holland* television appearance) and Seal (his second album). Their own second album in 1995, *Prayer 4 Unity*, included contributions from dub poet Linton Kwesi Johnson and Kenny Wellington, formerly horn player with Light Of The World.

● ALBUMS: *Good 4 We* (East West 1992)★★★, *Prayer 4 Unity* (East West 1995)★★★.

D-Train

This US soul group was formed in a Brooklyn, New York high school in the early 80s by Hubert Eaves III (keyboards) and James Williams (lead vocals). Having signed to the Epic/Prelude label, the group found greater success in the UK than in America. They enjoyed three UK Top 30 hits with 'You're The One For Me' (1982), 'Music, Part 1' (1983) and 'You're The One For Me (Remix)' (1985). D-Train's biggest US hit was the *Billboard* R&B Top 5 single 'Something's On Your Mind' (1983). However, the anticipated breakthrough in the USA never materialized and the group split in 1985 with Williams pursuing a solo career. Again, restricted to R&B chart success, Williams' three notable hits were 'Misunderstanding' (number 10, 1986), 'Oh, How I Love You (Girl)' (number 22, 1987) and 'In Your Eyes' (number 11, 1988).

● ALBUMS: *D-Train* (Prelude 1982)★★★, *Music* (Prelude 1983)★★★, *Something's On Your Mind* (Prelude

1984)★★, *You're The One For Me* (Prelude 1985)★★. Solo: James Williams *Miracles Of The Heart* (Columbia 1986)★★★, *In Your Eyes* (Columbia 1988)★★.

DAMAGE

Led by the striking figure of singer Andrez, Damage are one of several British R&B groups attempting to capitalize on Mark Morrison's international breakthrough. As their singer told the press in 1997: 'We're proud of being British. We've never pretended to be American. You know how it is in England, the DJs never support black British music. But they just can't hold it back any more because there's a massive market for it.' The quintet was formed at school at the beginning of the 90s, when the members were all teenagers. They sent a demo tape of a version of a Jackson Five song to Jazz Summers of Big Life Records in early 1995. Although Summers was impressed by the quality of their singing and harmonies, he waited 18 months before issuing their first record. 'Anything', composed by US songwriter Terri Robinson and featuring Little Caesar (of Junior MAFIA), was released in July 1996. Although it only charted at a lowly number 62, the record received excellent reviews (including Single Of The Week in *Blues & Soul* magazine). Encouraged by the response, Big Life set about establishing the group's name with a series of showcases and public appearances. Thereafter, they made quick inroads into the charts. Their second single, 'Love II Love', reached number 12, while the follow-up, 'Forever', was a number 6 hit during the lucrative Christmas period. Damage also supported teen sensations Boyzone at their Wembley Stadium performance. The group's excellent self-titled debut album followed, along with two further singles - 'Love Guaranteed' and a cover version of Eric Clapton's 'Wonderful Tonight'.

● ALBUMS: *Damage* (Big Life 1997)★★★★, *Forever* (Big Life 1997)★★★.

DANDERLIERS

This R&B vocal group was formed in 1955 in Chicago, Illinois, USA. The Danderliers were not a big-selling group, having only one national hit to their credit, 'Chop Chop Boom' (number 10 R&B 1955), but they had a pioneering influence in their home-town of Chicago. Eugene Record of the Chi-Lites was inspired to form a vocal group after hearing Danderliers songs. The members were Dallas Taylor (tenor and jump lead), James Campbell (tenor and ballad lead), first tenor Bernard Dixon, baritone Walter Stephenson, and bass Richard Thomas (replaced by Louis Johnson in 1956). 'Chop Chop Boom' was also a hit by a Canadian cover group, the Crew-Cuts, the same year. The song was a great jump number and unfairly obscured the Danderliers' tremendous reputation as masters of romantic ballads, notably 'My Autumn Love' (the flip-side to 'Chop Chop Boom'), 'May God Be With You' (1956) and 'My Love' (1956). The group broke up in 1957.

DANLEERS

This R&B vocal group from Brooklyn, New York, USA, consisted of Jimmy Weston (lead), Johnny Lee (first tenor), Willie Ephraim (second tenor), Nathaniel McCune (baritone) and Roosevelt Mays (bass). In 1957, the Danleers signed with composer/manager Danny Webb, who took the group and one of his songs, 'One Summer Night', to Amp-3 Records. 'One Summer Night' captured perfectly the teen angst of the rock 'n' roll era, and went to number 4 R&B and number 7 pop in 1957. Despite some equally evocative follow-ups on Mercury, the Danleers failed to have another hit, breaking up in 1959. Jimmy Weston continued his singing career in the Webtones, another recorded group managed by Danny Webb. The Webtones lasted until 1964.

● COMPILATIONS: *The Vocal Group Collection* (Mercury 1986)★★★, *One Summer Night* (Bear Family 1991)★★★.

DAVIS, 'BILLY' ROQUEL

b. 11 July 1937, Detroit, Michigan, USA. Davis as composer, producer and A&R man was one of the most significant behind-the-scenes talents of the soul era. His first musical association was as a member of a doo-wop group, the Five Jets, who recorded several records during 1953/4 that were barely heard outside of the Detroit area. Later, with Berry Gordy he wrote hit songs for Jackie Wilson under the name Tyran Carlo, notably 'Lonely Teardrops', 'To Be Loved', and 'That's Why (I Love You So)'. In 1956, he started an association with Chess Records, having his group the Four Aims (early Four Tops) record for the label, and providing two hit songs for the company, 'See Saw' (not the Don Covay hit) for the Moonglows and 'A Kiss From Your Lips' for the Flamingos. In 1958 with Berry Gordy's sister, Anna, he founded Anna Records, which had an early Detroit success, 'Money' by Barrett Strong. In 1961 Leonard Chess set up a label in Detroit for Davis to run, called Checkmate. Although it failed, the following year Chess brought Davis to Chicago to work as the chief A&R man for Chess Records. At this label Davis wrote and produced hit songs for artists such as Little Milton, the Dells, Fontella Bass, and Billy Stewart. Davis was the most instrumental person in forging the success of the label in the 60s, and after he left in 1968 the company went into decline. Davis joined the McCann Erickson Advertising Agency, where he established a successful career writing and producing jingles with an African-American slant.

DAVIS, CARL

b. Carl Adams, 4 April 1934, Chicago, Illinois, USA. Davis was the prime mover in the flourishing of Chicago as a soul centre during the 60s and early 70s. In 1961, while moonlighting from his Columbia Records promotion job, Davis, in partnership with Bill 'Bunky' Sheppard, established the Nat/Pam/Wes label complex. Shortly afterwards, he established himself as a producer to be reckoned with when he produced Gene Chandler's million-selling 'Duke Of Earl'. Columbia, seeing his talents were misplaced, in 1962 hired him as a producer, first for some acts on its own imprint and later on their moribund OKeh label. Within a year Davis had OKeh thriving again, producing hits with the help of Curtis Mayfield compositions and Johnny Pate arrangements. Notable artists that he made into national hitmakers were Major Lance, Billy

Butler And The Chanters, Walter Jackson, and the Artistics. Meanwhile, independently from OKeh he produced several hits for Gene Chandler on Constellation as well as Mary Wells' classic 'Dear Lover'. In 1965 he moved to the faltering Brunswick label and revived it with hits for Chandler, Jackie Wilson, Barbara Acklin, Tyrone Davis, and the Chi-lites. Davis established his own Chi-Sound label in 1976, but it was less successful as Davis struggled to keep up with the rapidly changing soul market, where vocal groups and stand-up southern-style soul singers were losing market share to self-contained funk bands. Davis still managed to place a few hits on the charts by old reliables such as Chandler, the Dells and Walter Jackson. Since the closing of Chi-Sound in 1984, Davis attempted several times to resurrect the company without success.

DAVIS, MARTHA

b. 14 December 1917, Wichita, Kansas, USA, and raised in Chicago. Davis was a notable R&B/jazz pianist and vocalist in the post-war years, with a touch of comedy in her act. She generally recorded as part of a trio, usually with her husband, bass player Calvin Ponder. She first recorded for the tiny Urban label in 1946. Later, recording for the equally small Jewel label, Davis reached the charts with 'Little White Lies' (number 11 R&B) in 1948. The recording giant Decca took notice, signed her, and on that label recorded two more hits in 1948, 'Don't Burn The Candle At Both Ends' (number 6 R&B) and 'Daddy-O' (number 9 R&B). One of her finest releases for Decca was 'Kitchen Blues' in 1947. Following a recording gap of four years Davis then recorded on the Coral label, but produced no more hits. Meanwhile, Davis and her husband created a touring stage act billed as Martha Davis And Spouse, which, with its combination of comedy and music, proved highly successful. During the 50s the duo made highly successful television appearances.

● COMPILATIONS: *You're On The Right Track Baby* (Jukebox Lil 1988)★★★.

DAVIS, TYRONE

b. 4 May 1938, Greenville, Mississippi, USA. One of the great unknowns of soul music, Davis has been a consistent chartmaker for over 20 years. This former Freddie King valet was discovered working in Chicago nightclubs by pianist Harold Burrage. 'Can I Change My Mind' (1968), Davis's first chart entry, was originally recorded as a b-side, but its success determined his musical direction. A singer in the mould of Bobby Bland and Z.Z. Hill, Davis was at his most comfortable with mid-paced material, ideal for the classic 'Windy City' orchestrations enhancing the mature delivery exemplified on 'Is It Something You've Got' and 'Turn Back The Hands Of Time', a US number 3. During the early 70s his producers began to tinker with this formula. 'I Had It All The Time' (1972) offered a tongue-in-cheek spoken introduction, while the beautifully crafted 'Without You In My Life' (1973), 'There It Is' (1973) and 'The Turning Point' (1975) emphasized rhythmic punch without detracting from Davis's feather-light vocals. The artist's work continued to enjoy success; 'In The Mood' (1979) and 'Are You Serious' (1982) were both substantial R&B hits and he has since remained an active performer. As the singer's extensive catalogue suggests, he is also greatly underrated.

● ALBUMS: *Can I Change My Mind* (Dakar 1969)★★★, *Turn Back The Hands Of Time* (Dakar 1970)★★★, *I Had It All The Time* (Dakar 1972)★★★, *Without You In My Life* (Dakar 1973)★★★, *It's All In The Game* (Dakar 1974)★★★, *Home Wrecker* (Dakar 1975)★★★, *Turning Point* (1976)★★★, *Love And Touch* (Columbia 1976)★★, *Let's Be Closer Together* (Columbia 1977)★★, *I Can't Go On This Way* (Columbia 1978)★★, *In The Mood With Tyrone Davis* (Columbia 1979)★★, *Can't You Tell It's Me* (Columbia 1979)★★, *I Just Can't Keep On Going* (1980)★★, *Tyrone Davis* (Highrise 1983)★★★, *Something Good* (1983)★★★, *Sexy Thing* (Future 1985)★★★, *Man Of Stone* (Future 1987)★★★, *Pacifier* (Future 1987)★★, *Flashin' Back* (Future 1988)★★, *Come On Over* (1990)★★, *I'll Always Love You* (Ichiban 1991)★★★, *Something's Mighty Wrong* (1992)★★★, *You Stay On My Mind* (Ichiban 1994)★★★, *Simply Tyrone Davis* (Malaco 1996)★★★.

● COMPILATIONS: *Greatest Hits* (Dakar 1972)★★★, *The Tyrone Davis Story* (Kent 1985)★★★, *In The Mood Again* (Charly 1989)★★★, *The Best Of Tyrone Davis* (Rhino 1992)★★★★.

DAWN, BILLY, QUARTETTE

One of many groups who started their careers harmonizing in the Crown Heights district of Brooklyn, New York, USA, this ill-fated doo-wop/R&B concern was initiated by Billy Dawn Smith (lead), his brother Tommy Smith (baritone), plus Donnie Myles (tenor) and Sonny Benton (bass). Future producer Al Browne also added piano and occasional baritone. 'This Is The Real Thing Now' was their debut release for the small Decatur Records label in 1952. It failed to sell, and as a result the quartet moved to Duke Records. Their single for the label, 'Why Can't I Have You', was released in the summer of 1952, but saw the band credited as the Mighty Dukes instead of the Billy Dawn Quartette. They then became the Four Dukes for their next single, a sprightly version of 'Crying In The Chapel' released in September 1953. Despite competition from a version by the Orioles, it achieved significant local sales. It was much to the group's surprise then, that Duke Records did not renew their option. A fourth single and a fourth name eventually arrived when they found a sympathetic ear at Herald Records. 'Eternal Love' was credited to the Heralds, and released in September 1954. Meanwhile, Billy Dawn Smith had secured himself an A&R position at this, the group's third label, through which he was able to find work backing several Ember and Herald Records artists in the studio. Eventually he saw his future as more in writing than in performance, and the Heralds broke up in 1956 without recording again (though in the interim they had enjoyed a regular slot on the *Spotlight On Harlem* television show). Billy Dawn found success with compositions for the Crests, Five Satins and Passions, as well as being a co-founder of Hull Records. Myles went on to work with the Victorians.

Day, Bobby

b. Robert Byrd, 1 July 1932, Fort Worth, Texas, USA, d. 27 July 1990. He moved to Los Angeles in 1947 and shortly afterwards formed the Flames, who recorded under a variety of names on numerous labels throughout the 50s. Oddly, it took until 1957 before they achieved their first and biggest hit as the Hollywood Flames with Day's song 'Buzz, Buzz, Buzz'. Simultaneously, the group were climbing the US charts as Bobby Day And The Satellites with another of his songs, 'Little Bitty Pretty One' on Class Records, although a cover version by Thurston Harris became a bigger hit. Day, who first recorded solo in 1955, took lone billing again in 1958 for the double-sided US number 2 hit 'Rockin' Robin' and 'Over And Over'. Despite releasing a string of further outstanding R&B/rock singles in the 50s, this distinctive singer-songwriter never returned to the Top 40. In the early 60s he formed Bob And Earl with ex-Hollywood Flame Earl Nelson, although he was replaced before the duo's hit 'Harlem Shuffle'. He later recorded without success under various names on Rendezvous, RCA and Sureshot and his own Bird Land label. He temporarily relocated to Australia before settling in Florida. Although his records were no longer selling, his songs were often revived, with Dave Clark taking 'Over And Over' to the top in 1965, Michael Jackson taking 'Rockin' Robin' to number 2 in 1972 and the Jackson Five reaching the Top 20 with the catchy 'Little Bitty Pretty One' in 1972. Day's long-awaited UK debut in 1989 was warmly received, although sadly he died of cancer in July 1990.

● ALBUMS: *Rockin' With Robin* (Class 1958)★★★.

Day, Margie

b. Margaret Hoeffler, 1926, Norfolk, Virginia, USA. Day had a giant impact in the R&B market for two years, 1950-51, when she hit with 'Street-Walkin' Daddy' (number 7 R&B) and 'Little Red Rooster' (number 5 R&B) as lead singer of the Griffin Brothers Orchestra. In 1952 she left the Griffin Brothers and joined the Paul Williams band. In 1964 she briefly retired from the music business and returned to Norfolk. There she joined the Dick Morgan Trio, and in the late 60s made two albums of standards for RCA. In 1969 after becoming ill she retired permanently from showbusiness.

● COMPILATIONS: *Riffin With The Griffin Brothers* (Ace 1985)★★★, *I'll Get A Deal* (Mr. R&B 1986)★★★.

Dazz Band

Bobby Harris masterminded the formation of the Dazz Band in the late 70s when he combined two Cleveland funk outfits, Bell Telefunk and the Kinsman Grill house band. The result was an eight-piece line-up, with Harris, Pierre DeMudd and Skip Martin III handling horns and vocals, and Eric Fearman (guitar), Kevin Frederick (keyboards), Kenny Pettus (percussion), Michael Wiley (bass) and Isaac Wiley (drums) providing the instrumental support.

Coining the word 'Dazz' as a contraction of 'danceable jazz', Harris initially named the band Kinsman Dazz, under which moniker they registered two minor US hits in 1978 and 1979. The following year, they signed to Motown Records, where their irresistible blend of dance rhythms and commercial melodies established them as one of the label's hottest acts of the 80s. Their early albums were firmly in the jazz-funk style pioneered by Earth, Wind And Fire and George Benson. They graduated towards a harder, less melodic funk sound, enjoying a US Top 10 hit with 'Let It Whip' in 1982, which won them a Grammy award for the best performance by an R&B Vocal Duo or Group. Notable British success followed with the tougher, sparse rhythm of 'Let It All Blow'. *Jukebox* marked a transition towards a more rock-orientated sound which brought them continued success in the specialist black music charts, though crossover recognition among pop fans proved more elusive. The band suffered two personnel changes in 1985, when Marlon McClain and Keith Harrison replaced Eric Fearman and Kevin Frederick. A switch to Geffen Records in 1986 proved unfulfilling, and the group quickly moved on to RCA Records, where they have yet to re-establish their hit-making form.

● ALBUMS: *Invitation To Love* (Motown 1980)★★★, *Let The Music Play* (Motown 1981)★★★, *Keep It Live* (Motown 1982)★★★, *On The One* (Motown 1983)★★★, *Joystick* (Motown 1983)★★★, *Jukebox* (Motown 1984)★★★, *Hot Spot* (Motown 1985)★★, *Wild And Free* (Geffen 1986)★★, *Rock The Room* (RCA 1988)★★, *Under The Streetlights* (Lucky 1996)★★★.

DeBarge

One sister, Bunny DeBarge, and four brothers, Mark, James, Randy and El DeBarge, combined to form this family group in Grand Rapids, Michigan, in 1978. Signed to Motown Records in 1979, they were viewed and marketed as successors to the young Jackson Five, a ploy helped by the physical similarity between El DeBarge and Michael Jackson. After several years of grooming from Motown's A&R department, the group (then known as the DeBarges) were launched with the album *The DeBarges* in March 1981, and gained their initial soul hit 18 months later. 'I Like It' repeated this success and crossed over into the pop charts, while two 1983 hits, 'All This Love' and 'Time Will Reveal', established DeBarge as one of America's most popular acts in the teenage market. A support slot on Luther Vandross's 1984 US tour brought them to a wider audience, and in 1985 they scored their biggest hit with the seductive 'Rhythm Of The Night', taken from the soundtrack to Motown's film *The Last Dragon*, in which the group also appeared. This single reached number 3 in the US charts, a success that the follow-up release, 'Who's Holding Donna Now?' came close to repeating. Lead vocalist Eldra DeBarge had become synonymous with the group's name, and his decision to go solo in February 1986 effectively sabotaged the group's career. In 1987, Bunny also departed when the rest of the group signed to Striped Horse Records. In the event, only Mark and James (who had briefly been married to Janet Jackson in the mid-80s) appeared on the resulting *Bad Boys*, by which time their commercial impetus had been lost. The group's wholesome image was seriously damaged by the arrest and conviction of their other brothers Bobby and Chico DeBarge in 1988 on cocaine trafficking charges.

● ALBUMS: *The DeBarges* (Gordy 1981)★★★, *All This Love* (Gordy 1982)★★★, *In A Special Way* (Gordy 1983)★★, *Rhythm Of The Night* (Gordy 1985)★★, *Bad Boys* (Striped Horse 1988)★★.

● COMPILATIONS: *Greatest Hits* (Motown 1986)★★★.

DeBarge, Bunny

b. Grand Rapids, Michigan, USA. Bunny DeBarge was a vocalist in the family group DeBarge from their inception in 1978 until 1987. She was the first member of the group to be married, and missed several national tours during her three pregnancies, although she appeared regularly on their Motown Records releases. In 1987, she chose to remain as a solo artist with the label rather than follow the rest of the group to Striped Horse Records. Her loyalty was rewarded when *In Love*, a light pop/soul concoction, was a minor US hit album, and 'Save The Best For Me' became a US Top 20 black music hit.

● ALBUMS: *In Love* (Motown 1987)★★.

DeBarge, Chico

b. Jonathan 'Chico' DeBarge, 1966, Grand Rapids, Michigan, USA. Chico DeBarge was too young to join the family group DeBarge in 1978, but he was signed to a solo contract with Motown Records in 1986, issuing a self-titled album in a harder, funk-rooted style than his brothers and sisters. His debut single, 'Talk To Me', was a major US hit, and he had four more black music chart entries up to 1988. His promising career was effectively ended when he and his brother Bobby DeBarge (a former member of the Motown group Switch) were arrested and then convicted on charges of trafficking cocaine in October 1988. Released after six years' imprisonment, DeBarge returned to music with *Long Time No See*.

● ALBUMS: *Chico DeBarge* (Motown 1986)★★★, *Long Time No See* (Universal 1998)★★★.

DeBarge, El

b. 4 June 1961, Grand Rapids, Michigan, USA. Eldra DeBarge became the lead singer of the family vocal group DeBarge from their formation in 1978. He was featured on all the group's hits between 1982 and 1985, when he elected to pursue a solo career, leaving DeBarge the following year. His debut album was an attractive mixture of pop and soul, fashioned in the style of Michael Jackson. He achieved a US number 1 black music hit in 1986 with 'Who's Johnny?', the theme song of the film *Short Circuit*, and re-emerged after a two-year pause in his career with 'Real Love' in 1989, which was soon followed by *Gemini*. In 1990 he co-wrote and sang lead on Quincy Jones's 'The Secret Garden', before moving to Warner Brothers.

● ALBUMS: *El DeBarge* (Gordy 1986)★★★, *Gemini* (Motown 1989)★★★, *Heart, Mind & Soul* (Warners/Reprise 1994)★★★.

Dees, Sam

b. 1945, Birmingham, Alabama, USA. One of only a handful of artists who remains a superb performer in his own right, and a writer of high-quality soul songs for many others, in the same way as the diverse, but equally talented, George Jackson, Frank O (Johnson), Ashford And Simpson, 'Joshie' Jo Armstead, Isaac Hayes, Eddie Hinton and Dees' long-standing friend Frederick Knight. After winning a song contest at the age of nine, Dees formed a group, the Bossanovians. Later, he travelled widely, and was 23 years old before he made his first recording in 1968 for Shelby Singleton's SSS-International label. Recorded in Nashville, and produced by William Crump, 'I Need You Girl' was a somewhat dated ballad, but 'Lonely For You Baby' was a strong mid-paced slice of southern-soul. In 1969 Dees moved on to Bob Groves' studio in Birmingham for the tough, self-penned 'Don't Keep Me Hanging On', coupled with the Marlin Greene/Eddie Hinton 'deepie', 'It's All Wrong' (originally intended as a vehicle for Percy Sledge). Both were released on Nate McCalla's Lola label, as were the very emotive ballad, 'Easier To Say Than Do', and the pacy Dees mover 'Soul Sister'. Already a prolific songwriter, in 1969 Dees formed his Moonsong Publishing Company, and by 1971, when he cut his two Chess singles, he was performing the roles of singer, writer and producer. He had been working with executive producer Lenny Sachs on Johnny Sanlin and Allman Brothers material in Macon, Georgia, when Sachs allowed Dees to cut the magnificent, slowish-paced 'Love Starvation' and 'Maryanna', followed by 'Can You Be A One Woman Man' and the storming 'Put You Back In Your Place', which were both recorded in a disused Birmingham church, and released by Chess. Still in Alabama, Dees cut the impressive 'dancer', 'I'm So Very Glad', for Clinton Moon's Clintone label, and the equally fine up-tempo 'Claim Jumpin'' (co-penned with Bill Brandon, who recorded for the sister Moonsong label). Dees was constantly writing material for other artists on these small labels, such as Rozetta Johnson and Black Haze Express. Atlantic leased a couple of Dees' Clintone productions, including the first a-side, a ballad, 'Just Out Of My Reach', and another single, with the gentle Dees/Brandon song, 'So Tied Up' as the top side, and one of Dees' greatest songs, 'Signed Miss Heroin', on the flip. The latter number was sparked by an anonymous drug-abuse newspaper article, and ranks with Esther Phillips' wonderful version of Gil Scott-Heron's 'Love Is Where The Hatred Is' as the finest ever soul song about that particular issue. Although mid-paced, the anti-heroin message is chilling. Dees went on to record another two singles, and the much sought-after *The Show Must Go On*. Surprisingly, 'Signed Miss Heroin' was not included on the album, although Dees pushed for its inclusion, along with another message song, 'Heritage Of A Blackman', but they were considered 'heavy', and too commercially risky. Although Dees continued to record, he also wrote some great songs for artists such as Loleatta Holloway ('Cry To Me'), Barbara Hall ('Drop My Heart Off At The Door'), and Margie Joseph ('Just As Soon As The Feeling's Over'). He also duetted with southern-soul singer Bettye Swann for Big Tree in Chicago in 1975, and cut a couple of fine sides at Tommy Couch's Malaco studios in 1978, which were initially issued on New London International, and re-released on Polydor. Dees' songs were also recorded by Malaco's own artists, such as Dorothy Moore ('Special Occasion'), and Denise LaSalle (the racy 'Keep Your Pants On'). He made demos of his material in LA for major A&M acts such as the Tavares, Rockie Robbins, Marilyn McCoo and Billy Davis. After recording a single in 1986 for the UK Move label, Dees formed his own Pen Pad outlet and released *Secret Admirer*, which spawned two US singles, 'Just Wait Until I Get You Home', and arguably Dees' greatest 80s song, 'After All', which was also released in 1989 by RCA. Dees is said to believe in keeping his sound 'contemporary' but always genuinely soulful, in a way that appeals to mature soul fans rather than to the rap-loving younger generation. More recently, he has joined the Ardent label and is still writing and recording great soul music.

● ALBUMS: *The Show Must Go On* (Atlantic 1975)★★★, *Secret Admirer* (Pen Pad 1988)★★★.

● COMPILATIONS: *Cry To Me* (Deep & Mellow Soul 1994)★★★, *Second To None* (Kent 1996)★★★.

DEL-SATINS

R&B artists the Del-Satins had few peers as practitioners of white doo-wop in the 60s. They were formed in 1958 in Manhattan, New York, USA, by Stan Ziska (lead), Fred Ferrara (baritone), his brother Tom Ferrara (bass), Leslie Cauchi (first tenor) and Bobby Fiela (second tenor). The Del-Satins was chosen as their name in open tribute to their principal influences, the Dells and Five Satins. Under the new name they secured a recording contract with End Records. Their debut single, 'I'll Pray For You', was released in 1961. New management was sought with Passions manager Jim Gribble, who found them a more permanent contract at Laurie Records. Their label star Dion was at the time grappling with diminishing chart returns after an impressive start, and wanted to replace his existing backing band, the Belmonts, with a 'rockier' troupe. The Del-Satins were instantly sent to work on Dion's new song, 'Runaround Sue', a two-week number 1 in the *Billboard* charts. Although their contribution to the hit was substantial, the Del-Satins received none of the credit. They stepped out on their own for 'Counting Teardrops' for Winn Records, before reuniting with Dion for 'The Wanderer', which stalled just one place short of the number 1 spot in the US charts. The follow-up, 'Lovers Who Wander', peaked at number 3, emphasizing the power of the Dion/Del-Satins coalition. While the combination was charting once more with the kazoo-led 'Little Dianne', the Del-Satins released 'Teardrops Follow Me', their first own-name outing to garner serious sales, after which they found regular work on television (Alan Freed) and radio (Freed and Murray The K). Back with Dion for the number 5 'Love Came To Me', the Del-Satins' own 'Does My Love Stand A Chance' did not fare well. In 1962 they moved to Columbia Records as part of Dion's new contract, which began with a version of the Drifters' 'Ruby Baby', another substantial hit at number 2. Still frustrated by their lack of recognition, in 1963 the Del-Satins auditioned for Phil Spector but declined his subsequent invitation to record with him. Meanwhile, in appreciation for their past efforts on his behalf, Dion wrote a song for the Del-Satins for single release, 'Feeling No Pain', but without his name to accompany it there was no chart return. Two more hits with their mentor followed, 'Donna The Prima Donna' and 'Drip Drop', before new manager Jay Fontana found the group a home at Mala Records. This relationship lasted for only one single, 'Two Broken Hearts', before three more efforts at B.T. Puppy Records. These included a rendering of the Drifters' 'Sweets For My Sweet', but afterwards Ziska left (for the Magnificent Men) and was temporarily replaced by Carl Parker. In 1966 the Vietnam War robbed the group of Cauchi and Tommy Ferrara, but the Del-Satins continued to play live with the addition of Richard Green, Mike Gregorio and Johnny Maestro (ex-Crests). When Cauchi returned he and the Del-Satins became Brooklyn Bridge. In 1991 the original Del-Satins re-formed for nostalgia shows.

● ALBUMS: *Out To Lunch* (BT Puppy 1972)★★.

DEL-VIKINGS

Formed by members of the US Air Force in 1955 at their social club in Pittsburg, Ohio, the Del-Vikings' place in history is primarily secured by their status as the first successful multiracial rock 'n' roll band, but their recorded legacy also stands the test of time. Another fact overlooked by many archivists is that they were in fact, at inception, an all-black troupe. They were formed at Pittsburgh airport in 1956 by Clarence Quick (bass), Corinthian 'Kripp' Johnson (b. 1933, USA, d. 22 June 1990; lead and tenor), Samuel Patterson (lead and tenor), Don Jackson (baritone) and Bernard Robertson (second tenor). They were invited to record by producer Joe Averback, but Air Force assignments in Germany dragged away both Patterson and Robertson, who were replaced by Norman Wright and Dave Lerchey, the latter the band's first white member. 'Come Go With Me' became the lead-off track on their debut single for Averback's Fee Bee Records, but was then nationally licensed to Dot Records. It reached number 4 in the *Billboard* charts in February 1957, the highest position thus far achieved by a mixed-race group. That mix was further refined when Jackson became the third member to be transferred to Air Force duties in Germany, at which time he was replaced by a second white member, Donald 'Gus' Backus. The group's second record, 'Down In Bermuda', was ignored, but 'Whispering Bells' was afforded a better reception, reaching number 9 in the US charts. Strange circumstances surrounded the subsequent disappearance of Johnson from the group; when their manager Al Berman took the Del-Vikings to Mercury Records, he was able to break their contract with Fee Bee because the musicians were under-age when they signed, apart from Johnson, who was legally bound being 21 years of age. William Blakely replaced him in the new line-up, which debuted with 'Cool Shake' in May 1957 (this entered the charts at about the same time as 'Whispering Bells', causing considerable confusion). Kripp Johnson retaliated by forming his own Del-Vikings with Arthur Budd, Eddie Everette, Chuck Jackson and original member Don Jackson, who had returned from his service endeavours in Germany. They released two singles, 'Willette' and 'I Want To Marry You', to little commercial recognition. Luniverse Records also muddied the picture by releasing an album of eight Del-Vikings songs that the group had originally placed with them in 1956 before Averback had signed them to Fee Bee. In order to clarify the situation, the next release on Dot Records was credited to the Dell-Vikings And Kripp Johnson, but this did not prevent Mercury Records suing to ensure that any use of the Del-Vikings name, whatever its spelling, belonged to it. Some of the confusion was abated when Kripp Johnson was able to rejoin the Del-Vikings when his contract with Fee Bee ran out in 1958 (by which time Donald Backus had become the fourth member of the group to lose his place due to an Air Force posting to Germany). Kripp sang lead on the group's last two Mercury singles, 'You Cheated' and 'How Could You'. Although recordings by the 'original Del-Vikings' were less forthcoming from this point, the group, now all discharged from the Air Force, toured widely throughout the 60s. They signed to a new label, ABC Paramount Records, in 1961, and began in promising style with 'Bring Back Your Heart'. Several excellent releases followed, but none revisited the chart action of old. The 70s saw them record a handful of one-off singles as they toured widely, including stints in Europe and the Far East.

● ALBUMS: *Come Go With The Del Vikings* (Luniverse 1957)★★★, *They Sing - They Swing* (Mercury 1957)★★★, *A Swinging, Singing Record Session* (Mercury 1958)★★, *Newies And Oldies* (1959)★★★, *The Del Vikings And The Sonnets* (Crown 1963)★★★, *Come Go With Me* (Dot 1966)★★★.

● COMPILATIONS: *Del Vikings* (Buffalo Bop 1988)★★★, *Cool Shake* (Buffalo Bop 1988)★★★, *Collectables* (Mercury 1988)★★★.

DELFONICS

Formed in Philadelphia, USA, in 1965 and originally known as the Four Gents, the Delfonics featured William Hart (b. 17 January 1945, Washington, DC, USA), Wilbert Hart (b. 19 October 1947, Philadelphia, Pennsylvania, USA), Randy Cain (b. 2 May 1945, Philadelphia, Pennsylvania, USA) and Ritchie Daniels. An instigator of the Philly Sound, the above line-up evolved out of an earlier group, the Veltones. The Delfonics' early releases appeared on local independent labels until their manager, Stan Watson, founded Philly Groove. Cut to a trio on Daniels' conscription, their distinctive hallmarks, in particular William Hart's aching tenor, were heard clearly on their debut hit, 'La La Means I Love You'. It prepared the way for several symphonic creations, including 'I'm Sorry', 'Ready Or Not Here I Come' (both 1968) and 'Didn't I (Blow Your Mind This Time)' (1970). Much of the credit for their sumptuous atmosphere was due to producer Thom Bell's remarkable use of brass and orchestration. It provided the perfect backdrop for Hart's emotive ballads. 'Trying To Make A Fool Out Of Me' (1970), the group's tenth consecutive R&B chart entry, marked the end of this relationship, although Bell later continued this style with the (Detroit) Spinners and Stylistics. The Delfonics, meanwhile, maintained a momentum with further excellent singles. In 1971 Cain was replaced by Major Harris, whose subsequent departure three years later coincided with the Delfonics' downhill slide. Unable to secure a permanent third member, the Harts were also bedevilled by Philly Groove's collapse. Singles for Arista (1978) and Lorimar (1979) were issued to negligible attention, consigning the group to the cabaret circuit.

● ALBUMS: *La La Means I Love You* (Philly Groove 1968)★★★, *The Sound Of Sexy Soul* (Philly Groove 1969)★★★, *The Delfonics* (Philly Groove 1970)★★★, *Tell Me This Is A Dream* (Philly Groove 1972)★★★, *Alive And Kicking* (Philly Groove 1974)★★.

● COMPILATIONS: *The Delfonics Super Hits* (Philly Groove 1969)★★★, *Symphonic Soul - Greatest Hits* (Charly 1988)★★★★, *Echoes - The Best Of The Delfonics* (Arista 1991)★★★★.

DELLS

A soul vocal and close harmony group formed in 1953 as the El-Rays, when the members - Johnny Funches (lead), Marvin Junior (b. 31 January 1936, Harrell, Arkansas, USA; tenor), Verne Allison (b. 22 June 1936, Chicago, Illinois, USA; tenor), Lucius McGill (b. 1935, Chicago, Illinois, USA; tenor), Mickey McGill (b. 17 February 1937, Chicago, Illinois, USA; baritone) and Chuck Barksdale (b. 11 January 1935, Chicago, Illinois, USA; bass) - were all high school students. As the El-Rays the group released one record on the Chess label, 'Darling Dear I Know', in 1953. After a name change they recorded 'Tell The World' in 1955, which was only a minor hit, but a year later they released 'Oh What A Night' (number 4 R&B chart), one of the era's best-loved black harmony performances and the Dells' last hit for 10 years. In 1965 they returned to the R&B chart with 'Stay In My Corner'. Three years later, under the guidance of producer Bobby Miller, a re-recorded version of this song effectively relaunched their career when it became a US Top 10 hit. An enchanting medley of 'Love Is Blue' and 'I Can Sing A Rainbow' (1969) was their sole UK hit in 1969, but a further re-recording, this time of 'Oh What A Night', introduced a string of successful releases in the USA, including 'Open Up My Heart' (1970), 'Give Your Baby A Standing Ovation' (1973) and 'I Miss You' (1974). The Dells continued to prosper through the 70s and 80s, surviving every prevalent trend in music, and in the early 90s they contributed music to the film *The Five Heartbeats*. Just as noteworthy was the members' own relationship which survived almost intact from their inception. Lucius McGill left when they were still known as the El-Rays and the only further change occurred in 1958 when Funches was replaced by ex-Flamingo Johnny Carter (b. 2 June 1934, Chicago, Illinois, USA). Marvin Junior took over as lead and Carter took first tenor. Funches gave his reason for leaving as being 'tired of the constant touring'. The Dells' enduring music is a tribute to their longevity.

● ALBUMS: *Oh What A Nite* (1959)★★★, *It's Not Unusual* (1965)★★★, *There Is* (Cadet 1968)★★★★, *Stay In My Corner* (Cadet 1968)★★★, *The Dells Musical Menu/Always Together* (Cadet 1969)★★★, *Love Is Blue* (Cadet 1969)★★★, *Like It Is, Like It Was* (Cadet 1970)★★★, *Oh, What A Night* (Cadet 1970)★★★, *Freedom Means* (Cadet 1971)★★★, *Dells Sing Dionne Warwick's Greatest Hits* (Cadet 1972)★★, *Sweet As Funk Can Be* (Cadet 1972)★★★, *Give Your Baby A Standing*

Ovation (Cadet 1973)★★★, with the Dramatics *The Dells Vs The Dramatics* (Cadet 1974)★★★, *The Mighty Mighty Dells* (Cadet 1974)★★★, *We Got To Get Our Thing Together* (Cadet 1975)★★★, *No Way Back* (Mercury 1975)★★★, *They Said It Couldn't Be Done, But We Did It* (Mercury 1977)★★, *Love Connection* (Mercury 1977)★★★, *New Beginnings* (ABC 1978)★★, *Face To Face* (ABC 1979)★★★, *I Touched A Dream* (20th Century 1980)★★★, *Whatever Turns You On* (20th Century 1981)★★, *One Step Closer* (1984)★★, *The Second Time* (Veteran 1988)★★, *Music From The Motion Picture: The Five Heartbeats* (Virgin 1991)★★★.
● COMPILATIONS: *The Dells Greatest Hits* (Cadet 1969)★★★, *The Best Of The Dells* (1973)★★★★, *Cornered* (1977)★★★, *Rockin' On Bandstand* (Charly 1983)★★★, *From Streetcorner To Soul* (Charly 1984)★★★, *Breezy Ballads And Tender Tunes* (Solid Smoke 1985)★★★, *On Their Corner/The Best Of*... (Chess/MCA 1992)★★★★.

DELTA 72

Comprising Gregg Foreman (guitar, vocals, harmonica), Jason Kourkounis (drums), Sarah Stolfa (Farfisa organ) and Kim Thompson (bass, vocals, ex-Cupid Car Club), the Washington, DC, USA band Delta 72 offer something of a throwback to the 50s and 60s. Like others such as Rocket From The Crypt and the Cramps, they match such period stylings with a ferocious, contemporary take on traditional R&B and rock 'n' roll. The group was originally formed in 1994 as a trio of Foreman, Stolfa and original drummer Benjamin Azzara. From then on they embarked on a massive touring schedule to establish the group, driving around the east coast and Midwest of America before returning home and recruiting bassist Kim Thompson in January 1995. Their debut single, 'On The Rocks'/'Got A Train To Catch'/'Hip Coat', was released as a joint venture between acclaimed indie labels Kill Rock Stars and Dischord Records in June. This was promoted by another exhaustive six-week tour that eventually proved too much for drummer Azzara, who was replaced by Kourkounis, formerly of Mule. The group's debut album was then recorded at Inner Ear Studios in Washington, DC, with Eli Janney (Girls Against Boys) and Don Zientra serving as engineers. Brendan Canty of Fugazi mixed the final results with the group. *The R&B Of Membership* proved an excellent introduction to the band, blending 12 R&B-styled, organ-driven songs with punk and blues guitar.
● ALBUMS: *The R&B Of Membership* (Touch And Go 1996)★★★, *The Soul Of A New Machine* (Touch And Go 1997)★★★.

DELTA RHYTHM BOYS

A vocal group formed in 1934 at Langston University, Oklahoma, USA. The classic line-up of the group was bass Lee Gaines (b. Otha Lee Gaines, Mississippi, USA, d. 15 July 1987), baritone Kelsey Pharr, first tenor lead Carl Jones, second tenor Traverse Crawford, and pianist/arranger Rene DeKnight. The Delta Rhythm Boys exuded a classy elegance and sophistication that made them the most renowned and respected of the 40s groups who sang a blend of jubilee, pop and swing. In 1936 the group transferred to Dillard University in New Orleans, Louisiana, and began singing under the name Frederick Hall Quintet, after their mentor, the school's musical director. By 1938 the group had made it to New York and were appearing in Broadway shows such as *Sing Out The News* and *The Hot Mikado* as the Delta Rhythm Boys. By 1940 the group, consisting of Gaines, Crawford, DeKnight and tenors Clinton Howard and Harry Lewis, had made its recording debut for Decca Records. During 1941 they had success with two of their most memorable recordings, 'Dry Bones' and 'Take The 'A' Train', and also with recordings backing Mildred Bailey. The Delta Rhythm Boys also appeared in films for Universal during 1943-45. Meanwhile, in 1943 Lewis was replaced by baritone Kelsey Pharr, and in 1944 Howard was replaced by Carl Jones. In 1945 the group were established on radio in programmes including *Amos And Andy* and *The Joan Davis Show*. In 1945 Decca teamed the Deltas with Ella Fitzgerald for some notable recordings. The group had one last hit for Decca in 1946 called 'Just A-Sittin' And A-Rockin' (number 3 R&B, number 17 pop), and in 1947 signed with RCA-Victor. While with Victor, the group established themselves as a first-rate jazz group, although no hits resulted. In 1949 they signed with Atlantic, and recorded some excellent R&B songs, notably 'If You See Tears In My Eyes' and 'I'd Rather Be Wrong Than Blue'. The group returned to Decca in 1950, and in 1952 recorded for Mercury. By that time, however, their music was becoming dated compared to the new R&B that was growing in popularity, but the Delta Rhythm Boys were rapidly developing a following in Europe, especially in France and the Scandinavian countries. Since 1949 they had been making regular tours to those countries and recording in Finnish and Swedish on each tour, and in 1956 they made Europe their permanent home. By 1960 only Gaines and Crawford remained from the classic group but they continued to perform with new members. Crawford died in 1975, and Gaines in 15 July 1987, after which the Delta Rhythm Boys disbanded.
● ALBUMS: *The Delta Rhythm Boys* (Mercury 1952)★★★, *Dry Bones* (RCA 1953)★★★, *The Delta Rhythm Boys* (Camden 1957)★★★, *The Delta Rhythm Boys* (Elektra 1957)★★★, *Delta Rhythm Boys In Sweden* (Jubilee 1957)★★★, *Swingin' Spirituals* (Coral 1961)★★★.
● COMPILATIONS: *Tall, Tan And Tender* (Dr. Horse 1992)★★★.

DEODATO

b. Eumir Deodato Almeida, 21 June 1942, Rio de Janeiro, Brazil. As a child, Deodato taught himself to play keyboards and graduated to playing in local pop bands in his teens. He also worked as a session musician (keybaords, bass, guitar) before recording under his own name. His first success came in Brazil, accompanying Astrud Gilberto. He won a prize at the Rio Song Festival for his composition, 'Spirit Of Summer', before emigrating to California in 1967. There he quickly established himself as a musical arranger, working with Roberta Flack's Chapter Two in 1970. He also appeared on recordings by

Frank Sinatra, Bette Midler, Aretha Franklin, Roberta Flack and others. He then signed as a solo artist to the New York-based CTI Records and found success with his first release, an adaptation of Richard Strauss's 'Also Sprach Zarathustra', which had recently been used as the title music to Stanley Kubrick's film *2001: A Space Odyssey*. Deodato's jazz version (originally intended for labelmate Bob James as *his* CTI debut) was an international smash, hitting number 2 on the US Top 100 and number 7 in the UK, and also collecting the 1973 Grammy award for 'Best Pop Instrumental Performance'. After two albums for CTI (*Prelude* and *Deodato 2*) and with the label in difficulties (ironically caused by the success of 'Also Sprach Zarathustra'), Deodato moved to MCA, recording *First Cuckoo*, *Whirlwinds* and *Very Together*, the latter causing dancefloor activity thanks to 'Peter Gunn'. A subsequent move to Warner Brothers Records revived his career, with 'Whistle Bump' and 'Night Cruiser' afforded almost anthem status in the UK. In 1979 he embarked on a highly successful production career, revitalizing the fortunes of Kool And The Gang with *Ladies Night* and *Celebration* in particular. After one further album for Warners in 1984 he switched to Atlantic, recording *Somewhere Out There* in 1989. The previous year he had produced the debut solo album from Dexys Midnight Runners star Kevin Rowland.

● ALBUMS: *Prelude* (CTI 1973)★★★, *Deodato 2* (CTI 1974)★★★, with Airto *In Concert* (CTI 1974)★★★, *Whirlwinds* (MCA 1974)★★, *Artistry* (MCA 1974)★★★, *First Cuckoo* (MCA 1975)★★★★, *Very Together* (MCA 1976)★★, *Love Island* (Warners 1978)★★, *Night Cruiser* (Warners 1980)★★, *Happy Hour* (Warners 1982)★★, *Motion* (Warners 1984)★★, *Somewhere Out There* (Atlantic 1989)★★.

DES'REE

b. *c*.1969, London, England. Des'ree had a convent school upbringing in Norwood, London. She signed to Sony subsidiary Dusted Records in 1991 after being spotted by A&R scout Lincoln Elias, and her first two singles, 'Feel So High' and 'Mind Adventures', both charted. 'Mind Adventures' was helped enormously by her appearance on the prime-time television programme *Wogan*. Its spiritual edge was fuelled by her lengthy apprenticeship in gospel choirs. On the strength of this she reached number 13 in the UK album chart with her debut. The first single from her second album, 'You Gotta Be', looked ready to repeat the success when it broke the UK Top 20 in February 1994, but when it was not played on BBC Television programme *Top Of The Pops* it fell straight out of the charts - a fate that also befell its successor. However, this was compensated for by an expanding international audience, with 'You Gotta Be' going Top 10 in the Australian charts. In America, her record company, 550 (an offshoot of Epic Records), promoted the single for no less than 32 weeks, an effort that paid off with a number 6 chart placing. Supporting Seal on tour helped her avoid the expected R&B bracket, and television appearances included *The Late Show With David Letterman* and *Tonight*. Afterwards, Des'ree toured with collaborator and co-writer Ashley Ingrams (ex-Imagination), and also wrote with the US hitmaker Brenda Russell.

● ALBUMS: *Mind Adventures* (Dusted 1992)★★, *I Ain't Movin'* (Sony 1994)★★★★.

DESANTO, SUGAR PIE

b. Umpeylia Marsema Balinton, 16 October 1935, Brooklyn, New York, USA. Raised in San Francisco, DeSanto was discovered at a talent show by Johnny Otis, who later dubbed her 'Little Miss Sugar Pie'. She recorded for Federal and Aladdin before 'I Want To Know' (1960) on Veltone reached the R&B charts. Signed to Checker in 1961, her first releases made little impact and for two years she toured as part of the James Brown Revue. 'Slip In Mules' (1964), an amusing 'answer' to Tommy Tucker's 'Hi-Heeled Sneakers', regained her chart position. It was followed by the sassy 'Soulful Dress', while an inspired pairing with Etta James produced 'Do I Make Myself Clear' (1965) and 'In The Basement' (1966). Although her recording career at Checker was drawing to a close, DeSanto's songs were recorded by such acts as Billy Stewart, Little Milton and Fontella Bass. DeSanto returned to San Francisco during the 70s where she continues to perform and record today.

● ALBUMS: *Sugar Pie* (Checker 1961)★★★, *Hello San Francisco* (1984)★★.

● COMPILATIONS: *Loving Touch* (Diving Duck 1987)★★★, *Down In The Basement - The Chess Years* (Chess 1988)★★★, *Sisters Of Soul* 12 tracks Sugar Pie DeSanto/14 tracks Fontella Bass (Roots 1990)★★★.

DESIRES

An R&B vocal group from Harlem, New York City, New York, USA, comprising lead Robert White, first tenor Charles Hurston, second tenor Jim Whittier, baritone Jerome Smith and bass Charles Powell. Whittier, the founder of the group, was a veteran of the doo-wop scene, having formed the Jive Tones, who recorded for Apt in 1958, in his native city of Rochester. The following year, Whittier moved to New York and immediately immersed himself in the flourishing doo-wop scene of Harlem. The Desires were signed to Bea Casalin's Hull label and recorded their one claim to fame, 'Let It Please Be You'. The song, featuring the child-tenor lead sound made popular by Frankie Lymon And The Teenagers, achieved a great deal of regional success on the east coast, and today it is one of the most beloved of the child-lead oldies. The death of Casalin served to put their record company in disarray and the Desires suffered as a result. Discouraged, the group broke up in 1961. As is true of many east coast doo-wop groups, the Desires have on occasion regrouped for revival shows.

DETROIT EMERALDS

Formed in Little Rock, Arkansas, USA, by the Tilmon brothers, Abrim, Ivory, Cleophus and Raymond, the Emeralds' first hit came in 1968 when 'Show Time' reached the US R&B Top 30. By the time 'Do My Right' (1971) reached the Soul Top 10, the line-up had been reduced to a trio of Abrim, Ivory and mutual friend James Mitchell (b. Perry, Florida, USA). The group secured their biggest US successes in 1972 with 'You Want It, You Got It' and 'Baby Let Me Take You (In My Arms)', but the following year 'Feel The Need In Me', which failed to crack *Billboard*'s Hot 100, peaked at number 4 in the UK chart. Three further UK hits followed, including, in 1977, a re-recorded version of their 1973 best-seller, but at home the Emeralds' career was waning. By 1977 Abrim Tilmon was the last remaining original member; sadly, he died from a heart attack five years later.

● ALBUMS: *Do Me Right* (Westbound 1971)★★, *You Want It, You Got It* (Westbound 1972)★★★, *I'm In Love With You* (Westbound 1973)★★★, *Feel The Need* (Westbound 1973)★★, *Abe James And Ivory* (1973)★★, *Let's Get Together* (Atlantic 1978)★★.

● COMPILATIONS: *Do Me Right/You Want It, You Got It* (Westbound 1993)★★★, *I'm In Love With You/Feel The Need* (Westbound 1993)★★★.

DETROIT SPINNERS

Formed in Ferndale High School, near Detroit, Michigan, USA, and originally known as the Domingoes, Henry Fambrough (b. 10 May 1935, Detroit, Michigan, USA), Robert 'Bobby' Smith (b. 10 April 1937, Detroit, Michigan, USA), Billy Henderson (b. 9 August 1939, Detroit, Michigan, USA), Pervis Jackson and George Dixon became the Spinners upon signing with the Tri-Phi label in 1961 (the prefix 'Motown' and/or 'Detroit' was added in the UK to avoid confusion with the Spinners folk group). Although not a member, producer and songwriter Harvey Fuqua sang lead on the group's debut single, 'That's What Girls Are Made For', which reached number 5 in the US R&B chart and broached the pop Top 30. Edgar 'Chico' Edwards then replaced Dixon, but although Fuqua took the quintet to Motown in 1963, they were overshadowed by other signings and struggled to gain a commercial ascendancy. 'I'll Always Love You' was a minor US hit in 1965, but it was not until 1970 that the Spinners achieved a major success when the Stevie Wonder composition 'It's A Shame' reached the Top 20 in both the USA and the UK. The following year the group moved to Atlantic on the suggestion of Aretha Franklin. However, lead singer G.C. Cameron, who had replaced Edwards, opted to remain at Motown and thus new singer Philippe Wynne (b. Philip Walker, 3 April 1941, Detroit, Michigan, USA, d. 14 July 1984) was added to the line-up. His expressive falsetto lent an air of distinctiveness to an already crafted harmony sound and, united with producer Thom Bell, the Spinners completed a series of exemplary singles that set a benchmark for sophisticated 70s soul. 'I'll Be Around', 'Could It Be I'm Falling In Love' (both 1972), 'One Of A Kind (Love Affair)' and 'Mighty Love Part 1' (both 1973) were each R&B chart-toppers, while 'Then Came You', a collaboration with Dionne Warwick, topped the US pop chart. 'Ghetto Child' (1973) and 'The Rubberband Man' (1976) provided international success as the quintet deftly pursued a sweet, orchestrated sound that nonetheless avoided the sterile trappings of several contemporaries. The early Atlantic singles featured smooth-voiced Smith as lead, but later singles featured the baroque stylings of Wynne. New lead John Edwards replaced Wynne when the latter left for Funkadelic in 1977, but the Spinners continued to enjoy hits, notably with 'Working My Way Back To You/Forgive Me Girl' which reached number 1 in the UK and number 2 in the USA. A medley of 'Cupid' and 'I've Loved You For A Long Time' reached both countries' respective Top 10s in 1980, but an ensuing unstable line-up undermined the group's subsequent career.

● ALBUMS: *Party - My Pad* (Motown 1963)★★, *The Original Spinners* (Motown 1967)★★★, *The Detroit Spinners* (Motown 1968)★★★, *Second Time Around* (V.I.P. 1970)★★★, *The (Detroit) Spinners* (Atlantic 1973)★★★★, *Mighty Love* (Atlantic 1974)★★★★, *New And Improved* (Atlantic 1974)★★★, *Pick Of The Litter* (Atlantic 1975)★★★★, *(Detroit) Spinners Live!* (Atlantic 1975)★★★, *Happiness Is Being With The (Detroit) Spinners* (Atlantic 1976)★★★, *Yesterday, Today And Tomorrow* (Atlantic 1977)★★, *Spinners/8* (Atlantic 1977)★★, *From Here To Eternally* (Atlantic 1979)★★, *Dancin' And Lovin'* (Atlantic 1980)★★, *Love Trippin'* (Atlantic 1980)★★, *Labor Of Love* (Atlantic 1981)★★, *Can't Shake This Feelin'* (Atlantic 1982)★★, *Grand Slam* (Atlantic 1983)★★, *Cross Fire* (Atlantic 1984)★★, *Lovin' Feelings* (Atco 1985)★★, *Down To Business* (Volt 1989)★★.

● COMPILATIONS: *The Best Of The Detroit Spinners* (Motown 1973)★★★★, *Smash Hits* (Atlantic 1977)★★★★, *The Best Of The Spinners* (Atlantic 1978)★★★★, *20 Golden Classics - The Detroit Spinners* (Motown 1980)★★★, *Golden Greats - Detroit Spinners* (Atlantic 1985)★★★, *A One Of A Kind Love Affair: The Anthology* (Atlantic 1991)★★★★.

DEVAUGHN, WILLIAM

An R&B vocalist from Washington, DC, USA. The impact of Curtis Mayfield on the soul market in the early 70s was most evident in the brief success of William DeVaughn, whose sound and style was uncannily similar to that of Mayfield. DeVaughn was a part-time entertainer, having left his job to record in Philadelphia with the support of the Philadelphia International Records house band, MFSB. DeVaughn was a one-hit-wonder with his massive success, 'Be Thankful For What You Got' (number 1 R&B, number 4 pop) from 1974. His 'Blood Is Thicker Is Water' made Top 10 R&B (number 43 pop) the same year on the strength of the previous hit. Another record released in 1974, 'Give The Little Man A Great Big Hand', was even less of a hit. DeVaughn only made the chart one more time, in 1980, with 'Figures Can't Calculate'.

● ALBUMS: *Be Thankful For What You Got* (Roxbury 1974)★★.

DIABLOS

From Detroit, Michigan, USA, the original members of this vocal group were lead Nolan Strong (b. 22 January 1934, Scottsboro, Alabama, USA, d. 21 February 1977), tenor Juan Guitierriez, baritone Willie Hunter, bass Quentin Eubanks, and guitarist Bob 'Chico' Edwards. The Diablos, with the Clyde McPhatter-sounding high tenor lead of Strong, created a body of music that had only minor success on the charts; nevertheless, they became one of the most renowned and beloved of all 50s groups among doo-wop aficionados. The group was formed in 1950, and in 1953 signed with Fortune Records, owned and operated by Jack and Devora Brown, the latter a poet and songwriter who supplied some of the group's best-known songs. They achieved local success with a Brown composition, 'Adios My Desert Love', in 1954. The group became famous for their next release, the scrumptious ballad, 'The Wind' (1954), which was a hit only in certain regional markets but over the years grew in appeal (it was remade with much success by the Jesters in 1960). After this record, two of Strong's brothers, George and Jimmy, replaced Eubanks and Guitierriez, respectively. The revamped Diablos found success on the national charts in 1956 with the scorching and bluesy 'Way You Dog Me Around' (number 12 R&B). The group stayed together while Nolan Strong was in the army during 1956-58, but upon his return the Diablos were never able to find a stable line-up and the group gradually disintegrated. Strong had a solo hit for Fortune with 'Mind Over Matter' in 1962, which went high on the charts in many regional markets. An *ad hoc* group of Diablos were touring the east coast in 1963, when they sold some a cappella practice tapes to a collector. An album of this material was released in 1972 on Relic called *Acappella Showcase*, in which the group was dubbed the Velvet Angels. The group had their last Fortune single released in 1964 and disbanded around the same time.

● ALBUMS: *Mind Over Matter* (Fortune 1963)★★★.

● COMPILATIONS: *Fortune Of Hits* (Fortune 1961)★★★, *Fortune Of Hits Vol 2.* (Fortune 1962)★★★, as the Velvet Angels *Acappella Showcase* (Relic 1972)★★★, with the Five Dollars *From The Beginning To Now!* (Fortune 1978)★★, *Daddy Rock* (Fortune 1984)★★.

DIAMONDS (CANADA)

The group comprised Dave Somerville (lead), Ted Kowalski (tenor), Bill Reed (bass) and Phil Leavitt (baritone), all born in Toronto, Canada. A white vocal group that specialized in cover versions of black R&B hits, the Diamonds were formed in 1953, and during the next two years, attracted a good deal of attention on the club circuit in America's Midwest states. In 1955 they recorded several sides for Decca's Coral label, including a cover version of the Cheers' Top 10 single, 'Black Denim Trousers And Motor Cycle Boots'. Early in the following year they moved to Mercury, a label already highly skilled in recreating existing hits, such as the Crew-Cuts' version of 'Sh-Boom' (1954), which was first released by the Chords. The Diamonds made their initial impact for Mercury with 'Why Do Fools Fall In Love', a Top 10 hit for Frankie Lymon And The Teenagers in 1956. The Diamonds' version made the US Top 20, and was followed in the same year by further successful substitutes for the originals, such as 'Church Bells May Ring' (Willows), 'Little Girl Of Mine' (Cleftones), 'Love, Love, Love' (Clovers), 'Ka Ding Dong' (G-Clefs)', 'Soft Summer Breeze' (Eddie Heywood) and 'A Thousand Miles Away' (Heartbeats). 'Little Darlin' (1957), written by Maurice Williams when he was lead singer with the Gladiolas and before he went on to the Zodiacs, gave the Diamonds their highest US chart entry (number 2), and subsequently became something of a rock 'n' roll classic. The group's remaining Top 40 hits in the 50s were 'Words Of Love', 'Zip Zip', 'Silhouettes' (also a million-seller for the Rays), 'The Stroll', 'High Sign', 'Kathy-O' (a ballad, in a more easy-listening style), 'Walking Along' and 'She Say Oom Dooby Doom'. In 1958 Phil Leavitt retired and was replaced by Michael Douglas, and, in the following year, two Californians, Evan Fisher and John Felton, took over from Bill Reed and Ted Kowalski. The 'new' Diamonds continued to record throughout the early 60s and had one Top 30 entry with 'One Summer Night' in 1961. After the group split up, Dave Somerville formed a double act with ex-Four Prep Bruce Belland, until the Diamonds re-formed in the early 70s. Despite Felton's death in an air crash in 1982, the group continued to tour, and was especially popular on the county fair circuit into the 90s.

● ALBUMS: *Collection Of Golden Hits* (Mercury 1956)★★★, *The Diamonds* (Mercury 1957)★★★, *The Diamonds Meet Pete Rugolo* (Mercury 1958)★★★, *The Diamonds Sing The Songs Of The Old West* (Mercury 1959)★★, *America's Famous Song Stylists* (Wing 1962)★★★, *Pop Hits By The Diamonds* (Wing 1962)★★.

● COMPILATIONS: *The Best Of The Diamonds* (Rhino 1984)★★★.

● FILMS: *The Big Beat* (1957).

DIAMONDS (USA)

The members of this vocal group from New York, USA, were lead Harold Wright (d. April 1996), first tenor Myles Hardy and bass Daniel Stevens. The Diamonds had moderate success in the early 50s specializing in deep-sounding ballads. The group was formed in 1948 as a trio - Wright, Hardy and Stevens - but in 1950 they added a guitarist, Ernest Ward, who also sang tenor. The group was discovered by Bobby Schiffman of the Apollo Theatre and he gave them their start by having them play the amateur shows at his theatre. As their manager he helped them to sign with Atlantic Records, which was enjoying great success with the Clovers at the time. The company released three singles by the group, the best-remembered being 'A Beggar For Your Kisses'. The unit broke up by 1954, and Wright joined the Regals, who recorded four tracks for Aladdin. When the other Regals became Sonny Til's new Orioles group, Wright formed the Metronomes, who recorded four tracks for Cadence Records.

DIDDLEY, BO

b. Otha Ellas Bates (later known as Ellas McDaniel), 28 December 1928, McComb, Mississippi, USA. After beginning his career as a boxer, where he received the sobriquet 'Bo Diddley', the singer worked the blues clubs of Chicago with a repertoire influenced by Louis Jordan, John Lee Hooker and Muddy Waters. In late 1954, he teamed up with Billy Boy Arnold and recorded demos of 'I'm A Man' and 'Bo Diddley'. Re-recorded at Chess Studios with a backing ensemble comprising Otis Spann (piano), Lester Davenport (harmonica), Frank Kirkland (drums) and Jerome Green (maracas), the a-side, 'Bo Diddley', became an R&B hit in 1955. Before long, Diddley's distorted, amplified, custom-made guitar, with its rectangular shape and pumping rhythm style became a familiar, much-imitated trademark, as did his self-referential songs with such titles as 'Bo Diddley's A Gunslinger', 'Diddley Daddy' and 'Bo's A Lumberjack'. His jive-talking routine with 'Say Man' (a US Top 20 hit in 1959) continued on 'Pretty Thing' and 'Hey Good Lookin'', which reached the lower regions of the UK charts in 1963. By then, Diddley was regarded as something of an R&B legend and found a new lease of life courtesy of the UK beat boom. The Pretty Things named themselves after one of his songs, while his work was covered by such artists as the Rolling Stones, Animals, Manfred Mann, Kinks, Yardbirds, Downliner's Sect and the Zephyrs. Diddley subsequently jammed on albums by Chuck Berry and Muddy Waters and appeared infrequently at rock festivals. His classic version of 'Who Do You Love' became a staple cover for a new generation of US acts ranging from Quicksilver Messenger Service to the Doors, Tom Rush and Bob Seger, while the UK's Juicy Lucy took the song into the UK Top 20.

Like many of his generation, Diddley attempted to update his image and in the mid-70s released *The Black Gladiator* in the uncomfortable guise of an ageing funkster. *Where It All Begins*, produced by Johnny Otis (whose hit 'Willie And The Hand Jive' owed much to Diddley's style), was probably the most interesting of his post-60s albums. In 1979, Diddley toured with the Clash and in 1984 took a cameo role in the film *Trading Places*. A familiar face on the revival circuit, Diddley is rightly regarded as a seminal figure in the history of rock 'n' roll. His continued appeal to younger performers was emphasized by Craig McLachlan's hit recording of 'Mona' in 1990. Diddley's sound and 'chunk-a-chunka-cha' rhythm continues to remain an enormous influence on pop and rock, both consciously and unconsciously. It was announced in 1995, after many years of relative recording inactivity, that Diddley had signed for Mike Vernon's Code Blue record label; the result was *A Man Amongst Men*. Even with the assistance of Richie Sambora, Jimmie Vaughan, Ronnie Wood, Keith Richards, Billy Boy Arnold, Johnny 'Guitar' Watson and the Shirelles, the anticipation was greater than the result.

● ALBUMS: *Bo Diddley* (Checker 1957)★★★, *Go Bo Diddley* (Checker 1958)★★★, *Have Guitar Will Travel* (Checker 1959)★★★, *Bo Diddley In The Spotlight* (Checker 1960)★★★, *Bo Diddley Is A Gunslinger* (Checker 1961)★★★, *Bo Diddley Is A Lover* (Checker 1961)★★★, *Bo Diddley* (Checker 1962)★★★, *Bo Diddley Is A Twister* (Checker 1962)★★★, *Hey Bo Diddley* (Checker 1963)★★★, *Bo Diddley And Company* (Checker 1963)★★★, *Bo Diddley Rides Again* (Checker 1963)★★★, *Bo Diddley's Beach Party* (Checker 1963)★★★, *Bo Diddley Goes Surfing* aka *Surfin' With Bo Diddley* (Checker 1963)★★★, *Hey Good Looking* (Checker 1964)★★★, with Chuck Berry *Two Great Guitars* (Checker 1964)★★★, *500% More Man* (Checker 1965)★★★, *Let Me Pass* (Checker 1965)★★★, *The Originator* (Checker 1966)★★★, *Boss Man* (Checker 1967)★★★, *Superblues* (Checker 1968)★★★, *The Super Super Blues Band* (Checker 1968)★★★, *The Black Gladiator* (Checker 1969)★★, *Another Dimension* (Chess 1971)★★★, *Where It All Begins* (Chess 1972)★★, *The Bo Diddley London Sessions* (Chess 1973)★★, *Big Bad Bo* (Chess 1974)★★★, *Got My Own Bag Of Tricks* (Chess 1974)★★★, *The 20th Anniversary Of Rock 'N' Roll* (1976)★★, *I'm A Man* (1977)★★, *Signifying Blues* (1993)★★★, *Bo's Blues* (1993)★★, *A Man Amongst Men* (Code Blue 1996)★★.
● COMPILATIONS: *Chess Master* (Chess 1988)★★★, *EP Collection* (See For Miles 1991)★★★★, *Bo Diddley: The Chess Years* 12-CD box set (Charly 1993)★★★★★, *Bo Diddley Is A Lover ... Plus* (See For Miles 1994)★★★, *Let Me Pass ... Plus* (See For Miles 1994)★★★.
● VIDEOS: *I Don't Sound Like Nobody* (Hendring Video 1990).
● FURTHER READING: *Where Are You Now Bo Diddley?*, Edward Kiersh. *The Complete Bo Diddley Sessions*, George White (ed.). *Bo Diddley: Living Legend*, George White.

Dillard, Moses

This southern-based performer is best recalled for 'My Elusive Dreams', his powerful soul-styled interpretation of a C&W favourite. Credited to 'Moses And Joshua Dillard', this irresistible single later became a Northern Soul favourite. The fictitious brother was, in fact, a member of Dillard's backing group, the Tex-Town Display, which included future singing star Peabo Bryson. In later years, Dillard pursued a backroom role and as featured songwriter and guitarist on Al Green's 1984 gospel album *Precious Lord*, he has since continued a career as a session musician.

Dillard, Varetta

b. 3 February 1933, Harlem, New York, USA, d. 4 October 1993, Brooklyn, New York, USA. Dillard was known for several hits of poppish R&B in a style very reminiscent of Ruth Brown. As the result of a bone deficiency she spent most of her childhood years in a hospital, where she discovered singing as a therapy. Encouraged and inspired by Carl Feaster, lead singer with the Chords, Dillard began entering talent shows, which led to two consecutive wins at the Apollo's amateur show. Signed to Savoy Records in 1951, she made her own records and duetted with H-Bomb Ferguson, enjoying success with 'Easy, Easy Baby' (number 8 R&B) in 1952, 'Mercy Mr. Percy' (number 6 R&B) in 1953, and after Johnny Ace's untimely demise, 'Johnny Has Gone' (number 6 R&B) in 1955. In 1956 Dillard switched to the RCA subsidiary label Groove, where, much to her distaste, she was coerced into capitalizing on James Dean's death with 'I Miss You Jimmy'. Later recordings for Triumph and MGM's Cub subsidiary failed to match her Savoy successes, and she ended her solo recording career in 1961, although she continued singing into the late 60s by joining her husband's group, the Tri-Odds.

● COMPILATIONS: *Double Crossing Daddy* (Mr. R&B 1984)★★★, *Mercy Mr. Percy* (Savoy Jazz 1988)★★★, *Got You On My Mind* (Bear Family 1989)★★★, *The Lovin' Bird* (Bear Family 1989)★★★.

Dixie Cups

Formed in New Orleans, Louisiana, USA, in 1963, the Dixie Cups were a female trio best known for the original recording of the hit 'Chapel Of Love' in the early 60s. The group consisted of sisters Barbara Ann Hawkins (b. 23 October 1943) and Rosa Lee Hawkins (b. 24 September 1944) and their cousin Joan Marie Johnson (b. January 1945, New Orleans, Louisiana, USA). Having sung together in church and at school, the girls formed a group called the Meltones for a high school talent contest in 1963. There they were discovered by Joe Jones, a New Orleans singer who had secured a hit himself with 'You Talk Too Much' in 1960. He became their manager and signed the trio with producers/songwriters Jerry Leiber and Mike Stoller, who were then starting their own record label, Red Bird, with industry veteran George Goldner. The Dixie Cups recorded Jeff Barry and Ellie Greenwich's 'Chapel Of Love' despite the fact that both the Ronettes and the Crystals had failed to have hits with the song, which was described by co-producer Mike Leiber as 'a record I hated with a passion'. Released as the debut Red Bird single, the trio's first single reached number 1 in the USA during the summer of 1964 (the trio later claimed that they received only a few hundred dollars for their part in the recording). Following that hit, the Dixie Cups toured the USA and released a number of follow-up singles for Red Bird, four of which charted. 'People Say', the second, made number 12 and the last, 'Iko Iko', a traditional New Orleans chant, reached number 20. The song was subsequently used in soundtracks for a number of films, in common with 'Chapel Of Love'. After Red Bird closed down in 1966, the Dixie Cups signed with ABC-Paramount Records. No hits resulted from the association, and the trio have not recorded since, although they continue to perform (the two sisters are the only originals still in the act).

● ALBUMS: *Chapel Of Love* (Red Bird 1964)★★★, *Iko Iko* reissue of first album (Red Bird 1965)★★★, *Ridin' High* (ABC/Paramount 1965)★★.

DIXIE FLYERS

The Dixie Flyers were the house band at Miami's Criteria Studio, purchased in 1970 by Atlantic Records. Their name derived from a literary reference to writer William Faulkner that likened him to a south-bound train, in the phrase 'When the Dixie Flyer comes down the track you'd better get out of the way'. Prior to their work for Atlantic at Criteria, the Flyers had performed on Tony Joe White's *Continued* 1969 album for Monument and then behind Betty LaVette on her remarkable 'He Made A Woman Out Of Me' for Lelan Roger's Silver Fox label, recorded the same year in Memphis. The group was assembled by pianist Jim Dickinson (b. James Luthor Dickinson), who had previously worked with producer Sam Phillips. Mike Utley (keyboards), Tommy McClure (bass) and Sammy Creason (drums) were joined by ex-Mar-Kay Charlie Freeman (guitar) in what was one of the last great house rhythm sections. Their finest sessions included those for Aretha Franklin's *Spirit In The Dark* and Brook Benton's 'Rainy Night In Georgia' (both 1970). However, the studio could not support a full-time group, as much of its work came from self-contained units, including the Allman Brothers Band and Derek And The Dominos. The group left their Miami enclave at the end of 1970, touring North America and Europe with Rita Coolidge. They disbanded in March 1972, leaving Dickinson's eclectic solo album *Dixie Fried* as a fitting testament to their skills. The pianist later returned to Memphis, where he has worked with such disparate acts as Big Star, Ry Cooder and Green On Red. Charlie Freeman died as a result of pulmonary edema on 31 January 1973 following years of narcotics abuse.

DO RAY ME TRIO

Like many R&B groups in the immediate post-World War II era, the Do Ray Me Trio (also called Do Ray And Me Trio) were a nightclub act that played a combination of vocal harmony ballads, jive numbers, jazz and blues. The group was formed in 1942 in California, USA, as the Al 'Stomp' Russell Trio, and consisted of Al Russell (tenor and piano), Joel Cowan (tenor and guitar) and William 'Doc Basso' Joseph (bass and bass fiddle). They recorded for Excelsior, Deluxe, and Queen without much success. In 1947 Joseph was replaced by Joe Davis and the group adopted the name Do Ray Me Trio. This new ensemble made their first recordings for the Commodore label and had a hit with 'Wrapped Up In A Dream' (number 2 R&B) at the end of 1947. Bassist Joe Davis was replaced in 1948 by Curtis Wilder, whose tenor made the group an all-tenor group. One of the trio's finest all-tenor recordings was the blow-harmony ballad 'Only One Dream', recorded for Ivory Records in 1949. When Cowan left in 1950 to join Camille Howard, the trio broke up. The Do Ray Me Trio was re-formed in 1951 with members Al Russell (piano), Al Moore (bass) and Buddy Hawkins (drums). This group recorded several singles for OKeh Records in 1951, then sporadically throughout the 50s for labels including Brunswick, Variety, Coral, Reet and Carlton. The trio recorded one album for the Stereophonic label in 1960, and it proved to be the group's last recording. The Do Ray Me Trio continued to play in nightclubs for several decades afterwards.

● ALBUMS: *The Do-Ray-Mi Trio* (Stereophonic 1960)★★★.

DOGGETT, BILL

b. 16 February 1916, Philadelphia, Pennsylvania, USA, d. 13 November 1996. In 1938 pianist Doggett formed his first band, partly drawing his sidemen from the band of Jimmy Goreham, with whom he had played for the past few years. Later that year he worked with Lucky Millinder, with whom he also played in the early 40s - Millinder having taken over leadership of Doggett's band. During this period Doggett wrote many arrangements for various bands, including Lionel Hampton and Count Basie, and also worked as staff arranger and accompanist with the popular vocal group the Ink Spots. He made a number of recordings with Buddy Tate and Illinois Jacquet, then worked with Willie Bryant, Johnny Otis and Louis Jordan. In the mid-40s he began playing organ, and when he formed his own R&B band in 1951, concentrated on this instrument. He had big hits with 'Honky Tonk', which reached number 1 in the R&B charts and number 2 in the US charts in 1956, and was in the Top 10 for 14 weeks with 'Slow Walk'. He showed his versatility by arranging and conducting Ella Fitzgerald's 1963 album

Rhythm Is Our Business. Doggett continued leading a swinging R&B-orientated band into the 80s.

● ALBUMS: *Bill Doggett - His Organ And Combo* (King 1955)★★★, *Bill Doggett - His Organ And Combo Vol 2* (King 1955)★★★, *All-Time Christmas Favorites* (King 1955)★★, *Sentimentally Yours* (King 1956)★★, *Moondust* (King 1957)★★, *As You Desire* (King 1957)★★★, *Hot Doggett* (King 1957)★★, with Earl Bostic *C'mon And Dance With Earl Bostic* (1957)★★★, *As You Desire* (King 1958)★★★, *A Salute To Ellington* (King 1958)★★★, *Goin' Doggett* (50s)★★★, *The Doggett Beat For Dancing Feet* (King 1958)★★★, *Candle Glow* (King 1958)★★★, *Dame Dreaming* (King 1958)★★★, *Everybody Dance To The Honky Tonk* (King 1958)★★★, *Man With A Beat* (1958)★★★, *Swingin' Easy* (King 1959)★★★, *Bill Doggett On Tour* (1959)★★★, *Dance Awhile With Doggett* (King 1959)★★, *Bill Doggett Christmas* (King 1959)★★, *Hold It* (King 1959)★★★, *High And Wide* (King 1959)★★★, *Big City Dance Party* (King 1959)★★★, *Bill Doggett On Tour* (King 1959)★★★, *For Reminiscent Lovers Romantic Songs* (King 1960)★★★, *Back Again With More Bill Doggett* (King 1960)★★★, *Focus On Bill Doggett* (1960)★★, *Bonanza Of 24 Songs* (King 1960)★★★, *The Many Moods Of Bill Doggett* (King 1963)★★, *American Songs In The Bossa Nova Style* (King 1963)★★, *Impressions* (King 1964)★★★, *Honky Tonk Popcorn* (King 1969)★★★, *Bill Doggett* iv (1971)★★★, *Lionel Hampton Presents Bill Doggett* (1977)★★★, *Bill Doggett* v (1978)★★★, *Midnight Shows Vol. 9* (1978)★★★.

● COMPILATIONS: with Buddy Tate *Jumpin' On The West Coast* (1947)★★★, *The Best Of Bill Doggett* (King 1964)★★★.

DOMINO, FATS

b. Antoine Domino, 26 February 1928, New Orleans, Louisiana, USA. From a large family, he learned piano from local musician Harrison Verrett who was also his brother-in-law. A factory worker after leaving school, Domino played in local clubs such as the Hideaway. It was there in 1949 that bandleader Dave Bartholomew and Lew Chudd of Imperial Records heard him. His first recording, 'The Fat Man', became a Top 10 R&B hit the next year and launched his unique partnership with Bartholomew who co-wrote and arranged dozens of Domino tracks over the next two decades. Like that of Professor Longhair, Domino's playing was derived from the rich mixture of musical styles to be found in New Orleans. These included traditional jazz, Latin rhythms, boogie-woogie, Cajun and blues. Domino's personal synthesis of these influences involved lazy, rich vocals supported by rolling piano rhythms. On occasion his relaxed approach was at odds with the urgency of other R&B and rock artists and the Imperial engineers would frequently speed up the tapes before Domino's singles were released. During the early 50s, Domino gradually became one of the most successful R&B artists in America. Songs such as 'Goin' Home' and 'Going To The River', 'Please Don't Leave Me' and 'Don't You Know' were bestsellers and he also toured throughout the country. The touring group included the nucleus of the band assembled by Dave Bartholomew for recordings at Cosimo Matassa's studio. Among the musicians were Lee Allen (saxophone), Frank Field (bass) and Walter 'Papoose' Nelson (guitar).

By 1955, rock 'n' roll had arrived and young white audiences were ready for Domino's music. His first pop success came with 'Ain't That A Shame' in 1955, although Pat Boone's cover version sold more copies. 'Bo Weevil' was also covered, by Teresa Brewer, but the catchy 'I'm In Love Again', with its incisive saxophone phrases from Allen, took Domino into the pop Top 10. The b-side was an up-tempo treatment of the 20s standard, 'My Blue Heaven', which Verrett had sung with Papa Celestin's New Orleans jazz band. Domino's next big success also came with a pre-rock 'n' roll song, 'Blueberry Hill'. Inspired by Louis Armstrong's 1949 version, Domino used his creole drawl to perfection. Altogether, Fats Domino had nearly 20 US Top 20 singles between 1955 and 1960. Among the last of them was the majestic 'Walking To New Orleans', a Bobby Charles composition that became a string-laden tribute to the sources of his musical inspiration. His track record in the *Billboard* R&B lists, however, is impressive, with 63 records reaching the charts. He continued to record prolifically for Imperial until 1963, maintaining a consistently high level of performance. There were original compositions such as the jumping 'My Girl Josephine' and 'Let the Four Winds Blow' and cover versions of country songs (Hank Williams' 'Jambalaya') as well as standard ballads such as 'Red Sails In The Sunset', his final hit single in 1963. The complex off-beat of 'Be My Guest' was a clear precursor of the ska rhythms of Jamaica, where Domino was popular and toured in 1961. The only unimpressive moments came when he was persuaded to jump on the twist bandwagon, recording a number titled 'Dance With Mr Domino'.

By now, Lew Chudd had sold the Imperial company and Domino had switched labels to ABC Paramount. There he recorded several albums with producers Felton Jarvis and Bill Justis, but his continuing importance lay in his tours of North America and Europe, which recreated the sound of the 50s for new generations of listeners. The quality of Domino's touring band was well captured on a 1965 live album for Mercury from Las Vegas with Roy Montrell (guitar), Cornelius Coleman (drums) and the saxophones of Herb Hardesty and Lee Allen. Domino continued this pattern of work into the 70s, breaking it slightly when he gave the Beatles' 'Lady Madonna' a New Orleans treatment. He made further albums for Reprise (1968) and Sonet (1979), the Reprise sides being the results of a reunion session with Dave Bartholomew.

In 1986 Domino was inducted into the Rock And Roll Hall Of Fame, and won Hall Of Fame and Lifetime Achievement awards at the 1987 Grammys. In 1991 EMI, which now owns the Imperial catalogue, released a scholarly box set of Domino's remarkable recordings. Two years later, Domino was back in the studio recording his first sessions proper for 25 years, resulting in his *Christmas Is A Special Day* set. 'People don't know what they've done for me', he reflected. 'They always tell me, "Oh Fats, thanks for so many years of good music". And I'll be thankin' them before they're finished thankin' me!'

He remains a giant figure of R&B and rock 'n' roll, both musically and physically.

● ALBUMS: *Carry On Rockin'* (Imperial 1955)★★★★, *Rock And Rollin' With Fats* (Imperial 1956)★★★★, *Rock And Rollin'* (Imperial 1956)★★★★, *This Is Fats Domino!* (Imperial 1957)★★★★, *Here Stands Fats Domino* (Imperial 1958)★★★★, *Fabulous Mr D* (Imperial 1958)★★★★, *Let's Play Fats Domino* (Imperial 1959)★★★★, *Fats Domino Swings* (Imperial 1959)★★★★, *Million Record Hits* (Imperial 1960)★★★★, *A Lot Of Dominos* (Imperial 1960)★★★★, *I Miss You So* (Imperial 1961)★★★, *Let The Four Winds Blow* (Imperial 1961)★★★★, *What A Party* (Imperial 1962)★★★, *Twistin' The Stomp* (Imperial 1962)★★★, *Just Domino* (Imperial 1962)★★★, *Here Comes Fats Domino* (ABC-Paramount 1963)★★★, *Walkin' To New Orleans* (Imperial 1963)★★★★, *Let's Dance With Domino* (Imperial 1963)★★★, *Here He Comes Again* (Imperial 1963)★★★, *Fats On Fire* (ABC 1964)★★★, *Fats Domino '65* (Mercury 1965)★★★, *Getaway With Fats Domino* (ABC 1965)★★★, *Fats Is Back* (Reprise 1968)★★★, *Cookin' With Fats* (United Artists 1974)★★★, *Sleeping On The Job* (Sonet 1979)★★★, *Live At Montreux* (Atlantic 1987)★★★, *Christmas Is A Special Day* (Right Stuff/EMI 1994)★★★.

● COMPILATIONS: *The Very Best Of Fats Domino* (Liberty 1970)★★★★, *Rare Domino's* (Liberty 1970)★★★, *Rare Domino's Vol. 2* (Liberty 1971)★★★, *Fats Domino - His Greatest Hits* (MCA 1986)★★★, *My Blue Heaven - The Best Of Fats Domino* (EMI 1990)★★★★,*They Call Me The Fat Man: The Legendary Imperial Recordings* 4-CD box set (EMI/Imperial 1991)★★★★★, *Out Of Orleans* 8-CD box set (Bear Family 1993)★★★★★, *The EP Collection Vol. 1* (See For Miles 1995)★★★★, *The Early Imperial Singles 1950-52* (Ace 1996)★★★★, *The EP Collection Vol. 2* (See For Miles 1997)★★★★.

● FILMS: *The Girl Can't Help It* (1956), *Jamboree* aka *Disc Jockey Jamboree* (1957), *The Big Beat* (1957).

DON AND JUAN

Don and Juan were a US R&B vocal duo who recorded one Top 10 doo-wop ballad: 'What's Your Name?' (1962). Don (b. Roland Trone) and Juan (b. Claude Johnson) were members of a vocal quartet called the Genies in Brooklyn, New York. In 1959 they released 'Who's That Knocking', which reached number 71 in the US charts on Shad Records. Unable to follow it with another hit, the group was dropped from the label, and subsequent recordings for Hollywood Records and Warwick Records also failed to chart. Trone and Johnson left the group and became house painters in the Long Island, New York area, until they were rediscovered, this time by an agent named Peter Paul, who arranged for the pair to sign with Big Top Records. Under their new name, they recorded 'What's Your Name', which reached number 7. Only one other single, 'Magic Wand', charted, although Don and Juan continued to record until 1967. Trone died in 1983 and Johnson rekindled the act with Alexander Faison, another former member of the Genies, as the new Don.

● COMPILATIONS: *What's Your Name* (Collectables 1995)★★★.

DOOTONES

The origins of vocal group the Dootones can be traced to Fremont High School in Los Angeles, California, USA, where singer and multi-instrumentalist H.B. Barnum played in a jazz band with his drumming friend Ronald Barrett. The Dootones were subsequently formed in 1954 when the duo added Charles Gardner and Marvin Wilkins. Their initial employment was as backing singers/musicians to the Meadowlarks and Penguins. They were titled the Dootones in 1955 by their manager, Dootsie Williams, and made their debut with 'Teller Of Fortune' in April. A pop-orientated take on R&B, it attracted local airplay, while further exposure came with Californian tours with Etta James and Jackie Wilson. Afterwards, Williams put the quartet together with Vernon Green, formerly of the Medallions, for a Canadian tour, and made his intentions to remodel the band as the new Medallions clear. The existing Dootones were evidently unhappy with this turn of events, and disbanded without issuing any further recordings. Barrett teamed up with the Meadowlarks, Gardner persevered with Green as yet another version of the Medallions, while Barnum joined the Robins, later working as an arranger with artists including Ray Charles and Lou Rawls. Charles Gardner became a minister in Pasadena. The Dootones recorded 'Down The Road' in 1962. Originally recorded in 1955, it backed a track entitled 'Sailor Boy' by a second, entirely different version of the Dootones assembled by Dootsie Williams. That formation had earlier released a single entitled 'Strange Love Affair'.

DORSEY, LEE

b. Irving Lee Dorsey, 24 December 1926, New Orleans, Louisiana, USA, d. 1 December 1986. An ex-boxer (nicknamed 'Kid Chocolate') turned singer, Dorsey first recorded for Joe Banashak's Instant label. One song, 'Lottie Mo', became a regional hit and led to a contract with Fury. The infectious 'Ya Ya' (1961) was a number 1 US R&B and pop Top 10 single. A year later a version by Petula Clark, retitled 'Ya Ya Twist', made the US Top 10 and reached the UK Top 20. Dorsey's next release 'Do-Re-Mi' (regularly performed by Georgie Fame and Dusty Springfield) was also a hit, although this time reaching no higher than 27 in the *Billboard* pop chart, and subsequent releases on Fury Records were less successful. His career stalled temporarily when Fury collapsed, but Dorsey re-emerged in 1965 with the classic 'Ride Your Pony' on the Amy label. Written by Allen Toussaint and produced by Marshall Sehorn, this combination created a series of impeccable singles that blended crisp arrangements with the singer's easy delivery. In 1966 he reached the peak of his success by gaining four Top 40 hits in the UK, including two Top 10 singles with 'Working In The Coalmine', featuring a wonderful bass riff, and 'Holy Cow', with a mix that enhances Dorsey's melancholic vocals. Both songs reached the US R&B and pop charts. The sweetly doom-laden 'Get Out Of My Life Woman' was another excellent song that deserved a better commercial fate. 'Everything I Do Gohn Be Funky (From Now On)' became Dorsey's last substantial hit in 1969, although the title track to his 'concept' album, 'Yes We Can', did reach the US R&B Top 50. Dorsey continued to record for Polydor and ABC and remained a popular figure, so much so that he guested on the 1976 debut album by Southside Johnny And The Asbury Dukes and supported the Clash on their 1980 tour of North America. Sadly, he died of emphysema in December 1986 and deserves to be remembered for his outstanding examples of melodic soul.

● ALBUMS: *Ya Ya* (Fury 1962)★★★, *Ride Your Pony* (Amy/Stateside 1966)★★★, *The New Lee Dorsey* (Amy/Stateside 1966)★★★★, *Yes We Can* (Polydor 1970)★★, *Night People* (ABC 1978)★★.

● COMPILATIONS: *The Best Of Lee Dorsey* (Sue 1965)★★, *All Ways Funky* (Charly 1982)★★★, *Gohn Be Funky* (Charly 1985)★★★, *Holy Cow! The Best Of Lee Dorsey* (1985)★★★★, *Am I That Easy To Forget?* (Charly 1987)★★★, *Can You Hear Me* (Charly 1987)★★★, *Ya Ya* (Relic 1992)★★★, *Working In A Coalmine* (1993)★★★, *Freedom For The Funk* (Charly 1994)★★★, *Wheelin' And Dealin': The Definitive Collection* (Arista 1997)★★★★.

DOVELLS

Originally called the Brooktones, this Philadelphia-based R&B vocal group comprised Len Barry (b. Leonard Borisoff, 6 December 1942, Philadelphia, Pennsylvania, USA), Jerry Summers (b. Jerry Gross), Mike Dennis (b. Michael Freda) and Danny Brooks (b. Jim Meeley). Signed to the Parkway Records label, the group had a US number 2 hit in 1961 with 'Bristol Stomp', succeeded the following year by the Top 40 hits 'Do The Continental', 'Bristol Twistin' Annie' and 'Hully Gully Baby', all of which became dance favourites of the era. Len Barry was responsible for introducing their contemporaneous friends, the Orlons, to Cameo Records, and after the departure of Brooks in 1962, the Dovells achieved another major US hit with a cover of the Phil Upchurch Combo hit 'You Can't Sit Down'. Barry departed from the group later that year and they continued as a trio. The Dovells recorded for MGM Records in the late 60s under the name of the Magistrates, but met with little success.

● ALBUMS: *The Bristol Stomp* (Parkway 1961)★★★, *All The Hits Of The Teen Groups* (Parkway 1962)★★★, *Don't Knock The Twist* film soundtrack (Parkway 1962)★★, *For Your Hully Gully Party* (Parkway 1963)★★, *You Can't Sit Down* (Parkway 1963)★★★, with Len Barry *Len Barry Sings With The Dovells* (Cameo 1964)★★★, *Discotheque* (1965)★★.

● COMPILATIONS: *Golden Hits Of The Orlons And The Dovells* (1963)★★★, *The Dovells' Biggest Hits* (1965)★★★, *Cameo/Parkway Sessions* (London 1979)★★★.

● FILMS: *Don't Knock The Twist* (1962).

DOWNING, WILL

b. New York, USA. Downing was an in-demand session singer during the late 70s, appearing on recordings by artists including Rose Royce, Billy Ocean, Jennifer Holliday and Nona Hendryx. The soul singer's career was really launched when he met producer/performer Arthur Baker in the mid-80s. This led to him joining Baker's group Wally Jump Jnr. And The Criminal Element, whose other members included Brooklyn-bred Wally Jump, Craig Derry (ex-Moments; Sugarhill Gang), Donny Calvin and Dwight Hawkes (both ex-Rockers Revenge), Rick Sher (ex-Warp 9), Jeff Smith, and the toasting pair Michigan And Smiley. After a spell with Wally Jump Jnr. recording for Baker's Criminal Records label, Downing secured a solo contract with Island Records and recorded his debut album in 1988 with Baker producing. The first release under Downing's own name was 'A Love Supreme', which set lyrics to one of John Coltrane's most famous compositions. The single reached number 1 in the UK, while his first album, produced by Baker, was a Top 20 hit. He had further hits with 'In My Dreams' and a remake of the Roberta Flack and Donny Hathaway duet 'Where Is The Love', on which he partnered Mica Paris. Downing himself produced the second album, co-writing tracks with Brian Jackson, Gil Scott-Heron's collaborator. Neither this nor *A Dream Fulfilled*, on which Barry J. Eastmond and Wayne Braithwaite co-produced, was able to approach the popularity of his debut. *Moods* put Downing firmly in the smooth late-night music category, and although his exquisite vocals were suitably melancholic, they came uncomfortably close to sounding merely lethargic.

● ALBUMS: *Will Downing* (4th & Broadway 1988)★★★★, *Come Together As One* (4th & Broadway 1989)★★, *A Dream Fulfilled* (4th & Broadway 1991)★★, *Love's The Place To Be* (4th & Broadway 1993)★★, *Moods* (4th & Broadway 1995)★★★.

DOZIER, LAMONT

b. 16 June 1941, Detroit, Michigan, USA. Schooled in the blossoming vocal group scene of the late 50s, Lamont Dozier sang alongside several Motown notables in the Romeos and the Voice Masters during 1957-58. He befriended local songwriter and producer Berry Gordy around this time, and was one of Gordy's first signings when he launched the Motown label at the end of the decade. Dozier issued his debut single, 'Let's Talk It Over', under the pseudonym 'Lamont Anthony' in 1960, and issued two further singles in the early 60s. In 1963, he recorded a one-off release with Motown songwriter Eddie Holland and was soon persuaded into a writing and production team with Eddie and his brother Brian Holland. The Holland/Dozier/Holland credit graced the majority of Motown's hit records for the next five years, as the trio struck up particularly successful working relationships with the Supremes and the Four Tops. Dozier contributed both lyrics and music to the partnership's creations, proving the initial impetus for hits such as 'Stop! In The Name Of Love' by the Supremes, 'Bernadette' by the Four Tops and 'Jimmy Mack' by Martha And The Vandellas. As a pianist, arranger and producer, Dozier was also prominent in the studio, supporting the central role of Brian Holland in the recording process.

Dozier and the Hollands left Motown in 1967, unhappy at the financial and artistic restrictions imposed by Gordy. The following year, they set up their own rival companies, Invictus and Hot Wax Records, who produced hits for artists such as Freda Payne and the Chairmen Of The Board. Dozier resumed his own recording career in 1972, registering a US hit with 'Why Can't We Be Lovers', and receiving critical acclaim for a series of duets with Brian Holland. The Holland/Dozier/Holland partnership was fragmenting, however, and in 1973 Dozier severed his ties with Invictus and signed to ABC. *Out Here On My Own* and *Black Bach* demonstrated the creative liberation Dozier felt outside the constraints of the HDH team, and he enjoyed major US hits in 1974 with 'Trying To Hold Onto My Woman', the anti-Nixon diatribe 'Fish Ain't Bitin'', and 'Let Me Start Tonite'. Dozier switched labels to Warner Brothers in 1976, issuing the highly regarded *Peddlin' Music On The Side* the following year. That album included the classic 'Goin' Back To My Roots', an avowal of black pride that became a big hit in the hands of Odyssey in the early 80s. Dozier also continued his production work, overseeing Aretha Franklin's *Sweet Passion* in 1977, plus recordings by Zingara and Al Wilson. In the late 70s and early 80s, Dozier's brand of soul music lost ground to the burgeoning disco scene. After several overlooked albums on Warners and A&M, he re-emerged in 1983 on his own Megaphone label, recording the muscular *Bigger Than Life*, and paying tribute to his own heritage with a remarkable 18-minute hits medley, 'The Motor City Scene'. Since then, he has remained out of the public eye, working sporadically on production projects with the Holland brothers.

● ALBUMS: *Out Here On My Own* (ABC 1973)★★, *Black Bach* (ABC 1974)★★, *Love And Beauty* (ABC 1975)★★, *Right There* (Warners 1976)★★, *Peddlin' Music On The Side* (Warners 1977)★★★, *Bittersweet* (Warners 1979)★★, *Working On You* (Columbia 1981)★★, *Lamont* (A&M 1982)★★★, *Bigger Than Life* (Megaphone 1983)★★.

Dr. Feelgood

The most enduring act to emerge from the much touted 'pub rock' scene, Dr. Feelgood was formed in 1971. The original line-up included Lee Brilleaux (b. 1953, d. 7 April 1994; vocals/harmonica), Wilko Johnson (b. John Wilkinson, 1947; guitar), John B. Sparks (b. 1953; bass), John Potter (piano) and 'Bandsman' Howarth (drums). When the latter pair dropped out, the remaining trio recruited a permanent drummer in John 'The Big Figure' Martin. Initially based in Canvey Island, Essex, on the Thames estuary, Dr. Feelgood broke into the London circuit in 1974. Brilleaux's menacing personality complemented Johnson's propulsive, jerky stage manner, while the guitarist's staccato style, modelled on Mick Green of the Pirates, emphasized the group's idiosyncratic brand of rhythm and blues. Their debut album, *Down By The Jetty*, was released in 1974, but despite critical approbation, it was not until the following year that the quartet secured due commercial success with *Stupidity*. Recorded live in concert, this raw, compulsive set topped the UK charts and the group's status seemed assured. However, internal friction led to Johnson's departure during sessions for a projected fourth album and although his replacement, John 'Gypie' Mayo, was an accomplished guitarist, he lacked the striking visual image of his predecessor. Dr. Feelgood then embarked on a more mainstream direction which was only intermittently successful. 'Milk And Alcohol' (1978) gave them their sole UK Top 10 hit, but they now seemed curiously anachronistic in the face of the punk upheaval. In 1981 Johnny Guitar replaced Mayo, while the following year both Sparks and the Big Figure decided to leave the line-up. Brilleaux meanwhile continued undeterred, and while Dr. Feelgood could claim a loyal audience, it was an increasingly small one. However, they remained a popular live attraction in the USA where their records also achieved commercial success. In 1993 Brilleaux was diagnosed as having lymphoma and, owing to the extensive treatment he was receiving, had to break the band's often-inexorable touring schedule for the first time in over 20 years. He died the following year.

● ALBUMS: *Down By The Jetty* (United Artists 1975)★★★★, *Malpractice* (United Artists 1975)★★★, *Stupidity* (United Artists 1976)★★★, *Sneakin' Suspicion* (United Artists 1977)★★, *Be Seeing You* (United Artists 1977)★★★, *Private Practice* (United Artists 1978)★★★, *As It Happens* (United Artists 1979)★★★, *Let It Roll* (United Artists 1979)★★, *A Case Of The Shakes* (United Artists 1980)★★, *On The Job* (Liberty 1981)★★, *Fast Women And Slow Horses* (Chiswick 1982)★★, *Mad Man Blues* (I.D. 1985)★★★, *Doctor's Orders* (Demon 1986)★★, *Brilleaux* (Demon 1986)★★, *Classic Dr. Feelgood* (Stiff 1987)★★, *Live In London* (Grand 1990)★★★, *The Feelgood Factor* (1993)★★, *Down At The Doctors* (Grand 1994)★★, *On The Road Again* (Grand 1996)★★★.

● COMPILATIONS: *Casebook* (Liberty 1981)★★, *Case History - The Best Of Dr. Feelgood* (EMI 1987)★★★, *Singles (The UA Years)* (Liberty 1989)★★★, *Looking Back* 4-CD box set (EMI 1995)★★★, *25 Years Of Dr. Feelgood* (Grand 1997)★★★★.

Dr. John

b. Malcolm John Rebennack, 21 November 1940, New Orleans, Louisiana, USA. Dr. John has built a career since the 60s as a consummate New Orleans musician, incorporating funk, rock 'n' roll, jazz and R&B into his sound. Rebennack's distinctive vocal growl and virtuoso piano playing brought him acclaim among critics and fellow artists, although his commercial successes have not equalled that recognition. Rebennack's musical education began in the 40s when he accompanied his father to blues clubs. At the age of 14 he began frequenting recording studios, and wrote his first songs at that time. By 1957 he was working as a session musician, playing guitar, keyboards and other instruments on recordings issued on such labels as Ace, Ric, Rex and Ebb. He made his first recording under his own name, 'Storm Warning', for Rex during that same year. His first album was recorded for Rex in 1958, and others followed on Ace and AFO Records with little success. In 1958 he also co-wrote 'Lights Out', recorded by Jerry Byrne, and toured with Byrne and Frankie Ford. By 1962 Rebennack had already played on countless sessions for such renowned producers as Phil Spector, Harold Battiste, H.B. Barnum and Sonny Bono (later of Sonny And Cher). Rebennack formed his own bands during the early 60s but they did not take off. By the mid-60s Rebennack had moved to Los Angeles, where he fused his New Orleans roots with the emerging west coast psychedelic sound, and he developed the persona Dr. John Creux, The Night Tripper. The character was based on one established by singer Prince La La, but Rebennack made it his own through the intoxicating brew of voodoo incantations and New Orleans heritage. An album, *Zu Zu Man*, for A&M Records, did not catch on when released in 1965. In 1968 Dr. John was signed to Atco Records and released *Gris Gris*, which received critical acclaim but did not chart. This exceptional collection included the classic 'Walk On Gilded Splinters' and inspired several similarly styled successors, winning respect from fellow musicians, and resulting in Eric Clapton and Mick Jagger guesting on a later album. The same musical formula and exotic image were pursued on follow-up albums, *Babylon* and *Remedies*. Meanwhile, he toured on the rock festival and ballroom circuit and continued to do session work. In 1971, Dr. John charted for the first time with *Dr. John, The Night Tripper (The Sun, Moon And Herbs)*. The 1972 *Gumbo* album, produced by Jerry Wexler, charted, as did the single 'Iko Iko'. His biggest US hit came in 1973 with the single 'Right Place, Wrong Time', which reached number 9; the accompanying album, *In The Right Place*, was also his best-selling, reaching number 24. These crafted, colourful albums featured the instrumental muscle of the Meters, but despite a new-found popularity, the artist parted from his record label, Atlantic, and subsequent work failed to achieve a similar status. During that year he toured with the New Orleans band the Meters, and recorded *Triumvirate* with Michael Bloomfield and John Hammond. The single 'Such A Night' also charted in 1973. Dr. John continued to record throughout the 70s and 80s for numerous labels, among them United Artists, Horizon and Clean Cuts, the latter releasing *Dr. John Plays Mac Rebennack*, a solo piano album, in 1981. In the meantime, he continued to draw sizeable audiences as a concert act across the USA, and added radio jingle work to his live and recorded work (he continued to play on many sessions). He recorded *Bluesiana Triangle* with jazz musicians Art Blakey and David 'Fathead' Newman and released *In A Sentimental Mood*, a collection of interpretations of standards including a moody duet with Rickie Lee Jones, on Warner Brothers Records. Despite employing a low-key approach to recording, Dr. John has remained a respected figure. His live appearances are now less frequent, but this irrepressible artist continues his role as a tireless champion of Crescent City music. In 1997 he signed to Parlophone Records, and recorded tracks with Spiritualized, Supergrass, Paul Weller and Primal Scream for a forthcoming album.

● ALBUMS: *Zu Zu Man* (A&M 1965)★★★, *Gris Gris* (Atco 1968)★★★★, *Babylon* (Atco 1969)★★★, *Remedies* (Atco 1970)★★★, *Dr. John, The Night Tripper (The Sun, Moon And Herbs)* (Atco 1971)★★★, *Dr. John's Gumbo* (Atco 1972)★★★★, *In The Right Place* (Atco 1973)★★★, with John Hammond, Mike Bloomfield *Triumvirate* (Columbia 1973)★★★, *Desitively Bonnaroo* (Atco 1974)★★★, *Hollywood Be Thy Name* (United Artists 1975)★★, *Cut Me While I'm Hot* (1975)★★, *City Lights* (Horizon 1978)★★★, *Tango Palace* (Horizon 1979)★★, with Chris Barber *Take Me Back To New Orleans* (1980)★★★, *Love Potion* (1981)★★, *Dr. John Plays Mac Rebennack* (Clean Cuts 1982)★★★, *The Brightest Smile In Town* (Clean Cuts 1983)★★★, *Such A Night - Live In London* (Spindrift 1984)★★★, *In A Sentimental Mood* (Warners 1989)★★, with Art Blakey, David 'Fathead' Newman *Bluesiana Triangle* (1990)★★★, *Going Back To New Orleans* (1992)★★★, *Television* (GRP 1994)★★, *Afterglow* (Blue Thumb 1995)★★, *Trippin' Live* (Eagle 1997)★★★.

● COMPILATIONS: *I Been Hoodood* (Edsel 1984)★★★, *In The Night* (Topline 1985)★★★, *Mos' Scocious* 2-CD set (Rhino 1994)★★★★, *The Best Of ...* (Rhino 1995)★★★★.

● VIDEOS: *Doctor John And Chris Barber, Live At The Marquee Club* (Jettisoundz 1986), *Live At The Marquee* (Hendring Video 1990).

● FURTHER READING: *Dr. John: Under A Hoodoo Moon*, Mac Rebennack with Jack Rummel.

DRAMATICS

This R&B vocal group was formed in Detroit in 1964 as the Sensations. They changed their name to the Dramatics in 1965 and originally consisted of lead Larry Reed, Rob Davis, Elbert Wilkins, Robert Ellington, Larry Demps (b. 23 February 1949) and Ron Banks (b. 10 May 1951, Detroit, Michigan, USA). Ellington quickly dropped out. The Dramatics were a typical 60s stand-up vocal group, specializing in romantic ballads, but ably made the transition to the disco era in the late 70s with aggressive dance numbers. They made their debut on the charts with a minor R&B hit in 1967, 'All Because Of You,' which, like all their releases in the 60s, was issued on a small Detroit label. Around 1968, Reed and Davis were replaced by William 'Wee Gee' Howard and Willie Ford (b. 10 July 1950), respectively. The reshaped quintet's fortunes flourished when Detroit producers Don Davis and Tony Hestor took command of their career and the group signed to the Memphis-based Stax Records in 1971. US hits with the label included 'Whatcha See Is Whatcha Get' (R&B number 3 and pop number 9, 1971), 'In The Rain' (R&B number 1 and pop number 5, 1972) and 'Hey You! Get Off My Mountain' (R&B number 5 and pop Top 50, 1973). In 1973 Howard left to establish his solo career as 'Wee Gee,' and new lead L.J. Reynolds (b. 1953, Saginaw, Michigan, USA), previously of Chocolate Syrup, was recruited by group leader Ron Banks, while Wilkins was replaced by Lenny Mayes. In 1974 the Dramatics left Stax, and the following year began an association with Los Angeles-based ABC while still recording in Detroit under Davis and Hestor. US hits at ABC included the ballad 'Me And Mrs. Jones' (R&B number 4 and pop Top 50, 1975), 'Be My Girl' (R&B number 3, 1976) and 'Shake It Well' (R&B number 4, 1977). Switching to MCA in 1979, the group secured their last Top 10 hit with 'Welcome Back Home' (R&B number 9, 1980). Shortly afterwards L.J. Reynolds left to establish a solo career, and in 1981 Craig Jones was recruited in his place, but they disbanded in 1982 after Ron Banks left to start a solo career. The Dramatics were reunited in the late 80s, and their grasp of superior soul remained as sure as ever.

● ALBUMS: *Whatcha See Is Whatcha Get* (Volt 1972)★★★★, *Dramatically Yours* (Volt 1973)★★★★, *A*

Dramatic Experience (Volt 1973)★★★★, with the Dells *The Dells vs. The Dramatics* (Cadet 1974)★★★, *The Dramatic Jackpot* (ABC 1975)★★★, *Drama V* (ABC 1975)★★★, *Joy Ride* (ABC 1976)★★★, *Shake It Well* (ABC 1977)★★★, *Do What You Wanna Do* (ABC 1978)★★★★, *Anytime Anyplace* (MCA 1979)★★★, *The Dramatic Way* (MCA 1980)★★★, *10 And A Half* (MCA 1980)★★★, *New Dimensions* (Capitol 1982)★★★, *Reunion* (Volt 1986)★★★, *The Dramatics - Live* (Volt 1988)★★, *Positive State Of Mind* (Volt 1989)★★★, *Stone Cold* (Volt 1990)★★★.
Solo: L.J. Reynolds *Travellin'* (Capitol 1982)★★★, *Lovin' Man* (Mercury 1984)★★★, *Tell Me You Will* (Fantasy 1987)★★★★.
● COMPILATIONS: *Best Of The Dramatics* (Stax 1976)★★★, *Whatcha See Is Whatcha Get/A Dramatic Experience* (Stax 1991)★★★★, *The ABC Years 1974-1980* (Ichiban 1996)★★★.

DREAMERS

R&B/doo-wop group the Dreamers formed in 1958 at a family wedding, attended by cousins Frank Cammarata (lead and tenor), Bob Malara (tenor), Luke 'Babe' Beradis (tenor and baritone) and Dominic Canzano (baritone and bass), with the only non-cousin John 'Buddy' Trancynger (baritone and bass). End Records promptly signed the band to its new offshoot, Goldisc. The sentimental ballad 'Teenagers Vow Of Love' proved popular in the New York area during 1960, when it was released as their debut recording. Afterwards Berardis and Canzano were replaced by Frank Nicholas (from the Meridians) and Frank DiGilio as the group found a new home at Cousins Records. Their first release there was a highly idiosyncratic version of Tony Bennett's 'Because Of You', but when it transferred mid-release to Cousins' May Records subsidiary, the momentum was lost, and with it the chance of an extended musical career. Afterwards, their opportunities to record disappeared as they concentrated on a stage show that proved particularly popular at service bases. They broke up in 1963, but re-formed briefly in the mid-80s.
● ALBUMS: *Yesterday Once More* (Dream 1987)★★★.

DRENNON, EDDIE

This American musician/arranger studied violin and composition at Howard University and worked with various people, such as the New Jersey Symphony and Bo Diddley. He recorded 20 tracks with Diddley and the electric violin sound that he invented was later 'borrowed' by the pioneering R&B band (and Diddley fans) the Yardbirds. As a soloist he recorded for Chess and RCA and also did a great deal of session work. In the 70s he was based in Washington and his 12-piece string section backed acts such as the O'Jays and the Stylistics when they came to town. His sole hit came with BBS Unlimited, an eight-piece group plus female vocalists and strings, which he formed in 1971. The disco hit 'Let's Do The Latin Hustle' was originally released in the USA on Friends & Co in 1975 and just made the R&B Top 40. Combining the sounds of MFSB and Barry White with a Latin dance beat, it topped the UK soul chart and made the Top 20. The song is perhaps best remembered because of its UK cover version (Drennon called it 'the counterfeit version') by Worcestershire group the M&O Band, who were accused of using part of Drennon's track on their record. His follow-up was 'Let's Do It Again', but the public did not take up the offer.
● ALBUMS: *Collage* (Pye 1976)★★.

DREW, PATTI

b. 29 December 1944, Charleston, South Carolina, USA, and raised in Evanston, Illinois. As lead singer of the Drew-vels, a group consisting of herself, her sisters Lorraine and Erma, and bass singer Carlton Black, she and the band had several local hits, notably 'Tell Him' (1963) and 'It's My Time' (1964). Drew became a solo artist two years later and achieved her biggest hits with a remake of 'Tell Him' (number 22 R&B, number 85), from 1967, and 'Workin' On A Groovy Thing' (number 34 R&B, number 62 pop), from 1968, a Neil Sedaka composition that was also a hit for the Fifth Dimension. After Drew's last record with Capitol Records in 1970, she essentially retired from the business a year later. She made one more record for Inovation in 1975. In the 80s she occasionally worked the local lounges in her home-town of Evanston with Carlton Black in a group called Front Line.
● ALBUMS: *Tell Him* (Capitol 1967)★★★, *Working On A Groovy Thing* (Capitol 1968)★★★, *I've Been Here All The Time* (Capitol 1969)★★★, *Wild Is Love* (Capitol 1970)★★★.
● COMPILATIONS: *Golden Classics* (Collectables 1994)★★★.

DRIFTERS

Formed in 1953 in New York, USA, at the behest of Atlantic Records, this influential R&B vocal group was initially envisaged as a vehicle for ex-Dominoes singer Clyde McPhatter. Gerhart Thrasher, Andrew Thrasher and Bill Pinkney completed the new quartet which, as Clyde McPhatter and the Drifters, achieved a number 1 R&B hit with their debut single, 'Money Honey'. Follow-up releases, including 'Such A Night', 'Lucille' and 'Honey Love' (a second chart-topper), also proved highly successful, while the juxtaposition of McPhatter's soaring tenor against the frenzied support of the other members provided a link between gospel and rock 'n' roll styles. The leader's interplay with bassist Pinkey breathed new life into 'White Christmas', the group's sixth R&B hit, but McPhatter's induction into the armed forces in 1954 was a blow that the Drifters struggled to withstand. The vocalist opted for a solo career upon leaving the services, and although his former group did enjoy success with 'Adorable' (number 1 R&B 1955), 'Steamboat' (1955), 'Ruby Baby' (1956) and 'Fools Fall In Love' (1957), such recordings featured a variety of lead singers, including David Baughn and Johnny Moore. A greater emphasis on pop material ensued, but tension between the group and their manager, George Treadwell, resulted in an irrevocable split. Having fired the extant line-up in 1958, Treadwell, who owned the copyright to the Drifters' name, invited another act, the Five Crowns, to adopt the appellation. Ben E. King (tenor), Charlie Thomas (tenor),

Doc Green Jnr. (baritone) and Elsbearry Hobbes (b. *c.*1936, d. 31 May 1996, New York, USA; bass), plus guitarist Reggie Kimber, duly became 'the Drifters', and declared their new-found role with 'There Goes My Baby'. Written and produced by Leiber And Stoller, this pioneering release featured a Latin rhythm and string section, the first time such embellishments had appeared on an R&B recording. The single not only topped the R&B chart, it also reached number 2 on the US pop listings, and anticipated the 'symphonic' style later developed by Phil Spector.

Further excellent releases followed, notably 'Dance With Me' (1959), 'This Magic Moment' (1960) and 'Save The Last Dance For Me', the last of which topped the US pop chart and reached number 2 in the UK. However, King left for a solo career following 'I Count The Tears' (1960), and was replaced by Rudy Lewis, who fronted the group until his premature death in 1964. The Drifters continued to enjoy hits during this period and songs such as 'Sweets For My Sweet', 'When My Little Girl Is Smiling', 'Up On The Roof' and 'On Broadway' were not only entertaining in their own right, but also provided inspiration, and material, for many emergent British acts, notably the Searchers, who took the first-named song to the top of the UK chart. Johnny Moore, who had returned to the line-up in 1963, took over the lead vocal slot from Lewis. 'Under The Boardwalk', recorded the day after the latter's passing, was the Drifters' last US Top 10 pop hit, although the group remained a popular attraction. Bert Berns had taken over production from Leiber and Stoller, and in doing so brought a soul-based urgency to their work, as evinced by 'One Way Love' and 'Saturday Night At The Movies' (1964). When he left Atlantic to found the Bang label, the Drifters found themselves increasingly overshadowed by newer, more contemporary artists and, bedevilled by lesser material and frequent changes in personnel, the group began to slip from prominence. However, their career was revitalized in 1972 when two re-released singles, 'At The Club' and 'Come On Over To My Place', reached the UK Top 10. A new recording contract with Bell was then secured and British songwriters/producers Tony Macauley, Roger Cook and Roger Greenaway fashioned a series of singles redolent of the Drifters' 'classic' era. Purists poured scorn on their efforts, but, between 1973 and 1975, the group, still led by Moore, enjoyed six UK Top 10 hits, including 'Come On Over To My Place', 'Kissin' In The Back Row Of The Movies', 'Down On The Beach Tonight' and 'There Goes My First Love'. This success ultimately waned as the decade progressed, and in 1982 Moore left the line-up. He was replaced, paradoxically, by Ben E. King, who in turn brought the Drifters back to Atlantic. However, despite completing some new recordings, the group found it impossible to escape its heritage, as evinced by the numerous 'hits' repackages and corresponding live appearances on the cabaret and nostalgia circuits. They were inducted into the Rock And Roll Hall Of Fame in 1988.

● ALBUMS: *Save The Last Dance For Me* (Atlantic 1961)★★★★, *The Good Life With The Drifters* (Atlantic 1964)★★★★, *The Drifters* (Clarion 1964)★★, *I'll Take You Where The Music's Playing* (Atlantic 1965)★★★, *Souvenirs* (Bell 1974)★★★, *Love Games* (Bell 1975)★★★, *There Goes My First Love* (Bell 1975)★★★, *Every Night's A Saturday Night* (Bell 1976)★★★, *Greatest Hits Live* (Astan 1984)★★, *Live At Havard University* (Showcase 1986)★★.

● COMPILATIONS: *Up On The Roof - The Best Of The Drifters* (Atlantic 1963)★★★★, *The Drifters Golden Hits* (Atlantic 1968)★★★★, *24 Original Hits* (Atlantic 1975)★★★★, *The Collection* (Castle 1987)★★★, *Diamond Series: The Drifters* (RCA 1988)★★★, *Best Of The Drifters* (Pickwick 1990)★★★, *Let The Boogie Woogie Roll - Greatest Hits (1953-58)* (Atlantic 1993)★★★, *All Time Greatest Hits And More (1959-65)* (Atlantic 1993)★★★★, *Up On The Roof, On Broadway & Under The Boardwalk* (Rhino/Pickwick 1995)★★★, *Rockin' And Driftin': The Drifters Box* 3-CD box set (Rhino 1996)★★★★, *Anthology One: Clyde & The Drifters* (Sequel 1996)★★★★, *Anthology Two: Rockin' & Driftin'* (Sequel 1996)★★★, *Anthology Three: Save The Last Dance For Me* (Sequel 1996)★★★★, *Anthology Four: Up On The Roof* (Sequel 1996)★★★★, *Anthology Five: Under The Boardwalk* (Sequel 1997)★★★★, *Anthology Six: The Good Life With The Drifters* (Sequel 1997)★★★, *Anthology Seven: I'll Take You Where The Music's Playing* (Sequel 1997)★★★★.

● FURTHER READING: *The Drifters: The Rise And Fall Of The Black Vocal Group*, Bill Millar. *Save The Last Dance For Me: The Musical Legacy 1953-92*, Tony Allan and Faye Treadwell.

Dru Hill

R&B group Dru Hill took their name from the historic Druid Hill Park complex in Baltimore, USA, where all four members were raised. They began their rise to fame in the mid-90s, largely through the intervention of Island Records' Hiriam Hicks - formerly manager of Boyz II Men. He was looking for a group to record a song, 'Tell Me', for the soundtrack to the film *Eddie*, to which Island held the rights. A tape of the quartet was passed to him by University Music president Haqq Islam. So impressed was Hicks after meeting the group that, not only did he ask them to perform a version of 'Tell Me' on the spot, but he also signed them to a worldwide contract with Island. At that time the group members - Jazz, Nokio, Woody and Sisquo, were all still in their teens. Nevertheless, their splendid self-titled debut album sounded impressively mature. The smoky jazz and R&B tracks benefited enormously from the input of producers Keith Sweat, Stanley Brown and Darryl Simmons, though Nokio also co-wrote and produced much of the contents. While the group's syncopated vocals were one highlight, Sisquo and Jazz also contributed heavily as musicians, playing keyboards, bass and trumpet between them.

● ALBUMS: *Dru Hill* (Island 1996)★★★.

Du Droppers

Although the Du Droppers formed in Harlem, New York, USA, in 1952, each member of the vocal quartet had already sung within their local gospel communities. Indeed, while doo-wop was primarily a young man's concern, the Du Droppers - J.C. 'Junior' Caleb Ginyard (b. 15 January 1910, St. Matthews, South Carolina, USA, d. 11

August 1978; lead), Harvey Ray (tenor/baritone), Willie Ray (tenor/baritone) and Eddie Hashew (bass) - had an average age of well over 40 at formation. Ginyard's previous experience was the most extensive, having sung with the Royal Harmony Singers, Jubalaires and Dixieaires. As the Du Droppers they rehearsed in basements until Paul Kapp, manager of the Delta Rhythm Boys, took over. They made their debut at the end of 1952 with a single for Bobby Robinson's Red Robin Records in Harlem, 'Can't Do Sixty No More'. This was an answer record to the Dominoes' 'Sixty Minute Man', but failed to replicate its success. After replacing Hashew with Bob Kornegay the group passed an audition for RCA Records, making their debut with 'I Want To Know (What You Do When You Go Round There)'. Released in March 1953, it made number 3 in the *Billboard* R&B charts. In retaliation Red Robin issued a single from masters that they still held, 'Come On And Love Me Baby'. However, its arrival was eclipsed by the Du Droppers' second release on RCA, 'I Found Out (What You Do When You Go Round There)', which continued firmly in the vein of their label debut. Continuing the parallels, it too hit number 3 in the R&B charts. 'Whatever You're Doin' was also an extension of the theme, but failed to break the charts, as did their first ballad, 'Don't Pass Me By'. RCA then initiated a new R&B subsidiary, Groove Records, and the Du Droppers gave the label its first release, 'Speed King'. For the subsequent 'How Much Longer', Prentice Moreland expanded the group to a quintet. He soon departed for spells in the Dominoes and Cadets, while the Du Droppers regrouped with the addition of Ravens singer Joe Van Loan. He did not last long, and was forced to 'leave' following record company politicking between Herald Records (who wanted to sign the Du Droppers, and who had Van Loan under contract anyway) and RCA (who wished to exercise their option for another year). Harvey Ray also left the fold. From then on the lead role was handled by Charlie Hughes (later of the Drifters) in the studio and Van Loan live. Hughes made his debut on the April 1955 single 'Give Me Some Consideration', after which Harvey Ray rejoined for a Canadian tour. One final single emerged amid all the confusion caused by the shifting personnel, 'You're Mine Already', before Ginyard left to join the Golden Gate Quartet. Though the other members struggled to carry on, this signalled the death knell for the Du Droppers.

● COMPILATIONS: *Can't Do Sixty No More* (Dr. Horse 1987)★★★.

Dubs

The original members of this vocal group from Harlem, New York, USA, were lead Richard Blandon, first tenor Billy Carlisle, tenor Cleveland Still, baritone James 'Jake' Miller, and bass Thomas Gardner. They came together in 1957 and were an amalgamation of members of two previous groups. Blandon and Carlisle had previously been with the Five Wings who had recorded for King (notably 'Teardrops Are Falling'), and Still, Miller and Gardner had come from the Scale-Tones, who had recorded for Jay-Dee. (Shortly after their first recordings, the Dubs replaced Gardner with former Five Wing Tommy Grate.) The Dubs never had any national hits, but several of their songs still resonate today as 'golden oldies', primarily because of their popularity on the east coast doo-wop scene. The group had five consecutive regional hits; 'Don't Ask Me To Be Lonely' (1957), 'Could This Be Magic' (1957), 'Beside My Love' (1958), 'Be Sure My Love' (1958) and 'Chapel Of Dreams' (1958). The group broke up in 1958, but like many such groups there were sporadic reunions and break-ups in subsequent years. In the 80s there were two different Dubs groups playing the east coast oldies circuit.

● ALBUMS: *The Dubs Meet The Shells* (Josie 1962)★★★.

● COMPILATIONS: *The Best Of The Dubs* (Collectables 1991)★★★, *The Unavailable 24 Tracks* (Juke Box Treasures 1993)★★.

Ducanes

Vocal group the Ducanes formed in New Jersey, USA. After sessions, the quintet - Louis Biscardi (lead), Eddie Brian (baritone), Jeff Breny (first tenor), Rick Scrofan (second tenor) and Dennis Buckley - began to harmonize popular doo-wop songs of the day, taking their main influence from the Flamingos. Phil Spector began to work with the Ducanes on 'Yes, I Love You'. Spector signed them to a production contract, but later overheard them practising Louis Lymon And The Teenchords' 'I'm So Happy'. This became their first and only single after Spector had worked his magic with it, including adding a guitar contribution from Jimi Hendrix. It reached number 109 in the *Billboard* charts during July 1961. Spector had different priorities by this time, and the Ducanes blew their only chance to return to the studio with him. Given a country song, 'Tennessee', to record by Liberty Records, the Ducanes responded by savagely lampooning its sentimental lyrics and adding barnyard noises. When the head of the record company learned of what they were planning, they were ejected from the studio. With Spector concentrating on launching his own label, Philles Records, the Ducanes' recording days were over. They were still just 16 years old. Only Eddie Brian recorded again, with the Connotations and Autumns in the mid-80s.

Duke, Doris

b. Doris Curry, 1945, Sandersville, Florida, USA. Duke emerged from a variety of gospel groups including the Raspberry Singers (which included Chuck Jackson), the David Sisters, the Evangelistic Gospel Singers and the Caravans. Between 1963 and 1967, Duke worked as a New York session singer, before recording a solo single under the name Doris Willingham. In 1968 she toured Europe with Nina Simone and subsequently came under the aegis of producer Jerry 'Swamp Dogg' Williams. Several superb records followed including 'I Don't Care Anymore' and 'To The Other Woman (I'm The Other Woman)' (1970), the latter reaching number 7 in the R&B charts. In spite of an excellent album, *I'm A Loser*, Doris Duke failed to achieve mainstream success and her recording career faltered in the latter half of the 70s. Duke briefly re-emerged in 1981 with a new album, *Funky Fox*.

● ALBUMS: *I'm A Loser* (Mojo 1969)★★★, *Woman*

(Contempo 1975)★★★, *A Legend In Her Own Time* (Contempo 1975)★★★, *Funky Fox* (1981)★★.

DUNCAN, DARRYL

b. Chicago, Illinois, USA. Duncan formed the funk group Cashmere in the mid-70s. Leaving the band prior to their chart successes on the Philly World label, he concentrated on songwriting, composing the attractive ballad 'Simply Beautiful' for Jerry Butler in 1982, and collaborating with artists including Chaka Khan and Maurice White. Moving to Los Angeles in 1986, he produced an album for Foxy Records, and opened his own recording career with a track on Motown's Police Academy IV film soundtrack. He signed a full-scale contract with Motown in 1987, and won immediate acclaim for the tribute single 'James Brown (Part 1)', and for the mix of funk and soul styles on his self-produced debut album.

● ALBUMS: *Heaven* (Motown 1988)★★★.

DUPREES

A rock 'n' roll vocal group from Jersey City, New Jersey, USA. One of the most pop-sounding of the Italian-American groups that were in abundance during the late 50s and early 60s, the Duprees specialized in recording updated versions of old pop hits in a smooth style with a slight rock 'n' roll feel. The group comprised lead vocalist Joseph (Joey Vann) Canzano (d. 28 February 1984), Mike Arnone, Tom Bialablow, John Salvato, and Joe Santollo (d. 3 June 1981). The Duprees signed with Coed, who with their other acts, notably the Rivieras, revived old pop hits using teenage vocal harmony groups to convey them to the new rock 'n' roll audience. The Duprees' biggest hit was their 1962 remake of the old Jo Stafford hit, 'You Belong To Me' (number 7 pop). The best of their other seven chart entries were 'My Own True Love' (number 13 pop, a vocal version of 'Tara's Theme') and 'Have You Heard' (number 18 pop), a remake of the decade-old Joni James hit. The Duprees' last national hit record was in 1965. Recording for Jerry Ross's Heritage/Colossus label complex during 1968/9, the Duprees failed to chart with the same formula of updating old pop hits, such as Bobby Helms' 'My Special Angel' and Don Rondo's 'Two Different Worlds'. The group's last recording was 'Delicious', a disco song for RCA in 1975. Santollo died in 1981 and Canzano in 1984, but remnants of the Duprees have subsequently built a successful career playing the oldies doo-wop circuit in the New York and New Jersey area.

● ALBUMS: *You Belong To Me* (Coed 1962)★★★, *Have You Heard* (Coed 1963)★★★, *Total Recall* (Heritage 1968)★★, *Take Me As I Am* (1st Choice 1984)★★, *Silver Anniversary* (1987)★★.

● COMPILATIONS: *The Best Of The Duprees* (Rhino 1990)★★★, *The Best Of The Duprees* (Collectables 1990)★★★, *The Best Of The Duprees* (Sequel 1993)★★★, *Delicious: The Heritage Years* (Sequel 1994)★★★, *The Complete Coed Masters* (Ace 1996)★★★.

DYER, ADA

b. USA. Dyer first recorded as a backing vocalist for soul performer Norman Connors in the early 80s, before joining the dance-rock group Warp 9. They scored several US hits under the aegis of producer Jellybean Benitez, first on the Prism label, and later for Motown. After recording *Fade In, Fade Out* in 1985, the group dissolved, and Dyer was signed to a solo contract with Motown, where she was teamed with producer James Anthony Carmichael. This partnership produced *Meant To Be* in 1988, which enjoyed some acclaim in dance music circles, and the USA disco hit 'I'll Bet Ya, I'll Let Ya'.

● ALBUMS: *Meant To Be* (Motown 1988)★★★.

DYKE AND THE BLAZERS

This Los Angeles-based unit evolved when Christian (b. Arlester 'Dyke' Christian, 1943, Buffalo, New York, USA, d. 1971) teamed with the Blazers, formerly the O'Jays' backing group. 'Funky Broadway', Dyke's own composition, gave his band its debut hit in 1967, but their performance was overshadowed by Wilson Pickett's more successful remade version. Dyke And The Blazers secured two minor chart places with 'So Sharp' (1967) and 'Funky Walk' (1968), before 'We Got More Soul' and 'Let A Woman Be A Woman - Let A Man Be A Man' reached the US R&B Top 10/pop Top 40 in 1969. The group's raw and energetic dancefloor style was continued with three singles on the R&B charts in 1970. Christian was shot dead the following year.

● ALBUMS: *The Funky Broadway* (Original Sound 1967)★★★.

● COMPILATIONS: *Dyke's Greatest Hits* (Original Sound 1969)★★★, *So Sharp* i (Kent 1983)★★★, *So Sharp* ii (Kent 1991)★★★.

DYNAMIC SUPERIORS

Joining forces in Washington, DC, in 1963, Tony Washington, George Spann, George Wesley Peterbank Jnr., Michael McCalpin and Maurice Washington had to wait a decade to win a recording contract. Motown Records president Ewart Abner spotted them performing at a talent show in Atlanta, Georgia, and signed them to the label in 1974. They were teamed with the Ashford And Simpson writing and production team, and their debut album was a lush collection of romantic soul ballads that produced two hits, 'Shoe Shoe Shine' and 'Leave It Alone'. Their second album, *Pure Pleasure*, added a disco feel to the Superiors' sound, and spawned two further chart entries. In 1977, the group enjoyed some success with a disco rearrangement of the Martha And The Vandellas' hit, 'Nowhere To Run', but they subsequently left Motown, and attempts to secure a major label recording contract elsewhere proved unsuccessful.

● ALBUMS: *The Dynamic Superiors* (Motown 1975)★★★, *Pure Pleasure* (Motown 1975)★★★, *You Name It* (Motown 1976)★★, *Give And Take* (Motown 1977)★★.

DYSON, RONNIE

b. 5 June 1950, Washington, DC, USA, d. 10 November 1990. Having played a leading role in the Broadway production of Hair, Dyson pursued his thespian ambitions in *Salvation*, a less infamous musical, from 1970. One of its songs, '(If You Let Me Make Love To You Then) Why

Can't I Touch You?', was a US Top 10 hit, while the singer reached the R&B chart with several subsequent singles, including 'I Don't Wanna Cry' (1970) and 'The More You Do It (The More I Like It Done To Me)' (1976). In 1971 'When You Get Right Down To It' reached the UK Top 40. Despite switching labels from Columbia to Cotillion, Dyson was unable to achieve another major success, and 'All Over Your Face' (1983) was his last chart entry.

● ALBUMS: *(If You Let Me Make Love To You Then) Why Can't I Touch You?* (Columbia 1970)★★, *One Man Band* (Columbia 1973)★★, *The More You Do It* (Columbia 1977)★★, *If The Shoe Fits* (Cotillion 1979)★★.

E

EAGLIN, SNOOKS

b. Fird Eaglin, 21 January 1936, New Orleans, Louisiana, USA. Eaglin was left blind after a childhood illness and was given the nickname Snooks after a character in a radio series. He played guitar and sang in Baptist churches before winning a local talent contest in 1947. During the 50s he was a street singer in New Orleans, performing a variety of pop, blues and folk material. However, his first recordings, made by Harry Oster for Folkways and Folk-Lyric in 1958, emphasized the country blues side of his repertoire. He was equally at home in R&B, however, and his 1960 records for Imperial were in this format. During the 60s, Eaglin was a popular artist in New Orleans, where he frequently accompanied Professor Longhair on guitar. Eaglin returned to a 'songster' mix of folk and pop when recorded in 1972 by Quint Davis, and his later records showed a versatility ranging from flamenco to swamp-pop. Eaglin's 80s albums for Black Top were produced by Hammond Scott and included Anson Funderburgh (guitar), Grady Gaines (saxophones) and Sam Myers (harmonica).

● ALBUMS: *Blues From New Orleans Vol. 1* (Storyville 1958)★★★★, *New Orleans Street Singer* (Folkways 1958)★★★★, *Snooks Eaglin* (Heritage 1961)★★★, *That's All Right* (Bluesville 1962)★★★, *Possum Up A Simmon Tree* (Arhoolie 1971)★★★, *Legacy Of The Blues* (1971)★★★, *Down Yonder* (Sonet 1978)★★★, *Baby You Can Get Your Gun!* (Black Top 1987)★★★, *Out Of Nowhere* (Black Top 1989)★★★, *Teasin' You* (Black Top 1992)★★, *Soul's Edge* (Black Top 1995)★★★, *Live In Japan* (Black Top 1997)★★★.

● COMPILATIONS: *The Legacy Of The Blues Volume 2* (Sonet 1988)★★★★, *Country Boy Down In New Orleans* (Arhoolie 1993)★★★, *The Complete Imperial Recordings* (Capitol 1996)★★★★.

EARL-JEAN

b. Ethel 'Earl-Jean' McCrea, North Carolina, USA. Together with Margie Hendrix and Pat Lyles she formed the Cookies, who first recorded on Lamp in 1954. They joined Atlantic in 1955 and were heard singing backing vocals on many hits on that label in the mid-50s. They had their own Top 10 R&B hit in 1956 with 'In Paradise' and shortly afterwards went to work with Ray Charles under the name the Raelettes. Earl-Jean re-formed the group with new members Dorothy Jones and Margaret Ross in 1962, and signed to Goffin And King's Dimension label as both artists and session singers. They had US Top 20 hits with 'Chains' (later recorded by the Beatles) and 'Don't Say Nothin' Bad (About My Baby)'. In 1964 Earl-Jean went solo on Colpix and her first single, 'I'm Into Something Good', another Goffin and King composition, became her only US hit, reaching the bottom of the Top 40. A year later, the song became a UK number 1 hit for Herman's Hermits. Earl-Jean's follow-up single, 'Randy', failed to chart, and although she continued to record as Darlene McCrae, she was unable to achieve consistent success.

EARTH, WIND AND FIRE

The origins of this colourful, imaginative group date back to the 60s and Chicago's black music session circle. Drummer Maurice White (b. 19 December 1941, Memphis, Tennessee, USA) appeared on sessions for Etta James, Fontella Bass, Billy Stewart and more, before joining the Ramsey Lewis Trio in 1965. He left four years later to form the Salty Peppers, which prepared the way for an early version of Earth Wind and Fire. The new group - Verdine White (b. 25 July 1951, Illinois, USA; bass), Michael Beale (guitar), Wade Flemmons (vocals), Sherry Scott (vocals), Alex Thomas (trombone), Chet Washington (tenor saxophone), Don Whitehead (keyboards) and Yackov Ben Israel (percussion) - embarked on a diffuse direction, embracing jazz, R&B and funk, as well as elements of Latin and ballad styles. The extended jam 'Energy', from their second album, was artistically brave, but showed a lack of cohesion within the group. White then abandoned the line-up, save his brother, and pieced together a second group around Ronnie Laws (b. 3 October 1950, Houston, Texas, USA; saxophone, guitar), Philip Bailey (b. 8 May 1951, Denver, Colorado, USA; vocals), Larry Dunn (b. Lawrence Dunhill, 19 June 1953, Colorado, USA; keyboards), Roland Battista (guitar) and Jessica Cleaves (b. 1948; vocals). He retained the mystic air of the original group but tightened the sound immeasurably, blending the disparate elements into an intoxicating 'fire'. Two 1974 releases, *Head To The Sky* and *Open Our Eyes*, established the group as an album act, while the following year 'Shining Star' was a number 1 hit in both the US R&B and pop charts. Their eclectic mixture of soul and jazz was now fused to an irresistible rhythmic pulse, while the songs themselves grew ever more memorable. By the end of the decade they had regular successes with such infectious melodious singles as 'Fantasy', 'September', 'After The Love Has Gone' and 'Boogie Wonderland', the latter an energetic collaboration with the Emotions. A further recording, 'Got To Get You Into My Life', transformed the song into the soul classic composer Paul McCartney had originally envisaged. The line-up of Earth, Wind And Fire remained unstable. Philip Bailey and Ronnie Laws both embarked on solo careers as new saxophonists, guitarists and percussionists were added. White's interest in Egyptology and mysticism provided a visual platform for the expanded group, particularly in their striking live performances. However, following 11 gold albums, 1983's *Electric Universe* was an unexpected commercial flop, and prompted a four-year break. A slimline core quintet, comprising the White brothers, Andrew Woolfolk, Sheldon Reynolds and Philip Bailey, recorded *Touch The World* in 1987 but they failed to reclaim their erstwhile standing. *Heritage* (1990) featured cameos from rapper MC Hammer and Sly Stone, in an attempt to shift White's vision into the new decade. Since 1987 White has no longer toured with the band, but regained his enthusiasm with 1997's *In The Name Of Love*, a back-to-basics album recorded for new label Eagle.

● ALBUMS: *Earth, Wind And Fire* (Warners 1971)★★, *The Need Of Love* (Warners 1972)★★, *Last Days And Time* (Columbia 1972)★★, *Head To The Sky* (Columbia 1973)★★★, *Open Our Eyes* (Columbia 1974)★★★★, *That's The Way Of The World* (Columbia 1975)★★★★, *Gratitude* (Columbia 1975)★★★, *Spirit* (Columbia 1976)★★★, *All And All* (Columbia 1977)★★★, *I Am* (ARC 1979)★★★, *Faces* (ARC 1980)★★★, *Raise!* (ARC 1981)★★★, *Powerlight* (Columbia 1983)★★★, *Electric Universe* (Columbia 1983)★★, *Touch The World* (Columbia 1987)★★★, *Heritage* (Columbia 1990)★★, *Millennium* (1993)★★★, *Greatest Hits Live, Tokyo Japan* (Rhino 1996)★★, *In The Name Of Love* (Eagle 1997)★★★.

● COMPILATIONS: *The Best Of Earth, Wind And Fire, Volume 1* (ARC 1978)★★★★, *The Collection* (K-Tel 1986)★★★, *The Best Of Earth, Wind And Fire, Volume 2* (Columbia 1988)★★★★, *The Eternal Dance* (1993)★★★, *The Very Best Of* (1993)★★★.

Ebonys

Formed in Camden, New Jersey, USA, and comprising Jenny Holmes, David Beasley, James Tuten and Clarence Vaughan, the Ebonys had minor success in the early 70s with a Dells-styled approach of baritone lead with answering falsetto second lead. The group was discovered by Gamble And Huff and recorded consistently for their Philadelphia International Records label in the early 70s, but achieved only two sizeable hits on the R&B charts, 'You're The Reason Why' (number 10 R&B, number 51 pop) from 1971, and 'It's Forever' (number 14 R&B, number 68 pop) from 1973. The group recorded for Buddah in 1976 with little success, with only a minor single, 'Making Love Ain't No Fun (Without The One You Love)' (number 83 R&B), making the charts. It was their last chart record.

● COMPILATIONS: *The Ebonys* (Philadelphia International Records 1971)★★★, *The Ebonys* (Soul From The Vaults 1991)★★★.

Eddy And The Soul Band

b. Eddy Conrad, 1959, Gary, Indiana, USA. Conrad grew up in Indiana obsessed by the sound of Isaac Hayes' 'Theme From Shaft'. The first record he ever purchased, Conrad would spend his pocket money continually attending reruns of the film at local cinemas. 'As a kid you always have heroes but with John Shaft [the film's protagonist] it was serious. He had that certain macho feeling that every kid wishes he had too.' In 1985 he fulfilled a long-held ambition by re-recording the track, which became a number 13 UK chart hit. It might well have charted higher had another version of 'Theme From Shaft' by Van Twist not been released at the same time. Afterwards, however, Conrad and his band disappeared from view completely.

Edsels

This R&B vocal ensemble from Campbell, Ohio, USA, led by George Jones Jnr. (lead vocal), also included Marshall Sewell, James Reynolds, and brothers Harry and Larry Greene. They were named after the popular make of car. In 1959 they auditioned for a local music publisher who helped them secure a recording contract. Their debut single was the fast doo-wop outing 'Rama Lama Ding Dong' (written by Jones), originally released under the incorrect title of 'Lama Rama Ding Dong'. It was a local hit but flopped nationally. Two years later, when Marcels had a big hit with the similar-sounding doo-wop version of 'Blue Moon', a disc jockey was reminded of 'Rama Lama Ding Dong' and started playing it. Demand grew and it was re-released under its correct title and became a hit in the USA. By this time the Edsels had moved on and could not capitalize on their success. Although the original failed in the UK the song was a hit in 1978 when it was covered by Rocky Sharpe And The Replays.

● COMPILATIONS: *Rama Lama Ding Dong* (Relic 1993)★★.

Edwards, Alton

b. Zimbabwe. Edwards' first musical experience came as a percussionist with an oil-drum band before he moved to Zambia to study the flute. In the early 70s he returned to Zimbabwe to join the soul band Sabu as vocalist and bass player. He subsequently formed his own band, Unity, before travelling once more. In 1978 he moved to Zurich in Switzerland where he wrote songs for the Superlove group. His stay there was short-lived, however, and within a year he had moved to Los Angeles to work with Motown Records producer Clay McMurray. He finally embarked on a solo career in 1981 after moving to England. After securing a contract with CBS Records' subsidiary Streetwave, he recorded a number of songs that he had written over preceding years. One of these, 'I Just Wanna (Spend Some Time With You)', became a UK Top 20 hit at the beginning of 1982. However, follow-up efforts such as 'Take Me' did not repeat its success.

EDWARDS, DENNIS

b. 3 February 1943, Birmingham, Alabama, USA. Dennis Edwards became a member of the Fireworks vocal group in the early 60s, before joining the Contours in 1965. After they split in 1967, he appeared occasionally with the Temptations, becoming a full member of the group when he replaced David Ruffin as lead vocalist in 1968. He remained with them until 1977, lending his dramatic tenor voice to hits such as 'Cloud Nine', 'I Can't Get Next To You' and 'Papa Was A Rolling Stone'. When the Temptations left Motown for Atlantic, he chose to remain with the label and begin a solo career. While he was still working on his debut album, the group returned to Motown, and Edwards resumed his position as their lead singer. In 1984, he again parted company with the group, notching up a major hit single, 'Don't Look No Further', a duet with Siedah Garrett. Three additional chart successes followed in 1985, and Edwards also issued two well-received albums. When his solo career ran into difficulties in 1987, he accepted the invitation to rejoin the Temptations, and was featured on their 1987 release, *Together Again*.

● ALBUMS: *Don't Look Any Further* (Gordy 1984)★★★, *Coolin' Out* (Gordy 1985)★★★.

EDWARDS, JACKIE

b. Wilfred Edwards, 1938, Jamaica, d. 15 August 1992. The honeyed tones of Jackie Edwards graced hundreds of ska, R&B, soul, rocksteady, reggae and ballad recordings, from the time he composed and sang 'Your Eyes Are Dreaming', a sentimental ballad, and the gentle Latin-beat 'Tell Me Darling', for future Island Records owner Chris Blackwell in 1959. In 1962, when Blackwell set up Island Records in London, Edwards made the trip to Britain with him. At Island in the early years, his duties included not only singing and songwriting, but also delivering boxes of ska records by bus to the capital's suburban shops. His persistence paid off when, in 1966, the Spencer Davis Group achieved two consecutive UK number 1 pop hits with his now classic compositions, 'Keep On Running' and 'Somebody Help Me'. In more recent years he continued to issue records whose standards of production were variable, but on which his crooning justified his soubriquet of 'the original cool ruler'.

● ALBUMS: *The Most Of ...* (Island 1963)★★★, *Stand Up For Jesus* (Island 1964)★★★, *Come On Home* (Island 1966)★★★, *By Demand* (Island 1967)★★★, *Premature Golden Sands* (Island 1967)★★★, *I Do Love You* (Trojan 1973)★★★, *Sincerely* (Trojan 1978)★★, *King Of The Ghetto* (Black Music 1983)★★, *Original Cool Ruler* (Vista Sounds 1983)★★. With Millie Small: *Pledging My Love* (1967)★★★, *The Best Of Jackie & Millie* (1968)★★★.

● COMPILATIONS: *The Best Of* (Island 1966)★★★.

EDWARDS, TOMMY

b. 17 February 1922, Richmond, Virginia, USA, d. 22 October 1969, Virginia, USA. This jazz/pop/R&B singer-songwriter began his professional career in 1931. He wrote the hit 'That Chick's Too Young To Fry' for Louis Jordan in 1946. A demo recording of his own 'All Over Again' later won Edwards an MGM contract. Early releases included 'It's All In The Game' (US number 18 in 1951), a tune based on a 1912 melody by future US Vice-President Charles Gates Dawes. Edwards re-recorded the song in 1958 in a 'beat-ballad' arrangement, hitting number 1 on both sides of the Atlantic and eventually selling 3.5 million. The song was covered many times and provided hits for Cliff Richard (1963-64) and the Four Tops (1970) and was a notable album track by Van Morrison (1979). Edwards himself enjoyed five more hits during the next two years, including 'Love Is All We Need' and remakes of earlier successes 'Please Mr. Sun' and 'The Morning Side Of The Mountain'.

● ALBUMS: *For Young Lovers* (MGM 1958)★★★, *Sings* (Regent 1959)★★, *It's All In The Game* (MGM 1959)★★★★, *Step Out Singing* (MGM 1960)★★★, *You Started Me Dreaming* (MGM 1960)★★★, *In Hawaii* (MGM 1960)★, *Golden Country Hits* (MGM 1961)★, *Stardust* (MGM 1962)★★★, *Soft Strings And Two Guitars* (MGM 1962)★★★, *Tommy Edwards* (1965)★★.

● COMPILATIONS: *Greatest Hits* (MGM 1961)★★★, *The Very Best Of* (MGM 1963)★★★, *It's All In The Game: The Complete Hits* (Epic 1995)★★★★.

8TH DAY

This multi-talented vocal and instrumental group had their biggest hit in 1971 on Holland/Dozier/Holland's Invictus label with the infectious, million-selling 'She's Not Just Another Woman', even though the track had, in fact, been recorded some two years earlier with Steve Mancha on lead vocals, making the number sound very like an early 100 Proof Aged In Soul release, a group led by Mancha. For the 1971 follow-up, 'You've Got To Crawl (Before You Walk)', lead vocalist Melvin Davis, a long-term Detroit drummer/singer, was recruited, and the rest of the regular line-up of the group became Tony Newton (bass), Carole Stallings (vocals, electric violin), Anita Sherman (vocals, vibes), Michael Anthony (lead guitar), Bruce Nazarian (rhythm guitar, keyboards), Jerry Paul (percussion), Lynn Harter (background vocals) and, somewhat later, Lymon Woodard (organ) and Larry Hutchison (vocals, guitar). Although 8th Day were always correctly regarded as a Detroit group, Stallings and Sherman were actually from the west coast. The group's first three releases reached the US charts and they also cut a superb cover version of 100 Proof's 'Too Many Cooks'; however, they soon developed a penchant for quasi-gospel message-songs, aesthetically very good but not commercially very successful. When Invictus began to fall apart, the group did likewise. Paul, Nazarian and Newton formed the short-lived Deliverance, cutting one single for NCI. Then founder-member Newton moved to the west coast, joining the Tony Williams' New Lifetime, and later playing with Gary Moore and G-Force and Thelma Hopkins. In the mid-90s Anita Sherman was providing background vocals for artists such as Joe Cocker.

● ALBUMS: *8th Day* (Invictus 1971)★★★, *Gotta Get Home* (Invictus 1972)★★.

● COMPILATIONS: *The Best Of 8th Day* (1992)★★★.

EL DORADOS

This Chicago, Illinois R&B vocal group achieved fame with one of the great jump tracks of the early rock 'n' roll era, 'At My Front Door', also called 'Crazy Little Mama'. Members on that hit were Pirkle Lee Moses (lead), Louis Bradley (second tenor), Jewel Jones (first tenor), James Maddox (baritone) and Richard Nickens (d. 1991; bass). The group was formed in 1952, and signed with Vee Jay Records in 1954. The El Dorados achieved nothing but local hits until finding success with 'At My Front Door' in 1955, when it went to number 2 R&B and number 17 pop. The group's only other chart record was the mid-tempo 'I'll Be Forever Loving You' (number 8 R&B 1956). The group reorganized in 1958, when Pirkle Lee Moses was abandoned by the other members and recruited new singers from another Vee Jay group, the Kool Gents, whose lead, Dee Clark, had just deserted them. The new El Dorados besides Moses were Doug Brown, John McCall and Teddy Long (d. 1991), but having no luck with further releases, this group broke up in 1959. Despite the El Dorados' meagre chart success most of their records have been cherished by doo-wop fans, who find the group not only one of the more soulful-sounding of the 50s doo-wop ensembles but equally adept at both ballads (notably 'I Began To Realize') and jumps (typically 'Bim Bam Boom'). The group took, perhaps unconsciously, a music that most observers consider nothing more than a commercial entertainment and created a profound and genuine folk art. Both Teddy Long and Richard Nickens died in 1991.

● ALBUMS: *Crazy Little Mama* (Vee Jay 1957)★★★, *Bim Bam Boom* (1981)★★★, *Low Milage - High Octane* (1984)★★★.

EL VENOS

A rare sextet in the 50s R&B scene, this Pittsburgh group's ranks featured Leon Daniels (lead), sister Anna Mae Jackson (lead), brother Joey Daniels (baritone), Daniel Jackson (first tenor), Leon Taylor (second tenor) and Bernard Palmer (bass). They began on the familiar street-corner career route in 1955, eventually signing with RCA Records, where they were placed on their Groove Records R&B subsidiary. A few months later 'Geraldine', written by Taylor, was released to instant favour. The song was played on Dick Clark's *American Bandstand* television show, but the possibility of a live appearance was lost when the members were unable to raise the finance for the journey to Philadelphia. Instead the El Venos were forced to content themselves with local shows, often conducted with major artists such as the Heartbeats who were passing through Pittsburgh. They transferred to a second RCA affiliate, Vik Records, for their second single, 'You Must Be True', but this failed to match the impact of their debut. The next two years were spent raising money in order to travel to New York for auditions. However, Calico Records chose not to release the two songs the El Venos recorded with them. The same fate befell two more songs recorded for Mercury Records' Amp 3 subsidiary. Dispirited, the group broke up, with Anna Mae Jackson changing her name to Anne Keith and releasing a solo record, backed by the Altairs (the band formed by their erstwhile sponsor, Pittsburgh disc jockey Bill Powell).

ELBERT, DONNIE

b. 25 May 1936, New Orleans, Louisiana, USA, d. 31 January 1989. Elbert's prolific career began in the 50s as a member of the Vibraharps. His first solo hit, 'What Can I Do?', was released in 1957, but the singer's career was interrupted by a spell in the US Army. Discharged in 1961, recordings for Parkway Records and Checker then followed, before Elbert founded his own labels, Gateway/Upstate, in 1964. His reputation was secured by 'Run Little Girl' and 'A Little Piece Of Leather', compulsive performances highlighting Donnie's irrepressible falsetto. The latter single became a standard in UK soul clubs when it was released on the Sue label and on the strength of this popularity Elbert went to the UK where he married and settled. The singer pursued his career with several releases, including an album of Otis Redding cover versions, *Tribute To A King*. Elbert returned to the USA in 1970 although his pounding version of the Supremes' 'Where Did Our Love Go?' (1972) was recorded in London. A hit on both sides of the Atlantic, it was followed in 1972 by 'I Can't Help Myself', another reworking of a Tamla/Motown classic. Elbert's last UK chart entry came with a new, but inferior, version of 'A Little Bit Of Leather' (1972), although he continued to appear in the US R&B listings up until 1977. Elbert later moved to Canada where he became an A&R director with Polygram Records.

● ALBUMS: *The Sensational Donnie Elbert Sings* (King 1959)★★★, *Tribute To A King* (1968)★★, *Where Did Our Love Go* (All Platinum 1971)★★, *Have I Sinned* (1971)★★, *Stop In The Name of Love* (Avco 1972)★★, *A Little Bit Of Leather* (1972)★★, *Roots Of Donnie Elbert* (1973)★★★, *Dancin' The Night Away* (1977)★★.

ELGINS

US-born Johnny Dawson, Cleo Miller and Robert Fleming, later replaced by Norbert McClean, sang together in three Detroit vocal groups in the late 50s, the Sensations, the Five Emeralds and the Downbeats. Under the last of these names, they recorded two singles for Motown in 1959 and 1962. Also in 1962, Saundra Mallett (later Saundra Mallett Edwards) issued 'Camel Walk' for Tamla, backed by the Vandellas. Motown suggested that she join forces with the Downbeats, and the new group was named the Elgins after the title originally used by the Temptations when they first joined Motown. In the fiercely competitive climate of Motown Records in the mid-60s, the Elgins were forced to wait three years before they could issue a single, but 'Darling Baby' - written and produced by Holland/Dozier/ Holland - reached the US R&B Top 10 early in 1966. 'Heaven Must Have Sent You', which also exhibited the traditional Motown sound of the period, matched that success, but after one further hit in 1967, the group broke up. In 1971, the group enjoyed two unexpected UK Top 20 hits when Motown reissued 'Heaven Must Have Sent You' and the former b-side 'Put Yourself In My Place'. The Elgins re-formed to tour

Britain, with Yvonne Allen (a former session vocalist) taking the place of Saundra Mallett, but plans for the revitalized group to renew their recording career foundered. In 1989 Yvonne Allen, Johnny Dawson, Norman Mclean and Jimmy Charles recorded a new arrangement of 'Heaven Must Have Sent You' for producer Ian Levine. They continued working for his Motor City label in the 90s, releasing *Take The Train* and *Sensational*. The original lead vocalist on all their Motown material, Saundra Edwards, was also recording for the same label.

● ALBUMS: *Darling Baby* (VIP 1966)★★★, *Take The Train* (Motor City 1990)★★, *Sensational* (Motor City 1991)★★.

ELLIOTT, MISSY

b. *c*.1971, Virginia, USA. Hip-hop/R&B songwriter Missy 'Misdemeanor' Elliott has become one of the most esteemed composers in the New York 90s hip-hop firmament, providing material for artists including MC Lyte, Adina Howard and Jodeci. In 1997, she launched a solo career with the album *Supa Dupa Fly* and attendant single 'The Rain (Supa Dupa Fly)'. The well-connected Elliott was provided with immediate exposure for the song via rotation play of its Hype Williams-directed video on MTV. Co-produced with long-time collaborator Timbaland and producer DJ Magic, the album received excellent reviews, though Elliott was reluctant to commit herself fully to a career as a performer: 'I don't want to get caught up and be an artist always on the go, because once you do that, it's hard to get into the studio and do what I do.' The album also featured cameo appearances from Aaliyah and Busta Rhymes (Elliott has written songs for both). Despite her growing reputation and success, Elliott is still based in her home-town in Virginia, where she lives with her mother.

● ALBUMS: *Supa Dupa Fly* (East West 1997)★★★.

ELLIS, SHIRLEY

b. New York, New York, USA. Before striking out on a solo career in 1963, Ellis served an apprenticeship singing with an unsuccessful vocal group, the Metronones. Her strong voice was used to good effect on dance-floor ravers 'The Nitty Gritty' (number 4 R&B and number 8 pop in 1963) and '(That's) What The Nitty Gritty Is' (number 14 R&B 1964), and her future looked bright. Ellis, however, soon found herself in novelty song territory with catchy ditties written by her manager Lincoln Chase, namely, 'The Name Game' (number 4 R&B and number 3 pop in 1965) and 'The Clapping Song (Clap Pat Clap Slap)' (number 16 R&B and number 8 pop in 1965). The latter was the only UK success for Ellis, amazingly hitting twice, in 1965, when it reached number 6, and on an EP in 1978. The Belle Stars successfully revived 'The Clapping Song' in 1982.

● ALBUMS: *In Action* (Congress 1964)★★, *The Name Game* (Congress 1965)★★★, *Sugar, Let's Shing A Ling* (Columbia 1967)★★.

● COMPILATIONS: *The Very Best Of ...* (Taragon 1995)★★★.

ELLISON, LORRAINE

b. 1943, Philadelphia, Pennsylvania, USA, d. 17 August 1985. Although only associated with a few minor hits in the history of R&B, Ellison's intense, dramatic and highly gospelized vocal delivery helped define deep soul as a particular style. Ellison recorded with two gospel groups, the Ellison Singers and the Golden Chords, but left the latter in 1964 to pursue a solo career in R&B music. 'I Dig You Baby' (number 22 R&B) in 1965 was her first chart entry, but it was the powerful 'Stay With Me' (number 11 R&B, number 64 pop) in 1966 that established her reputation. Written and produced by Jerry Ragovoy, the song, featuring Ellison's awe-inspiring vocal pleas, ultimately proved to be a spectacular one-off performance. Nothing in her subsequent recordings emulated its naked emotion, and even the excellent 'Heart Be Still' (number 43 R&B, number 89 pop), from 1967, was something of an anti-climax. Ellison never charted again, not even with the original version of 'Try Just A Little Bit Harder' (1968), which rock singer Janis Joplin later remade with great success. Ellison's compositions, on which she often collaborated with her manager, Sam Bell (of Garnet Mimms And The Enchanters fame), were recorded by Howard Tate and Garnet Mimms.

● ALBUMS: *Heart And Soul* (Warners 1966)★★, *Stay With Me* (Warners 1970)★★★, *Lorraine Ellison* (Warners 1974)★★.

● COMPILATIONS: *The Best Of Philadelphia's Queen* (1976)★★★, *Stay With Me* (1985)★★★.

EMOTIONS

The Hutchinson sisters, Wanda (b. 17 December 1951; lead vocal), Sheila and Jeanette, first worked together in Chicago, Illinois, USA, as the Heavenly Sunbeams, then as the Hutchinson Sunbeams up to 1968. They recorded for several local companies prior to arriving at Stax on the recommendation of Pervis Staples of the Staple Singers. Their debut release for the label, 'So I Can Love You' (1969), reached the US Top 40, and introduced a series of excellent singles, including 'Show Me How' (1971) and 'I Could Never Be Happy' (1972). Although Jeanette was briefly replaced by a cousin, Theresa Davis, she latterly returned to the line-up, while a fourth sister, Pamela, came into the group when Davis left. The Emotions moved to Columbia Records in 1976 and began working under the aegis of Maurice White of Earth, Wind And Fire. 'Best Of My Love' was a US number 1 the following year while the singers secured further success with 'Boogie Wonderland' in 1979, an energetic collaboration with White's group. The Emotions continued to record into the 80s and if their material was sometimes disappointing, their harmonies remained as vibrant as ever.

● ALBUMS: *So I Can Love You* (Stax 1970)★★★, *Songs Of Love* (Stax 1971)★★★, *Untouched* (Stax 1972)★★★, *Flowers* (Columbia 1976)★★★, *Rejoice* (Columbia 1977)★★★, *Sunshine* (Stax 1977)★★★, *Sunbeam* (Columbia 1978)★★★, *Come Into Our World* (ARC 1979)★★★, *New Affair* (ARC 1981)★★, *If I Only Knew* (Motown 1985)★★.

● COMPILATIONS: *Chronicle: Greatest Hits*

(Stax/Fantasy 1979)★★★★, *Heart Association - The Best Of The Emotions* (Columbia 1979)★★★★.

En Vogue

Vocal dance/R&B outfit consisting of Dawn Robinson (b. *c.*1965, Connecticut, USA), Terry Ellis (b. *c.*1966, Texas, USA), Cindy Herron (b. *c.*1963, San Francisco, California, USA) and Maxine Jones (b. *c.*1962, Patterson, New Jersey, USA). They formed in Oakland, California, where they were auditioned by Denzil 'Denny' Foster and Thomas McElroy. The duo had worked together in both the Timex Social Club and Club Nouveau (who enjoyed big hits with 'Rumours' in 1986 and 'Lean On Me', a hip-hop version of Bill Withers' 70s classic, and a Grammy winner, in 1987). Afterwards they decided to write and produce under their own steam: 'When Tommy and I bumped into each other in the early 80s, we had the same notion. Everyone was saying R&B was tired and worn out. The new era was hip-hop and rap. But we thought: why not combine the two eras? Put good songs - and the 70s were loaded with good songs - over the new grooves.' En Vogue were formed in October 1988 after the duo auditioned to establish their own 'girl group'. Of the four selected, only Cindy Herron had previous 'showbiz' experience, winning Miss San Francisco and Miss Black California pageants, and also working as an actress. The group remained primarily responsible for their own image and songs, but they were groomed for success by joining Hammer's 1990 tour, and that of Freddie Jackson a year later. They went on to enjoy singles success with 'Hold On' and 'Lies' in 1990. The latter introduced female rapper Debbie T, and added a new, post-feminist outlook to traditional R&B concerns. Their second album, meanwhile, featured two Curtis Mayfield cover versions, and produced further hits in 'Free Your Mind' and 'Give It Up, Turn It Loose'. Heavily influenced by Chaka Khan, En Vogue, in turn, helped to start the New Jill Swing movement, which has thrown up the likes of SWV, Jade and TLC. They were approached by Roseanne Barr and her then-husband Tom Arnold to appear in their own sitcom. These distractions did not affect their singing or their commercial appeal into the mid-90s. Following a lengthy break from recording, during which Robinson left to pursue a solo career, they returned to a competitive market with the classy *EV3*.

● ALBUMS: *Born To Sing* (Atlantic 1990)★★★, *Remix To Sing* (Atlantic 1991)★★★, *Funky Divas* (East West 1992)★★★★, *Runaway Love* mini album (East West 1993)★★★, *EV3* (East West 1997)★★★.
Solo: Terry Ellis *Southern Gal* (East West 1995)★★.

Enchantment

Five-piece vocal group formed in Detroit, Michigan, in 1966 comprising Emanuel (EJ) Johnson, David Banks, Joe (Jobie) Thomas, Ed (Mickey) Clanton and Bobby Green. Their career did not take off, however, until they moved to Los Angeles in the 70s, signing to United Artists and recording an excellent debut album and hitting the Top 30 of the pop charts with 'Gloria'. They subsequently signed with Roadshow (via RCA) and returned to the singles chart with 'It's You That I Need' and 'Sunshine'. They also performed the soundtrack to the film *Deliver Us From Evil*. In 1983 they signed for Columbia, releasing one album before negotiating a new contract with Prelude, for whom they issued one single, 'Feel Like Dancing', in 1984.

● ALBUMS: *Enchantment* (United Artists 1978)★★★★, *Journey To The Land Of Enchantment* (Roadshow 1979)★★★, *Soft Lights, Sweet Music* (Roadshow 1980)★★★, *Utopia* (Columbia 1983)★★★.

Ertegun, Ahmet

b. Turkey. The son of the Turkish ambassador to Washington, USA, Ahmet Ertegun moved to New York upon his father's death in 1944. Although a philosophy graduate, he was drawn towards a musical career via his passion for jazz and blues, of which he was an inveterate collector. With friend and partner Herb Abramson, he founded two unsuccessful labels, Quality and Jubilee, before inaugurating Atlantic Records in 1947. Early releases featured recordings by jazz artists Errol Garner and Tiny Grimes, but Ertegun decided to pursue an R&B-styled policy and the label enjoyed its first notable hit with Granville 'Stick' McGhee's 'Drinking Wine Spo-De-O-Dee', which Ertegun produced. He continued to fulfil that role when Jerry Wexler arrived at Atlantic. The pair were responsible for producing early seminal releases for Clyde McPhatter and the Drifters, including 'Money Honey' and 'Such A Night'. Ahmet also proved himself a skilled composer, co-penning 'Chains Of Love' and 'Sweet Sixteen', the first two hits for 1949 signing Big Joe Turner. Many of his subsequent compositions were credited to the anagrammatical pseudonym, 'Nutgere'.

During the 50s Atlantic established itself as a leading independent through the signings of Ray Charles and Bobby Darin. Ertegun and Wexler produced Ray Charles together, while Ahmet took sole charge for Darin, notably on his first hit, 'Splish Splash'. The label was quick to capitalize on the long-player format and Ertegun passed responsibility for transferring 78s to the new medium to his older brother, Nesuhi. The Coasters and a revitalized Drifters ensured Atlantic's success rate was maintained and with many contemporaries now experiencing financial difficulties, Ertegun entered the 60s as a music industry survivor. Indeed, in 1965 he assisted producer/songwriter Bert Berns in establishing the Bang label. Although Jerry Wexler is credited with shaping Atlantic's mid-60s policies, in particular its arrangements with Stax and Fame, Ahmet signed white 'southern-styled' acts Dr. John, Delaney And Bonnie and Jessie Davis to the label. However, his greatest achievement was a deliberate decision to broaden Atlantic's R&B image with pop and rock signings. Ertegun brought Sonny And Cher to the company, a faith repaid immediately when 'I Got You Babe' became one of the bestselling singles of 1965. That same year he launched the (Young) Rascals, who gained 17 US Top 20 hits until leaving for Columbia in 1969. Meanwhile, another Ahmet acquisition, Vanilla Fudge, found success with their dramatic rearrangements of popular songs, notably 'You Keep Me Hanging On'. He introduced Neil Young and Stephen Stills to the public via Buffalo Springfield, who struck gold with 'For What It's Worth' and won critical acclaim for three excellent albums. Ahmet kept faith with Stills upon the quintet's disintegration, trading band member Richie Furay for David Crosby and securing a release for the Hollies' Graham Nash. The resultant 'supergroup', Crosby, Stills And Nash, became one of the era's leading attractions. Another Ertegun signing, Iron Butterfly, did not receive the same critical approbation, but *In A Gadda Da Vida* was, for a spell, the biggest-selling album in history.

Ertegun's vision proved equally astute with respect to UK acts. A licensing agreement with Polydor ensured Atlantic had first option on its British roster. He took up the Bee Gees and Cream, as well as the solo careers of the latter's ex-members following their split. Eric Clapton proved an important coup. Ertegun signed Led Zeppelin directly to US Atlantic; his faith was rewarded when the quartet became one of rock's most successful bands. Ahmet's instincts proved sure when he took up the rights to the soundtrack of the up-and-coming Woodstock Festival, and in 1970, Ahmet persuaded the Rolling Stones that Atlantic was the natural home for their own record label. By this point, however, his company's autonomy had been effected. In 1967 Ertegun and Wexler allowed Warner Brothers to purchase Atlantic stock in return for an executive position in a conglomerate known as WEA with the acquisition of Elektra. Although Ertegun has remained at his label's helm, it has subsequently lost its distinctive qualities. He has concurrently pursued other interests and a passion for soccer led to his becoming a director of the New York Cosmos, to which he attracted such luminaries as Pele and Franz Bekenbauer. Even if his profile is less apparent than in previous years, Ahmet Ertegun has left an indelible mark on the development of popular music through his entrepreneurial and musical gifts.

ERVIN, DIFOSCO

(see Irwin, Big Dee)

ESCORTS

An R&B vocal group formed in Rahway State Prison, New Jersey, USA. The members were lead Reginald Hayes, Laurence Franklin, Robert Arrington, William Dugger, Stephen Carter, Frank Heard and Marion Murphy. Producer George Kerr discovered them and under his supervision the group made a moderate impact on the charts with classic soul harmony singing. Kerr launched the group with an album recorded live at Rahway, *All We Need Is Another Chance* (1973). It produced two chart singles, 'Look Over Your Shoulder' (number 45 R&B) and 'I'll Be Sweeter Tomorrow' (number 83 R&B), both songs written by Kerr and both recorded by the O'Jays years earlier when they were being produced by Kerr. A second album, *3 Down 4 To Go*, was a studio recording made when three of the members were out of prison. The album featured more originals and produced two more chart singles, 'Disrespect Can Wreck (number 61 R&B) and 'Let's Make Love At Home Sometime' (number 58 R&B). The group could not sustain itself on its modest sales and soon thereafter broke up. Hayes surfaced in 1986 with a self-produced solo album that failed to return him to the public eye. The Escorts reunited in 1992 and released *Back To Love*, which only elicited interest in the UK.

● ALBUMS: *All We Need Is Another Chance* (Alithia 1973)★★★, *3 Down 4 To Go* (Alithia 1974)★★★, *Back To Love* (1992)★★★.
Solo: Reginald Hayes *On Wings Of Love* (Escort 1986)★★.

ESQUIRES

Formed in Milwaukee, USA, in 1957 with a line-up featuring Gilbert Moorer, Alvis Moorer and Betty Moorer. Originally conceived as a doo-wop group, the Esquires were briefly augmented by Harvey Scales before Sam Pace joined in 1961. In 1965 Betty Moorer was replaced by Shawn Taylor. The group then moved to Chicago where they signed to the Bunky label. An original song, 'Get On Up', was recorded with the help of Millard Edwards, who sang its distinctive bass line. Edwards became a permanent member when this infectious single was an R&B hit in 1967. Shawn Taylor left before a similar-sounding follow-up, 'And Get Away', was issued, but rejoined in 1971. That same year, 'Girls In The City', featuring Taylor as lead, was a Top 20 US R&B hit. The opportunistic 'Get Up '76' was the Esquires' most recent hit; by the early 80s only Gilbert and Alvis Moorer remained from the group's heyday.

● ALBUMS: *Get On Up And Get Away* (Bunky 1967)★★★, with the Marvelows *Chi-Town Showdown* (1982)★★★.

ETERNAL

This UK pop dance quartet originally comprised lead singer Easther Bennett plus sister Vernie Bennett, Louise Nurding and Kelle Bryan. Nurding and Bryan both attended the Italia Conti stage school, and the Bennett sisters sang in a Croydon Baptist church. It was through Nurding that they came to the attention of manager Dennis Ingoldsby (co-owner of management agency and record label First Avenue). Their first two singles, 'Stay' and 'Save Our Love', made an immediate impact on the UK charts and launched the group as one of the teen phenomena of 1993. However, much more strident and demanding of the listener was their third single, 'Just A Step From Heaven', the accompanying video for which depicted gangs of youths populating scenes of urban desolation, before switching to a woman giving a lecture on self-awareness beneath the symbol of the Black Panther movement. It was perhaps a little disappointing, then, to learn that Eternal's songs were not of their own creation, and written instead by backroom staff. Nevertheless, *Always And Forever* spawned no less than six Top 15 UK hit singles (another record). By the time sole white member Nurding left amicably in the summer of 1995 to forge a solo career (billed simply as Louise), Eternal had become Britain's most successful all-female group since Bananarama. *Power Of A Woman* became Ingoldsby's first serious attempt to break the group in America, writing material around a formula that drew obvious comparisons to modern R&B stars such as En Vogue. The title track was taken from the album as the group's first single

as a trio, entering the UK Top 10 in October 1995 (joining Louise's first solo single). For the first time, too, roughly half the songs on the album were self-composed. *Before The Rain* confirmed the trio's soul credentials, but suffered from a shortage of stand-out tracks.
● ALBUMS: *Always And Forever* (First Avenue/EMI 1994)★★, *Power Of A Woman* (First Avenue/EMI 1995)★★★, *Before The Rain* (EMI 1997)★★.
● COMPILATIONS: *Greatest Hits* (EMI 1997)★★★.
● VIDEOS: *Always And Forever* (1994).

EVANS, TERRY

b. *c.*1944, Vicksburg, Mississippi, USA. Having spent more than a decade as one of Los Angeles' foremost session singers, in recent years Evans has taken firm steps towards a solo career. As a teenager, he sang with a high school vocal group, the Knights, who from time to time sang with the Red Tops, a big band popular in Clarksdale and Jackson and around the Delta. Evans was 22 when he moved to Los Angeles. For several years, he held a day job and at weekends sang in small clubs around South Central LA, including the Cotton Club and the Road Runner. He met Bobby King through a mutual friend and the pair rehearsed together. In 1976, King secured a contract with Warner Brothers and called Evans when Ry Cooder asked for backing singers while recording *Chicken Skin Music*. Both men worked on further Cooder albums and toured with him. When not on tour, Evans gigged locally with his own five-piece group, which formed the basis of the studio band for their two albums. During that time, he also sang on albums by Boz Scaggs, Maria Muldaur, John Fogerty and John Lee Hooker. Evans' own debut album came about through one of his songs being used on Pops Staples' debut solo album. Produced by Cooder, it draws on a studio band that includes Frankie Ford, Robert Ward, Jim Keltner, the Paramount Singers and Cooder himself. He has subsequently released two albums for Audioquest.
● ALBUMS: with Bobby King *Live And Let Live* (Rounder/Special Delivery 1988)★★★, with King *Rhythm, Blues, Soul & Grooves* (Rounder/Special Delivery 1990)★★★, *Blues For Thought* (PointBlank 1994)★★★, *Puttin' It Down* (Audioquest 1995)★★★, *Come To The River* (Audioquest 1997)★★★.

EVERETT, BETTY

b. 23 November 1939, Greenwood, Mississippi, USA. Having moved to Chicago in the late 50s, Everett recorded unsuccessfully for several local labels, including Cobra, C.J. and One-derful, and briefly sang lead with the all-male group the Daylighters. Her hits came on signing to Vee Jay Records where 'You're No Good' (1963) and 'The Shoop Shoop Song (It's In His Kiss)' (1964) established her pop/soul style. A duet with Jerry Butler, 'Let It Be Me' (1964), consolidated this position, but her finest moment came with 'Getting Mighty Crowded', a punchy Van McCoy song. Her career faltered on Vee Jay's collapse in 1966, and an ensuing interlude at ABC Records was unproductive, despite producing classic tracks such as 'Love Comes Tumbling Down'. However, in 1969, 'There'll Come A Time' reached number 2 in the R&B charts, a momentum that continued into the early 70s with further releases on UNI and Fantasy Records. Everett's last chart entry was in 1978 with 'True Love (You Took My Heart)'. Cher took her version of 'The Shoop Shoop Song' to the top of the charts in 1991.
● ALBUMS: *You're No Good* (Vee Jay 1964)★★★, *It's In His Kiss* (Vee Jay/Fontana1964)★★★, with Jerry Butler *Delicious Together* (Vee Jay 1964)★★★, *There'll Come A Time* (Uni 1969)★★, *Love Rhymes* (1974)★★, *Black Girl* (1974)★★, *Happy Endings* (1975)★★.
● COMPILATIONS: *The Very Best Of Betty Everett* (Vee Jay 1965)★★★, *Betty Everett* (1974)★★★, *Hot To Handle* (1982)★★★, with Lillian Offitt *1957-1961* (Flyright 1986)★★, *The Real Thing* (Charly 1987)★★★★, *The Shoop Shoop Song* (1993)★★★, *Love Rhymes/Happy Endings* (1993)★★★.

EXCITERS

Formed in the Jamaica district of Queens, New York City, this aptly named group, which included Herb Rooney (b. 1941, New York City, New York, USA), Brenda Reid (b. 1945), Carol Johnson (b. 1945) and Lillian Walker (b. 1945), first came to prominence with the vibrant 'Tell Him', a US Top 5 hit in 1962 (also a hit in the UK for Billie Davis in 1963). Produced by Leiber And Stoller and written by Bert Berns (under his pseudonym Bert Russell), the single's energy established the pattern for subsequent releases. 'Do Wah Diddy' (later a hit by Manfred Mann) and 'He's Got The Power' took elements from both uptown soul and the girl-group genre, but later singles failed fully to exploit this powerful combination. The group had lesser hits with 'I Want You To Be My Boy' (1965), a revival of 'A Little Bit Of Soap' (1966) and 'You Don't Know What You're Missing (Till It's Gone)' (1969), but failed to recapture the verve of those first releases. The group re-entered the UK charts in 1975 with 'Reaching For The Best'. Ronnie Pace and Skip McPhee later replaced Johnson and Walker, while Rooney and Reid (his wife) had a minor 1978 hit as Brenda And Herb, releasing one album in 1979, *In Heat Again*.
● ALBUMS: *Tell Him* (United Artists 1963)★★★, *The Exciters* (Roulette 1965)★★★, *Caviar And Chitlins* (1969)★★, *Black Beauty* (1971)★★, *Heaven Is Where You Are* (1976)★★, *The Exciters* (1977)★★.
● COMPILATIONS: *The Hit Power Of The Exciters* (1986)★★★, *Tell Him* (EMI 1991)★★★.
● FILMS: *Bikini Beach* (1964).

EXQUISITES

Vocal group the Exquisites were formed in 1981 in Long Island, New York, USA, by former Gino And The Dells baritone Pete Chacona and tenor Bernie Festo, after Chacona had attended an audition for Festo's then group. Through local newspaper advertising, John O'Keefe (first tenor) and Bob Thomas (lead, ex-Fascinations) were recruited, while familial ties brought in bass singer George Chacona, Pete's brother. Rehearsing material by the Moonglows, Flamingos and Harptones, they set about performing at local shows and nostalgia rallies. When O'Keefe left to join the Teenchords in 1983, he was replaced on first tenor by Mike Paccione. Their first recording came in early 1985 when their version of the Shirelles' 'Dedicated To The One I Love' was released on Avenue D Records, followed by an update of the El Dorados' 'At My Front Door'. After sending a tape to local R&B revival disc jockey Don K. Reed's *Doo-Wop Shop* show in 1985, they found their version of the Solitaires' 'Walking Along' earn a regular slot as opening theme to the highly influential oldies programme. When Paccione departed in 1987, George Santiago (ex-Eternals) came on board, with the line-up also expanded by the arrival of Al Pretea (ex-Dolphins). A little later Zeke Suarez replaced Festo. The group embarked on sessions for their debut album in 1990 with Crystal Ball Records, recording versions of songs by the Drifters, Jive Five and El Dorados, as well as the doo-wop standard 'Over The Rainbow'.

● ALBUMS: *The Exquisites* (Crystal Ball 1991)★★★.

FAIR, YVONNE

b. 1942, Virginia, USA, d. March 1994, Las Vegas, Nevada, USA. Fair joined the Chantels in the early 60s before touring for five years as a member of James Brown's revue, and recording two singles with Brown for King. After recording one unsuccessful single for Motown's Soul subsidiary in 1970, she spent three years as part of Chuck Jackson's band, before returning to Motown in 1974. Fair teamed up with producer Norman Whitfield, who brought her raucous vocal talents to his song 'Funky Music Sho' Nuff Turns Me On', a 1974 R&B hit, followed later that year by 'Walk Out The Door If You Wanna'. It was the b-side of the latter single - a fiery revival of Gladys Knight's 1968 hit, 'It Should've Been Me' - that brought her most attention, when it belatedly charted in Britain early in 1976. Fair had already left the Motown stable, and was unable to capitalize on this success. She appeared in the film *Lady Sings The Blues*, and before her untimely death in 1994, she worked with Dionne Warwick.

● ALBUMS: *The Bitch Is Black* (1975)★★★.

● FILMS: *Lady Sings The Blues*.

FAITH HOPE AND CHARITY

An R&B vocal trio from Tampa, Florida, USA, Faith Hope And Charity, with a solid background from the soul era, became a moderately successful unit during the disco period, when they married exuberant, gospel-styled vocals with a disco beat. Original members were lead Zulema Cusseaux, Brenda Hilliard and Albert Bailey. After two hits on the Maxwell label in 1970, 'So Much Love' (number 14 R&B, number 51 pop) and 'Baby Don't Take Your Love' (number 36 R&B, number 96 pop), Cusseaux left the group in 1971 (Cusseaux built a moderately successful solo career in the early 70s under the name Zulema). A new third member, Diane Destry, was not added until 1974, and at that time the group was signed to the RCA label under the production aegis of Van McCoy. He gave them their biggest hit in 1975 with 'To Each His Own' (number 1 R&B, number 50 pop). Nothing they subsequently recorded came close and their last chart record was 'Don't Pity Me' (number 20 R&B) for 20th Century in 1978. In the UK they reached the charts in 1976 with a revival of Doris Troy's old hit, 'Just One Look' (number 38). In 1978 Destry left and Hilliard and Bailey carried on for another album before fading.

● ALBUMS: *Faith, Hope And Charity* (RCA 1975)★★★, *Life Goes On* (RCA 1976)★★, *Don't Pity Me* (20th Century 1977)★★, *Faith, Hope & Charity* (20th Century 1978)★★.

FALCONS

This R&B vocal group from Detroit, Michigan, USA, helped define soul music in the early 60s. The great legacy of music left by the Falcons has unfortunately been obscured by the group's reputation as the genesis of so many great talents. The group has at one time claimed as members Eddie Floyd (b. 25 June 1935, Montgomery, Alabama, USA), Wilson Pickett (b. 18 March 1941, Prattville, Alabama, USA), Joe Stubbs (b. Joe Stubbles), brother of the Four Tops' Levi Stubbs and later a member of the Contours and then the Originals, Mack Rice, the original singer of 'Mustang Sally', and guitarists Lance Finnie and Robert Ward successively, whose bluesy guitar work helped immeasurably to raise the reputation of the group. The Falcons' chart success was surprisingly slim, with only five releases making the chart, the best-known being 'You're So Fine', a proto-soul number led by Stubbs that went to number 2 R&B (number 17 pop) in 1959, and 'I Found A Love', the incredibly torrid secular gospel number led by Wilson Pickett that went to number 6 R&B (number 75 pop) in 1962.

The original Falcons formed in 1955 and comprised lead Eddie Floyd, Bob Manardo, Arnett Robinson, Tom Shetler, and Willie Schofield. In 1956 they met Detroit producer Robert West and for the next three years issued releases by the Falcons on several labels, including his own Flick label, but without achieving any national success. After Joe Stubbs and Mack Rice replaced Shetler, Manardo and Robinson in 1957, and guitarist Lance Finnie joined the group, the classic group of Falcons were together, blending gospel fervour to rhythm and blues harmony, as reflected in their 'You're So Fine' hit of 1959. They managed two more hits with Stubbs as lead with 'Just For Your Love' (number 26 R&B 1959) and 'The Teacher' (number 18 R&B 1960), before Wilson Pickett replaced Stubbs in 1960. The memorable 'I Found A Love', and several other Falcons records, featured as backing the Dayton group the Ohio Untouchables, cen-

tred on the great guitar of Robert Ward. In the 70s the Ohio Untouchables had emerged as the premier funk group the Ohio Players, and Ward re-emerged from 25 years' retirement in 1991 to release a well-received blues album. The Falcons disbanded in 1963, but the name continued with another Detroit ensemble, consisting of Carlis 'Sonny' Monroe, James Gibson, Johnny Alvin and Alton Hollowell. This group made the R&B chart in 1966 with 'Standing On Guard'.
● COMPILATIONS: *You're So Fine* (Relic 1985)★★★, *I Found A Love* (Relic 1985)★★★, *Marv Johnson/The Falcons* (1986)★★★.

FANTASTIC FOUR

Formed in Detroit in 1965 by 'Sweet' James Epps, Wallace Childs and Ralph and Joseph Pruitt. This excellent quartet's early releases were influenced by the hoarse, urgent style of the Four Tops. After three of the group's singles, 'The Whole World Is A Stage', 'You Gave Me Something' (both 1967) and 'I Love You Madly' (1968), reached the US R&B Top 20 on the Ric Tic label, the Fantastic Four were acquired by Motown, but the label was less successful in promoting them. The group, whose later members included Cleveland Horne and Ernest Newsome, later moved to the Eastbound/Westbound complex, where their releases, including 'Alvin Stone (The Birth And Death Of A Gangster)' (1975) and 'I Got To Have Your Love' (1977), enjoyed intermittent success.
● ALBUMS: *Alvin Stone (The Life And Death Of A Gangster)* (Westbound 1975)★★★, *Night People* (Westbound 1976)★★★, *Got To Have Your Love* (Westbound 1977)★★★, *BYOF (Bring Your Own Funk)* (1978)★★.
● COMPILATIONS: *Best Of The Fantastic Four* (1969)★★★.

FANTASTIC JOHNNY C

b. Johnny Corley, 28 April 1943, Greenwood, South Carolina, USA. Fantastic Johnny C hit the US charts in 1967 with the infectious soul mover 'Boogaloo Down Broadway'. His 'Wilson Pickett-like' vocal delivery, powered by a heavy percussion and a horn section similar to the Stax/Atlantic sound, took three months to make the US Top 10. It was written and produced by songwriter Jesse James, as was the flip-side, 'Look What Love Can Make You Do', which used the same backing track, but with different lyrics. The chart performance of the follow-up, 'Got What You Need', proved disappointing. He recorded a sequel to Cliff Nobles And Co.'s US hit 'The Horse', titled 'Hitch It To The Horse', both written by James, which became his final US Top 40 hit in August 1968.

FARRIS, DIONNE

b. 1969, Bordentown, New Jersey, USA. Dionne Farris took a brave decision in 1994 to leave Grammy award winners Arrested Development, where she was an 'extended family member', choosing instead to set out on a solo trail with an album that spanned funk, rock, soul and jazz. Her first single, 'I Know', charted strongly in both the Hot 100 and Adult Contemporary *Billboard* charts. The only problem was that certain R&B stations and magazines did not respond to the presence of guitars in her work, while rock outlets thought her too 'pop'. Nevertheless, the album ended up in many critics' picks of 1994, while her marketing problems were addressed the following year by touring both alternative and urban R&B clubs on alternate nights. An appearance on the television programme *Saturday Night Live* preceded the May release of 'Don't Ever Touch Me (Again)'. Her debut album was an assured collection of highly charged songs, played with her group of musicians who include the highly original guitarist/musical arranger David Harris. The varied content underlines Farris's influences - she cites James Taylor, Nancy Wilson and Chaka Khan - hence the disparate yet cohesive content. From the Beatles' 'Blackbird' to her own gutsy 'Passion', complete with heavy metal guitar, Farris is an exciting prospect.
● ALBUMS: *Wild Seed - Wild Flower* (Columbia 1994)★★★★.

FASCINATIONS

Formed in 1960 in Detroit, Michigan, USA, the Fascinations were a female vocal quartet who were produced by Curtis Mayfield. The group was originally called the Sabre-ettes, and included lead singer Shirley Walker and Martha Reeves (b. 18 July 1941, Alabama, USA), who went on to lead Martha And The Vandellas. After several personnel changes, the group comprised Walker, new lead vocalist Bernadine Boswell Smith, her sister Joanne Boswell Levell, and Fern Bledsoe. They moved to Chicago and were discovered there by members of the Impressions, who brought them to Mayfield's attention. Their first two singles were recorded for the ABC-Paramount label in 1962-63, and did not sell well. That label dropped them, but Mayfield did not forget the group and in 1966, when he started his own Mayfield label, he signed the Fascinations, eventually releasing five singles by the group. Of those, three made the US R&B charts, with the second of those, 'Girls Are Out To Get You', rising to number 13 (it also made number 92 on the pop chart). When the Fascinations' contract came up for renewal in 1969, Mayfield did not sign them again, and the Fascinations disbanded. In 1971, they reunited for a tour of England but split permanently after that tour.
● COMPILATIONS: *Out To Getcha!* (Sequel 1997)★★★★.

FATBACK BAND

There are many, including genuine authorities such as Afrika Bambaataa, who state that 'King Tim III (Personality Jock)' by Fatback, released on Spring Records in 1979, is the first true hip-hop record. 'King Tim' was actually the b-side to 'You're My Candy Sweet', before radio programmers and listeners made it the more popular selection. The rap was delivered by the band's master of ceremonies/warm-up act, King Tim III. After appearing solo on 'Charley Says! (Roller Boogie Baby)', backed by Fatback, he would disappear into the mists of hip-hop mythology. Archivists may like to note that 'King Tim III' is included on the Fatback XII album. Elsewhere, Fatback remained a predominantly R&B-based funk band. They were originally formed by Johnny King (guitar), Earl Shelton (saxophone), George Williams (trumpet), George Adam (flute), Johnny Flippin (bass) and Bill Curtis (drums). Later members included Saunders McCrae (keyboards) and Richard Cromwell (trombone).

● ALBUMS: As Fatback Band: *Raising Hell* (Event 1976)★★★, *Night Fever* (Spring 1976)★★★. As Fatback: *Fired Up 'N' Kickin'* (Spring 1978)★★★, *Fatback XII* (Spring 1979)★★★, *Hot Box* (Spring 1980)★★★, *14 Karat* (Spring 1980)★★★, *Tasty Jam* (Spring 1981)★★★, *Gigolo* (Spring 1982)★★.

FAT LARRY'S BAND

'Fat' Larry James (b. 2 August 1949, Philadelphia, Pennsylvania, USA, d. 5 December 1987; drums) formed this funk/disco outfit in Philadelphia following his spell as a back-up musician for the Delfonics and Blue Magic. The group comprised Art Capehart (trumpet, flute), Jimmy Lee (trombone, saxophone), Doug Jones (saxophone), Erskine Williams (keyboards), Ted Cohen (guitar), Larry LaBes (bass), Darryl Grant (percussion). James found success easier in the UK than in his homeland, having a UK Top 40 hit with 'Center City' in 1977, and in 1979 achieving a Top 50 with 'Boogie Town' under the title of FLB. That same year, one of James's other projects, the studio group Slick, had two UK hit singles with 'Space Bass' and 'Sexy Cream'. These two releases established them with the disco market. However, it was not until 1982 that the group secured a major national hit, with a recording of the Commodores' song 'Zoom' taking them to number 2 in the UK charts, although it only managed to scrape into the US soul chart at 89. It proved, however, to be the band's last success of any note, and hope of a regeneration was cut short on their founder's death in 1987.

● ALBUMS: *Feel It* (WMOT 1977)★★, *Off The Wall* (1978)★★, *Stand Up* (Fantasy 1980)★★, *Breakin' Out* (Virgin 1982)★★, *Straight From The Heart* (1983)★★, *Nice* (1986)★★.

● COMPILATIONS: *Bright City Lights* (Fantasy 1980)★★, *Close Encounters Of A Funky Kind* (Southbound/Ace 1995)★★★.

FIAGBE, LENA

b. *c.*1969, Ladbroke Grove, London, England. Lena Fiagbe is a talented, soul-inspired singer whose demo cassette inspired a bidding war among the major record companies in 1993, with the U2-backed Mother label emerging as the victor. Fiagbe's father had been a huge fan of Lena Horne (hence his daughter's name), and Flagbe's microphone performance certainly incorporates some of the dynamism of that artist. Her debut single, 'You Come From Earth', which thematically shared Jamiroquai's wide-eyed wonder at the universe, was inspired by a documentary about space travel, but flopped. In light of this, the record company insisted on some remixes. Fiagbe herself was unhappy with the house mixes applied to the follow-up single, 'Gotta Get It Right (One World)', which grazed the UK Top 20: 'The only thing I dislike is if by putting out dance mixes people start seeing me as a dance artist, then I can't handle it. That's not what I'm about.' After this she toured with Lenny Kravtiz and Daryl Hall, co-writing 'Borderline' on the latter's *Soul Alone* set, and earned further critical praise for her debut album, *Visions* (limited editions of which contained a free seven-track acoustic CD - as if to confirm Fiagbe's status as a singer-songwriter).

● ALBUMS: *Visions* (Mother 1994)★★★.

FIELDS, RICHARD 'DIMPLES'

b. San Francisco, California, USA. Fields earned the nickname 'Dimples' from a female admirer who remarked that he was always smiling. Fields began singing in the early 70s, purchasing a San Francisco cabaret, the Cold Duck Music Lounge, and installing himself as its entertainment. He began recording for his own DRK Records label during this period. Each of his three albums for DRK sold reasonably well and Fields signed to Boardwalk Records in 1981. His first chart single was that year's 'Earth Angel', a remake of the 1954 Penguins ballad. His biggest hit was 1982's 'If It Ain't One Thing . . . It's Another', an R&B number 1, which became his only crossover pop chart hit. Two albums, 1981's *Dimples* and the following year's *Mr. Look So Good!*, also reached the charts, but Boardwalk folded as his third album for the company, *Give Everybody Some!*, was released in 1983, destroying any chance of success. Fields signed with RCA Records in 1984 and recorded two albums for that label before he was dropped. Fields' US career ended with his association with RCA.

● ALBUMS: *It's Finger Looking Good* (DRK *c.*70s)★★★, *Ready For Anything* (DRK *c.*70s)★★★, *Spoiled Rotten* (DRK *c.*70s)★★★, *Dimples* (Boardwalk 1981)★★★★, *Mr. Look So Good!* (Boardwalk 1982)★★★, *Give Everybody Some!* (Boardwalk 1983)★★, *Mmm* (RCA 1984)★★, *Dark Gable* (RCA 1985)★★★.

FIFTH DIMENSION

Originally known as the Versatiles and later as the Vocals, Marilyn McCoo (b. 30 September 1943, Jersey City, New Jersey, USA), Florence LaRue (b. 4 February 1944, Philadelphia, Pennsylvania, USA), Billy Davis Jnr. (b. 26 June 1940, St. Louis, Missouri, USA), Lamont McLemore (b. 17 September 1940, St. Louis, Missouri, USA) and Ron Townsend (b. 29 January 1941, St. Louis, Missouri, USA) were a soul-influenced harmony group, based in Los Angeles. They sprang to fame in 1967 as an outlet for the then unknown talents of songwriter Jimmy Webb. Ebullient singles on the pop charts, including 'Go Where You Wanna', 'Up Up And Away' and 'Carpet Man', established their fresh voices, which wrapped themselves around producer Bones Howe's dizzy arrangements. Having completed two albums containing a number of Webb originals, the group then took to another composer, Laura Nyro, whose beautiful soul-styled songs 'Stoned Soul Picnic', 'Sweet Blindness' (both 1968), 'Wedding Bell Blues' (1969) and 'Save The Country' (1970) continued the Fifth Dimension's success and introduced the group to the R&B charts. These popular recordings were punctuated by 'Aquarius/Let The Sunshine In', a medley of songs from the rock musical *Hair*, which topped the US chart in 1969 and reached number 11 in Britain that same year. In 1971 the group reached number 2 in the USA with the haunting 'One Less Bell To Answer'. From then on, however, the MOR elements within their style began to take precedence and the quintet's releases grew increasingly bland. In 1976 McCoo and Davis (who were now married) left for a successful career both as a duo and as solo artists. They had a US number 1 hit together in 1976 with 'You Don't Have To Be A Star', which was followed up in 1977 by their last Top 20 hit, 'Your Love'. McCoo went on to host the US television show *Solid Gold* for much of the early 80s.

● ALBUMS: *Up Up And Away* (Soul City 1967)★★★, *The Magic Garden* (Soul City 1967)★★★, *Stoned Soul Picnic* (Soul City 1968)★★★, *The Age Of Aquarius* (Soul City 1969)★★★, *Fantastic* (1970)★★, *Portrait* (Bell 1970)★★, *Love's Lines, Angles And Rhymes* (Bell 1971)★★★, *The 5th Dimension Live!* (Bell 1971)★★, *Individually And Collectively* (Bell 1972)★★, *Living Together, Growing Together* (Bell 1973)★★, *Earthbound* (ABC 1975)★★.

● COMPILATIONS: *Greatest Hits* (Soul City 1970)★★★, *The July 5th Album* (Soul City 1970)★★★, *Reflections* (Bell 1971)★★★, *Greatest Hits On Earth* (Arista 1972)★★★, *Anthology* (Rhino 1986)★★★, *Greatest Hits* (1988)★★★, *The Definitive Collection* (Arista 1997)★★★.

FINAL FOUR

R&B vocal quartet the Final Four are unusual for their genre in that the contents of their independently released debut album were largely self-written and produced. Comprising Jimmy, Gee, E.J. and Rich, the group formed in Indianapolis as a result of each member meeting on the local church and club-singing scene. As Jimmy told *Billboard* magazine in 1996, 'Each of the groups we were in at the time was pretty good, but there were members in each of them that weren't as committed as they should have been. So the four of us joined forces, which made for a unit that wanted to do this more than just for a hobby.' The group began by playing local gigs and winning a series of talent contests. After signing to Our Turn Records in 1996, the group abandoned plans to release 'Swangin'', a collaboration with rapper Tim Dog, as their first single. They were concerned that this might give a wrong impression of the group, who were keen to be seen to represent the 'wholesome' side of R&B.

● ALBUMS: *Final Four* (Our Turn 1996)★★★.

FIRST CHOICE

Part of the Philadelphia sound of the mid-70s, this female vocal group's biggest success was 'Armed And Extremely Dangerous'. Rochelle Fleming (b. 11 February 1950, Philadelphia, Pennsylvania, USA), Joyce Jones (b. 30 July 1949) and Annette Guest (b. 19 November 1954, Chester, Pennsylvania, USA) were originally known as the Debronettes. Local DJ Georgie Woods introduced the trio to Norman Harris, guitarist with MFSB, to produce their debut single, 'This Is The House Where Love Died'. Although it sold poorly, the record led to a new contract with Philly Groove and 'Armed and Extremely Dangerous'. Also produced by Harris, the song was a hit first in the UK, where it reached the Top 20 on Bell. US success followed and the later singles, 'Smarty Pants' and 'The Player', sold equally well. While producer Harris was associated with numerous hits during the disco boom of the late 70s, the only later chart entry for First Choice was 'Dr Debbie Martine' and in 1984 First Choice split up. In 1987 Fleming re-formed the group with her cousin Laconya Fleming and Lawrence Cottel to record 'Love Itch' (Prelude). In the same year a reissue of the 1977 track 'Let No Man Put Asunder' was a dancefloor hit in the UK.

● ALBUMS: *Armed And Extremely Dangerous* (Philly Groove 1973)★★★, *Smarty Pants* (Philly Groove 1974)★★★, *So Let Us Entertain You* (Warners 1976)★★★, *Delusions* (Gold Mind 1977)★★★, *Dr Love* (Gold Mind 1977)★★★, *Hold Your Horses* (Gold Mind 1979)★★★.

FIVE BLIND BOYS OF MISSISSIPPI

This vocal gospel group, consisting of Archie Brownley (lead), Joseph Ford, Lawrence Abrams and Lloyd Woodard, was formed in 1936 by blind students of the Piney Woods School, Jackson, Mississippi. They began singing together in their school grounds and called themselves the Cotton Blossom Singers. By the mid-40s the group had moved to New Orleans and had added Melvin Henderson as their second lead. He was in turn replaced by (the sighted) Percell Perkins, whereupon the band became the Five Blind Boys Of Mississippi. Ford left the group in 1948 and was replaced by J.T. Clinkscales (also blind). The group moved to Houston, Texas, in the 50s and signed to Peacock Records. 'Our Father' was their biggest hit, and became a gospel classic. It also reached number 10 in the R&B chart. Dozens of 45s and at least five albums emerged on Peacock during the 60s as the group toured constantly. Perkins left in order to devote himself to the ministry and became Reverend Perkins. His replacements included Reverend Samy Lewis, Reverend George Warren and Tiny Powell. Brownley died in New Orleans in 1960 and Roscoe Robinson took over as lead, and Willmer 'Little Axe' Broadnax joined as second lead. Woodard died in the mid-70s and Lawrence Abrams in 1982, but the Five Blind Boys continued to tour with new members. Brownley is one of the pivotal influences in the development of black soul music in the 50s and 60s, with both Ray Charles and James Brown taking their cue from his strident vocal performances.

● ALBUMS: *My Desire* (Peacock *c.*60s), *There's A God* (Peacock *c.*60s), *Best Of The Five Blind Boys Of Mississippi Vol. 1* (MCA *c.*70s), *Best Of The Five Blind Boys Of Mississippi Vol. 2* (MCA *c.*70s), *Soon I'll Be Done* (MCA *c.*70s).

FIVE CROWNS

The Five Crowns were formed at Wadleigh Junior High School in Harlem, New York, USA, in 1952. The group comprised Wilbur 'Yunkie' Paul (lead), brothers James 'Poppa' Clark, Claudie 'Nicky' Clark and John 'Sonny Boy' Clark (all tenor) and Doc Green (bass/baritone). Their distinctive sound (not least because of the presence of four tenors) brought them to the attention of Rainbow Records in July 1952. They found instant success in October when 'You're My Inspiration' became a major regional R&B hit. However, they failed to follow up this breakthrough, with successive singles such as 'Who Can Be True', 'Why Don't You Believe Me' and 'Alone Again' faring poorly. Finding themselves in dispute with an evidently disappointed Rainbow Records, they moved to the Old Town label in July 1953. However, neither 'You Could Be My Love' nor 'Lullaby Of The Bells' revived fortunes. In the aftermath they returned to Rainbow on its subsidiary label Riviera Records. A creative renaissance was witnessed by the powerful 'You Came To Me', but this again failed to translate into commercial sales. The group disbanded later that year. Green then put together a new Five Crowns who released one single, 'God Bless You', for Gee Records. He was also the only original member remaining in the reshuffled line-up who released 'I Can't Pretend' for Transworld Records. Titled simply the Crowns by 1958, the formation that recorded 'Kiss And Make Up' was ironically closer to the original Five Crowns, with James Clark rejoining, plus the presence of Benjamin Nelson (later known as Ben E. King), Elsbury Hobbs and Charlie Thomas. This was the only record ever to be released on Doc Pomus's R&B Records label. Afterwards, they performed at the Apollo Theatre and so impressed George Treadwell that he immediately sacked the members of his band the Drifters, and replaced them in a straight swap with the Crowns.

FIVE DUTONES

Formed in St. Louis, Missouri, USA, around 1957, by Robert Hopkins, Leroy Joyce, Willie Guest, Oscar Watson and James West. Originally a doo-wop group, the Five Dutones moved to Chicago in the early 60s. By that time Hopkins and Watson had been replaced by Frank McCurry and Andrew Butler, respectively. Their exhilarating single 'Shake A Tail Feather' was released in 1963. Later revived by James And Bobby Purify and Mitch Ryder, this definitive early version was a US Top 30 R&B hit. James West died of a heart attack in 1963 and was replaced by David Scott. The Five Dutones recorded a total of nine singles, most of which were based on local dance crazes, but split in 1967. The group's back-up musicians, the Exciters, became a minor charting band, the South Shore Commission, which featured as vocalists McCurry and Scott, both latter-day members of the Five Dutones. Scott later joined the Chi-Lites in the late 70s while Leroy Joyce changed his name to Leroy Brown and worked with the Eddy Clearwater Blues Band.

● COMPILATIONS: *Shake A Tail Feather* (1979)★★★.

FIVE KEYS

This US R&B vocal group helped shape the rhythm and blues revolution of the early 50s. The ensemble was formed as the Sentimental Four in Newport News, Virginia, USA, in the late 40s, and originally consisted of two sets of brothers - Rudy West (b. 25 July 1932, Newport News, Virginia, USA) and Bernie West (b. 4 February 1930, Newport News, Virginia, USA), and Ripley Ingram (b. 1930, d. 23 March 1995, Newport News, Virginia, USA) and Raphael Ingram. After Raphael Ingram left and Maryland Pierce (b. 1933) and Dickie Smith became members in 1949, the name of the group was changed to Five Keys. With Pierce doing the lead work, the Five Keys joined Los Angeles-based Aladdin Records in 1951, and the same year had a hit with a remake of the old standard 'Glory Of Love', which became a US R&B number 1. Despite recording an appealing combination of old standards and R&B originals, further chart success on Aladdin eluded the Five Keys. In 1952 Rudy West went into the army, and was replaced by Ulysses K. Hicks, and in 1954 Dickie Smith left and was replaced with Ramon Loper. This new line-up of Five Keys was signed to Capitol Records, which brought the group to stardom, albeit with some modification in their style from a deep rhythm and blues sound to a more pop vein with greater instrumentation in support. The group's first hit for Capitol was the novelty pop jump 'Ling Ting Tong' (US R&B number 5 and pop Top 30 in 1955). Following the first Capitol recording session, Rudy West rejoined the Five Keys in October 1954, replacing the ailing Hicks, who died a few months later. Further hits on Capitol included some spectacular R&B ballads: the Chuck Willis-composed 'Close Your Eyes' (R&B number 5, 1955), 'The Verdict' (R&B number 13, 1955) and 'Out Of Sight, Out Of Mind' (R&B number 12 and pop Top 30 in 1956). The Capitol material also featured old standards, such as a marvellous remake of the Ink Spots' 'The Gypsy' (1957). Rudy West retired in 1958. An unsuccessful period at King Records from 1958-61 produced more personnel changes and no hits, and few songs that could compete with the new rock 'n' roll sounds. Periodic sessions were recorded by various reunion groups in subsequent years, but the basic legacy of the Five Keys rests in their Aladdin, Capitol and King sessions.

● ALBUMS: *The Best Of The Five Keys* (Aladdin 1956)★★★, *The Five Keys On The Town* (Score 1957)★★, *The Five Keys On Stage* (Capitol 1957)★, *The Five Keys* (King 1960)★★★, *Rhythm And Blues Hits Past And Present* (King 1960)★★★, *The Fantastic Five Keys* (Capitol 1962)★★★.

● COMPILATIONS: *The Five Keys* (King 1978)★★, *The Five Keys And The Nitecaps* (Detour 1988)★★★, *The Five Keys: Capitol Collector's Series* (Capitol 1989)★★★, *Dream On* (Charly 1991)★★★, *The Five Keys: The Aladdin Years* (EMI 1991)★★★.

FIVE RED CAPS

An African-American vocal/instrumental combo from Los Angeles, California, USA. Members were Steve Gibson (b. 17 October 1914, Lynchburg, Virginia, USA; guitar, bass singer), Emmett Matthews (b. *c.*1902, St. Louis, Missouri, USA; saxophone, tenor singer), Dave Patillo (b. Marshall, Texas, USA, d. 1966; bass, vocals), Jimmy Springs (b. 5 September 1911, Mattoon, Illinois, USA, d. 1987; drums, tenor singer) and Romaine Brown (d. 1986; piano). The Five Red Caps, in their long history, represent virtually every facet of black popular music from the 30s through to the 50s, from crooning ballads, rousing jumps, and humorous jive tunes, to rock 'n' roll. They began as the Four Toppers in 1938 and in 1942 became the Five Red Caps. They signed with Joe Davis and his Beacon label in 1943 and gained their first and biggest hit with 'I've Learned A Lesson I'll never Forget' (number 3 R&B) in early 1944. Three other records that year made the charts, namely 'Boogie-Woogie Ball', 'Just For You' and 'No One Else Will Do'. In 1946 the group moved to Mercury Records and, recording under the name Steve Gibson And The Red Caps, achieved a hit in 1948 with 'Wedding Bells Are Breaking Up That Old Gang Of Mine' (number 21 pop). In 1950 the group signed with RCA and with the addition of Damita Jo (b. Damita Jo DuBlanc, 5 August 1930, Austin, Texas, USA), the group had their last hit with the ballad 'I Went To Your Wedding' (number 20 pop) in 1952. The Red Caps, however, found it increasingly hard to compete during the rock 'n' roll revolution, and disbanded in 1956. Damita Jo went on to pursue a highly successful career as a nightclub chanteuse. Gibson formed a new Red Caps group, recruiting brothers Peck and Joe Furness and Emmett Matthews from the original unit. They recorded more in the rock 'n' roll vein and had minor success with a cover version of the Rays' 'Silhouettes' (1957). Gibson kept various Red Caps ensembles together until 1966, when Dave Patillo died.

● COMPILATIONS: *You're Driving Me Crazy* (Mercury 1954)★★★, *Blueberry Hill* (Mercury 1954)★★★, *It's So Good* (Krazy Kat 1986)★★★, *Boogie Woogie On A Saturday Night* (Bear Family 1990)★★★★, *Blueberry Hill* (Dr. Horse 1990)★★★.

5 ROYALES

The 5 Royales were hugely successful exponents of southern vocal R&B throughout the 50s, although they started their career in a different style as the Royal Sons Gospel Group of Winston-Salem, North Carolina, USA. This quintet variously featured the brothers Clarence, Curtis and Lowman Pauling (d. 26 December 1973, Brooklyn, New York, USA), Otto Jeffries, Johnny Tanner, Obadiah Carter (d. July 1994, Winston-Salem, North Carolina, USA), James Moore and William Samuels. The Pauling brothers had started out supporting their father, Lowman Pauling Snr., on local North Carolina stages, while his namesake son reputedly built his first guitar out of cigar-boxes. Lowman Pauling Jnr. was the group's musical arranger and springboard, while Johnny Tanner usually handled lead vocals. At the suggestion of local radio producer Robert Woodward, the group contacted New York label Apollo Records, headed by Bess Berman and Carl Le Bowe. There the group sang spirituals as the Royal Sons Quintet, until Le Bowe rechristened them 5 Royales for the purposes of recording R&B music. Having elected to pursue the latter style, Johnny Holmes, the final member of the Royal Sons who graced their 'Bedside Of A Neighbour' debut, departed. This left a core 5 Royales line-up of Lowman Pauling (guitar), Johnny Tanner (lead), Moore (tenor), Carter (tenor) and Jeffries (baritone). Typical of their background, their first single, 'Give Me One More Chance' (coupled with 'Too Much Of A Little Bit'), was a spiritual standard energized into a raunchy R&B number. By 1953 Eugene Tanner (b. 1936, d. 29 December 1994, Winston-Salem, North Carolina, USA; baritone/bass) had replaced Jeffries, the oldest member of the group by over 10 years, who was no longer capable of performing the group's energetic stage routines, instead becoming manager. Together they achieved their first major success with 'Baby Don't Do It', which made number 1 in the US R&B charts in January 1953. The follow-up single, 'Help Me Somebody', stayed at number 1 on the same chart for five weeks, while the band's powerful and frequent live performances, now completely divorced from their gospel background, built them a formidable reputation. Their new-found fame also resulted in a lawsuit when they discovered that the Royals of Detroit were the first of several groups to impersonate them. The band's first appearance at the Apollo followed in January 1953, appearing for a week alongside Willy Mabon and Gene Ammons. In August 'Too Much Lovin'' became another sizeable R&B hit, although it was the b-side, 'Laundromat Blues', with its sexually suggestive lyric, that provoked most attention. By 1954 the group had signed to King Records, following Le Bowe's defection to that label. However, the 5 Royales were never as successful again. Though over 40 singles were issued under their name up to 1965, usually of good quality, they seldom reached the charts. 'Tears Of Joy' and 'Think', from 1957 and 1959, respectively, were two notable exceptions. 'Think' was their first national US pop chart success, at number 66, although 'Dedicated To The One I Love', later covered by the Shirelles and Mamas And The Papas, also reached number 81 on the same chart in 1961. This was a revised version of a Chester Mayfield composition, 'I Don't Want You To Go', which Mayfield had written while a member of fellow North Carolina R&B group the Casanovas, also signed to Apollo. Their membership included William Samuels, Lowman Pauling's brother-in-law and formerly of the Royal Sons himself. However, after leaving King Records in 1960 the band failed to reach the charts again, despite recording for several labels with variable line-ups. Lowman Pauling left the group between stints at Home Of The Blues Records and Todd Records, replaced by Robert 'Pee Wee' Burris on guitar. Tanner also departed in December 1963, and was replaced by Eudell Graham. Graham, who became the focus of the touring 5 Royales, was later jailed for armed robbery. After the group broke up, Clarence Pauling rechristened himself Clarence Paul, and became the A&R director at Motown Records where he helped to shape the careers of Stevie Wonder and Marvin Gaye. The 5 Royales' influence on R&B, meanwhile, proved fundamental to the music of James Brown, with whom the band had frequently worked in their heyday. Lowman Pauling, whose uninhibited guitar style was also a major influence on the style of Eric Clapton, died in 1973 while working as a custodian at a Brooklyn synagogue.

● ALBUMS: *The Five Royales* (Apollo 1953)★★★, *The Five Royales Sing For You* (King 1959)★★★.

● COMPILATIONS: *Sing Baby Don't Do It* (Relic 1987)★★, *Sing Laundromat Blues* (Relic 1987)★★, *Monkey, Hips And Rice: The 5 Royales Anthology* (Rhino 1997)★★★.

FIVE SATINS

This R&B vocal group was formed in New Haven, Connecticut, USA, in 1955. The Five Satins' first hit, 'In The Still Of The Night' (US R&B number 3 and pop Top

30 in 1956), was one of the definitive songs of the early rock 'n' roll era, with its strong chanting of doo-wop riffs in the background and impassioned lead work. The group on this record consisted of lead Fred Parris, Al Denby, Ed Martin, bass Jim Freeman and pianist Jessie Murphy. Parris, who wrote the song, brought valuable experience to the Five Satins, having formed the Scarlets (Parris, Denby, Bill Powers, Sylvester Hopkins and Nate Mosely) in 1953, a group that hit regionally with 'Dear One' in 1954. The long-cherished national success for Parris was initially denied him, as he was in the army stationed in Japan when 'In The Still Of The Night' became a hit, and the wonderful follow-up, 'To The Aisle' (US R&B number 5 and pop Top 30 in 1957), featured a reorganized group with Bill Baker (b. Auburn, Alabama, USA, d. 10 August 1994, New Haven, Connecticut, USA) as lead. Parris returned from Japan in 1958 and again reorganized the Five Satins, recruiting tenor Richie Freeman (b. December 1940), second tenor West Forbes (b. 1937), Sylvester Hopkins (b. 1938) and Lou Peeples. This group was not able to secure another big hit, although 'Shadows' (US R&B number 27, 1959) kept their name visible. Their profile was significantly enhanced with the release of Art Laboe's first *Oldies But Goodies*, which included 'In The Still Of The Night'. As a result, the song helped to create the doo-wop revival in the early 60s and re-entered the national pop chart in 1961. The Five Satins broke up in the early 60s, but re-formed and became a perennial on the oldies circuit in the 70s. The new group consisted of Parris, Richie Freeman, Jimmy Curtis and Nate Marshall. Under the name Black Satin, they had a number 49 R&B hit in 1975 with 'Everybody Stand And Clap Your Hands (For The Entertainer)'.

● ALBUMS: *The Five Satins Sing* (Ember 1957)★★★, *Encore, Volume 2* (Ember 1960)★★★.

● COMPILATIONS: *The Best Of The Five Satins* (Celebrity Show 1971)★★★, *In The Still Of The Night* (1990)★★★.

FIVE SHARPS

Formed in the early 50s in Jamaica, New York, USA, the Five Sharps were a vocal harmony group whose sole claim to fame is the fact that their only record, Harold Arlen's 'Stormy Weather', is acknowledged by collectors to be the rarest in the world. The group consisted of Ronald Cuffey (lead vocals), Clarence Bassett and Robert Ward (both tenors), Mickey Owens (bass vocals) and Tom Duckett (piano). In late 1952 the group recorded the standard 'Stormy Weather' for Jubilee Records. The record failed to gain any significant airplay or sales and the Five Sharps broke up. Virtually no one remembered their recording until a collector found a 78 rpm copy at a Brooklyn record store in 1961. When no others turned up, the value of the surviving original rose steadily; a second copy was finally located in 1977 and sold for nearly $4,000. No 45s were ever discovered and should another 78 appear in the 90s, its value is now estimated by experts to be over $10,000.

FIVE STAIRSTEPS

A Chicago group comprised of Burke family members Clarence Jnr. (b. 1951), James (b. 1952), Aloha (b. 1950), Kenneth (b. 1954) and Dennis (b. 1953). Discovered and produced by Curtis Mayfield, this young quintet enjoyed a consistent run of R&B chart success, with releases on the Windy C, Curtom and Buddah labels. The unit's material - 'You Waited Too Long' (1966), 'World Of Fantasy' (1966), 'Come Back' (1966) and 'Danger, She's A Stranger' (1967) - ranged from gentle dance songs to orchestrated ballads, and their fledgling talent was recognized in 1967 with a NATRA award as that year's outstanding R&B group. For two years the group's name was expanded to include five-year-old sibling Cubie, but when the newcomer left in 1969, the line-up reverted to the 5 Stairsteps, later dropping the '5' altogether. Paradoxically, the 5 Stairsteps' biggest hit, 'O-o-h Child' (1970), a US Top 10 entry, came on parting with Mayfield. Instrumentally self-contained, the quintet pursued a direction similar to Sly And The Family Stone, but they were unable to capitalize on this new-found position. The group broke up in 1972, but whereas the majority entered full-time education, Clarence Jnr. and Kenneth became session musicians. In 1976 the duo resumed work with brothers Dennis and James, securing a contract with George Harrison's Dark Horse label at the behest of singer Billy Preston. Although the Stairsteps returned to the soul Top 10 with 'From Us To You', they split up again soon afterwards. Clarence Jnr. subsequently formed the Invisible Man's Band, who recorded two albums, *The Invisible Man's Band* (1980) and *Really Wanna See You* (1981). While Kenneth, latterly known as Keni Burke, enjoyed a successful career as a solo artist and producer.

● ALBUMS: as the Five Stairsteps *The Five Stairsteps* (Windy City 1967)★★★, *Second Resurrection* (1976)★★; as the 5 Stairsteps And Cubie *Our Family Portrait* (Buddah 1968)★★★, *Love's Happening* (Curtom 1969)★★★; as the Stairsteps *Stairsteps* (Buddah 1970)★★★, *The Stairsteps* (Buddah 1971)★★★.

● COMPILATIONS: *Step By Step By Step* (Buddah 1970)★★★, *Comeback - The Best Of The 5 Stairsteps* (Sequel 1990)★★★, *Greatest Hits, Featuring Keni Burke* (Sequel 1995)★★★★.

FIVE STAR

This commercial pop act was formed by the five siblings of the Pearson family, all of whom shared vocal duties and were born in Romford, Essex, England; Deniece (b. 13 June 1968), Doris (b. 8 June 1966), Lorraine (b. 10 August 1967), Stedman (b. 29 June 1964) and Delroy (b. 11 April 1970). Their father, Buster, had been a professional guitarist with a variety of acts including Wilson Pickett, Desmond Dekker and Jimmy Cliff. After his retirement from the live circuit he formed reggae label K&B, then the more commercially disposed Tent Records. His daughters persuaded him to let them record a version of his recently written composition, 'Problematic'. It showed promise and he decided to throw his weight behind their career as manager, while the brothers elected to expand the group to a five-piece.

Although 'Problematic' failed to chart, Buster secured a licensing agreement for Tent with RCA Records, but follow-ups 'Hide And Seek' and 'Crazy' also missed out. However, when Nick Martinelli took over production duties, 1985's 'All Fall Down' reached the charts. Heavy promotion, and the group's choreographed dance routines, ensured that next single, 'Let Me Be The One', followed it into the Top 20. By the time the band's debut album was released, they had worked through six different producers and countless studios. Despite the relative disappointment of chart placings for subsequent singles 'Love Take Over' and 'R.S.V.P.', the band departed for a major US promotional tour. The Walt Disney organization immediately stepped in to offer the band their own show, but Buster declined. Back in the UK, 'System Addict', the seventh single milked from *Luxury Of Life*, became the first to break the Top 10. Both 'Can't Wait Another Minute' and 'Find The Time' repeated the feat, before the band acquired the sponsorship of Crunchie Chocolate Bars for their UK tour. Their next outings would attract the sponsorship of Ultrabite toothpaste, much to the derision of critics who were less than enamoured by their 'squeaky clean' image. Meanwhile, *Silk And Steel*, the second album, climbed slowly to the top of the UK charts. It would eventually earn triple platinum status, unleashing another steady stream of singles. The most successful of these, 'Rain And Shine', achieved their best placing in the singles chart, at number 2. Continued success allowed the family to move from Romford, Essex, to a mansion in Sunningdale, Berkshire, where they installed a massive studio complex. Ever a favourite for media attacks, Buster was variously accused of keeping his offspring in a 'palatial prison', and of spending wanton sums of money on trivia. However, as their records proved increasingly unsuccessful, the family were the subject of several media stories concerning their financial instability. These hit a peak when the band were forced to move from their home in 1990. Attempts to resurrect their career in America on Epic failed, with their fortunes hitting an all-time low in October 1991 when Stedman Pearson was fined for public indecency.

● ALBUMS: *Luxury Of Life* (Tent 1985)★★, *Silk And Steel* (Tent 1986)★★★, *Between The Lines* (Tent 1987)★★, *Rock The World* (Tent 1988)★★, *Five Star* (Tent 1990)★★.

● COMPILATIONS: *Greatest Hits* (Tent 1989)★★★.

Flack, Roberta

b. 10 February 1937, Asheville, North Carolina, USA. Born into a musical family, Flack graduated from Howard University with a BA in music. She was discovered singing and playing jazz in a Washington nightclub by pianist Les McCann, who recommended her talents to Atlantic Records. Two classy albums, *First Take* and *Chapter Two*, garnered considerable acclaim for their skilful, often introspective, content before Flack achieved huge success with a poignant version of folk-singer Ewan MacColl's ballad, 'First Time Ever I Saw Your Face'. Recorded in 1969, it was a major international hit three years later, following its inclusion in the film *Play Misty For Me*. Further hits came with 'Where Is The Love?' (1972), a duet with Donny Hathaway, and 'Killing Me Softly With His Song' (1973), where Flack's penchant for sweeter, more MOR-styled compositions gained an ascendancy. Her cool, almost unemotional style benefited from a measured use of slow material, although she seemed less comfortable on up-tempo songs. Flack's self-assurance wavered during the mid-70s, but further duets with Hathaway, 'The Closer I Get To You' (1978) and 'You Are My Heaven' (1980), suggested a rebirth. She was shattered when her partner committed suicide in 1979, but in the 80s Flack enjoyed a fruitful partnership with Peabo Bryson that reached a commercial, if sentimental, peak with 'Tonight I Celebrate My Love' in 1983. *Set The Night To Music* was produced by the highly respected Arif Mardin, but the bland duet with Maxi Priest on the title track was representative of this soulless collection of songs. Still, Roberta Flack remains a crafted, if precisionist, performer.

● ALBUMS: *First Take* (Atlantic 1970)★★★★, *Chapter Two* (Atlantic 1970)★★★, *Quiet Fire* (Atlantic 1971)★★, with Donny Hathaway *Roberta Flack And Donny Hathaway* (Atlantic 1972)★★★, *Killing Me Softly* (Atlantic 1973)★★, *Feel Like Making Love* (Atlantic 1975)★★, *Blue Lights In The Basement* (Atlantic 1978)★★, *Roberta Flack* (Atlantic 1978)★★, with Hathaway *Roberta Flack Featuring Donny Hathaway* (Atlantic 1980)★★★, with Peabo Bryson *Live And More* (Atlantic 1980)★★, *Bustin' Loose* (MCA 1981)★★, *I'm The One* (Atlantic 1982)★★, with Bryson *Born To Love* (Capitol 1983)★★★, *Oasis* (Atlantic 1989)★★, *Set The Night To Music* (Atlantic 1991)★★, *Roberta* (Atlantic/East West 1995)★★★.

● COMPILATIONS: *The Best Of Roberta Flack* (Atlantic 1980)★★★, *Softly With These Songs: The Best Of ...* (Atlantic 1993)★★★.

● FURTHER READING: *Roberta Flack: Sound Of Velvet Melting*, Linda Jacobs.

● FILMS: *Body Rock* (1984).

Flamingos

This R&B vocal group, formed in Chicago, Illinois, USA, in 1951, was renowned for producing the tightest and most gorgeous harmonies of the rock 'n' roll era. For much of their history they consisted of Zeke Carey (b. 24 January 1933, Bluefield, Virginia, USA), Jake Carey (b. 9 September 1926, Pulaski, Virginia, USA), Paul Wilson (b. 6 January 1935, Chicago, Illinois, USA, d. May 1988) and Johnny Carter (b. 2 June 1934, Chicago, Illinois, USA). The group's first lead was Sollie McElroy (b. 16 July 1933, Gulfport, Mississippi, USA, d. 15 January 1995), who brought the group regional fame on 'Golden Teardrops' for the Chance label in 1954. He was replaced by Nate Nelson (b. 10 April 1932, Chicago, Illinois, USA, d. 10 April 1984) who brought the group into the rock 'n' roll era with the magnificent ballad 'I'll Be Home', a number 5 R&B hit in 1956 on the Chess label. There then followed a period of disarray, in which Carter and Zeke Carey were lost to the draft. The Flamingos brought into the group Tommy Hunt (b. 18 June 1933, Pittsburgh, Pennsylvania, USA) and Terry Johnson (b. 12 November 1935, Baltimore, Maryland, USA) and moved to New York where they signed with End Records in 1958. At End the

Flamingos had their biggest US hits, 'Lovers Never Say Goodbye' (R&B number 25 in 1958), 'I Only Have Eyes For You' (R&B number 3 and pop number 11 in 1959), 'Nobody Loves Me Like You' (R&B number 23 and pop Top 30 in 1960), the latter song written by Sam Cooke. One of the group's last outstanding records was 'I Know Better' (1962), a Drifters' sound-alike that captured top spots in many markets. During the early 60s the Flamingos lost the rest of their original members, except for Jake and Zeke Carey. The cousins managed to achieve some minor hits during the soul era, notably 'Boogaloo Party', which was the group's only UK chart hit when it reached number 26 in 1969 (three years earlier it was a US R&B number 22 hit). The Flamingos' last US chart record was 'Buffalo Soldier' in 1970 (R&B Top 30). Nate Nelson died in 1984 and Paul Wilson in 1988. Sollie McElroy, after leaving the Flamingos in 1955, joined the Moroccos, with whom he recorded for three years, and Johnny Carter joined the Dells in 1960.

● ALBUMS: *The Flamingos* (Checker 1959)★★★, *Flamingos Serenade* (End 1959)★★★, *Flamingos Favorites* (End 1960)★★★, *Requestfully Yours* (End 1960)★★★, *The Sound Of The Flamingos* (End 1962)★★★, *The Spiritual And Folk Moods Of The Flamingos* (1963)★★, *Their Hits - Then And Now* (Philips 1966)★★, *Flamingos Today* (1971)★★.

● COMPILATIONS: *Collectors Showcase: The Flamingos* (Constellation 1964)★★★, *Golden Teardrops* (1982)★★★, *Flamingos* (Chess 1984)★★★★, *The Chess Sessions* (Chess 1987)★★★, *The Best Of The Flamingos* (Rhino 1990)★★★★, *The Flamingos: I Only Have Eyes For You* (Sequel 1991)★★★, *The Flamingos Meet The Moonglows: The Complete 25 Chance Recordings* (Vee Jay 1993)★★★.

● FILMS: *Go Johnny Go* (1958).

FLARES

From Los Angeles, California, USA, the members of this vocal group were Aaron Collins, Willie Davis, Tommy Miller and George Hollis. The Flares were a one-hit-wonder, but they had a extensive pedigree in the music field long before their one hit. Collins and Davis had been members of the Cadets/Jacks during the 50s and had built the Flares on the ashes of that group. Miller and Hollis had been members of the Flairs, who were stable-mates with the Cadets/Jacks on the label complex owned by the Bihari brothers. The Flares signed with the small Felsted label in 1960 and on their third release they reached the charts with 'Footstompin'' (number 20 R&B, number 25 pop) in 1961 (the song was covered by David Bowie in 1975 on *Fame*). Capitol Records took notice and picked up the group for their Press subsidiary, releasing an album and a spate of dance-related songs. The group disbanded not long after the release of their last Press single in 1963.

● ALBUMS: *Encore Of Footstompin' Hits* (Press 1961)★★★.

FLEMONS, WADE

b. 25 September 1940, Coffeyville, Kansas, USA, d. 13 October 1993. Flemons made a brief impact on the R&B scene in the late 50s and early 60s, recording hits for the Chicago-based Vee Jay Records. He was raised in Wichita, Kansas, until the age of 15, when he moved with his parents to Battle Creek, Michigan. There he formed a vocal group, the Newcomers, and was discovered by Vee Jay Records in 1958. On Flemons's first hit, 'Here I Stand' (number 19 R&B, number 80 pop), the company billed the act as Wade Flemons And The Newcomers. As a solo artist, he charted again in 1960 with 'Easy Lovin'' (number 10 R&B, number 70 pop), but the b-side, 'Woops Now', received solid airplay in many areas. Flemons's remake of the Percy Mayfield song 'Please Send Me Someone To Love' (number 20 R&B), in 1961, was his last chart record. Flemons deserved to chart in 1964 with his definitive version of 'I Knew You When', which Billy Joe Royal put high on the pop charts a year later. Flemons was a co-writer for one of the Dells' biggest hits, 'Stay In My Corner'. In the early 70s he played keyboards for Earth, Wind And Fire, who then recorded for Warner Brothers, but was not a part of the group after they signed with Columbia in 1973.

● ALBUMS: *Wade Flemons* (Vee Jay 1960)★★★.

FLETCHER, DARROW

b. 23 January 1951, Inkster, Michigan, USA, and raised in Chicago, Illinois. Fletcher's only hit was 'The Pain Gets A Little Deeper' (number 23 R&B), released in early 1966 on the Groovy label, when he was still a freshman in high school. He toured with Stevie Wonder before recording with his stepfather, Johnny Haygood, who operated the small Jacklyn label in Chicago. No more national hits followed, but Fletcher enjoyed a big local hit with 'Sitting There That Night' (1966), a perfect example of Chicago-style, soft, mid-tempo soul, with its Curtis Mayfield-style lyrical guitar. Further singles were released on the Revue, UNI, Congress and Genna labels. His last chart record was in 1976 for Ray Charles's Crossover label, but it provoked little interest.

FLIRTATIONS

A British-based R&B female group, who originally came from New York City, New York, USA. The Supremes were extremely popular during the late 60s, and record companies were keen to record any female groups who sounded like them. The Flirtations were the beneficiaries of this phenomenon. The members were sisters Shirley and Earnestine Pearce and Viola Billups. The Pearce sisters had earlier been in the Gypsies, but after minor success the group broke up. Recording in England for the Deram label, the Flirtations had a notable hit in 1969 with a Supremes-styled number, 'Nothing But A Heartache' (number 34 pop), which sounded rather retrograde in the soul market, where it did not chart.

● ALBUMS: *Love Makes The World Go Round* (Deram 1969)★★.

FLOATERS

Originally from Detroit, USA, Charles Clark (Libra), Larry Cunningham (Cancer), Paul Mitchell (Leo), Ralph Mitchell (Aquarius) and latterly, Jonathan 'Mighty Midget' Murray, who joined the group in 1978, were responsible for one of soul's more aberrant moments.

'Float On', with its astrological connotations and Barry White-influenced machismo, was saved from utter ignominy by a light, almost ethereal melody line that was effective enough to provide the group with a US number 2 and a UK number 1 hit single in 1977. The Floaters could not survive the gimmick and although two further singles reached the R&B Top 50, this often-ridiculed performance remains their lasting testament.

● ALBUMS: *Floaters* (ABC 1977)★★★, *Magic* (ABC 1978)★★, *Into The Future* (ABC 1979)★★.

FLOYD, EDDIE

b. 25 June 1935, Montgomery, Alabama, USA. A founder-member of the Detroit-based Falcons, Floyd was present on both their major hits, 'You're So Fine' (1959) and 'I Found A Love' (1962). He then recorded solo for Lupine in Detroit and Safice in Washington, DC, before moving to Memphis in 1965 to join the Stax organization. He first made his mark there as a composer, penning Wilson Pickett's '634-5789', among others. During Floyd's recording tenure at Stax, he enjoyed the use of the session bands Booker T. And The MGs and the Mar-Keys. He opened his account with 'Things Get Better' (1965), followed by the anthem-like 'Knock On Wood' (1966), one of soul's enduring moments, and probably the only time 'lightning' and 'frightening' have been coupled without sounding trite. Although subsequent releases failed to match its success, a series of powerful singles, including 'Love Is A Doggone Good Thing' (1967) and 'Big Bird' (1968), confirmed Floyd's stature both as a performer and songwriter. Although his compositions were recorded by several acts, his next US Top 20 pop hit came with Sam Cooke's 'Bring It On Home To Me' in 1968. Floyd stayed with Stax until its bankruptcy in 1975, whereupon he moved to Malaco Records. His spell there was thwarted by commercial indifference and he left the label for Mercury in 1977, but met with no better results. Briefly relocated to London, he recorded under the aegis of Mod resurrectionists Secret Affair, before surfacing in New York with the album *Try Me*. In 1988, Floyd linked up with William Bell's Wilbe venture and issued his *Flashback* album. In 1990 Floyd appeared live with a re-formed Booker T. And The MGs.

● ALBUMS: *Knock On Wood* (Stax 1967)★★★, *I've Never Found A Girl* (Stax 1968)★★★, *You've Got To Have Eddie* (Stax 1969)★★★, *California Girl* (Stax 1970)★★, *Down To Earth* (Stax 1971)★★, *Baby Lay Your Head Down* (Stax 1973)★★, *Soul Street* (Stax 1974)★★, *Experience* (Malaco 1977)★★, *Try Me* (1985)★★, *Flashback* (Wilbe 1988)★★.

● COMPILATIONS: *Rare Stamps* (Stax 1968)★★★, *Chronicle* (1979)★★★, *The Best Of Eddie Floyd* (Stax/Ace 1988)★★★★, *I've Never Found A Girl* (1992)★★★, *Rare Stamps/I've Never Found A Girl* (1993)★★★.

FORD, FRANKIE

b. Francis Guzzo, 4 August 1939, Gretna, Louisiana, USA. A rocker from a suburb of New Orleans, Frankie Ford is second cousin to that other New Orleans legend Dr. John. His first major appearance was on *Ted Mack's Amateur Hour Talent Show*, where he sang with Carmen Miranda and Sophie Tucker. After winning a scholarship to South Eastern College, Hammond, he started his first band with schoolfriends. By 1958 he was singing with the Syncopators, when he was asked to audition for Ace Records. Subsequently, he released his first single, 'Cheatin' Woman', as Frankie Ford. Fellow musician Huey 'Piano' Smith (b. 26 January 1934, New Orleans, Louisiana, USA) had previously recorded with his group the Clowns a self-penned song called 'Sea Cruise', but Ace persuaded him to let Ford record a new vocal over Bobby Marcham's original. They also added a few extra effects such as paddle-steamer whistle blows, which altered the song enough for Ford to claim a co-writing credit. Released under the title Frankie Ford with Huey 'Piano' Smith and his Clowns, it sold over a million copies and docked in the national Top 20. It was perceived in retrospect as a rock 'n' roll classic, and was revived by Jerry Lee Lewis, Herman's Hermits, Sha Na Na, John Fogerty and Shakin' Stevens. Both 'Sea Cruise' and its follow-up, 'Alimony', were taken from original tapes recorded by composer Huey Smith with the Clowns; the lead vocals were then erased and Ford's singing superimposed. As Morgus And The Ghouls, Ford and the Clowns also recorded 'Morgus The Magnificent', a novelty tribute to a local television personality. There was also an unissued homage to Fats Domino, written and recorded by Ford and Dave Bartholomew. Ford left Ace in 1960 to form his own Spinet Records and signed to Liberty in 1960, but never repeated the success of 'Sea Cruise'. He also formed a 'supergroup' with Huey Smith, Robert Parker (hitmaker of 'Barefootin'') and Dr. John (under various pseudonyms due to contractual problems), and they recorded various New Orleans favourites. He continued to record for obscure labels throughout the 70s. In 1971, he opened a club in New Orleans' French Quarter where he became a cabaret fixture and tourist attraction. Moreover, he still looked youthful enough to play his younger self in the 1978 movie *American Hot Wax*, set in the late 50s. As part of a package, he toured the UK in 1985 along with Rick Nelson, Bobby Vee and Bo Diddley. Ford resents the term one-hit-wonder, and rightly pointed out that his four recordings of 'Sea Cruise' have now sold over 30 million copies worldwide.

● ALBUMS: *Let's Take A Sea Cruise* (Ace 1959)★★, *Frankie Ford* (1976)★★.

● COMPILATIONS: *New Orleans Dynamo* (Ace 1989)★★★.

● FILMS: *American Hot Wax* (1978).

FORMATIONS

This Philadelphia-based soul group comprised Jerry Akines, Johnny Bellmon, Reginald Turner and Victor Drayton. Originally formed by Akines and Drayton as the Extremes, they were renamed when Bellmon replaced Ernie Brooks in 1965. They recorded for Thom Bell at Cameo, but nothing was released. In 1968, 'At The Top Of The Stairs', produced in New York by John Madara and ex-Danny And The Juniors member Danny White on MGM Records, gave them a minor US hit. After a couple of less successful releases, they changed their name to the Corner Boys and recorded on Gamble And Huff's Neptune label, with 'Gang War' making the R&B Top 50 in

1969. In 1971 they had their biggest success as the writers of Wilson Pickett's Top 20 hit 'Don't Let The Green Grass Fool You'. They then changed their name again and recorded as the Silent Majority on Holland/Dozier/Holland's Hot Wax label. As recording artists they enjoyed their biggest success in 1971 when the Motown-influenced 'At The Top Of The Stairs' was re-released in the UK and made the Top 30.

FORREST

This US soul group was based around lead singer Forrest Thomas (b. 1953, USA). Despite finding little success in the US national pop or R&B charts, in 1983, the group achieved two UK hits on CBS with 'Rock The Boat' (formerly a hit for the Hues Corporation in 1974) which reached number 4, and the follow-up, 'Feel The Need In Me', reached the Top 20 that same year (previously a hit for the Detroit Emeralds in 1973). By the end of the year, Forrest's brief chart success came to a halt when 'One Lover (Don't Stop The Show)' failed to climb higher than number 67. Subsequently, Thomas (and Forrest) faded from the scene.

● ALBUMS: *Forrest* (Columbia 1983)★★.

FORTUNE RECORDS

Formed in 1951 by husband and wife Jack and Devora Brown, Fortune Records was an R&B record label based in Detroit, Michigan, USA. The Browns had begun a music publishing company in 1947 and decided to expand into recordings four years later. The label's top act became the soulful vocal group Nolan Strong and the Diablos, who began recording for Fortune in 1956. Their singles, including 'The Wind' and 'Mind Over Matter', are highly prized by R&B record collectors. The group placed only one single, 'Way You Dog Me Around', on the R&B charts. Another artist, Andre Williams, recorded his best-known track, 'Bacon Fat', in 1955 before it was leased to Epic Records and became a Top 10 R&B hit. Another Fortune single, 'Village Of Love' by Nathaniel Mayer And The Fabulous Twilights, was also leased, to United Artists, although the Top 20 R&B placing went to the Fortune version. The label stopped issuing new releases by the 70s, but has survived by reissuing its earlier recordings, which are anxiously bought by devoted R&B collectors.

FOUNDATIONS

Formed in January 1967, the Foundations were discovered by London record dealer Barry Class as they rehearsed in the Butterfly, a club situated in a basement below his office. He introduced the group to songwriters Tony Macauley and John MacLeod, whose composition 'Baby, Now That I've Found You' became the group's debut release. An engaging slice of commercial pop/soul, the single soared to the top of the UK charts and by February 1968 had reached number 9 in the USA, with global sales eventually exceeding three million. The group's multiracial line-up included Clem Curtis (b. 28 November 1940, Trinidad, West Indies; vocals), Alan Warner (b. 21 April 1947, London, England; guitar), Tony Gomez (b. 13 December 1948, Colombo, Sri Lanka; organ), Pat Burke (b. 9 October 1937, Jamaica, West Indies; tenor saxophone, flute), Mike Elliot (b. 6 August 1929, Jamaica, West Indies; tenor saxophone), Eric Allan Dale (b. 4 March 1936, Dominica, West Indies; trombone), Peter Macbeth (b. 2 February 1943, London, England; bass) and Tim Harris (b. 14 January 1948, London, England; drums). Dale was a former member of the Terry Lightfoot and Alex Welsh jazz bands, while Elliot had backed Colin Hicks, brother of British rock 'n' roll singer Tommy Steele. This mixture of youth and experience drew much contemporary comment. The Foundations scored a second multi-million-seller in 1968 with 'Build Me Up, Buttercup'. Written by Macauley in partnership with Manfred Mann's Michael D'Abo, this compulsive song reached number 2 in Britain before topping the US chart for two weeks. The group enjoyed further success with several similarly styled releases, including 'Back On My Feet Again' and 'Any Old Time' (both 1968), but their momentum faltered when Curtis embarked on an ill-starred solo career. He was replaced by Colin Young (b. 12 September 1944, Barbados, West Indies), but the departure of Elliot signalled internal dissatisfaction. 'In The Bad Bad Old Days' (1969) returned the group to the UK Top 10, but that year's minor hit, 'Born To Live And Born To Die', was their last chart entry. The septet split up in 1970 when the rhythm section broke away to form the progressive group Pluto. A completely new line-up later resurrected the Foundations' name with little success.

● ALBUMS: *From The Foundations* (Pye 1967)★★, *Rocking The Foundations* (Pye 1968)★★, *Digging The Foundations* (Pye 1969)★★.

● COMPILATIONS: *Back To The Beat* (PRT 1983)★★, *The Best Of The Foundations* (PRT 1987)★★★, *Foundations Greatest Hits* (Knight 1990)★★★.

● FILMS: *The Cool Ones* (1967).

FOUR BLAZES

The most famous line-up of this group from Chicago, Illinois, USA, was Tommy Braden (d. 1957; lead vocals, bass), William 'Shorty' Hill (vocals, guitar), Floyd McDaniels (vocals, guitar), and Paul Lindsley 'Jelly' Holt (vocals, drums). The Four Blazes became hit-makers in the early 50s with a mélange of jive, ballad, and jazz sounds that combined vocal harmony with their own instrumental support. This type of group was common in the 40s, when acts such as Cats And The Fiddle and Five Red Caps held sway, and the Four Blazes were one of the last of this breed to have R&B hits. The group was formed in 1940 by Holt, who recruited Hill, McDaniels, and bassist Prentice Butler, and they soon became perennials in Chicago clubs. They became the Five Blazes when they added pianist and lead vocalist Ernie Harper in 1946. They first recorded for Aristocrat in 1947, but were unable to garner more than a few local plays for their records. In 1950, after Butler died and Harper left the group. Holt recruited Tennessee bassist Tommy Braden, who became the new lead singer of the renamed Four Blazes. In 1952 they signed with United and immediately achieved a number 1 R&B hit in 1952 with the Braden-composed 'Mary Jo'. Tenor saxophonist Eddie Chamblee was prominently featured on the record and in effect became a part of the group both while touring and recording. 'Mary Jo' was followed with two more charting records, 'Please Send Her Back To Me' (number 7 R&B) and 'Perfect Woman' (number 5 R&B), both from 1953. Another record that received strong regional sales was 'My Hat's On The Side Of My Head' (1953). Braden left the group in late 1954, and neither he nor the group could return to the charts. Holt recruited new members and continued to play Chicago clubs as the Five Blazes until disbanding the group in 1957. Braden died in 1957.

● COMPILATIONS: *Swingin' & Singin'* six tracks, remainder by the Dozier Boy (P-Vine 1982)★★★.

FOUR BUDDIES

The Four Buddies, from Baltimore, Maryland, USA, were one of the best representatives of the smooth, deep-sounding vocal harmony style that was popular in the early 50s. The group members were Leon Harrison (lead, first tenor), Gregory Carroll (second tenor), Bert Palmer (baritone) and Tommy Smith (bass). The group was discovered and signed by Savoy Records in 1951 and managed by Friz Pollard (the famed All-American football star from Brown in 1915). They first recorded as the Metronomes with Johnny Otis on Savoy. Then as the Four Buddies they had one R&B hit, 'I Will Wait' (number 2 R&B), in 1951, but other outstanding songs included 'My Summer's Gone' and 'Don't Leave Me Now'. The group toured extensively from Las Vegas to the chitlin' circuit theatres of the Apollo and the Howard. When the Four Buddies' contract at Savoy expired in 1953, the group broke up. Gregory joined the Orioles a year later, but Harrison formed a new group, the Buddies, which included second tenor Luther Dixon (who later produced and wrote for Scepter, Wand), baritone Roger Wainwright and bass Danny Ferguson. During 1954 the Buddies recorded for Glory and as the Barons for Decca, but without any chart success.

FOUR FELLOWS

Formed in Brooklyn, New York, USA, the group consisted of Jimmy McGowan, Larry Banks, Davy Jones and Teddy Williams. McGowan and Williams began their careers in the late 40s when they were a part of a gospel and jubilee group, the Starlight Toppers. That unit broke up around 1951, but in 1953 McGowan and Williams joined Banks and Jones to form the Four Fellows. The group's debut for Derby went unnoticed, and they next signed with Glory Records. They recorded a fine record, 'I Wish I Didn't Love You', but it, too, went unnoticed. The Four Fellows' third record was a song that Banks had written while serving in the Korean War, 'Soldier Boy' (not be confused with the Shirelles' later hit of the same title), and it finally reached number 4 R&B in 1955. The following year, after the group recorded the fine ballad 'Darling You', Jones left and joined the Rays. He was replaced by Jimmy Mobley. The Four Fellows never returned to the charts and broke up in 1957. Banks later wrote the hit 'Go Now', which was first recorded by his wife, Bessie Banks, and became a hit for the Moody Blues in 1964. McGowan wrote and published his memoirs in 1983 under the title *Here Today! Here To Stay!*.

FOUR TOPS

Levi Stubbs (b. *c.*1938, Detroit, Michigan, USA), Renaldo 'Obie' Benson (b. 1937, Detroit, Michigan, USA), Lawrence Peyton (b. *c.*1938, Detroit, Michigan, USA, d. 10 June 1997) and Abdul 'Duke' Fakir (b. *c.*1938, Detroit, Michigan, USA), first sang together at a party in Detroit in 1954. Calling themselves the Four Aims, they began performing at supper clubs in the city, with a repertoire of jazz songs and standards. In 1956, they changed their name to the Four Tops to avoid confusion with the popular singing group the Ames Brothers, and recorded a one-off single for the R&B label Chess. Further unsuccessful recordings appeared on Red Top, Columbia and Riverside between 1958 and 1962, before the Four Tops were signed to the Motown jazz subsidiary Workshop, in 1963. Motown boss Berry Gordy elected not to release their initial album, *Breaking Through*, in 1964, and suggested that they record with the label's Holland/Dozier/Holland writing and production team. The initial release from this liaison was 'Baby I Need Your Loving', which showcased the group's strong harmonies and the gruff, soulful lead vocals of Levi Stubbs; it reached the US Top 20. The following year, another Holland/Dozier/Holland song, 'I Can't Help Myself', topped the charts, and established the Four Tops as one of Motown's most successful groups. Holland/Dozier /Holland continued to write and produce for the Four Tops until 1967. The pinnacle of this collaboration was 'Reach Out I'll Be There', a transatlantic hit in 1966. This represented the pinnacle of the traditional Motown style, bringing an almost symphonic arrangement to an R&B love song; producer Phil Spector described the record as 'black (Bob) Dylan'. Other major hits such as 'It's The Same Old Song' and 'Bernadette' were not as ambitious, although they are still regarded as Motown classics today. In 1967, the Four Tops began to widen their appeal with soul-tinged versions of pop hits, such as the Left Banke's 'Walk Away Renee' and Tim Hardin's 'If I Were A Carpenter'. The departure of Holland, Dozier and Holland from Motown later that year brought a temporary halt to the group's progress, and it was only in 1970, under the aegis of producer/writers like Frank Wilson and Smokey Robinson, that the Four Tops regained their hit status with a revival of the Tommy Edwards hit 'It's All In The Game', and the socially aware ballad 'Still Waters'. That same year, they teamed up with the Supremes for the first of three albums of collaborations. Another revival, Richard Harris's hit 'MacArthur Park', brought them success in 1971, while Renaldo Benson also co-wrote Marvin Gaye's hit single 'What's Going On'. However, after working with the Moody Blues on 'A Simple Game' in 1972, the Four Tops elected to leave Motown when the corporation relocated its head office from Detroit to California. They signed a contract with Dunhill, and immediately restored their chart success with records that marked a return to their mid-60s style, notably the theme song to the 'blaxploitation' movie *Shaft In Africa*, 'Are You Man Enough'. Subsequent releases were less dynamic, and for the remainder of the 70s the Four Tops enjoyed only sporadic chart success, although they continued touring and performing their Motown hits. After two years of inactivity at the end of the decade, they joined Casablanca Records, and immediately secured a number 1 soul hit with 'When She Was My Girl', which revived their familiar style. Subsequent releases in a similar vein also charted in Britain and America.

In 1983, the group performed a storming medley 'duel' of their 60s hits with the Temptations during the Motown 25th Anniversary television special. They re-signed to the label for the aptly titled *Back Where I Belong*, one side of which was produced by Holland/Dozier/Holland. However, disappointing sales and disputes about the group's musical direction led them to leave Motown once again for Arista, where they found immediate success in 1988 with the singles 'Indestructible' and 'Loco In Acapulco', the latter taken from the soundtrack to the film *Buster*. The Four Tops retained a constant line-up from their inception up until Peyton's death in June 1997. Their immaculate choreography and harmonies have ensured them ongoing success as a live act from the mid-60s to the present day - notably in the UK and Europe, where they have always been held in higher regard than in their homeland.

● ALBUMS: *Four Tops* (Motown 1965)★★★, *Four Tops No. 2* (Motown 1965)★★★★, *Four Tops On Top* (Motown 1966)★★★★, *Four Tops Live!* (Motown 1966)★★★, *Four Tops On Broadway* (Motown 1967)★★★, *Four Tops Reach Out* (Motown 1967)★★★★, *Yesterday's Dreams* (Motown 1968)★★★, *Four Tops Now!* (Motown 1969)★★★, *Soul Spin* (Motown 1969)★★★, *Still Waters Run Deep* (Motown 1970)★★★, *Changing Times* (Motown 1970)★★★, with the Supremes *The Magnificent Seven* (Motown 1970)★★★★, with the Supremes *The Return Of The Magnificent Seven* (Motown 1971)★★, with the Supremes *Dynamite* (Motown 1972)★★★, *Nature Planned It* (Motown 1972)★★★, *Keeper Of The Castle* (Dunhill 1972)★★★, *Shaft In Africa* film soundtrack (Dunhill 1973)★★, *Main Street People* (Dunhill 1973)★★, *Meeting Of The Minds* (Dunhill 1974)★★, *Live And In Concert* (Dunhill 1974)★★, *Night Lights Harmony* (ABC 1975)★★, *Catfish* (ABC 1976)★★, *The Show Must Go On* (ABC 1977)★★, *At The Top* (MCA 1978)★★, *The Four Tops Tonight!* (Casablanca 1981)★★, *One More Mountain* (Casblanca 1982)★★, *Back Where I Belong* (Motown 1983)★★, *Magic* (Motown 1985)★★, *Hot Nights* (Motown 1986)★★, *Indestructible* (Arista 1988)★★.

● COMPILATIONS: *Four Tops Greatest Hits* (Motown 1967)★★★★★, *Four Tops Greatest Hits, Vol. 2* (Motown 1971)★★★★, *Four Tops Story* (Motown 1973)★★★★, *Four Tops Anthology* (Motown 1974)★★★★★, *Best Of The Four Tops* (K-Tel 1982)★★★, *Collection: Four Tops* (Castle 1992)★★★.

FOUR TUNES

The Four Tunes, like many African-American groups of the 40s and early 50s, were a pop rather than a R&B ensemble. The group had its origin in the Brown Dots, and were formed by Ivory 'Deek' Watson after he left the Ink Spots in 1945. The remainder of the group was Pat Best, Jimmy Gordon and Jimmy Nabbie. While still with the Brown Dots, Best, Gordon and Nabbie joined with Danny Owens in 1946 to record on the Manor label as the Sentimentalists, changing their name shortly afterwards to the Four Tunes. They backed Savannah Churchill on her 1947 hit 'I Want To Be Loved (But Only By You)', but did not attain any national hits of their own while with Manor. In 1948 they finally left the Brown Dots and a year later signed with RCA. Their two big chart hits came after with Jubilee in 1953 with 'Marie' (number 2 R&B, number 13 pop) from 1953, and 'I Understand (Just How You Feel)' (number 7 R&B, number 6 pop) from 1954. The Four Tunes made their last recordings in 1956 and finally broke up in 1963. Their musical legacy was remembered in 1961 when the G-Clefs had a big hit with 'I Understand (Just How You Feel)' and in 1965 when the Bachelors had success with 'Marie'.

● ALBUMS: *The Four Tunes: 12 X 4* (Jubilee 1957)★★★.

● COMPILATIONS: *The Complete Jubilee Sessions* (Sequel 1992)★★★.

FOUR VAGABONDS

A vocal group formed in St. Louis, Missouri, USA. In the wake of the success of the Mills Brothers, a number of African-American groups emerged who specialized in harmonized pop songs flavoured by imitation horn sounds, and the Four Vagabonds were one of the most outstanding. Unlike the Mills Brothers, however, the group throughout its career was not primarily a recording group, but instead radio performers. For most of their career they were based in Chicago and consisted of lead John Jordan, tenor Robert O'Neal, baritone Narval Taborn and bass and guitarist Ray 'Happy Pappy' Grant Jnr. They formed the group at Vashon High in 1933 and soon began singing on St. Louis radio stations. In 1936 they moved to Chicago and became regulars on the popular radio show *Don McNeal's Breakfast Club*, on which for the next decade they sang pop tunes and spirituals. Radio exposure for the group expanded rapidly in the years that followed, and they appeared on programmes such as *Club Matinee*, hosted by Durwood Kirby and Gary Moore, ABC's *Tin Pan Alley*, the *Curt Massey Show*, the *Chesterfield Supper Club* with Perry Como, and a programme with Danny Thomas. The Four Vagabonds first recorded in 1941. Their one hit was 'It Can't Be Wrong' (number 3 R&B), from 1943. The group made its last record in 1949 and broke up in 1952.

● COMPILATIONS: *Yesterday's Memories* (Relic 1988)★★★.

FOXX, INEZ AND CHARLIE

Inez Foxx (b. 9 September 1942, Greensboro, North Carolina, USA) and Charlie Foxx (b. 23 October 1939, Greensboro, North Carolina, USA). A brother and sister duo, Inez was a former member of the Gospel Tide Chorus. Her first solo single, 'A Feeling', was issued on Brunswick Records, credited to 'Inez Johnston'. Charlie was, meanwhile, a budding songwriter and his reworking of a nursery rhyme, 'Mockingbird', became their first single together. Released on the Sue label subsidiary Symbol, it was a US Top 10 hit in 1963, although it was not until 1969 that the song charted in the UK Top 40. Their immediate releases followed the same contrived pattern, but later recordings for Musicor/Dynamo, in particular 'I

Stand Accused', were more adventurous. However, their final hit together, '(1-2-3-4-5-6-7) Count The Days' (1967), was modelled closely on that early style. Solo again, Inez continued to record for Dynamo before signing with Stax/Volt in 1972. Although apparently uncomfortable with their recording methods, the results, including the *Inez Foxx In Memphis* album, were excellent.

● ALBUMS: *Mockingbird* (Sue 1963)★★★, *Inez And Charlie Foxx* (Sue 1964)★★★, *Come By Here* (Musicor/Dynamo 1965)★★★.
Solo: Inez Foxx *Inez Foxx In Memphis* (Volt 1972)★★★★, *At Memphis And More* (Ace 1990)★★★. Charlie Foxx *Foxx/Hill* (Foxx/Hill 1982)★★★.

● COMPILATIONS: *The Best Of Charlie And Inez Foxx* (Stateside 1986)★★★, *Count The Days* (Charly 1995)★★★, *Greatest Hits* (Musicor/Dynamo 1996)★★★★.

FRANKLIN, ARETHA

b. 25 March 1942, Memphis, Tennessee, USA. Aretha Franklin's music is steeped in the traditions of the church. Her father, C.L. Franklin, was a Baptist preacher who, once he had moved his family to Detroit, became famous throughout black America for his fiery sermons and magnetic public appearances. He knew the major gospel stars Mahalia Jackson and Clara Ward, who in turn gave his daughter valuable tutelage. At the age of 12, Aretha was promoted from the choir to become a featured soloist. Two years later she began recording for JVB and Checker. Between 1956 and 1960, her output consisted solely of devotional material, but the secular success of Sam Cooke encouraged a change of emphasis. Franklin auditioned for John Hammond, who signed her to Columbia. Sadly, the company was indecisive on how best to showcase her remarkable talent. They tried blues, cocktail jazz, standards, pop songs and contemporary soul hits, each of which wasted the singer's natural improvisational instincts. There were some occasional bright spots - 'Running Out Of Fools' (1964) and 'Cry Like A Baby' (1966) - but in both cases content succeeded over style. After a dozen albums, a disillusioned Franklin joined Atlantic Records in 1966, where the magnificent 'I Never Loved A Man (The Way I Loved You)', recorded in January 1967 in New York, declared her liberation. The album was scheduled to be made in Muscle Shoals, but Franklin's husband Ted White had an argument with the owner of Fame Studios, Rick Hall. At short notice Jerry Wexler flew the musicians to New York. The single soared into the US Top 10 and, coupled with the expressive 'Do Right Woman – Do Right Man', only the backing track of which was recorded in Alabama, it announced the arrival of a major artist. The releases that followed – 'Respect', 'Baby I Love You', '(You Make Me Feel Like) A Natural Woman', 'Chain Of Fools' and '(Sweet Sweet Baby) Since You've Been Gone' – many of which featured the Fame rhythm section 'borrowed' by Wexler for sessions in New York, confirmed her authority and claim to being the 'Queen Of Soul'. The conditions and atmosphere created by Wexler and the outstanding musicians gave Franklin such confidence that her voice gained power and control. Despite Franklin's professional success, her personal life grew confused. Her relationship with husband and manager White disintegrated, and while excellent singles such as 'Think' still appeared, others betrayed a discernible lethargy. She followed 'Think' with a sublime cover version of Hal David and Burt Bacharach's 'I Say A Little Prayer', giving power and authority to simple yet delightful lyrics: 'the moment I wake up, before I put on my make-up, I say a little prayer for you'. Following a slight dip in her fortunes during the late 60s, she had regained her powers in 1970 as 'Call Me', 'Spirit In The Dark' and 'Don't Play That Song' ably testified. *Aretha Live At Fillmore West* (1971), meanwhile, restated her in-concert power. The following year, another live appearance resulted in *Amazing Grace*, a double gospel set recorded with James Cleveland and the Southern California Community Choir. Its passion encapsulated her career to date. Franklin continued to record strong material throughout the early 70s and enjoyed three R&B chart-toppers, 'Angel', 'Until You Come Back To Me (That's What I'm Gonna Do)' and 'I'm In Love'. Sadly, the rest of the decade was marred by recordings that were at best predictable, at worst dull. It was never the fault of Franklin's voice, merely that the material was often poor and indifferent. Her cameo role in the film *The Blues Brothers*, however, rekindled her flagging career. Franklin moved to Arista Records in 1980 and she immediately regained a commercial momentum with 'United Together' and two confident albums, *Aretha* and *Love All The Hurt Away*. 'Jump To It' and 'Get It Right', both written and produced by Luther Vandross, and *Who's Zoomin' Who?*, continued her rejuvenation. From the album, produced by Narada Michael Walden, Franklin had hit singles with 'Freeway Of Love', 'Another Night' and the superb title track. In the mid-80s, she made the charts again, in company with Annie Lennox ('Sisters Are Doin' It For Themselves') and George Michael ('I Knew You Were Waiting (For Me)'), which went to number 1 in the the USA and UK in 1987. Franklin's *Through The Storm*, from 1989, contained more powerful duets, this time with Elton John on the title track, James Brown ('Gimme Some Lovin'', remixed by Prince for 12-inch), and Whitney Houston ('It Isn't, It Wasn't, It Ain't Never Gonna Be'). The album also included a remake of her 1968 US Top 10 title, 'Think'. In 1991, her *What You See Is What You Sweat* was criticized for its cornucopia of different styles: a couple of tracks by Burt Bacharach and Carole Bayer Sager; a collaboration with Luther Vandross; a fairly thin title ballad; and the highlight, 'Everyday People', a mainstream disco number, written by Sly Stone and brilliantly produced by Narada Michael Walden. Franklin may now lack the instinct of her classic Atlantic recordings, but as her 'return to gospel' *One Lord One Faith One Baptism* (released in 1987) proved, she is still a commanding singer. Franklin possesses an astonishing voice that has often been wasted on a poor choice of material. She is rightfully heralded as the Queen of Soul, even though that reputation was gained in the 60s. There are certain musical notes that can be played on a saxophone that are chilling; similarly, there are sounds above the twelfth fret on a guitar that are orgasmic - Aretha Franklin is better than any instrument, as she can hit notes that do not exist in instrumental terms. The 4-CD box set *Queen Of Soul*, highlighting the best of her Atlantic recordings, confirmed her position as one of the greatest voices in recording history.

● ALBUMS: *Aretha* (Columbia 1961)★★, *The Electrifying Aretha Franklin* (Columbia 1962)★★, *The Tender, The Moving, The Swinging Aretha Franklin* (Columbia 1962)★★, *Laughing On The Outside* (Columbia 1963)★★, *Unforgettable* (Columbia 1964)★★, *Songs Of Faith* (Checker 1964)★★, *Running Out Of Fools* (Columbia 1964)★★, *Yeah!!!* (Columbia 1965)★★, *Queen Of Soul* (1965)★★★, *Once In A Lifetime* (1965)★★★, *Soul Sister* (Columbia 1966)★★★, *Take It Like You Give It* (Columbia 1967)★★★, *I Never Loved A Man The Way That I Love You* (Atlantic 1967)★★★★★, *Aretha Arrives* (Atlantic 1967)★★★★, *Take A Look* early recordings (Columbia 1967)★★★, *Aretha: Lady Soul* (Atlantic 1968)★★★★★, *Aretha Now* (Atlantic 1968)★★★★★, *Aretha In Paris* (Atlantic 1968)★★★, *Aretha Franklin: Soul '69* (Atlantic 1969)★★★★, *Today I Sing The Blues* (Columbia 1969)★★★★, *Soft And Beautiful* (Columbia 1969)★★★, *I Say A Little Prayer* (1969)★★★, *Aretha Franklin Live* (1969)★★★, *This Girl's In Love With You* (Atlantic 1970)★★★, *Spirit In The Dark* (Atlantic 1970)★★★, *Two Sides Of Love* (1970)★★★, *Aretha Live At Fillmore West* (Atlantic 1971)★★★, *Young, Gifted And Black* (Atlantic 1972)★★★, *Amazing Grace* (Atlantic 1972)★★★, *Hey Now Hey (The Other Side Of The Sky)* (Atlantic 1973)★★, *Let Me Into Your Life* (Atlantic 1974)★★★, *With Everything I Feel In Me* (Atlantic 1974)★★★, *You* (Atlantic 1975)★★, *Sparkle* (Atlantic 1976)★★, *Sweet Passion* (Atlantic 1977)★★, *Satisfaction* (1977)★★★, *Almighty Fire* (Atlantic 1978)★★, *La Diva* (Atlantic 1979)★★, *Aretha* (Arista 1980)★★, *Love All The Hurt Away* (Arista 1981)★★, *Jump To It* (Arista 1982)★★, *Get It Right* (Arista 1983)★★, *Who's Zoomin' Who?* (Arista 1985)★★★, *Aretha* (Arista 1986)★★★, *One Lord, One Faith, One Baptism* (Arista 1987)★★, *Through The Storm* (Arista 1989)★★, *What You See Is What You Sweat* (Arista 1991)★★.

● COMPILATIONS: *Aretha Franklin's Greatest Hits* Columbia recordings 1961-66 (Columbia 1967)★★★, *Aretha's Gold* (Atlantic 1969)★★★★, *Aretha's Greatest Hits* (Atlantic 1971)★★★★, *In The Beginning/The World Of Aretha Franklin 1960-1967* (Columbia 1972)★★★, *The Great Aretha Franklin: The First 12 Sides* (Columbia 1973)★★★, *Ten Years Of Gold* (Atlantic 1976)★★★★, *Legendary Queen Of Soul* (Columbia 1983)★★★★, *Aretha Sings The Blues* (Columbia 1985)★★★, *The Collection* (Castle 1986)★★★★, *Never Grow Old* (Chess 1987)★★★, *20 Greatest Hits* (Warners 1987)★★★★, *Aretha Franklin's Greatest Hits 1960-1965* (Columbia 1987)★★★★, *Queen Of Soul: The Atlantic Recordings* 4-CD box set (Rhino/Atlantic 1992)★★★★★, *Aretha's Jazz* (1993)★★★, *Greatest Hits 1980-1994* (Arista 1994)★★★, *Love Songs* (Rhino/Atlantic 1997)★★★.

● VIDEOS: *Queen Of Soul* (Music Club 1988), *Live At Park West* (PVE 1995).

● FURTHER READING: *Aretha Franklin*, Mark Bego.

● FILMS: *The Blues Brothers* (1980).

FRANKLIN, C.L., REV.

b. Clarence LaVaughn Franklin, 22 January 1915, Sunflower County, Mississippi, USA, d. 24 July 1984. Although his own career was eclipsed by that of his daughter, Aretha Franklin, the Rev. C.L. Franklin was a popular religious recording artist in his own right. Franklin began singing in church at the age of 12 and began preaching two years later. He attended college and gained a ministerial degree, preaching in Mississippi, New York and Tennessee before being named pastor of the New Bethel Baptist Church in Detroit, Michigan, USA, in 1946. He began recording 78s featuring his sermons, for the J-V-B label in 1953, some of which were leased to Chess Records for more widespread distribution. He recorded over a dozen singles for the label. Each summer, daughter Aretha would accompany her father on the road, where he participated in gospel revues; much of her exposure to the gospel singing style came during those tours. In the 60s the Rev. Franklin became active in the civil rights movement and helped organize the 1963 March on Washington, at which Dr. Martin Luther King delivered his famous 'I have a dream' speech. Also the father of Erma Franklin and Carolyn Franklin, the Rev. Franklin was shot by burglars entering his home in 1979. He lapsed into a coma from which he never recovered.

● ALBUMS: *A Wild Man Meets Jesus* (1968)★★★, *Man On The Moon* (1970)★★★.

FRANKLIN, CAROLYN

b. 13 May 1944, Memphis, Tennessee, USA, d. 25 April 1988, Bloomfield Hills, Detroit, Michigan, USA. The younger sister of Aretha and Erma Franklin, Carolyn was born while her pastor father Rev. C.L. Franklin was in charge of the New Salem Baptist Church in Memphis. Subsequently, the family moved to Buffalo in New York State, and then to Detroit, where she and her sisters and two brothers grew up. From an early age, Carolyn played the piano, sang, and wrote her own music and lyrics. She cut some demos in a 'late-night supper-club' style for Lloyd Price's Double L label around 1963/4, and these were released in 1970 on a UK Joy album, *The First Time I Cried*. It included Carolyn's early 60s version of 'Don't Catch The Dog's Bone', which her sister Erma later recorded for Shout. Backing Aretha on her early recordings, alongside Erma and cousin Brenda Bryant (later Corbett), introduced Carolyn to 'big time' secular music, and her own solo recording career did not take off properly until after the early peak of Aretha's post-Columbia success with Atlantic between 1967 and 1969, and Erma's somewhat secondary success for Bert Berns' Shout label during the same period. Her first two albums, *Baby Dynamite* (1969) and *Chain Reaction* (1970), were both produced by Jimmy Radcliffe. Neither album included a hit single, although they contained two songs, 'All I Want To Be Is Your Woman' and 'It's True I'm Gonna Miss You', that became minor R&B hits. Franklin's 1973 album *I'd Rather Be Lonely* was named after a Radcliffe song, and he started out as the album's producer, but died later in the year. He was still credited as co-producer of Franklin's final solo album, *If You Want Me*, due to its inclusion of some earlier material. As well as singing back-up, Carolyn wrote several songs for Aretha, including 'Baby Baby Baby', 'Without Love', 'Sing It Again - Say It Again', 'I Was Made For You', 'Ain't No Way', 'Save Me', 'As Long As You Are There', and the big hit, 'Angel'. In 1980, along with Brenda Corbett and Margaret Branch, she was seen backing her sister during the 'Think' sequence in the successful cult film *The Blues Brothers*, and in 1987, with Erma and Brenda, she supported Aretha's second 'return to gospel' album, *One Lord, One Faith, One Baptism*, recorded at the Franklin family's New Bethel Baptist Church. The same year, in a very different venture, Carolyn sang backing vocals on British singer Paul King's album *Joy*, produced by her close friend Dan Hartman. By this time, Carolyn had cancer, but doggedly pursued her desire to obtain a college degree in entertainment law, which she received some 10 days before she died at Aretha's Bloomfield Hills home in April 1988.

● ALBUMS: *Baby Dynamite* (Shout 1969)★★★, *Chain Reaction* (Shout 1970)★★★, *I'd Rather Be Lonely* (1973)★★★, *If You Want Me* (RCA 1976)★★★.

● COMPILATIONS: *The First Time I Cried* (1970)★★★.

FRANKLIN, ERMA

b. 1943, Memphis, Tennessee, USA. The younger sister of Aretha Franklin, this excellent singer's career has been overshadowed by that of her illustrious sibling. Erma's most celebrated moment came in 1967 with 'Piece Of My Heart', an intense uptown soul ballad co-written and produced by Bert Berns. The song was adopted by Janis Joplin, but Franklin's own progress faltered with the collapse of her record label. Although she did secure a minor 1969 hit with 'Gotta Find Me A Lover (24 Hours A Day)', her later work failed to match that early promise. During the past three decades much of her time has been spent running Boysville, a child care charity in Detroit. In 1992 Levi's chose 'Piece Of My Heart' for one of their television advertisements, and in predictible fashion it scaled the charts and gave Aretha's often overlooked sister her true moment of (belated) glory.

● ALBUMS: *Her Name Is Erma* (Epic 1962)★★★, *Soul Sister* (Brunswick 1969)★★★.

● COMPILATIONS: *Piece Of My Heart - The Best Of* (Epic 1992)★★★, *Golden Classics* (1993)★★★.

FREEEZ

This British funk group was led by John Rocca (b. 23 September 1960, London, England), and included Peter Maas (bass), Andy Stennet (keyboards) and Paul Morgan (drums). Rocca, a former van salesman for the dance music specialist shop Disc Empire, formed the group in 1978. They released their first single, 'Keep In Touch', on their own Pink Rythm (sic) label (one of the first British acts to form their own label), and it narrowly missed the UK Top 40 in 1980 when picked up by Calibre. After moving to Beggars Banquet Records in 1981 they hit the UK Top 10 with 'Southern Freeze', which included vocals by Ingrid Mansfield-Allman (b. London, England). The album of the same name reached the Top 20. The group expanded to a seven piece with the addition of Gordon Sullivan, George Whitmore and new vocalist Alison Gordon. Later reduced to the basic duo of Rocca and Maas, they had their biggest success in 1983 with 'I.O.U.', written and produced in the USA by Arthur Baker with mixing assistance from Jellybean. In 1985 Rocca and Stennet recorded as Pink Rhythm while Freeez continued with Maas, Morgan, Billy Crichton and Louis Smith and recorded on Siren in 1986. As a solo artist Rocca had a US dance number 1 with 'I Want To Be Real' in 1987; the same year a remix of Freeez's 'I.O.U.' on Citybeat made the UK Top 30. Rocca later recorded on Who'd She Coo and Cobra (where he re-recorded 'Southern Freeze') and reappeared in 1991 as Midi Rain on Vinyl Solution.

● ALBUMS: *Southern Freeze* (Beggars Banquet 1981)★★★, *Gonna Get You* (Beggars Banquet 1983)★★★.

FUNKADELIC

George Clinton (b. 22 July 1940, Kannapolis, North Carolina, USA), established this inventive, experimental group out of the 1969 line-up of the Parliaments - Raymond Davis (b. 29 March 1940, Sumter, South Carolina, USA), Grady Thomas (b. 5 January 1941, Newark, New Jersey, USA), Calvin Simon (b. 22 May 1942, Beckley, West Virginia, USA), Clarence 'Fuzzy' Haskins (b. 8 June 1941, Elkhorn, West Virginia, USA), plus the backing group; Bernard Worrell (b. 19 April 1944, Long Beach, New Jersey, USA; keyboards), William Nelson Jnr. (b. 28 January 1951, Plainfield, New Jersey, USA; bass), Eddie Hazel (b. 10 April 1950, Brooklyn, New York, USA, d. 23 December 1992; lead guitar), Lucius Ross (b. 5 October 1948, Wagram, North Carolina, USA; rhythm guitar) and Ramon 'Tiki' Fulwood (b. 23 May 1944, Philadelphia, Pennsylvania, USA; drums) - when contractual problems prevented the use of their original name. Bandleader Clinton seized the opportunity to reconstruct his music and the result laced hard funk with a heady dose of psychedelia, hence the name Funkadelic. Primarily viewed as an album-orientated vehicle, the group's instinctive grasp of such contrasting styles nonetheless crossed over into their singles. Although few managed to enter the R&B Top 30, Funkadelic consistently reached the chart's lower placings. In 1977 Clinton moved from the Westbound label to Warner Brothers Records and the following year the compulsive 'One Nation Under A Groove' was a million-seller. By this point the distinctions between Funkadelic and Parliament were becoming increasingly blurred and the former secured another major hit in 1979 with '(Not Just) Knee Deep'. Several offshoot projects, Bootsy's Rubber Band, Parlet and the Brides Of Funkenstein, also emanated from within the burgeoning corporation, but a protracted contractual wrangle with Warners ended with legal action. Three long-time associates, Clarence Haskins, Calvin Simon and Grady Thomas, then broke away, taking the Funkadelic name with them. Despite an early R&B hit, 'Connections And Disconnections', they were unable to maintain their own direction and the group later dissolved. In 1993 the band were favourably reappraised and courted by the soul and dance cognoscenti. Now recording as the P-Funk All Stars, Clinton's 1996 album *The Awesome Power Of A Fully Operational Mothership* was a superb blend of the Funkadelic and Parliament sounds.

● ALBUMS: *Funkadelic* (Westbound 1970)★★★, *Free Your Mind ... And Your Ass Will Follow* (Westbound 1970)★★★, *Maggot Brain* (Westbound 1971)★★★★, *America Eats Its Young* (Westbound 1972)★★★, *Cosmic Slop* (Westbound 1973)★★★, *Standing On The Verge Of Getting It On* (Westbound 1974)★★★, *Let's Take It To The Stage* (Westbound 1975)★★★★, *Tales Of Kidd Funkadelic* (Westbound 1976)★★★, *Hardcore Jollies* (Warners 1976)★★★, *One Nation Under A Groove* (Warners 1978)★★★★, *Uncle Jam Wants You* (Warners 1979)★★★, *Connections And Disconnections* (LAX 1981)★★, *The Electric Spanking Of War Babies* (Warners 1981)★★★★.
● COMPILATIONS: *Funkadelic's Greatest Hits* (Westbound 1975)★★★, *The Best Of The Early Years - Volume One* (Westbound 1977)★★★★, *The Best Of ... 1976-1981* (Charly 1994)★★★★, *Parliament-Funkadelic Live 1976-1993* 4-CD box set (Sequel 1994)★★★, *Funkadelic's Finest* (Westbound 1997)★★★★.

FUNKMASTERS

A collection of UK funk musicians (sometimes including members of Gonzalez), vocalists and rapper Bo Kool, masterminded by reggae radio disc jockey Tony Williams. Williams, who was then heard regularly on Radio London, produced several records under this name, including 'Love Money' in 1982, one of the earliest UK rap tracks. It came out on his own Tania label, and created some interest on the US dance scene. The act's only chart success came in 1984 with 'It's Over', a Tony Williams song that made the UK Top 10 on his Master Funk label. The hit introduced the public to the voice of Julie Roberts (b. 1962, London, England), who had started in Black Jade and had previously recorded as a soloist on the label Red Bus. Roberts was working in the USA when the record charted and had to be substituted for all promotion work. She later recorded many singles for Bluebird Records and sang with Courtney Pine's Jazz Warriors as well as Working Week. She also later helped to host the UK version of television's *Soul Train*.

FUQUA, HARVEY

b. 27 July 1929, Louisville, Kentucky, USA. Alternate lead and founder of the famed vocal group the Moonglows, Fuqua began moving towards A&R and production work in 1959 while still singing with the group. In 1960 he disbanded the Moonglows and moved to Detroit to work with Gwen Gordy, Berry Gordy's sister, at her Anna label. The following year, he and Gwen Gordy, soon to be husband and wife, formed the Harvey and Tri-Phi labels. They had only moderate success with the labels, but managed to sign some top talents, including the Detroit Spinners, Shorty Long, Johnny Bristol, and Junior Walker And The All Stars. In 1963 Fuqua closed down the labels and joined Berry Gordy's growing Motown operation as writer, producer and promotion man, bringing with him several of the Harvey and Tri-Phi acts to the company. Fuqua was responsible for Motown's Artist Development section, which groomed Motown acts in their stage performances and public behaviour. In 1970 Fuqua left Motown and formed his own production company. He drew talent from both Louisville and Detroit to form a staple of artists - the Niteliters, New Birth, and Love, Peace & Happiness. The Niteliters were a funk instrumental group, New Birth was the Niteliters with a vocal ensemble, and Love, Peace & Happiness a vocal spin-off from New Birth. In 1971 he placed these artists with RCA, and enjoyed hits with all three. New Birth, which lasted the longest, remained on the charts to 1979. In the late 70s Fuqua established a production company in San Francisco and produced disco hits for Sylvester for Fantasy Records. In the early 80s he produced most of Marvin Gaye's Columbia material
● FILMS: *Go Johnny Go* (1958).

G-CLEFS

This US doo-wop-styled vocal group consisted of brothers Teddy, Chris, Timmy and Arnold Scott and friend Ray Gibson, all from Roxbury, Massachusetts, USA. The quintet, who began singing gospel, were spotted by Pilgrim Records' Jack Gould and in 1956 their first release, 'Ka Ding Dong' (on which Freddy Cannon is reputed to have played guitar), reached the R&B Juke Box Top 10 and the US Top 40 pop chart. It probably would have been a bigger hit but for cover versions by two name acts, the Diamonds and Hilltoppers. Following another release on Pilgrim and two on Paris they decided to put their singing careers on ice and finish their schooling. After the youngest member Arnold left school in 1960 they re-formed and, with help from Gould, joined Terrace Records. Their first release, a version of the Four Tunes' song 'I Understand' cleverly combined with the chorus of 'Auld Lang Syne', gave them their only US Top 10 entry and five months later (around New Year) their sole UK Top 20 hit. The follow-up 'A Girl Has To Know' charted, but later releases including ones on Loma, Regina and Veep brought them no further success. Freddie And The Dreamers had a UK Top 5 hit with a cover version of their arrangement of 'I Understand' in 1964.

G.Q.

This quartet formed in New York and comprised Keith 'Sabu' Crier (who subsequently changed his name and enjoyed solo success as Keith Sweat) on bass and vocals, Emmanuel Rahiem LeBlanc (guitar, lead vocals), Paul Service (drums, vocals) and Herb Lane (keyboards, vocals). Crier and LeBlanc had previously worked as Sabu and the Survivors, Sons of Darkness and Third Chance before linking up with Lane and drummer Kenny Banks as The Rhythm Makers and signing with Vigor (part of the De-Lite label). Their one album, *Soul On Your Side*, attracted considerable import interest in the UK, thanks to the hypnotic single 'Zone', in 1976. Following the departure of Banks, Paul Service was drafted in as replacement and the group became 'G.Q.' (which stood for Good Quality) upon the suggestion of their manager, Tony Lopez. They played one of their tapes to producer Beau Ray Fleming and he in turn invited Larkin Arnold, Senior Vice-President of Arista, to audition the group in a South Bronx basement. One cut in particular from their audition stood out; 'Disco Nights (Rock Freak)', which they were made to play several times. Two weeks later G.Q. were in the studio recording their debut album for the company. The single peaked at number 12 on the US Top 100 (and number 42 in the UK), earning a gold disc and propelling their debut album to gold status. Their second album spawned another hit single in 'Standing Ovation', after which Paul Service left and the group continued as a trio for their final album for Arista. They recorded one final single, 'You Are The One For Me', for the independent Stadium label and then disbanded permanently following Crier's decision to pursue a solo career.

● ALBUMS: *Disco Nights* (Arista 1979)★★★, *GQ Two* (Arista 1980)★★★, *Face To Face* (Arista 1981)★★.

Gabrielle

The corporate record industry's new soul diva of the 90s, Gabrielle has earned a high commercial profile via a series of perfectly realized, expertly pitched releases. Visually distinguished by a black eye patch, she tore up the charts with her debut single, 'Dreams', in 1993. Equally accessible was a follow-up, 'Going Nowhere' The album that followed was assembled by seven different producers, including the Boilerhouse (Cox and Steele of the Fine Young Cannibals) and Steve Jervier (famed for his work with Take That). She was fêted at various awards ceremonies, and became such a celebrity that she was invited to appear at the Armani fashion show in Milan. During the break between her albums she gave birth to a child. Ten of the tracks on *Gabrielle* were written by Andy Dean and Ben Wolff, and they shared the production with Foster & McElroy. The Motown pastiche 'Give Me A Little More Time' was a Top 5 UK hit in the spring of 1996, and was followed in November by the number 2 single 'If You Ever' (with East 17).

● ALBUMS: *Find Your Way* (Go! Beat 1994)★★★, *Gabrielle* (Go! Beat 1996)★★★.

Gaines, Grady

b. 14 May 1934, Waskom, Texas, USA. By the time his family moved to Houston, the 12-year-old Gaines was already intent upon following Louis Jordan's example by becoming a saxophonist. He took lessons and at the E.L. Smith Junior High School, he met Calvin Owens, a student music teacher at the time. While in senior high school, he met Little Richard at the Club Matinee and played with his band, the Tempo Toppers. Gaines worked on studio sessions for Duke/Peacock until 1955, when Little Richard asked him to join his touring band. The association lasted for three years, during which time they recorded 'Keep A Knockin'' and appeared in *Don't Knock The Rock*, *The Girl Can't Help It* and *Mister Rock And Roll*. When Little Richard renounced rock 'n' roll in favour of religion in 1958, Gaines and the band named themselves the Upsetters and hired Dee Clark to be their singer. They also worked and recorded with Little Willie John and Sam Cooke, appearing on the latter's 'Twisting The Night Away'. During the 70s, Gaines worked with Joe Tex, Little Johnny Taylor, Curtis Mayfield and Millie Jackson. He left the music business in 1980 but made a comeback five years later that resulted in a contract with Black Top. His records call on the services of veterans such as Carol Fran and Clarence Hollimon, Teddy Reynolds and Lloyd Lambert, as well as featuring his regular vocalist, Big Robert Smith.

● ALBUMS: *Full Gain* (Black Top 1987)★★★, *Gulf Coast Blues Vol. 1* (Black Top 1990)★★★, *Black Top Blues-A-Rama Vol. 4* (Black Top 1990)★★★, *Horn Of Plenty* (Black Top 1992)★★★.

Gale, Eric

b. 20 September 1938, Brooklyn, New York, USA, d. 25 May 1994, Baja California, Mexico. Gale studied chemistry at Niagara University. He took up the double bass when he was 12 years old and also played tenor saxophone, trombone and tuba before he chose the guitar. The basis of his style was formed on the 50s and 60s R&B circuit. He was with the Drifters, Jackie Wilson, the Flamingos and Maxine Brown, before playing in the 60s with King Curtis, Jimmy Smith, David 'Fathead' Newman, Mongo Santamaría and Aretha Franklin. In the early 70s Gale became the house guitarist with Creed Taylor's new CTI label and worked with Stanley Turrentine's band. He took four years off on his Ohio farm and went to Jamaica where he assimilated the reggae style. On his return to New York in 1976 he was a founder of the influential funk band Stuff along with artists including Steve Gadd, Cornell Dupree and Richard Tee. They played regularly at Mikell's in Manhattan with only minimal rehearsal. In the early 90s he performed as a regular band member in several US television shows. Gale thought like a frontline musician and played like a saxophonist.

● ALBUMS: *Stuff* (1977)★★★, *Ginseng Woman* (Columbia 1977)★★★, *Multiplication* (Columbia 1979)★★★, *Forecast* (Columbia 1979)★★★, *Part Of You* (Columbia 1979)★★★, *Touch Of Silk* (Columbia 1980)★★, *Blue Horizon* (Elektra 1982)★★★, *Island Breeze* (Elektra 1984)★★.

● COMPILATIONS: *The Best Of Eric Gale* (Columbia 1980)★★★.

Gamble And Huff

This exceptional songwriting and production team first met while working on 'The 81', a 1964 single by Candy And The Kisses. Leon Huff (b. 1942, Camden, New Jersey, USA), an established session musician, played piano on the recording, while the songwriter Kenny Gamble (b. 11 August 1943, Philadelphia, Pennsylvania, USA) was also a member of the Romeos, a Philadelphia group Huff would later join. The duo achieved a US Top 10 hit in 1967, producing 'Expressway To Your Heart' for the Soul Survivors. However, their work with the Intruders ('(Love Is Like A) Baseball Game') gave a better indication of subsequent developments. The homely lyrics, tightened rhythm and sweetening strings, so prevalent on the team's later recordings, were already present on these 1968 recordings. Gamble and Huff productions also provided hits for Archie Bell And The Drells ('I Can't Stop Dancing'), Jerry Butler ('Only The Strong Survive') and, later, Wilson Pickett ('Don't Let The Green Grass Fool You'). Having disbanded their Excel and Gamble outlets, the duo formed a third label, Neptune, where they pieced together an impressive roster of acts, many of whom were retained when its successor, Philadelphia International, was founded in 1971. This definitive company was responsible for many of the decade's finest soul singles, including 'If You Don't Know Me By Now' (Harold Melvin And The Blue Notes), 'Backstabbers' (O'Jays) and 'Me And Mrs Jones' (Billy Paul). Gamble and Huff had, by now, defined their art. Their music formed a natural stepping-stone between Tamla/Motown and disco, but this pre-eminent position was undermined by a 1975 payola scandal which accused the label of offering bribes in return for airplay. Although the charges against Huff were dismissed, Gamble was fined $2,500. By coincidence or not, the pair's work suffered following the indictment. Their records became increasingly formula-bound, imitative of a now-passing golden era, but lacking flair and innovation. Their last consistent commercial success came with Teddy Pendergrass, but the singer's horrific car accident forestalled his career. McFadden And Whitehead's 1979 single, 'Ain't No Stoppin' Us Now', was a proud promulgation, but the Philly-soul sound was unable to adapt to the new decade. Nonetheless, Gamble and Huff remain one of the most important, and successful, writing/production teams to emerge from black music.

GAP BAND

This septet was led by three brothers, Charles, Ronnie and Robert Wilson. They took their name from the initials of three streets, Greenwood, Archer and Pine, in their home-town of Tulsa, Oklahoma, USA. After two minor US hits in 1977, this post-Sly Stone funk band hit the R&B Top 10 with 'Shake', 'Steppin' (Out)' and 'I Don't Believe You Want To Get Up And Dance'. The last release is better known by its subtitle, 'Oops, Up Side Your Head' and this infectious dance-based song reached the UK Top 10 in 1980. The Gap Band continued to score substantial soul/dance hits; 'Burn Rubber (Why Do You Wanna Hurt Me)' (1980), 'You Dropped A Bomb On Me' and 'Party Train' (both 1982), all topped that particular chart, while 'Big Fun' reached the UK Top 5 in 1986. Three years later they recorded the theme song to the film *I'm Gonna Git You Sucka*, a pastiche of 70s 'blaxplotation' movies. Written by Norman Whitfield, the song was mixed by Frankie Knuckles, and as such confirmed the Gap Band's unerring ability to adapt to current musical fashions.

● ALBUMS: *The Gap Band* (Mercury 1977)★★★, *The Gap Band II* (Mercury 1979)★★★★, *The Gap Band III* (Mercury 1980)★★★, *The Gap Band IV* (Total Experience 1982)★★★★, *Gap Band V - Jammin'* (Total Experience 1983)★★★, *The Gap Band VI* (Total Experience 1985) ★★★, *The Gap Band VII* (Total Experience 1986)★★★, *The Gap Band VIII* (Total Experience 1986)★★, *Straight From The Heart* (Total Experience 1987)★★, *I'm Gonna Git You Sucka* (1989)★★, *Round Trip* (Capitol 1989)★★, *Live And Well* (Intersound 1996)★★.

● COMPILATIONS: *Gap Gold/Best Of The Gap Band* (Mercury 1985)★★★★, *The 12" Collection* (Mercury 1986)★★★.

GAYE, MARVIN

b. Marvin Pentz Gay Jnr., 2 April 1939, Washington, DC, USA, d. 1 April 1984, Los Angeles, USA. Gaye was named after his father, a minister in the Apostolic Church. The spiritual influence of his early years played a formative role in his musical career, particularly from the 70s onwards, when his songwriting shifted back and forth between secular and religious topics. He abandoned a place in his father's church choir to team up with Don Covay and Billy Stewart in the R&B vocal group the Rainbows. In 1957, he joined the Marquees, who recorded for Chess under the guidance of Bo Diddley. The following year the group was taken under the wing of producer and singer Harvey Fuqua, who used them to re-form his doo-wop outfit the Moonglows. When Fuqua moved to Detroit in 1960, Gay went with him: Fuqua soon joined forces with Berry Gordy at Motown, and Gay became a session drummer and vocalist for the label. In 1961, he married Gordy's sister, Anna, and was offered a solo recording contract. Renamed Marvin Gaye, he began his career as a jazz balladeer, but in 1962 he was persuaded to record R&B, and notched up his first hit single with the confident 'Stubborn Kind Of Fellow', a Top 10 R&B hit. This record set the style for the next three years, as Gaye enjoyed hits with a series of joyous, dance-flavoured songs that cast him as a smooth, macho, Don Juan figure. He also continued to work behind the scenes at Motown, co-writing Martha And The Vandellas' hit 'Dancing In The Street', and playing drums on several early recordings by Little Stevie Wonder. In 1965, Gaye dropped the call-and-response vocal arrangements of his earlier hits and began to record in a more sophisticated style. 'How Sweet It Is (To Be Loved By You)' epitomized his new direction, and it was followed by two successive R&B number 1 hits, 'I'll Be Doggone' and 'Ain't That Peculiar'. His status as Motown's best-selling male vocalist left him free to pursue more esoteric avenues on his albums, which in 1965 included a tribute to the late Nat 'King' Cole and a collection of Broadway standards.

To capitalize on his image as a ladies' man, Motown teamed Gaye with their leading female vocalist, Mary Wells, for some romantic duets. When Wells left Motown in 1964, Gaye recorded with Kim Weston until 1967, when she was succeeded by Tammi Terrell. The Gaye/Terrell partnership represented the apogee of the soul duet, as their voices blended sensuously on a string of hits written specifically for the duo by Ashford And Simpson. Terrell developed a brain tumour in 1968, and collapsed onstage in Gaye's arms. Records continued to be issued under the duo's name, although Simpson allegedly took Terrell's place on some recordings. Through the mid-60s, Gaye allowed his duet recordings to take precedence over his solo work, but in 1968 he issued the epochal 'I Heard It Through The Grapevine' (written by Whitfield/Strong), a song originally released on Motown by Gladys Knight And The Pips, although Gaye's version had actually been recorded first. With its tense, ominous rhythm arrangement, and Gaye's typically fluent and emotional vocal, the record represented a landmark in Motown's history - not least because it became the label's biggest-selling record to date. Gaye followed up with another number 1 R&B hit, 'Too Busy Thinking 'Bout My Baby', but his career was derailed by the insidious illness and eventual death of Terrell in March 1970.

Devastated by the loss of his close friend and partner, Gaye spent most of 1970 in seclusion. The following year, he emerged with a set of recordings that Motown at first refused to release, but which eventually formed his most successful solo album. On 'What's Going On', a number 1 hit in 1971, and its two chart-topping follow-ups, 'Mercy Mercy Me (The Ecology)' and 'Inner City Blues', Gaye combined his spiritual beliefs with his increasing concern about poverty, discrimination and political corruption in American society. To match the shift in subject matter, Gaye evolved a new musical style that influenced a generation of black performers. Built on a heavily percussive base, Gaye's arrangements mingled jazz and classical influences into his soul roots, creating a fluid instrumental backdrop for his sensual, almost despairing vocals. The three singles were all contained on *What's Going On*, a conceptual masterpiece on which every track contributed to the spiritual yearning suggested by its title. After making a sly comment on the 1972 US presidential election campaign with the single 'You're The Man', Gaye composed the soundtrack to the 'blaxploitation' thriller *Trouble Man*. His primarily instrumental score highlighted his interest in jazz, while the title song provided him with another hit single. Gaye's next project saw him shifting his attention from the spiritual to the sexual with *Let's Get It On*, which included a quote from T.S. Eliot on the sleeve and devoted itself to the art of talking a woman into bed. Its explicit sexuality marked a sea-change in Gaye's career; as he began to use cocaine more and more regularly, he became obsessed with his personal life, and rarely let the outside world figure in his work. Paradoxically, he continued to let Motown market him in a traditional fashion by agreeing to collaborate with Diana Ross on a sensuous album of duets in 1973 - although the two singers allegedly did not actually meet during the recording of the project. The break-up of his marriage to Anna Gordy in 1975 delayed work on his next album. *I Want You* was merely a pleasant reworking of the *Let's Get It On* set, albeit cast in slightly more contemporary mode. The title track was another number 1 hit on the soul charts, however, as was his 1977 disco extravaganza, 'Got To Give It Up'. Drug problems and tax demands interrupted his career, and in 1978 he fled the US mainland to Hawaii in a vain attempt to salvage his second marriage. Gaye devoted the next year to the *Here My Dear* double album, a bitter commentary on his relationship with his first wife. Its title was ironic: he had been ordered to give all royalties from the project to Anna as part of their divorce settlement.

With this catharsis behind him, Gaye began work on an album to be called *Lover Man*, but he cancelled its release after the lukewarm sales of its initial single, the sharply self-mocking 'Ego Tripping Out', which he had presented as a duet between the warring sides of his nature. In 1980, under increasing pressure from the Internal Revenue Service, Gaye moved to Europe where he began work on an ambitious concept album, *In My Lifetime*. When it emerged in 1981, Gaye accused Motown of remixing and editing the album without his consent, of removing a vital question-mark from the title, and of parodying his original cover artwork. The relationship between artist and record company had been shattered, and Gaye left Motown for Columbia in 1982. Persistent reports of his erratic personal conduct and reliance on cocaine fuelled pessimism about his future career, but instead he re-emerged in 1982 with a startling single, 'Sexual Healing', which combined his passionate soul vocals with a contemporary electro-disco backing. The subsequent album, *Midnight Love*, offered no equal surprises, but the success of the single seemed to herald a new era in Gaye's music. He returned to the USA, where he took up residence at his parents' home. The intensity of his cocaine addiction made it impossible for him to work on another album, and he fell into a prolonged bout of depression. He repeatedly announced his wish to commit suicide in the early weeks of 1984, and his abrupt shifts of mood brought him into heated conflict with his father, rekindling animosity that had festered since Gaye's adolescence. On 1 April 1984, another violent disagreement provoked Marvin Gay Snr. to shoot his son dead, a tawdry end to the life of one of soul music's premier performers.

Motown and Columbia collaborated to produce two albums based on Gaye's unfinished recordings. *Dream Of A Lifetime* mixed spiritual ballads from the early 70s with sexually explicit funk songs from a decade later, while *Romantically Yours* offered a travesty of Gaye's original intentions in 1979 to record an album of big band ballads. Although Gaye's weighty canon is often reduced to a quartet of 'I Heard It Through The Grapevine', 'Sexual Healing', *What's Going On* and *Let's Get It On*, his entire recorded output signifies the development of black music from raw rhythm and blues, through sophisticated soul to the political awareness of the early 70s, and the increased concentration on personal and sexual politics thereafter. Gaye's remarkable vocal range and fluency remains a touchstone for all subsequent soul vocalists, and his 'lover man' stance has been frequently copied as well as parodied.

● ALBUMS: *The Soulful Moods Of Marvin Gaye* (Tamla 1961)★★★, *That Stubborn Kind Of Fella* (Tamla 1963)★★★★, *Recorded Live: On Stage* (Tamla 1964)★★★, *When I'm Alone I Cry* (Tamla 1964)★★★, with Mary

Wells *Together* (Motown 1964)★★★, *Hello Broadway This Is Marvin* (Tamla 1965)★★★, *How Sweet It Is To Be Loved By You* (Tamla 1965)★★★, *A Tribute To The Great Nat King Cole* (Tamla 1965)★★★, *Moods Of Marvin Gaye* (Tamla 1966)★★★, with Kim Weston *Take Two* (Tamla 1966)★★★, with Tammi Terrell *United* (Tamla 1967)★★★, *In The Groove* (Tamla 1968)★★★, with Terrell *You're All I Need* (Tamla 1968)★★★, with Terrell, Weston, Wells *Marvin Gaye And His Girls* (Tamla 1969)★★★, with Terrell *Easy* (Tamla 1969)★★★, *M.P.G.* (Tamla 1969)★★★, *That's The Way Love Is* (Tamla 1970)★★★, *What's Going On* (Tamla 1971)★★★★★, *Trouble Man* film soundtrack (Tamla 1972)★★, *Let's Get It On* (Tamla 1973)★★★★★, with Diana Ross *Diana And Marvin* (Motown 1973)★★★, *Marvin Gaye Live!* (Tamla 1974)★★, *I Want You* (Tamla 1976)★★★, *Marvin Gaye Live At The London Palladium* (Tamla 1977)★★★, *Here My Dear* (Tamla 1978)★★★, *In Our Lifetime* (Tamla 1981)★★★, *Midnight Love* (Columbia 1982)★★★, *Dream Of A Lifetime* (Columbia 1985)★★★, *Romantically Yours* (Columbia 1985)★★★, *The Last Concert Tour* (Giant 1991)★★, *For The Very Last Time* (1994)★★, *Vulnerable* (Motown 1997)★★★.

● COMPILATIONS: *Marvin Gaye's Greatest Hits* (Tamla 1964)★★★★, *Marvin Gaye's Greatest Hits Vol. 2* (Tamla 1967)★★★, with Tammi Terrell *Marvin Gaye & Tammi Terrell: Greatest Hits* (Tamla 1970)★★★, *Super Hits* (Tamla 1970)★★★, *Anthology* (Motown 1974)★★★, *Marvin Gaye's Greatest Hits* (Tamla 1976)★★★★, *Every Great Motown Hit Of Marvin Gaye* (Motown 1983)★★★★, *Motown Remembers Marvin Gaye* (Tamla 1986)★★★, *18 Greatest Hits* (Motown 1988)★★★★, *Love Songs* (Telstar 1990)★★★★, *The Marvin Gaye Collection* 4-CD box set (Tamla/Motown 1990)★★★★★, *Night Life* (1993)★★★, *The Master: 1961-1984* 4-CD box set (Motown 1995)★★★, *Early Classics* (Spectrum 1996)★★★.

● FURTHER READING: *Divided Soul: The Life Of Marvin Gaye*, David Ritz. *I Heard It Throught The Grapevine: Marvin Gaye, The Biography*, Sharon Davis.

GAYLE, MICHELLE

b. London, England. Immediately recognizable to fans of pop culture through her role as Hattie Tavernier in BBC Television soap opera *EastEnders*, Michelle Gayle's crossover to the music charts was one of the most viable amid a slew of sorry cash-ins: 'I wasn't even going to do *EastEnders*. I was going to turn it down because I just wanted to focus on music. I was in a band, Amorphous, at the time and basically agreed to play Hattie to help make some money to pay for demos and equipment for the group.' She had started writing songs at the age of 13, following advice from her music teacher, by which time she had already appeared in another BBC Television programme, *Grange Hill*. Certainly, her attempts to convince the press that her real calling had always been music were backed up by a voice with impressive range and control, best demonstrated on the hit singles 'Looking Up' and 'Sweetness'. Taken under the wing of Dennis Ingoldsby at First Avenue Management (Eternal, Dina Carroll, Judy Cheeks), he helped to procure a series of suitable musical compositions for her chart forays, over which Gayle would customize lyrics. Although the selection of material on her debut was certainly limited, the best of it was undoubtedly first-class pop soul. Its reward was gold status in the UK charts, as Gayle became a major star via widespread UK touring in support of Eternal. After a quiet period, Gayle resurfaced in 1997 with a strong modern R&B collection, *Sensational*.

● ALBUMS: *Michelle Gayle* (RCA 1994)★★★, *Sensational* (RCA 1997)★★★.

GAYNOR, GLORIA

b. 7 September 1947, Newark, New Jersey, USA. The 'Queen Of The Discotheques' spent several years struggling on the east coast circuit prior to finding success. A 1965 single, produced by Johnny Nash, preceded her spell as a member of the Soul Satisfiers. Gaynor was discovered singing in a Manhattan nightclub by her future manager, Jay Ellis. He teamed with producers Tony Bongiovia and Meco Monardo to create an unswerving disco backbeat that propelled such exemplary Gaynor performances as 'Never Can Say Goodbye' (1974) and 'Reach Out I'll Be There' (1975). Her crowning achievement followed in 1979 when 'I Will Survive' topped both the UK and US charts. This emotional, almost defiant performance, later adapted as a gay movement anthem, rose above the increasingly mechanical settings her producers were fashioning for the disco market. 'I Am What I Am', another song with militant implications, was a UK hit in 1983, but the singer was too closely tied to a now dying form and her later career suffered as a result. 'I Will Survive' has been re-released successfully several times.

● ALBUMS: *Never Can Say Goodbye* (MGM 1975)★★★, *Experience Gloria Gaynor* (MGM 1975)★★★, *I've Got You* (Polydor 1976)★★, *Glorious* (Polydor 1977)★★, *Love Tracks* (Polydor 1979)★★★, *I Have A Right* (Polydor 1979)★★★, *Stories* (Polydor 1980)★★, *I Kinda Like Me* (Polydor 1981)★★, *Gloria Gaynor* (Polydor 1982)★★, *I Am Gloria Gaynor* (Chrysalis 1984)★★, *The Power Of Gloria Gaynor* (Stylus 1986)★★.

● COMPILATIONS: *Greatest Hits* (Polydor 1982)★★★, *I Will Survive: Greatest Hits* (1993)★★★.

GAYTEN, PAUL

b. 29 January 1920, New Orleans, Louisiana, USA, d. 29 March 1991. This R&B bandleader and producer began his professional career when he formed a combo in the late 30s. Gayten made his first sides for the New Jersey-based Deluxe label in 1947 and immediately had a US R&B hit with '(You Don't Love Me) True' (number 5). The follow-up, 'Since I Fell For You' (number 3, 1947), featured vocalist Annie Laurie, who would lead on many other Gayten hits, including 'Cuttin' Out' (number 6, 1949) and 'I'll Never Be Free' (number 4, 1950). Another chart record, 'Goodnight Irene' (number 6, 1950), featured the Coleman Brothers ensemble on vocals. By 1949 Gayten had expanded his combo into a nine-piece orchestra and switched to the Regal label. Besides his own hits on the label, he backed and produced Larry Darnell on a spate of hits. He moved to OKeh Records in 1951. In 1954 Gayten moved to Chess Records, and began production and A&R work in New Orleans for the company, producing records on various New Orleans artists, namely Clarence 'Frogman' Henry, Sugar Boy Crawford, TV Slim and Bobby Charles, as well as for himself. His most successful records were a revival of 'Music Goes Round And Round' (1956) and the instrumental 'Nervous Boogie' (1957). In 1960 he moved to Los Angeles to open a Chess office there. Gayten left Chess in 1968 and retired from the music business in 1978. *Creole Gal* is a retrospective of Gayten's late 40s and early 50s material and the 1989 album is a retrospective of his Chess years.

● COMPILATIONS: *Creole Gal* (Route 66 1978)★★★, *Chess King Of New Orleans* (Chess 1989)★★★, with Annie Laurie *Regal Records In New Orleans* (Ace 1992)★★★.

GEMS

Formed in Chicago in 1961 and originally known as the Lovettes, the group comprised Raynard Miner, Vandine Harris, Theresa Washum, Dorothy Hucklebee and Jessica Collins. Students at Marshall High School on Chicago's West Side, the Lovettes progressed from amateur talent contests to a contract with Chess Records. A sixth member, Bertha Watts, was added in 1962. The group recorded two singles as the Lovettes, 'The Crush' and 'Hands Off', before becoming the Gems. Under this name they would issue a further six singles, of which 'I Can't Help Myself' was arguably the best. By that time (1964), Bertha Watts had dropped out again and Vandine Harris had been replaced by Minnie Riperton. The group was used as backing singers on sessions by the Dells, Billy Stewart and Etta James. Miner was, meanwhile, developing a songwriting talent and he collaborated on 'Rescue Me' (Fontella Bass), 'We're Gonna Make It' (Little Milton) and 'Higher And Higher' (Jackie Wilson). Following the Gems' final single, 'Happy New Love', Riperton issued a solo single in 1966 under the name of Andrea Davis, while the other group members became back-up singers for several Chess recording artists. A regrouped Gems was formed in 1967. Now called the Starlets, Riperton, Washum, Jessica Edmund and Dorothy Martin released two singles for Chess before breaking up for good. Riperton then joined Rotary Connection before achieving fame as a solo artist under her own name in the mid-70s. Miner later wrote material for Invictus/Hot Wax label acts Chairmen Of The Board, Honey Cone, Freda Payne and Flaming Ember. In 1974 he wrote and produced 'Shortage' for Coda, which included Martin and Edmund from the Starlets.

GENTRYS

Formed in 1963 in Memphis, Tennessee, USA, the Gentrys forged their early reputation playing high school dances. The group - Larry Raspberry (vocals, guitar), Bruce Bowles (vocals), Jimmy Hart (vocals), Bobby Fisher (tenor saxophone, piano, guitar), Jimmy Johnson (trumpet, organ), Pat Neal (bass) and Larry Wall (drums) - later won the city's 'Battle Of The Bands' contest and within months had secured a recording contract with the independent Youngstown label. Their first release, 'Sometimes', was coupled with the infectious 'Keep On Dancing', an R&B track that attracted more interest than the a-side. The major label MGM Records picked up the national distribution rights to the single, resulting in the single reaching number 4 in the US charts, subsequently selling in excess of one million copies. The song was later covered by the Bay City Rollers, giving them their first chart hit in 1971. The Gentrys were unable to repeat their early success, but remained a popular live attraction throughout America's southern states. After the break-up of the group in 1970, Jimmy Hart resuscitated the Gentrys' name by forming a new line-up with Steve Speer (bass), Dave Beaver (keyboards), Jimmy Tarbutton (guitar) and Mike Gardner (drums). This incarnation achieved some success with minor placings in the singles chart. Late-period member Rick Allen resurfaced in the Box Tops, while Raspberry later embarked on a solo career, leading a new group, the High-Steppers.

● ALBUMS: *Keep On Dancing* (MGM 1965)★★★, *Time* (MGM 1966)★★★, *The Gentrys* (Sun 1970)★★.

● COMPILATIONS: *Gentrys* (MGM 1966)★★★.

● FILMS: *It's A Bikini World* (1967).

GEORGE, BARBARA

b. 16 August 1942, New Orleans, Louisiana, USA. Barbara George is best remembered for her 1961 R&B number 1 hit 'I Know', released on the small AFO (All For One) label. George was discovered by Jessie Hill, another New Orleans R&B artist, himself known for the hit 'Ooh Poo Pah Doo'. Hill brought George to AFO, where label head Harold Battiste at first did not see much potential in the girl. They recorded 'I Know' in spite of this and it was heard by Sue Records owner Juggy Murray, who agreed to distribute the record. 'I Know' not only reached the top of the R&B chart but was an enormous success in the US pop charts. George was unable to follow her hit with any other significant records, however, and by the end of the 60s she had retired from music, save for a brief return in the early 80s.

● ALBUMS: *I Know You Don't Love Me Anymore* (AFO 1962)★★★.

GEORGIO

b. Georgio Allentini, 1966, San Francisco, USA. Georgio launched his musical career in Los Angeles in 1986, when he began working as a disc jockey. He then financed the recording and release of his debut single, 'Sexappeal'. This track was picked up for release by Motown, and became a national hit, followed by a US Top 10 black music smash, 'Tina Cherry'. Both releases emphasized his debt to the music of Prince, whose sexual outrageousness is imitated by Georgio. This stance was maintained for later singles, 'Lover's Lane' and 'Bedrock', which also reached the US charts.

● ALBUMS: *Georgio* (Motown 1987)★★.

GEYER, RENEE

Geyer is Australia's most established rock/soul solo vocalist, having recorded 11 albums since the early 70s. She first came to notice as vocalist on jazz rock band Sun's 1972 album. Next came a more lauded combo, Mother Earth, who also provided backing for her first solo album, which consisted mostly of cover versions. She charted with 'It's A Man's Man's World'. The band Sanctuary, composed of seasoned rock and session players, became her regular backing band, also writing songs for her. The mid-70s provided several hit singles and successful albums and also established her as Australia's premier female soul vocalist. In 1976 she went to the USA for the first time, and over the next decade split her time between the USA and Australia, steadily releasing records and playing live with self-titled bands put together from the cream of Australia's musicians for the duration of the tour. By the mid-80s Geyer was ensconced in Los Angeles, writing and doing session work. An album with Easy Pieces was recorded in 1988 but sunk rapidly. Unfortunately as yet, she has not been able to demonstrate her talent to the international market.

● ALBUMS: *Renee Geyer* (1973)★★★, *It's A Man's Man's World* (1974)★★★, *Ready To Deal* (1975)★★★, *Winner* (1975)★★, *Really Love You* (1976)★★★, *Moving Along* (1977), *Blues Licence* (1979)★★★, *So Lucky* (1981)★★, *Renee Live* (1983)★★, *Sing To Me* (1985)★★★, *Live In The Basement* (1986)★★★.

GILL, JOHNNY

b. Washington, DC, USA. Gill's expertly delivered soul vocal chords have been working since an early age. At the age of seven he was singing with his three brothers in the gospel quartet the Wings Of Faith. His debut album was recorded when he was only 16. Following his meeting and subsequent recording with Stacey Lattisaw (*Perfect Combination*), she proffered his rough demo to Ahmet Ertegun at Atlantic Records, resulting in 1985's *Chemistry*. Although Gill failed to dent the charts he had built a considerable reputation with his voice, and replaced Bobby Brown in New Edition towards the end of their heyday, singing on their comeback hit 'If It Isn't Love' in 1988. He reinvented himself once again, following a similar pattern: working with Lattishaw, followed by another self titled solo album, this time on Motown Records. The mix was favourable, having been produced by Jimmy Jam And Terry Lewis and LA And Babyface. The album was a major success and established him as a potential modern R&B giant, spawning a number of US hits including 'Rub You The Right Way', 'My My My' and 'Fairweather Friend'. Futher success came as a featured vocalist with Shanice ('Silent Prayer') and Shabba Ranks ('Slow And Sexy'). 'This Floor' kept his profile alive in 1993, together with Provocative, but is was not until 1996 that a new solo album was released, three years after his last.

● ALBUMS: *Johnny Gill* (Cotillion 1983)★★, with Stacey Lattishaw *Perfect Combination* (Cotillion 1984)★★, *Chemistry* (Atlantic 1985)★★★, *Johnny Gill* (Motown 1990)★★★★, *Provocative* (Motown 1993)★★★, *Let's Get The Mood Right* (Motown 1996)★★★.

GISCOMBE, JUNIOR

b. Norman Giscombe, 10 November 1961, England. Known simply as Junior, this young performer promised much in his early years when he achieved a UK Top 10 hit with 'Mama Used To Say' (picking up a Grammy award). The follow-up, 'Too Late', was his last Top 20 hit in the UK. The tag he was given as 'the future of UK soul' hung heavily around him, and his career ended up being handled by a variety of labels from Mercury and London to MCA. Each one found difficulty, despite good reviews, in breaking Giscombe. He did make a brief return to the UK Top 10 in April 1987 when he duetted with Kim Wilde on 'Another Step Closer To You'. He became involved with the formation of Red Wedge in 1986 with Billy Bragg, Jimmy Somerville and Paul Weller. During the 90s he recorded as Junior Giscombe.

● ALBUMS: *JI* (Mercury 1982)★★★, *Inside Lookin' Out* (Mercury 1983)★★★, *Acquired Taste* (London 1986)★★★, *Sophisticated Street* (MCA 1988)★★, *Stand Strong* (MCA 1990)★★★, *Renewal* (MCA 1992)★★.

GLASS HOUSE

Tyrone 'Ty' Hunter (b. 1943, USA, d. 24 February 1981), Scherrie Payne (b. 14 November 1944, Detroit, Michigan, USA), Larry Mitchell, Pearl Jones and Eric Dunham made up this Detroit-based group. Hunter's prolific career had begun in the Voice Masters, after which he followed a solid, if unspectacular, solo path. Pearl Jones, meanwhile, was a back-up singer for several acts, including Billy Stewart and Mitch Ryder. Glass House secured a US R&B hit in 1969 with 'Crumbs Off The Table', but despite minor hits between 1970 and 1972, Payne's concurrent solo releases accelerated their demise. Scherrie, sister of singer Freda, joined the Supremes in 1975 and stayed there for two years. She later returned to the R&B chart in 1987 with 'Incredible' (a duet with Phillip Ingram) and 'Testify'. Hunter had, meanwhile, replaced C.P. Spencer in the Originals but died, almost forgotten, in February 1981.

● ALBUMS: *Inside The Glass House* (Invictus 1971)★★★, *Thanks, I Needed That* (Invictus 1972)★★★.

GLENN, GARRY

Born in Detroit, Michigan, USA, Garry Glenn is the brother of the gospel singer Beverly Glenn, with whom he toured as a teenager. He subsequently submitted songs to various soul acts, the Dramatics being the first to record his work. In the early 80s, he worked as an arranger and keyboard player for Al Hudson and the Soul Partners, and wrote material for Earth, Wind And Fire. His major breakthrough came when Anita Baker recorded his song 'Caught In The Rapture' and invited him to play keyboards with her touring band in 1984/5. He then performed a similar role for Billy Ocean, before quitting live work to produce an album for Freddie Jackson in 1986. That same year, he was signed to Motown after contributing a song to the *Police Academy IV* soundtrack. He scored immediate success as a solo artist with 'Do You Have To Go' in 1987, which showcased his falsetto vocals. A follow-up hit, 'Feels Good To Feel Good', matched him with Sheila Hutchinson of the Emotions.

● ALBUMS: *Feels Good To Feel Good* (Motown 1987)★★★.

GOINS, HERBIE

Goins, like Geno Washington, was a former US serviceman who remained in the UK when his military service ended. In 1963 he joined Alexis Korner's Blues Incorporated and was featured vocalist on several of this seminal band's releases, including *Red Hot From Alex* and *At The Cavern*. In 1965 he left to lead Herbie Goins And The Night Timers, which became a highly popular attraction in London's clubs. The group was signed to Parlophone Records, for whom they recorded several excellent dance-orientated soul singles, including 'The Music Played On' (1965), 'Number One In Your Heart' and 'Incredible Miss Brown' (both 1966). In 1967 the Night Timers recorded their only album. *Number One In Your Heart* is an exciting set, with swinging versions of such club standards as 'Pucker Up Buttercup', 'Knock On Wood' and 'Look At Granny Run', but it was deemed anachronistic when compared with the contemporary psychedelic trends. The group broke up in 1968.

● ALBUMS: *Number One In Your Heart* (Parlophone 1967)★★★.

GOLDNER, GEORGE

b. 1919, near Turtle Bay, Manhattan, USA, d. 15 April 1970. Goldner's long association with New York music circles began in the early 50s. Although initially employed at Tico, a label specializing in Latin music, he switched to R&B in 1953 with the formation of Rama. Its roster included vocal groups the Crows and Harptones, establishing a pattern for Goldner's subsequent outlets, Gee, Gone/End and Roulette. Drawing on New York's profligate street-corner harmony acts, the entrepreneur launched the careers of Frankie Lymon And The Teenagers, Little Anthony And The Imperials and the Chantels, but subsequently sold his interests in each of the companies. Goldner re-emerged in 1964, partnering songwriters/producers Jerry Leiber and Mike Stoller in Red Bird Records. The label enjoyed a highly successful initial period with hits by the Dixie Cups, Jelly Beans and Shangri-Las, and Goldner later bought out his partners when they tired of administrative roles. Despite a promotional acumen, he was unable to maintain the outlet's position and it folded in 1966. In keeping with many contemporaries faced with a new generation of self-sufficient acts, Goldner was unable to exert the same influence in pop's post-Beatles history and later dropped out of music.

GOLDWAX RECORDS

A label founded in Memphis in 1964 that recorded some of the classic deep soul sounds of the south. It was founded by a pharmacist, Rudolph 'Doc' Russell, and an air conditioner salesman, Quinton Clauch. Clauch was the experienced half of the team, having supervised some recording sessions at Sun Records and then become a co-founder of Hi Records. Goldwax's most notable artists were James Carr, Spencer Wiggins, and the Ovations, a vocal group whose leader sounded like Sam Cooke. The label briefly had O.V. Wright, who recorded the song 'That's How Strong My Love Is' before Otis Redding covered it and brought it acclaim. The company closed its doors in 1969. Clauch revived the label in 1991, recording a few acts, notably, Ruby Andrews and James Carr.

GONZALEZ

Gonzalez were a very loose UK-based group of some 15 to 30 itinerants (many of whom also played in Georgie Fame's Blue Flames), who assembled in England during 1971 to play a blend of funky soul music. The key members were keyboardist Roy Davies (also in the Butts Band with ex-Doors Robbie Krieger and John Densmore), Mick Eve (former saxophone player with Herbie Goins' Night-Timers and Georgie Fame's Blue Flames), Chris Mercer (former saxophone player with John Mayall, Keef Hartley and Juicy Lucy), Steve Gregory (former saxophone player with Tony Colton's Crawdaddies, Geno Washington's Ram Jam Band and Riff Raff), Gordon Hunte (ex-guitar with Johnny Nash), Lisle Harpe (ex-bass with the Night-Timers, Juicy Lucy and Stealers Wheel) and Rosko Gee (later to play bass with Traffic). They released a self-titled album in 1974 but it was not a great success. In 1977, however, with the line-up standing at Davies, Hunte, Eve, Mercer, plus Ron Carthy (trumpet), Geoffrey 'Bud' Beadle (saxophone), Colin Jacas (trombone), Alan Sharp, Godfrey McLean, and Bobby 'John' Stigmac (percussion), John Giblin (bass), Richard Bailey and Preston Heyman (drums), and Lenny Zakatek (vocals), they recorded the Gloria Jones-penned 'I Haven't Stopped Dancing Yet' for EMI Records' soul label Sidewalk. It was not issued until 1979 when it gave the band a surprise hit. The follow-up, 'Ain't No Way To Treat A Lady', flopped. They later recorded for PRT and by the mid-80s were on the Tooti Fruiti label. Having undergone many more personnel changes, the band finally disintegrated in 1986 after the death of founding member Roy Davies.

● ALBUMS: *Gonzalez* (1974)★★, *Shipwrecked* (Capitol1979)★★★.

GOODFELLAZ

A contemporary R&B act formed in Los Angeles, California, USA, in the mid-90s, Goodfellaz comprises DeLouie Avant, Angel Vasquez and Ray Vencier. Prior to signing to A&M Records subsidiary Avatar, the trio 'shopped' for a record contract with a collection of demo tracks that were considered sufficiently strong to comprise their debut album. After securing a contract, Family Stand founders Jeff Smith and Peter Lord were enrolled as producers for this self-titled project. Justifying their appeal to the press in an already-crowded market for vocal R&B, Vasquez told *Billboard* magazine: 'It's our distinct vocals that sets us apart from other guy groups. Ray has a really big voice, mine has a lighter, falsetto tone to it, and Louie has a really soulful feel. When you hear our tracks, you can pick each of us out easily.' The album was promoted with the release of a single, 'Sugar Honey Ice Tea', which secured heavy rotation on R&B-themed television and radio stations.

● ALBUMS: *Goodfellaz* (Avatar/A&M 1997)★★★.

GOODING, CUBA

b. 27 April 1944, New York, USA. Gooding began his professional musical career in 1971, when he was chosen to replace the late Donald McPherson in the Main Ingredient. His easy, soulful vocals fitted in immediately with the group's cabaret-based style, and the first release by the new line-up, 'Everybody Plays The Fool', was a major hit in the USA. Gooding was showcased on 10 further chart entries, before electing to begin a solo career at Motown in 1978. The ambitiously titled *The First Cuba Gooding Album* suggested that his solo work might rival the popularity of the Main Ingredient, but the poor reception of *Love Dancer* and his subsequent singles blighted this promise. Gooding was subsequently dropped by Motown in 1983. His son is rapper and actor Cuba Gooding Jr., who won an Academy Award in 1997 for his role in the film *Jerry Maguire*.

● ALBUMS: *The First Cuba Gooding Album* (Motown 1978)★★★, *Love Dancer* (Motown 1979)★★.

GORDON, ROBERT

b. 1947, Washington, DC, USA. Gordon was briefly a leading light during the 70s rediscovery of pop's roots. His own preferences for rockabilly and soul became apparent on stage when, after moving to New York in 1970, he began singing with various groups including Tuff Darts, with whom he was heard among other acts on a concert album from the celebrated CBGB's club. As a solo artist, he was produced by Richard Gottehrer and signed to Private Stock. On a 1977 album with Link Wray, the ghost of the 50s faced the spirit of the 70s in state-of-the-art workouts of old chestnuts such as 'Summertime Blues', Frankie Ford's 'Sea Cruise' and the tie-in single, 'Red Hot'. Hopes of a hit via Bruce Springsteen's 'Fire', the single from *Fresh Fish Special*, were dashed by a cover version from the better-known Pointer Sisters but, transferring to RCA, Gordon tried again with help from Gottehrer, Chris Spedding and the cream of Nashville session players on *Rock Billy Boogie*, which contained 'The Catman', a self-penned tribute to Gene Vincent. A promotional tour of North America and Europe stoked up much revivalist fervour, and guaranteed a fair hearing for *Bad Boy*, highlighted by arrangements of Conway Twitty's 'It's Only Make Believe' and Joe Brown's 'A Picture Of You'. However, most consumers favoured the original sounds to Gordon's remakes and stylized homages - though few quarrelled over his integrity and taste. He recorded one more album for RCA in 1981.

● ALBUMS: with Link Wray *Robert Gordon With Link Wray* (Private Stock 1977)★★★, with Link Wray *Fresh Fish Special* (Private Stock 1978)★★★, *Rock Billy Boogie* (RCA 1979)★★, *Bad Boy* (RCA 1980)★★, *Are You Gonna Be The One* (RCA 1981)★★, *Live At Lone Star* (New Rose 1989)★★.

● COMPILATIONS: *Too Fast To Live, Too Young To Die* (1982)★★, *Robert Gordon Is Red Hot* (Bear Family 1989)★★★, *Black Slacks* (Bear Family 1990)★★★, *Red Hot 1977-1981* (Razor & Tie 1995)★★★.

GORDON, ROSCO

b. 23 December 1933, Memphis, Tennessee, USA. A self-taught pianist with no acknowledged influences other than a presumed awareness of the work of Amos Milburn and Little Willie Littlefield. Gordon was part of the Beale Streeters group in the late 40s, alongside Johnny Ace, B.B. King and later, Bobby Bland. Ike Turner, then a freelance producer and talent scout, recognized the potential of Gordon's powerful singing and recorded him for Modern. He was still a teenager when he first recorded at Sam Phillips' Memphis Recording Service in January 1951. Phillips sold masters to both Chess Records in Chicago and RPM in Los Angeles, and thus, Gordon's 'Booted' appeared on both labels, a possible factor in its becoming the number 1 R&B hit in the spring of 1952. The follow-up, 'No More Doggin'', was another Top 10 R&B hit and typified what became known as 'Rosco's Rhythm', a loping boogie shuffle rhythm that predated and perhaps influenced Jamaican ska and blue-heat music. Gordon signed to Phillips' own Sun label in 1955, recording a regional hit, 'The Chicken', which led to his appearance in the film *Rock Baby, Rock It* two years later. Moving to New York, he formed the duo Rosco and Barbara, making singles for Old Town. Many tracks recorded during this time remained unissued until the 70s and 80s. His most well-known song reached number 2 in the R&B charts and was recorded in 1960 for the Chicago-based label Vee Jay. With its catchy sax-driven riff, 'Just A Little Bit' captured the imaginations of British R&B groups as well as black record buyers. A version by Merseybeat band the Undertakers was a minor hit in 1964. Further records for ABC, Old Town, Jomada, Rae-Cox and Calla made little impression and in 1970, Gordon created his own label, Bab-Roc, issuing records by himself and his wife Barbara. An album of new compositions plus remakes of his hits was recorded for Organic Productions in 1971 but never released. A brief visit to England in 1982 brought an onstage reunion with B.B. King at London's 100 Club. At that time he was financing recordings from his own cleaning business.

● COMPILATIONS: *The Legendary Sun Performers: Rosco Gordon* (Charly 1977)★★★, *Best Of Rosco Gordon Vol. 1* (Ace 1980)★★★, *Rosco Gordon Vol. 2* (Ace 1982)★★★, *Keep On Diggin'* (Mr R&B 1981)★★★, *The Memphis Masters* (Ace 1982)★★★, *Rosco Rocks Again* (JSP 1983)★★★, *Bootin' Boogie* (1990)★★★, *Lets Get High* (Charly 1990)★★★.

● FILMS: *Rock Baby, Rock It* (1957).

GORDY, BERRY

b. Berry Gordy Jnr., 28 November 1929, Detroit, Michigan, USA. Gordy took his first tentative steps into the music business in 1955, when he opened a jazz record store in Detroit. When it folded, he returned to the automobile assembly lines until he met the manager of young R&B singer Jackie Wilson. Gordy wrote Wilson's first major hit, the novelty and now classic 'Reet Petite', and joined the singer's entourage, composing four further chart successes over the next two years. In 1958, Gordy set himself up as an independent producer, working with young unknowns such as the Miracles, Marv Johnson and Eddie Holland. That year he formed the Jobete Music company to handle songs by himself and his associates. At the suggestion of the Miracles' vocalist Smokey Robinson, Gordy went a stage further in 1959 by launching his own record company, Tamla Records. This was merely the first of a succession of labels gathered under his Motown Records umbrella, which rapidly became one of America's most important independent concerns.

Gordy masterminded Motown from the outside, choosing the artist-roster, writing and producing many of the early releases, and chairing weekly meetings that determined every aspect of the company's artistic direction. Having co-produced and co-written Motown's first major hit, the Miracles' 'Shop Around' in 1960, Gordy was also responsible for hits such as 'Do You Love Me' and 'Shake Sherry' by the Contours, 'Fingertips (Part 2)' by Stevie Wonder, 'Try It Baby' by Marvin Gaye and 'Shotgun' by Junior Walker And The All Stars. As Motown's influence and reputation grew, Gordy groomed a school of producers and writers to create the style that he dubbed 'The Sound of Young America'. Gradually his own artistic input lessened, although he continued to collaborate on Supremes hits such as 'Love Child' and 'No Matter What Sign You Are' until the end of the decade. His time was primarily devoted to increasing Motown's market share, and to dealing with a series of bitter clashes between artists and company, which threatened to halt the label's progress by the early 70s. Anxious to secure new power bases, Gordy shifted Motown's main offices from Detroit to California, and inaugurated a new films division with the highly acclaimed *Lady Sings The Blues*. This movie starred former Supreme Diana Ross, with whom Gordy had long been rumoured to be enjoying a romantic liaison. Their relationship was part of the company's backbone, and her eventual decision to leave Motown in the early 80s was read as an indicator of the label's declining fortunes. Having lost many of its major creative talents, Motown subsisted through the 70s and early 80s on the backs of several unique individuals, notably Stevie Wonder and Lionel Richie. Gordy was no longer finding significant new talent, however. Ironically, one of his company's most successful newcomers of the 80s was his own son, Rockwell. Gordy's personal career has long since been synonymous with the fortunes of his company, and he surprised the industry when he sold Motown Records to MCA in 1988 - just weeks after he had been inducted into the Rock 'n' Roll Hall Of Fame in recognition of his pioneering talents as a major songwriter, impresario and executive. In the 90s, new label head Andre Harrell attempted to reassert the label as a leading force in black music, achieving notable success with acts such as Johnny Gill, Boyz II Men and Queen Latifah. In 1997 Gordy sold 50% of his Jobete music publishing to EMI. This catalogue of the golden age of Motown contains many of the finest songs of the era, and is unquestionably worth the purchase price of $135 million.

● FURTHER READING: *Movin' Up*, Berry Gordy. *To Be Loved*, Berry Gordy. *Where Did Our Love Go?*, Nelson George.

GRAHAM CENTRAL STATION

Formed in San Francisco in late 1972 by Larry Graham (b. 14 August 1946, Beaumont, Texas, USA), erstwhile bassist in Sly And The Family Stone. The core of the group - David Vega (lead guitar), Hershall Kennedy (keyboards), Willie Sparks and Patrice Banks (both drums) - consisted of former members of Hot Chocolate (USA), a local band Graham was producing, while a second keyboard player, Robert Sam, was drafted in from Billy Preston's touring ensemble. Musically, Graham Central Station emulated the rhythmic funk of Sly And The Family Stone, but lacked their perception. Renowned as one of the era's flashiest live attractions, the group's shows included light panels programmed to oscillate in time to their pulsating sound. Although their initial albums enjoyed critical and commercial success, later releases failed to capitalize on this in-concert popularity and in 1980 Graham embarked on a solo career.

● ALBUMS: *Graham Central Station* (Warners 1974)★★★, *Release Yourself* (Warners 1974)★★★, *Ain't No 'Bout-A-Doubt It* (Warners 1975)★★★, *Mirror* (Warners 1976)★★★, *Now Do U Wanta Dance* (Warners 1977)★★★. As Larry Graham & Graham Central Station *My Radio Sure Sounds Good To Me* (Warners 1978)★★★, *Star Walk* (Warners 1979)★★.

GRAHAM, JAKI

b. Birmingham, England. Graham is a soul artist who sang at school before taking a secretarial position. In the evenings she continued her singing in a band called Ferrari with David 'Dee' Harris (later of Fashion), before moving on to the Medium Wave band. She was spotted there by Rian Freshwater, who managed David Grant (ex-Linx) and singer/producer Derek Bramble (b. 1962, London, England), formerly of Heatwave, who became her producer and songwriter. She signed to EMI, who released her debut 45 'What's The Name Of Your Game' (1984). Her first chart appearance came via a duet with production stablemate David Grant on 'Could It Be I'm Falling In Love' in 1985. She followed that success with the solo hits 'Round And Round' and 'Heaven Knows', before another Grant duet, 'Mated' (written by Todd Rundgren). The second album provided a trio of hits; 'Set Me Free', 'Breaking Away' and 'Step Right Up'. Her highest chart entry since then has been 1994's 'Ain't Nobody' (number 44).

● ALBUMS: *Heaven Knows* (EMI 1985)★★★, *Breaking Away* (EMI 1986)★★★, *From Now On* (EMI 1989)★★.

● VIDEOS: *Set Free* (PMI 1986).

GRAHAM, LARRY

b. 14 August 1946, Beaumont, Texas, USA. Graham moved to Oakland, California while still a child and by his late teens had established a proficiency on several instruments. A member of Sly And The Family Stone between 1967 and 1972, he left to form Graham Central Station, one of the era's most popular funk bands. In 1980 he embarked on a solo career which opened successfully with 'One In A Million You', a US Top 10 hit. The singer enjoyed R&B hits with 'When We Get Married' (1980) and

'Just Be My Lady' (1981), while his most recent chart entry was 'If You Need My Love Tonight', a 1987 duet with Aretha Franklin.

● ALBUMS: *One In A Million You* (Warners 1980)★★★, *Just Be My Lady* (Warners 1981)★★★, *Sooner Or Later* (Warners 1982)★★, *Victory* (Warners 1983)★★, *Fired Up* (1985)★★★.

GRANT, AMY

b. 25 November 1960, Augusta, Georgia, USA. A huge influence on the development of modern gospel music, Grant's perennially youthful but always convincing vocal has imbued her many recordings with a purity of spirit and performance that can be awe-inspiring. Songs such as 'Angels', 'Raining On The Inside' and 'Find A Way', scattered through a consistently high-quality recording career, have endeared her to her massive contemporary and gospel audience as well as critics. Though originally a primarily religious performer, her material also blends in rhythms derived from modern R&B and soul, while her lyrics contemplate subjects outside of the average gospel singer's repertoire. However, when secular subjects are tackled, there is an abiding spirituality to Grant's treatment of them that ensures her position as a gospel singer despite her 90s R&B success: 'The point of my songs is never singer-focused. It's experience focused. When I go in the studio, I'm taking my experience as a wife and a mother with me.' Married to country singer-songwriter Gary Chapman, her audience is now as varied as her songwriting: 'When I was in high school, I listened to Aretha Franklin and the Jackson Five. I remember discovering R&B music then and Joni Mitchell too.' Though earlier albums had flirted with pop, rock, soul and country, her first truly secular release arrived in 1991 with *Heart In Motion*. With a major hit in 'Baby Baby', this move into the contemporary pop world was rewarded with platinum sales, spending 52 consecutive weeks on the US album chart. Long-term collaborators Keith Thomas and Michael Omartian were again in place for the follow-up, *House Of Love*. Boosted by a strong duet with Vince Gill on the title track and the presence of another hit single, 'Lucky One', this collection also included a cover version of the Joni Mitchell standard, 'Big Yellow Taxi'. Grant took a giant leap in credibility with *Behind The Eyes* in 1997. This was an album of much greater depth that dispelled the perception of her as merely a vacuous pop diva.

● ALBUMS: *My Father's Eyes* (Myrrh/Reunion 1979)★★★, *Never Alone* (Myrrh/Reunion 1980)★★★, *In Concert* (Myrrh/Reunion 1981)★★★★, *In Concert Volume Two* (Myrrh/Reunion 1981)★★★, *Age To Age* (Myrrh/Reunion 1982)★★★★, *Straight Ahead* (A&M 1984)★★★★, *Unguarded* (A&M 1985)★★★, *A Christmas Album* (Myrrh/Reunion 1988)★★★, *Lead Me On* (A&M 1988)★★★, *Heart In Motion* (A&M 1991)★★★, *Home For Christmas* (A&M 1992)★★★, *House Of Love* (A&M 1994)★★★, *Behind The Eyes* (A&M 1997)★★★★.

● COMPILATIONS: *The Collection* (Myrrh/Reunion 1986)★★★★.

● VIDEOS: *Building The House Of Love* (A&M 1994).

GRANT, DAVID

b. 8 August 1956, Kingston, Jamaica, West Indies. By the time everyone realized that Linx was not the spearhead of a new UK soul movement, singer David Grant had swapped his glasses and moustache for a sweatband and aerobics gear and gone solo. Suddenly he was Britain's answer to Michael Jackson. He could dance, he was pretty and his voice was high, and 'Stop And Go', 'Watching You Watching Me' and 'Love Will Find A Way' all made the UK Top 30 in 1983. His songwriting partnership with Derek Bramble developed, resulting in the Steve Levine-produced self-titled album. More memorable, however, were his duets with Jaki Graham in 1985, on the Spinners' 'Could It Be I'm Falling In Love' and Todd Rundgren's 'Mated'. 'Hopes And Dreams' was an altogether weightier offering, with contributions from Aswad and Go West, but it just made the Top 100. Grant penned further hits for Gavin Christopher, Cheryl Lynn and Hot Chocolate. He maintained a loyal club following for a time, where his energetic 'soul' music was highly popular. In the 90s he has done session work, acting and has been a television presenter.

● ALBUMS: *David Grant* (Chrysalis 1983)★★★, *Hopes And Dreams* (Chrysalis 1985)★★, *Change* (Polydor 1987)★★, *Anxious Edge* (4th & Broadway 1990)★★.

● COMPILATIONS: *The Best Of David Grant And Linx* (Chrysalis 1993)★★★.

GRAY, DOBIE

b. Leonard Victor Ainsworth, 26 July 1942, Brookshire, Texas, USA. Although Gray had already been recording for a number of years, the anthem-like 'The In Crowd' (1965) was his first major hit. This compulsive, if boastful, single was followed by 'See You At The Go-Go' (1965), but it was eight years before the singer secured another chart entry. In the intervening period, Gray worked as an actor, appearing in productions of *Hair* and the controversial play *The Beard*. In the early 70s Gray sang lead for a hard rock group, Pollution; they recorded three albums that were well received, but were commercial failures. He also recorded several demos for songwriter Paul Williams, whose brother Mentor, a producer, was responsible for relaunching Dobie's singing career. The superbly crafted 'Drift Away' (a US Top 5 in 1973), provided an artistic and commercial success that the singer followed with further examples of progressive southern rock/soul. However, despite minor successes for the Capricorn and Infinity labels, Gray was unable to find a distinctive direction and his new-found promise was left unfulfilled.

● ALBUMS: *Drift Away* (Decca 1973)★★★, *Loving Arms* (MCA 1973)★★, *Hey Dixie* (MCA 1974)★★, *New Ray Of Sunshine* (Capricorn 1975)★★, *Dobie Gray* (Capricorn 1976)★★, *Midnight Diamond* (Infinity 1979)★★.

● COMPILATIONS: *Sings For In Crowders That Go-Go* (Kent 1987)★★★.

GREAVES, R.B.

b. Ronald Bertram Aloysius Greaves III, 28 November 1944, Georgetown, British Guyana. This singer, half north

American Indian, made his greatest impact with the 1969 single, 'Take A Letter Maria'. A nephew of Sam Cooke, Greaves had built a career both in the Caribbean and in the UK, where he performed as Sonny Childs with his group the TNTs. His biggest hit had been recorded by both Tom Jones and Stevie Wonder before the author recorded it himself at the insistence of Atlantic Records president Ahmet Ertegun, who produced it. The ska-flavoured soul song peaked at number 2 in the US charts in late 1969. Greaves recorded a series of cover records as follow-ups, including Burt Bacharach and Hal David's '(There's) Always Something There To Remind Me', James Taylor's 'Fire And Rain' and Procol Harum's 'Whiter Shade Of Pale'. All charted, as did his self-titled 1970 album. Greaves left the label in the 70s when Ertegun could no longer spare time to work with him directly. He recorded briefly for MGM and then turned to country music without much commercial success.

● ALBUMS: *Greaves* (Atco 1969)★★★, *R.B. Greaves* (Atco 1970)★★★.

GREEN, AL

b. Al Greene, 13 April 1946, Forrest City, Arkansas, USA. Having served his musical apprenticeship in the Greene Brothers, a fraternal gospel quartet, this urbane singer made his first recordings in 1960. Four years later he helped form the Creations with Curtis Rogers and Palmer Jones. These two companions subsequently wrote and produced 'Back Up Train', a simple, effective ballad and a 1967 R&B hit for his new group, Al Greene And The Soul Mates. Similar releases fared less well, prompting Green's decision to work solo. In 1969 he shared a bill with bandleader Willie Mitchell, who took the singer to Hi Records. The combination of a crack house band, Mitchell's tight production and Green's silky, sensuous voice, resulted in some of soul's definitive moments. The combination took a little time to gel, but with the release of 'I Can't Get Next To You' (1970), they were clearly on course. Previously a hit for the Temptations, this slower, blues-like interpretation established an early pattern. However, the success of 'Tired Of Being Alone' (1971), a Green original, introduced a smoother perspective. A US number 11 and a UK number 4, it was followed by 'Let's Stay Together' (1971), 'I'm Still In Love With You' (1972), 'Call Me (Come Back Home)', 'Here I Am (Come And Take Me)' (both 1973), each of which increased Green's stature as a major artist. His personal life, however, was rocked in October 1974. Following an argument, his girlfriend, Mary Woodson, burst in while the singer was taking a bath and poured boiling grits over his back. She then shot herself dead. Although he occasionally recorded gospel material, a scarred and shaken Green vowed to devote more time to God. His singles, meanwhile, remained popular, 'L-O-V-E (Love)' and 'Full Of Fire' were both R&B chart toppers in 1975, but his work grew increasingly predictable and lacked the passion of his earlier records. The solution was drastic. The partnership with Mitchell was dissolved and Green opened his own recording studio, American Music. The first single was the majestic 'Belle' (a US R&B Top 10 hit), although the accompanying album was a departure from his commercial formula and something of a 'critics favourite', as were the later Hi collections. The failure of further singles suggested that the problem was more than simply a tired working relationship. In 1979 Green fell from a Cincinnati stage, which he took as a further religious sign. *The Lord Will Make A Way* was the first of several gospel-only recordings, which included a 1985 reunion with Mitchell for *He Is The Light*. Green has since continued to record sacred material. A practising minister, he nonetheless reached the UK singles chart in 1989 with the distinctly secular 'Put A Little Love In Your Heart'. His Hi albums, *Al Green Gets Next To You*, *Let's Stay Together*, *I'm Still In Love With You* and *Call Me*, are particularly recommended. *Greatest Hits* and *Take Me To The River - Greatest Hits Volume Two* offer the simplest overview, with the former being reissued on CD in an expanded form with 15 tracks. *Truth 'N' Time* (1978) best represents the post-Mitchell, pre-gospel recordings. *Don't Look Back* was a sparkling return after many years away from recording new R&B/soul material, and some critics rated it as high as albums such as *Let's Stay Together*. The US release was delayed for nearly three years, until *In Good Hands* was issued, containing eight tracks from *Don't Look Back*.

● ALBUMS: *Back Up Train* (1967)★★★, *Green Is Blues* (Hi 1970)★★★, *Al Green Gets Next To You* (Hi 1971)★★★★, *Let's Stay Together* (Hi 1972)★★★★, *Al Green* (Bell 1972)★★★, *I'm Still In Love With You* (Hi 1972)★★★★, *Call Me* (Hi 1973)★★★★, *Livin' For You* (Hi 1973)★★★★, *Al Green Explores Your Mind* (Hi 1974)★★★★, *Al Green Is Love* (Hi 1975)★★★, *Full Of Fire* (Hi 1976)★★★, *Have A Good Time* (Hi 1976)★★★, *The Belle Album* (Hi 1977)★★★★, *Truth 'N' Time* (Hi 1978)★★★★, *The Lord Will Make A Way* (Myrrh 1980)★★★, *Higher Plane* (Myrrh 1981)★★★, *Tokyo Live* (Hi 1981)★★★★, *Precious Lord* (Myrhh 1982)★★, *I'll Rise Again* (Myrrh 1983)★★★, *Trust In God* (Myrrh 1984)★★★, *He Is The Light* (A&M 1985)★★★, *Going Away* (A&M 1986)★★★, *White Christmas* (Hi 1986)★★, *Soul Survivor* (A&M 1987)★★★, *I Get Joy* (A&M 1989)★★★, *Don't Look Back* (RCA 1993)★★★, *In Good Hands* (MCA 1995)★★★.

● COMPILATIONS: *Greatest Hits* (Hi 1975)★★★★★, *Greatest Hits, Volume 2* (Hi 1977)★★★★, *The Cream Of Al Green* (Hi 1980)★★★★, *Spotlight On Al Green* (PRT 1981)★★★★, *Take Me To The River (Greatest Hits Volume 2)* (Hi 1987)★★★★, *Hi-Life - The Best Of Al Green* (K-Tel 1988)★★★, *Love Ritual: Rare & Previously Unreleased 1968-1976* (Hi 1989)★★★★, *You Say It!* (Hi 1990)★★★, *Christmas Cheers* nine tracks plus 12 by Ace Cannon (Hi 1991)★★, *One In A Million* (Word/Epic 1991)★★★★, *The Flipside Of Al Green* (1993)★★★.

● VIDEOS: *Gospel According To Al Green* (Hendring Video 1990).

GREEN, GARLAND

b. 24 June 1942, Dunleath, Mississippi, USA. Green used his most distinctive of baritones, plaintive with a blues feel, to create a marvellous body of typical Chicago-style uptown soul during the late 60s and early 70s. He came to Chicago in 1958, and found work in a corn-starch factory while singing on weekends in local clubs. He was discovered by Jo Armstead in 1967, who was intrigued by the 'pleading quality' of his voice, which was in the same vein as fellow Chicagoan Tyrone Davis, Green was quickly put into a recording studio. He first made a mark with the beautiful 'Girl I Need You', with a Chicago-style mid-tempo approach, but it failed to chart. Fame came with the later 'Jealous Kind Of Fellow', which went to number 5 R&B and number 20 pop in 1969. 'Plain And Simple Girl' (US R&B number 17, 1971) was his next most successful release, but he continued to produce top-quality songs, such as 'Let The Good Times Roll' (US R&B number 65, 1974) and 'Bumpin' And Stompin'' (US R&B number 72, 1975), despite modest chart success. Green moved to Los Angeles in 1979 and had one more minor chart record in 1983 with 'Tryin' To Hold On' (US R&B number 6), a remake of an earlier Lamont Dozier hit. An excellent compilation of his best work was recently issued using the same title as his debut album.

● ALBUMS: *Jealous Kind Of Fellow* (Gamma 1969)★★★, *Love Is What We Came Here For* (Uni 1977)★★★, *Garland Green* (Revue 1983)★★★.

● COMPILATIONS: *Jealous Kind Of Fellow* (Varese 1996)★★★★.

Greer, 'Big' John

b. John Marshall Greer, 21 November 1923, Hot Springs, Arkansas, USA, d. 12 May 1972. Greer, who performed both as a vocalist and a tenor saxophonist, is a perfect representative of the flowering of the saxophone in the post-World War II era as an R&B instrument. He first made his mark in the music business leading his own quintet in 1948 and made some favourably received recordings. In late 1948 he joined the Lucky Millinder Band, with whom he recorded as both a vocalist and sax soloist, but in April 1949 he was again making solo recordings for the RCA label. Over the following years he had releases both as a member of the Millinder band and as a solo artist. 'Got You On My Mind' from 1952 was his only national R&B hit. RCA released him from his contract in 1955, and after a short stay at King Records in 1956, he never made another recording.

● COMPILATIONS: *R&B In New York City* (Official 1988)★★★, *Rockin' With Big John* (Bear Family 1992)★★★.

Groove Theory

A USA-based duo of Bryce Wilson and Amel Larrieux, Groove Theory offer a close reading of old soul and R&B influences, combined with modern production techniques drawn from hip-hop and contemporary artists such as D'Angelo. Wilson's professional grounding was in hip-hop, having appeared on the 1990 Mantronix hits 'Got To Have Your Love' and 'Take Your Time' under the alias Bryce Lover. However, frustrated by the lack of creative opportunities that group offered, he left to start teaching himself basic production technique while guesting on projects with Reach and Kenny Thomas. Through a publishing contract with Rondor Music he met songwriter Larrieux, who had attended the same school as Boyz II Men, and Groove Theory were formed in 1993. Wilson's ex-room-mate Paris Davis was then hired as an A&R executive by Epic Records, and signed the group to the label. As well as contributing to recordings by established R&B acts such as Chanté Moore, Toni Braxton, Chaka Khan and Tracie Spencer, the group embarked on sessions for their debut album. The first release to be taken from it, 'Tell Me', reached number 4 in the US *Billboard* charts and also reached the UK Top 40. Their subsequent self-titled debut featured co-production from Jimmy Henchman and various others.

● ALBUMS: *Groove Theory* (Epic 1996)★★★.

Guthrie, Gwen

b. 1950, Newark, New Jersey, USA. Prior to her involvement within the reggae industry, Guthrie was a classically trained pianist while at school and a fine vocalist, culminating in her joining the Ebonettes and the Matchmakers alongside the lead singer from Cameo, Larry Blackmon. After graduating, Guthrie pursued a career in teaching but later returned to the recording studios as a session vocalist. As well as demonstrating her vocal skills she found time to collaborate with Patrick Grant writing songs for Sister Sledge and Ben E. King. In 1976 Guthrie embarked on a US tour with Roberta Flack, which led to a long association, including sessions with Donny Hathaway. By 1978 Guthrie relocated to Jamaica, although she occasionally returned to the USA for session work. Her presence on the island resulted in her providing a soulful vocal contribution behind Peter Tosh for the release of *Bush Doctor*, *Mystic Man* and *Wanted Dread And Alive*. Tosh's 1981 release *Wanted* included a duet with Guthrie, 'Nothing But Love', but the song failed to make a significant impression, partly due to Tosh's militant image. In 1982 her work with Tosh and Word Sound And Power led to sessions for a Sly And Robbie-produced album which was originally intended to showcase the diversity of the Taxi Gang. Her predominant vocals resulted in the album being released as her debut, *Gwen Guthrie*, which spawned the crossover hits 'It Should Have Been You' and 'For You (With A Melody Too)'. The following year saw the release of 'Hopscotch' and 'You're The One', lifted from her second album with the Rhythm Twins. She was obliged to promote her new-found success while pregnant with her second child, which led to a period of recording inactivity. By the mid-80s she reappeared on the reggae scene for a duet with Boris Gardiner, who had enjoyed a phenomenal revival in his career with the 1986 chart-topping hit, 'I Want To Wake Up With You'. He followed his hit with two less successful releases and in 1987 recruited Guthrie to perform on 'Friends And Lovers', produced by Willie Lindo and Sly Dunbar. While maintaining her notoriety as an R&B performer ('Ain't Nothin' Goin' On But The Rent' hit number one on the R&B charts in 1986), Guthrie continued to release the occasional reggae single. In 1996 she released 'Girlfriend's Boyfriend', which was produced in Jamaica and topped most of the international reggae charts.

● ALBUMS: *Gwen Guthrie* (Island 1982)★★★, *Portrait* (Island 1983)★★★, *Good To Go Lover* (Polydor 1986)★★★.

Guy

Widely applauded as the originators of Swing Beat, a fusion of hip-hop beats with gospel/soul vocals, Guy comprised Teddy Riley (ex-R&B group Kids At Work) and brothers Aaron and Albert Damion Hall. At the close of the 80s the New York trio broke big by combining Aaron's talented larynx with the studio know-how of producer Riley. The sound and image was much copied both by artists and consumers. Riley went on to become a multimillionaire, for his sins, though his acrimonious split from former business partner Gene Griffin helped to sour a couple of the more rap-based tracks on the band's follow-up album. However, as with many of Riley's projects, the group did not replicate their US success in Britain. Aaron Hall's first solo album, *The Truth*, was released in 1993, including the swing classic 'Don't Be Afraid'. Riley would go on to produce, among several other projects, Michael Jackson's *Dangerous* in 1991.

● ALBUMS: *Guy* (Uptown 1989)★★★, *The Future* (Uptown 1990)★★★.

Gypsies

A female R&B group from New York City, New York, USA, comprising sisters Betty, Shirley and Earnestine Pearce, and Lestine Johnson. The group's only hit was 'Jerk It' (number 33 R&B) from 1965. In 1965 Shirley and Earnestine joined with Viola Billups to form the Flirtations, which had considerable success in 1969 with a Supremes-styled number, 'Nothing But A Heartache' (number 34 pop), which sounded somewhat retrograde in the soul market where it did not chart. A Flirtations album, *Love Makes The World Go Round*, surfaced in 1975 to no great acclaim.

Gyrlz

The first genuine 'New Jill Swing' act, the Gyrlz were formed in the USA during 1987 by Terri, Monica and Tara. Their initial demo tapes were produced by the omnipresent Teddy Riley and Kyle West. 'When we recorded our demos with Teddy he was still living in the St. Nicholas Projects in Harlem. Those were the good old days', remembers Terri. They then met up with Uptown Records' representative Andre Harrell, who asked them, via the intervention of Heavy D, to record an album. They enjoyed minor success with 'Wishing You Were Here', before joining Al. B. Sure as backing singers on his Heartbreak tour. From there they became the opening act for Bobby Brown and New Edition, but split at the end of the tour. 'We were lost rebels without much of a cause and with nowhere to go', is how Monica painfully recalls the experience. Terri returned to New York, briefly singing for Key West, another Uptown band who never released an album, before moving back to Philadelphia. There she decided to reunite with Monica, as Terri And Monica, with Tara becoming their manager.

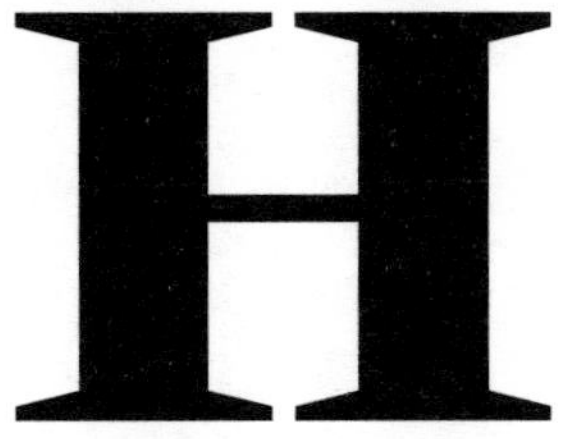

Hairston, Curtis

b. 1962, Winston Salem, North Carolina, USA. Curtis was the son of an early member of the Platters and started singing semi-professionally when aged only 13. In 1981 he was the first act signed to Pretty Pearl, a label owned by ex-New York Knickerbockers basketball star Earl 'Earl The Pearl' Monroe. Hairston moved to New York in 1982 when his first single, 'Summertime', was released. The follow-up 'I Want You (All Tonight)' was a big UK club hit and narrowly missed the Top 40 in 1983. The dance classic 'I Want Your Lovin (Just a Little Bit)' was his most successful release and graced the UK Top 20 in 1985 and also became one of his three minor US R&B charters. The soulful singer, who is better known in Britain than his homeland, joined Atlantic in 1986 and had his last UK hit that year with 'Chillin' Out'. He has also sung on albums by BB&Q (he was the lead on their UK Top 40 hit 'Genie') as well as singing backing vocals for Change.

● ALBUMS: *Curtis Hairston* (Atlantic 1986)★★★.

Hall And Oates

Like their 60s predecessors the Righteous Brothers (and their 90s successor Michael Bolton), Hall And Oates' string of hits was proof of the perennial appeal of white soul singing. The duo achieved their success through the combination of Hall's falsetto and Oates' warm baritone. A student at Temple University, Daryl Hall (b. Daryl Franklin Hohl, 11 October 1949, Pottstown, Pennsylvania, USA) sang lead with the Temptones and recorded a single produced by Kenny Gamble in 1966. Hall subsequently made solo records and formed soft-rock band Gulliver with Tim Moore, recording one album for Elektra. In 1969 he met Oates (b. 7 April 1949, New York, USA), a former member of Philadelphia soul band the Masters. The two began to write songs together and were discovered by Tommy Mottola, then a local representative of Chappell Music. He became their manager and negotiated a recording contract with Atlantic. Their three albums for the label had star producers (Arif Mardin on *Whole Oates* and Todd Rundgren for *War Babies*) but sold few copies. However, *Abandoned Luncheonette* included the first version of one of Hall And Oates' classic soul ballads, 'She's Gone'. The duo came to national prominence with the million-selling 'Sara Smile', their first single for RCA. It was followed by the tough 'Rich Girl', which reached number 1 in the USA in 1977. However, they failed to capitalize on this success, dabbling unimpressively in the then fashionable disco style on *X-Static*. The turning point came with the Hall and Oates-produced *Voices*. The album spawned four hit singles, notably a remake of the Righteous Brothers' 'You've Lost That Lovin' Feelin''. It also included the haunting 'Every Time You Go Away', a big hit for Paul Young in 1985. For the next five years the pair could do no wrong, as hit followed hit. Among their best efforts were 'Maneater', the pounding 'I Can't Go For That (No Can Do)', 'Out Of Touch' (co-produced by Arthur Baker) and 'Family Man' (a Mike Oldfield composition). On *Live At The Apollo* they were joined by Temptations members Eddie Kendricks and David Ruffin. This was the prelude to a three-year hiatus in the partnership, during which time Hall recorded his second solo album with production by Dave Stewart. Reunited in 1988, Hall And Oates had a big US hit with 'Everything Your Heart Desires' on Arista. On the 1990 hit 'So Close', producers Jon Bon Jovi and Danny Kortchmar added a strong rock flavour to their sound. The duo did not record together again until 1997's *Marigold Sky*, by which time their slick brand of soul was sounding increasingly dated.

● ALBUMS: *Whole Oates* (Atlantic 1972)★★, *Abandoned Luncheonette* (Atlantic 1973)★★★, *War Babies* (Atlantic 1974)★★, *Hall & Oates* (RCA 1975)★★, *Bigger Than Both Of Us* (RCA 1976)★★, *Beauty On A Back Street* (RCA 1977)★★★, *Livetime* (RCA 1978)★★, *Along The Red Ledge* (RCA 1978)★★★, *X-Static* (RCA 1979)★★, *Voices* (RCA 1980)★★★, *Private Eyes* (RCA 1981)★★★★, *H_2O* (RCA 1982)★★★★, *Bim Bam Boom* (RCA 1984)★★★, with Eddie Kendrick, David Ruffin *Live At The Apollo* (RCA 1985)★★★, *Ooh Yeah!* (Arista 1988)★★, *Change Of Season* (Arista 1990)★★, *Really Smokin'* (1993)★★, *Marigold Sky* (Push/BMG 1997)★★.
Solo: Daryl Hall *Sacred Songs* (RCA 1980)★★, *Three Hearts In The Happy Ending Machine* (RCA 1986)★★, *Soul Alone* (Epic 1993)★★★.

● COMPILATIONS: *No Goodbyes* (Atlantic 1977)★★★, *The Atlantic Collection* (Rhino 1996)★★★★.

HALL, RICK

b. 31 January 1932, Franklin County, Mississippi, USA. Hall played in Carmol Taylor And The Country Pals before forming the Hallmarks. In 1958 he joined the Fairlanes, which included another successful producer-to-be, Billy Sherrill, with whom he started Spar Music and the Florence Alabama Music Enterprises (FAME), together with Tom Stafford. In 1961, differences forced a split; shortly afterwards, Arthur Alexander took a song, 'You Better Move On', to Stafford, who in turn sent Alexander along to Rick Hall. The result was a hit record in 1962, once Hall had managed to lease the master to Dot Records, who then promptly whisked Alexander away from Hall. However, although he had 'lost' Alexander, with the money he made from the singer's initial hit record, Hall was able to lease a studio at Avalon Boulevard, Muscle Shoals. However, it was his success in producing hits at Fame for other nationally distributed independent labels such as Atlantic and Chess that really established Hall's and Muscle Shoals' considerable reputation. A major part in that achievement was played by the several wonderful rhythm sections that Hall recruited to play at his studios, and who would feature on major hits by artists including Clarence Carter, Wilson Pickett, Arthur Conley, Etta James and, later, Candi Staton. Perhaps the best-known line-up of Fame musicians stemmed from the 1966/7 period and comprised Spooner Oldham (keyboards), Jimmy Johnson (guitar), Junior Lowe/David Hood (bass) and Roger Hawkins (drums), with Oldham soon to be replaced by Florida émigré Barry Beckett. It was Oldham, Johnson and Hawkins who played on Aretha Franklin's first and only session at Fame in January 1967, which produced 'I Never Loved A Man (The Way I Love You)'; Jerry Wexler then 'borrowed' the same musicians for the New York sessions that produced her subsequent Atlantic successes. Many of the early Fame-originated songs came from writers such as Dan Penn, Spooner Oldham, and Donnie Fritts, with Penn in particular also playing an important role as a quasi-producer/A&R representative. After Penn's departure his role at Fame was taken on first by Jimmy Johnson (who also often engineered sessions) and later by multi-talented blind soulman Clarence Carter; however, it was Rick Hall who always remained 'the boss'. In the 70s Hall produced smash hits for acts including the Osmonds, Paul Anka and Bobbie Gentry. In the 80s he returned to country music and is now one of the most successful producers in that field.

● FURTHER READING: *Sweet Soul Music*, Peter Guralnick. *Say It One More Time For The Brokenhearted*, Barney Hoskyns. *Music Fell On Alabama*, Christopher S. Fuqua.

HAMILTON, ROY

b. 16 April 1929, Leesburg, Georgia, USA, d. 20 July 1969. Hamilton's booming baritone voice made him a 50s hit-maker singing gospel-flavoured pop songs. In the late 40s Hamilton honed his singing skills in a church choir and as a member of its offshoot quartet, the Searchlight Singers. He won a talent contest at the Apollo Theatre in 1947, but it was not until 1953 that he was discovered singing in a New Jersey club by Bill Cook, an influential local disc jockey who became the singer's manager. Hamilton's very first record for Columbia's subsidiary Epic, 'You'll Never Walk Alone', became an R&B number 1 and national US Top 30 hit in 1954, and it shot Hamilton to fame (the song would also later become a UK hit for Gerry And The Pacemakers in 1963). There followed for Hamilton a long string of singles that reached both R&B and pop audiences, notably 'If I Loved You', 'Ebb Tide' and 'Hurt' (all three 1954), and 'Unchained Melody' (an R&B number 1, 1955). Hamilton's songbook was built from the most popular entertainments of the day; 'You'll Never Walk Alone' and 'If I Loved You' were two Rodgers And Hammerstein songs taken from their musical *Carousel*, and 'Unchained Melody' came from a Warner Brothers film, *Unchained*. Hamilton retired during 1956-58 due to exhaustion, but when he came back he had adopted the harder gospel sound of his youth to compete with rock 'n' roll and the emerging soul sound. Best reflecting the change in style were the singles 'Don't Let Go' (1958) and his last hit record, 'You Can Have Her' (1961), plus the album *Mr. Rock And Soul* in 1962. The Epic label treated Hamilton as a major pop star and issued 16 albums by the artist. During the mid-60s, his

career sank while recording with MGM and then RCA.
● ALBUMS: *Roy Hamilton* (Epic 1956)★★★, *You'll Never Walk Alone* (Epic 1956)★★★, *The Golden Boy* (Epic 1957)★★★, *With All My Love* (Epic 1958)★★★, *Why Fight The Feeling?* (Epic 1959)★★, *Come Out Swingin'* (Epic 1959)★★★, *Have Blues, Must Travel* (Epic 1959)★★, *Roy Hamilton Sings Spirituals* (Epic 1960)★★★, *Soft 'N' Warm* (Epic 1960)★★★, *You Can Have Her* (Epic 1961)★★★, *Only You* (Epic 1961)★★★, *Mr. Rock And Soul* (Epic 1962)★★★, *The Great Golden Grooves* (1963)★★, *Warm Soul* (1963)★★★, *Sentimental, Lonely And Blue* (1964)★★, *The Impossible Dream* (1966)★★★.
● COMPILATIONS: *Roy Hamilton At His Best* (Epic 1960)★★★, *Roy Hamilton's Greatest Hits* (Epic 1962)★★★, *The Voice Of Roy Hamilton* (1967)★★★, *Unchained* (Charly 1988)★★★, *Golden Classics* (1991)★★★.

HAMMOND, CLAY

b. 21 June 1936, Roseback, Texas, USA. Clay was the older brother of Walter Hammond, singer with the original Olympics. Initially achieving success as a songwriter, Clay's composition 'Part Time Love' was a number 1 R&B single for 'Little' Johnny Taylor. Hammond later recorded for several labels, including Galaxy and Duo Disc, before settling with Kent in 1967. His releases included two superb southern soul ballads, 'You Messed Up My Mind' (1966) and 'I'll Make It Up To You' (1968). Clay's subsequent recordings were more irregular, although a successful Japanese tour did produce an album, *These Arms Of Mine*. In 1981 he joined the Rivingtons, who were still working the oldies circuit on the strength of their novelty hit 'Papa Oom Mow Mow'. Hammond later sang with one of the many different Drifters groups.
● ALBUMS: *These Arms Of Mine* (1980)★★★, *Streets Will Love You* (Evejim 1988)★★.
● COMPILATIONS: *Taking His Time* (Kent 1988)★★★.

HANCOCK, HUNTER

A San Antonio, Texas disc jockey on station KMAC, Hancock moved to California and worked as a jazz presenter on radio station KFVD (latterly KPOP) in Los Angeles in 1943. Switching exclusively to what later developed into R&B, Hancock launched his *Harlem Matinee* radio show in June 1948, and became known for his wild hollering and screaming. In playing the new music at that time, he predated Alan Freed by several years. Hancock was soon a popular figure at the many black clubs on Central Avenue. He became good friends with Johnny Otis and presided over many shows at Otis's Barrelhouse club. In 1951, Hancock presented two concert shows, *The Blues & Rhythm Midnight Matinee*, from the Olympic Auditorium, showcasing local black artists such as Floyd Dixon, Big Jay McNeely, Maxwell Davis and Peppermint Harris. The results have recently been issued for the first time on Sweden's Route 66 label. Hancock remained an advocate for R&B throughout the 50s, moving to KGFJ and KFOX and back to KPOP, and in February 1959 he formed his own Swingin' label, based near Sunset Boulevard. His first release was 'There Is Something On Your Mind' by Big Jay McNeely which had been recorded two years earlier, but nevertheless reached number 5 on the R&B charts. Swingin', and its sister label Magnum, ceased business in late 1964 after several dozen R&B and vocal group releases by such artists as Marvin & Johnny, Joe Houston and Rochell And The Candles. At this time Hancock was still a disc jockey on KGFJ; he retired from the music business in 1968.
● ALBUMS: *Hunter Hancock Presents 'Blues & Rhythm Midnight Matinee'* (1985)★★★.

HARPTONES

An R&B vocal group formed in 1953 in Harlem, New York City, New York, USA. The members were lead Willie Winfield, first tenor Nick Clark, second tenor William Dempsey, baritone Bill 'Dicey' Galloway, bass Billy Brown and pianist/arranger Raoul J. Cita. The Harptones were one of the smoothest and most polished R&B vocal groups to emerge during the early rock 'n' roll era. Although considered a part of the doo-wop phenomenon, they rarely employed nonsense syllables. Instead, the chorus would answer in words employing a special 'opened mouth harmony' devised by Cita. The Harptones were giants on the east coast but virtually unknown elsewhere in the country. Among their best numbers (all ballads) are 'Sunday Kind Of Love' (1954), 'My Memories Of You' (1954) and 'Life Is But A Dream" (1955); none of their jump songs were particularly convincing. By 1956, with the death of Brown, the group was beginning to break up, and during this time Jimmy Beckum appeared on many of the tracks recorded for George Goldner's Rama/Gee complex. Top notch songs during this period included 'On Sunday Afternoon' and 'Shrine Of St. Cecilia'. Their final recordings were released in 1957. During the 70s and 80s Winfield and Cita made up various permutations of a Harptones group to play the east coast oldies circuit.
● COMPILATIONS: *The Paragons Meet The Harptones* (Musicnote 1963)★★★, *The Harptones Featuring Willie Winfield* (Relic 1971)★★★, *Echoes Of A Rock Era* 12 tracks by the Harptones, 12 by the Crows (Roulette 1972)★★★, *The Harptones Featuring Willie Winfield Vol. 2* (Relic 1973)★★★, *Golden Classics: The Goldner Recordings, 1956-57* (Collectables 1991)★★★★, *A Sunday Kind Of Love* (Relic 1992)★★★.

HARRIS, BETTY

b. 1943, Orlando, Florida, USA. A former maid to Big Maybelle, with whom she would duet onstage, Harris was subsequently signed to Jubilee Records where her version of Solomon Burke's hit, 'Cry To Me', reached the US R&B Top 10 and national Top 30 in 1963. A follow-up, 'His Kiss', was a minor success, but this expressive singer matured upon signing to the New Orleans outlet Sansu. She proceeded to record a series of exemplary Allen Toussaint songs that combined the Crescent City kick of Lee Dorsey with traces of uptown soul. Indeed, Irma Thomas notwithstanding, it could be argued that Toussaint's work reached an apogee with such excellent records as 'What A Sad Feeling', 'I Don't Want To Hear It' and 'What'd I Do Wrong'. Paradoxically, a simpler ballad, 'Nearer To You' (1967), was Harris's only other hit and

this accomplished singer has not achieved the commercial success her talent deserved.
● ALBUMS: *Betty Harris* (London 1963)★★★★, *Soul Perfection* (Action 1969)★★★.
● COMPILATIONS: *In The Saddle* (1981)★★★★.

HARRIS, MAJOR

b. 9 February 1947, Richmond, Virginia, USA. A former member of several groups, including the Jarmels, Harris joined the Delfonics in 1971, where he remained for three years. On his departure the singer inaugurated the Major Harris Boogie Blues Band with Allison Hobbs, Phyllis Newman and Karen Dempsey, but it was as a solo act for Atlantic Records that he found success. 'Love Won't Make Me Wait' (1975), an R&B chart hit and US pop Top 5, was notorious for the impassioned groans of a female accompanist. Harris enjoyed further success with 'I Got Over Love' and 'Jealousy', but his career faltered until 1983, when 'All My Life' was a minor R&B hit. In the late 80s, Major returned to the reactivated Delfonics line-up.
● ALBUMS: *My Way* (Atlantic 1975)★★★, *Jealousy* (Atlantic 1976)★★★, *How Do You Take Your Love* (RCA 1978)★★.

HARRIS, THURSTON

b. 11 July 1931, Indianapolis, Indiana, USA, d. 1990, California, USA. After serving an apprenticeship touring with Jimmy Liggins, Harris settled in Los Angeles, where he made his recording debut in 1953 as a member of the Lamplighters. The group released over a dozen, now highly sought-after, singles, but to no success. Harris returned to Indianapolis and achieved fame as a solo act with his 1957 US Top 10 hit 'Little Bitty Pretty One'. This irresistible slice of tongue-in-cheek R&B reached the Top 10 in both US R&B and pop charts and was later immortalized by several British beat groups who covered the song during the 60s. Although Harris enjoyed another, albeit minor, hit the following year with 'Do What You Did', he was unable to sustain a consistent recording career, drifting from label to label, as well as suffering a troubled personal life, which at one time involved drug addiction. In 1990 he died of a heart attack in California.
● COMPILATIONS: *Little Bitty Pretty One* (Pathe Marconi 1984)★★★, *Thurston Harris* (Aladdin 1987)★★★.

HARRIS, WYNONIE

b. 24 August 1915, Omaha, Nebraska, USA, d. 14 June 1969. As a youth Harris played drums in and around his home-town before moving to Los Angeles in the early 40s. There he played, danced, sang and worked in several non-musical capacities in various clubs and theatres, also appearing in a film, *Hit Parade Of 1943*. Along with many other singers of the time, Harris was heavily influenced by Louis Jordan and, after a spell with the Lucky Millinder big band, he went solo as an R&B singer. He had already had a minor hit with Millinder, 'Who Threw The Whiskey In The Well?', and followed this with 'Bloodshot Eyes' and 'Good Rocking Tonight'. Unfortunately for his career prospects, audiences were turning towards the emerging and very much younger rock 'n' roll singers. Harris regularly worked with jazz-orientated groups, including those led by Illinois Jacquet, Lionel Hampton and Charles Mingus. Essentially a contemporary urban blues singer with an extrovert, jumping style, Harris had the misfortune to appear at a time when the music scene did not embrace his particular style of blues. In the early 50s he retired, but attempted a comeback in the early 60s and again in 1967. The times were a little more receptive to Harris's undoubted talent, but by that time he had developed lung cancer, from which he died in 1969. His son, Wesley Devereaux, is singer who has inherited his father's feeling for the blues.
● ALBUMS: with Amos Milburn *Party After Hours* (Aladdin 1955)★★★.
● COMPILATIONS: with Roy Brown *Battle Of The Blues* (King 1958)★★★★, *Mr Blues Meets The Master Saxes* recorded 1945-46 (1959)★★★★, *Good Rockin' Blues* recorded 1947-52 (King 1970)★★★★.
● FURTHER READING: *Rock Mr. Blues: The Life And Music Of Wynonie Harris*, Tony Collins.

HARRISON, WILBERT

b. 5 January 1929, Charlotte, North Carolina, USA, d. 26 October 1994, Spencer, North Carolina, USA. Although Harrison first recorded as early as 1953, it was not until the end of the decade that the singer established his reputation with a superb jump blues-styled adaptation of the perennial 'Kansas City'. This memorable single eventually rose to number 1 in the US pop and R&B charts, despite the attention of several competing versions. The singer then unleashed a series of similarly excellent releases including the compulsive 'Let's Stick Together', which was revived many years later by Bryan Ferry. Harrison continued to record, rather unsuccessfully, throughout the 60s, until 'Let's Work Together', a regenerated reading of that former release, returned him to the public eye. Harrison subsequently appeared in London with Creedence Clearwater Revival, but the song ultimately became better known with Canned Heat's hit version, a number 2 in the UK and a number 17 in the USA. Its originator, meanwhile, made several excellent albums in the wake of his new-found popularity, but was unable to gain any consistent commercial appeal.
● ALBUMS: *Kansas City* (Sphere Sound 1965)★★★, *Let's Work Together* (Sue 1970)★★★, *Shoot You Full Of Love* (Juggernaut 1971)★★, *Anything You Want* (1971)★★, *Wilbert Harrison* (Buddah 1971)★★, *Soul Food Man* (Chelsea 1976)★★, *Lovin' Operator* (Charly 1985)★★, *Small Labels* (Krazy Kat 1986)★★, *Listen To My Song* (Savoy Jazz 1987)★★.
● COMPILATIONS: *Kansas City* (Relic 1990)★★★★.

HATHAWAY, DONNY

b. 1 October 1945, Chicago, Illinois, USA, d. 13 January 1979. Originally schooled in the gospel tradition, this versatile artist majored in musical theory before performing in a cocktail jazz trio. Hathaway was then employed as a producer with Curtis Mayfield's Curtom label, while a duet with June Conquest, 'I Thank You Baby', became his first hit in 1969. The following year he was signed by Atlantic for whom he recorded several imaginative singles, including 'The Ghetto (1970) and 'Love Love Love'

(1973). His crafted compositions were recorded by such acts as Aretha Franklin and Jerry Butler, but Hathaway is best remembered for his duets with Roberta Flack. Their complementary voices were honed to perfection on 'Where Is The Love' (1972) and 'The Closer I Get To You' (1978), both of which reached the US Top 5. Why this gifted musician should have taken his own life remains unexplained, but on 13 January 1979, Hathaway fell from the fifteenth floor of New York's Essex House hotel. In 1980, Hathaway achieved a posthumous UK number 3 hit with another Roberta Flack duet, 'Back Together Again'.

● ALBUMS: *Everything Is Everything* (Atco 1970)★★★, *Donny Hathaway* (Atco 1971)★★★, *Donny Hathaway Live* (Atco 1972)★★, *Come Back Charleston Blue* film soundtrack (1972)★, with Roberta Flack *Roberta Flack And Donny Hathaway* (Atlantic 1972)★★★, *Extension Of A Man* (Atco 1973)★★, with Flack *Roberta Flack Featuring Donny Hathaway* (Atlantic 1980)★★★, *In Performance* (1980)★★★.

● COMPILATIONS: *Best Of Donny Hathaway* (Atco 1978)★★★.

HAWKINS, EDWIN, SINGERS

As directors of music at their Berkeley church, the Ephresian Church of God in Christ, Edwin Hawkins (b. August 1943, Oakland, California, USA) and Betty Watson began in 1967 to absorb the leading soloists from other San Franciso-based choirs to inaugurate the North California State Youth Choir. In 1969, the 50-strong ensemble recorded an album to boost their funds, and when San Francisco DJ Tom Donahue began playing one of its tracks, 'Oh Happy Day', the assemblage found itself with both a record contract with the Buddah label and a surprise international hit. Although renamed the Edwin Hawkins Singers, the featured voice belonged to Dorothy Combs Morrison (b. 1945, Longview, Texas) and much of the single's attraction comes from her powerful delivery. The singer subsequently embarked on a solo career which failed to maintain its initial promise while Hawkins, deprived of such an important member, struggled in the wake of this 'novelty' hit, although they enjoyed a period of great demand for session singing. One such session put them back into the US charts in 1970 while guesting on Melanie's Top 10 hit 'Lay Down (Candle In The Wind)'. It was their last chart appearence to date and eventually the group's fortunes faded. The Singers, now somewhat reduced in numbers, continue to tour and occasionally record.

● ALBUMS: *Oh Happy Day* (Fixit 1969)★★★, *Lets Us Go Into The House Of The Lord* (1969)★★★, *Peace Is Blowing In The Wind* (1969)★★★, *Live At The Yankee Stadium* (1969)★★, *I'd Like To Teach The World To Sing* (Buddah 1972)★★★, New World (1973)★★★, *Live - Amsterdam* (1974)★★★, *Live At The Bitter End, N.Y.* (1974)★★★, *Wonderful* (1977)★★★, *Love Alive II* (1979)★★★, *Imagine Heaven* (Fixit 1982)★★★, *Live With The Oakland Symphony Orchestra* (1982)★★★, *Give Us Peace* (1982)★★★, *Imagine Heaven* (Fixit 1989)★★★, *Face To Face* (Fixit 1991)★★★.

Solo: Edwin Hawkins *Children (Get Together)* (1971)★★★, *Love Alive* (1977)★★★.

● COMPILATIONS: *The Best Of The Edwin Hawkins Singers* (1985)★★★, *The Very Best Of The Edwin Hawkins Singers* (Camden 1998)★★★.

HAWKINS, 'SCREAMIN' JAY'

b. Jalacy Hawkins, 18 July 1929, Cleveland, Ohio, USA. Reportedly raised in Cleveland by a tribe of Blackfoot Indians, young Jalacy became interested in music at an early age, teaching himself piano at the age of six and, having mastered the keyboard, he then learned to play saxophone in his early teens. Hawkins was also an adept young boxer, winning an amateur *Golden Gloves* contest at the age of 14 and becoming Middleweight Champion of Alaska in 1949. He judged music to be the easier option, and became a professional musician, playing piano with artists such as Gene Ammons, Arnett Cobb, Illinois Jacquet, James Moody, Lynn Hope, and on one occasion, Count Basie. In 1950, Hawkins began developing an act based more on his almost operatic bass-baritone voice, and the following year he joined Tiny Grimes' Rocking Highlanders as pianist and occasional vocalist, making his recording debut with the band for Gotham Records in 1952 (the record was withdrawn after three weeks) and for Atlantic Records in 1953 (the results remain unissued). Leaving Grimes, Hawkins was befriended by blues shouter Wynonie Harris, who brought the young musician to New York City as his protégé. At this point, Hawkins' fortunes began to take an upswing, first with his debut records under his own name for the Timely label, followed by superior efforts for Mercury/Wing and Grand Records. In 1956, Screamin' Jay (as he was now known) signed with Columbia's reactivated OKeh subsidiary and enjoyed enormous success with his manic - and apparently drunken - rendition of his own 'I Put A Spell On You', which he had recorded earlier as a ballad for Grand Records. Released in October 1956, the original version was quickly withdrawn as a result of the public outrage caused by the 'suggestive and cannibalistic' sound effects provided by Hawkins. A suitably truncated substitution was soon made. Despite these efforts, an airplay ban remained in force, but the record sold over a million copies regardless, becoming a classic of rock music and invoking hundreds of cover versions from Nina Simone to the Alan Price Set and Creedence Clearwater Revival. Remaining with OKeh until 1958, Hawkins ran the gamut of his weird-but-wonderful repertoire with recordings of straight R&B songs such as 'Little Demon' and 'Person To Person', tongue-in-cheek, semi-operatic standards such as 'I Love Paris' and 'Temptation', and the unclassifiable and uniquely bizarre 'Hong Kong', 'Alligator Wine' and 'There's Something Wrong With You'. To enhance this ghoulish strangeness, on his tours with rock 'n' roll package shows, Hawkins was encouraged by Alan Freed to use macabre props such as skulls, snakes and shrunken heads and to begin his act from the inside of a coffin. Again, uproar followed, resulting in a largely unrepresentative album release and, worse still, Hawkins' only 50s film appearance in *Mister Rock 'N' Roll* being cut out in case parents boycotted the film's release. Shunned by the mass media, Hawkins spent most of the 60s playing one-nighters and tired rock 'n' roll revival gigs, making the occasional one-off recording agreement with tiny independent labels. *The Night And Day Of Screaming Jay Hawkins*, recorded in London for producer Shel Talmy's Planet label, was more conservative in tone. A brace of late 60s albums extended his idiosyncratic reputation and it was during these sessions that Hawkins recorded the original 'Constipation Blues', a lavatorial performance destined to become an intrinsic part of his stage act. He enjoyed a cameo role in the much-praised film *American Hot Wax*, and later won a starring role as the laconic hotel desk clerk in Jim Jarmusch's *Mystery Train*. Hawkins later collaborated with modern garage band the Fleshtones. A 1991 release, *Black Music For White People*, which included readings of two Tom Waits compositions, 'Ice Cream Man' and 'Heart Attack And Vine', as well as a rap interpretation of 'I Put A Spell On You', revealed an undiminished power. His influence on other performers, notably Screaming Lord Sutch, Arthur Brown and Alice Cooper, should not be underestimated. Touring and recording steadily through the 70s and 80s, Hawkins has recently formed a new band, the Fuzztones, and has made successful tours of Europe and the USA.

● ALBUMS: *At Home With Screamin' Jay Hawkins* (Epic 1958)★★★, *I Put A Spell On You* (Epic 1959)★★★★, *The Night & Day Of Screamin' Jay Hawkins* (Planet 1965)★★★, *What That Is* (Philips 1969)★★, *Screamin' Jay Hawkins* (Philips 1970)★★★, *A Portrait Of A Man & His Woman* (1972)★★★, *I Put A Spell On You* (1977)★★★, *Frenzy* (Edsel 1982)★★, *Real Life* (Charly 1983)★★, *Midnight* (1985)★★, *Live And Crazy* (Midnight Music 1986)★★★, *Feast Of The Mau Mau* (Edsel 1988)★★, *Real Life* (Charly 1989)★★★, *I Is* (1989)★★★, *I Want To Do It In A Cave!* (1990)★★★, *Voodoo Jive* (1990)★★★, *Black Music For White People* (Demon 1991)★★★, *Stone Crazy* (Demon 1993)★★★, *Somethin' Funny Goin' On* (Demon 1994)★★★.

● COMPILATIONS: *I Put A Spell On You* (Direction 1969)★★★, *Screamin' The Blues* (Red Lightin' 1982)★★★, *Frenzy* (Edsel 1986)★★★, *I Put A Spell On You* (Charly 1989)★★★, *Spellbound 1955-1974* (Bear Family 1990)★★★, *Voodoo Jive: The Best Of Screamin' Jay Hawkins* (Rhino 1990)★★★, *Cow Fingers And Mosquito Pie* (Epic 1991)★★★, *Screamin' Jay Hawkins - 1952-1955* (Magpie 1991)★★★, *From Gotham And Grand* (SJH 1992)★★★, *Portrait Of A Man* (Edsel 1995)★★★, *Alligator Wine* (Music Club 1997)★★★.

● FILMS: *American Hot Wax* (1976), *Mystery Train* (1989).

HAYES, ISAAC

b. 20 August 1942, Covington, Tennessee, USA. Hayes' formative years were spent playing piano and organ in various Memphis clubs. He fronted several groups, including Sir Isaac And The Doo-dads, the Teen Tones and Sir Calvin And His Swinging Cats, and recorded a handful of rudimentary singles. However, it was not until 1964 that he was able to attract the attention of the city's premier soul outlet, Stax Records. Having completed a session with Mar-Keys saxophonist Floyd Newman, Hayes was invited to remain as a stand-in for Booker T. Jones. He then established a songwriting partnership with David Porter and enjoyed success with Sam And Dave's 'Hold On I'm Comin'', 'Soul Man' and 'When Something Is Wrong With My Baby'. The team also wrote for Carla Thomas ('B-A-B-Y') and Johnnie Taylor ('I Had A Dream', 'I Got To Love Somebody's Baby'). They were responsible for the formation of the Soul Children as a vehicle for their songwriting. Hayes, nonetheless, remained a frustrated performer, and an after-hours, jazz-based spree resulted in his debut, *Presenting Isaac Hayes*, in 1967. *Hot Buttered Soul*, released in 1969, established the artist's reputation - its sensual soliloquies and shimmering orchestration combined in a remarkable, sophisticated statement. The artist also attained notoriety for his striking physical appearance - his shaven head and gold medallions enhanced a carefully cultivated mystique. However, *The Isaac Hayes Movement*, *To Be Continued* (both 1970) and *Black Moses* (1971) were less satisfying artistically as the style gradually degenerated into self-parody. *Shaft* was a highly successful film soundtrack released in 1971, and is considered by many to be Hayes' best work. Its theme also became an international hit single and its enduring qualities were emphasized when the song was covered by Eddy And The Soul Band in 1985, and reached number 13 in the UK charts. However, subsequent film scores, *Tough Guys* (1973) and *Truck Turner* (1974), were less interesting. Hayes left Stax in 1975 following a much publicized row over royalties, and set up his own Hot Buttered Soul label. Declared bankrupt the following year, he moved to Polydor and Spring labels, where his prolific output continued. In 1981, however, he retired for five years before re-emerging with 'Ike's Rap', a Top 10 US R&B single that partially revitalized his reputation. Many of Hayes' original Enterprise albums have been reissued in CD format by UK Ace under their reactivated Stax logo. Although trumpeted as a return to form, Hayes' mid-90s albums for Pointblank indicated little progress.

● ALBUMS: *Presenting Isaac Hayes* later reissued as *In The Beginning* (Stax 1967)★★, *Hot Buttered Soul* (Enterprise 1969)★★★★, *The Isaac Hayes Movement* (Enterprise 1970)★★, *To Be Continued* (Enterprise 1970)★★, *Shaft* (Enterprise 1971)★★★★, *Black Moses* (Enterprise 1971)★★, *Live At The Sahara Tahoe* (Enterprise 1973)★★, *Joy* (Enterprise 1973)★★, *Tough Guys* film soundtrack (Enterprise 1974)★★, *Truck Turner* film soundtrack (Enterprise 1974)★★, *Chocolate Chip* (HBS 1975)★★★, *Use Me* (Enterprise 1975)★★, *Disco Connection* (HBS 1976)★★, *Groove-A-Thon* (HBS 1976)★, *Juicy Fruit (Disco Freak)* (HBS 1976)★, with Dionne Warwick *A Man And A Woman* (HBS 1977)★, *New Horizon* (Polydor 1977)★, *Memphis Movement* (1977)★, *Hot Bed* (Stax 1978)★★, *For The Sake Of Love* (Polydor 1978)★, *Don't Let Go* (Polydor 1979)★★, with Millie Jackson *Royal Rappin's* (Polydor 1979)★★, *And Once Again* (Polydor 1980)★★, *Light My Fire* (1980)★★, *A Lifetime Thing* (Polydor 1981)★★, *U Turn* (Columbia 1984)★★, *Love Attack* (Columbia 1988)★★, *Branded* (Pointblank 1995)★★, *Raw And Refined* (Pointblank 1995)★★.

● COMPILATIONS: *The Best Of Isaac Hayes* (Enterprise 1975)★★★, *The Isaac Hayes Chronicle* (1978)★★★,

Enterprise - His Greatest Hits (Stax 1980)★★★★, *Best Of Isaac Hayes, Volumes 1 & 2* (Stax 1986)★★★, *Isaac's Moods* (Stax 1988)★★★, *Greatest Hit Singles* (Stax 1991)★★★, *The Collection* (Connoisseur Collection 1995)★★★.

HAYWOOD, LEON

b. 11 February 1942, Houston, Texas, USA. This Los Angeles-based soul vocalist and keyboardist launched his career as a conventional entertainer with great success in the 60s, having over 20 singles on the US R&B charts from 1965. In his teens, he performed with a local Houston group and accompanied blues artist Guitar Slim for some time. He relocated to Los Angeles in the early 60s and worked with saxophonist Big Jay McNeely, who arranged for him to record his first single, 'Without A Love', an instrumental on the small Swingin' label. After that, he joined Sam Cooke's band as keyboardist until the singer's untimely death. Haywood next recorded two singles for Fantasy Records, and subsequently moved to Imperial Records, where he recorded the single 'She's With Her Other Love', which made the R&B charts in 1965. He was part of two session bands organized by Los Angeles disc jockey Magnificent Montegue which issued the instrumental hits 'Hole In The Wall' (R&B number 5/pop Top 50, 1965) under the name of the Packers, and 'Precious Memories' (R&B number 31, 1967) as the Romeos. In 1967, Haywood secured his first big solo hit with the marvellous 'It's Got To Be Mellow' (R&B number 21) on Decca. He played on further recording sessions with the Packers and Dyke And The Blazers, then returned to recording under his own name. He found only sporadic success, most notably with 'It's Got To Be Mellow' and 'Keep It In The Family'. After recording for Columbia Records, he moved over to MCA Records. He emerged as a star in the 70s by adeptly modifying his style to incorporate the emerging funk and disco idioms. He joined 20th Century Records in 1974 and was immediately successful, notably with the psychedelicized 'I Want'a Do Something Freaky To You' (R&B number 7/pop number 15, 1975), 'Strokin' (Pt. II)' (R&B number 13, 1976) and 'Party' (R&B number 24, 1978). In 1980, Haywood revived the shuffle beat of 50s rock 'n' roll with the compelling 'Don't Push It Don't Force It' (number 2 R&B, US Top 50, UK Top 20). His last R&B chart record was 'Tenderoni' (number 22 R&B) in 1984. After a few more chart singles, for Casablanca Records and Modern Records, Haywood disappeared from the charts, but in the late 80s became associated in an executive/production capacity with the Los Angeles-based Edge label.

● ALBUMS: *Soul Cargo* (Vocalion 1966)★★★, *The Mellow Mellow Leon Haywood* (Galaxy 1967)★★★, *It's Got To Be Mellow* (MCA 1967)★★★, *Back To Stay* (Pye 1973)★★★, *Keep It In The Family* (20th Century 1974)★★★, *Come And Get Yourself Some* (20th Century 1975)★★★, *Intimate* (1976)★★★, *Double My Pleasure* (MCA 1978)★★★, *Energy* (1980)★★, *Naturally* (20th Century 1980)★★★, *It's Me Again* (1983)★★.

● COMPILATIONS: *The Best Of Leon Haywood* (Mercury 1996)★★★.

HEAD, ROY

b. 1 September 1941, Three Rivers, Texas, USA. This respected performer first formed his group, the Traits, in 1958, after moving to San Marcos. The line-up included Jerry Gibson (drums), who later played with Sly And The Family Stone. Head recorded for several local labels, often under the supervision of famed Texas producer Huey P. Meaux, but it was not until 1965 that he had a national hit when 'Treat Her Right' reached number 2 on both the US pop and R&B charts. This irresistible song, with its pumping horns and punchy rhythm, established the singer alongside the Righteous Brothers as that year's prime blue-eyed soul exponent. Head's later releases appeared on a variety of outlets, including Dunhill and Elektra Records, and embraced traces of rockabilly ('Apple Of My Eye') and psychedelia ('You're (Almost) Tuff'). However, by the 70s he had honed his style and was working as a country singer, and in 1975 he earned a notable US C&W Top 20 hit with 'The Most Wanted Woman In Town'.

● ALBUMS: *Roy Head And The Traits* (TNT 1965)★★★, *Treat Me Right* (Scepter 1965)★★★, *A Head Of His Time* (Dot 1968)★★, *Same People* (Dunhill 1970)★★, *Dismal Prisoner* (1972)★★, *Head First* (Dot 1976)★★, *Tonight's The Night* (ABC 1977)★★, *Boogie Down* (1977)★★, *Rock 'N' Roll My Soul* (1977)★★, *In Our Room* (1979)★★, *The Many Sides Of Roy Head* (1980)★★.

● COMPILATIONS: *His All-Time Favourites* (1974)★★★, *Treat Her Right* (Bear Family 1988)★★★, *Slip Away: His Best Recordings* (Collectables 1993)★★, *Treat Her Right: Best Of Roy Head* (Varèse Vintage 1995)★★★★.

HEARTBEATS

This doo-wop vocal quartet was formed in Queens, New York, USA, in 1954, originally named simply the Hearts. Three of the band members, Albert Crump (lead), Wally Roker (bass) and Vernon Seavers (baritone), met while attending Woodrow Wilson High School. They completed the line-up with Robby Tatum from a neighbouring school. They acquired a new lead in the shape of James Sheppard (d. 24 January 1970, Long Island, New York, USA) and Crump then sang first tenor. The group made their recording debut on Philadelphia's Network Records with Sheppard's 'Tormented'. Receiving scant promotion, it brought the group little exposure and fewer sales. More productive would be a liaison with Hull Records. This began in September 1955 with 'Crazy For You', a strong regional seller, and continued with 'Darling How Long' in February of the following year. One of the most fondly remembered records of the whole doo-wop era, 'Your Way', like all their previous releases was written by Sheppard. Though it did not chart at the time, it has subsequently become one of the most popular songs of the period. Their star rising, the group's next recording was 'Oh Baby Don't', but it sold mainly on the strength of Sheppard's plangent b-side composition, 'A Thousand Miles Away'. This quickly became a nationwide hit, peaking at number 53 in the *Billboard* charts. The Heartbeats sought to confirm their popularity with nationwide tours in the company of Ray Charles, B.B.

King and others. After a publishing dispute with Hull Records, the Heartbeats' next single emerged on Rama Records in 1957. 'I Won't Be The Fool Anymore' was followed by 'Everybody's Somebody's Fool', which returned them to the lower reaches of the charts. Spells at Gee and Roulette Records (two singles each) preceded the band's break-up in 1958, at which time the members divided into two factions. The rest of the band were allegedly none too impressed when Sheppard fell asleep at the microphone one night in Philadelphia, and other bouts of unshackled egotism exacerbated the situation. The momentum was lost, and all bar Sheppard returned to regular employment. Their erstwhile lead put together Shep And The Limelites, who released a number of singles, though only one, 'Daddy's Home', enjoyed major success (US number 2 in 1961). Sheppard was found dead in his car in 1970 after being shot and robbed.

● COMPILATIONS: *The Best Of The Heartbeats Including Shep & The Limelites* (Rhino 1990)★★★★.

HEATWAVE

Although based in Britain, Heatwave was formed by the Wilder brothers, Johnnie and Keith, on their discharge from the US Army. An advertisement in a music paper yielded Hull, England-born songwriter Rod Temperton, while further members recruited were two more Americans, Eric Johns and Jessie Whitten, a Czech, Ernest Berger, and a Spaniard, Mario Mantese. Between 1977 and 1981 the group enjoyed a series of hit singles in both the UK and USA, including 'Boogie Nights', 'Always And Forever' and 'Mind Blowing Decisions'. Despite maintaining some links, Temperton officially left the band in 1977 to forge an impressive songwriting career. His compositions have been recorded by George Benson, Herbie Hancock and Michael Jackson, and included the title song to the multi-million selling album *Thriller*. Heatwave's own progress was marred by a series of tragedies. Whitten was stabbed to death, Mantese left the group following a severe car crash, while Johnnie Wilder was paralyzed from the neck down as a result of a further road accident. Johnnie Wilder courageously remained at the group's helm, producing their work and singing in the studio, while another vocalist, J.D. Nicholas, took his place onstage. However, Heatwave were unable to withstand these traumas and in 1984 Nicholas opted to join the Commodores.

● ALBUMS: *Too Hot To Handle* (Epic 1977)★★★★, *Central Heating* (Epic 1978)★★★, *Hot Property* (Epic 1979)★★, *Candles* (Epic 1980)★★★, *Current* (Epic 1982)★★.

● COMPILATIONS: *Best Of* (Epic 1993)★★★★.

HEAVEN AND EARTH

Heaven And Earth, from Chicago, Illinois, USA, represented the last gasp of regionalism in the R&B recording industry, having emerged as local hitmakers during the late 70s. Original members were brothers Dwight (falsetto lead) and James Dukes (bass), Keith Steward (tenor) and Michael Brown (baritone). Their marvellous 'I Can't Seem To Forget You', featuring the falsetto lead of Dwight Dukes, was played like the national anthem in Chicago in 1976, but seemingly nowhere else. Baritone Dean Williams replaced Brown in 1978 and, as the group's new lead, radically changed the group's sound with the urbane 'Guess Who's Back In Town' (number 42 R&B). Greg Rose replaced Williams in 1979 for yet another change in sound with the funk dance hit 'I Feel A Groove Under My Feet' (number 78 R&B). Heaven And Earth recorded in Philadelphia in 1981 and reached the charts with 'I Really Love You' (number 47 R&B) before breaking up. Steward remained in Philadelphia to form Cashmere in 1982. Greg Rose later became a part of the highly successful vocal quartet Rose Brothers, who had a spate of southern-made hits during 1986/7.

● ALBUMS: *I Can't Seem To Forget You* (G.E.C. 1976)★★★, *Heaven And Earth* (Mercury 1978)★★★, *Fantasy* (Mercury 1979)★★.

HEBB, BOBBY

b. 26 July 1941, Nashville, Tennessee, USA. An accomplished musician and songwriter, Hebb appeared on the *Grand Ole Opry* at 12 and studied guitar with Chet Atkins. He later moved to New York, ostensibly to play with Mickey And Sylvia. When that duo split, a new combination emerged: Bobby And Sylvia. This short-lived partnership was followed by several solo Hebb releases that culminated in 'Sunny' (1966). Written in memory of his brother Hal, who died the day after the assassination of John F. Kennedy, this simple, melancholic song reached number 2 in the USA and number 12 in the UK. It was recorded by many artists, including Cher and Georgie Fame, whose version reached number 13 in the UK in 1966. Despite his tag as 'the song a day man', Hebb chose the country standard 'A Satisfied Mind' as the follow-up. It fared less well commercially, although the singer later secured a reputation in UK northern soul circles with 'Love Me' and 'Love Love Love', which reached the Top 40 in the UK in 1972. Hebb returned to the fringes of the soul chart with 'Sunny 76', a reworking of his best-known moment.

● ALBUMS: *Sunny* (Philips 1966)★★.

HELMS, JIMMY

b. 1944, Florida, USA. A versatile individual, Helms was a member of the Fort Jackson Army Band during his spell in the forces. He forged a singing career after his national service, and was a frequent performer on the popular *Merv Griffin* US televison show. He also appeared in the hippie musical *Hair*. Helms' only notable chart success came in 1973 with the smooth and soulful 'Gonna Make You An Offer You Can't Refuse', the title of which was taken from a line in the Francis Ford Coppola movie *The Godfather*. The record faltered in the US charts but reached the UK Top 10. He was, however, unable to repeat this one-off hit.

● ALBUMS: *Gonna Make You An Offer* (Cube 1974)★★★, *Songs I Sing* (1975)★★.

HENDERSON, FINIS

Finis Henderson III was raised in Chicago, USA, the son of a vice-president of Sammy Davis Enterprises. He was a founder-member of the urban Chicago soul band

Weapons Of Peace, who had three minor hits on Playboy Records in 1976/7 before disbanding. Moving to Los Angeles, Henderson began working as a comedian, contributing material to Richard Pryor, who invited him to tour as his support. Choosing to follow his musical ambitions, however, Henderson formed a soul group called Prophesy, before signing to Motown Records in 1982. His debut, *Finis*, highlighted his ballad style, and produced the hit single 'Skip To My Lou'. Motown were disappointed with sales of the album, and subsequently dropped him from their roster. Since then, he has been unable to secure a major contract.

● ALBUMS: *Finis* (Motown 1983)★★★.

HENDRICKS, BOBBY

b. 22 February 1938, Columbia, Ohio, USA. Having forged his reputation in two singing groups, the Swallows and the Flyers, Hendricks joined the Drifters in 1958, but left for a solo career the same year. 'Itchy Twitchy Feeling', on which he was backed by the Coasters, gave Hendricks a US Top 30 pop hit, but he was unable to secure a consistent profile. He briefly entered the lower regions of the US pop charts in 1960 with 'Psycho'. Hendricks rejoined the Drifters in 1964, where his subsequent path was obscured by the myriad of changes affecting the act's turbulent history.

HENRY, CLARENCE 'FROGMAN'

b. 19 March 1937, Algiers, Louisiana, USA. Henry began performing during the 50s with a New Orleans-based R&B group led by Bobby Mitchell. The singer later began work with bandleader Paul Gayten who accompanied him on his 1957 smash 'Ain't Got No Home'. However, it was not until 1961 that 'But I Do' provided a follow-up to this novelty song, earning Henry a US number 4 and UK number 3 hit. Co-written by Bobby Charles, the song featured several seasoned New Orleans musicians, including the young Allen Toussaint, and relaunched Henry's career. The same year a further international success, 'You Always Hurt The One You Love' - previously a hit for the Mills Brothers in 1944 - echoed the same effortless style. The following single fared better in the UK, with 'Lonely Street'/'Why Can't You' narrowly missing the Top 40, but it was the artist's last substantial hit. He continued to record for a variety of companies, and a 1969 collection, *Is Alive And Well And Living In New Orleans*, was acclaimed as a fine example of the 'Crescent City' style. Since then, Henry has remained a popular live attraction in his adopted city.

● ALBUMS: *You Always Hurt The One You Love* (Pye 1961)★★★, *Is Alive And Well And Living In New Orleans* (1969)★★★, *New Recordings* (Clarence Frogman Henry 1979)★★, *Little Green Frog* (Bear Family 1987)★★.

● COMPILATIONS: *Legendary Clarence 'Frogman' Henry* (Silvertown 1983)★★★, *But I Do* (Charly 1989)★★★★.

HENRY, PAULINE

The former vocalist with the Scottish band the Chimes, whose solo work brought about a reassessment of her career: 'After the Chimes, I took a while to think about what I really wanted to do with my career. I got my head down writing and had 25 songs. I learned my craft live, as opposed to being 'created' in the studio. I didn't know much about studios until I joined the Chimes.' As she idolizes Tina Turner, it was doubtless no accident that her debut album included compositions such as 'Can't Take Your Love', co-written with Terry Britten, who had penned many of Turner's biggest hits. There was also a cover version of Bad Company's 'Feel Like Making Love', revealing her R&B roots.

● ALBUMS: *The Harder They Come* (Sony 1993)★★★, *Pauline* (Soho Square 1994)★★★.

HI RECORDS

Formed in Memphis, Tennessee, USA, in 1957 by Ray Harris, a rockabilly singer, Hi Records - the letters originally stood for Hit Instrumentals - became a key black music label in the 70s, primarily as the home of soul/gospel giant Al Green. Harris launched the company for an investment of $3.50. Hi's first major hit came in late 1959 with 'Smokie Part 2' by the Bill Black Combo and crystallized the following year with Black's Top 10 'White Silver Sands'. In 1961 Black's saxophonist, Ace Cannon, began a short string of Hi hits with the US Top 20 single 'Tuff'. The mid-60s found soul singer Willie Mitchell, leader of Hi's house band, as the label's biggest seller with nine chart hits, none of which made the Top 20. Mitchell purchased Hi in 1970, the same year he brought Green to the label. Green eventually placed 16 Hi singles on the charts, seven of which were US Top 10 hits (including the 1972 number 1 hit 'Let's Stay Together'). Ann Peebles was the last notable Hi artist, best known for the 1973 Top 10 single 'I Can't Stand The Rain'. Hi was sold to Cream Records in the late 70s but failed to survive the disco era. Today Hi records are being reissued by Demon Records in the UK and MCA in the USA.

● COMPILATIONS: *The Greatest Hits From Memphis* (1969)★★★, *Hi Records - The Early Years* (1987)★★★, *Hi Records - The Early Years, Volume Two* (1988)★★★, *Hi Rhythm & Blues* (1988)★★★, *The Soul Years* (1988)★★★★, *Hi Records - The Blues Sessions* (1988)★★★, *The Hi Records Story* (1989)★★★★.

HIGGINS, CHUCK

b. Charles Williams Higgins, 17 April 1924, Gary, Indiana, USA. Higgins was an R&B singer best known for his recording 'Pachuko Hop' in 1952. The son of a preacher who also played trombone, Higgins learned to play the trumpet at the age of 10. In 1940 he moved to Los Angeles, where he played the trumpet in his high-school band. While attending the Los Angeles Music Conservatory, Higgins formed a band with pianist Frank Dunn, saxophonist Johnny Parker and others on bass and drums. After a series of personnel changes, Higgins took over the saxophone position and wrote 'Pachuko Hop', featuring a squealing solo on that instrument. It became a highlight of his stage show and was heard by Vernon 'Jake' Porter, owner of Combo Records. Porter released the single ('pachuko' was a slang word denoting a Mexican-American dressed fashionably in baggy pants, with a long key chain), with the b-side 'Motorhead Baby', another raw R&B rocker (and later the inspiration for the nickname of Frank Zappa sideman James 'Motorhead' Sherwood, and subsequently, the heavy metal band Motorhead). Although the record was not a big seller outside the Los Angeles area, it made Higgins a local favourite and he secured concert bookings with Charlie Parker, Nat 'King' Cole, Johnny Ace, Little Richard and the Orioles. Among Higgins' band members at the time was Johnny 'Guitar' Watson, who then left for a successful blues solo career. Higgins never signed an exclusive recording contract, so his records were released on numerous labels, including Aladdin Records, Caddy, Lucky, Recorded in Hollywood, Specialty Records and Dootone. Primarily an instrumentalist, Higgins also recorded some music featuring singers. He retired from performing in the early 60s and went on to teach music at Los Angeles high schools and colleges. He attempted a comeback briefly in the mid-70s, performing in a disco style, but achieved no success. Two albums recorded in the late 70s returned him to his earlier style and attracted a small European following. In 1983 he toured the UK and later returned to performing in his original style at Los Angeles nightclubs during the 80s. A collection of his early rare singles, *Yak A Dak*, was released on the Swedish Saxophonograph label in 1990.

● ALBUMS: *Pachuko Hop* (1956)★★★, *Rock 'N' Roll Versus Rhythm And Blues* (1959)★★★, *Motor Head Chuck* (1977)★★★, *Chuck Higgins Is A Ph.D.* (1979)★★.

● COMPILATIONS: *Yak A Dak* (Saxophonograph 1990)★★★, *Pachuko Hop* (Ace/Specialty 1992)★★★.

Higgins, Monk

b. Milton Bland, 17 October 1936, Menifee, Arkansas, USA, d. 3 July 1986, Los Angeles, California, USA. Higgins began his career as a highly successful producer and arranger in Chicago, first with the One-Derful label complex, then with St. Lawrence, and finally with Chess Records. While at St. Lawrence he recorded a number of appealing instrumentals, notably the national hit 'Who-Dun-It?' (number 30 R&B) and a double-sided local hit, 'Ceatrix Did It'/'Who-Dun-It?'. Higgins moved to Los Angeles in 1969, and arranged and produced acts on the United Artists/Imperial/Minit complex of labels, and recorded himself on a number of singles and albums. He hit the national charts again with 'Gotta Be Funky' (number 22 R&B) in 1972. During the 70s, with ex-Stax head Al Bell, he produced many successful records for Bobby Bland.

High Inergy

Barbara Mitchell, Linda Howard, Michelle Rumph and Vernessa Mitchell formed High Energy in April 1976, when all four singers were accepted into the Bicentennial Performing Arts Program in Pasadena, California, USA. They were discovered by Gwen Gordy-Lupper, sister of Motown Records boss Berry Gordy, who signed them to his Gordy label in 1977. Renamed High Inergy and promoted as 'the new Supremes', the vocal combo found immediate success with 'You Can't Turn Me Off (In The Middle Of Turning Me On)', a Top 20 hit in the USA in September 1977. By 1983, they had notched up eight further soul hits, without crossing over into the pop market. Vernessa Mitchell left the group in 1979 to pursue a career in gospel. High Inergy disbanded in 1984 when lead singer Barbara Mitchell went solo. She had already duetted with Smokey Robinson on a minor hit single, 'Blame It On Love', in 1983, but her 1984 debut, *Get Me Through The Night*, provoked little public response.

● ALBUMS: *Turnin' On* (Gordy 1977)★★★, *Steppin' Out* (Gordy 1978)★★, *Shoulda Gone Dancin'* (Gordy 1979)★★★, *Frenzy* (Gordy 1979)★★★, *Hold On* (Gordy 1981)★★, *So Right* (Gordy 1982)★★, *Groove Patrol* (Gordy 1983)★★.

Solo: Barbara Mitchell *Get Me Through The Night* (1984)★★.

Hightower, Rosetta

b. 23 June 1944, USA. This vocalist achieved fame as a member of the Orlons, a Philadelphia-based vocal group which enjoyed success with 'The Wah Watusi' and 'Don't Hang Up'. The unit disbanded in 1968 when Hightower went to the UK to pursue a career as a session singer. She contributed to Joe Cocker's international smash hit 'With A Little Help From My Friends', and her later appearances included Muddy Waters' *London Sessions* (1972), Dana Gillespie's *Wasn't Born A Man* (1973), Doris Troy's *Stretching Out* and Kevin Ayers' *Confessions Of Dr. Dream* (both 1974). During this period Hightower was also a member of Charge, a short-lived studio group that also featured former Grease Band stalwarts Neil Hubbard, Alan Spenner and Chris Stainton. Her only solo album was produced by Ric Grech.

● ALBUMS: *Hightower* (Columbia 1971)★★.

Highway QC's

Manager Charles Copeland put together gospel group the Highway QC's in 1945 in Chicago, Illinois, USA. He enlisted Spencer Taylor Jnr. (lead), Sam Cooke (lead and first tenor), Lee Richardson (second tenor), Creadell Copeland (baritone) and Charles Richardson (bass). Their name was taken from the Q.C. High School they all attended and the Highway Baptist Church where they rehearsed. Cooke was then recruited by the Soul Stirrers and replaced by Johnnie Taylor, formerly singer with the Five Echoes. Their belated recording career began in 1955 after being placed on the local Vee Jay Records label. 'Somewhere To Lay My Head' was their debut single, followed by several further sides and an album. Most of these tracks were recorded without the aid of Copeland or the Richardson brothers, who had been replaced by James Walker (bass), Ray Crume (tenor), James Davis (tenor and second lead) and Chris Flowers (baritone). Spencer Taylor Jnr. was now the sole lead following his namesake Johnnie Taylor's 1956 departure to replace the solo-bound Cooke in the Soul Stirrers. Johnnie Taylor subsequently enjoyed a solo career himself, working primarily in the blues medium and scoring a number 1 hit with 'Who's Makin' Love' in 1968. The Highway QC's continued in the interim, with the addition of Will Rogers on second lead in 1961 (he, too, would go on to join the Soul Stirrers). One album for ABC Dunhill in 1973 preceded a long spell at Savoy Records, where they recorded seven albums between 1976 and 1983. This was their most fertile period in commercial terms, but into the 90s a touring version of the group was still active (and still fronted by Spencer Taylor Jnr.). In 1995 they celebrated 50 years in the music business.

● ALBUMS: *Somewhere To Lay My Head* (VeeJay 1963)★★★, *Be At Rest* (Peacock 1966)★★★, *Stay With God* (Savoy 1976)★★★.

● COMPILATIONS: *The Best Of The Highway QC's* (Capitol/Chameleon 1990)★★★★.

HILL, JESSIE

b. 9 December 1932, New Orleans, Louisiana, USA, d. 17 September 1996. Jessie Hill's primary claim to fame was the classic New Orleans R&B hit 'Ooh Poo Pah Doo - Part II' in 1960. His first musical experience was as a drummer at the age of seven. At 15 he played in a Dixieland band and at 20 formed an R&B group called the House Rockers. He briefly worked with Professor Longhair and Huey Smith in the mid-50s before re-forming the House Rockers in 1958, abandoning the drums to sing. After Hill performed 'Ooh Poo Pah Doo' as a joke at his gigs, Joe Banashak of Minit Records heard the song and agreed to record it. Arranged by Allen Toussaint, it eventually reached number 3 on the R&B charts and number 28 on the national pop charts. Hill had only one other minor chart single before moving to Los Angeles, where he wrote songs performed by Sonny And Cher, Ike And Tina Turner and Iron Butterfly. He recorded one album later in his career and there is a collection of his Minit sides on Charly Records.

● ALBUMS: *Naturally* (1972)★★.

● COMPILATIONS: *Y'all Ready Now?* (Charly 1980)★★★, *Golden Classics* (Collectables)★★★.

HILL, Z.Z.

b. Arzel Hill, 30 September 1935, Naples, Texas, USA, d. 27 April 1984. A singer in the mould of Bobby 'Blue' Bland, Hill served his musical apprenticeship in Dallas lounge bars. He recorded for his brother Matt's MH label before signing to Kent Records in 1964. A string of mature, sophisticated singles followed, including 'Hey Little Girl' (1965) and 'I Found Love' (1966). More 'adult' than contemporaries at Stax, such records struggled for acceptance outside the south and failed to reach the R&B chart. Although Hill left Kent in 1968, the label continued to release his material and three years later secured a Top 30 R&B hit with his 1964 recording, 'I Need Someone (To Love Me)'. The artist enjoyed similar success with the engaging 'Don't Make Me Pay For His Mistakes', which peaked at number 17 (US R&B). Other releases were less fortunate, but the singer's work with Jerry 'Swamp Dogg' Williams improved the situation. Later spells with Hill/United Artists and Columbia were marred by corporate indecision. In 1981, Hill signed with Malaco, a company devoted to classic southern soul. His albums there, including *Down Home*, *The Rhythm And The Blues* and *I'm A Blues Man*, proved his most artistically satisfying. Hill died of a heart attack in April 1984.

● ALBUMS: *A Whole Lot Of Soul* (Kent 1969)★★★, *The Brand New Z.Z. Hill* (Mankind 1972)★★★, *Dues Paid In Full* (Kent 1972)★★★, *The Best Thing That's Ever Happened To Me* (Mankind 1972)★★★★, *Keep On Loving You* (1975)★★★, *Let's Make A Deal* (Columbia 1978)★★★, *Mark Of Z.Z.* (1979)★★★, *Z.Z. Hill* (Malaco 1981)★★★, *Down Home* (Malaco 1982)★★★★, *The Rhythm And The Blues* (Malaco 1983)★★★★, *I'm A Blues Man* (Malaco 1984)★★★, *Bluesmaster* (Malaco 1984)★★★.

● COMPILATIONS: *Dues Paid In Full* (Kent 1984)★★★, *In Memorium 1935-1984* (Malaco 1985)★★★, *Whoever's Thrilling You (Is Killing Me)* (Stateside 1986)★★★, *Greatest Hits* (Malaco 1986)★★★★, *The Best Of Z.Z. Hill* (Malaco 1986)★★★, *The Down Home Soul Of Z.Z. Hill* recorded 1964-68 (1992)★★★.

HILLSIDE

A contemporary soul trio from Los Angeles, California, USA, Hillside launched their recording career in 1996 with a self-titled collection released on their own Organized Fun label. Comprising Anthony 'Rox' Brown, Wayne Cockerham and Eric 'Junx' Jenkins, their album highlighted the group's tasteful blend of traditional vocal R&B harmonies with rhythms and melodies inspired by the soul and funk traditions. They had initially found the music industry disinterested in what they described as 'the live, instrumental thing', so the group set up Organized Fun, distributed by Bellmark, and produced *Hillside* themselves. The accent on live drums rather than a drum machine helped distinguish the group's 'classicist' intentions from the plethora of male R&B groups, as did the absence of samples and their preference for their own musicianship (keyboards, bass and drums). The album was promoted by the release of a single, 'Pearl'.

● ALBUMS: *Hillside* (Organized Fun 1996)★★★.

HINES, SIMONE

b. *c.*1975, New Jersey, USA. Another of a seemingly endless roll-call of female soul/R&B singers to emerge in the mid-90s, Simone Hines released her self-titled debut for Epic Records in 1997. Hines' career began as a club singer who graduated to sharing a stage with Queen Latifah and Michael Bolton. She also appeared alongside Aretha Franklin at New York's Apollo Theatre during a 1992 Democratic Party fund-raiser. The producers on her debut album included Narada Michael Walden, Harvey Mason Jnr. and Rodney Jerkins. A highly polished collection of sensual R&B ballads, three of the album's tracks were co-written by the artist. It also included a cover version of the Emotions' 'Best Of My Love'. In addition to the release of a single, 'Yeah! Yeah! Yeah!', Hines increased her profile by recording a track alongside Foxy Brown for Puff Daddy's 1997 album, a huge international seller.

● ALBUMS: *Simone Hines* (Epic 1997)★★★.

HINTON, EDDIE

b. Edward Craig Hinton, 15 June 1944, Jacksonville, Florida, USA, d. 28 July 1995, Birmingham, Alabama, USA. Guitarist Eddie Hinton's professional reputation was largely built around his session work. Having originally played on the club circuit of the southern states of America, he moved to Muscle Shoals, Alabama, in the mid-60s. Between 1967 and 1971 he was a principal member of the Muscle Shoals Sound house band, performing with Aretha Franklin, Wilson Pickett, Otis Redding, Elvis Presley, Percy Sledge, Solomon Burke, Joe Tex and many more. Although best known for his skilful guitar playing, Hinton was also proficient on several other instruments, including bass, drums and keyboards. His studio expertise saw him work as a producer, and he also wrote songs for others. His compositions included 'Choo Choo Train' (Box Tops), 'Breakfast In Bed' (Dusty Springfield and UB40) and 'It's All Wrong, But It's All Right' (Percy Sledge). He released a debut solo album in 1978, but *Very Extremely Dangerous* failed to sell. Afterwards, Hinton, long considered by associates to be a troubled soul, experienced a period of depression that culminated in his admittance to the Alabama Rescue Mission. He returned to recording in the late 80s with an album for Swedish label Almathea, before signing a new contract with Rounder Records. Two albums followed, but in 1995 he was discovered dead in the locked bathroom of his parents' home.

● ALBUMS: *Very Extremely Dangerous* (Capricorn 1978)★★, *Letters From Mississippi* (Almathea 1988)★★★, *Cry And Moan* (Rounder 1991)★★★, *Very Blue Highway* (Rounder 1993)★★★.

HINTON, JOE

b. 15 November 1929, Evansville, Indiana, USA, d. 13 August 1968, Boston, USA. Hinton recorded a string of R&B singles for the Texas-based Back Beat label in the late 50s and 60s, the best-known of which, a cover version of Willie Nelson's 'Funny', reached the Top 20 in the USA in August 1964. Hinton first applied his falsetto to gospel music with the Blair Singers and the Spirit Of Memphis Quartet. He moved to Memphis, Tennessee, to work with the latter group, who recorded for the Peacock label. In 1958 Peacock president Don Robey convinced Hinton to switch to secular music and in 1958 signed him to the Back Beat subsidiary. Hinton's first single for the label was 'Ladder of Love', which did not sell well. It was not until the 1963 'You Know It Ain't Right' that Hinton reached the charts, at number 20. After one other minor chart single, 'Better To Give Than Receive', Hinton had his greatest success with the Nelson ballad, which rose to number 13 in 1964. There was one further single in the charts that year, 'I Want A Little Girl', but Hinton's career declined after that. He recorded for Backbeat until 1968, when he died of skin cancer.

● ALBUMS: *Funny (How Time Slips Away)* (Backbeat 1965)★★★, *Duke-Peacock Remembers Joe Hinton* (Duke 1969)★★★, *Joe Hinton* (1973)★★★.

HOLDEN, RON

b. 7 August 1939, Seattle, Washington, USA, d. 22 January 1997. Holden's career had a unique beginning: he had been arrested for driving with alcohol and marijuana in his possession and was in the police station when a police officer heard him singing. The officer, Larry Nelson, told Holden that he was planning on quitting the police department for a career in music and gave Holden his phone number. The teenager called Nelson upon his release from jail and Nelson recorded Holden singing his own composition 'Love You So'. The ballad was issued on Nelson's Nite Owl label and then sold to the larger Donna label, reaching the US Top 10 in the summer of 1960. An album was released on Donna but further singles on that and other labels did not recapture the flavour of the hit and Holden retired from the music business.

● ALBUMS: *Love You So* (Donna 1960)★★★.

HOLIDAY, JIMMY

b. 24 July 1934, Durant, Mississippi, USA, d. 15 February 1987. This versatile singer first came to prominence in 1963 with the self-penned 'How Can I Forget?' which was covered at the same time by Ben E. King. Holiday later joined the Minit label where he made several excellent recordings, ranging from the 'Memphis'-influenced R&B of 'You Won't Get Away' to the urban soul of 'I'm Gonna Move To The City'. His biggest hit on Minit was 'Baby I Love You' (1966), a bigger hit for Little Milton in 1970. Holiday also recorded with former Raelette Clydie King, and later pursued a career as a songwriter on his departure from the label. A partnership with Randy Myers and Jackie DeShannon produced several excellent compositions, including the much-covered 'Put A Little Love In Your Heart', recorded successfully in 1989 by Al Green and Annie Lennox. Holiday died of heart failure in 1987.

● ALBUMS: *Turning Point* (1967)★★★, *Spread Your Love* (1968)★★.

● COMPILATIONS: *Everybody Needs Help* (Stateside 1986)★★★.

HOLLAND, BRIAN

b. 15 February 1941, Detroit, Michigan, USA. A mainstay of black music in Detroit since the mid-50s, Brian Holland emerged as the lead vocalist of the Satintones, before touring as pianist with Barrett Strong in 1960. He joined Strong at Motown Records in 1961, enjoying immediate success as the co-writer and producer of the label's biggest hit to date, the Marvelettes' 'Please Mr Postman'. In 1962 he formed a production team with Lamont Dozier and Freddy Gorman; a year later, Gorman was replaced by Holland's brother Eddie. Working as Holland/Dozier/Holland, the trio masterminded a remarkable series of hits for Motown during the remainder of the 60s. In 1967, they clashed with the label's head, Berry Gordy, and left to set up the Invictus and Hot Wax labels. Throughout this period, Brian Holland was the partnership's chief voice in the studio, while his colleagues were responsible for composing the majority of the trio's hits. Holland scored a rare solo hit himself in 1972, 'Don't Leave Me Starvin' For Your Love', plus two chart duets with Lamont Dozier. Since the demise of Invictus in the mid-70s, he has featured in periodic production projects with his brother.

HOLLAND, EDDIE

b. 30 October 1939, Detroit, Michigan, USA. Like his brother Brian Holland, Eddie was active in the Detroit music scene from the mid-50s onwards, leading the Fideltones vocal group, and producing demo recordings for Jackie Wilson. In 1958, he met Berry Gordy, who produced a series of solo singles for Holland on Mercury and United Artists. Gordy signed Holland to his fledgling Motown Records concern in 1961, and was rewarded when Holland's 'Jamie', an affectionate parody of Jackie Wilson, became a US Top 30 hit. Holland achieved three further chart successes in 1964, among them 'Leaving Here', which proved popular among British R&B bands. That year he also helped to inaugurate the Holland/Dozier/Holland partnership, Motown's most successful writing and production team of all time. Working mostly as the trio's lyricist, Holland was involved in a chain of hits for artists such as the Supremes and the Four Tops. He also collaborated with writer/producer Norman Whitfield on a series of singles by the Temptations, notably 'I'm Losing You' and 'Beauty Is Only Skin Deep'. The same pairing evolved 'He Was Really Saying Something' and 'Needle In A Haystack' for the Velvelettes, while Holland also co-wrote Shorty Long's dancefloor classic, 'Function At The Junction'. Eddie Holland continued to compose and produce with his brother and Lamont Dozier when the trio formed the Invictus and Hot Wax labels in 1968. Since then he has continued to work periodically with both his former partners.

● ALBUMS: *Eddie Holland* (Motown 1962)★★★.

HOLLAND/DOZIER/HOLLAND

Brothers Eddie Holland (b. 30 October 1939, Detroit, Michigan, USA) and Brian Holland (b. 15 February 1941, Detroit, Michigan, USA), and Lamont Dozier (b. 16 June 1941, Detroit, Michigan, USA) formed one of the most successful composing and production teams in popular music history. Throughout the mid-60s, they almost single-handedly fashioned the classic Motown sound, creating a series of hit singles that revolutionized the development of black music. All three men were prominent in the Detroit R&B scene from the mid-50s, Brian Holland as lead singer with the Satintones, his brother Eddie with the Fideltones, and Dozier with the Romeos. By the early 60s, they had all become part of Berry Gordy's Motown concern, working both as performers and as writers/arrangers. After masterminding the Marvelettes' 1961 smash 'Please Mr Postman', Brian Holland formed a production team with his brother Eddie, and Freddy Gorman. In 1963, Gorman was replaced by Dozier, and the trio made their production debut with a disregarded record by the Marvelettes, 'Locking Up My Heart'. Over the next five years, the triumvirate wrote and produced scores of records by almost all the major Motown artists, among them a dozen US number 1 hits. Although Smokey Robinson can claim to have been the label's first true auteur, Holland/Dozier/Holland created the records that transformed Motown from an enthusiastic Detroit soul label into an international force. Their earliest successes came with Marvin Gaye, for whom they wrote 'Can I Get A Witness?', 'Little Darling', 'How Sweet It Is (To Be Loved By You)' and 'You're A Wonderful One', and Martha And The Vandellas, who had hits with the trio's 'Heatwave', 'Quicksand', 'Nowhere To Run' and 'Jimmy Mack'. Impressive although these achievements were, they paled alongside the team's run of success with the Supremes. Ordered by Berry Gordy to construct suitable vehicles for the wispy, feminine vocal talents of Diana Ross, they produced 'Where Did Our Love Go?', a simplistic but irresistible slice of lightweight pop-soul. The record reached number 1 in the USA, as did its successors, 'Baby Love', 'Come See About Me', 'Stop! In The Name Of Love' and 'Back In My Arms Again' - America's most convincing response to the otherwise overwhelming success of British beat groups in 1964 and 1965. These Supremes hits charted the partnership's growing command of the sweet soul idiom, combining unforgettable hooklines with a vibrant rhythm section that established a peerless dance groove. The same process was apparent - albeit with more sophistication - on the concurrent series of hits that Holland/Dozier/Holland produced and wrote for the Four Tops. 'Baby I Need Your Loving' and 'I Can't Help Myself' illustrated their stylish way with up-tempo material; '(It's The) Same Old Song' was a self-mocking riposte to critics of their sound, while 'Reach Out I'll Be There', a worldwide number 1 in 1966, pioneered what came to be known as 'symphonic soul', with a towering arrangement and a melodic flourish that was the peak of their work at Motown. Besides the Supremes and the Four Tops, the trio found success with the Miracles ('Mickey's Monkey' and 'I'm The One You Need'), Kim Weston ('Take Me In Your Arms'), and the Isley Brothers ('This Old Heart Of Mine', 'Put Yourself In My Place' and 'I Guess I'll Always Love'). Their long-standing commitments continued to bring them recognition in 1966 and 1967, however, as the Supremes reached the top of the US charts with 'You Can't Hurry Love', 'You Keep Me Hanging On', 'Love Is Here And Now You're Gone', and the mock-psychedelic 'The Happening', and the Four Tops extended their run of success with 'Bernadette' and 'Standing In The Shadows Of Love'.

In 1967, when Holland/Dozier/Holland effectively commanded the US pop charts, they split from Berry Gordy and Motown, having been denied more control over their work and more reward for their labours. Legal disputes officially kept them out of the studio for several years, robbing them of what might have been their most lucrative period as writers and producers. They were free, however, to launch their own rival to Motown, in the shape of the Invictus and Hot Wax labels. Neither concern flourished until 1970, and even then the names of the company's founders were absent from the credits of their records - although there were rumours that the trio were moonlighting under the names of their employees. On the evidence of Invictus hits by artists such as the Chairmen Of The Board and Freda Payne, the case was convincing, as their records successfully mined the familiar vein of the trio's Motown hits, at a time when their former label was unable to recapture that magic without them. Business difficulties and personal conflicts gradually wore down the partnership in the early 70s, and in 1973 Lamont Dozier left the Holland brothers to forge a solo career. Invictus and Hot Wax were dissolved a couple of years later, and since then there have been only occasional reunions by the trio, none of which have succeeded in rekindling their former artistic fires. The

Holland/Dozier/Holland partnership will be remembered for its five halcyon years of success in the 60s, not the two decades or more of disappointment and unfulfilled potential that followed.

● COMPILATIONS: *The Very Best Of The Invictus Years* (Deep Beats 1997)★★★.

HOLLIDAY, JENNIFER

b. 19 October 1960, Houston, Texas, USA. This powerful vocalist first attracted attention as lead in the Broadway show *Your Arm's Too Short To Box With God*. She is, however, better known for her Tony-winning role in the musical *Dreamgirls*, a thinly disguised adaptation of the Supremes' story, which former member Mary Wilson took as the title of her autobiography. The show's undoubted highlight was Holliday's heart-stopping rendition of 'And I Am Telling You I'm Not Going', one of soul's most emotional, passionate performances. The single's success in 1982 prompted Holliday's solo career, but subsequent work was overshadowed by that first hit. She returned to the stage in 1985 in *Sing, Mahalia Sing* and has also acted in the television series *The Love Boat*. Holliday was also part of the backing choir on Foreigner's 1984 UK number 1 hit single, 'I Wanna Know What Love Is'. *Say You Love Me* won her a second Grammy award in 1985. She appeared in the musical *Grease* in the 90s and has recorded only sporadically. Holliday possesses an outstandingly powerful and emotional voice, the range of which has seen her compared to Aretha Franklin.

● ALBUMS: with Loretta Devine, Cleavant Derricks *Dreamgirls* Original Broadway Cast (Geffen 1982)★★★, *Feel My Soul* (Geffen 1983)★★★, *Say You Love Me* (Geffen 1985)★★★, *Get Close To My Love* (Geffen 1987)★★★, *I'm On Your Side* (Arista 1991)★★★, *On And On* (Inter Sound 1994)★★★.

● COMPILATIONS: *The Best Of Jennifer Holliday* (Geffen 1996)★★★★.

HOLLOWAY, BRENDA

b. 21 June 1946, Atascadero, California, USA. Brenda Holloway began her recording career with three small Los Angeles labels, Donna, Catch and Minasa, in the early 60s, recording under the aegis of producer Hal Davis. In 1964, Holloway made an impromptu performance at a disc jockeys' convention in California, where she was spotted by a Motown Records talent scout. She signed to the label later that year, becoming its first west coast artist. Her initial Tamla single, 'Every Little Bit Hurts', established her bluesy soul style, and was quickly covered by the Spencer Davis Group in Britain. She enjoyed further success in 1964 with 'I'll Always Love You', and the following year with 'When I'm Gone' and 'Operator'. Her consistent record sales led to her winning a place on the Beatles' 1965 US tour, but subsequent Tamla singles proved less successful. Holloway began to devote increasing time to her songwriting, forming a regular writing partnership with her sister Patrice, and Motown staff producer Frank Wilson. This combination produced her 1968 single 'You've Made Me So Very Happy', a song that proved more successful via the million-selling cover version by the white jazz-rock group Blood, Sweat And Tears. In 1968, Holloway's contract with Motown was terminated. The label issued a press release stating that the singer wished to sing for God, although Holloway blamed business differences for the split. She released a gospel album in 1983 and worked with Ian Levine from 1987. She teamed with Jimmy Ruffin in 1989 for a duet, 'On The Rebound'.

● ALBUMS: *Every Little Bit Hurts* (Tamla 1964)★★★, *The Artistry Of Brenda Holloway* (Motown 1968)★★★, *All It Takes* (1991)★★★.

● COMPILATIONS: *Greatest Hits And Rare Classics* (1991)★★★.

HOLLOWAY, LOLEATTA

b. November 1946, Chicago, Illinois, USA. With her full-bodied gospelized vocals, which lent tremendous energy to her disco recordings, Holloway, as one of the leading disco divas, epitomized like no other singer of her day the transition of African-American popular music from soul to disco in the late 70s. She started in the church singing gospel, and sang with the famed Caravans from 1967-71. She was first recorded by her manager/husband Floyd Smith in Chicago on his Apache label, releasing 'Rainbow 71'. In 1973 she signed with GRC's Aware label and achieved a double-sided chart record with 'Mother Of Shame'/'Our Love' (number 43 R&B). These songs came from her debut album, *Loleatta*, which was recorded in Chicago and Atlanta. 'Cry To Me' (number 10 R&B, number 68 pop), a 1975 remake of the Solomon Burke hit, was pure, heartfelt soul and her biggest hit, effectively launching her second album, *Cry To Me*. In 1976 she moved to Philadelphia producer Norman Harris's Gold Mind label and recorded *Loleatta*, which featured a healthy tension between her earthy, soulful, gospelized roots and the Philly rhythm section. It produced her first disco hit, 'Hit And Run' (number 56 R&B), in 1977. *Queen Of The Night*, one of her most successful albums, consolidated her position in the disco galaxy of stars, but at the expense of the soulful sides of her artistry. *Loleatta Holloway*, with production help from Smith, brought her back to a more balanced presentation of deep soul and disco, but was notable for her disco groove 'All About The Paper'. *Love Sensation*, under the production aegis of Dan Hartman, featured soulful workouts, such as the splendid remake of Otis Redding's hit 'I've Been Loving You Too Long', and disco numbers such as 'Love Sensation', a dancehall classic that was much sampled by rappers years later. Holloway's last chart single was 'Crash Goes Love' for Streetwise in 1984. During the 80s she confined her recording to small independent labels such as DJ International and Saturday Records.

● ALBUMS: *Loleatta* (Aware 1973)★★★, *Cry To Me* (Aware 1975)★★★★, *Loleatta* (Gold Mind 1976)★★★, *Queen Of The Night* (Gold Mind 1978)★★★, *Loleatta Holloway* (Gold Mind 1979)★★★, *Love Sensation* (Gold Mind 1980)★★★.

HOLLYWOOD FLAMES

Formed as the Flames in 1949, this R&B group went through a variety of name changes - Four Flames, Hollywood Four Flames, Jets, Ebbtides and Satellites -

during its career. However, it was as the Hollywood Flames that they had their biggest success, the 1957 hit 'Buzz, Buzz, Buzz'. The song was written by founding member Bobby Byrd, who also had a solo career as Bobby Day. The vocal on the song was not by Day, however, but by group member Earl Nelson, who also recorded as Jackie Lee and as half of Bob And Earl. The other members of the group at the time of the hit, which reached number 11 in the US pop charts and number 5 in the R&B charts, were founding member David Ford and baritone Curtis Williams, co-writer of the hit 'Earth Angel' and a former member of the group that recorded it, the Penguins. 'Buzz, Buzz, Buzz' was released on Ebb Records, run by Lee Rupe, wife of Specialty Records owner Art Rupe. Released in November 1957, the single spent 17 weeks in the charts. Follow-up singles were issued under Day's name, but by 1959 Ebb had folded. The group continued to record with various personnel for several years.

● COMPILATIONS: *The Hollywood Flames* (Specialty 1992)★★★.

HOLMAN, EDDIE

b. 3 June 1946, Norfolk, Virginia, USA. Holman's claim to fame was the 1969 soul ballad 'Hey There Lonely Girl', sung in a piercing falsetto style. Holman began playing keyboards and guitar as a child and studied music at schools in New York City and Pennsylvania. He first recorded in 1962 for the small Leopard Records and later with the Cameo/Parkway company. He collected minor chart hits for that company and then signed with ABC in 1968. 'Hey There Lonely Girl' was a remake of a song originally recorded by Ruby And The Romantics as 'Hey There Lonely Boy'. Holman changed the gender and took the song to number 2 in the US charts in 1970. Four years later the song reached number 4 in the UK. He continued to have lesser R&B hits on the Parkway label with 'This Can't Be True' (1965) and 'I'm A Loser' (1966). Releases during the early 70s kept the singer in the US soul chart while his career enjoyed a brief revival in 1977 with 'This Will Be A Night To Remember' and 'You Make My Life Complete'. He recorded on such labels as Polydor and Salsoul in the 70s and recorded for his own label, Agape, as a Christian artist in the early 90s.

● ALBUMS: *I Love You* (ABC 1969)★★★, *Night To Remember* (1977)★★, *United* (New Cross 1985)★★.

HONEY CONE

The product of various Los Angeles female groups, Carolyn Willis (b. 1946, Los Angeles, USA), Edna Wright (b. 1944, Los Angeles, USA) and Shellie Clark (b. 1943, Brooklyn, New York, USA), first came together as Honey Cone to work on the Andy Williams television show. Each was an established singer: Willis in the Girlfriends, Clark in the Ikettes, while Wright had sung in the Blossoms alongside her sister, Darlene Love. Early Honey Cone singles, 'While You're Out Looking For Sugar' and 'Girls It Ain't Easy', were R&B hits in 1969, before two 1971 soul chart-toppers, 'Want Ads' and 'Stick Up', established the trio. Stylistically, such songs invoked a saltier Supremes, and this gritty approach was confirmed on 'One Monkey Don't Stop No Show' and 'Sittin' On A Time Bomb (Waitin' On The Hurt To Come)'. The group broke up in 1973 when later singles were less successful, leaving Edna Wright free to resume her career as a session singer.

● ALBUMS: *Honey Cone* (Hot Wax 1969)★★★, *Take Me With You* (Hot Wax 1970)★★★, *Sweet Replies* (Hot Wax 1971)★★★, *Soulful Tapestry* (Hot Wax 1971)★★★, *Love, Peace And Soul* (Hot Wax 1972)★★★.

● COMPILATIONS: *Girls It Ain't Easy* (HDH 1984)★★★, *Are You Man Enough?* (HDH 1992)★★★★.

HOT STREAK

Jazz-disco fusion quartet from New Jersey, USA, comprising Derrick Dupree (vocals), Al Tanner (lead guitar), Jacob Dixon (bass) and Ricci Burgess (drums). The group started in the gospel field and entered the R&B arena in 1982. They were originally called A Different Flavour and then became Special Forces and had a single, 'Stroke It', released on Salsoul. They worked with Curtis Hudson and his wife Lisa Stevens who, apart from being members of Pure Energy, had penned Madonna's huge hit 'Holiday'. The duo renamed the foursome Hot Streak and wrote 'Body Work' for them. The New York disco label Easy Street snapped up the single and had it remixed by John 'Jellybean' Benitez. The record, which included a well-known US army chant, became a favourite in US discos, and perhaps not surprisingly, in health clubs. In the UK it shot to the top of the club charts and also went into the Top 20. Despite the good start, the group never continued their hot streak.

● FILMS: *Breakdance - The Movie* (1984).

HOUSTON, CISSY

b. Emily Drinkard, 1933, Newark, New Jersey, USA. Houston's singing career began in a family gospel group, the Drinkard Singers, which also featured her nieces Dee Dee and Dionne Warwick. The trio was later employed as backing singers for many artists, including Solomon Burke and Wilson Pickett. While Dionne began recording as a solo artist, Houston continued this backroom work. Between 1967 and 1970 she was lead vocalist with the Sweet Inspirations, an impressive quartet who sang on countless releases, primarily for Atlantic Records. Houston's subsequent solo releases included 'I'll Be There' (1970), 'Be My Baby' (1971) and 'Think It Over' (1978), but her career failed to match expectations and was later eclipsed by the success of her daughter Whitney Houston. Cissy has now returned chiefly to the gospel fold, as a major figure in the New Hope Baptist Church Choir of Newark, New Jersey, although in 1992 she shared a secular Shanachie CD with Chuck Jackson.

● ALBUMS: *Presenting Cissy Houston* (Major Minor 1970)★★★, *The Long And Winding Road* (Pye 1971)★★, *Cissy Houston* (Private Stock 1977)★★★, *Think It Over* (Private Stock 1978)★★, *Warning - Danger* (Private Stock 1979)★★, *Step Aside For A Lady* (EMI 1980)★★, with Chuck Jackson *I'll Take Care Of You* (Shanachie 1992)★★, *Face To Face* (House Of Blues 1996)★★★.

● COMPILATIONS: *Mama's Cookin'* (Charly 1987)★★★, *Midnight Train To Georgia: The Janus Years* (Ichiban 1995)★★★.

HOUSTON, THELMA

Thelma Houston left her home-town of Leland, Mississippi, USA, in the late 60s to tour with the gospel group the Art Reynolds Singers. Her impassioned vocal style and innate mastery of phrasing brought her to the attention of the prodigal writer/arranger Jimmy Webb in 1969. He composed and produced *Sunshower*, a remarkable song cycle that also included an adaptation of the Rolling Stones' 'Jumpin' Jack Flash'. The album transcended musical barriers, mixing the fluency of jazz with the passion of soul, and offering Houston the chance to bite into a sophisticated, witty set of lyrics. *Sunshower* won great critical acclaim, and helped her to secure a contract with Motown Records. Initially, the company made inadequate use of her talents, failing to provide material that would stretch her vocal capacities to the full. The stasis was broken in 1976 when Houston reworked 'Don't Leave Me This Way', previously a hit for Harold Melvin And The Bluenotes. Her disco interpretation brought a refreshing touch of class to the genre, and achieved impressive sales on both sides of the Atlantic. Ever enthusiastic to repeat a winning formula, Motown made several attempts to reproduce the verve of the hit single. Houston issued a series of interesting, if slightly predictable, albums in the late 70s, and also collaborated on two efforts with Jerry Butler, in an attempt to echo Motown's great duets of the 60s. The results were consistent sellers among the black audience, without ever threatening to rival Houston's earlier pop success. A switch to RCA failed to alter her fortunes. Houston enjoyed wider exposure in the late 70s with film roles in *Death Scream, Norman ... Is That You?* and *The Seventh Dwarf*, and for a while it seemed as if acting would become her main source of employment. She retired from recording during the mid-80s, re-emerging in 1987 on MCA with a critically acclaimed but commercially disappointing album. An album for Reprise in 1990 suffered the same fate. Houston's inconsistent chart record over the last two decades belies the impressive calibre of her vocal talents.

● ALBUMS: *Sunshower* (Stateside 1969)★★, *Thelma Houston* (Mowest 1973)★★, *Anyway You Like It* (Tamla 1976)★★, with Jerry Butler *Thelma And Jerry* (Motown 1977)★★, *The Devil In Me* (Tamla 1977)★★, with Butler *Two To One* (Motown 1978)★★, *Ready To Roll* (Tamla 1978)★★, *Ride To The Rainbow* (Tamla 1979)★★, *Breakwater Cat* (RCA 1980)★★, *Never Gonna Be Another One* (RCA 1981)★★, *I've Got The Music In Me* (RCA 1981)★★, *Qualifying Heats* (MCA 1987)★★★, *Throw You Down* (Reprise 1990)★★★.

● COMPILATIONS: *Best Of Thelma Houston* (Motown 1991)★★★.

HOUSTON, WHITNEY

b. 9 August 1963, Newark, New Jersey, USA. This pop and soul singer followed the traditions of her mother Cissy and cousin Dionne Warwick by beginning her vocal career in gospel. There was much diversity in her early performances, however. These included engagements as backing singer with established acts, such as Chaka Khan, as well as lead vocals on the Michael Zager Band's single 'Life's A Party'. She also appeared as a model in various magazines and as an actress in television shows such as *Give Me A Break*. By 1983 she had entered a worldwide contract with Arista Records, and the following year had her first commercial success when 'Hold Me', a duet with Teddy Pendergrass, crept into the US Top 50. However, the rest of that year was taken up with the recording of a debut album. Clive Davis, the head of Arista, who had taken a strong personal interest in the vocalist, insisted on selecting the best songwriters and producers in search of the definitive debut album. *Whitney Houston* was finally released in March 1984, from which time it would begin its slow stalking of the album charts, topping them early the next year. Its steady climb was encouraged by the success of the singles 'You Give Good Love' and 'Saving All My Love For You', which hit numbers 3 and 1, respectively. The latter single also saw her on top of the charts in the UK and much of the rest of the world. The disco-influenced 'How Will I Know' and the more soul-flavoured 'Greatest Love Of All', both topped the US charts in rapid succession. Her domination was acknowledged by a series of prestigious awards, notably a Grammy for 'Saving All My Love For You' and an Emmy for Outstanding Individual Performance In A Variety Program On US TV. 'I Want To Dance With Somebody (Who Loves Me)', released in 1987, topped the charts on both sides of the Atlantic once more, paving the way for *Whitney* to become the first album by a female artist to debut at number 1 on the US album charts, a feat it also achieved in the UK. The album included a version of 'I Know Him So Well', sang as a duet with her mother Cissy, and the ballad 'Didn't We Almost Have It All' which became her fifth successive US number 1 shortly afterwards. However, even this was surpassed when 'So Emotional' and 'Where Do Broken Hearts Go' continued the sequence, breaking a record previously shared by the Beatles and the Bee Gees. In 1988 she made a controversial appearance at Nelson Mandela's 70th Birthday Party, where other acts accused her of behaving like a prima donna. By September 'Love Will Save The Day' had finally broken the winning sequence in the USA where it could only manage number 9. Another series of awards followed, including Pop Female Vocal and Soul/R&B Female Vocal categories in the American Music Awards, while rumours abounded of film offers alongside Robert De Niro and Eddie Murphy. Her recording of the title track to the 1988 Olympics tribute, *One Moment In Time*, restored her to prominence, while 'I'm Your Baby Tonight' put her back on top of the singles chart. Despite the relatively modest success of the album of the same name (number 3 in the US charts), 'All The Man That I Need' compensated by becoming her ninth number 1. She became permanently enshrined in the hearts of the American public, however, when she took the microphone to perform 'The Star Spangled Banner' at Super Bowl XXV in Miami. The public response ensured that the version emerged as a single shortly afterwards. She also performed the song at Houston as she welcomed back US troops returning from the Gulf War. Such open displays of patriotism have not endeared her to all, but her remarkably rich voice looks set to continue as a fixture of the charts in the 90s, although critics claim that her masterful vocal technique is not equalled by her emotional commitment to her music. In 1992, Houston married singer Bobby Brown (the relationship would prove tempestous). The same year she made a credible acting debut in the film *The Bodyguard*. Two songs recorded by her were lifted from the phenomenally successful soundtrack album - cover versions of Dolly Parton's powerful 'I Will Always Love You', which topped the US chart for 12 weeks and the UK charts for nine, and Chaka Khan's 'I'm Every Woman'.

● ALBUMS: *Whitney Houston* (Arista 1985)★★★★, *Whitney* (Arista 1987)★★★★, *I'm Your Baby Tonight* (Arista 1990)★★★, various artists *The Bodyguard* film soundtrack (Arista 1992)★★★, *The Preacher's Wife* film soundtrack (Arista 1996)★★.

HOWARD, ADINA

b. Grand Rapids, Michigan, USA. With her 1995 debut, *Do You Wanna Ride?*, assertive soul singer Adina Howard managed to achieve commercial success as well as raising eyebrows with her volatile cocktail of sexually potent imagery and effusive R&B. The mainstream success of the attendant single, 'Freak Like Me', helped pave the way for other upfront female R&B singers, including Foxy Brown and Lil' Kim. Peaking at number 7 in the *Billboard* R&B charts, the debut album's sales profile of over half a million copies was encouraging. The follow-up, 1997's *Welcome To Fantasy Island*, opted for sensuality over sexuality: '(the lyrics) are not vulgar. I may say some things straight out, but for the most part, it's a pretty mature album.' Howard was also more closely involved in the creative process, writing four of the songs and co-producing two others. However, the promotional single, '(Freak) And U Know It', at least maintained some of the titular traditions of the previous album.

● ALBUMS: *Do You Wanna Ride?* (Mecca Don/Elektra 1995)★★★, *Welcome To Fantasy Island* (Mecca Don/Elektra 1997)★★★.

HOWARD, CAMILLE

b. 29 March 1914, Galveston, Texas, USA. Howard took over the stool from Betty Hall Jones as pianist with Roy Milton's Solid Senders in the early 40s. She recorded with Milton on all his prime recordings for Specialty Records and his own Roy Milton/Miltone labels of the 40s and early 50s, and was occasionally featured singing her 'Groovy Blues', 'Mr Fine', 'Thrill Me' and 'Pack Your Sack, Jack', among others. Remaining with Milton, Howard simultaneously pursued her own recording career from 1946 when she recorded for the small Pan American label with James Clifford's band and, more notably, with her own sessions for Specialty, which resulted in her successful instrumental boogies (including her biggest hit 'X-temperaneous Boogie') and small band R&B vocals (like the similarly successful 'Money Blues'). In 1953 Howard was signed to Federal for two west coast sessions and she went to Chicago and Vee Jay for her final single in 1956. Camille Howard still lives in Los Angeles, where her voice and keyboard skills are reserved only for spiritual performances. Her reissued material on Ace Records covers her most interesting work.

● COMPILATIONS: with Edith Mackey, Priscilla Bowman, Christine Kittrell *Rock 'N' Roll Mamas* (1985)★★★, with Lil Armstrong And Dorothy Donegan *Brown Gal 1946-1950* (Krazy Kat 1987)★★★, *X-Temperaneous Boogie* (1989)★★★, *Rock Me Daddy: Camille Howard Vol 1* (Ace 1993)★★★★, *X-Temporaneous Boogie: Camille Howard Vol 2* (Ace 1996)★★★★.

HOWARD, MIKI

The soul singer Miki Howard combines spiritual soul music with touches of jazz singing. Before turning solo, she was a jazz session singer, working with, among others, Grover Washington Jnr., Philip Bailey and Billy Cobham. *Come Share My Love* attracted comparisons with Regina Belle, while *Love Confessions* introduced a slick R&B sound and included 'That's What Love Is', a duet with Gerald LeVert, as well as her familiar jazz stylings, best represented by her version of Earth, Wind And Fire's 'Reasons'. On *Miki Howard*, the singer tackled a variety of styles, including a swingbeat reworking of Aretha Franklin's 'Until You Come Back To Me (That's What I'm Gonna Do)'. Her ballads revealed an emotional depth to match her vocal range and technical abilities. *Femme Fatale* included versions of Billie Holiday's 'Good Morning Heartache', Dinah Washington's 'This Bitter Earth' and Sly Stone's 'Thank You'. She also co-wrote three songs herself, and dueted with Christopher Williams on 'I Hope That We Can Be Together Soon'. Following the album she concentrated on pursuing an acting career, appearing in 1993's *Malcolm X* biopic (as Billie Holiday) and co-starring in John Singleton's *Poetic Justice*.

● ALBUMS: *Come Share My Love* (Atlantic 1986)★★, *Love Confessions* (Atlantic 1987)★★★, *Miki Howard* (Atlantic 1989)★★★, *Femme Fatale* (Giant 1992)★★★.

● FILMS: *Malcom X* (1993).

HUES CORPORATION

Formed in 1969 in Los Angeles, California, USA. Their name was taken as a pun on the Howard Hughes billion-dollar corporation. They had been performing for five years when their biggest hit, 'Rock The Boat', arrived. The vocal trio consisted of Hubert Ann Kelly (b. 24 April 1947, Fairchild, Alabama, USA; soprano), St. Clair Lee (b. Bernard St. Clair Lee Calhoun Henderson, 24 April 1944, San Francisco, California, USA; baritone) and Fleming Williams (b. Flint, Michigan, USA; tenor). Their first record, 'Goodfootin'', was recorded for Liberty Records in 1970 but failed to hit. They signed with RCA Records in 1973 and made the charts with a song called 'Freedom For The Stallion'. 'Rock The Boat', originally a forgotten album track, was released in 1974 as the next single and reached number 1 in the US pop charts and number 6 in the UK, becoming one of the first significant disco hits. Tommy Brown (b. Birmingham, Alabama, USA) replaced Williams after the single hit and their only other chart success came later that same year with 'Rockin' Soul', which peaked at number 18 in the US chart and reached the Top 30 in the UK. The group continued to record into the late 70s, but they were unable to repeat their earlier success. However, in 1983 'Rock The Boat' made another chart appearance when Forrest took the single to the UK Top 5 position.

● ALBUMS: *Freedom For The Stallion* (RCA 1974)★★, *Love Corporation* (RCA 1975)★★, *I Caught Your Act* (Warners 1977)★★, *Your Place Or Mine* (Warners 1978)★★.

● COMPILATIONS: *Best Of The Hues Corporation* (RCA 1976)★★★.

HUGHES, JIMMY

b. 1938, Leighton, Alabama, USA, d. 4 January 1997. This former member of the Singing Clouds abandoned the gospel field following the success of Arthur Alexander and recorded a handful of secular songs. When his producer, Rick Hall, was unable to secure an outlet for one such master, 'Steal Away', he issued it himself, inaugurating the Fame label. The prototype country-soul ballad, it became a US Top 20 R&B hit in 1964. Hughes enjoyed even greater success with 'Neighbor Neighbor' (1966) and 'Why Not Tonight?' (1967), but was unable to sustain the momentum. Two 1968 singles on Atlantic and Stax/Volt, 'It Ain't What You Got' and 'I Like Everything About You', achieved only minor placings. He later retired from music altogether, dying of cancer in January 1997. *Why Not Tonight* is an excellent representation of his later Fame recordings, while *Soul Neighbors*, shared with Joe Simon, offers some of his earlier work.

● ALBUMS: *Steal Away* (Fame 1964)★★★, *Why Not Tonight* (Fame 1967)★★★★, *Something Special* (1969)★★★.

● COMPILATIONS: *A Shot Of Rhythm And Blues* (Charly 1980)★★★, with Joe Simon *Soul Neighbors* (Charly 1984)★★★, *Something Special* 13 tracks plus nine by Joe Hicks (1993)★★★.

HUNT, TOMMY

b. Charles Hunt, 18 June 1933, Pittsburgh, Pennsylvania, USA. Hunt's dramatic pop-soul vocals, on string-drenched ballads, perfectly represented the Brill Building sound of the early 60s. He had a long career in vocal groups prior to his solo career of the early 60s. In 1952 and 1953 he was a member of the Chicago-based Five Echoes along with future soul superstar Johnnie Taylor. He was a member of the Flamingos from 1958 to 1961. His biggest hit was 'Human' (number 5 R&B, number 48 pop) in 1961, recorded for Scepter Records. He recorded other top-notch material for the company, including 'I Am A Witness' (1963) and the original version of 'I Just Don't Know What To Do For Myself', which later became a hit for Dusty Springfield. His last hit was the wonderful Luther Dixon-produced hit 'The Biggest Man', for the Dynamo label in 1967. He moved to England in the 70s and recorded for Polydor in 1972 and Pye in 1974. In the late 70s he was a star on the northern soul circuit, and had a hit with a revival of Roy Hamilton's 'Crackin' Up' on the Spark label, the first of three UK hits. He recorded two albums while in England, *Live At The Wigan Casino* (1975), a collection of 60s soul songs, and *A Sign Of The Times* (1976), a collection of songs that reflected the tastes of northern soul fans.

● ALBUMS: *I Just Don't Know What To Do With Myself* (Scepter 1962)★★★, *Live At The Wigan Casino* (Spark 1975)★★, *A Sign Of The Times* (Spark 1976)★★★.

● COMPILATIONS: *Tommy Hunt's Greatest Hits* (Dynamo 1967)★★★★, *Your Man* (Kent 1986)★★★, *Human: His Golden Classics* (Collectables 1991)★★★, *The Biggest Man* (Kent 1997)★★★★.

HUNTER, IVORY JOE

b. 10 October 1911, Kirbyville, Texas, USA, d. 8 November 1974. Although Hunter was a well-known figure in Texas through his radio shows, it was not until the 40s, when he moved to the west coast, that his career flourished. He established his own record companies, Ivory and Pacific, the latter of which provided the outlet for Hunter's first R&B chart-topper, 'Pretty Mama Blues'. Hunter continued his success with several singles recorded with sidemen from the Duke Ellington Orchestra before one of his most enduring compositions, 'I Almost Lost My Mind', became a second R&B number 1 in 1950. A re-recorded version also proved popular when the singer moved to the Atlantic label later in the decade, but Pat Boone's opportunistic cover version was a greater commercial success. However, a further fine Hunter original, 'Since I Met You Baby', then swept to the top of the R&B chart in 1956 and to number 12 in the national pop chart. Unhappy at being labelled an R&B act, this talented and prolific artist was equally adept with pop, ballad and spiritual styles and in later years became a popular C&W attraction, so much so that a benefit concert was held for him at Nashville's *Grand Ole Opry* shortly before his death in 1974, as a result of lung cancer.

● ALBUMS: *I Get That Lonesome Feeling* (1957)★★★, *Ivory Joe Hunter* (Sound 1957)★★★, *Ivory Joe Hunter* (Atlantic 1958)★★★, *Ivory Joe Hunter Sings The Old And The New* (Atlantic 1958)★★★, *Ivory Jo Hunter* (Sage 1959)★★★, *The Fabulous Ivory Joe Hunter* (1961)★★★, *This Is Ivory Joe Hunter* (1964)★★★, *The Return Of Ivory Joe Hunter* (Epic 1971)★★★, *I've Always Been Country* (1974)★★★.

● COMPILATIONS: *Sixteen Of His Greatest Hits* (1958)★★★★, *Ivory Joe Hunter's Greatest Hits* (1963)★★★, *7th Street Boogie* (Route 66 1980)★★★, *The Artistry Of Ivory Joe Hunter* (Bulldog 1982)★★★, *This Is Ivory Joe* (Ace 1984)★★★★, *I Had A Girl* (Route 66 1987)★★★, *Jumping At The Dewdrop* (Route 66 1987)★★★, *Since I Met You Baby* (Mercury 1988)★★★, *I'm Coming Down With The Blues* (Home Cooking 1989)★★★, *Sings 16 Greatest Hits* (1992)★★★★.

HUTSON, LEROY

b. 4 June 1945, Newark, New Jersey, USA. This African-American instrumentalist, composer, arranger, producer and multi-talented performer generated a host of affiliations, but never achieved a level of success commensurate with his talent. He first formed a vocal group in his native New Jersey, but emerged as a soul music talent while attending Howard University in 1970. There with his room-mate Donny Hathaway, he collaborated on 'The Ghetto', a hit for Hathaway in early 1970. Hutson and Hathaway also sang in the Mayfield Singers, who released one single for Curtis Mayfield in 1967. Later Hutson teamed up with Deborah Rollins to form Sugar And Spice, recording several singles with no success. In 1971 Hutson replaced Mayfield in the Impressions and recorded two unsatisfactory albums with the group. Hudson began his solo career on Curtom in 1973 and through 1980 established himself with a moderately successful recording career, recording seven albums and charting with some 13 singles in the USA. On most of his work, he wrote, produced, arranged and played multiple instruments, but Hutson never made a truly top-notch album. His best charted singles were 'All Because Of You' (1975), 'Feel The Spirit' (1976), 'I Do I Do' (1976), 'Where Did Love Go' (1978), and 'Right Or Wrong' (1979). When Curtom went out of business in 1980, Hutson's career was essentially behind him and he soon disappeared from the music world.

● ALBUMS: *Love O' Love* (Curtom 1973)★★★, *Leroy Hutson, The Man* (Curtom 1975)★★★, *Le Roy Hutson* (Curtom 1975)★★, *Feel The Spirit* (Curtom 1976)★★★, *Hutson II* (Curtom 1976)★★★, *Closer To The Source* (Curtom 1978)★★, *Unforgettable* (RSO/Curtom 1979)★★.
● COMPILATIONS: *The Very Best Of* (Deep Beats 1997)★★★.

Hyman, Phyllis

b. Pittsburgh, Pennsylvania, USA, d. 30 June 1995. A singer, actress and fashion model, Hyman was one of several acts nurtured by vocalist Norman Connors. Although she had already secured a minor R&B hit with 'Baby I'm Gonna Love You' in 1976, a duet with Connors the following year, covering the Stylistics hit 'Betcha By Golly Wow', brought the artist a wider audience. Although Hyman failed to reach the US pop Top 100, over the next 10 years she enjoyed 13 soul hits, including 'You Know How To Love Me' (1979) and 'Can't We Fall In Love Again' (1981). The latter release coincided with the singer's appearance in the Broadway musical *Sophisticated Ladies*.

● ALBUMS: *Phyllis Hyman* (Buddah 1977)★★, *Somewhere In My Lifetime* (Arista 1979)★★★, *Sing A Song* (Buddah 1979)★★★, *You Know How To Love Me* (Arista 1979)★★★★, *Can't We Fall In Love Again* (Arista 1981)★★★★, *Goddess Of Love* (Arista 1983)★★★, *Living All Alone* (Philadelphia International 1986)★★★, *Prime Of My Life* (Philadelphia International 1991)★★★.
● COMPILATIONS: *The Best Of Phyllis Hyman* (Arista 1986)★★★, *The Legacy Of Phyllis Hyman* (Arista 1996)★★★★, *Sweet Music* (Camden 1998)★★★.

Ideals

An R&B vocal group from Chicago, Illinois, USA. Formed in 1952, the outfit scuffled for many years with several personnel changes before recording in 1961 on the local Paso label. The Ideals at this time consisted of Reggie Jackson, Leonard Mitchell, Robert Tharp and Sam Steward (bass). In 1963 the group added a fifth member, lead Eddie Williams, and with his rough-hewn, soulful delivery they recorded their most successful record, 'The Gorilla'; its 'monkey dance' theme was designed to reap sales from the success of the dance fad. It never reached any national charts but nonetheless received national exposure, partly in the pop market, and earned the group its first national tour. In 1965 the Ideals reorganized as a trio with Jackson, Mitchell and Steward, and they finally reached the R&B charts with 'Kissin'' in 1966, although the record did not, in fact, sell as well as 'The Gorilla'. A notable song in 1966 was 'You Lost And I Won', which neatly married the group's doo-wop past with the sound of soul. However, the group broke up a short time later. Most of the members did not join other acts after their Ideals association, except for Tharp and Mitchell. Tharp, under the name Tommy Dark, joined Jerry Murray in 1964 to form a dance duo called Tom And Jerrio, specializing in Boogaloo records. They had a hit with 'Boo-Ga-Loo' (number 10 R&B) in 1965. Leonard Mitchell continued to record by joining with Jerome Johnson and Robert Thomas to form the Channel 3, who released one single, to no great acclaim.

Ikettes

This female R&B trio was formed by Ike Turner as part of his revue and was used for chorusing. Throughout the 60s and 70s, there were several line-ups of Ikettes, each of which provided a stunning visual and aural complement on stage to the performances of Ike And Tina Turner. Ike Turner occasionally recorded the group, with results that emhasized their tough, soulful R&B sound, much like his work with Tina. The original group was formed from the Artettes - Robbie Montgomery, Frances Hodges and Sandra Harding - who were the backing vocalists for the St. Louis singer Art Lassiter. They provided the chorus sound to Ike And Tina Turner's first hit, 'A Fool In Love.' On the first recordings of the Ikettes in 1962, the group consisted of Delores Johnson (lead), Eloise Hester and 'Joshie' Jo Armstead. They recorded the hit 'I'm Blue (The Gong-Gong Song)' (number 3 R&B, number 19 pop) for Atco in 1962. The best-known group of Ikettes were Vanetta Fields, Robbie Montgomery and Jessie Smith, a line-up formed in the St. Louis area around 1963. They recorded for the Modern label, including the hits 'Peaches 'N' Cream' (number 28 R&B, number 36 pop) and 'I'm So Thankful' (number 12 R&B, number 74 pop), both in 1965. This group left Turner in 1968 and enjoyed a big hit as the Mirettes in 1968 with a remake of the Wilson Pickett hit, 'In The Midnight Hour' (number 18 R&B, number 45 pop). Later line-ups of Ikettes included several singers who developed careers of their own, notably P.P. Arnold, Claudia Lennear and Bonnie Bramlett (who formed the duo Delany And Bramlett).

● ALBUMS: *Soul Hits* (Modern 1965)★★, *Gold And New* (United Artists 1974)★★, as the Mirettes *In The Midnight Hour* (Revue 1968)★★, *Whirlpool* (Uni 1969)★★.

● COMPILATIONS: *Fine Fine Fine* (Kent 1992)★★.

IMAGINATION

One of the most successful British funk bands of the early 80s, Imagination were formed by the idiosyncratically named Lee John (b. John Lesley McGregor, 23 June 1957, Hackney, London, England; vocals), Ashley Ingram (b. 27 November 1960, Northampton, England; guitar) and Errol Kennedy (b. Montego Bay, West Indies). John (of St. Lucian descent) was educated in New York, where he also became a backing vocalist for the Delfonics and Chairmen Of The Board. He met Ingram, who played bass for both bands, and they formed a duo called Fizzz. Back in England, John, who had already appeared on *Junior Showtime* as a child, enrolled at the Anna Scher Theatre School where he studied drama. Kennedy was an experienced singer with Jamaican bands and learnt the drums through the Boys Brigade and later the Air Training Corps band. He had also spent some time in the soul group Midnight Express. Kennedy met John and Ingram in early 1981, after which they formed Imagination as a pop/soul three-piece. They made an immediate impact with their debut 'Body Talk', and further Tony Swain-produced hits followed, including UK Top 5 entries with 'Just An Illusion' and 'Music And Lights'. However, the run of hits dried up by 1984, when John returned to acting. He had already appeared in the *Dr Who* story *Enlightenment* in 1983. Having switched to RCA Records in 1986, Imagination made a minor comeback in 1988 with 'Instinctual'.

● ALBUMS: *Body Talk* (R&B 1981)★★★, *In The Heat Of The Night* (R&B 1982)★★, *Night Dubbing* (R&B 1983)★★, *Scandalous* (R&B 1983)★★, *Imagination* (RCA 1989)★★.

● COMPILATIONS: *Imagination Gold* (Stylus 1984)★★★.

IMAGINATIONS

Formed in Bellmore, Long Island, New York, USA, in 1961, doo-wop group the Imaginations consisted of Frank Mancuso (lead), Bobby Bloom (first tenor), Phil Agtuca (second tenor), Pete Agtuca (baritone) and Richard LeCausi (bass). In April 1961, Music Makers released the group's 'Goodnight Baby', which featured King Curtis on saxophone. The Imaginations' second studio engagement came as back-up singers for Darlene Day, and, with studio time remaining, they also recorded two of their own songs, 'Guardian Angel' and 'Hey You'. When the tracks formed their second single, both sides attracted airplay, and the record was licensed to Duel Records, although too late, apparently, to allow it a chance to reach the national charts. Despite this, 'Hey You', primarily through repeated radio plays, became established as one of the most popular vocal group records in the New York area throughout the early 60s. However, that impetus was stalled when Mancuso joined the air forces, and Music Makers closed down. Bobby Caupin took over on lead as the group switched to a new title, the Ebonaires. A single was recorded ('Chapel Bells') but never released. Still not dispirited, Bobby Bloom took over on lead as the group then reverted to their former name for 'Wait A Little Longer Son', issued on new label Ballad Records. Again a release of genuine quality, it too was picked up for extended distribution, this time by Laurie Records. By 1963 the group had broken up, but they re-formed when producers Pete Antell and John Linde took an interest in their careers. Bloom, Phil Agtuca and LeCausi were then joined by John Governale (first tenor) and Pete Lanzetta (baritone) in the Expressions. As well as backing Tommy Boyce in the studio, the Expressions released a debut single in 1963, 'On The Corner' - a eulogy to the origins of doo-wop on street corners. However, it flopped, and the group broke up once again. Bloom, however, persevered as a solo artist, and was rewarded in 1970 when his 'Montego Bay' became a national Top 10 hit (number 3 in England). Despite further chart appearances he committed suicide on 28 February 1974.

IMMATURE

Starting out as MCA Records' answer to the teenage R&B boy band boom, Immature have belied both these inauspicious beginnings and their own choice of moniker by prospering as a commercial act in the 90s. A trio comprising lead singer Marques 'Batman' Houston (b. *c.*1982, USA), Jerome 'Romeo' Jones (b. *c.*1982, USA) and Kelton 'LDB' Kessee (b. *c.*1981, USA), they became regulars on the pages of the American teen press from their inception in the late 80s. However, they enjoyed their biggest commercial success in 1994 with 'Never Lie', a number 5 hit on *Billboard*'s R&B chart. The attendant album, *We Got It*, peaked at number 14 in the equivalent album chart, and sold close to half a million copies. Their 1997 release, *The Journey*, was their most ambitious to date, and paired them with R&B songwriting/production veterans Keith Sweat, Rodney Jerkins and Marc Gordon of Levert. The up-tempo, party-orientated atmosphere was further embossed by the presence of rappers Bizzy Bones (Bone Thugs N'Harmony) and Daz (the Dogg Pound). In the same year the group also recorded a pilot for their own television show, entitled *Keepin' It Real*, said to be a 'funkier take on *The Wonder Years*'.

● ALBUMS: *We Got It* (MCA 1994)★★★, *The Journey* (MCA 1997)★★★.

IMPALAS

With sweet-voiced lead singer Joe 'Speedo' Frazier (b. 5 September 1943, New York City, New York, USA), this New York doo-wop group had an overnight success with their first record, '(Sorry) I Ran All The Way Home'. From the Carnesie section of Brooklyn, the rest of the Impalas were Richard Wagner, Lenny Renda and Tony Calouchi. They were discovered by disk jockey Alan Freed and Artie Zwirn, who co-wrote the bright, brash novelty tune with Gino Giosasi (of the Gino and Gina vocal duo). With an arrangement by Ray Ellis, '(Sorry) I Ran All The Way Home' was released in 1959 on the MGM subsidiary label Cub, reaching number 2 in America and entering the UK Top 30. The follow-up, 'Oh What A Fool' was a smaller hit. The Impalas made later records for Hamilton and 20th Century Fox before splitting up. Frazier went on to sing with Love's Own in 1973.

● ALBUMS: *Sorry I Ran All The Way Home* (Cub 1959)★★★.

IMPERIAL RECORDS

Formed in Los Angeles, California, USA, by Lew Chudd in 1947, Imperial emerged as one of the most influential independent R&B labels of the 50s. Despite the company's devotion to the R&B market, for many years their only major hit was by the C&W artist Slim Whitman, with 'Indian Love Call' in 1952. Having secured the New Orleans R&B bandleader Dave Bartholomew as house producer, a former Bartholomew band member, Fats Domino, was signed to record for the label, and his first release, 'The Fat Man' became a US R&B chart hit. The subsequent and consistent success of Domino's career in the national US chart between 1955 and 1962 was, for some time, crucial to Imperial's ability to promote other R&B artists, such as Roy Brown ('Let The Four Winds Blow'), Smiley Lewis ('I Hear You Knockin''), Chris Kenner ('Sick And Tired') and Ernie Freeman ('Raunchy'). In 1957 Chudd found his new pop star in Rick Nelson, who provided the label with a string of 16 hits up until 1962. An effort to cash in on Phil Spector's Teddy Bears success with 'To Know Him Is To Love Him' (having been recorded on the Dore label) came to nought, except that the group did release their only (and very rare) album on the Imperial label. Other US hits during this period were supplied by Garry Mills (a 1960 Top 30 hit with 'Look For A Star - Part 1') and the rock 'n' roll drummer Sandy Nelson, with his instrumental hits 'Let There Be Drums' (1961) and 'Drums Are My Beat' (1962). Throughout this time the label was well served by the steady success of Slim Whitman, particularly in the UK, where the Imperial label was licensed to London Records.

In the early 60s Chudd acquired the New Orleans label Minit. He sold the company to Liberty Records in 1963, after which Imperial concentrated more on the mainstream pop market, releasing many British acts in the USA, including Billy J. Kramer (a Top 10 hit with 'Little Children'/'Bad To Me' in 1964), Georgie Fame (a Top 30 hit in 1965 with 'Yeh Yeh') and the Hollies (notably, two Top 10 hits in 1966 with 'Bus Stop' and 'Stop Stop Stop'). Cher had begun her solo career with Imperial, achieving five US Top 40 hits between 1965 and 1967, including 'Bang Bang (My Baby Shot Me Down)' (number 2) and 'You Better Sit Down Kids' (number 9), and former rock 'n' roll singer-turned-MOR act Johnny Rivers had an impressive string of 13 hit singles from 1964-67, including the number 1 'Poor Side Of Town' in 1966. A link with the R&B past was maintained with Irma Thomas's Top 20 hit 'Wish Someone Would Care' (1964) and with Mel Carter's three Top 40 hits during 1965-66, which included the Top 10 'Hold Me, Thrill Me, Kiss Me' (1965). Songwriter Jackie DeShannon's occasional excursion into the recording studio rewarded Imperial with two Top 10 hits with the classic Burt Bacharach song 'What The World Needs Now Is Love' (1965) and 'Put A Little Love In Your Heart' (1969). Classic IV rounded off the label's list of Top 10 hits during 1968-69 with 'Spooky' (number 3), 'Stormy' (number 5) and 'Traces' (number 2). By the end of the 60s, the machinations of the corporate music industry had forced Liberty and Imperial to merge with the United Artists label who, in turn, were swallowed up by the giant EMI conglomerate by 1979.

● COMPILATIONS: *Imperial Rockabillies* (1977)★★★★, *Imperial Rockabillies Volume 2* (1979)★★★, *Imperial Rockabillies Volume 3* (1980)★★★, *Imperial Musicians 1951-1962: The Rhythm In Rhythm & Blues* (1987)★★★★.

IMPRESSIONS

Formed in Chicago in 1957 and originally known as the Roosters, this group comprised Jerry Butler (b. 8 December 1939, Sunflower, Mississippi, USA), Curtis Mayfield (b. 3 June 1942, Chicago, Illinois, USA), Sam Gooden (b. 2 September 1939, Chattanooga, Tennessee, USA), and brothers Richard Brooks and Arthur Brooks (both born in Chattanooga, Tennessee, USA). Mayfield and Butler first met in the choir of the Travelling Soul Spiritualists Church, from where they formed the Modern Jubilaires and Northern Jubilee Singers. The two teenagers then drifted apart, and while Mayfield was involved in another group, the Alphatones, Butler joined Gooden and the Brooks brothers in the Roosters. Mayfield was subsequently installed as their guitarist. Dubbed the Impressions by their manager, the group's first single for Abner/Falcon, 'For Your Precious Love', was a gorgeous ballad and a substantial hit, reaching number 11 in the US pop chart in 1958. The label credit, which read 'Jerry Butler And The Impressions', caused internal friction and the two sides split after one more release. While Butler's solo career gradually prospered, that of his erstwhile colleagues floundered. He and Mayfield were later reconciled on Butler's 1960 single 'He Will Break Your Heart', the success of which (and of other Mayfield-penned songs) rekindled the Impressions' career. Signed to ABC-Paramount in 1961, they had a hit with the haunting 'Gypsy Woman'. Subsequent releases were less well received until 'It's All Right' (1963) soared to number 1 in the R&B chart and to number 4 in the pop chart. The group was now a trio of Mayfield, Gooden and Fred Cash, and their rhythmic harmonies were set against Johnny Pate's stylish arrangements. Magnificent records – including 'I'm So Proud', 'Keep On Pushing', 'You Must Believe Me' (all 1964) and 'People Get Ready' (1965) – showed how Mayfield was growing as an incisive composer, creating lyrical songs that were alternately poignant and dynamic. During this period the Impressions had what was to be their last US pop Top 10 hit, 'Amen', which was featured in the film *Lilies Of The Field*. Mayfield then set up two short-lived record companies, Windy C in 1966, and Mayfield in 1967. However, it was the singer's third venture, Curtom, that proved most durable. In the meantime, the Impressions had emerged from a period when Motown had provided their prime influence. 'You Been Cheatin'' (1965) and 'You Always Hurt Me' (1967), however good in themselves, lacked the subtlety of their predecessors, but represented a transition in Mayfield's musical perceptions. Statements that had previously been implicit were granted a much more open forum. 'This Is My Country' (1968), 'Mighty Mighty Spade And Whitey' (1969) and 'Check Out Your Mind' (1970) were tougher, politically based performances, while his final album with the group, the quintessential *Young Mod's Forgotten Story*, set the framework for his solo work. Mayfield's replacement, Leroy Hutson, left in 1973. Reggie Torian and Ralph Johnson were subsequently added, and the new line-up topped the R&B chart in 1974 with 'Finally Got Myself Together (I'm A Changed Man)'. 'First Impressions' (1975) became their only British hit, but the following year Johnson left. Although Mayfield, Butler, Cash and Gooden have, on occasions, re-formed, the latter pair have also kept active their version of the Impressions.

● ALBUMS: *The Impressions* (ABC-Paramount 1963)★★★, *The Never Ending Impressions* (ABC-Paramount 1964)★★★, *Keep On Pushing* (ABC-Paramount 1964)★★★, *People Get Ready* (ABC-Paramount 1965)★★★, *One By One* (ABC-Paramount 1965)★★★, *Ridin' High* (ABC-Paramount 1966)★★★, *The Fabulous Impressions* (ABC 1967)★★★, *We're A Winner* (ABC 1968)★★, *This Is My Country* (ABC 1968)★★, *The Versatile Impressions* (1969)★★, *The Young Mod's Forgotten Story* (Curtom 1969)★★, *Check Out Your Mind* (Curtom 1970)★★, *Times Have Changed* (Curtom 1972)★★, *Preacher Man* (Curtom 1973)★★, *Finally Got Myself Together* (Curtom 1974)★★, *Three The Hard Way* (1974)★★, *First Impressions* (Curtom 1975)★★★, *It's About Time* (Cotillion 1976)★★, *Loving Power* (Curtom 1976)★★, *Come To My Party* (1979)★★, *Fan The Fire* (20th Century 1981)★★.

● COMPILATIONS: *The Impressions Greatest Hits* (ABC-Paramount 1965)★★★★, *The Best Of The Impressions* (ABC 1968)★★★★, *16 Greatest Hits* (ABC 1971)★★★★, *Curtis Mayfield/His Early Years With The Impressions* (ABC 1973)★★★, with Butler and Mayfield solo tracks *The Vintage Years - The Impressions Featuring Jerry Butler And Curtis Mayfield* (Sire 1977)★★★, *Your Precious Love* (Topline 1981)★★★★, *The Definitive Impressions* (Kent 1989)★★★★, *The Impressions Greatest Hits* (MCA 1989)★★★★, as Curtis Mayfield And The Impressions *The Anthology 1961 - 1977* (1992)★★★★, *All The Best* (Pickwick 1994)★★★★.

INCOGNITO

Incognito were among the most prolific and popular of the 90s UK jazz funk generation, though their origins can be traced back to the previous decade's Brit Funk movement. The mainstay of the group is Jean Paul 'Bluey' Maunick, a veteran of Light Of The World. His original co-conspirator in Incognito was Paul 'Tubs' Williams, plus a loose collection of friends and associates including Ganiyu 'Gee' Bello, Ray Carless, Jef Dunn, Vin Gordon and Peter Hinds. Incognito made their debut when a demo single, 'Parisienne Girl', received such strong club and radio support that it was made an official release, peaking at number 73 in the UK charts in 1980. However, this early incarnation of the group was a brief one, and yielded just a single album for Ensign Records. Williams joined The Team, a funk group assembled by Bello, also working with Maunick on his Warriors side project. However, at the prompting of Gilles Peterson of Talkin' Loud Records, Incognito reconvened in the 90s with Maunick again at the helm. This time, a variety of guest singers were included in the package. 'Always There' (1991) featured the vocals of Jocelyn Brown, and was also remixed by David Morales (though Maunick was none too happy with the experiment). It reached number 6 in the UK charts. Maysa Leak, who had begun by guesting on their 1991 single 'Crazy For You', left the band amicably in June 1994. She was previously best known for her contribution to Stock, Aitken And Waterman's 'Roadblock'. The highly rated *Positivity* sold 350,000 copies in the USA, a market where Maunick was also beginning to enjoy success as a producer (Ray Simpson, Chaka Khan, George Benson). For 1995's fifth album the new vocal recruits were Joy Malcolm (ex-Young Disciples) and Pamela Anderson (a relative of sisters Carleen and Jhelisa Anderson). This time the sound veered from jazz funk to include Philly soul-styled orchestral arrangements and more luxuriant vocal interplay.

● ALBUMS: *Jazz Funk* (Ensign 1981)★★, *Inside Life* (Talkin' Loud 1991)★★★, *Tribes Vibes And Scribes* (Talkin' Loud 1992)★★★, *Positivity* (Talkin' Loud 1993)★★★★, *100° And Rising* (Talkin' Loud 1995)★★★★, *Beneath The Surface* (Talkin' Loud 1996)★★★.

INCREDIBLES

The original members of this vocal group from Los Angeles, California, USA, were lead Cal Waymon (b. 1942, Houston, Texas, USA), Carl Gilbert (b. 1943, Toledo, Ohio, USA) and Jean Smith (b. 1945, Arkansas, USA), all graduates of Los Angeles' Jefferson High School. Waymon, the writer and producer of the group, had a background as a folk-singer, and had for a time lived in New York, where he played guitar and sang topical songs in Greenwich Village coffee-houses. On his return to Los Angeles in 1966, he formed the Incredibles, and within months had a moderate national R&B success with 'I'll Make It Easy (If You'll Come On Home)' (number 39 R&B). The group then added a fourth member, Alda Denise Erwin (b. St. Louis, Missouri, USA), and the following year achieved another moderate hit with a remake of the old standard 'Heart And Soul' (number 45 R&B). The Incredibles - featuring Waymon, Erwin, and new member Don Rae Simpson, from Montreal, Canada - were still recording and touring in 1969, when their only album was released, but their career was behind them. The Incredibles boasted a smooth, relaxed sound that had an enduring power - their songs are still eminently listenable decades later.

● ALBUMS: *Heart & Soul* (Audio Arts 1969)★★.

INDEPENDENTS

This Chicago-based group consisted of Charles 'Chuck' Jackson (22 March 1945, Greenville, South Carolina, USA), Maurice Jackson - no relation (b. 12 June 1944, Chicago, Illinois, USA), Eric Thomas (b. 1951, Chicago, Illinois, USA) and Helen Curry (b. Clarksdale, Mississippi, USA). Chuck Jackson (no relation to the 'Any Day Now' artist of the same name) was at one time an art director at *Playboy* magazine and also found time to write occasional sermons for his brother, the civil rights leader and politician Reverend Jesse Jackson. Fired with an ambition to put his words into song, Chuck joined Jerry Butler's writers workshop and teamed up with Marvin Yancey. The duo's talents were recognized by Butler, who recorded two of their compositions for his 1971 album, *JB Sings Assorted Songs*. Encouraged by this, the duo recorded one of their own songs, 'Just As Long As You Need Me', and discovered that they had a moderate success on their hands, enough to prompt them to form a group as a vehicle for their talents. They recruited from the Chicago club scene Maurice Jackson and Helen Curry (who had previously worked together as a duo, and prior to which Maurice had recorded with the vocal group Mark 4), and finally, Eric Thomas. Yancey preferred to stay behind the scenes to write and produce, occasionally performing live and playing keyboards. Between 1972 and 1974 they had a run of eight R&B Top 40 entries, including 'Leaving You' (1973), a million-selling single that peaked at number 21 in the US pop chart. Despite this consistency, the quartet was unable to break into the Top 20 pop chart, a factor that precipitated their demise. Yancey and Chuck Jackson continued working together and subsequently guided the early career of singer Natalie Cole.

● ALBUMS: *The First Time We Met* (Wand 1973)★★★, *Helen, Eric, Chuck, Maurice* (Wand 1973)★★.

● COMPILATIONS: *Discs Of Gold* (1974)★★★, *The First Time We Met - The Greatest Hits* (Charly 1986)★★★.

INGRAM, JAMES

b. 16 February 1956, Akron, Ohio, USA. A singer, composer and multi-instrumentalist, Ingram moved to Los Angeles in the early 70s where he played keyboards for Leon Haywood, and formed his own group, Revelation Funk. He also served as demo singer for various publishing companies, an occupation that led to his meeting and working with Quincy Jones. Ingram's vocals were featured on 'Just Once' and 'One Hundred Ways' from *The Dude* (1981), one of Jones's last albums for A&M Records. Both tracks made the US Top 20. Signed to Jones's own Qwest label, Ingram had a US number 1 in 1982, duetting with Patti Austin on 'Baby, Come To Me', which became the theme for the popular television soap *General Hospital*. In the same year, he released *It's Your Night*, an album that eventually spawned the hit single 'Ya Mo B There' (1984), on which he was joined by singer-songwriter Michael McDonald, and made the US Top 20 again when he teamed with Kenny Rogers and Kim Carnes for 'What About Me?'. Ingram's subsequent albums, *Never Felt So Good*, produced by Keith Diamond, and *It's Real*, on which he worked with Michael Powell and Gene Griffin, failed to live up to the promise of his earlier work, although he continued to feature in the singles chart with 'Somewhere Out There', a duet with Linda Ronstadt from Steven Spielberg's animated movie *An American Tail*, and 'I Don't Have The Heart', which topped the US chart in 1990. Also in that year, Ingram was featured, along with Al B. Sure!, El DeBarge and Barry White, on 'The Secret Garden (Sweet Seduction Suite)', from Quincy Jones's album *Back On The Block*. Ingram has also served as a backing singer for several other big-name artists, such as Luther Vandross and the Brothers Johnson. His compositions include 'P.Y.T. (Pretty Young Thing)', which he wrote in collaboration with Quincy Jones for Michael Jackson's 1982 smash hit album *Thriller*.

● ALBUMS: *It's Your Night* (Qwest 1983)★★, *Never Felt So Good* (Qwest 1986)★★, *It's Real* (Qwest 1989)★★, *Always You* (Qwest 1993)★★.

● COMPILATIONS: *The Power Of Great Music* (Qwest 1991)★★★.

INGRAM, LUTHER

b. Luther Thomas Ingram, 30 November 1944, Jackson, Tennessee, USA. This singer-songwriter's professional career began in New York with work for producers Jerry Leiber and Mike Stoller. Several unsuccessful singles followed, including 'I Spy For The FBI', which failed in the wake of Jamo Thomas's 1966 hit version. Ingram then moved to Koko Records, a tiny independent label later marketed by Stax. Ingram's career flourished in the wake of this arrangement. With Mack Rice, he helped to compose 'Respect Yourself' for the Staple Singers, while several of his own releases were R&B hits. The singer's finest moment came with his 1972 recording of the classic Homer Banks, Raymond Jackson and Carl Hampton song, '(If Loving You Is Wrong) I Don't Want To Be Right'. This tale of infidelity was later recorded by Rod Stewart, Millie Jackson and Barbara Mandrell, but neither matched the heartbreaking intimacy Ingram brought to his superb original version. It went on to sell over a million copies and reached number 3 in the US pop charts. The haunting 'I'll Be Your Shelter (In Time Of Storm)' then followed as the artist proceeded to fashion a substantial body of work. His undoubted potential was undermined by Koko's financial problems, but after eight years in the commercial wilderness, Ingram returned to the R&B chart in 1986 with 'Baby Don't Go Too Far'.

● ALBUMS: *I've Been Here All The Time* (Koko 1972)★★, *(If Loving You Is Wrong) I Don't Want To Be Right* (Koko 1972)★★★, *Let's Steal Away To The Hideaway* (Koko 1976)★★★, *Do You Love Somebody* (Koko 1977)★★, *It's Your Night* (QWest 1983)★★, *Luther Ingram* (Profile 1986)★★.

● COMPILATIONS: *Greatest Hits* (The Right Stuff 1996)★★★.

INK SPOTS

The original line-up consisted of Jerry Franklin Daniels (b. 1916, d. 7 November 1995, Indianapolis, Indiana, USA; lead tenor, guitar), Orville 'Hoppy' Jones (b. 17 February

1905, Chicago, Illinois, USA, d. 18 October 1944; bass), Charlie Fuqua (d. 1979; baritone, guitar) and Ivory 'Deek' Watson (d. 1967; second tenor). Most sources state that this enormously popular black vocal quartet was formed in the early 30s when they were working as porters at the Paramount Theatre in New York. Early in their career the Ink Spots played 'hot' numbers, and travelled to England in the mid-30s where they performed with the Jack Hylton Band. When they returned to the USA, Daniels became ill and was replaced by Bill Kenny (b. 1915, d. 23 March 1978). The new combination changed their style, slowed down the tempos, and had a big hit in 1939 with 'If I Didn't Care', which featured Kenny's impressive falsetto and a deep-voiced spoken chorus by bass singer Jones. This record set the pattern for their future success, mixed with only a few slightly more up-tempo items, such as 'Java Jive', 'Your Feet's Too Big', and two of several collaborations with Ella Fitzgerald, 'Cow-Cow-Boogie' and 'Into Each Life Some Rain Must Fall'. The latter sold more than a million copies. Throughout the 40s their US hits included 'Address Unknown' (number 1), 'My Prayer', 'Bless You', 'When The Swallows Come Back To Capistrano', 'Whispering Grass', 'We Three' (number 1), 'Do I Worry?', 'I Don't Want To Set The World On Fire', 'Don't Get Around Much Any More', 'I'll Get By', 'Someday I'll Meet You Again', 'I'm Making Believe' (number 1) and 'I'm Beginning To See The Light' (both with Ella Fitzgerald), 'The Gypsy' (number 1 and a million-seller), 'Prisoner Of Love', 'To Each His Own' (number 1 and another million-seller), 'It's A Sin To Tell A Lie', 'You Were Only Fooling (While I Was Falling In Love)' and 'You're Breaking My Heart' (1949). The group were also popular on radio, in theatres, and made guest appearances in movies such as *The Great American Broadcast* and *Pardon My Sarong*. Orville Jones died in 1944 and was replaced by Bill Kenny's twin brother Herb (b. Herbert Cornelius Kenny, 1915, d. 11 July 1992, Columbia, Maryland, USA). A year later, founder-member Watson recruited Jimmie Nabbie (b. 1920, Tampa, Florida, USA, d. 15 September 1992, Atlanta, Georgia, USA) as lead tenor, and then Watson himself was replaced by Billy Bowen. Subsequent personnel changes were many and varied. There was some confusion in 1952 when two different groups began using the Ink Spots' name, Charlie Fuqua and Bill Kenny each owning 50 per cent of the title. Fuqua's Inkspots consisted of himself, Watson, Harold Jackson, and high tenor Jimmy Holmes. Other members included Isaac Royal, Leon Antoine and Joseph Boatner (d. 8 May 1989, Laconia, New Hampshire, USA). In the early 50s the Ink Spots had further chart success with 'Echoes', 'Sometime' and 'If', and Bill Kenny also had US hits in his own name, including 'It Is No Secret' (with the Song Spinners) and '(That's Just My Way Of) Forgetting You'. It is said that, over the years, many other groups worked under the famous name, including one led by Al Rivers (d. 17 February 1993, aged 65) who sang with the Ink Spots in the late 40s and 50s, and another fronted by Stanley Morgan (d. 21 November 1989, aged 67), an occasional guitar player with the quartet in the 30s. In 1988 the original group's first hit, 'If I Didn't Care', was awarded a Grammy, and a year later the Inkspots were inducted into the Rock And Roll Hall Of Fame. Jimmie Nabbie's Inkspots appeared extensively worldwide for many years through to the early 90s, until Nabbie's death in 1992 following double bypass heart surgery. Gregory Lee took over as frontman when the group co-starred with Eartha Kitt in the UK tour of *A Night At The Cotton Club*, during which, according to one critic, 'they reproduced the sedate four-part harmonies with skill and just enough spontaneity to satisfy their long-term fans'. In 1995, when the Inkspots were in cabaret at London's Café Royal, the line-up was Grant Kitchings (lead tenor), Sonny Hatchett (second lead tenor), Ellis Smith (baritone and guitar) and Harold Winley (bass). The latter is said to have worked with the group for more than 40 years.

● ALBUMS: *Americas Favorite Music* (Waldorf Music 1950)★★★, *The Ink Spots Volume 1* (Decca 1950)★★★★, *The Ink Spots Volume 2* (Decca 1950)★★★★, *Precious Memories* (Decca 1951)★★★, *Street Of Dreams* (Decca 1954)★★★★, *If I Didn't Care* (1956)★★★, *Time Out For Tears* (Decca 1957)★★★, *Something Old, Something New* (King 1958)★★★, *Sincerely Yours* (1958)★★★, *Torch Time* (Decca 1958)★★★, *Songs That Will Live Forever* (King 1959)★★★, *Favourites* (1960)★★★, *Lost In A Dream* (1965)★★★, *Stanley Morgan's Ink Spots In London* (1977)★★★, *Just Like Old Times* (Open Sky 1982)★★★.

● COMPILATIONS: *Golden Favourites* (Decca 1962)★★★★, *Best Of* (Decca 1965)★★★★, *Greatest Hits Vols. 1 & 2* (Grand Award 1956)★★, *The Best Of The Ink Spots* (MCA 1980)★★★★, *Golden Greats: Ink Spots* (MCA 1986)★★★, *Swing High! Swing Low!* (Happy Days 1989)★★★. In addition, there are a great many compilations available under the title of *Greatest Hits* or *Best Of*.

INMATES

The Inmates - Bill Hurley (vocals), Peter Gunn (b. Peter Staines; guitar), Tony Oliver (guitar), Ben Donnelly (bass) and Jim Russell (drums) - emerged in the late 70s as a UK R&B group in the style of Dr. Feelgood. Their adaptation of 'Dirty Water', a garage-band classic originally recorded by the Standells, led to the Inmates' debut album. In common with several similarly styled groups, the quintet was unable to transfer their live excitement onto record, and despite other promising collections, the band was restricted to a narrow, pub rock-influenced ghetto. Singer Bill Hurley recorded the solo *Double Agent* in 1985, but its gritty mixture of soul and R&B classics fared no better than those of the parent group. *Meet The Beatles, Live In Paris* is a set of Beatles songs performed in a hard R&B and Chicago blues vein.

● ALBUMS: *First Offence* (Polydor 1979)★★★, *Shot In The Dark* (Radar 1980)★★★, *Heatwave In Alaska* (1982)★★★, *True Live Stories* (1984)★★★, *Five* (Lolita 1984)★★★, *Meet The Beatles, Live In Paris* (1988)★★★, *Fast Forward* (Sonet 1989)★★★, *Inside Out* (New Rose 1991)★★★, *Wanted* (1993)★★★.

INSTANT FUNK

Based in Philadelphia, USA, Instant Funk comprised James Carmichael (vocals), George Bell (guitar), Kim Miller (guitar), Scotty Miller (drums), Raymond Earl (bass), Dennis Richardson (keyboards), Charles Williams (percussion), Larry Davis (trumpet) and John Onderline (sax). They were ostensibly the musical vehicle for noted producer/writer Bunny Sigler, who used them for the instrumentation on his own albums and subsequently secured them a contract with T.S.O.P. Records. Their debut album, *Get Down With The Philly Jump*, received considerable attention, thanks to the success of the single, 'It Ain't Reggae (But It's Funky)'. Their biggest breakthrough was achieved through 'I Got My Mind Made Up', a number 20 US hit and gold disc for Salsoul Records in 1979. They recorded further albums for that label without coming close to repeating this success, and eventually surfaced in 1985, recording 'Tailspin' for the Pop Art label.

● ALBUMS: *Get Down With The Philly Jump* (T.S.O.P. 1976)★★★, *I Got My Mind Made Up* (Salsoul 1978)★★★, *Instant Funk* (Salsoul 1979)★★★, *Witch Doctor* (Salsoul 1979)★★, *The Funk Is On* (Salsoul 1980)★★, *Kinky* (Salsoul 1983)★★, *Instant Funk* (Salsoul 1983)★★.

Intrigue

An R&B vocal trio comprising Audley Wiggan Jnr., and brothers Jason and Anthony Harper, Intrigue piloted a new musical hybrid in the mid-90s that they themselves described as 'acoustic soul'. An attempt to stamp out a new musical identity in a crowded R&B marketplace, the same epithet served as the title of the group's 1995 debut album. Co-produced with Ali Dee, the album favoured traditional instrumentation - strings, keyboards, piano, horns and upright bass - to provide a sympathetic melodic backdrop to the vocalists' oscillating melodies. *Acoustic Soul* was promoted by a single, 'If You've Ever Been In Love', a typically lush, evocative example of the album's contents. Previous singles had included 'Dance With Me', a cover version of the Drifters hit, which gave a strong indication of the trio's influences. The group confirmed their commitment to a traditional style of vocal R&B by performing an all-acoustic tour of trade conventions, benefits and parades through the early months of 1997.

● ALBUMS: *Acoustic Soul* (GRV/Universal 1995)★★★.

Intruders

Formed in Philadelphia in 1960, Eugene 'Bird' Daughtry (b. 29 October 1939, Kinston, North Carolina, USA, d. 25 December 1994), Phil Terry (b. 1 November 1943, Philadelphia, Pennsylvania, USA), Robert 'Big Sonny' Edwards (b. 22 February 1942, Philadelphia, Pennsylvania, USA) and Sam 'Little Sonny' Brown have enjoyed the benefit of a long-standing relationship with producers Gamble And Huff. Signed to the duo's Excel/Gamble outlet, the group scored several minor hits, notably '(We'll Be) United' (1966) and 'Together' (1967). In 1968 'Cowboys To Girls', a prototype for the emergent Philly-soul sound, became their first million-seller, peaking at number 6 in the national US pop chart. The follow-up, '(Love Is Like A) Baseball Game', was another R&B smash, as well as one of soul's best sporting metaphors, Mel And Tim's 'Backfield In Motion' notwithstanding. In 1970, the Intruders replaced lead Sam Brown with Bobby Starr (b. 19 January 1937, Baltimore, Maryland, USA), and subsequently reached the charts with 'When We Get Married' (1970), '(Win, Place Or Show) She's A Winner' (1971) and 'I'll Always Love My Mama' (1973). Despite an undeniable quality, the Intruders' releases were overshadowed by those of stablemates the O'Jays and Harold Melvin And The Blue Notes.

● ALBUMS: *Cowboys To Girls* (Gamble 1968)★★★, *When We Get Married* (Gamble 1970)★★★, *Save The Children* (Gamble 1973)★★★★, *Energy Of Love* (Gamble 1974)★★★.

● COMPILATIONS: *The Intruders Greatest Hits* (Gamble 1969)★★★, *Cowboys To Girls: The Best Of The Intruders* (Sony/Legacy 1996)★★★★.

Invincibles

An R&B vocal trio from Los Angeles, California, USA. The falsetto lead in soul music was especially strong in the genre of stand-up vocal groups, and from the groups of the 60s, the Invincibles were perhaps one of the greatest practitioners of the falsetto-edged vocal harmony style. The group members were David Richardson, Lester Johnson and Clifton Knight. Richardson was originally from Louisiana and brought a background in gospel singing to the group, and Johnson and Knight both came from Texas. The Invincibles' best work was demonstrated on two superb hits, 'Heart Full Of Love' (number 31 R&B) from 1965, and 'Can't Win' (number 38 R&B) from 1966, both of which went beyond mere sweetness to exhibit deep, soulful feeling. However, the Invincibles faded after these two records.

Invisible Man's Band

(see Five Stairsteps)

Irwin, Big Dee

b. Difosco Ervin, 4 August 1939, New York City, New York, USA, d. 27 August 1995, Las Vegas, Nevada, USA. The corpulent R&B singer first made his mark as lead for the doo-wop group the Pastels, who had successes with two sumptuous ballads, 'Been So Long' (1957) and 'So Far Away' (1958). As a solo artist, he is recalled for a series of tongue-in-cheek singles, the most successful of which was a version of the Bing Crosby hit 'Swingin' On A Star' in 1963, an irreverent performance on which he was joined by a perky Little Eva. Irwin's other releases included 'Everybody's Got A Dance But Me', on which he begrudged the dance-based releases of other artists, and 'Happy Being Fat', where Eva, once again, provided the spiky interjections. Irwin later enjoyed intermittent success as a songwriter, including 'What Kind Of Boy', recorded on the Hollies' debut album. He died in 1995 of heart failure.

Isley Brothers

Three brothers, O'Kelly (b. 25 December 1937, d. 31 March 1986), Rudolph (b. 1 April 1939) and Ronald Isley (b. 21 May 1941), began singing gospel in their hometown of Cincinnati, USA, in the early 50s, accompanied by their brother Vernon, who died in a car crash around

1957. Moving to New York the following year, the trio issued one-off singles before being signed by the RCA Records production team, Hugo And Luigi. The Isleys had already developed a tight vocal unit, with Rudolph and O'Kelly supporting Ronald's strident tenor leads in a call-and-response style taken directly from the church. The self-composed 'Shout' - with a chorus based on an ad-libbed refrain that had won an enthusiastic response in concert - epitomized this approach, building to a frantic crescendo as the brothers screamed out to each other across the simple chord changes. 'Shout' sold heavily in the black market, and has since become an R&B standard, but RCA's attempts to concoct a suitable follow-up were unsuccessful. The group switched labels to Wand in 1962, where they enjoyed a major hit with an equally dynamic cover version of the Top Notes' 'Twist And Shout', an arrangement that was subsequently copied by the Beatles. In the fashion of the times, the Isleys were forced to spend the next two years recording increasingly contrived rewrites of this hit, both on Wand and at United Artists. A brief spell with Atlantic Records in 1964 produced a classic R&B record, 'Who's That Lady?', but with little success. Tired of the lack of control over their recordings, the Isleys formed their own company, T-Neck Records, in 1964 - an unprecedented step for black performers. The first release on the label, 'Testify', showcased their young lead guitarist, Jimi Hendrix, and allowed him free rein to display his virtuosity and range of sonic effects. However, the record's experimental sound went unnoticed at the time, and the Isleys were forced to abandon both T-Neck and Hendrix, and sign a contract with Motown Records. They were allowed little involvement in the production of their records and the group were teamed with the Holland/Dozier/Holland partnership, who effectively treated them as an extension of the Four Tops, and fashioned songs for them accordingly. This combination reached its zenith with 'This Old Heart Of Mine' in 1966, a major hit in the USA, and a belated chart success in Britain in 1968. UK listeners also reacted favourably to 'Behind A Painted Smile' and 'I Guess I'll Always Love You' when they were reissued at the end of the 60s. Such singles were definitive Motown: a driving beat, an immaculate house band and several impassioned voices; but although the Isleys' records always boasted a tougher edge than those by their stablemates, little of their work for Motown exploited their gospel and R&B heritage to the full.

Tired of the formula and company power games, the Isleys reactivated T-Neck in 1969, along with a change of image from the regulation mohair suits to a freer, funkier 'west coast' image, reflected in their choice of repertoire. At this point too, they became a sextet, adding two younger brothers, Ernie (b. 7 March 1952; guitar) and Marvin (bass), as well as a cousin, Chris Jasper (keyboards). While their mid-60s recordings were enjoying overdue success in Britain, the Isleys were scoring enormous US hits with their new releases, notably 'It's Your Thing' and 'I Turned You On'. These records sported a stripped-down funk sound, inspired by James Brown And The JBs, and topped with the brothers' soaring vocal harmonies. They issued a succession of ambitious albums in this vein between 1969 and 1972, among them a live double set that featured extended versions of their recent hits, and *In The Beginning*, a collection of their 1964 recordings with Jimi Hendrix. In the early 70s, the Isleys incorporated into their repertoire a variety of rock material by composers such as Bob Dylan, Stephen Stills and Carole King. Their dual role as composers and interpreters reached a peak in 1973 on *3+3*, the first album issued via a distribution agreement with CBS Records. The record's title reflected the make-up of the group at that time, with the three original vocalists supported by the new generation of the family. Ernie Isley's powerful, sustained guitarwork, strongly influenced by Jimi Hendrix, became a vital ingredient in the Isleys' sound, and was featured heavily on the album's lead single, 'That Lady', a revamped version of their unheralded 1964 single on Atlantic. *3+3* also contained soft soul interpretations of material by Seals And Croft, James Taylor and the Doobie Brothers. An important key track was the Isleys' own 'Highway Of My Life', which demonstrated Ronald's increasing mastery of the romantic ballad form. Having established a winning formula, the Isleys retained it throughout the rest of the 70s, issuing a succession of slick, impressive soul albums that were divided between startlingly tough funk numbers and subdued Ronald Isley ballads. *The Heat Is On* in 1975 represented the pinnacle of both genres; the angry lyrics of 'Fight The Power', a US Top 10 single, contrasted sharply with the suite of love songs on the album's second side, aptly summarized by the title of one of the tracks, 'Sensuality'. 'Harvest For The World' (1976) proved to be one of the Isleys' most popular recordings in Britain, with its stunning blend of dance rhythm, melody and social awareness (the song hit the charts in 1988 for the Christians). In the late 70s, the increasing polarization of the rock and disco markets ensured that while the Isleys continued to impress black record buyers, their work went largely unheard in the white mainstream. 'The Pride', 'Take Me To The Next Phase', 'I Wanna Be With You' and 'Don't Say Goodnight' all topped the specialist black music charts without registering in the US Top 30, and the group responded in kind, concentrating on dance-flavoured material to the exclusion of their ballads. 'It's A Disco Night', a UK hit in 1980, demonstrated their command of the idiom, but a growing sense of self-parody infected the Isleys' music in the early 80s. Conscious of this decline, Ernie and Marvin Isley and Chris Jasper left the group in 1984 to form the successful Isley, Jasper, Isley combination. The original trio soldiered on, but the sudden death of O'Kelly Isley from a heart attack on 31 March 1986 brought their 30-year partnership to an end. Ronald and Rudolph dedicated their next release, *Smooth Sailin'*, to him, and the album produced another black hit in Angela Wimbush's ballad, 'Smooth Sailin' Tonight'. Wimbush now assumed virtual artistic control over the group, and she wrote and produced their 1989 release *Spend The Night*, which was effectively a Ronald Isley solo album. The artistic innovations of the Isley Brothers, continued by the second generation of the family in Isley, Jasper, Isley, belie the conservatism of their releases since the late 70s. Their 1996 release *Mission To Please* attempted to move them into the same smooth urban soul territory as Keith Sweat and Babyface. The group represented the apogee of gospel-inspired soul on their early hits, they pioneered the ownership of record labels by black artists, and invented a new funk genre with their blend of dance rhythms and rock instrumentation in the early 70s. Their series of US hits from the 50s to the 90s is one of the major legacies of black American music.

● ALBUMS: *Shout* (RCA Victor 1959)★★★, *Twist And Shout* (Wand 1962)★★★★, *The Fabulous Isley Brothers-Twisting And Shouting* (Wand 1964)★★, *Take Some Time Out-The Famous Isley Brothers* (United Artists 1964)★★, *This Old Heart Of Mine* (Tamla 1966)★★, *Soul On The Rocks* (Tamla 1967)★★, *It's Our Thing* (T-Neck 1969)★★★, *Doin' Their Thing* (Tamla 1969)★★★, *The Brothers: Isley* (T-Neck 1969)★★★, with Brooklyn Bridge and Edwin Hawkins *Live At Yankee Stadium* (T-Neck 1969)★★, *Get Into Something* (T-Neck 1970)★★★, *Givin' It Back* (T-Neck 1971)★★★, *Brother Brother Brother* (T-Neck 1972)★★★, *The Isleys Live* (T-Neck 1973)★★★, *3+3* (T-Neck 1973)★★★★, *Live It Up* (T-Neck 1974)★★★, *The Heat Is On* (T-Neck 1975)★★★★, *Harvest For The World* (T-Neck 1976)★★★, *Go For Your Guns* (T-Neck 1977)★★★, *Showdown* (T-Neck 1978)★★★, *Winner Takes All* (T-Neck 1979)★★★, *Go All The Way* (T-Neck 1980)★★★, *Grand Slam* (T-Neck 1981)★★★, *Inside You* (T-Neck 1981)★★★, *The Real Deal* (T-Neck 1982)★★★, *Between The Sheets* (T-Neck 1983)★★★, *Masterpiece* (Warners 1985)★★★, *Smooth Sailin'* (Warners 1987)★★★, as Isley Brothers Featuring Ronald Isley *Spend The Night* (Warners 1989)★★, *Tracks Of Life* (Warners 1992)★★★, *Live* (Elektra 1993)★★, *Mission To Please* (Island 1996)★★.

● COMPILATIONS: *In The Beginning: With Jimi Hendrix* (T-Neck 1970)★★, *Isleys' Greatest Hits* (T-Neck 1973)★★★★, *Rock Around The Clock* (Camden 1975)★★, *Super Hits* (Motown 1976)★★★, *Forever Gold* (T-Neck 1977)★★★★, *The Best Of The Isley Brothers* (United Artists 1978)★★★, *Timeless* (Epic 1979)★★★, *Let's Go* (Stateside 1986)★★, *Greatest Motown Hits* (Motown 1987)★★★, *The Complete UA Sessions* (EMI 1990)★★★, *The Isley Brothers Story/Volume 1: The Rockin' Years (1959-1968)* (Rhino 1991)★★★, *The Isley Brothers Story/Volume 2: T-Neck Years (1968-1985)* (Rhino 1991)★★★★, *Beautiful Ballads* (Epic Legacy 1995)★★, *Funky Family* (Epic Legacy 1995)★★, *Early Classics* (Spectrum 1996)★★★.

ISLEY, JASPER, ISLEY

This trio broke away from the Isley Brothers in 1984. Instrumentalists Ernie Isley, Chris Jasper and Marvin Isley had augmented the latter group during its highly successful 70s reign, but their own subsequent career confirmed their deft vocal abilities. The group's early releases were overshadowed by their former achievements, but a soul chart topper, 'Caravan Of Love' (1985), successfully covered in the UK by the Housemartins, proclaimed their new identity. Later singles were, however, less popular, and two years later Jasper began recording as a solo act and his 'Superbad' reached the R&B Top 3.

● ALBUMS: *Broadway's Closer To Sunset Boulevard* (Columbia 1985)★★★, *Caravan Of Love* (Columbia 1985)★★★, *Different Drummer* (Columbia 1987)★★★. Solo: Chris Jasper *Superbad* (Epic 1988)★★.

IVY, QUIN

b. 1938, Oxford, Mississippi, USA. Although Rick Hall was perhaps chiefly responsible for putting Muscle Shoals-recorded soul music on the map with his fine 60s and early 70s productions at Fame Studios, Quin Ivy, who entered the business just after Hall, deserves credit, not only for the consistent run of hits he had with his mainstay artist Percy Sledge, but for the other fine southern-soul music he recorded with lesser-known musicians and singers at his Quinvy Studio in nearby Sheffield, Alabama. A white sharecropper's son, Ivy's first interest was country music, but he switched to R&B in the mid-50s after hearing records by artists such as LaVern Baker and Ivory Joe Hunter, as well as the Nashville 'black music' shows of Hoss Allen and John R. He began working in radio at the tiny local Oxford station, before moving to WMPS in Memphis, and several other stations, including WLAY in Muscle Shoals, Alabama, where Sam Phillips had been a DJ. In 1963, he used the name Tune Town (a previous Shoals-area record label owned by James Joiner) for his new record store in nearby Sheffield. Quin and Rick Hall began writing songs, including two for Jimmy Hughes: his first a-side, 'I'm Qualified', leased to the Guyden label, and 'Lollipops, Lace And Lipstick', the b-side of his first hit 'Steal Away' (and the first ever single on the Fame label). In 1966 Ivy opened his first Quinvy Studio across the street from his Sheffield record store, using an old rewired console discarded by the WLAY radio station, an equally old Ampex recorder bought in Nashville and some dilapidated A7 speakers. He tried to persuade Fame regular Dan Penn to work as his engineer, but instead settled for Marlin Greene. Quin offered Greene 10% of the business, and besides engineering, he played guitar, arranged strings, and even designed the new company logo. The first ever session held at the Quinvy studio was for a local singer, Donna Thatcher (later a backing singer, as Donna Godchaux, with Grateful Dead), but it was the second session that propelled Ivy into the big time when he recorded a black male nurse who worked at the nearby Colbert County Hospital. The nurse was Percy Sledge and the record was 'When A Man Loves A Woman'. Jerry Wexler of Atlantic Records leased the track from Ivy (with some assistance from Rick Hall) and it became a US number 1 in 1966. The steady sales of Sledge's many records over the next few years financed several other fine soul artists on Ivy's own labels, Quinvy and South Camp (distributed by Atco/Atlantic). Quin Ivy's artists had the cream of the late 60s Shoals-based musicians to support them, including Roger Hawkins, Junior Lowe, Spooner Oldham, David Hood, Eddie Hinton, Jimmy Johnson and Marlin Greene. Stand-out tracks included Don Varner's UK northern dance favourite, the pulsating 'Tearstained Face', and the equally superb up-tempo soul of Tony Borders' 'What Kind Of Spell'. There were also many prime examples of southern deep soul, including Borders' 'Cheaters Never Win', the young Z.Z. Hill's

'Faithful & True', and three tracks in particular by the outstanding Bill Brandon: 'Self Preservation', 'One Minute Woman' (unissued at the time), and the first, and arguably best, recording of a deep ballad called 'Rainbow Road', written by Dan Penn and Donnie Fritts for and about Arthur Alexander, who recorded it himself some years later for Warner. Most of these sides appeared on Quinvy or South Camp, but Ivy also leased product to other small labels (in addition to the Sledge material and one Z.Z. Hill single to Atlantic, and an Eddie Bradford single to Chess). These included Tower, Revue, Nugget, Diamond and Uni. Their relative lack of success, combined with an eventual decline in the sales of Percy Sledge records, caused Ivy to sell the studio to his engineer, David Johnson, in 1973. It was renamed Broadway Sound, and Percy Sledge recorded two further albums there in 1974 and 1983, and James Govan and Freddie North recorded in the studio during the 70s. Quin Ivy gained an MA degree at Mississippi University before returning to the Shoals area to teach accountancy. Virtually the complete Quinvy-South Camp soul output (excluding the Sledge material) was released in 1989 by the UK Charly label on five separate albums, followed by a 27-track selective CD that also included four sides not on the albums.

● COMPILATIONS: *Tear Stained Soul* (Charly 1989)★★★, *High On the Hog* (Charly 1989)★★★, *You Better Believe It!* (Charly 1989)★★★, *More Power To Ya!* (Charly 1989)★★★, *Rainbow Road* (Charly 1989)★★★, *Rare Soul From Alabama - The South Camp Quinvy CD* (Charly 1989)★★★★.

Jackie And The Starlites

Jackie And The Starlites were perhaps the most extreme example of overt emotionalism in doo-wop, in which lead Jackie Rue would scream out the lyrics in the most anguished, heartbreaking voice, and in the middle of the songs break down sobbing. The members, besides Rue, were Alton Thomas, John Felix and Billy Montgomery. Rue began singing with the Five Wings, a group in Harlem, New York, in 1955, and made two haunting singles for the King label, most notably 'Teardrops Are Falling' (a stunning remake appeared in the 1990 John Waters film *Cry Baby*). In 1960 Rue surfaced again with the Starlights and signed with Bobby Robinson's Fury label. Their first record was 'Valerie', and it quickly became something of a phenomenon on the east coast. Their best follow-up, 'I Found Out Too Late', made the national charts in 1962, but later records for Robinson failed to find favour. The Starlites recorded unsuccessfully for the Hull label during 1962-63 before breaking up. With a scruffy and rough image, Rue and his group were not destined to attain middle-class respectability. In 1961 two members of the group killed a man in an armed robbery and received extensive jail sentences. Rue died of a drug overdose some time in the late 60s or early 70s.

● COMPILATIONS: *The Kodaks Versus The Starlites* (Sphere Sound 1965)★★★, *Valerie* (Relic 1991)★★★, *Jackie & The Starlites Meet The Bopchords* (Collectables 1991)★★★.

Jacks

(see Cadets)

Jackson Five

The Jackson Five comprised five brothers, Jackie (b. Sigmund Esco Jackson, 4 May 1951), Tito (b. Toriano Adaryll Jackson, 15 October 1953), Jermaine (b. Jermaine Lajuan Jackson, 11 December 1954), Marlon (b. 12 March 1957) and Michael Jackson (b. 29 August 1958). Raised in Gary, Indiana, USA, by their father Joe, a blues guitarist, they began playing local clubs in 1962, with youthful prodigy Michael as lead vocalist. Combining dance routines influenced by the Temptations with music inspired by James Brown, they first recorded for the Indiana-based Steeltown label before auditioning for Motown Records in 1968. Bobby Taylor recommended the group to Motown, although the company gave Diana Ross public credit for their discovery. A team of Motown writers known as the Corporation composed a series of songs for the group's early releases, all accentuating their youthful enthusiasm and vocal interplay. Their debut single for Motown, 'I Want You Back', became the fastest-selling record in the company's history in 1969, and three of their next five singles also topped the American chart. Michael Jackson was groomed for a concurrent solo recording career, which began in 1971, followed by similar excursions for Jermaine and elder brother Jackie. As the group's appeal broadened, they became the subjects of a cartoon series on American television, *The Jackson 5*, and hosted a television special, *Goin' Back To Indiana*. After the dissolution of the Corporation in 1971, the group recorded revivals of pop and R&B hits from the 50s, and cover versions of other Motown standards, before being allowed to branch out into more diverse material, such as Jackson Browne's 'Doctor My Eyes'. They also began to record their own compositions in the early 70s, a trend that continued until 1975, by which time they were writing and producing most of the songs on their albums. The Jackson Five reached the peak of their popularity in Britain when they toured there in 1972, but after returning to America they suffered decreasing record sales as their music grew more sophisticated. By 1973, they had dropped the teenage stylings of their early hits, concentrating on a cabaret approach to their live performances, while on record they perfected a harder brand of funk. The group's recording contract with Motown expired in 1975. Feeling that the label had not been promoting their recent records, they signed to Epic Records. Jermaine Jackson, however, who was married to the daughter of Motown boss Berry Gordy, chose to leave the group and remain with the company as a solo artist. Gordy sued the Jackson Five for alleged breach of contract in 1976, and the group were forced to change their name to the Jacksons. The case was settled in 1980, with the brothers paying Gordy $600,000, and allowing Motown all rights to the 'Jackson Five' name.

● ALBUMS: *Diana Ross Presents The Jackson 5* (Motown 1970)★★★, *ABC* (Motown 1970)★★★★, *Third Album* (Motown 1970)★★★, *Christmas Album* (Motown 1970)★★, *Maybe Tomorrow* (Motown 1971)★★, *Goin' Back To Indiana* (Motown 1971)★★, *Lookin' Through The Windows* (Motown 1972)★★★, *Skywriter* (Motown 1973)★★★, *Get It Together* (Motown 1973)★★★, *Dancing Machine* (Motown 1974)★★★, *Moving Violation* (Motown 1975)★★★, *Joyful Jukebox Music* (Motown 1976)★★★.

● COMPILATIONS: *Jackson 5 Greatest Hits* (Motown 1971)★★★★, *Jackson Five Anthology* 3-LP set (Motown 1976)★★★★, *Soulstation! - 25th Anniversary Collection* 4-CD box set (Motown 1995)★★★★, *Early Classics* (Spectrum 1996)★★★.

● FURTHER READING: *Jackson Five*, Charles Morse. *The Jacksons*, Steve Manning. *Pap Joe's Boys: The Jacksons' Story*, Leonard Pitts. *The Magic And The Madness*, J. Randy Taraborrelli. *The Record History: International Jackson Record Guide* , Ingmar Kuliha.

JACKSON, BULLMOOSE

b. Benjamin Clarence Jackson, 1919, Cleveland, Ohio, USA, d. 31 July 1989, Cleveland, Ohio, USA. Jackson become interested in music at an early age, and received singing and violin lessons by the age of four. In high school he learned to play the saxophone, and upon his graduation in the late 30s he was hired by legendary trumpeter Freddie Webster to play alto and tenor with his Harlem Hotshots. Living briefly in Buffalo, New York, in the early 40s, Jackson returned to Cleveland to a job at the Cedar Gardens, where in 1944, he was discovered by bandleader Lucky Millinder who needed a musician to replace tenor saxophonist Lucky Thompson. Initially recording simply as a talented accompanist with Millinder's orchestra on Decca and as a guest musician with Big Sid Catlett's band on Capitol, Jackson astounded his colleagues by substituting for blues shouter Wynonie Harris one night in Lubbock, Texas. He remained a part of the Millinder aggregation until June 1948 with the huge success of his R&B hit 'I Love You, Yes I Do'. He began making records under his own name from 1945 with King/Queen and Superdisc, as well as appearing on Millinder's Decca tracks. He also made an appearance in the 1948 musical film *Boarding House Blues*. Jackson enjoyed great success on King Records between 1947 and 1954 with ballads such as 'I Love You, Yes I Do' (which spawned innumerable cover versions for every conceivable market), 'All My Love Belongs To You' and 'Little Girl Don't Cry'. Bullmoose was also responsible for some of the hottest, most suggestive R&B ever recorded, and it is these titles - 'Big Ten-Inch (Record)', 'I Want A Bow-Legged Woman', 'Nosey Joe' and 'Oh John' - that found favour with the later crop of jump and R&B revival bands. Jackson moved to Chess's short-lived Marterry subsidiary in 1955, switched to the tiny Encino label in 1956, and was reduced to making re-recordings of his old hits in the early 60s for Warwick and 7 Arts. By that time he had taken a job with a catering firm during the week and only played the occasional weekend gig. In 1974 he made a cameo appearance in the dramatic film *Sincerely The Blues*, led a jazz band at the Smithsonian Institute in 1976, and went on to tour France and North Africa with Buck Clayton's Quartet. In 1983 Jackson was tracked down by the Pittsburgh-based band the Flashcats, who had been covering his risqué R&B songs, and after 35 years he was big news again with a sell-out tour, a new recording contract with Bogus Records, a celebrated show at Carnegie Hall and a European tour with the Johnny Otis Show in 1985.

● ALBUMS: *Big Fat Mamas Are Back In Style Again* (Route 66 1980)★★★, *Moosemania!* (Bogus 1985)★★★, *Moose On The Loose* (Bogus 1985)★★★.

● FILMS: *Sincerely The Blues* (1974).

JACKSON, CHUCK

b. 22 July 1937, Latta, South Carolina, USA. Jackson travelled the traditional 50s route into soul music via a spell in the gospel group the Raspberry Singers. In 1957, he joined the hit doo-wop group the Del-Vikings, taking a prominent role on their US Top 10 success 'Whispering Bells'. His strong baritone vocals enabled him to launch a solo career with Beltone Records in 1960, before signing to the more prestigious Wand label the following year. Jackson's early 60s singles for Wand epitomized the New York uptown soul style, with sophisticated arrangements - often crafted by Burt Bacharach - supporting his sturdy vocals with female vocalists and orchestras. He enjoyed enormous success in the R&B market for several years with a run of hits that have become soul classics, such as 'I Don't Want To Cry', 'I Wake Up Crying', 'Any Day Now' and 'Tell Him I'm Not Home', although only the majestic 'Any Day Now', co-written by Bacharach, crossed into the US Top 30. In 1965 he was teamed with Maxine Brown on a revival of Chris Kenner's R&B favourite, 'Something You Got', the first of three hit duets over the next two years. Their partnership was severed in 1967 when Jackson joined Motown, a decision he later described as 'one of the worst mistakes I ever made in my life'. Although he notched up a minor hit with Freddie Scott's 'Are You Lonely For Me Baby?' in 1969, the majority of his Motown recordings found him pitched against unsympathetic backdrops in a vain attempt to force him into the label's formula. Jackson left Motown in 1971 for ABC, where again he could only muster one small hit, 'I Only Get This Feeling', in 1973. Another switch of labels, to All-Platinum in 1975, produced the chart entry 'I'm Wanting You, I'm Needing You' in his traditional style. In 1980, he joined EMI America, where his most prominent role was as guest vocalist on two hit albums by Gary 'U.S.' Bonds. In the late 80s Jackson was one of many ex-Motown artists signed to Ian Levine's Motor City label, with whom he released two singles. He released an album with Cissy Houston in 1992.

● ALBUMS: *I Don't Want To Cry* (Wand 1961)★★★, *Any Day Now* (Wand 1962)★★★★, *Encore* (Wand 1963)★★★, *Chuck Jackson On Tour* (Wand 1964)★★★, *Mr Everything* (Wand 1965)★★★, with Maxine Brown *Saying Something* (Wand 1965)★★★, *A Tribute To Rhythm And Blues* (Wand 1966)★★★, *A Tribute To Rhythm And Blues Vol. 2* (Wand 1966)★★★, with Brown *Hold On We're Coming* (Wand 1966)★★★, *Dedicated To The King* (Wand 1966)★★★, *The Early Show* (1967)★★★, *Chuck Jackson Arrives* (Motown 1968)★★★, *Goin' Back To Chuck Jackson* (Motown 1969)★★★, *Teardrops Keep Falling On My Heart* (Motown 1970)★★★, *Through All Times* (ABC 1974)★★★, *Needing You, Wanting You* (All Platinum 1975)★★★, *The Great Chuck Jackson* (Bulldog 1977)★★★, *I Wanna Give You Some Love* (EMI America 1980)★★★, *After You* (EMI America 1980)★★, with Cissy Houston *I'll Take Care Of You* (Shanachie 1992)★★.

● COMPILATIONS: *Chuck Jackson's Greatest Hits* (Wand 1967), *Mr. Emotion* (Kent 1985)★★★, *A Powerful Soul* (Kent 1987)★★★, *Good Things* (Kent 1991)★★★, *I Don't Want To Cry/Any Day Now* (Ace 1993)★★★, *Encore/Mr Everything* (Ace 1994)★★★, *The Great Recordings* (Tomato 1995)★★★.

Jackson, Freddie

b. 2 October 1956, Harlem, New York, USA. A singer-songwriter, who was especially successful in the late 80s, Jackson was brought up in Harlem, and sang at the White Rock Baptist church while he was still a young child. Later, he worked in a bank before joining the group LJE, along with the singer, songwriter and producer Paul Laurence. In the early 80s, Jackson moved to California and became lead singer with the R&B vocal/instrumental group Mystic Merlin. He sang on their *Full Moon*, which featured the popular soul/dance track 'Mr Magician'. In 1984, Jackson returned to the east coast where he was spotted singing in a New York club by Melba Moore. After serving as a backing vocalist for Moore, Evelyn 'Champagne' King, and others, Jackson signed a solo contract with Capitol Records, and issued *Rock Me Tonight* in 1985. Both the album, and its title track, 'Rock Me Tonight (For Old Times Sake)', which Jackson had written with Paul Laurence, made the US Top 20, and also did well in the UK. Subsequent singles from *Rock Me Tonight*, such as 'You Are My Lady' and 'He'll Never Love You (Like I Do)', proved to be ideally suited for the burgeoning soul club scene on both sides of the Atlantic. In 1986, Jackson duetted with Melba Moore on 'A Little Bit More' from her album *A Lot Of Love*, and issued his own *Just Like The First Time*, which included three more successful dance sides, 'Have You Ever Loved Somebody', 'Tasty Love', and 'Jam Tonight'. Jackson's subsequent albums did not fare so well, and were sometimes critized for their 'sameness'. Nevertheless, *Don't Let Love Slip Away* contained two UK hits, 'Nice 'N' Slow' and 'Crazy (For Me)', and *Time For Love* was given extra interest by the inclusion of guest artists such as Audrey Wheeler, Will Downing and Naje. *Here It Is* was released on RCA Records. Jackson's song-writing activities, mostly in collaboration with Paul Laurence, resulted in numbers such as 'Trust Me' for Lilo Thomas, 'Keepin' My Lover Satisfied' for Melba Moore, and 'Jam Song' for Howard Johnson.

● ALBUMS: *Rock Me Tonight* (Capitol 1985)★★★, *Just Like The First Time* (Capitol 1986)★★, *Don't Let Love Slip Away* (Capitol 1988)★★, *Do Me Again* (Capitol 1990)★★★, *Time For Love* (Capitol 1992)★★, *Here It Is* (RCA 1993)★★.

● COMPILATIONS: *The Greatest Hits Of ...* (Capitol 1993)★★★.

Jackson, George

b. 1946, Greenville, Mississippi, USA. Jackson has a quietly emotional country-soul delivery that could have made him a southern-soul singing star in his own right, but as he only recorded 15 singles over a 22-year period between 1963 and 1985 (and, more recently, a fine album), it is as a prolific and highly skilled songwriter that he is most respected. When Jackson was 14, he offered some of his songs to Ike Turner when Turners' Revue was playing Greenville, and went with him to Cosimo's famous studio in New Orleans to record 'Nobody Wants To Cha Cha With Me'/'Who Was That Guy' for Turner's Prann label. Later, Jackson travelled extensively, trying to promote himself and his songs. He was rejected by the fast-growing Stax Records, but in 1965, while in Memphis, Jackson linked up with the Ovations on the newly formed Goldwax label, penning their biggest hit, 'It's Wonderful To Be In Love'. Goldwax soon recognized Jackson's writing ability and he provided material for other artists on the label, including 'Old Friend' and 'He's Too Old' for Spencer Wiggins, and 'Coming Back To Me Baby' for James Carr. He also joined fellow singer-songwriter Dan Greer to cut the Goldwax single 'Good Times'/'You Didn't Know It But You Had Me' as George And Greer. By 1968, Jackson had left Goldwax for the nearby Hi label, where he initially recorded one single, 'I'm Gonna Wait'/'So Good To Me'. While still involved with Hi, Jackson appeared as Bart Jackson on a Decca release, 'Wonderful Dream'/'Dancing Man', and, shortly afterwards, moved across to Muscle Shoals and Rick Hall's Fame studio at the instigation of Nashville producer (and an old friend of Hall's) Billy Sherrill. This was Fame's peak soul period, and Hall engaged Jackson as a 'house' writer. He found immediate success with Clarence Carter's 'Too Weak To Fight' and Wilson Pickett's 'A Man And A Half'. Later Jackson songs for Fame included many of Candi Staton's superb early recordings, such as 'I'm Just A Prisoner', 'I'd Rather Be An Old Man's Sweetheart (Than A Young Man's Fool)', the racy 'Get It When I Want It', 'Evidence', 'Too Hurt To Cry', 'Freedom Is Just Beyond The Door' and the beautiful 'How Can I Put Out The Flame'. These songs are widely regarded as examples of some of the finest southern soul ever recorded by a female artist, with lyrics that were full of meaning and innuendo, a hallmark of Jackson's best work. He wrote for other Fame artists, and recorded three singles himself, two appearing on Fame, and one later leased out to Chess. By the early 70s Rick Hall's Fame productions for 'out-of-town' artists were increasingly 'pop'-orientated. The Osmonds recorded there, and Jackson gave them their first ever hit on MGM, the massive-selling early 1971 US chart-topper, 'One Bad Apple', which he had originally written with the Jackson Five in mind. Meanwhile, Jackson 'the performer' fleetingly rejoined Willie Mitchell at Hi, and in 1972/3 released two more singles of his own, including the beautiful southern country/soul song 'Aretha, Sing One For Me', a paean to the great female soul singer. It had little commercial impact, and Jackson soon linked up with MGM, for whom he had effectively launched the Osmonds pop act. While still writing for others, Jackson also recorded three singles for the label in 1973/4, the best being the punchy '(If I Could Get On That) Soul Train'. One more followed in 1976 for Er Music ('Talkin' About The Love I Have For You') and then, in 1979, Jackson cut 'Fast Young Lady' for Muscle Shoals Sounds. After Bob Seger had a big hit in 1979 with Jackson's 'Old Time Rock And Roll', the singer-songwriter formed his own publishing company, Happy Hooker Music, and gained further financial rewards in 1981 from another Seger success, 'Trying To Live My Life Without You', originally cut some years earlier by Otis Clay for Hi. Jackson then recorded several more obscure singles for his own Washataw and Happy Hooker labels in 1984/5, before joining the burgeoning southern blues and soul label Malaco as a staff writer. Jackson's successful compositions for the label included the huge seller for the late Z.Z. Hill, 'Down Home Blues', which he originally wrote some 10 years earlier. With the likes of Bobby 'Blue' Bland, Johnnie Taylor, Latimore and Denise LaSalle all recording for Malaco, Jackson's brand of southern soul songwriting has plenty of scope. In March 1991, he recorded an excellent album, *Heart To Heart Collect*, for Senator Jones' Hep' Me Records, and wrote all of the 10 tracks. Recorded at IRS studio in Pearl, Mississippi, it was released in the UK on CD in 1993 on Gary Cape's Black Grape label.

● ALBUMS: *Heart To Heart Collect* (Hep' Me 1991)★★★★.

● COMPILATIONS: *Hi Records The Blue Sessions* one track (1988), *Hi Records The Soul Years* two tracks (1988), *The History Of Hi Records Rhythm & Blues Volume 1* one track (1988), *River Town Blues* one track (1988), *The Hi Records Story* one track (1989), *Hi R&B And Soul* two tracks (1992), *The Hi Records 45's Collection Volume 2* five tracks (1992).

JACKSON, JACKIE

b. Sigmund Esco Jackson, 4 May 1951, Gary, Indiana, USA. Jackie has spent his entire professional career as a member of the Jackson Five (later known as the Jacksons). He was a founder of the family troupe in 1962, and has remained a relatively sheltered figure within the group ever since. Like his brothers Michael and Jermaine, he was groomed for a solo career at the height of the group's American popularity in the early 70s. When his solitary album flopped, he resumed his place as a backing singer for his younger brothers. By the late 70s, he had won some measure of artistic involvement in the Jacksons' recordings, and he co-wrote the hit singles 'Destiny', 'Can You Feel It?', 'Walk Right Now' and 'Torture' between 1978 and 1982. Since then, he has surfaced only occasionally in the media, expressing his frustration at being overshadowed by the success of his brother Michael.

● ALBUMS: *Jackie Jackson* (Motown 1973)★★.

JACKSON, JANET

b. Janet Damita Jackson, 16 May 1966, Gary, Indiana, USA. Jackson was the youngest of the nine children in the family that produced the Jackson Five (including Michael Jackson, Jermaine Jackson and LaToya Jackson). When Janet was four years old, the family moved to the Los Angeles area; three years later she made her performing debut in Las Vegas with her brothers. At the age of nine, she joined them on a television special. She was cast in the US television programmes *Good Times* from 1977-79 and *Diff'rent Strokes* from 1981-82. She signed to A&M Records in 1982 and recorded her self-titled debut album, followed by *Dream Street* in 1984. Both albums sold only moderately, although they each yielded one US Top 10 single. Jackson's breakthrough came in 1986 with *Control*, which reached number 1 and produced an astonishing five US Top 10 singles and three UK Top 10 singles. The album was ultimately certified quadruple platinum for sales of over four million copies in the USA. Jackson followed up in 1989 with *Janet Jackson's Rhythm Nation 1814*, another quadruple platinum album, which yielded chart-topping singles such as 'Miss You Much' and 'Rhythm Nation'. Jackson undertook her first concert tour in 1990. By the end of the year she had scooped eight *Billboard* awards, including Top R&B Albums and Singles Artist, Best Pop and R&B Album Award for *Rhythm Nation*, and Top Hot 100 Singles Artist. The success of the *Rhythm Nation* album continued into 1991 when, in January, Jackson became the first artist in history to have culled from one album seven Top 5 singles in the *Billboard* chart. Jackson's commercial peak continued into the 90s with the unprecedented performance of *Janet*, which entered the US album chart at number 1, beating brother Michael's sales record by selling 350,000 copies in its first week. The compilation album *Design Of A Decade* was another huge seller, and followed her collaboration with brother Michael on 'Scream'. Her first studio set in four years, *The Velvet Rope* was a deeply personal album that dealt frankly with her much self-publicized emotional breakdown.

● ALBUMS: *Janet Jackson* (A&M 1982)★★, *Dream Street* (A&M 1984)★★★, *Control* (A&M 1986)★★★★, *Control: The Remixes* (A&M 1987)★★★, *Janet Jackson's Rhythm Nation 1814* (A&M 1989)★★★, *Janet* (Virgin 1993)★★★★, *The Velvet Rope* (Virgin 1997)★★★.

● COMPILATIONS: *Janet Remixed* (Virgin 1995)★★★, *Design Of A Decade 1986/1996* (A&M 1995)★★★.

● VIDEOS: *Janet* (Virgin 1994), *Design Of A Decade 86-96* (VVL 1995).

● FURTHER READING: *Out Of The Madness (The Strictly Unauthorised Biography Of ...)*, Andrew Bart and J. Randy Taraborrelli (eds.).

JACKSON, JERMAINE

b. Jermaine Lajuan Jackson, 11 December 1954, Gary, Indiana, USA. Jermaine was one of five brothers who made up the Jackson Five in 1962. Besides playing bass, he acted as vocal counterpoint to his younger brother Michael Jackson, a musical relationship that continued after the group were signed to Motown Records in 1968. Jermaine contributed occasional lead vocals to their albums in the early 70s, and his performance of 'I Found That Girl' on *Third Album* was one of their most affecting ballads. Like his brothers Michael and Jackie, Jermaine was singled out by Motown for a solo career, and he had an immediate US Top 10 hit with a revival of Shep And The Limeliters' doo-wop classic 'Daddy's Home', in 1972. Later releases were less favourably received, but he consolidated his position within the company in 1973 with his marriage to Hazel, the daughter of Motown boss Berry Gordy. His new family connections entailed a stark conflict of interest when the other members of the Jackson Five decided to leave the label in 1975. Given the choice of deserting either his brothers or his father-in-law, he elected to remain with Motown, where his solo releases were subsequently given a higher priority than before. Despite heavy promotion, Jermaine's late 70s recordings failed to establish him as a distinctive soul voice, and he faced constant critical comparisons with the Jacksons' work on Epic. His career was revitalized by the intervention of Stevie Wonder, who wrote and produced the 1979 hit 'Let's Get Serious' in 1979, which successfully echoed the joyous funk of Wonder's own recordings. The gentle soul of 'You Like Me Don't You' brought him another hit in 1981, while the US Top 20 single 'Let Me Tickle Your Fancy' the following year featured an unlikely collaboration with new wave band Devo. Jackson's increased public profile won him a more generous contract with Motown in the early 80s. He formed his own production company, launching Michael Lovesmith as a recording artist and overseeing the career development of Syreeta. But this increased freedom was not enough to keep him at Motown, and in 1983 he signed with Arista Records. The following year, he was reconciled with his brothers: he joined the Jacksons on the *Victory* album and tour, and his own *Jermaine Jackson* featured a sparkling duet with Michael Jackson on 'Tell Me We're Not Dreaming'. He subsequently collaborated with Pia Zadora on the theme from the film *Voyage Of The Rock Aliens*, and with Whitney Houston on his 1986 project *Precious Memories*. In that same year, he formed his own label, WORK Records, and accepted an offer to portray the late Marvin Gaye in a biopic that was never completed. He has continued to work with the Jacksons and as a soloist since then, although his recent projects have been overshadowed by the media circus surrounding his brother Michael, a subject touched upon in Jermaine's 'Word To The Badd!!'.

● ALBUMS: *Jermaine* (Motown 1972)★★, *Come Into My Life* (Motown 1973)★★, *My Name Is Jermaine* (Motown 1976)★★, *Feel The Fire* (Motown 1977)★★, *Frontier* (Motown 1978)★★, *Let's Get Serious* (Motown 1980)★★★, *Jermaine* (Motown 1980)★★, *I Like Your Style* (Motown 1981)★★, *Let Me Tickle Your Fancy* (Motown 1982)★★, *Jermaine Jackson* (USA) *Dynamite* (UK) (Arista 1984)★★★, *Precious Moments* (Arista 1986)★★, *Don't Take It Personal* (Arista 1989)★★, *You Said* (La Face 1991)★★.

JACKSON, LATOYA

b. 29 May 1956, Gary, Indiana, USA. As a member of the singing Jackson family, LaToya served her apprenticeship as a backing vocalist to the Jacksons group along with her sisters, Rebbie and Janet Jackson. LaToya embarked on a solo career in 1980, signing to the Polydor label. Despite the family connection, LaToya's solo career found difficulty in emulating the success of her younger sister Janet; her highest single chart position was with the US number 56, 'Hearts Don't Lie' (1984) on her new label, Private I/Epic. A later label change to RCA Records did not alter her fortunes. She later exacerbated family relations with a somewhat scurrilous autobiography in 1991, and by refusing to sanction the 1992 ABC mini-series *The Jacksons: An American Dream*.

● ALBUMS: *LaToya Jackson* (Polydor 1980)★★, *My Special Love* (Polydor 1981)★★, *Heart Don't Lie* (Private Stock 1984)★★, *Imagination* (Private Stock 1985)★★, *You're Gonna Get Rocked* (RCA 1988)★★.

● FURTHER READING: *LaToya Jackson*, LaToya Jackson with Patricia Romanowski.

JACKSON, MICHAEL

b. Michael Joseph Jackson, 29 August 1958, Gary, Indiana, USA. Jackson has spent almost his entire life as a public performer. He was a founder-member of the Jackson Five at the age of four, soon becoming the group's lead vocalist and frontman. Onstage, he modelled his dance moves and vocal styling on James Brown, and portrayed an absolute self-confidence on stage that belied his shy, private personality. The Jackson Five were signed to Motown Records at the end of 1968; their early releases, including chart-toppers 'I Want You Back' and 'I'll Be There', illustrated his remarkable maturity. Although Michael was too young to have experienced the romantic situations that were the subject of his songs, he performed with total sincerity, showing all the hallmarks of a great soul artist. Ironically, his pre-adolescent vocal work carried a conviction that he often failed to recapture later in his career. When MGM Records launched the Osmonds as rivals to the Jackson Five in 1970, and singled out their lead singer, 13-year-old Donny Osmond, for a solo career, Motown felt duty bound to reply in kind. Michael Jackson's first release as a solo performer was the aching ballad 'Got To Be There', a major US and UK hit. A revival of Bobby Day's rock 'n' roll novelty 'Rockin' Robin' reached the top of the US charts in 1972, while the sentimental film theme 'Ben' repeated that achievement later in the year. Motown capitalized on Jackson's popularity with a series of hurried albums, which mixed material angled towards the teenage market with a selection of the label's standards. They also stockpiled scores of unissued tracks, which were released in the 80s to cash in on the success of his Epic recordings. As the Jackson Five's sales slipped in the mid-70s, Michael's solo career was put on hold, and he continued to reserve his talents for the group after they were reborn as the Jacksons in 1976. He re-entered the public eye with a starring role in the film musical *The Wiz*, collaborating on the soundtrack album with Quincy Jones. Their partnership was renewed in 1979 when Jones produced *Off The Wall*, a startlingly successful collection of contemporary soul material that introduced the world to the adult Michael Jackson. In his new incarnation, Jackson retained the vocal flexibility of old, but added a new element of sophistication and maturity. The album topped the charts in the UK and USA, and contained two number 1 singles, 'Don't Stop Till You Get Enough' (for which Jackson won a Grammy award) and 'Rock With You'. Meanwhile, Motown capitalized on his commercial status by reissuing a recording from the mid-70s, 'One Day In Your Life', which duly topped the UK charts. Jackson continued to tour and record with the Jacksons after this solo success, while media speculation grew about his private life. He was increasingly portrayed as a figure trapped in an eternal childhood, surrounded by toys and pet animals, and insulated from the traumas of the real world. This image was consolidated when he was chosen to narrate an album based on the 1982 fantasy film *ET - The Extra Terrestrial*. The record was quickly withdrawn because of legal complications, but still won Jackson another Grammy award. In 1982 *Thriller*, Jackson's second album with Quincy Jones, was released, and went on to become one of the most commercially successful albums of all time. It also produced a run of successful hit singles, each accompanied by a promotional video that widened the scope of the genre. 'The Girl Is Mine', a duet with Paul McCartney, began the sequence in relatively subdued style; it reached number 1 in the USA and UK, but merely set the scene for 'Billie Jean', an effortless mix of disco and pop that spawned a series of answer records from other artists. The accompanying video was equally spectacular, portraying Jackson as a master of dance, a magician who could transform lives, and a shadowy figure who lived outside the everyday world. Its successor, 'Beat It', established another precedent, with its determinedly rock-flavoured guitar solo by Eddie Van Halen making it the first black record to receive rotation airplay on the MTV video station. Its promo film involved Jackson at the centre of a choreographed street battle, a conscious throwback to the set pieces of *West Side Story*. However, even this was a modest effort compared to 'Thriller', a rather mannered piece of disco-funk accompanied by a stunning long-form video that placed Jackson in a parade of Halloween horrors. This promo clip spawned a follow-up, *The Making Of 'Thriller'*, which in turn sold more copies than any other home video to date.

The *Thriller* album and singles won Jackson a further seven Grammies; amidst this run of hits, Jackson slotted in 'Say Say Say', a second chart-topping duet with Paul McCartney. He accepted the largest individual sponsorship deal in history from Pepsi-Cola in 1983; the following year, his involvement in the Jacksons' 'Victory Tour' sparked the greatest demand for concert tickets in the history of popular music. Jackson had by now become an almost mythical figure, and like most myths he attracted hyperbole. A group of Jehovah's Witnesses announced that he was the Messiah; he was said to be taking drugs to change his skin colour to white; it was claimed that he had undergone extensive plastic surgery to alter his appearance; and photographs were published that suggested he slept in a special chamber to prevent himself ageing. More prosaically, Jackson began 1985 by co-writing and performing on the USA For Africa benefit single 'We Are The World', another international number 1. He then spent $47.5 million in purchasing the ATV Music company, who controlled the songs of John Lennon and Paul McCartney, thus effectively sabotaging his musical relationship with his erstwhile partner. Later that year he took part in *Captain Eo*, a short film laden with special effects that was only shown at the Disneyworld amusement park; he also announced plans to write his autobiography. The book was delayed while he recorded *Bad*, another collaboration with Quincy Jones that finally appeared in 1987. It produced seven Top 10 singles, among them the title track, which again set fresh standards with its promotional video. The album suffered by comparison with his previous work, however, and even its multi-million sales were deemed disappointing after the phenomenal success of *Thriller*. In musical terms, *Bad* certainly broke no fresh ground; appealing though its soft funk confections were, they lacked substance, and represented only a cosmetic advance over his two earlier albums with Jones. Unabashed, Jackson continued to work in large scale. He undertook a lengthy world concert tour to promote *Bad*, utilizing stunning visual effects to capture the atmosphere of his videos. At the same time, he published his autobiography, *Moonwalker*, which offered little personal or artistic insight; neither did the alarmingly expensive feature film that accompanied it, and which buttressed his otherworldly image. The long-awaited *Dangerous* arrived at the end of 1991 and justifiably scaled the charts. This was a *tour de force* of gutsy techno pop, with Teddy Riley contributing to a number of tracks. Although the customarily sweet pop was sharpened to a hard point, it still displayed the unmistakable Jackson sound. By maintaining a leisurely working schedule, Jackson had guaranteed that every new project was accompanied by frenzied public anticipation.

Until 1992, his refusal to undergo probing interviews had allowed the media to portray him as a fantasy figure, a hypochondriac who lived a twilight existence cut off from the rest of humanity. He attempted to dispel this image, and succeeded to a degree, with a carefully rehearsed interview with US chat show host Oprah Winfrey in 1992. The televised programme was shown all over world, during which viewers saw his personal funfair in the back garden, and watched as Jackson spoke of his domineering father. However, the unthinkable happened in 1993, just as Jackson's clean image was at its peak. Allegations of sexual abuse were made by one of Jackson's young friends and the media had a riotous time. Jackson's home was raided by police while he was on tour in the Far East and the artist, clearly disturbed, cancelled a number of performances due to dehydration. No charges were made, and things began to quieten down until November 1993, when Jackson left the USA and went into hiding. Additionally, he confessed to being addicted to painkillers and was seeking treatment. After this admission, Jackson's long-time sponsors Pepsi-Cola decided to pull out of their contract with the now damaged career of the world's most popular superstar. The media were handed more bait when he married Lisa Marie Presley on 26 May 1994, perhaps in an attempt to rebuild his image. The marriage collapsed nineteen months later, giving further rise to allegations that it was merely a set-up to improve his soiled image. He did, however, enhance his reputation with *HIStory Past, Present And Future, Book 1*. One half of the double set chronicled his past hits, but there was the equivalent of a new album forming the second half. Lyrically, the new material was strong, and Jackson very cleverly gave himself a forum to respond to his critics. Although not breaking any new ground musically, the sound was refreshingly varied and, as ever, highly polished. The downside of this return was a sickening display of self-aggrandizement at the 1996 BRIT Awards. Controversy surrounded Jarvis Cocker (of Pulp), who invaded the stage in protest while Jackson, dressed in Messiah-white, was surrounded by, among others, worshipping children and a rabbi. *Blood On The Dancefloor - HIStory In The Mix* was a collection of remixes and new material that spawned further hit singles. It appeared that, despite the allegations of child abuse and the constant media attacks, particularly surrounding his unexpected second marriage and the birth of his child, Jackson's fans remained loyal to the 'King of Pop'.

● ALBUMS: *Got To Be There* (Motown 1971)★★★, *Ben* (Motown 1972)★★★, *Music And Me* (Motown 1973)★★★, *Forever, Michael* (Motown 1975)★★★, *Off The Wall* (Epic 1979)★★★★, *One Day In Your Life* (Motown 1981)★★★, *Thriller* (Epic 1982)★★★★★, *ET - The Extra Terrestrial* (MCA 1983)★★, *Farewell My Summer Love* 1973 recording (Motown 1984)★★★, *Looking Back To Yesterday* (Motown 1986)★★★, *Bad* (Epic 1987)★★★, *Dangerous* (Epic 1991)★★★, *HIStory Past, Present & Future, Book 1* (Epic 1995)★★★★, *Blood On The Dance Floor - HIStory In The Mix* (Epic 1997)★★★.

● COMPILATIONS: *The Best Of Michael Jackson* (Motown 1975)★★★, *Michael Jackson 9 Single Pack* (Epic 1983)★★★, *The Michael Jackson Mix* (Stylus 1987)★★★, *Souvenir Singles Pack* (1988)★★★, *Anthology* (Motown 1993)★★★★, *Ghosts* (Epic 1998)★★★.

● VIDEOS: *The Making Of Thriller* (Vestron Music Video 1986), *The Legend Continues* (Video Collection 1988), *Moonwalker* (1992), *Dangerous - The Short Films* (1994), *HIStory Past, Present & Future, Book 1* (1995).

● FURTHER READING: *Michael Jackson*, Stewart Regan. *The Magic Of Michael Jackson*, No editor listed. *Michael Jackson*, Doug Magee. *The Michael Jackson Story*, Nelson George. *Michael In Concert*, Phyl Garland. *Michael Jackson: Body And Soul: An Illustrated Biography*, Geoff Brown. *Michael!: The Michael Jackson Story*, Mark Bego. *On The Road With Michael Jackson*, Mark Bego. *Sequins & Shades: The Michael Jackson Reference Guide*, Carol D. Terry. *Michael Jackson: Electrifying*, Greg Quill. *Moonwalk*, Michael Jackson, *Michael Jackson: The Magic And The Madness*, J. Randy Taraborrelli. *Michael Jackson: The Man In The Mirror*, Todd Gold. *Sequins And Shades*, Carol D. Terry. *Michael Jackson: The King Of Pop*, Lisa D. Campbell. *Michael Jackson: In His Own Words*, Michael Jackson. *The Visual Documentary*, Adrian Grant. *Michael Jackson Unauthorized*, Christopher Andersen.

JACKSON, MILLIE

b. 15 July 1944, Thompson, Georgia, USA. A former model, Millie Jackson's controversial singing career began professionally in 1964 at a club in Hoboken, New Jersey, USA. Her first recordings followed in 1970; over the next three years she made several excellent, if traditional, soul singles, which included two US R&B Top 10 entries, with 'Ask Me What You Want' and 'My Man A Sweet Man'. 'Hurts So Good', a song from a pseudo-feminist 'blaxploitation' film, *Cleopatra Jones*, was Jackson's biggest hit to date, but her subsequent direction was more fully shaped in 1974 with the release of *Caught Up*. With backing from the Muscle Shoals rhythm section, the tracks included a fiery interpretation of '(If Lovin' You Is Wrong) I Don't Wanna Be Right'. The accompaniment intensified the sexual element in her work as Millie embraced either the pose of adultress or of wronged wife. A further collection, *Still Caught Up*, continued the saga, but Jackson's style later verged on self-parody as she progressed down an increasingly blind alley. The raps became longer and more explicit, and two later albums, *Feelin' Bitchy* and *Live And Uncensored*, required warning stickers for public broadcast. Despite excursions into C&W and a collaboration with Isaac Hayes, Jackson seemed unable to abandon her 'bad mouth' role, exemplified in 80s titles such as 'Sexercise Pts 1 & 2' and 'Slow Tongue (Working Your Way Down)'. Despite her strong cult following, the only occasion on which Jackson has made any significant impact on the UK singles market was in 1985 when duetting with Elton John on 'Act Of War', which reached the Top 40. She possesses one of soul's outstanding voices, yet sadly chooses to limit its obvious potential. Nearly all of Jackson's Spring albums saw CD release in the 90s on UK Ace's Southbound label.

● ALBUMS: *Millie Jackson* (Spring 1972)★★★, *It Hurts So Good* (Spring 1973)★★★, *Caught Up* (Spring 1974)★★★★, *Soul Believer* (Spring 1974)★★★, *Still Caught Up* (Spring 1975)★★★, *Free And In Love* (Spring 1976)★★★, *Lovingly Yours* (Spring 1977)★★★, *Feelin' Bitchy* (Spring 1977)★★★★, *Get It Out 'Cha System* (Spring 1978)★★★, *A Moment's Pleasure* (Spring 1979)★★★, with Isaac Hayes *Royal Rappin's* (Polydor 1979)★★, *Live And Uncensored* (Spring 1979)★★★, *For Men Only* (Spring 1980)★★★, *I Had To Say It* (Spring 1981)★★, *Just A Lil' Bit Country* (1981)★★, *Live And Outrageous* (Spring 1982)★★, *Hard Times* (Spring 1982)★★, *E.S.P. (Extra Sexual Persuasion)* (Sire 1984)★★, *An Imitation Of Love* (Jive 1986)★★★, *The Tide Is Turning* (Jive 1988)★★★, *Back To The Sh.t* (Jive 1989)★★★.

● COMPILATIONS: *Best Of Millie Jackson* (Spring 1976)★★★★, *21 Of The Best* (Southbound/Ace 1994)★★★.

JACKSON, WALTER

b. 19 March 1938, Pensacola, Florida, USA, d. 20 June 1983. Crippled by polio as a child, Jackson spent much of his life on crutches. This disability imbued his work with a greater pathos. Jackson recorded in 1959 as a member of the Velvetones, but his solo career unfolded on signing to the OKeh label. 'It's All Over' (1964), a Curtis Mayfield-penned ballad, was Jackson's first R&B hit. It was followed by exceptional performances such as 'Welcome Home' (1965) and 'It's An Uphill Climb To The Bottom' (1966), both of which reached the soul Top 20. However, the singer's definitive, towering version of 'My Ship is Comin' In' (first recorded by Jimmy Radcliffe and later by the Walker Brothers) sadly failed to chart. Walter later recorded for Cotillion and Brunswick, but between 1973 and 1976 he retired from active performing. Jackson returned with a series of minor hits, including an interpretation of Morris Albert's 'Feelings', but his health was deteriorating. He died of a cerebral haemorrhage in 1983.

● ALBUMS: *It's All Over* (OKeh 1964)★★★, *Welcome Home: The Many Moods Of Walter Jackson* (OKeh 1965)★★★, *Speak Her Name* (OKeh 1967)★★, *Feeling Good* (Chi-Sound 1976)★★★, *I Want To Come Back As A Song* (Chi-Sound 1977)★★, *Good To See You* (Chi-Sound 1978)★★, *Send In The Clowns* (1979)★★, *Tell Me Where It Hurts* (1981)★★, *A Portrait Of Walter Jackson* (Bluebird 1984)★★★.

● COMPILATIONS: *Walter Jackson's Greatest Hits* compiles 12 of his OKeh recordings (Epic 1987)★★★.

JACKSONS

Jackie (b. Sigmund Esco Jackson, 4 May 1951, Gary, Indiana, USA), Tito (b. Toriano Adaryll Jackson, 15 October 1953, Gary), Marlon (b. Marlon David Jackson, 12 March 1957, Gary), Michael (b. Michael Joseph Jackson, 29 August 1958, Gary) and Randy Jackson (b. Steven Randall Jackson, 29 October 1962, Gary) changed their collective name from the Jackson Five to the Jacksons in March 1976, following their departure from Motown Records. At the same time, Randy Jackson replaced his brother Jermaine, handling percussion and backing vocals. The group's new recording contract with Epic offered them a more lucrative agreement than they had enjoyed with Motown, although at first they seemed to have exchanged one artistic strait-jacket for another. Their initial releases were written, arranged and produced by Gamble And Huff, whose expertise ensured that the Jacksons sounded professional, but slightly anonymous. 'Enjoy Yourself' and 'Show You The Way To Go' were both major hits in the US charts, and the latter also topped the UK sales listing. The group's second album with Gamble And Huff, *Goin' Places*, heralded a definite decline in popularity. *Destiny* saw the Jacksons reassert control over writing and production, and produced a string of worldwide hit singles. 'Blame It on The Boogie' caught the mood of the burgeoning disco market, while the group's self-composed 'Shake Your Body (Down To The Ground)' signalled Michael Jackson's growing artistic maturity. The success of Michael's first adult solo venture, *Off The Wall* in 1979, switched his attention away from the group. On *Triumph*, they merely repeated the glories of their previous album, although the commercial appeal of anything bearing Michael's voice helped singles such as 'Can You Feel It?', 'Heartbreak Hotel' and 'Lovely One' achieve success on both sides of the Atlantic. The Jacksons' 1981 US tour emphasized Michael's dominance over the group, and the resulting *Live* included many of his solo hits alongside the brothers' joint repertoire. Between 1981 and the release of *Victory* in 1984, Michael issued *Thriller*, until recently the bestselling album of all time. When the Jacksons' own effort was released, it became apparent that he had made only token contributions to the record, and its commercial fortune suffered accordingly. 'State Of Shock', which paired Michael with Mick Jagger, was a US hit, but sold in smaller quantities than expected. Hysteria surrounded the group's 'Victory Tour' in the summer of 1984; adverse press comment greeted the distribution of tickets, and the Jacksons were accused of pricing themselves out of the reach of their black fans. Although they were joined onstage by their brother Jermaine for the first time since 1975, media and public attention was focused firmly on Michael. Realizing that they were becoming increasingly irrelevant, the other members of the group began to voice their grievances in the press; as a result, Michael Jackson stated that he would not be working with his brothers in the future. The Jacksons struggled to come to terms with his departure, and it was five years before their next project was complete. *2300 Jackson Street* highlighted their dilemma: once the media realized that Michael was not involved, they effectively boycotted its release. Randy Jackson was sentenced to a one-month jail sentence in November 1990 for assaulting his wife. In 1992, ABC aired the five-hour mini-series *The Jacksons: An American Dream*.

● ALBUMS: *The Jacksons* (Epic 1976)★★★, *Goin' Places* (Epic 1977)★★★, *Destiny* (Epic 1978)★★★★, *Triumph* (Epic 1980)★★★, *The Jacksons Live* (Epic 1981)★★★, *Victory* (Epic 1984)★★★, *2300 Jackson Street* (Epic 1989)★★.

JAGUARS

An R&B vocal group from Los Angeles, California, USA. The Jaguars were one of the few Los Angeles groups that could sing standards in the spirit and style of pop music, but added a hard rock 'n' roll edge. The members of this black-white-Hispanic group were Sonny Chaney (lead), Val Poliuto (tenor), Manual Chavez (baritone) and Charles Middleton (bass). The group began recording for a small label in Los Angeles in 1955, and the following year found success with a doo-wop remake of the Jerome Kern standard 'The Way You Look Tonight'. The group lost Middleton in 1958, and the following year the remaining three, with freelance vocalists Tony Allen and Richard Berry, recorded as the Velvetones. The record was not a success and the group disbanded. Chavez and Chaney went on to record as a duo.

● COMPILATIONS: *The Way You Look Tonight* (Earth Angel 1988)★★★.

JAI

b. Jason Roe, *c*.1973, Yeovil, Somerset, England. A contemporary pop singer-songwriter, Jai's first musical experience came as part of a Somerset band that featured PJ Harvey collaborators Rob Ellis and Steve Vaughan. He signed to the M&G subsidiary label Wired Recordings in 1995. Despite a high media profile, including appearances on the *National Lottery Live* and features in both mainstream and teenage pop magazines, his first two singles, 'I Believe' and 'Don't Give Me Away', flopped. In truth, his record company were struggling to find the correct marketing formula for a young singer with a mature, soulful voice. After first targeting a younger pop audience, M&G attempted to build his profile on the club circuit by employing remixers including the Psychonauts, Carl Mackintosh and UNKLE. He also toured in support of Olive and Gabrielle, in an attempt to broaden his audience. As he told *Music Week* in 1997, 'I was uncomfortable with being promoted as a pop act. I understand it though, because I'm not doing anything majorly leftfield.' Despite minimal sales returns on his early recordings, his management decided to launch him in America, where his soul-based style was not restricted to such a niche audience. His blend of classic and contemporary soul (his influences include Marvin Gaye, Stevie Wonder and Soul II Soul) and the use of real instruments had by now earned him comparisons to David McAlmont. His debut album, *Heaven*, was co-written by producer Joel Bogen, who provided a series of sumptuous arrangements as a backdrop to Jai's arresting falsetto. The only cover version was a contemporary interpretation of the Arthur Hamilton standard, 'Cry Me A River'.

● ALBUMS: *Heaven* (Wired Recordings 1997)★★★.

JAMES, COLIN, AND THE LITTLE BIG BAND

b. Colin James Munn, 1964, Regina, Saskatchewan, Canada. The son of Quaker parents, James's first musical love was folk, but by his early teens he had developed a keen interest in the blues. His school work suffered as he proceeded to master blues guitar, and upon leaving school at the age of 16, he moved to Winnipeg and formed the HooDoo Men. In 1983 James befriended Stevie Ray Vaughan who became a mentor to the young Canadian. Having impressed a Virgin Records executive by literally dancing on his table at a gig, he was signed and released *Colin James* in 1988. His band at this time comprised John Ferreira (saxophone), Dennis Marenko (bass), Rick Hopkins (keyboards) and Darrel Mayes (drums). The debut, although competent, did not fully convey the excitement of his live gigs. Much more satisfying and gutsy was *Sudden Stop*, with a sound undoubtedly aided by Z.Z. Top's producer Joe Hardy. 'Just Came Back' from the album became a major hit in Canada and he duetted with Bonnie Raitt on another track. James gigged solidly for 18 months promoting this successful album and it was not until the end of 1993 that he found enough time to issue a new release. *The Little Big Band* was a powerful and tasteful jump-blues and R&B excursion showcasing great brass and James's fluid guitar style. The line-up included Chuck Leavell on piano and utilized the Roomful Of Blues horn section in addition to the continuing presence of Ferreira on sax. In 1994 he signed to Elektra Records and the following year a much more mainstream rock album, *Bad Habits*, was released.

● ALBUMS: *Colin James* (Virgin 1988)★★★, *Sudden Stop* (Virgin 1990)★★★, *Colin James And The Little Big Band* (Pointblank 1993)★★★, *Bad Habits* (Elektra 1995)★★.

JAMES, ETTA

b. Jamesetta Hawkins, 25 January 1938, Los Angeles, California, USA. James's introduction to performing followed an impromptu audition for Johnny Otis backstage at San Francisco's Fillmore Auditorium. 'Roll With Me Henry', her 'answer' to the Hank Ballard hit 'Work With Me Annie', was retitled 'The Wallflower' in an effort to disguise its risqué lyric and became an R&B number 1. 'Good Rockin' Daddy' provided another hit, but the singer's later releases failed to chart. Having secured a contract with the Chess group of labels, James, also known as Miss Peaches, unleashed a series of powerful songs, including 'All I Could Do Was Cry' (1960), 'At Last' (1961), 'Trust In Me' (1961), 'Don't Cry Baby' (1961), 'Something's Got A Hold On Me' (1962), 'Stop The Wedding' (1962) and 'Pushover' (1963). She also recorded several duets with Harvey Fuqua. Heroin addiction sadly blighted both her personal and professional life, but in 1967 Chess took her to the Fame studios. The resultant *Tell Mama* was a triumph, and pitted James's abrasive voice with the exemplary Muscle Shoals house band. Its highlights included the proclamatory title track, a pounding version of Otis Redding's 'Security' (both of which reached the R&B Top 20) and the despairing 'I'd Rather Go Blind', which was later a UK Top 20 hit for Chicken Shack. The 1973 album *Etta James* earned her a US Grammy nomination, despite her continued drug problems, which she did not overcome until the mid-80s. A 1977 album, *Etta Is Betta Than Evah*, completed her Chess contract, and she moved to Warner Brothers. A renewed public profile followed her appearance at the opening ceremony of the Los Angeles Olympics in 1984. *Deep In The Night* was a critics' favourite. The live *Late Show* albums, released in 1986, featured Shuggie Otis and Eddie 'Cleanhead' Vinson, and were followed by *Seven Year Itch*, her first album for Island Records, in 1989. This, and the subsequent release, *Stickin' To My Guns*, found her back on form, aided and abetted once more by the Muscle Shoals team. She was inducted into the Rock And Roll Hall Of Fame in 1993. Her ability to take and shape a song demonstrates the depth of her great ability to 'feel' the essence of the lyric and melody. All her cover versions, from 'Need Your Love So Bad' to 'The Night Time Is The Right Time', are given her indelible stamp. Following the use in a television advertisement of her version of Muddy Waters' 'I Just Want To Make Love To You', she unexpectedly found herself near the top of the UK charts in 1996. She is both emotional and 'foxy', yet still remains painfully underexposed; this hit may open the door to her extraordinary voice, which was showcased to great effect on 1997's *Love's Been Rough On Me*.

● ALBUMS: *Miss Etta James* (Crown 1961)★★★★, *At*

Last! (Argo 1961)★★★★, *Second Time Around* (Argo 1961)★★★★, *Twist With Etta James* (Crown 1962)★★★★, *Etta James* (Argo 1962)★★★★, *Etta James Sings For Lovers* (Argo 1962)★★★★, *Etta James Top Ten* (Argo 1963)★★★, *Etta James Rocks The House* (Argo 1964)★★★, *The Queen Of Soul* (Argo 1965)★★★★, *Call My Name* (Cadet 1967)★★★, *Tell Mama* (Cadet 1968)★★★★★, *Etta James Sings Funk* (Cadet 1970)★★★, *Losers Weepers* (Cadet 1971)★★★, *Etta James* (Chess 1973)★★★, *Come A Little Closer* (Chess 1974)★★★, *Etta Is Betta Than Evah!* (Chess 1977)★★★, *Deep In The Night* (Warners 1978)★★★★, *Changes* (MCA 1980)★★★, *Red, Hot And Live* (1982)★★★, *The Heart And Soul Of* (1982)★★★, with Eddie 'Cleanhead' Vinson *Blues In The Night: The Early Show* (Fantasy 1986)★★★, *Blues In The Night: The Late Show* (Fantasy 1986)★★★, *Seven Year Itch* (Island 1989)★★★, *Stickin' To My Guns* (Island 1990)★★★★, *Something's Gotta Hold On Me (Etta James Vol. 2)* (Roots 1992)★★★, *The Right Time* (Elektra 1992)★★★, *Mystery Lady: Songs Of Billie Holiday* (Private Music 1994)★★★, *Love's Been Rough On Me* (Private Music 1997)★★★.

● COMPILATIONS: *The Best Of ...* (Crown 1962)★★★★, *The Soul Of Etta James* (Ember 1968)★★★★, *Golden Decade* (Chess 1972)★★★★, *Peaches* (Chess 1973)★★★★, *Good Rockin' Mama* (Ace 1981)★★★★, *Chess Masters* (Chess 1981)★★★, *Tuff Lover* (Ace 1983)★★★★, *Juicy Peaches* (Chess 1985)★★★, *R&B Queen* (Crown 1986)★★★, *Her Greatest Sides, Volume One* (Chess/MCA 1987)★★★★, *R&B Dynamite* (Ace 1987)★★★★, *Rocks The House* (Charly 1987)★★★, *The Sweetest Peaches: The Chess Years, Volume 1 (1960-1966)* (Chess/MCA 1988)★★★★, *The Sweetest Peaches: The Chess Years, Volume 2 (1967-1975)* (Chess/MCA 1988)★★★★, *Tell Mama* (1988)★★★★, *Chicago Golden Years* (Vogue 1988)★★★, *Come A Little Closer* (Charly 1988)★★★, *Juicy Peaches* (Charly 1989)★★★★, *The Gospel Soul Of Etta James* (AJK 1990)★★★, *Legendary Hits* (Jazz Archives 1992)★★★, *Back In The Blues* (Zillion 1992)★★★, *The Soulful Miss Peaches* (Charly 1993)★★★★, *I'd Rather Go Blind - The World Of Etta James* (Trace 1993)★★★, *Something's Got A Hold* (Charly 1994)★★★, *Blues In The Night, The Early Show* (Fantasy 1994)★★★, *Blues In The Night, The Late Show* (Fantasy 1994)★★★, *Miss Peaches Sings The Soul* (That's Soul 1994)★★★, *Live From San Francisco '81* (Private Music 1994)★★★, *The Genuine Article: The Best Of* (MCA/Chess 1996)★★★★.

● VIDEOS: *Live At Montreux* (Island Visual Arts 1990), *Live At Montreux: Etta James* (Polygram Music Video 1992).

● FURTHER READING: *Rage To Survive*, Etta James with David Ritz.

JAMES, JIMMY, AND THE VAGABONDS

Jimmy James (b. September 1940, Jamaica), enjoyed local success with two self-composed singles, 'Bewildered And Blue' and 'Come Softly To Me', before arriving in England in 1964. He joined the multiracial Vagabonds - Wallace Wilson (lead guitar), Carl Noel (organ), Matt Fredericks (tenor saxophone), Milton James (baritone saxophone), Phillip Chen (bass), Rupert Balgobin (drums) and Count Prince Miller (vocals/MC) - and the new unit became a leading attraction at UK soul venues during the 60s. The group was managed and produced by the early Who mentor Peter Meaden. Although they failed to secure a substantial chart hit, the Vagabonds' early albums were impressive, infectious reinterpretations of contemporary releases, featuring material by the Impressions, the Miracles and Bobby Bland. Such a function, however enthusiastic, lost its impetus when the original artists gained popular acclaim. 'Red Red Wine' gave the group a belated, if minor, success in 1968, but the unit was latterly dubbed *passé*. Chen later enjoyed a fruitful association with Rod Stewart, while James enjoyed two hits in 1976 alongside another set of Vagabonds with 'I'll Go Where The Music Takes Me' and 'Now Is The Time', the latter of which reached the UK Top 5. The singer has since pursued a career as a cabaret attraction.

● ALBUMS: *The New Religion* (1966)★★★, *Open Up Your Soul* (1968)★★★, one side only *London Swings* (1968), *You Don't Stand A Chance If You Can't Dance* (Pye 1975)★★, *Now* (Pye 1976)★★, *Life* (Pye 1977)★★, *Dancin' Till Dawn* (PRT 1979)★★.

● COMPILATIONS: *This Is Jimmy James* (1968)★★★, *Golden Hour Of Jimmy James* (Golden Hour 1979)★★.

JAMES, RICK

b. James Johnson, 1 February 1948, Buffalo, New York, USA. The nephew of Temptations vocalist Melvin Franklin, James pioneered a crossover style between R&B and rock in the mid-60s. In 1965, he formed the Mynah Birds in New York with two future members of the Buffalo Springfield, Neil Young and Bruce Palmer, plus Goldie McJohn, later with Steppenwolf. Motown Records signed the band as a riposte to the British wave of R&B artists then dominating the charts, before their career was aborted when James was arrested for draft evasion. Resuming his career in Britain in the early 70s, James formed the funk combo Main Line. Returning to the USA, he assembled a like-minded group of musicians to perform a dense, brash brand of funk, influenced by Sly Stone and George Clinton. Signed to Motown in 1977, initially as a songwriter, he rapidly evolved a more individual style, which he labelled 'punk funk'. His first single, 'You And I', typified his approach, with its prominent bass riffs, heavy percussion, and sly, streetwise vocals. The record reached the US Top 20 and topped the specialist soul charts - a feat that its follow-up, 'Mary Jane', came close to repeating, though the song's blatant references to marijuana cut short any hopes of radio airplay. James chose to present himself as a social outlaw, with outspoken views on drugs and sex. In a move subsequently echoed by Prince, he amassed a stable of artists under his control at Motown, using the Stone City Band as his backing group, and the Mary Jane Girls as female pawns in his macho master-plan. James also produced records by actor Eddie Murphy, vocalist Teena Marie, Val Young, and Process and the Doo-Rags. His own recordings, predominantly in the funk vein, continued to corner the disco market, with 'Give It To Me Baby' and

'Super Freak', on which he was joined by the Temptations, achieving notable sales in 1981. Both tracks came from *Street Songs*, a Grammy-nominated record that catapulted James into the superstar bracket. Secure in his commercial standing, he revealed that he preferred recording ballads to the funk workouts that had made his name, and his drift towards a more conservative image was heightened when he duetted with Smokey Robinson on the hit single 'Ebony Eyes', and masterminded the Temptations' reunion project in 1983. James's flamboyant lifestyle took its toll on his health and he was hospitalized several times between 1979 and 1984. His career continued unabated, and he had major hits in 1984 and 1985 with the more relaxed '17' and 'The Glow'. The latter also provided the title for a highly acclaimed album, which reflected James's decision to abandon the use of drugs, and move towards a more laid-back soul style. He was angered by constant media comparisons of his work with that of Prince, and cancelled plans to star in an autobiographical film called *The Spice Of Life* in the wake of the overwhelming commercial impact of his rival's *Purple Rain*. After releasing *The Flag* in 1986, James ran into serious conflict with Motown over the status of his spin-off acts. When they refused to release any further albums by the Mary Jane Girls, James left the label, signing to Reprise Records, where he immediately achieved a soul number 1 with 'Loosey's Rap', a collaboration with Roxanne Shante. James's drug problems had not disappeared and following years of abuse he was jailed in 1991, together with his girlfriend Tanya Hijazi, for various offences including dealing cocaine, assault and torture. The King Of Funk confessed to *Rolling Stone* that at least by being in prison he 'could not do drugs'. He was released in 1996.

● ALBUMS: *Come Get It!* (Gordy 1978)★★★, *Bustin' Out Of L Seven* (Gordy 1979)★★★, *Fire It Up* (Gordy 1979)★★★, *In 'n' Out* (Gordy 1980)★★, *Garden Of Love* (Gordy 1980)★★, *Street Songs* (Gordy 1981)★★★★, *Throwin' Down* (Gordy 1982)★★★, *Cold Blooded* (Gordy 1983)★★, *Glow* (Gordy 1985)★★, *The Flag* (Gordy 1986)★★, *Wonderful* (Reprise 1988)★★.

● COMPILATIONS: *Reflections: All The Great Hits* (Gordy 1984)★★★★, *Greatest Hits* (Motown 1993)★★★, *Bustin' Out: The Best Of Rick James* (Motown 1994)★★★, *Greatest Hits* (Spectrum 1996)★★★.

JAMIROQUAI

Jason 'Jay' Kay's UK funk group Jamiroquai (named after the Iroquois tribe whose pantheism inspired him) made a rapid impact - they were signed to Sony Records for an eight-album contract on the strength of just one single for Acid Jazz Records - 'When You Gonna Learn?'. Kay (b. *c.*1969, London, England) was brought up in Ealing, London, England, by his jazz-singer mother, Karen Kay. Inspired by Sly Stone, Gil Scott-Heron and Roy Ayers, he integrated those influences into a 90s pop format that also combined 'new age' mysticism and the growing urban funk movement, which took its name from the Acid Jazz label. However, as a former breakdancer, he had already recorded in a hip-hop style, releasing a single with a sampler and drum machine for Morgan Khan's Streetsounds label in 1986. His first major label single, 'Too Young To Die', immediately broke into the UK Top 10, while the debut album entered the chart at number 1 (it has since gone on to worldwide sales of over two million). However, a press backlash soon followed, not helped by Kay's naïve statements about the environment after he had blown his advance on petrol-guzzling cars. Despite the healthy sales, his case was not helped by a less than spectacular debut album, which came with an order form for his own brand clothing (seven per cent of profits going to Greenpeace), although there were strong compositions such as 'If I Like It, I Do It'. The second album was a considerable improvement, with the previous emphasis on his media relations now switched to his music. Songs such as 'Kids', 'Return' and 'Morning Glory' gave his obvious vocal talents better service, adding ghetto hip-hop rhythms to the previous acid jazz and funk backdrops. *Travelling Without Moving* confirmed Jamiroquai as a highly commercial act, selling to date over five and a half million copies worldwide, and winning four trophies at the 1997 MTV Awards.

● ALBUMS: *Emergency On Planet Earth* (Sony 1993)★★★, *The Return Of The Space Cowboy* (Sony 1994)★★★★, *Travelling Without Moving* (Sony 1996)★★★★.

JARMELS

One of the era's many 'one-hit wonders', the Jarmels were formed in Richmond, Virginia, USA, by Nathaniel Ruff (b. 1939), Ray Smith (b. 1941), Paul Burnett (b. 1942), Earl Christian (b. 1940) and Tom Eldridge (b. 1941). They scored a major chart entry in 1961 with 'A Little Bit Of Soap', a song that retained an enduring appeal when composer Bert Berns recorded further versions with the Exciters and deep soul singer Garnet Mimms. British rock 'n' roll revivalists Showaddywaddy later took this favoured composition into the UK Top 5 in 1978. Despite appearances to the contrary, the Jarmels continued to record, although they were never able to recapture that early success. A later version of the group featured singer Major Harris, who subsequently joined the Delfonics prior to launching his solo career.

● COMPILATIONS: *The Complete Jarmels* (Ace 1986)★★★.

JARREAU, AL

b. 12 March 1940, Milwaukee, Wisconsin, USA. Although Jarreau sang from childhood, it was many years before he decided to make singing his full-time occupation. Working outside music for most of the 60s, he began to sing in small west coast clubs and eventually achieved enough success to change careers. By the mid-70s he was becoming well known in the USA, and, via records and a European tour, greatly extended his audience. Singing a highly sophisticated form of vocalese, Jarreau's style displays many influences. Some of these come from within the world of jazz, notably the work of Jon Hendricks, while others are external. He customarily uses vocal sounds that include the clicks of African song and the plosives common in oriental speech and singing patterns. This range of influences makes him both hard to classify and more accessible to the wider audience for crossover music. More commercially successful than most jazz singers, Jarreau's work in the 70s and 80s consistently appealed to young audiences attuned to fusions in popular music. By the early 90s, when he was entering his 50s, his kinship with youth culture was clearly diminishing, but his reputation was by this time firmly established.

● ALBUMS: *1965* (1965)★★, *We Got By* (Reprise 1975)★★★, *Glow* (Reprise 1976)★★, *Look To The Rainbow: Live In Europe* (Warners 1977)★★, *All Fly Home* (Warners 1978)★★, *This Time* (Warners 1980)★★★, *Breakin' Away* (Warners 1981)★★★, *Jarreau* (Warners 1983)★★★, *Spirits And Feelings* (Happy Bird 1984)★★★, *Ain't No Sunshine* (Blue Moon 1984)★★★, *High Crime* (Warners 1984)★★, *Al Jarreau In London* (Warners 1984)★★, *You* (Platinum 1985)★★★, *L Is For Lover* (Warners 1986)★★★, *Hearts Horizon* (Reprise 1988)★★★, *Manifesto* (Masters 1988)★★★, *Heaven And Earth* (Reprise 1992)★★★, *Tenderness* (Warners 1994)★★★.

● FILMS: *Breakdance - The Movie* (1984).

JAYHAWKS

The R&B novelty song 'Stranded In The Jungle' was a hit in 1956 for two US groups. The Cadets' version remains the best-known (although the New York Dolls' 70s cover version is also highly regarded by some), but the Jayhawks actually beat them to the US charts by one week. The doo-wop quartet consisted of lead Jimmy Johnson, baritone Dave Govan, tenor Carl Fisher and bass Carver Bunkum. They formed while in high school in Los Angeles, USA, in the early 50s. 'Stranded In The Jungle' was co-written by Johnson and friend Ernest Smith. It reached number 18 while the Cadets' cover version landed three positions higher. Subsequent records by the group failed and by 1960, with a few personnel changes, they had metamorphosed into the Vibrations, who had success with the dance hit 'The Watusi' (1961) and 'My Girl Sloopy' (1964), the latter adapted by the McCoys as 'Hang On Sloopy'. The Vibrations also moonlighted in 1961 as the Marathons, another one-hit-wonder with the novelty tune 'Peanut Butter'.

JAZZIE B.

b. Beresford Romeo, 26 January 1963, London, England. The larger-than-life svengali Jazzie B. began his musical apprenticeship on the London sound system circuit before helming the enormous international success of Soul II Soul. As such, Jazzie B. is widely credited with having pioneered a renaissance in British soul music in the late 80s - certainly his group were the first of their generation to make a serious impact on the US R&B charts. By the advent of Soul II Soul's fifth album, Jazzie B. had signed a new contract with Island Records' subsidiary 4th And Broadway, following six successful years with Virgin Records. Island also provided a home for his record label, production and publishing company, Soul II Soul Records, and an artist roster including Yorker, Backroom, the Funki Dreds and EFUA. Although his publishing agreement with EMI Publishing for the Jazzie B. Music, Soul II Soul and Mad Music catalogues also expired in 1996, his music remained omnipresent in the UK media, including advertisements for Renault and Levi's. Indeed, his only significant setback has been the clothes stores opened in the late 80s under the Soul II Soul banner, which have since closed. While waiting to conclude record company business and begin work on the new Soul II Soul album, Jazzie B. continued to occupy himself by running his studio complex in Camden, north London.

JESSIE, OBIE DONMELL 'YOUNG'

b. 28 December 1936, Dallas, Texas, USA. Inspired by Roy Brown and Joe Williams, Young Jessie teamed up with fellow Jefferson High School alumni - Johnny Watson, Richard Berry and Cornell Gunter - in the early 50s to set up a vocal group. In 1953, the Debonaires were signed to the Bihari's Flair label and rechristened the Flairs. During 1954-55, Jessie began carving out a solo career on Modern Records, with whom he had his biggest hit, 'Mary Lou' in 1955. The song was later covered successfully by Ronnie Hawkins on Roulette. At Modern, Jessie also recorded a classic of black rock 'n' roll, 'Hit Git & Split' before moving on to a brief spell with the Coasters and resuming his solo career on Atlantic/Atco (1957), Capitol (1959), Mercury (1961), Vanessa (1962) and Bit (1964). In the early 70s Jessie sang with the group Seeds Of Freedom and toured Europe the following decade as both an R&B performer and a jazz singer. He currently lives with his wife, singer Barbara Prince, near Venice Beach.

● COMPILATIONS: *Hit Git & Split* (Ace 1982)★★★, *Shuffle In The Gravel* (Mr R&B 1986)★★★, *Shufflin' & Jivin'* (Ace 1987)★★★.

JESTERS

The Jesters were representative of the classic New York style of doo-wop characterized as 'greasy', in which the vocal harmony was in a rock 'n' roll style, extremely expressive, loaded with exotic flourishes, and usually supporting a falsetto lead. The members of the Jesters were Lenny McKay (lead), Adam Jackson (d. 21 February 1995; lead), Anthony 'Jimmy' Smith (second tenor), Leo Vincent (baritone) and Noel Grant (bass). The group came together in 1955, and was signed by Paul Winley for his Winley label in 1957. They were regularly teamed with another local group, the Paragons, in live mock-competitions. Their first release, 'So Strange'/'Love No One But You', was a double-sided hit in the New York area in the summer of 1957. In the autumn they hit again locally with 'Please Let Me Love You'. 'The Plea', a remake of the Chantels' hit, made it to number 74 of the *Billboard* pop chart in 1958, but, like the other records, it mainly sold in New York. 'I Laughed'/'Now That You're Gone' from the summer of 1958 was the last record to feature the original group. In 1960 a new line-up of Jackson, Smith, Melvin Lewis and Don Lewis recorded the Jesters' most successful song, 'The Wind', a remake of the 1954 Diablos hit.

● COMPILATIONS: *The Paragons Meet The Jesters* (Jubilee 1959)★★★, *The Paragons Meet The Jesters* (Collectables 1990)★★★, *'War': The Paragons Vs The*

Jesters (Sting Music Ltd. 1993)★★★, *The Best Of The Jesters* (Collectables 1993)★★★.

JEWELS

Formed in 1961 as the Impalas, this Washington, DC, USA-based all-female quartet was comprised of Carrie Mingo, Sandra Bears, Grace Ruffin and Margie Clark. As the Impalas, they came under the wing of Bo Diddley, who recorded the group in his personal studio and played guitar on their debut single, 'I Need You So Much'. Diddley secured a recording contract with Chess Records, but nothing emerged. They were then taken on by manager/producer Bob Lee, who changed their name to the Four Jewels in 1962. They issued five tracks on Start and then others for Chess, as well as background vocals for Billy Stewart, Ruffin's cousin. By 1964, having released another failed single on Tec Records, Mingo left, and was replaced by Martha Harvin. The group shortened its name to the Jewels and recorded a song called 'Opportunity' for Carole King's Dimension label. The record reached number 64 in 1964 and was their only charting release. In 1965 they joined James Brown's revue for a year. They broke up three years later. In the early 80s Mingo sang and recorded with a neo-doo-wop group, the Velons, who released *Moonlight And Music* on the Sold Smoke label in 1984. A year later, Mingo was reunited with the other Jewels - Bears, Ruffin, and Clark - and played in the Washington area. They released an album of re-recorded songs from their Start and Chess singles, *Loaded With Goodies*.

● ALBUMS: *Loaded With Goodies* (BJM 1985)★★★.

JIMMY JAM AND TERRY LEWIS

Based in Minneapolis, Minnesota, USA, Jimmy 'Jam' Harris and Terry Lewis are prolific producers of contemporary R&B The two first worked together in the early 80s as members of Time (formerly Flyte Time), and subsequently, Harris (keyboards) and Lewis (bass) became black music's most consistently successful production duo. They formed their own record label, Tabu, in 1980, which enjoyed enormous success with artists such as the S.O.S. Band throughout the 80s. Among the other early bands and artists to benefit from the duo's writing and production skills were Change, Cherrelle, the Force MD's, Johnny Gill and the former Time singer Alexander O'Neal. Their greatest success, however, came as the creative catalysts behind Janet Jackson's career. The first album they recorded with her, *Control*, included five hit singles, and the follow-up, *Rhythm Nation 1814*, was similarly successful. In 1990 Jam and Lewis recorded once again with Time, who had re-formed to make *Pandemonium*, which was released on Prince's Paisley Park Records. Though the reunion was not widely regarded as a success, the duo's productions remained in the higher reaches of the charts. Their continued association with Janet Jackson was never surpassed commercially but many others benefited from their expertise, especially with their pioneering work in what would become known as swingbeat, and cross-genre productions with artists ranging from the Human League to Sounds Of Blackness. In the 90s they also established a new record label, Perspective Records, distributed by A&M Records.

JIVE BOMBERS

This New York R&B group was formed in 1948 from elements of two earlier acts, the Tinney Brothers (founded during the mid-30s) and the Palmer Brothers (founded late 20s). The group, recording for Coral as the Sparrows in 1949 and as the Jive Bombers after 1952, were from the same era as the Mills Brothers and Ink Spots. Thus, their age and repertoire of old songs kept them in staid nightclubs during most of their career, and their appearance in the teen rock 'n' roll market was very brief. When the group had a hit with 'Bad Boy' in 1957, the members were Earl Johnson (b. 30 November 1932, New York City, New York, USA; tenor vocals), Al Tinney (b. 28 May 1929, Ansonia, Connecticut, USA; piano), William 'Pee Wee' Tinney (b. 25 September 1930, New York City, New York, USA; drums, guitar) and Clarence Palmer (b. 2 January 1919, Pawtucket, Rhode Island, USA; bass fiddle). 'Bad Boy' went to number 7 on the R&B chart and number 36 on the pop chart. It was written and recorded by Lillian Armstrong as 'Brown Gal' in 1936, and had been recorded by the Jive Bombers twice before, in 1949 and 1952, as 'Brown Boy'. The Jive Bombers failed to reach the charts again, despite recording excellent material such as a remake of Don Redman's 'Cherry'. Although Palmer left in 1959, the Jive Bombers stayed together until 1968.

● ALBUMS: *Bad Boy* (Savoy Jazz 1984)★★★★

JIVE FIVE

From Brooklyn, New York City, New York, USA, the Jive Five were one of the last doo-wop groups to have a national hit and one of the few to make a successful transition to the soul era. The group members were Eugene Pitt (b. 6 November 1937; lead), Jerome Hanna (first tenor), Richard Harris (second tenor), Billy Prophet (baritone) and Norman Johnson (d. 1970; bass). Their biggest hit was 'My True Story' (number 1 R&B, number 3 pop) from 1961, which was something of a neo-doo-wop sound. A particularly outstanding feature of the group's approach was the counterpointing exchanges between lead Pitt and bass Johnson. Continuing with the same sound, the group had lesser hits during the next two years with 'Never Never' (number 74 pop), 'What Time Is It' (number 67 pop) and 'These Golden Rings' (number 27 R&B). By 1964 the group had developed a soul sound and had joined United Artists Records. At this point Pitt and Johnson were supported by new members Casey Spencer (second tenor), Beatrice Best (baritone), and Webster Harris (first tenor). The group found success in 1965 with 'I'm A Happy Man' (number 26 R&B, number 36 pop), and followed with 'A Bench In The Park', which received good airplay in Washington, DC, but nowhere else. The group left United Artists in 1966, and their last chart record was in 1970, for Decca. In the 80s Eugene Pitt And The Jive Five made two fine albums for Ambient Sound, who were unable to break the group out of the limited audience for doo-wop harmony.

● ALBUMS: *The Jive Five* (United Artists 1965)★★★,

Here We Are (Ambient Sound 1982)★★★, *Way Back* (Ambient Sound 1985)★★★.
● COMPILATIONS: *Our True Story* Beltone recordings (Ace 1991)★★★, *My True Story* Beltone recordings (Relic 1991)★★★, *The Complete United Artists Recordings: I'm A Happy Man* (1992)★★★.

Jodeci

Among the more eloquent practitioners of New Jack Swing or swingbeat, Jodeci have enjoyed more success in the USA in the genre during the 90s than any other act, with the possible exceptions of R. Kelly and Bobby Brown. The group consists of two pairs of brothers: Joel 'JoJo' and Gedric 'K-Ci' Hailey, and 'Mr' Dalvin and Donald 'DeVante Swing' DeGrate Jnr. The latter is also responsible for most of the group's writing and production. They began their musical career by harmonizing in their local Tiny Grove, North Carolina church services. They signed to prominent swingbeat stable Uptown Records in 1991, and the initial results were impressive. Their silky, soulful vocals were stretched over sparse hip-hop beats to produce a debut album that was at once tough and elegant. It sold two million copies and earned Jodeci numerous accolades. *Diary Of A Mad Band*, much in the vein of their debut, also went multi-platinum, and earned the group an appearance on MTV's *Unplugged* showcase - a rare recognition afforded a band working in their territory. For 1995's third album the group slightly altered their musical backdrop, adopting the G-Funk beats made prevalent by Dr Dre and his various acolytes. However, this softer, more resonant sound was once again subordinate to the group's dynamic sense of harmony. They featured on 2 Pac's (Tupac Shakur) number 1 single 'How Do You Want It' in June 1996.
● ALBUMS: *Forever My Lady* (Uptown/MCA 1991)★★★★, *Diary Of A Mad Band* (Uptown/MCA 1993)★★★, *The Show, The After Party, The Hotel* (Uptown/MCA 1995)★★★, as K-Ci & JoJo *Love Always* (MCA 1997)★★★.

John, Little Willie

b. William Edgar John, 15 November 1937, Cullendale, Arkansas, USA, d. 26 May 1968. The brother of singer Mable John, Willie was one of the most popular 50s R&B performers. His first hit, 'All Around The World', also known as 'Grits Ain't Groceries', was followed by a spectacular double-sided smash, 'Need Your Love So Bad'/'Home At Last' in 1956. The a-side of this successful coupling was later recorded by Fleetwood Mac and Gary Moore. It was followed by 'Fever'/'Letter From My Darling', both sides of which also reached the US R&B Top 10. 'Fever', written by Otis Blackwell (as 'Davenport') and Eddie Cooley, was a million-selling single in its own right, topping that particular chart in May 1956. However, the song is more closely associated with Peggy Lee, who took the song into the US and UK charts in 1958. 'Talk To Me, Talk To Me' gave Little Willie John another gold disc that year, while in 1959 he enjoyed further success with 'Leave My Kitten Alone', a favoured song of British beat groups. The singer's professional career faltered during the 60s while his private life ended in tragedy. Convicted of manslaughter in 1966, John died of a heart attack in Washington State Prison in 1968. He was posthumously inducted into the Rock And Roll Hall Of Fame in 1996.
● ALBUMS: *Fever* (King 1956)★★★★, *Talk To Me* (King 1958)★★★★, *Mister Little Willie John* (King 1958)★★★★, *Action* (King 1960)★★★★, *Sure Things* (King 1961)★★★, *The Sweet, The Hot, The Teen Age Beat* (King 1961)★★★, *Come On And Join* (Ling 1962)★★★, *These Are My Favourite Songs* (King 1964)★★, *Little Willie John Sings All Originals* (King 1966)★★.
● COMPILATIONS: *Free At Last* (King 1970)★★★★, *Grits And Soul* (Charly 1985)★★★★, *Fever* (Charly 1990)★★★★, *Sure Things* (King 1990)★★★, *Fever - The Best Of ...* (1994)★★★★.

John, Mable

b. 3 November 1930, Bastrop, Louisiana, USA. The elder sister of Little Willie John, author of 'Leave My Kitten Alone', Mable John was an early signing to Berry Gordy's Tamla-Motown label. She appeared on the first Motortown Revue in 1959, and recorded four singles for the company. After an interlude working in a small Chicago outlet, Four Brothers, she signed to Stax in 1966. Here Mable specialized in 'deep' ballads, pitting her emotive pleas against a complementary Booker T. And The MGs/Mar-Keys backing. 1966's 'Your Good Thing (Is About To End)', a tale of infidelity and the consequences thereof, which Lou Rawls later took into the pop chart, was the first of seven releases. In 1968 she joined Ray Charles' Raelettes, and ceased performing as a solo artist. Her distinctive voice is nonetheless audible on several of the group's Tangerine recordings. Mable John subsequently worked as an advisor on *Lady Sings The Blues*, Berry Gordy's film biography of Billie Holiday.
● COMPILATIONS: *Stay Out Of The Kitchen* (Stax Sessions 1992)★★★.

Johnnie And Joe

This US R&B duo featured Johnnie Louise Richardson (d. 25 October 1988) and Joe Rivers (b. Charleston, South Carolina, USA). Emerging from the Bronx, New York, USA, they were famed for their sublime doo-wop-flavoured ballads, notably 'Over The Mountain, Across The Sea' (number 3 R&B/number 8 pop, 1957), one of the most memorable and enduring early rock 'n' roll hits. Richardson was the daughter of Zelma 'Zell' Sanders, the owner of J&S Records. Sanders teamed her up with Rivers and one of the great blends of voices was born. Most of the duo's records were leased to the Chicago-based Chess Records, who were able to distribute the records nationally. Other great Johnnie And Joe singles included their first hit, 'I'll Be Spinning' (number 10 R&B, 1957) and 'My Baby's Gone, On, On' (number 15 R&B, 1957). Johnnie And Joe songs were especially popular in the Hispanic community, particularly 1960's 'Across The Sea'. After a brief association in the Jaynetts girl group in 1964, Richardson resumed her career with Rivers and the pair made records throughout the 60s. During the 70s and 80s they performed in oldies concerts, and made a critically acclaimed album in 1982.
● ALBUMS: *Kingdom Of Love* (1982)★★★.

JOHNSON, JOHNNY, AND THE BANDWAGON

Formed in 1967 and originally known simply as the Bandwagon, this popular soul group consisted of four former solo singers who decided to pool their resources. John Johnson (b. 1945, Florida, USA), Terry Lewis (b. 1946, Baltimore, Ohio, USA), Arthur Fullilove (b. 1947, New York City, USA) and Billy Bradley (b. 1945, Rochester, New York, USA) had a hit with their debut UK release when 'Breaking Down The Walls Of Heartache' reached number 4 in October 1968. This pulsating dance song was the quartet's biggest hit, but two years later they enjoyed further success with 'Sweet Inspiration' and 'Blame It On The Pony Express', both of which reached the UK Top 10. The group was latterly based in Britain where, unlike in America, they had been well received. Johnson assumed leadership as original members dropped out, until the billing eventually read 'Johnny Johnson And His Bandwagon'. However the singer's frenetic vocal style proved inflexible and as the band's recordings grew increasingly predictable, so their commercial success waned.

● ALBUMS: *Johnny Johnson And The Bandwagon* (Direction 1968)★★, *Soul Survivor* (Bell 1970)★★.

JOHNSON, LOU

b. 1941, USA. A singer in the mould of Ben E. King, Johnson was a former member of the Zionettes. Their single 'Talking About The Man' enjoyed sufficient local interest to prompt his solo ambitions. Signed to the Big Top/Big Hill group of labels, Johnson recorded a series of superb Burt Bacharach/Hal David compositions, including 'Reach Out For Me' (1963) and '(There's) Always Something There To Remind Me' (1964). Both reached the lower rungs of the R&B chart. Sandie Shaw's recording of the latter became a UK number 1 while the former song provided Dionne Warwick with a US Top 20 hit. Johnson's 'Kentucky Bluebird (Send A Message To Martha)' later became a hit for Adam Faith and was subsequently revamped by Dionne Warwick as 'A Message To Michael'. Johnson's last chart record was 'A Time To Love, A Time To Cry' (1965), a vocal version of Sidney Bechet's 'Petite Fleur'. Johnson's later work for other outlets was also promising, but the singer failed to realize his full potential.

● ALBUMS: *With You In Mind* (1971)★★★.

JOHNSON, MARV

b. Marvin Earl Johnson, 15 October 1938, Detroit, Michigan, USA, d. 16 May 1993, Columbia, South Carolina, USA. The gospel training that Johnson received as a teenager in the Junior Serenaders was a major influence on his early R&B releases. In 1958, he formed a partnership with the young Berry Gordy, who was then working as a songwriter and producer for Jackie Wilson. Gordy produced Johnson's earliest releases on Kudo, and launched his Tamla label with Johnson's single 'Come To Me', which became a hit when it was licensed to United Artists. Johnson remained with the label until 1965, scoring a run of chart entries in the early 60s with 'You Got What It Takes', 'I Love The Way You Move' and 'Move Two Mountains' - all produced by Gordy. Johnson's tracks showcased his delicate tenor vocals against a female gospel chorus, and he maintained this style when he signed to Gordy's Motown stable in 1965. His initial release on the Gordy Records label, the soul favourite 'I Miss You Baby', was a US hit, although it proved to be a false dawn. His subsequent US releases failed, and Johnson eventually abandoned his recording career in 1968. Ironically, the UK Tamla-Motown label chose this moment to revive Johnson's 1966 recording 'I'll Pick A Rose For My Rose', which became an unexpected Top 20 hit amidst a dramatic revival in the label's popularity in Britain. Johnson quickly travelled to the UK to capitalize on this success, before retiring to become a sales executive at Motown. After almost two decades working behind the scenes in the music business, he returned to performing in 1987, touring with the 'Sounds Of Motown' package and re-recording his old hits for the Nightmare label. He was teamed with Carolyn Gill (of the Velvelettes) by record producer Ian Levine to release 'Ain't Nothing Like The Real Thing' in 1987. He released *Come To Me* on Levine's Motor City label. Johnson collapsed and died at a concert in South Carolina on 16 May 1993.

● ALBUMS: *Marvellous Marv Johnson* (United Artists 1960)★★★, *More Marv Johnson* (United Artists 1961)★★, *I Believe* (United Artists 1966)★★, *I'll Pick A Rose For My Rose* (Motown 1969)★★, *Come To Me* (Motor City 1990)★★.

● COMPILATIONS: *The Best Of Marv Johnson - You Got What It Takes* (1992)★★★, *The Very Best* (Essential Gold 1996)★★★.

JOHNSON, RUBY

b. 19 April 1936, Elizabeth City, North Carolina, USA. To many soul fans, Johnson is still chiefly remembered for her wonderful deep-soul Volt recording, 'I'll Run Your Hurt Away', released in March 1966, but some of her other material from the same era confirms that she was a high-quality soul singer. Although African-American, Johnson was raised in North Carolina in the quasi-Jewish Temple Beth-El faith. One of nine children, she grew up singing a cappella at the local temple, but aspired to emulate the power-soul style of Aretha Franklin and Etta James. After singing with Samuel Latham And The Rhythm Makers at Virginia Beach, she moved to Washington, DC, and became show-opener at the popular Spa Club. Never Duncan, manager of Bobby Parker (of 'Watch Your Step' fame), signed her first to the Philadelphia-based V-Tone label (for which Parker was also recording), and then to his own Nebs outlet. Subsequently, ex-Washington disc jockey Al Bell signed Johnson to Stax/Volt when he moved to Memphis in 1965. For Volt, Johnson cut several excellent cover versions of other artists' soul titles, such as Theola Kilgore's 'The Love Of My Man' and Ben E. King's 'Don't Play That Song'. She also recorded songs by in-house Stax writers, including Isaac Hayes and David Porter. Porter's 'I'll Run Your Hurt Away' is said to have reduced him to tears as he wrote it; at times it seems that Johnson was so completely immersed in her performance that she might also break down - her rendition of the song represents a mesmerizing masterpiece of soul. Although never a commercial recording artist, Johnson remained a popular club singer until 1974 when she opted out of the 'disco' boom to take a regular government job. In 1993 she was employed in Maryland, recruiting volunteers to work with handicapped children.

● COMPILATIONS: *I'll Run Your Hurt Away* (1993)★★★.

JOHNSON, SYL

b. Sylvester Thompson, 1 July 1936, Holly Springs, Mississippi, USA. Johnson was the youngest of three children and his family moved to Chicago during the late 40s. An elder brother, Mac Thompson, played bass with the Magic Sam Blues Band. Having learned guitar and harmonica, Johnson began frequenting the city's southside blues clubs, playing alongside Howlin' Wolf, Muddy Waters and Junior Wells. His first recordings were made in 1956 accompanying Billy Boy Arnold, after which Johnson appeared on sessions for Shakey Jake, Junior Wells and Jimmy Reed. In 1959 Federal released Johnson's first solo single, 'Teardrops', and he recorded unsuccessfully for several independents until signing with Twilight (later changed to Twinight) in 1967. His debut there, 'Come On Sock It To Me', reached number 12 in the R&B chart. Johnson's musical activities, however, were not solely confined to performing. He also produced several local acts including Tyrone Davis and Otis Clay, while the Deacons, his backing group, featuring brother Jimmy Johnson on guitar, enjoyed a minor hit on the singer's Shama label. Johnson was then spotted by Willie Mitchell and 'Dresses Too Short' (1968) was recorded with the Mitchell's Hi Records house band. The remaining Twinight sessions were divided between Memphis and Chicago. Johnson remained with the label until 1971, recording two albums in the process. Free to sign with Hi, he began a series of releases that matched for excellence those of labelmate Al Green. Brash, up-tempo topsides, including 'Back For A Taste Of Your Love' and 'We Did It', contrasted with the often-reflective couplings, of which 'Anyway The Wind Blows' and 'I Hear The Love Chimes' were particularly emotive. The third of his exemplary albums for Hi, *Total Explosion*, produced Johnson's only substantial R&B hit when his version of 'Take Me To The River' (1975) reached number 7. However, his final years at Hi were dogged by internal problems and towards the end of the decade he reactivated his Shama label. A contemporary blues/soul collection, *Ms Fine Brown Frame*, was licensed to Boardwalk, while a French album, *Suicide Blues*, followed in 1984. By the mid-80s, he had semi-retired from the music business and opened a string of fast-food fish restaurants. He returned to performing in 1992 and in 1994 with an excellent album *Back In The Game*.

● ALBUMS: *Dresses Too Short* (Twinight 1968)★★★, *Is It Because I'm Black?* i (Twinight 1970)★★★, *Back For A Taste Of Your Love* (Hi 1973)★★★★, *Diamond In The Rough* (Hi 1974)★★★, *Total Explosion* (Hi 1976)★★★★, *Uptown Shakedown* (Shama 1979)★★★, *Brings Out The Blues In Me* (Shama 1980)★★★, *Ms Fine Brown Frame* (Boardwalk 1983)★★★, *Suicide Blues* (1984)★★★, *Foxy Brown* (Shama 1988)★★★, *Back In The Game* (Delmark 1994)★★★.

● COMPILATIONS: *Brings Out The Blues In Me* (Flyright 1986)★★★, *Is It Because I'm Black?* ii (Charly 1986)★★★★, *The Love Chimes* (Hi 1986)★★★, *Stuck In Chicago* (Hi 1989)★★★.

JONES GIRLS

This US vocal trio comprised Brenda Jones, Shirley Jones and Valerie Jones, and first came to public attention after backing Diana Ross on tour. In the past they had opened for artists including B.B. King, the Four Tops and Little Richard. It was through Ross that they gained their first studio session, but it was not until 1977 that they released their debut single, produced by Kenny Gamble of Gamble And Huff; 'You Gonna Make Me Love Somebody Else' reached the US Top 40. Surpassing all original criticisms that they were too derivative of the Emotions, the trio established their own exquisite style with melodic and soulful vocals, luscious strings, tight horns and slick rhythms. However, owing to bad luck with two record companies that both collapsed, their chart success was wrecked; however, during the early 90s they returned with the release of *Coming Back*.

● ALBUMS: *The Jones Girls* (Philadelphia International 1979)★★★★, *At Peace With Woman* (Philadelphia International 1980)★★★, *Get As Much Love As You Can* (Philadelphia International 1982)★★★, *On Target* (RCA 1983)★★★, *Keep It Comin'* (Philadelphia International 1984)★★★, *Coming Back* (1992)★★★.

● COMPILATIONS: *Artists Showcase: The Jones Girls* (DM Streetsounds 1986)★★★.

JONES, BOOKER T.

(see Booker T. And The MG's)

JONES, JIMMY

b. 2 June 1937, Birmingham, Alabama, USA. Jones, who had spent a long apprenticeship singing in R&B doo-wop groups, became a rock 'n' roll star in the early 60s singing 'Handy Man' and other hits with a dramatic and piercingly high falsetto. He began his career as a tap dancer, and in 1955 joined a vocal group, the Sparks Of Rhythm. In 1956 Jones formed his own group, the Savoys, which were renamed the Pretenders in 1956. With all these groups, tracks were recorded in the prevailing doo-wop manner but with no discernable success beyond a few local radio plays in the New York/New Jersey area. Success finally came when Jones launched a solo career, signing with MGM's Cub subsidiary in 1959 and hitting with his debut, 'Handy Man' (number 3 R&B/number 2 pop chart in 1960). Retaining the same falsetto style, he followed up with 'Good Timin'' (number 8 R&B/number 3 pop chart in 1960), but the decline in sales was considerable for his two other US chart entries, 'That's When I Cried' (number 83 pop chart in 1960) and 'I Told You So' (number 85 pop chart in 1961). In the UK, Jones's chart success was exceptional compared to most of his US contemporaries. In 1960 'Handy Man' reached number 3, 'Good Timin'' number 1, 'I Just Go For You' number 35,

'Ready For Love' number 46 and 'I Told You So' number 33. 'Handy Man' was revived on the charts twice, by Del Shannon in 1964 and by James Taylor in 1977.

● ALBUMS: *Good Timin'* (MGM 1960)★★★.

JONES, JOE

b. 12 August 1926, New Orleans, Louisiana, USA. Jones was a pianist and vocalist who made his mark in 1960 with the R&B/novelty single 'You Talk Too Much'. His career began in the mid-40s as a valet and bandleader for B.B. King. Jones recorded under his own name as early as 1954 and went on the road as a pianist for Shirley And Lee. Jones's big hit was co-written with pianist Reginald Hall, and recorded for the small local label Ric Records. However, as the record began to take off, it was discovered that Jones had already recorded the song for the larger, New York-based Roulette Records. They lodged an injunction and the Ric version was withdrawn. Jones was unable to follow that hit and went into publishing, production and management, his greatest success in that area being with the Dixie Cups and, to a lesser degree, Alvin Robinson.

● ALBUMS: *You Talk Too Much* (Roulette 1961)★★★.

JONES, LINDA

b. 14 January 1944, Newark, New Jersey, USA, d. 14 March 1972, New York City, New York, USA. This soulful song stylist started in her family's gospel group the Jones Singers at the age of six. Her first recording was 'Lonely Teardrops' under the name Linda Lane, on Cub Records in 1963, and she had unsuccessful singles on Atco in 1964 and Blue Cat the following year. In 1967 she worked with writer/producer George Kerr and signed to Russ Regan's Loma label in 1967. This resulted in her biggest hit, 'Hypnotized', which narrowly missed the US Top 20. She later had releases on Warner 7-Arts, Cotique and Gamble And Huff's Neptune label before joining Sylvia Robinson's Turbo Records in 1971. A sufferer of diabetes, Jones collapsed backstage at the Apollo in New York on 14 March 1972 and died shortly afterwards in hospital. She was way ahead of her time and made melisma (spreading a syllable over several notes) an art form. This unique singer, who has influenced scores of R&B artists, was aptly described in *Black Music* magazine as 'perhaps the most soulful singer in the history of R&B music'.

● ALBUMS: *Hypnotized* (Loma 1967)★★★.

● COMPILATIONS: *20 Golden Classics* (Collectables 1988)★★★★.

JONES, QUINCY

b. Quincy Delight Jones Jnr., 14 March 1933, Chicago, Illinois, USA. Jones began playing trumpet as a child and also developed an early interest in arranging, studying at the Berklee College Of Music. When he joined Lionel Hampton in 1951 it was as both performer and writer. With Hampton he visited Europe in a remarkable group that included rising stars Clifford Brown, Art Farmer, Gigi Gryce and Alan Dawson. Leaving Hampton in 1953, Jones wrote arrangements for many musicians, including some of his former colleagues and Ray Anthony, Count Basie and Tommy Dorsey. He mostly worked as a freelance but had a stint in the mid-50s as musical director for Dizzy Gillespie, one result of which was the 1956 album *World Statesman*. Later in the 50s and into the 60s Jones wrote charts and directed the orchestras for concerts and record sessions by several singers, including Frank Sinatra, Billy Eckstine, Brook Benton, Dinah Washington (an association that included the 1956 album *The Swingin' Miss 'D'*), Johnny Mathis and Ray Charles, whom he had known since childhood. He continued to write big band charts, composing and arranging albums for Basie, *One More Time* (1958-59) and *Li'l Ol' Groovemaker...Basie* (1963). By this time, Jones was fast becoming a major force in American popular music. In addition to playing he was busy writing and arranging, and was increasingly active as a record producer. In the late 60s and 70s he composed scores for around 40 feature films and hundreds of television shows. Among the former were *The Pawnbroker* (1965), *In Cold Blood* (1967) and *In The Heat Of The Night* (1967), while the latter included the long-running *Ironside* series and *Roots*. Other credits for television programmes include *The Bill Cosby Show*, *NBC Mystery Series*, *The Jesse Jackson Series*, *In The House* and *Mad TV*. He continued to produce records featuring his own music played by specially assembled orchestras. As a record producer Jones had originally worked for Mercury's Paris-based subsidiary Barclay, but later became the first black vice-president of the company's New York division. Later, he spent a dozen years with A&M Records before starting up his own label, Qwest. Despite suffering two brain aneurysms in 1974 he showed no signs of reducing his high level of activity. In the 70s and 80s, in addition to many film soundtracks, he produced successful albums for Aretha Franklin, George Benson, Michael Jackson, the Brothers Johnston and other popular artists. With Benson he produced *Give Me The Night*, while for Jackson he helped to create *Off The Wall* and *Thriller*, the latter proving to be one of the best-selling albums of all time. He was also producer of the 1985 number 1 charity single 'We Are The World'. Latterly, Jones has been involved in film and television production, not necessarily in a musical context. As a player, Jones was an unexceptional soloist; as an arranger, his attributes are sometimes overlooked by the jazz audience, perhaps because of the manner in which he has consistently sought to create a smooth and wholly sophisticated entity, even at the expense of eliminating the essential characteristics of the artists concerned (as some of his work for Basie exemplifies). Nevertheless, with considerable subtlety he has fused elements of the blues and its many offshoots into mainstream jazz, and has found ways to bring soul to latter-day pop in a manner that adds to the latter without diminishing the former. His example has been followed by many although few have achieved such a level of success. A major film documentary, *Listen Up: The Lives Of Quincy Jones*, was released in 1990, and five years later Jones received the Jean Hersholt Humanitarian Award at the Academy Awards ceremony in Los Angeles. This coincided with *Q's Jook Joint*, a celebration of his 50 years in the music business with re-recordings of selections from his extraordinarily varied catalogue. The album lodged itself at the top

of the *Billboard* jazz album chart for over four months.
● ALBUMS: *Quincy Jones With The Swedish/U.S. All Stars* (Prestige 1953)★★★, *This Is How I Feel About Jazz* (ABC-Paramount 1957)★★★, *Go West Man* (ABC-Paramount 1957)★★★, *The Birth Of A Band* (Mercury 1959)★★★, *The Great Wide World Of Quincy Jones* (Mercury 1960)★★★, *Quincy Jones At Newport '61* (Mercury 1961)★★★, *I Dig Dancers* (Mercury 1961)★★★, *Around The World* (Mercury 1961)★★★, *The Quintessence* (Impulse 1961)★★★, *Big Band Bossa Nova* (Mercury 1962)★★★, *Quincy Jones Plays Hip Hits* (Mercury 1963)★★★, *The Boy In The Tree* (1963)★★★, *Quincy's Got A Brand New Bag* (Mercury 1964)★★★, *Quincy Jones Explores The Music Of Henry Mancini* (Mercury 1964)★★★, *Golden Boy* (Mercury 1964)★★★, *The Pawnbroker* (Mercury 1964)★★★, *Quincy Plays For Pussycats* (Mercury 1965)★★★, *Walk Don't Run* (Mainstream 1966)★★★, *The Slender Thread* (Mercury 1966)★★★, *The Deadly Affair* (Verve 1967)★★★, *Enter Laughing* (Liberty 1967)★★★, *In The Heat Of The Night* film soundtrack (United Artists 1967)★★★, *In Cold Blood* film soundtrack (Colgems 1967)★★★, *Banning* (1968)★★★, *For The Love Of Ivy* (ABC 1968)★★★, *The Split* (1968)★★★, *Jigsaw* (1968)★★★, *A Dandy In Aspic* (1968)★★★, *The Hell With Heroes* (1968)★★★, *MacKennas Gold* (RCA 1969)★★★, *The Italian Job* film soundtrack (Paramount 1969)★★★, *The Lost Man* (1969)★★★, *Bob & Carol & Ted & Alice* (Bell 1969)★★★, *John And Mary* (A&M 1969)★★★, *Walking In Space* (A&M 1969)★★★, *Gula Matari* (A&M 1970)★★★, *The Out Of Towners* (United Artists 1970)★★★, *Cactus Flower* (Bell 1970)★★★, *The Last Of The Hot Shots* (1970)★★★, *Sheila* (1970)★★★, *They Call Me Mr Tibbs* (United Artists 1970)★★★, *Smackwater Jack* (A&M 1971)★★★, *The Anderson Tapes* (1971)★★★, *Dollars* (1971)★★★, *Man And Boy* (1971)★★★, *The Hot Rock* (Prophesy 1972)★★★, *Ndeda* (Mercury 1972)★★★, *The New Centurians* (1972)★★★, *Come Back Charleston Blue* (Atco 1972)★★★, *You've Got It Bad Girl* (A&M 1973)★★★, *Body Heat* (A&M 1974)★★★, *This Is How I Feel About Jazz* (Impulse 1974)★★★, *Mellow Madness* (A&M 1975)★★★, *I Heard That!* (A&M 1976)★★★, *Roots* (A&M 1977)★★★, *Sounds ... And Stuff Like That* (A&M 1978)★★★, *The Wiz* (MCA 1978)★★★, *The Dude* (A&M 1981)★★★, *The Color Purple* film soundtrack (Qwest 1985)★★★, *Back On The Block* (Qwest 1989)★★★, *Listen Up, The Lives Of Quincy Jones* (Qwest 1990)★★★, with Miles Davis *Live At Montreux* recorded 1991 (Reprise 1993)★★★★, *Q's Jook Joint* (Qwest 1995)★★★★.
● COMPILATIONS: *Compact Jazz: Quincy Jones* (Phillips/Polygram 1989)★★★★.
● VIDEOS: *Miles Davis And Quincy Jones: Live At Montreux* (1993).
● FURTHER READING: *Quincy Jones*, Raymond Horricks.
● FILMS: *Listen Up: The Lives Of Quincy Jones* (1990).

JONESES

An R&B vocal group from Pittsburgh, Pennsylvania, USA, the Joneses were typical of the vocal group renaissance of the early 70s, recording in the soft-soul mode that featured a falsetto lead, pretty harmonies and fully orchestrated arrangements. The original group started in Pittsburgh in 1969, but the recording group arrived at its final line-up after moving to New York to record for V.M.P. Records in the early 70s. The members of the V.M.P. group featured falsetto lead Cy Brooks, Glenn Dorsey, Sam White and brothers Reginald and Wendell Noble, and on that label they had a New York hit with 'Pretty Pretty'. Moving to the Pride label in 1973, they had another local hit, 'Pull My String'. Mercury Records then took notice and signed them. Brooks left at this point and his lead spot was taken by baritone Harold Taylor (who had earlier been with the group in Pittsburgh). At Mercury the Joneses first hit locally in Baltimore with 'Baby Don't Do It', but in 1974 they began a string of national hits with 'Hey Babe' (number 18 R&B). They then followed with their only crossover hit, 'Sugar Pie Guy' (number 10 R&B, number 47 pop), also in 1974. They also had considerable success with 'I Can't See What You See In Me' (number 28 R&B) in 1975. The Joneses broke up in 1975, but in the following years there were four resurrections of the group, the first in 1977 and the last in 1992, and each time the only constant in the new line-ups was Glenn Dorsey. These new Joneses groups recorded with Epic, Spring, Collectables and Atlantic Records with varying success.
● ALBUMS: *Keeping Up With* (Mercury 1974)★★★, *The Joneses* (Epic 1977)★★★, *Hard* (Atlantic 1990)★★.
● COMPILATIONS: *Golden Soul Classics From The Early Years* contains one new track, the rest are their pre-Mercury releases (Collectables 1994)★★★.

JOSEPH, MARGIE

b. Margaret Marie Joseph, 1950, Pascagoula, Mississippi, USA. Having recorded unsuccessfully for the OKeh label, this excellent singer endured two further flops before an Aretha Franklin-influenced ballad, 'Your Sweet Lovin'', reached the R&B chart in 1970. The following year Joseph's ambitious reworking of the Supremes' 'Stop! In The Name Of Love' was trimmed down to six minutes to provide her with a second hit. Another interpretation, this time of Paul McCartney's 'My Love', became Margie's best-selling single in 1974. Further releases, including 'Words (Are Impossible)' (1974) and 'What's Come Over Me?' (1975), a duet with the sweet-soul group Blue Magic, kept her name alive in the R&B chart. To date, Joseph has been unable to reap the full benefit of her undoubted potential.
● ALBUMS: *Margie Joseph Makes A New Impression* (Volt 1971)★★★, *Margie Joseph - Phase Two* (Volt 1971)★★, *Sweet Surrender* (Atlantic 1974)★★★, *Margie* (1975)★★, *Hear The Words, Feel The Feeling* (Cotillion 1976)★★★, *Feeling My Way* (Atco 1978)★★★, *Knockout* (Jive 1983)★★, *Stay* (Ichiban 1988)★★★.
● COMPILATIONS: *In The Name Of Love* (Stax 1988)★★★.

JUNIOR

(see Giscombe, Junior)

K-Doe, Ernie

b. Ernest Kador Jnr., 22 February 1936, New Orleans, Louisiana, USA. Previously a singer with touring gospel groups, K-Doe's earliest non-secular recordings were made in the mid-50s as a member of the Blue Diamonds. His first solo record, 'Do Baby Do', was released on Specialty in 1956. The singer's biggest hit came with the Allen Toussaint song 'Mother-In-Law' (1961), which reached number 1 in the US pop charts. This pointed 'novelty' song was followed by 'Te-Ta-Te-Ta-Ta', and a strong double-sided release, 'I Have Cried My Last Tear'/'A Certain Girl'. The latter track proved popular in Britain where it was covered by the Yardbirds and the Paramounts. Further K-Doe singles included 'Popeye Joe' and 'I'm The Boss', but it was not until 1967 that he returned to the R&B chart with two singles for the Duke label, 'Later For Tomorrow' and 'Until The Real Thing Comes Along'. He remains a popular, energetic performer and occasional recording artist in New Orleans.

● ALBUMS: *Mother-In-Law* (Minit 1961)★★★★.
● COMPILATIONS: *Burn, K-Doe, Burn!* (Charly 1989)★★★★.

Kaye, Carol

b. Carol Everett, 1935, Washington, USA. Bass guitarist Kaye was one of the few women musicians, as opposed to vocalists, prospering in the enclosed Los Angeles session fraternity. During the 60s she joined, among others, Glen Campbell, Tommy Tedesco, Billy Strange (guitars) and Larry Knechtal (piano) as a member of a group affectionately known as Hal Blaine's Wrecking Crew. Kaye contributed to innumerable recordings, the most notable of which were with Phil Spector protégées the Crystals, the Ronettes and Darlene Love. Her bass work also appeared on many west coast Tamla/Motown sessions and, by contrast, *Freak Out*, the first album by the Mothers Of Invention. Her affinity with soul/blues-influenced artists was exemplified in appearances on Joe Cocker's *With A Little Help From My Friends* (1969) and Robert Palmer's *Some People Can Do What They Like* (1976). Classical-styled sessions for David Axelrod contrasted with singer-songwriter work with Dory Previn and exemplified the versatility of this talented and prolific musician. The milestone singles on which Kaye claims to have played (there is some dispute that James Jamerson was on the final mix) are: 'River Deep Mountain High' (Ike And Tina Turner), 'Theme From Shaft' (Isaac Hayes), 'Get Ready' (Temptations), 'Reach Out I'll Be There' (Four Tops), 'I Was Made To Love Her' (Stevie Wonder), 'Everybody's Talkin'' (Nilsson), 'Homeward Bound' (Simon And Garfunkel), 'Good Vibrations' (Beach Boys), 'It's My Party' (Lesley Gore), 'Light My Fire' (Doors), 'You Can't Hurry Love' (Supremes) and 'Young Girl' by Gary Puckett.

KC And The Sunshine Band

This racially integrated band was formed in Florida, USA, in 1973 by Harry Wayne (KC) Casey (b. 31 January 1951, Hialeah, Florida, USA; vocals, keyboards) and Richard Finch (b. 25 January 1954, Indianapolis, Indiana, USA; bass). Arguably the cornerstone of the Miami-based TK label, the duo wrote, arranged and produced their own group's successes, as well as those of singer George McCrae. The Sunshine Band enjoyed several hits, including 'Queen Of Clubs' (1974, UK Top 10), three consecutive US number 1s with 'Get Down Tonight', 'That's The Way (I Like It)' (both 1975) and '(Shake, Shake, Shake), Shake Your Body' (1976), each of which displayed an enthusiastic grasp of dance-based funk. The style was exaggerated to almost parodic proportions on 'I'm Your Boogie Man' (1977, a US number 1) and 'Boogie Shoes' (1978), but a crafted ballad, 'Please Don't Go', in 1979, not only reversed this bubblegum trend, but was a transatlantic smash in the process (and a UK number 1 in 1992 for K.W.S.). That same year KC duetted with Teri DeSario on the US number 2 hit 'Yes, I'm Ready', on the Casablanca label. Although the group numbered as many as 12 on its live appearances, its core revolved around Jerome Smith (b. 18 June 1953, Hialeah, Florida, USA; guitar), Robert Johnson (b. 21 March 1953, Miami, Florida, USA; drums) and its two songwriters. The team moved to Epic/CBS Records after the collapse of the TK organization in 1980. Any benefit this accrued was hampered by a head-on car crash in January 1982 that left Casey paralyzed for several months. Their fortune changed the following year when the group found themselves at the top of the UK charts with 'Give It Up'. It did not reach the US charts until the following year, and was by then credited to 'KC'. Casey and Finch subsequently seem to have lost the art of penning radio-friendly soul/pop.

● ALBUMS: *Do It Good* (TK 1974)★★★, *KC And The Sunshine Band* (TK 1975)★★★, as the Sunshine Band *The Sound Of Sunshine* (TK 1975)★★, *Part 3* (TK 1976)★★★★, *I Like To Do It* (Jay Boy 1977)★★★, *Who Do Ya (Love)* (TK 1978)★★, *Do You Wanna Go Party* (TK 1979)★★, *Painter* (Epic 1981)★★, *All In A Night's Work* (Epic 1983)★★, *Oh Yeah!* (ZYX 1993)★★, *Get Down Live!* (Intersound 1995)★★.
Solo: Wayne Casey/KC *Space Cadet* (Epic 1981)★★, *KC Ten* (Meca 1984)★★.
● COMPILATIONS: *Greatest Hits* (TK 1980)★★★, *The Best Of KC And The Sunshine Band* (Rhino 1990)★★★★.

Kelly Brothers

(see King Pins)

Kelly, R.

b. Robert Kelly, *c.*1969, Chicago, Illinois, USA. Dance/R&B artist who made his first impact with the release of a debut album in 1991, with his band, Public Announcement. Kelly grew up in the housing projects of

Chicago's South Side, but channelled his energies away from fast money-making schemes and into long-term musicianship. He had a natural flair for most instruments, eventually becoming, more by accident than design, a useful busking act. It earned the young Kelly a living, until constant police disruptions forced him to reconsider his employment. He put together the R&B group MGM, and went on to win a national talent contest on the *Big Break* television show, hosted by Natalie Cole. Unfortunately, that group's energy dissipated, and his next major break came when manager Barry Hankerson spotted him while auditioning for a play at the Regal Theatre in Chicago. He soon had Kelly acting as musical co-ordinator/producer for a slew of acts, including Gladys Knight, David Peaston, Aaliyah and the Hi-Five (who had a number 1 single, 'Quality Time', with Kelly at the controls). His diversity was confirmed with his work with the Winans gospel family, notably a duet with Ronald Winans on 'That Extra Mile'. However, all this would be surpassed by the success of his second album, which stayed on top of the R&B charts for nine weeks. Two huge singles were included on the set, the tearaway hits 'She's Got That Vibe' and 'Bump 'N Grind'. As if from nowhere, despite a long apprenticeship, Kelly seemed to have acquired the Midas touch. 'I Believe I Can Fly' became a massive hit when it was featured as the theme for the 1997 movie *Space Jam*.

● ALBUMS: *Born Into The '90s* (Jive 1991)★★★, *12 Play* (Jive 1994)★★★★, *R. Kelly* (Jive 1995)★★★.

● VIDEOS: *12 Play-The Hit Videos Vol. 1* (Jive 1994), *Top Secret Down Low Videos* (6 West 1996).

KENDRICKS, EDDIE

b. 17 December 1939, Union Springs, Alabama, USA, d. 5 October 1992, Alabama, USA. Kendricks was a founder-member of the Primes in the late 50s, an R&B vocal group that moved to Detroit in 1960 and formed the basis of the Temptations. His wavering falsetto vocals were an essential part of the group's sound throughout their first decade on Motown Records. He was singled out as lead vocalist on their first major hit, 'The Way You Do The Things You Do', and was also given a starring role on the 1966 US number 29 'Get Ready'. David Ruffin gradually assumed the leadership of the group, but in 1971 Kendricks was showcased on 'Just My Imagination', one of their most affecting love ballads. Kendricks chose this moment to announce that he was leaving the Temptations, weary of the production extravaganzas that Norman Whitfield was creating for the group. His initial solo albums failed to establish a distinctive style, and it was 1973 before he enjoyed his first hit, with an edited version of the disco classic 'Keep On Truckin''. The accompanying album, *Eddie Kendricks*, was in more traditional style, while *Boogie Down!* had Kendricks displaying emotion over a succession of dance-oriented backing tracks. Rather than repeat a winning formula, Kendricks bravely chose to revise his sound on *For You* in 1974. The first side of the album was a masterful arrangement of vocal harmonies, with Kendricks submerged by the backing. 'Shoeshine Boy' was extracted as a single, and followed 'Keep On Truckin'' and 'Boogie Down' to the summit of the soul charts. *The Hit Man* and *He's A Friend* repeated the experiment with less conviction, and by the time he left Motown for Arista in 1978, Kendricks had been forced to submit to the prevailing disco current. After a run of uninspiring efforts, *Love Keys* on Atlantic in 1981 was a welcome return to form, teaming the singer with the Muscle Shoals horns and the Holland/Dozier/Holland production team. Poor sales brought this liaison to an end, and Kendricks returned to the Temptations fold for a reunion tour and album in 1982. When this venture was completed, he formed a duo with fellow ex-Temptation David Ruffin, and the pair were showcased at Live Aid as well as on a live album by Hall And Oates. This exposure allowed them to secure a contract as a duo, and *Ruffin And Kendricks* in 1988 represented the most successful blending of their distinctive vocal styles since the mid-60s. Kendricks died of lung cancer in 1992, after having already had his right lung removed the previous year.

● ALBUMS: *All By Myself* (Tamla 1971)★★★, *People...Hold On* (Tamla 1972)★★★, *Eddie Kendricks* (Tamla 1973)★★★, *Boogie Down!* (Tamla 1974)★★★, *For You* (Tamla 1974)★★★, *The Hit Man* (Tamla 1975)★★★, *He's A Friend* (Tamla 1976)★★★, *Goin' Up In Smoke* (Tamla 1976)★★★, *Slick* (Tamla 1977)★★★, *Vintage '78* (Arista 1978)★★, *Something More* (Arista 1979)★★, *Love Keys* (Atlantic 1981)★★★, with David Ruffin *Ruffin And Kendricks* (RCA 1988)★★★.

● COMPILATIONS: *At His Best* (Motown 1990)★★★.

KENNER, CHRIS

b. 25 December 1929, Kenner, Louisiana, USA, d. 25 January 1976. This New Orleans-based artist had a US Top 20 R&B hit in 1957 on the Imperial label with his own composition, 'Sick And Tired', a song later revived by Fats Domino. Kenner was one of the first signings to the Instant label, on which he recorded his three best-known songs. In 1961, a song co-written with Fats Domino, 'I Like It Like That, Part 1', reached number 2 in the US pop charts. Kenner later received a Grammy nomination for the song. This was followed by 'Something You Got' and 'Land Of A 1,000 Dances' (1963). The latter, based on a gospel song, 'Children Go Where I Send You', later became a hit for Cannibal And The Headhunters (1965) and Wilson Pickett (1966 - US Top 10/UK Top 30). Although Kenner was beset throughout much of his career by alcohol problems, received a prison sentence in 1968 for statutory rape of a minor, and to a lesser degree, had a reputation as a poor live performer, he managed to record some of the best R&B to emanate from the Crescent City. He died of a heart attack in January 1976.

● ALBUMS: *Land Of 1,000 Dances* (Atlantic 1966)★★★.

● COMPILATIONS: *I Like It Like That* (Charly 1987)★★★.

● FILMS: *Be My Guest* (1965).

KHAN, CHAKA

b. Yvette Marie Stevens, 23 March 1953, Great Lakes Naval Training Station, Illinois, USA. Having sung with several Chicago club bands, including Lyfe, Lock And Chains and Baby Huey And The Babysitters, Chaka Khan became acquainted with Ask Rufus, a group formed from the remnants of hit group the American Breed. When Khan replaced original singer Paulette McWilliams, the line-up truncated its name to Rufus and as such released a succession of superior funk singles. Khan's stylish voice was the group's obvious attraction and in 1978 she began recording as a solo act. 'I'm Every Woman' topped the US R&B chart that year while subsequent releases, 'What Cha' Gonna Do For Me' (1981) and 'Got To Be There' (1982), consolidated this position. However, a 1984 release, 'I Feel For You', established the singer as an international act when it reached number 2 in the USA and number 1 in the UK pop charts. This exceptional performance was written by Prince and featured contributions from Stevie Wonder and Melle Mel. It not only led to a platinum-selling album, but won a Grammy for Best R&B Female Performance. Khan has since continued to forge a successful career, working with David Bowie and Robert Palmer, and duetting with Steve Winwood on his international smash, 'Higher Love'. In 1985 she enjoyed two Top 20 UK chart entries with 'This Is My Night' and 'Eye To Eye', while four years later a remix of 'I'm Every Woman' reached the Top 10 in the UK. She collaborated with Gladys Knight, Brandy and Tamia on the minor hit single 'Missing You' in 1996, taken from the Queen Latifah film *Set It Off*.

● ALBUMS: *Chaka* (Warners 1978)★★★, *Naughty* (Warners 1980)★★★, *What Cha' Gonna Do For Me* (Warners 1981)★★★, *Echoes Of An Era* (Elektra 1982)★★★, *Chaka Khan* (Warners 1982)★★★, *I Feel For You* (Warners 1984)★★★, *Destiny* (Warners 1986)★★, *CK* (Warners 1988)★★★, *Life Is A Dance - The Remix Project* (Warners 1989)★★, *The Woman I Am* (Warners 1992)★★★.

● COMPILATIONS: *Epiphany: The Best Of ... Vol. 1* (Reprise 1996)★★★★.

● FILMS: *Breakdance - The Movie* (1984).

King Floyd

b. 13 February 1945, New Orleans, Louisiana, USA. This itinerant singer first began performing at the age of 11, but his reputation was established by several mid-60s recordings produced by Harold Battiste. Floyd's first major hit came in 1970 with the excellent 'Groove Me', which reached the US Top 10, and he enjoyed two further Top 5 R&B singles with 'Baby Let Me Kiss You' (1971) and 'Woman Don't Go Astray' (1972). He continued to enjoy limited success throughout the first half of that decade, but 'Body English', released in 1976, was his last chart entry to date.

● ALBUMS: *King Floyd - A Man In Love* (1967)★★★, *King Floyd* (1971)★★★, *Think About It* (1973)★★, *Well Done* (1974)★★★, *Body English* (1976)★★.

King Pins

An R&B vocal group from Clarksdale, Mississippi, USA, the King Pins were essentially a secularized gospel group, and thus their early 60s records display some of the incipient sounds of the soul revolution. Members were three Kelly brothers - Andrew, Curtis and Robert - Charles Lee and Offee Reece. Curtis and Robert were the two leads in the group. They had one hit as the King Pins, 'It Won't Be This Way Always' (number 13 R&B, number 89 pop), from 1963, and one as the Kelly Brothers, 'Falling In Love Again' (number 39 R&B), from 1966. The group returned to their gospel roots in the 70s.

● ALBUMS: *It Won't Be This Way Always* (King 1963)★★★, as the Kelly Brothers *Sweet Soul* (President 1968)★★★.

● COMPILATIONS: as the Kelly Brothers *Sanctified Southern Soul* (Kent 1996)★★★.

King Pleasure And The Biscuit Boys

One of several UK groups devoted to reviving the jump-jive music pioneered in the 40s by Louis Jordan, they gathered a strong following across Europe in the late 80s. The group was formed in the Birmingham area in 1986 by ex-rockabilly bassist King Pleasure (b. 13 March 1966, Wednesbury, West Midlands, England; vocals, saxophone) and Bullmoose K. Shirley (b. 6 December 1967, Bilston, West Midlands, England; guitar). Other founder-members were P. Popps Martin (b. 23 February 1968, Wednesfield, West Midlands, England; saxophone), Piano-Man Skan (b. 22 March 1962, Birmingham, West Midlands, England; keyboards), Slap Happy (b. 5 November 1970, Rugby, Warwickshire, England; double bass), 'Bam Bam' Beresford (b. 25 March 1968; drums) and Lisa 'Sugar' Lee (vocals). They signed to local label Big Bear in 1988, following their debut album with a cover version of Jordan's 'Ain't Nobody Here But Us Chickens'. The band played support gigs to B.B. King and Cab Calloway as well as appearing in 10 European countries. In 1991, Lee and Skan left to be replaced by Ivory Dan McCormack (b. 1974, Norton, Cleveland, England; piano), ex-Big Town Playboy Big Al Nichols (b. 1964, Wrexham, North Wales; tenor saxophone) and Cootie Alexander (b. 6 September 1969, Birmingham, West Midlands, England; trumpet). They are one of the most exciting live bands and are leaders in waving the flag for 40s jump R&B.

● ALBUMS: *King Pleasure And The Biscuit Boys* (Big Bear 1988)★★★, *This Is It!* (Big Bear 1990)★★★, *Better Beware!* (Big Bear 1991)★★★, *Blues And Rhythm Revue, Volume 1* (Big Bear 1995)★★★.

King, Ben E.

b. Benjamin Earl Nelson, 28 September 1938, Henderson, North Carolina, USA. King began his career while still a high-school student singing in a doo-wop group, the Four B's. He later joined the Five Crowns who, in 1959, assumed the name the Drifters. King was the featured lead vocalist and occasional composer on several of their recordings including 'There Goes My Baby' and 'Save The Last Dance For Me' (written by Doc Pomus and Mort Shuman). After leaving the group in 1960, he recorded the classic single 'Spanish Harlem' (1961), which maintained the Latin quality of the Drifters' work and deservedly reached the US Top 10. The follow-up, 'Stand By Me' (1961), was even more successful and was followed by further hits including 'Amor' (1961) and 'Don't Play That Song (You Lied)' (1962). Throughout this period, King's work was aimed increasingly at the pop audience. 'I (Who Have Nothing)' and 'I Could Have

Danced All Night' (both 1963) suggested showbusiness rather than innovation, although Bert Berns' 'It's All Over' (1964) was a superb song. 'Seven Letters' and 'The Record (Baby I Love You)' (both 1965) prepared the way for the rhetorical 'What Is Soul?' (1967), which effectively placed King alongside such soul contemporaries as Otis Redding, Wilson Pickett and Joe Tex. Unfortunately, King's commercial standing declined towards the end of the 60s when he left the Atlantic/Atco group of labels. Unable to reclaim his former standing elsewhere, King later re-signed with his former company and secured a US Top 5 hit in 1975 with 'Supernatural Thing Part 1'. In 1977, a collaboration with the Average White Band resulted in two R&B chart entries and an excellent album, *Benny And Us*. However, King's later recordings, including *Music Trance* (1980) and *Street Tough* (1981), proved less successful. In 1986, 'Stand By Me' was included in a film of the same name and once more became an international hit, reaching the US Top 10 and number 1 in the UK, thereby briefly revitalizing the singer's autumnal career.

● ALBUMS: *Spanish Harlem* (Atco 1961)★★★, *Ben E. King Sings For Soulful Lovers* (Atco 1962)★★★, *Don't Play That Song* (Atco 1962)★★★, *Young Boy Blues* (Clarion 1964), *Seven Letters* (Atco 1965)★★★, *What Is Soul* (Atco 1967)★★★, *Rough Edges* (1970)★★★, *Beginning Of It All* (1971)★★★, *Supernatural* (Atco 1975)★★★, *I Had A Love* (Atco 1976)★★, with the Average White Band *Benny And Us* (Atlantic 1977)★★★, *Let Me Live In Your Life* (Atco 1978)★★, *Music Trance* (Atlantic 1980)★★, *Street Tough* (Atlantic 1981)★★, *Save The Last Dance For Me* (EMI 1988)★★★.

● COMPILATIONS: *Greatest Hits* (1964)★★★, *Here Comes The Night* (Edsel 1984)★★★, *Stand By Me: The Best Of Ben E. King* (Atlantic 1986)★★★, *The Ultimate Collection: Ben E. King* (Atlantic 1987)★★★★, *Anthology One: Spanish Harlem* (RSA 1996)★★★, *Anthology Two: For Soulful Lovers* (RSA 1996)★★★, *Anthology Three: Don't Play That Song* (RSA 1996)★★★, *Anthology Four: Seven Letters* (RSA 1997)★★★, *Anthology Five: What Is Soul?* (RSA 1997)★★★, *Anthology Six: Supernatural* (RSA 1997)★★★, *Anthology Seven: Benny And Us* (RSA 1997)★★.

King, Earl

b. Earl Silas Johnson IV, 7 February 1934, New Orleans, Louisiana, USA. The son of a blues pianist, King became an accomplished guitarist and singer with local bands before making his first recordings in 1953 for Savoy ('Have You Gone Crazy') and Specialty ('A Mother's Love'). Strongly influenced by Guitar Slim (Eddie Jones), during the mid-50s he worked with Huey Smith's band and recorded his biggest hit, 'Those Lonely Lonely Nights', with Smith on piano; this was on Johnny Vincent's Ace label, for whom King was house guitarist. In 1958, he made a version of 'Everyone Has To Cry Sometime' as Handsome Earl. He went on to record for Rex and Imperial where he made 'Come On' and the R&B hit 'Trick Bag' (1962) which featured King's influential guitar figures. He was also starting to enjoy success as a songwriter, composing the Lee Dorsey hit 'Do Re Mi', 'He's Mine' for Bernadine Washington, 'Big Chief' recorded by Professor Longhair and 'Teasin' You', Willie Tee's 1965 R&B hit. Jimmy Clanton, Dr. John and Fats Domino were others who recorded King compositions. During the 60s and early 70s, King himself made recordings for Amy, Wand, Atlantic and Motown, although the Allen Toussaint-produced Atlantic session was not released until 1981 and the Motown tracks remain unissued. King remained active into the 80s, recording with Roomfull Of Blues for Black Top. His Imperial tracks were reissued by EMI in 1987.

● ALBUMS: *New Orleans Rock 'N' Roll* (Sonet 1977)★★★, *Street Parade* (Charly 1981)★★★, with Roomfull Of Blues *Glazed* (Black Top 1988)★★★, *Sexual Telepathy* (Black Top 1990)★★★, *Hard River To Cross* (1993)★★★.

● COMPILATIONS: *Soul Bag* (Stateside 1987)★★★.

King, Evelyn 'Champagne'

b 1 July 1960, Bronx, New York, USA. A former office cleaner at Gamble And Huff's Sigma Sound studios, King was nurtured by T. Life, a member of the company's writing and production staff. He coached the aspiring singer on recording technique and was instrumental in preparing King's career. Her debut single, 'Shame', was released in 1977 and after considerable success on the dance/club circuit - since regarded as a classic of its kind - it finally broke into the national pop charts the following year, reaching the US Top 10/UK Top 40. Evelyn's second hit, 'I Don't Know If It's Right', became the artist's second gold disc and she later enjoyed international hits with 'I'm In Love' (1981) and a UK Top 10, 'Love Come Down' (1982). After a disappointing period during the mid-80s, her 1988 album *Flirt* was generally considered to be a return to form. King has remained a popular performer on the soul/dance music charts.

● ALBUMS: *Smooth Talk* (RCA 1977)★★★, *Music Box* (RCA 1979)★★★, *Call On Me* (RCA 1980)★★★, *I'm In Love* (RCA 1981)★★★, *Get Loose* (RCA 1982)★★★, *Face To Face* (RCA 1983)★★, *So Romantic* (RCA 1984)★★, *A Long Time Coming* (RCA 1985)★★, *Flirt* (EMI 1988)★★★.

● COMPILATIONS: *The Best Of Evelyn 'Champagne' King* (RCA 1990)★★★, *The Essential Works Of* (1992)★★★.

King, Solomon

This US singer came to prominence in 1968 with the powerful hit ballad 'She Wears My Ring'. It was based on a classical piece of music called *Golandrina (The Swallow)*. King was signed by manager/entrepreneur Gordon Mills but failed to emulate the phenomenal success of his stablemates Tom Jones and Engelbert Humperdinck. He continued to record well into the 70s, and his version of 'Say A Little Prayer' (1970) is a prized rarity among soul fans.

● ALBUMS: *She Wears My Ring* (Columbia 1968)★★★, *You'll Never Walk Alone* (Columbia 1971)★★.

Kinney, Fern

b. Jackson, Mississippi, USA. In the late 60s, Kinney replaced Patsy McClune in the Poppies, a female pop/R&B trio whose 'Lullabye Of Love' on Epic had been a minor US hit in 1966. Together with Rosemary Taylor and Dorothy Moore (also a successful solo artist later), she remained in the group for two years. In the 70s, she worked as a session singer for two local studios, Malaco and North American. During this time she backed singers including Jean Knight, King Floyd, Frederick Knight and her old friend Dorothy Moore. Kinney's first solo recording was 'Your Love's Not Reliable' on Atlantic in 1968, but it was not until 1979 that she had her only US success, which came with a revival of King Floyd's 'Groove Me', an R&B chart-topper from 1970. It reached the R&B Top 30, number 54 on the US pop chart and was a club hit in the UK. In 1980, her revival of UK singer-songwriter Ken Leray's 1977 recording 'Together We Are Beautiful' gave the singer, with her thin, high voice, a surprise UK number 1 hit. Oddly, the record had no impact in her homeland and, after various follow-ups failed to restore her to the UK chart, she returned to session singing and family life.

● ALBUMS: *Groove Me* (Warners 1980)★★★, *Fern* (Warners 1981)★★.

KIRKLAND, EDDIE

b. 16 August 1928, Kingston, Jamaica, West Indies. The career of guitarist Eddie Kirkland spans 40 years and a variety of musical styles. Soon after his birth the family relocated to the southern states of America and at the age of 15 he took a day job at the Ford Motor Company in Detroit. He met John Lee Hooker and became his regular accompanist both on the club circuit and on record, proving to be one of the few who could follow Hooker's erratic style. Kirkland's first recordings were made in 1952 and throughout the decade he recorded for RPM, King, Cobra, Fortune and Lupine. In 1961 he made his first deviation from 'down-home' blues when he recorded with King Curtis and Oliver Nelson for Prestige. In the mid-60s he moved to Macon, Georgia, where he turned to soul music, eventually signing to Otis Redding's enterprise Volt, in 1965. Redding used Kirkland in his touring band, but Kirkland's role as a soul artist was never more than minor. In the 70s, he returned to his blues roots, recording for Pete Lowery's Trix label, both solo and with small bands, and has since maintained a heavy touring schedule at home and in Europe.

● ALBUMS: *The Devil And Other Blues Demons* (Trix 1972)★★★, *Pickin' Up The Pieces* (GRP 1981)★★★, *The Way It Was* (Red Lightnin' 1983)★★★, *Have Mercy* (Pulsar 1993)★★★, *All Around The World* (Deluge 1993)★★★, *Some Like It Raw* (Deluge 1994)★★★, *Where You Get Your Sugar?* (Deluge 1995)★★★, *Front And Center* (Trix 1995)★★★.

KIRKLAND, LEROY

b. 10 February 1906, South Carolina, USA, d. 6 April 1988, New York, USA. Raised in Jacksonville, Florida, Kirkland was a butcher before he moved to New York in 1942. He became an arranger whose career spanned the eras of big band jazz, R&B, rock 'n' roll and soul. Kirkland played guitar in southern jazz bands in the 20s and during the 30s worked as arranger and songwriter for Erskine Hawkins. He joined Tommy and Jimmy Dorsey in the 40s and later in that decade began arranging music at Savoy Records in New York. He continued to arrange R&B artists for OKeh Records, Mercury Records and other companies, working with such groups as the Five Satins, the Ravens and the Everly Brothers. He managed Ruby And The Romantics during the 60s, and in the last few years of his life concentrated on gospel music.

KITTRELL, CHRISTINE

b. 11 August 1929, Nashville, Tennessee, USA. Kittrell made a number of attractive and moderately successful records for local labels during the 50s. A choir member as a child, her voice lacked the distinctive nuance that might have brought her more durable success. Her first record, 'Old Man You're Slipping' (Tennessee 117), was backed by tenor saxophonist Louis Brooks and his band, with whom she had made her professional debut six years earlier in 1945. Fats Domino sidemen Buddy Hagans and Wendell Duconge played on her first and biggest hit, 'Sittin' Here Drinking' (Tennessee 128), which brought her a six-week engagement at the Pelican Club in New Orleans. Kittrell had toured with the Joe Turner band in 1951 but she preferred to work around Nashville, at clubs such as the New Era and the Elks. Engaged as singer with Paul 'Hucklebuck' Williams' band in December 1952, *Billboard* noted that the 'five-foot-six chirp' was the 'blues find of the decade'. She made her west coast debut in 1954 with Earl Bostic and later Johnny Otis. Several releases on the Republic label at this time led to only regional success. One session that included 'Lord Have Mercy' (Republic 7096) is reputed to feature Little Richard on piano. In August 1954, *Billboard* announced her departure from the R&B field to sing with the Simmons Akers spiritual singers. In the early 60s she recorded for Vee Jay but her original version of 'I'm A Woman' was covered by Peggy Lee. She re-recorded an old Republic song, 'Call His Name' (Federal 12540), in 1965, and spent the next few years touring army bases in south-east Asia entertaining US troops. Subsequently, she retired to her Ohio home.

● COMPILATIONS: *Nashville R&B, Vol 2* (1986)★★★.

KNIGHT BROTHERS

An R&B duo from Washington, DC, USA, consisting of Richard Dunbar (b. 31 May 1939) and Jimmy Diggs (b. 1937), the Knight Brothers reflected the emergence of a new entity in R&B music in the early 60s - the impassioned gospel duos - the most significant being the Righteous Brothers and Sam And Dave. Their one hit was 'Temptation 'Bout To Get Me' (number 12 R&B, number 70 pop) from 1965, for Chess Records. The Knight Brothers never managed to reach the charts again, however, and after an unsuccessful stay at Mercury Records, the duo broke up in 1969. Dunbar went on to sing with a revived Orioles group during the 70s and 80s. Dunbar's joining of the placid-sounding Orioles was not entirely anomalous, as the singer had started his career as a member of a doo-wop group, the Starfires, who recorded on several labels from 1958-61.

KNIGHT, CURTIS

b. 1945, Fort Scott, Kansas, USA. Having completed his national service, Knight settled in California where he hoped to pursue a career in music. He appeared in a low-budget film, *Pop Girl*, before relocating to New York during the early 60s. Knight then recorded for several minor labels, but these releases have been eclipsed by the singer's collaborations with Jimi Hendrix, who joined Curtis's group, the Squires, in 1965. Hendrix's tenure there was brief, but the contract he signed with Knight's manager, Ed Chalpin, had unfortunate repercussions, particularly as the guitarist ill-advisedly undertook another recording session in 1967. His spells with Knight yielded 61 songs, 26 studio and 35 live, which have since been the subject of numerous exploitative compilations. Although some of this material is, in isolation, worthwhile, such practices have undermined its value. As Curtis Knight continued to pursue his career throughout the 60s using whatever musicians were available, he increasingly relied on his Hendrix association, and in 1974 published *Jimi*, 'an intimate biography'. By this point Knight was based in London where he led a new group, Curtis Knight - Zeus. This band comprised Eddie Clarke (guitar; later in Motörhead), Nicky Hogarth (keyboards), John Weir (bass) and Chris Perry (drums). They completed two albums, but only one was issued in the UK. The singer undertook a European tour and an unremarkable album before returning to the USA.

● ALBUMS: *Down The Village* (1972)★★, *Second Coming* (1974)★★, *Live In Europe* (1989)★★. Selected recordings with Jimi Hendrix *Get That Feeling* (Capitol 1967)★, *Strange Things* (1968)★★, *Flashing/Jimi Hendrix Plays Curtis Knight Sings* (1968)★★, *The Great Jimi Hendrix In New York* (1968)★★, *In The Beginning* (1973)★, *Looking Back With Jimi Hendrix* (1975)★, *My Best Friend* (1981)★, *Second Time Around* (1981)★★, *Hush Now* (1981)★ *Last Night* (1981)★, *Mr. Pitiful* (1981)★★, *Welcome Home* (1981)★.

● FURTHER READING: *Jimi*, Curtis Knight.

KNIGHT, FREDERICK

b. 15 August 1944, Alabama, USA. Knight had a Top 30 hit in both the USA and UK with 'I've Been Lonely For So Long', a light, but deceptively memorable single. This 1972 release on the Stax label was the singer's only major success, although 'I Betcha Didn't Know That' (1975) and 'The Old Songs' (1981) reached the minor R&B placings. In the interim, however, the artist had written and produced singles for Anita Ward, including her international smash 'Ring My Bell', and had formed his own Junta and Park Place labels in the late 70s and mid-80s, respectively. Knight continues to pursue an active career.

● ALBUMS: *I've Been Lonely For So Long* (Stax 1972)★★★, *Let The Sunshine In* (1979)★★★, *Knight Time* (Timeless 1981)★★, *Knight Rap* (Timeless 1987)★★.

● COMPILATIONS: *Timeless Soul Collection* (Timeless 1987)★★★, *I've Been Lonely For So Long* (Stax 1992)★★★.

KNIGHT, GLADYS, AND THE PIPS

Gladys Knight (b. 28 May 1944, Atlanta, Georgia, USA), her brother Merald 'Bubba' (b. 4 September 1942, Atlanta, Georgia, USA), sister Brenda and cousins Elenor Guest and William Guest (b. 2 June 1941, Atlanta, Georgia, USA) formed their first vocal group in their native Atlanta in 1952. Calling themselves the Pips, the youngsters sang supper-club material in the week, and gospel music on Sundays. They first recorded for Brunswick in 1958, with another cousin of the Knights, Edward Patten (b. 2 August 1939), and Langston George making changes to the group line-up the following year when Brenda and Elenor left to get married. Three years elapsed before their next sessions, which produced a version of Johnny Otis's 'Every Beat Of My Heart' for the small Huntom label. This song, which highlighted Knight's bluesy, compelling vocal style, was leased to Vee Jay Records when it began attracting national attention, and went on to top the US R&B charts. By this time, the group, now credited as Gladys Knight And The Pips, had signed a long-term contract with Fury Records, where they issued a re-recording of 'Every Beat Of My Heart' which competed for sales with the original release. Subsequent singles such as 'Letter Full Of Tears' and 'Operator' sealed the group's R&B credentials, but a switch to the Maxx label in 1964 - where they worked with producer Van McCoy - brought their run of successes to a halt. Langston George retired from the group in the early 60s, leaving the quartet line-up that survived into the 80s.

In 1966, Gladys Knight and the Pips were signed to Motown's Soul subsidiary, where they were teamed up with producer/songwriter Norman Whitfield. Knight's tough vocals left them slightly out of the Motown mainstream, and throughout their stay with the label the group were regarded as a second-string act. In 1967, they had a major hit single with the original release of 'I Heard It Through The Grapevine', an uncompromisingly tough performance of a song that became a Motown standard in the hands of its author Marvin Gaye in 1969. 'The Nitty Gritty' (1968) and 'Friendship Train' (1969) proved equally successful, while the poignant 'If I Were Your Woman' was one of the label's biggest-selling releases of 1970. In the early 70s, the group slowly moved away from their original blues-influenced sound towards a more middle-of-the-road harmony blend. Their new approach brought them success in 1972 with 'Neither One Of Us (Wants To Say Goodbye)'. Later that year, Knight and The Pips elected to leave Motown for Buddah, unhappy at the label's shift of operations from Detroit to Hollywood. At Buddah, the group found immediate success with the US chart-topper 'Midnight Train To Georgia', an arresting soul ballad, while major hits such as 'I've Got To Use My Imagination' and 'The Best Thing That Ever Happened To Me' mined a similar vein. In 1974, they performed Curtis Mayfield's soundtrack songs for the film *Claudine*; the following year, the title track of *I Feel A Song* gave them another soul number 1. Their smoother approach was epitomized by the medley of 'The Way We Were/Try To Remember' which was the centrepiece of *Second Anniversary* in 1975 - the same year that saw Gladys and the group host their own US television series. Gladys made her acting debut in *Pipedream* in 1976, for which the group recorded a soundtrack album. Legal problems then dogged their career until the end of the decade, forcing Knight and the Pips to record separately until they could sign a new contract with CBS. *About Love* in 1980 teamed them with the Ashford And Simpson writing/production partnership, and produced a strident piece of R&B social comment in 'Bourgie Bourgie'. Subsequent releases alternated between the group's R&B and MOR modes, and hits such as 'Save The Overtime (For Me)' and 'You're Number One In My Book' (1983) and, after a move to MCA Records, 'Love Overboard' (1988), demonstrated that they could work equally well in either genre. The latter song earned them a Grammy award for the Best R&B performance in early 1989. Following this, Knight and the Pips split. Merald remained with Gladys Knight when she achieved a UK Top 10 that year with the James Bond movie song 'Licence To Kill', and released *A Good Woman* the following year. She collaborated with Chaka Khan, Brandy and Tamia on the minor hit single 'Missing You' in 1996, taken from the Queen Latifah film *Set It Off*.

● ALBUMS: *Letter Full Of Tears* (Fury 1961)★★, *Gladys Knight And The Pips* (Maxx 1964)★★, *Everybody Needs Love* (Soul 1967)★★★, *Feelin' Bluesy* (Soul 1968)★★★, *Silk 'N' Soul* (Soul 1969)★★★, *Nitty Gritty* (Soul 1969)★★★, *All In A Knight's Work* (Soul 1970)★★★, *If I Were Your Woman* (Soul 1971)★★★, *Standing Ovation* (Soul 1972)★★★, *Neither One Of Us* (Soul 1973)★★★★, *All I Need Is Time* (Soul 1973)★★★, *Imagination* (Buddah 1973)★★★★, *Knight Time* (Soul 1974)★★, *Claudine* (Buddah 1974)★★★, *I Feel A Song* (Buddah 1974)★★★, *A Little Knight Music* (Soul 1975)★★★, *Second Anniversary* (Buddah 1975)★★★, *Bless This House* (Buddah 1976)★★, *Pipe Dreams* film soundtrack (Buddah 1976)★★, *Still Together* (Buddah 1977)★★★, *The One And Only* (Buddah 1978)★★★, *About Love* (Columbia 1980)★★, *Touch* (Columbia 1981)★★★, *That Special Time Of Year* (Columbia 1982)★★, *Visions* (Columbia 1983)★★★, *Life* (Columbia 1985)★★★, *All Our Love* (MCA 1987)★★★.
Solo: Gladys Knight *Miss Gladys Knight* (Buddah 1979)★★, *Good Woman* (MCA 1991)★★★. The Pips *At Last - The Pips* (Casablanca 1979)★★, *Callin'* (Casablanca 1979)★★.

● COMPILATIONS: *Gladys Knight And The Pips Greatest Hits* (Soul 1970)★★★★, *Anthology* (Motown 1974)★★★★, *The Best Of Gladys Knight And The Pips* (Buddah 1976)★★★★, *30 Greatest* (K-Tel 1977)★★★, *The Collection - 20 Greatest Hits* (1984)★★★, *The Best Of Gladys Knight And The Pips: The Columbia Years* (Columbia 1988)★★★, *Every Beat Of My Heart: The Greatest Hits* (Chameleon 1989)★★★, *The Singles Album* (Polygram 1989)★★★, *Soul Survivors: The Best Of Gladys Knight And The Pips* (Rhino 1990)★★★★, *17 Greatest Hits* (1992)★★★.

KNIGHT, JEAN

b. 26 June 1943, New Orleans, Louisiana, USA. Knight's early releases with producer Huey P. Meaux were overshadowed by 'Mr. Big Stuff' in 1971, one of soul's most popular releases. Released on Stax and produced by Wardell Quezerque at the same session that yielded the King Floyd hit 'Groove Me', Knight's performance was rewarded with a US number 2 pop hit and R&B number 1. The combination of the irresistible rhythms of southern and New Orleans dance styles indicated the emergence of a new-found style; however, despite several excellent follow-up singles, including 'You Think You're Hot Stuff' and 'Carry On', the studio team were unable to develop this style further. The singer did re-emerge during the 80s with 'You Got The Papers (But I Got The Man)' (1981) and a version of the perennial, if suggestive, favourite, 'My Toot Toot' (1985).

● ALBUMS: *Mr. Big Stuff* (Stax 1971)★★★, *Keep It Comin'* (1981)★★★, *My Toot Toot* (Mirage 1985)★★.

● COMPILATIONS: *Mr. Big Stuff* (Ace 1990)★★★.

KODA, CUB

b. Michael Koda, 1 August 1948, Detroit, Michigan, USA. Guitarist Michael 'Cub' Koda led the hard-rock/soul trio Brownsville Station during the 70s and later released a string of roots-oriented solo albums for various labels. Koda took his nickname from a character on television's *Mickey Mouse Club*, Cubby. Raised listening to jazz records as a child, he began playing drums at the age of five, switching to guitar at the age of 13. His first high-school band, the Del-Tinos, recorded three singles and a number of unreleased tracks later collected on an album. In 1969, he formed Brownsville Station, at first a 50s-rock-orientated group, with Mike Lutz (guitar), Tony Diggins (bass) and T.J. Cronley (drums). Their claim to fame was the 1973/4 US number 3/UK Top 30 single 'Smokin' In The Boys' Room' (successfully covered by Mötley Crüe in 1985). Brownsville Station had two more chart singles for Big Tree and two for Private Stock, as well as one other chart album, before breaking up in 1979. Koda then formed the Points and later the Bone Gods, as well as releasing solo albums spotlighting rockabilly music, blues, Chuck Berry and Bo Diddley, and one on which he acted as a disc jockey, playing his favourite records and providing between-song patter. He currently writes a regular record review column for the US record collector magazine *Goldmine*.

● ALBUMS: *Cub Koda And The Points* (1980)★★★, *It's The Blues, Volume 1* (1981)★★, *That's What I Like About The South* (1984)★★★, *Go! Go! With The Del-Tinos* (1984)★★★, *The Cub Koda Crazy Show* (1984)★★★, *Let's Get Funky* (1985)★★, *Cub Digs Chuck* (1989)★★★, *Cub Digs Bo* (1991)★★★.

KODAKS

An R&B vocal group from Newark, New Jersey, USA, the original members were lead Pearl McKinnon, first tenor James Patrick, second tenor William Franklin, baritone Larry Davis and bass William Miller. The Kodaks were representative of the pre-teen lead sound, featuring a girlish and innocent, pre-pubescent male voice. When the pre-teen leads first became popular, it was assumed that they were all male, but research conducted in the 70s into the history of many such groups discovered that some were led by females, notably Pearl McKinnon of the Kodaks and Faith Taylor of the Sweet Teens. The Kodaks came together in 1957 and signed with Bobby Robinson's Fury label. The first release paired a terrific jump, 'Little Boy And Girl', with the touching ballad 'Teenager's Dream', and received significant local airplay. The second release, in the spring of 1958, the exhilarating 'Oh Gee, Oh Gosh', was their most sizeable hit, winning air time on the entire east coast and some in the Midwest. The b-side, 'Make Believe World', was especially appealing, with creatively harmonized choruses. At this time, Davis and Franklin left to form the Sonics, who would later record 'This Broken Heart'. They were replaced with Richard Dixon and Harold Jenkins. Two more singles followed, the last one being the excellent jump 'Runaround Baby' (1958), but it did not attract the public who were evidently tiring of the Frankie Lymon sound. McKinnon left the group around 1959 and a reorganized Kodaks recorded some more singles for first J&S and then Wink before finally disbanding in 1961. Meanwhile, McKinnon became lead of a new group, Pearl And The Deltars, who released a fine single on Fury in 1961 that met with little success. McKinnon in the 70s was the amazing 'Frankie Lymon' lead in the reunited Teenagers group, and those who heard her Kodaks tracks in the 50s could easily understand how she managed the deception.

● COMPILATIONS: *The Kodaks Versus The Starlites* (Sphere Sound 1965)★★★, *Oh Gee Oh Gosh* (Relic 1992)★★★.

Kokomo

Formed in 1973, this blue-eyed soul band was made up from the remnants of several British groups. Vocalists Dyan Birch, Paddie McHugh and Frank Collins were ex-members of Arrival, a superior pop harmony band, while Neil Hubbard (guitar) and Alan Spenner (bass) had previously worked with Joe Cocker's Grease Band. The line-up was completed by further formidable musicians, Tony O'Malley (piano), Jim Mullen (guitar), Terry Stannard (drums), Joan Linscott (congas) and journeyman saxophonist Mel Collins. A popular live attraction, Kokomo's acclaimed debut album suggested a future akin to that of the Average White Band. However, the group failed to sustain its promise and quickly ran out of inspiration, possibly because of the conflict of so many strong musical ideas and styles. This line-up split in January 1977, but a reconstituted version of the band appeared on the London gig circuit in the early 80s and recorded one album. The fluctuating activity of the group saw yet another reunion in the latter part of the 80s. This incarnation faltered when Alan Spenner died in August 1991.

● ALBUMS: *Kokomo* (Columbia 1975)★★★, *Rise And Shine!* (Columbia 1976)★★, *Kokomo* (Columbia 1982)★★. Solo: Tony O'Malley *Naked Flame* (Jazz House 1995)★★★.

● COMPILATIONS: *The Collection* (1992)★★★.

Kool And The Gang

Originally formed as a quartet, the Jazziacs, by Robert 'Kool' Bell (b. 8 October 1950, Youngstown, Ohio, USA; bass), Robert 'Spike' Mickens (b. Jersey City, New Jersey, USA; trumpet), Robert 'The Captain' Bell - later known by his Muslim name Amir Bayyan (b. 1 November 1951, Youngstown, Ohio, USA; saxophone, keyboards) and Dennis 'D.T.' Thomas (b. 9 February 1951, Jersey City, New Jersey, USA; saxophone). Based in Jersey City, this aspiring jazz group opened for acts such as Pharaoh Sanders and Leone Thomas. They were later joined by Charles 'Claydes' Smith (b. 6 September 1948, Jersey City, New Jersey, USA; guitar) and 'Funky' George Brown (b. 5 January 1949, Jersey City, New Jersey, USA; drums), and as the Soul Town Band, moderated their early direction by blending soul and funk, a transition completed by 1969 when they settled on the name Kool And The Gang. The group crossed over into the US pop chart in 1973 and initiated a run of 19 stateside Top 40 hits on their own De-Lite label starting with 'Funky Stuff', a feat consolidated the following year with a couple of Top 10 hits, 'Jungle Boogie' and 'Hollywood Swinging'. They continued to enjoy success although their popularity momentarily wavered in the latter half of the 70s as the prominence of disco strengthened. In 1979 the Gang added vocalists James 'J.T.' Taylor (b. 16 August 1953, Laurens, South Carolina, USA) and Earl Toon Jnr., with Taylor emerging as the key member in a new era of success for the group, which coincided with their employment of an outside producer. Eumire Deodato refined the qualities already inherent in the group's eclectic style and together they embarked on a series of highly successful international hits including 'Ladies Night' (1979), 'Too Hot' (1980) and the bubbling 'Celebration', a 1980 platinum disc and US pop number 1 - later used by the media as the home-coming theme for the returning American hostages from Iran. Outside the USA they achieved parallel success and proved similarly popular in the UK where 'Get Down On It' (1981), 'Joanna' (1984) and 'Cherish' (1985) each reached the Top 5. The arrival of Taylor also saw the group's albums achieving Top 30 status in their homeland for the first time, with *Celebrate!* reaching the Top 10 in 1980. Their longevity was due, in part, to a settled line-up. The original six members remained with the group into the 80s and although newcomer Toon left, Taylor blossomed into an ideal frontman. This core was later supplemented by several auxiliaries, Clifford Adams (trombone) and Michael Ray (trumpet). This idyllic situation was finally undermined by Taylor's departure in 1988 and he was replaced by three singers, former Dazz Band member Skip Martin plus Odeen Mays and Gary Brown. Taylor released a solo album in 1989, *Sister Rosa*, while the same year the group continued recording with the album *Sweat*. The compilation set *The Singles Collection* shows that Taylor left behind him one of the most engaging and successful of soul/funk catalogues.

● ALBUMS: *Kool And The Gang* (1969)★★, *Live At The Sex Machine* (De-Lite 1971)★★, *Live At P.J.s* (De-Lite 1971)★★, *Music Is The Message* (1972)★★, *Good Times* (De-Lite 1973)★★★, *Wild And Peaceful* (De-Lite 1973)★★★, *Light Of Worlds* (De-Lite 1974)★★★, *Spirit Of The Boogie* (De-Lite 1975)★★, *Love And Understanding* (De-Lite 1976)★★, *Open Sesame* (De-Lite 1976)★★, *The*

Force (De-Lite 1977)★★, *Everbody's Dancin'* (1978)★★, *Ladies' Night* (De-Lite 1979)★★★, *Celebrate!* (De-Lite 1980)★★★, *Something Special* (De-Lite 1981)★★, *As One* (De-Lite 1982)★★, *In The Heart* (De-Lite 1983)★★★★, *Emergency* (De-Lite 1984)★★, *Victory* (Curb 1986)★★, *Forever* (Mercury 1986)★★, *Sweat* (Mercury 1989)★★, *Kool Love* (Telstar 1990)★★, *State Of Affairs* (Curb 1996)★★.

● COMPILATIONS: *The Best Of Kool And The Gang* (De-Lite 1971)★★, *Kool Jazz* (De-Lite 1974)★★, *Kool And The Gang Greatest Hits!* (De-Lite 1975)★★★, *Spin Their Top Hits* (De-Lite 1978)★★★★, *Kool Kuts* (De-Lite 1982)★★★, *Twice As Kool* (De-Lite 1983)★★★★, *The Singles Collection* (De-Lite 1988)★★★★, *Everything's Kool And The Gang: Greatest Hits And More* (Mercury 1988)★★★★, *Great And Remixed 91* (Mercury 1992)★★★, *Collection* (Spectrum 1996)★★★.

Kool Gents

The Kool Gents were one of the numerous underexposed doo-wop groups that never had a hit, but who, decades later, became appreciated as great disseminators of R&B harmony. The group was formed in Chicago, Illinois, USA, in 1952, by Cicero Blake from among his classmates at Marshall High School, and after a number of changes in personnel, including the loss of Blake, the recording group consisted of lead Dee Clark, John McCall (first tenor), Doug Brown (second tenor), Teddy Long (baritone) and Johnny Carter (bass). They signed with Vee Jay Records and the first releases in 1954 featured John McCall as lead and lacked distinctiveness. A switch to Clark proved most dramatic, as the group produced three beautiful ballads during 1956, namely 'I Just Can't Help Myself', 'Just Like A Fool' and 'When I Call On You'. Also in 1956, the Kool Gents recorded a novelty number called 'The Convention', on which they were billed as the Delegates. Vee Jay were alerted to Clark's talents, pulled him out of the Kool Gents, and launched him as one the company's most successful recording acts (on most Dee Clark albums there are songs he recorded as a member of the Kool Gents). The remaining Kool Gents joined Pirkle Lee Moses (who had just lost his group, the El Dorados) and formed a new El Dorados group that made a few records for Vee Jay. Blake, who started the ball rolling, became a moderately successful soul-blues singer.

Kreuz

Hailed as the future of UK swingbeat when they first appeared in 1992, Kreuz were the first artists to be signed to Motown's new UK division. The trio of Sean Cummings (vocals), Wayne Lawes (bass) and Ricardo Reid (keyboards, vocals) based themselves in London, with their initial demos being funded by a local community arts project. Hardly new to the music scene, Lawes had undertaken production work for Mica Paris, Loose Ends and the Jones Girls among others, Reid was an in-demand session keyboardist, and all three had contributed to Vanessa Simon's 1992 release *Family Madness*. Already signed to ARP, Kreuz released the popular club track 'Hush Hush' and finalized a contract with Motown to release their debut *New Generation*. The album featured a statement of intent with 'UK Swing', but there was actually little to differentiate their sound from American swingbeat acts such as Boyz II Men.

● ALBUMS: *New Generation* (Motown 1992)★★★.

Kubota, Toshi

b. *c*.1962, Japan. Arguably the most successful Japanese artist to transfer American-styled soul and urban R&B into an Oriental vernacular, in 1995 Toshi made a serious push to gain international acceptance. *Sunshine Moonlight* featured noted collaborators such as Nile Rodgers, Omar Hakim and Caron Wheeler, with whom he performed a duet cover version of Bill Withers' 'Just The Two Of Us'. The lead-off single, 'Funk It Up', was remixed for the US market by leading house music producer David Morales, and also featured on a mini-album of remixes of previously Japanese-only singles. Resident in New York since 1993, the album was recorded there with Toshi as producer, along with three tracks completed in Los Angeles sessions with Christian Warren. Describing the results as 'pop, but with a black flavour', Toshi was coached in the presentation of lyrics to make them more accessible to native English speakers.

● ALBUMS: *Sunshine Moonlight* (Sony/Columbia 1995)★★★.

Kut Klose

Formed in Atlanta, Georgia, USA, by the female trio of Tabitha Duncan, Athena Cage and LaVonn Battle, Kut Klose specialize in a sassy brand of urban R&B pop, primarily mounted on their smooth harmonies. Their debut album, *Surrender*, was the second to be released on Keith Sweat's Keia Records label (the first being Silk's platinum-selling debut), and merged pop sensibilities with hip-hop beats and simplistic but effective lyrics - as Battle puts it: 'A little hip hop, a little rhythm and blues, a little soulful and a little youthful.' Comprising ballads such as 'I Like' and 'Giving You My Love' alongside the 'new Jill swing' of 'Don't Change', the opening single was 'Get Up On It', a duet with Sweat himself. The album was written and produced by Sweat, Eric McCaine (of Entouch) and the group themselves, and recorded at the Sweat Shop, the state-of-the-art studio built by Sweat in his Atlanta home.

● ALBUMS: *Surrender* (Keia 1995)★★★.

L.A. And Babyface

US songwriters and producers who have become the Chinn And Chapman of black pop/dance in the 90s. Sharing a knack for knowing what is palatable both on radio and in clubland, L.A. Reid (also of the Deele) and Babyface (b. Kenneth Edmonds, 10 April 1959, Indianapolis, Indiana, USA, ex-Manchild and the Deele) began a glittering career when helming Pebbles' instant smash, 'Girlfriend', in 1988. Reid later married the San Franciscan diva, while Babyface boasts kinship with Kevon and Melvin Edmonds of After 7. Their output is typified by hard, fast rhythms, and an up-tempo approach enhanced by the strong melodic abilities of their chosen vocalists. These have included Bobby Brown, Paula Abdul, the Boys, Midnight Star, Toni Braxton and the Jacksons. Babyface, meanwhile, has also released a succession of smooth, lovers' rock albums. His 1991 set included duets recorded for albums by Pebbles and Karyn White. Babyface won a Grammy award for Producer of the Year in 1995.

L.V.

b. Larry Sanders, Los Angeles, California, USA. His stage name an acronym for Large Variety, engaging gospel/soul singer L.V. first came to prominence through his contribution to the huge international success of rapper Coolio's 'Gangsta's Paradise'. For many, it was L.V.'s soaring vocal refrain that made the song so memorable, as much as Coolio's bleak, understated narrative. L.V. grew up the youngest of six brothers, his interest in music fired by his father's skills in singing gospel and R&B, while still working as a carpenter. He sang in talent shows throughout his high school years, usually covering classic soul material. When he attended college he majored in music and joined the gospel group Voices Of South Central. However, in the mid-80s he became the innocent victim of a mistaken identity shooting, and was shot nine times at close range outside his home in South Central, Los Angeles. Hospitalized for two months, he spent the next two years in a wheelchair. Although already religious, the event hardened his spiritual resolve. When 'Gangsta's Paradise' became a major hit, it was due in no small part to Stevie Wonder's allowing L.V. and Coolio to adapt the song from his 'Pastime Paradise'. All three later appeared on stage together to sing the song at the 1995 *Billboard* Awards ceremony. He followed up this collaborative success with the release of his own single, 'Throw Your Hands Up', featuring Naughty By Nature, and his first album, *I Am L.V.*

● ALBUMS: *I Am L.V.* (Tommy Boy 1996)★★★.

LaBelle

This popular soul act evolved from two friends, Patti LaBelle (b. Patricia Holte, 24 May 1944, Philadelphia, Pennsylvania, USA) and Cindy Birdsong (b. 15 December 1939, Camden, New Jersey, USA), who sang together in a high school group, the Ordettes. In 1962, they teamed up with two girls from another local attraction, the Del Capris - Nona Hendryx (b. 18 August 1945, Trenton, New Jersey, USA) and Sarah Dash (b. 24 May 1942, Trenton, New Jersey, USA). Philadelphia producer Bobby Martin named the quartet after a local label, Bluebell Records, and the group became Patti LaBelle And The Blue-Belles. Infamous for their emotional recordings of 'You'll Never Walk Alone', 'Over The Rainbow' and 'Danny Boy', the quartet also wrung a fitting melodrama from 'I Sold My Heart To The Junkman' and 'Down The Aisle (Wedding Song)'. This almost kitchen-sink facet has obscured their more lasting work, of which 'Groovy Kind Of Love' (later a hit for the Mindbenders) is a fine example. Cindy Birdsong left the group in 1967 to replace Florence Ballard in the Supremes, but the remaining trio stayed together despite failing commercial fortunes. Expatriate Briton Vicki Wickham, a former producer on UK television's pop show *Ready Steady Go!*, became their manager and suggested the trio drop their anachronistic name and image and embrace a rock-orientated direction. Having supported the Who on a late 60s concert tour, LaBelle then accompanied Laura Nyro on *Gonna Take A Miracle*, a session that inspired their album debut. One of the few female groups to emerge from the passive 60s to embrace the radical styles of the next decade, their album releases won critical praise, but the trio did not gain commercial success until the release of *Nightbirds*. The 1975 single 'Lady Marmalade (Voulez-Vous Coucher Avec Moi Ce Soir?)' was an international hit single produced by Allen Toussaint and composed by Bob Crewe and Kenny Nolan. Subsequent singles, however, failed to emulate this achievement. *Phoenix* and *Chameleon* were less consistent, although the group continued to court attention for their outlandish, highly visual stage costumes. LaBelle owed much of its individuality to Nona Hendryx, who emerged as an inventive and distinctive composer. Her sudden departure in 1976 was a fatal blow and the group broke apart. Patti LaBelle embarked on a solo career and has since enjoyed considerable success.

● ALBUMS: as Patti LaBelle And The Blue-Belles *Sweethearts Of The Apollo* (Atlantic 1963)★★★, *Sleigh Bells, Jingle Belles* (Atlantic 1963)★★, *On Stage* (Atlantic 1964)★★, *Over The Rainbow* (Atlantic 1966)★★; as LaBelle *LaBelle* (1971)★★★, *Moonshadow* (1972)★★★, *Pressure Cookin'* (1973)★★★★, *Nightbirds* (Epic 1974)★★★★, *Phoenix* (Epic 1975)★★, *Chameleon* (Epic 1976)★★.

● COMPILATIONS: *The Early Years* (1993)★★★, *Over The Rainbow - The Atlantic Years* (1994)★★★.

LaBelle, Patti

b. Patricia Holte, 24 May 1944, Philadelphia, Pennsylvania, USA. The former leader of Labelle began her solo career in 1976. Although her first releases showed promise, she was unable to regain the profile enjoyed by her former group and at the beginning of the 80s, Patti agreed to tour with a revival of the stage play *Your Arms Are Too Short To Box With God*. The production reached Broadway in 1982 and, with Al Green as a co-star, became one of the year's hits. Having made her film debut as a blues singer in *A Soldier's Story* (1984), Patti LaBelle resumed recording with 'Love Has Finally Come At Last', a magnificent duet with Bobby Womack. Two tracks from 1984's box-office smash *Beverly Hills Cop*, 'New Attitude' (US Top 20) and 'Stir It Up', also proved popular. 'On My Own', a sentimental duet with Michael McDonald, was a spectacular hit in 1986. This million-selling single confirmed LaBelle's return and although some commentators criticize her almost operatic delivery, she remains a powerful and imposing performer. She made a return to the US stage in 1989, performing in various states with the 'lost' Duke Ellington musical *Queenie Pie*, and has continued to release strong albums throughout the 90s.

● ALBUMS: *Patti LaBelle* (Epic 1977)★★★, *Tasty* (Epic 1978)★★★, *It's Alright With Me* (Epic 1979)★★★, *Released* (Epic 1980)★★★, *The Spirit's In It* (Philadelphia International 1981)★★★, *I'm In Love Again* (Philadelphia International 1983)★★★, *Patti* (Philadelphia International 1985)★★★, *The Winner In You* (MCA 1986)★★★, *Be Yourself* (MCA 1989)★★, *Starlight Christmas* (MCA 1990)★★★, *Burnin'* (MCA 1991)★★★, *Live!* (MCA 1992)★★, *Gems* (MCA 1994)★★★, *Flame* (MCA 1997)★★★.

● COMPILATIONS: *Best Of ...* (Epic 1986)★★★, *Greatest Hits* (MCA 1996)★★★.

LAKESIDE

Formed in 1969, US vocalists Tiemeyer McCain, Thomas Oliver Shelby, Otis Stokes and Mark Woods were augmented by an instrumental unit consisting of Steve Shockley (guitar), Norman Beavers (keyboards), Marvin Craig (bass), Fred Alexander (drums) and Fred Lewis (percussion). Originally based in Dayton, Ohio, USA, this funk group secured its first hit in 1978 with 'It's All The Way Live'. Released on the Solar label, it was the first of a series of popular singles including 'Fantastic Voyage' (1980), 'I Want To Hold Your Hand' (1982) and 'Outrageous' (1984), all of which reached the US R&B Top 10. Although guitarist Shockley was an integral part of the Solar house band, Lakeside lacked the profile of label-mates Shalamar. A three-year chart hiatus ended in 1987, but that year's 'Bullseye' remains the group's last chart entry to date.

● ALBUMS: *Shot Of Love* (Solar 1978)★★★, *Rough Riders* (Solar 1979)★★★, *Fantastic Voyage* (Solar 1980)★★★, *Keep On Moving Straight Ahead* (Solar 1981)★★, *Your Wish Is My Command* (Solar 1982)★★, *Untouchables* (Solar 1983)★★★, *Outrageous* (Solar 1984)★★.

LAMPLIGHTERS

This vocal R&B outfit was formed in 1952 at Jordan High School in Los Angeles, California, USA, but was always too erratic and plagued with personal problems to be destined for success in the long haul. Leon Hughes, Matthew Nelson and Willie Ray Rockwell comprised the initial trio, who entered a talent show at Johnny Otis's Barrell House but came second to singer Thurston Harris. They set about convincing him to join forces with them, and he eventually agreed. Al Frazier, formerly vocalist with the Mellomoods, helped choreograph their rough stage act. Their performances soon evolved into some of the most exciting and wild events on the west coast R&B circuit, with acrobatics and audience participation that predated the rock 'n' roll boom. Frazier, too, was persuaded to join the group. After losing Leon Hughes the unit secured a contract at Federal Records, having been once more reduced to a quartet. Their debut single, a powerful ballad titled 'Part Of Me', failed to garner its just reward, though it did introduce them as the Lamplighters (Federal boss Ralph Bass had chosen the name in the absence of any band decision). A second single emerged, 'Bee Bop Wino', but its title ironically mirrored the slide of several members of the band into alcoholism. Indeed, Rockwell later died after drunkenly crashing his car into a telephone pole. In 1954, following the release of 'Sad Life', 'Smootchie', 'I Used To Cry Mercy, Mercy' and 'Salty Dog', the group embarked on a major tour, with Eddie Jones and Harold Lewis deputizing for Rockwell and Nelson. Harris quit halfway through the tour because of a disagreement over money, and that appeared to be the end of the story. However, back in Los Angeles, Frazier put together a new version of the band with Carl White, Sonny Harris and a returning Matthew Nelson. The new formation christened itself the Tenderfoots. Four singles, beginning with 'Kissing Bug' in March 1955, failed to bring any success, and they returned to the Lamplighters name after renewing their friendship with Thurston Harris. Three final singles emerged on Federal between 1955 and 1956. However, Thurston Harris's old behaviour problems resurfaced and he was soon replaced by Turner Wilson III. After this, the group changed names again to become the Sharps, while Thurston Harris enjoyed one major solo single, 'Little Bitty Pretty One' (which ironically featured the Sharps as uncredited backing band).

LANCE, MAJOR

b. 4 April 1939, Winterville, Mississippi, USA, d. 3 September 1994, Decatur, Georgia, USA. A former amateur boxer and a dancer on the Jim Lounsbury record-hop television show, Lance also sang with the Five Gospel Harmonaires and for a brief period with Otis Leavill and Barbara Tyson in the Floats. His 1959 Mercury release, 'I Got A Girl', was written and produced by Curtis Mayfield, a high school contemporary, but Lance's career was not truly launched until he signed with OKeh Records three years later. 'Delilah' opened his account there, while a further Mayfield song, the stylish 'The Monkey Time' in 1963, gave the singer a US Top 10 hit. The partnership between singer and songwriter continued through 1963-64 with a string of US pop chart hits: 'Hey Little Girl', 'Um Um Um Um Um Um', 'The Matador' and 'Rhythm'. Although Lance's range was more limited than that of his associate, the texture and phrasing mirrored that of Mayfield's work with his own group, the Impressions. 'Ain't That A Shame', in 1965, marked a pause in their relationship as its commercial success waned. Although further vibrant singles followed, notably 'Investigate' and 'Ain't No Soul (In These Rock 'N' Roll Shoes)', Lance left OKeh for Dakar Records in 1968 where 'Follow The Leader' was a minor R&B hit. Two 1970 releases on Curtom, 'Stay Away From Me' and 'Must Be Love Coming Down', marked a reunion with Mayfield. From there, Lance moved to Volt, Playboy and Osiris, the last of which he co-owned with Al Jackson, a former member of Booker T. And The MGs. These spells were punctuated by a two-year stay in Britain (1972-74), during which Lance recorded for Contempo and Warner Brothers. Convicted of selling cocaine in 1978, the singer emerged from prison to find his OKeh recordings in demand as part of America's 'beach music' craze, where aficionados in Virginia and the Carolinas maintained a love of vintage soul. A heart attack in September 1994 proved fatal for Lance.

● ALBUMS: *Monkey Time* (OKeh 1963)★★★, *Major Lance's Greatest Hits - Recorded 'Live' At The Torch* (OKeh 1973)★★, *Now Arriving* (Motown 1978)★★, *The Major's Back* (1983)★★, *Live At Hinkley* (1986)★★.

● COMPILATIONS: *Um Um Um Um Um - The Best Of Major Lance* (OKeh 1964)★★★, *Major's Greatest Hits* (OKeh 1965)★★★, *The Best Of* ... (Epic 1976)★★★, *Monkey Time* recorded 60s (Edsel 1983)★★★, *Swing'est Hits Of* ... (1984)★★★, *Best Of* ... (1994)★★★.

LARKS

Originally known as Don Julian And The Meadowlarks, and formed in 1953, this US group consisted of Julian (lead), Ronald Barrett, (tenor) Earl Jones (baritone) and Randy Jones (bass). Barrett was replaced with Glen Reagan by the time the group recorded its first single, 'Heaven And Paradise', for the Dootone label. That record failed to make the R&B charts and Julian went on to record under various names for the next decade. In 1965, Julian wrote a dance song, 'The Jerk', after seeing a group of children doing a new dance by that name. He assembled a new group, consisting of Charles Morrison, Ted Waters and himself, and called it the Larks; the group's back-up band assumed the Meadowlarks name. Released on the Money label, the single climbed to number 7 in early 1965. The group was unable to follow it with another hit, although other bands, such as the Capitols and the Miracles, capitalized on the new dance craze by recording, respectively, 'Cool Jerk' and 'Come On And Do The Jerk'.

● ALBUMS: *The Jerk* (Money 1965)★★★, *Soul Kaleidoscope* (Money 1966)★★★, *Superslick* (Money 1967)★★★.

LARKS (APOLLO)

An R&B vocal group from Raleigh, North Carolina, USA. The members were Eugene Mumford (tenor/lead), Thurmon Ruth (baritone/lead), Alden Bunn (baritone/lead/guitar), Raymond Barnes (tenor), Hadie Rowe Jnr. (baritone) and David McNeil (bass). The group began as a gospel ensemble, the Jubilators, who were formed in 1950 by Ruth and Bunn after they had withdrawn from the Selah Jubilee Singers (a New York City gospel group that Ruth had formed and led since 1927). The Jubilators went to New York City and to obtain seed money, immediately recorded gospel with four different companies under four different names; the Selah Singers for Jubilee, Jubilators for Regal, Four Barons for Savoy and Southern Harmonaires for Apollo. The latter wanted the group to record some secular tracks and so the group became the Larks to record R&B. It was with the Larks' tracks that the group obtained lasting success and fame. They made their first impact with romantic ballads using as lead the beautiful voice of Mumford, and initial hits in early 1951 were 'Hopefully Yours' (backed with the masterful 'When I Leave These Prison Walls') and 'My Reverie'. The blues side of the group, with Bunn as lead and on guitar, came to the forefront on their next tracks, when in the last half of 1951 they had hits with a Sonny Boy Williamson song, 'Eyesight To The Blind' (number 5 R&B), and 'Little Side Car' (number 10 R&B). These were the group's last hits, and in 1952 the Larks disbanded. Mumford joined the Golden Gate Quartet, and in 1954 formed a new Larks group, but the magic was gone and the records they made were poor. The new Larks disbanded in 1955, and Mumford joined Billy Ward And The Dominoes and sang lead on their 'Stardust' and 'Deep Purple' hits. Alden Bunn organized the Wheels ('My Heart's Desire') before later carving out a career as blues singer Tarhill Slim. He also made some successful duet recordings with Little Ann.

● COMPILATIONS: *My Reverie* (Relic 1988)★★★, *When I Leave These Prison Walls* (Relic 1988)★★★.

LASALLE, DENISE

b. Denise Craig, 16 July 1939, LeFlore County, Mississippi, USA. Having moved to Chicago in 1954 to pursue a career as a fiction writer, LaSalle turned to songwriting and by the late 60s had begun to record for Billy 'The Kid' Emerson's Tarpon label, on which she achieved a sizeable local hit, 'A Love Reputation', in 1967. In 1969, she formed Crajon productions with her husband, Bill Jones, and also began working with producer Willie Mitchell in Memphis. After a period writing and producing for other artists, LaSalle returned to recording her own compositions, and one of the first results, 'Trapped By A Thing Called Love', released not on her own label but on Westbound in 1971, reached number 1 in the US R&B charts and climbed to the US pop Top 20. Several excellent, sometimes uncompromising, singles followed, including 'Man Sized Job' (1972), 'Married, But Not To Each Other' (1976) and 'What It Takes To Get A Good Woman' (1973). A stylist in the mould of Laura Lee, Ann Peebles and Millie Jackson, LaSalle continued to enjoy hits during the late 70s, but is now better known for her 1985 UK Top 10 novelty hit, 'My Toot Toot'. Her 1997 album *Smokin' In Bed* was an unexpected commercial success.

● ALBUMS: *Trapped By A Thing Called Love* (Westbound 1972)★★★, *On The Loose* (Westbound 1973)★★★, *Here I Am Again* (Westbound 1975)★★★, *Second Breath* (ABC/Dot 1976)★★★, *The Bitch Is Bad* (ABC 1977)★★, *Under The Influence* (ABC 1978)★★, *Unwrapped* (MCA 1979)★★★, *I'm So Hot* (MCA 1980)★★, *And Satisfaction*

Guaranteed (MCA 1981)★★★, *A Lady In The Streets* (Malaco 1983)★★★, *Right Place, Right Time* (Malaco 1984)★★★, *Love Talkin'* (Malaco 1985)★★★, *My Toot Toot* (Malaco 1985)★★★, *Rain And Fire* (Malaco 1986)★★★, *It's Lying Time Again* (Malaco 1987)★★★, *Hittin' Where It Hurts* (Malaco 1988)★★★, *Holding Hands With The Blues* (Malaco 1989)★★★, *Still Trapped* (Malaco 1990)★★★, *Smokin' In Bed* (Malaco 1997)★★★.
● COMPILATIONS: *Doin' It Right* (Malaco 1973)★★★★.

LATIMORE

b. Benjamin Latimore, 7 September 1939, Charleston, Tennessee, USA. This singer, who performed under his surname only, brought a blues feeling to 70s soul music. His passionate vocal delivery and keyboard-dominated style was particularly popular with his female audience. Latimore sang gospel music as a child in his family's Baptist church but did not sing professionally until his first year of college, where he worked with a group called the Hi-Toppers. The group had already recorded for Excello Records when Latimore took over the piano position; he never recorded with the group but remained with them until 1962. At that time he joined Joe Henderson's revue as pianist, and with that group backed artists such as Ben E. King, Slim Harpo and Jimmy Reed in concert. Latimore left Henderson in 1964 and worked as an opening act for teen-idol Steve Alaimo. He also recorded some unsuccessful singles for the Dade label at this time, but finally achieved a hit in 1973 for the related Glades label, with a remake of 'T-Bone' Walker's 'Stormy Monday'. The following year Latimore reached his commercial height with a number 1 R&B single, 'Let's Straighten It Out'. He charted with 13 singles in total for Glades during the 70s, reaching the R&B Top 10 twice more. In 1982, he switched to Malaco Records, for whom he continues to record.
● ALBUMS: *Latimore* (Glades 1973)★★★, *More, More, More* (Glades 1974)★★★, *Latimore III* (Glades 1975)★★★★, *It Ain't Where You Been . . .* (Glades 1977)★★★, *Dig A Little Deeper* (Glades 1978)★★★, *Singing In The Key Of Love* (Malaco 1982)★★★, *Good Time Man* (Malaco 1985)★★★, *Every Way But Wrong* (Malaco 1988)★★★, *I'll Do Anything For You* (Malaco 1988)★★★, *Slow Down* (Malaco 1989)★★★, *The Only Way Is Up* (1992)★★★, *Catchin' Up* (1994)★★★.
● COMPILATIONS: *Sweet Vibrations - The Best Of ...* (Sequel 1991)★★★★.

LATTIMORE, KENNY

b. USA. Lattimore first entered the music industry at the age of 14 when he joined the R&B vocal group Maniquin, who recorded briefly for Epic Records in the 80s. When that group broke up, Lattimore remained in the industry as a songwriter for artists including Glenn Jones and Jon Lucien. As a solo artist, Lattimore and new label Columbia Records were keen to project a more mature, sophisticated image, though one still rooted in a traditional R&B style. The reward was substantial sales for his solo debut, which marked him out as a strong male R&B voice, sympathetic towards but stylistically opposed to the hold hip-hop had taken on the genre. As he told the press: 'I have an appreciation for hip-hop and what it's about, but that's not the life I live. I grew up listening to Earth, Wind And Fire albums, and that's what I know. I'm more into listening to the music my parents listened to.' He also stressed his wish to address the negative portrayal of African-American males in the media, and the music industry in particular. Columbia's marketing of Lattimore was certainly targeted at the mainstream, with support slots for R&B/soul traditionalists such as Chaka Khan and Barry White. In the meantime, Lattimore achieved his biggest singles success in the autumn of 1997 with 'For You'.
● ALBUMS: *Kenny Lattimore* (Columbia 1997)★★★.

LATTISAW, STACY

b. 25 November 1966, Washington, DC, USA. Lattisaw emerged as a child prodigy in the late 70s, touring with Ramsey Lewis at the age of 11 and recording her first album for Cotillion Records a year later. Her light and breezy pop-disco style was epitomized by her 1980 US hits, 'Dynamite' and 'Let Me Be Your Angel', produced by Van McCoy and Narada Michael Walden, respectively. She enjoyed success in 1982 with the novelty record 'Attack Of The Name Game', but her subsequent Cotillion releases failed to match the sparkle of her early work. An album of duets with fellow teenager Johnny Gill in 1984 was well received in the disco market, but her solo career was only revived after she signed to Motown in 1986 and enjoyed a major dance hit with 'Nail It To The Wall'.
● ALBUMS: *Young And In Love* (Cotillion 1979)★★★, *Let Me Be Your Angel* (Cotillion 1980)★★★, *With You* (Cotillion 1981)★★★, *Sneakin' Out* (Cotillion 1982)★★★, *16* (Cotillion 1983)★★★, with Johnny Gill *Perfect Combination* (Cotillion 1984)★★, *I'm Not The Same Girl* (1985)★★, *Take Me All The Way* (Motown 1986)★★★, *Personal Attention* (Motown 1988)★★★.

LAVETTE, BETTY

b. Betty Haskin, 1946, Muskegon, Michigan, USA. She gained her first professional experience as part of the touring review run by soul singers Don Gardner and Dee Dee Ford in the early 60s. Her passionate vocal style won her a solo contract with Atlantic Records, where she adopted her stage name for the 1962 R&B hit 'My Man - He's A Loving Man', one of the finest early examples of southern soul. However, she was unable to build on this success, and only made sporadic recordings with small labels during the rest of the decade. Her torch ballad 'Let Me Down Easy' was an R&B hit in 1965, written by country 'rebels' Jim and Tompall Glaser, the song was later covered by the Spencer Davis Group. Lavette recorded material by other country writers, and her version of Mickey Newbury's 'Just Dropped In (To See What Condition My Condition Is In)' in 1969 was later picked up by Kenny Rogers. She enjoyed two further chart successes in 1969-70 with country/soul recordings on Lelan Rogers' Silver Fox label, most notably with the superb, if risqué, 'He Made A Woman Out Of Me', turned into a pop release for Bobbie Gentry. After singles for SSS-International and TCI, LaVette next returned to the Atlantic fold to record two 1971/2 singles for their Atco label. Of these, her searing version of Joe Simon's 'Your Time To Cry' (retitled 'Your Turn To Cry') became yet another high point in a career of little-known but aesthetically sublime recordings. The mid- to late 70s saw singles on Epic and a disco-influenced outing for West End, while LaVette also starred in the Broadway musical *Bubbling Brown Sugar*. In the early 80s, renewed interest in her early recordings led to her being offered a contract with Motown. There she recorded the acclaimed *Tell Me A Lie*, one of the label's few ventures into southern soul. Besides the R&B hit 'Right In The Middle (Of Falling in Love)', the album included impressive remakes of 'I Heard It Through The Grapevine' and 'If I Were Your Woman'. Lavette remains a cult figure among soul fans in the UK, and many of her 60s recordings have been reissued in recent years. In 1992 Lavette recorded two singles and *Not Gonna Happen Twice* on Ian Levine's Motor City label.

● ALBUMS: *Tell Me A Lie* credited as Bettye Lavette (Motown 1980)★★★, *Not Gonna Happen Twice* (Motor City 1992)★★★.

● COMPILATIONS: *Easier To Say* (Charly 1980)★★★, *I'm In Love* (Charly 1985, reissued in 1991 as *Nearer To You* with extra tracks)★★★.

Leach, Lillian, And The Mellows

The original members of the line-up were lead Lillian Leach, first tenor Johnny Wilson, second tenor Harold Johnson and bass Norman Brown. This 50s vocal harmony group from the Bronx, New York, USA, never had a national R&B hit, but enjoyed a number of regional hits on the east coast on the strength of the lead voice of Leach, who possessed one of the warmest and most sensual voices in the history of doo-wop. The group was formed in 1954 and soon signed a contract with veteran Joe Davis on his Jay Dee label. They made their biggest impact with their second release, the exquisitely romantic 'Smoke From A Cigarette', from early 1955. It achieved substantial local success, and during the neo-doo-wop renaissance of the early 60s became one of the most requested oldies. The next release, another remarkable ballad, 'I Still Care' (1955), received modest airplay. Its b-side featured another wonderful ballad, 'I Was A Fool To Care'. The last release for Jay Dee was 'Yesterday's Memories', another underappreciated masterpiece of its time. In 1956 the Mellows moved to the Celeste label, and at this point Norman Brown left and vocal group veterans Arthur Crier and Gary Morrison were added. Commercial success at Celeste was not forthcoming, even for the outstanding 'My Darling'. The group left the company in 1957, and completed one more recording session for Apollo in 1958 (which was left in the can) before disbanding. Johnson and Crier went on to form the Halos, who backed Curtis Lee on 'Pretty Little Angel Eyes'. Lillian Leach And The Mellows probably attained greater fame after the record collecting community rediscovered the group's recordings during the 60s and lionized them, making them perennials on oldies shows for decades afterwards.

● COMPILATIONS: *Yesterday's Memories* (Relic 1992)★★★.

Leavill, Otis

b. Otis Leavill Cobb, 8 February 1941, Atlanta, Georgia, USA. Brought up on Chicago's west side, Leavill came to music through his family's gospel group, the Cobb Quartet. He later formed the short-lived Floats with a childhood friend, Major Lance, and Barbara Tyson. Leavill's first solo single was issued in 1963 and coupled 'Rise Sally Rise' with 'I Gotta Right To Cry', an early Curtis Mayfield song. The singer's reputation was secured with a 1964 release, 'Let Her Love Me', written by Billy Butler and produced by Major. Although he continued to record for several companies, Leavill's principal task was undertaken at OKeh where he assisted producer Carl Davis. The partners would subsequently form the Dakar label in 1967. Leavill recorded four singles for the company, two of which, 'I Love You' and 'Love Uprising', were written by Eugene Record of the Chi-Lites. Leavill later returned to a backroom role working with Davis at Brunswick, and later Chi-Sound, which folded in 1984.

Lee, Jackie

b. Earl Nelson, 8 September 1928, Lake Charles, Louisiana, USA. Lee had an impressive success in 1965 with the dance hit 'The Duck' (number 4 R&B, number 14 pop), but his presence in the R&B scene was far more ubiquitous than was indicated by that one hit. He sang lead on the Hollywood Flames' hit, 'Buzz Buzz Buzz', and was part of the duo of Bob And Earl that had a hit with 'Harlem Shuffle' (number 3 R&B, number 44 pop) in 1964. After 'The Duck', a follow-up, 'Would You Believe', did not make any of the national charts but was highly successful in regional markets across the USA. Lee had a minor success with 'African Boo-Ga-Loo' in 1968 and his last chart record was 'The Chicken' in 1970.

● ALBUMS: *The Duck* (Mirwood 1965)★★.

Lee, Laura

b. Laura Lee Newton, 9 March 1945, Chicago, Illinois, USA. A member of her adopted mother's, Ernestine Rundless's, gospel group the Meditation Singers, Lee's first secular recording was made for the Detroit-based Ric-Tic label. She was signed to Chess Records in 1966, who, after failing to find success with a Chicago-recorded single, sent her to Rick Hall's Fame Studio in Muscle Shoals where 'Dirty Man' and the Fame-cut 'Uptight Good Man' became two 1967 R&B hits. She recorded many fine, assertive sides for Chess, before beginning her most prolific period when she joined Hot Wax. 'Wedlock Is A Padlock', 'Women's Love Rights' (both 1970), 'Rip Off' and 'If You Can Beat Me Rockin' (You Can Have My Chair)' (both 1972), continued the singer's uncompromising demands, but such declarations were inverted on 'I'll Catch You When You Fall' (1973) and 'I Can't Make It Alone' (1974) as Lee broadened her canvas. The singer left Hot Wax in 1975, but despite enjoying an R&B hit with 'You're Barking Up The Wrong Tree' (1976), her later output was largely unsuccessful. Laura Lee returned to the gospel field in 1983 with *Jesus Is The Light Of My Life*, which she co-produced with singer Al Green.

● ALBUMS: *Women's Love Rights* (Hot Wax 1971)★★★,

The Two Sides Of Laura Lee (Hot Wax 1972)★★★, *I Can't Make It Alone* (Invictus 1974)★★★, *Jesus Is The Light Of My Life* (1983)★★★.
● COMPILATIONS: *Best Of ...* (1972)★★★, *Love More Than Pride* (1972)★★★, *The Rip Off* (HDH 1984)★★★, *Uptight Good Woman* (1984)★★★, *That's How It Is - The Chess Years* (Chess/MCA 1990)★★★, *Greatest Hits* (HDH/Fantasy 1991)★★★, *Love Rights And Wrongs* (Deep Beats 1997)★★★.

LESTER, KETTY

b. Revoyda Frierson, 16 August 1934, Hope, Arkansas, USA. Ketty Lester began her singing career on completing a music course at San Francisco State College. A residency at the city's Purple Onion club was followed by a successful tour of Europe before she joined bandleader Cab Calloway's revue. Later domiciled in New York, Lester's popular nightclub act engendered a recording contract, of which 'Love Letters' was the first fruit. The singer's cool-styled interpretation of this highly popular standard, originally recorded by Dick Haymes, reached the Top 5 in both the USA and UK in 1962, eventually selling in excess of one million copies. The song has been covered many times, with notable successes for Elvis Presley and Alison Moyet. Its attractiveness was enhanced by a memorable piano figure but Lester was sadly unable to repeat the single's accomplished balance between song, interpretation and arrangement. She later abandoned singing in favour of a career as a film and television actress, with appearances in *Marcus Welby MD*, *Little House On The Prairie*, *The Terminal Man* and *The Prisoner Of Second Avenue*, to name but a few. She was later coaxed back into the studio, but only on her stipulation that it would be exclusively to perform sacred music.
● ALBUMS: *Love Letters* (Era 1962)★★, *Soul Of Me* (RCA Victor 1964)★★, *Where Is Love* (RCA Victor 1965)★★, *When A Woman Loves A Man* (1967)★★, *I Saw Him* (1985)★★.

LEVERT

From Philadelphia, USA, contemporary R&B band LeVert derived their name from the surname of brothers Sean and Gerald Levert, the offspring of O'Jays founder Eddie Levert. The predominantly vocal trio additionally included schoolfriend Marc Gordon. Their debut album, *I Get Hot*, produced the US R&B hit 'I'm Still', but marketing at the small independent Tempre Records failed to satisfy their ambitions. A year later they signed to Atlantic Records and struck number 1 in the US R&B charts with '(Pop, Pop, Pop) Goes My Mind', taken from *Bloodline*. The similarity of Gerald's voice to that of his father's was unmistakable, yet LeVert were undoubtedly a product of the 80s with their advanced production techniques and layered rhythms. The follow-up album, *Bloodline*, went gold and yielded a further substantial crossover pop hit with 'Cassanova'. *Just Coolin'*, accompanied by a successful single of the same title, kept up the commercial momentum, but failed to match the impact of the group's earlier work. With Gerald freelancing as a producer for several other R&B acts, *Rope-A-Dope* again achieved gold status, despite apparent creative stagnation. The group was put on temporary hold when Gerald announced the launch of a solo career in 1991, but he returned for *For Real Tho'*. However, with their lead singer's busy schedule taking centrestage, it appeared for some time that LeVert's absence would become permanent, until the release of *The Whole Scenario* in 1997.
● ALBUMS: *I Get Hot* (Tempre 1985)★★★, *Bloodline* (Atlantic 1986)★★★, *The Big Throwdown* (Atlantic 1987)★★★, *Just Coolin'* (Atlantic 1988)★★★, *Rope-A-Dope* (Atlantic 1990)★★, *For Real Tho'* (Atlantic 1992)★★, *The Whole Scenario* (Atlantic 1997)★★★.

LEVERT, GERALD

b. Philadelphia, USA. Bridging the gap between traditional and contemporary R&B, Gerald Levert has a fine vocal technique first heard in 1985 with the release of the debut album by the group LeVert. By the time that group's *Just Coolin'* had become a major US success, Gerald had already taken time off from the parent group to produce a number of artists with Marc Gordon, including Stephanie Mills, James Ingram, Miki Howard, the O'Jays and Troop. He also wrote 'Whatever It Takes' for Anita Baker's platinum-selling *Compositions* album. *Rope-A-Dope* also went gold for the group, while as head of Atlantic Record's Trevel Productions, Gerald worked with new vocal groups Rude Boy and Men At Large. All these endeavours preceded the announcement of his solo career in 1991. The timing had been carefully planned, and paid huge rewards when 'School Me', 'Can You Handle It', 'Baby Hold On To Me' (featuring his father, Eddie Levert of the O'Jays) and the title track of the parent album *Private Line* achieved major success. The songs, written in conjunction with new partner Tony Nicholas, established him as a major force in contemporary R&B and soul, with an equal emphasis on up-tempo dance numbers and balladeering. Afterwards, Gerald returned to work with LeVert (the band), and their fifth album, *For Real Tho*, earned another gold disc. Further production work with Barry White, Little Joe (lead singer of Rude Boy), Drama and Men At Large interrupted preparations for a second solo set, which finally followed in 1994. *Groove On* was envisaged by the artist as 'a 90s version of a 60s soul show, with a band, a whole horn section, the works'. Once more working with Nicholas, this time the ballads included 'I'd Give Anything', which became the album's first hit single, produced by Grammy award-winning hit-maker David Foster, and the 'issue' song 'How Many Times', which dealt with a woman suffering physical and emotional abuse. The reconstruction of a traditional soul dynamic was enshrined by the presence of Gerald's father as co-producer on 'Same Time, Same Place', while 'Can't Help Myself' was originally written for the Forest Whitaker film *Strapped*. In 1995 he enjoyed further international success with 'Answering Service', confirming Levert as one of the leading lights of modern soul and vocal R&B. The same year also produced a well-received collection of duets performed with his father, titled *Father And Son* (see Levert, Gerald And Eddie).
● ALBUMS: *Private Line* (Atlantic 1991)★★★★, *Groove On* (Atlantic 1994)★★★.

LEVERT, GERALD AND EDDIE

The 1995 release of *Father And Son* paired two legends of soul music, singer and producer Gerald Levert (of LeVert) and his father Eddie, lead singer and founding member of the O'Jays. The album featured a combination of original songs written expressly for the purpose by the duo and a selection of cover versions, including several O'Jays remakes. Produced by Gerald and Tony Nicholas, a co-writer on the project who had worked extensively with Gerald in the past, the album was prompted by requests from fans after the father and son team had performed together in concert on several occasions. With 10 gold and four platinum albums between them, it was a partnership bound to appeal to fans of soul and R&B. The pair had first recorded a duet, 'Baby Hold On To Me', for Gerald's 1991 debut solo album, *Private Line*. It reached the top of the US R&B singles chart in January 1992. In addition to the customary accompanying promotional tour for *Father And Son*, the duo also announced details of a new national scholarship fund overseen by Eddie's 100 Black Men collective.

● ALBUMS: *Father And Son* (East West 1995)★★★.

LEWIS, BARBARA

b. 9 February 1943, Salem, Michigan, USA. Signed to Atlantic Records in 1961, Lewis enjoyed several regional hits before the sensual 'Hello Stranger' established her light but enthralling style. Recorded in Chicago, the performance was enhanced by the vocal support of the Dells. Further singles included the vibrant 'Someday We're Gonna Love Again' (1965), while 'Baby I'm Yours' and 'Make Me Your Baby' (both 1966) maintained her smooth, individual approach. Barbara remained with the label until 1968, but the following year moved to the Stax subsidiary Enterprise. Internal problems sadly doomed the album she made there, and having completed a handful of singles, Lewis withdrew from music altogether.

● ALBUMS: *Hello Stranger* (Atlantic 1963)★★★, *Snap Your Fingers* (Atlantic 1964)★★★, *Baby I'm Yours* (Atlantic 1965)★★★, *It's Magic* (Atlantic 1966)★★★, *Workin' On A Groovy Thing* (Atlantic 1968)★★★, *The Many Grooves Of Barbara Lewis* (Enterprise 1970)★★★.

● COMPILATIONS: *The Best Of ...* (Atlantic 1971)★★★, *Hello Stranger* (Solid Smoke 1981)★★★, *Golden Classics* (Collectables 1987)★★★, *The Many Grooves Of Barbara Lewis* (1992)★★★, *Hello Stranger: The Best Of ...* (Rhino/Atlantic 1994)★★★.

LEWIS, RAMSEY

b. 27 May 1935, Chicago, Illinois, USA. Lewis started playing piano at the age of six. He graduated from school in 1948, after winning both the American Legion Award as an outstanding scholar and a special award for piano services at the Edward Jenner Elementary School. He began his career as an accompanist at the Zion Hill Baptist Church, an experience of gospel that never left him. He later studied music at Chicago Music College with the idea of becoming a concert pianist, but left at the age of 18 to marry. He found a job working in a record shop and joined the Clefs, a seven-piece dance band. In 1956, he formed a jazz trio with the Clefs' rhythm section (whom he had known since high school) - bassist Eldee Young and drummer Isaac 'Red' Holt. Lewis made his debut recordings with the Argo record label, which later became Chess. He also had record dates with prestigious names such as Sonny Stitt, Clark Terry and Max Roach. In 1959, he played at Birdland in New York City and at the Randall's Island Festival. In 1964, 'Something You Got' was a minor hit, but it was 'The In Crowd', an instrumental cover version of Dobie Gray's hit, that made him famous, reaching number 5 in the US charts and selling over a million copies by the end of 1965. Lewis insisted on a live sound, complete with handclaps and exclamations, an infectious translation of a black church feel into pop. His follow-up, 'Hang On Sloopy', reached number 11 and sold another million. These hits set the agenda for his career. Earnings for club dates increased tenfold. His classic 'Wade In The Water' was a major hit in 1966, and became a long-standing encore number for Graham Bond. The rhythm section left and resurfaced as a funk outfit in the mid-70s, variously known as Redd Holt Unlimited and Young-Holt Unlimited. Lewis had an astute ear for hip, commercial sounds: his replacement drummer Maurice White left in 1971 to found the platinum mega-sellers Earth, Wind And Fire. Lewis never recaptured this commercial peak; he attempted to woo his audience by using synthesizers and disco rhythms, and continued securing *Billboard* Top 100 hits well into the 70s. His album success was a remarkable achievement, with over 30 of his albums making the *Billboard* Top 200 listings. *The In Crowd* stayed on the list for almost a year, narrowly missing the top spot. *Mother Nature's Son* was a tribute to the Beatles, while the *Newly Recorded Hits* in 1973 was a dreadful mistake: the originals were far superior. By the 80s he was producing middle-of-the-road instrumental albums and accompanying singers, most notably Nancy Wilson. Nevertheless, it is his 60s hits - simple, infectious and funky - that will long endure.

● ALBUMS: *Down To Earth* (EmArcy 1958)★★★, *Gentleman Of Swing* (Argo 1958)★★★, *Gentlemen Of Jazz* (Argo 1958)★★★, *An Hour With The Ramsey Lewis Trio* (Argo 1959)★★★, *Stretching Out* (Argo 1960)★★★, *The Ramsey Lewis Trio In Chicago* (Argo 1961)★★★, *More Music From The Soil* (Argo 1961)★★★, *Sound Of Christmas* (Argo 1961)★★★, *The Sound Of Spring* (Argo 1962)★★★, *Country Meets The Blues* (Argo 1962)★★★, *Bossa Nova* (Argo 1962)★★★, *Pot Luck* (Argo 1962)★★★, *Barefoot Sunday Blues* (Argo 1963)★★★, *The Ramsey Lewis Trio At The Bohemian Caverns* (Argo 1964)★★★, *Bach To The Blues* (Argo 1964)★★★, *More Sounds Of Christmas* (Argo 1964)★★★, *You Better Believe It* (Argo 1965)★★★★, *The In Crowd* (Argo 1965)★★★★, *Hang On Ramsey!* (Cadet 1965)★★★★, *Swingin'* (Cadet 1966)★★★★, *Wade In The Water* (Cadet 1966)★★★★, *Goin' Latin* (Cadet 1967)★★, *The Movie Album* (Cadet 1967)★★, *Dancing In The Street* (Cadet 1967)★★★, *Up Pops Ramsey Lewis* (Cadet 1968)★★★, *Maiden Voyage* (Cadet 1968)★★★, *Mother Nature's Son* (Cadet 1969)★★, *Another Voyage* (Cadet 1969)★★, *Ramsey Lewis: The Piano Player* (Cadet 1970)★★★, *Them Changes* (Cadet

1970)★★★, *Back To The Roots* (Cadet 1971)★★★, *Upendo Ni Pamoja* (Columbia 1972)★★★, *Funky Serenity* (Columbia 1973)★★, *Sun Goddess* (Columbia 1974)★★★, *Don't It Feel Good* (Columbia 1975)★★★, *Salongo* (Columbia 1976)★★★, *Love Notes* (Columbia 1977)★★★, *Tequila Mockingbird* (Columbia 1977)★★★, *Legacy* (Columbia 1978)★★★, *Routes* (Columbia 1980)★★★, *Three Piece Suite* (Columbia 1981)★★★, *Live At The Savoy* (Columbia 1982)★★★, *Les Fleurs* (1983)★★, *Chance Encounter* (Columbia 1983)★★, with Nancy Wilson *The Two Of Us* (Columbia 1984)★★★, *Reunion* (Columbia 1984)★★★, *Fantasy* (1986)★★, *Keys To The City* (Columbia 1987)★★, *Classic Encounter* (Columbia 1988)★★, with Billy Taylor *We Meet Again* (Columbia 1989)★★★, *Urban Renewal* (Columbia 1989)★★★, *Electric Collection* (Columbia 1991)★★★, *Ivory Pyramid* (GRP 1992)★★, with King Curtis *Instrumental Soul Hits* (1993)★★, *Between The Keys* (GRP 1996)★★.

● COMPILATIONS: *Choice! The Best Of The Ramsey Lewis Trio* (Cadet 1965)★★★, *The Best Of Ramsey Lewis* (Cadet 1970)★★★, *Ramsey Lewis' Newly Recorded All-Time, Non-Stop Golden Hits* (Columbia 1973)★★★, *The Greatest Hits Of Ramsey Lewis* (Chess 1988)★★★, *20 Greatest Hits* (1992)★★★, *Collection* (More Music 1995)★★★.

● FILMS: *Gonks Go Beat* (1965).

LEWIS, SMILEY

b. Overton Amos Lemons, 5 July 1913, DeQuincy, Louisiana, USA, d. 7 October 1966. While failing to gain the commercial plaudits his work deserved, this New Orleans-based artist was responsible for some of that city's finest music. He made his recording debut, as Smiling Lewis, in 1947, but his strongest work appeared during the 50s. 'The Bells Are Ringing' (1952) took him into the US R&B chart, and his biggest hit came three years later with 'I Hear You Knocking'. This seminal slice of Crescent City blues featured pianist Huey 'Piano' Smith and bandleader Dave Bartholomew, and was revived successfully in 1970 by Dave Edmunds. Smiley's career was dogged by ill luck. His original version of 'Blue Monday' was a hit in the hands of Fats Domino, while Elvis Presley took another song, 'One Night', and by altering its risqué lyric, secured a massive pop hit in the process. A further powerful Lewis performance, 'Shame, Shame, Shame', has subsequently become an R&B standard and it was even covered by the Merseybeats on their EP *On Stage* in 1964. This underrated artist continued recording into the 60s, but died of cancer in 1966.

● ALBUMS: *I Hear You Knocking* (Imperial 1961)★★★.

● COMPILATIONS: *Shame Shame Shame* (1970)★★★, *The Bells Are Ringing* (1978)★★★, *Caledonia's Party* (KC 1986)★★★, *New Orleans Bounce - 30 Of His Best* (Sequel 1991)★★★.

LIGGINS, JOE

b. 9 July 1916, Guthrie, Oklahoma, USA, d. 26 July 1987, Los Angeles, California, USA. After attempting to learn various brass instruments, Joe Liggins settled down to study musical composition and piano arrangement. After moving to California, he began writing for and playing with local bands, graduating in the 40s to the respected units of Cee Pee Johnson and Sammy Franklin, the latter of whom he was working with when, in 1945, he left to form his own group, the Honeydrippers. Joe Liggins And His Honeydrippers first recorded for Exclusive, with whom they had 10 hits between 1945 and 1949 - including the huge crossover hits 'The Honeydripper' and 'I've Got A Right To Cry'; he followed his brother Jimmy to Specialty Records in 1950 where the hits continued with 'Rag Mop' and the hugely successful 'Pink Champagne' (*Billboard*'s number 1 blues record of the year). Leaving Specialty in 1954, Liggins went briefly to Mercury (1954) and Aladdin Records (1956) before returning to Mercury to record an album in 1962. Later singles appeared on tiny independents such as his own Honeydripper label and Jimmy Liggins' Duplex Records, and he was enjoying something of a renaissance at the time of his death in 1987.

● ALBUMS: *Honeydripper* (Mercury 1962)★★★★, *Great R&B Oldies* (1972)★★★, with Jimmy Liggins *Saturday Night Boogie Woogie Man* (1974)★★★, *Darktown Strutters' Ball* (1981)★★★, *Joe Liggins & His Honeydrippers* (1985)★★★, *The Honeydripper* (Jukebox Lil 1988)★★★, *Joe Liggins & The Honeydrippers* (Ace 1989)★★★★, *Vol. 2: Drippers Boogie* (Ace 1993)★★★★.

LIGHT OF THE WORLD

Pioneering Brit funk band Light Of The World were formed in London in 1978, the original line-up comprising Jean Paul 'Bluey' Maunick (guitar), Neville 'Breeze' McKreith (guitar), Everton McCalla (drums), Chris Etienne (percussion), Paul 'Tubs' Williams (bass), Peter Hinds (keyboards), Canute Wellington (trumpet) and David 'Baps' Baptiste (trumpet). Taking their name from a Kool And The Gang album, they signed to Ensign Records in 1979, achieving an immediate dancefloor hit with their debut single 'Swingin''. The release of their self-titled debut album was marred by the death of Etienne during a promotional tour. Nigel Martinez, Nat Augustin and Gee Bello were added to the line-up for *Round Trip* (produced by Augie Johnson), but following further minor hits the band split up in 1981. Wellington, Baptiste and McKreith became Beggar & Co., while Maunick, Hinds and Williams formed Incognito. There was a brief Light Of The World reunion when Augustin, Bello and Tubbs collaborated on an album for EMI in 1982. Hinds went on to become a respected R&B/soul producer, including work with the Chimes. Light Of The World reformed in 1990, recording for Chrysalis Records.

● ALBUMS: *Light Of The World* (Ensign 1979)★★★ *Round Trip* (Ensign 1980)★★★ *Check Us Out* (EMI 1982)★★.

● COMPILATIONS: *Best Of Light Of The World* (Ensign 1985)★★★.

LIGHTHOUSE FAMILY

UK soul band the Lighthouse Family consists of the Newcastle-based duo of Tunde Baiyewu (b.1969), a vocalist of Nigerian descent, and London-born songwriter and musician Paul Tucker (b. 1969, England). They met while working at nightclub bars in the north-east of

England, at which time Tucker was also recording his own compositions at home in his spare time. They formed a partnership in early 1993 after being introduced by a local soul DJ. After hearing a tape of the group's 'Ocean Drive' played down the phone, Polydor Records A&R director Colin Barlow recognized their potential, particularly in the mainstream album market, and signed them to a long-term development contract. Influenced by artists such as Bob Marley, Stevie Wonder and Marvin Gaye, the duo made their debut in June 1995 with 'Lifted', which entered the lower reaches of the UK chart. This, like their debut album, was produced by Mike Peden, formerly of UK soul band the Chimes and producer for Shara Nelson and Darryl Hall. 'Ocean Drive', also the title of the debut album, was placed on the soundtrack to the Richard E. Grant film *Jack And Sarah* before being released as their second single. Determined not to see a good song die, 'Lifted' was reissued in 1996 and this time caught the mood of the public by becoming a major hit. 'Goodbye Heartbreak' and 'Loving Every Minute' completed the duo's impressive run of hit singles. The 1997 follow-up *Postcards From Heaven* confirmed Lighthouse Family's status as one of Britain's biggest new bands, and featured the huge-selling singles 'Raincloud' and 'High'.

● ALBUMS: *Ocean Drive* (Polydor 1995)★★★, *Postcards From Heaven* (Wild Card/Polydor 1997)★★★.

Limmie And The Family Cooking

Led by Limmie Snell (b. Dalton, Alabama, USA), this vocal trio was hugely popular on the UK disco scene in the mid-70s. Snell's first musical influence was gospel but at the age of 11 he made a series of novelty records as Lemmie B. Good. He next formed a singing group with his sisters Jimmy and Martha. After an initial recording for Phil Spector's Scepter label, they were signed to Avco, where Steve Metz and Sandy Linzer produced the catchy 'You Can Do Magic', a UK Top 10 hit in 1973. This was followed by the less successful 'Dreamboat', but the next year the trio had another UK bestseller with a revival of the Essex's 1963 hit 'A Walking Miracle'. More pop than soul, Limmie And the Family Cooking next recorded a version of the 50s hit 'Lollipop'. Despite its failure, the group remained a favourite with British disco audiences and appeared on soul revival bills in the UK over the next decade.

Linx

One of the leading lights in the brief but high-profile Brit-funk movement of the early 80s (with Light Of The World, its spin-offs Beggar And Co, Imagination and Freeez), Linx were based around the duo of David Grant (b. 8 August, 1956, Kingston, Jamaica, West Indies; vocals) and Sketch Martin (b. 1954, Antigua, West Indies; bass), and completed by Bob Carter (keyboards) and Andy Duncan (drums). Grant's family moved to the UK in the late 50s and he grew up in north London. Sketch was taken to the UK when he was four, and was based in West Ham, east London. They met while working in a hi-fi shop. Grant later opened a record shop with his cousin, and became a junior reporter on a local paper, before working at Island Records' press office. Martin worked for the civil service, a film company, and the Performing Rights Society. They had their debut single, 'You're Lying', released as a private pressing (1,000 copies) and sold through a specialist funk shop before Chrysalis Records picked up on it and enabled it to be a hit. They were the first of the Brit Funk bands to make an impression in the USA, when 'You're Lying' made the R&B charts. Further singles included 'Intuition' and 'So This Is Romance'. The video for 'Intuition' featured the late Bertice Reading, while their stage performances harked back to the best traditions of the Glitter Band and Adam And The Ants by employing twin drummers. Grant moved on to a solo career with Chrysalis and had hit duets with Jaki Graham. He moved to Polydor Records in 1987 then Fourth and Broadway in 1990.

● ALBUMS: *Intuition* (Chrysalis 1981)★★★, *Go Ahead* (Chrysalis 1981)★★.

● COMPILATIONS: *The Best Of David Grant And Linx* (Chrysalis 1993)★★★.

Little Anthony And The Imperials

Formed in Brooklyn, New York, USA, in 1957, and originally called the Chesters, the group comprised 'Little' Anthony Gourdine (b. 8 January 1940, Brooklyn, New York, USA), Ernest Wright Jnr. (b. 24 August 1941, Brooklyn, New York, USA), Clarence Collins (b. 17 March 1941, Brooklyn, New York, USA), Tracy Lord and Glouster Rogers (b. 1940). A vital link between doo-wop and sweet soul, the Imperials were the prototype for the Delfonics and Stylistics. Gourdine first recorded in 1956 as a member of the Duponts. From there he helped form the Chesters, who became the Imperials on signing to the End label. The 'Little Anthony' prefix was subsequently added at the suggestion of the influential disc jockey Alan Freed. The group's first hit, the haunting 'Tears On My Pillow' (1958), encapsulated the essence of street-corner harmony. Further success came with 'So Much' (1959) and 'Shimmy Shimmy Ko-Ko-Bop' (1960), before Gourdine was persuaded to embark on an ill-fated solo career. In 1964, he formed a 'new' Imperials around Wright, Collins and Sammy Strain (b. 9 December 1940). Their first hit, 'I'm On The Outside (Looking In)', showcased Gourdine's dazzling falsetto, a style continued on 'Goin' Out Of My Head' and 'Hurt So Bad' (both of which reached the US pop Top 10). Complementing these graceful releases were such up-tempo offerings as 'Better Use Your Head' and 'Gonna Fix You Good' (both 1966). The line-up later drifted apart and in 1974 Sammy Strain replaced William Powell in the O'Jays. Three years later, Collins formed his own 'Imperials', touring Britain on the strength of two hit singles, a reissued 'Better Use Your Head', and a new recording, 'Who's Gonna Love Me'. In the 80s Gourdine released *Daylight* on the religious outlet Songbird.

● ALBUMS: *We Are Little Anthony And The Imperials* (End 1959)★★★, *Shades Of The 40's* (End 1961)★★★, *I'm On The Outside Looking In* (DCP 1964)★★★, *Goin' Out Of My Head* (DCP 1965)★★★, *Paying Our Dues* (Veep 1967)★★★, *Reflections* (Veep 1967)★★, *Movie Grabbers* (Veep 1968)★★, *Out Of Sight, Out Of Mind* (United

Artists 1969)★★, *On A New Street* (Avco 1974)★★. Solo: Anthony Gourdine *Daylight* (Songbird 1980)★★.
● COMPILATIONS: *Little Anthony And The Imperials Greatest Hits* (Roulette 1965)★★★, *The Best Of Little Anthony And The Imperials* (DCP 1966)★★★, *The Best Of Little Anthony And The Imperials* (Rhino 1989)★★★.

Little Beaver

b. William Hale, 15 August 1945, Forest City, Arkansas, USA. Little Beaver, a singer and guitarist, made his mark on the tail-end of the soul era in the early 70s, with a typical southern-style body of work that included both blues and soul traditions. Little Beaver grew up in Arkansas but as a teenager moved to Florida. He recorded some local hits for various labels, with a Bobby Bland-style gospel-blues voice. He then joined Henry Stone's TK complex of labels in 1971, and penned some hits for Betty Wright as well as playing on innumerable sessions. By the time Little Beaver first recorded on his own for TK's Cat subsidiary in 1972, he had found his own voice and style and had a national hit with 'Joey' (number 48 R&B). His biggest hit was 'Party Down' (number 2 R&B) from 1974. His deep southern sound was not all that compatible with the emerging disco and funk trends and Beaver had his last chart record in 1976.
● ALBUMS: *Joey* (Cat 1972)★★★★, *Black Rhapsody* (Cat 1973)★★★, *Little Beaver* (Cat 1974)★★★, *Party Down* (Cat 1975)★★, *When Was The Last Time* (Cat 1977)★★.
● COMPILATIONS: *Party Down* (Collectables 1994)★★★, *The Very Best Of ...* (Sequel 1997)★★.

Little Eva

b. Eva Narcissus Boyd, 29 June 1943, Bellhaven, North Carolina, USA. Discovered by songwriters Carole King and Gerry Goffin, Little Eva shot to fame in 1962 with the international hit 'The Loco-Motion', a driving, dance-based song. Its ebullient, adolescent approach was muted on a follow-up single, 'Keep Your Hands Off My Baby', but although further releases from the following year, 'Let's Turkey Trot' and 'Old Smokey Locomotion', revived its novelty appeal, they lacked its basic excitement. Eva continued to record until 1965, but her only other substantial hit came with 'Swinging On A Star', a duet with Big Dee Irwin, on which she was, unfortunately, uncredited. She made a UK chart comeback in 1972 with a reissue of 'The Loco-Motion', which peaked at number 11, and the song's lasting appeal was reaffirmed in 1988 when Kylie Minogue emulated Eva's original UK chart position.
● ALBUMS: *L-L-L-L-Loco-Motion* (Dimension 1962)★★.
● COMPILATIONS: *Lil' Loco'Motion* (Rock Echoes 1982)★★, *The Best Of Little Eva* (1988)★★★, *Back On Track* (1989)★★★.

Little Joe And The Thrillers

This R&B vocal group came from Philadelphia, Pennsylvania, USA. The group was formed in 1956 by Joe Cook (b. 29 December 1922, Philadelphia, Pennsylvania, USA), who had made his first record in 1949 as lead of a gospel group, the Joe Cook Quartet. While recording as a member of a later gospel group, the Evening Star Quartet, Cook formed the Thrillers, which besides Cook consisted of Farris Hill (tenor), Richard Frazier (tenor), Donald Burnett (baritone) and Harry Pascle (bass). Their only real claim to fame was 'Peanuts', which entered the US Top 30 in 1957 on the OKeh label. Cook's piercing falsetto lead became the standard for many R&B doo-wop groups from the late 50s through the 70s. The first release by the group was a dance number called 'The Slop', which achieved some local east coast recognition in 1956. The Thrillers never hit the charts after 'Peanuts' and they broke up, Little Joe continued recording up to 1966 on various small Philadelphia labels. In 1964, Cook organized an all-girl group, the Sherrys, two of whom were his daughters, and enjoyed a Top 40 national hit with 'Pop Pop Pop-Pie'.
● ALBUMS: *Little Joe Cook-In* (1981)★★★.

Little Milton

b. James Milton Campbell Jnr., 7 September 1934, Inverness, Mississippi, USA. Having played guitar from the age of 12, Little Milton (he legally dropped the James when he discovered that he had a brother of the same name on his father's side) made his first public appearances as a teenager in the blues bars and cafés on Greenville's celebrated Nelson Street. He first appeared on record accompanying pianist Willie Love in the early 50s, then appeared under his own name on three singles issued on Sam Phillips' Sun label under the guidance of Ike Turner. Although their working relationship continued throughout the decade, it was on signing to Chicago's Chess/Checker outlet that Milton's career flourished. An R&B-styled vocalist in the mould of Bobby Bland and 'T-Bone' Walker, his work incorporated sufficient soul themes to maintain a success denied to less flexible contemporaries. Propelled by an imaginative production, Milton had a substantial hit in 1965 with the optimistic 'We're Gonna Make It', and followed it with other expressive performances, including 'Who's Cheating Who?' (1965), plus the wry 'Grits Ain't Groceries' (1968). Campbell remained with Chess until 1971, whereupon he switched to Stax. 'That's What Love Will Do' returned the singer to the R&B chart after a two-year absence, but despite his appearance in the pivotal *Wattstax* film, Little Milton was unable to maintain a consistent recording career. A series of ill-fitting funk releases from the late 70s reinforced the perception that the artist was at his peak with blues-edged material, something proved by his excellent contemporary work for Malaco Records. In the 90s he was with Delmark Records and experienced something of a resurgence during the most recent blues boom.
● ALBUMS: *We're Gonna Make It* (Checker 1965)★★★, *Little Milton Sings Big Blues* (Checker 1966)★★★, *Grits Ain't Groceries* (Chess 1969)★★★, *If Walls Could Talk* (Chess 1970)★★★, *Waiting For Little Milton* (Stax 1973)★★★, *Blues 'N' Soul* (Stax 1974)★★★, *Montreux Festival* (Stax 1974)★★★, *Me For You, You For Me* (Glades 1976)★★★, *Friend Of Mine* (Glades 1976)★★★, shared with Jackie Ross *In Perspective* (1981)★★★, *I Need Your Love So Bad* (MCA 1982)★★★, *Age Ain't Nothing But A Number* (MCA 1983)★★★, *Playin' For Keeps* (Malaco 1984)★★★, *Annie Mae's Cafe* (Malaco 1987)★★★, *Movin' To The Country* (Malaco 1987)★★★, *I Will Survive*

(Malaco 1988)★★★, *Too Much Pain* (Malaco 1990)★★★, *Reality* (1992)★★★, *I'm A Gambler* (Malaco 1994)★★★, *Live At Westville Prison* (Delmark 1995)★★★, *Cheatin' Habit* (Malaco 1996)★★★.

● COMPILATIONS: *Little Milton's Greatest Hits* (Chess 1972)★★★★, *Little Milton* (1976)★★★, *Sam's Blues* (Charly 1976)★★★, *Walkin' The Back Streets* (1981)★★★, *Raise A Little Sand* (Red Lightnin' 1982)★★★, *Little Milton Sings Big Blues* (Chess 1987)★★★, *His Greatest Hits* (Chess 1987)★★★, *Chicago Golden Years* (Vogue 1988)★★★, *Hittin' The Boogie (Memphis Days 1953-1954)* (Zu Zazz 1988)★★★, *We're Gonna Make It* (Charly 1990)★★★★, *The Sun Masters* (Rounder 1990)★★★, *Blues In The Night* (Dillon 1992)★★★★, *Welcome To The Club: The Essential Chess Recordings* (MCA 1994)★★★★, *Little Milton's Greatest Hits* (Malaco 1995)★★★★, *The Complete Stax Singles* (Ace 1995)★★★★.

LITTLE RICHARD

b. Richard Wayne Penniman, 5 December 1935, Macon, Georgia, USA. The wildest and arguably the greatest and most influential of the 50s rock 'n' roll singers and songwriters. He first recorded in late 1951 in Atlanta for RCA, cutting eight urban blues tracks with his mentor Billy Wright's Orchestra, 'Taxi Blues' being the first of four unsuccessful single releases on the label. He moved to Houston, Texas, in 1953, and with the Tempo Toppers (vocals) and the Duces of Rhythm (backing) recorded four R&B tracks including 'Ain't That Good News'. Eight months later he recorded another four with Johnny Otis's Orchestra but none of these were released at the time. In February 1955, at the suggestion of Lloyd Price, he sent a demo to Specialty Records who realized his potential, and in September, under the guidance of producer Robert 'Bumps' Blackwell, recorded a dozen tracks in New Orleans. The classic 'Tutti Frutti', which was among them, gave him his first R&B and pop hit in the USA. The follow-up, 'Long Tall Sally', topped the R&B chart and was the first of his three US Top 10 hits, despite being covered by Pat Boone, whose previous record, a cover version of 'Tutti Frutti', was still charting. Richard's string of Top 20 hits continued with the double-sider 'Rip It Up'/'Ready Teddy', the former being his first UK release and chart entry in late 1956. Richard's frantic, unrestrained performance of his first two hits 'Long Tall Sally' and 'Tutti Frutti' in the film *Don't Knock The Rock* undoubtedly helped push his next UK single, which coupled the tracks, into the Top 3.

His next film and single was *The Girl Can't Help It*, the title song of which missed the US Top 40 but together with its b-side, 'She's Got It' (a reworking of his earlier track 'I Got It'), gave him two more UK Top 20 hits. The remainder of 1957 saw him notch up three more huge transatlantic hits with the rock 'n' roll classics 'Lucille', 'Keep A Knockin'' (he featured both in the movie *Mr. Rock & Roll*) and 'Jenny Jenny' and a Top 20 album with *Here's Little Richard*. At the very height of his career, the man with the highest pompadour in the business shocked the rock world by announcing, during an Australian tour, that he was quitting music to go into a theological college. In 1958, previously recorded material such as the transatlantic Top 10 hit 'Good Golly Miss Molly' kept his name on the chart, and a year later he had his biggest UK hit with a 1956 recording of the oldie 'Baby Face' which reached number 2. Between 1958 and 1962 Richard recorded only gospel music for Gone, Mercury (with producer Quincy Jones) and Atlantic. In late 1962, Richard toured the UK for the first time and the now short-haired wild man who pounded pianos and pierced eardrums with his manic falsetto was a huge success. In 1963, he worked in Europe with the Beatles and the Rolling Stones, who were both great admirers of his music. His first rock recordings in the 60s were made back at Specialty and resulted in the UK Top 20 hit 'Bama Lama Bama Loo'. In 1964, he signed with Vee Jay where he re-recorded all his hits, revived a few oldies and cut some new rockers - but the sales were unimpressive. In the mid-60s, soul music was taking hold worldwide and Richard's soulful Vee Jay tracks, 'I Don't Know What You've Got But It's Got Me' (which featured Jimi Hendrix on guitar) and 'Without Love', although not pop hits, were among the best recordings of the genre. For the rest of the 60s he continued to draw the crowds, singing his old hits, and in the studios he mixed 50s rock and 60s soul for Modern in 1965, OKeh a year later and Brunswick in 1967. The best of these were his OKeh tracks, which included 'Poor Dog', 'Hurry Sundown' and the UK-recorded 'Get Down With It' (which gave Slade their first hit in the 70s).

Reprise Records, whom he joined in 1970, tried very hard to return him to the top, and under the expertise of producer Richard Perry he managed minor US hits 'Freedom Blues' and 'Greenwood, Mississippi', but his three albums sold poorly. The rest of the 70s was spent jumping from label to label, recording in supergroup-type projects and playing oldies shows. When he desired, he could still 'out-rock' anyone, but there was often too much Las Vegas glitter, excessive posturing and an element of self-parody. In 1976, he rejoined the church and for the next decade preached throughout America. In 1986, Richard was one of the first artists inducted into the Rock And Roll Hall of Fame and he successfully acted in the film *Down And Out In Beverly Hills*, which included the rocking 'Great Gosh A'Mighty', which just missed the US Top 40. Renewed interest spurred WEA to sign him and release *Lifetime Friend*, which included the chart record 'Operator'. Since the mid-80s he has become a frequent visitor on chat shows, an in-demand guest on other artist's records and a familiar face in videos (by acts ranging from Hank Williams Jnr. to Living Colour to Cinderella). He even has his own star on the Hollywood Walk of Fame and a boulevard named after him in his home-town. Nowadays a regular presenter of music awards, he has also been the star of Jive Bunny hits. The leader of rebellious 50s rock 'n' roll, and the man who shook up the music business and the parents of the period, is now a much-loved personality accepted by all age groups.

● ALBUMS: *Little Richard* (Camden 1956)★★★, *Here's Little Richard* (Specialty 1957)★★★★★, *Little Richard Volume 2* (Specialty 1957)★★★★★, *The Fabulous Little Richard* (Specialty 1958)★★★★★, *Sings Gospel* (20th Century 1959)★★, *It's Real* (Mercury 1961)★★, *Little*

Richard Sings Freedom Songs (Crown 1963)★★, *Coming Home* (Coral 1963)★★, *King Of The Gospel Singers* (Wing 1964)★, *Little Richard Is Back* (Vee Jay 1965)★★, *The Explosive Little Richard* (Columbia 1967)★★★, *Good Golly Miss Molly* (Specialty 1969)★★★, *The Little Richard Story* (Joy 1970)★★★, *Well Alright* (Specialty 1970)★★★, *Rock Hard Rock Heavy* (Specialty 1970)★★, *You Can't Keep A Good Man Down* (Union Pacific 1970)★★, *The Rill Thing* (Reprise 1970)★★, *Mr Big* (Joy 1971)★★, *Cast A Long Shadow* (Epic 1971)★★, *King Of Rock 'n' Roll* (Reprise 1971)★★★, *The Original Little Richard* (Specialty 1972)★★★, *The Second Coming* (Warners 1973)★★★, *Rip It Up* (Joy 1973)★★, *Slippin' And Slidin'* (Joy 1973)★★, *Good Golly Miss Molly* (Hallmark 1974)★★★, *Greatest Hits Recorded Live* (Embassy 1974)★★★, *Keep A Knockin'* (Rhapsody 1975)★★, *Dollars Dollars* (Charly 1975)★★, *The Great Ones* (MFP 1976)★★, *Little Richard And Jimi Hendrix Together* (Ember 1977)★, *Whole Lotta Shakin' Goin' On* (DJM 1977)★★★, *Little Richard Now* (Creole 1977)★★, *The Georgia Peach* (Charly 1980)★★★, *Little Richard And His Band* (Specialty 1980)★★, *Ooh! My Soul* (Charly 1982)★★★, *Whole Lotta Shakin'* (Bulldog 1982)★★★, *Get Down With It* (Edsel 1982)★★, *The Real Thing* (Magnum Force 1983)★★★, *Little Richard* (Cambra 1983)★★★, *He's Got It* (Topline 1984)★★, *Lifetime Friend* (Warners 1986)★★★.

● COMPILATIONS: *His Biggest Hits* (Specialty 1963)★★★★, *Little Richard's Greatest Hits* (Vee Jay 1965)★★★★, *Little Richard's Greatest Hits* (OKeh 1967)★★★★, *Little Richard's Greatest Hits* (Joy 1968)★★★, *Little Richard's Grooviest 17 Original Hits* (Specialty 1968)★★★★, *20 Original Greatest Hits* (Specialty 1976)★★★★, *The Essential Little Richard* (Specialty 1985)★★★★, *18 Greatest Hits* (Rhino 1985)★★★★, *20 Classic Cuts* (Ace 1986)★★★★, *Shut Up! A Collection Of Rare Tracks (1951 - 1964)* (Rhino 1988)★★★, *The Collection* (Castle 1989)★★★★, *The Specialty Sessions* 6-CD box set (Specialty 1990)★★★★★, *The Formative Years, 1951-53* (Bear Family 1989)★★★, *The EP Collection* (See For Miles 1993)★★★★★.

● FURTHER READING: *The Life And Times Of Little Richard: The Quasar Of Rock*, Charles White.

● FILMS: *The Girl Can't Help It* (1956), *Don't Knock The Rock* (1956), *Catalina Caper* (1967).

LIZZIE

b. Sweden. Swedish soul singer Lizzie earned immediate comparisons to Kate Bush with her sultry debut single 'Impossible'. Released by MNW Records in 1993, it was not her first attempt to make a career in the music industry. In the mid-80s she had sung with Houses And Gardens - a briefly successful band noted for its exuberant live performances. She was also previously half of the Master Twins duo, who worked with some of London's top producers.

LONG, SHORTY

b. Frederick Earl Long, 20 May 1940, Birmingham, Alabama, USA, d. 29 June 1969, Detroit, Michigan, USA. Multi-instrumentalist Long received tutelage from W.C. Handy and Alvin Robinson before joining Harvey Fuqua's Tri-Phi label in 1961. This Detroit-based company was later acquired by Tamla/Motown and Long acted as master of ceremonies on his new outlet's touring revues before recording 'Devil With The Blue Dress On' in 1964 for the Motown subsidiary Soul. The singer's slow, blues-based interpretation was not a hit, but the song became successful in the hands of Mitch Ryder and Bruce Springsteen. Long enjoyed minor chart entries with 'Function At The Junction' (1966) and 'Night Fo' Last' (1968), before reaching the US Top 5 in 1968 with a version of 'Here Comes The Judge'. His premature death as a result of a boating accident on the Detroit River robbed Motown of an ebullient, but sadly unfulfilled, talent.

● ALBUMS: *Here Comes The Judge* (Soul 1968)★★, *The Prime Of Shorty Long* (Soul 1969)★★.

LOOSE ENDS

Formed in 1982 by Jane Eugene, Steve Nichol and Carl McIntosh, Loose End were the first all-black UK band to be signed to the Virgin label. After several unsuccessful singles they changed their name to Loose Ends, enlisted producer Nick Martinelli, and started to make an impression on the soul/dance scene with a series of excellent releases. Their major breakthrough came with the Top 20 singles 'Hangin' On A String (Contemplating)' and 'Magic Touch', and their second album *So Where Are You*, featuring backing vocals by American singer Joanna Gardner. Subsequent singles and albums were not as successful, but they developed a busy sideline as songwriters and producers (Juliet Roberts, Five Star, Lavine Hudson). Following the disbandment of the original line-up, McIntosh returned in 1990 with new members Linda Carriere and Sunay Suleyman, breaking into the Top 20 with 'Don't Be A Fool'.

● ALBUMS: *A Little Spice* (Virgin 1984)★★★, *So Where Are You* (Virgin 1985)★★★, *Zagora* (Virgin 1986)★★★, *The Real Chuckeeboo* (Virgin 1988)★★★, *Look How Long* (Ten 1990)★★.

LOST GENERATION

An R&B vocal group from Chicago, Illinois, USA. The Lost Generation bucked the early 70s major trend in sweet falsetto-led vocal groups by providing a fresh sound of a dry, hard lead. The members were Lowrell Simon (lead, ex-Vondells), his brother Fred Simon, Larry Brownlee (d. 1978; ex-CODs) and Jesse Dean (ex-Vondells). The Lost Generation established themselves with 'The Sly, Slick, And The Wicked' (number 14 R&B, number 30 pop) in 1970, and although they were never able to penetrate the national pop charts again, they managed to sustain themselves on R&B hits for the next several years, notably with 'Wait A Minute' (number 25 R&B) in 1970, and 'Talking The Teenage Language' (number 35 R&B) in 1971. The group broke up after their last chart record in 1974. Lowrell Simon, under the name of 'Lowrell', went on to establish a solo career, having a solid hit with 'Mellow Mellow Right On' (number 32 R&B) in 1979, and AVI released *Lowrell* the same year.

● ALBUMS: *The Sly, Slick And The Wicked* (Brunswick 1970)★★★, *Young, Tough And Terrible* (Brunswick 1971)★★.

LOVE, DARLENE

b. Darlene Wright, 26 July 1938, Los Angeles, California, USA. A prolific vocalist, Love began her career in 1957 as a founder-member of the Blossoms. This influential girl-group not only enjoyed an extensive recording career in its own right, but also appeared on scores of sessions and as the resident singers on US television's *Shindig*. Love also enjoyed a fruitful association with producer Phil Spector, and sang lead vocals on the Crystals' 'He's A Rebel' and 'Zip-A-Dee-Doo-Dah' by Bob B. Soxx And The Blue Jeans. Love completed six singles in her own right for Spector's Philles label, including 'Christmas (Baby Come Home)', '(Today I Met) The Boy I'm Gonna Marry' and 'Wait Til' My Bobby Gets Home', the latter reaching the US Top 30 in 1963. Love subsequently pursued her solo career on a variety of outlets before being reunited with Spector in 1977 for 'Lord, If You're A Woman'. She continued her demanding session-singer schedule and in the 80s branched into acting with film roles in *Lethal Weapon* and *Lethal Weapon 2*, as well as the Royal Shakespeare Company's co-production of Stephen King's horror-novel *Carrie*. In 1990, Love completed the long-awaited *Paint Another Picture*, before touring the USA as a back-up vocalist for Cher. Together with Marianne Faithfull and Merry Clayton she performed a female vocal cabaret as '20th Century Pop' in 1996. In March 1997 she was awarded considerable back-royalties for singing on a number of Spector's records, claiming that she was not rewarded financially because she did not have any formal contract.

● ALBUMS: *Darlene Love* (1981)★★, *Paint Another Picture* (Columbia 1990)★★.

● COMPILATIONS: *Masters* (1981)★★★, *The Best Of Darlene Love* (1992)★★★.

LOVE UNLIMITED

Formed in 1969 in San Pedro, California, USA, under the aegis of singer/producer Barry White, the group consisted of Diane Taylor, Linda James and her sister Glodean James, who married White on 4 July 1974. The trio had an early hit with 'Walkin' In The Rain With The One I Love' (1972), an imaginatively arranged performance which married contemporary soul to the aura of the now-passed girl-group genre, reminiscent of the Shangri-Las. Love Unlimited's later releases included 'It May Be Winter Outside (But In My Heart It's Spring)' (1973) and 'Under The Influence Of Love' (1974), both of which White had previously recorded with Felice Taylor. The care the producer lavished on such releases equalled that of his own, but despite further R&B hits, 'I Belong To You' (1974) was the trio's final US pop chart entry.

● ALBUMS: *Love Unlimited* (Uni 1972)★★, *Under The Influence Of...* (20th Century 1973)★★, *In Heat* (20th Century 1974)★★, *He's All I Got* (Unlimited Gold 1977)★★, *Love Is Back* (Unlimited Gold 1980)★★.

LOVE UNLIMITED ORCHESTRA

This 40-piece orchestra was pieced together by singer Barry White to back his girl trio protégées, Love Unlimited. The unit also supplied the silky backing to several of White's singles and enjoyed an international hit in 1974 in their own right with 'Love Theme'. Later releases, including 'Rhapsody In White' and 'Satin Soul', were less successful, although they did provide the theme song to the Dino DeLaurentis remake of *King Kong* (1977). One member, saxophonist Kenny G, later embarked on a solo career.

● ALBUMS: *Rhapsody In White* (20th Century 1974)★★, *Together Brothers* (20th Century 1974)★★, *White Gold* (20th Century 1974)★, *Music Maestro Please* (20th Century 1976)★, *My Sweet Summer Suite* (20th Century 1976)★, *My Musical Bouquet* (20th Century 1978)★, *Super Movie Themes* (20th Century 1979)★, *Let 'Em Dance* (Unlimited Gold 1981)★, *Welcome Aboard* (Unlimited Gold 1981)★, *Rise* (1983)★.

LOVELITES

An R&B female group from Chicago, Illinois, USA. The Lovelites epitomized a Chicago approach to soul music that married teenage voices to bright-sounding horn arrangements and mid-tempos. The architect of the group was Patti Hamilton, who was the principal songwriter and whose emotive lead voice helped immeasurably ensure the success of the Lovelites. She formed the original group in 1967, with herself, her sister Rozena Petty, and Barbara Peterman. Ardell McDaniel replaced Peterman in 1968, who in turn was replaced by Rhonda Grayson in 1971. Petty was replaced by Joni Berlmon in 1970. The trio had two magnificent hits, 'How Can I Tell My Mom And Dad' (number 15 R&B) from 1969, and 'My Conscience' (number 36 R&B) from 1971. Their one album, *With Love From The Lovelites*, only yielded one national hit, yet was loaded with fine songs that were frequently played in many locales. The group broke up in 1973.

● ALBUMS: *With Love From The Lovelites* (Uni 1970)★★★.

LOWRELL

(see Lost Generation)

LUCAS, CARRIE

b. Carmel, California, USA. This sensuous soul and disco stylist started as a backing singer with the Whispers and did backing vocals on record for D.J. Rogers. She also wrote songs recorded by R&B acts the Whispers, the Soul Train Gang and South Shore Commission before joining the Soul Train label in 1976. Her first chart record and biggest hit was the disco smash 'I Gotta Keep Dancin'', released simply under the name Carrie in 1977. Two years later 'Dance With You' on Solar, (formerly Soul Train) also made the lower reaches of the Top 100 and gave her a UK Top 40 entry. Over the next six years she registered four US Top 200 album entries and a further five R&B chart singles, the biggest of these being her revival (with the Whispers) of Barbara Lewis's 'Hello Stranger', which reached the Top 20 in 1985 on Constellation Records. Lucas, who is married to Solar Records head Dick Griffey, has now put her singing career on ice.

● ALBUMS: *Simply Carrie* (Soul Train 1977)★★★, *Carrie*

Lucas In Danceland (Solar 1979)★★, *Portrait Of Carrie* (Solar 1980)★★, *Still In Love* (Solar 1982)★★★.

LUTCHER, NELLIE

b. 15 October 1915, Lake Charles, Louisiana, USA. A singer/pianist notable for her percussive piano-playing and distinctive scat-vocal approach. Initially, Lutcher played in a big band with her bass-playing father before moving on to join the Southern Rhythm Boys band. She played clubs on the west coast during the late 30s/early 40s and signed to Capitol Records in 1947 following an appearance on a *March Of Dimes* charity show. Her first release, the R&B-styled 'Hurry On Down', became a US Top 20 hit that same year and was followed by 'He's A Real Gone Guy', 'The Song Is Ended' and 'Fine Brown Frame'. The latter was a cover version of an earlier hit by bandleader Buddy Johnson. She later moved on to Liberty Records, recording a highly rated album, *Our New Nellie*. However, her popularity had faded, and during the late 60s and early 70s she took a staff job with the Hollywood Local Branch of the Musicians' Union, still occasionally playing clubs such as the New York Cookery.

● ALBUMS: *Real Gone* (1954)★★★, *Our New Nellie* (Liberty 1955)★★★★.

● COMPILATIONS: *Real Gone Gal* (Stateside 1985)★★★, *My Papa's Got To Have Everything* (Jukebox Lil 1985)★★★, *Ditto From Me To You* (Jukebox Lil 1987)★★★.

LYMON, FRANKIE, AND THE TEENAGERS

b. 30 September 1942, Washington Heights, New York, USA, d. 28 February 1968, New York City, New York, USA. Often billed as the 'boy wonder', Lymon first entered the music business after teaming up with a local all-vocal quartet, the Premiers. The latter comprised Jimmy Merchant (b. 10 February 1940, New York, USA), Sherman Garnes (b. 8 June 1940, New York, USA, d. 26 February 1977), Herman Santiago (b. 18 February 1941, New York, USA) and Joe Negroni (b. 9 September 1940, New York, USA, d. 5 September 1978). Lymon joined them in 1954 and soon afterwards they were signed to the Gee label as the Teenagers. Their debut, the startling 'Why Do Fools Fall In Love?', was issued on 1 January 1956 and soon climbed into the US Top 10, alongside the early recordings of Elvis Presley and Carl Perkins. The song went on to reach number 1 in the UK and sold two million copies. Lymon soon left school and the group toured extensively. For their second single, 'I Want You To Be My Girl', the 13-year-old boy wonder was given superior billing to the group. With their use of high tenor, deep bass and soprano and teenage-orientated lyrics, the Teenagers boasted one of the most distinctive sounds in 50s pop. After registering chart entries in the USA with 'I Promise To Remember' and 'The ABCs Of Love', they found greater acclaim in England. The soaring 'I'm Not A Juvenile Delinquent' (from the film *Rock Rock Rock*) hit the UK Top 12 and Lymon was afforded the honour of appearing at the London Palladium. So strong was his appeal at this point that the single's b-side, 'Baby Baby', received separate promotion and outshone the a-side by climbing to number 4. During his celebrated UK tour, Lymon recorded as a soloist with producer Norrie Paramor and the resulting 'Goody Goody' reached the Top 30 on both sides of the Atlantic. By the summer of 1957, he had split from the Teenagers, and thereafter, his career prospects plummeted. He enjoyed the excesses of stardom, smoking cigars, drinking heavily and enjoying under-age sex with women old enough to be his mother. Despite recording a strong album, his novelty appeal waned when his voice broke. By 1961, the teenager was a heroin addict and entered Manhattan General Hospital on a drug rehabilitation programme. Although he tried to reconstruct his career with the help of Dizzy Gillespie and even took dancing lessons and studied as a jazz drummer, his drug habit remained. In 1964, he was convicted of possessing narcotics and his finances were in a mess. His private life was equally chaotic and was punctuated by three marriages. In February 1968, he was discovered dead on the bathroom floor of his grandmother's New York apartment with a syringe by his side. The Teenager who never grew up was dead at the tragically young age of 25. His former group continued to record sporadically and in the 80s, surviving members Santiago and Merchant formed a new Teenagers and Pearl McKinnon took Lymon's part. They were inducted into the Rock And Roll Hall Of Fame in 1993.

● ALBUMS: *The Teenagers Featuring Frankie Lymon* (Gee 1957)★★★, *The Teenagers At The London Palladium* (Roulette 1958)★★, *Rock 'N' Roll Party With Frankie Lymon* (Guest 1959)★★★.

● COMPILATIONS: *Frankie Lymon And The Teenagers* 61-track set (Murray Hill 1987)★★★, *The Best Of Frankie Lymon And The Teenagers* (Roulette 1990)★★★.

LYMON, LOUIS, AND THE TEEN-CHORDS

This vocal group from New York City, New York, USA, consisted of Louis Lymon (lead), Ralph Vaughan (first tenor), Rossilio Rocca (second tenor), Lyndon Harold (baritone) and David Little (bass). Lymon, the youngest brother of the great Frankie Lymon, built a remarkably top-notch group modelled on the pre-teen girlish sound of his brother and his group the Teenagers, even though he lacked the range and commanding stage presence of Frankie. The Teen-Chords never secured a national hit, but were extremely popular on the east coast, where doo-wop groups attracted their biggest following. The group was formed in 1956 and was signed by Bobby Robinson; he formed the Fury label to launch the group. They achieved two New York hits for Robinson, with 'I'm So Happy' (1956) and 'Honey Honey' (1957), and the group was subsequently signed to George Goldner's End label. They promoted their first End release, 'Your Last Chance', by making an imposing appearance in a quirky rock 'n' roll film, *Jamboree*. However, that was the peak of their success. After having a hit with 'Dance Girl' in 1958, the group, disillusioned by their lack of national success, broke up.

● COMPILATIONS: *I'm So Happy* (Relic 1992)★★★.

● FILMS: *Jamboree a.k.a. Disc Jockey Jamboree* (1957).

LYNN, BARBARA

b. Barbara Lynn Ozen, 16 January 1942, Beaumont, Texas, USA. Lynn was signed up by producer Huey P. Meaux after hearing a demo tape and watching her perform in a Texas club. Her early records were recorded at Cosimo's New Orleans studio and leased to the Jamie label. Composed by Lynn, 'You'll Lose A Good Thing' (1962) was an R&B chart-topper and pop Top 10 hit in the USA, and was followed by 'You're Gonna Need Me' and 'Oh! Baby (We Got A Good Thing Goin')'. The last of these was revived by the Rolling Stones on *Out Of Our Heads*. Barbara issued several singles on Meaux's own label, Tribe, among which was her version of 'You Left The Water Running' (1966). Subsequent releases for Atlantic Records included 'This Is The Thanks I Get' (1968) and '(Until Then) I'll Suffer' (1972), both of which reached the R&B chart for this accomplished singer, songwriter and guitarist, who continued to tour, including visits to Japan, and also recorded albums for Ichiban and Rounder/Bullseye.

● ALBUMS: *You'll Lose A Good Thing* (Jamie 1962)★★★★, *Here Is Barbara Lynn* (Atlantic 1968)★★★, *You Don't Have To Go* (Ichiban 1988)★★★, *Barbara Lynn Live In Japan* (1993)★★★, *So Good* (Bullseye Blues 1994)★★.

● COMPILATIONS: *The Barbara Lynn Story* (1965)★★★, *We Got A Good Thing Goin'* (1984)★★, *Barbara Lynn* (Good Thing 1989)★★★, *You'll Lose A Good Thing* (Sound Of The Fifties 1992)★★★, *The Atlantic Years* (Ichiban/Soul Classics 1994)★★★.

LYNN, CHERYL

b. Cheryl Lynn Smith, 11 March 1957, Los Angeles, California, USA. The full-throated Lynn became a hit-maker at the height of disco's popularity, singing dance tunes that retained the gospel vocal approach of classic soul. Lynn grew up in the church where her mother was a minister of music. Her break into the music business came in 1976 after she won as a contestant on the US television amateur talent show *The Gong Show*. Before signing with Columbia, however, she spent half a year with a touring company of *The Wiz*, a black musical based on the *Wizard Of Oz* story. Lynn achieved a million-seller with her very first record, 'Got To Be Real', reaching number 1 R&B and number 12 pop in 1978. Other chart entries followed, notably 'Shake It Up Tonight' (US R&B number 5), 'Encore' (US R&B number 1), and 'If You Were Mine' (US R&B number 11). She also enjoyed success in 1982 with an excellent remake of the Marvin Gaye and Tammi Terrell hit, 'If This World Was Mine' (US R&B number 4), on which she duetted with Luther Vandross. Her success in the UK was minimal, with only 'Encore' briefly entering the charts in 1984.

● ALBUMS: *Cheryl Lynn* (Columbia 1978)★★, *In Love* (Columbia 1980)★★★, *In The Night* (Columbia 1981)★★★, *Instant Love* (Columbia 1982)★★, *Preppie* (Columbia 1984)★★, *It's Gonna Be Right* (Columbia 1985)★★, *Start Over* (Manhattan 1987)★★, *Whatever It Takes* (1989)★★.

MABLEY, MOMS 'JACKIE'

b. Loretta Mary Aiken, 19 March 1894, Brevard, North Carolina, USA, d. 23 May 1975. Mabley was raised in Washington, DC. Her maudlin 1969 recitation of the Dion hit 'Abraham, Martin And John' somewhat obscured her history as the most successful comedienne on the black theatre circuit. The song made her a one-hit-wonder when it made number 18 R&B and number 35 pop, yet she had been performing for almost 40 years and had already charted with 13 comedy albums on the pop album charts. She was masterful at blue humour but less effective with suitable family fare. Mabley entered the Chitlin' Circuit in 1921 when she toured with Butterbeans And Susie. She also had minor roles in films, such as *Emperor Jones* (1933), *Killer Diller* (1947) and *Boarding House Blues* (1948). *Amazing Grace* (1974) was her only starring appearance.

● ALBUMS: *Moms Mabley At The UN* (Chess 1961)★★★, *Moms Mabley Onstage* (Chess 1961)★★★, *Moms Mabley At The Playboy Club* (Chess 1961)★★★, *Moms Mabley At Geneva Conference* (Chess 1962)★★★, *Moms Mabley Breaks It Up* (Chess 1963)★★★, *Young Men, Si - Old Men, No* (Chess 1963)★★★, *I Got Somethin' To Tell You!* (Chess 1963)★★★, *The Funny Sides Of Moms Mabley* (Chess 1964)★★★, *Out On A Limb* (Mercury 1964)★★★, *Moms Wows* (Chess 1964)★★★, *Moms The Word* (Mercury 1964)★★★, *Now Hear This* (Mercury 1965)★★★, *The Youngest Teenager* (Mercury 1969)★★★.

MACEO AND THE KING'S MEN

This group was formed in 1970 by Maceo Parker (b. 14 February 1943, Kinston, North Carolina, USA; tenor saxophone) and Melvin Parker (b. Kinston, North Carolina, USA; drums). Former members of various high school bands, the brothers joined the James Brown revue in 1964, and were featured on several of the artist's seminal recordings before embarking on an independent career in March 1970. The new group, Maceo And The King's Men, was completed by other defecting members of Brown's troupe. Richard 'Kush' Griffiths (trumpet), Joseph 'Joe' Davis (trumpet), L.D. 'Eldee' Williams (tenor saxophone), Jimmy 'Chank' Nolen (guitar), Alphonso 'Country' Kellum (guitar) and Bernard Odum (bass) were all serving members of the James Brown Orchestra, and similarities between both groups' music were thus inevitable. Despite this, however, neither of the King's Men albums sold well, and several musicians drifted back to their former employer. Both Maceo and Melvin also rejoined Brown, but in deference to their obvious frustration, he wrote, arranged and produced several tracks for a spin-off project, Maceo And The Macks. Two singles, 'Party - Part 1' and 'Soul Power 74 - Part 1', reached the R&B Top 30, before an album entitled *Us*, credited solely to Maceo, was released in 1974. The brothers left the fold again in 1976, whereupon the saxophonist joined George Clinton's Funkadelic empire. Maceo did, however, rejoin Brown briefly in the 80s. 'Cross The Track (We Better Go Back)', a track by Maceo And The Macs, was reissued in 1987 and reached number 54 in the UK chart. In the early 90s Maceo Parker joined with fellow Brown alumni, tenor saxophonist Pee Wee Ellis and trombonist Fred Wesley, to make the well-received *Roots Revisited* and *Mo' Roots*.

● ALBUMS: as Maceo And The King's Men *Doing Their Own Thing* (House Of Fox 1970)★★★, *Funky Music Machine* (People 1974)★★. As Maceo *Us* (Polydor 1974)★★★★. As Maceo Parker *For All The King's Men* (4th & Broadway 1989)★★★, *Roots Revisited* (Verve 1990)★★★★, *Mo' Roots* (Verve 1991)★★★, *Life On Planet Groove* (1992)★★★, *Southern Exposure* (1993)★★★.

Mack, Lonnie

b. Lonnie McIntosh, 18 July 1941, Harrison, Indiana, USA. Lonnie Mack began playing guitar while still a child, drawing early influence from a local blues musician, Ralph Trotts, as well as established figures Merle Travis and Les Paul. He later led a C&W act, Lonnie And The Twilighters, and by 1961 was working regularly with the Troy Seals Band. The following year, Mack recorded his exhilarating instrumental version of Chuck Berry's 'Memphis'. By playing his Gibson 'Flying V' guitar through a Leslie cabinet, the revolving device that gives the Hammond organ its distinctive sound, Mack created a striking, exciting style. 'Memphis' eventually reached the US Top 5, while an equally urgent original, 'Wham', subsequently broached the Top 30. *The Wham Of That Memphis Man* confirmed the artist's vibrant skill, which drew on blues, gospel and country traditions. Several tracks, notably 'I'll Keep You Happy', 'Where There's A Will' and 'Why', also showed Mack's prowess as a soulful vocalist, and later recordings included a rousing rendition of Wilson Pickett's 'I Found A Love'. The guitarist also contributed to several sessions by Freddy King and appeared on James Brown's 'Kansas City' (1967). Mack was signed to Elektra in 1968 following a lengthy appraisal by Al Kooper in *Rolling Stone* magazine. *Glad I'm In The Band* and *Whatever's Right* updated the style of early recordings and included several notable remakes, although the highlight of the latter set was the extended 'Mt. Healthy Blues'. Mack also added bass to the Doors' *Morrison Hotel* (1970) and undertook a national tour prior to recording *The Hills Of Indiana*. This low-key, primarily country album was the prelude to a six-year period of seclusion that ended in 1977 with *Home At Last*. Mack then guested on Michael Nesmith's *From A Radio Engine To The Photon Wing*, before completing *Lonnie Mack And Pismo*, but this regeneration was followed by another sabbatical. He re-emerged in 1985 under the aegis of Texan guitarist Stevie Ray Vaughan, who co-produced the exciting *Strike Like Lightning*. Released on the Alligator label the album rekindled this talented artist's career, a rebirth that was maintained on the fiery *Second Sight*.

● ALBUMS: *The Wham Of That Memphis Man* (Fraternity 1963)★★★★, *Glad I'm In The Band* (Elektra 1969)★★★, *Whatever's Right* (Elektra 1969)★★★, *The Hills Of Indiana* (Elektra 1971)★★★, *Home At Last* (Capitol 1977)★★, *Lonnie Mack With Pismo* (Capitol 1977)★★, *Strike Like Lightning* (Alligator 1985)★★★, *Second Sight* (Alligator 1987)★★★, *Live! Attack Of The Killer V* (Alligator 1990)★★.

● COMPILATIONS: *For Collectors Only* (Elektra 1970)★★★, *The Memphis Sound Of Lonnie Mack* (1974)★★★, *Roadhouses And Dance Halls* (Epic 1988)★★★.

Mad Lads

From Memphis, Tennessee, USA, the Mad Lads comprised John Gary Williams, Julius Green, William Brown and Robert Phillips. Although not one of the premier Stax/Volt acts, this quartet enjoyed seven R&B hits between 1965 and 1969. After changing their name from the Emeralds, their first single, 'The Sidewalk Surf', flopped, but the group placed three singles in the R&B Top 20 in 1965-66, the best-known being 'I Want Someone'. Their first hit, 'Don't Want To Shop Around', was curiously anachronistic, owing more to doo-wop than southern soul. Later releases, including the perky 'Sugar Sugar', were more typical, but the group was increasingly obscured by its more successful counterparts. In 1966, Williams and Brown were drafted and replaced by Sam Nelson and Quincy Clifton Billops Jnr. A version of the Jimmy Webb standard 'By The Time I Get To Phoenix' proved to be the Mad Lads' last chart entry in 1969, after which they broke up. A new line-up was assembled in 1972, but disbanded after completing one album. Former member Billops joined another Stax group, Ollie And The Nightingales, and from there moved into a re-formed version of the Ovations. A new Mad Lads built around Williams and Gary formed in 1984, with a new Volt album, *Madder Than Ever*, released in 1990.

● ALBUMS: *In Action* (Volt 1966)★★★, *The Mad, Mad, Mad, Mad, Mad Lads* (Volt 1969)★★★, *A New Beginning* (Volt 1972)★★, *New Directions* (Express 1985)★★, *Madder Than Ever* (Volt 1990)★★.

● COMPILATIONS: *Their Complete Early Recordings* (Volt/Ace 1997)★★★, *The Best Of The Mad Lads* (Volt/Ace 1997)★★★.

Magnificent Men

A white R&B vocal septet from York and Harrisburg, Pennsylvania, USA, the Magnificent Men (often abbreviated to the 'Mag Men') drew their members from doo-wop groups called the Endells (who released one single, 'Vicky', in 1963) and the Del-Chords (who released 'Everybody's Gotta Lose Someday' in 1964). From the latter band were culled singers Dave Bupp and Buddy King, with instrumental backing provided by the former Endells (Jim Seville, Bob Angelucci, Tom Hoover, Terry Crousare and Tom Pane). They signed to Capitol Records and 'Peace Of Mind' was released in 1965. The follow-up single was 'Maybe, Maybe Baby', radio exposure for which brought them to the Apollo Theatre in New York. Their legendary performance here drew James Brown up from the audience, joining them in a 45-minute set. However, the group was facing difficulty in outgrowing their local popularity, with 'Stormy Weather' failing and 'I Could Be So Happy' only managing a meagre number 93 in the *Billboard* charts. Joining the Motortown Revue as its only white act, their next effort was 'The Sweet Soul Medley', a version of the Arthur Conley standard reworked to include nods to their favourite groups of the day. The rest of their Capitol singles failed significantly to embellish their reputation (despite a strong reading of Jimmy Webb's 'By The Time I Get To Phoenix) and in 1969 the Magnificent Men moved to Mercury Records. Both 'Holly Go Softly' and a version of Bob Dylan's 'Lay Lady Lay' also stalled. When Bupp left he was replaced by Stan Sommers (ex-Del-Satins) but the group did not record again.

● ALBUMS: *The Magnificent Men* (Capitol 1967)★★★, *The Magnificent Men Live!* (Capitol 1967)★★★.

Magnificents

Formed in 1953 in Chicago, Illinois, USA, the group members were Johnny Keyes, Thurman 'Ray' Ramsey, Fred Rakestraw and Willie Myles. In their up-tempo songs, the Magnificents brought rock 'n' roll to their doo-wop, and in their ballads they stayed true to their R&B roots. Singing as the Tams, they were discovered by disc jockey Magnificent Montague, who gave them their name and became their manager. Their one hit, 'Up On The Mountain' (number 9 R&B), in 1956, has come to be remembered as a golden oldie, but equally outstanding was their great ballad b-side, 'Why Did She Go', led by Ramsey. However, Ramsey left to be replaced by L.C. Cooke (brother of Sam Cooke), and Barbara Arrington was added to the group as lead. The successful sound of the group was subsequently lost on the next record, 'Caddy Bo'. The third single, 'Off The Mountain', deserved to restore the group to prominence, but it was not to be. Keyes and the rest of the group broke from Montague, who then formed a new Magnificents, the identity of whose members remains unknown. Their 'Don't Leave Me' is one of the most beloved of the doo-wop oldies that were never actually hits.

● COMPILATIONS: *Magnificents & Rhythm Aces: 15 Cool Jewels* (Solid Smoke 1984)★★★.

Main Ingredient

This New York-based trio, Donald McPherson (b. 9 July 1941, d. 4 July 1971), Luther Simmons Jnr. (b. 9 September 1942) and Tony Sylvester (b. 7 October 1941, Panama) made their recording debut in 1965. One of several groups using the name 'the Poets', they decided to become the Main Ingredient and signed with producer Bert DeCoteaux, whose lush arrangements provided the requisite foil for their excellent harmonies. This skill was particularly apparent on such early releases as 'I'm So Proud' (1970), 'Spinning Around (I Must Be Falling In Love)' and 'Black Seeds Keep On Growing' (both 1971). McPherson died from leukaemia in 1971 and, ironically, it was his replacement, Cuba Gooding, who sang on the group's million-seller 'Everybody Plays The Fool'. Although the Ingredient went on to enjoy further commercial success, their work grew increasingly bland and lacked the purpose of those early releases. Gooding embarked on a solo career with Motown in 1977, but reunited with Sylvester and Simmons in 1979, continuing to record under the Main Ingredient name into the 80s. Simmons was replaced by Jerome Jackson in the late 80s, following which the group moved to Polydor Records.

● ALBUMS: *The Main Ingredient L.T.D.* (RCA 1970)★★★, *Tasteful Soul* (RCA 1971)★★, *Black Seeds* (RCA 1971)★★★, *Bitter Sweet* (RCA 1972)★★★, *Afrodisiac* (RCA 1973)★★, *Euphrates River* (RCA 1974)★★, *Rolling Down A Mountainside* (RCA 1975)★★★, *Shame On The World* (RCA 1975)★★, *Music Maxiums* (RCA 1977)★★, *Ready For Love* (RCA 1980)★★, *I Only Have Eyes For You* (RCA 1981)★★, *I Just Wanna Love You* (Polydor 1989)★★.

Majors

Formed in Philadelphia, Pennsylvania, USA, in 1959, the Majors were an R&B quintet who crossed over to the US pop charts three times in 1962, most notably with their debut, 'A Wonderful Dream'. The group consisted of lead singer Rick Cordo, Ron Gathers, Gene Glass, Idella Morris and Frank Troutt; their recordings were produced by the influential Jerry Ragovoy - 'A Wonderful Dream' was his first Top 40 success. The Majors had their roots in a harmony group called the Premiers. Upon recording their first single, 'Lundee Dundee', for Rocal Records in 1960, they changed their name to the Versatiles. The next time the group entered the studio was in 1962 for the Ragovoy-produced tracks for Imperial Records. During 1963, they recorded eight singles for the label, as well as one album. The group resurfaced with a single on ABC-Paramount in 1966, under the name the Performers. They toured throughout the 60s but split by the end of that decade.

● ALBUMS: *Meet The Majors* (Imperial 1962, reissued as *A Golden Classics Edition* on Collectables in 1991)★★★.

Malone, J.J.

b. 20 August 1935, Pete's Corner, Alabama, USA. Malone was playing guitar and harmonica before his thirteenth birthday, and he began performing at dances and parties when he was 17. In the mid-50s he spent a year in the Air Force and formed his first band, the Rockers, later called Tops In Blues. Once out of the armed services in 1957, he formed the Rhythm Rockers in Spokane, Washington, and they worked all over the west coast. In 1966, he settled in Oakland, California, and recorded for the Galaxy label, enjoying a hit with 'Its A Shame' in 1972; he subsequently had records issued by the Red Lightnin', Cherrie, Paris Album and Eli Mile High labels. Malone is a soulful vocalist, adept on both piano and guitar and equally convincing at straight blues or rocking R&B material.

● ALBUMS: with Troyce Key *I've Gotta New Car* (Red Lightnin' 1980)★★★, *Bottom Line Blues* (1991)★★★.

Mancha, Steve

b. Clyde Wilson, 25 December 1945, Walhall, South Carolina, USA. Mancha probably achieved his most significant commercial success as lead vocalist of the group 100 Proof Aged In Soul on their big 1970 hit 'Somebody's

Been Sleeping'; however, soul fans, and especially Detroit soul fans, remember him from his days as writer and performer Clyde Wilson in Detroit, where his family had settled in 1954. Signing first with Harvey Fuqua, together with friend Wilbert Jackson, Wilson and Jackson performed as the Two Friends for Fuqua's HPC label. Soon, this and other Fuqua labels were incorporated by Berry Gordy into his fledgling Motown empire, and in 1965, Wilson moved to the Wheelsville label, owned by Don Davis, where he recorded 'Did My Baby Call' coupled with 'Whirlpool'. In 1966 he had a hit as a member of the Holidays (other members were J.J. Barnes and Edwin Starr) with 'I'll Love You Forever' (number 7 R&B). That year Clyde Wilson became Steve Mancha, and joined Don Davis's Groovesville Records as a solo artist in 1966, together with J.J. Barnes and Melvin Davis. Mancha recorded five singles for the label, with 'I Don't Wanna Lose You' and 'Don't Make Me A Storyteller' making the national R&B charts. Davis subsequently formed Groove City, for whom Mancha cut just one single, 'Hate Yourself In The Morning'/'A Love Like Yours'. Six of these Groovesville and Groove City sides appeared on the Stax/Volt album *Rare Stamps*, after Don Davis began leasing his product to the Memphis-based label (the other tracks on the album were Davis-produced items by J.J. Barnes). Mancha then signed for Holland/Dozier/Holland's Hot Wax, which the famous trio had formed on splitting with Motown. Here, Mancha became lead vocalist on all but three of 100 Proof Aged In Soul's recordings, as well as co-writing seven of their sides. When Holland/Dozier/Holland moved to California, Mancha stayed in Detroit and became involved in gospel music, returning to the secular scene in 1986 when UK soul entrepreneur Ian Levine recorded him on 'It's All Over The Grapevine' for EMI.

● COMPILATIONS: *Rare Stamps* one side by J.J. Barnes (Stax 1969)★★★, *Don Davis Presents The Sound Of Detroit* six tracks (1993).

MANHATTANS

Formed in 1962 in Jersey City, New Jersey, USA, about 10 miles south of New York City's borough of Manhattan, the Manhattans were a soul group whose greatest success came during the 70s. The original members were lead vocalist George Smith, bass singer Winfred 'Blue' Lovett (b. 16 November 1943), tenor Edward Bivins (b. 15 January 1942), tenor Kenneth Kelley (b. 9 January 1943) and baritone Richard Taylor (b. 1940, d. 7 December 1987). Specializing in smooth ballads, the group recorded first for the Newark, New Jersey-based Carnival label, on which they placed eight singles on the US R&B charts, beginning with 1965's 'I Wanna Be (Your Everything)'. In 1969, they changed to Deluxe Records, on which they recorded their first Top 10 R&B hit, 'One Life To Live', in 1972. In 1971, Smith died, and was replaced by Gerald Alston (b. 8 November 1942). The group left Deluxe for Columbia in 1973, where their now-sweetened soul style resulted in a string of Top 10 R&B hits, including the 1976 number 1 'Kiss And Say Goodbye', which also made number 1 on the pop charts, and 1980's 'Shining Star' (number 4 R&B/number 5 pop). After 1983's number 4 'Crazy', the group's chart popularity waned, although they continued to release recordings for Columbia. Taylor left the group in 1976 and was not replaced; he died in 1987. Alston left in 1988 for a solo career, following which the group switched to the Valley Vue label.

● ALBUMS: *Dedicated To You* (Carnival 1964)★★★, *For You And Yours* (Carnival 1965)★★★, *With These Hands* (Deluxe 1970)★★★, *A Million To One* (Deluxe 1972)★★★, *There's No Me Without You* (Columbia 1973)★★★, *Summertime In The City* (1974)★★★, *That's How Much I Love You* (Columbia 1975)★★★, *The Manhattans* (Columbia 1976)★★★★, *It Feels So Good* (Columbia 1977)★★★, *There's No Good In Goodbye* (Columbia 1978)★★★★, *Love Talk* (Columbia 1979)★★★, *After Midnight* (Columbia 1980)★★★, *Black Tie* (Columbia 1981)★★★, *Follow Your Heart* (Columbia 1981)★★★, *Forever By Your Side* (Columbia 1983)★★★, *Too Hot To Stop It* (Columbia 1985)★★★, *Back To Basics* (Columbia 1986)★★, *Sweet Talk* (Valley Vue 1989)★★, *Now* (1994)★★.

Solo: Gerald Alston *Gerald Alston* (Motown 1989)★★, *Open Invitation* (Motown 1990)★★★.

● COMPILATIONS: *Manhattans Greatest Hits* (Columbia 1980)★★★★, *Best Of The Manhattans* (Columbia 1984)★★★★, *Best Of The Manhattans* (Pickwick 1992)★★★, *Collection* (Castle 1992)★★★, *Dedicated To You/For You And Yours* (Collectables 1993)★★★.

MAR-KEYS

Formed in Memphis, Tennessee, USA, and originally known as the Royal Spades, the line-up comprised Steve Cropper (b. 21 October 1941, Willow Spring, Missouri, USA; guitar), Donald 'Duck' Dunn (b. 24 November 1941, Memphis, Tennessee, USA; bass), Charles 'Packy' Axton (tenor saxophone), Don Nix (b. 27 September 1941, Memphis, Tennessee, USA; baritone saxophone), Wayne Jackson (trumpet), Charlie Freeman (b. Memphis, Tennessee, USA; guitar), Jerry Lee 'Smoochy' Smith (organ) and Terry Johnson (drums). Although their rhythmic instrumental style was not unique in Memphis (Willie Mitchell followed a parallel path at Hi Records), the Mar-Keys were undoubted masters. Their debut hit, 'Last Night', reached number 3 in the US *Billboard* pop chart during the summer of 1961, establishing Satellite, its outlet, in the process. Within months, Satellite had altered its name to Stax and the Mar-Keys became the label's house band. Initially all-white, two black musicians, Booker T. Jones (organ) and Al Jackson (drums), had replaced Smith and Johnson by 1962. The newcomers, along with Cropper and Dunn, also worked as Booker T. And The MGs. A turbulent group, the Mar-Keys underwent several changes. Freeman left prior to the recording of 'Last Night' (but would later return for live work), Nix and Axton also quit, while Joe Arnold and Bob Snyder joined on tenor and baritone saxophone. They, in turn, were replaced by Andrew Love and Floyd Newman, respectively. Although commercial success under their own name was limited, the group provided the backbone to sessions by Otis Redding, Sam And Dave, Wilson Pickett, Carla Thomas and many others, and were the pulsebeat to countless classic records. Axton, the son of

Stax co-founder Estelle, later fronted the Packers, who had a hit with 'Hole In The Wall' (1965). The single, released on Pure Soul, featured a not-inconspicuous MGs. Line-ups bearing the Mar-Keys' name continued to record despite the desertion of most of the original members. Nix later became part of the Delaney And Bonnie/Leon Russell axis while Charlie Freeman was later part of the Dixie Flyers, one of the last traditional house bands. Both he and Axton died in the early 70s, victims, respectively, of heroin and alcohol abuse. Jackson, Love and Newman, meanwhile, continued the Mar-Keys' legacy with releases on Stax and elsewhere, while simultaneously forging a parallel career as the Memphis Horns.

● ALBUMS: *Last Night* (Atlantic 1961)★★★, *Do The Popeye With The Mar-Keys* (London 1962)★★★, *The Great Memphis Sound* (Atlantic 1966)★★★, with Booker T. And The MGs *Back To Back* (Stax 1967)★★★, *Mellow Jello* (Atlantic 1968)★★★, *Damifiknow* (Stax 1969)★★, *Memphis Experience* (1971)★★.

MARATHONS

The brief history of the Marathons is shrouded in mystery and confusion. Long thought to be a pseudonym for the Olympics, the US R&B group that had recorded 'Western Movies' in 1958, the Marathons was actually a pseudonym for the Vibrations, a Los Angeles vocal group who had a 1961 dance hit with 'The Watusi', and in a previous incarnation, as the Jayhawks who hit the US singles charts in 1956 with 'Stranded In The Jungle'. The convoluted story of the Marathons' only hit, 1961's 'Peanut Butter', is that the Olympics' record company, Arvee, needed a new release from the group while they were on the road. In the Olympics' place, Arvee hired the Vibrations to record 'Peanut Butter', a virtual soundalike of the Olympics' own '(Baby) Hully Gully'. 'Peanut Butter' reached number 20 on Arvee, but when the Vibrations' own label discovered that its group had been moonlighting, it took over distribution of the record, issuing it on both the Chess and Argo labels. With that decision, the career of the non-existent Marathons came to an end. However, an attempt by Arvee to cash in on the success of the group resulted in a bogus version of the Marathons, along with an album and a series of single releases, including 'C. Percy Mercy Of Scotland Yard' and 'Tight Sweater'.

● COMPILATIONS: *The Olympics Meet The Marathons* (Ace 1985)★★★.

MARCELS

The Marcels were one of several doo-wop-influenced American vocal groups to achieve success in the early 60s, despite the passing of the genre's golden age. Cornelius 'Nini' Harp (lead singer), Ronald 'Bingo' Mundy (tenor), Fred Johnson (bass), Gene Bricker (tenor) and Richard Knauss (baritone), all native to Pittsburg, Pennsylvania, USA, achieved fame for their distinctive version of Richard Rodgers/Lorenz Hart's classic 'Blue Moon', previously a UK Top 10 hit for Elvis Presley in 1956, which topped both the US and UK charts in 1961. Johnson's distinctive bass introduction to the song has remained one of the most enduring vocal phrases of the time. The quartet scored a further US Top 10 hit that year with 'Heartaches', but its personnel was unstable, with Allen Johnson (d. 28 September 1995) replacing Knauss, and Walt Maddox replacing Bricker. Mundy walked out on the group during this same period, which did little to prepare them for the ever-changing trends prevalent during the early 60s, and eventually undermined the Marcels' long-term aspirations.

● ALBUMS: *Blue Moon* (Colpix 1961)★★★.

● COMPILATIONS: *Heartaches* (Colpix 1987)★★★, *Rare Items* (Colpix 1988)★★, *The Best Of The Marcels* (Roulette 1990)★★★, *The Complete Colpix Sessions* (Sequel 1994)★★★★.

MARCHAN, BOBBY

b. 30 April 1930, Youngstown, Ohio, USA. Marchan was a New Orleans entertainer who had moderate success both as a rock 'n' roller and soul singer. His long-time career as a female impersonator reflected a time-honoured tradition in black entertainment, originating in medicine shows. He began performing in Ohio as a comic drag singer, and in 1954 made his way to New Orleans as a member of a drag-queen troupe called the Powder Box Revue. Also in that year, he made his first records for California-based Aladdin Records. In 1957, he joined Huey 'Piano' Smith and the Clowns as lead vocalist and, with his distinctive vocals and pianist Smith's boogie-woogie stylings, recorded a succession of infectious rock 'n' roll hits, notably 'Rocking Pneumonia And The Boogie Woogie Flu' and 'Don't You Just Know It'. Marchan left the Clowns in 1960 after leaping onto the charts with a melodramatic version of 'There Is Something On Your Mind' (number 1 R&B and number 31 pop), a cover version of Big Jay McNeely's hit of the previous year. Marchan's version made an impact through its impassioned recitation involving sexual jealousy and murder, lifted from an earlier New Orleans hit, Larry Darnell's 'I'll Get Along Somehow' from 1949. Marchan had a moderate hit in 1966 with 'Shake Your Tambourine' (number 14 R&B). He continued to record into the mid-70s, but with no further success. In-between singing engagements, Marchan worked as a female impersonator on New Orleans' Bourbon Street, and was a master of ceremonies at many clubs.

● ALBUMS: *There's Something On Your Mind* (Fire 1964)★★★.

● COMPILATIONS: *Golden Classics* (Collectables 1988)★★★.

MARIE, TEENA

b. Mary Christine Brocker, 1957, Santa Monica, California, USA. A singer, songwriter, multi-instrumentalist, arranger and producer, Teena Marie is one of the few white artists to sustain a consistent career in the US soul market. Spotted by Motown Records' Berry Gordy in the 70s, he linked her up with funk star and labelmate Rick James, and her early career strongly reflected their joint influences. The highly commercial *Wild And Peaceful* saw her backed by James and the Stone City Band on a set that included their hit duet, 'I'm A Sucker For Your Love'. She returned the favour by partnering James on 'Fire

And Desire' on his *Street Songs* album in 1981. Afterwards, Marie took increasing control of her career and songwriting, singing both ballads and funk. Both 'I Need Your Lovin'' and 'Square Biz' reached the Top 20 of the US *Billboard* charts in 1980 and 1981, respectively. In the UK, 'Behind The Groove', a surprise disco smash at number 6 in the singles chart, led to confusion in public minds over her and the similarly titled Kelly Marie (it also, accidentally, picked up on the prevalent UK disco trend for songs with 'Groove' in the title). However, her greatest success followed her move to Epic Records, which some saw as an assertion of her independence, with the number 4-peaking US hit, 'Lovergirl'. Afterwards, her chart career declined. *Emerald City* was a funky outing, notable particularly for Stevie Ray Vaughan's guitar solo on 'You So Heavy'. Demonstrating her talent for modernizing her technique with the advent of each new instalment in R&B's development, *Ivory* was produced by Soul II Soul's Jazzie B.

● ALBUMS: *Wild And Peaceful* (Gordy 1979)★★★, *Lady T* (Gordy 1980)★★★, *Irons In The Fire* (Gordy 1980)★★★, *It Must Be Magic* (Gordy 1981)★★★★, *Robbery* (Epic 1983)★★★, *Starchild* (Epic 1984)★★★, *Emerald City* (Epic 1986)★★★, *Naked To The World* (Epic 1988)★★★, *Ivory* (Epic 1990)★★★★.

● COMPILATIONS: *Greatest Hits* (Motown 1985)★★★★, *Greatest Hits* different track-listing to Motown issue (Epic 1991)★★★★.

MARKHAM, PIGMEAT

b. Dewey Markham, 1904, Durham, North Carolina, USA, d. 13 December 1981. Best known as a comedian, Markham began his long career in 1917, dancing in travelling shows. He travelled the southern 'race' circuit with blues singer Bessie Smith and later appeared on burlesque bills with Milton Berle, Red Buttons and Eddie Cantor. By the 50s, Markham was one of black America's most popular entertainers through his shows at the Regal in Chicago, the Howard in Washington and, in particular, New York's famed Apollo. Despite being black, he applied burnt cork make-up to his face, a device that caused many of his fans to believe he was actually white. He later made several successful appearances on the influential *Ed Sullivan* television show and was signed by Chess during the 60s. The Chicago-based label issued several in-concert albums and his 1968 novelty hit, 'Here Comes The Judge'. This tongue-in-cheek recording was inspired by the artist's catch-phrase, which was used extensively on the American television comedy series *Rowan And Martin's Laugh-In*. Although hampered by a competitive version by Shorty Long, Markham enjoyed a Top 20 hit in the USA and UK. Although this was a one-off achievement, Pigmeat Markham remained a well-known figure until his death in December 1981.

MARTHA AND THE VANDELLAS

Martha Reeves (b. 18 July 1941, Alabama, USA), with Annette Sterling Beard, Gloria Williams and Rosalind Ashford, formed the Del-Phis in 1960, one of the scores of female vocal groups then operating in Detroit, Michigan, USA. After Reeves began working as a secretary at Motown Records, they were offered a one-off single release on the label's Melody subsidiary, on which they were credited as the Vels. Gloria Williams left the group when the single flopped, but the remaining trio were allowed a second opportunity, recording 'I'll Have To Let Him Go' in late 1962, when the artist for whom it had been intended, Mary Wells, failed to arrive for the session. Renamed Martha And The Vandellas, the group divided their time between backing other Motown artists and recording in their own right. They were featured on Marvin Gaye's 1962 hit 'Stubborn Kind Of Fellow', before the US Top 30 success of their own release, 'Come And Get These Memories', brought their career as second-string vocalists to an end. Their next single, the dynamic 'Heat Wave', was masterminded by the Holland/Dozier/Holland production team, and epitomized the confidence and verve of the Vandellas' finest work. 'Quicksand' repeated the hit formula with a US Top 10 chart placing, while it was 'Dancing In The Street' that represented the pinnacle of their sound. The song, co-written by Marvin Gaye and Mickey Stevenson, was an anthemic invitation to party, given added bite by the tense political situation in the black ghettos. Holland/Dozier/Holland's production exploited all the potential of the music, using clunking chains to heighten the rhythmic feel, and a majestic horn riff to pull people to their feet. 'Dancing In The Street' was the most exciting record Motown had yet made, and it was a deserved number 2 hit in America.

Nothing the Vandellas recorded thereafter reached quite the same peak of excitement, although not for want of trying. 'Nowhere To Run' in 1965 was an irresistible dance hit, which again was given political connotations in some quarters. It introduced a new group member, former Velvelette Betty Kelly, who replaced Annette Sterling Beard. This line-up scored further Top 10 hits with 'I'm Ready For Love' and the infectious 'Jimmy Mack', and celebrated Motown's decision to give Reeves individual credit in front of the group's name with another notable success, 'Honey Chile'. Reeves was taken seriously ill in 1968, and her absence forced the group to disband. By 1970, she was able to resume her career, recruiting her sister Lois and another former Velvelette, Sandra Tilley, to form a new Vandellas line-up. No major US hits were forthcoming, but in Britain they were able to capitalize on the belated 1969 success of 'Dancing In The Street', and had several Top 30 entries in the early 70s. When Motown moved their headquarters from Detroit to Hollywood in 1972, Reeves elected to stay behind. Disbanding the group once again, she fought a lengthy legal battle to have her recording contract annulled, and was eventually free to begin an abortive solo career. Her sister Lois joined Quiet Elegance, while Sandra Tilley retired from the music business, and died in 1982. Motown retained the rights to the Vandellas' name, but chose not to sully the memory of their early 60s hits by concocting a new version of the group without Martha Reeves.

● ALBUMS: *Come And Get These Memories* (Gordy 1963)★★★, *Heat Wave* (Gordy 1963)★★★, *Dance Party* (Gordy 1965)★★★, *Watchout!* (Gordy 1967)★★, *Martha*

& The Vandellas Live! (Gordy 1967)★. As Martha Reeves And The Vandellas *Ridin' High* (Gordy 1968)★★, *Sugar 'n' Spice* (Gordy 1969)★★, *Natural Resources* (Gordy 1970)★★, *Black Magic* (Gordy 1972)★★.
● COMPILATIONS: *Greatest Hits* (Gordy 1966)★★★★, *Anthology* (Motown 1974)★★★★, *Compact Commmand Performances* (Motown 1992)★★★, *24 Greatest Hits* (Motown 1992)★★★★, *Live Wire, 1962-1972* (Motown 1993)★★★★, *Milestones* (Motown 1995)★★★★.

MARVELETTES

The Marvelettes' career epitomized the haphazard progress endured by many of the leading girl-groups of the early 60s. Despite enjoying several major US hits, they were unable to sustain a consistent line-up, and their constant shifts in personnel made it difficult to overcome their rather anonymous public image. The group was formed in the late 50s by five students at Inkster High School in Michigan, USA: Gladys Horton, Georgeanna Marie Tillman (d. 6 January 1980), Wanda Young, Katherine Anderson and Juanita Grant. They were spotted at a school talent show by Robert Bateman of the Satintones, who introduced them to Berry Gordy, head of the fledgling Motown organization. Bateman co-produced their early releases with Brian Holland, and the partnership found immediate success with 'Please Mr Postman' - a US number 1 in 1961, and Motown's biggest-selling record up to that point. This effervescent slice of pop-R&B captivated teenage audiences in the USA, and the song was introduced to an even wider public when the Beatles recorded a faithful cover version on their second album.

After a blatant attempt to repeat the winning formula with 'Twistin' Postman', the Marvelettes made the Top 20 again in 1962 with 'Playboy' and the chirpy 'Beechwood 4-5789'. The cycle of line-up changes was already underway, with Juanita Grant's departure reducing the group to a four-piece. The comparative failure of the next few singles also took its toll, and by 1965, Tillman had also left. The remaining trio, occasionally augmented by Florence Ballard of the Supremes, was paired with producer/writer Smokey Robinson. He tailored a series of ambitious hit singles for the group, the most successful of which was 'Don't Mess With Bill' in 1966 - although 'The Hunter Gets Captured By The Game' was arguably a more significant achievement. Gladys Horton, the Marvelettes' usual lead singer, left the group in 1967, to be replaced by Anne Bogan. They continued to notch up minor soul hits for the remainder of the decade, most notably 'When You're Young And In Love', before disintegrating in 1970. Wanda Young completed the group's recording commitments with an album, *The Return Of The Marvelettes*, which saw her supported by session vocalists. In 1989 original members Wanda Rogers and Gladys Horton, plus Echo Johnson and Jean McLain, recorded for Ian Levine's Motor City label, issuing the disco-sounding 'Holding On With Both Hands' and *Now*. Johnson and McLain were replaced by Jackie and Regina Holleman for subsequent releases.
● ALBUMS: *Please Mr Postman* (Tamla 1961)★★★★, *The Marvelettes Sing Smash Hits Of 1962* (Tamla 1962)★★★, *Playboy* (Tamla 1962)★★★, *The Marvellous Marvelettes* (Tamla 1963)★★★★, *Recorded Live: On Stage* (Tamla 1963)★★, *The Marvelettes* (Tamla 1967)★★★, *Sophisticated Soul* (Tamla 1968)★★★, *In Full Bloom* (Motown 1969)★★, *The Return Of The Marvelettes* (Motown 1970)★★, *Now* (Motor City 1990)★★.
● COMPILATIONS: *The Marvelettes Greatest Hits* (Tamla 1963)★★★★, *Anthology* (Motown 1975)★★★★, *Compact Command Perfomances - 23 Greatest Hits* (Motown 1992)★★★★, *Deliver The Singles 1961-1971* (Motown 1993)★★★★, *The Very Best* (Essential Gold 1996)★★★.

MARVELLOS

An R&B vocal group from Los Angeles, California, USA, comprising Jesse Harris, Milton Hayes, Harold Harris, Willie Holley and Lance Porter. The group was formed in 1963 and first found success locally with 'She Told Me Lies' for Exodus. It raised enough interest for Warner Brothers to pick it up and release it on its Reprise label. The formation of Warner Brothers' R&B subsidiary, Loma, saw the Marvellos joining that label in 1965. The group immediately succeeded with 'We Go Together', styled after the Temptations' 'It's Growing'. Nothing more happened after 'We Go Together' had run its course and members of the Marvellos spent many years as background session singers. However, in 1975, Jesse Harris and Milton Hayes found new success in a highly respected vocal group, Street Corner Symphony, which had evolved out of the session group in which they were working. The outfit released *Harmony Grits* (1975) and *Little Funk Machine* (1976), reprising old songs and singing new material in a neo-doo-wop style.

MARVELOWS

Formed in Chicago Heights, Illinois, USA, in 1959, Melvin Mason, Willie 'Sonny' Stevenson, Frank Paden and Johnny Paden were originally known as the Mystics. They became the Marvelows in 1964, following the addition of Jesse Smith. The group was then signed to ABC Records, and enjoyed a hit the following year with the euphoric 'I Do', which combined equal traces of doo-wop and Chicago soul (this excellent song was later revived in 1977 by the J. Geils Band). The Marvelows replaced Jesse Smith with Andrew Thomas in 1967, and the following year hit with a soft ballad, 'In The Morning'. The Marvelows broke up in 1969, but reformed briefly in 1974.
● ALBUMS: *The Mighty Marvelows* (ABC-Paramount 1968)★★★.
● COMPILATIONS: with the Esquires *Chi-Town Showdown* (1982)★★★.

MARVIN AND JOHNNY

From Los Angeles, California, USA, Marvin Phillips (b. 23 October 1931, Guthrie, Oklahoma, USA) and Emory 'Johnny' Perry (b. 1 March 1928, Sherman, Texas, USA) made a brief impact on the rock 'n' roll scene when Los Angeles was a major centre of the R&B recording scene during the late 40s and early 50s. Phillips and Perry had known each other since 1949, when they both played saxophones in the Richard Lewis Band. When Phillips formed the Marvin Phillips And His Men From Mars combo, Perry joined him. Meanwhile, Phillips gained his first success in the recording business when he teamed with Jesse Belvin in a duo called Marvin And Jesse, reaching the charts with the dreamy ballad 'Dream Girl' (number 2 R&B) in 1952 for Specialty Records. After Belvin was drafted into the army in 1953, Phillips, at the behest of Specialty, recruited a new partner, his old friend Perry, to form Marvin And Johnny. The duo immediately had a hit with 'Baby Doll' (number 9 R&B) in 1953. They moved to Modern in 1954 and released 'Tick Tock' (number 9 R&B). However, they are best remembered for 'Cherry Pie', the b-side to 'Tick Tock', which, although not making any national charts, possibly achieved more radio airplay. The song was revived by Skip And Flip in 1960 on the Brent label, putting it high on the pop charts.

● ALBUMS: *Marvin And Johnny* (Crown 1963)★★★.

● COMPILATIONS: *Flipped Out* (Specialty 1992)★★★.

Maskman And The Agents

An R&B vocal group from Washington, DC, USA, Maskman And The Agents achieved success based on the nexus of two popular culture phenomena: soul music and the spy craze. The group members were Harmon Bethea, Tyrone Gay, Paul Williams and Johnny Hood. Bethea was a 25-year veteran of the R&B business, having been in the group the Cap-Tans; in 1967, he formed from the remnants of his old group Maskman And The Agents. The outfit sang novelty soul songs and Bethea appeared masked, reflecting the period when *I Spy* and *Get Smart* were popular US television spy shows, and James Bond films were highly successful. In the same period Edwin Starr had a hit with 'Agent Double-O Soul' and Jamo Thomas with 'I Spy (For The F.B.I.)'. Mask Man And The Agents succeeded with two moderately sized hits, 'One Eye Open' (number 20 R&B) in 1968, and 'My Wife, My Dog, My Cat' (number 22 R&B) in 1969. They never charted nationally again.

● ALBUMS: *One Eye Open* (Dynamo 1968)★★★, *Got To Find A Sweet Name* (Musicor 1970)★★.

Mason, Barbara

b. 9 August 1947, Philadelphia, Pennsylvania, USA. Mason first recorded for Crusader Records in 1964, but did not achieve success until she began recording for the Philadelphia-based Artic label the following year. With her voice sounding young and innocent in its thinness and flatness, Mason reached the US charts with the marvellous 'Yes, I'm Ready' (R&B number 2, 1965), and excellent follow-ups, 'Sad, Sad Girl' (R&B number 12/pop Top 30, 1965), 'I Need Love' (R&B number 25, 1966) and 'Oh, How It Hurts' (R&B number 11, 1968). A brief stay at the National Records label yielded one moderate hit, 'Raindrops Keep Fallin' On My Head' (R&B number 38, 1970), a cover version of the B.J. Thomas hit. In 1972, Mason signed with Buddah Records and moved into recording more mature material, such as 'Give Me Your Love' (R&B number 9/pop Top 40, 1972), a Curtis Mayfield song from the movie *Superfly*, 'From His Woman To You' (R&B number 3/pop Top 30, 1974), and 'Shackin Up' (R&B number 9, 1975); however, she sounded much less interesting as a singer. She still had her thin-sounding voice, but what was fetching in an 18-year-old sounded weak and undeveloped for a woman in her late 20s. Additionally, her habit of including recitations ('raps') in songs about man-woman relationships strongly dated her later material, most typically on 'She's Got The Papers (But I Got The Man)' (R&B number 29, 1981). Mason's last chart record was 'Another Man' (R&B number 68, 1984), which was the singer's only UK chart entry, reaching number 45 the same year.

● ALBUMS: *Yes, I'm Ready* (Artic 1965)★★★, *If You Knew Him Like I Do* (1970)★★★, *Lady Love* (Buddah 1973)★★, *Give Me Your Love* (Buddah 1973)★★★, *Transition* (Buddah 1974)★★, *Love's The Thing* (Buddah 1975)★★★, *Locked In This Position* (Curtom 1977)★★, *I Am Your Woman, She Is Your Wife* (Prelude 1978)★★, *A Piece Of My Life* (WMOT 1980)★★, *Tied Up* (West End 1984)★★.

● COMPILATIONS: *Philadelphia's Lady Love* (Sequel 1990)★★★, *Yes I'm Ready* (1994)★★★, *The Very Best Of Barbara Mason* (Sequel 1996)★★★.

Matassa, Cosimo

Of Italian ancestry, Matassa ran a New Orleans juke-box company and a record store, J&M Amusement Services, in the early 40s. In 1945 he opened a small recording studio behind the shop. For the next 20 years, Cosimo's studios were the focus of recording activity in the city. Among the first to produce at Cosimo's was Dave Bartholomew, who recorded Roy Brown for De Luxe and Tommy Ridgley for Imperial. In 1949, Bartholomew began recording Fats Domino at the studio, and in 1952, he recorded Lloyd Price. There were other hits from J&M by Shirley And Lee. By the mid-50s, a studio band had emerged to accompany the growing number of singers working there. Led by saxophonists Red Tyler and Lee Allen, its members included Earl Palmer (drums) and Frank Fields (bass). In 1956, the studio moved to larger premises and was renamed Cosimo's. Soon afterwards, Little Richard made some of his most famous recordings there. During this time, Matassa had been engineer and studio owner but in 1957 he moved into management with white pop singer Jimmy Clanton. Two years later he started his own, short-lived, label, Rex. Among its roster of artists was Mickey Gilley, Earl King, Jerry McCain and Mac Rebennack (Dr. John). Matassa returned to his recording work on hits such as Barbara Lynn's 'You'll Lose A Good Thing' (1962) until 1966, when he set up Dover Records, an ambitious distribution company for local New Orleans labels. There were big successes with Robert Parker ('Barefootin'') and Aaron Neville ('Tell It Like It Is'), but by 1968 Dover too had become bankrupt. Afterwards, Matassa remained a part-owner of the Jazz City Studios in New Orleans, as well as working at Sea-Saint studios and forming the Jefferson Jazz company with Marshall Sehorn.

Maurice And Mac

(Maurice McAlister and Green McLauren). One of the long lost soul duos of the 60s, Chicago-based Maurice And

Mac's output for the Checker label between 1967 and 1970 contained both upbeat and slow-tempo examples of gospel-based soul as good as anything by better-known duos such as Sam And Dave or James And Bobby Purify. Maurice And Mac were founder-members of the fine Chicago R&B/early soul group, the Radiants, who began recording for Chess in 1962. The group itself stemmed from the young people's choir of the local Greater Harvest Baptist Church. Both McAlister and McLauren sang with the choir, but Maurice McAlister first came to notice in gospel circles as early as 1956 when he formed the Golden Gospeltones quartet together with Leonard Caston. Caston, the son of famous bluesman Leonard 'Baby Doo' Caston, and a long-time associate of Willie Dixon, later wrote and produced for ex-Temptation Eddie Kendricks at Motown, and formed Caston And Majors. In 1960, Caston and McAlister joined a doo-wop group, the Radiants, with McAlister on lead, plus Wallace Sampson, Jerome Brooks, Elzie Butler and Charles Washington, later replaced by Green 'Mac' McLauren. In 1962, they signed for Chess, and recorded 'One Day I'll Show You', which combined doo-wop with soul, and 'Father Knows Best'. On the strength of their first secular recording, they appeared at Harlem's Apollo, but were still members of the Greater Harvest Baptist Church choir, who recorded a gospel album and two singles for the Sharp label in the same year (1962), with McAlister taking lead on 'Steal Away' and McLauren on 'What A Difference In My Life'. By early 1963 they had left the Church, and a further nine Radiants Chess singles, chiefly featuring McAlister on lead, appeared up until 1966. Green McLauren enlisted in the US armed forces in late 1963, and was replaced for a time by Frank McCollum, before the Radiants continued to work as a trio. The group had some sucess in 1965 with 'Voice Your Choice' and 'It Ain't No Big Thing', both of which made the R&B and Hot 100 Charts. There were two further hits in 1967/8, but with a different Radiants line-up. Maurice McAlister left to go solo in mid-1966, and made one recording for Chess later that year ('Baby Hang On'), but after it flopped, he teamed up with the newly demobbed Green 'Mac' McLauren. As Maurice And Mac they were allotted to the Checker label and sent south to Rick Hall's 'Fame' studio in Muscle Shoals. The initial recordings contrasted the duo's churchy vocals with the sympathetic sound of Fame's premier soul-loving rhythm section. They included the ultra-deep 'Lean On Me' and 'You're The One', the slightly pacier but still deep cover version of Ben E. King's 'So Much Love', the lilting mid-tempo of 'Why Don't You Try Me', the driving soul of 'Try Me', and an excellent version of the much-covered 'You Left The Water Running', first recorded by Billy Young. They were followed by other great cuts such as the rhythmic 'Love Power', which was re-released on the superb 1984 Japanese P-Vine album, containing all of Maurice And Mac's best material. Poor promotion by Chess/Checker affected those and subsequent issues, such as their Chicago sides, which included the deep *crie de coeur* 'What Am I Gonna Do', 'Lay It On Me', 'Oh What A Time', 'Baby You're The One' (arguably the duo's most beautiful deep ballad), 'Kick My Cat, I'll Beat Your Dog', and the very churchy, slow-building deepie, 'But You Know I Love You'. The latter single was released on Checker in 1970, and in the following year the Chess label reissued 'Lay It On Me' coupled with 'You Can't Say I Didn't Try'. McAlister's high pitched tenor and McLauren's deeper, gospel-style baritone combined on one last single for Brown Sugar in 1972 ('Use That Good Thing'/'Ain't No Harm To Moan'), before the pair split up. McLauren disappeared completely from the music scene, and McAlister spent some time making television jingles, before working as an appliance-repairman in Chicago. In the 80s, he was reported to be playing a few local clubs with a newly formed band.

● COMPILATIONS: *Lean On Me* (1984)★★★★.

MAXWELL

b. 1974, Brooklyn, New York, USA. Half West Indian, half Puerto Rican soul singer Maxwell had to suffer the ignominy of his record company sitting on his debut album for a year, ignoring his traditional soul style in favour of the hip-hop-influenced singers dominating the R&B charts. Finally released in April 1996, *Maxwell's Urban Hang Suite* was a concept album about monogamy that eschewed male braggadocio to explore old-fashioned, romantic love. Featuring a collaboration with Leon Ware, co-writer of Marvin Gaye's *I Want You*, the album proved to be an unexpected critical and commercial success. Maxwell was voted Best R&B Artist by *Rolling Stone* magazine, and *Urban Hang Suite* was nominated for a Grammy. At the 11th Annual Soul Train Awards in March 1997, Maxwell won both Best Male R&B/Soul Album and Single (for 'Ascension'), and Best R&B/Soul or Rap New Artist. The same month, *Urban Hang Suite* went platinum.

● ALBUMS: *Maxwell's Urban Hang Suite* (Columbia 1996)★★★★.

MAYE, ARTHUR LEE

b. 11 December 1934, Tuscaloosa, Alabama, USA. Maye had one of the most engaging lead voices on the west coast doo-wop scene and he put it to terrific use on many fine songs, usually recorded with his group the Crowns. His career was a unique dual one - as a baseball player (as Lee Maye) and as a singer - and he was only able to record and tour during the off-seasons. In 1954, the same year he joined a Milwaukee Braves' minor league club, he formed a trio in Los Angeles with bass Johnny Coleman and bass/baritone Richard Berry. They made some records for the Flair label that were released as being by the Rams and the '5' Hearts. At the end of the 1954 baseball season, Maye organized the Crowns, which other than himself included Berry and Coleman, with new members Charles Colbert (tenor), Johnny Morris (tenor) and Joe Moore (baritone). Occasionally, bass Randy Jones would substitute for Berry. The records they made for the RPM label were excellent, notably the classic 'Truly' and 'Love Me Always', but the Crowns only managed local success with them. After the 1955 baseball season, Maye And The Crowns then joined the Specialty label, recording one of their finest songs, 'Gloria'. No hits resulted and at the end of the 1956 baseball season, Maye began an association with Johnny Otis, touring with him in a vocal ensemble called the Jayos. They recorded for Otis's Dig label without much success, but Maye also brought the Crowns to the label, recording several tracks, most notably 'This Is The Night For Love' (1956). Maye And The Crowns made further tracks in 1957 for Flip and in 1959 for Cash. In 1959 Maye was brought up from the minor leagues to play major league baseball for the Milwaukee Braves. This served to end Maye's career with the Crowns, but as Maye played for various major league teams through 1971, each off-season allowed him time to record some solo numbers. He made his last record for Dave Antrell's Antrell label in 1985.

MAYER, NATHANIEL

b. 10 February 1944, Detroit, Michigan, USA. Mayer was a typical transitional artist, whose vocal intensity evoked both the doo-wop past and the emerging soul music. This style was magnificently realized in his lone hit, 'Village Of Love', which went to number 16 R&B and number 22 pop in 1962. It was recorded for a small Detroit company, Fortune, and proved to be the biggest hit the label ever had (after being leased to United Artists). Mayer started singing in high school, and recorded his first record, the wonderful 'My Last Dance With You', with a pick-up group, the Fabulous Twilights. It failed to attract buyers, but the follow-up, 'Village Of Love', also recorded with the group, gave him a national audience. Later releases, notably 'Leave Me Alone' (1962) and 'Going Back To The Village Of Love' (1964), could not return Mayer to the charts, probably because the primitive production of Fortune's records made them sound uncompetitive next to the increasingly sophisticated recording methods employed by rival firms. Mayer never recorded again after his stay at Fortune Records.

● ALBUMS: *Going Back To The Village Of Love* (Fortune 1964)★★★.

MAYFIELD, CURTIS

b. 3 June 1942, Chicago, Illinois, USA. As songwriter and vocalist with the Impressions, Mayfield established an early reputation as one of soul music's most intuitive talents. In the decade between 1961 and 1971, he penned a succession of exemplary singles for his group, including 'Gypsy Woman' (1961), 'It's All Right' (1963), 'People Get Ready' (1965), 'We're A Winner' (1968) and 'Choice Of Colours' (1969), the subjects of which ranged from simple, tender love songs to broadsides demanding social and political equality. Years later Bob Marley lifted lines from the anthemic 'People Get Ready' to populate his own opus, 'One Love'. Two independent record companies, Windy C and Curtom, emphasized Mayfield's statesman-like role within black music, while his continued support for other artists - as composer, producer or session guitarist - enhanced a virtually peerless reputation. Jerry Butler, Major Lance, Gene Chandler and Walter Jackson are among the many Chicago-based singers benefiting from Mayfield's involvement. Having parted company with the Impressions in 1970, the singer began his solo career with '(Don't Worry) If There's A Hell Below We're All Going To Go', a suitably astringent protest song. The following year Mayfield enjoyed his biggest UK success when 'Move On Up' reached number 12, a compulsive dance song that surprisingly did not chart in the USA. There, the artist's commercial ascendancy was maintained with 'Freddie's Dead' (US R&B number 2/number 4 pop hit) and the theme from 'Superfly' (1972), a 'blaxploitation' film that he also scored. Both singles and the attendant album achieved gold status, inspiring further excursions into motion picture soundtracks, including *Claudine*, *A Piece Of The Action*, *Sparkle* and *Short Eyes*, the last of which featured Mayfield in an acting role. However, although the singer continued to prove popular, he failed to sustain this high profile, and subsequent work, including his production of Aretha Franklin's 1978 album, *Almighty Fire*, gained respect rather than commercial approbation. In 1981, he joined the Boardwalk label, for which he recorded *Honesty*, his strongest album since the halcyon days of the early 70s. Sadly, the death of the label's managing director Neil Bogart left an insurmountable gap, and Mayfield's career was then blighted by music industry indifference. The singer nonetheless remained a highly popular live attraction, particularly in Britain where '(Celebrate) The Day After You', a collaboration with the Blow Monkeys, became a minor hit. In 1990, a freak accident, in which part of a public address rig collapsed on top of him during a concert, left Mayfield permanently paralyzed from the neck down. The effects, both personal and professional, proved costly, but not completely devastating in terms of his musical career . The material for *BBC Radio 1 Live In Concert* was gathered from the gig at London's Town And Country Club during Mayfield's 1990 European tour. In 1993 Warner Brothers released *A Tribute To Curtis Mayfield* featuring various artists, including Lenny Kravitz, Whitney Houston, Aretha Franklin, Bruce Springsteen, Rod Stewart, Elton John and Steve Winwood, which was an excellent tribute to the Mayfield songbook. Winwood contributed the album's highlight, a sparkling version of 'It's All Right!' A year later Charly Records reissued the majority of Mayfield's 70s albums on CD as well as several compilations. The icing on the cake came in 1996 when Rhino Records collated the best package in a three-CD box set. At the end of 1996 a new album, *New World Order*, was released to excellent reviews. The album stands up to repeated listening, but some particularly enthusiastic critics may have been swayed by their affection for such an important man, together with sympathy for his tragic disability. During the recording Mayfield had to lie on his back in order to give some gravitational power to his singing. His contribution to soul music has been immense; whatever the limitations of his disability, his voice, however, remains perfect and unique.

● ALBUMS: *Curtis* (Buddah 1970)★★★, *Curtis/Live!* (Buddah 1971)★★★, *Roots* (Buddah 1971)★★★★, *Superfly* film soundtrack (Buddah 1972)★★★★★, *Back To The World* (Buddah 1973)★★★★, *Curtis In Chicago* (Buddah 1973)★★★, *Sweet Exorcist* (Buddah 1974)★★★, *Got To Find A Way* (Buddah 1974)★★★, *Claudine* (Buddah 1975)★★, *Let's Do It Again* (Curtom 1975)★★★, *There's No Place Like America Today* (Curtom 1975)★★★,

Sparkle (Curtom 1976)★★, *Give, Get, Take And Have* (Curtom 1976)★★, *Short Eyes* (Curtom 1977)★★, *Never Say You Can't Survive* (Curtom 1977)★★, *A Piece Of The Action* (Curtom 1978)★★, *Do It All Night* (Curtom 1978)★★★, *Heartbeat* (RSO 1979)★★★, with Linda Clifford *The Right Combination* (RSO 1980)★★, *Something To Believe In* (RSO 1980)★★, *Love Is The Place* (Boardwalk 1981)★★, *Honesty* (Boardwalk 1983)★★★★, *We Come In Peace With A Message Of Love* (CRC 1985)★★★, *Live In Europe* (Ichiban 1988)★★★, *People Get Ready* (Essential 1990)★★★, *Take It To The Streets* (Curtom 1990)★★★, *BBC Radio 1 Live In Concert* (Windsong 1994)★★, *New World Order* (Warners 1996)★★★.

● COMPILATIONS: *Of All Time* (Curtom 1990)★★★, *Get Down To The Funky Groove* (1994)★★★, *Groove On Up* (1994)★★★, *Tripping Out* (Charly 1994)★★★, *A Man Like Curtis - The Best Of* (1994)★★★, *Living Legend* (Curtom Classics 1995)★★★, *People Get Ready: The Curtis Mayfield Story* 3-CD box set (Rhino 1996)★★★★, *Love Peace And Understanding* (Sequel 1997)★★★.

● VIDEOS: *Curtis Mayfield At Ronnie Scott's* (Hendring Video 1988).

● FILMS: *Superfly* (1973), *The Groove Tube* (1974).

Mayfield, Percy

b. 12 August 1920, Minden, Louisiana, USA, d. 11 August 1984. A gifted performer, Percy Mayfield's first success came in 1950 with 'Please Send Me Someone To Love' on the Specialty label. A massive US R&B hit, it reportedly sold well in excess of one million copies and became an enduring composition through its many cover versions. Further chart entries, 'Lost Love' (1951) and 'Big Question' (1952), confirmed Mayfield's status, but it was nine years before he secured another bestseller with 'River's Invitation'. 'Hit The Road Jack' enhanced Mayfield's standing as a gifted composer when it became an international hit for Ray Charles. This influential musician recorded several of Mayfield's songs; Mayfield, in turn, pursued his career on Charles's Tangerine outlet. The talented artist remained an active performer throughout the 70s and early 80s, and his later work appeared on several different labels. His death from a heart attack in 1984 robbed R&B of one of its most individual voices. Johnny Adams released an excellent tribute album in 1989 titled *Walking On A Tightrope*.

● ALBUMS: *My Jug And I* (HMV 1962)★★★, *Percy Mayfield* (1969)★★★, *Bought Blues* (1969)★★★, *Tightrope* (1969)★★★, *Percy Mayfield Sings* (1970)★★★, *Weakness Is A Thing Called Man* (RCA 1970)★★, *Blues - And Then Some* (1971)★★, *Please Send Me Someone To Love* (Intermedia 1982)★★★, *Live* (Winner 1992)★★★.

● COMPILATIONS: *The Best Of Percy Mayfield* (Specialty 1970)★★★★, *The Incredible Percy Mayfield* (1972)★★★, *My Heart Is Always Singing Sad Songs* (Ace 1985)★★★, *The Voice Within* (Route 66 1988)★★★, *Percy Mayfield: Poet Of The Blues* (Specialty 1990)★★★, *Percy Mayfield Vol. 2: Memory Pain* (Ace 1992)★★★.

● VIDEOS: *John Lee Hooker/Lowell Fulson/Percy Mayfield* (1992).

Maze (featuring Frankie Beverly)

Frankie Beverly (b. 6 December 1946, Philadelphia, Pennsylvania, USA) had an apprenticeship in several Philadelphia groups. One such unit, Frankie Beverly And The Butlers, recorded several well-received singles in the 60s, but never managed to attract more than local play. By the early 70s, however, impressed by Santana and Sly And The Family Stone, he formed a self-contained band, Raw Soul, and they moved to San Francisco where they became the house band at a local club, the Scene. Discovered by a girlfriend of Marvin Gaye, the group subsequently supported the singer in concert, and it was he who suggested they change their name in deference to their now cooler sound. The septet, which featured Wayne aka Wuane Thomas, Sam Porter, Robin Duke, Roame Lowery, McKinley Williams, Joe Provost plus Beverly, thus became Maze. Their debut album was issued in January 1977, since which time Maze have remained one of soul's most consistent live attractions. Indeed, the group sold out six consecutive nights at London's Hammersmith Odeon during their 1985 tour. However, Beverly's brand of funk/R&B has failed to achieve the wider recognition it deserves and he remains something of a cult figure.

● ALBUMS: *Maze Featuring Frankie Beverly* (Capitol 1977)★★★, *Golden Time Of Day* (Capitol 1978)★★★, *Inspiration* (Capitol 1979)★★★, *Joy And Pain* (Capitol 1980)★★★, *Live In New Orleans* (Capitol 1981)★★★, *We Are One* (Capitol 1983)★★★, *Can't Stop The Love* (Capitol 1985)★★★, *Live In Los Angeles* (Capitol 1986)★★★★, *Silky Soul* (Warners 1989)★★★, *Back To Basics* (1993)★★★.

● COMPILATIONS: *Lifelines Volume One* (Capitol 1989)★★★.

McCall, Cash

b. Maurice Dollison, 28 January 1941, New Madrid, Missouri, USA. McCall was a songwriter, session musician and vocalist in the R&B and gospel fields. Best known for his 1966 R&B hit 'When You Wake Up', McCall began singing with the gospel Belmont Singers at the age of 12. Moving to Chicago in the 60s, he played guitar for the Five Blind Boys of Mississippi, Pilgrim Jubilee Singers and Gospel Songbirds. His secular recording career began in 1963 for One-derful Records. He next signed to the small Thomas label, for which he recorded his only R&B chart hit. Subsequent releases for labels such as Checker, Ronn, Paula and Columbia Records did not fare as successfully. In 1967, McCall wrote 'That's How Love Is', a hit for Otis Clay, and also penned songs for artists including Etta James and Tyrone Davis.

● ALBUMS: *Omega Man* (Paula 1973)★★★, *No More Doggin'* (L&R 1983)★★★.

McCall, Toussaint

b. 1934, Monroe, Louisiana, USA. McCall's haunting hypnotic 'Nothing Takes The Place Of You' (number 5 R&B) was one of the highlights of a golden year in soul, 1967. Six other singles followed and one album but McCall could not recapture the magic of that one hit. He attempted to revive his career in 1976 with an album on McGowan, but it met with little acceptance. In 1988 he made a surprise appearance in the John Waters film *Hairspray*, where his lip-sync cameo to 'Nothing Can Take The Place Of You', was a most memorable moment, even if it was outside the timeframe of the movie.

● ALBUMS: *Nothing Takes The Place Of You* (Ronn 1967)★★★, *Make Love To Me* (McGowan 1976)★★.

McCLAIN, MIGHTY SAM

b. 15 April 1943, Monroe, Louisiana, USA. Raised as one of 13 children, McClain first began singing in his mother's small gospel group when he was five, before starting work as a cotton picker. However, following disputes with his stepfather he ran away from home and the plantation at the age of 13. Eventually he found employment as valet to Little Melvin Underwood, taking over the singing role in his band when original vocalist Little Sonny Green left. Eventually the band settled in Penascola, Florida, where he started to sing part-time in the Dothan Sextet. Through disc jockey Papa Don Schroeder he was invited to record at Fame Studios in Muscle Shoals in Alabama. He subsequently built his reputation via a series of powerful soul singles released between 1966 and 1971 for labels such as Amy, Malaco and Atlantic Records. Among these singles were versions of Buster Brown's 'Fannie Mae', the country ballad 'Sweet Dreams' (in opposition to a 'white' version of the same song by Tommy McLain) and the Dan Penn/Spooner Oldham composition, 'In The Same Old Way' - three songs considered by many to be among the best southern soul 45s ever released. He also appeared three times at the Apollo Theatre. Afterwards, however, his career went into freefall, and through much of the 70s and 80s he subsisted on the streets of Penascola, Florida, as a dope pedlar. It was only in 1983 that he made a comeback, when producer Carlo Ditta invited him to return to the studio and record 'Pray'. This was followed by an EP, *Your Perfect Companion*, for the Orleans label. With interest in his lost career reborn, the Japanese label Dead Ball followed that release with a live recording of one of his shows in Tokyo. McClain also made a series of guest appearances on an album recorded by Hubert Sumlin for Black Top Records in 1987, before spending the next five years working on a failed real estate venture with his third wife in Houston. Nothing more was heard until he re-emerged on AudioQuest Records in 1993 with a stunning new album, *Give It Up To Love*. Featuring McClain originals alongside two cover versions (of Al Green and Carlene Carter songs), it attracted rave reviews in the soul and R&B music press, and was followed up two years later by *Keep On Movin'*, as McClain at last began to enjoy the fruits of his labours and talent.

● ALBUMS: *Give It Up To Love* (AudioQuest 1993)★★★★, *Keep On Movin'* (AudioQuest 1995)★★★, *Sledgehammer Soul And Down Home Blues* (Audioquest 1997)★★★.

● COMPILATIONS: *Nothing But The Truth* (Charly 1988)★★★.

McCLINTON, DELBERT

b. 4 November 1940, Lubbock, Texas, USA. This white R&B artist honed his craft working in a bar band, the Straitjackets, backing visiting blues giants such as Sonny Boy Williamson, Howlin' Wolf, Lightnin' Hopkins and Jimmy Reed. McClinton made his first recordings as a member of the Ron-Dels, and was noted for his distinctive harmonica work on Bruce Channel's 'Hey Baby', a Top 3 single in the UK and number 1 in the USA in 1962. Legend has it that on a tour of the UK with Channel, McClinton met a young John Lennon and advised him on his harmonica technique, resulting in the sound heard on 'Love Me Do'. Relocating to Los Angeles in the early 70s, McClinton emerged in a partnership with fellow Texan Glen Clark, performing country/soul. They achieved a degree of artistic success, releasing two albums before splitting, with McClinton embarking on a solo career. His subsequent output reflects several roadhouse influences. Three gritty releases, *Victim Of Life's Circumstances*, *Genuine Cowhide* and *Love Rustler*, offered country, R&B and southern-style funk, while a 1979 release, *Keeper Of The Flame*, contained material written by Chuck Berry and Don Covay, as well as several original songs, including loving remakes of two compositions from the Delbert And Glen period. Emmylou Harris had a C&W number 1 with McClinton's 'Two More Bottles Of Wine' in 1978, and 'B Movie Boxcar Blues' was used in the John Belushi/Dan Aykroyd film *The Blues Brothers*. His 1980 album, *The Jealous Kind*, contained his solitary hit single, a Jerry Williams song, 'Givin' It Up For Your Love', which reached the US Top 10. After a rest-period during much of the 80s, this rootsy and largely underrated figure made a welcome return in 1989 with the fiery *Live From Austin*. His most recent collection, the assured *One Of The Fortunate Few*, was arguably his finest recording to date.

● ALBUMS: as Delbert And Glen *Delbert And Glen* (1972)★★, as Delbert And Glen *Subject To Change* (1973)★★, *Victim Of Life's Circumstances* (ABC 1975)★★★, *Genuine Cowhide* (ABC 1976)★★★, *Love Rustler* (ABC 1977)★★★, *Second Wind* (ABC 1978)★★, *Keeper Of The Flame* (Capricorn 1979)★★, *The Jealous Kind* (Capitol 1980)★★★, *Plain' From The Heart* (Capitol 1981)★★★, *Live From Austin* (Alligator 1989)★★★, *I'm With You* (Curb 1990)★★★, *Never Been Rocked Enough* (Curb 1992)★★★, *One Of The Fortunate Few* (Rising Tide 1997)★★★★.

● COMPILATIONS: *Very Early Delbert McClinton With The Ron-Dels* (1978)★★, *The Best Of Delbert McClinton* (MCA 1981)★★★.

McCLURE, BOBBY

b. 21 April 1942, Chicago, Illinois, USA, d. 13 November 1992, Los Angeles, California, USA. McClure's family moved to East St. Louis when he was two years old, and he was singing in church by the time he was nine. A year later, he provided the unbroken high-tenor lead in the otherwise all-female Spirit Of Illinois gospel group, who went on to tour the 'programs' with better-known gospel quartets such as the Swan Silvertones, the Pilgrim Travellers and the Soul Stirrers, for whom McClure's idol

Sam Cooke was singing lead. By the late 50s, McClure was involved in R&B, and formed the doo-wop group Bobby And The Vocals. Subsequently, he sang with East St. Louis drummer Big Daddy Jenkins' band, before replacing vocalist Bernard Mosley with Oliver Sain's famous revue. Sain launched two other major blues/soul names, Little Milton and Fontella Bass. Bass and McClure duetted on his first recording, 'Don't Mess Up A Good Thing', which was released in January 1965 on Checker, and made the US Top 30. In the mid-60s, McClure moved to Chicago to gig with the likes of Otis Clay and Little Milton, but by the early 70s he was back in East St. Louis singing for Sain, sometimes duetting with Shirley Brown, and recording for Sain's Vanessa label as well as February 15 Records. He also cut for Sedgwick, Klondike, and Willie Mitchell's by now predominantly soul-orientated Memphis-based Hi label, for whom he recorded four good, but unsuccessful, sides. By the 80s McClure was working as a correction officer in an Illinois penitentiary, but still recorded two singles for B-Mac, before quitting his job and moving to Los Angeles where he recorded for Jerry 'Swamp Dogg' Williams and for ex-Stax man Al Bell's Edge Records. Sadly, Bobby McClure was only 50 when he died from a stroke following a brain aneurysm.

● ALBUMS: *The Cherry LP* (Edge 1988)★★★.

● COMPILATIONS: *The Rough Edge* two tracks (1989)★★★, *Bobby McClure & Willie Clayton* eight tracks (1992)★★★.

McCoo, Marilyn

b. 30 September 1943, Jersey City, New Jersey, USA. McCoo first reached stardom as a founding member of the Fifth Dimension. That group was formed in Los Angeles in 1965 as the Versatiles, and enjoyed a number of Top 10 hits between 1967 and 1972, including 'Up-Up And Away', 'Stoned Soul Picnic', 'Aquarius/Let The Sunshine In' and 'Wedding Bell Blues'. McCoo married Fifth Dimension member Billy Davis Jnr in 1969, and together they left the group in 1975 to form an act as a duo. Signed to ABC Records, their first single, 'I Hope We Get To Love In Time', was a minor chart entry in 1976, but the album of the same title yielded 'You Don't Have To Be A Star (To Be In My Show)', a number 1 hit. The couple then hosted their own television show for six weeks in 1977. They released two further albums together in 1977 and 1978, and both recorded solo albums in the 80s. In 1981, McCoo hosted the popular television musical programme *Solid Gold*, with which she remained until 1984, returning once more in 1987-88. She released a gospel-orientated album in 1991.

● ALBUMS: *Solid Gold* (1981)★★, *The Me Nobody Knows* (1991)★★★. With Billy Davis Jnr. *I Hope We Get To Love In Time* (ABC 1976)★★★, *The Two Of Us* (ABC 1977)★★, *Marilyn & Billy* (Columbia 1978)★★.

McCoy, Van

b. 6 January 1944, Washington, DC, USA, d. 6 July 1979. This successful artist had been a member of several groups prior to announcing his solo career with 'Hey Mr DJ'. Released in 1959, the single was distributed by Sceptre Records, with whom McCoy subsequently served in an A&R capacity. He also branched out into writing and production work, making contributions to hits by the Drifters, Gladys Knight And The Pips and Barbara Lewis. Following that, McCoy embarked on a fruitful relationship with Peaches And Herb. In 1968, he established VMP (Van McCoy Productions) and enjoyed further success with Jackie Wilson ('I Get The Sweetest Feeling') and Brenda And The Tabulations ('Right On The Tip Of My Tongue'). He later became the musical arranger for the Stylistics, on the departure of Thom Bell, and emphasized the sweet, sentimental facets of their sound. McCoy was also encouraged to record under his own name and, fronting the Soul Symphony, secured an international smash in 1975 with the multi-million-selling disco-dance track, 'The Hustle'. This perky performance set the pattern for further releases but the style quickly grew anonymous. McCoy continued his successful production career with, among others, Faith, Hope And Charity, until his premature death from a heart attack in 1979.

● ALBUMS: *Soul Improvisations* (1972)★★, *From Disco To Love* (Buddah 1972)★★★, *Disco Baby* (Avco 1975)★★★, *The Disco Kid* (Avco 1975)★★, *The Real McCoy* (H&L 1976)★★★, *The Hustle* (H&L 1976)★★★, *Rhythms Of The World* (1976)★★, *My Favourite Fantasy* (MCA 1978)★★, *Van McCoy And His Magnificent Movie Machine* (1978)★★, *Sweet Rhythm* (H&L 1979)★★, *Lonely Dancer* (MCA 1979)★★.

● COMPILATIONS: *The Hustle And Best Of Van McCoy* (H&L 1976)★★★.

McCracklin, Jimmy

b. James David Walker, 13 August 1921, St. Louis, Missouri, USA. A former professional boxer, McCracklin began his singing career in 1945. Four years later he formed his own band, the Blues Blasters, in San Francisco, but almost a decade passed before the artist secured minor fame for his single 'The Walk'. This gritty slice of R&B crossed over into the pop charts via Dick Clark's *American Bandstand* show where it was favoured by the resident dancers. In the wake of this success, McCracklin continued to enjoy intermittent chart success. 'Just Got To Know' (1961) and 'Think' (1965) reached the US R&B Top 10, but later blues/soul-styled releases fared less well and confined this underrated performer's appeal to a more specialist audience.

● ALBUMS: *Jimmy McCracklin Sings* (Crown 1961)★★★, *I Just Gotta Know* (Imperial 1961)★★★, *Twist With Jimmy McCracklin* (Crown 1962)★★★, *Every Night, Every Day* (Imperial 1965)★★★, *Think* (Imperial 1965)★★★, *My Answer* (Imperial 1966)★★★, *New Soul Of Jimmy McCracklin* (Imperial 1966)★★★, *A Piece Of Jimmy McCracklin* (Minit 1968)★★★, *Let's Get Together* (Minit 1968)★★★, *Stinger Man* (Minit 1969)★★★, *High On The Blues* (Stax 1971)★★, *Yesterday Is Gone* (Stax 1972)★★, *Same Lovin'* (Evejim 1989)★★, *A Taste Of The Blues* (Bullseye Blues 1994)★★★.

● COMPILATIONS: *The Best Of* (Imperial 1966)★★★★, *Jimmy McCracklin And His Blues Blasters* (Pinnacle 1981)★★★, *Blues And Soul* (Stateside 1986)★★★, *I'm Gonna Have My Fun* (Route 66 1986)★★★, *You Deceived Me* (Crown Prince 1986)★★★, *Blast 'Em Dead* (Ace

1988)★★★, *Everybody Rock!* (Charly 1989)★★★, *The Mercury Recordings* 1958-60 recordings (Bear Family 1992)★★★★, *The Walk: Jimmy McCracklin At His Best* (Razor & Tie 1997)★★★★.

McCrae, George

b. 19 October 1944, West Palm Beach, Florida, USA. A member of a vocal group, the Stepbrothers, while at elementary school, McCrae later joined the Jivin' Jets. This unit broke up on his induction into the US Navy, but was re-formed by the singer on completing his service in 1967. McCrae's wife, Gwen McCrae, joined the line-up, but after six months the couple began work as a duo. Together they recorded two singles, the second of which, 'Lead Me On', won Gwen a contract as a solo artist with Columbia Records. She received sole credit on the song's ensuing re-release which reached the R&B Top 40. McCrae then began managing his wife's career, but following an R&B Top 20 hit with 'For Your Love' (1973), the pair resumed their singing partnership. McCrae was responsible for one of soul's most memorable releases when Gwen failed to arrive for a particular studio session. He was obliged to sing lead on 'Rock Your Baby', a melodic composition written and produced by Harry Wayne (KC) Casey and Rick Finch, the two protagonists of KC And The Sunshine Band. This soaring, buoyant song topped both the US and UK charts, while two further releases, 'I Can't Leave You Alone' (1974) and 'It's Been So Long' (1975) also reached the UK Top 10. McCrae's work was less well received at home but he continued to record with and manage his wife, appearing on her US number 1 R&B hit 'Rockin' Chair' (1975). In 1984, George McCrae enjoyed a final minor UK chart entry with 'One Step Closer (To Love)', but continued to record and tour in the mid-90s.

● ALBUMS: *Rock Your Baby* (TK 1974)★★★, *George McCrae* i (TK 1975)★★★, *Diamond Touch* (TK 1977)★★★, *George McCrae* ii (TK 1978)★★★, *We Did It* (TK 1979)★★★, with Gwen McCrae *Together* (Cat 1975)★★★, *One Step Closer To Love* (President 1984)★★.

● COMPILATIONS: *The Best Of George McCrae* (President 1984)★★★, *The Best Of George And Gwen McCrae* (1993)★★★.

McCrae, Gwen

b. 21 December 1943, Pensacola, Florida, USA. The wife of George McCrae, Gwen made her mark in the mid-70s with a delightful series of southern-style soul numbers produced by Steve Alaimo and Clarence Reid for Henry Stone's Miami-based TK operation. She first found success with a remarkable remake of the old Bobby Bland gospel-blues, 'Lead Me On' (R&B number 32, 1970). The record was recorded for TK Records, but leased to Columbia. The following year, now on TK's subsidiary label Cat, she followed with an equally remarkable remake of the Ed Townsend oldie, 'For Your Love' (R&B number 17). McCrae had her only pop hit with 'Rockin' Chair' in 1975, when the number 1 R&B hit crossed over to reach the US Top 10. 'Love Insurance' (R&B number 16) was a respectable follow-up in 1975. TK collapsed in 1980, and McCrae moved to New Jersey, and while there signed with Atlantic, after which she entered the charts with 'Funky Sensation' (number 22 R&B) in 1981. McCrae's last US chart record was in 1984, but in the UK she had a hit with 'All This Love That I'm Giving' (number 63), in 1988.

● ALBUMS: *Gwen McCrae* (Cat 1974)★★★, *Rockin' Chair* (Cat 1975)★★★★, with George McCrae *Together* (Cat 1975)★★★, *Something So Right* (Cat 1976)★★★, *Let's Straighten It Out* (Cat 1978)★★★, *Melody Life* (Cat 1979)★★, *Gwen McCrae* (Atlantic 1981)★★★, *On My Way* (Atlantic 1982)★★, *Psychic Hotline* (Goldwax 1996)★★★.

● COMPILATIONS: *The Best Of Gwen McCrae* (Sequel 1992)★★★★, *The Best Of George And Gwen McCrae* (1993)★★★.

McDaniel, Floyd

b. 21 July 1915, USA, d. 22 July 1995, Chicago, Illinois, USA. Singer and guitarist McDaniel took his first professional engagement in the late 30s with the Rhythm Rascals. After becoming leader of the Cotton Club Tramp Band in New York he found his most famous and enduring professional commitment with the Five Blazes, beginning in 1941. Fusing jazz and R&B, the group stayed together through the war years and into the mid-50s, proving an ever popular attraction on the east coast of America. After their dissolution McDaniel continued to work as a session and live musician. He sang back-up vocals for Sam Cooke for a period before joining one of the numerous line-ups of the Ink Spots for over 10 years. In the 90s he was still active, recording music with the Blues Swingers for Delmark Records as late as 1994 and played at the 1995 Chicago Blues Festival. He died of cancer a year later aged 80.

● ALBUMS: *Let Your Hair Down* (Delmark 1995)★★★.

McDaniels, Gene

b. Eugene B. McDaniels, 12 February 1935, Kansas City, Kansas, USA. A former gospel singer and bandleader, McDaniels completed studies at Omaha's Conservatory of Music before embarking on a recording career. Signed to Liberty in the late 50s, he enjoyed several local hits, including 'In Times Like These' and 'The Green Door', prior to securing two US Top 5 entries in 1961 with 'A Hundred Pounds Of Clay' and 'Tower Of Strength'. Both singles fared less well in Britain, where cover versions by Craig Douglas and Frankie Vaughan took the plaudits, but McDaniels' influence on British music was acknowledged by his appearance in the film *It's Trad, Dad*. McDaniels' last US chart entry came the following year with 'Point Of No Return', a smooth, jazz-based performance and arguably the singer's finest release. He sadly fell from favour when tastes changed following the rise of the Beatles and his subsequent efforts at soul, tinged with social consciousness, paled beside these early recordings.

● ALBUMS: *In Times Like These* (Liberty 1960)★★★, *Sometimes I'm Happy (Sometimes I'm Blue)* (Liberty 1960)★★★, *100 lbs Of Clay* (Liberty 1961)★★★★, *Gene McDaniels Sings Movie Memories* (Liberty 1962)★★, *Tower Of Strength* (Liberty 1962)★★★★, *Spanish Lace* (Liberty 1963)★★, *The Wonderful World Of Gene*

McDaniels (Liberty 1963)★★, *Facts Of Life* (1968)★★, *Outlaw* (Atlantic 1970)★★, *Headless Heroes Of The Apocalypse* (Atlantic 1971), *Natural Juices* (1975)★★.
● COMPILATIONS: *Hit After Hit* (1962)★★★, *Another Tear Falls* (Charly 1986)★★★.
● FILMS: *It's Trad, Dad* aka *Ring-A-Ding Rhythm* (1962).

McDonald, Michael

b. 2 December 1952, St. Louis, Missouri, USA. Following his departure from the Doobie Brothers in 1982, McDonald, the former Steely Dan keyboard player, embarked on a popular solo career. He had already won a Grammy for his song, co-written with Kenny Loggins, 'What A Fool Believes', but during the 80s he had his compositions recorded by numerous artists, including Aretha Franklin, Millie Jackson and Carly Simon. He almost made the top of the US charts in 1982 with his soulful 'I Keep Forgettin' (Every Time You're Near)'. It is not often that a white singer is able to write and sing black soul music with such conviction and integrity. His 'Yah Mo B There', recorded with James Ingram in 1984, is a modern soul classic. The 1985 album *No Lookin' Back* was a dance favourite, shortly to be followed by his epic number 1 hit with Patti LaBelle, 'On My Own'. During that year, he enjoyed an international hit with the theme from the film *Running Scared*, the graceful 'Sweet Freedom'. McDonald has one of the most powerful voices in modern soul/rock, and has honed his ability to become a major, although not always completely consistent, songwriter.
● ALBUMS: *If That's What It Takes* (Warners 1982)★★★★, *No Looking Back* (Warners 1985)★★★, *Lonely Talk* (Warners 1989)★★★, *Take It To Heart* (Reprise 1990)★★★, *Blink Of An Eye* (1993)★★.
● COMPILATIONS: *Sweet Freedom: Best Of Michael McDonald* (Warners 1986)★★★.

McFadden And Whitehead

Gene McFadden and John Whitehead (both b. 1948, Philadelphia, Pennsylvania, USA), were former members of the Epsilons, a group managed by Otis Redding, prior to joining the Philadelphia International label. Here they forged a career as producers, playing a major role in the development of the label's 'sound' and as songwriters, penning hits for Harold Melvin And The Blue Notes ('Bad Luck', 'Wake Up Everybody') and the O'Jays ('Back Stabbers'), ultimately being responsible for over 20 gold discs. As performers, MacFadden and Whitehead enjoyed an international smash with 'Ain't No Stoppin Us Now' (1979), a defiant, post-disco anthem, highlighted by the latter's magnificent, exhorting delivery. The duo's later releases, however, were less successful, and, after serving time in prison for tax evasion, Whitehead embarked on a solo career in 1988.
● ALBUMS: *McFadden And Whitehead* (Philadelphia International 1979)★★★, *I Heard It In A Love Song* (TSOP 1980)★★.

McNeely, Big Jay

b. Cecil James McNeely, 29 April 1927, Los Angeles, California, USA. As a tenor saxophonist McNeely was one of the pioneers of the wild, honking style that emerged in the dancehalls during the late 40s. The definitive tune of this style was 'Deacon's Hop', which reached number 1 R&B in 1949. His 'Wild Wig', which went to number 12 R&B the same year, was McNeely's only other chart record in this style. He returned to the charts in 1959 with the classic 'There Is Something On Your Mind' (number 5 R&B/number 44 pop), but vocalist Sonny Warner was the focus rather than McNeely. During the 80s McNeely revived his career with a series of reissue albums.
● ALBUMS: *Big Jay McNeely* (Federal 1954)★★★★, *A Rhythm And Blues Concert* (Savoy 1955)★★★, *Big Jay McNeely In 3-D* (Federal 1956)★★★, *Big Jay McNeely* (Warners1963)★★, *People Will Be People* (Big J 1996)★.
● COMPILATIONS: *Road House Boogie* (Saxophonograph 1985)★★★, *Best Of Big Jay McNeely* (Saxophonograph 1986)★★★, *From Harlem To Camden* (Ace 1987)★★★, *Golden Classics* (1989)★★★, *Live At Birdland 1957* (Big J 1989)★★★, *Welcome To California* (1990)★★★, *Live And Rare* (Earth Angel 1991)★★, *Blow The Wall Down* (1991)★★★.

McPhatter, Clyde

b. Clyde Lensley McPhatter, 15 November 1932, Durham, North Carolina, USA, d. 13 June 1972, New York City, New York, USA. For three years, McPhatter was the lead singer in the seminal R&B vocal group Billy Ward And His Dominoes. He left in 1953 to form the Drifters, whose early releases were enhanced by the singer's emotional, gospel-drenched delivery. In 1954 McPhatter was drafted into the US Army, where he entertained fellow servicemen. Such work prompted a solo career, and the vibrant 'Seven Days' (1956) was followed by several other superb performances, many of which, including 'Treasure Of Love', 'Without Love (There Is Nothing)' and 'A Lover's Question', became R&B standards. A hugely influential figure, McPhatter inspired a generation of singers. His work was covered by Elvis Presley, Ry Cooder and Otis Redding, but his departure from the Atlantic label to MGM in 1959 precipitated an artistic decline. Although he had several minor hits during the early 60s, arguably his finest work was the US Top 10 hit 'Lover Please' in 1962. The follow-up, 'Little Bitty Pretty One', became standard fodder for many UK beat groups in the early 60s (recorded by the Paramounts). The singer became increasingly overshadowed by new performers and his career started to wane in the mid-60s. Beset by personal problems, he came to Britain in 1968, but left two years later without an appreciable change in his fortunes. A 1970 album on Decca, *Welcome Home*, was his last recording. McPhatter, one of R&B's finest voices, died from a heart attack as a result of alcohol abuse in 1972.
● ALBUMS: *Clyde McPhatter And The Drifters* (Atlantic 1958)★★★★, *Love Ballads* (Atlantic 1958)★★★★, *Clyde* (Atlantic 1959)★★★, *Let's Start Over Again* (MGM 1959)★★★, *Ta Ta* (Mercury 1960)★★★, *Golden Blues Hits* (1962)★★★, *Lover Please* (Mercury 1962)★★★★, *May I Sing For You* (Wing 1962)★★★, *Rhythm And Soul* (Mercury 1963)★★★, *Songs Of The Big City* (Mercury 1964)★★, *Live At The Apollo* (Mercury 1964)★★, *Welcome Home* (Decca 1970)★★.

● COMPILATIONS: *Greatest Hits* (MGM 1960)★★★, *The Best Of Clyde McPhatter* (Atlantic 1963)★★★, *Greatest Recordings* (1972)★★★, *A Tribute To Clyde McPhatter* (1973)★★★, *Rock And Cry* (Charly 1984)★★★, *Rhythm And Soul* 8-LP box set of MGM/Mercury recordings (Bear Family 1987)★★★★, *Deep Sea Ball - The Best Of Clyde McPhatter* (Atlantic 1991)★★★★, *Love Ballads* (Sequel 1997)★★★.

McWilliams, Brigitte

b. Chicago, Illinois, USA. An R&B singer of distinctive vocal quality and strength, Brigitte McWilliams made her debut for Virgin Records in 1994 with a lacklustre set entitled *Take Advantage Of Me*. Although it received generally favourable reviews in the soul/R&B papers, the artist later complained that she enjoyed 'zero creative control' in its conception and birth. She addressed this artistic impasse with the follow-up set, 1997's *Too Much Woman*, assembling a band of old-school R&B veterans to help her. These included guitarist Al McKay and keyboardist Larry Dunn (Earth, Wind And Fire), guitarist Jimmy Macon (Gap Band), Bobby Watson (Rufus) and Billy Preston. Recorded in informal 'jam' sessions, the results of employing such first-rate genre performers were immediately satisfying. McWilliams herself contributed three songs to the collection, part of a shift of emphasis towards a female view of relationship issues, rather than the more hackneyed R&B stereotype outlined on her debut.

● ALBUMS: *Take Advantage Of Me* (Virgin 1994)★★, *Too Much Woman* (Virgin 1997)★★★.

Medallions

The Medallions were formed by lead singer Vernon Green (b. Denver, Colorado, USA) in Los Angeles, California, USA, after record company boss Dootsie Williams commented on the quality of his voice as he was walking down the street one day. The rest of the group - Andrew Blue (tenor), Randolph Bryant (baritone) and Ira Foley (bass) - were built around Green's strong vocal abilities, and took their collective name from their leader's fondness for jewellery. Williams was as good as his word and signed the group to Dootone Records, a relationship that began with the release of 'The Letter'. The b-side, 'Buick 59', was particularly well received on Los Angeles radio, and started a trend of naming singles after car types ('Coupe De Ville Baby', '59 Volvo', etc.). Willy Graham replaced Andrew Blue, while the group expanded to a quintet in 1955 with the addition of Donald Woods. However, the group broke up after the release of their third single, 'Speedin''. Abandoning Green, the other four members formed the Vel-Aires and signed with Flip Records. Green responded by putting together a new Medallions featuring Kenneth Williams and Frank Marshall, issuing 'Only For You'. This formation did not last, however, and Williams then placed Green as singer with another of his groups, the Dootones (who shared the name of the label). They were still titled the Medallions, but their first release together was as back-up group to Johnny Morisette on October 1955's 'My Pretty Baby'. However, a month later they debuted in their own right with 'Dear Darling' then 'I Want A Love'. Their next release saw their billing extended to Vernon Green And The Medallions. They released three singles for Dootone's Dooto subsidiary between 1956 and 1957 in this manner. None of these singles, which again featured fluctuating line-ups, were successful. Green left to form the Phantoms, a masked group who recorded briefly for Specialty Records, but then returned in 1957 to front another version of the Medallions. Five further singles emerged (three for Dooto, one for Minit and one for Pan World Records), while the band continued to tour widely. The most interesting of these singles was the second, 'Magic Mountain'/'59 Volvo'. The latter track was expressly commissioned by a local disc jockey whose brother owned a Volvo dealership. The band was then put on hold for nine years following an automobile accident that incapacitated Green. He returned to front the Medallions for a final 1973 single for Dooto, 'Can You Talk', and again in 1989 at the inaugural Doo-wop Society show.

Medley, Bill

b. 19 September 1940, Santa Ana, California, USA. After several successful years with the Righteous Brothers, Medley embarked on a solo career in late 1967. Several relatively barren years followed, until Medley received a major push from A&M in 1971. Again, no hits were forthcoming, and in 1974, the Righteous Brothers reunited. Medley's second attempt at a solo career took place in 1981, five years after the mysterious murder of his wife Karen. This time he enjoyed some minor hits, which reached fruition during the second half of the 80s with his contribution to the movie *Dirty Dancing*. Collaborating with Jennifer Warnes, Medley found the perfect song in '(I've Had) The Time Of My Life', which reached number 1 in the US charts. Further film-related material saw Medley enjoy minor successes, most notably with a cover version of the Hollies' 'He Ain't Heavy, He's My Brother' from the soundtrack of *Rambo III*.

● ALBUMS: Bill Medley *100%* (MGM 1968)★★★, *Soft And Soulful* (MGM 1969)★★★, *A Song For You* (A&M 1971)★★★, *Sweet Thunder* (1981)★★, *Right Here And Now* (Planet 1982)★★.

● COMPILATIONS: *The All-Time Greatest Hits Of Bill Medley* (RCA 1988)★★★.

Mel And Tim

Cousins Mel Hardin and Tim McPherson were born and raised in Holly Springs, Mississippi, USA, and later moved to St. Louis, Missouri. They were signed to Gene Chandler's Bamboo label and reached the US Top 10 with 'Backfield In Motion' (1969). A vibrant single, it was followed by 'Good Guys Only Win In The Movies', after which Mel And Tim switched to Stax. The sumptuous 'Starting All Over Again', later covered by Johnnie Taylor, was another major R&B hit, but further singles, including 'I May Not Be What You Want' (from the film *Wattstax*), had less success.

● ALBUMS: *Good Guys Only Win In The Movies* (Bamboo 1969)★★, *Starting All Over Again* (Stax 1972)★★★, *Mel And Tim* (Stax 1973)★★.

MELENDES, LISA

b. East Harlem, New York, USA. This tiny Puerto Rican singer found immediate success in 1988's soul/dance scene when she made her debut with 'Make Noise', assisted by producer Carlo Berrios. 'Make Noise' was the result of her experiments with a new hybrid of street/dance music, which she christened 'new school'. A second hit single, 'Together Forever', sold nearly half a million copies, and topped the *Billboard* Dance and Hot 100 charts. Afterwards her career stalled, though an attempt to revive her fortunes was made in 1994 with *True To Life*, produced by hip-hop artist Greg Nice (Nice And Smooth). Preceded by the single 'Goody Goody', it heralded Melendes's new image - sultry looks and free-flowing dresses contrasting with heavy combat boots.

● ALBUMS: *True To Life* (Fever 1994)★★.

MELLO-KINGS

The Mello-Kings were responsible for one of the most durable doo-wop hits of the 50s. Despite the fact that their only hit, 'Tonite Tonite', never climbed higher than number 77 in the US charts, that single is still considered one of the most popular group harmony recordings of the era, more than three decades after its initial release. The group consisted of brothers Jerry and Bob Scholl, Eddie Quinn, Neil Arena and Larry Esposito. The quintet was formed in 1956 at a high school in Mount Vernon, New York, USA, under the guidance of manager Dick Levister. Originally named the Mellotones, the group was signed to the Herald label. 'Tonite Tonite' was written by Billy Myles, a staff composer for the label. The group was forced to change its name after the single's release, as another group had already claimed Mellotones. The record lasted only 10 weeks in the US charts, and the group was never able to repeat this success, although 'Tonite Tonite' returned in 1961, reaching number 95, due to a resurgence of interest in the doo-wop sound, and has been consistently voted among the top five doo-wop records of all time in radio polls, particularly in the New York area. A new Mello-Kings led by Jerry Scholl, whose brother Bob died on 27 August 1975, was still touring the rock 'n' roll revival circuit in the early 90s.

● COMPILATIONS: *Tonite, Tonite* (Relic 1991)★★★, *Greatest Hits* (Collectables 1992)★★★.

MELLOWMOODS

An R&B vocal group from Harlem, New York City, New York, USA. The Mellowmoods began at the dawn of the doo-wop era, and made a brief impression on the recording scene with their deep street-corner sound. The members were Ray 'Buddy' Wooten, Bobby Williams, Monteith 'Monte' Owens, Alvin 'Bobby' Baylor, and Jimmy Bethea. Their one hit was 'Where Are You? (Now That I Need You)' (number 7 R&B) for Bobby Robinson's Robin label in 1951. They failed on their subsequent releases, 'I Couldn't Sleep A Wink Last Night' for Red Robin in 1952, and two more releases on Prestige. The group broke up after their last record in 1953, and Owens and Williams became members of the newly formed Solitaires.

MELLOWS

One of the rare 50s R&B groups to be led by a female vocalist, the Mellows comprised Lillian Leach (lead), Johnny 'Tiny' Wilson (first tenor), Harold Johnson (second tenor) and Norman 'Polecat' Brown (bass). The three boys had met as teenagers at the Morris High School in the Bronx, New York, USA. They encountered Leach at a party in 1954 when she joined their harmonizing. The revised blend was an instant hit, and the sound it produced gave the quartet their name (having learned that their original choice, the Mello-Tones, had already been employed elsewhere). Johnson started seeking a contract, eventually finding one with Jay Dee Records (he had previously worked for that label with Dean Barlow and the Crickets). Johnson also penned their first single, 'How Sentimental Can I Be?', but this pop-orientated ballad failed to find a suitable audience due to a lack of promotion and airplay. They had more success with their second record, the seductive 'Smoke From Your Cigarette', which became a regional hit. However, neither 'I Still Care' nor 'Yesterday's Memories' were substantial enough to build on this impact, and the group was also weakened by the loss of Norman Brown (replaced on bass by Gary Morrison). They then added a fifth member, Arthur Crier of the Chimes. The Mellows moved over to Celeste Records in 1955, but both the singles released on the label flopped. Candlelight Records was their next port of call, although 'You're Gone'/'Men Of Silver' marked the end of their career. They broke up in 1957. Johnson and Crier went on to the Halos, who backed several notable artists and enjoyed a hit under their own steam with 'Nag'. A reunion of the Mellows took place in 1984 with three of the original members, and the group have continued to peddle sweet R&B pop on the nostalgia circuit ever since.

MELTDOWN

Meltdown are a five-piece band formed by ex-Yardbirds drummer Jim McCarty. Previously responsible for writing epochal songs for the latter band, including 'Shapes Of Things', 'Still I'm Sad' and 'Over Under Sideways Down', McCarty started Meltdown in the 90s as an avenue for full-blooded R&B, mixing original material with blues classics written by Freddie King, Johnny Winter, Peter Green and others. The cast list behind Meltdown was certainly impressive; Ray Majors (guitar, vocals) was formerly with Mott The Hoople and the British Lions, and had previously worked with McCarty as part of Box Of Frogs in 1984. He then joined the drummer's pre-Meltdown combo, the McCarty Band, for live work, replacing Top Topham. Sam Johnson provides expressive slide guitar. Despite his tender years Johnson had already worked with Pete Hogman of the Five Dimensions and Dick Taylor of the Pretty Things. The other youngster in the band is keyboard player Steve Corley, a jazz prodigy from the Royal Academy Of Music. Female bass player/vocalist Nikki Racklin had already recorded solo and opened shows for Naked Truth and James. The group then set about a series of live UK dates, before mini-tours of Sweden and France.

MELVIN, HAROLD, AND THE BLUE NOTES

Formed in Philadelphia in 1954, the Blue Notes - Harold Melvin (b. 25 June 1939, Philadelphia, Pennsylvania, USA, d. 24 March 1997), Bernard Wilson, Jesse Gillis Jnr., Franklin Peaker and Roosevelt Brodie - began life as a doo-wop group. In 1960, they enjoyed a minor hit with a ballad, 'My Hero', but failed to make a significant breakthrough despite several excellent singles. By the end of the decade only Melvin and Wilson remained from that early group, with John Atkins and Lawrence Brown completing the line-up. Two crucial events then changed their fortunes. Theodore 'Teddy' Pendergrass (b. 26 March 1950, Philadelphia, Pennsylvania, USA), drummer in the Blue Notes' backing band, was brought into the frontline as the featured vocalist in place of the departing Atkins. A fifth singer, Lloyd Parkes, also joined the group, which was then signed by producers Gamble And Huff, whose sculpted arrangements and insistent rhythm tracks provided the perfect foil for the Pendergrass voice. His imploring delivery was best heard on 'If You Don't Know Me By Now' (1972), an aching ballad that encapsulated the intimacy of a relationship. Further singles, including 'The Love I Lost (1973) and 'Where Are All My Friends' (1974), enhanced Pendergrass's reputation and led to his demand for equal billing in the group. Melvin's refusal resulted in the singer's departure. However, while Pendergrass remained contracted to Philadelphia International and enjoyed considerable solo success, Melvin And The Blue Notes, with new singer David Ebo, moved to ABC Records. Despite securing a UK Top 5 hit with 'Don't Leave Me This Way' and a US R&B Top 10 hit with 'Reaching For The World' in 1977, the group was unable to recapture its erstwhile success. By the early 80s, they were without a recording contract, but continued to enjoy an in-concert popularity. They signed to Philly World in 1984, achieving minor UK hit singles the same year with 'Don't Give Me Up' and 'Today's Your Lucky Day'.

● ALBUMS: *Harold Melvin And The Blue Notes* (Philadelphia International 1972)★★★, *Black And Blue* (Philadelphia International 1973)★★★★, *To Be True* (Philadelphia International 1975)★★★★, *Wake Up Everybody* (Philadelphia International 1975)★★★★, *Reaching For The World* (ABC 1977)★★★★, *Now Is The Time* (ABC 1977)★★, *Blue Album* (Source 1980)★★, *All Things Happen In Time* (MCA 1981)★★, *Talk It Up* (Philly World 1984)★★.

● COMPILATIONS: *All Their Greatest Hits!* (Philadelphia International 1976)★★★★, *Golden Highlights Of Harold Melvin* (Columbia 1986)★★★, *Satisfaction Guaranteed - The Best Of Harold Melvin And The Blue Notes* (Philadelphia International 1992)★★★, *Collection Gold* (1993)★★★, *If You Don't Know Me By Now* (Epic Legacy 1995)★★★★.

MEMORY

Formed by members of the New York Life Assurance company in Lebanon, New Jersey, USA, in the autumn of 1976, Memory's music was more colourful than either those origins or their lacklustre choice of name would suggest. Comprising six multiracial computer database operatives, Jaime de Jesus (lead), Lesley Uhl (falsetto), Herb 'Iceman' Olson (baritone), Lou 'Big Lou' Benito (bass), Bobby 'Bobby Hep' Hepburn (first tenor) and Otis 'Big O' Harper (second tenor), they would meet after working hours in the company boardroom and practise their harmony singing. Perfecting oldies by the Drifters and other doo-wop groups of the 50s, their debut performance came at their employer's Christmas party in 1976. Afterwards they moved onto the local New Jersey club circuit, where they would spend several years cultivating an audience. Their first recording, 'Street Corner Serenade', was released in March 1981, at which time Olson was replaced on baritone by Greg Restivo. A second single, a cover version of the Drifters' 'Under The Boardwalk', followed, but it was to be their final release. They continued to perform, however, to appreciative doo-wop fans throughout their native New Jersey and nearby cities, until 1987. Afterwards the members returned to their seats behind VDU screens, although four of the band had taken new jobs outside the insurance industry.

MEMPHIS HORNS

The Memphis Horns, an offshoot of the Mar-Keys, boasted a fluid line-up throughout its history. The mainstays, trumpeter Wayne Jackson and tenor saxophonist Andrew Love, guided the group through its period at the Stax and Hi studios. Augmented by James Mitchell (baritone saxophone), Jack Hale (trombone) and either Ed Logan or Lewis Collins (tenor saxophone), the Horns appeared on releases by Al Green, Ann Peebles, Syl Johnson and many others. The group's eponymous debut album featured several members of the Dixie Flyers and, during the mid-70s, the Horns secured four R&B hits including 'Get Up And Dance' and 'Just For Your Love'. The 1978 album *Memphis Horns II*, featured as guest vocalists Michael McDonald, Anita Pointer and James Gilstrap. The Memphis Horns are, however, better recalled for their contributions to many of southern soul's finest moments. Andrew Love and Wayne Jackson maintained the Memphis Horns' name throughout the 80s and made appearances on U2's *Rattle And Hum* and Keith Richards' *Talk Is Cheap* (both in 1988). In 1990 the duo supported Robert Cray, and in 1991, 1992 and 1994 they played at the annual Porretta Terme Soul Festival in Italy which regularly attracts top soul acts from the Memphis area.

● ALBUMS: *Memphis Horns* (Cotillion 1970)★★★, *Horns For Everything* (Million 1972)★★★, *High On Music* (RCA 1976)★★, *Get Up And Dance* (RCA 1977)★★, *Memphis Horns Band II* (RCA 1978)★★★, *Welcome To Memphis* (RCA 1979)★★, *Flame Out* (Lucky 7 1992)★★★.

MEN OF VIZION

Comprising George Spencer III, Corley Randolph, Desmond T. Greggs, Brian L. Dermus and lead singer Prathan 'Spanky' Williams, Men Of Vizion formed in New York, USA, in the early 90s. Their sophisticated vocal R&B harmonies impressed Michael Jackson, and they signed with his record label, MJJ, after a demo tape was played to him by producer Teddy Riley in 1993. Men Of

Vizion made their long-playing debut in 1996 with *Personal*, a sumptuous blend of vocal R&B and 90s production techniques. As Greggs told *Billboard*, 'We're here to prove that intimate songwriting in R&B is coming back. We're writing songs that everyone will understand.' The first single, 'House Keeper', was a cover version of the 1977 Jackson Five song 'Show You The Way To Go', and was included on the *Money Train* soundtrack.

● ALBUMS: *Personal* (MJJ 1996)★★★.

Meters

This fundamental quartet, Art Neville (b. Arthur Lanon Neville, 17 December 1937, New Orleans, Louisiana, USA; keyboards), Leo Nocentelli (guitar), George Porter (bass) and Joseph 'Zigaboo/Ziggy' Modeliste (drums), came together during informal sessions held in various New Orleans nightclubs. Initially known as Art Neville and the Neville Sounds, they were spotted by producers Allen Toussaint and Marshall Sehorn, who signed the unit to their Sansu label to work on sessions for the duo's other artists, including Lee Dorsey and Betty Harris. Redubbed the Meters, the group's first singles, 'Sophisticated Cissy' and 'Cissy Strut', reached the US R&B Top 10 in 1969. These tough instrumentals mixed the bare-boned approach of Booker T. And The MGs with the emergent funk of Sly Stone, a style consolidated on several further releases and the unit's three albums for the Josie label. This canvas was broadened on a move to Warner Brothers/Reprise in 1972, where a series of critically acclaimed albums, including *Cabbage Alley* and *Rejuvenation*, reinforced their distinctive, sinewy rhythms. Such expertise was also heard on many sessions, including those for Robert Palmer, Dr. John and Paul McCartney, while in 1975, the group supported the Rolling Stones on their North American tour. Cyril Neville (vocals, percussion) was added to the line-up at this time, but the Meters found it difficult to make further commercial progress. In 1976, Art and Cyril joined Charles and Aaron Neville on a project entitled the Wild Tchoupitoulas. Led by an uncle, George Landry (Big Chief Jolly), this was the first time the brothers had played together. When the Meters split the following year, the quartet embarked on a new career, firstly as the Neville Family Band, then as the Neville Brothers.

● ALBUMS: *The Meters* (Josie 1969)★★★, *Look-Ka Py Py* (Josie 1970)★★★★, *Struttin'* (Josie 1970)★★★★, *Cabbage Alley* (Reprise 1972)★★★★, *Rejuvenation* (Reprise 1974)★★★★, *Fire On The Bayou* (Reprise 1975)★★★, *Trick Bag* (Reprise 1976)★★, *New Directions* (Warners 1977)★★★, *Uptown Rulers! Live On The Queen Mary* 1975 recording (Rhino 1992)★★★.

● COMPILATIONS: *Cissy Strut* (Island 1974)★★★, *Good Old Funky Music* (Pye 1979)★★★, *Second Line Strut* (Charly 1980)★★★, *Here Come The Meter Men* (Charly 1986)★★★★, *Funky Miracle* (Charly 1991)★★★★, *The Meters Jam* (Rounder 1992)★★★★.

MFSB

'Mother, Father, Sister, Brother' or MFSB (and there was a less flattering alternative), was the house band employed by producers Gamble And Huff. Jesse James, Bobby Martin, Norman Harris, Ronnie Baker, Earl Young, Roland Chambers and Karl Chambers came to prominence as the uncredited performers on 'The Horse', a hit for Cliff Nobles And Co. in 1968. As the James Boys, the septet replicated that hit with a cash-in release, 'The Mule', and the unit also recorded under other names, including the Music Makers and Family. It was as the instrumental muscle behind the Philadelphia International stable and artists such as the O'Jays and Harold Melvin And The Blue Notes that the group garnered its reputation. 'TSOP (The Sound Of Philadelphia)', the theme from television's *Soul Train* show, was a million-selling single in 1974, but later releases failed to match its exuberance and purpose. Undeniably rhythmic and undoubtedly competent, MFSB nonetheless lacked the focal point that the Three Degrees' voices provided on those early successes.

● ALBUMS: *MFSB* (Philadelphia International 1973)★★, *Love Is The Message* (Philadelphia International 1974)★★, *Universal Love* (Philadelphia International 1975)★★, *Philadelphia Freedom!* (Philadelphia International 1975)★★★, *Summertime* (Philadelphia International 1976)★★, *The End Of Phase 1* (Philadelphia International 1977)★★, *The Gamble-Huff Orchestra* (Philadelphia International 1979)★★, *Mysteries Of The World* (Philadelphia International 1981)★★.

● COMPILATIONS: *Love Is The Message: The Best Of MSFB* (Sony Legacy 1996)★★★.

Mickey And Sylvia

McHouston 'Mickey' Baker (b. 15 October 1925, Louisville, Kentucky, USA) and Sylvia Vanderpool (b. 6 March 1936, New York City, New York, USA). This popular duo began recording together in 1956 and enjoyed an US R&B chart-topper that year with 'Love Is Strange', which peaked at number 11 in the US pop chart the following year. This enduring call-and-response song is rightly regarded as a classic of its genre, and later became a minor UK hit when recorded by the Everly Brothers. Mickey and Sylvia had further success with 'There Oughta Be A Law' (1957) and, after a brief hiatus as a duo, 'Baby You're So Fine' (1961), but their career together was undermined by commitments elsewhere. Prolific session work for Atlantic, Savoy, King and Aladdin earned the former the epithet Mickey 'Guitar' Baker, while the latter had made her recording debut with jazz trumpeter Oran 'Hot Lips' Page as early as 1950. In 1973, she began recording as Sylvia, and later achieved notable success as an entrepreneur through her ownership of Sugar Hill Records, early champions of the rap/hip-hop scene.

● ALBUMS: *New Sounds* (Vix 1957)★★, *Love Is Strange* (Camden 1965)★★.

● COMPILATIONS: *Love Is Strange And Other Hits* (RCA 1989)★★★, *The Willow Sessions* (Sequel 1996)★★★.

Mighty Clouds Of Joy

Gospel quartet the Mighty Clouds Of Joy formed at Jefferson High School in Los Angeles, California, USA, in 1960. Joe Ligon (b. Troy, Alabama, USA; lead), Johnny Martin (b. Los Angeles, California, USA; tenor), Richard Wallace (b. Georgia, USA; baritone) and Elmo Franklin (b.

Louisiana, USA; bass) became the band's first permanent line-up. After a series of small-scale gospel concerts in local churches, the group were recruited by the Houston-based label Peacock Records. Throughout the 60s the group recorded a series of albums for the label that all sold well in the gospel market, although later they would change tempo to adapt to the prevailing musical climate, leading them into soul, R&B and rock 'n' roll. 'Time', on ABC Records, produced by Gamble And Huff, became a number 32 R&B hit in 1974. 'Mighty Cloud Of Joy' also achieved minor success, but their highest chart placing came with the release of '(Ride The) Mighty High' in February 1976. However, the glamour of the pop world never completely tore the group away from their religious beliefs, a fact confirmed by the title of their Grammy-nominated 1978 album, *God Is Not Dead*. The same year's *Live And Direct* won a Grammy award, as did the subsequent *Changing Times* (produced by Frank Wilson, former Jackson 5 associate). By 1980 the group had moved to Word Records and earned another Grammy nomination for *Cloudburst*, this time produced by Al McKay of Earth, Wind And Fire. At this time the group also included Paul Beasley (ex-Keynotes) and Michael Cook. None of this activity, however, slowed the band's frenetic touring and recording pace, and two further Grammy nominations were awarded in 1982 for *Miracle Man* and *The Mighty Clouds Above*. When Johnny Martin died in 1987, first Dwight Gordon and then Michael McGowan stepped in. By the mid-90s they were still to be found performing hundreds of concerts a year, with over thirty albums to their name.

● ALBUMS: *A Bright Side* (Peacock 1960)★★★, *It's Time* (ABC 1974)★★★, *Kickin'* (ABC 1976)★★★, *God Is Not Dead* (ABC 1978)★★★, *Live And Direct* (ABC 1978)★★★★, *Changing Times* (Epic 1979)★★★, *Cloudburst* (Word 1980)★★★★, *Miracle Man* (Word 1982)★★★, *Mighty Clouds Above* (Word 1982)★★★, *Power* (Intersound 1995)★★★.

● COMPILATIONS: *The Best Of The Mighty Clouds Of Joy Vol. 1* (MCA 1973)★★★★, *The Best Of The Might Clouds Of Joy Vol. 2* (MCA 1973)★★★, *Request Line* (ABC 1982)★★★.

Mighty Sam

b. Sam McClain, 15 April 1943, Monroe, Louisiana, USA. Introduced to gospel as a child, McClain served his apprenticeship in a schoolfriend's R&B group. In 1963, he joined the Dothan Sextet and remained their lead singer for the next three years. Disc jockey 'Papa' Don Schroeder 'discovered' Sam and signed him to the Bell subsidiary Amy, where the artist recorded eight singles. The Fame studio house band provided the perfect accompaniment to McClain's rasping interpretations, which evoked those of Bobby Bland and Little Milton. Ballads such as 'In The Same Old Way' (1967) and 'When She Touches Me' (1967), and the deep country soul of 'Sweet Dreams' (1968) stand among his finest offerings. In 1970, following Schroeder's retirement, Mighty Sam joined Atlantic Records for two excellent singles before switching to Malaco Records for a solitary release. After years of neglect, during which the singer was almost penniless, he re-emerged on the Orleans label. A *Live In Japan* set followed. McClain's distinctive growl can also be heard on *Hubert Sumlin's Blues Party*, one of the finest blues collections of the late 80s. *Give it Up To Love* demonstrated his voice reaching a glorious peak and is probably his finest album. It is a great pity, however, that this man has not received wider success and recognition.

● ALBUMS: *Mighty Soul* (Amy 1969)★★★, *Your Perfect Companion* (1986)★★★, *Live In Japan* (Orleans 1987)★★★, *Give It Up To Love* (Audioquest 1996)★★★★, *Sledgehammer Soul And Down Home Blues* (Audioquest 1997)★★★.

● COMPILATIONS: *Nothing But The Truth* (Charly 1988)★★★.

Milburn, Amos

b. 1 April 1927, Houston, Texas, USA, d. 3 January 1980, Houston, Texas, USA. After service in the US Navy in World War II, Milburn formed his own blues and R&B band in Houston in which he played piano and sang, and in 1946 he was offered a contract by the Aladdin label. Between November 1948 and February 1954 he and his band, the Aladdin Chicken Shackers, had an extraordinary run of 19 consecutive Top 10 hits on the *Billboard* R&B chart, including four number 1s ('Chicken Shack Boogie', 'A&M Blues', 'Roomin' House Boogie' and 'Bad, Bad Whiskey'). His romping boogies about drinking and partying were hugely popular and for two years (1949 and 1950) he was voted Top R&B Artist by *Billboard*. Following the break-up of his band in 1954 he never achieved the same level of success, and he left Aladdin in 1956. He then recorded as part of a duo with Charles Brown for the Ace label, and in 1963 recorded an album for Motown Records. In the 60s he played clubs around Cincinnati and Cleveland, Ohio, drawing heavily on his catalogue of old hits, but did not have any more hit records. In 1970 he suffered the first of a series of strokes. In 1972 he retired and returned to his home-town of Houston where he died eight years later.

● ALBUMS: with Wynonie Harris *Party After Hours* (Aladdin 1955)★★★, *Rockin' The Boogie* (Aladdin 1955)★★★, *Let's Have A Party* (Score 1957)★★★, *Amos Milburn Sings The Blues* (Score 1958)★★★, *The Blues Boss* (Motown 1963)★★★, *13 Unreleased Masters* (Pathé-Marconi 1984)★★.

● COMPILATIONS: *Million Sellers* (Imperial 1962)★★★★, *Greatest Hits* Aladdin recordings (Official Records 1988)★★★★, *Blues & Boogie: His Greatest Hits* (Sequel 1991)★★★★, *Down The Road Apiece: The Best Of ...* (EMI 1994)★★★★, *The Complete Aladdin Recordings Of Amos Milburn* (Mosaic 1995)★★★★.

Miles, Buddy

b. George Miles, 5 September 1945, Omaha, Nebraska, USA. A teenage prodigy, this powerful, if inflexible drummer was a veteran of several touring revues prior to his spell with soul singer Wilson Pickett. In 1967, Miles joined the Electric Flag at the behest of guitarist Mike Bloomfield, whose subsequent departure left the drummer in control. Although the group collapsed in the wake of a disappointing second album, Miles retained its horn section for his next venture, the Buddy Miles Express. This exciting unit also included former Mitch Ryder guitarist Jim McCarthy. Their first album, *Expressway To Your Skull*, was full of driving, electric soul rhythms that had the blessing of Jimi Hendrix, who produced the album and wrote the sleeve notes. In 1969, Miles joined Jimi Hendrix in the ill-fated Band Of Gypsies. The drummer then continued his own career with the Buddy Miles Band and the rumbustious *Them Changes* album, the title track of which was a minor US hit. As an integral part of the artist's career, the song was not only featured on the *Band Of Gypsies* album, but provided one of the highlights of Miles's 1972 collaboration with Carlos Santana, which was recorded live in an extinct Hawaiian volcano. Having participated in an ill-fated Electric Flag reunion, the drummer continued his prolific rock/soul output with a variety of releases. Despite enjoying a seemingly lower profile during the 80s, Miles has been the guiding musical force behind the phenomenally successful California Raisins, a cartoon group inspired by television advertising. In the mid-90s Miles reappeared with an accomplished album on Ryko that included his interpretations of 'All Along The Watchtower' and 'Born Under A Bad Sign'. It was alleged in 1996 that Miles had once again fallen upon hard times.

● ALBUMS: as the Buddy Miles Express *Expressway To Your Skull* (Mercury 1968)★★★★, as the Buddy Miles Express *Electric Church* (Mercury 1969)★★★, as the Buddy Miles Band *Them Changes* (Mercury 1970)★★★, as the Buddy Miles Band *We Got To Live Together* (Mercury 1970)★★★, as the Buddy Miles Band *A Message To The People* (Mercury 1971)★★★, as the Buddy Miles Band *Buddy Miles Live* (Mercury 1971)★★, with Carlos Santana *Carlos Santana And Buddy Miles! Live!* (Columbia 1972)★★★, as the Buddy Miles Band *Chapter VII* (Columbia 1973)★★, as the Buddy Miles Express *Booger Bear* (Columbia 1973)★★, *All The Faces Of Buddy Miles* (1974)★★★, *More Miles Per Gallon* (Casablanca 1975)★★, *Bicentennial Gathering* (1976)★★, *Sneak Attack* (Atlantic 1981)★★, *Hell And Back* (Ryko 1994)★★★.

Mills, Stephanie

b. 1959, Brooklyn, New York, USA. Mills found fame when aged just nine, winning an influential talent show at Harlem's famous Apollo Theatre for six weeks running. Soon afterwards, she appeared on Broadway in the play *Maggie Flynn*. She toured with the Isley Brothers, and in 1973, recorded her debut, *Movin' In The Right Direction*, for the Paramount label. Her debut single - 'I Knew It Was Love' - was issued in 1974. Already an established performer, Mills was still in her teens when, in 1975, she was offered the part of Dorothy in the stage show *The Wiz* - the all-black reworking of *The Wizard Of Oz*. It was a role she retained for several years, and she had hoped to continue it in the film version, until Diana Ross usurped her position. During her run in the show, Mills was recommended to Motown's Berry Gordy by Jermaine Jackson and recorded an album for the label. *For The First Time* was written and produced by Burt Bacharach and Hal David. Motown chose not to continue its association with Mills, and she signed to 20th Century for three albums, the second of which spawned the huge worldwide hit 'Never Knew Love Like This' in 1980. That same year, Mills married Jeffrey Daniels of Shalamar, though the marriage was short-lived. After working with Teddy Pendergrass in 1981, and charting with the duet 'Two Hearts', Mills signed a new contract with Casablanca, and in 1983, received her own daytime television show on NBC. She reclaimed her role as Dorothy in a revival of *The Wiz* and had a further hit with 'The Medicine Song' from *I've Got The Cure*. This album was produced by David 'Hawk' Wolinski, formerly with the group Rufus. In 1985 she moved to MCA, where she enjoyed further hits including 'Stand Back' and 'Comfort Of A Man'.

● ALBUMS: *For The First Time* (Motown 1976)★★, *Whatcha Gonna Do With My Lovin'?* (20th Century 1979)★★★, *Sweet Sensation* (20th Century 1980)★★★★, *Stephanie* (20th Century 1981)★★★★, *Tantalizingly Hot* (Casablanca 1982)★★★, *Merciless* (Casablanca 1983)★★★, *I've Got The Cure* (Casablanca 1984)★★, *Stephanie Mills* (MCA 1985)★★★, *If I Were Your Woman* (MCA 1987)★★★, *Home* (MCA 1989)★★, *Something Real* (1993)★★★.

Milton, Roy

b. 31 July 1907, Wynnewood, Oklahoma, USA, d. 18 September 1983, Los Angeles, California, USA. Growing up on his Chickasaw grandmother's reservation, Milton encountered blues music when his family moved to Tulsa. In the late 20s, he was a vocalist with the Ernie Fields Orchestra; while on tour in Texas, he replaced the band's drummer after the latter was arrested. He left the Fields band in 1933 and moved to Los Angeles. After a couple of years he formed Roy Milton And The Solid Senders with pianist Camille Howard, Buddy Floyd and Hosea Sapp. In December 1945 they recorded 'R.M. Blues', which became an immediate hit, establishing both Roy Milton and Specialty Records and spearheading the wave of small R&B units that tolled the death knell of the big bands. Milton remained with Specialty for 10 years, recording ballads and pop tunes alongside more popular blues and boogie material such as 'Milton's Boogie', 'Hop, Skip And Jump', 'T-Town Twist' and 'Best Wishes'. After Specialty, he recorded for Dootone, King and Warwick, but by the end of the 60s his style of music had become outdated. He appeared with Johnny Otis at the 1970 Monterey Jazz Festival and resumed a solo career that also brought him to Europe. He fell ill in 1982 and was confined to his home until his death a year later.

● COMPILATIONS: *Big Fat Mama* (Jukebox Lil 1985)★★★, *Grandfather Of R&B* (Jukebox Lil 1987)★★★, *Roy Milton And His Solid Senders* (Specialty/Ace 1990)★★★, *Groovy Blues* (Specialty/Ace 1992)★★★, *Blowin' With Roy* (Specialty/Ace 1994)★★★.

Mimms, Garnet, And The Enchanters

b. Garrett Mimms, 26 November 1933, Ashland, West Virginia, USA. A former member of Philadelphia-based gospel groups the Evening Stars and the Norfolk Four, Mimms formed a secular quintet, the Gainors, in 1958.

The line-up included future soul star Howard Tate, as well as Sam Bell, Willie Combo and John Jefferson. Over the next three years, the Gainors made several singles for Cameo Records, Mercury Records and Tally-Ho which, although unsuccessful, betrayed a contemporary soul feel. The group subsequently evolved into Garnet Mimms And The Enchanters, where the singer and Sam Bell were joined by Charles Boyer and Zola Pearnell. Signed to United Artists in 1963, they came under the tutelage of writer/producer Jerry Ragovoy. His inspired work helped create some of urban R&B's finest moments. The impassioned 'Cry Baby' was an immediate US hit, while 'Baby Don't You Weep' and 'For Your Precious Love' consolidated their arrival. The group split in 1964, when Mimms embarked on a solo career. Although the Enchanters found a new vocalist and continued to record, they were overshadowed by their former leader. Mimms' subsequent releases, 'Look Away', 'It Was Easier To Hurt Her' and 'I'll Take Good Care Of You', were artistic triumphs, pitting the singer's church roots against Ragovoy's sophisticated backdrop. Such excellent records were not always well received, and in 1967, Mimms was demoted to United Artists' subsidiary Veep. 'My Baby' and 'Roll With The Punches' followed, but the singer's tenuous position was confirmed when the latter was only released in Britain. Ragovoy then took Mimms to Verve Records (where he was also producing Howard Tate), but the four singles that appeared, although good, found little favour. It was not until 1977 that the singer returned to the chart. Credited to Garnet Mimms And The Truckin' Company, 'What It Is' was a minor R&B hit and even clipped the UK chart at number 44. Mimms is now a born-again Christian and has not recorded for many years.

● ALBUMS: with the Enchanters *Cry Baby And 11 Other Hits* (United Artists 1963)★★★, *As Long As I Have You* (United Artists 1964)★★★, *I'll Take Good Care Of You* (United Artists 1966)★★, *Garnet Mimms Live* (United Artists 1967)★★, *Garnet Mimms Has It All* (Arista 1978)★★.

● COMPILATIONS: *Garnet Mimms And Maurice Monk* (United Artists 1963)★★★, *Sensational New Star* (United Artists 1963)★★★, *Warm And Soulful* (United Artists 1966)★★★, *Roll With The Punches* (Charly 1986)★★★, *Cry Baby* (1991)★★★, *Garnet Mimms And The Enchanters* (1991)★★★, *The Best Of ... Cry Baby* (1993)★★★.

MINIT RECORDS

Synonymous with both the New Orleans soul scene and the outstanding producer, writer and musician Allen Toussaint, Minit Records took its name from the original intention to supply disc jockeys with short (i.e., Minit) records that maximized the possibility of playing advertisements in-between. In fact, Toussaint was not present at the label's inception in 1959, when Joe Banashak and Larry McKinley formed the company. The first release was 'Bad Luck And Trouble', by Boogie Jake. However, Boogie's moniker drew resistance from radio stations, ensuring that its local popularity did not translate to national acclaim, despite Chess Records' licensing it for that purpose. Chess then reneged on its future options, although neither Boogie's follow-up (this time released under his real name, Matthew Jacobs) or a further single by Noland Pitts provided success. At this stage a twist in fortunes helped shape Minit's future. Regular A&R representative Harold Batiste temporarily left, leaving Banashak and McKinley to recruit Toussaint, who had already successfully auditioned as a musician. When Batiste failed to return, the post became Toussaint's on a permanent footing. Toussaint went on to define the Minit sound - writing much of the artistic repertoire, as well as arranging, producing and playing on the sessions. Minit's first hit, however, arrived with a rare artist's-own composition - Jessie Hill's 'Ooh Poo Pah Doo'. Reaching number 28 in the *Billboard* charts and number 3 in its R&B division, it was followed by a second, lesser hit, 'Whip It On Me'. Meanwhile, Toussaint had begun to shape the careers of Minit's roster. Ernie K-Doe was a veteran of the Blue Diamonds, and later recorded for Specialty and Ember Records as a solo artist. K-Doe broke through with his third release for the label, a Toussaint composition entitled 'Mother-In-Law'. This rose to number 1 in the main *Billboard* charts and gave New Orleans its first ever such success. Follow-ups included 'Te-Ta-Te-Ta-Ta' and 'I Cried My Last Tear'. The latter was a double a-side featuring another Toussaint composition, 'A Certain Girl', which was later covered by the Yardbirds. Benny Speelman, who had provided additional vocals on K-Doe's 'Mother-In-Law' hit, was also a fellow Minit intern. He found fame under his own name with the 1962 double a-side, 'Lipstick Traces (On A Cigarette)'/'Fortune Teller'. The first-named title was later revived by both the O'Jays and Ringo Starr. More enduringly, Aaron Neville also began his career at Minit, beginning with 1960's 'Over You'. One of many songs Toussaint composed in tandem with Allen Orange (who also recorded solo for the label), it was a precursor to the artist's major breakthrough six years later with 'Tell It Like It Is'. Another staple of the early catalogue was the subsequently popular Irma Thomas, while the Showmen achieved a 1961 hit for the label with 'It Will Stand'; leader General Johnson found subsequent success with Chairman Of The Board. However, by the time the Showmen's '30-21-46 (You)' had become another hit in 1963, Minit Records was in trouble. This coincided with Toussaint being drafted into the services, as well as the sale of Imperial Records (who distributed Minit) to Liberty Records. Minit was thus inactive until 1966, at which time Imperial revived the label, using it as a more generic soul outlet, effectively meaning that the subsidiary was now no longer dealing with exclusively New Orleans-based acts. The new roster included the Players, Jimmy Holiday, Jimmy McCracklin, Vernon Greene And The Medallions and the O'Jays, who moved over from Imperial. Ike And Tina Turner were also drafted from the parent label, and enjoyed their biggest success with Minit via the Beatles' cover version, 'Come Together'. Another important name, that of Bobby Womack, was also added to the discography in his guise as lead singer of the Valentinos, before staying with the label when he became a solo artist. Minit's death came in 1971, when Liberty merged with

United Artists and all subsidiary labels surrendered their artist rosters to the new conglomeration. A beautifully designed package was issued in 1994 with a full history.
● COMPILATIONS: *The Mint Records Story* (EMI 1994)★★★★.

MINT CONDITION

One of a myriad of R&B-inspired groups who dot the musical landscape in the 90s, Mint Condition comprises Larry Wadell (keyboards), Homer O'Dell (guitar), Stokley Williams (vocals, drums), Jeff Allen (saxophone, keyboards), Kerri Lewis (keyboards) and Ricky Kinchen (bass). The group was formed in 1989, and two years later found itself signed to Terry Lewis's Perspective Records, for whom they released their *Meant To Be* debut. Despite including the hit singles 'Breakin' My Heart (Pretty Brown Eyes)' and 'Forever In Your Eyes', it failed to achieve a mainstream breakthrough for the group. The same fate befell *From The Mint Factory*, released two years later. This time the hit single, 'U Send Me Swingin'', reached number 2 in *Billboard*'s Hot R&B chart. A concerted effort was then made to propel the group's third album, *Definition Of A Band*, higher up the charts. Whether or not the attempt to convert Mint Condition into an 'album act' succeeds, few critics quibbled with the standard of the writing and production displayed on this set, especially on the compulsive first single, 'What Kind Of Man Would I Be?'.
● ALBUMS: *Meant To Be* (Perspective 1991)★★, *From The Mint Factory* (Perspective 1993)★★★, *Definition Of A Band* (Perspective 1996)★★★.

MINT JULEPS

This a cappella soul group from London, England, consisted of sisters Debbie, Lizzie, Sandra and Marcia Charles, plus their friends Debbie and Julie. They all formerly worked together at the Half Moon Theatre in Putney, where they decided to form a group. They played at various benefits and toured with Sister Sledge and Billy Bragg, and worked as backing singers for Bob Geldof, the Belle Stars and Dr. Feelgood. They signed to Stiff Records, and were managed by former Darts members Rita Ray and Rob Fish. The Mint Juleps recorded vocal versions of Neil Young's 'Only Love Can Break Your Heart', Robert Palmer's 'Every Kinda People', and the original 'Girl To The Power Of 6' (produced by Trevor Horn). They later moved away from a cappella into a style of lightweight rap. They appeared on the ex-Grateful Dead drummer Mickey Hart's *Mystery Box* in 1996.
● ALBUMS: *One Time* (Stiff 1985)★★★.

MIRACLES

Of all the R&B vocal groups formed in Detroit, Michigan, USA, in the mid-50s, the Miracles proved to be the most successful. They were founded at the city's Northern High School in 1955 by Smokey Robinson (b. William Robinson, 19 February 1940, Detroit, Michigan, USA), Emerson Rogers, Bobby Rogers (b. 19 February 1940, Detroit, Michigan, USA), Ronnie White (b. 5 April 1939, Detroit, Michigan, USA, d. 26 August 1995) and Warren 'Pete' Moore (b. 19 November 1939, Detroit, Michigan, USA). Emerson Rogers left the following year, and was replaced by his sister Claudette, who married Smokey Robinson in 1959. Known initially as the Matadors, the group became the Miracles in 1958, when they made their initial recordings with producer Berry Gordy. He leased their debut, 'Got A Job' (an answer record to the Silhouettes' major hit 'Get A Job'), to End Records, produced a duet by Ron (White) And Bill (Robinson) for Argo, and licensed the classic doo-wop novelty 'Bad Girl' to Chess in 1959. The following year, Gordy signed the Miracles directly to his fledgling Motown label. Recognizing the youthful composing talents of Smokey Robinson, he allowed the group virtual free rein in the studio, and was repaid when they issued 'Way Over There', a substantial local hit, and then 'Shop Around', which broke both the Miracles and Motown to a national audience. The song demonstrated the increasing sophistication of Robinson's writing, which provided an unbroken series of hits for the group over the next few years. Their raw, doo-wop sound was further refined on the Top 10 hit 'You Really Got A Hold On Me' in 1962, a soulful ballad that became a worldwide standard after the Beatles covered it in 1963. Robinson was now in demand by other Motown artists: Gordy used him as a one-man hit factory, to mastermind releases by the Temptations and Mary Wells, and the Miracles' own career suffered slightly as a result. They continued to enjoy success in a variety of different styles, mixing dancefloor hits such as 'Mickey's Monkey' and 'Going To A Go-Go' with some of Robinson's most durable ballads, such as 'Oooh Baby Baby' and 'The Tracks Of My Tears'. Although Robinson sang lead on almost all the group's recordings, the rest of the group provided a unique harmony blend behind him, while guitarist Marv Tarplin - who co-wrote several of their hits - was incorporated as an unofficial Miracle from the mid-60s onwards. Claudette Robinson stopped touring with the group after 1965, although she was still featured on many of their subsequent releases. Exhausted by several years of constant work, Robinson scaled down his writing commitments for the group in the mid-60s, when they briefly worked with Holland/Dozier/Holland and other Motown producers. Robinson wrote their most ambitious and enduring songs, however, including 'The Tears Of A Clown' in 1966 (a belated hit in the UK and USA in 1970), 'The Love I Saw In You Was Just A Mirage', and 'I Second That Emotion' in 1967. These tracks epitomized the strengths of Robinson's compositions, with witty, metaphor-filled lyrics tied to aching melody lines and catchy guitar figures, the latter often provided by Tarplin. Like many of the veteran Motown acts, the Miracles went into a sales slump after 1967 - the year when Robinson was given individual credit on the group's records. Their slide was less noticeable in Britain, where Motown gained a Top 10 hit in 1969 with a reissue of 'The Tracks Of My Tears', which most listeners imagined was a contemporary record. The success of 'The Tears Of A Clown' prompted a revival in fortune after 1970. 'I'm The One You Need' became another reissue hit in Britain the following year, while 'I Don't Blame You At All', one of their strongest releases to date, achieved chart success on both sides of the Atlantic.

In 1971, Robinson announced his intention of leaving the Miracles to concentrate on his position as vice-president of Motown Records. His decision belied the title of his final hit with the group, 'We've Come Too Far To End It Now' in 1972, and left the Miracles in the unenviable position of having to replace one of the most distinctive voices in popular music. Their choice was William 'Bill' Griffin (b. 15 August 1950, Detroit, Michigan, USA), who was introduced by Robinson to the group's audiences during a 1972 US tour. The new line-up took time to settle, while Smokey Robinson launched a solo career to great acclaim in 1973. The group responded with *Renaissance*, which saw them working with Motown luminaries such as Marvin Gaye and Willie Hutch. The following year, they re-established the Miracles as a hit-making force with 'Do It Baby' and 'Don'tcha Love It', dance-orientated singles that appealed strongly to the group's black audience. In 1975, 'Love Machine' became the Miracles' first US chart-topper, while the concept album *City Of Angels* was acclaimed as one of Motown's most progressive releases. This twin success proved to be the Miracles' last commercial gasp. Switching to Columbia Records in 1977, they lost Billy Griffin, who set out on a little-noticed solo career. Donald Griffin briefly joined the group in his place, but the Miracles ceased recording in 1978. Thereafter, Ronnie White and Bill Rogers steered the outfit into the new decade as a touring band, before the Miracles disbanded without any fanfares, only to be re-formed by Bobby Rogers in 1982. He enlisted Dave Finlay and Carl Cotton as the new Miracles. Former members Billy Griffin and Claudette Robinson (ex-wife of Smokey) recorded solo tracks for Ian Levine's Motor City label during 1988-91. Another re-formed group comprising Billy Griffin, Robinson, Rogers, Donald Griffin, Cotton and Finlay also recorded for Levine, remaking 'Love Machine' in 1990. White died in 1995 after losing his battle with leukaemia.

● ALBUMS: *Hi, We're The Miracles* (Tamla 1961)★★★, *Cookin' With The Miracles* (Tamla 1962)★★★★, *I'll Try Something New* (Tamla 1962)★★★, *The Fabulous Miracles* (Tamla 1963)★★★, *Recorded Live: On Stage* (Tamla 1963)★★, *Christmas With The Miracles* (Tamla 1963)★★, *The Miracles Doin' 'Mickey's Monkey'* (Tamla 1963)★★★, *Going To A Go-Go* (Tamla 1965)★★★★, *I Like It Like That* (Tamla 1965)★★★, *Away We A Go-Go* (Tamla 1966)★★★, *Make It Happen* (Tamla 1967)★★★, *Special Occasion* (Tamla 1968)★★★, *Live!* (Tamla 1969)★★, *Time Out For Smokey Robinson And The Miracles* (Tamla 1969)★★★, *Four In Blue* (Tamla 1969)★★★, *What Love Has Joined Together* (Tamla 1970)★★★, *A Pocket Full Of Miracles* (Tamla 1970)★★★, *The Season For Miracles* (Tamla 1970)★★★, *One Dozen Roses* (Tamla 1971)★★★, *Flying High Together* (Tamla 1972)★★★, *Renaissance* (Tamla 1973)★★★, *Do It Baby* (Tamla 1974)★★★, *Don't Cha Love It* (Tamla 1975)★★, *City Of Angels* (Tamla 1975)★★, *The Power Of Music* (Tamla 1976)★★, *Love Crazy* (Columbia 1977)★★, *The Miracles* (Columbia 1978)★★.

● COMPILATIONS: *Greatest Hits From The Beginning* (Tamla 1965)★★★★, *Greatest Hits Vol. 2* (Tamla 1968)★★★★, *1957-72* (Tamla 1972)★★★★, *Smokey Robinson And The Miracles' Anthology* (Motown 1973)★★★★, *Compact Command Performances* (Motown 1987)★★★★, *The Greatest Hits* (Motown 1992)★★★★, *The 35th Anniversary Collection* 4-CD box set (Motown Masters 1994)★★★★.

● FURTHER READING: *Smokey: Inside My Life*, Smokey Robinson and David Ritz.

MITCHELL, BOBBY

b. 16 August 1935, Algiers, Louisiana, USA, d. 17 March 1989, New Orleans, Louisiana, USA. After studying music in high school, Mitchell formed a vocal group, the Toppers, in June 1950. The group comprised various high school friends and they entered local talent shows. After being discovered by Dave Bartholomew in 1952, the group began recording for Imperial until they split up in 1955 upon graduation, leading Mitchell to a solo career and his biggest hit the following year, 'Try Rock And Roll'. This reached number 14 on *Billboard*'s R&B chart - although he is probably better known as the originator of 'I'm Gonna Be A Wheel Someday' which was later covered by Fats Domino. Leaving Imperial in 1958, he recorded infrequently for small local labels such as Ronn, Sho-Biz and Rip, and by the late 60s, he was working outside the music business.

● COMPILATIONS: *I'm Gonna Be A Wheel Someday* (Mr R&B 1987)★★★.

MITCHELL, MCKINLEY

b. 25 December 1934, Jackson, Mississippi, USA, d. 1986, USA. A formative soul singer with George Leaner's early 60s Chicago-based One-derful label, Mitchell came from the Chicago blues-club scene to launch that label with his fine, self-penned 'The Town I Live In', later re-recorded during an even more productive soul period in the 70s with the Malaco subsidiary Chimneyville. After leading the Hearts Of Harmony gospel group at the age of 16, Mitchell tried secular music with a quintet in Springfield, Massachusetts, before moving to Philadelphia to front his own gospel group, the Mitchellairs. Subsequently, he travelled to Chicago, where he sang at several blues clubs, and worked with Muddy Waters at Pepper's Lounge. Ironically, his first recording, 'Rock Everybody Rock', was in a rock 'n' roll style, cut with members of Howlin' Wolf's band for the Boxer label in 1959. In the local clubs, Mitchell had become known as McKinley 'Soul' Mitchell by the time he brought 'The Town I Live In' to Leaner in 1962. Despite this number 8 R&B hit, Mitchell's subsequent records for One-derful, although good examples of early 'tough' soul, sold poorly, and Mitchell embarked on a Chicago label-hopping exercise with the likes of St Lawrence, Chess, Spoonful, Sandman, Black Beauty and Big 3, often being produced by Chicago bluesman Willie Dixon. In 1976, Mitchell's Big 3 recording, 'Trouble Blues', received good southern coverage from Jackson's Malaco label, and it was followed by other superior soul sides for the same company's Chimneyville label, including the beautiful 'The End Of The Rainbow' and 'The Same Old Dream', as well as the fine remake of 'The Town I Live In'. A good Chimneyville album, *McKinley Mitchell*, was also released in 1978. In the 80s, Mitchell worked for James Bennett's Rettas label where he cut three singles and an album. Earlier material was reissued on both US and Japanese labels. Mitchell died prematurely from a heart attack in 1986, and was buried in his native Jackson.

● ALBUMS: *McKinley Mitchell* (Chimneyville 1978)★★★, *I Won't Be Back For More* (Rettas 1984)★★★, *The Last Of McKinley Mitchell* (1988)★★.

● COMPILATIONS: *McKinley 'Soul' Mitchell* (1979)★★★, *The Complete Malaco Collection* (1992)★★★.

Mitchell, Willie

b. 3 January 1928, Ashland, Mississippi, USA. A veteran of several Memphis-based bands, Mitchell rose to prominence in the late 50s with an outfit that formed the basis for his production work and early solo recordings. The line-up included Lewis Steinberg and Al Jackson, both of whom would later appear in Booker T. And The MGs. By the 60s, Mitchell was leading the Hi Records house band. The company was established on the success of Bill Black, the one-time Elvis Presley bassist whose economical instrumental singles suggested the style later forged at the Stax studio. Although Black died in 1965, releases bearing his name continued, with Mitchell's group supplying the music. Mitchell's own recording career prospered with such classic Memphis offerings as '20-75' and 'Percolatin'' (both 1964), as well as the Junior Walker-influenced groove of 'That Driving Beat' and 'Everything Is Gonna' Be Alright' (both 1966). 'Soul Serenade' was a Top 10 US R&B single in 1968, but his releases were latterly obscured by his work with other artists. Mitchell became vice-president at Hi in 1970, and proceeded to mould its 70s sound with production work for Al Green, Syl Johnson and Ann Peebles. Other sessions at his Royal Studio included those of Bobby Bland, Otis Clay and O.V. Wright. During the early part of the decade, Mitchell's classic band - the Hodges brothers, Charles (organ), Teeny (guitar) and Leroy (bass), Howard Grimes or Al Jackson (drums) and the Memphis Horns - defined post-Stax southern soul, but the formula grew sterile as time progressed. Treasured moments still occurred, but the loss of Green, then Johnson, suggested an internal dissatisfaction. Mitchell resigned from Hi in 1979, three years after its acquisition by the Los Angeles-based Cream label, and joined the Bearsville label as a producer and artist. During the 80s he became a partner in a video production company and set up his Wayco outlet. In 1985, he was reunited with Al Green for the latter's *He Is The Light* and the following year's *Going Away*. In 1987, he produced Scottish pop group Wet Wet Wet.

● ALBUMS: *20-75* (Hi 1964)★★★, *It's Dance Time* (Hi 1965)★★★, *That Driving Beat* (Hi 1966)★★★, *It's What's Happening* (Hi 1966)★★★, *Willie Mitchell Live* (Hi 1968)★★, *Soul Serenade* (Hi 1968)★★, *Solid Soul* (Hi 1969)★★, *On Top* (Hi 1969)★★, *Soul Bag* (Hi 1970)★★, *Robbins Nest* (Hi 1970)★★, *Hold It* (Hi 1971)★★★, *Listen Dance* (Hi 1971)★★.

● COMPILATIONS: *The Best Of Willie Mitchell* (Hi 1977)★★★.

MN8

Comprising the pseudonymous KG, G-Man, Kule T and Dee-Tails, UK black pop group MN8 made a major breakthrough in 1994 with the release of 'I've Got A Little Something For You'. A strangely threatening swingbeat tune, it nevertheless saw the group, who are based in Surrey, become firm favourites with the nation's teenagers. The follow-up single was 'If You Only Let Me In', another example of the group's catchy swingbeat soul. The accompanying video featured the group's lascivious dance routines - already one of their most recognizable traits. They subsequently joined Janet Jackson on her European tour and continued to appear regularly on UK television. The group's 1995 debut album, *To The Next Level*, demonstrated a greater versatility than might have been anticipated from the group's singles, and included a Disney-style ballad in 'Pathway To The Moon' alongside more soul-based material such as 'Lonely' and 'Happy'.

● ALBUMS: *To The Next Level* (Columbia 1995)★★★.

Modern Records

Modern Records was founded in Los Angeles, California, USA, in 1945 by brothers Jules, Saul And Joe Bihari. They secured early success with Hadda Brooks and Johnny Moore's Three Blazers, and within two years Modern had become one of the leading post-war R&B labels on the west coast, alongside Imperial Records and Aladdin Records. The Biharis manufactured their own records, building one of the largest pressing plants in the region, and an agreement with a network of independent distributors ensured Modern's releases enjoyed national distribution. Etta James's 'Wallflower', Jessie Belvin's 'Goodnight My Love' and the Cadets' 'Stranded In The Jungle' were some of the label's most successful recordings during the early 50s. John Lee Hooker, Lightnin' Hopkins and Willie 'Smokey' Hogg also recorded for Modern but its eminent position was undermined by its practice of 'covering' other R&B hits. Nevertheless, the Biharis were able to establish several subsidiary companies, including RPM, founded in 1950, and Flair, founded in 1953. B.B. King was RPM's most important signing, as this seminal blues singer/guitarist remained with the company until the 60s. Rosco Gordon ('No More Doggin'') and Johnny 'Guitar' Watson ('Those Lonely, Lonely Nights') were among the other artists enjoying success on this outlet. Meanwhile, Richard Berry's influential 'Louie Louie' was first issued on Flair. In 1951, armed with a Magnechord tape recorder, Joe Bihari undertook the first of several field trips to Mississippi. He made several important juke-joint blues recordings on location, notably with impassioned slide guitarist Elmore James. In 1952 Modern set up the Meteor label in Memphis, Tennessee, USA. It was managed by a fourth Bihari brother, Lester. By the end of the 50s the Modern group was being eclipsed by newer independent companies, notably Atlantic Records. The Biharis opted to concentrate on a newly founded budget line, Crown Records, which, following bankruptcy, was succeeded by Kent Records. These outlets revived recordings from Modern's halcyon era, but the entire operation ceased trading during the 80s following the death of Jules Bihari. The best of its catalogue has since been repacked for compact disc by UK licensees Ace Records.

MOMENTS

Formed in Hackensack, New Jersey, USA, in the late 60s, this distinctive sweet soul trio comprised Al Goodman (b. 31 March 1947, Jackson, Mississippi, USA; ex-Vipers and Corvettes), Harry Ray (b. 15 December 1946, Longbranch, New Jersey, USA, d. 1 October 1992; ex-Sounds Of Soul and Establishment) and William Brown (b. 30 June 1946, Perth Amboy, New Jersey, USA; ex-Broadways and Uniques). The falsetto-led, 50s-style harmony vocal group recorded for Sylvia Robinson's Stang label. According to Goodman, the original group led by Mark Greene was replaced by Ray, Goodman and Brown in 1969, after their first hit 'Not On The Outside'. It was this trio's fourth R&B Top 20 hit, 'Love On A Two-Way Street', in 1970, that gave them their biggest pop hit, reaching number 3 in the US charts. They had a further 21 R&B chart records, which included their self-penned Top 20 hit 'Sexy Mama' in 1973, and the R&B number 1 'Look At Me (I'm In Love)' in 1975. Their first UK success came in 1975 with 'Girls', made with fellow Stang group the Whatnauts. They had two further UK Top 10s: 'Dolly My Love' in 1975 and 'Jack In The Box' in 1977, neither of which charted in the USA. In 1979, they joined Polydor as Ray, Goodman And Brown.

● ALBUMS: *Not On The Outside* (Stang 1969)★★★, *A Moment With The Moments* (Stang 1970)★★★, *The Moments Live At The New York State Woman's Prison* (Stang 1971)★★, *Love At The Miss Black America Pageant* (Stang 1971)★★, *Those Sexy Moments* (Stang 1974)★★★, *Look At Me* (Stang 1975)★★★, with the O'Jays *The O'Jays Meet The Moments* (Philadelphia International 1975)★★★, *Moments With You* (Stang 1976)★★, *Sharp* (Stang 1978)★★.

● COMPILATIONS: *Moments Greatest Hits* (Stang 1971)★★★, *Best Of The Moments* (Stang 1974)★★★, *Greatest Hits* (Chess 1987)★★★, *Moments* (1988)★★★, *Late Night Soul* (Sequel 1992)★★★, *Lucky Me* (Collectables 1997)★★★.

MONITORS

Sandra Fagin, John 'Maurice' Fagin, Warren Harris and Richard Street formed the Monitors in the early 60s, having each performed with Detroit-based vocal groups since the late 50s. In 1965, they were signed to Motown's VIP subsidiary, for whom they issued six singles and an album over the next four years. Their doo-wop-influenced style was epitomized by the 1966 R&B hit 'Say You', and their cover of the Valadiers' 'Greetings (This Is Uncle Sam)' later that year - the most successful recording of this sly piece of social comment that was taped by several artists on the Motown roster. The Monitors were unable to establish themselves among the label's frontline artists, however, and they dissolved in 1969. Richard Street replaced Eddie Kendricks in the Temptations in 1971. In 1990 the band re-formed with original members Harris and Fagin, Hershell Hunter (who joined the group in 1968), Darrell Littlejohn (who recorded for Motown as half of Keith & Darrell) and Harris's daughter Leah. They recorded with Ian Levine's Motor City label releasing *Grazing In The Grass*.

● ALBUMS: *Greetings ... We're The Monitors* (VIP 1968)★★★, *Grazing In The Grass* (Motor City 1990)★★.

MONOTONES

Formed in 1955 in Newark, New Jersey, USA, the Monotones recorded one of the most memorable doo-wop novelty songs of the 50s, 'Book Of Love'. The group was a sextet, Warren Davis, George Malone, Charles Patrick, Frank Smith, and John and Warren Ryanes. They had sung in the same church choir as Dionne Warwick and Cissy Houston before forming their own group. In 1956, they appeared on the *Ted Mack's Amateur Hour* television programme, singing the Cadillacs' 'Zoom'. They won first prize and began to think more seriously about a career in music. Inspired by a television commercial for toothpaste ('You'll wonder where the yellow went when you brush your teeth with Pepsodent'), Patrick, Malone and Davis wrote 'Book Of Love' to a similar melody. They recorded it at Bell Studio in New York and it was released on the small Mascot label, a subsidiary of Hull Records. It was then picked up by Argo Records for national distribution and ultimately reached number 5 in the USA. The group was touring when their record entered the charts, and months passed before they had a chance to record a follow-up. A single called 'Tom Foolery' was released but failed to chart; the third, 'The Legend Of Sleepy Hollow', was a fine record and is still played on doo-wop radio programmes today, but it also failed to chart in its own time. After a few more singles, the Monotones gave up, although some of the original members performed under that name in the 90s. John Ryanes died on 30 May 1972.

● COMPILATIONS: *Who Wrote The Book Of Love?* (Collectables 1992)★★★.

MONTCLAIRS

This R&B vocal group from East St. Louis, Illinois, USA, comprised lead Phil Perry, David Frye, George McLellan, Kevin Sanlin and Clifford 'Scotty' Williams. The Montclairs were representative of the vocal group renaissance of the early 70s when falsetto lead and sweet-sound vocals were fashionable. The group recorded their first single in 1969, which was only distributed in the St. Louis area, and the following year began recording for bandleader/producer Oliver Sain at his Archway Studio. Sain arranged for the group to be signed with Paula Records, based in Shreveport, Louisiana. Their outstanding hits for the label were 'Dreaming Out Of Season' (number 34 R&B) from 1972, and 'Make Up For Lost Time' (number 46 R&B) from 1974. Their last chart record was 'Baby You Know (I'm Gonna Miss You)' from 1974. After the Montclairs left Paula in 1975 they disbanded.

● ALBUMS: *Dreaming Out Of Season* (Paula 1972)★★★.

MONTRELL, ROY

b. 27 February 1928, New Orleans, Louisiana, USA. Guitarist Montrell joined Roy Milton's Solid Senders upon his discharge from the US Army in 1951, but soon returned to New Orleans where he formed a trio called the Little Hawkettes, which worked various clubs along Bourbon Street. After touring with Lloyd Price, he began to do session work in New Orleans for Ace and Specialty, recording with artists including Edgar Blanchard and Little Richard. He only had two releases under his own name: one on Specialty in 1956 - the black rock 'n' roll classic 'Ooh Wow That Mellow Saxophone' - and another on Minit in 1960. The most renowned New Orleans session guitarist by 1960, Montrell played with Allen Toussaint's band and Harold Battiste's AFO combo, and in 1962 he took over from Walter Nelson as Fats Domino's guitarist, becoming Domino's bandleader in the late 60s.

MOONGLOWS

This R&B vocal group was formed in Cleveland, Ohio, USA, in 1952. If there were any group that best signalled the birth of rock 'n' roll - by which R&B emerged out of its black subculture into mainstream teen culture - it was the Moonglows. The group's career paralleled that of their mentor, legendary disc jockey Alan Freed, who in his rise in rock 'n' roll made the Moonglows the mainstays of his radio programmes, motion pictures and stage shows. Their membership comprised lead singer Bobby Lester (b. 13 January 1930, Louisville, Kentucky, USA, d. 15 October 1980), Harvey Fuqua (b. 27 July 1929, Louisville, Kentucky, USA), Alexander 'Pete' Graves (b. 17 April 1930, Cleveland, Ohio, USA), and Prentiss Barnes (b. 12 April 1925, Magnolia, Mississippi, USA). After recording for Freed's Champagne label in 1953, the group signed with Chicago-based Chance, where they managed to secure a few regional hits, most notably a cover version of Doris Day's 'Secret Love' in 1954. Freed used his connections to sign the Moonglows to a stronger Chicago label, the fast-rising Chess Records, and the group enjoyed a major hit with 'Sincerely' (number 1 R&B/number 20 pop 1954). Joining the group at this time was guitarist Billy Johnson (b. 1924, Hartford, Connecticut, USA, d. 1987).

Using a novel technique they called 'blow harmony', other great hits followed: 'Most Of All' (number 5 R&B 1955), 'We Go Together' (number 9 R&B 1956), 'See Saw' (number 6 R&B/number 25 pop 1956), all which featured Lester on lead; and a remake of Percy Mayfield's 'Please Send Me Someone To Love' (number 5 R&B/number 73 pop 1957) and 'Ten Commandments Of Love' (number 9 R&B/number 22 pop 1958), which featured Fuqua on lead. The original Moonglows disbanded in 1958, and Fuqua put together a new group that included Marvin Gaye. In 1960 Fuqua disbanded this group and he and Gaye went to Detroit to work in the industry there. Fuqua worked with Berry Gordy's sister, Gwen Gordy on the Anna label and Gaye joined Berry Gordy's Motown operation. Fuqua carved out a very successful career as a producer and record executive, working with Motown artists in the 60s and a stable of Louisville artists in the 70s on the RCA label.

● ALBUMS: *Look! It's The Moonglows* (Chess 1959)★★★, *The Return Of The Moonglows* (RCA Victor 1972)★★★, *The Moonglows On Stage* (Relic 1992)★★.

● COMPILATIONS: *The Best Of Bobby Lester And The Moonglows* (Chess 1962)★★★, *The Flamingos Meet The Moonglows* (Vee Jay 1962)★★★, *The Moonglows* (Constellation 1964)★★★, *Moonglows* (Chess 1976)★★★, *Their Greatest Sides* (Chess 1984)★★★, *Blue Velvet: The Ultimate Collection* (MCA/Chess 1993)★★★★, *The Flamingos Meet The Moonglows: The Complete 25 Chance Recordings* (Vee Jay 1993)★★★, *Their Greatest Hits* (MCA 1997)★★★.

MOORE, DOROTHY

b. 13 October 1947, Jackson, Mississippi, USA. Moore was one of the last great southern soul singers finding success in the late 70s when disco and funk were making deep soul increasingly a marginalized form limited to the south. She began her career at Jackson State University where she formed an all-female group called the Poppies. The group recorded for Columbia Records' Date subsidiary but never reached the national charts. She established a solo career in 1976 with a series of remarkable ballads for Malaco Records, hitting in 1976 with 'Misty Blue' (number 2 R&B, number 3 pop) and 'Funny How Time Slips Away' (the Willie Nelson song, number 7 R&B, number 58 pop), and 'I Believe You' (number 5 R&B, number 27 pop) in 1977. Moore's recordings in the next few years were not nearly as successful as she succumbed increasingly to the disco trend. She left the business for several years, but in 1986 recorded a fine gospel album in Nashville, *Giving It Straight To You* for the Rejoice label. It yielded a masterful remake of Brother Joe May's 'What Is This' that became a Top 10 gospel hit. Moore returned to secular music in 1988, recording, in a deep-soul style, two albums for the Volt subsidiary of Fantasy. In 1990 she began recording for her original label, Malaco.

● ALBUMS: as the Poppies *Lullaby Of Love* (Epic 1966)★★★, *Misty Blue* (Malaco 1976)★★★, *Dorothy Moore* (Malaco 1977)★★★, *Once More With Feeling* (Malaco 1978)★★★, *Definitely Dorothy* (Malaco 1979)★★★, *Talk To Me* (Malaco 1980)★★★, *Giving It Straight To You* (Rejoice 1986)★★★, *Time Out For Me* (Volt 1988)★★★, *Winner* (Volt 1989)★★★, *Feel The Love* (Malaco 1990)★★★, *Stay Close To Home* (Malaco 1992)★★★.

MOORE, JACKIE

b. 1946, Jacksonville, Florida, USA. This powerful soul singer moved to Philadelphia in the late 60s and, with help from top local R&B disc jockey Jimmy Bishop, had two releases on Shout and one on Wand. When success was not forthcoming she returned to Jacksonville and, partly owing to her cousin, noted producer Dave Crawford, joined Atlantic in 1970. Crawford produced and co-wrote 'Precious, Precious', which, after lying dormant for some months on a b-side, eventually sold a million and in 1970 became her only US Top 40 pop hit. After six Top 40 R&B hits she joined Kayvette Records in 1975 when she achieved her biggest R&B success, 'Make Me Feel Like A Woman', which was produced by Brad Shapiro. Moore moved to Columbia in 1978 and continued to sell records in the US soul market. She also had her only UK hit with 'This Time Baby', which narrowly missed the Top 40 in 1979. A consistent R&B hitmaker for over a decade, she increased her tally of US R&B chart entries to 15 in 1983 when she recorded on Catawba.

● ALBUMS: *Sweet Charlie Babe* (Atlantic 1973)★★★, *Make Me Feel Like A Woman* (Kayvette 1975)★★★★, *I'm On My Way* (Columbia 1979)★★★, *With Your Love* (Columbia 1980)★★★.

● COMPILATIONS: *Precious Precious: The Best Of ...* (1994)★★★★.

MOORE, JOHNNY

b. John Dudley Moore, 20 October 1906, Austin, Texas, USA, d. 6 January 1969, Los Angeles, California, USA. The elder brother of guitarist Oscar Moore, Johnny began playing guitar with his violinist father's string band in 1934 and moved to the west coast, where Oscar joined Nat 'King' Cole's Trio and Johnny Moore joined a group called the Blazes. Fired by that group in 1942, Moore decided to form his own group, which he christened the Three Blazers. This featured Eddie Williams on bass and, briefly, pianist Garland Finney. When Finney left the trio the following year, Moore hired Charles Brown, a singer and pianist he had seen at an amateur talent show, and the Blazers began recording in 1944 for the small Atlas label. This was followed in 1945-48 by extensive recording for Exclusive, Philo/Aladdin and Modern. During this period the Blazers became a household name with huge hits such as 'Driftin' Blues', 'Merry Christmas Baby', 'Sunny Road' and 'More Than You Know'. When Oscar Moore joined the group in 1947, it was the start of several major problems that ultimately resulted in a split, and Moore tried to replace Charles Brown with a succession of soundalikes. The most successful of these was Billy Valentine, who took the Blazers back to the R&B charts with RCA-Victor's 'Walkin' Blues' in 1949. After his 1949-50 association with Victor, Johnny Moore's Blazers recorded for the gamut of Los Angeles labels, but were successful only with 1953's novelty 'Dragnet Blues' on Modern and 1955's morbid 'Johnny Ace's Last Letter' on Hollywood. Johnny Moore and Charles Brown were reconciled in the mid-50s and the real Three Blazers reunited for records on Aladdin, Hollywood and Cenco; however, by that time, Moore's cool, sophisticated, melodic blues guitar was out of favour with R&B fans. He was an inspiration to most of the electric blues guitarists of the late 40s and early 50s and his solos on recordings by Ivory Joe Hunter, Floyd Dixon and Charles Brown, as well as tracks with his own group, bear witness that he was one of the unsung greats of his instrument.

● COMPILATIONS: with Charles Brown *Sunny Road* (Route 66 1980)★★★, with Brown *Race Track Blues* (Route 66 1981)★★★, with Brown *Sail On Blues* (Jukebox Lil 1989)★★★, *This Is One Time, Baby* (Jukebox Lil 1989)★★★, *Why Johnny Why?* (Route 66 1989)★★★, with Brown *Drifting And Dreaming* (Ace 1995)★★★.

MOORE, MELBA

b. Melba Hill, 29 October 1945, New York City, New York, USA. Based in New York, Melba Moore first attracted attention in the Broadway production of *Hair*. Although she has continued her thespian inclinations, winning an award for her performance in the musical *Purlie*, Moore has also forged a successful singing career. 'This Is It', reached the UK Top 10 in 1976, and although her hits have since been inconsistent, Moore remained a fixture on the R&B lists over the following decade.

● ALBUMS: *Look What You're Doing To The Man* (Mercury 1971)★★, *Peach Melba* (Buddah 1975)★★★, *This Is It* (Buddah 1976)★★, *Melba* (Buddah 1976)★★, *A Portrait Of Melba* (Buddah 1978)★★, *Melba* (Epic 1978)★★, *Burn* (Epic 1979)★★, *Dancin' With Melba Moore* (Buddah 1979)★★, *What A Woman Needs* (Capitol 1981)★★, *The Other Side Of The Rainbow* (Capitol 1982)★★, *Never Say Never* (Capitol 1983)★★, *Read My Lips* (Capitol 1985)★★, *A Lot Of Love* (Capitol 1987)★★, *I'm In Love* (Capitol 1988)★★.

● COMPILATIONS: *The Best Of* (Razor & Tie 1995)★★★, *This Is It* (Camden 1998)★★★.

● FILMS: *Def By Temptation*.

MORELLS

Formed in Springfield, Missouri, USA, in 1982, the Morells recorded only one album, *Shake And Push*, on Borrowed Records. Although it never charted, this roots-rock group built a devoted following on the US alternative circuit. Consisting of bassist Lou Whitney (who had once performed with soul singer Arthur Conley), his wife Maralie (keyboards), D. Clinton Thompson (guitar) and Ron Gremp (drums), the group started in the late 70s as the Skeletons and then the Original Symptoms before settling in as the Morells, combining within their sound rockabilly, soul, blues and jazz. The group disbanded in the mid-80s. Lou Whitney went on to produce the debut album by New York rockers the Del-Lords before re-forming the Skeletons in 1988 with Thompson.

● ALBUMS: *Shake And Push* (Borrowed 1982)★★★.

MOROCCOS

This R&B vocal ensemble were from Chicago, Illinois, USA. With the impassioned lead work of the great Sollie McElroy (d. 1995), the Moroccos proved to be one of the finest doo-wop groups to come out of Chicago. They formed in 1952, and by 1954, when they were signed to United Records, the line-up consisted of Ralph Vernon (lead), George Prayer (d. 1992; baritone), Melvin Morrow (d. 1982; tenor), and Fred Martin (d. 1986; bass). Only after they added the ex-lead of the Flamingos, Sollie McElroy, did United release their recordings. The Moroccos' remake of the Harold Arlen/E.Y. 'Yip' Harburg tune, 'Somewhere Over The Rainbow' (1955), gave the group their biggest sales, but only regionally. Other fine regional hits were 'Pardon My Tears' (1955), 'What Is A Teen-Ager's Prayer' (1956) and 'Sad Sad Hours' (1957). On the latter, George Prayer had been replaced with Calvin Baron from the Sun Ra organization. The Moroccos broke up in 1957. In 1966 soul singer Joe Simon had a big hit with 'Teenager's Prayer', a remake of the Moroccos' song.

MORRISON, MARK

b. 1973, Leicester, Leicestershire, England. Although the swingbeat or urban R&B sound of R. Kelly, SWV, TLC and others had made a huge impression among British record buyers, until the breakthrough of Mark Morrison in 1995 the UK had failed to provide a credible domestic alternative. Morrison had grown up in Leicester and Palm Beach, Florida, USA, and was thus better disposed to adopt the style than most. His debut single, 1995's 'Crazy', saw him announce himself as the 'UK King Of Swing', and brought immediate chart success. His irresistible March 1996 single 'Return Of The Mack' was highly derivative of his American peers in style, language and content, but again brought major chart success both in the UK and USA. It was followed by an album of the same title which was co-produced with Phil Chill. He was found guilty of threatening behaviour with a gun and was sentenced to three months' imprisonment in May 1997.

● ALBUMS: *Return Of The Mack* (WEA 1996)★★★.

Motor Town Revue

The celebrated Motor Town Revue was instigated by Motown Records founder Berry Gordy as an adjunct to his activities as label boss, manager (through International Talent Management) and publisher (Jobete) of his many talented artists. Indeed, some have suggested that this was an attempt to bring every aspect of their performance under his personal remit. The idea for the revue came as a result of discussions between Gordy, Thomas 'Bean' Bowles and Esther Gordy Edwards. The first show was scheduled for 2 November 1962 at the Boston Arena, before sweeping across the US mainland playing 19 further major cities in 23 days. Promoted by Henry Wynne's Supersonic Attractions, the Motor Town Revue gave the lie to the carefully projected impression of a 'happy family' at Motown. In the touring buses musicians were separated from artists. With musicians at the back and artists at the front, the sections of the bus were analogized as 'Broadway' (front) and 'Harlem' (back) by some of the incredulous travellers. Artists including the Supremes, Stevie Wonder, the Temptations, the Marvelettes, and Martha And The Vandellas were among those taking part, but they encountered significant resistance when they travelled through America's Deep South. The artists found themselves playing in the firmament of the civil rights movement, and they were often refused entry to 'white only' restaurants as they travelled. Bowles' task as road manager became increasingly frenetic, and on Thanksgiving Day 1962 he was seriously injured in a car crash that killed driver Ed McFarland Jnr. Luckily, the tour proceeds he was carrying, some $12,000, still found their way back to Motown headquarters. With Bowles confined to hospital, it then looked likely that the tour would collapse, but Esther Gordy Edwards immediately took over his responsibilities to stabilize the situation. The tour finally finished in triumph with 11 dates at Harlem's Apollo Theatre. Motown learned the lessons of the tour well, making sure that subsequent revues were better orchestrated and regulated. A UK Motor Town Revue of 1965 (with Georgie Fame as special 'guest star') also proved problematic, although it too was a relative success and helped to develop a major international fanbase for Motown's galaxy of stars.

Motown Records

The history of Motown Records remains a paradigm of success for independent record labels, and for black-owned industry in the USA. The corporation was formed in 1959 by Berry Gordy, a successful R&B songwriter who required an outlet for his initial forays into production. He used an $800 loan to finance the release of singles by Marv Johnson and Eddie Holland on his Tamla label, one of a series of individual trademarks that he eventually included under the Motown umbrella. Enjoying limited local success, Gordy widened his roster, signing acts including the Temptations and Marvelettes in 1960. That year, the Miracles' 'Shop Around' gave the company its first major US hit, followed in 1961 by their first number 1, the Marvelettes' 'Please Mr Postman'. Gordy coined the phrase 'The Sound Of Young America' to describe Motown's output, and his apparently arrogant claim quickly proved well founded. By 1964, Motown was enjoying regular hits via the Supremes and the Four Tops, while Mary Wells' 'My Guy' helped the label become established outside the USA. The label's vibrant brand of soul music, marked by a pounding rhythm and a lightness of touch that appealed to both pop and R&B fans, provided America's strongest response to the massive impact of the British beat group invasion in 1964 and 1965. At the same time, Gordy realized the importance of widening his commercial bases; in 1965, he overtly wooed the middle-of-the-road audience by giving the Supremes a residency at the plush Copa nightclub in New York - the first of many such ventures into traditional showbiz territory. The distance between Motown's original fans and their new surroundings led to accusations that the company had betrayed its black heritage, although consistent chart success helped to cushion the blow.

In 1966, Motown took three steps to widen its empire, snapping up groups such as the Isley Brothers and Gladys Knight And The Pips from rival labels, opening a Hollywood office to double its promotional capabilities, and snuffing out its strongest opposition in Detroit by buying the Golden World and Ric-Tic group of R&B companies. Throughout these years, Gordy maintained a vice-like grip over Motown's affairs; even the most successful staff writers and producers had to submit their work to a weekly quality control meeting, and faced the threat of having their latest creations summarily rejected. Gradually, dissent rose within the ranks, and in 1967 Gordy lost the services of his A&R controller, Mickey Stevenson, and his premier writing/production team, Holland/Dozier/Holland. Two years of comparative failure followed before Motown regained its supremacy in the pop market by launching the career of the phenomenally successful Jackson Five in 1969. Gordy made a bold but ultimately unsuccessful attempt to break into the rock market in 1970 with his Rare Earth label, one of a variety of spin-off companies launched in the early part of the decade. This was a period of some uncertainty for the company; several major acts either split up or chose to seek artistic freedom elsewhere, and the decision to concentrate the company's activities in its California office in 1973 represented a dramatic break from its roots. At the same time, Gordy masterminded the birth of Motown's film division, with the award-winning biopic about Billie Holiday, *Lady Sings The Blues*. The burgeoning artistic and commercial success of Stevie Wonder kept the record division on course, although outsiders noted a distinct lack of young talent to replace the company's original stalwarts.

The mid-70s proved to be Motown's least successful period for over a decade; only the emergence of the Commodores maintained the label as a contemporary musical force. Motown increasingly relied on the strength of its back catalogue, with only occasional releases, such as the Commodores' 'Three Times A Lady' and Smokey Robinson's 'Being With You', rivalling the triumphs of old. The departure of Marvin Gaye and Diana Ross in the early 80s proved a massive psychological blow, and, despite the prominence of Commodores leader Lionel Richie, the company failed to keep pace with the fast-moving developments in black music. From 1986, there were increasing rumours that Berry Gordy was ready to sell the label; these were confirmed in 1988, when Motown was bought by MCA, with Gordy retaining some measure of artistic control over subsequent releases. After more than a decade of disappointing financial returns, Motown remains a record industry legend on the strength of its remarkable hit-making capacities in the 60s. Some realignment was tackled in the 90s by the new label chief Andre Harrell; his brief was to make Motown the leading black music label once again. New releases from Horace Brown, Johnny Gill, Queen Latifah and Boyz II Men started the rebirth.

● COMPILATIONS: *Motown Chartbusters Volumes 1 - 10* (Motown 1968-1977), *20th Anniversary Album* (Motown 1986)★★★★, *Hitsville USA: The Motown Singles Collection 1959 - 1971* 4-CD box set (Motown 1993)★★★★★, *This Is Northern Soul! 24 Tamla Motown Rarities* (Debutante 1997)★★★.

● VIDEOS: *The Sounds Of Motown* (PMI 1985), *The Sixties* (CIC Video 1987), *Time Capsule Of The 70s* (CIC Video 1987), *Motown 25th: Yesterday, Today, Forever* (MGM/UA 1988).

Muscle Shoals

Situated in Alabama between the focal centres of Nashville and Memphis, Muscle Shoals was the natural melting pot for southern country soul. During the 50s the Fairlanes, who included Rick Hall (b. 31 January 1932, Franklin County, Mississippi, USA) and Billy Sherrill in the line-up, were one of many groups performing in the area. In 1958 the two musicians formed a partnership with Tom Stafford, who ran a basic recording studio in a room above his father's drugstore. Entitled 'Fame: Florence Alabama Music Enterprises', the rudimentary company fell apart two years later, but the terms of the split left Hall with the name while Sherrill travelled to Nashville where he became a successful producer. Hall then purchased a tobacco warehouse in Muscle Shoals and transformed it into a four-track studio. He assembled a house band with David Briggs (piano), Terry Thompson (guitar), Norbert Putnam (bass) and Jerry Carrigan (drums) - and gained a smash hit with Arthur Alexander's 'You Better Move On'. Having sold the master to Dot Records, Rick moved to larger premises at 603 East Avalon Avenue, where the studio remains situated. Over the next few years Hall established Fame as both a record label and recording centre. Hits for the Tams and Joe Tex cemented its reputation, although the departure to Nashville of Briggs, Putnam and Carrigan was a serious blow. A second classic house band was forged around Jimmy Johnson (guitar), Jimmy Lowe (bass), Spooner Oldham (piano) and Roger Hawkins (drums). Jerry Wexler took Wilson Pickett to Fame in 1966, inaugurating a fruitful period for his Atlantic label and the studio. Many superb sessions followed, including those for Aretha Franklin, King Curtis and Arthur Conley, while newer musicians - Roger Hood (bass) and Duane Allman (guitar) - were drawn into the circle. However, Hall's autocratic approach resulted in a second defection, when Hawkins, Beckett, Johnson and Hood left *en masse* to found their own set-up, Muscle Shoals Sound, in 1969. Hall continued undeterred but by the 70s, the studio was being increasingly used for pop and country productions. He closed down the Fame label in 1974, and, tired of losing rhythm sections, latterly worked as an executive producer for his song publishing empire. The rival Muscle Shoals Sound was situated at 3614 Jackson Highway in nearby Florence. The new studio initially acquired many of Atlantic's R&B contracts, but diversified into other areas when the label directed its work to Criteria in Miami. Paul Simon, Rod Stewart, the Rolling Stones and Bob Seger were among the many acts to record successfully at Muscle Shoals, enabling the studio to move to a larger site on the banks of the Tennessee River.

NATHAN, SYDNEY

b. 1904, Cincinnati, Ohio, USA, d. 1968. Nathan learned to play drums and piano in his childhood with the help of local black musicians, but entered the record-selling business in the 30s, although he still became a successful songwriter under the pseudonym of 'Lois Mann'. In November 1943 his King Records was launched with releases by local hillbilly acts. These initial releases failed to sell due to the poor pressings; Nathan then decided to learn how to press his own records. As a result, King Records became known as an outlet for hillbilly music, and had success early on with hits by the Delmore Brothers and Cowboy Copas. One year later, Nathan started his Queen Records subsidiary as a showcase for jazz and R&B acts, making particular use of his friend Lucky Millinder's Orchestra, with releases by Bullmoose Jackson, Annisteen Allen, David 'Panama' Francis and Sam Taylor - all Millinder alumni. In 1946 Queen Records began recording, issuing some fine gospel music by such artists as Swan's Silvertone Singers and Wings Over Jordan Choir. Nathan's name became synonymous with peerless gospel and exciting R&B thereafter. By August 1947 the Queen label was discontinued and all output - new and old - was issued or reissued on King Records. This switch brought about a change of luck for Nathan; success came almost immediately with three big hits in Bullmoose Jackson's 'I Love You, Yes I Do', Lonnie Johnson's 'Tomorrow Night' and Wynonie Harris' version of 'Good Rockin' Tonight', and at about the same time, Nathan began leasing or acquiring masters from smaller independents such as DeLuxe, Miracle and Gotham. During the 50s and early 60s, King Records went from strength to strength with top-selling R&B artists such as Tiny Bradshaw, Earl Bostic, Bill Doggett, Sonny Thompson, Little Willie John and James Brown, and on the new subsidiary label Federal with the Dominoes, Freddie King and others, but by 1964 Nathan's search for innovative recording talent was virtually at an end. King settled down to focus on James Brown's career and to repackage much of its back-catalogue on album. In 1968 Nathan merged with Don Pierce's Starday record company. After Nathan's death, Starday/King and all its offshoots were sold to Gusto Records of Nashville, Tennessee.

NATURAL FOUR

The Natural Four, who had a series of moderate-sized hits during the soul era, recorded a soft style of soul in two configurations, both led by Chris James. The original members, from Oakland, California, USA, were Chris James, Allen Richardson, John January and Al Bowden. This group first recorded in 1968 on a small local label called Boola-Boola. From there they went to ABC Records, and reached the national charts in 1969 with 'Why Should We Stop Now' (number 31 R&B). The group was unable to repeat their success. Before breaking up in 1971, they recorded an unnoticed single for Bay Area producer Ron Carson that was released on Chess Records. James organized a new group - Darryl Canady, Steve Striplin and Delmos Whitney - and signed with Curtis Mayfield's Curtom label in 1972, and the following year had a sizable hit with 'Can This Be Real' (number 10 R&B, number 31 pop), written by Leroy Hutson. Subsequent records were not nearly so engaging and the group faded. Their last chart record was in 1976.

● ALBUMS: *Natural Four* (ABC 1970)★★★, *Natural Four* (Curtom 1974)★★★, *Heaven Right Here On Earth* (Curtom 1975)★★, *Nightchaser* (Curtom 1976)★★.

NDEGÉ OCELLO, ME'SHELL

b. 1969, Berlin, West Germany. Introduced by her PR machine as a female equivalent to Prince, Me'Shell Ndegé Ocello has embarked on a solo career that embraces both the hip-hop and R&B markets. Like Prince, she is a multi-instrumentalist, and writes, produces and plays on all her songs. Her name is Swahili, meaning 'Free Like A Bird'. After a nomadic life as the child of a US forces man, her first love was art rather than the jazz skills of her father and brother. Much of her youth was spent in Washington's 'go-go' scene, where at one point she was actually shot at while on stage with Little Bennie and the Masters, at the Cherry Atlantic Skating Rink. Her interest in music blossomed when her brother started playing guitar in a local band; when the bass player left his instrument lying around after rehearsal, Me'Shell was a quick convert. At the age of 19, she left for New York 'with my baby and my bass'. There she joined Living Colour's Black Rock Coalition, and recorded sessions for artists of the calibre of Caron Wheeler and Steve Coleman. She was the musical director for Arrested Development's *Saturday Night Live* appearance, though her own demos attracted little response. Madonna subsequently stepped in, inviting her to become one of the first artists signed to her Maverick empire. A palpable maturity was revealed on her debut, with a combination of acid jazz and R&B rhythms backing her beat poetry. She gained a breakthrough hit with 'If That's Your Boyfriend (He Wasn't Last Night)', a provocative post-feminist statement. Despite the sexual overtones of her packaging, she was not averse to strong political statements, with material such as 'Step Into The Projects' retaining a strong cutting edge, and lines such as 'The white man shall forever sleep with one eye open' (from 'Shoot'n Up And Gett'n High') suggesting overtones of Public Enemy. The album was produced by A Tribe Called Quest's Bob Power, alongside guests including DJ Premier (Gang Starr) and Geri Allen (Blue Note). Although she attracted some criticism for espousing the corporate rebellion angle, her connections with Maverick hardly passing unobserved, there was substance and fire in the best of her work. In 1994 she had a US Top 3 hit with 'Wild Night' a duet with John Mellencamp. *Peace Beyond Passion* reverted to 70s-style retro-funk.

● ALBUMS: *Plantation Lullabies* (Maverick/Reprise 1993)★★★★, *Peace Beyond Passion* (Maverick 1996)★★★.

NELSON, JIMMY 'T-99'

b. 7 April 1928, Philadelphia, Pennsylvania, USA. Nelson joined his brother (who later became famous as a singer with the Johnny Otis Orchestra under the stage-name Redd Lyte) on the west coast in the mid-40s, and began shouting the blues after seeing Big Joe Turner. While singing with the Peter Rabbit Trio in 1951, Nelson was signed to Modern's RPM subsidiary, with whom he had big R&B hits with 'T-99 Blues' and 'Meet Me With Your Black Dress On'. In 1955 Nelson moved to Houston, Texas, where he recorded for Chess and a host of small Texas and California independent labels. From the mid-60s he worked outside the music business until he was recorded with Arnett Cobb's band by Roy Ames in 1971 for Home Cooking Records. In recent years he has resumed performing and has toured Europe.

● COMPILATIONS: *Jimmy 'Mr T-99' Nelson* (Ace 1981)★★★, *Watch That Action!* (Ace 1987)★★★, with Arnett Cobb And His Mobb *Sweet Sugar Daddy* (1990)★★★.

NELSON, SHARA

b. London, England. Nelson, formerly vocalist for Massive Attack, began her solo career with 'Down That Road' on Cooltempo Records in July 1993 after returning to London from Bristol. Both Paul Oakenfold and Steve Osbourne were involved in remixing the single, which marketed her as the 'new Aretha Franklin'. She readily admitted to her Motown influences, and the arrangements on her debut album were sumptuous affairs, with heaped strings and gushing choruses. However, she did not desert her dance/hip-hop roots entirely, with co-writing credits for Prince B of PM Dawn ('Down That Road'), Adrian Sherwood (the title track) and Saint Etienne ('One Goodbye In Ten') offering a good balance. The latter track was the second single to be taken from the album, bringing her first major hit. *What Silence Knows'* commercial performance was something of a breakthrough for British R&B, and it was among the nominations for 1994's Mercury Music Prize and two categories in the BRIT Awards. In 1995 *Friendly Fire* firmly established her as an international soul artist, a fact at least partly attributable to Nelson's ability to write lyrics of much greater depth than is generally associated with the genre. The production assistance of Tim Simenon (Bomb The Bass) and Mike Peden (ex-Chimes) and musicianship of Skip McDonald (Sugarhill Gang, etc.), Pressure Drop, Ashley Beadle and the ubiquitous Jah Wobble also contributed greatly to an exemplary collection of cool, resonant soul songs.

● ALBUMS: *What Silence Knows* (Cooltempo 1993)★★★, *Friendly Fire* (Cooltempo 1995)★★★★.

NEVILLE BROTHERS

The Nevilles represented the essence of 40 years of New Orleans music distilled within one family unit. The Nevilles comprised Art (b. Arthur Lanon Neville, 17 December 1937, New Orleans, Louisiana, USA; keyboards, vocals), Charles (b. 28 December 1938, New Orleans, Louisiana, USA; saxophone, flute), Aaron (b. 24 January 1941, New Orleans, Louisiana, USA; vocals, keyboards) and Cyril (b. 10 January 1948, New Orleans, Louisiana, USA; vocals). Each member was also a capable percussionist. They have, individually and collectively, been making an impression on R&B, rock 'n' roll, soul, funk and jazz since the early 50s. Art was the leader of the Hawkettes, whose 1954 Chess Records hit 'Mardi Gras Mambo' has become a New Orleans standard, reissued every year at Mardi Gras time. From 1957 he released solo singles on Specialty Records, and in the early 60s, both he and Aaron worked (separately) for the legendary producer Allen Toussaint. Aaron had emerged from vocal group the Avalons, and although he had a minor R&B hit in 1960 with Toussaint's 'Over You', it was not until 1967 that he achieved fame with the soul ballad 'Tell It Like It Is', a million-seller that reached number 2 in the charts. Charles Neville, meanwhile, had been working - on the road and back home as part of the Dew Drop Inn's house band - with many legendary names: B.B. King, Bobby Bland and Ray Charles, among them. In 1968 Art formed the Meters, one of the Crescent City's most innovative and respected outfits. Featuring Leo Nocentelli (guitar), George Porter (bass), Joseph Modeliste (drums) and, later, Cyril Neville (percussion), they were New Orleans' answer to Booker T. And The MGs, and besides their own albums, they could be heard on early 70s releases by Paul McCartney, Robert Palmer, LaBelle and Dr. John. *The Wild Tchoupitoulas* was a transitional album, featuring the Meters' rhythm section and all four Neville Brothers; by 1978 they were officially a group. Despite a considerable 'cult' following, particularly among fellow musicians, it took them until 1989 and the release of the Daniel Lanois-produced *Yellow Moon*, to find a wider audience. A single, 'With God On Our Side', was extracted and became a minor hit; Aaron, duetting with Linda Ronstadt, achieved his greatest chart success since 'Tell It Like It Is', when 'Don't Know Much' reached US and UK number 2 and won them the first of two Grammy awards. In 1990, as a band, they released *Brother's Keeper* and appeared on the soundtrack of the movie *Bird On A Wire*. *Family Groove* was a more pedestrian offering, but was followed by a compelling live set that played to the group's strengths. *Mitakuye Oyasin Oyasin* was a new studio album that featured Aaron's strong cover version of Bill Withers' 'Ain't No Sunshine'.

● ALBUMS: as the Wild Tchoupitoulas *The Wild Tchoupitoulas* (Antilles 1976)★★★, *The Neville Brothers* (Capitol 1978)★★★, *Fiyo On The Bayou* (A&M 1981)★★★★, *Neville-ization* (Black Top 1984)★★★★, *Live At Tipitina's* (Spindletop 1985)★★★, *Neville-ization II* (1987)★★★, *Uptown* (EMI America 1987)★★, *Live At Tipitina's Volume 2* (Demon 1988)★★★, *Yellow Moon* (A&M 1989)★★★★, *Brother's Keeper* (A&M 1990)★★★★,

Family Groove (A&M 1992)★★★, *Live On Planet Earth* (A&M 1994)★★★, *Mitakuye Oyasin Oyasin/All My Relations* (A&M 1996)★★★.
● COMPILATIONS: *Treacherous: A History Of The Neville Brothers 1955-1985* (Rhino 1987)★★★★, *Legacy: A History Of The Nevilles* (Charly 1990)★★★★, *Treacherous Too!* (Rhino 1991)★★★, *With God On Our Side* 2-CD set (A&M 1997)★★★.
● VIDEOS: *Tell It Like It Is* (BMG Video 1990).

NEVILLE, AARON

b. 24 January 1941, New Orleans, Louisiana, USA. Neville began performing in the Hawkettes, a group that also featured his brother Art. Aaron was signed to Minit Records as a solo artist, but despite a minor hit with 'Over You' (1960), he remained largely unknown until the release of 'Tell It Like It Is' (1966) on Par-Lo. This simple, haunting ballad showcased the singer's delicate delivery while the song's slogan-like title echoed the sentiments of the rising Black Power movement. Par-Lo went bankrupt, and despite subsequent strong releases, Neville was unable to repeat its commercial success. In 1978, following the break-up of the Meters, Aaron joined Art, Cyril and Charles in the Neville Family Band, later renamed the Neville Brothers. He continued a parallel solo career and in 1989 enjoyed an international hit with 'Don't Know Much', a duet with Linda Ronstadt. *Warm Your Heart* was a strong collection, but subsequent albums have failed to do justice to Neville's astonishing voice.
● ALBUMS: *Tell It Like It Is* (Par-Lo 1967)★★, *Orchid In The Storm* mini-album (Demon 1986)★★★, *Warm Your Heart* (A&M 1991)★★★, *The Grand Tour* (A&M 1993)★★, *Soulful Christmas* (A&M 1993)★★, *The Tattooed Heart* (A&M 1995)★★, *. . . To Make Me Who I Am* (A&M 1997)★★.
● COMPILATIONS: *Like It 'Tis* (Minit 1967)★★, *Humdinger* (Stateside 1986)★★, *Make Me Strong* (Charly 1986)★★★, *Show Me The Way* (Charly 1989)★★★, *Greatest Hits* (Curb 1990)★★★, *My Greatest Gift* a collection of late 60s/early 70s recordings (Rounder 1990)★★★.

NEVILLE, ART

b. Arthur Lanon Neville, 17 December 1937, New Orleans, Louisiana, USA. Neville first attracted attention as a member of the Hawkettes, a Crescent City act that achieved notable local success in 1954 with 'Mardi Gras Mambo'. Although ostensibly a keyboard player - he appeared as session pianist on Jerry Byrne's 'Lights Out' - Neville also undertook a singing career and, having signed with the renowned Specialty Records, enjoyed a regional hit with his debut single, 'Cha Dooky-Doo'. This progress was interrupted by a spell in the US armed forces, but upon being discharged, he completed a series of low-key singles for the Minit/Instant label. Neville later achieved considerable acclaim as a member of the Meters, which in turn evolved into the equally compulsive Neville Brothers, where Art was joined by siblings Cyril, Charles and Aaron Neville.
● COMPILATIONS: *Mardi Gras Rock 'N' Roll* (Ace 1986)★★★, *Rock 'N' Roll Hootenanny* (Charly 1988)★★★.

NEVILLE, IVAN

b. New Orleans, Louisiana, USA. The son of singer Aaron Neville, Ivan made his debut in 1988 with *If My Ancestors Could See Me Now*, recorded with Fabulous Thunderbirds and Billy Joel producer Danny Kortchmar and featuring Jeff Porcaro on drums. Despite garnering a strong critical reaction as a contemporaneous R&B/soul album, Neville left Polydor Records shortly after its release, citing managerial changes at the label as the reason for the debut's lack of commercial success. Certainly, it contained two high-quality singles in 'Falling Out Of Love' (a duet with Bonnie Raitt) and 'Not Just Another Girl'. Afterwards, Neville concentrated on touring and recording with the Neville Brothers, also working with Rufus (Chaka Khan), the Rolling Stones (singing backing vocals on *Voodoo Lounge*) and with Keith Richards' Expensive Winos group. His second album, *Thanks*, followed in 1995 for the independent Iguana Records (who also licensed his debut for reissue). It featured 'After All This Time', a duet with father Aaron.
● ALBUMS: *If My Ancestors Could See Me Now* (Polydor 1988)★★★, *Thanks* (Iguana 1995)★★★.

NEW EDITION

Upbeat US teenage pop stars New Edition were formed by Maurice Starr, who modelled them on the Jackson 5. He recruited five handsome young men, Bobby Brown (b. 5 February 1969, Roxbury, Massachusetts, USA), Ralph Tresvant (b. 16 May 1968, Boston, Massachusetts, USA), Michael Bivins (b. 10 August 1968, Boston, Massachusetts, USA), Ricky Bell (b. 18 September 1967, Boston, Massachusetts, USA), and Ronnie DeVoe (b. 17 November 1967, Boston, Massachusetts, USA), who originally performed high-quality mainstream pop with soul overtones. As their careers progressed, however, they began to incorporate the sound and style of hip-hop, inadvertently becoming forerunners for the New Jack Swing (aka swingbeat) hybrid that Teddy Riley then developed. Following the success of *Candy Girl*, New Edition fired Starr, who then repeated the trick and earned a good deal of money by masterminding the career of New Kids On The Block. The first rap exchanges occurred on *New Edition*, their MCA Records debut, where the quintet proved particularly effective on tracks such as 'School'. Shortly afterwards, Brown left for a hugely successful solo career that still embraced hip-hop as well as harmonic soul ballads. New Edition continued with an idiosyncratic album of doo-wop cover versions, before the arrival of Johnny Gill for *Heart Break*, which was produced by Jimmy Jam And Terry Lewis. With sales and interest slumping, the remaining members set out on more successful solo projects. Bell Biv DeVoe comprised the adventures of the three named founder-members, while both Gill and Tresvant followed the solo trail. A total reverse in their fortunes occurred in 1996, when their first album in many years entered the *Billboard* album chart at number 1, a remarkable comeback.
● ALBUMS: *Candy Girl* (Streetwise 1983)★★, *New Edition* (MCA 1984)★★★, *All For Love* (MCA 1985)★★★, *Christmas All Over The World* (MCA 1985)★★, *Under The*

Blue Moon (MCA 1986)★★, *Heart Break* (MCA 1988)★★★, *Home Again* (MCA 1996)★★★.
● COMPILATIONS: *New Edition's Greatest Hits* (MCA 1991)★★★★.

New York City

New York City (from the city of the same name) were one of the finest representatives of the renaissance of vocal harmony groups and the explosion of the Philadelphia recording scene during the early 70s. The group members were Tim McQueen, John Brown (earlier a member of the Five Satins), Ed Shell and Claude Johnson. The group first recorded for Buddah as Triboro Exchange, but it was not until their name change in 1972 and their signing to Chelsea Records that the group became successful. Under the aegis of Philadelphia producer/arranger Thom Bell, the group flourished on the charts with such hits as 'I'm Doin' Fine Now' (number 14 R&B, number 17 pop), 'Quick, Fast, In A Hurry' (number 19 R&B, number 79 pop) and 'Happiness Is' (number 20 R&B). Their last chart record was in 1975, a time when stand-up vocal groups were becoming less of a factor in R&B. Their legacy was recalled in 1992 when in the UK the Pasadenas had a number 1 hit with 'I'm Doing Fine Now'.
● ALBUMS: *I'm Doing Fine Now* (Chelsea 1973)★★★, *Soulful Road* (Chelsea 1974)★★★.
● COMPILATIONS: *Best Of New York City* (Chelsea 1976)★★★, *I'm Doing Fine Now* (Collectables 1993)★★★.

New York Skyy

This eight-piece soul/funk band were formed in New York. Known as Skyy in America, they were led by Randy Muller. The other members were Anibal Anthony (guitar), Gerald Le Bon (bass), Tommy McConnel (drums), Larry Greenberg (keyboards), Denise Dunning-Crawford (vocals), Delores Dunning-Milligan (vocals) and Bonnie Dunning (vocals). They gained an underground cult following and reached the lower regions of the UK chart in 1982 with the exuberant 'Let's Celebrate'. Always a favourite on the dance/soul charts, they found crossing over to mainstream singles and albums a hard task and only achieved limited success. Very similar to Earth, Wind And Fire, they were primarily a visual act, who released a number of albums containing some rather mediocre tracks.
● ALBUMS: *Skyy* (Salsoul 1979)★★, *Skyway* (Salsoul 1979)★★, *Skyyport* (Salsoul 1980)★★, *Skyline* (Salsoul 1981)★★, *Skyyjammers* (Salsoul 1982)★★, *Skyylight* (Salsoul 1983)★★, *Inner City* (Salsoul 1984)★★, *From The Left Side* (Capitol 1986)★★, *Start Of A Romance* (Atlantic 1988)★★.
● COMPILATIONS: *Greatest Hits* (DM Streetsounds 1987)★★★.

Newberry, Booker, III

b. 19 January 1956, Youngstown, Ohio, USA. This rotund soul singer started performing in his local group, Mystic Nights, in 1971. He moved to nearby Philadelphia to find fame and in the mid-70s formed and fronted the quintet Sweet Thunder. They had a Top 40 R&B hit in 1978 with 'Baby, I Need Your Love Today' which they recorded for WMOT Records and which was picked up by Fantasy Records. The group recorded three albums for WMOT: *Above The Clouds* (1976), *Sweet Thunder* (1978), which made the US Top 200, and *Horizons* (1979). The group split in 1979 and for a time Newberry worked with the group Impact. In 1983 he signed with Boardwalk Records and his recording of 'Love Town', though only a minor US R&B hit, shot into the UK Top 20 in its first week of release, peaking at number 6. His follow-up, 'Teddy Bear', narrowly missed the UK Top 40 and he then quickly faded from the public eye. He recorded on Malaco in 1984 and returned to the spotlight, albeit briefly, in 1986, when 'Take A Piece Of Me' on Omni put his name back on the US R&B chart.
● ALBUMS: *Love Town* (Boardwalk 1984)★★.

Newman, David 'Fathead'

b. 24 February 1933, Dallas, Texas, USA. Newman is a tenor/baritone/soprano saxophone player and flautist, whose work contains elements of both jazz and R&B. In the early 50s he toured with Texan blues guitarist 'T-Bone' Walker and recorded the classic 'Reconsider Baby' with Lowell Fulson in 1954. For the next 10 years Newman was part of Ray Charles's orchestra, appearing on landmark recordings such as 'I Got A Woman', 'What'd I Say' and 'Lonely Avenue'. Other tenures have included the saxophone position in Herbie Mann's Family Of Mann (1972-74). He has recorded some two dozen albums as a leader since 1958, most tending towards mainstream and post-bop jazz with a funk edge, and has worked extensively as an accompanist in the blues, rock and jazz fields. He worked on Natalie Cole's bestselling *Unforgettable* (1990), and enjoyed much acclaim for his involvement in the *Bluesiana Triangle* benefit projects in aid of the homeless. *Blue Greens And Beans* was a collection of bop standards also featuring another Texan player, Marchel Ivery.
● ALBUMS: as leader *Lonely Avenue* (1971)★★★, *Mr. Fathead* (1976)★★★, *Fire! Live At the Village Vanguard* (Atlantic 1989)★★★, *Blue Greens And Beans* (Timeless 1991)★★★, *Blue Head* (Candid 1991)★★★, with Art Blakey, Dr. John *Bluesiana Triangle* (1990)★★★, *Return To The Wide Open Spaces* (Meteor 1993)★★★.
● COMPILATIONS: *Back To Basics* (1990)★★★.

Nightingale, Maxine

b. 2 November 1952, Wembley, London, England. Although Nightingale made her recording debut in 1968, early acclaim was garnered from a series of roles in the stage productions of *Hair*, *Jesus Christ Superstar* and *Godspell*. She resumed a solo career during the 70s, achieving an international hit with the compulsive 'Right Back Where We Started From'. This infectious performance, featured heavily in Paul Newman's cult movie *Slapshot*, reached number 8 in the UK and number 2 in the USA, but although 'Love Hit Me' also reached the UK Top 20, the singer was unable to sustain consistent success. 'Lead Me On', a flop at home, climbed to number 5 in the USA in 1979, but proved to be her last substantial release.
● ALBUMS: *Right Back Where We Started From* (United

Artists 1976)★★★, *Love Hit Me* (United Artists 1977)★★★, *Night Life* (United Artists 1977)★★, *Love Lines* (United Artists 1978)★★, *Lead Me On* (United Artists 1979)★★, *Bittersweet* (Liberty 1981)★★, *It's A Beautiful Thing* (Highrise 1982)★★.

NIX, DON

b. 27 September 1941, Memphis, Tennessee, USA. Saxophonist Nix was one of several aspiring high-school musicians forming the basis of the Mar-Keys. This renowned instrumental group enjoyed several R&B-styled bestsellers and became the house band for the Stax record company during the mid-60s, performing on sessions for Otis Redding, Rufus Thomas, Wilson Pickett and Sam And Dave. Nix moved to California in 1965 where he became acquainted with several 'southern' expatriates, notably Leon Russell and Delaney And Bonnie. Nix produced the latter's *Home*, then subsequently worked with Albert King and John Mayall, and completed several uneven, yet endearing, albums. In 1972 he toured with the ambitious Alabama State Troupers, an *ad hoc* musical carnival that also included Lonnie Mack, Jeannie Greene, Marlin Greene and Furry Lewis. Although never a well-known figure, Nix retained the respect of his contemporaries.

● ALBUMS: *In God We Trust* (Shelter 1971)★★★, *Living By The Days* (Elektra 1971)★★★, *Hobos, Heroes And Street Corner Clowns* (Stax 1974)★★★, *Gone Too Long* (1976)★★, *Skyrider* (1979)★★★.

● FURTHER READING: *Road Stories And Recipes*, Don Nix.

NOBLES, CLIFF (AND CO.)

Cliff Nobles (b. 1944, Mobile, Alabama, USA) had a background as a gospel singer. In an effort to break into something more commercial, he moved to Philadelphia and won a contract with Atlantic Records. He was dropped from the label after three unsuccessful singles, 'My Love Is Getting Stronger', 'Let's Have A Good Time' and 'Your Love Is All I Need', whereupon independent producer Jesse James took him on and recorded 'The More I Do For You' on the Phil LA Of Soul label. 'The Horse' (1968), Nobles' US number 2 hit, was originally the b-side to the undistinguished 'Love Is Alright'. Ironically, the former track did not feature the artist's regular group - Bobby Tucker (guitar), Benny Williams (bass) and Tommy Soul (drums) - but, instead, the James Boys, a collection of emergent Philadelphia session musicians put together by producer Leon Huff. This unit then rushed out a complementary single, 'The Mule', which had the same version of 'The Horse' on the reverse. Despite minimal input, Nobles' name still graced such follow-up singles as 'Horse Fever', although he later secured a minor R&B success with 'Feeling Of Loneliness' (1973). The James Boys - Jesse James, Bobby Martin, Norman Harris, Roland Chambers, Nat Chambers, Ronnie Baker and Karl Young - became MFSB, the Sigma Sound studio house band.

● ALBUMS: *The Horse* (Phil LA Of Soul 1968)★★.

NORMAN, JIMMY

b. 12 August 1937, Nashville, Tennessee, USA. Norman is one of many talented and ubiquitous R&B performers who have had a modest but memorable impact on the music scene. His first professional experience was as a member of the Los Angeles group the Chargers, who recorded a couple of doo-wop records for RCA during 1958-59. The Chargers broke up in 1959 and Norman began recording as a solo act under producer H.B. Barnum. In 1960 he and Barnum, in an *ad hoc* group called the Dyna-Sores, recorded a successful cover version of the Hollywood Argyles' song 'Alley Oop', and their version made it to number 59 on the pop charts. Norman's solo career then took off when he achieved a regional success with the haunting 'Here Comes The Night' in 1961. The following year he reached the national charts with the memorable New Orleans-styled 'I Don't Love You No More' (number 21 R&B, number 47 pop). He never again matched these achievements, but his delightful 'Love Is Wonderful' was an east coast hit in 1963. Norman had one other national chart record, 'Can You Blame Me' (number 35 R&B), in 1966. In the 70s and 80s he performed as a member of the Cornell Gunther-led Coasters group, one of several competing on the revival circuit during that time. In the early 70s Norman recorded several singles for this Coasters group on the Turntable label, and made some records as lead singer in Eddie Palmieri's Latin-R&B fusion group, the Harlem River Drive. In 1975 he returned to solo recording, releasing some singles for Buddah Records. Norman recorded his first album in 1987 for the tiny Badcat label.

● ALBUMS: *Home* (Badcat 1987)★★★.

NORTH, FREDDIE

b. 28 May 1939, Nashville,Tennessee, USA. In the mid-50s the soulful singer formed the Rookies, who recorded 'Money, Money, Money' on Federal. North later became a demo singer (often singing country songs) for a Nashville publisher. In 1959, under the future hit producer Billy Sherrill, he recorded a single on Sam Phillips' Phillips label. North's record 'Okay, So What', on University in 1960, led to his appearing on *Bandstand*, but no hit resulted. In 1962 he moved to Capitol and two years later recorded on Ric Records. In the mid-60s he joined Nashboro working in their stockroom. This led to his recording on their A-Bet label in 1968 where he released his debut, *The Magnetic North*. In 1970 he moved to the Nashboro-distributed Mankind label and, produced by owner producer/songwriter Jerry Williams Jnr. (aka Swamp Dogg and Raw Spitt), had his first and biggest hit, 'She's All I Got', an R&B Top 10 hit that made the US Top 40 in 1971. A year later, while working as Nashboro's national director of promotion, he had his second and last chart hit with 'You And Me Together Forever'.

● ALBUMS: *The Magnetic North* (A-Bet 1968)★★★, *Friend* (Mankind 1972)★★★, *Cuss The Wind* (Nashboro 1974)★★★, *I'm Your Man* (Broadway Sounds 1977)★★★.

● COMPILATIONS: *I'm Your Man* (Charly R&B 1989)★★★.

NOTATIONS

An R&B vocal group from Chicago, Illinois, USA, the original group members were Clifford Curry, LaSalle Matthews, Bobby Thomas and Jimmy Stroud (replaced by Walter Jones in 1973). The Notations featured a delightful upbeat sound and made a modest impact during the 70s. The group was formed in the late 60s and recorded unsuccessfully for a few local labels before achieving a hit nationally on the Twinight label with 'I'm Still Here' (number 26 R&B). They were signed by Curtom Records in 1975 to the company's Gemigo subsidiary and had hits with 'It Only Hurts For A Little While' (number 27 R&B) and 'It's Alright (This Feeling)' (number 42 R&B). The Notations left Curtom in 1977, and three of the members - Curry, Matthews and Thomas - made one more single, 'Judy Blue Eyes', for Mercury, before breaking up in 1978.

● ALBUMS: *Notations* (Gemigo 1976)★★★.

NU COLOURS

Widely regarded as one of the UK's premier R&B vocal groups, Nu Colours are led by Lawrence Johnson and were the first act signed to Polydor Records' rap/soul division Wild Card. They made a minor impact in 1992 with two singles, 'Tears' and 'Power', both gaining positions in the lower regions of the UK's Top 75. After a third single, 'What In The World', they gained their biggest success with a 1993 re-release of 'Power', which reached number 40. However, the attendant album was, by the group's own admission, rather disjointed and unconvincing, although their appearance as backing singers on M People's *Elegant Slumming* confirmed their technical abilities. Having failed to make the transition to chart status that Wild Card anticipated, the group spent much of 1994 and 1995 working with a variety of different producers and collaborators in order to mould their obvious talents into a more cohesive direction. Original member Priscilla Mae-Jones was reunited with the band too, in an effort to consolidate the vocal power of lead singer Fazay Simpson. Working with producers such as Simon Law, Ian Green, Joel Kipnes and Dinky Bingham, the resulting suite of songs became the basis for the group's second album release in 1996.

● ALBUMS: *Unlimited* (Wild Card/Polydor 1993)★★, *Nu Colours* (Wild Card/Polydor 1996)★★★.

NUNN, BOBBY

b. Buffalo, New York, USA. Nunn made his initial funk recordings at home in the mid-70s, forming his own label to handle their distribution. The results impressed new Motown signing Rick James, who invited Nunn to play on his debut *Come Get It*. Nunn subsequently moved to Los Angeles, where he formed the dance band Splendor, who recorded one album for CBS Records. When this venture failed, Rick James arranged for him to sign with Motown in 1981. The label encouraged comparisons between the two singers, which were fulfilled by the suggestive lyrics and rhythmic funk of Nunn's debut singles, 'She's Just A Groupie' and 'Got To Get Up On It'. A collaboration with Tata Vega on 'Hangin' Out At The Mall' was a dance hit in 1983, but this success was short-lived; Motown refused to issue the projected *Fresh*, and he was later dropped from the label.

● ALBUMS: *Second To Nunn* (Motown 1982)★★★, *Private Party* (Motown 1983)★★.

NUTMEGS

The Nutmegs comprised lead Leroy Griffin, first tenor James 'Sonny' Griffin, second tenor James Tyson, baritone Billy Emery and bass Leroy McNeil. The group was formed in New Haven, Connecticut, USA, in 1954. The Nutmegs are famed for just two records, 'Story Untold' (number 2 R&B) and the follow-up, 'Ship Of Love' (number 13 R&B), both from 1955. The songs, with their exotic warbling, are a working definition of 'rockaballad', a valuable term of the era that anticipated the rock 'n' roll revolution. Most notable among the lesser songs are 'Whispering Sorrows', 'My Story', and the west coast-sounding 'My Sweet Dream'. Surviving less well in the Nutmegs' canon were the rock 'n' roll jumps, which were mostly routine. After several years of declining fortunes and many personnel changes, the group broke up in 1962. The Nutmegs were one of the cult groups of the east coast collecting scene, and during the early 60s, a cappella practice versions of their songs launched a craze for a cappella doo-wop recordings. The group, without lead Leroy Griffin (who died years earlier), worked the doo-wop revival circuit on the east coast during the 70s.

● COMPILATIONS: *The Nutmegs Featuring Leroy Griffin* (Relic 1971)★★★, *Story Untold* (Relic 1993)★★★.

O'JAYS

The core of this long-standing soul group, Eddie Levert (b. 16 June 1942) and Walter Williams (b. 25 August 1942) sang together as a gospel duo prior to forming the Triumphs in 1958. This doo-wop-influenced quintet was completed by William Powell, Bill Isles and Bobby Massey and quickly grew popular around its home-town of Canton, Ohio, USA. The same line-up then recorded as the Mascots before taking the name the O'Jays after Cleveland disc jockey Eddie O'Jay, who had given them considerable help and advice. Having signed to Imperial Records in 1963, the O'Jays secured their first hit with

'Lonely Drifter', which was followed by an imaginative reworking of Benny Spellman's 'Lipstick Traces' (1965) and 'Stand In For Love' (1966). Despite gaining their first R&B Top 10 entry with 'I'll Be Sweeter Tomorrow (Than I Was Today)' (1967), the group found it difficult to maintain a consistent profile, and were reduced to a four-piece following Isles' departure. However, they were in demand as session singers, backing artists including Nat 'King' Cole and the Ronettes. In 1968 the group met producers (Kenny) Gamble And (Leon) Huff with whom they recorded, unsuccessfully, on the duo's short-lived Neptune label. The line-up was reduced further in 1972 when Bobby Massey left. Paradoxically, the O'Jays then began their most fertile period when Gamble And Huff signed them to Philadelphia International Records. The vibrant 'Back Stabbers', a US Top 3 hit, established the group's style, but the preachy 'Love Train', with its plea for world harmony, introduced the protest lyrics that would be a feature of their later releases 'Put Your Hands Together' (1973) and 'For The Love Of Money' (1974). *Back Stabbers*, meanwhile, rapidly achieved classic status and is regarded by many as Gamble And Huff's outstanding work. In 1975 Sammy Strain joined the line-up from Little Anthony And The Imperials when ill health forced William Powell to retire from live performances. This founder-member continued to record with the group until his death on 25 April 1976. 'Message In Our Music' (1976) and 'Use Ta Be My Girl' (1977) confirmed the O'Jays' continued popularity as they survived Philly soul's changing fortunes, with *So Full Of Love* (1978) achieving platinum sales. However, as the genre felt the ravages of fashion so the group also suffered. The early 80s were commercially fallow, until *Love Fever* (1985) restated their direction with its blend of funk and rap. Two years later, the O'Jays were unexpectedly back at the top of the soul chart with 'Lovin' You', confirming their status as one of soul music's most durable groups. The commercial resurrection was due in no small part to their renewed relationship with Gamble And Huff. Their output in the 90s has failed to equal the success of their 70s releases, although Eddie's son, Gerald Levert, both as a member of Levert and solo, has kept the family name alive. In 1995 Eddie, who had previously appeared alongside his son on several occasions, recorded an album of duets with Gerald for release as *Father And Son*. He is also the spokesperson for the social/business collective 100 Black Men, reaffirming the O'Jays' long-standing commitment to social change. *Love You To Tears* was their best album in many years, probably because it echoed the lush romantic sound of their heyday with Gamble And Huff in the early 70s.

● ALBUMS: *Comin' Through* (Imperial 1965)★★★, *Soul Sounds* (Imperial 1967)★★★, *O'Jays* (Minit 1967)★★★, *Full Of Soul* (Minit 1968)★★★, *Back On Top* (Bell 1968)★★★, *The O'Jays In Philadelphia* (Neptune 1969)★★★, *Back Stabbers* (Philadelphia International 1972)★★★★, *Ship Ahoy* (Philadelphia International 1973)★★★★, *The O'Jays Live In London* (Philadelphia International 1974)★★, *Survival* (Philadelphia International 1975)★★★, *Family Reunion* (Philadelphia International 1975)★★, with the Moments *The O'Jays Meet The Moments* (Philadelphia International 1975)★★★, *Message In The Music* (Philadelphia International 1976)★★★, *Travelin' At The Speed Of Thought* (Philadelphia International 1977)★★, *So Full Of Love* (Philadelphia International 1978)★★★, *Identify Yourself* (Philadelphia International 1979)★★★, *The Year 2000* (TSOP 1980)★★, *Peace* (Phoenix 1981)★★, *My Favourite Person* (Philadelphia International 1982)★★, *When Will I See You Again* (Epic 1983)★★, *Love And More* (Philadelphia International 1984)★★★, *Love Fever* (Philadelphia International 1985)★★★, *Close Company* (Philadelphia International 1985)★★★, *Let Me Touch You* (EMI Manhattan 1987)★★★, *Serious* (EMI 1989)★★, *Emotionally Yours* (EMI 1991)★★, *Heartbreaker* (EMI 1993)★★, *Love You To Tears* (Global Soul/BMG 1997)★★★★.

● COMPILATIONS: *Collectors' Items: Greatest Hits* (Philadelphia International 1977)★★★, *Greatest Hits* (Philadelphia International 1984)★★★★, *From The Beginning* (Chess 1984)★★★, *Working On Your Case* (Stateside 1985)★★★, *Reflections In Gold 1973-1982* (Charly 1988)★★★, *Love Train: The Best Of ...* (Columbia/Legacy 1995)★★★★.

O'Neal, Alexander

b. 14 November 1953, Natchez, Mississippi, USA. O'Neal was one of the best-known soul crooners of the late 80s. In 1978, he joined Flyte Tyme with future producers Jimmy Jam And Terry Lewis. The group became the backing band for Prince, although O'Neal was soon dismissed for insubordination. During the early 80s he began a solo career as a vocalist, making his first recordings with Jam and Lewis producing in 1984. The resulting album was issued by the local Tabu label, and contained R&B hits with 'A Broken Heart Could Mend', 'Innocent' (a duet with Cherrelle) and 'If You Were Here Tonight'. The latter reached the UK Top 20 in 1986, after Cherrelle's 'Saturday Love' (which featured O'Neal) had been an even bigger success there. His career was interrupted by treatment for drug and alcohol addiction, but O'Neal broke through to the mainstream US audience in 1987-88 with his second album and the singles 'Fake' and 'Never Knew Love Like This', another collaboration with Cherrelle. He remained very popular in the UK with live performances (including a Prince's Trust concert) and a BBC Television special. When, in 1991, he released his first album of new material for three years, it went straight into the UK Top 10. Jam and Lewis were again the producers.

● ALBUMS: *Alexander O'Neal* (Tabu 1985)★★★, *Hearsay* (Tabu 1987)★★★★, *My Gift To You* (Tabu 1988)★★★, *All Mixed Up* (Tabu 1989)★★★, *All True Man* (Tabu 1991)★★★★, *Love Makes No Sense* (Tabu 1993)★★★, *Lovers Again* (One World/EMI Premier 1996)★★★.

● COMPILATIONS: *This Thing Called Love, The Greatest Hits* (Tabu 1992)★★★★.

Ocean, Billy

b. Leslie Sebastian Charles, 21 January 1950, Trinidad, West Indies. Raised in England, Ocean worked as a session singer simultaneously with his employment at the

Dagenham Ford Motor Company plant, before being signed by the GTO label as a solo artist. His early hits included 'Love Really Hurts Without You' (1976) and 'Red Light Spells Danger' (1977), two purposeful, if derivative, performances. The singer's subsequent releases fared less well, and for four years between 1980 and 1984, Ocean was absent from the UK charts. Paradoxically, it was during this period that he began to win an audience in America. Ocean moved there at the turn of the decade and several R&B successes prepared the way for 'Caribbean Queen (No More Love On The Run)', his first national US pop number 1. Now signed to the Jive label, this million-selling single introduced an impressive run of hits, including two more US chart toppers, 'There'll Be Sad Songs (To Make You Cry)' (1986) and 'Get Outta My Dreams, Get Into My Car' (1988). Despite securing a UK number 1 with 'When The Going Gets Tough, The Tough Get Going' (which was featured in the film *The Jewel Of The Nile*), Ocean's luck in Britain constantly fluctuated. However, his popular appeal secured him three UK Top 5 albums during this period, including the *Greatest Hits* collection in 1989.

● ALBUMS: *Billy Ocean* (GTO 1977)★★, *City Limit* (GTO 1980)★★, *Nights (Feel Like Getting Down)* (GTO 1981)★★★, *Inner Feelings* (GTO 1982)★★★, *Suddenly* (Jive 1984)★★★, *Love Zone* (Jive 1986)★★, *Tear Down These Walls* (Jive 1988)★★, *Time To Move On* (Jive 1993)★★.

● COMPILATIONS: *Greatest Hits* (Jive 1989)★★★, *Lover Boy* (Spectrum 1993)★★★.

ODYSSEY

Formed in New York City, vocalists Lillian, Louise and Carmen Lopez were originally known as the Lopez Sisters. Their parents came from the Virgin Islands, but they were born and raised in Stamford, Connecticut, USA. Carmen left the group in 1968 and was replaced by Tony Reynolds (b. Manila), who, after the group's first album, was replaced by Bill McEachern. Odyssey's 1977 release, 'Native New Yorker', reached the US Top 20, but the song proved more popular in the UK where it peaked at number 5. It was not until 1980 that Odyssey appeared again in the UK chart with the first of several UK hits. 'Use It Up And Wear It Out' topped the chart in June of that year, while the beautiful, soulful ballad 'If You're Looking For A Way Out' gave them their third Top 10 hit. Two more effortless pop/soul offerings, 'Going Back To My Roots' (1981) and 'Inside Out' (1982), reached the Top 5. However, the lack of sustained success at home hampered the group's wider progress and they latterly broke up.

● ALBUMS: *Odyssey* (RCA 1977)★★★, *Hollywood Party Tonight* (RCA 1978)★★★, *Hang Together* (RCA 1980)★★★, *I Got The Melody* (RCA 1981)★★, *Happy Together* (RCA 1982)★★, *A Piping Journey* (Mannick Music 1987)★★.

● COMPILATIONS: *Best Of Odyssey* (RCA 1981)★★★, *Magic Touch Of Odyssey* (Telstar 1982)★★, *Magic Moments With Odyssey* (RCA 1984)★★★, *Greatest Hits* (Stylus 1987)★★★, *Greatest Hits* (RCA 1990)★★★.

OHIO PLAYERS

Formed in Dayton, Ohio, USA, in 1959, this multi-talented unit originated from three members of the Ohio Untouchables, Leroy 'Sugarfoot' Bonner, Clarence 'Satch' Satchell and Marshall Jones. They forged a reputation as a powerful instrumental group by providing the backing to the Falcons, whose R&B classic 'I Found A Love' (1962) featured singer Wilson Pickett. The Players began recording in their own right that same year, but did not achieve a notable success until the following decade when they embarked on a series of striking releases for the Westbound label after brief sessions for both Compass and Capitol Records. The group's experimental funk mirrored the work George Clinton had forged with Funkadelic for the same outlet and in 1973 the septet - Bonner, Satchell, Jones, Jimmy 'Diamond' Williams, Marvin 'Merv' Pierce, Billy Beck and Ralph 'Pee Wee' Middlebrook - enjoyed a massive R&B smash with the irrepressible 'Funky Worm'. The Players later switched to Mercury where their US hits included 'Fire' (1974) and 'Love Rollercoaster' (1975), both of which topped the soul and pop charts. 'Who'd She Coo?' became the group's last substantial hit the following year and although success did continue throughout the rest of the 70s, their releases grew increasingly predictable. The group had become renowned for their sexually explicit album covers, suggesting the possibilities of a jar of honey, or depicting macho males dominating scantily clad subservient females - and vice versa. However, their musical credibility was such that the unit's version of 'Over The Rainbow' was played at Judy Garland's funeral. Williams and Beck left the line-up in 1979 to form a new group, Shadow. A reshaped Ohio Players recorded throughout the 80s, and scored a minor soul hit in 1988 with 'Sweat'. They have continued touring into the 90s.

● ALBUMS: *First Impressions* (1968)★★, *Observations In Time* (1968)★★, *Pain* (Westbound 1972)★★★, *Pleasure* (Westbound 1973)★★★, *Ecstasy* (Westbound 1973)★★★, *Skin Tight* (Mercury 1974)★★, *Climax* a collection of outtakes (Westbound 1974)★★, *Fire* (Mercury 1974)★★★★, *Honey* (Mercury 1975)★★★★, *Contradiction* (Mercury 1976)★★★, *Angel* (Mercury 1977)★, *Mr. Mean* (Mercury 1977)★★, *Jass-Ay-Lay-Dee* (Mercury 1978)★★, *Everybody Up* (Arista 1979)★★, *Tenderness* (Boardwalk 1981)★★, *Ouch!* (Epic 1982)★★, *Graduation* (Air City 1985)★★.

● COMPILATIONS: *Ohio Players Greatest Hits* (Westbound 1975)★★★, *Rattlesnake* (Westbound 1975)★★, *Ohio Players Gold* (Mercury 1976)★★★★, *Ohio Players* (Capitol 1977)★★, *The Best Of The Westbound Years* (Westbound 1991)★★★, *Orgasm* (Westbound 1993)★★★, *Funk On Fire: The Mercury Anthology* (Mercury 1997)★★★.

OLDHAM, SPOONER

b. Lindon Dewey Oldham. Oldham first came to prominence as an in-house pianist at the Fame recording studio. Here he met Dan Penn and the resultant songwriting partnership was responsible for scores of southern soul compositions, including hits for James And Bobby Purify ('I'm Your Puppet'), Clarence Carter ('She

Ain't Gonna Do Right') and Percy Sledge ('Out Of Left Field'). Oldham later moved to California where he became a fixture as a session musician, appearing on albums by Jackson Browne, Maria Muldaur, Linda Ronstadt and the Flying Burrito Brothers. He also maintained his relationship with Penn and the duo subsequently formed an independent production company. During the 70s/80s Oldham appeared with Neil Young as a member of the Gone With The Wind Orchestra and the International Harvesters.

OLLIE AND JERRY

The R&B duo of Ollie Brown and Jerry Knight came from Los Angeles, California, USA. This dance music producing and writing team briefly charted courtesy of two soundtrack items from the motion picture *Breakin'*. Their 'Breakin' . . . There's No Stopping Us' went to number 3 in the US R&B chart and number 9 national in 1984, and later in the year 'Electric Boogie' proved to be a minor R&B hit at number 45. In the UK, 'Breakin' . . . There's No Stopping Us' went to number 5 in 1984, and 'Electric Boogaloo' went to number 57 in 1985. The Ollie and Jerry team was somewhat of an outgrowth of their work together on several albums for Ray Parker, Jnr., and his Raydio group. Brown continued his career in Detroit in 1975, playing drums with Edwin Starr, Stevie Wonder and the Rolling Stones, and beginning in 1978 as guest drummer for Raydio. By the early 80s he was producing for such acts as Patti Austin and Klique. Knight began his musical career as bass player in Bill Withers' band, and then moved to Raydio, where he sang the high parts as well as played bass. He charted with three albums, *Jerry Knight* (1980), *Perfect Fit* (1981) and *Love's On Our Side* (1983) and six singles, notably 'Overnight Sensation' (US R&B number 17, 1980) and 'Perfect Fit' (1981), before teaming up with Ollie Brown on the soundtrack titles for *Breakin'*.

● FILMS: *Breakdance - The Movie* (1984).

OLYMPICS

Originally known as the Challengers, this adaptable vocal group, Walter Ward (b. 1940, Jackson, Mississippi, USA; lead), Eddie Lewis (b. 1937, Houston, Texas, USA; tenor), Charles Fizer (b. 1940, Shreveport, Louisiana, USA, d. August 1972; baritone) and Walter Hammond (baritone) was formed in Compton, California, in 1954. The Olympics' finest moment came with 'Western Movies' (1958), a humorous novelty disc in the vein of the Coasters and the Clovers, which reached the Top 10 in the USA and Top 20 in the UK. The song was produced and co-written by Fred Smith, who later worked with Bob And Earl. The same was true of 'Private Eye', another laconic tribute to 50s pulp-fiction culture, but it was 1960 before the group claimed another US hit with 'Big Boy Pete', by which time Melvin King (b. 1940, Shreveport, Louisiana, USA), had replaced Walter Hammond. Meanwhile, the sacked lead vocalist Fizer, whose troubled life had already resulted in a prison sentence for drugs possession, was shot by the National Guard during the Watts riots in 1965. A reshaped Olympics later went on to have hits with such dancefloor favourites as 'The Bounce' (1963), 'Good Lovin'' (1965 - later successfully covered by the Young Rascals) and 'Baby Do The Philly Dog' (1966), before being drawn towards the 'oldies' circuit.

● ALBUMS: *Doin' The Hully Gully* (Arvee 1960)★★★, *Dance By The Light Of The Moon* (Arvee 1961)★★, *Party Time* (Arvee 1961)★★, *Do The Bounce* (Tri-Disc 1963)★★, *Something Old Something New* (Mirwood 1966)★★, *Soul Music* (1968)★★.

● COMPILATIONS: *Greatest Hits* (1971)★★★, *The Official Record Album Of The Olympics* (1984)★★★, *The Olympics Meet The Marathons* (Ace 1985)★★★.

OMAR

b. Omar Lye Fook, 1969, Canterbury, England. Omar was born the son of a Chinese Jamaican father and an Indian Jamaican mother. A former principle percussionist of the Kent Youth Orchestra, he would later graduate from the Guildhall School Of Music. His debut singles were 'Mr Postman' and 'You And Me' (featuring backing vocals from Caron Wheeler), before his debut album was released, via Harlesden's Black Music Association's Kong Dance label, on a slender budget. Nevertheless, it reached the Top 60. In its wake, Omar's name suddenly began to crop up everywhere, be it as a singer, writer or producer. Following a high-profile Hammersmith Odeon concert in December 1990, Gilles Peterson of Talkin' Loud persuaded financial backers Phonogram to open their wallets. The debut album was slightly remixed and re-released, the title track having already earned its stripes as a club favourite. Although by definition a soul artist, Omar's use of reggae, ragga and particularly hip-hop has endeared him to a wide cross-section of the dance community. RCA won the scramble to sign Omar after departing from Talkin' Loud in January 1993. Since then, Omar has continued to collaborate with a number of premier R&B artists - songwriter Lamont Dozier, keyboard player David Frank (famed for his contribution to Chaka Khan's 'I Feel For You'), bass player Derek Bramble (ex-Heatwave), Leon Ware (arranger for Marvin Gaye) and no less than Stevie Wonder himself, who contacted Omar after hearing his 'Music' cut.

● ALBUMS: *There's Nothing Like This* (Kongo Dance 1990)★★★, *For Pleasure* (RCA 1994)★★★, *This Is Not A Love Song* (RCA 1997)★★★.

ONE-DERFUL RECORDS

A Chicago record company founded by George Leaner in 1962 to record the hard soul sounds of the city. George Leaner, with his brother Ernie Leaner (d. 17 April 1990, Kalamazoo, Michigan, USA), had been operating a distribution firm, United Distributors, since 1950. The One-derful/Midas/M-Pac/Mar-V-lus label complex secured notable national hits with McKinley Mitchell's 'The Town I Live In', the Five Dutones' 'Shake A Tail Feather', Harold Burrage's 'Got To Find A Way' and Otis Clay's 'That's How It Is', all of which epitomized Leaner's hard-soul vision for the label. His most successful artist, however, was a recording act that could not sing, Alvin Cash And The Crawlers. Rather, leader Cash chanted his way through such giant hits as 'Twine Time', 'The Barracuda', and 'Philly Freeze'. Leaner recorded his acts in One-derful's house studio at 1825 S. Michigan, using such producer talents as Monk Higgins (Milton Bland) and Andre Williams, and songwriting talents such as Otis Hayes, Eddie Silvers and Larry Nestor. The label folded in 1968, but brother Ernie and nephew Tony Leaner continued the family's involvement in the record business by founding the Toddlin' Town label, signing some of the artists who had previously been on One-derful. It lasted until 1971.

100 Proof Aged In Soul

This short-lived quartet was formed in Detroit around Steve Mancha (b. Clyde Wilson, 25 December 1945, Walhalla, South Carolina, USA), Joe Stubbs, Don Hatcher and Eddie Anderson. The group was the culmination of several individual careers. Joe Stubbs, the brother of Four Tops' singer Levi, was the featured voice on the Falcons' hit 'You're So Fine', prior to his spells in the Originals and the Contours. Mancha had recorded several solo singles and, with Eddie Anderson, was a member of the Holidays. 100 Proof made their soul chart debut with 'Too Many Cooks (Spoil The Soup)' in 1969. The nursery-rhyme simplicity of 'Somebody's Been Sleeping' gave them a US Top 10 hit the following year. '90 Day Freeze' (1971) introduced a revamped group of Mancha, Hatcher, Ron Bykowski, Dave Case and Darnell Hughes, which remained intact until their outlet, Hot Wax, was wound down. Mancha revived his solo career under his real name as a gospel singer and also became involved in production work. A new 100 Proof appeared in 1976, but none of the original cast were involved.

● ALBUMS: *Somebody's Been Sleeping In My Bed* (Hot Wax 1970)★★★.

● COMPILATIONS: *Greatest Hits* (HDH/Fantasy 1990)★★★★.

Originals

Freddie Gorman, Walter Gaines, C.P. Spencer (aka Crathman Spencer and Spencer Craftman), Henry 'Hank' Dixon and Joe Stubbs first recorded as the Originals in 1966. Several members were already an integral part of Detroit's music history. Gorman, who released several solo singles, also co-wrote 'Please Mr. Postman' for the Marvelettes, while Stubbs was a former singer with both the Falcons and the Contours. Between 1965 and 1969, the quintet was used primarily as a backing group before their career blossomed with 'Baby I'm For Real', a number 1 R&B single co-written and produced by Marvin Gaye. The singer's involvement continued on two further releases, 'The Bells' and 'We Can Make It Pretty Baby', but despite several excellent records, including *California Sunset*, a collection of Lamont Dozier songs, the group was unable to sustain this momentum. Reduced to a quartet following Stubbs' departure for 100 Proof Aged In Soul, the Originals underwent further changes prior to their departure from Motown in 1978. By this point, Ty Hunter, former singer with the Voice Masters and Glass House, had joined the line-up, but his death three years later effectively marked the end of this group. The original line-up teamed with the Supremes for 'Back By Popular Demand' on Ian Levine's Motor City label in 1992. Former members C.P. Spencer, Freddie Gorman and Joe Stubbs were also signed to Levine's label.

● ALBUMS: *Green Grow The Lilacs* aka *Baby I'm For Real* (Soul 1969)★★★, *Portrait Of The Originals* (Soul 1970)★★★★, *Naturally Together* (Soul 1970)★★★, *Def.I.Ni.Tions* (Soul 1972)★★★, *Game Called Love* (Soul 1974)★★★, *California Sunset* (Soul 1975)★★★★, *Communique* (Soul 1976)★★★, *Down To Love Town* (Soul 1977)★★, *Another Time Another Place* (Fantasy 1978)★★, *Come Away With Me* (Fantasy 1979)★★, *Yesterday And Today* (1981)★★.

Orioles

This R&B vocal group was formed in 1947 in Baltimore, Maryland, USA. Along with the Ravens, the Orioles were considered the pioneers of rhythm and blues vocal harmony. All born in Baltimore, the group members were Sonny Til (b. Earlington Carl Tilghman, 18 August 1928, d. 9 December 1981; lead), Alexander Sharp (tenor), George Nelson (baritone), Johnny Reed (bass) and guitarist Tommy Gaither. Gaither died in a car accident in 1950 and was replaced by Ralph Williams, and Nelson left in 1953 and was succeeded by Gregory Carroll. The Orioles launched their career with the quiet, languorous ballad 'It's Too Soon To Know', which went to number 1 in the R&B charts (number 13 pop) in 1948. The song was written by Deborah Chessler, the group's manager, and she wrote many of their subsequent hits. Most Orioles hits followed the same formula of Til's impassioned tenor lead with sleepy vocal support and almost invisible instrumental accompaniment in which the music was felt rather than heard. These included the US R&B hits '(It's Gonna Be A) Lonely Christmas' (number 8, 1948), 'Tell Me So' (number 1, 1949), 'Forgive And Forget' (number 5, 1949), 'Crying In The Chapel' (number 1 - and a pop number 11, 1953), and their last R&B chart record, 'In The Mission Of St. Augustine' (number 7, 1953). In 1955 the Orioles broke up, with Sharp and Reed joining various Ink Spots groups. Til formed a new Orioles group from members of another group, the Regals, but could not revive the fortunes of the Orioles. George Nelson died around 1959, Alexander Sharp some time in the 60s, and Sonny Til on 9 December 1981.

● ALBUMS: *The Cadillacs Meet The Orioles* (1961)★★, *Modern Sounds Of The Orioles Greatest Hits* (1962)★★★, *Sonny Til Returns* (1970)★★★, *Old Gold/New Gold* (1971)★★★, *Visit Manhattan Circa 1950's* (1981)★★★.

● COMPILATIONS: *The Orioles Sing: Their Greatest Hits, 1948-1954* (Collectables 1988)★★★, *Hold Me, Thrill Me, Kiss Me* (1991)★★, *Greatest Hits* (1991)★★★, *The Jubilee Recordings* 7-CD box set (Bear Family 1993)★★★★.

Orlons

A mixture of schoolfriends and neighbours, this Philadelphia-based group was formed by Shirley Brickley (b. 9 December 1944), Steve Caldwell (b. 22 November 1942), Rosetta Hightower (b. 23 June 1944, USA) and Marlena Davis (b. 4 October 1944). Introduced to Cameo Records by the lead singer of the Dovells, Len Barry, the Orlons' first hits, 'The Wah Watusi', 'Don't Hang Up' and 'South Street', cleverly exploited the male/female aspect of the group. Each of these releases reached the US Top 5, but their potential was undermined when 'Cross Fire!' (1963) and 'Rules Of Love' (1964) were only minor hits. Any lingering impetus was lost when Davis and Caldwell left the line-up, but although Audrey Brickley took their place, the Orlons broke up in 1968 when Rosetta Hightower moved to the UK to become a session singer.

● ALBUMS: *The Wah-Watusi* (Cameo 1962)★★, *All The Hits* (Cameo 1963)★★, *South Street* (Cameo 1963)★★★, *Not Me* (Cameo 1964)★★, *Down Memory Lane* (Cameo 1964)★★★.

● COMPILATIONS: *Biggest Hits* (Cameo 1963)★★, *Golden Hits Of The Orlons And The Dovells* (1963)★★★, *Cameo Parkway Sessions* (London 1978)★★.

Osborne, Jeffrey

b. 9 March 1948, Providence, Rhode Island, USA. Osborne sang with LTD (Love, Togetherness And Devotion) from 1970 until its disbandment 12 years later. However, he remained subject to the LTD contract with A&M Records for whom he recorded five albums as a solo soul executant. Under George Duke's supervision, the first of these contained the singles 'I Really Don't Need No Light' and 'On The Wings Of Love' which both reached the US Top 40 - and the latter was a 'sleeper' hit in the UK, when 'Don't You Get So Mad' and the title track of *Stay With Me Tonight* had made slight headway there. In 1984 'Don't Stop' was, nevertheless, his last UK chart entry. The album of the same name featured a duet with Joyce Kennedy - duplicated on her *Lookin' For Trouble*, which was produced by Osborne. *Emotional* was a strong album, as were the subsequent singles, one of which, 'You Should Be Mine (The Woo Woo Song)', reached number 13, becoming his biggest US hit. For two years, he chose - perhaps unwisely - to rest on his laurels. He returned with *One Love One Dream* (co-written with Bruce Roberts) and, just prior to a transfer to Arista Records, he teamed up with Dionne Warwick for 1990's 'Love Power'. Airplay for his increasingly more predictable output was no longer automatic - and consumers had not restored him, even temporarily, to his former moderate glory.

● ALBUMS: *Jeffrey Osborne* (A&M 1982)★★★, *Stay With Me Tonight* (A&M 1983)★★★, *Don't Stop* (A&M 1984)★★★, *Emotional* (A&M 1986)★★★, *One Love One Dream* (A&M 1988)★★, *Only Human* (Arista 1991)★★★.

Otis, Johnny

b. 28 December 1921, Vallejo, California, USA. Born into a family of Greek immigrants, Otis was raised in a largely black neighbourhood where he thoroughly absorbed the prevailing culture and lifestyle. He began playing drums in his mid-teens and worked for a time with some of the locally based jazz bands, including, in 1941, Lloyd Hunter's orchestra. In 1943 he gained his first name-band experience when he joined Harlan Leonard for a short spell. Some sources suggest that, during the difficult days when the draft was pulling musicians out of bands all across the USA, Otis then replaced another ex-Leonard drummer, Jesse Price, in the Stan Kenton band. In the mid-40s Otis also recorded with several jazz groups, including Illinois Jacquet's all-star band and a septet led by Lester Young, which also featured Howard McGhee and Willie Smith. In 1945 Otis formed his own big band in Los Angeles. In an early edition assembled for a recording session, he leaned strongly towards a blues-based jazz repertoire and hired such musicians as Eli Robinson, Paul Quinichette, Teddy Buckner, Bill Doggett, Curtis Counce and singer Jimmy Rushing. This particular date produced a major success in 'Harlem Nocturne'. He also led a small band, including McGhee and Teddy Edwards, on a record date backing Wynonie Harris. However, Otis was aware of audience interest in R&B and began to angle his repertoire accordingly. Alert to the possibilities of the music and with a keen ear for new talent, he quickly became one of the leading figures in the R&B boom of the late 40s and early 50s. Otis also enjoyed credit for writing several songs, although, in some cases, this was an area fraught with confusion and litigation. Among his songs was 'Every Beat Of My Heart', which was a minor hit for Jackie Wilson in 1951 and a massive hit a decade later for Gladys Knight. Otis was instrumental in the discovery of Etta James and Willie Mae 'Big Mama' Thornton. A highly complex case of song co-authorship came to light with 'Hound Dog', which was recorded by Thornton. Otis, who had set up the date, was listed first as composer, then as co-composer with its originators, Leiber And Stoller. After the song was turned into a multi-million dollar hit by Elvis Presley other names appeared on the credits and the lawyers stepped in. Otis had a hit record in the UK with an updated version of 'Ma, He's Making Eyes At Me' in 1957. During the 50s Otis broadcast daily in the USA as a radio disc jockey, and had a weekly television show with his band and also formed several recording companies, all of which helped to make him a widely recognized force in west coast R&B. During the 60s and 70s, Otis continued to appear on radio and television, touring with his well-packaged R&B-based show. His son, Johnny 'Shuggie' Otis Jnr., appeared with the show and at the age of 13 had a hit with 'Country Girl'. In addition to his busy musical career, Otis also found time to write a book, *Listen To The Lambs*, written in the aftermath of the Watts riots of the late 60s.

● ALBUMS: *Mel Williams And Johnny Otis* (1955)★★★, *Rock 'N' Roll Parade, Volume 1* (Dig 1957)★★★, *The Johnny Otis Show* (Capitol 1958)★★★★, *Cold Shot* (Kent 1968)★★★★, *Cuttin' Up* (Epic 1970)★★, *Live At Monterey* (Epic 1971)★★, *The New Johnny Otis Show* (Alligator 1981)★★, *Spirit Of The Black Territory Bands* (1993)★★.

● COMPILATIONS: *The Original Johnny Otis Show* (Savoy1985)★★★★, *The Capitol Years* (Capitol 1989)★★★★.

● FURTHER READING: *Upside Your Head! Rhythm And Blues On Central Avenue*, Johnny Otis.

Otis, Shuggie

b. John Otis Jnr., 30 November 1953, Los Angeles, California, USA. A precociously talented guitarist, Otis was encouraged by his bandleader father, Johnny Otis, who had him playing bass and lead guitar onstage in his early teens. Johnny Otis featured him on his 1969 Kent album, *Cold Shot*, and through that Al Kooper espoused his cause and recorded his debut album for Columbia.

Father and son then both signed to Epic, and Shuggie appeared on his father's albums, *Cuttin' Up* and *The Johnny Otis Show Live At Monterey!*, as well as doing session work for Sugarcane Harris and playing bass on one track on Frank Zappa's *Hot Rats*. Three further solo albums of indifferent quality were issued before Otis retired at the grand old age of 22. In the years that followed, he continued to do session work for his father but drug problems hampered his efforts at reviving his own career. An album recorded for Big Bear in 1991, *At The Blues Summit*, remains unissued.

● ALBUMS: *Kooper Session: Al Kooper Introduces Shuggie Otis* (Columbia 1969)★★★, *Here Comes Shuggie Otis* (Epic 1970)★★, *Freedom Flight* (Epic 1971)★★, *Inspiration Information* (Epic 1975)★★, *Omaha Bar-B-Q* (Epic 1976)★★, *Shuggie's Boogie: Shuggie Otis Plays The Blues* (Epic/Legacy 1994)★★★.

OVATIONS

An R&B vocal group from Memphis, Tennessee, USA. The lead singer Louis Williams sounded very much like Sam Cooke, and the group built their career on a merger of the Sam Cooke sound with southern gospel harmonies. Recording for the Goldwax label, their first hit in 1965 was 'It's Wonderful To Be In Love' (number 22 R&B, number 61 pop). Although producing a score of southern hits, they had only one other national hit on Goldwax with 'Me And My Imagination' (number 40 R&B) in 1967. The original group soon broke up, and Williams formed a new Ovations group with three former members of Ollie And The Nightingales, Rochester Neal, Bill Davis and Quincy Billops Jnr. They reached the charts again with the MGM-subsidiary label Sounds Of Memphis. Reverting to the parent label, the group had its biggest hit in 1973 by fully exploiting Williams' ability to sound like Sam Cooke with a remake of the singer's 1962 hit, 'Having A Party' (number 7 R&B, number 56 pop). The group never was able to hit the charts again and soon disbanded.

OVERBEA, DANNY

b. 3 January 1926, Philadelphia, Pennsylvania, USA, d. 11 May 1994, Chicago, Illinois, USA. Guitarist and singer Overbea, who came out of the Chicago R&B scene, was one of the earliest pioneers of rock 'n' roll. He began his musical career in 1946 and first recorded in 1950 as a vocalist on an Eddie Chamblee track. Overbea joined Chess Records in 1952, producing his best-known songs, 'Train Train Train' (number 7 R&B) and '40 Cups Of Coffee', the following year. Both were essentially rock 'n' roll songs before the concept of 'rock 'n' roll' had even emerged. In the pop market, 'Train Train Train' was covered by Buddy Morrow and '40 Cups Of Coffee' by Ella Mae Morse. By 1955, when rock 'n' roll was making its breakthrough on the pop charts, Bill Haley And His Comets recorded '40 Cups Of Coffee', which, even though it did not chart, proved to be one of the group's better efforts. Famed disc jockey Alan Freed featured Overbea many times in his early rock 'n' roll revues in Ohio and New York; his acrobatic back-bend to the floor while playing the guitar behind his head was always a highlight of the shows. Overbea was also a talented ballad singer (in the mode of Billy Eckstine), having most success with 'You're Mine' (also recorded by the Flamingos) and 'A Toast To Lovers'. Overbea made his last records in 1959 and retired from the music business in 1976.

OWENS, JAY

b. Jerome Owens, 1947, Lake City, Florida, USA. Blind singer and guitarist Owens purveys music that is accurately described by the title of his first album. His first musical inspiration was his uncle Clarence Jenkins, a popular local blues musician, whom Owens quickly learned to accompany on the bass strings of his first guitar. Further tuition in chords and tunings came from Ink Spots guitarist Jimmy McLin, who lived nearby. In high school he joined Albert Wright And The Houserockers, a revue band that also featured shake dancers. Although both parents were ministers in the Pentecostal Church, they encouraged their son's musical education. He joined Chuck Mills' band, the Barons, and travelled throughout America, working with Al Green, O.V. Wright, Donny Hathaway, Little Milton and Bobby Womack. He also worked with Faith Hope And Charity, a vocal group whose lead singer, Zulema Cusseaux, left to pursue a solo career in New York, taking Owens with her. After several years, he left to form a series of his own bands, including Soundtrack And The Pocket, a blues trio that gigged at New York venues such as Manny's Car Wash and the Lone Star Cafe. He was introduced to Mike Vernon through Lazy Lester; Vernon heard his songs and invited him to England, where he was a surprise hit at the 1992 Burnley Blues Festival. *The Blues Soul Of...*, consisting entirely of original material that skilfully blended blues, soul and gospel influences, was well received. Moving to Code Blue, *Movin' On* repeated the same feat, proving the emergence of a serious songwriting talent.

● ALBUMS: *The Blues Soul Of...* (Indigo/Code Blue 1992/1994)★★★, *Movin' On* (Code Blue 1995)★★★★.

OZONE

Ozone were formed in Nashville, Tennessee, USA, in 1977 by three former members of the funk band the Endeavors, Benny Wallace, Jimmy Stewart and Charles Glenn. This trio recruited Thomas Bumpass, William White, Ray Woodard, Greg Hargrove and Paul Hines to lend them instrumental and vocal support. The group perfected a mix of up-tempo dance material and romantic ballads that was heavily influenced by the Commodores, and they were signed to the same record label as their mentors in 1979. Motown initially used Ozone as backing musicians for artists including Billy Preston and Syreeta, before allowing them to record the first in a series of low-key albums in 1980. The instrumental 'Walk On' brought them an initial taste of chart success, but like their subsequent black-music hits, it failed to cross over into the pop market.

● ALBUMS: *Walk On* (Motown 1980)★★★, *Jump On It* (Motown 1981)★★, *Send It* (Motown 1981)★★, *Li'l Suzy* (Motown 1982)★★, *Glasses* (Motown 1983)★★.

PALMER, EARL

b. 25 October 1924, New Orleans, Louisiana, USA. Palmer's mother was a vaudeville performer, and from an early age he began entertaining as a singer and dancer. Playing drums in his school band, he started listening to jazz drummers such as Big Sid Catlett and Panama Francis, and joined Dave Bartholomew's band in 1947. He recorded with the Bartholomew band and went on to play on many of his productions for Imperial Records, notably Fats Domino's classic records. Palmer is probably featured on virtually every other Crescent City classic, including those Specialty rockers by Little Richard and Lloyd Price, but in 1956 Aladdin Records hired him as a session arranger to handle their New Orleans sessions. In February 1957, he moved out to Los Angeles to work for Aladdin until the company was liquidated. He remained one of the busiest session drummers on the west coast throughout the 60s and 70s, recording with everyone from Lightnin' Hopkins to Marvin Gaye and subsequently wrote movie scores and advertising jingles.

PARAGONS

An R&B vocal group from Brooklyn, New York, New York, USA. With their high false falsetto and exotic warbling, the Paragons represented a rock 'n' roll doo-wop sound - sometimes called 'greasy' - that was extremely popular on the east coast in the late 50s. The members were lead Julius McMichael, Ben Frazier, Al Brown, Donald Travis and Ricky Jackson. The group was signed by Paul Winley in 1957 and their first record on the Winley label, 'Florence'/'Hey Little School Girl' was a local New York hit in early 1957. Later that year they followed that hit with another remarkable ballad, 'Let's Start Over Again'. The group had no more hits, but continued to record fine music into the 60s.

● COMPILATIONS: *The Paragons Meet The Jesters* (Jubilee 1959)★★★, *The Paragons Vs. The Harptones* (Musicnote 1963)★★★, *Simply The Paragons* (Rare Bird 1974)★★★, *The Paragons Meet The Jesters* (Collectables 1990)★★★, *The Best Of The Paragons* (Collectables 1990)★★★, *'War': The Paragons Vs The Jesters* (Sting Music Ltd 1993)★★★.

PARIS, MICA

b. Michelle Wallen, 27 April 1969, London, England. Having written, recorded and produced with the aid of heavyweights including Nile Rodgers (Chic), Prince and Rakim (Eric B And Rakim), Paris remains one of the UK's biggest talents never to have made the great leap forward. It has not been for want of effort or ability, but so far, no-one has been able to maximize the potential of one of the world's most delightful soul-dance performers. Stronger material would certainly help. There are examples from her debut album when she hits a perfect beat, as when she matches for dexterity the tenor sax of Courtney Pine on 'Like Dreamers Do'. Her second album used new, hot producers as a remedy (Charles Mantronik of Mantronix, and Dancin' Danny D of D-Mob); however, a sense of frustration still pervades her career.

● ALBUMS: *So Good* (4th & Broadway 1989)★★★, *Contribution* (4th & Broadway 1990)★★.

● VIDEOS: *Mica Paris* (Island Visual Arts 1991).

PARKER, 'LITTLE' JUNIOR

b. Herman Parker Jnr., 3 March 1927, West Memphis, Arkansas, USA, d. 18 November 1971, Blue Island, Illinois, USA. Despite his later fame, some confusion still exists regarding the parentage and birth details of Little Junior Parker (Clarksdale, Mississippi, and 1932 are sometimes quoted, and his parents' names have variously been cited as Herman Snr., Willie, Jeanetta or Jeremeter). It is certain that they were a farming family situated near enough to West Memphis for Little Junior (who had started singing in church) to involve himself in the local music scene at an early age. His biggest influence in the early days was Sonny Boy 'Rice Miller' Williamson, in whose band Parker worked for some time before moving on to work for Howlin' Wolf, later assuming the leadership of the latter's backing band. He was a member of the *ad hoc* group the Beale Streeters, with Bobby Bland and B.B. King, prior to forming his own band, the Blue Flames, in 1951, which included the well-regarded guitarist Auburn 'Pat' Hare. His first, fairly primitive, recordings were made for Joe Bihari and Ike Turner in 1952 for the Modern label. This brought him to the attention of Sam Phillips and Sun Records, where Parker enjoyed some success with his recordings of 'Feeling Good', although the period is better recalled for the downbeat 'Mystery Train', which was later covered by the young Elvis Presley. His greatest fame on record stemmed from his work on Don Robey's Duke label operating out of Houston, Texas, and it was along with fellow Duke artist Bobby 'Blue' Bland that Little Junior headed the highly successful Blues Consolidated Revue, which quickly became a staple part of the southern blues circuit. His tenure with Robey lasted until the mid-60s, with his work moving progressively away from his hard blues base. In his later days, Parker appeared on such labels as Mercury, United Artists and Capitol, enjoying intermittent chart success with 'Driving Wheel' (1961), 'Annie Get Your Yo-Yo' (1962) and 'Man Or Mouse' (1966). His premature death in 1971 occurred while he was undergoing surgery for a brain tumour and robbed R&B of one of its most influential figures.

● ALBUMS: with Bobby Bland *Blues Consolidated* (Duke 1958)★★★, with Bland *Barefoot Rock And You Got Me* (Duke 1960)★★★, *Driving Wheel* (Duke 1962)★★★★, *Like It Is* (Mercury 1967)★★★, *Honey-Drippin' Blues* (1969)★★★, *Blues Man* (1969)★★★, *The Outside Man* (1970)★★★, *Dudes Doing Business* (1971)★★, *Blue Shadows Falling* (Groove Merchant 1972)★★, *Good*

Things Don't Happen Every Day (Groove Merchant 1973)★★, *I Tell Stories, Sad And True ...* (1973)★★, *You Don't Have To Be Black To Love The Blues* (People 1974)★★, *Love Ain't Nothin' But A Business Goin' On* (1974)★★★.

● COMPILATIONS: *The Best Of Junior Parker* (Duke 1966)★★★★, *Sometime Tomorrow My Broken Heart Will Die* (1973)★★★, *Memorial* (Vogue 1973)★★★, *The ABC Collection* (1976)★★★★, *The Legendary Sun Performers - Junior Parker And Billy 'Red' Love* (Charly 1977)★★★, *I Wanna Ramble* (Ace 1982)★★★, *Junior's Blues: The Duke Recordings Vol. 1* (1993)★★★★.

Parker, Bobby

b. 31 August 1937, Lafayette, Louisiana, USA. With a reputation based upon one record from 1961, guitarist Parker spent 30 years in obscurity before recording his first album. His family moved to east Los Angeles in 1943 and Parker acquired his first guitar three years later. While still in high school, he formed a band with future rockers Don Harris and Dewey Terry. After winning a talent contest at Johnny Otis's Barrelhouse club, he was offered the guitar spot with Otis Williams & The Charms. From there, he worked in Bo Diddley's touring band for three years and then joined Paul 'Hucklebuck' Williams' orchestra. While with them he made his first single, 'Blues Get Off My Shoulder', for Vee Jay in Chicago. The b-side, 'You Got What It Takes', became a hit for Marv Johnson but featured composer credits for Berry Gordy and Billy Davis. In 1961 Parker settled in Washington, DC, and released his first and only hit, 'Watch Your Step' on V-Tone, basing the tune on Dizzy Gillespie's 'Manteca'. The Spencer Davis Group covered it in England and John Lennon revealed that the Beatles' 'Day Tripper' was based on a variation of its main riff. In 1969 he toured England and recorded 'It's Hard But It's Fair' for Blue Horizon. Sessions for Lillian Clayborn's DC label and for producer Mitch Corday in the 60s are also rumoured to exist. Parker gave up music for five years during the 80s, but returned in 1989. *Bent Out Of Shape* showed that his talent was undiminished; *Livin' Blues* accurately described Parker's style of stringing notes together as 'tight as a suspension bridge'.

● ALBUMS: *Bent Out Of Shape* (Black Top 1993)★★★, *Shine Me Up* (Black Top 1995)★★★.

Parker, Maceo

(see Maceo And The King's Men)

Parker, Ray, Jnr.

b. 1 May 1954, Detroit, Michigan, USA. This accomplished musician gained his reputation during the late 60s as a member of the house band at the 20 Grand Club. This Detroit nightspot often featured Tamla/Motown acts, one of which, the (Detroit) Spinners, was so impressed with the young guitarist's skills that they added him to their touring group. Parker was also employed as a studio musician for the emergent Invictus/Hot Wax stable and his choppy style was particularly evident on 'Want Ads', a number 1 single for Honey Cone. Parker also participated on two Stevie Wonder albums, *Talking Book* and *Innervisions*, an association that prompted a permanent move to Los Angeles. Here Parker continued his session work (Marvin Gaye, Boz Scaggs, Labelle, Barry White and Love Unlimited) until 1977, when he formed Raydio with other Detroit musicians Arnell Carmichael (synthesizer), Jerry Knight (bass), Vincent Bonham (piano), Larry Tolbert, Darren Carmichael and Charles Fearing. 'Jack And Jill', a pop/soul reading of the nursery rhyme, gave the group an international hit, while further releases consistently reached the R&B charts. 'A Woman Needs Love (Just Like You Do)', credited to Ray Parker Jnr. And Raydio, was a US Top 5 hit in 1981, while the following year the leader embarked on a solo path with 'The Other Woman'. In 1984 Parker secured a multi-million-selling single with the theme song to the film *Ghostbusters*, although its lustre was somewhat tarnished by allegations that he had plagiarized a Huey Lewis composition, 'I Want A New Drug'. Nonetheless, Parker's success continued as the song secured him a 1984 Grammy award for Best Pop Instrumental Performance. In 1986 he moved to the Geffen label, releasing *After Dark* the following year. A single from the album, 'I Don't Think That Man Should Sleep Alone', was a Top 20 hit in the UK. After producing New Edition's debut album, Parker moved to the MCA label and released the disappointing *I Love You Like You Are*.

● ALBUMS: as Raydio *Raydio* (Arista 1977)★★★, *Rock On* (Arista 1979)★★★. As Ray Parker Jnr. And Raydio *Two Places At The Same Time* (Arista 1980)★★★, *A Woman Needs Love* (Arista 1981)★★★. As Ray Parker *The Other Woman* (Arista 1982)★★, *Woman Out Of Control* (Arista 1983)★★, *Sex And The Single Man* (Arista 1985)★★, *After Dark* (Geffen 1987)★★★, *I Love You Like You Are* (MCA 1991)★★.

● COMPILATIONS: *Greatest Hits* (Arista 1982)★★★★, *Chartbusters* (Arista 1984)★★★, *The Collection* (Arista 1986)★★★.

Parker, Robert

b. 14 October 1930, New Orleans, Louisiana, USA. An accomplished saxophonist, this versatile musician was first heard on numerous recordings by pianist Professor Longhair. Parker also appeared on sessions for Irma Thomas, Ernie K-Doe and Joe Tex while at the same time embarking on a singing career. His early releases were largely unsuccessful until 'Barefootin'', an irresistible dance record, became a hit in the USA and the UK during 1966. The singer continued this instinctive blend of soul and New Orleans R&B on several further releases, but 'Tip Toe' (1967) was his only further chart entry.

● ALBUMS: *Barefootin'* (Island 1966)★★.

● COMPILATIONS: *Get Ta Steppin'* (Charly 1987)★★.

Parliament

This exceptional US vocal quintet was formed in 1955 by George Clinton (b. 22 July 1940, Kannapolis, North Carolina, USA), Raymond Davis (b. 29 March 1940, Sumter, South Carolina, USA), Calvin Simon (b. 22 May 1942, Beckley, West Virginia, USA), Clarence 'Fuzzy' Haskins (b. 8 June 1941, Elkhorn, West Virginia, USA) and Grady Thomas (b. 5 January 1941, Newark, New Jersey, USA). George Clinton's interest in music did not fully emerge until his family moved to the urban setting of Plainfield, New Jersey. Here, he fashioned the Parliaments after the influential doo-wop group Frankie Lymon And The Teenagers. Two singles, 'Poor Willie' and 'Lonely Island', mark this formative era, but it was not until 1967 that Clinton was able to secure a more defined direction with the release of '(I Wanna) Testify'. Recorded in Detroit, the single reached the US Top 20, but this promise was all but lost when Revilot, the label to which the band was signed, went out of business. All existing contracts were then sold to Atlantic, but Clinton preferred to abandon the Parliaments' name altogether in order to be free to sign elsewhere. Clinton took the existing line-up and its backing group to Westbound Records, where the entire collective recorded as Funkadelic. However, the outstanding problem over their erstwhile title was resolved in 1970, and the same musicians were signed to the Invictus label as Parliament. This group unleashed the experimental and eclectic *Osmium* before securing an R&B hit with the irrepressible 'Breakdown'. For the next three years the 'Parliafunkadelicament Thang' would concentrate on Funkadelic releases, but disagreements with the Westbound hierarchy inspired Parliament's second revival. Signed to the Casablanca label in 1974, the group's first singles, 'Up For The Down Stroke', 'Chocolate City' and 'P. Funk (Wants To Get Funked Up)' were marginally more mainstream than the more radical material Clinton had already issued, but the distinctions became increasingly blurred. Some 40 musicians were now gathered together under the P. Funk banner, including several refugees from the James Brown camp including Bootsy Collins, Fred Wesley and Maceo Parker, while live shows featured elements from both camps. Parliament's success within the R&B chart continued with 'Give Up The Funk (Tear The Roof Off The Sucker)' (1976), and two 1978 bestsellers, 'Flashlight' and 'Aqua Boogie (A Psychoalphadiscobetabioaquadoloop)', where the group's hard-kicking funk was matched by the superlative horn charts and their leader's unorthodox vision. Their last chart entry was in 1980 with 'Agony Of Defeet', after which Clinton decided to shelve the Parliament name again when problems arose following Polygram's acquisition of the Casablanca catalogue.

● ALBUMS: *Osmium* (Invictus 1970)★★★, *Up For The Down Stroke* (Casablanca 1974)★★★★, *Chocolate City* (Casablanca 1975)★★★, *Mothership Connection* (Casablanca 1976)★★★★, *The Clones Of Doctor Funkenstein* (Casablanca 1976)★★★★, *Parliament Live - P. Funk Earth Tour* (Casablanca 1977)★★★, *Funkentelechy Vs The Placebo Syndrome* (Casablanca 1977)★★★★, *Motor-Booty Affair* (Casablanca 1978)★★★★, *Gloryhallastoopid (Or Pin The Tale On The Funky)* (Casablanca 1979)★★★, *Trombipulation* (Casablanca 1980)★★★, *Dope Dogs* (Hot Hands 1995)★★★.

● COMPILATIONS: *Parliament's Greatest Hits* (Casablanca 1984)★★★★, *The Best Of Parliament* (Club 1986)★★★, *Rhenium* (Demon 1990)★★★, *Tear The Roof Off 1974-80* (Casablanca 1993)★★★★, *Parliament-Funkadelic Live 1976-93* 4-CD box set (Sequel 1994)★★★★.

PASADENAS

UK soul band formed in 1987 by three brothers - Jeff Aaron Brown(b. 12 December 1964), Michael Milliner (b. 15 February 1962), and David Milliner (b. 16 February 1962), plus Hamish Seelochan (b. 11 August 1964) and Andrew Banfield (b. 4 December 1964). They had previously been performing since 1982 in an outfit titled Finesse. Finesse danced on videos by Animal Nightlife, Freez and others, appearing in the film *Absolute Beginners*. The band's debut 45, 'Right On', was a paean to artists such as Marvin Gaye. Follow-ups, including 'Riding On A Train', 'Enchanted Lady' and 'I'm Doing Fine Now' (UK number 4 in February 1992), established them as a chart act proper. As well as the traditions of doo-wop, the band were heavily influenced by the spirit and style of the decade, despite their own acknowledgement that 'being black in the 50s was not a nice thing'.

● ALBUMS: *To Whom It May Concern* (Columbia 1988)★★★, *Elevate* (Columbia 1991)★★★, *Yours Sincerely* (Columbia 1992)★★★.

PASSIONS

This rock 'n' roll vocal group from Brooklyn, New York, USA, comprised lead Jimmy Gallagher, second tenor Albie Galione, first tenor Tony Armato and baritone Vinny Acierno. The Passions were one of the first Italian-American vocal ensembles to make their presence felt on the rock 'n' roll scene, and typically of such groups, their sound was smooth and sincere. The Passions were formed in 1958, and after signing with the local Audicon label in 1959 immediately found success with 'Just To Be With You' (USA number 69 pop) in 1959. It would be the group's only national hit, but in the New York metropolitan area the Passions were seen as local stars, and, therefore, their impact was far greater. Their double-sided follow-up in 1960, 'I Only Want You'/'This Is My Love', is still cherished by doo-wop fans. At this time Vinny Acierno was replaced by Lou Rotondo. The Passions' next single was a smooth version of the Cadillacs' classic ballad 'Gloria' (1960), which, although only achieving local success, became an enduring legacy for the group and something of a doo-wop standard. The group was unable to sustain success with the singles it recorded in the next two years, and in 1964 the Passions disbanded.

● COMPILATIONS: *Just To Be With You* (Clifton 1990)★★★, *Legendary Hits* (Crystal Ball 1991)★★★, *Just To Be With You* (Relic 1992)★★★.

PASTELS

This R&B vocal group formed at a US Air Force base in Narsarssuak, Greenland, in 1954, and comprised Big Dee Irwin, Richard Travis, Tony Thomas and Jimmy Willingham. Members were later transferred to Washington, DC, and the Pastels were discovered by the New York-based Hull Records in 1957. They were signed to the company's subsidiary label, Mascot, but after their first hit, 'Been So Long', all their records were leased to the Chess (Records) brothers' Argo label in Chicago. 'Been So Long', an R&B number 5 and pop Top 30 hit, was an utterly sublime doo-wop with haunting chorusing, and for decades later was a staple on oldies radio shows. By 1958 all the Pastels had left the service, and the group was ready to exploit the success of their hit with follow-ups; however, they instead suffered a severe failure, with a lack of national chart success in 1958 for the sublime 'So Far Away', their third and final release. The following year the Pastels disbanded but Dee Irwin continued in the music business. In 1964 he enjoyed a Top 40 national pop hit with 'Swingin' On A Star', accompanied by the uncredited Little Eva. He continued behind the scenes as a songwriter, composing for artists such as Ray Charles, Arthur Prysock, Esther Phillips and Isaac Hayes.

PATE, JOHNNY

b. 1923, Chicago Heights, Illinois, USA. Pate was one of the most important producers and arrangers in the creation of the Chicago sound in soul music during the 60s. With his highly lyrical horn arrangements Pate was able to suggest a gospel-tinged feeling with the utmost in subtlety and nuance. This deft approach probably derived from his 50s career as a bassist in his own cocktail lounge jazz combo, which worked Chicago clubs for many years. He first began performing in these clubs with Coleridge Davis and Stuff Smith in the late 40s. By the early 50s Pate had formed his own unit. In 1958, performing as the Johnny Pate Quintet, he achieved a national hit with 'Swingin' Sheppard Blues' (number 17 R&B, number 43 pop), a cover version of the hit by the Moe Koffman Quartet. By the end of the 50s the nightclubs in the black community were closing down and the call for cocktail lounge jazz was greatly diminished, so Pate began working freelance for various Chicago R&B labels as an arranger and producer. Beginning in 1962 he began writing most of the arrangements for the horn-driven OKeh Records' hits of Major Lance and Billy Butler produced by Carl Davis. A year later Pate started production and arrangement work with the Impressions on ABC Records. At ABC he served as A&R man and produced and arranged hits for another Chicago-based group, the Marvelows. When the Impressions moved to the Curtom label in 1970 so did Pate, but he only stayed until 1972, when he moved to the west coast.

● ALBUMS: *Johnny Pate At The Blue Note* (Stepheny 1957)★★★, *Jazz Goes Ivy League* (King 1958)★★★, *Swingin' Flute* (King 1958)★★★, *A Date With Johnny Pate* (King 1959)★★★.

PATTERSON, RAHSAAN

b. *c.*1974, New York City, New York, USA. Progressive urban R&B vocalist Rahsaan Patterson attracted strong reviews upon the release of his self-titled 1997 debut album. A collection of ballads combining strong melodic and rhythmic elements, critics were impressed both by his sonorous voice and the maturity of the songwriting. Born in New York but resident in Los Angeles, the ambitious, engaging young artist was keen to state that his lyrics reflected the life he saw around him in urban California: 'The theme of my album circles around life's everyday experiences, so there's no contrived notions or gimmicks on it', he told *Billboard* magazine. Although *Rahsaan Patterson* was his first recording, the artist could already boast of considerable experience in the entertainment industry. As a child, he was a featured performer on *Kids Incorporated*, a televised variety series. He had also sung backing vocals extensively, and co-wrote two hit singles - 'Back To The World', written with Keith Crouch for Tevin Campbell, and 'Baby', written with Les Pierce for Brandy. Pierce and Crouch both reappeared on his solo debut, alongside Jammy Jaz, Ira Schick and Dinky Bingham.

● ALBUMS: *Rahsaan Patterson* (MCA 1997)★★★★.

PAUL, BILLY

b. Paul Williams, 1 December 1934, Philadelphia, Pennsylvania, USA. Although Paul had been an active singer in the Philadelphia area since the 50s, singing in jazz clubs and briefly with Harold Melvin And The Blue Notes, it was not until he met producer Kenny Gamble that his career prospered. After signing to the Neptune label, he enjoyed a successful spell on the Philadelphia International label. His instinctive, jazz-based delivery provided an unlikely foil for the label's highly structured, sweet-soul sound but Paul's impressive debut hit, 'Me And Mrs Jones', nonetheless encapsulated the genre. A classic confessional tale of infidelity, Paul's unorthodox style enhanced the ballad's sense of guilt. His later releases included 'Thanks For Saving My Life' (1974), 'Let's Make A Baby' (1976) and 'Let 'Em In' (1977), the last of which adapted the Paul McCartney hit to emphasize lyrical references to Dr. Martin Luther King. Paul continued to make excellent records, but his last chart entry to date came in 1980 with 'You're My Sweetness'.

● ALBUMS: *Ebony Woman* (Neptune 1970)★★, *Going East* (Philadelphia International 1971)★★★, *360 Degrees Of Billy Paul* (Philadelphia International 1972)★★★, *Feelin' Good At The Cadillac Club* (Philadelphia International 1973)★★★, *War Of The Gods* (Philadelphia International 1973)★★★, *Live In Europe* (Philadelphia International 1974)★★, *Got My Head On Straight* (Philadelphia International 1975)★★★, *When Love Is New* (Philadelphia International 1975)★★★, *Let 'Em In* (Philadelphia International 1977)★★, *Only The Strong Survive* (Philadelphia International 1978)★★, *First Class* (Philadelphia International 1979)★★, *Lately* (Total Experience 1985)★★★, *Wide Open* (Ichiban 1988)★★★.

● COMPILATIONS: *Best Of Billy Paul* (Philadelphia International 1980)★★★★, *Billy Paul's Greatest Hits* (Philadelphia International 1983)★★★.

PAUL, CLARENCE

b. Clarence Pauling, 19 March 1928, Winston-Salem, North Carolina, USA, d. 6 May 1995, Los Angeles, California, USA. One of Motown Records' best-known producers, Pauling's work was synonymous with the early career of Stevie Wonder. He also produced several other stars, including Marvin Gaye and the Temptations. Together with brother Lowman Pauling, Clarence's musical apprenticeship came in the gospel choirs of North Carolina, before forming the Royal Sons with

Lowman (they would later become the 5 Royales after Clarence left). In the 50s he joined two further gospel aggregations, Wings Over Jordan and the Coleman Brothers, between his service for the US Army in North Korea. Afterwards, he launched a career in secular music, with R&B 45s for Federal, Roulette and Hannover Records, but with little success. By the late 50s, he had established himself as a songwriter, notably for Roy Hamilton. As Lowman Pauling was also pursuing this route, it was at that time that he changed his name to Clarence Paul to avoid confusion. He moved to Detroit in the early 60s, befriending Stevie Wonder while he was still known as Steveland Morris. It was largely through Paul that Wonder secured a contract with Tamla Motown in 1961. Wonder's success reflected on Paul, and he was commissioned by Motown as a full-time producer and songwriter. He also duetted on some of Wonder's early recordings, including 'La La La La La' and 'Blowing In The Wind'. They also wrote songs together, including 'Fingertips'. He then became assistant to Motown A&R director Mickey Stevenson, but when Stevenson relocated to Los Angeles in the early 70s to inaugurate Venture Records, Paul followed him, taking up a new post in Venture's A&R department. Wonder was by his bedside before his death after a short illness in 1995, after which his body was returned to Winston-Salem for burial next to his brother Lowman.

PAYNE, FREDA

b. Freda Charcilia Payne, 19 September 1945, Detroit, Michigan, USA. Schooled in jazz and classical music, this urbane singer attended the Institute Of Musical Arts and worked with Pearl Bailey prior to recording her debut album in 1963 for MGM Records. Payne signed to Holland/Dozier/Holland's label Invictus and her first recording, 'The Unhooked Generation', introduced a new-found soul style, but it was the magnificent follow-up, 'Band Of Gold' (1970), that established Payne's reputation. This ambiguous wedding-night drama was a US number 3 and UK number 1 and prepared the way for several more excellent singles in 'Deeper And Deeper', 'You Brought The Joy' and 'Bring The Boys Home', an uncompromising anti-Vietnam anthem. Ensuing releases lacked her early purpose and were marred by Payne's increasingly unemotional delivery. The singer moved to ABC/Dunhill (1974), Capitol (1976) and Sutra (1982), but Payne was also drawn to television work and would later host a syndicated talk show, *For You Black Woman*. In 1990 she recorded for Ian Levine's Motor City label.

● ALBUMS: *After The Lights Go Down And Much More* (MGM 1963)★★, *How Do You Say I Don't Love You Anymore* (1966)★★★, *Band Of Gold* (Invictus 1970)★★★, *Contact* (Invictus 1971)★★★, *Reaching Out* (Invictus 1973)★★★, *Payne And Pleasure* (Dunhill 1974)★★, *Out Of Payne Comes Love* (ABC 1975)★★, *Stares And Whispers* (Capitol 1977)★★, *Supernatural High* (Capitol 1978)★★, *Hot* (Capitol 1979)★★.

● COMPILATIONS: *The Best Of Freda Payne* (Invictus 1972)★★★, *Bands Of Gold* (HDH/Demon 1984)★★★, *Deeper And Deeper* (HDH/Demon 1989)★★★, *The Best Of* (Castle 1997)★★★.

PAYNE, SCHERRIE

b. 14 November 1944, Detroit, Michigan, USA. The sister of soul singer Freda Payne, Scherrie forsook her teaching position at Detroit's Grayling Observatory to join the Glass House. This short-lived group enjoyed a series of minor US hits, the most notable of which was 'Crumbs Off The Table', a US R&B Top 10 entry in 1969. Several unsuccessful solo singles followed upon the unit's demise, but Payne achieved a higher profile upon replacing Jean Terrell in the Supremes. She remained with the trio between 1974 and 1976, contributing to *High Energy* and *Mary, Scherrie And Susaye* (both 1976). After the break-up of the group, she made one unsuccessful album with fellow ex-Supreme Susaye Green, in 1979, before resuming her own career with 'Incredible'. A duet with Philip Ingram and 'Testify' reached the lower reaches of the R&B chart during 1987, but the singer failed to consolidate her early promise.

● ALBUMS: with Susaye Green *Partners* (1979)★★.

PEACHES AND HERB

Herb Fame (b. Herbert Feemster, 1 October 1942) and Francine Barker (b. Francine Hurd, 1947). These two Washington-based singers were signed separately to the same record label, Date, and met on a promotional tour. Producer Dave Kapralik put the couple together, and their easy, if unexceptional, voices took 'Close Your Eyes' into the US Top 10 in 1967. The duo continued to figure in the charts with 'United' (1968) and 'When He Touches Me (Nothing Else Matters)' (1969). However, although Barker was featured on these records, she had been replaced for live performances by former session singer Marlene Mack (b. 1945, Virginia, USA). The 'sweethearts of soul' were ostensibly disbanded in July 1970 when a disillusioned Herb Fame left music in favour of the Police Department, although a 'bogus' duo hurriedly stepped in to fill the gap. Herb resumed recording in 1976 with a new 'Peaches', Linda Greene (b. Washington, DC, USA). Following a brief spell at MCA Records, the reconstituted couple moved to Polydor where they enjoyed a major hit with 'Shake Your Groove Thing' (1978). The following year, 'Reunited' reached number 1 in the USA and number 4 in the UK. They continued to enjoy success into the 80s, but these later releases lacked the charm of their early work.

● ALBUMS: *Let's Fall In Love* (Date 1967)★★★, *For Your Love* (Date 1967)★★★, *Peaches And Herb* (1977)★★, *2 Hot!* (Polydor 1978)★★, *Twice The Fire* (Polydor 1979)★★, *Worth The Wait* (Polydor 1980)★★, *Sayin' Something!* (Polydor 1981)★★, *Remember* (1983)★★.

● COMPILATIONS: *Peaches And Herb's Greatest Hits* (Date 1968)★★★.

PEBBLES

b. Perri Alette McKissack, Oakland, California, USA. This female singer, nicknamed 'Pebbles' by her family for her resemblance to the cartoon character Pebbles Flintstone, is based in San Francisco, California, and enjoyed substantial success after teaming up with black pop's hottest production team, L.A. Reid And Babyface. Before their meeting she had spent her teenage years and early professional career with Con Funk Shun in the early 80s. She sprang to fame in 1988 with 'Girlfriend', a debut smash both for her and her production team. This was quickly followed by the US number 2-peaking 'Mercedes Boy'. From that time, both parties made the most of her success, with Pebbles' second album, *Always*, showcasing a particularly effective demonstration of L.A. and Babyface's studio technique (for the first time in the backroom duo's history, Pebbles was awarded a co-production credit), with hard, propulsive rhythms and irresistible hooks. Singles such as 'Giving You The Benefit' continued to scale the US charts. Pebbles, whose cousin is vocalist Cherrelle, subsequently married L.A. Reid, after which her output became noticeably less prolific. Her January 1991 single, 'Love Makes Things Happen', featuring backing vocals by Babyface, reached number 13 in the US charts, but she has not enjoyed sustained success since. Her 1995 album, *Straight From My Heart*, featured writing contributions from Tony Rich, among others, but was released in the aftermath of her separation from Reid and fared poorly in the charts.

● ALBUMS: *Pebbles* (MCA 1988)★★★, *Always* (MCA 1990)★★★, *Straight From My Heart* (MCA 1995)★★.

PEEBLES, ANN

b. 27 April 1947, East St. Louis, Missouri, USA. An impromptu appearance at the Rosewood Club in Memphis led to Peebles' recording contract. Bandleader Gene Miller took the singer to producer Willie Mitchell, whose skills fashioned an impressive debut single, 'Walk Away' (1969). Peebles' style was more fully shaped with 'Part Time Love' (1970), an irresistibly punchy reworking of the Clay Hammond-penned standard, while powerful original songs, including 'Slipped Tripped And Fell In Love' (1972) and 'I'm Gonna Tear Your Playhouse Down' (1973), later recorded by Paul Young and Graham Parker, confirmed her promise. Her work matured with the magnificent 'I Can't Stand The Rain', which defined the Hi Records sound and deservedly ensured the singer's immortality. Don Bryant, Peebles' husband and a songwriter of ability, wrote that classic as well as '99 lbs' (1971). Later releases, '(You Keep Me) Hangin' On' and 'Do I Need You', were also strong, but Peebles was latterly hampered by a now-established formula and sales subsided. 'If You Got The Time (I've Got The Love)' (1979) was the singer's last R&B hit, but her work nonetheless remains among the finest in the 70s soul canon. After a return to the gospel fold in the mid-80s, Peebles bounced back in 1990 with *Call Me*. In 1992 the fine, back-to-the-Memphis-sound *Full Time Love* was issued. She appeared that summer at the Porretta Terme Soul Festival in Italy and her riveting performance was captured on a CD of the festival, *Sweet Soul Music - Live!*, released by Italian label 103.

● ALBUMS: *This Is Ann Peebles* (Hi 1969)★★★, *Part Time Love* (Hi 1971)★★★, *Straight From The Heart* (Hi 1972)★★★, *I Can't Stand The Rain* (Hi 1974)★★★★, *Tellin' It* (Hi 1976)★★★, *If This Is Heaven* (Hi 1978)★★★, *The Handwriting On The Wall* (Hi 1979)★★★, *Call Me* (Waylo 1990)★★★, *Full Time Love* (Rounder/Bullseye 1992)★★★, *Fill This World With Love* (Bullseye 1996)★★★.

● COMPILATIONS: *I'm Gonna Tear Your Playhouse Down* (Hi 1985)★★★★, *99 lbs* (Hi 1987)★★★, *Greatest Hits* (Hi 1988)★★★★, *Lookin' For A Lovin'* (Hi 1990)★★★, *Straight From The Heart/I Can't Stand The Rain* (1992)★★★, *Tellin' It/If This Is Heaven* (1992)★★★, *This Is Ann Peebles/The Handwriting On The Wall* (1993)★★★, *The Flipside Of ...* (1993)★★★, *U.S. R&B Hits* (1995)★★★.

PENDERGRASS, TEDDY

b. Theodore Pendergrass, 26 March 1950, Philadelphia, Pennsylvania, USA. Pendergrass joined Harold Melvin And The Blue Notes in 1969, when they invited his group, the Cadillacs, to work as backing musicians. Initially their drummer, Pendergrass had become the featured vocalist within a year. His ragged, passionate interpretations brought distinction to such releases as 'I Miss You' and 'If You Don't Know Me By Now'. Clashes with Melvin led to an inevitable split and in 1976 Pendergrass embarked on a successful solo career, remaining with the Philadelphia International label. His skills were most apparent on slower material, which proved ideal for the singer's uncompromisingly sensual approach, which earned him a huge following among women. 'The Whole Town's Laughing At Me' (1977), 'Close The Door' (1978) and 'Turn Off The Lights' (1979) stand among the best of his early work and if later releases were increasingly drawn towards a smoother, more polished direction, Pendergrass was still capable of creating excellent records, including a moving rendition of 'Love TKO', a haunting Womack And Womack composition. However, his life was inexorably changed in 1982, following a near-fatal car accident that left the singer confined to a wheelchair, although his voice was intact. Nonetheless, after months of physical and emotional therapy, he was able to begin recording again. 'Hold Me' (1984), Pendergrass's debut hit on his new outlet, Asylum Records, also featured Whitney Houston, while further success followed with 'Love 4/2' (1986), 'Joy' and '2 A.M.' (both 1988). In 1991, 'It Should've Been You' did much to reinstate him in people's mind's as a major artist. He moved to a new label in 1996 after a lengthy gap in his career.

● ALBUMS: *Teddy Pendergrass* (Philadelphia International 1977)★★★, *Life Is A Song Worth Singing* (Philadelphia International 1978)★★★, *Teddy* (Philadelphia International 1979)★★★★, *Teddy Live! (Coast To Coast)* (Philadelphia International 1979)★★, *T.P.* (Philadelphia International 1980)★★★★, *It's Time For Love* (Philadelphia International 1981)★★★, *This One's For You* (Philadelphia International 1982)★★★, *Heaven Only Knows* (Philadelphia International 1983)★★★, *Love Language* (Asylum 1984)★★, *Workin' It Back* (Asylum 1985)★★★, *Joy* (Elektra 1988)★★★, *Truly Blessed* (Elektra 1991)★★★, *Little More Magic* (Elektra 1993)★★★, *You And I* (BMG/Surefire 1997)★★★.

● COMPILATIONS: *Greatest Hits* (Philadelphia International 1984)★★★★, *The Philly Years* (Repertoire 1995)★★★★.

● VIDEOS: *Teddy Pendergrass Live* (Columbia-Fox 1988).

PENGUINS

Formed in 1954 in Fremont High School, Los Angeles, California, USA, the Penguins were one of the most important R&B vocal groups from the west coast in the early 50s. Their hit ballad 'Earth Angel' remains one of the most fondly recalled 'doo-wop' recordings. The group consisted of lead vocalist Cleveland 'Cleve' Duncan (b. 23 July 1935, Los Angeles, California, USA), Bruce Tate (baritone), Curtis Williams (first tenor) and Dexter Tisby (second tenor). Williams learned 'Earth Angel' from Los Angeles R&B singer Jesse Belvin, and passed it on to his group. Some sources give co-writing credit to Williams, Belvin and Gaynel Hodge, a member of vocal group the Turks. Hodge won a 1956 lawsuit recognizing his role in the writing of the song. However, most reissues of 'Earth Angel' still list only either Belvin, Williams or both. The Penguins, who took their name from a penguin on a cigarette packet, signed with the local DooTone Records, owned by Dootsie Williams. Their first recording date was as a backing group for a blues singer, Willie Headon. They next recorded 'Hey Sinorita', an up-tempo number. 'Earth Angel' was chosen as their first single's b-side but when both sides were played on LA radio station KGJF, listeners called in to request that 'Earth Angel' be played again. It ultimately reached number 1 in the US *Billboard* R&B chart. It also reached the pop Top 10, but was eclipsed by a cover version by the white group the Crew-Cuts. The song has also charted by Gloria Mann (1955), Johnny Tillotson (1960), the Vogues (1969) and New Edition (1986). The Penguins continued to record other singles for DooTone (plus one album for the related Dooto label) and then Mercury Records, before disbanding in 1959. Members Williams and Tate have since died, Tisby retired from music, and Duncan later formed new bands under the name Penguins; he was still performing under that name in the early 90s.

● ALBUMS: *The Cool, Cool Penguins* (Dooto 1959)★★★, side 1 only *The Best Vocal Groups: Rhythm And Blues* (Dooto 1959)★★★, *Big Jay McNeely Meets The Penguins* (Ace 1984)★★★, *Earth Angel* (Ace 1988)★★★, *The Authentic Golden Hits Of The Penguins* (Juke Box 1993)★★★.

PENISTON, CE CE

b. Cecelia Peniston, 6 September 1969, Phoenix, Arizona, USA. Peniston started acting at school when in her early teens. She went on to appear in numerous talent contests and also won the beauty pageants Miss Black Arizona and Miss Galaxy. She worked as a backing singer and while still at school wrote 'Finally', which would become her first solo single. Fresh out of college, and with only the faintest hopes of a music career, she nevertheless sprang into the Top 10 lists of both the UK and USA on the back of a speculative demo. The music that backed 'Finally' bore more than a passing resemblance to the Ce Ce Rogers underground hit, 'Someday'. A singer and dancer slightly reminiscent of late 70s soul, most of her compositions are piano-based with strong similarities to Aretha Franklin and Whitney Houston. While her modelling career has been put on the backburner, her attitude to singing remains refreshingly uncomplicated: 'What I know best is singing my lil' old heart out'. 'We Got A Love Thang' became a second hit early in 1992, as did the re-released 'Finally', before the release of her debut album, which was somewhat disjointed. She has also sung backing vocals on Kym Sims' 'Too Blind To See'. Her second album included contributions from house gurus David Morales and Steve 'Silk' Hurley, but was generally more urban R&B-focused. This trend continued with *Movin' On*.

● ALBUMS: *Finally* (A&M 1992)★★, *Thought Ya Knew* (A&M 1994)★★★, *Movin' On* (A&M 1996)★★★.

PENN, DAN

b. Wallace Daniel Pennington, 16 November 1941, Vernon, Alabama, USA. His reputation as a songwriter was secured when one of his early compositions, 'Is A Bluebird Blue?', was a hit for Conway Twitty in 1960. Penn also led a local group, the Mark V, which included David Briggs (piano), Norbert Putnam (bass) and Jerry Carrigan (drums). Also known as Dan Penn And The Pallbearers, these musicians later formed the core of the first Fame studio house band. Their subsequent departure for a more lucrative career in Nashville left room for a second session group, among whose number was pianist Spooner Oldham. Over the next few years, Penn's partnership with this newcomer produced scores of excellent southern soul compositions, including 'Out Of Left Field', 'It Tears Me Up' (Percy Sledge), 'Slippin' Around' (Clarence Carter) and 'Let's Do It Over' (Joe Simon) and 'Dark End Of The Street', a classic guilt-laced 'cheating' ballad, first recorded by James Carr. Penn subsequently left Fame to work at the rival American Sound studio where he joined studio-owner Chips Morman, with whom he had also struck up a songwriting partnership (their 'Do Right Woman - Do Right Man' was the b-side of Aretha Franklin's first hit single for Atlantic Records). Later at American Studios, Penn would also be responsible for producing hit group the Box Tops, but in 1969 he broke away to form his own studio, Beautiful Sounds. The 70s, however, were much less prolific. Having flirted with a singing career with several one-off releases, he finally produced a fine solo album, *Nobody's Fool*, which included the first version of 'I Hate You', later covered by Bobby Bland. Penn also maintained his friendship with Oldham, but by the time the duo formed their own independent production company, the changing face of popular music rendered their talents anachronistic. However, in 1991 Oldham and Penn reunited to appear at the New York Bottom Line's In Their Own Words songwriter series. This live performance of self-penned songs was so successful that it inspired Penn to record a new album of his own work, both old and new, the critically acclaimed *Do Right Man*. To promote the album he played a further series of live dates, including the 1994 Porretta Terme Soul Festival in Italy, and then at London's South Bank Centre as part of a salute to southern songwriters under the banner The American South, which also included Allen Toussaint and Joe South.

● ALBUMS: *Nobody's Fool* (1973)★★★, *Do Right Man* (Sire/Warners Brothers 1994)★★★★.

PENTAGONS

The members of this vocal group from San Bernadino, California, USA, were Joe Jones (lead), Carl McGinnis (bass), Otis Munson (tenor) and the brothers Ted (tenor) and Ken Goodloe (baritone, piano). The Pentagons helped to make the early 60s the era of neo-doo-wop renaissance, in which they sang classic 50s vocal harmonies that evoked the past, but with full orchestrated support that reflected the coming soul era. The original Pentagons group, which was assembled in 1958, consisted of the Goodloe brothers, McGinnis, plus Bill James as tenor and Johnny Torrence as lead. They recorded one unsuccessful single for Specialty Records, and then Torrence and James departed to be replaced by Jones and Munson, respectively. Another single for Modern was released under the name of the Shields, and then in 1961 the group had a big hit with a Ken Goodloe song, 'To Be Loved (Forever)' (number 48 pop). It was released on Bob Keane's Donna label, but after one follow-up on Donna the group moved to the Jamie label. They reached the charts again during 1961 with another Goodloe composition, 'I Wonder (If Your Love Will Ever Belong To Me)' (number 84 pop). Ricky Nelson was so impressed with the song he recorded it in 1964. Later Pentagons releases failed to make the charts, and the group broke up in 1962. The Goodloes put together another outfit in 1964, but this, too, disbanded in 1966 after a few failed singles. Ken Goodloe died on 4 August 1991.

● COMPILATIONS: *The Pentagons* (True Gems 1986)★★★, *Golden Classics* (Collectables 1990)★★★.

PERSUADERS

An R&B vocal group from New York, New York, USA, the original members were lead Douglas 'Smokey' Scott, Willie Holland, James 'B.J' Barnes and Charles Stodghill. The Persuaders were one of a myriad of stand-up vocal groups that helped to make the early 70s an era of vocal harmony renaissance, one that significantly shaped the popular music of the day. The arresting dry lead of Scott, set against the pristine sweet harmonizing of the rest of the group, gave the Persuaders a distinctive sound. The group was organized in 1968 as the Internationals and soon met Richard and Robert Poindexter, who owned a small label and began recording the group. In 1971, the Internationals redubbed themselves the Persuaders and had a hit with 'Thin Line Between Love And Hate' (number 1 R&B, number 15 pop), a fabulous composition by the Poindexters. They followed with an almost equally attractive song, 'Love Gonna Pack Up (And Walk Out)' (number 8 R&B, number 64 pop). The 1972 hit 'Peace In The Valley Of Love' (number 21 R&B) featured a revised line-up, with Barnes and Stodghill being replaced by John Tobias and Thomas Lee Hill. The Persuaders gained their second-biggest hit in 1973 with 'Some Guys Have All The Luck' (number 7 R&B, number 39 pop), and competed with Gladys Knight And The Pips on the charts in 1974 with a rival version of 'Best Thing That Ever Happened To Me' (number 29 R&B, number 85 pop). The Persuaders' last chart record was in 1977, and by that time only Scott remained from the original line-up.

● ALBUMS: *Thin Line Between Love And Hate* (Win Or Lose 1972)★★★, *The Persuaders* (Atco 1973)★★★, *Best Thing That Ever Happened To Me* (Atco 1974)★★★, *It's All About Love* (Calla 1976)★★.

PERSUASIONS

Formed in the Bedford-Stuyvesant area of New York City, this talented group has continued the a cappella tradition despite prevalent trends elsewhere. Jerry Lawson (b. 23 January 1944, Fort Lauderdale, Florida, USA; lead), Joseph 'Jesse' Russell (b. 25 September 1939, Henderson, North Carolina, USA; tenor), Little Jayotis Washington (b. 12 May 1941, Detroit, Michigan, USA; tenor), Herbert 'Tubo' Rhoad (b. 1 October 1944, Bamberg, South Carolina, USA, d. 8 December 1988; baritone) and Jimmy 'Bro' Hayes (b. 12 November 1943, Hopewell, Virginia, USA; bass) began working together in 1966. Having recorded for Minit, the Persuasions gained prominence four years later with *Accapella*, a part live/part studio album released on Frank Zappa's Straight label. Their unadorned voices were later heard on several superb collections, including *Street Corner Symphony* and *Chirpin'*, while the group also supplied harmonies on Joni Mitchell's *Shadows And Light* (1980). During 1973-74, Willie C. Daniel replaced Jayotis Washington in the group. In 1988 Rhoad died, leaving a four-man group. The Persuasions continue to pursue this peerless path, winding sinewy harmonies around such varied songs as 'Slip Sliding Away', Five Hundred Miles' and 'Under The Boardwalk'.

● ALBUMS: *Accapella* (Straight 1970)★★★, *We Came To Play* (Capitol 1971)★★★, *Street Corner Symphony* (Capitol 1972)★★★★, *Spread The Word* (Capitol 1972)★★★, *We Still Ain't Got No Band* (MCA 1973)★★★, *More Than Before* (A&M 1974)★★, *I Just Wanna Sing With My Friends* (A&M 1974)★★, *Chirpin'* (Elektra 1977)★★★★, *Comin' At Ya* (Flying Fish 1979)★★★, *Good News* (Rounder 1983)★★, *No Frills* (Rounder 1986)★★★, *Stardust* (Catamount 1987)★★★, *Right Around The Corner* (Bullseye 1994)★★★, *Sincerely* (Bullseye 1996)★★★.

● COMPILATIONS: *Man, Oh Man* (EMI 1997)★★★★.

PHAJJA

Pronounced 'fah-jah', the name being Arabic for 'new beginning', this trio of female singers was convened in Los Angeles, California, USA, in the mid-90s. Featuring Karen Johnson and sisters Nakia and Kena Epps, the group were signed by Warner Brothers Records in 1996 in an attempt to gain a foothold in the R&B market. Their first single, 'What Are You Waiting For?', was released in April 1997, and preceded a huge promotional push on the part of their label. The group themselves were confident about their prospects: 'Even though we consider this a very romantic album, we made sure that the lyrics do more than scrape the surface of love themes.' Whether or not *Seize The Moment* helps them to realize Warners' ambitions is open to question, its contents displaying little originality, although the group's talent for harmonies masked some of the songwriting deficiencies.

● ALBUMS: *Seize The Moment* (Warners 1997)★★.

PHILADELPHIA INTERNATIONAL RECORDS

Founded in Philadelphia, Pennsylvania, USA, in 1971, this much-respected record company defined the sweet, melodic style of early 70s urban soul. Initiators Gamble And Huff were already renowned songwriters and producers through collaborations with Jerry Butler, the Soul Survivors and the Intruders, although several early ventures into label ownership, notably with Gamble and Neptune, had folded prematurely. They nevertheless established a distinctive sound that eschewed Tamla/Motown's cavernous basslines in favour of a smooth, string-laden, silky approach, fashioned on Burt Bacharach's early work with Dionne Warwick, but embellished with lush orchestration and arrangements often obscuring the punch of a crack rhythm section. Armed with a marketing and distribution agreement with Columbia Records, Gamble and Huff founded Philadelphia International knowing that the parent company would exploit the white market, leaving the duo free to concentrate their energies on black radio stations. The result was a series of marvellous crossover hits, including 'Love Train' and 'Backstabbers' (the O'Jays), 'Me And Mrs Jones' (Billy Paul) and 'If You Don't Know Me By Now' (Harold Melvin And The Blue Notes), while the label's cool, sculpted formula was echoed by Blue Magic, the (Detroit) Spinners and the Stylistics. The duo's house band - Roland Chambers and Norman Harris (guitars), Vince Montana (vibes), Ronnie Baker (bass) and Earl Young (drums) - also appeared on releases by the Delfonics and First Choice, while David Bowie used their Sigma Sound studio to record *Young Americans*. The rise of disco undermined the freshness of 'Philly Soul', but a recurrent controversy of payola allegations did more to undermine the company's collective confidence. Charges against Huff - that he offered inducements in exchange for airplay - were dropped in 1976, but Gamble was fined $2,500, although commentators have viewed the indictment as racially motivated. Philadelphia International continued to function in the 80s, but its pre-eminent position was usurped by a new generation of black acts. It nonetheless set benchmarks for quality and style in the same way as Motown had done during the previous decade.

● COMPILATIONS: *Philadelphia Classics* (1978)★★★, *The Philadelphia Story* 14-LP box set (1986)★★★★, *TSOP: The Sound Of Philadelphia* (1988)★★★, *The Philadelphia Years, Volume One* (1989)★★★★, *The Philadelphia Years Volume 2* (1989)★★★, *The Philly Sound* 3-CD box set (Epic/Legacy 1998)★★★★.

PHILLIPS, ESTHER

b. Esther Mae Jones, 23 December 1935, Galveston, Texas, USA, d. 7 August 1984, Carson, California, USA. This distinctive vocalist was discovered by bandleader Johnny Otis. She joined his revue in 1949 where, as 'Little Esther', the teenage singer recorded two number 1 R&B singles, 'Double Crossing Blues' and 'Mistrustin' Blues'. She then worked solo following the band's collapse, but by the middle of the decade Phillips was chronically addicted to drugs. In 1954 she retired to Houston to recuperate and did not fully resume recording until 1962. Phillips' version of 'Release Me', a country standard that was later a hit for Engelbert Humperdinck, mirrored the blend of black and white music found, contemporaneously, in Ray Charles and Solomon Burke. An album, *Release Me! - Reflections Of Country And Western Greats*, consolidated this style, but when Phillips moved to the Atlantic label, her recordings assumed a broader aspect. Polished interpretations of show tunes and standards contrasted a soul-based perspective shown in her retitled version of the John Lennon/Paul McCartney song, 'And I Love Him', a performance showcased on the syndicated television show *Around The Beatles*. Her unique, nasal intonation was perfect for her 1966 hit, 'When A Woman Loves A Man', while her several collaborations with the Dixie Flyers, the highly respected Criteria studio house band, were artistically successful. The singer moved to Kudu Records in 1972 where she recorded the distinctly biographical 'Home Is Where The Hatred Is', an uncompromising Gil Scott-Heron composition. The same label provided 'What A Diff'rence A Day Makes' (1975), which reached the US Top 20 and the UK Top 10. She also completed two exceptional albums at this time, *From A Whisper To A Scream* and *Alone Again Naturally*, but was increasingly pushed towards a specialist rather than popular audience. Ill health sadly undermined this artist's undoubted potential, and in August 1984, Phillips died of liver and kidney failure.

● ALBUMS: *Memory Lane* (1956)★★★, *Down Memory Lane With Little Esther* (King 1959)★★★, *Release Me! - Reflections Of Country And Western Greats* (Lenox 1963)★★, *And I Love Him* (Atlantic 1965)★★★★, *Esther* (Atlantic 1966)★★★, *The Country Side Of Esther Phillips* (Atlantic 1966)★★, *Burnin' - Live At Freddie Jett's Pied Piper LA* (Atlantic 1970)★★★, *From A Whisper To A Scream* (Kudu 1972)★★★★, *Alone Again Naturally* (Kudu 1972)★★★★, *Black-Eyed Blues* (Kudu 1973)★★, *Performance* (Kudu 1974)★★★, with Joe Beck *What A Difference A Day Makes* (Kudu 1975)★★★, *Confessin' The Blues* (Atlantic 1975)★★★, *For All We Know* (1976)★★★, *Capricorn Princess* (Kudu 1976)★★★, *You've Come A Long Way Baby* (Mercury 1977)★★★, *All About Esther* (Mercury 1978)★★, *Here's Esther ... Are You Ready* (Mercury 1979)★★, *A Good Black Is Hard To Crack* (Mercury 1981)★★.

● COMPILATIONS: *Little Esther Phillips - The Complete Savoy Recordings* 1949-59 recordings (Savoy Jazz 1984)★★★★.

PIANO RED

b. William Lee Perryman, 19 October 1911, Hampton, Georgia, USA, d. 8 January 1985. The younger brother of blues artist Rufus 'Speckled Red' Perryman, this powerful keyboard player enjoyed several R&B bestsellers from 1950-51, including 'Rockin' With Red' and 'Red's Boogie'. He subsequently assumed another identity, Dr. Feelgood, and with his backing group, the Interns, secured further success with a series of pounding performances. His most influential releases included 'Right String Baby But The Wrong Yo Yo', the eponymous 'Doctor Feelgood', beloved of British beat groups, and 'Mister Moonlight', which was recorded by both the Beatles and the Merseybeats. Another of Perryman's whimsical offerings, 'Bald Headed Lena', was covered by the Lovin' Spoonful, but none of these versions matched the wry insistency of the originals. Perryman remained a popular live attraction, particularly in Europe, until his death in 1985.

● ALBUMS: *Piano Red In Concert* (Groove 1956)★★★, *Happiness Is Piano Red* (King 1970)★★★, *All Alone With His Piano* (1972)★★★, *Piano Red - Ain't Going To Be Your Low-Down Dog No More* (1974)★★, as Dr. Feelgood *All Alone* (1975)★★★, *Percussive Piano* (1979)★★, *Dr. Feelgood* (Black Lion 1979)★★★, with the Interns *What's Up Doc* (1984)★★, *Music Is Medicine* (1988)★★.

Pic And Bill

Charles Edward Pickens and Bill(y) Mills (b. North Carolina, USA). Male soul duos were extremely popular in the 60s and 70s - Sam And Dave and James And Bobby Purify were perhaps the best-known and most commercially successful examples. Pickens and Mills, along with several others such as the Knight Brothers, Maurice And Mac, Eddie And Ernie, Sam And Bill, and Van And Titus, were less well known but no less emotive, and were raised in the gospel hotbed of North Carolina. From 1965 they were based for five years in Fort Worth, Texas, where they recorded extensively for Major Bill Smith, owner of the local Le Cam, Soft, Charay and Shalimar labels. Smith had sustained his small empire on the back of three massive 60s pop and country hits that he had successfully leased out to bigger labels: Paul And Paula's teen-love anthem 'Hey Paula', Bruce Channel's 'Hey Baby', and J. Frank Wilson's million-selling country hit 'The Last Kiss'. However, Pic And Bill were two big-voiced gospel and soul artists, and Charles Pickens had a hand in the production of their 11 singles and one album from this era, as well as writing many of the songs. They began in 1966 with the poppish 'What Would I Do' for Charay, followed by the superb deep-soul 'All I Want Is You', 'It's Not You' and 'Nobody But My Baby'. 'Just A Tear'/'Sad World Without You' was a big double-sided seller in the southern states, and 'A Man Without A Woman' was a cover version of a side already recorded for Major Bill Smith by another of his male duos, Matt And Robert. In the late 60s, Charles Pickens went solo with his own soul-ballad, 'How Many Times', which was followed by the duo's cover version of Joe Hinton's 'Funny How Time Slips Away', the disappointing 'Together Till the End Of Time', and an impressive 1968 version of Sam And Dave's much-covered 'deep' classic, 'When Something Is Wrong With My Baby'. Major Bill then leased three Pic And Bill singles to the Mercury subsidiary Smash and one to Blue Rock. One of the Smash releases was a straight reissue of an earlier single, but the new recordings included a great, soulful version of Paul McCartney's 'Yesterday', along with 'Don't Put Me Down', 'Moments Like These' and the 1955 ballad, 'Love Is A Many Splendoured Thing'. The Blue Rock single consisted of another deep ballad, 'Soul Of A Man' (not the Fontella Bass number), and the slightly funky 'Gonna Give It To You'. Major Bill also issued a Pic And Bill album, *Thirty Minutes Of Soul*, which was first released on Charay, and then, in the 70s, on both LeCam and Twelve O'Clock. Also in the 70s, their 'All I Want Is You' Charay side surfaced again on both LeCam and Zuma. Billy Mills recorded some solo material for Major Bill that was not released at the time, and went on to record a session for the Nashville label Sound Stage 7, but no more was heard of Charles Pickens for some time. Then, in 1987, the duo reunited for the Bandit label in Ashville, North Carolina, and recorded the Dave Smith-produced 'Hang On In There Baby'; the latter was a 12-inch single release and this, plus nine other sides cut for Bandit, appeared on the Japanese Vivid Sound CD, *Taking Up The Slack*. Much of the best of Pic And Bill's 'prime' output from their time with Major Bill Smith appeared on the 1988 UK Charly release, *Givin' It To You*.

● ALBUMS: *Thirty Minutes Of Soul* (Charay 1969)★★★, *Taking Up the Slack* (Vivid Sound 1987)★★★.

● COMPILATIONS: *Givin' It To You* (Charly 1988)★★★★.

Pickett, Wilson

b. 18 March 1941, Prattville, Alabama, USA. Raised in Detroit, Pickett sang in several of the city's R&B groups. He later joined the Falcons, an act already established by the million-selling 'You're So Fine'. Pickett wrote and sang lead on their 1962 hit 'I Found A Love', after which he launched his solo career. A false start at Correctone was overturned by two powerful singles, 'If You Need Me' and 'It's Too Late', recorded for Lloyd Price's Double L outlet. The former track's potential was undermined by Solomon Burke's opportunistic cover version on Atlantic Records, the irony of which was compounded when Pickett moved to that same label in 1964. An inspired partnership with guitarist Steve Cropper produced the classic standard 'In The Midnight Hour', as well as 'Don't Fight It' (both 1965), '634-5789 (Soulsville, USA)', 'Land Of A 1,000 Dances' (written by Chris Kenner), 'Mustang Sally' (all 1966) and 'Funky Broadway' (1967). The singer's other collaborators included erstwhile Falcon Eddie Floyd and former Valentino, Bobby Womack. The latter partnership proved increasingly important as the 60s progressed. A 1968 album, *The Midnight Mover*, contained six songs featuring Womack's involvement. Deprived of the Stax house band due to their break with Atlantic, Pickett next recorded at Fame's Muscle Shoals studio. A remarkable version of 'Hey Jude', with Duane Allman on guitar, was the highlight of this period. A further experiment, this time with producers Gamble And Huff, resulted in two hits, 'Engine Number 9' (1970) and 'Don't Let The Green Grass Fool You' (1971), while a trip to Miami provided 'Don't Knock My Love', his last Top 20 hit for Atlantic. Wilson switched to RCA in 1972, but his previous success was hard to regain. A mercurial talent, Pickett returned to Muscle Shoals for *Funky Situation* (1978), issued on his own Wicked label. More recently, he worked alongside Joe Tex, Don Covay, Ben E. King and Solomon Burke in a revamped Soul Clan. Pickett was the invisible figure and role model in the award-winning soul music film *The Commitments* in 1991. Since then, Pickett has found life a struggle and has been arrested and charged with various drug offences.

● ALBUMS: *It's Too Late* (Double-L 1963)★★, *In The*

Midnight Hour (Atlantic 1965)★★★★, *The Exciting Wilson Pickett* (Atlantic 1966)★★★★, *The Wicked Pickett* (Atlantic 1966)★★★★, *The Sound Of Wilson Pickett* (Atlantic 1967)★★★★, *I'm In Love* (Atlantic 1968)★★★, *The Midnight Mover* (Atlantic 1968)★★★, *Hey Jude* (Atlantic 1969)★★★, *Right On* (Atlantic 1970)★★★, *Wilson Pickett In Philadelphia* (Atlantic 1970)★★, *If You Need Me* (Joy 1970)★★, *Don't Knock My Love* (Atlantic 1971)★★, *Mr. Magic Man* (RCA 1973)★★, *Miz Lena's Boy* (RCA 1973)★★, *Tonight I'm My Biggest Audience* (RCA 1974)★★, *Live In Japan* (1974)★★, *Pickett In Pocket* (RCA 1974)★★, *Join Me & Let's Be Free* (RCA 1975)★★, *Chocolate Mountain* (Wicked 1976)★★, *A Funky Situation* (Wicked 1978)★★, *I Want You* (EMI America 1979)★★, *The Right Track* (EMI America 1981)★★, *American Soul Man* (Motown 1987)★★.

● COMPILATIONS: *The Best Of Wilson Pickett* (Atlantic 1967)★★★★, *The Best Of Wilson Pickett Vol. 2* (Atlantic 1971)★★★★, *Wilson Pickett's Greatest Hits* i (Atlantic 1973)★★★★, *Collection* (Castle 1992)★★★, *A Man And A Half: The Best Of Wilson Pickett* (Rhino/Atlantic 1992)★★★★★.

PILGRIM TRAVELERS

Primarily known today as one of soul singer Lou Rawls' first groups, the close-harmony group the Pilgrim Travelers was formed in 1936 in Houston, Texas, USA, as an offshoot of the Pleasantgrove Baptist Church. The founder-members were Joe Johnson, Kylo Turner, Keith Barber and Rayfield Taylor. They won a talent contest in 1944, the prize for which was a national tour with the Soul Stirrers. After the tour the group moved to Los Angeles, California, and added J.W. Alexander as tenor, and Jessie Whitaker as baritone. After brief spells with Big Town and Swing Time, the Pilgrim Travelers moved to Specialty Records in the late 40s. In addition to gospel standards such as 'The Old Rugged Cross', their most fondly remembered track from this period was 'Jesus Met The Woman At The Well'. When Rayfield Taylor departed in the 50s he was replaced by George McCurn. By 1957 Kylo Turner and Keith Barber had also left, and they were replaced by Ernest Booker and Lou Rawls (ex-Teenage Kings Of Harmony and Holy Wonders). With Rawls, Whitaker and Booker alternating leads the group released a string of singles for Andex Records in the 50s, with Sam Cooke guesting on recording sessions and some touring dates. However, after Booker left in 1957 the group abbreviated their name to simply the Travelers and recorded more secular material for a time. The group ground to a halt two years later, with Rawls going on to a successful R&B career and Alexander partnering Sam Cooke in the formation of Sar Records.

PIXIES THREE

The Pixies Three, an all-female trio from Hanover, Pennsylvania, USA, comprised lead Midge Bollinger, Debbie Swisher (b. 1948) and Kaye McCool (b. 1946). The group enjoyed brief success during the peak years of the 'girl group' phenomenon, in which raucous and strident-sounding female voices became one of the favourite sounds in rock 'n' roll. Swisher and McCool founded the Pixies Three in 1957 while still in grade school, bringing Bollinger into the group after several months singing as a duo. They served a long five-year apprenticeship performing at weddings, civic clubs, and private parties before they gained their professional break in 1962 when they were signed by producers John Madara and David White (of Danny And The Juniors) to a recording contract with Mercury Records. The Pixies Three's 1963 debut, 'Birthday Party', was an exuberant workout that evoked Claudine Clark's 'Party Lights' from the previous year. It was a number 1 hit in many markets but fared more modestly nationwide (number 40 pop). The follow-up in late 1963 was a double-sided chart record, and as usual in such cases, the record's chart career suffered from split airplay. The a-side '442 Glenwood Avenue' (number 56 pop) was in the rock 'n' roll mode of their first hit, and the b-side, 'Cold Cold Winter' (number 79 pop), was a subdued ballad. After this record, Bollinger left the group. Swisher switched to lead and recruited Bonnie Long, a friend from Hanover, to maintain the trio. The re-formed Pixies in 1964 reached the charts with 'Gee' (number 89 pop), a remake of the 1954 hit by the Crows. Following minor regional interest for 'Summertime U.S.A.' (1964), the Pixies Three broke up. Debbie Swisher was the only member of the group to continue in the music business, singing lead for the Angels from 1966-68 (she was lead on their RCA tracks). In the 90s the Pixies Three appeared at occasional reunion concerts.

● ALBUMS: *Party With The Pixies Three* (Mercury 1964)★★★.

PLATTERS

One of the leading R&B vocal groups of the 50s, they were the first black group to be accepted as a major chart act and, for a short time, were the most successful vocal group in the world. The Platters were formed in Los Angeles in 1953 by entrepreneur/songwriter Buck Ram (b. 21 November 1907, Chicago, Illinois, USA, d. 1 January 1991). Through his ownership of the Platters' name, Ram was able to control the group throughout their career, and his talent for composing and arranging enabled the Platters to make a lasting impression upon popular music. Their original line-up, Tony Williams (b. 5 April 1928, Elizabeth, New Jersey, USA, d. 14 August 1992, New York, USA; lead tenor), David Lynch (b. 1929, St. Louis, Missouri, USA, d. 2 January 1981; tenor), Alex Hodge (baritone) and Herb Reed (b. 1931, Kansas City, Missouri, USA; bass), recorded unsuccessfully in 1954, precipitating the arrival of two new members, Paul Robi (b. 1931, New Orleans, Louisiana, USA, d. 2 January 1989), who replaced Hodge, and Zola Taylor (b. 1934; contralto). Signed to Mercury Records, the Platters secured their first hit in 1955 when 'Only You' reached the US Top 5, an effortlessly light performance that set the pattern for subsequent releases, including 'The Great Pretender', 'My Prayer' and 'Twilight Time', each of which reached number 1 in the US charts. 'Smoke Gets In Your Eyes' (previously a hit for Paul Whiteman in 1934), which was an international number 1 hit single in 1958-59, highlighted their smooth delivery and arguably remains the group's best-loved release. Lead singer Williams left for a solo career in 1961, taking with him much of the Platters' distinctive style. His departure led to further changes, with Sandra Dawn and Nate Nelson replacing Taylor and Robi. With Sonny Turner as the featured voice, the group began embracing a more contemporary direction, seen in such occasional pop hits as 'I Love You 1000 Times' (1966) and 'With This Ring' (1967). During the late 60s, and for a long time afterwards, personnel changes brought much confusion as to who were the legitimate Platters. Sonny Turner and Herb Reed formed their own version, while Tony Williams did likewise. The Platters' legacy has since been undermined by the myriad of line-ups performing under that name, some of which had no tangible links to the actual group. This should not detract from those seminal recordings that bridged the gap between the harmonies of the Mills Brothers and the Ink Spots and the sweet soul of the ensuing decade. In the late 80s, Buck Ram continued to keep an eagle eye on the Platters' sold-out appearances at Las Vegas and other US cities. The group were inducted into the Rock And Roll Hall Of Fame in 1990, but Ram died the following year.

● ALBUMS: *The Platters* (Federal 1955)★★★★, also released on King as *Only You* and Mercury labels, *The Platters, Volume 2* (Mercury 1956)★★★★, *The Flying Platters* (Mercury 1957)★★★, *The Platters On Parade* (Mercury 1959)★★★, *Flying Platters Around The World* (Mercury 1959)★★★, *Remember When* (Mercury 1959)★★★, *Reflections* (Mercury 1960)★★★, *Encore Of Golden Hits* (Mercury 1960)★★★, *More Encore Of Golden Hits* (Mercury 1960)★★★, *The Platters* (Mercury 1960)★★★, *Life Is Just A Bowl Of Cherries* (Mercury 1961)★★★, *The Platters Sing For The Lonely* (Mercury 1962)★★★, *Encore Of The Golden Hits Of The Groups* (Mercury 1962)★★★, *Moonlight Memories* (Mercury 1963)★★★, *Platters Sing All The Movie Hits* (Mercury 1963)★★, *Platters Sing Latino* (Mercury 1963)★★, *Christmas With The Platters* (Mercury 1963)★★★, *New Soul Campus Style Of The Platters* (Mercury 1965)★★, *I Love You 1000 Times* (Musicor 1966)★★, *Going Back To Detroit* (Stateside 1967)★★★, *I Get The Sweetest Feeling* (1968)★★★, *Sweet Sweet Lovin'* (1968)★★, *Our Way* (Pye International 1971)★★★, *Encore Of Broadway Golden Hits* (1972)★★★, *Live* (1974)★★.

● COMPILATIONS: *The Original Platters - 20 Classic Hits* (Mercury 1978)★★★★, *Platterama* (Mercury 1982)★★★★, *The Platters: Anthology* (Rhino 1986)★★★★, *Smoke Gets In Your Eyes* (Charly 1991)★★★★, *Magic Touch: An Anthology* (Polygram 1992)★★★★, *Greatest Hits* (1993)★★★★.

● FILMS: *Carnival Rock* (1957), *Girl's Town* aka *The Innocent And The Damned* (1959).

PLAYERS

An R&B vocal group from Chicago, Illinois, USA. The original members of the group were lead Herbert Butler, Collis Gordon and John Thomas. The Players were formed in 1966 when Gordon and Thomas recruited Butler to sing lead for them on a song they had written, 'He'll Be Back', a marvellous lament about the plight of a girl whose boyfriend was fighting in the jungles of Vietnam. The trio was recorded by Calvin Carter, the long-time producer at Vee Jay Records, and signed with the west coast-based Minit subsidiary of Imperial Records. In the middle of the session Carter replaced Gordon and Thomas in the background with the veteran Dells. 'He'll Be Back' became a national hit (number 24 R&B), deservedly so, but the follow-up, 'I'm Glad I Waited' (number 32 R&B), lacking the back-up talent of the Dells and the songwriting talents of Gordon and Thomas, was a pale reflection of the previous hit. The Players made an album and toured with a new line-up of Butler, Joe Brackenridge, Otha Lee Givens and Tommie Johnson, but with no more forthcoming hits, they eventually faded.

● ALBUMS: *He'll Be Back* (Minit 1966)★★.

POINTER SISTERS

These four sisters, Anita (b. 23 January 1948), Bonnie (b. 11 July 1951, East Oakland, California, USA), Ruth (b. 1946) and June (b. 1954), were all born and raised in Oakland, California, USA, and first sang together in the West Oakland Church of God where their parents were ministers. Despite their family's reservations, Bonnie, June and Anita embarked on a secular path that culminated in work as backing singers with several of the region's acts including Cold Blood, Boz Scaggs, Elvin Bishop and Grace Slick. Ruth joined the group in 1972, a year before their self-named debut album was released. During this early period the quartet cultivated a nostalgic 40s image, where feather boas and floral dresses matched their close, Andrews Sisters-styled harmonies. Their repertoire, however, was remarkably varied and included versions of Allen Toussaint's 'Yes We Can Can' and Willie Dixon's 'Wang Dang Doodle', as well as original compositions. One such song, 'Fairytale', won a 1974 Grammy for Best Country Vocal Performance. However, the sisters were concerned that the typecast, nostalgic image was restraining them as vocalists. They broke up briefly in 1977, but while Bonnie Pointer embarked on a solo career, the remaining trio regrouped and signed with producer Richard Perry's new label, Planet. 'Fire', a crafted Bruce Springsteen composition, was a million-selling single in 1979, and the group's rebirth was complete. The Pointers' progress continued with two further gold discs, 'He's So Shy' and the sensual 'Slow Hand', while two 1984 releases, 'Jump (For My Love)' and 'Automatic', won further Grammy awards. June and Anita also recorded contemporaneous solo releases, but although 'Dare Me' gave the group another major hit in 1985, their subsequent work lacked the sparkle of their earlier achievements.

● ALBUMS: *The Pointer Sisters* (Blue Thumb 1973)★★★, *That's A Plenty* (Blue Thumb 1974)★★, *Live At The Opera House* (Blue Thumb 1974)★★, *Steppin'* (Blue Thumb 1975)★★, *Havin' A Party* (Blue Thumb 1977)★★, *Energy* (Planet 1978)★★★, *Priority* (Planet 1979)★★★, *Special Things* (Planet 1980)★★★, *Black And White* (Planet 1981)★★★, *So Excited!* (Planet 1982)★★★, *Break Out* (Planet 1983)★★★, *Contact* (RCA 1985)★★★, *Hot Together* (RCA 1986)★★, *Serious Slammin'* (RCA 1988)★★, *Right Rhythm* (Motown 1990)★★, *Only Sisters Can Do That* (1993)★★.

Solo: Anita Pointer *Love For What It Is* (RCA 1987)★★. June Pointer *Baby Sitter* (Planet 1983)★★.
● COMPILATIONS: *The Best Of The Pointer Sisters* (Blue Thumb 1976)★★★★, *Pointer Sisters' Greatest Hits* (Planet 1982)★★★, *Jump - The Best Of The Pointer Sisters* (RCA 1989)★★★★, *The Collection* (1993)★★★.

POINTER, BONNIE

b. 11 July 1951, East Oakland, California, USA. One of the four siblings who made up the successful R&B vocal group the Pointer Sisters, Bonnie Pointer was featured on two of the group's major hit singles, 'Yes We Can Can' and 'How Long', and on five albums between 1973-78. She then signed a solo contract with Motown, where she substituted a modern disco style for the 40s-influenced jazz she had recorded with her sisters. 'Free Me From My Freedom' was a major black music hit in 1978, followed a year later by a sterling rendition of the Elgins' 'Heaven Must Have Sent You'. The latter was the linchpin of *Bonnie Pointer II*, an ambitious set of revivals of classic Motown hits. Pointer's increasingly outspoken attitude towards the label's hierarchy led to her contract being cancelled in 1981. After two years of legal battles, she signed to Private I Records, where she attained a succession of minor hits in the mid-80s.
● ALBUMS: *Bonnie Pointer* (Motown 1978)★★, *Bonnie Pointer II* (Motown 1979)★★★, *If The Price Is Right* (Private I 1984)★★★.

PORTER, DAVID

b. 21 November 1941, Memphis, Tennessee, USA. Although better recalled for his partnership with Isaac Hayes, Porter had been an active, if unsuccessful, performer prior to their meeting, recording for several labels including Savoy and Hi Records. The singer was also present on several early Stax sessions. Porter first encountered his future colleague when he tried to sell Hayes life insurance, but the pair soon combined in one of the 60s soul era's most electric songwriting teams. Rightly applauded for their songs for Sam And Dave, including 'Hold On I'm Comin'', 'Soul Man' and 'When Something Is Wrong With My Baby', the duo also provided hits for Carla Thomas ('B-A-B-Y') and Johnnie Taylor ('I Had A Dream'). Their friendship was strained when Hayes secured an international bestseller with his *Hot Buttered Soul*. Porter then relaunched his solo career and in 1970 had a Top 30 US R&B hit with 'Can't See You When I Want To'. His only other chart entry came in 1972 when 'Ain't That Loving You (For More Reasons Than One)' was a minor success. Credited to 'Isaac Hayes And David Porter', it ostensibly marked the end of their collaboration.
● ALBUMS: *Gritty, Groovy And Gettin' It* (Enterprise 1970)★★, *David Porter: Into A Real Thing* (Enterprise 1971)★★, *Victim Of The Joke* (1974)★★.

PORTER, N.F.

Though Porter's name hardly ranks with the greats of the soul music tradition, he was responsible for producing one of the northern soul movement's most enduring classics. 'Keep On Keepin' On', released in 1971, featured production from Gabriel Mekler (a collaborator with Steppenwolf) and strings to sweeten its driving rhythm - exactly what was demanded by the notorious all-night dancers on the northern soul scene. Later, DJ Richard Searling persuaded Joy Division to reshape the song into 'Interzone'. The easiest access to this exclusive rarity these days is by way of the *Golden Torch Story* CD, released on Goldmine Records.

POSITIVE FORCE

This eight-piece jazz funk act was formed in Pennsylvania, USA, by Brenda Reynolds and Albert Williams. Producer Nate Edmunds discovered them and brought them to Sylvia Robinson's Sugarhill label. Edmunds produced their first single, 'We Got The Funk', which he had co-written with Reynolds and Williams. The record vanished without trace in their homeland, although it became a big club hit in the UK and spent a week in the Top 20 in 1979. Despite appearances on shows such as *Top Of The Pops* in the UK, it was to be the sole taste of success for Reynolds and the group's other vocalist, Vicki Drayton. They were, however, positive about the situation, saying that they truly enjoyed their five minutes of fame: 'For once in our lives we had been treated like someone special'. Positive Force made a brief reappearance in the UK Top 75 the following year when 'We Got The Funk' was featured in the club/disco medley hit from Calibre Cuts.

POWELL, BOBBY

b. *c*.1941. From Baton Rouge, Louisiana, Powell was a heavily gospel-influenced soul artist, who achieved modest success in the 60s and 70s recording for small southern labels. He began his career in the church and singing in gospel groups, and in 1965 began recording for Lionel Whitfield's Whit label in Shreveport, Louisiana. Powell secured his biggest success in 1965 with 'C.C. Rider' (number 1 on the *Cash Box* R&B chart), a remake of a 20s blues standard. He obtained another hit with the funky 'Do Something For Yourself' (number 21 R&B) from 1966, but his most impressive recording that year was 'I'm Gonna Leave You' (number 34 R&B), which with its stinging blues guitar and a shouting gospel chorus ranked as one of the funkiest, most down-home soul records in history. Powell achieved some regional success in 1969 with 'In Time', and reached the charts again in 1971 with a remake of Baby Washington's 'The Bells' (number 14 R&B). Beginning in the late 70s, Powell began recording for the Hep Me label, but despite some sizeable regional successes failed to reach the national charts. During the 80s he functioned as a perennial opening act in Baton Rouge - regardless of who came to town, Powell performed the opening gig. By the early 90s Powell had abandoned R&B to sing exclusively gospel music.
● ALBUMS: *Thank You* (Excello 1973)★★★, *Bobby Powell Explains The Glory Of Love* (Hep Me 1981)★★, *Down By The Riverside* (Hep Me 80s)★★.
● COMPILATIONS: *A Fool For You* (Charly 1988)★★★, *In Time* (P-Vine 1992)★★★, *Especially For You* (Ace 1993)★★★.

PRESTON, BILLY

b. 9 September 1946, Houston, Texas, USA. Preston's topsy-turvy musical career began in 1956 when he played organ with gospel singer Mahalia Jackson and appeared in the film *St Louis Blues* as a young W.C. Handy. As a teenager he worked with Sam Cooke and Little Richard, and it was during the latter's 1962 European tour that Preston first met the Beatles, with whom he would later collaborate. Preston established himself as an adept instrumentalist recording in his own right, especially on the driving 'Billy's Bag'. He also frequently appeared as a backing musician on the US television show *Shindig*. After relocating to Britain as part of the Ray Charles revue, he was signed to Apple in 1969. George Harrison produced his UK hit 'That's The Way God Planned It', and Preston also contributed keyboards to the Beatles' 'Get Back' and *Let It Be*. The following year he made a guest appearance at the Concert For Bangla Desh. He subsequently moved to A&M Records, where he had a successful run of hit singles, with 'Outa-Space' (1972), a US number 1 in 1973 with 'Will It Go Round In Circles', 'Space Race' (1973), and another US number 1 in 1974 with 'Nothing From Nothing'. His compositional talents were also in evidence on 'You Are So Beautiful', a US Top 10 hit for Joe Cocker. Preston, meanwhile, continued as a sideman, most notably with Sly And The Family Stone and on the 1975 Rolling Stones US tour. A sentimental duet with Syreeta, 'With You I'm Born Again', was an international hit in 1980. In 1989 Preston toured with Ringo Starr's All Star Band and recorded for Ian Levine's Motor City label in 1990-91, including further collaborations with Syreeta. He was arrested on a morals charge in the USA during 1991 and six years later he was sentenced to three years for a drugs possession offence.

● ALBUMS: *Gospel In My Soul* (1962)★★, *16 Year Old Soul* (Derby 1963)★★, *The Most Exciting Organ Ever* (Vee Jay 1965)★★★, *Early Hits Of 1965* (Vee Jay 1965)★★, *The Apple Of Their Eye* (1965)★★, *The Wildest Organ In Town!* (Vee Jay 1966)★★★, *That's The Way God Planned It* (Apple 1969)★★★, *Greazee Soul* (Apple 1969)★★★, *Encouraging Words* (Apple 1970)★★, *I Wrote A Simple Song* (A&M 1972)★★★, *Music Is My Life* (A&M 1972)★★★, *Everybody Likes Some Kind Of Music* (A&M 1973)★★, *The Kids & Me* (A&M 1974)★★★, *Live European Tour* (A&M 1974)★★, *It's My Pleasure* (A&M 1975)★★★, *Do What You Want* (A&M 1976)★★, *Billy Preston* (A&M 1976)★★, *A Whole New Thing* (A&M 1977)★★, *Soul'd Out* (A&M 1977)★★, with Syreeta *Fast Break* film soundtrack (Motown 1979)★★, *Late At Night* (Motown 1980)★★★, *Behold* (Myrrh 1980)★★, *Universal Love* (1980)★★, *The Way I Am* (Motown 1981)★★, with Syreeta *Billy Preston & Syreeta* (Motown 1981)★★, *Pressin' On* (Motown 1982)★★, *Billy's Back* (NuGroov 1995)★★.

● COMPILATIONS: *The Best Of Billy Preston* (A&M 1988)★★★, *Collection* (Castle 1989)★★★.

PRICE, LLOYD

b. 9 March 1933, Kenner, Louisiana, USA. Price, who launched his career in the early 50s performing rocking R&B, New Orleans-style, was - like his Crescent City compatriot Fats Domino - made for the rock 'n' roll era. He did not have to modify his approach at all to become a rock 'n' roll hitmaker in the late 50s. Price formed his own band in New Orleans in 1949 and in 1952 was signed with the Los Angeles-based Specialty Records, who made a practice of recording New Orleans artists. His first hit, 'Lawdy Miss Clawdy' (US R&B number 1, 1952), established his career in the R&B field and he followed with four more Top 10 hits. Military service intervened and took Price out of action from 1954-56. On returning to civilian life he settled in Washington, DC, and set up a record company with Harold Logan. Price regained his place on the chart in 1957 with 'Just Because' (US R&B number 3 and pop Top 30). Signed to ABC-Paramount, the company transformed their R&B veteran into a rock 'n' roll hitmaker for the new teen market. He and Logan revamped an old blues, 'Stack-O-Lee', that had been a hit for Ma Rainey in the 20s, and made it one of his biggest successes (US R&B and pop number 1, 1959). In the UK, it entered the Top 10. Price's chart career peaked in 1959, with such hits as 'Where Were You (On Our Wedding Day)' (US R&B number 4 and pop Top 30), 'Personality' (US R&B number 1 and pop number 2) and 'I'm Gonna Get Married' (US R&B number 1 and pop number 3), all of which were similarly successful in the UK. The hits continued, to a lesser extent, the following year with 'Lady Luck' (US R&B number 3 and pop Top 20) and 'Question' (US R&B number 5 and number 19 pop). Three years later Price resurfaced on the Double-L label (owned by Price and Logan), briefly making an impact on the emerging soul market with his reworking of jazz standards 'Misty' (US R&B number 11 and pop Top 30) and 'Bill Bailey' (US R&B Top 40 and pop Top 100 as 'Billy Baby'). Double-L also released Wilson Pickett's first solo sides, and in the late 60s Price began another label called Turntable for which Howard Tate, among others, recorded. Price's last chart record was in 1976 on the LPG label, a label he formed in partnership with the notorious boxing promoter Don King.

● ALBUMS: *Lloyd Price* (Specialty 1959)★★★★, *The Exciting Lloyd Price* (ABC 1959)★★★★, *Mr. Personality* (ABC 1959)★★★★, *Mr. Personality Sings The Blues* (ABC 1960)★★★★, *The Fantastic Lloyd Price* (ABC 1960)★★★, *Lloyd Price Sings The Million Sellers* (ABC 1961)★★★, *Cookin' With Lloyd Price* (ABC 1961)★★, *The Lloyd Price Orchestra* (Double L 1963)★★, *Misty* (Double L 1963)★★, *Lloyd Swings For Sammy* (Monument 1965)★★, *Lloyd Price Now* (Jad 1969)★★, *To The Roots And Back* (1972)★★, *The Nominee* (1978)★★.

● COMPILATIONS: *Mr. Personality's Big 15* (ABC 1960)★★★★, *The Best Of Lloyd Price* (1970)★★★★, *Lloyd Price's 16 Greatest Hits* (ABC 1972)★★★★, *Original Hits* (1972)★★★, *The ABC Collection* (ABC 1976)★★★★, *Mr. Personality Revisited* (Charly 1983)★★★, *Lloyd Price* (Specialty 1986)★★★, *Personality Plus* (Specialty 1986)★★★, *Walkin' The Track* (Specialty 1986)★★, *Lawdy!* (Specialty 1991)★★★, *Stagger Lee & All His Other Greatest Hits* (1993)★★★★, *Greatest Hits* (MCA 1995)★★★★.

PRIMES

Formed in Birmingham, Alabama, in 1958, the Primes comprised Eddie Kendricks (b. 17 December 1939, Union Springs, Alabama, USA, d. 5 October 1992, Alabama, USA), Paul Williams and Kel Osborn. Unable to secure a recording contract for their R&B-styled vocal group material in Alabama, the group moved to Detroit in 1959, where they became established in the black neighbourhood housing projects. They encouraged a group of female friends to form a sister group called the Primettes; however, the Primes disbanded in 1961 when Kendricks and Williams joined three members of another Detroit group, the Distants, to form the Temptations.

PRIMETTES

This US vocal group comprised Diana Ross (b. 26 March 1944, Detroit, Michigan, USA), Mary Wilson (b. 6 March 1944, Greenville, Mississippi, USA), Florence Ballard (b. 30 June 1943, Detroit, Michigan, USA, d. 22 February 1976) and Betty Travis (b. *c.*1944), and was formed in Detroit in 1959 as a sister group to the Primes (who subsequently merged with the Distants to become the Temptations). They auditioned for Berry Gordy at Motown in 1960, but he declined to sign them. Instead, they made a series of recordings for the Lu-Pine label in Detroit, most of which remained unissued until 1968. They also appeared as backing vocalists on records by Eddie Floyd, Don Revel and Gene Martin. Betty Travis was replaced in 1960 by Barbara Martin, and this line-up requested a second chance from Gordy. They were finally signed to Motown in 1961, whereupon they were renamed the Supremes.

● ALBUMS: *The Roots Of Diana Ross* (1973)★★.

PRINCE

b. Prince Rogers Nelson, 7 June 1958, Minneapolis, Minnesota, USA. A prodigiously talented singer-songwriter, multi-instrumentalist and producer, Prince was named after the Prince Roger Trio, of whom his father, John Nelson, was a member. After running away from his mother and stepfather he briefly joined up with John, who bought him his first guitar. He was later adopted by the Andersons, and became a close friend of Andre Anderson (later Andre Cymone). Prince was already conversant with piano and guitar and had written his own material from an early age. Together with Anderson he joined the latter's cousin, Charles Smith, in a junior high school band titled Grand Central. As Prince progressed to high school, Grand Central became Champagne, and he introduced original material into his sets for the first time. His musical development continued with the emergence of 'Uptown', a musical underground scene that included Flyte Time, as well as other important influences including Jellybean Johnson, Terry Lewis and Alexander O'Neal. Prince's first demos were recorded in 1976 with Chris Moon, who gave him guidance in the operation of a music studio, and free reign to experiment at weekends. Moon also introduced him to backer Owen Husney, after which Prince provided interested parties with a superior-quality demo. Husney and his partner Levinson set about a massive 'hyping' campaign, the results of which secured him a long-term, flexible contract with Warner Brothers Records after a great deal of scrambling amongst the majors.

Debuting with *Prince For You*, Prince sent shock waves through his new sponsors by spending double his entire advance on the production of a single album. It sold moderately (USA number 163), with the single 'Soft And Wet' making a big impact in the R&B charts. The album's blend of deep funk and soul was merely an appetizer in comparison to his later exploits, but enough to reassure his label that their investment had been a solid one. By 1979 Prince had put together a firm band (his debut had been recorded almost exclusively by himself). This featured Cymone (bass), Gayle Chapman and Matt Fink (both keyboards), Bobby Z (drummer) and Dez Dickerson (guitar). Despite lavishing considerably less time and money on it than its predecessor, *Prince* nevertheless charted (USA number 22) and boasted two successful singles, 'Why You Wanna Treat Me So Bad?' and 'I Wanna Be Your Lover'. A succession of live dates promoting the new album *Dirty Mind* saw Lisa Coleman replacing Chapman. The album was the first fully to embody Prince's sexual allure, and the phallic exhortations on his Fender Telecaster and explicit material such as 'Head' appalled and enticed in equal proportions. Artists such as Rick James, whom Prince supported in 1980, were among those who mistrusted Prince's open, androgynous sexuality. Returning to Minneapolis after an aborted UK tour, Cymone departed for a solo career while former members of Flyte Time and others released a self-titled album under the band name the Time. It transpired later that their songs had been written by Prince, who was the motivation behind the entire project. Prince was nothing if not prolific, and both *Controversy* and *1999* followed within 12 months. *Controversy* attempted to provide a rationale for the sexual machinations that dominated *Dirty Mind*, falling unhappily between the two stools of instinct and intellect. It was a paradox not entirely solved by *1999*, a double album that had enough strong material to make up two sides of excellence but no more. The promotional tour featured a special revue troupe: Prince And The Revolution headlined above the Time and Vanity 6 (an all-girl Prince creation). The single 'Little Red Corvette' was lifted from the album and was the first to gain significant airplay on MTV. The song was almost entirely constructed for this purpose, using a strong 'white' metaphor as leverage. After internal disputes with the Time, Prince began work on the *Purple Rain* film, a glamorized autobiographical piece in which he would star. The potent social commentary of 'When Doves Cry' was lifted from the soundtrack and became the first Prince song to grace the top of the US charts. 'Let's Go Crazy' and 'Purple Rain' (numbers 1 and 2, respectively) further established him as a figurehead for the 80s. The latter saw him turn his hand to Jimi Hendrix pyrotechnics and textures in the song. After the end of a huge and successful tour, Prince returned to the studio for a duet with Apollonia, the latest in a seemingly endless succession of female protégées. He also found time to revitalize the career of Scottish pop singer Sheena Easton by composing her US Top 10 effort 'Sugar Walls'. When *Around The World In A Day* emerged in 1985 it topped the US charts for a three-week run, despite a deliberate lack of promotion. Drowning in quasi-psychedelia and 60s optimism, it was a diverting but strangely uneventful, almost frivolous, jaunt. It preceded the announcement that Prince was retiring from live appearances. Instead, he had founded the studio/label/complex Paisley Park in central Minneapolis, which would become the luxurious base for his future operations. As work began on a second movie, *Under The Cherry Moon*, 'Kiss' was released to become his third US number 1. Held one place beneath it was the Bangles' 'Manic Monday', written by Prince under one of his numerous pseudonyms, in this case, Christopher.

He quickly overturned his decision not to perform live, and set out on the *Parade* tour to promote the number 1 album of the same name. Unfortunately, although 'Kiss' and 'Girls And Boys' represented classic Prince innuendo, the rest of the album lacked focus. The shows, however, were spectacular even by Prince standards, but his backing band the Revolution were nevertheless disbanded at the end of the tour. In 1987 Prince instituted a new line-up for the latest live engagements. While retaining the backbone of the Revolution (Fink, Leeds, Brooks and Safford) he added Sheila E, Marco Weaver, and Seacer. The new album was to be a radical departure from the laconic, cosseted atmosphere that pervaded *Parade*. 'Sign 'O' The Times', the title track, was a hard-hitting testimony to urban dystopia, drug-related violence and human folly. The vast majority of tracks on the double album revisited the favoured territory of sex and sensuality. The follow-up album would elaborate on the darker shades of *Sign 'O' The Times*' apocalyptic vision. However, the *Black Album* was recalled by Prince before it reached the shops. Combining primal funk slices with sadistic overtones, Prince's decision to suspend it ensured that it would become the 80s' most coveted bootleg. The mythology surrounding its non-release has it that the *Black Album* was the work of Prince's 'dark' side - 'Spooky Electric'. This was given credence by the subsequent *Lovesexy*, apparently the result of the pre-eminence of 'Camille' - Prince's 'good' side. Playing both albums side by side certainly reveals a sharp dichotomy of approach. His next tour, meanwhile, saw the inclusion of a huge Pink Cadillac as a mobile part of the set. Exhausted musicians testified to the difficulty of backing their leader, rushing from orchestrated stadium performances to private club dates where entire sets would be improvised, all of which Prince, naturally, took in his stride. 1989 closed with a duet with Madonna, who, alongside Michael Jackson, was the only artist able to compete with Prince in terms of mass popularity. The following year was dominated by the soundtrack album for the year's biggest film, *Batman*. If the album was not his greatest artistic success, it proved a commercial smash, topping the US charts for six weeks. He had also written and produced an album for singer Mavis Staples. At first glance it seemed an unlikely combination, but Prince's lyrics tempered the sexual with the divine in a manner that was judged acceptable by the grand lady of gospel. In February 1990 Sinead O'Connor recorded a version of Prince's composition 'Nothing Compares 2 U', which topped both the US and UK charts. In September 1990 he released *Graffiti Bridge*, which accompanied a film release of the same title. The album was composed entirely of Prince compositions of which he sang just over half - other guests included Tevin Campbell, Mavis Staples and the Time. Both album and film were critical and commercial failures, however. *Graffiti Bridge* was his first commercial let-down for some time, peaking at number 6 in the USA (although it made number 1 in the UK). Prince, as usual, was already busy putting together new projects. These included his latest backing outfit, the New Power Generation, featuring Tony M (rapper), Rosie Gaines (vocals), Michael Bland (drums), Levi Seacer (guitar), Kirk Johnson (guitar), Sonny T (bass) and Tommy Barbarella (keyboards). They were in place in time for the sessions for *Diamonds And Pearls*, a comparatively deliberate and studied body of work. The album was released in October 1991, and showcased the new backing band. Greeted by most critics as a return to form, the New Power Generation were considered his most able and vibrant collaborators since the mid-80s. Taken from it, 'Cream' became a US number 1. 1992's 'Money Don't Matter 2 Night' featured a video directed by film-maker Spike Lee, while 'Sexy MF' was widely banned on UK radio because of its suggestive lyrics. Both 'Sexy MF' and 'My Name Is Prince' were included on the *Love Symbol Album* - which introduced the cryptic 'symbol' that he would legally adopt as his name in June 1993. Much of the attention subsequently surrounding the artist concerned his protracted battle against his record company, Warner Brothers. His behaviour became increasingly erratic - speaking only through envoys, he appeared at the 1995 BRIT Awards ceremony with the word 'slave' written across his forehead as a protest. In October he abandoned the symbol moniker and from that point was known as 'The Artist Formerly Known As Prince'. Naturally, this produced enough running gags to fill a book and his credibility was in serious danger. In 1995 he released *The Gold Experience*, a return to the raunchy funk of his 80s prime in tracks such as 'Pussy Control' and 'I Hate You'. It also included the smoothly accessible 'The Most Beautiful Girl In The World', his bestselling single for many years. Following the release of *Chaos And Disorder* in July 1996, he sacked the New Power Generation and announced that he would not be touring, preferring to spend more time with his wife and new baby (who tragically died months after birth). He celebrated his release from the Warner Brothers contract with the sprawling *Emancipation*.

Although 'The Artist Formerly Known As Prince' has yet to provide the definitive album of which he is so obviously capable, the continued flow of erratic, flawed gems suggests that the struggle will continue to captivate his audience through the 90s. It it universally hoped that he reverts to his real name.

● ALBUMS: *Prince - For You* (Warners 1978)★★★, *Prince* (Warners 1979)★★★, *Dirty Mind* (Warners 1980)★★★, *Controversy* (Warners 1981)★★★, *1999* (Warners 1982)★★★★, *Purple Rain* film soundtrack (Warners

1984)★★★★, *Around The World In A Day* (Paisley Park 1985)★★★, *Parade - Music From Under The Cherry Moon* film soundtrack (Paisley Park 1986)★★★, *Sign 'O' The Times* (Paisley Park 1987)★★★★, *Lovesexy* (Paisley Park 1988)★★★, *Batman* film soundtrack (Warners 1989)★★★, *Graffiti Bridge* (Paisley Park 1990)★★, *Diamonds And Pearls* (Paisley Park 1991)★★★, *Symbol* (Paisley Park 1993)★★★, *Come* (Paisley Park 1994)★★, *The Gold Experience* (Warners 1995)★★★, *Chaos And Disorder* (Warners 1996)★★, *Emancipation* (New Power Generation 1996)★★.

● COMPILATIONS: *The Hits: Volume I & II* (Paisley Park/Warners 1993)★★★★.

● VIDEOS: *Double Live* (Polygram 1986), *Prince And The Revolution; Live* (Channel 5 1987), *Sign O' The Times* (Palace Video 1988), *Lovesexy Part 1* (Palace Video 1989), *Lovesexy Part 2* (Palace Video 1989), *Get Off* (Warner Music Video 1991), *Prince: The Hits Collection* (1993), *3 Chains O' Gold* (Warner Reprise 1994), *Billboards* (Warner Vision 1994).

● FURTHER READING: *Prince: Imp Of The Perverse*, Barney Hoskyns. *Prince: A Pop Life*, Dave Hill. *Prince By Controversy*, The 'Controversy' Team. *Prince: A Documentary*, Per Nilsen. *Prince: An Illustrated Biography*, John W. Duffy. *Prince*, John Ewing.

Prince La La

b. Lawrence Nelson. The brother of Walter 'Papoose' Nelson, a respected session musician, this New Orleans-based singer/guitarist was signed to AFO ('All For One'), a local label owned by Harold Battiste. The Prince enjoyed a US R&B Top 30 hit with 'She Put The Hurt On Me' (1961), an enchanting slice of classic Crescent City backbeat, originally intended for singer Barbara George. It was later recorded by the Spencer Davis Group. Prince La La's promising career was tragically cut short when he was murdered shortly after the release of his second single. Through the legacy of his music, he nevertheless remained an influential figure and his voodoo, 'night-tripper' persona was later adopted by Dr. John.

Prisonaires

As their name suggests, this doo-wop group were formed in 1940 while each member was in the State Penitentiary, Tennessee, USA. The founding member was second tenor Ed Thurman, and he took on Johnny Bragg (lead), John Drue (first tenor), William Stuart (baritone and guitar) and Marcell Sanders (bass). The group was paraded around a variety of receptions and civic functions as demonstration of the jail's enlightened rehabilitation programme, where they played a mix of blues, gospel and pop songs under armed guard. Edwards then arranged for two talent scouts from Sam Phillips' Sun Records to see the group. They were subsequently driven down to Memphis in June 1953 to record a song written by Bragg and fellow inmate Robert Riley, 'Just Walkin' In The Rain'. The record took hold first on radio and then became a major seller, moving over 250,000 copies, despite a competing version from Johnny Ray that sold eight times that amount. Still, the Prisonaires had arrived, and found themselves in demand for a series of television and concert appearances. They gradually became high-status figures in Tennessee, and never betrayed the trust placed in them by trying to escape their guards on their numerous forays outside the prison (on one occasion they were said to have lost their escorts but nevertheless travelled back to the prison under their own guidance). A second single followed in August 1953, the highly spiritual 'My God Is Real', followed by 'I Know' and its autobiographical b-side, 'A Prisoner's Prayer'. While recording it they made the acquaintance of Elvis Presley, who later visited them in prison. By now some of his colleagues had become eligible for parole, so Bragg formed a new version of the band titled the Sunbeams with Hal Hebb, Willy Wilson, Al Brooks and Henry 'Dishrag' Jones. This group lasted only until 1955, when the group was retitled the Marigolds and scored a number 8 R&B chart success with 'Rollin' Stone'. However, by 1956 Bragg had been released and he recorded a series of singles under his own name for Decca Records. He was then arrested for 'parole violation' in 1960 when found in the back seat of a car with a white woman (his wife). His penalty was to return to prison for an incredible six and a half years. Despite this second injustice, Bragg put together another version of the Prisonaires with new inmates, but they never recorded again. On release, he worked in a cemetery.

● COMPILATIONS: *Five Beats Behind Bars* (Charly 1978)★★★.

Professor Longhair

b. Henry Roeland Byrd, 19 December 1918, Bogalusa, Louisiana, USA, d. 30 January 1980. Byrd grew up in New Orleans where he was part of a novelty dance team in the 30s. He also played piano, accompanying John Lee 'Sonny Boy' Williamson. After wartime service, Byrd gained a residency at the Caldonia club, whose owner christened him Professor Longhair. By now, he had developed a piano style that combined rumba and mambo elements with more standard boogie-woogie and barrelhouse rhythms. Particularly through his most ardent disciple, Dr John, Longhair has become recognized as the most influential New Orleans R&B pianist since Jelly Roll Morton. In 1949 he made the first record of his most famous tune, 'Mardi Gras In New Orleans', for the Star Talent label, which credited the artist as Professor Longhair And His Shuffling Hungarians. He next recorded 'Baldhead' for Mercury as Roy Byrd and his Blues Jumpers and the song became a national R&B hit in 1950. Soon there were more singles on Atlantic (a new version of 'Mardi Gras' and the well-known 'Tipitina' in 1953) and Federal. A mild stroke interrupted his career in the mid-50s and for some years he performed infrequently apart from at Carnival season when a third version of his topical song, 'Go To The Mardi Gras' (1958), received extensive radio play. Despite recording Earl King's 'Big Chief' in 1964, Longhair was virtually inactive throughout the 60s. He returned to the limelight at the first New Orleans Jazz & Heritage Festival in 1971 when, accompanied by Snooks Eaglin, he received standing ovations. (A recording of the concert was finally issued in 1987.) This led to European tours in 1973 and 1975 and to recordings with Gatemouth Brown and for Harvest. Longhair's final album, for Alligator, was completed shortly before he died of a heart attack in January 1980. In 1991 he was posthumously inducted into the Rock And Roll Hall Of Fame.

● ALBUMS: *New Orleans Piano* reissue (Atco 1972)★★★★, *Rock 'N' Roll Gumbo* (1974)★★★★, *Live On The Queen Mary* (Harvest 1978)★★★, *Crawfish Fiesta* (Alligator 1980)★★★, *The London Concert* (JSP 1981)★★★, *The Last Mardi Gras* (Atlantic 1982)★★★★, *Houseparty New Orleans Style (The Lost Sessions 1971-1972)* (Rounder 1987)★★★, *Live In Germany* (1993)★★★, *Go To The Mardi Gras* (Wolf 1997)★★★.

● COMPILATIONS: *Fess: The Professor Longhair Anthology* (Rhino 1994)★★★★.

● FURTHER READING: *A Bio-discography*, John Crosby.

PURIFY, JAMES AND BOBBY

Formed in 1965, this high-powered soul duo consisted of James Purify (b. 12 May 1944, Pensacola, Florida, USA) and Robert Lee Dickey (b. 2 September 1939, Tallahassee, Florida, USA). Unfairly tarnished as a surrogate Sam And Dave, the duo's less frenetic style was nonetheless captivating. During the early 60s Dickey worked as a singer/guitarist in the Dothan Sextet, a group fronted by Mighty Sam McClain. When Florida disc jockey 'Papa' Don Schroeder offered Sam a solo career, Dickey introduced his cousin, James Purify, as a replacement. Their onstage duets became so popular that Schroeder added them to his fast-growing roster. Their first single, 'I'm Your Puppet', was recorded at Fame in Muscle Shoals and released on Bell. Written by Dan Penn and Spooner Oldham, this simple, poignant ballad became the duo's only US Top 10 hit in September 1966. Rather than follow their own path, the cousins were tempted towards cover versions including 'Shake A Tail Feather' and 'I Take What I Want'. In spite of the undoubted quality of these releases, many critics dubbed them 'contrived'. In 1967 'Let Love Come Between Us' became their last US Top 30 hit, although several strong records followed. When Dickey retired in 1970 James found another 'Bobby' in Ben Moore and it was this new combination that secured a 1976 British hit with a remake of 'I'm Your Puppet'. Unable to sustain this rejuvenation, the duo parted, although Moore resurfaced in 1979 with a solo album, *Purified*. The pick of the original duo's Bell recordings can be found on *100% Purified Soul*.

● ALBUMS: *James And Bobby Purify* (Bell 1967)★★★, *The Pure Sound Of The Purifys* (Bell 1968)★★★, *You And Me Together Forever* (Casablanca 1978)★★.

● COMPILATIONS: *100% Purified Soul* (Charly 1988)★★★★.

Q-TIPS

Fronted by Paul Young (b. 17 January 1956, Luton, Bedfordshire, England), Q-Tips was one of the most renowned live bands on the UK club circuit in the early 80s, playing an estimated 800 gigs in under three years. The group was formed in 1979 by Young and other ex-members of Streetband, John Gifford (guitar, vocals) and Mick Pearl (bass, vocals). In place of their former band's rock sound, Q-Tips was organized as a classic soul group with an experienced brass section of Tony Hughes (trumpet) and saxophonists Steve Farr and Stewart Blandamer (both ex-Johnny Wakelin's Kinshasa Band, Jimmy James And The Vagabonds and the Flirtations). Other members were Barry Watts (drums) and Ian Kewley (keyboards) from Samson and latterly hard rock band Limey. With matching suits and arrangements out of the Tamla/Motown and Stax songbooks, Q-Tips were seen as part of a mod revival. After releasing a frantic version of Joe Tex's 'SYSLJFM (The Letter Song)' on the Shotgun label, the group signed to Chrysalis Records and covered the Miracles' 'Tracks Of My Tears'. By this time, Clifford had been replaced by Garth Watt-Roy (ex-Greatest Show On Earth, Fuzzy Duck, Marmalade and Limey). The debut album included Blandamer originals such as 'A Man Can't Lose' as well as cover versions, but its lack of sales led to Chrysalis dropping the band. The group then signed to Rewind Records, who chose a version of Boudleaux Bryant's 'Love Hurts' as a single. Although this failed to sell, it brought Young to the notice of CBS Records, who signed him as a solo artist at the start of 1982. The Q-Tips disbanded after a farewell tour and the release of a live album. *Live At Last* included 'Broken Man', the first song co-written by Young and Kewley, who continued their partnership during the first phase of the Young's triumphant solo career.

● ALBUMS: *Q-Tips* (Chrysalis 1980)★★★, *Live At Last* (Rewind 1982)★★★, *BBC Radio 1 Live In Concert* (Windsong 1991)★★.

QUEST, J.

b. *c.*1967, New York, USA. J. Quest began singing in public at the age of 10 when he toured the USA as soloist with the New York Boys' Choir. In 1993, he met Lisa Lisa while in the studio with his manager and through her he was introduced to the producer Junior Vasquez, who asked Quest to sing on several tracks he was working on, two of which later appeared on his debut album ('Brand New Luv' and 'Behind The Scenes'). On *The Quest Is On*

Quest also sang with Pudgee The Phat Bastard (the first US single, 'Anything') and Ill Al Skratch ('Up And Down'). The latter was a remix of a song that had originally appeared on the soundtrack to the film *Jason's Lyric*. The music combined urban hip-hop with R&B in a manner most readily reminiscent of R. Kelly.

● ALBUMS: *The Quest Is On* (Mercury 1995)★★★.

Quin-Tones

Formed in 1957 in Philadelphia, Pennsylvania, USA, the Quin-Tones were a doo-wop sextet (five vocalists and a pianist) with one Top 20 single to its name, 1958's 'Down The Aisle Of Love'. The group consisted of Roberta Haymon (lead) and Phyllis Carr, Jeannie Crist, Carolyn Holmes and Kenny Sexton, plus Ronnie Scott (piano), who also arranged their material. Originally called the Quinteros, they were taken under the wing of disc jockey Paul Landersman, who secured the group a recording contract under their new name Quin-Tones (the hyphen was to avoid confusion with another Quintones group), with Chess Records. Their debut, 1958's 'Ding Dong', did not attract attention, and neither did the follow-up, 'Down The Aisle Of Love', on Red Top. However, after Dick Clark aired the song on *American Bandstand* and agreed to purchase the song's publishing rights, it was re-released on Hunt Records. This time it sold, giving the group its one taste of success. The group disbanded in 1960.

● COMPILATIONS: *There's Gonna Be Joy* (1993)★★★.

Radiants

An R&B vocal group from Chicago, Illinois, USA, the Radiants were a typical transitional group of the early 60s, bringing doo-wop harmonies into the soul era with gospel-inspired vocal treatments. The group began in 1960 when Maurice McAlister (b. 11 January 1940, Mississippi, USA) distilled a vocal group from members of the Greater Harvest Baptist Church choir. The original group besides McAlister (lead) were Wallace Sampson (baritone), Jerome Brooks (second tenor), Elzie Butler (bass) and Green McLauren (first tenor), and their first hit (and record) for Chess Records was the Miracles-styled 'Father Knows Best' (1962), but the superior b-side, 'One Day I'll Show You', received much regional play. 'Heartbreak Society' and 'Shy Guy', both 1963, failed to generate sales outside the Chicago area, and the group reorganized as a trio - McAlister, Sampson and Leonard Caston Jnr. The trio format introduced a unique pronounced switch-off lead style, in which the vocal interplay worked as a constant flux of voices slipping in and out of the musical mix, most evident on 'Voice Your Choice' (number 16 R&B), from 1964, and 'It Ain't No Big Thing' (number 14 R&B), from 1965. Another reorganization took place in 1965, in which McAlister left the group, and the Radiants then had a hit with 'Feel Kind Of Bad' (number 47 R&B); after yet another reorganization, they secured a hit with 'Hold On' (number 35 R&B). The Radiants broke up in 1972. In 1966, meanwhile, McAlister and McLauren formed a duo, Maurice And Mac, who, recording in Muscle Shoals, Alabama, achieved several southern R&B hits, notably with 'You Left The Water Running' (number 43 R&B) in 1968.

Raelettes

This vocal group was formed in the USA around Margie Hendrix, and was previously known as the Cookies, whose R&B backing voices appeared on numerous 50s sessions and inspired the new group's inception. Founded to provide responsive vocals for singer Ray Charles, this female trio provided the launching pad for several careers. Merry Clayton, Mable John, Minnie Riperton, Clydie King and Estella Yarbrough were all members at some point, although Hendrix provided a long-serving consistency. The Raelettes did have several minor hits via Charles's Tangerine label, but their constantly changing personnel denied them a more constructive recording career. Hendrix, however, who had had early solo exposure on the Lamp label, also recorded on her own in the 60s, for Tangerine, Mercury and Sound Stage 7.

● ALBUMS: *Souled Out* (Tangerine 1969)★★★, *Yesterday, Today And Tomorrow* (Tangerine 1972)★★.

● FILMS: *Blues for Lovers* aka *Ballad In Blue* (1964).

Ragovoy, Jerry

b. 4 September 1930, Philadelphia, Pennsylvania, USA. Ragovoy's career as a songwriter and producer began in the doo-wop era of the early 50s. His first successful act was the Castelles, who had a hit with 'My Girl Awaits Me' in 1953. In 1959 he began a partnership with entrepreneur Bill Fox that resulted in several collaborations with the Majors, one of the latter's successful acts. Ragovoy produced several of the group's releases, including the US Top 30 hit 'A Wonderful Dream', co-writing them under the pseudonym 'Norman Meade'. This appellation also appeared on 'Time Is On My Side', recorded by Irma Thomas in 1964 and later revived successfully by the Rolling Stones. Ragovoy also enjoyed a fruitful partnership with fellow black music producer Bert Berns and together the duo guided the career of deep soul singer Garnet Mimms. In 1966 Ragovoy wrote and produced 'Stay With Me Baby' for Lorraine Ellison, one of the decade's most compulsive vocal performances, before supervising a series of excellent releases by Howard Tate. His anthem-like recording, 'Get It While You Can', was later adopted by Janis Joplin, who covered several Ragovoy compositions including 'Piece Of My Heart', originally written for Erma Franklin. In the mid-60s he also became east coast A&R chief for Warner Brothers' then recently formed soul subsidiary Loma, where he wrote songs for and produced artists including the Olympics, the Enchanters (ex-Garnet Mimms), Carl Hall, Lonnie Youngblood, Roy Redmond, Ben Aiken and (once again) Lorraine Ellison. In 1973 Ragovoy formed his own Rags production company and leased product to Epic, most notably that by Howard Tate and Lou Courtney, the latter's *I'm In Need Of Love*. In the late 70s/early 80s, Ragovoy began writing for and producing artists as diverse as Bonnie Raitt, Dionne Warwick, Essra Mohawk, Major Harris and Peggi Blu. In 1988 he produced some songs for Irma Thomas's album that year for Rounder and his name still apears occasionally on the credits of songs performed by many different artists. In his book *Off The Record*, Joe Smith (ex-Warner President and then President of Capitol/EMI) gave Ragovoy's major contribution to soul music long overdue recognition when he said: 'You might not know him but he produced and wrote some of the best rhythm and blues of the sixties - and he's not black - he's a man with a sense of soul.'

RAINBOWS

R&B vocal group the Rainbows were formed in the early 50s in Washington, DC, USA, by John Berry (lead and second tenor), Ronald 'Poosie' Miles (lead and second tenor), Henry 'Shorty' Womble (first tenor; ex-Serenaders), James 'Sally' Nolan (baritone) and Frank 'Jake' Hardy (bass; also ex-Serenaders). They were signed by Bobby Robinson of Red Robin Records in 1955 after unsuccessfully auditioning a year earlier. 'Mary Lee', their debut, followed in June, and proved popular both in New York and Boston (where it was licensed to Pilgrim Records). After a young Marvin Gaye and soul star Billy Stewart had sung with the group, Henry Womble's impending college career meant the group had a vacancy; it was filled by two new members, Don Covay and Chester Simmons. However, only two further Rainbows singles emerged. 'Shirley' and 'Minnie' continued their use of female names as titles. By 1957 the group had broken up, allowing Nolan and Simmons to join with Gaye and Reese Palmer to form the Marquees before becoming the new Moonglows. A new Rainbows was formed in 1961 with Miles now joined by Duval Potter (tenor), Joe Walls (tenor), Layton McDonald (baritone) and Victor English (bass). Two singles were released in 1963, 'I Know' and 'It Wouldn't Be Right'. Neither charted and the group folded once more with members scattering in various directions. Covay became a major songwriting talent. Simmons worked for the Reflection Sound studio before joining Reese in 70s group Choice Of Color. The other members retired from the music industry.

RARE EARTH

Saxophonist Gil Bridges and drummer Pete Rivera (Hoorelbeke) formed their first R&B band, the Sunliners, in Detroit in 1961. Bassist John Parrish joined in 1962; guitarist Rod Richards and keyboards player Kenny James followed in 1966. Other members included Ralph Terrana (keyboards), Russ Terrana (guitar) and Fred Saxon (saxophone). After years of playing in local clubs and releasing unspectacular records on MGM, Hercules and Golden World, they were signed to Verve Records and released *Dreams And Answers*. They signed to Motown Records in 1969, where they had the honour of having a newly formed progressive rock label named after them (following their hopeful suggestion to Motown executives). Rare Earth Records enjoyed an immediate success with a rock-flavoured version of the Temptations' hit 'Get Ready', which reached the US Top 10. The single was edited down from a 20-minute recording that occupied one side of their debut Motown album; it showcased the band's instrumental prowess, but also typified their tendency towards artistic excess. A cover version of another Temptations' classic, '(I Know) I'm Losing You', brought them more success in 1970, as did original material such as 'Born To Wander' and 'I Just Want To Celebrate'. The band had already suffered the first in a bewildering series of personnel changes that dogged their progress over the next decade, as Rod Richards and Kenny James were replaced by Ray Monette and Mark Olson, respectively, and Ed Guzman (b. *c*.1944, d. 29 July 1993) was added on percussion. This line-up had several minor US hits in the early 70s, until internal upheavals in 1973 led to a complete revamp of the band's style. The Temptations' mentor, Norman Whitfield, produced the highly regarded *Ma* that year. By the release of *Back To Earth* in 1975, he in turn had been supplanted by Jerry La Croix. Subsequent releases proved commercially unsuccessful, though the band continued to record and tour into the 80s. Former members Pete Rivera (Hoorelbeke) and Michael Urso later combined with Motown writer/producer Tom Baird as Hub for two albums on Capitol Records, *Hub* and *Cheeta*. At the turn of the decade the line-up comprised Gil Bridges, Ray Monette, Edward Guzman, Wayne Baraks, Rick Warner, Dean Boucher and Randy Burghdoff. They joined Ian Levine's Motor City label in 1990 and issued 'Playing To Win' and 'Love Is Here And Now You've Gone'. During the mid-90s Pete Hoorelbeke/Rivera was playing with the Classic Rock All Stars, a band that comprised Spencer Davis, Mike Pinera (ex-Blues Image and Iron Butterfly) and Jerry Corbetta (Sugarloaf).

● ALBUMS: *Dreams And Answers* (Verve 1968)★★★, *Get Ready* (Rare Earth 1969)★★★, *Ecology* (Rare Earth 1970)★★★, *One World* (Rare Earth 1971)★★★, *Rare Earth In Concert* (Rare Earth 1971)★★, *Willie Remembers* (Rare Earth 1972)★★★, *Ma* (Rare Earth 1973)★★★, *Back To Earth* (Rare Earth 1975)★★★, *Midnight Lady* (Rare Earth 1976)★★, *Rare Earth* (Prodigal 1977)★★, *Band Together* (Prodigal 1978)★★, *Grand Slam* (Prodigal 1978)★★, *Made In Switzerland* (Line 1989)★★, *Different World* (Koch 1993)★★.

● COMPILATIONS: *The Best Of Rare Earth* (Rare Earth 1972)★★★, *Rare Earth: Superstars Series* (Motown 1981)★★★, *Greatest Hits And Rare Classics* (Motown 1991)★★★, *Earth Tones: The Essential Rare Earth* (Motown 1994)★★★, *Anthology* (Motown 1995)★★★.

RAVENS

An African-American vocal group from New York City, New York, USA. Formed in 1945, the Ravens are considered the first of the 'bird groups' and their success was highly influential in ushering in an avalanche of vocal groups in the post-World War II R&B revolution. The original members were Ollie Jones (tenor), Leonard Puzey (tenor), Warren Suttles (baritone) and Jimmy Ricks (bass). After Maithe Marshall replaced Jones in 1946, the Ravens featured two leads, Ricks, who used his outstanding bass with terrific rhythmic bounce on the mid-tempo tunes, and Marshall, whose soaring falsetto tenor lent great poignancy to the ballads. The group also used with great effectiveness the switchover lead between Marshall and Ricks, which gave the Ravens a unique sound until it was widely imitated by other vocal ensembles. The Ravens first recorded for the Hub label in 1946, but only after they signed with National did they reach the charts, with the Ricks-led 'Write Me A Letter' (number 5 R&B) in 1948. Memorable recordings by the group at this time also included the Marshall-led songs 'September Song' and 'Searching For Love'. Their 1948 hit versions of 'Silent Night' (number 8 R&B) and 'White Christmas' (number 9 R&B) paved the way for later R&B vocal groups to interpret Christmas standards with an R&B flavour (the Ravens' vocal arrangement of 'White Christmas' was lifted for Clyde McPhatter And The Drifters' version from 1955). The Ravens' last chart record was in 1952 on Mercury with 'Rock Me All Night Long' (number 4 R&B). The group's last notable recording was 'Give Me A Simple Pray' in 1955 on the Argo label. With Ricks' departure for a solo career in 1956 the group faded from the scene.

● COMPILATIONS: *The Ravens* (Harlem Hit Parade 1973)★★★, *The Greatest Group Of Them All* (Savoy 1978)★★★★, *Old Man River* (Savoy Jazz 1985)★★★.

RAWLS, LOU

b. 1 December 1935, Chicago, Illinois, USA. Briefly a member of the acclaimed gospel group the Pilgrim Travellers, this distinctive singer began forging a secular career following his move to California in 1958. An association with Sam Cooke culminated in 'Bring It On Home To Me', where Rawls' throaty counterpoint punctuated his colleague's sweet lead vocal. Rawls' own recordings showed him comfortable with either small jazz combos or cultured soul, while an earthier perspective was shown on his 1965 release, *Live!*. He achieved two Top 20 singles with 'Love Is A Hurtin' Thing' (1966) and 'Dead End Street' (1967), and enjoyed further success with a 1969 reading of Mable John's 'Your Good Thing (Is About To End)'. Several attempts were made to mould Rawls into an all-round entertainer, but while his early 70s work was generally less compulsive, the singer's arrival at Philadelphia International signalled a dramatic rebirth. 'You'll Never Find Another Love Like Mine', an international hit in 1976, matched the classic Philly sound with Rawls' resonant delivery, and prepared the way for a series of exemplary releases including 'See You When I Git There' (1977) and 'Let Me Be Good To You' (1979). The singer maintained his association with producers Gamble And Huff into the next decade. His last chart entry, 'I Wish You Belonged to Me', came in 1987 on the duo's self-named label, since which time he has recorded for the jazz outlet Blue Note. Rawls has also pursued an acting career and provided the voice for several Budweiser beer commercials.

● ALBUMS: *Lou Rawls Sings, Les McCann Ltd Plays Stormy Monday* (1962)★★★, *Black And Blue* (Capitol 1963)★★★, *Tobacco Road* (Capitol 1963)★★★, *Nobody But Lou Rawls* (Capitol 1965)★★★, *Lou Rawls And Strings* (Capitol 1965)★★, *Lou Rawls Live!* (Capitol 1966)★★★, *Lou Rawls Soulin'* (Capitol 1966)★★★, *Lou Rawls Carryin' On!* (Capitol 1967)★★★, *Too Much!* (Capitol 1967)★★★, *That's Lou* (Capitol 1967)★★★, *Merry Christmas Ho! Ho! Ho!* (Capitol 1967)★, *Feeling Good* (Capitol 1968)★★★, *You're Good For Me* (Capitol 1968)★★★, *The Way It Was - The Way It Is* (Capitol 1969)★★★, *Close-Up* (Capitol 1969)★★★, *Your Good Thing* (Capitol 1969)★★★, *You've Made Me So Very Happy* (Capitol 1970)★★, *Bring It On Home To Me* (1970)★★★, *Natural Man* (MGM 1971)★★, *Silk And Soul* (MGM 1972)★★, *All Things In Time* (Philadelphia International 1976)★★★, *Unmistakably Lou* (Philadelphia International 1977)★★★★, *When You Hear Lou, You've Heard It All* (Philadelphia International 1977)★★★★, *Lou Rawls Live* (Philadelphia International 1978)★★★, *Let Me Be Good To You* (Philadelphia International 1979)★★★★, *Sit Down And Talk To Me* (Philadelphia International 1980)★★★, *Shades Of Blue* (Philadelphia International 1981)★★★, *Now Is The Time* (Portrait 1982)★★★, *When The Night Comes* (Epic 1983)★★★, *Close Company* (Epic 1984)★★★, *Love All Your Blues Away* (Epic 1986)★★★, *At Last* (Blue Note 1989)★★★, *Portrait Of The Blues* (1992)★★★.

● COMPILATIONS: *The Best Of Lou Rawls: The Capitol/Blue Note Years* (Capitol 1968)★★★, *Soul Serenade* (Stateside 1985)★★★, *Stormy Monday* (See For Miles 1985)★★★, *Classic Soul* (Blue Moon 1986)★★★, *Greatest Hits* (Curb 1990)★★★, *Greatest Hits In Concert* (1993)★★★, *For You My Love* (1994)★★★, *The Philly Years* (Repertoire 1995)★★★★.

RAY, GOODMAN AND BROWN

Al Goodman (b. 31 March 1947, Jackson, Mississippi, USA), Harry Ray (b. 15 December 1946, Longbranch, New Jersey, USA; d. 1 October 1992) and William Brown (b. 30 June 1946, Perth Amboy, New Jersey, USA). This smooth soul trio had 27 R&B hits as the Moments. While waiting for the outcome of legal wranglings with Sylvia Robinson's Stang Records, they recorded backing vocals on two successful Millie Jackson albums. When it was decided that Stang owned the name the Moments, the trio joined Polydor in 1979 under their own surnames. Their first single, their own composition, 'Special Lady', reached the US Top 5 and their debut album, which they co-produced with Vince Castellano, made the Top 20. *Ray, Goodman & Brown II* made the US Top 100 and their revival of the Platters' 'My Prayer' narrowly missed the Top 40. Ray left in 1982 and made an unsuccessful solo album on Sylvia Robinson's Sugar Hill label. He rejoined the trio in 1983 and they had some success with Panoramic Records. In 1986 they signed to EMI America when they had their last R&B Top 10 hit with 'Take It To The Limit'.

● ALBUMS: *Ray, Goodman & Brown* (Polydor 1980)★★★, *Ray, Goodman & Brown II* (Polydor 1980)★★★, *Stay* (Polydor 1982)★★.

Ray, Johnnie

b. 10 January 1927, Dallas, Oregon, USA, d. 24 February 1990, Los Angeles, California, USA. Known at various times in his career as the Prince of Wails, the Nabob of Sob and the Howling Success because of his highly emotional singing and apparent ability to cry at will, Ray is rated an important influence in the development of 50s and early 60s popular music. Of North American Indian origin, he became deaf in his right ear at the age of 12, which caused him to wear a hearing-aid throughout his career. He was heavily influenced by gospel and R&B music and performed in bars and clubs around Detroit in the late 40s, singing to his own piano accompaniment. Signed by Columbia Records in 1951, his first two releases were on their small OKeh label, usually reserved for black artists. His first record, 'Whiskey And Gin', was followed by 'Cry'. Unsophisticated, full of anguish, despair and a good deal of sobbing, it shocked a pop world accustomed to male singers crooning in front of big bands, and streaked to the top of the US charts, complete with Ray's own composition, 'The Little White Cloud That Cried', on the b-side. 'Cry' became his 'identity' song, and a multi-million-seller.

Ray was then transferred to the Columbia label, and during the next couple of years, he had several massive US hits including 'Please Mr Sun', 'Here Am I - Broken Hearted', 'Walkin' My Baby Back Home' and 'Somebody Stole My Gal'. His stage performances, with their overt sexuality and hysterical audience reaction, made him *persona non grata* to parents of teenagers worldwide. For a few years during the 50s, he enjoyed phenomenal success, revolutionizing popular music and symbolizing teenagers' frustrations and desires. Always acknowledging his gospel roots, Ray recorded several tracks associated with black artists, including the Drifters' R&B hit 'Such a Night' (1954), which was banned on several US radio stations, and 'Just Walkin' In the Rain' (1956), which climbed to number 2 in the US charts, and was originally recorded by the Prisonaires. By contrast, in 1954, he played a young singer who decides to become a priest in Irving Berlin's musical film *There's No Business Like Show Business*. Ray sang the gospel-styled 'If You Believe' and 'Alexander's Ragtime Band'. During the late 50s in the USA, rumours were rife concerning his possible homosexuality and drug-taking, and as a result he became more popular abroad than at home. In the UK, in person and on record, he had been a favourite since 1952. Three of his US hits reached UK number 1, including 'Yes Tonight Josephine' (1957). Other UK successes included 'Faith Can Move Mountains', 'Hey There' and 'Look Homeward Angel'. Ray also duetted with Doris Day ('Ma Says Pa Says', 'Full Time Job', 'Let's Walk That-Away') and Frankie Laine ('Good Evening Friends'). In the early 60s, suffering from financial problems and alcoholism, and left behind as the musical climate rapidly changed, he turned to cabaret in the USA. During the 70s he began to revive his career, leaning heavily on his old material for its nostalgic appeal. Always in demand in the UK, he was headlining there until the late 80s. His last performance is said to have been in his home-town on 7 October 1989, and he died of liver failure a few months later in Los Angeles. As to his influence and legacy, one writer concluded: 'Ray was the link between Frank Sinatra and Elvis Presley, re-creating the bobby-sox mayhem that elevated "The Voice" while anticipating the sexual chaos that accompanied Presley.'

● ALBUMS: *Johnnie Ray* (Columbia 1951)★★★, *At The London Palladium* (Philips 1954)★★, *I Cry For You* (Columbia 1955)★★★, *Johnnie Ray* (Epic 1955)★★★, *The Voice Of Your Choice* (Philips 1955)★★★, *Johnnie Ray Sings The Big Beat* (Columbia 1957)★★★★, *Johnnie Ray At The Desert Inn In Las Vegas* (Columbia 1959)★★★, *A Sinner Am I* (Philips 1959)★★, *'Til Morning* (Columbia 1959)★★, *Johnnie Ray On The Trail* (Columbia 1959)★★, *I Cry For You* (1960)★★, *Johnnie Ray* (Liberty 1962)★★, *Yesterday, Today And Tomorrow* (Celebrity 1980)★★, *Yesterday - The London Sessions 1976* (1993)★★.

● COMPILATIONS: *Showcase Of Hits* (Philips 1958)★★★★, *Johnnie Ray's Greatest Hits* (Columbia 1959)★★★★, *The Best Of Johnny Ray* (Realm 1966)★★★★, *An American Legend* (Columbia 1978)★★★★, *Portrait Of A Song Stylist* (Masterpiece 1989)★★★★, *Greatest Hits* (Pickwick 1991)★★★.

● FURTHER READING: *The Johnnie Ray Story*, Ray Sonin.

Rayber Voices

This early Motown backing vocal group came from Detroit, Michigan, USA. The ensemble was established in 1958 and directed by Berry Gordy's second wife, Raynoma Gordy (b. Raynoma Mayberry, 8 March 1937, Detroit, Michigan, USA). There was no established line-up, but the most regular participants were Robert Bateman (bass), Sonny Sanders (b. William Sanders, 6 August 1939, Chicago Heights, Illinois, USA; tenor), Brian Holland (b. 15 February 1941, Detroit, Michigan, USA; baritone) and Raynoma Gordy (soprano). The group made their debut on Herman Griffin's 'I Need You' (1958), and toured with Marv Johnson the following year after his 'Come To Me' achieved a modicum of success. Joining the voices at this time was Gwendolyn Murray. As Gordy's Motown empire grew the Rayber Voices eventually included members of the Temptations, Martha And The Vandellas, and the Miracles. However, the days of using *ad hoc* ensembles soon ended and by the early 60s the Rayber Voices was replaced by a full-time back-up group, the Andantes.

Raydio

(see Parker, Ray, Jnr.)

Rays

This R&B group consisted of Harold Miller (b. 17 January 1931), tenor Walter Ford (b. 5 September 1931), second tenor Davey Jones (b. 1931) and baritone Harry James (b. 1932). It was formed in New York in 1955, when two refugees from the Four Fellows (of 'Soldier Boy' fame), Miller and Jones, teamed up with James and Ford. They first recorded for Chess with no success, then moved to the Philadelphia-based Cameo label in 1957 and achieved lasting fame, albeit as one-hit-wonders, with 'Silhouettes.' The song went to number 3 both R&B and pop in late 1957. The flip-side, the rousing jump led by Ford, 'Daddy Cool', received solid play and briefly charted. These songs are much better known than the Rays, having been remade innumerable times. Herman's Hermits in 1965 and Cliff Richard in 1990 both took 'Silhouettes' up the charts, while British revivalist band Darts, in 1977, and Boney M in 1976, each took 'Daddy Cool' into the UK Top 10.

REAL BREAKS

A sophisticated female vocal quartet, Real Breaks have thus far failed to convert a strong live following into sales for their multi-textured R&B-flavoured songs. The group comprises Josina Elder, Wendi Williams, LaTanyia Baldwin and Necia Bray. They made their debut in 1994 with *A Natural Thing* for A&M Records. Despite a major-label push, this failed to rise higher than number 80 in the *Billboard* R&B charts. Despite some elegant harmonics, the blame was laid by critics on the flimsy material chosen, which undid the group's best efforts. The group recovered to tour as backing vocalists to Stevie Wonder in 1995, leading to a new contract with Arista Records' subsidiary, Rowdy. Their second album was produced by big names including Dallas Austin, the founder of Rowdy Records, Daryl Simmons and Mario Winans. It was promoted by the classy, elegant R&B singles 'Like I Do' and 'Hold Me'.

● ALBUMS: *A Natural Thing* (A&M 1994)★★, *Free* (Rowdy/Arista 1996)★★★.

REAL THING

This Liverpool-based group had its origins in the Mersey boom. Lead singer Eddie Amoo was a former member of the Chants, whose excellent beat singles garnered considerable praise. Although they failed to chart, the Chants continued to record for various labels until the name was ultimately dropped. The Real Thing emerged in 1976 with 'You To Me Are Everything', which reached number 1 in the UK. Their next release, 'Can't Get By Without You' continued their brand of commercial sweet-soul, but later singles were less successful until a more forthright performance in 1979 with the *Star Wars*-influenced 'Can You Feel The Force', took the group back into the Top 5, establishing their popularity with the British disco audience. Subsequent material fared less well, although remixes of those first two hits charted 10 years after their initial release.

● ALBUMS: *The Real Thing* (Pye 1976)★★, *Four From Eight* (Pye 1977)★★, *Step Into Our World* (Pye 1978)★★, *Can You Feel The Force* (Pye 1979)★★.

● COMPILATIONS: *Greatest Hits* (K-Tel 1980)★★★, *100 Minutes Of The Real Thing* (PRT 1982)★★, *Best Of The Real Thing* (West 5 1986)★★, *Heart And Soul Of The Real Thing* (Heart And Soul 1990)★★, *A Golden Hour Of The Real Thing* (Knight 1991)★★.

REDDING, OTIS

b. 9 September 1941, Dawson, Georgia, USA, d. 10 December 1967. The son of a Baptist minister, Redding assimilated gospel music during his childhood and soon became interested in jump blues and R&B. After resettling in Macon, he became infatuated with local luminary Little Richard, and began singing on a full-time basis. A high-school friend and booking agent, Phil Walden, then became his manager. Through Walden's contacts Redding joined Johnny Jenkins And The Pinetoppers as a sometime singer and occasional driver. Redding also began recording for sundry local independents, and his debut single, 'She's Alright', credited to Otis And The Shooters, was quickly followed by 'Shout Ba Malama'. Both performances were firmly in the Little Richard mould. The singer's fortunes blossomed when one of his own songs, 'These Arms Of Mine', was picked up for the Stax subsidiary Volt. Recorded at the tail-end of a Johnny Jenkins session, this aching ballad crept into the American Hot 100 in May 1963. Further poignant releases, 'Pain In My Heart', 'That's How Strong My Love Is' and 'I've Been Loving You Too Long', were balanced by brassy, uptempo performances including 'Mr. Pitiful', 'Respect' and 'Fa Fa Fa Fa Fa Fa (Sad Song)'. He remained something of a cult figure until 1965 and the release of the magnificent *Otis Blue*, in which original material nestled beside the Rolling Stones' 'Satisfaction' and two songs by another mentor, Sam Cooke. Redding's version of the Temptations' 'My Girl' then became a UK hit, while the singer's popularity was further enhanced by the tour of the *Hit The Road Stax* revue in 1967. 'Tramp', a duet with Carla Thomas, also provided success, while Redding's production company, Jotis, was responsible for launching Arthur Conley. A triumphant appearance at the Monterey Pop Festival suggested that Redding was about to attract an even wider following but tragedy struck on 10 December 1967. The light aircraft in which he was travelling plunged into Lake Monona, Madison, Wisconsin, killing the singer, his valet, the pilot and four members of the Bar-Kays. The wistful '(Sittin' On) The Dock Of The Bay', a song Redding recorded just three days earlier, became his only million-seller and US pop number 1. The single's seeming serenity, as well as several posthumous album tracks, suggested a sadly unfulfilled maturity. Although many now point to Redding's limited range, his emotional drive remains compelling, while the songs he wrote, often with guitarist Steve Cropper, stand as some of soul's most enduring moments. Redding is rightly regarded as a giant of soul music.

● ALBUMS: *Pain In My Heart* (Atco 1964)★★★★, *The Great Otis Redding Sings Soul Ballads* (Volt 1965)★★★★, *Otis Blue/Otis Redding Sings Soul* (Volt 1965)★★★★★, *The Soul Album* (Volt 1966)★★★★, *Complete And Unbelievable ... The Otis Redding Dictionary Of Soul* (Volt 1966)★★★★, with Carla Thomas *The King & Queen* (Stax 1967)★★★★, *Otis Redding Live In Europe* (Volt 1967)★★★★, *Here Comes Some Soul From Otis Redding And Little Joe Curtis* pre-1962 recording (Marble Arch

1967)★, *The Dock Of The Bay* (Volt 1968)★★★, *The Immortal Otis Redding* (Atco 1968)★★★, *Otis Redding In Person At The Whiskey A Go Go* (Atco 1968)★★★, *Love Man* (Atco 1969)★★★, *Tell The Truth* (Atco 1970)★★★, shared with Jimi Hendrix *Monterey International Pop Festival* (Reprise 1970)★★★★, *Live Otis Redding* (Atlantic 1982)★★★, *Remember Me* (1992)★★★, *Good To Me* (1993)★★★.

● COMPILATIONS: *History Of Otis Redding* (Volt 1967)★★★★, *The Best Of Otis Redding* (Atco 1972)★★★★, *Pure Otis* (Atlantic 1979)★★★, *Come To Me* (Charly 1984)★★, *Dock Of The Bay - The Definitive Collection* (Atlantic 1987)★★★★, *The Otis Redding Story* 4-LP box set (Atlantic 1989)★★★★, *Remember Me* US title *It's Not Just Sentimental* UK title (Stax 1992)★★★, *Otis!: The Definitive Otis Redding* 4-CD box set (Rhino 1993)★★★★★.

● VIDEOS: *Remembering Otis* (Virgin 1990).

● FURTHER READING: *The Otis Redding Story*, Jane Schiesel.

Reed, Dalton

b. 1954, Lafayette, Louisiana, USA, d. 23 September 1994, Minneapolis, Minnesota, USA. As a child in Lafayette, Reed often attended church gatherings, his family having played the church organ and piano over several generations. He played trumpet during high school before working with a number of local R&B bands, either singing or playing trumpet, trombone or piano. His first own-name band, Dalton Reed And The Musical Journey Band, performed regularly around Lafayette, in addition to several dates backing zydeco legend Rockin' Sidney. It was not until 1986 that he had the chance to record his first single, however, and it was then released on his own Sweet Daddy Records label. 'Givin' On In To Love'/'Strange Things' sold well locally but was not immediately followed up as Reed concentrated on his day job as a master welder. He had to wait until he and his brother formed another label, Reed Brothers Records, before he released his second single, 'Chained And Bound'. It was at this juncture that Reed's career picked up some belated momentum. He was signed to Rounder Records' Bullseye Blues subsidiary by producer Scott Billington, a contract that resulted in two albums. Though neither *Louisiana Soul Man* nor *Willing & Able* spread his reputation much further than his native city, both were excellent collections of dynamic, emotive contemporary R&B. Shortly after the second of these releases Reed died of heart failure.

● ALBUMS: *Louisiana Soul Man* (Bullseye Blues 1992)★★★, *Willing & Able* (Bullseye Blues 1994)★★★.

Reese, Della

b. Dellareese Taliaferro, 6 July 1932, Detroit, Michigan, USA. Reese is a renowned gospel singer, working with Mahalia Jackson and Clara Ward before becoming lead singer with the Meditation Singers. Her place was taken by Laura Lee when she left to join the Erskine Hawkins orchestra in 1956. Reese began a solo recording career with Jubilee in 1957, releasing the Top 20 hit 'And That Reminds Me' and a version of Cole Porter's 'In The Still Of The Night'. Now established as a gospel-influenced ballad singer, she signed to RCA in 1959 where Hugo And Luigi produced 'Don't You Know', based on an aria from Puccini's opera *La Bohème*. It reached number 2 and was followed by the Top 20 single 'Not One Minute More'. Later RCA singles included revivals of 'Someday (You'll Want Me To Want You)' (1960) from 1946 and the 20s standard 'Bill Bailey' (1961). During the 60s and 70s, she worked frequently in cabaret, recording for ABC and Avco, where she had a minor disco hit with 'If It Feels Good Do It' in 1972. In 1980, Reese returned to RCA to record an album of songs adapted from the classics.

● ALBUMS: *The History Of The Blues* (London 1959)★★★, *Della* (RCA 1960)★★★★, *Della Della Cha-Cha-Cha* (RCA 1960)★★★★, *Special Delivery* (RCA 1961)★★★, *The Classic Della* (RCA 1962)★★★, *Della On Stage* (RCA 1962)★★★, *Waltz With Me Della* (RCA 1964)★★★, *At Basin Street East* (RCA 1965)★★★, *Moody* (RCA 1965)★★★, *C'mon And Hear It* (HMV 1965)★★★, *I Like It Like Dat* (HMV 1966)★★★, *Della Reese Live* (ABC 1966)★★, *One More Time* (HMV 1967)★★★, *Let Me Into Your Life* (1975)★★★, *The Classical Della* (RCA 1980)★★, *Della By Starlight* (RCA 1982)★★★, *Sure Like Lovin' You* (President 1985)★★★.

● COMPILATIONS: *The Best Of* (1973)★★★, *And That Reminds Me: The Jubilee Years* (Collectors Choice 1996)★★★, *The Best Thing For You* (Jasmine 1997)★★★.

Reeves, Dianne

b. 1956, Detroit, Michigan, USA. A vocalist with an international reputation and following, Dianne Reeves made her name in the late 80s, when she was discovered by Blue Note Records during a worldwide revival of interest in jazz. A gifted technician with a genuine swing feel, Reeves' career has tended to reflect the difficult fortunes of the singer trying to find a voice in contemporary jazz, without succumbing to the financially dominant worlds of soul or R&B. Born in Detroit but raised from the age of two in Denver, Reeves was still in high school, singing with the high-school big band, when she was spotted by swing trumpeter Clark Terry at the National Association of Jazz Educators Conference in Chicago. Terry's encouragement and advice led her to study at the University of Colorado, where she was able to perform with him, and later to move to California and pursue music full-time. In Los Angeles in the mid-70s, Reeves' range and rich, expressive natural voice, led her quickly into the west coast's famous studio scene, where she became very much in demand, recording for drummer Lenny White, saxophonist Stanley Turrentine and drummer Alphonzo Johnson. Between 1978 and 1980, she worked full-time with Los Angeles-based pianist Billy Childs, whom Reeves still credits for giving her a chance to experiment and grow, while working almost nightly. Still studying (under vocal coach Phil Moore), she gained her first big international exposure in 1981, touring with Sergio Mendes. Reeves recorded her first album a year later. *Welcome To My Love*, co-produced by Childs and released on Palo Alto Jazz, set the trend for the original material that helped distinguish much of Reeves' work in later years. But it was in 1987 that she had her biggest break, when Blue Note Records president Bruce Lundvall spotted her at an Echoes Of Ellington concert in Los Angeles, and wasted no time in setting up her first major session. The resulting *Dianne Reeves* featured George Duke, Freddie Hubbard, Herbie Hancock, Tony Williams, Stanley Clarke and her old friend Billy Childs, and rocketed Reeves onto the international festival circuit. Despite a long-running flirtation with R&B and soul (her discography is split almost exactly down the middle), Reeves has managed to retain her jazz credibility, in 1995 releasing *Quiet After The Storm*, a superb world music-influenced jazz record with guest contributions by saxophonist Joshua Redman, trumpeter Roy Hargrove, flautist Hubert Laws, guitarist Kevin Eubanks and percussionist Airto Moreira.

● ALBUMS: *Welcome To My Love* (Palo Alto Jazz 1982)★★★, *For Every Heart* (Palo Alto Jazz 1985)★★★, *Dianne Reeves* (Blue Note 1987)★★★, *Never Too Far* (EMI 1989)★★★, *I Remember* (EMI 1990)★★★, *Art And Survival* (EMI 1994)★★★, *Quiet After The Storm* (Blue Note 1995)★★★★, *The Grand Encounter* (Blue Note 1996)★★★★.

Reeves, Martha

b. 18 July 1941, Alabama, USA. Reeves was schooled in both gospel and classical music, but it was vocal group R&B that caught her imagination. She began performing in the late 50s under the name Martha Lavaille, briefly joining the Fascinations and then the Del-Phis. In 1961 she joined the fledgling Motown organization in Detroit, where she served as secretary to William Stevenson in the A&R department. Her other duties included supervising Little Stevie Wonder during office hours, and singing occasional backing vocals on recording sessions. Impressed by the power and flexibility of her voice, Berry Gordy offered her the chance to record for the label. She reassembled the Del-Phis quartet as the Vels for a single in 1962, and later that year she led the group on their debut release under a new name, Martha And The Vandellas. From 1963 onwards, they became one of Motown's most successful recording outfits, and Reeves' strident vocals were showcased on classic hits such as 'Heat Wave', 'Dancing In The Street' and 'Nowhere To Run'. She was given individual credit in front of the group from 1967 onwards, but their career was interrupted the following year when she was taken seriously ill, and had to retire from performing. Fully recovered, Reeves emerged in 1970 with a new line-up of Vandellas. After two years of episodic success, she reacted bitterly to Motown's decision to relocate from Detroit to Hollywood, and fought a legal battle to be released from her contract. The eventual settlement entailed the loss of her use of the Vandellas' name, but left her free to sign a solo contract with MCA in 1973. Her debut album was the result of lengthy recording sessions with producer Richard Perry. It earned much critical acclaim but was commercially disappointing, failing to satisfy either rock or soul fans with its hybrid style. Moving to Arista Records in 1977, she was submerged by the late 70s disco boom on a series of albums that allowed her little room to display her talents. Her subsequent recording contracts have proved unproductive, and since the early 80s she has found consistent work on package tours featuring former Motown artists. During the late 80s she toured with a 'fake' Vandellas before being reunited with the original group (Annette Sterling and Rosalind Holmes) on Ian Levine's Motor City label. They released 'Step Into My Shoes' in 1989 while ex-Vandella Lois Reeves also recorded for Levine's label.

● ALBUMS: *Martha Reeves* (MCA 1974)★★★, *The Rest Of My Life* (Arista 1977)★, *We Meet Again* (Milestone 1978)★, *Gotta Keep Moving* (Fantasy 1980)★.

● COMPILATIONS: *We Meet Again/Gotta Keep Moving* (1993)★, *Early Classics* (Spectrum 1996)★★.

Regents

A rock 'n' roll vocal group from the Bronx, New York, USA. The Regents were part of the explosion of Italian-American vocal groups from the New York area who made their impact during the early 60s, before the British invasion and the rise of self-contained bands made them passé. The group comprised Guy Villari (lead), Sal Cuomo, Charles Fassert, Don Jacobucci and Tony Gravagna, and was formed in 1958. They first recorded a demo of 'Barbara-Ann', but when no company showed interest in the song they broke up. Three years later, the small Cousins label released the demo with some bass dubbing and the record became a hit (number 13 pop). The Regents re-formed without their lead, Villari, and enjoyed a moderate hit with 'Runaround' (number 28 pop) in 1961, but could not sustain themselves beyond that. Villari and Fassert with Ronnie Lapinsky and Sal Corrente formed the Runarounds in 1964 and found some local success with 'Carrie'. The memory of the Regents was sustained in 1966 when the Beach Boys made 'Barbara-Ann' a hit again, and during the 70s the Regents re-formed and became regulars on the east coast revival doo-wop circuit.

● ALBUMS: *Barbara-Ann* (Gee 1961)★★★, *Live At The AM/PM Discotheque* (Capitol 1964)★★★.

Reid, L.A.

(see L.A. And Babyface)

Rhodes, Todd Washington

b. 31 August 1900, Hopkinsville, Kentucky, USA, d. 4. June 1965, Detroit, Michigan, USA. Pianist Rhodes first came to prominence in the late 20s as a founder-member of McKinney's Cotton Pickers, recording several dozen tracks for RCA Victor between 1928 and 1931. Leaving the Cotton Pickers in 1934, Rhodes became a popular act on the Detroit jazz scene and formed his own band in the early 40s, recording for the local Sensation label between 1947 and 1950. He hit the R&B charts with 'Bell Boy Boogie', and gave Alan Freed his famous signature tune 'Blues For The Red Boy'. Rhodes' material was leased to Vitacoustic in Chicago and King in Cincinnati. In 1951, Todd Rhodes And His Toddlers began recording for King Records proper, and for the following three years produced some of the best R&B of the 50s, both alone and as backing band for artists including Wynonie Harris and Dave Bartholomew. Rhodes was also instrumental in giving R&B singer LaVern Baker her big break. Rhodes disbanded his group in 1957, although he continued to play as a solo act until his death in 1965. Many of his sidemen and associates progressed to become respected jazz musicians or session players for the mighty Motown empire.

● ALBUMS: *Your Daddy's Doggin' Around* (Jukebox Lil 1985)★★★, *Dance Music That Hits The Spot* (Swingtime 1988)★★★.

RIBITONES

The Ribitones, from Brooklyn, New York, USA, were formed in 1978 by Freddy 'Frogs' Toscano, a veteran of Fourth Dimension, an offbeat vocal pop group who had recorded for Columbia Records in the 60s. He then became a member of several jazz and fusion bands in the intervening years, but the Ribitones was intended as a vehicle to allow him to return to his early rock 'n' roll roots. To this end he recruited Lou Benevento (lead), Fil Spina (baritone), Anthony Carbone (first tenor) and Carmine De Sena (second tenor) initially, until Jim Pace and Frank Russo replaced De Sena and Spina. Russo, Benevento and Carbone had already worked together on the streets of Brooklyn in the early 60s singing amateur doo-wop harmonies. This new collaboration sparked into life with the 1979 release of 'Most Of All', an a cappella treatment of the old Moonglows standard, backed with a version of the El Dorados' 'At My Front Door' - rechristened 'Crazy Little Mama'. It was about this time that critics started to cite the Ribitones as the original 'rock-apella' group, due to their use of a rhythm guitar behind a strong vocal presence. A second single by the group was credited to Freddy Frogs And The BMTS when Toscano re-released 'Crazy Little Mama' on his own Off The Wall Records (it became a surprise minor hit in the UK). This led to touring engagements in England, plus long stints on the road back in their home territory. However, by 1984 the group was no more, as Toscano formed an off-shoot group with Lou Ligreori (ex-Riffs), Mike Paquette (ex-Dedications) and Larry Critelli and Bill Walsh (both ex-Velvet Riffs).

● ALBUMS: *Patty And The Street-Tones Meet The Ribitones* (Clifton 1980)★★★.

RICH, TONY, PROJECT

b. Detroit, Michigan, USA. Influenced in his youth by a wide range of music from Madonna and Bruce Springsteen to the Gap Band, Funkadelic and Motown Records, Rich grew up in the video age and modelled himself after its more expansive performers. Born to a musical father, it was not long before he began writing his own songs on a keyboard borrowed from his brother. By his early teens he was playing in local R&B and jazz fusion bands, 'learning how to make a band work'. He also worked with several gospel groups and choirs while collaborating with local songwriters and helping them to produce demos. He might well have continued to neglect his own material had it not been for the input of John Salley, later the star of basketball team Miami Heat, but at that time a member of the Detroit Pistons and a well-known member of the local music community. He encouraged Rich to pursue a solo career, and also put him in touch with several local rappers who used his production and writing expertise. This employment helped him to purchase his own studio equipment, but more importantly, while in Salley's studio he was offered the chance to meet pop svengali Babyface. Rich then contributed several songs to an album by Pebbles, which in turn led to a meeting in Atlanta with her husband L.A. Reid. Reid listened with enthusiasm to his four-track demos and immediately offered him a contract with LaFace Records. Rich moved to Atlanta full-time in 1993. Among his first production commitments was a session with Elton John and the Sounds Of Blackness on a tribute record to Curtis Mayfield. He produced half an album for Savvy Records' group 4.0 and 'I Sit Away' for the multi-platinum-selling Boyz II Men. He also produced for Johnny Gill and conducted remixes on material by Toni Braxton ('You Mean The World To Me') and TLC ('Red Light Special'). In 1994 he began work in earnest on his own debut. *Words* was a sophisticated blend of R&B and soul with some unusual elements - including a country song, 'Billy Goat'. The first single, 'Nobody Knows', included a guest role for brother Joe - whose keyboard Rich had originally purloined at the inception of his career many years previously. Although its success in US markets was widely anticipated, it also broke through in the UK, reaching the Top 10 in May 1996.

● ALBUMS: *Words* (LaFace/Arista 1996)★★★★.

RICHIE, LIONEL

b. 20 June 1949, Tuskegee, Alabama, USA. Richie grew up on the campus of Tuskegee Institute, where he formed a succession of R&B groups in the mid-60s. In 1968 he became the lead singer and saxophonist with the Commodores. They signed to Atlantic Records in 1968 for a one-record contract, before moving to Motown Records, being schooled as support act to the Jackson Five. The Commodores became established as America's most popular soul group of the 70s, and Richie was responsible for writing and singing many of their biggest hits, specializing in romantic, easy-listening ballads such as 'Easy', 'Three Times A Lady' and 'Still'. His mellifluous vocal tones established him as the most prominent member of the group, and by the late 70s he had begun to accept songwriting commissions from other artists. He composed Kenny Rogers' 1980 number 1 'Lady', and produced his *Share Your Love* the following year. Also in 1981, he duetted with Diana Ross on the theme song for the film *Endless Love*. Issued as a single, the track topped the UK and US charts, and became one of Motown's biggest hits to date. Its success encouraged Richie to branch out into a fully fledged solo career in 1982. His debut, *Lionel Richie*, produced another chart-topping single, 'Truly', which continued the style of his ballads with the Commodores. In 1983, he released *Can't Slow Down*, which catapulted him into the first rank of international superstars, eventually selling more than 15 million copies worldwide. The set also won two Grammy awards, including Album Of The Year. It spawned the number 1 hit 'All Night Long', a gently rhythmic dance number that was promoted by a startling video, produced by former

Monkee Michael Nesmith. Several more Top 10 hits followed, the most successful of which was 'Hello', a sentimental love song that showed how far Richie had moved from his R&B roots. Now described by one critic as 'the black Barry Manilow', Richie wrote and performed a suitably anodyne theme song, 'Say You, Say Me', for the film *White Nights* - winning an Oscar for his pains. He also collaborated with Michael Jackson on the charity single 'We Are The World' by USA For Africa. In 1986, he released *Dancing On The Ceiling*, another phenomenally popular album that produced a run of US and UK hits. The title track, which revived the sedate dance feel of 'All Night Long', was accompanied by another striking video, a feature that has played an increasingly important role in Richie's solo career. The critical consensus was that this album represented nothing more than a consolidation of his previous work, though Richie's collaboration with the country group Alabama on 'Deep River Woman' did break new ground. Since then, his ever more relaxed schedule has kept his recording and live work to a minimum. He broke the silence in 1996 with *Louder Than Words*, on which he resisted any change of style or the musical fashion-hopping of the past decade. Instead, he stayed with his chosen path of well-crafted soul music, which in the intervening years has become known as 'Urban R&B'.

● ALBUMS: *Lionel Richie* (Motown 1982)★★★, *Can't Slow Down* (Motown 1983)★★★★, *Dancing On The Ceiling* (Motown 1986)★★★, *Back To Front* (Motown 1992)★★, *Louder Than Words* (Mercury 1996)★★.

● COMPILATIONS: *Truly: The Love Songs* (Motown 1998)★★★.

● VIDEOS: *All Night Long* (RCA/Columbia 1986), *Dancing On The Ceiling* (Hendring Video 1988).

● FURTHER READING: *Lionel Richie: An Illustrated Biography*, David Nathan.

RIDGLEY, TOMMY

b. 30 October 1925, New Orleans. Originally a pianist, Ridgley played with a Dixieland group and Earl Anderson's band in 1949 before his powerful R&B voice made him one of New Orleans' most respected singers for nearly three decades. His first record was 'Shrewsbury Blues', named after a district of the city and produced by Dave Bartholomew for Imperial in 1949. He also recorded the humorous 'Looped' before Ahmet Ertegun's Atlantic label came to record in New Orleans in 1953. The label recorded Ridgley singing 'I'm Gonna Cross That River' and 'Ooh Lawdy My Baby', with Ray Charles on piano. Both were highly popular locally. 'Jam Up', an instrumental with Ridgley on piano, later appeared on anthology albums. In 1957, it was the turn of Al Silver of the New York-based Ember label to fish in the New Orleans talent pool. He recorded Ridgley in a more mellow blues ballad style on 'When I Meet My Girl' and 'I've Heard That Story Before'. At this point, Ridgley turned down a booking at New York's Apollo because 'the money they was offering didn't match up to the money down here'. By now, Ridgley and his band the Untouchables were resident at the New Orleans Auditorium, backing touring rock 'n' roll package shows when they reached Louisiana. Several young singers also started their careers with his group, notably Irma Thomas. In the early 60s, Ridgley recorded for the local Ric label, owned by Joe Ruffino. Among his singles were 'In The Same Old Way' and Ivory Joe Hunter's 'I Love You Yes I Do'. Later tracks were produced by Wardell Quezergue while in 1973, Ridgley turned to production, having a local hit with 'Sittin' And Drinkin' by Rose Davis. He remained a familiar figure on the New Orleans music scene throughout the 70s and 80s when Rounder recorded him. His debut for Black Top featured gutsy horns and support from Snooks Eaglin (guitar) and George Porter Jr. (bass).

● ALBUMS: *Through The Years* reissue (1984)★★★, *New Orleans King Of The Stroll* (Rounder 1988)★★★, *Since The Blues Began* (Black Top 1995)★★★.

RIGHTEOUS BROTHERS

Despite their professional appellation, Bill Medley (b. 19 September 1940, Santa Ana, California, USA) and Bobby Hatfield (b. 10 August 1940, Beaver Dam, Wisconsin, USA) were not related. They met in 1962 at California's Black Derby club, where they won the approbation of its mixed-race clientele. By blending Medley's sonorous baritone with Hatfield's soaring high tenor, this white duo's vocal style invoked that of classic R&B, and a series of excellent singles, notably 'Little Latin Lupe Lu', followed. They achieved national fame in 1964 following several appearances on US television's highly popular *Shindig*. Renowned producer Phil Spector then signed the act to his Philles label and proceeded to mould his 'Wagerian' sound to their dramatic intonation. 'You've Lost That Lovin' Feelin'' justifiably topped the US and UK charts and is rightly lauded as one the greatest pop singles of all time. A similar passion was extolled on 'Just Once In My Life' and 'Ebb Tide', but the relationship between performer and mentor rapidly soured. The Righteous Brothers moved outlets in 1966, but despite gaining a gold disc for '(You're My) Soul And Inspiration', a performance modelled on their work with Spector, the duo was unable to sustain the same success. They split in 1968, with Medley beginning a solo career and Hatfield retaining the name with new partner Jimmy Walker, formerly of the Knickerbockers. This short-lived collaboration ended soon afterwards, but the original pair were reunited in 1974 for an appearance on *The Sonny And Cher Comedy Hour*. They scored a US Top 3 hit that year with the maudlin 'Rock 'n' Roll Heaven', but were unable to regain former glories and have subsequently separated and re-formed on several occasions. In 1987 Medley enjoyed an international smash with '(I've Had) The Time Of My Life', a duet with Jennifer Warnes taken from the film *Dirty Dancing*, while a reissue of 'Unchained Melody', a hit for the Righteous Brothers in 1965, topped the UK chart in 1990 after it featured in the film *Ghost*.

● ALBUMS: *The Righteous Brothers - Right Now!* (Moonglow 1963)★★, *Some Blue-Eyed Soul* (Moonglow 1965)★★, *You've Lost That Lovin' Feelin'* (Philles 1965)★★★★, *Just Once In My Life* (Philles 1965)★★★★, *Back To Back* (Philles 1965)★★★★, *This Is New!* (Moonglow 1965)★★, *In Action* (Sue 1966)★★, *Soul And Inspiration* (Verve 1966)★★★★, *Go Ahead And Cry*

(Verve 1966)★★★, *Sayin' Somethin'* (Verve 1967)★★★, *Souled Out* (Verve 1967)★★★, *Standards* (Verve 1967)★★★, *One For The Road* (Verve 1968)★★★, *Rebirth* (Verve 1970)★★, *Give It To The People* (Haven 1974)★★, *The Sons Of Mrs Righteous* (Haven 1975)★★.

● COMPILATIONS: *The Best Of The Righteous Brothers* (Moonglow 1966)★★, *Greatest Hits* (Verve 1967)★★★★, *Greatest Hits Volume 2* (Verve 1969)★★★, *2 By 2* (MGM 1973)★★★, *Best Of The Righteous Brothers* (Verve 1987)★★★★, *Anthology (1962-1974)* (Rhino 1989)★★★★, *Best Of The Righteous Brothers* (Curb 1990)★★★, *Unchained Melody: The Very Best Of The Righteous Brothers* (Polygram 1990)★★★★, *The Moonglow Years* (Polygram 1991)★★★.

● VIDEOS: *21st Anniversary Celebration* (Old Gold 1990).

● FILMS: *Beach Ball* (1964).

RILEY, TEDDY

Widely regarded as not only the originator, but the motivating force behind New Jack Swing, Riley remains arguably the most successful and revered producer in commercial dance music. His writing, remixing and production credits include numerous Bobby Brown records, and work with Keith Sweat, Jazzy Jeff And The Fresh Prince, Wreckx-N-Effect, James Ingram and Michael Jackson (*Dangerous*). Despite this prolificacy, he maintains, 'I don't work with anyone who isn't a real singer. I've turned down a lot of artists who are big but who I reckon don't have the ability.' His 'swing' groups included the originals, Guy, with whom he sang vocals, as well as Jodeci, Mary J. Blige, and soundtrack work on *New Jack City* and *Do The Right Thing*. His origins were in the R&B group Kids At Work, and his stepfather was Gene Griffin, who released one of the earliest rap tracks in Trickeration's 'Rap, Bounce, Rollerskate'. Riley's own rap connections included an uncredited appearance on Doug E. Fresh's 'The Show', but by the turn of the decade he would be a multi-millionaire. He returned to the group format in 1994 for his latest project, BLACKstreet, which also boasted Chauncey 'Black' Hannibal (an original member of Jodeci), Levi Little (bass, guitar, keyboards) and David Hollister (formerly backing vocalist for Mary J. Blige, Al B. Sure!, Patti LaBelle and 2Pac).

RIPERTON, MINNIE

b. 8 November 1947, Chicago, Illinois, USA, d. 12 July 1979, Los Angeles, California, USA. A former singer with the Gems, Riperton recorded under the name Andrea Davis prior to joining the Rotary Connection. She remained with this black pop/psychedelic group between 1967 and 1970, before embarking on a solo career. In 1973 the singer began working with Wonderlove, Stevie Wonder's backing group. Two years later he returned this compliment, producing Riperton's *Perfect Angel*, and contributing two original compositions to the selection. However, it was 'Loving You', a song written by Riperton and her husband Richard Rudolph, that brought international success, (US number 1/UK number 2) in 1975. This delicate performance featured the artist's soaring multi-octave voice, but set a standard later releases found hard to emulate. Riperton died from cancer in July 1979.

● ALBUMS: *Perfect Angel* (Epic 1974)★★★, *Come To My Garden* recorded in 1969 (Janus 1974)★★, *Adventures In Paradise* (Epic 1975)★★, *Stay In Love* (Epic 1977)★★, *Minnie* (Capitol 1979)★★, *Love Lives Forever* (Capitol 1980)★★.

● COMPILATIONS: *The Best Of Minnie Riperton* (1981)★★.

RIVERS, JOHNNY

b. John Ramistella, 7 November 1942, New York City, New York, USA. Johnny Rivers enjoyed a succession of pop hits in the 60s and 70s, initially by remaking earlier R&B songs and eventually with his own compositions. His singles were spirited creations, some recorded live in front of an enthusiastic, hip Los Angeles audience. His father moved the family to Baton Rouge, Louisiana, in 1945, where Rivers began playing guitar at the age of eight. By the age of 13, having become enamoured of the local rock 'n' roll and R&B artists, he was fronting his own group. In 1958 he ventured to New York to make his first recording. Top disc jockey Alan Freed met the singer and gave him his new name, Johnny Rivers, and also recommended to the local Gone Records label that they sign Rivers. They did, and his first single, 'Baby Come Back', was issued that year. At 17 Rivers moved to Nashville, where he wrote songs with another aspiring singer, Roger Miller, and recorded demo records for Elvis Presley, Johnny Cash and others, including Ricky Nelson, who recorded Rivers' 'Make Believe' in 1960. Rivers relocated to Los Angeles at that time. Between 1959 and his 1964 signing to Imperial Records he recorded singles for small labels such as Guyden, Cub and Dee Dee, as well as the larger Chancellor, Capitol Records, MGM Records, Coral Records and United Artists Records, none with any chart success.

In late 1963 Rivers began performing a three-night stand at the LA club Gazzari's, which was so successful it was extended for weeks. He then took up residency at the popular discotheque the Whisky A-Go-Go, where his fans began to include such stars as Johnny Carson, Steve McQueen and Rita Hayworth. His first album for Imperial, *Johnny Rivers At The Whisky A Go Go*, was released in the summer of 1964 and yielded his first hit, Chuck Berry's 'Memphis', which reached number 2. Further hits during 1964-65 included Berry's 'Maybelline', Harold Dorman's 'Mountain Of Love', the traditional folk song 'Midnight Special', Willie Dixon's 'Seventh Son' and Pete Seeger's 'Where Have All The Flowers Gone', each delivered in a rousing, loose interpretation that featured Rivers' nasal vocal, his concise, soulful guitar-playing and sharp backing musicians. Relentlessly rhythmic, the tracks were produced by Lou Adler, working his way towards becoming one of the city's most formidable hitmakers. Rivers started 1966 with 'Secret Agent Man', the theme song from a popular television spy thriller. Later that year he achieved his only number 1 record with his own 'Poor Side Of Town' (co-written with Adler), an uncharacteristic ballad using top studio musicians such as Hal Blaine, James Burton and Larry Knechtel. Rivers also launched his own Soul City record label in 1966, signing the popular Fifth Dimension, who went on to have four Top 10 singles on the label. Retreating from the party atmosphere of his earlier recordings for Imperial, Rivers had hits in 1967 with two Motown cover versions, the Four Tops' 'Baby I Need Your Lovin'' and Smokey Robinson's 'The Tracks Of My Tears'. Following an appearance at the Monterey Pop Festival, another soulful ballad, the James Hendricks-penned 'Summer Rain', became Rivers' last major hit of the 60s. The latter also appeared on Rivers' bestselling album, *Realization*. Early 70s albums such as *Slim Slo Slider*, *Home Grown* and *LA Reggae* were critically lauded but not commercially successful, although the latter gave Rivers a Top 10 single with Huey 'Piano' Smith's 'Rockin' Pneumonia - Boogie Woogie Flu'. A version of the Beach Boys' 'Help Me Rhonda' (with backing vocal by Brian Wilson) was a minor success in 1975, and two years later Rivers landed his final Top 10 single, 'Swayin' To The Music (Slow Dancin')'. Rivers recorded a handful of albums in the 80s, including a live one featuring the old hits, but none reached the charts.

● ALBUMS: *Johnny Rivers At The Whisky A Go Go* (Imperial 1964)★★★★, *The Sensational Johnny Rivers* (Capitol 1964)★★★★, *Go, Johnny, Go* (1964)★★★, *Here We A-Go-Go Again* (Imperial 1964)★★★, *Johnny Rivers In Action!* (Imperial 1965)★★★, *Meanwhile Back At The Whisky A Go Go* (Imperial 1965)★★★★, *Johnny Rivers Rocks The Folk* (Imperial 1965)★★, *... And I Know You Wanna Dance* (Imperial 1966)★★★, *Changes* (Imperial 1966)★★★, *Rewind* (Imperial 1967)★★★, *Realization* (Imperial 1968)★★★, *Johnny Rivers* (Sunset 1968)★★★, *A Touch Of Gold* (Imperial 1969)★★★, *Slim Slo Slider* (Imperial 1970)★★★, *Rockin' With Johnny Rivers* (Sunset 1971)★★★, *Non-Stop Dancing At The Whisky A Go Go* (United Artists 1971)★★★, *Home Grown* (United Artists 1971)★★★, *L.A. Reggae* (United Artists 1972)★★★, *Johnny Rivers* (United Artists 1972)★★★, *Blue Suede Shoes* (United Artists 1973)★★★, *Last Boogie In Paris* (Atlantic 1974)★★★, *Rockin' Rivers* (1974)★★★, *Road* (Atlantic 1975)★★★, *New Lovers And Old Friends* (Epic 1975)★★★, *Help Me Rhonda* (Epic 1975)★★★, *Wild Night* (United Artists 1976)★★★, *Outside Help* (Big Tree 1978)★★, *Borrowed Time* (RSO 1980)★★, *The Johnny Rivers Story* (1982)★★★, *Portrait Of* (1982)★★★, *Not A Through Street* (Priority 1983)★★.

● COMPILATIONS: *Johnny Rivers' Golden Hits* (Imperial 1966)★★★, *The History Of Johnny Rivers* (Liberty 1971)★★★, *Go Johnnny Go* (Hallmark 1971)★★★, *Greatest Hits* re-recordings (MCA 1985)★★, *The Best Of Johnny Rivers* (EMI America 1987)★★★, *Anthology 1964-1977* (Rhino 1991)★★★★.

Rivieras

This R&B vocal group came from Englewood, New Jersey, USA. The members were Homer Dunn (lead), Charles Allen (bass), Ronald Cook (tenor) and Andrew Jones (baritone). The group specialized in singing doo-wop versions of old big band hits, especially those of Glenn Miller. Dunn formed his first group, the Bob-O-Links, in 1952 in Hackensack, New Jersey. Moving to Englewood, New Jersey, Dunn formed the Rivieras in 1955, and they managed to stay together for three years playing local gigs before being eventually signed to the Coed label. The Rivieras' principal hits were 'Count Every Star' (1958), which was previously a 1950 hit for Ray Anthony, and 'Moonlight Seranade' (1959), a Miller hit in 1939. Other outstanding releases issued before the group disbanded in 1961 were 'Our Love' (1959) and 'Moonlight Cocktail' (1960), previously hits for Tommy Dorsey and Miller, respectively.

● ALBUMS: with the Duprees *Jerry Blavat Presents Drive-In Sounds* (Lost Nite 1965)★★★, *The Rivieras Sing* (Post 1971)★★.

● COMPILATIONS: *Moonlight Cocktails* (Relic 1992)★★★.

Roachford

This UK soul/funk band is comprised of Andrew Roachford (vocals, keyboards, percussion), Chris Taylor (drums), Hawi Gondwe (guitars) and Derrick Taylor (bass). Andrew Roachford performed from the age of 14 when he played in London's Soho jazz clubs. The band was assembled in 1987, and by early 1988 was touring with Terence Trent D'Arby and the Christians, gaining a reputation for excellent live shows. Strong live support was instrumental to their breakthrough and CBS Records beat many other labels to sign the band. Two singles and an album came out in late 1988, but it was not until early 1989 that 'Cuddly Toy' was re-released to become a massive hit, closely followed by 'Family Man'. The self-titled album was also rediscovered and the band started to make inroads into the American market. Sessions for their second album took place in Britain and at Prince's Paisley Park studios. Although named after Andrew Roachford, he has always maintained that 'Roachford is a whole band, not a group of session guys backing me up'. None of the singles released from 1994's *Permanent Shade Of Blue* managed to break the Top 20, but the album was an acclaimed fusion of blues and funk stylings. After a three-year hiatus Roachford returned with the more mainstream-orientated *Feel*, to mixed reviews.

●ALBUMS: *Roachford* (Columbia 1988)★★★, *Get Ready!* (Columbia 1991)★★, *Permanent Shade Of Blue* (Columbia 1994)★★★, *Feel* (Columbia 1997)★★.

Robert And Johnny

This R&B duo came from the Bronx, New York, USA. Robert Carr and Johnny Mitchell grew up in the same neighbourhood and attended high school together. Upon their signing to Old Town Records in 1956, their duets captured the sound of the then popular doo-wop groups. 'I Believe in You', with the duo's trademark approach of sighing and pausing, where one took the lead and then the two came together on the choruses, established their name in New York City, but no further west than the Hudson River. 'We Belong Together', however, established the duo as rock 'n' roll immortals, reaching number 12 R&B and number 32 pop in 1958. Robert and Johnny, alas, were fated to be one-hit-wonders and ended their recording career in 1962. 'We Belong Together' fared far better, being revived on the charts in 1966 by Dee Brown and Lola Grant and in 1968 by the Webs.

● COMPILATIONS: *We Belong Together* (Ace 1986)★★.

Roberts, Bruce

b. New York, USA. Los Angeles, California-based songwriter Bruce Roberts has written songs for many of the greats - including Aretha Franklin, Ashford And Simpson, Elton John, Barbra Streisand, Heart, k.d. lang, Bette Midler, Patti LaBelle, Dionne Warwick, the Pointer Sisters, Natalie Cole, Alice Cooper, Dolly Parton and Whitney Houston. After working on jingle production in his youth Roberts attended the Juilliard music school. This led to a summer job at Chappell Music and, subsequently, employment by Warner Brothers in their copyright department. Asked if he could write songs, he furnished the company with his first composition, 'I'll Make You Music', which he now describes as 'horrible'. Nevertheless, it became a US Top 20 hit for the Beverly Bremers. Further songs were written, and in 1980 he released his first, self-titled album for Elektra Records. Although it received strong notices and precipitated a second album, for the rest of the decade he returned to writing songs for other artists. It was 1995 before he resumed his own recording career, conceding to the press: 'I decided that I really had a passion to become an artist.' *Intimacy* was the result, a set of soul-based ballads recorded in his bedroom with the help of friends such as k.d. lang, Elton John (on the attendant single, 'When The Money's Gone'), Luther Vandross, All-4-One and Ashford And Simpson.

● ALBUMS: *Bruce Roberts* (Elektra 1980)★★★, *Intimacy* (Atlantic 1995)★★★.

Roberts, Joe

Roberts is a Manchester-based soul-dance vocalist, and an ex-mod who was brought up in a commune (when his parents moved from London to Karling in Norfolk, his father switching jobs from economist to carpenter). This background can be gauged in his lyrics, which come heavily laden with 'peace and love' metaphors, but also reflect the early influence of Sly Stone, Al Green and Marvin Gaye, who were introduced to him by later collaborator Eric Gooden. He had also learned the piano from the age of eight, and this was reflected in the musicianship of his club music. After moving to Manchester in 1981, he became a member of local covers band the Risk, who evenutally used Roberts' own songs. He hit sprightly single form on cuts such as 'Love Is Energy' - recorded with the aforementioned Gooden, whom he had met at college, and is his current songwriting partner - and 'Back In My Life'.

● ALBUMS: *Looking For The Here And Now* (London 1994)★★★.

Roberts, Juliet

The term house diva does not fully cover the career or capabilities of Juliet Roberts, who is in addition a proficient singer-songwriter, and a veteran of the early days of British soul. Unlike many in the field, she did not learn her craft at the church choir, having instead been brought up in the more restrained Catholic faith. However, music was still in her blood. Her father was formerly a member of the calypso band the Nightingales, and took her to various concerts. Her first performances came as a member of reggae band Black Jade, before she signed solo to Bluebird Records in 1980, a label set up by her local record shop in Paddington, north London. Two tracks, a cover version of the Police's 'The Bed's Too Big Without You' and 'Fool For You', emerged, while she was still engaged in her day job as a sports tutor. They were enough to attract the attention of fellow Londoners the Funk Masters. She appeared as lead singer on their Top 10 hit 'It's Over', in 1983. After a year's sabbatical in the USA she embarked on her music career proper, and, within a week of returning to British shores, was enlisted as singer for Latin jazz band Working Week. When that group floundered (after several noble releases), she finally signed to Cooltempo as a solo artist.

● ALBUMS: *Natural Thing* (Cooltempo 1994)★★★.

Robey, Don

b. 1 November 1903, Houston, Texas, USA, d. 16 June 1975, Houston, Texas, USA. Houston businessman and impresario Don Robey bought his nightclub, the Bronze Peacock, in 1945, and it soon became a centre for developing local talent as well as bringing in big names from across the country. Soon afterwards, he opened a record shop, which eventually became the base of operations for his Peacock Records, one of the first ever labels in the USA to have a black owner. Peacock developed as one of the most important R&B and gospel labels, featuring artists such as Gatemouth Brown, Johnny Ace and Big Mama Thornton, as well as the Dixie Hummingbirds and Five Blind Boys. Robey then bought the Duke label from Memphis, which became another major outlet, especially for Bobby Bland and Junior Parker. Another label, Songbird, also issued gospel records for many years.

Robins

An R&B vocal group from Los Angeles, California, USA, formed in 1947. The original members were 'Ty' Terrell Leonard, twins Billy and Roy Richard, and Bobby Nunn. The group recorded some tracks for Aladdin before they hooked up with bandleader Johnny Otis in 1949, when they won second place at a talent contest at his club, The Barrelhouse. Their first chart record, in 1950 for Savoy Records, was the mid-tempo 'If It's So, Baby' (number 10 R&B), recorded with the Johnny Otis Orchestra. Its excellent ballad b-side, 'If I Didn't Love You So', received much more airplay in many areas. Otis also used the Robins to back his young prodigy, Little Esther, on the hit 'Double Crossing Blues' in 1950. The Savoy recordings were made in a bluesy modulated style of the period and did nothing to set apart the Robins from other groups. During 1950-52 the group recorded for Modern, RPM (as the Nic Nacs), and Recorded In Hollywood without notable success. In 1953 the Robins, with the addition of tenor lead Grady Chapman, were signed to RCA and came under the production aegis of the up-and-coming songwriting team of Leiber And Stoller. Jerry Leiber and Mike Stoller began to radically transform the Robins into a proto-rock 'n' roll group with an exuberant beat-infected sound. No hits resulted on RCA, but in 1954, with a move to Leiber and Stoller's own Spark label, and with Carl Gardner having replaced Grady Chapman, the Robins found success with 'Riot In Cell Block No. 9'. The song, which used the menacing bass of Richard Berry and machine-gun sound-effects, was one of the most controversial records of 1954. It sold well in California and a few other locales but failed to chart nationally because of poor distribution. The group successfully followed it with another regional hit, 'Framed' (1954), and in 1955 hit with 'Smokey Joe's Cafe'. Fast-rising independent Atlantic Records took notice of sales in California and assumed distribution, making it a national hit (number 10 R&B) on their Atco subsidiary. The Robins, however, split up, with Gardner and Nunn joining with Billy Guy and Leon Hughes to form the Coasters to record for Atlantic. Under the aegis of producers Leiber And Stoller, the Coasters flourished. The Robins - with newcomer H.B. Barnum and with returning Grady Chapman - continued to record, on the Whippet and other labels, albeit unsuccessfully, until breaking up some time in the early 60s.

● ALBUMS: *Rock 'N' Roll With The Robins* (Whippet 1958)★★★.

● COMPILATIONS: *The Best Of The Robins* collects their Whippet recordings (GNP-Crescendo 1975)★★★, *The Roots Of Rock 'N Roll* collects their Savoy recordings (Savoy Jazz 1987)★★★.

ROBINSON, ALVIN

b. 1937, d. 24 January 1989. Robinson was a New Orleans-based session guitarist, and secured a minor hit in 1964 with a recording of a Chris Kenner song, 'Something You Got'. The single was released on Tiger Records, a short-lived outlet owned by Jerry Leiber and Mike Stoller, who then took Robinson to their next venture, Red Bird. His first release there, 'Down Home Girl', was an inspired amalgamation of New York pop and Crescent City R&B. Later covered by the Rolling Stones, Robinson's single was one of the finest to appear on this impressive label. It was followed by a reshaped version of 'Let The Good Times Roll', but the artist was unable to find another success. Robinson moved to the west coast in 1969 and was one of several expatriate musicians who played on Dr. John's New Orleans 'tribute' album, *Gumbo*. He returned to New Orleans in 1985 and died in 1989.

● COMPILATIONS: *Shine On* (Charly 1989)★★★.

ROBINSON, BOBBY

Robinson opened a record shop in Harlem, New York City, USA, shortly after World War II, and became an authority on the music scene. His advice was sought by many independent labels. In November 1951 he formed his first record company, Robin Records - which swiftly became Red Robin Records when a southern independent of the same name threatened legal action. He began producing and releasing records by such artists as Morris Lane, Tiny Grimes and Wilbert 'Red' Prysock, but found greater success with the birth of the New York doo-wop groups, and such acts as the Mello Moods, Vocaleers and the Du Droppers. Red Robin was dissolved in 1956, but many more labels were to follow through to the 60s - Whirlin Disc, Fury, Fire, Fling, Enjoy and Everlast - mainly issuing classic vocal group numbers by acts such as the Channels, Velvets, Scarlets, Teenchords, the Delfonics and Gladys Knight And the Pips. These labels occasionally achieved success with single R&B stars such as Wilbert Harrison ('Kansas City'), Buster Brown ('Fannie Mae'), Bobby Marchan ('There Is Something On Your Mind'), Lee Dorsey ('Ya Ya'), Lightnin' Hopkins, Elmore James and King Curtis. In the early 70s Bobby Robinson started a new label, Front Page Records, and reactivated his Enjoy label.

ROBINSON, FREDDIE

b. 24 February 1939, Arkansas, USA. As 'Fred Robertson', he recorded with Little Walter (Jacobs) in the late 50s and by the early 60s he had become a noted guitarist in Chicago, where he recorded for the Queen, M-Pac/One-Der-Ful and Chess labels. After moving to Los Angeles around 1968, he maintained his links with producer/musician Milton Bland (aka Monk Higgins) and recorded in a jazz context for World Pacific in 1969 and as a blues and soul guitarist for Enterprise (the Stax subsidiary label) a few years later. In 1977 he recorded for ICA, with whom he also worked as a session guitarist, writer and arranger, mostly in a soul vein. In the 80s he toured and recorded with Louis Myers.

● ALBUMS: *The Coming Atlantis* (Pacific Jazz 1969)★★★, *At The Drive-In* reissued as *Black Fox* (Enterprise 1972)★★★, *Off The Cuff* (1973)★★★.

ROBINSON, ROSCOE

b. 22 May 1928, Dumont, Alabama, USA. Robinson was a soul and gospel singer in the mid-60s and 70s. After moving to Gary, Indiana, at the age of 10, Robinson's singing career began in the early 40s with the gospel group Joiner's Five Trumpets and he became a member of various gospel groups throughout the rest of the decade. He first recorded for Trumpet Records in 1951 with the Southern Sons. In the early 50s, after a spell in the army, he continued working with gospel groups including the Five Blind Boys Of Mississippi. Switching to secular music in 1965, Robinson first recorded 'What Makes A Man Do Wrong' for Tuff Records. His biggest hit came in 1966 with 'That's Enough', a Top 10 R&B single for Wand Records. Moving over to the Sound Stage 7 label in 1967 did not yield any chart successes and there was one final R&B chart single in 1969 on Atlantic Records. In 1971, Robinson signed Stan Lewis's Jewel/Paula/Ronn concern, and six singles for Paula appeared over the next two years, while a fine gospel album was released on Jewel in 1972. Gospel reclaimed Robinson after this, with outings on Gospel Roots in 1977, a re-association with the Original Five Blind Boys on their 1982 Peace International album, and a fine solo gospel set for Savoy the following year.

● ALBUMS: *He Still Lives In Me* (Jewel 1972)★★★★, *Time To Live* (Gospel Roots 1977)★★★, *High On Jesus* (Savoy 1983)★★★.

● COMPILATIONS: *Why Must It End* Sound Stage 7 and Paula secular recordings (Charly 1987)★★★.

ROBINSON, SMOKEY

b. William Robinson, 19 February 1940, Detroit, Michigan, USA. A founding member of the Miracles at Northern High School, Detroit, in 1955, Robinson became one of the leading figures in the local music scene by the end of the decade. His flexible tenor voice, which swooped easily into falsetto, made him the group's obvious lead vocalist, and by 1957 he was composing his own variations on the R&B hits of the day. That year he met Berry Gordy, who was writing songs for R&B star Jackie Wilson, and looking for local acts to produce. Vastly impressed by Robinson's affable personality and promising writing talent, Gordy took the teenager under his wing. He produced a series of Miracles singles in 1958 and 1959, all of which featured Robinson as composer and lead singer, and leased them to prominent R&B labels. In 1960 he signed the Miracles to his Motown stable, and began to groom Robinson as his second-in-command. In Motown's early days, Robinson was involved in every facet of the company's operations, writing, producing and making his own records, helping in the business of promotion and auditioning many of the scores of young hopefuls who were attracted by Gordy's growing reputation as an entrepreneur. Robinson had begun his career as a producer by overseeing the recording of the Miracles' 'Way Over There', and soon afterwards he was charged with developing the talents of Mary Wells and the Supremes. Wells soon became Robinson's most successful protégée: Robinson wrote and produced a sophisticated series of hit singles for her between 1962 and 1964. These records, such as 'You Beat Me To The Punch', 'Two Lovers' and 'My Guy', demonstrated his growing confidence as a writer, able to use paradox and metaphor to transcend the usual banalities of the teenage popular song. A measure of Robinson's influence over Wells' career is the fact that she was unable to repeat her chart success after she elected to leave Motown, and Robinson, in 1964.

Although Robinson was unable to turn the Supremes into a hit-making act, he experienced no such failure in his relationship with Motown's leading male group of the mid-60s, the Temptations. Between 1964 and 1965, Robinson was responsible for the records that established their reputation, writing lyrical and rhythmic songs of a calibre that few writers in pop music have equalled since. 'The Way You Do The Things You Do' set the hit sequence in motion, followed by the classic ballad 'My Girl' (later equally popular in the hands of Otis Redding), the dance number 'Get Ready', 'Since I Lost My Baby' and the remarkable 'It's Growing', which boasted a complex lyric hinged around a series of metaphorical images. During the same period, Robinson helped to create two of Marvin Gaye's most enduring early hits, 'Ain't That Peculiar' and 'I'll Be Doggone'. Throughout the 60s, Smokey Robinson combined this production and A&R work with his own career as leader of the Miracles. He married fellow group member Claudette Rogers in 1959, and she provided the inspiration for Miracles hits such as 'You've Really Got A Hold On Me' and 'Oooh Baby Baby'. During the mid-60s, Robinson was apparently able to turn out high-quality songs to order, working with a variety of collaborators including fellow Miracle Ronnie White, and Motown guitarist Marv Tarplin. As the decade progressed, Bob Dylan referred to Robinson apparently without irony, as 'America's greatest living poet'; as if to justify this assertion, Robinson's lyric-writing scaled new heights on complex ballads such as 'The Love I Saw In You Was Just A Mirage' and 'I Second That Emotion'. From 1967 onwards, Robinson was given individual credit on the Miracles' releases. For the next two years, their commercial fortunes went into a slide, which was righted when their 1965 recording of 'The Tracks Of My Tears' became a major hit in Britain in 1969, and the four-year-old 'The Tears Of A Clown' achieved similar success on both sides of the Atlantic in 1970. At the end of the decade, Robinson briefly resumed his career as a producer and writer for other acts, collaborating with the Marvelettes on 'The Hunter Gets Captured By The Game', and the Four Tops on 'Still Water'. Business concerns were occupying an increasing proportion of his time, however, and in 1971 he announced that he would be leaving the Miracles the following year, to concentrate on his role as Vice-President of the Motown corporation. A year after the split, Robinson launched his solo career, enjoying a hit single with 'Sweet Harmony', an affectionate tribute to his former group, and issuing the excellent *Smokey*. The album included the epic 'Just My Soul Responding', a biting piece of social comment about the USA's treatment of blacks and American Indians. Robinson maintained a regular release schedule through the mid-70s, with one new album arriving every year. Low-key and for the most part lushly produced, they made little impact, although Robinson's songwriting was just as consistent as it had been in the 60s. He continued to break new lyrical ground, striking the banner for non-macho male behaviour on 1974's 'Virgin Man', and giving name to a new style of soft soul on 1975's *A Quiet Storm*. Singles such as 'Baby That's Backatcha' and 'The Agony And The Ecstasy' sold well on the black market, but failed to achieve national airplay in the USA, while in Britain Robinson was regarded as a remnant from the classic era of Motown. His first film soundtrack project, *Big Time*, in 1977, won little praise, and it appeared as if his creative peak was past. Instead, he hit back in 1979 with 'Cruisin'', his biggest chart success since 'The Tears Of A Clown' nine years earlier. A sensuous ballad in the musical tradition of his 60s work, the record introduced a new eroticism into his writing, and restored faith in his stature as a contemporary performer. Two years later, he gained his first UK number 1 with 'Being With You', a touching love song that came close to equalling that achievement in the USA. 'Tell Me Tomorrow' enjoyed more Stateside success in 1982, and Robinson settled into another relaxed release schedule that saw him ride out the 80s on a pattern of regular small hits and consistent album sales. Robinson was contributing significantly less new material, however, and his 1988 autobiography, *Smokey*, revealed that he had been battling against cocaine addiction for much of the decade. Although his marriage to Claudette failed, he returned to full health and creativity, and enjoyed two big hits in 1987, 'Just To See Her' and 'One Heartbeat'.

Voted into the Rock And Roll Hall Of Fame in 1988, Smokey Robinson is now one of the senior figures in popular music, a writer and producer still best remembered for his outstanding work in the 60s, but who has seldom betrayed the responsibility of that legacy since then.

● ALBUMS: *Smokey* (Tamla 1973)★★★, *Pure Smokey* (Tamla 1974)★★★, *A Quiet Storm* (Tamla 1975)★★★, *Smokey's Family Robinson* (Tamla 1976)★★★, *Deep In My Soul* (Tamla 1977)★★★, *Big Time* (Tamla 1977)★★★, *Love Breeze* (Tamla 1978)★★★, *Smokin'* (Tamla 1978)★★★, *Where There's Smoke* (Tamla 1979)★★★, *Warm Thoughts* (Tamla 1980)★★★★, *Being With You* (Tamla 1981)★★★★, *Yes It's You Lady* (Tamla 1982)★★★, *Touch The Sky* (Tamla 1983)★★★, *Blame It On Love* (Tamla 1983)★★★, *Essar* (Tamla 1984)★★★, *Smoke Signals* (Tamla 1985)★★★, *One Heartbeat* (Motown 1987)★★★, *Love, Smokey* (Motown 1990)★★★, *Double Good Everything* (SBK 1991)★★.

● COMPILATIONS: with the Miracles *The Greatest Hits* (Motown 1992)★★★★, with the Miracles*The 35th Anniversry Collection* 4-CD box set (Motown Masters 1994)★★★★, *Early Classics* (Spectrum 1996)★★★★.

● FURTHER READING: *Smokey: Inside My Life*, Smokey Robinson and David Ritz.

Rochell And The Candles

From Los Angeles, California, USA, this vocal group comprised first tenor lead Johnny Wyatt (b. 1938, Texacali, Texas; d. 1983), tenor lead Rochell Henderson, baritone Melvin Sasso, and bass T.C. Henderson. Their one hit, 'Once Upon A Time' (number 20 R&B, number 26 pop), from 1961, was part of the early 60s neo-doo-wop phenomenon when doo-wop experienced a resurgence of interest on the charts. The novelty of the falsetto lead of Wyatt plus the name of 'Rochell' gave many listeners the false impression that the group was led by a female. The follow-up, 'So Far Away' (1961), likewise featured Wyatt's high pitched lead, but despite its excellence, failed to dent the charts. Other singles followed, both on Swingin' and Challenge, but the Candles could not return to the charts. Their last recording, a sublime remake of the Olympics' 'Big Boy Pete' was released in 1964 to an indifferent world. Wyatt went on to become lead of the soul-era group Johnny And The Expressions, who hit the charts with 'Something I Want To Tell You' in 1966. He also made some singles as a solo artist for Bronco during 1966-67.

● COMPILATIONS: *The Golden Groups: The Best Of Swingin' Records* features 10 tracks by Rochell And The Candles, four by the Hollywood Saxons (Relic 1985)★★★.

Rock 'n' Roll Revue

Jazz and R&B performers were at the fore of this 1956 film, despite its grossly misleading title. Also known as *Harlem Rock 'n' Roll*, it was shot at New York's fabled Apollo Theatre. Lionel Hampton, Duke Ellington and Nat 'King' Cole headed a star-studded cast that also featured the Clovers, Joe Turner and Ruth Brown. Shot in sepia-inspired yellow and brown - known as Wondercolour - the film captures several performers at their peak and provides a fascinating insight into several acts inspiring, but not recording, rock 'n' roll. Curiously, the portion featuring Dinah Washington was cut from the UK print, but *Rock 'n' Roll Revue* remains highly interesting feature.

Rocket 88

This part-time attraction was drawn from the ranks of the UK's finest R&B/jazz musicians. Formed in 1979, the unit revolved around singer/guitarist Alexis Korner, bassist/vocalist Jack Bruce and three members of the Rolling Stones' circle, Ian Stewart (piano), Bill Wyman (bass) and Charlie Watts (drums). The unit took its name from a 1951 recording by Jackie Brenson, often cited as the first rock 'n' roll single, although the music offered by this *ad hoc* collective invoked the earlier boogie-woogie style of Meade 'Lux' Lewis. Their lone album, recorded live in Hannover, Germany, included versions of 'St. Louis Blues' and 'Roll 'Em Pete' and, while undeniably low-key, was nonetheless an enthralling glimpse into the artistic preferences of musicians freed from perceived commercial restraints. Korner's premature death ended speculation that Rocket 88 might blossom into a full-time commitment.

● ALBUMS: *Rocket 88* (Atlantic 1981)★★★.

Rockin' Sidney

b. Sidney Semien, 9 April 1938, Lebeau, Louisiana, USA. The full range of black south Louisiana music - blues, R&B, swamp pop and zydeco - can be found in the work of Rockin' Sidney, who was born and grew up in the French-speaking part of that state. Many of his records are characterized by a light approach - even his blues tracks frequently opt for melody rather than emotional expression. Nevertheless, he has recorded regularly for over 30 years, from early singles on the local Jin and Goldband labels to albums self-produced in his own studio. In the early 80s, he achieved a wider profile through the success of his song 'Toot Toot'. So far he has not managed to recapture its novelty appeal, despite evident hard work: his recent recordings have featured Semien playing all of the instruments. His infectious and accessible songs have done much to broaden the appeal of zydeco music in Europe.

● ALBUMS: *They Call Me Rockin'* (Flyright 1975)★★★, *Boogie Blues 'N' Zydeco* (Maison De Soul 1984)★★★, *My Toot Toot* mini-album (Epic 1985)★★★★, *Creola* (ZBC 1987)★★★, *Crowned Prince Of Zydeco* (Maison De Soul 1987)★★★, *Give Me A Good Time Woman* (Maison De Soul 1987)★★★, *A Celebration Holiday* (ZBC 1987)★★★, *Hotsteppin* (JSP 1987)★★★, *My Zydeco Shoes* (Maison De Soul 1987)★★★★, *Live With The Blues* (JSP 1988)★★★, *Mais Yeah Chere* (1993)★★★★.

Rockwell

Kenneth Gordy (b. 15 March 1964, Detroit, Michigan, USA) was the son of Berry Gordy, the head of Motown Records. Nepotism was not an immediate factor in his career, as he was signed to Motown as a soloist without his father's knowledge. Using the name of his school band, Rockwell made his debut in 1984 with the eerie funk song 'Somebody's Watching Me', which featured backing vocals by Michael and Jermaine Jackson. Only after the record reached number 2 in the US charts was Rockwell's identity revealed, as he was determined that his music should be judged on its merits, not his parentage. His second single, 'Obscene Phone Caller', was another Top 40 hit, but 'He's A Cobra' in 1985 failed to breach the Top 100, despite a cameo appearance by Stevie Wonder. Subsequent recordings demonstrated the limitations of his synth-based arrangements and inflexible vocals.

● ALBUMS: *Somebody's Watching Me* (Motown 1984)★★★, *Captured* (Motown 1985)★★, *Genie* (Motown 1986)★★.

RONETTES

Veronica 'Ronnie' Bennett (b. 10 August 1943, New York, USA), her sister Estelle (b. 22 July 1944, New York, USA) and cousin Nedra Talley (b. 17 January 1946, New York, USA) began their career as a dance act, the Dolly Sisters. By 1961 they had become the resident dance troupe at the famed Peppermint Lounge, home of the twist craze, and having taken tuition in harmony singing, later secured a recording contract. The trio's first single, 'I Want A Boy', was credited to Ronnie And The Relatives, but when 'Silhouettes' followed in 1962, the Ronettes appellation was in place. They recorded four singles for the Colpix/May group and appeared on disc jockey Murray The K's *Live From The Brooklyn Fox* before a chance telephone call resulted in their signing with producer Phil Spector. Their first collaboration, the majestic 'Be My Baby' defined the girl-group sound as Spector constructed a cavernous accompaniment around Ronnie's plaintive, nasal voice. The single reached the Top 5 in the USA and UK before being succeeded by the equally worthwhile 'Baby I Love You', another Top 20 entrant in both countries. The producer's infatuation with Ronnie - the couple were later married - resulted in some of his finest work being reserved for her, and although ensuing singles, including 'The Best Part of Breaking Up', 'Walking In The Rain' (both 1964) and 'Is This What I Get For Loving You' (1965), failed to recapture the Ronettes' early success, they are among the finest pop singles of all time. The group's career was shelved during Spector's mid-60s 'retirement', but they re-emerged in 1969 with 'You Came, You Saw You Conquered'. Credited to 'The Ronettes Featuring The Voice Of Veronica', this excellent single was nonetheless commercially moribund and Ronnie's aspirations were again sublimated. She separated from Spector in 1973 and joined Buddah Records, founding a new group with vocalists Denise Edwards and Chip Fields. Ronnie And The Ronettes made their debut that year with 'Lover Lover', before changing their name to Ronnie Spector and the Ronettes for 'I Wish I Never Saw The Sunshine', an impassioned remake of a song recorded by the original line-up, but which remained unissued until 1976. The group's name was then dropped as its lead singer pursued her solo ambitions.

● ALBUMS: *Presenting The Fabulous Ronettes Featuring Veronica* (Philes 1964)★★★.

● COMPILATIONS: *The Ronettes Sing Their Greatest Hits* (Phil Spector International 1975)★★★, *Their Greatest Hits - Vol. II* (1981)★★, *The Colpix Years 1961-63* (Murray Hill 1987)★★★, *The Best Of* (ABKCO 1992)★★★.

ROOGALATOR

One of the first of the 70s UK R&B revivalist bands (along with Dr Feelgood), Roogalator were led by American Danny Adler (b. 1949, Cincinnati, Ohio, USA). He left the USA in the early 70s having played guitar for Bootsy Collins and various jazz and blues musicians. He arrived in London and in 1972 put together the first line-up of Roogalator. Over the years numerous personnel were involved including key names such as Paul Riley (of Chilli Willi And The Red Hot Peppers) and Bobby Irwin (of the Strutters, the Sinceros, and various Nick Lowe bands). They came under the management of Robin Scott (later the brains behind M) and in 1973 recorded their best-known track - 'Cincinatti Fat Back' - for a BBC radio session. This was eventually released as an EP by Stiff in 1976. Scott then formed the Do It label in order to release an album by the band, whose new line-up was Adler (guitar, vocals), Nick Plytas (keyboards), Julian Scott (bass) and Justin Hilkdreth (drums). Adler also pursued a simultaneous career with the De Luxe Blues Band.

● ALBUMS: *Play It By Ear* (Do It 1978)★★★.

ROSE ROYCE

Formed in the USA as a multi-purpose backing group, the original nine-piece worked under a variety of names. In 1973 Kenji Brown (guitar), Victor Nix (keyboards), Kenny Copeland, Freddie Dunn (trumpets), Michael Moore (saxophone), Lequient 'Duke' Jobe (bass), Henry Garner and Terrai Santiel (drums) backed Edwin Starr as Total Concept Limited, before supporting Yvonne Fair as Magic Wand. This line-up later became the regular studio band behind the Undisputed Truth and Temptations, before embarking on their own recording career following the addition of singer Gwen Dickey. The group took the name Rose Royce in 1976 when they recorded the successful soundtrack to the motion picture *Car Wash*, the title song of which was a platinum-selling single. Two further songs from the film reached the R&B Top 10 before the band joined producer Norman Whitfield's label. Two atmospheric releases, 'Wishing On A Star' and 'Love Don't Live Here Anymore' (both 1978), reached the Top 3 in the UK despite disappointing sales at home. This feature continued the following year with 'Is It Love You're After', another UK Top 20 record. Their popularity in the UK was verified in 1980 when the *Greatest Hits* collection reached number 1 in the album charts. Since then the group has continued to record, but their releases have only made the lower reaches of the charts.

● ALBUMS: *Car Wash* (MCA 1976)★★★★, *Rose Royce II/In Full Bloom* (Whitfield 1977)★★★★, *Rose Royce III/Strikes Again!* (Whitfield 1978)★★★, *Rose Royce IV/Rainbow Connection* (Whitfield 1979)★★, *Golden Touch* (Whitfield 1981)★★, *Jump Street* (Warners 1981)★★, *Stronger Than Ever* (Epic 1982)★★, *Music Magic* (Streetwave 1984)★★, *The Show Must Go On* (Streetwave 1985)★★, *Fresh Cut* (Carrere 1987)★★.

● COMPILATIONS: *Greatest Hits* (Whitfield 1980)★★★★, *Is It Love You're After* (Blatant 1988)★★★.

Rosie And The Originals

Formed in 1960 in San Diego, California, USA, Rosie And The Originals were 15-year-old Rosalie 'Rosie' Hamlin (b. Alaska, USA), Noah Tafolla (guitar), Carl Van Guida (drums), Tony Gomez (saxophone) and David Ponci (guitar). Hamlin wrote their only hit song, 'Angel Baby' (wrongly credited to Ponci), as a poem to her first boyfriend, then set it to music on a piano. They recorded the doo-wop ballad and then found a local label, Highland Records, to issue it. The record became a local sensation on Los Angeles radio station KFWB before breaking nationally in late 1960, eventually climbing to the US Top 5. Rosie And The Originals recorded no albums but, with the assistance of Jackie Wilson, Hamlin later recorded for Brunswick Records, including *Lonely Blue Nights* in 1961. She subsequently married Tafolla, then divorced and later appeared in 'oldies' shows, performing with a band, the LA Rhythm Section.

Ross, Diana

b. 26 March 1944, Detroit, Michigan, USA. While still in high school Ross became the fourth and final member of the Primettes, who recorded for Lu-Pine in 1960, signed to Motown Records in 1961 and then changed their name to the Supremes. She was a backing vocalist on the group's early releases, until Motown supremo Berry Gordy insisted that she become their lead singer, a role she retained for the next six years. In recognition of her prominent position in the Supremes, she received individual billing on all their releases from 1967 onwards. Throughout her final years with the group, Ross was being groomed for a solo career under the close personal supervision of Gordy, with whom she was rumoured to have romantic links. In late 1969, he announced that Ross would be leaving the Supremes, and she played her final concert with the group in January 1970. Later that year Ross began a long series of successful solo releases with the chart-topping 'Ain't No Mountain High Enough'. In April 1971, she married businessman Robert Silberstein, but they were divorced in 1976 after renewed speculation about her relationship with Gordy.

As she continued to enjoy success with lightweight love songs in the early 70s, Motown's plan to widen Ross's appeal led her to host a television special, *Diana!*, in 1971. In 1972, she starred in Motown's film biography of Billie Holiday, *Lady Sings The Blues*, winning an Oscar nomination for her stirring portrayal of the jazz singer's physical decline into drug addiction. However, subsequent starring roles in *Mahogany* (1975) and *The Wiz* (1978) drew a mixed critical response. In 1973, Ross released an album of duets with Marvin Gaye, though allegedly the pair did not meet during the recording of the project. She enjoyed another US number 1 with 'Touch Me In The Morning', and repeated that success with the theme song from *Mahogany* in 1975. 'Love Hangover' in 1976 saw her moving into the contemporary disco field, a shift of direction that was consolidated on the 1980 album *Diana*, produced by Nile Rodgers and Bernard Edwards of Chic. Her choice of hit material continued to be inspired and the 80s started with a major hit, 'Upside Down', which rooted itself at the top of the US chart for a month; similar but lesser success followed with 'I'm Coming Out' and 'It's My Turn'. The following year a collaboration with Lionel Richie produced the title track to the film *Endless Love*; this tear-jerker spent more than two months at the top of the US chart. By now, Ross was as much a media personality as a soul singer, winning column inches for her liaison with Gene Simmons of Kiss. There was also intense speculation about the nature of her relationship with Michael Jackson, whose career she had helped to guide since 1969.

After months of rumour about her future, Ross left Motown in 1981, and signed contracts with RCA for North America, and Capitol for the rest of the world. She formed her own production company and had further hits. A reworking of Frankie Lymon's 'Why Do Fools Fall In Love' and Michael Jackson's 'Muscles' confirmed her pre-eminence in the field of disco-pop. During the remainder of the 80s only 'Missing You', a tribute to the late Marvin Gaye, brought her the success to which she had become accustomed. In Britain, however, she achieved a number 1 hit in 1986 with 'Chain Reaction', an affectionate recreation of her days with the Supremes, written and produced by the Bee Gees. In 1986, Ross married a Norwegian shipping magnate, effectively quashing renewed rumours that she might wed Berry Gordy and return to Motown. Since then, she has won more publicity for her epic live performances than for her sporadic releases of new material, which continue to occupy the lighter end of the black music market.

● ALBUMS: *Diana Ross* (Motown 1970)★★★, *Everything Is Everything* (Motown 1970)★★★, *Diana!* (Motown 1971)★★★, *Surrender* (Motown 1971)★★★, *Lady Sings The Blues* (Motown 1972)★★★★, *Touch Me In The Morning* (Motown 1973)★★★, with Marvin Gaye *Diana And Marvin* (Motown 1973)★★★, *Last Time I Saw Him* (Motown 1973)★★★, *Diana Ross Live At Caesar's Palace* (Motown 1974)★★★, *Mahogany* (Motown 1975)★★, *Diana Ross* (Motown 1976)★★★, *An Evening With Diana Ross* (Motown 1977)★★★, *Baby It's Me* (Motown 1977)★★★, *Ross* (Motown 1978)★★★, *The Boss* (Motown 1979)★★★, *Diana* (Motown 1980)★★★, *To Love Again* (Motown 1981)★★★, *Why Do Fools Fall In Love* (RCA 1981)★★★, *Silk Electric* (RCA 1982)★★, *Ross* (RCA 1983)★★, *Swept Away* (RCA 1984)★★, *Eaten Alive* (RCA 1985)★★, *Red Hot Rhythm 'N' Blues* (RCA 1987)★★★, *Working Overtime* (Motown 1989)★★, *Greatest Hits Live* (Motown 1989)★★★, *Force Behind The Power* (Motown 1991)★★, *Live, Stolen Moments* (1993)★★, with Placido Domingo, José Carreras *Christmas In Vienna* (Sony 1993)★★, *Take Me Higher* (Motown 1995)★★.

● COMPILATIONS: *All The Great Hits* (Motown 1981)★★★★, *Diana Ross Anthology* (Motown 1983)★★★★, *One Woman, The Ultimate Collection* (EMI 1993)★★★★, *Voice Of Love* (EMI 1996)★★★★.

● VIDEOS: *The Visions Of Diana Ross* (PMI 1986), *One Woman - The Video Collection* (1993), *Stolen Moments* (1994).

● FURTHER READING: *Diana Ross*, Leonore K. Itzkowitz. *Diana Ross*, Patricia Mulrooney Eldred. *Diana*

Ross: Supreme Lady, Connie Berman. *I'm Gonna Make You Love Me: The Story Of Diana Ross*, James Haskins. *Diana Ross: An Illustrated Biography*, Geoff Brown. *Dreamgirl: My Life As A Supreme*, Mary Wilson. *Call Her Miss Ross*, J. Randy Taraborrelli. *Supreme Faith: Someday We'll Be Together*, Mary Wilson with Patricia Romanowski. *Secrets Of The Sparrow*, Diana Ross.

Ross, Jackie

b. 30 January 1946, St. Louis, Missouri, USA. This cool, stylish singer made her debut on Sam Cooke's Sar label in 1962. 'Selfish One' (1964), her first single for Chess, showcased a mature delivery that further releases, including 'I've Got The Skill' (1964) and 'Take Me For A Little While' (1965), amplified. Tailor-made for producer Billy Davis's imaginative arrangements, she found it hard to maintain this standard on the several labels - Brunswick, Scepter, Mercury and more - to which she had later turned. An interlude on Jerry Butler's Fountain label resulted in 'Who Could Be Loving You' (1969), an alluring, mid-paced ballad subsequently revived by Dusty Springfield. Ross was last heard on a 1981 album by Little Milton.

● ALBUMS: *Full Bloom* (Chess 1964)★★★, *A New Beginning* (1980)★★, shared with Little Milton *In Perspective* (1981)★★★.

Royalettes

A female R&B vocal group from Baltimore, Maryland, USA, consisting of sisters Anita and Sheila Ross (lead), Terry Jones and Veronica Brown. The group was discovered in 1962 when they won a talent contest sponsored by legendary Baltimore disc jockey Buddy Deane. Their prize was a recording contract with Chancellor Records, but the two releases did not click with the public. A single for Warner Brothers did nothing either. In 1964 the Royalettes were signed to MGM and were teamed up with arranger/producer Teddy Randazzo, and he applied a little of the same magic that he used in recording all the Little Anthony And The Imperials hits for DCP during the 60s. The result was the girls' first national hit with 'It's Gonna Take A Miracle' (number 28 R&B, number 41 pop), from 1965, on which Randazzo created a sound that was indistinguishable from Little Anthony. The girls broke out of the Little Anthony mode with their second hit 'I Want To Meet Him' (number 26 R&B, number 72 pop), also from 1965. The Royalettes were not able to reach the charts again, despite the release of some excellent songs, notably 'Only When You're Lonely' (1966). It failed to chart, possibly because Chicago-based singer Holli Maxwell had already had success in several markets with her version of the song. After a single for Roulette in 1967 failed to attract an audience, the Royalettes broke up.

● ALBUMS: *It's Gonna Take A Miracle* (MGM 1965)★★★, *The Elegant Sound Of The Royalettes* (MGM 1966)★★★.

● COMPILATIONS: *It's Gonna Take A Miracle: The MGM Sides* (Ichiban 1996)★★★.

Ruby And The Romantics

Edward Roberts (first tenor), George Lee (second tenor), Ronald Mosley (baritone) and Leroy Fann (bass) had been working as the Supremes prior to the arrival of Ruby Nash Curtis (b. 12 November 1939, New York City, New York, USA) in 1962. Curtis had met the group in Akron, Ohio, and took on the role as their lead singer. They subsequently secured a contract with the New York label Kapp and at the suggestion of the company, changed their name to Ruby And The Romantics. By the following year they had taken the evocative 'Our Day Will Come' to the top of the US pop chart, earning them a gold disc. Over the next 12 months the group enjoyed a further six hits including the original version of 'Hey There Lonely Boy' which, with a change of gender, was later revived by Eddie Holman. After three years at Kapp, the group signed to the ABC label. In 1965 'Does He Really Care For Me', the Romantics' last chart entry, preceded a wholesale line-up change. Ruby brought in a new backing group; Richard Pryor, Vincent McLeod, Robert Lewis, Ronald Jackson and Bill Evans, but in 1968 the forthright Curtis replaced this version with Denise Lewis and Cheryl Thomas.

● ALBUMS: *Our Day Will Come* (Kapp 1963)★★★, *Till Then* (Kapp 1963)★★★, *Ruby And The Romantics* (ABC 1967)★★, *More Than Yesterday* (ABC 1968)★★.

● COMPILATIONS: *Greatest Hits Album* (Kapp 1966)★★★, *The Very Best Of ...* (Target 1995)★★★.

Ruffin, David

b. 18 January 1941, Meridian, Mississippi, USA, d. 1 June 1991. The younger brother of Jimmy Ruffin and the cousin of Melvin Franklin of the Temptations, David Ruffin was the son of a minister, and began his singing career with the gospel group the Dixie Nightingales. He combined the roles of vocalist and drummer in the doo-wop combo the Voice Masters from 1958, before signing to the Anna label in Detroit as a soloist in 1960. His releases there and on Check-Mate in 1961 proved unsuccessful, though they demonstrated the raw potential of his vocal skills. In 1963, Ruffin replaced Eldridge Bryant as tenor vocalist in the Temptations. At first, he played a supporting role behind the falsetto leads of Eddie Kendricks. From 1965 onwards he was allowed to take the spotlight on hits such as 'My Girl' and 'I Wish It Would Rain', which illustrated his commanding way with a ballad, and raunchier R&B material such as 'I'm Losing You' and 'Ain't Too Proud To Beg'. Adopting the role of frontman, Ruffin was soon singled out by the media as the key member of the group, though his erratic behaviour caused some tension within the ranks. The Motown hierarchy slowly began to ease him out of the line-up, achieving their aim when they refused to give him solo billing in front of the group's name in 1968. Still under contract to the label, he embarked on an episodic solo career. 'My Whole World Ended', a Top 10 hit in 1969, re-established his credentials as a great soul singer, under the tutelage of producers Harvey Fuqua and Johnny Bristol. Subsequent releases failed to utilize his talents to the full, and an album of duets with his brother Jimmy also proved disappointing. After three years of comparative silence, Ruffin re-emerged in 1973 with the first of a series of workmanlike albums which spawned one Top 10 single, the Van McCoy-produced 'Walk Away From Love', and a batch of minor hits. In 1979, he left Motown for Warner Brothers Records, where his career fell into decline. In the early 80s he was briefly jailed for tax evasion, and his slide was only halted when a Temptations reunion in 1983 brought him back into contact with Eddie Kendricks. After the project was complete, Ruffin and Kendricks established a regular partnership, which was boosted when they were showcased in a prestigious concert at New York's Apollo by long-time Temptations fans, Hall And Oates. This event was captured on a 1985 live album, and Ruffin and Kendricks also joined the rock duo at the Live Aid concert in Philadelphia. They subsequently recorded a well-received album of duets for RCA, which revived memories of their vocal interplay with the Temptations two decades earlier. He recorded with Ian Levine's Motor City label in 1990 including 'Hurt The One You Love' and toured with Eddie Kendricks and Dennis Edwards as Tribute To The Temptations on a package tour in 1991. A few weeks after the last performance he died in tragic circumstances after an overdose of crack cocaine.

● ALBUMS: *My Whole World Ended* (Motown 1969)★★★, *Feelin' Good* (Motown 1969)★★, with Jimmy Ruffin *I Am My Brother's Keeper* (Motown 1970)★★, *David Ruffin* (Motown 1973)★★, *Me'n'Rock'n'Roll Are Here To Stay* (Motown 1974)★★, *Who I Am* (Motown 1975)★★, *Everything's Coming Up Love* (Motown 1976)★★, *In My Stride* (Motown 1977)★★, *So Soon We Change* (Warners 1979)★, *Gentleman Ruffin* (Warners 1980)★★, with Kendrick *Ruffin And Kendrick* (RCA 1987)★★★.

● COMPILATIONS: *David Ruffin At His Best* (Motown 1978)★★★.

RUFFIN, JIMMY

b. 7 May 1939, Collinsville, Mississippi, USA. The son of a minister, Ruffin was born into a musical family: his brother, David Ruffin, and cousin, Melvin Franklin, both became mainstays of the Temptations. Ruffin abandoned his gospel background to become a session singer in the early 60s, joining the Motown stable in 1961 for a one-off single before he was drafted for national service. After leaving the US Army, he returned to Motown, turning down the opportunity to join the Temptations and instead recommending his brother for the job. His commercial breakthrough came in 1966 with the major US and UK hit 'What Becomes Of The Broken-Hearted', which displayed his emotional, if rather static, vocals. After three smaller hits, Ruffin found success in the USA hard to sustain, concentrating instead on the British market. 'I'll Say Forever My Love' and 'It's Wonderful' consolidated his position in the UK, and in 1970 he was voted the world's top singer in one British poll. Ruffin left Motown in the early 70s after an unsuccessful collaboration with his brother, and achieved minor success with singles on Polydor and Chess. Despite his popularity as a live performer in Britain, he enjoyed no significant hits until 1980, when 'Hold On To My Love', written and produced by Robin Gibb of the Bee Gees, brought him his first US Top 30 hit for 14 years. A duet with Maxine Nightingale, 'Turn To Me', was a big seller in 1982, while Ruffin's only other success of note in the 80s was the British chart-contender 'There Will Never Be Another You' in 1985. He joined Ian Levine's Motor City label in 1988 and recorded two singles with Brenda Holloway.

● ALBUMS: *Top Ten* (Soul 1967)★★★, *Ruff'n'Ready* (Soul 1969)★★, *The Groove Governor* (1970)★★, with David Ruffin *I Am My Brother's Keeper* (Motown 1970)★★, *Jimmy Ruffin* (1973)★★, *Love Is All We Need* (Polydor 1975)★★, *Sunrise* (RSO 1980)★★★.

● COMPILATIONS: *Greatest Hits* (Tamla Motown 1974)★★★, *20 Golden Classics* (Motown 1981)★★★, *Greatest Motown Hits* (Motown 1989)★★★, *Early Classics* (Spectrum 1996)★★.

RUFUS

This Chicago-based group evolved from the American Breed when three original members, Al Ciner (guitar), Charles Colbert (bass) and Lee Graziano (drums), were joined by Kevin Murphy (keyboards), Paulette McWilliams (vocals), Ron Stockard and Dennis Belfield. Initially known as Smoke, then Ask Rufus, it was several months before a stable unit evolved. Graziano made way for Andre Fisher, but the crucial change came when Chaka Khan (b. Yvette Marie Stevens, 23 March 1953, Great Lakes Naval Training Station, Illinois, USA) joined in place of McWilliams. The group, now known simply as Rufus, signed with the ABC label in 1973, but made little headway until a chance encounter with Stevie Wonder during sessions for a second album. Impressed by Khan's singing, he donated an original song, 'Tell Me Something Good', which, when issued as a single, became a gold disc. It began a run of exceptional releases, including 'You Got The Love' (1974), 'Sweet Thing' (1975) and 'At Midnight (My Love Will Lift You Up)' (1977), all of which topped the R&B chart. By this time Rufus had stabilized around Khan, Murphy, Tony Maiden (guitar), Dave Wolinski (keyboards), Bobby Watson (bass) and John Robinson (drums), but it was clear that the singer was the star attraction. She began recording as a solo act in 1978, but returned to the fold in 1980 for *Masterjam*, which contained 'Do You Love What You Feel', another number 1 soul single. Khan continued to pursue her own career and perform with Rufus, who secured an international hit in 1983 with 'Ain't Nobody'. The song was written by Wolinski, by now an established figure in soul circles through his work on Michael Jackson's *Off The Wall*. The distinction between Chaka Khan's successful solo recordings and her work with Rufus has become blurred over the years, but it remains arguable whether or not she achieved the same empathy elsewhere.

● ALBUMS: *Rufus* (ABC 1973)★★, *Rags To Rufus* (ABC 1974)★★★★, *Rufusized* (ABC 1975)★★★★, *Rufus Featuring Chaka Khan* (ABC 1975)★★★, *Ask Rufus* (ABC 1977)★★★, *Street Player* (ABC 1978)★★★, *Numbers* (ABC 1979)★, *Masterjam* (MCA 1979)★★★, *Party 'Til You're Broke* (MCA 1981)★★, *Camouflage* (MCA 1981)★★, *Live - Stompin' At The Savoy* (Warners 1983)★★.

● FILMS: *Breakdance - The Movie* (1984).

RuPaul

b. Rupaul Andre Charles, 17 November 1960, Dan Diego, California, USA. A seven-foot tall (in heels), transsexual American diva package. At the age of 15 RuPaul took himself (as he then was) off to Atlanta, where he associated with the B-52's and appeared on cable television. Moving to New York, he would become part of the Wigstock counter-culture that also gave birth to Deee-Lite. He subsequently became a figurehead for the US gay movement when his debut album crossed over to the mainstream, and was a chat show favourite. He has been keen to tackle the role, leading a demonstration against the Ku Klux Klan in full drag. He obtained his own television series, and helped to present the 1994 BRIT Awards alongside a dwarfed Elton John.

● ALBUMS: *Supermodel Of The World* (Tommy Boy 1993)★★, *Foxy Lady* (1996)★★.

● FURTHER READING: *Lettin' It All Hang Out: An Autobiography*, RuPaul.

Rushen, Patrice

b. 30 September 1954, Los Angeles, California, USA. Rushen grew up in Los Angeles and attended the University of Southern California. She started learning classical piano when she was three, and turned to jazz in her teens. A group with which she was playing won an award for young musicians at Monterey in 1972. She played with a host of artists, including Abbey Lincoln, Donald Byrd and Sonny Rollins, before joining Lee Ritenour's group in 1977. Her career as a solo singing artist, which commenced in the late 70s as a pop/soul artist, bore fruit on the Elektra label. The US R&B Top 20 hit 'Hang It Up' (1978) was followed by 'Haven't You Heard' (US R&B number 7/US pop Top 30, 1979). The latter, plus 'Never Gonna Give You Up (Won't Let You Be)' were minor UK hits in the early 80s, but were eclipsed by the Top 10 'Forget Me Nots'. Despite a tailing off in UK/US pop chart action from that point, Rushen continued to appear regularly on the US R&B/soul charts. She gained notable chart success with 'Feel So Real (Won't Let Go)' (number 3, 1984) and 'Watch Out (number 9, 1987). After a period of label change, to Arista Records, she has focused increased attention on her singing, and her predominantly bop-based playing has given way to fusion and urban R&B styles. In 1988 she played with the Wayne Shorter/Carlos Santana group.

● ALBUMS: *Prelusion* (1974)★★★, *Before The Dawn* (1975)★★★, with Sonny Rollins *The Way I Feel* (Original Jazz Classics 1976)★★★, *Shout It Out* (Prestige 1977)★★★, with Lee Ritenour *Sugarloaf Express* (Elite 1978)★★, with John McLaughlin *Johnny McLaughlin, Electric Guitarist* (Columbia 1978)★★★★, *Patrice* (Elektra 1979)★★★, *Pizzazz* (Elektra 1979)★★★, *Let There Be Funk* (Elektra 1980)★★★, *Posh* (Elektra 1980)★★★, *Straight From The Heart* (Elektra 1982)★★★, *Now* (Elektra 1984)★★★, *Breaking All The Rules* (1986)★★★, *Watch Out!* (Arista 1987)★★★, *Signature* (Discovery 1997)★★★.

● COMPILATIONS: *The Best Of Patrice Rushen* (Rhino 1996)★★★★.

S.O.S. Band

Formed in Atlanta, Georgia, USA, in 1977, the S.O.S. Band enjoyed a long run of hits on the US R&B charts during the 80s. The group originally consisted of Mary Davis (vocals, keyboards), Jason 'T.C.' Bryant (keyboards), Billy R. Ellis (saxophone) and James Earl Jones III (drums). They performed regularly, as Sounds Of Santa Monica, at Lamar's Regal Room in Atlanta where they were discovered by Milton Lamar, the club's owner, who later became their manager. The group were signed to the independent Tabu Records and soon added new members Willie 'Sonny' Killebrew (saxophone, flute), John Simpson III (bass, keyboards) and Bruno Speight (guitar). The group then changed its name to the S.O.S. Band. Performing in the then popular funk style, the band began to amass a catalogue of US hits in 1980, with 'Take Your Time (Do It Right) Part 1' rising to number 1 on the R&B chart and number 3 on the national pop chart. They returned to the pop singles chart four more times throughout their career, but never again came close to that initial position. On the R&B chart, however, they were mainstays through 1987, returning to the Top 10 four more times - in 1983 with 'Just be Good To Me' (number 2) and 'Tell Me If You Still Care' (number 5), in 1984 with 'Just The Way You Like It' (number 6), and in 1986 with 'The Finest' (number 2). Five S.O.S. Band albums also charted in the USA, the debut, *S.O.S.*, faring the best at number 12. There were a number of personnel changes throughout the decade, with vocalist Davis leaving for a solo career in 1987. The band released an album on Arista in 1991.

● ALBUMS: *S.O.S.* (Tabu 1980)★★, *Too* (Tabu 1981)★★, *S.O.S. III* (Tabu 1982)★★, *On The Rise* (Tabu 1983)★★★, *Just The Way You Like It* (Tabu 1984)★★★, *Sands Of Time* (Tabu 1985)★★★, *Diamonds In the Raw* (Tabu 1989)★★, *One Of Many Nights* (Arista 1991)★★★.

● COMPILATIONS: *The Way You Like It* (Columbia 1988)★★★.

Sade

b. Helen Folasade Adu, 16 January 1959, Ibadan, Nigeria. Sade's sultry jazz-tinged vocals made her one of the most successful international stars of the 80s. Of mixed Nigerian/English parentage, Sade grew up in Clacton, Essex, England, writing songs as a teenager. While an art student in London, she joined Arriva, where she met guitarist Ray St. John with whom she composed 'Smooth Operator'. From 1981-83, Sade fronted the funk band Pride, leaving the following year to form her own band with ex-Pride members Stewart Matthewman (saxophone), Andrew Hale (keyboards) and Paul Denman (bass). The line-up was completed by drummer Paul Cook. The group gained a following on the London club scene and in 1984 its first single, the lilting 'Your Love Is King' was a Top 10 hit. This was followed by the Robin Millar-produced *Diamond Life*, which was to become one of the biggest-selling debut albums of the decade, with over six million copies sold worldwide. Sade's next album, with all songs written by group members, included the US number 1 'Promise' as well as further hit singles, 'The Sweetest Taboo' and 'The First Time'. Sade also contributed music to the soundtrack of *Absolute Beginners*, a 1987 film in which she had a cameo role. With ex-Wham! backing singer Leroy Osbourne added to the group, Sade began a world tour in 1988 to coincide with the release of her third album, from which 'Paradise' headed the R&B chart in the USA. Sade took her time in delivering *Love Deluxe*. Although it was another mature work, and included two excellent hit singles in 'No Ordinary Love' and 'Feel No Pain', the fickle British public were lukewarm. The album briefly dented the UK top 30, while in the USA it was a million-seller, peaking at number 3. A greatest hits package was released in 1994, indicating by implication that the artist's best compositions are already behind her. Her band have recorded separately as Sweetback. In 1997 she gave birth to her first child.

● ALBUMS: *Diamond Life* (Epic 1984)★★★★, *Promise* (Epic 1985)★★★★, *Stronger Than Pride* (Epic 1988)★★★★, *Love Deluxe* (Epic 1992)★★★.

● COMPILATIONS: *The Best Of Sade* (Epic 1994)★★★★.

● VIDEOS: *Life Promise Pride Love* (1993), *Sade Live* (SMV 1994), *Live Concert Home Video* (Epic 1994).

Sain, Oliver

b. 1 March 1932, Dundee, Mississippi, USA. Working out of St. Louis, saxophonist Sain first established himself as a bandleader and producer, but later in his career made a name for himself as a disco star. After forming his band in St. Louis in 1960, he developed a considerable local reputation playing at all the clubs in the city and across the Mississippi in East St. Louis and other communities. Members of his band have included Fontella Bass, Bobby McClure and Little Milton. He made his first records in 1962 for the tiny Bobbin label, featuring Fontella Bass on vocals and piano and Little Milton on guitar. In 1966 he founded Archway Studio and occasionally recorded himself as well as a host of St. Louis/East St. Louis acts. Sain never achieved any national recognition, however, until the early 70s, when he began recording instrumentals for the Nashville-based Abet label, establishing himself as an unlikely disco star. His most renowned hits were 'Bus Stop' (number 47 R&B) in 1974 and 'Party Hearty' (number 16 R&B) in 1976. His last chart record a year later was 'I Feel Like Dancin'' (number 74 R&B). Sain's albums, unlike his singles, were broader than disco in appeal, containing, besides rousing dance grooves, some warm, southern-style, soulful saxophone playing. During the 80s and 90s he established himself as a producer of blues acts, notably Larry Davis, Eddie Kirkland, David Dee and Johnnie Johnson.

● ALBUMS: *Main Man* (Abet 1973)★★★, *Bus Stop* (Abet 1974)★★★, *Blue Max* (Abet 1975)★★, *So Good In The Morning* (Houston Connection 1981)★★.

● COMPILATIONS: *Disco King* (Soul Posters 1976)★★★, *At His Best* (Abet 1977)★★★.

Sam And Bill

An R&B vocal duo formed in Newark, New Jersey, USA, consisting of Bill Johnson (b. 16 October 1932, Augusta, Georgia, USA) and Sam Gary (b. Columbus, South Carolina, USA). Sam And Bill were fine representatives of an interesting early 60s phenomenon in the soul revolution - that is, the emergence of highly gospelized vocal duos such as Sam And Dave, the Righteous Brothers and Knight Brothers. Johnson first recorded for Sun Records in a group called the Steps Of Rhythm. Gary was originally the guitarist for a group called the Soul Brothers. The two teamed up in 1962 and had hits with deep soul reworkings of two pop ballads, 'For Your Love' (number 14 R&B, 1965), which was a remake of Ed Townsend's 1958 hit, and 'Fly Me To The Moon' (number 38 R&B, 1966). Their record company JoDa then folded and the duo broke up. Johnson recruited Sam Davis Jnr. (b. 10 December 1940, Winston-Salem, North Carolina, USA) to be the new Sam. This duo in 1967 recorded for Brunswick Records without success.

Sam And Dave

Samuel David Moore (b. 12 October 1935, Miami, Florida, USA) and David Prater (b. 9 May 1937, Ocilla, Georgia, USA, d. 9 April 1988). Sam And Dave first performed together in 1961 at Miami's King Of Hearts club. Moore originally sang in his father's Baptist church before joining the Melonaires, while Prater, who had worked with the Sensational Hummingbirds, was also gospel-trained. Club-owner John Lomelo became the duo's manager and was instrumental in securing their contract with Roulette. Five singles and one album subsequently appeared between 1962 and 1964, produced by R&B veteran Henry Glover, but it was not until Jerry Wexler signed Sam And Dave to Atlantic Records that their true potential blossomed. For political reasons, their records appeared on Stax; they used the Memphis-based house band, while many of their strongest moments came from the Isaac Hayes/David Porter staff writing team. 'You Don't Know Like I Know', 'Hold On I'm Comin' (both 1966), 'Soul Man' (1967) and 'I Thank You' (1968), featuring Prater's gritty delivery and Moore's higher interjections, were among the genre's finest. When Stax and Atlantic separated in 1968, Sam And Dave reverted to the parent company, but a disintegrating personal relationship seemed to mirror their now decaying fortune. The amazing 'Soul Sister, Brown Sugar' (1969) delayed the slide, but the duo split briefly the next year when Sam Moore began his own career. Three solo singles followed, but the pair were reunited by a contract with United Artists. A renewed profile, on the strength of the Blues Brothers' success with 'Soul Man', faltered when the differences between the two men proved irreconcilable. By 1981, Moore was again pursuing an independent direction, but his sole chart success came when he was joined by Lou Reed for a remake of 'Soul Man' six years later.

Prater found a new foil in the 'Sam' of Sam & Bill, but before they were able to consolidate this new partnership, Prater died in a car crash on 9 April 1988. Arguably soul's definitive duo, Sam And Dave released records that combined urgency with an unbridled passion.

● ALBUMS: *Sam And Dave* i (Roulette/King 1966)★★, *Hold On, I'm Comin'* (Stax 1966)★★★★, *Double Dynamite* (Stax 1967)★★★★, *Soul Men* (Stax 1967)★★★★, *I Thank You* (Atlantic 1968)★★★, *Double Trouble* (Stax 1969)★★★, *Back At 'Cha* (United Artists 1976)★★, *Sam And Dave* ii 1962-63 recordings (Edsel 1994)★★.

● COMPILATIONS: *The Best Of Sam And Dave* (Atlantic 1969)★★★★, *Can't Stand Up For Falling Down* (Edsel 1984)★★★, *Greatest Hits* (Castle 1986)★★★, *Wonderful World* (Topline 1987)★★★, *Sweet Funky Gold* (Gusto 1988)★★★, *Sweat 'N' Soul: Anthology 1968 - 1971* (Rhino 1993)★★★★, *The Very Best Of ...* (Rhino 1995)★★★★.

SANDPEBBLES

From New York City, New York, USA, this vocal group comprised Calvin White, Andrea Bolden and Lonzine Wright. White had been a member of the Gospel Wonders in the early 60s and he brought some robust gospel-style singing to the Sandpebbles when he formed the group. Under the aegis of New York producer Tony Vann, the Sandpebbles enjoyed big hits with 'Forget It' (number 10 R&B, number 81 pop) and 'Love Power' (number 14 R&B, number 22 pop) for the Calla label in 1967. The Sandpebbles changed their name to C & The Shells in 1968, and produced by Jerry Williams, had a hit with a softer-styled 'You Are The Circus' (number 28 R&B) in 1969. C & The Shells left Cotillion in 1970, and joined the tiny Zanzee label, where they recorded with little success. The last release by the group was in 1973.

SAPPHIRES

A vocal trio from Philadelphia, Pennsylvania, USA, consisting of Carol Jackson (lead), George Gainer and Joe Livingston. The group purveyed an infectious pop-soul girl-group sound that was typical of east coast African-American acts during the early 60s. Their one big hit was 'Who Do You Love' (number 9 R&B, number 25 pop) in 1964, but they recorded other excellent numbers in 'Oh So Soon' and 'Where Is Johnny Now'. Moving to ABC later in the decade, they failed to return to the charts but created several cherished singles that later found favour in the UK on the northern soul scene, such as 'Gotta Have Your Love' and 'Slow Fizz'.

● ALBUMS: *Who Do You Love* (Swan 1964)★★★.

● COMPILATIONS: *Who Do You Love* (Collectables 1989)★★★, *The Best Of ...* (Sequel 1995)★★★.

SATINTONES

An R&B vocal group from Detroit, Michigan, USA. The Satintones are known not so much for their recordings but for their early association with the famed Motown organization, and for producing future talents in the Detroit recording scene. The original members were Robert Bateman, Chico Laverett, James Ellis and Sonny Sanders, who came together in 1957. They were the first group signed to one of Berry Gordy's labels, when 'Going To The Hop' was issued on Tamla in 1959, followed by the first single on Motown Records, 'Sugar Daddy'. After three further singles for Motown, all in the R&B vocal group style of the late 50s, the group disbanded, with Robert Bateman becoming a producer for the label. He worked on the Marvelettes' hit single 'Please Mr. Postman' in 1962, before leaving Motown and setting up as an independent producer in Detroit. In 1967, Bateman produced the solo recordings by the former Supreme, Florence Ballad. Sonny Sanders had the most impressive post-Satintones career, working as an arranger, producer and bandleader in Detroit and later Chicago. In Detroit, he arranged and produced several big hits for Ric Tic, notably Edwin Starr's 'Stop Her On Sight' and the Reflections' 'Just Like Romeo And Juliet'. In Chicago, working under producer Carl Davis, he arranged such hits as Mary Wells's 'Dear Lover', the Artistics' 'I'm Gonna Miss You', Barbara Acklin's 'Love Makes A Woman', and Gene Chandler's 'The Girl Don't Care'. Sanders was one of the key backroom talents in the success of the Brunswick label during the late 60s and early 70s.

SAYLES, JOHNNY

b. 9 February 1937, Winnsboro, Texas, USA, d. 17 August 1993, Chicago, Illinois, USA. Sayles was arguably one of the finest 'tough-soul' singers of the earliest (early 60s) soul era, and several of his recordings for George Leaner's Chicago-based Mar-V-Lus label are as potent and telling as anything recorded by far better-known singers, such as Wilson Pickett and Otis Clay. Sayles only had four sides released at the time, but several others were reissued later on a superb Japanese album. At the age of 18, he moved to St. Louis and worked with Eugene Neal's Rocking Kings, Ike Turner's local Kings Of Rhythm, and fronted his own band at Chuck Berry's Paradise Club. After quitting music for a time to study in Houston, in 1963 he joined the Five Dutones' Review tour, playing the role of Little Johnny Taylor, who had a current R&B number 1 hit with 'Part Time Love'. His first recording for Leaner the fine, up-tempo 'Don't Turn Your Back On Me', which featured Sayles' driving, tough-soul vocal, and was coupled with 'You Told A Lie', a great Bobby 'Blue' Bland-style, 'bluesoul' track. His second release, 'You Did Me Wrong' (May 1964), with its metronomic slow, plodding beat, appealed equally to both blues and deep-soul lovers. It was backed by 'Got You On My Mind', an even slower and more bluesy number. Further Mar-V-Lus releases included the mid-paced 'Tell Me Where I Stand' and 'The Girl That I Love', Subsequently, Sayles joined a Lou Rawls show in Alaska, and his later Leaner recordings were not available until the 80s Japanese P-Vine album. After leaving Rawls, Sayles joined ex-Leaner producer Monk Higgins, and recorded the outstanding 'Nothing But Hard Rocks', which was released on Chi-Town. He worked for several other labels, including St Lawrence, Chess and Minit, where his 'Anything For You' became a UK northern-soul favourite when it was issued on Liberty. For the Dakar label, Sayles recorded 'Somebody's Changing My Sweet Baby's Mind', which had been intended as a follow-up to Tyrone Davis's first hit for the label, 'Can I Change My Mind', and *Man On The Inside*, but continued to eschew recording in favour of live performances. Reported to have always wanted to sing 'sweet' like Roy Hamilton, his vocal power was immense, and at times, his stage presence was said to have rivalled even that of James Brown.

● ALBUMS: *Man On the Inside* (Dakar 80s)★★★.

● COMPILATIONS: *Soul On Fire* nine tracks (1981)★★★.

SCAGGS, BOZ

b. William Royce Scaggs, 8 June 1944, Ohio, USA. Scaggs was raised in Dallas, Texas, where he joined fellow guitarist Steve Miller in a high-school group, the Marksmen. The musicians maintained this partnership in the Ardells, a group they formed at the University of Wisconsin, but this early association ended when Scaggs returned to Texas. He then formed an R&B unit, the Wigs, whom he took to London in anticipation of a more receptive audience. The group broke up when this failed to materialize, and the guitarist headed for mainland Europe where he forged a career as an itinerant folk-singer. Scaggs was particularly successful in Sweden, where he recorded a rudimentary solo album, *Boz*. This interlude in exile ended in 1967 when he received an invitation from his erstwhile colleague to join the fledgling Steve Miller Band. Scaggs recorded two albums with this unit but left for a solo career in 1968. *Boz Scaggs* was a magnificent offering and featured sterling contributions from Duane Allman, particularly on the extended reading of Fenton Robinson's 'Loan Me A Dime'. Over the next five years, Scaggs pursued an exemplary soul/rock direction with several excellent albums, including *My Time* and *Slow Dancer*. Skilled production work from Glyn Johns and Johnny Bristol reinforced its high quality, but it was not until 1976 and the smooth *Silk Degrees* that this was translated into commercial success. A slick session band, which later became Toto, enhanced some of Scaggs' finest compositions, including 'Lowdown' (a US chart number 3 hit), 'What Can I Say?' and 'Lido Shuffle', each of which reached the UK Top 30. The album also featured 'We're All Alone', which has since become a standard. Paradoxically the singer's career faltered in the wake of this exceptional album and despite enjoying several hit singles during 1980, Scaggs maintained a low profile during the subsequent decade. It was eight years before a new selection, *Other Roads*, appeared and a further six before *Some Change*. The latter was an uninspired collection. Scaggs took heed of the failings of that release and moved back to his roots with *Come On Home*, an earthy collection of R&B classics that went some way in removing the gloss of his recent work.

● ALBUMS: *Boz* (1966)★★, *Boz Scaggs* (Atlantic 1969)★★★, *Moments* (Columbia 1971)★★★, *Boz Scaggs And Band* (Columbia 1971)★★★, *My Time* (Columbia 1972)★★★, *Slow Dancer* (Columbia 1974)★★★, *Silk Degrees* (Columbia 1976)★★★★, *Down Two Then Left* (Columbia 1977)★★, *Middle Man* (Columbia 1980)★★★, *Other Roads* (Columbia 1988)★★★, *Some Change* (Virgin 1994)★★, *Come On Home* (Virgin 1997)★★★★.

● COMPILATIONS: *Hits!* (Columbia 1980)★★★, *My Time: A Boz Scaggs Anthology (1969-1987)* (Columbia 1997)★★★★.

SCALES, HARVEY, AND THE SEVEN SOUNDS

An R&B band formed in Milwaukee, Wisconsin, USA, in 1961. The members were lead vocalist and guitarist Harvey Scales (b. 1941, Arkansas, USA), Monny Smith, Bill Purtie, Rudy Jacobs, Al Vance, Bill Stonewall and Ray Armstead. Superstar James Brown was sweeping the charts in the late 60s with his new kind of hard soul called 'funk', and under his influence, Harvey Scales And The Seven Sounds, like numerous other groups at that time, made their presence felt recording new funk sounds. The group's one hit, 'Get Down' (number 32 R&B, 1967), was recorded on Lenny LeCour's Magic Touch label. The b-side, 'Love-itis', was later recorded by the rock group J. Geils Band. After signing with Chess Records, Scales and his group had a regional hit with the LeCour-produced 'The Yolk' in 1969. Later, under the aegis of Detroit producer Don Davis, the group recorded for Stax Records with little success. In 1976, for southern soul hit-maker Johnnie Taylor, Scales co-wrote the massive hit 'Disco Lady'. That success secured Scales a recording contract with Casablanca, with whom the artist released two albums. Scales was still recording in the early 90s.

● ALBUMS: *Confidential Affair* (Casablanca 1978)★★★, *Hot Foot* (Casablanca 1979)★★, *All In A Night's Work* (Earthtone 1991)★★.

SCHOOLBOYS

An R&B vocal group from Harlem, New York City, New York, USA. With a remarkable series of pleading ballads in 1957, the Schoolboys typified the east coast pre-teen soprano sound, but like most such groups their career was short-lived. The group members were Leslie Martin (lead), Roger Hayes (tenor), James McKay (baritone) and Renaldo Gamble (bass), and their entry into the recording business was facilitated by famed New York disc jockey Tommy 'Dr. Jive' Smalls, who was introduced to the group at the behest of their manager. Smalls then arranged for the group to be signed to OKeh Records. The Schoolboys' first success was a double-sided hit, 'Please Say You Want Me' (number 13 R&B)/'Shirley' (number 15 R&B), in early 1957. The group broke up soon afterwards, but 'Carol' made a strong impression later in the year on the east coast, even though it failed to make the national charts. The Schoolboys' last record on OKeh, 'Pearl', featured Martin in the lead, who was supported by some members of the Cadillacs. Gamble had gone to join the Kodaks (another pre-teen group) and Hayes joined the Collegians of 'Zoom Zoom Zoom' fame. The Schoolboys made one more record, for Juanita, 'Angel Of Love', in 1958, before ending their career.

● COMPILATIONS: *Little Joe And The Thrillers Meet The Schoolboys* contains six tracks by the Schoolboys (Collectables 1991)★★★.

SCOTT, FREDDIE

b. 24 April 1933, Providence, Rhode Island, USA. Scott was a contract songwriter with Screen Gems/Columbia, and had also recorded for a score of minor New York labels. His 1963 hit, 'Hey Girl', was issued on Colpix, but after two lesser hits, Scott signed to Shout Records. 'Are You Lonely For Me', later recorded by Chuck Jackson, was a US R&B number 7 in 1966. Scott subsequently issued emotional versions of Solomon Burke's 'Cry To Me', Van Morrison's 'He Ain't Give You None' and a powerful Bert Berns/Jeff Barry composition, 'Am I Grooving You'. Shout latterly folded and the singer moved between several companies. His last chart hit came on Probe in 1970 with 'I Shall Be Released'.

● ALBUMS: *Freddie Scott Sings* (Colpix 1964)★★★, *Everything I Have Is Yours* (Columbia 1964)★★★, *Lonely Man* (Columbia 1967)★★, *Are You Lonely For Me?* (Shout 1967)★★★, *I Shall Be Released* (Probe 1970)★★.

SCOTT, MARYLIN

Other than her records, almost nothing is known about Marylin Scott. One of her record companies had an address for her in Norfolk, Virginia, USA, and her first recording session was held in Charlotte, North Carolina, so a background in the south-eastern states of the USA seems likely. Between 1945 and 1951 she recorded blues and R&B as Scott, and gospel as Mary Deloach. There was also a further gospel record in the mid-60s. Some of her records feature acoustic instruments and a fairly traditional sound, while others are in a more contemporary vein, with a small band for the R&B numbers, and organ and backing vocals for the gospel. In whatever setting, she performed with skill and conviction, and seemed to have few problems reconciling the sacred and secular sides of her musical personality.

● ALBUMS: *The Uneasy Blues* (1988)★★★, *I Got What Daddy Like* (1988)★★★.

SCOTT, PEGGY, AND JO JO BENSON

Duo comprising Peggy Scott (b. Peggy Stoutmeyer, 25 June 1948, Opp, Alabama, USA) and Jo Jo Benson (b. 1940, Columbia, Ohio, USA). Scott, a former gospel singer, toured with Ben E. King, until a car accident forced her to seek a residency in a local group, the Swinging Sextet. Here she met Benson, who had sung with the Chuck Willis show, the Upsetters and the Enchanters. Scott and Benson enjoyed a major US hit in 1968 with 'Lover's Holiday', but despite other success with 'Pickin' Wild Mountain Strawberries' and 'Soul Shake', the duo were unable to sustain a career together. Both subsequently recorded as solo acts, with Scott cutting some fine performances for Old Town, Mercury, Malaco, RCA and SSS-International, for whom her cover version of Brenda Holloway's 'Every Little Bit Hurts' was outstanding. The two singers briefly reunited in the early 80s, for *Nothing Can Stand In Our Way*.

● ALBUMS: *Soul Shake* (SSS International 1969)★★★, *Lover's Heaven* (SSS International 1969)★★, *Nothing Can Stand In Our Way* (Gulf Coast 1983)★★★.

● COMPILATIONS: *Soul Shake* (Charly 1986)★★★, *The Best Of Peggy Scott & Jo Jo Benson* (Ichiban 1996)★★★.

SCOTT-ADAMS, PEGGY

b. Peggy Stoutmeyer, 25 June 1948, Opp, Alabama, USA. After forming her own gospel group, the Gospel Harmonettes, while still at school, Scott-Adams became the featured vocalist with Ben E. King's band. She then briefly sang with The Sextet, a trio formed by James and Bobby Purify, and survived a near-fatal car crash that threatened her career. Relocating to Jackson, Mississippi, Scott-Adams recorded a series of highly successful R&B singles with Jo Jo Benson for the SSS label in the late 60s, including 'Pickin' Wild Mountain Berries', 'Lover's Holiday' and 'Soul Shake'. In 1970 the duo moved to Atlantic Records, and recorded with Jerry Wexler at Muscle Shoals Studios, but their successful run of singles had by now dried up. Scott-Adams also released two solo singles for Atco, before the duo broke up in 1971. She went on to record for Old Town, Mercury and RCA, before reuniting with Benson and achieving moderate success with *Nothing Can Stand In Our Way* in the early 80s. She subsequently disappeared from the music business, working in her husband's funeral home, reappearing briefly to duet with Ray Charles on his *Would You Believe* and *Strong Love Affair* albums. She came out of her musical 'retirement' with the release of a new album, *Help Yourself*, in 1996. As she wryly told *Billboard* magazine shortly after its release: 'I had this quiet little life just five months ago. You know, being a mortician's wife, well, it's a very serene business. Then all hell broke loose.' Her breakthrough with *Help Yourself* had much to do with the success of the attendant single, 'Bill', on local blues and R&B radio stations. The song, which described the loss of a lover, not to another woman, but to a man, was written by Jimmy Lewis, the owner of Miss Butch Records. Scott-Adams had initially been reluctant to record such a potentially controversial single; however, she was pleased with the attendant publicity, which helped to promote album sales. *Help Yourself* included other strong tracks, particularly the tender soul ballad 'I'll Take Care Of You', which reminded many of her late 60s peak.

● ALBUMS: *Great Scott* (Old Town 1975)★★★, *Help Yourself* (Miss Butch/Mardi Gras 1996)★★★★.

SEARS, ZENAS 'DADDY'

b. *c.*1914, d. 4 October 1989, Atlanta, Georgia, USA. A respected white Atlanta jazz and pop disc jockey, Sears began programming jump blues and R&B records in January 1946. Two years later he took a job at the state-owned radio station WGST, on the condition that he would be allowed a nightly blues show, *The Blues Caravan*. Owing to his success with this format, he was able to expand the show to include talent shows, which he broadcast live from Atlanta theatres such as Decatur Street's 81 Theatre. Here he discovered local singers such as Tommy Brown, Billy Wright, Chuck Willis (whom he managed in the early to mid-50s, and secured him his first recording contract with OKeh Records) and Little Richard. These artists were invariably backed by the Blues Caravan All Stars, a group of local musicians that included John Peek and Roy Mays. In 1954, Georgia's new governor banned Sears' programme from the WGST, and Sears formed WAOK. He continued with his policy to play the best of black music - in 1959 he recorded Ray Charles's set at the WAOK 5th Anniversary Party which Atlantic issued as the bestselling *Ray Charles In Person*. In the late 50s and 60s, Sears became involved with Dr Martin Luther King and the SCLC, and his position with the radio station allowed him to spread his views on integration and equal rights.

Sensations

This Philadelphia R&B ensemble featured the warm, chirpy lead of Yvonne Mills Baker (b. Philadelphia, Pennsylvania, USA). The group was formed in 1954, and in 1956 they had two minor ballad hits, a remake of the old standard 'Yes Sir That's My Baby' (US R&B number 15) and 'Please Mr. Disc Jockey' (US R&B number 13) for the Atlantic subsidiary label Atco. The group included lead Baker, alternate lead Tommy Wicks and bass Alphonso Howell. The Sensations failed to register further hits and disbanded. In 1961 Howell persuaded Baker to re-form the group and they added Richard Curtain (tenor) and Sam Armstrong (baritone). Through their mentor and producer, Philadelphia disc jockey Kae Williams, the Sensations won a contract with the Chess subsidiary label Argo. Singing with greater robustness and at a faster pace, the group had success first with a remake of the Teresa Brewer oldie, 'Music Music Music' (US R&B number 12 in 1961). The following year they struck gold with 'Let Me In' (US R&B number 2 and pop number 4). The last chart record for the Sensations was a remake of the Frankie Laine hit 'That's My Desire' (US pop Top 75 in 1962). The group disbanded around 1964 and Baker continued making records for a few more years in the soul idiom.

● ALBUMS: *Let Me In* (Argo 1963)★★★.

702

A vocal R&B trio named after its Las Vegas, Nevada, USA home area code, 702 made their long-playing debut for Michael Bivins in 1996. Bivins first became acquainted with the group (which was originally a quartet) after they improvised an audition piece for him at the music industry's Jack The Rapper convention. Comprising sisters Irish and Lemisha Grinstead and Kameelah Williams, the group members were only aged between 11 and 13 when they took this momentous step. However, it was five years before they released *No Doubt*, an album that made strong use of their elegant harmonies and their varied musical influences, ranging from gospel to blues, jazz and hip-hop. In the interim, Grinstead sang on the 1995 hit 'This Lil' Game We Play', by fellow Biv 10 recording artists, Subway. 702's first single, 'Steevo', utilized a slang expression for 'personal style and attitude', and made a strong impression on regional R&B stations. It was followed by a second single, 'Get It Together', in December 1996.

● ALBUMS: *No Doubt* (Biv 10/Motown 1996)★★★.

7669

Four New York 'New Jill Swingers' (they prefer the term 'new ghetto revolutionary music') with the hardcore attitude of rap, 7669 arrived on the scene in 1994 amid a swirl of deliberately provocative press shots, notably topless poses astride large motorcycles, which also graced the album cover. Less readily apparent was the fact that the backdrop of shrubbery was in fact a 'field of pot'. Their name was taken from the year of US independence (1776) crossed with the 'date' of the sexual revolution (1969). The members, Shorti-1-Forti (b. Marcy Roberts), Big Ange (b. Angela Hunte), El Boog-E (b. El-Melek A. Moore) and Thicknezz (b. Mallore Irvine), proferred songs with dubious titles such as '69 Ways To Love A Black Man' and 'Cloud 69', the duplicity of lascivious titles being an obvious clue to the lack of imagination inherent in the project. However, the production, helmed by Kangol, Ali Dee and Forceful, was enough to make proceedings listenable.

● ALBUMS: *East From A Bad Block* (Motown/Polydor 1994)★★.

Sexton, Ann

b. 5 February 1950, Greenville, South Carolina, USA. One of several lesser-known southern-soul female artists, Sexton made a string of quality records for legendary Nashville soul DJ/label-owner, the late John Richbourg aka John R. Born into a South Carolina family steeped in gospel music, she married at a young age, and, with her husband Melvin Burton (who later played saxophone in Moses Dillard's band), soon progressed from gospel to secular club singing, where she was spotted in 1971 by songwriter David Lee. In a local studio, Sexton recorded Lee's impassioned 'You're Letting Me Down', coupled with the future UK northern-soul favourite 'You've Been Gone Too Long'. Released initially on Lee's tiny Impel label, it was later issued by John R on his Seventy-Seven outlet. After a couple of Nashville sessions, Sexton's records were then chiefly cut in Memphis, some produced by Lee and John R and others by Gene 'Bowlegs' Miller, who had earlier discovered Ann Peebles. By 1976, John R was recording Sexton's versions of songs by the fine southern-soul writer/singer Frank O (Johnson) at Clayton Ivey's Wishbone studio in Muscle Shoals. After John R's Seventy Seven label folded, Sexton recorded the highly regarded *The Beginning* in 1977 for the Monument subsidiary Sound Stage 7, but to no commercial impact.

● ALBUMS: *The Beginning* (Sound Stage 7 1977)★★★.

● COMPILATIONS: *Love Trials* (Charly 1987)★★★, *You're Gonna Miss Me* (1993)★★★.

Shades

Female R&B quartet Shades features Monique Peoples, Danielle Andrews, Tiffanie Cardwell and Shannon Walker Williams. They formed after meeting at Northeastern University, Boston, Massachusetts, USA, in the early 90s. After signing with Motown Records they released an impressive 1996 single, 'Tell Me', before embarking on sessions for a self-titled debut album. This was promoted with the release of a second single, 'Serenade', which also made the US R&B charts. The latter featured a looped sample from Spandau Ballet's 'True' (previously employed by PM Dawn on 'Set Adrift On Memory Bliss'), and was also issued in a Spanish-language version in an attempt to broaden the group's appeal.

● ALBUMS: *Shades* (Motown 1997)★★★.

SHADES OF BLUE

From Detroit, Michigan, USA, Shades Of Blue are known for just one hit, 'Oh How Happy', which, with its singalong simplicity and good cheer, raced up the chart in 1966, reaching number 12. The members of the group were Nick Marinelli, Linda Allan, Bob Kerr and Ernie Dernai. They were discovered and produced by soul singer Edwin Starr, who was looking for a white group to record 'Oh How Happy', a song he had written years earlier. After the group were turned down by another Detroit company, Starr took them to Harry Balk's small Impact operation, and with 'Oh How Happy', Impact achieved its only national hit. The group could not give Balk another big record, as their two subsequent records in 1966 - 'Lonely Summer' and 'Happiness' - stalled on the lower reaches of the charts.

● ALBUMS: *Happiness Is The Shades of Blue* (Impact 1966)★★.

SHAI

Comprising singers Carl Martin, Marc Gay, Garfield Bright and Darnell Van Rensalier, US R&B group Shai made a strong impact with their 1992 debut album, *If I Ever Fall In Love*. It peaked at number 3 in the *Billboard* R&B charts, and at number 6 in the pop chart, and included the hit singles 'Comforter' and 'Baby I'm Yours'. Recorded in only six weeks, in retrospect it sounded a little rushed. In comparison, 1993's *Right Back At Cha*, which featured remixes and alternative versions of songs from the debut, was a commercial disappointment. It sold less than a tenth of the copies that the debut had sold. The group's second album proper was not released until 1995. *Blackface*, recorded over nine months, was a mature, sophisticated collection of original R&B material, boasting evident refinement in the group's songwriting. As Bright accurately summarized, 'It's more rhythm-oriented than our last album. The drum patterns are more funky and the hooks are more melodic, so it swings a little better.'

● ALBUMS: *If I Ever Fall In Love* (Gasoline Alley/MCA 1992)★★★, *Right Back At Cha* (Gasoline Alley/MCA 1993)★★, *Blackface* (Gasoline Alley/MCA 1995)★★★.

SHAKATAK

This UK group were one the original benefactors of the early 80s British jazz/funk boom (alongside contemporaries Level 42). The group comprised Bill Sharpe (keyboards), George Anderson (bass), Keith Winter (guitar), Roger Odell (drums), Nigel Wright (keyboards, synthesizers) and Gil Seward (vocals). Between 1980 and 1987, Shakatak had 14 UK chart singles. Since their chart debut with 'Feels Like The First Time' on Polydor Records (a long-standing partnership), other notable hits have been 'Easier Said Than Done' (1981), 'Night Birds' (UK Top 10 - 1982), 'Dark Is The Night' (1983) and 'Down On The Street' (UK Top 10 - 1984). This understated group proved their reputation as one of the finest purveyors of classy jazz/funk with the successful K-Tel compilation *The Coolest Cuts*. The latter half of the 80s showed Shakatak leaving behind the demands of instant pop chart hits and allowing themselves to mature, honing their jazz influences - most evidently on the 1989 set *Turn The Music Up*, their first studio effort in almost five years. In addition to releasing a solo album in 1988, Sharpe also collaborated with Gary Numan on the one-off single 'Change Your Mind', in 1985. On reaching the UK Top 20, it was not until four years later that the duo released a full album, *Automatic*.

● ALBUMS: *Drivin' Hard* (Polydor 1981)★★★, *Nightbirds* (Polydor 1982)★★★, *Invitations* (Polydor 1982)★★★, *Out Of This World* (Polydor 1983)★★★, *Down On The Street* (Polydor 1984)★★★, *Live!* (Polydor 1985)★★, *Turn The Music Up* (Polydor 1989)★★★, *Bitter Sweet* (Polydor 1991)★★★, *Street Level* (1993)★★.
Solo: Bill Sharpe *Famous People* (Polydor 1988)★★, with Gary Numan *Automatic* (Polydor 1989)★★.

● COMPILATIONS: *The Coolest Cuts* (K-Tel 1988)★★★, *The Remix Best Album* (1992)★★.

SHALAMAR

This group was created by Dick Griffey, booking agent for US television's *Soul Train* show, and Simon Soussan, a veteran of Britain's 'northern soul' scene. The latter produced 'Uptown Festival', a medley of popular Tamla/Motown favourites, which was issued on Griffey's Solar label. Although credited to 'Shalamar', the track featured session musicians, but its success inspired Griffey to create a performing group. Jody Watley (b. 30 January 1959, Chicago, Illinois, USA), Jeffrey Daniels and Gerald Brown were recruited via *Soul Train* in 1977, although Brown was replaced the following year by Howard Hewitt (b. Akron, Ohio, USA). 'The Second Time Around' gave the trio an R&B chart topper in 1979, but subsequent releases were better received in the UK, where lightweight soul/disco offerings, including 'I Can Make You Feel Good', 'A Night To Remember' and 'There It Is', provided three Top 10 entries in 1982. Daniels and Watley then left the group to pursue solo careers. Their replacements, Delisa Davis and Micki Free, joined in 1984. The group won a Grammy award for 'Don't Get Stopped In Beverly Hills', a track from *Heartbreak* used in the Eddie Murphy film *Beverly Hills Cop*, but Hewitt's departure in 1986 eroded any new-found confidence. Sidney Justin restored the group to a trio, continuing to have further, albeit minor, hit singles. By now, Shalamar's golden, if brief, period had ended; nevertheless, the Shalamar name survived into the late 80s when Justin, along with Free and Davis, recorded *Circumstantial Evidence* (produced by L.A. Reid and Babyface) and *Wake Up*.

● ALBUMS: *Uptown Festival* (Soul Train 1977)★★, *Disco Gardens* (Solar 1978)★★, *Big Fun* (Solar 1979)★★★, *Three For Love* (Solar 1981)★★★, *Go For It* (Solar 1981)★★★, *Friends* (Solar 1982)★★★, *The Look* (Solar 1983)★★★, *Heartbreak* (Solar 1984)★★, *Circumstantial Evidence* (Solar 1987)★★, *Wake Up* (Solar 1990)★★.

● COMPILATIONS: *Shalamar's Greatest Hits* (Solar 1982)★★★, *The Greatest Hits* (Stylus 1986)★★★, *Here It Is - The Best Of* (MCA 1992)★★★ *A Night To Remember* (Spectrum 1995)★★.

● FILMS: *Footloose* (1984).

SHANICE

b. Shanice Wilson, 14 May 1973, McKees Rocks, Pittsburgh, Pennsylvania, but raised in Los Angeles, California, USA. Shanice began singing on stage with her mother Crystal and her aunt Penni, who now jointly oversee her career. Afterwards, she found her way into the modelling industry, appearing in television commercials, including one with Ella Fitzgerald, and performing in local musicals before reaching her teens. One particular performance in *Get Happy* led to her first recording contract when she was just 11 years old, with A&M Records. By 1990 she had been signed to Motown Records by president Jheryl Busby. Partnered with producer Narada Michael Walden, the resulting chemistry produced a 1992 gold-certified album, *Inner Child*, which featured the international hit single 'I Love Your Smile'. Two other US Top 10 hits were also featured: 'Silent Prayer' (which saw accompaniment from labelmate Johnny Gill) and 'I'm Crying'. Nominated for a Grammy as Best R&B Female Vocalist in her own country and awarded the Golden Lion Award as Best International Artist in Germany, Shanice built on the breakthrough with extensive international touring. Meanwhile, she found time to collaborate with Kenny Loggins on his *Live From The Redwoods* album and contributed to three film soundtracks, *Beverley Hills 90210* (which gave Shanice another Top 5 US hit with 'Saving Forever For You'), the Eddie Murphy film *Boomerang* ('Don't Wanna Love You') and *Meteor Man* (which included her US R&B number 1 'It's For You'). *21 Ways ... To Grow* moved to a more up-tempo style, with harder grooves inspired by hip-hop and the usual array of soulful ballads. If featured another hit single in 'I Like', with remixes from Kenny 'Dope' Gonzalez, while the album's production team included Jermaine Dupri (Kris Kross, Xscape) and Chris Stokes. She duetted with Jon Secada in 1995 on 'If I Never Knew You' from the highly successful Disney movie *Pocahontas*.

● ALBUMS: as Shanice Wilson *Discovery* (A&M 1987)★★, *Inner Child* (Motown 1992)★★★, *21 Ways ... To Grow* (Motown 1994)★★★.

SHANNON

b. Brenda Shannon Greene, 1958, Washington, DC, USA. Shannon was best known for her 1984 US Top 10/UK Top 20 dance single 'Let The Music Play'. She grew up in Brooklyn, New York, and studied both singing and dance as a child. Shannon was attending York University when she recorded 'Let The Music Play', originally for Emergency Records, in 1983. Mirage Records, a division of the larger Atlantic Records, picked up distribution of the single and it made its way to number 2 on the US R&B charts and number 8 pop. The follow-up, 'Give Me Tonight', also reached the R&B Top 10 but did not make the pop Top 40. In the UK, she gained two further chart hits with 'Give Me Tonight' and 'Sweet Somebody' both reaching the Top 30 in 1984. Shannon had one final pop chart single, 'Do You Wanna Get Away', in 1985, but continued to place on the R&B charts for another year, finally achieving a total of seven singles on that chart. Her debut album, *Let The Music Play*, also charted, but by the late 80s Shannon's name had disappeared from the US music scene.

● ALBUMS: *Let The Music Play* (Mirage 1984)★★★, *Do You Wanna Get Away* (Mirage 1985)★★.

● COMPILATIONS: *Dancefloor Artists Volume 8* (Deep Beats 1996)★★★.

SHANNON, PRESTON

b. Memphis, Tennessee, USA. A contemporary soul singer whose songs are mixed with discernible elements of southern funk and blues, Preston Shannon made his Bullseye Blues Records debut in 1994 with *Break The Ice*. With a voice clearly modelled on Otis Redding, this saw him combine classic soul phrasing with guitar work drawing on the Delta blues style of Albert King. It won over numerous critics, many of whom saw his style as a powerful distillation of the traditions at work behind twentieth-century music in Memphis. The follow-up set, 1996's *Midnight In Memphis*, was recorded at Willie Mitchell's Royal Studio with brothers Ron and Willi Levy on production. Featuring a full horn section, the title track was a joint Shannon/Levy composition. Once again, the album provoked critical approbation.

● ALBUMS: *Break The Ice* (Bullseye Blues 1994)★★★, *Midnight In Memphis* (Bullseye Blues 1996)★★★.

SHARP, DEE DEE

b. Dione LaRue, 9 September 1945, Philadelphia, Pennsylvania, USA. A backing vocalist for the Cameo-Parkway labels, Dee Dee Sharp was the uncredited voice on Chubby Checker's 'Slow Twistin'' single. Her own debut, 'Mashed Potato Time', was recorded at the same session and, thanks to the power of Dick Clark's *American Bandstand* television show, this energetic, exciting song became an immediate success. Cameo sadly chose to milk its dance-based appeal and releases such as 'Gravy (For My Mashed Potatoes)' and 'Do The Bird' packaged her as a temporary novelty act at the expense of an untapped potential. Dee Dee resurfaced in the 70s on the TSOP/Philadelphia International labels. Married to producer Kenny Gamble, she enjoyed two minor soul hits with 'I'm Not In Love' (1976 - a cover of the 10cc hit) and 'I Love You Anyway' (1981).

● ALBUMS: *It's Mashed Potato Time* (Cameo 1962)★★★, *Songs Of Faith* (Cameo 1962)★★, with Chubby Checker *Down To Earth* (Cameo 1962)★★, *Do The Bird* (Cameo 1963)★★★, *All The Hits* (Cameo 1963)★★, *Down Memory Lane* (Cameo 1963)★★, *What Color Is Love* (1978)★★★.

● COMPILATIONS: *Biggest Hits* (Cameo 1963)★★★, *18 Golden Hits* (Cameo 1964)★★★.

● FILMS: *Don't Knock The Twist* (1962).

SHARPEES

The line-up comprised Vernon Guy (b. 21 March 1945), Stacy Johnson (b. 13 April 1945), Herbert Reeves (b. 1947, d. 1972) and early member Horise O'Toole (b. 1943), all from St. Louis, Missouri, USA. George Leaner's Chicago-based One-derful label recruited several acts from the St. Louis area via local representatives, A&R man Mack McKinney and house writer/arranger Eddie Silvers. One such act was the Sharpees, named after the St. Louis guitarist/bandleader/revue-director, Benny Sharp. Johnson was the first to be recruited in 1961 after Sharp heard him perform solo with the Arabians. He was joined by Vernon Guy (ex-Seven Gospel Singers and Cool Sounds), and O'Toole, then with the Originals. They first worked as the New Breed, but had become the Sharpees by the time they backed (Little Miss) Jessie Smith in 1961 on 'My Baby's Gone' for the Mel-O label. Then, in late 1962, Guy and Johnson left Sharp to join the Ike And Tina Turner Review and to record solo singles for Ike Turner's Teena, Sonja and Sony labels in 1963. They both also appeared on the 1964 Kent live album *The Ike & Tina Turner Review*, before Johnson moved to Los Angeles. Later that year, while on the west coast, Johnson was back with Turner, who produced his 'Consider Yourself' for the Modern label. By the time the Sharpees arrived at Oliver Sain's St. Louis studio to record their first single, 'Do The 45', which was released on George Leaner's One-derful label, the line-up consisted of two of the original members, Guy and O'Toole, plus a new man, Herbert Reeves, ex-leader of the Arabians. The record was similar to Junior Walker's 'Shotgun', and was a strong 'dance' seller in northern US markets. While on tour, O'Toole contracted tuberculosis, and was replaced by the other founder-member, Stacy Johnson. The Sharpees' 'Tired Of Being Lonely' (1965), recorded in Chicago with Reeves' strong but soulful lead, made the upper reaches of the Hot 100 early in 1966. After two flop singles, the Sharpees remained a very popular live act on the chitlin' circuit through to 1967, with Johnson cutting a solo single for another of Leaner's labels, M-Pac, in 1966 under the aegis of Harold Burrage. The group effectively disbanded in 1967, although a new pact with Sharp resulted in one more record a year later, on Midas, another Leaner label. They stayed together until 1972, when Herbert Reeves was tragically shot dead. In the early 80s, Guy and Johnson formed a new Sharpees group with Bobby Wilson and Guy's nephew, Paul Grady, and they continued to gig around the St. Louis area.

SHAW, MARLENA

b. Marlina Burgess, 1944, New Rochelle, New York, USA. Shaw was a cocktail lounge-type jazz singer who occasionally ventured onto the soul music charts. She began her career in 1963, and was discovered by Chess Records in 1966 while singing on the Playboy lounge circuit. On Chess's Cadet subsidiary, under the aegis of producer Richard Evans, she performed vocal counterparts of jazz hits such as 'Mercy Mercy Mercy' (number 33 R&B, number 58 pop) by Cannonball Adderley and 'Wade In The Water' by Ramsey Lewis Trio. Chess released two albums and a series of singles before Shaw left the company in 1968. For the next five years she performed periodically with Count Basie, and after signing with Blue Note in 1972 built a solidly based jazz recording career. Her most popular album for the company was *Who Is This Bitch, Anyway?*, but her last Blue Note release in 1976, *Just A Matter Of Time*, saw a more disco-driven result that yielded a modest chart single, 'It's Better Than Walkin' Out' (number 74 R&B). A move to Columbia in 1977 resulted in her biggest chart success with *Sweet Beginnings* and a hit single, 'Go Away Little Boy' (number 21 R&B), a remake of Steve Lawrence's 'Go Away Little Girl'. From an album for South Bay, *Let Me In Your Life*, she achieved her last chart single, 'Never Give Up On You' (number 91 R&B), but has remained active in the 90s.

● ALBUMS: *Out Of Different Bags* (Cadet 1967)★★★, *The Spice Of Life* (Cadet 1968)★★★, *From The Depths Of My Soul* (Blue Note 1973)★★★, *Live At Montreaux* (Blue Note 1974)★★★, *Who Is This Bitch Anyway?* (Blue Note 1975)★★★, *Just A Matter Of Time* (Blue Note 1976)★★, *Sweet Beginnings* (Columbia 1977)★★★, *Acting Up* (Columbia 1978)★★★, *Take A Bite* (Columbia 1979)★★★, *Let Me In Your Life* (South Bay 1983)★★★, *Love Is In Flight* (Polydor 1988)★★, *Dangerous* (Concord 1996)★★★.

SHELLS

This US, Brooklyn-based R&B vocal group was formed in 1957. The Shells were noted for their typical New York doo-wop stylings, in which the use of a prominent bass, piercing falsetto, and strong vocal riffing in support of a romantic lead, made for one of the great folk acts of the 50s. The group cut their first record, 'Baby Oh Baby', in 1957, which did little upon its release on the local Johnson label. The Shells broke up, but the following year, lead Nathaniel 'Little Nate' Bouknight formed a new ensemble, bringing in Bobby Nurse (first tenor), Shade Randy Alston (second tenor), Gus Geter (baritone), and Danny Small (bass). Subsequent records did nothing, but as a result of the resurgence of doo-wop on the charts in the early 60s owing to the promotion efforts of record collectors Wayne Stierle and Donn Fileti, the career of the Shells was far from dead. Stierle and Fileti began promoting 'Baby Oh Baby' in 1960 and were able to make it a Top 20 hit on the national pop charts (it went to number 11 on *Cash Box*'s R&B chart). The group re-formed and Stierle started acting as producer, coming out with some great sides, notably two excellent ones with new lead Ray Jones, 'Happy Holiday' (1962) and 'Deep In My Heart' (1962). However, the Shells failed to reach the charts and broke up. In 1966, Stierle reassembled the group for one last a cappella session using the four remaining members, without a lead.

● COMPILATIONS: *Acappela Session With The Shells* (1972)★★★, *The Greatest Hits Of The Shells* (1973)★★★, *Baby Oh Baby: Golden Classics* (1989)★★★.

SHELTON, ROSCOE

b. 22 August 1931, Lynchburg, Tennessee, USA. Based in Nashville, Shelton, with his high tenor voice, made his mark in the mid-60s with a style that reflected both gospel and country music influences and modestly rode on the back of the popularity for southern-style deep soul. Shelton served a long apprenticeship singing for the Fireside Gospel Singers and, more importantly, for the famed Fairfield Four, before recording blues for Excello in the 50s. For John Richbourg's Sound Stage 7 operation, he released two deep-soul ballads, 'Strain On My Heart' (number 25 R&B, 1965) and 'Easy Going Fellow' (number

32 R&B, 1965), both written by New Orleans' Allen Orange. An appealing album followed, *Soul In His Music, Music In His Soul*, which featured more fine compositions by Orange. Shelton, however, could not sustain his career, despite later recording some outstanding songs, notably Dan Penn's 'There's A Heartbreak Somewhere'.

● ALBUMS: *Music In His Soul, Soul In His Music* (Sound Stage 7 1966)★★★, *She's The One* (Appaloosa 1995)★★★.

● COMPILATIONS: *Strain On Your Heart* (Charly 1987)★★★, *Roscoe Shelton Sings* (P-Vine Sings 1995)★★★★.

SHEP AND THE LIMELITES

This R&B vocal group came from New York City, New York, USA. James Sheppard (b. *c.*1936, Queens, New York, USA, d. 24 January 1970, Long Island, New York, USA) was lead and songwriter successively for two R&B groups, the Heartbeats and Shep and the Limelites. He created the first 'song cycle' (i.e., a string of songs constituting a musical and literary unit) in rock 'n' roll. With the Limelites he attained his only Top 10 pop success with 'Daddy's Home', making him a one-hit-wonder. However, that song was part of a long cycle of songs, among the most distinctive being 'A Thousand Miles Away' (US R&B number 5 and pop Top 60 in 1956), '500 Miles To Go' (1957), recorded with the Heartbeats, 'Daddy's Home' (US R&B number 4 and pop number 2 in 1961), 'Ready For Your Love' (US pop Top 50 in 1961), 'Three Steps From The Altar' (US pop Top 60 in 1961), 'Our Anniversary' (US R&B number 7 in 1962) and 'What Did Daddy Do' (1962). The song-cycle first emerged in the nineteenth century as part of the German *lied* tradition, and many critics have thought that the Beatles, with *Sgt. Pepper's Lonely Heart's Club Band* in 1967, had created the first rock 'n' roll song cycle. The Heartbeats were formed in New York City in 1954, and first recorded the following year. Members on the first record were James Sheppard (tenor/baritone lead), Albert Crump (first tenor), Vernon Seavers (baritone), Robby Tatum (baritone) and Wally Roker (bass). The group distinguished itself with smooth tight harmony and a knack for creating great nonsense vocal riffs. Their sound was the ultimate in romantic doo-wop balladry. In 1960 the group broke up, and the following year Sheppard formed a new group, Shep And The Limelites, with two veterans of the New York doo-wop scene, first tenor Clarence Bassett and second tenor Charles Baskerville. A rarity among doo-wop groups, using no bass and relying on two-part harmony, Shep and the Limelites magnificently continued the great smooth romantic sound of the Heartbeats, albeit with less flavourful harmonies. The group broke up in 1966. Sheppard was shot dead on 24 January 1970. Bassett continued singing, firstly in the Flamingos, and later in Creative Funk. Wally Roker became a successful executive in the music business.

● ALBUMS: *Our Anniversary* (Hull 1962)★★★.

● COMPILATIONS: *Echoes Of The Rock Era* (1972)★★★, with the Heartbeats *The Best Of The Heartbeats Including Shep & The Limelites* (Rhino 1990)★★★★.

SHEPPARDS

This R&B vocal group was formed in 1959 in Chicago, Illinois, USA. The Sheppards created a marvellous transitional style of R&B during the early 60s, drawing much of its character from earlier doo-wop, yet incorporating instrumentation and vocal stylings that in later years would inform soul music. They were named after their producer Bill 'Bunky' Sheppard. The members were lead and bass Millard Edwards, lead and top tenor Murrie Eskridge, baritone Jimmy Allen, bass and fifth tenor James Dennis Isaac, second tenor O.C. Perkins and guitarist Kermit Chandler. The group's most famous song was the doo-wop ballad 'Island Of Love' (1959), but later tracks included 'The Glitter In Your Eyes' (1961) and 'Tragic' (1962). All the members had been veterans of the R&B scene for several years before joining together as the Sheppards. Eskridge and Perkins were members of the Palms on United in 1957, and Edwards, Allen and Isaac were members of the Bel Aires on Decca in 1958. Edwards left the group in 1967 to join the Esquires, another Sheppard-produced group. The Sheppards broke up in 1969. Jimmy Allen died in 1980, and Kermit Chandler in 1981.

● ALBUMS: *The Sheppards* (1964)★★★.

● COMPILATIONS: *Golden Classics* (1989)★★★.

SHIELDS

This R&B vocal group came from Los Angeles, California, USA. The Shields were an *ad hoc* group formed in 1958 by producer George Motola to record a cover version of the Slades' 'You Cheated'. The membership of that particular group has always been conjectural, but it is generally accepted to have comprised lead Frankie Ervin (b. 27 March 1926, Blythe, California, USA), falsetto Jesse Belvin (b. 15 December 1932, San Antonio, Texas, USA), Johnny 'Guitar' Watson (b. 3 February 1935, Houston, Texas, USA), Mel Williams and Buster Williams. 'You Cheated', which went to number 11 R&B and number 12 pop in 1958, was the group's only hit, and the song remains one of the most enduring legacies of the age of doo-wop.

SHIRELLES

Formed in Passaic, New Jersey, USA, the Shirelles are arguably the archetypal 'girl-group'; Shirley Owens (b. 10 June 1941), Beverly Lee (b. 3 August 1941), Doris Kenner (b. 2 August 1941) and Addie 'Micki' Harris (b. 22 January 1940, d. 10 June 1982) were initially known as the uncomfortably named Poquellos. Schoolfriends for whom singing was simply a pastime, the quartet embarked on a professional career when a classmate, Mary Jane Greenberg, recommended them to her mother. Florence Greenberg, an aspiring entrepreneuse, signed them to her Tiara label, on which the resultant single, 'I Met Him On A Sunday', was a minor hit. This inspired the inauguration of a second outlet, Scepter, where the Shirelles secured pop immortality with 'Will You Love Me Tomorrow'. Here, Alston's tender, aching vocal not only posed the crucial question, but implied that she already had decided 'yes' to her personal dilemma. One of pop's most treasured recordings, it was followed by a series of exceptional singles, 'Mama Said' (1961), 'Baby It's You' (1962) and 'Foolish Little Girl' (1963), which confirmed their exemplary position. The Shirelles' influence on other groups, including those in Britain, is incalculable, and the Beatles, the Merseybeats and Manfred Mann are among those who covered their work. The quartet's progress was dealt a crucial setback when producer and arranger Luther Dixon left to take up another post. Newer Scepter acts, including Dionne Warwick, assumed the quartet's one-time prime position, while a punitive record contract kept the group tied to the label. By the time the Shirelles were free to move elsewhere, it was too late to enjoy a contemporary career and the group was confined to the 'oldies' circuit. Alston left for a solo career in 1975. Harris died of a heart attack in June 1982 following a performance in Atlanta. By combining sweetening strings with elements of church music and R&B, the Shirelles exerted an unconscious pivotal influence on all female vocal groups. They were inducted into the Rock And Roll Hall Of Fame in 1996.

● ALBUMS: *Tonight's The Night* (Scepter 1961)★★★, *The Shirelles Sing To Trumpets And Strings* (Scepter/Top Rank 1961)★★★, *Baby It's You* (Scepter/Stateside 1962)★★★★, *Twist Party* (Scepter 1962)★★★, *Foolish Little Girl* (Scepter 1963)★★★, *It's A Mad Mad Mad Mad World* (Scepter 1963)★★, *The Shirelles Sing The Golden Oldies* (Scepter 1964)★, with King Curtis *Eternally Soul* (Wand 1970)★★★, *Tonight's The Night* (Wand 1971)★★★, *Happy In Love* (RCA 1972)★★, *The Shirelles* (RCA 1973)★★, *Let's Give Each Other Love* (RCA 1976)★★, *Spontaneous Combustion* (Scepter 1997)★★.
Solo: Shirley Alston (Owens) *With A Little Help From My Friends* (Strawberry 1975)★★, *Lady Rose* (Strawberry 1977)★★.

● COMPILATIONS: *The Shirelles Hits* (Scepter/Stateside 1963)★★★★, *The Shirelles Greatest Hits Vol. 2* (Scepter 1967)★★★, *Remember When Vol. 1* (Wand 1972)★★★, *Remember When Vol 2* (Wand 1972)★★★, *Golden Hour Of The Shirelles* (Golden Hour 1973)★★★, *Juke Box Giants* (Audio Fidelity 1981)★★★, *The Shirelles Anthology (1959-1967)* (Rhino 1984)★★★★, *Soulfully Yours* (Kent/Ace 1985)★★★, *Sha La La* (Impact/Ace 1985)★★★, *The Shirelles Anthology (1959-1964)* (Rhino 1986)★★★★, *Lost And Found* (Impact/Ace 1987)★★★, *Greatest Hits* (Impact/Ace 1987)★★★★, *16 Greatest Hits* (Gusto 1988)★★★★, *The Collection* (Castle 1990)★★★★, *The Best Of* (Ace 1992)★★★★, *Lost And Found: Rare And Unissued* (1994)★★★, *The Very Best Of ...* (Rhino 1994)★★★★, *The World's Greatest Girls Group* (Tomato/Rhino 1995)★★★★.

● FURTHER READING: *Girl Groups: The Story Of A Sound*, Alan Betrock.

Shirley And Lee

New Orleans-based duo Shirley Goodman (b. 19 June 1936, New Orleans, Louisiana, USA) and Leonard Lee (b. 29 June 1936, d. 23 October 1976) began recording together in 1952. Billed as 'The Sweethearts Of The Blues', they enjoyed a series of US R&B hits, including 'I'm Gone' (1952) and 'Feel So Good' (1955), marked by the juxtaposition between Shirley's shrill, child-like intonation and Lee's bluesy counterpoint. In 1956 they crossed over into the US pop Top 20 with 'Let The Good Times Roll', a charming, infectious performance, written and arranged by Lee. The song became the first million-seller for the Aladdin label and is now regarded as an R&B standard. Shirley And Lee enjoyed minor hits with 'I Feel Good' (1956) and 'When I Saw You' (1957), before parting company in 1963. Shirley moved to the west coast, where she appeared on sessions for producer Harold Battiste and Dr. John, while Lee pursued a low-key solo career. His death in 1976 paradoxically coincided with Goodman's new-found popularity as leader of Shirley And Company.

● ALBUMS: *Let The Good Times Roll* (Aladdin 1956)★★★, *Let The Good Times Roll* (Imperial 1962)★★★.

● COMPILATIONS: *Legendary Masters Shirley & Lee* (EMI 1974)★★★, *Happy Days* (Manhattan 1980)★★, *Respectfully Yours* (Manhattan 1980)★★, *The Best Of Shirley & Lee* (Ace 1982)★★★.

Showmen

An R&B vocal group from Norfolk, Virginia, USA. The Showmen were a classic early 60s transitional group who represented some of the dying gasps of doo-wop and the first stirrings of the soul revolution. The members were General Norman Johnson (b. 23 May 1943, Norfolk, USA), Milton Wells, Gene and Dorsey Wright, and Leslie Felton. The group signed with the New Orleans-based Minit label in 1961 and had an immediate hit with a perky rock 'n' roll/R&B anthem called 'It Will Stand' (number 40 R&B, number 61 pop). The b-side, 'Country Fool', received solid airplay in many parts of the country. The staying power of 'It Will Stand' was most evident when it made a modest return to the charts in 1964 (number 80 pop). In 1963, the Showmen found success in many markets with the delightful '39-21-46', and this, too, proved to have staying power over the years. The Showmen moved to the Philadelphia-based Swan label in 1965, but the singles they released were uninspired. The group's last record was in 1967, recorded in the Carolinas for the tiny Jokers Three label. In 1968 Johnson moved to Detroit and formed the Chairman Of The Board to record on the Invictus label. The Showmen's legacy lived on in the Carolinas, where their classic hits 'It Will Stand' and '39-21-46' have become Beach standards. For decades, Johnson pursued a lucrative career in that region as a Beach artist, long after his popularity in the black community had faded.

● COMPILATIONS: *Some Folks Don't Understand It* (Charly 1991)★★★.

Showstoppers

This US group was formed in Philadelphia by the younger brothers of R&B singer Solomon Burke. The unit comprised Laddie Burke (b. 1950, Philadelphia, Pennsylvania, USA) and Alex Burke (b. 1949, Philadelphia, Pennsylvania, USA). The group was completed by another set of brothers, Earl Smith (b. 1949, Massachusetts, USA) and Timmy Smith (b. 1950,

Massachusetts, USA). Having met while studying at Germantown High School, this electrifying unit, initially influenced by the vocal group the Vibrations, is best recalled for 'Ain't Nothing But A Houseparty' (1968), a vibrant, infectious song beloved in discotheques. A minor pop hit in the USA, the single proved far more popular in Britain, reaching number 11 on its first release before re-entering the charts in 1971. The backing musicians on this song included Carl Chambers, who was later drummer with Gladys Knight And The Pips, and Joe Thomas, who went on to become the guitarist with the Impressions. Two tracks, 'Eeny Meeny', a UK Top 40 entry in 1968, and 'Shake Your Mini', followed, but the Showstoppers were unable to repeat their early success.

SIFFRE, LABI

b. London, England. The son of an English mother and Nigerian father. Siffre first took employment as a minicab driver and delivery man but practised guitar whenever he could, going on to study music harmonics. He played his first gigs as one of a trio of like-minded youngsters, before taking up a nine-month residency at Annie's Rooms. His tenure completed, he travelled to Cannes, France, and played with a variety of soul musicians and bands. He returned to the UK in the late 60s and enjoyed solo hits in 1971 with 'It Must Be Love' (later covered by Madness) and 'Crying, Laughing, Loving, Lying'. Although 'Watch Me' in 1972 was his last hit of the 70s, he made a spectacular comeback in 1987 with the anthemic '(Something Inside) So Strong'. In recent years Siffre has devoted most of his time to his poetry and has shown a sensitive and intelligent grasp of world issues. His relaxed nature and engaging personality has made his poetry readings more popular than his songs.

● ALBUMS: *Labi Siffre* (1970)★★★, *Singer And The Song* (Pye 1971)★★★, *Crying, Laughing, Loving, Lying* (Pye 1972)★★★, *So Strong* (Polydor 1988)★★★, *Make My Day* (Connoisseur 1989)★★★.

● COMPILATIONS: *The Labi Siffre Collection* (Conifer 1986)★★★.

SIGLER, BUNNY

b. Walter Sigler, 27 March 1941, Philadelphia, Pennsylvania, USA. Sigler first made a name for himself singing a medley of old R&B hits, finding success in 1967 with 'Let The Good Times Roll & Feel So Good' (number 20 R&B and number 22 pop) and 'Lovey Dovey & You're So Fine'. Earlier in his career he had belonged to a doo-wop vocal group, the Opals, who recorded in 1959 for the Philadelphia V-Tone label, with little success. After his late 60s records, Sigler abandoned recording for several years to concentrate on songwriting, and wrote songs for Jackie Moore, Joe Simon, the Three Degrees, O'Jays, Intruders and Billy Paul, most of whom were Philadelphia International Records (PIR) artists. In 1973 Sigler returned to the charts on PIR with a remake of Bobby Lewis's old hit 'Tossin' And Turnin'' (number 38 R&B). By the late 70s he had moved into disco on the Gold Mind label, and in 1978 secured his biggest hits with 'Let Me Party With You' (number 8 R&B and number 43 pop) and 'Only You' (number 11 R&B and number 87 pop), the latter recorded with Loleatta Holloway.

● ALBUMS: *Let The Good Times Roll* (Parkway 1967)★★★, *That's How Long I'll Be Loving You* (Philadelphia International 1974)★★★, *Keep Smilin'* (Philadelphia International 1975)★★★, *My Music* (Philadelphia International 1976)★★★, with Barbara Mason *Locked In This Position* (1977)★★★, *Let Me Party With You* (Gold Mind 1978)★★★, *I've Always Wanted To Sing...Not Just Write Songs* (Gold Mind 1979)★★★, *Let It Snow* (1980)★★★.

SILHOUETTES

Formed in 1956 in Philadelphia, Pennsylvania, USA, the Silhouettes recorded one of the classics of the doo-wop era of rock 'n' roll, 'Get A Job'. The song was written by tenor Rick Lewis while he was in the US Army, stationed in Germany. Upon returning home, Lewis joined a singing group called the Parakeets. He left them to front a band called the Gospel Tornadoes, comprising lead singer Bill Horton, bass singer Raymond Edwards and baritone Earl Beal. When the gospel group changed to secular music, it took on a new name, the Thunderbirds. A disc jockey, Kae Williams, signed the group to his own Junior Records in 1958 and 'Get A Job' was recorded as the b-side to the ballad 'I'm Lonely'. The group's name was changed to the Silhouettes and the record was released on the larger Ember label. 'Get A Job' received more attention than the ballad side and ultimately found its way to number 1 in the USA, becoming, in time, one of the best-known up-tempo doo-wop records. The non-sense phrase 'sha-na-na-na', part of its lyric, was borrowed in the late 60s by the rock 'n' roll revival group Sha Na Na. The Silhouettes recorded a number of follow-ups but never again returned to the charts. With numerous personnel changes, the group managed to stay afloat until 1968. Four original members reunited in 1980 and were still working the revival circuit in the early 90s.

● ALBUMS: *The Original And New Silhouettes - '58-'68 Get A Job* (1968)★★★.

SILK

Comprising Gary 'Big G' Glenn, Gary 'Little G' Jenkins, Jonathan Rasboro, Jimmy Gates Jnr. and Timothy Cameron, Silk formed in Atlanta, Georgia, USA, in the early 90s. Their 1992 debut album, *Lose Control*, was a smooth collection of contemporary soul songs produced by Keith Sweat; it quickly rose to number 1 on the *Billboard* Top R&B albums chart and sold nearly two million copies. It featured three US R&B Top 10 hits, including 'Freak Me', which stayed at number 1 on the chart for eight weeks in 1993. Sweat had discovered the group and signed them to his own Keia label. However, with a view to extending their career beyond the confines of sexually suggestive material such as 'Freak Me', the group left Sweat and moved to Elektra Records for 1995's self-titled second album. As well as three of their own songs, *Silk* included contributions from several top-flight R&B writers, plus renowned production teams including Dave Hall, Soul Shock and Gerald LeVert.

● ALBUMS: *Lose Control* (Keia 1992)★★★, *Silk* (Elektra 1995)★★★.

SIMON, JOE

b. 2 September 1943, Simmesport, Louisiana, USA. Simon's professional career began following his move to Oakland, California, where a 1962 release, 'My Adorable One', was a minor hit. In 1964, Joe met John Richbourg, a Nashville-based disc jockey who began guiding the singer's musical path, initially on the Sound Stage 7 label. 'Let's Do It Over' (1965), Simon's first R&B hit, emphasized Richbourg's preference for a blend of gentle soul and country, and the singer's smooth delivery found its niche on such poignant songs as 'Teenager's Prayer', 'Nine Pound Steel' (both 1967) and 'The Chokin' Kind', a US R&B number 1 in 1969. The following year, Simon moved to the Polydor subsidiary Spring. He maintained his ties with Richbourg until 1971, when a Gamble And Huff production, 'Drowning In The Sea Of Love', was an R&B number 3. Further success came with 'The Power Of Love' (1972), 'Step By Step' (1973 - his only UK hit), 'Theme From Cleopatra Jones' (1973) and 'Get Down Get Down (Get On The Floor)' (1975), but the artist increasingly sacrificed his craft in favour of the dancefloor. His late 70s releases were less well received and in 1980 he returned to Nashville. From that time, Simon's work was restricted to local labels.

● ALBUMS: *Simon Pure Soul* (Sound Stage 1967)★★★, *No Sad Songs* (Sound Stage 1968)★★★, *Simon Sings* (Sound Stage 1969)★★★, *The Chokin' Kind* (Sound Stage 1969)★★★, *Joe Simon - Better Than Ever* (Sound Stage 1969)★★★, *The Sounds Of Simon* (Spring 1971)★★★, *Drowning In The Sea Of Love* (Spring 1972)★★★, *Power Of Love* (Spring 1973)★★★, *Mood, Heart And Soul* (Spring 1974)★★★, *Simon Country* (Spring 1974)★★★, *Get Down* (Spring 1975)★★★, *Joe Simon Today* (Spring 1976)★★★, *Easy To Love* (Spring 1977)★★★, *Bad Case Of Love* (Spring 1978)★★, *Love Vibration* (Spring 1979)★★, *Happy Birthday Baby* (Spring 1979)★★, *Soul Neighbors* (Compleat 1984)★★, *Mr. Right* (Compleat 1985)★★★.

● COMPILATIONS: *Joe Simon* 1962/3 Hush/Vee Jay recordings (1969), *Joe Simon's Greatest Hits* (1972)★★★, *The Best Of Joe Simon* (Sound Stage 1972)★★★, *The World Of ...* (Sound Stage 1973)★★★★, *The Best Of ...* (1977)★★★, *Lookin' Back - The Best Of Joe Simon 1966-70* (Charly 1988)★★★, *Mr Shout* (Ace 1997)★★★, *Music In My Bones - The Best Of Joe Simon* (Rhino 1997)★★★.

SIMONE, NINA

b. Eunice Waymon, 21 February 1933, Tyron, North Carolina, USA. An accomplished pianist as a child, Simone later studied at New York's Juilliard School Of Music. Her jazz credentials were established in 1959 when she secured a hit with an emotive interpretation of George Gershwin's 'I Loves You Porgy'. Her influential 60s work included 'Gin House Blues', 'Forbidden Fruit' and 'I Put A Spell On You', while another of her singles, 'Don't Let Me Be Misunderstood', was later covered by the Animals. The singer's popular fortune flourished upon her signing with RCA. 'Ain't Got No - I Got Life', a song lifted from the mock-hippie musical *Hair*, was a UK number 2, while her searing version of the Bee Gees' 'To Love Somebody' reached number 5. In America, her own composition, 'To Be Young, Gifted And Black', dedicated to her late friend, the playwright Lorraine Hansberry, reflected Simone's growing militancy. Releases then grew infrequent as her political activism increased. A commanding, if taciturn live performer, Simone's appearances were increasingly focused on benefits and rallies, although a fluke UK hit, 'My Baby Just Cares For Me', pushed the singer, momentarily, into the commercial spotlight when it reached number 5 in 1987. Tired of an America she perceived as uncaring, Simone settled in France. An uncompromising personality, Nina Simone's interpretations of soul, jazz, blues and standards are both compulsive and unique.

● ALBUMS: *Little Girl Blue* (Bethlehem 1959)★★, *Nina Simone And Her Friends* (Bethlehem 1959)★★, *The Amazing Nina Simone* (Colpix 1959)★★★, *Nina Simone At The Town Hall* (Colpix 1959)★★★, *Nina Simone At Newport* (Colpix 1960)★★★, *Forbidden Fruit* (Colpix 1961)★★★, *Nina Simone At The Village Gate* (Colpix 1961)★★★, *Nina Simone Sings Ellington* (Colpix 1962)★★★, *Nina's Choice* (Colpix 1963)★★★, *Nina Simone At Carnegie Hall* (Colpix 1963)★★★★, *Folksy Nina* (Colpix 1964)★★★, *Nina Simone In Concert* (Philips 1964)★★★, *Broadway ... Blues ... Ballads* (Philips 1964)★★★, *I Put A Spell On You* (Philips 1965)★★★, *Tell Me More* (1965)★★★, *Pastel Blues* (Philips 1965)★★★, *Let It All Out* (Philips 1966)★★★, *Wild Is The Wind* (Philips 1966)★★★, *Nina With Strings* (Colpix 1966)★★★, *This Is* (1966)★★★, *The High Priestess Of Soul* (Philips 1966)★★★, *Nina Simone Sings The Blues* (RCA Victor 1967)★★★★, *Sweet 'N' Swinging* (1967)★★★, *Silk And Soul* (RCA Victor 1967)★★★, *'Nuff Said* (RCA Victor 1968)★★★, *And Piano!* (1969)★★★, *To Love Somebody* (1969)★★★, *Black Gold* (RCA 1970)★★★, *Here Comes The Sun* (RCA 1971)★★★, *Heart And Soul* (1971)★★★, *Emergency Ward* (RCA 1972)★★★, *It Is Finished* (RCA 1972)★★★, *Gifted And Black* (Mojo 1974)★★★, *I Loves You Porgy* (1977)★★★, *Baltimore* (CTI 1978)★★★, *Cry Before I Go* (Manhattan 1980)★★★, *Nina Simone* (Dakota 1982)★★★, *Fodder On My Wings* (IMS 1982)★★★, *Nina's Back* (VPI 1986)★★★, *Live At Vine Street* (Verve 1987)★★★, *Live At Ronnie Scott's* (Windham Hill 1988)★★★, *Live* (Zeta 1990)★★, *The Blues* (Novus/RCA 1991)★★★, *In Concert* (1992)★★★, *A Single Woman* (1993)★★, *The Great Show Of Nina Simone: Live In Paris* (Accord 1996)★★.

● COMPILATIONS: *The Best Of Nina Simone* (Philips 1966)★★★★, *The Best Of Nina Simone* (RCA 1970)★★★★, *Fine And Mellow* (Golden Hour 1975)★★★, *The Artistry Of Nina Simone* (RCA 1982)★★★, *Music For The Millions* (Phillips 1983)★★★, *My Baby Just Cares For Me* (Charly 1984)★★★★, *Lady Midnight* (Connoisseur 1987)★★★, *The Nina Simone Collection* (Deja Vu 1988)★★★★, *The Nina Simone Story* (Deja Vu 1989)★★★, *16 Greatest Hits* (1993)★★★★, *Anthology: The Colpix Years* (Rhino 1997)★★★★, *Saga Of The Good Life And The Hard Times* 1968 sessions (RCA 1997)★★★, *The Great Nina Simone* (Music Club 1997)★★★★, *Ultimate* (Verve 1998)★★★.

● VIDEOS: *Live At Ronnie Scott's* (Hendring 1988).

● FURTHER READING: *I Put A Spell On You: The Autobiography Of Nina Simone*, Nina Simone with Stephen Cleary.

Simply Red

This 80s soul-influenced group was led by Manchester-born vocalist Mick Hucknall (b. Michael James Hucknall, 8 June 1960, Denton, Gt. Manchester, England). Hucknall's first recording group was the punk-inspired Frantic Elevators, who recorded a handful of singles, including an impressive vocal ballad, 'Holding Back The Years'. When they split up in 1983, the vocalist formed Simply Red with a fluid line-up that included Ojo, Mog, Dave Fryman and Eddie Sherwood. After signing to Elektra Records the group had a more settled line-up featuring Hucknall, Tony Bowers (bass), Fritz McIntyre (b. 2 September 1958; keyboards), Tim Kellett (brass), Sylvan Richardson (guitar) and Chris Joyce (drums). Their debut album *Picture Book* climbed to number 2 in the UK charts, while their enticing cover version of the Valentine Brothers' 'Money's Too Tight To Mention' was a Top 20 hit. Although the group registered a lowly number 66 with the follow-up 'Come To My Aid', they rediscovered the hit formula with a sterling re-recording of the minor classic 'Holding Back The Years', which peaked at number 2. The song went on to top the US charts, ushering in a period of international success. Their next album, *Men And Women*, included collaborations between Hucknall and former Motown Records composer Lamont Dozier (of Holland/Dozier/Holland fame). Further hits followed with 'The Right Thing', 'Infidelity' and a reworking of the Cole Porter standard, 'Ev'ry Time We Say Goodbye'. Having twice reached number 2 in the album charts, Simply Red finally scaled the summit in 1989 with the accomplished *A New Flame*. The album coincided with another hit, 'It's Only Love', which was followed by a splendid reworking of Harold Melvin And The Bluenotes' 'If You Don't Know Me By Now', which again climbed to number 2 in the UK. Since then, Simply Red (now effectively Hucknall and various backing musicians) have consolidated their position as one of the most accomplished blue-eyed soul outfits to emerge from the UK in recent years. The 1991 album *Stars* pursued hip-hop-inspired rhythms, alongside their usual soul style. It topped the British charts over a period of months, outselling much-hyped efforts by Michael Jackson, U2, Dire Straits and Guns N' Roses. The much awaited follow-up *Life* was also a big seller, although it showed little sign of creative development. The band returned to the charts in 1996 and 1997 with cover versions of Aretha Franklin's 'Angel' and Gregory Isaacs' 'Night Nurse'.

● ALBUMS: *Picture Book* (Elektra 1985)★★★, *Men And Women* (Warners 1987)★★, *A New Flame* (Warners 1989)★★★, *Stars* (East West 1991)★★★★, *Life* (East West 1995)★★★.

● COMPILATIONS: *Greatest Hits* (East West 1996)★★★.

● VIDEOS: *Greatest Video Hits* (Warner Vision 1996).

● FURTHER READING: *Simply Mick: Mick Hucknall Of Simply Red. The Inside Story*, Robin McGibbon and Rob McGibbon. *The First Fully Illustrated Biography*, Mark Hodkinson.

Simpson, Valerie

b. 26 August 1946, The Bronx, New York, USA. This career of this superior singer and songwriter is inexorably linked to that of her partner Nicholas Ashford. Billed as Valerie And Nick, the couple made their recording debut in 1964 with 'I'll Find You', but achieved greater distinction for a series of excellent compositions, often in partnership with 'Joshie' Jo Armstead. Among the many artists to record the team's songs were Ray Charles, Maxine Brown and Chuck Jackson. In 1966 Ashford And Simpson were signed to the staff of Tamla/Motown. The latter supposedly deputized, uncredited, for singer Tammi Terrell while she was too ill to complete duets with Marvin Gaye. Simpson's voice, she controversially claims, was featured on 'The Onion Song', a UK Top 10 hit, which in part inspired the resumption of her recording career. 'Silly Wasn't I' reached the R&B Top 30 in 1972, but the following year she and Ashford rekindled their performing partnership and, as Ashford And Simpson, enjoyed a prolonged spell of chart success.

● ALBUMS: *Valerie Simpson Exposed* (Tamla 1971)★★, *Valerie Simpson* (Tamla 1972)★★.

● COMPILATIONS: *Keep It Comin'* (Tamla 1977)★★.

Sister Sledge

Debra (b. 1955), Joan (b. 1957), Kim (b. 1958) and Kathie Sledge (b. 1959) were all born and raised in Philadelphia, Pennsylvania, USA. They started their recording career in 1971 and spent a short time working as backing singers before enjoying a series of minor R&B hits between 1974 and 1977. Two years later they entered a fruitful relationship with Chic masterminds Nile Rodgers and Bernard Edwards that resulted in several sparkling singles, including 'He's The Greatest Dancer', 'We Are Family' and 'Lost In Music', each of which reached the the UK Top 20 in 1979. The Sisters then left the Chic organization and began to produce their own material in 1981. Although success in the USA waned, the quartet retained their UK popularity and two remixes of former hits served as a prelude to 'Frankie', a simple but irrepressible song which reached number 1 in 1985. Since then, however, Sister Sledge have been unable to maintain this status.

● ALBUMS: *Circle Of Love* (Atco 1975)★★, *Together* (Cotillion 1977)★★, *We Are Family* (Cotillion 1979)★★★, *Love Somebody Today* (Cotillion 1980)★★, *All American Girls* (Cotillion 1981)★★, *The Sisters* (Cotillion 1982)★★, *Bet Cha Say That To All The Girls* (Cotillion 1983)★★, *When The Boys Meet The Girls* (Atlantic 1985)★★.

● COMPILATIONS: *Greatest Hits* (Atlantic 1986)★★★, *The Best Of...* (Rhino 1992)★★★★.

Six Teens

An R&B vocal group from Los Angeles, California, USA. In the wake of the success of Frankie Lymon And The Teenagers, many east coast groups emerged with a preteen lead sound. The Six Teens diverged slightly from the pattern by virtue of their west coast origin and the use of a female to sing the 'adolescent teen boy' part. The members were Trudy Williams (lead), Ed Wells (lead), Richard

Owens, Darryl Lewis, Beverly Pecot and Louise Williams. Their one hit was the fetching 'A Casual Look' (number 7 R&B, number 25 pop), from 1956, on which Williams' youth was most telling and appealing. The group's follow-up, 'Send Me Flowers', was a regional hit in Hawaii, and 'Only Jim' and 'Arrow Of Love' likewise achieved regional sales. The group's last recordings were made in 1958, and Owens became a member of the Vibrations.

● COMPILATIONS: *A Casual Look* (Official 1989)★★★.

SLEDGE, PERCY

b. 25 November 1941, Leighton, Alabama, USA. An informal, intimate singer, Sledge led a popular campus attraction, the Esquires Combo, prior to his recording debut. Recommended to Quin Ivy, owner of the Norala Sound studio, Sledge arrived with a rudimentary draft of 'When A Man Loves A Woman'. A timeless single, its simple arrangement hinged on Spooner Oldham's organ sound and the singer's homely, nasal intonation. Released in 1966, it was a huge international hit, setting the tone for Sledge's subsequent path. A series of emotional, poignant ballads followed, poised between country and soul, but none achieved a similar commercial profile. 'It Tears Me Up', 'Out Of Left Field' (both 1967) and 'Take Time To Know Her' (1968) nonetheless stand among southern soul's finest achievements. Having left Atlantic Records, Sledge re-emerged on Capricorn in 1974 with *I'll Be Your Everything*. Two 80s collections of re-recorded hits, *Percy* and *Wanted Again*, confirm the singer's intimate yet unassuming delivery. Released in Britain following the runaway success of a resurrected 'When A Man Loves A Woman', they are not diminished by comparison. In 1994 Sledge recorded his first all-new set for some time, the excellent *Blue Night* on Sky Ranch/Virgin, which capitalized on the Sledge 'strong suit', the slow-burning countrified soul-ballad, even although the sessions were recorded in Los Angeles. The appearance of musicians such as Steve Cropper and Bobby Womack helped to ensure the success of the album.

● ALBUMS: *When A Man Loves A Woman* (Atlantic 1966)★★★★, *Warm And Tender Soul* (Atlantic 1966)★★★★, *The Percy Sledge Way* (Atlantic 1967)★★★, *Take Time To Know Her* (Atlantic 1968)★★★, *I'll Be Your Everything* (Capricorn 1974)★★★, *If Loving You Is Wrong* (Charly 1986)★★★, *Percy!* (Monument 1987)★★★, *Wanted Again* (Demon 1989)★★, *Blue Night* (Sky Ranch 1994)★★★★.

● COMPILATIONS: *The Best Of Percy Sledge* (Atlantic 1969)★★★★, *The Golden Voice Of Soul* (Atlantic 1975)★★★, *Any Day Now* (Charly 1984)★★★, *Warm And Tender Love* (Blue Moon 1986)★★★, *When A Man Loves A Woman (The Ultimate Collection)* (Atlantic 1987)★★★★, *It Tears Me Up: The Best Of ...* (Rhino 1992)★★★★, *Greatest Hits* (1993)★★★★.

SLICK

(see Fat Larry's Band)

SLY AND THE FAMILY STONE

This US group was formed in San Francisco, California, in 1967 and comprised Sly Stone (b. Sylvester Stewart, 15 March 1944, Dallas, Texas, USA), Freddie Stone (b. 5 June 1946, Dallas, Texas, USA; guitar), Rosie Stone (b. 21 March 1945, Vallejo, California, USA; piano), Cynthia Robinson (b. 12 January 1946, Sacramento, California, USA; trumpet), Jerry Martini (b. 1 October 1943, Colorado, USA; saxophone), Larry Graham (b. 14 August 1946, Beaumont, Texas, USA; bass) and Greg Errico (b. 1 September 1946, San Francisco, California, USA; drums). Sly Stone's recording career began in 1948. A child prodigy, he drummed and added guitar to 'On The Battlefield For My Lord', a single released by his family's group, the Stewart Four. At high school he sang harmony with the Vicanes, but by the early 60s he was working the bars and clubs on San Francisco's North Beach enclave. Sly learned his trade with several bands, including Joe Piazza And The Continentals, but he occasionally fronted his own. 'Long Time Away', a single credited to Sylvester Stewart, dates from this period. He also worked as a disc jockey at stations KSOL and KDIA. Sly joined Autumn Records as a songwriter/house-producer, and secured a 1964 success with Bobby Freeman's 'C'mon And Swim'. His own opportunistic single, 'I Just Learned How To Swim', was less fortunate, a fate that also befell 'Buttermilk Pts 1 & 2'. Stone's production work, however, was exemplary; the Beau Brummels, the Tikis and the Mojo Men enjoyed a polished, individual sound. In 1966 Sly formed the Stoners, a short-lived group that included Cynthia Robinson. The following year Sly And The Family Stone made its debut on the local Loadstone label with 'I Ain't Got Nobody'. The group was then signed to Epic, where their first album proclaimed itself *A Whole New Thing*. However, it was 1968 before 'Dance To The Music' became a Top 10 single in the USA and UK. 'Everyday People' topped the US chart early the following year, but Sly's talent was not fully established until a fourth album, *Stand!*, was released. Two million copies were sold, while tracks including the title song, 'I Want To Take You Higher' and 'Sex Machine', transformed black music forever. Rhythmically inventive, the whole band pulsated with a crazed enthusiasm that pitted doo-wop, soul, the San Francisco sound, and more, one on top of the other. Contemporaries, from Miles Davis to George Clinton and the Temptations, showed traces of Sly's remarkable vision. A sensational appearance at the Woodstock Festival reinforced his popularity. The new decade began with a double-sided hit, 'Thank You (Falettinme Be Mice Elf Agin)'/'Everybody Is A Star', an R&B and pop number 1, but the optimism suddenly clouded. Sly began missing concerts; those he did perform were often disappointing and when *There's A Riot Goin' On* did appear in 1971, it was dark, mysterious and brooding. This introverted set nevertheless reached number 1 in the US chart, and provided three successful singles, 'Family Affair' (another US R&B and pop number 1), 'Running Away' and 'Smilin'', but the joyful noise of the 60s was now over. *Fresh* lacked Sly's erstwhile focus while successive releases, *Small Talk* and *High On You*, reflected a waning power. The Family Stone was also crumbling: Larry Graham left to form Graham Central Station, while Andy Newmark replaced Greg Errico. However, the real undermining factor was the leader's drug dependency, a constant stumbling block to Sly's recurrent 'comebacks'. A 1979 release, *Back On The Right Track*, featured several original members, but later tours were dogged by Sly's addiction problem. Jailed for possession of cocaine in 1987, this innovative artist closed the decade fighting further extradition charges. There has been little of any note heard of Stone in the 90s.

● ALBUMS: *A Whole New Thing* (Epic 1967)★★★, *Dance To The Music* (Epic 1968)★★★★, *Life* (USA) *M'Lady* (UK) (Epic/Direction 1968)★★★★, *Stand!* (Epic 1969)★★★★, *There's A Riot Going On* (Epic 1971)★★★★, *Fresh* (Epic 1973)★★★, *Small Talk* (Epic 1974)★★★, *High On You* (Epic 1975)★★, *Heard Ya Missed Me, Well I'm Back* (Epic 1976)★★, *Back On The Right Track* (Warners 1979)★★★, *Ain't But The One Way* (Warners 1982)★★.

● COMPILATIONS: *Greatest Hits* (Epic 1970)★★★★, *High Energy* (Epic 1975)★★★★, *Ten Years Too Soon* (Epic 1979)★★, *Anthology* (Epic 1981)★★★★, *Takin' You Higher: The Best Of Sly And The Family Stone* (Sony 1992)★★★★, *Precious Stone: In The Studio With Sly Stone 1963-1965* (Ace 1994)★★.

SMITH, HUEY 'PIANO'

b. 26 January 1934, New Orleans, Louisiana, USA. Pianist Smith drew his pulsating style from a variety of musical sources, including the boogie-woogie of Albert Ammons and jazz of Jelly Roll Morton. Having served in bands led by Earl King and Eddie 'Guitar Slim' Jones, Smith became a session musician before embarking on an independent recording career. Leading his own group, the Clowns, which at its peak included Gerry Hall, Eugene Francis, Billy Roosevelt and vocalist Bobby Marchan, he achieved two million-selling singles in 1957 with 'Rockin' Pneumonia And The Boogie Woogie Flu' and 'Don't You Just Know It'. Both releases showcased classic New Orleans rhythms as well as the leader's vibrant, percussive technique. The pianist was also featured on 'Sea Cruise', a 1959 smash for Frankie Ford, whose speeded-up vocal was overdubbed onto an existing Clowns tape. However, despite other excellent releases, Huey Smith did not enjoy another hit and, having become a Jehovah's Witness, forsook music in favour of preaching.

● ALBUMS: *Having A Good Time* (Imperial 1959)★★★, *For Dancing* (Imperial 1961)★★, *T'was The Night Before Christmas* (Imperial 1962)★★, *Rock 'N' Roll Revival* (Imperial 1963)★★★.

● COMPILATIONS: *Rockin' Pneumonia And The Boogie Woogie Flu* (1965)★★★, *Huey 'Piano' Smith's Rock And Roll Revival* (1974)★★★, *Rockin' Pneumonia And The Boogie Woogie Flu* different from previous entry (Ace 1979)★★★, *Rockin' And Jivin'* (Charly 1981)★★★, *The Imperial Sides 1960/1961* (Pathe Marconi 1984)★★★, *Somewhere There's Honey For The Grizzly* (Ace 1984)★★★, *Serious Clownin' - The History Of Huey 'Piano' Smith And The Clowns* (Rhino 1986)★★★★, *Pitta Pattin'* (Charly 1987)★★★.

SMITH, O.C.

b. Ocie Lee Smith, 21 June 1932, Mansfield, Louisiana, USA. O.C. Smith was raised in Los Angeles, where he began singing jazz and standards in clubs at the end of the 40s. After serving five years in the US Air Force, he signed with Cadence Records in 1956, enjoying some success the following year with the sophisticated 'Lighthouse'. He remained predominantly a club performer until 1961, when he replaced Joe Williams in the Count Basie Band. He resumed his solo career in 1963, finally attaining a commercial breakthrough in 1968 with Dallas Frazier's unusual story-song, 'The Son Of Hickory Holler's Tramp', recorded at Fame Studios in Muscle Shoals, and a major hit in Britain. In the USA, this record was overshadowed by his rendition of Bobby Russell's 'Little Green Apples', which outsold a rival hit version by Roger Miller, although in Britain, it lost out to a home-grown release by Leapy Lee. 'Daddy's Little Man' in 1969 provided Smith's final taste of US Top 40 success, though the soul-flavoured 'La La Peace Song' proved popular in 1974, and 'Together' was an unexpected chart entry in 1977. During the decade in which he was most successful, Smith issued a series of impressive albums that showcased his fluent, soulful vocal style.

● ALBUMS: *The Dynamic O.C. Smith* (1966)★★★, *Hickory Holler Revisited* (Columbia 1968)★★★, *For Once In My Life* (Columbia 1969)★★★, *O.C. Smith At Home* (Columbia 1969)★★★, *Help Me Make It Through The Night* (Columbia 1971)★★★, *La La Peace Song* (Columbia 1974)★★, *Together* (Columbia 1977)★★.

● COMPILATIONS: *O.C. Smith's Greatest Hits* (Columbia 1970)★★★, *The O.C. Smith Collection* (Pickwick 1980)★★★.

SOLITAIRES

From Harlem, New York, USA, the Solitaires, like no other vocal group of the 50s, sang lushly harmonized doo-wop with a dreamy romantic feeling, and rank as one of the great groups of the 50s. Formed in 1953, the group originally comprised veterans of the doo-wop scene and consisted of lead Herman Curtis (ex-Vocaleers), tenor Buzzy Willis and bass Pat Gaston (both ex-Crows), tenor/guitarist Monte Owens and baritone Bobby Baylor (both of whom had recorded with the Mellomoods), and pianist Bobby Williams. They signed with Hy Weiss's Old Town label in 1954, and with Curtis's haunting falsetto on 'Wonder Why', 'Blue Valentine', 'Please Remember My Heart' and 'I Don't Stand A Ghost Of A Chance', the group quickly established themselves locally if not nationally. Their deep, yet crisp and clean, R&B sound set a standard for other groups. Curtis left in 1955 and, with the wonderfully flavourful tenor of new recruit Milton Love, the group entered their most commercially successful period. With such great records as 'The Wedding' (1955), 'The Angels Sang' (1956), 'You've Sin' (1956) and 'Walking Along' (1957), the latter covered by the Diamonds, they became a rock 'n' roll phenomenon. By the time the Solitaires left Old Town in 1960, however, they had metamorphosed into a Coasters-sounding group, and by the time of their last recording in 1964 personnel changes had left little that was recognizable from the classic group. In the following decades, various ensembles of the Solitaires would appear on revival shows.

● COMPILATIONS: *Walking Along With* (Ace 1992)★★★.

Sons Of Champlin

Bill Champlin (vocals, trumpet) and Tim Caine (saxophone) formed this enigmatic white-soul aggregation in 1965. They were initially joined by Terry Haggerty (lead guitar), Al Strong (bass) and Jim Myers (drums), but when a horn player, Geoff Palmer, was added, Champlin switched to guitar. Draft victim Myers was then replaced by Bill Bowen. Originally dubbed the Masterbeats, then the Sons Of Father Champlin, the group adopted their more familiar name in 1966. A confident debut single, 'Sing Me A Rainbow', preceded their transformation from besuited aspirants to chemical proselytizers. Now established on the San Francisco scene, a sprawling double album, *Loosen Up Naturally*, encapsulated their unique blend of love, peace, happiness and funk. A second album, named after the group's now truncated title, the Sons, refined a similar mixture before they embarked on one of their periodic implosions, during which time various members joined, and left such ensembles as the Rhythm Dukes and the Nu-Boogaloo Express. A reconstituted line-up, shorn of its horn section, reappeared on *Follow Your Heart*. Champlin, Haggerty and Palmer were joined by David Shallock (guitar) and Bill Vitt (drums) in a new venture, Yogi Phlegm, but this unfortunate/wonderful appellation was then abandoned. The quintet later reclaimed the Sons Of Champlin name, but although they secured some commercial success, it was tempered by mismanagement and misfortune. Bill Champlin embarked on a solo career during the late 70s. He appeared as a backing singer on a score of releases and co-wrote 'After The Love Is Gone' for Earth, Wind And Fire. Having completed two solo albums, *Single* and *Runaway*, this expressive vocalist joined Chicago in 1982.

● ALBUMS: *Loosen Up Naturally* (Capitol 1969)★★★, as The Sons*The Sons* (Capitol 1969)★★, *The Sons Minus Seeds And Stems* (Capitol 1970)★★, *Follow Your Heart* (Capitol 1971)★★★, *Welcome To The Dance* (Columbia 1973)★★, *The Sons Of Champlin* (Ariola America 1975)★★, *A Circle Filled With Love* (Ariola America 1976)★★, *Loving Is Why* (Ariola America 1977)★★.

● COMPILATIONS: *Marin County Sunshine* (Decal 1988)★★★.

Soul Children

This group was formed as a vehicle for the songwriting talents of Isaac Hayes and David Porter in Memphis, Tennessee, USA. Comprising Anita Louis (b. 24 November 1949, Memphis, Tennessee, USA), Shelbra Bennett (b. Memphis, Tennessee, USA), John 'Blackfoot' Colbert (b. 20 November 1946, Greenville, Mississippi, USA) and Norman West (b. 30 October 1939, Monroe, Louisiana, USA), they first surfaced in 1968 with 'Give 'Em Love'. This excellent Hayes/Porter composition established their startling vocal interplay, which, at times, suggested a male/female Sam And Dave. Although artistically consistent, only three of the group's singles, 'The Sweeter He Is' (1969), 'Hearsay' (1970) and 'I'll Be The Other Woman' (1973), reached the US R&B Top 10. The Soul Children were later reduced to a trio and moved to Epic when their former outlet, Stax, went into liquidation. Colbert later found fame under the name J. Blackfoot when one of his releases, 'Taxi', was a 1983 hit in both the USA and UK.

● ALBUMS: *Soul Children* (Stax 1969)★★★, *Best Of Two Worlds* (Stax 1971)★★★, *Genesis* (Stax 1972)★★★, *Friction* (Stax 1974)★★★, *The Soul Years* (1974)★★★, *Finders Keepers* (Epic 1976)★★★, *Where Is Your Woman Tonight?* (Epic 1977)★★★, *Open Door Policy* (1978)★★★.

● COMPILATIONS: *Soul Children/Genesis* (Stax 1990)★★★, *Friction/Best Of Two Worlds* (Stax 1992)★★★, *The Singles Plus Open Door Policy* (1993)★★★★.

Soul For Real

A highly commercial swingbeat/urban R&B concern, signed to Uptown Records prior to Andre Harrell's defection to Motown Records, Soul For Real made their debut with *Candy Rain* in 1995. Comprising four brothers, Soul For Real are led by their eldest sibling, Chris 'Choc' Dalyrimple (b. *c*.1971, USA). The other Dalyrimple brothers are Andre (b. *c*.1974, USA), Brian (b. *c*.1976, USA) and Jason (b. *c*.1980, USA). Despite the record label turbulence that accompanied the departure of Harrell, *Candy Rain* earned platinum status, though the group insisted they could have sold many more copies had the record been given sufficient promotion. However, it unquestionably served to launch Soul For Real's career, housing three hit singles in 'Every Little Thing I Do', 'Candy Rain' and 'If You Want It'. With the advent of the 1996 follow-up, *For Life*, it had become obvious that both the group and Uptown were gearing up to ensure the act reached its projected multi-platinum status. In order to achieve this, the group embraced a much more mature sound, replacing the bubblegum pop of its forerunner with a considered, slightly forced R&B feel.

● ALBUMS: *Candy Rain* (Uptown 1995)★★★, *For Life* (Uptown 1996)★★★.

Soul II Soul

This highly successful UK rap, soul and R&B group originally consisted of Jazzie B (b. Beresford Romeo, 26 January 1963, London, England; rapper), Nellee Hooper (musical arranger) and Philip 'Daddae' Harvey (multi-instrumentalist). The early definition of the group was uncomplicated: 'It's a sound system, an organisation (which) came together to build upon making careers for people who had been less fortunate within the musical and artistic realms.' The name Soul II Soul was first used to describe Jazzie B and Harvey's company supplying disc jockeys and PA systems to dance acts. They also held a number of warehouse raves, particularly at Paddington Dome, near Kings Cross, London, before setting up their own venue. There they met Hooper, formerly of the Wild Bunch and subsequently a member of Massive Attack. Joining forces, they took up a residency at Covent Garden's African Centre before signing to Virgin Records' subsidiary Ten Records. Following the release of two singles, 'Fairplay' and 'Feel Free', the band's profile grew with the aid of fashion T-shirts, two shops and Jazzie B's slot on the then pirate Kiss-FM radio station. However, their next release would break not only them but vocalist Caron Wheeler, when 'Keep On Movin'' reached number 5 in the UK charts. The follow-up, 'Back To Life (However Do You Want Me)', once more featured Wheeler, and was taken from their debut *Club Classics Volume One*. The ranks of the Soul II Soul collective had swelled to incorporate a myriad of musicians, whose input was evident in the variety of styles employed. Wheeler soon left to pursue a solo career, but the band's momentum was kept intact by 'Keep On Movin'' penetrating the US clubs and the album scaling the top of the UK charts. 'Get A Life' was a further expansion on the influential, much copied stuttering rhythms that the band had employed on previous singles, but Jazzie B and Hooper's arrangement of Sinead O'Connor's UK number 1, 'Nothing Compares To You', was a poignant contrast. Other artists who sought their services included Fine Young Cannibals and Neneh Cherry. The early part of 1990 was spent in what amounted to business expansion, with a film company, a talent agency and an embryonic record label. The band's second album duly arrived halfway through the year, including Courtney Pine and Kym Mazelle in its star-studded cast. However, despite entering the charts at number 1 it was given a frosty reception by some critics who saw it as comparatively conservative. Mazelle would also feature on the single 'Missing You', as Jazzie B unveiled his (ill-fated) new label Funki Dred, backed by Motown Records. Although *Volume III, Just Right* made its debut at number 3 in the UK album charts, it proffered no substantial singles successes, with both 'Move Me No Mountain' and 'Just Right' stalling outside the Top 30. Jazzie B would spend the early months of 1993 co-producing James Brown's first album of the 90s, *Universal James*, and Virgin issued a stop-gap singles compilation at the end of the year. The group's fourth studio album was not available until July 1995, as Caron Wheeler returned to the fold. However, the accompanying hit single, 'Love Enuff', was sung by ex-Snap! singer Penny Ford.

● ALBUMS: *Club Classics Volume I* (Ten 1989)★★★★, *Volume II: 1990 A New Decade* (Ten 1990)★★★, *Volume III, Just Right* (Ten 1992)★★★, *Volume V - Believe* (Virgin 1995)★★★, *Time For Change* (Island 1997)★★★.

● COMPILATIONS: *Volume IV - The Classic Singles 88-93* (Virgin 1993)★★★★.

Soul Stirrers

One of gospel's renowned vocal groups, the Soul Stirrers first performed in the early 30s, but their ascendancy began the following decade under the leadership of Rebert H. Harris. Eschewing the accustomed quartet format, Harris introduced the notion of a fifth member, a featured vocalist, thus infusing a greater flexibility without undermining traditional four-part harmonies. Harris left the group in 1950, tiring of what he perceived as non-spiritual influences. His replacement was Sam Cooke, late of the Highway QCs, a singer already groomed as a likely successor by Soul Stirrer baritone R.B. Robinson. This particular line-up was completed by Silas Roy Crain (b. 1911, Texas, USA, d. 14 September 1996), Jesse J. Farley, T.L. Bruster and Paul Foster (d. 20 August 1995), although Bob King replaced Bruster in 1953. Cooke's silky delivery brought the group an even wider appeal, while his compositions, including 'Nearer To Thee' and 'Touch The Hem Of His Garment', anticipated the styles he would follow on embracing secular music in 1956. Cooke's replacement, Johnnie Taylor, was also drawn from the ranks of the Highway QCs. The newcomer bore an obvious debt to the former singer as the group's work on Cooke's Sar label attested. Taylor also embarked on a solo career, but the Stirrers continued to record throughout the 60s with Willie Rogers, Martin Jacox and Richard Miles assuming the lead role in turn. Like the Staple Singers before them, the veteran group latterly began to include material regarded as inspirational (for example 'Let It Be'), as opposed to strictly religious. In the late 80s and early 90s UK Ace released a series of fine CD reissues of Specialty material, chiefly featuring Sam Cooke as lead singer.

● ALBUMS: with Sam Cooke *The Soul Stirrers Featuring Sam Cooke* (Specialty 1959)★★★★, with Cooke *The Wonderful World Of Sam Cooke* (Keen 1965)★★★, *Going Back To The Lord Again* (Specialty 1972)★★★, *Strength, Power And Love* (1974)★★★, *Tribute To Sam Cooke* (Chess/MCA 1986)★★★, *Resting Easy* (Chess/MCA 1986)★★★, *In the Beginning* (1989)★★★, with Cooke *Sam Cooke With The Soul Stirrers* (Specialty 1991)★★★★, *The Soul Stirrers Featuring R.H. Harris Shine On Me* (Ace 1992)★★★, *Jesus Gave Me Water* (Ace 1993)★★★, *Heaven Is My Home* (Ace 1993)★★★, *The Last Mile Of The Way* (Ace 1994)★★.

Soul Survivors

Vocalists Kenneth Jeremiah, Richard Ingui and Charles Ingui were a New York-based singing group, the Dedications, prior to adding backing musicians Paul Venturini (organ), Edward Leonetti (guitar) and Joey Forgione (drums). The sextet took the name the Soul Survivors in 1966 and secured a US Top 5 hit the following year with 'Expressway To Your Heart'. This all-white group was produced by the emergent Gamble And Huff team, but subsequent releases, including the similar-sounding 'Explosion In Your Soul', were less successful and they split up. The Ingui brothers resurrected the name during the 70s, but despite signing to their former mentor's TSOP label, were unable to rekindle their former profile. Jeremiah later joined Shirley Goodman in Shirley & Company.

● ALBUMS: *When The Whistle Blows Anything Goes* (Crimson 1967)★★★, *Take Another Look* (Crimson 1968)★★★, *Soul Survivors* (TSOP 1974)★★★.

Soul, Jimmy

b. James McCleese, 24 August 1942, Weldon, North Carolina, USA, d. 25 June 1988. A former boy preacher, McCleese acquired his 'Soul' epithet from his congregations. He subsequently toured southern US states as a member of several gospel groups, including the famed Nightingales, wherein Soul was billed as 'The Wonder Boy', before discovering a forte for pop and R&B. He became a popular attraction around the Norfolk area of

Virginia where he was introduced to songwriter/producer Frank Guida, who guided the career of Gary 'U.S.' Bonds. Soul joined Guida's S.P.Q.R. label and enjoyed a Top 20 US R&B hit with his debut single, 'Twistin' Matilda', before striking gold with his second release, 'If You Wanna Be Happy', which topped the US pop chart in 1963. Both songs were remakes of popular calypso tunes, reflecting Guida's passion for West Indian music. The song also became a minor hit in Britain, and was latterly covered by the Peter B's, a group that included Peter Bardens, Peter Green and Mick Fleetwood. It sadly proved Soul's final chart entry although he nonetheless remained a popular entertainer until his death in June 1988.

● ALBUMS: *If You Wanna Be Happy* (S.P.Q.R. 1963)★★★, *Jimmy Soul And The Belmonts* (S.P.Q.R. 1963)★★★.

● COMPILATIONS: *If You Wanna Be Happy: The Very Best Of* (Ace 1996)★★★.

SOUNDS OF BLACKNESS

Led by bodybuilder Gary Hines, a former Mr Minnesota, Sounds Of Blackness are a gospel/soul 40-piece choir whose work has also revolutionized the dance charts. Stranger still, perhaps, was the fact that they broke through so late in their career. They were 20 years old as an outfit when they came to prominence in 1991. Hines took them over from their original incarnation as the Malcalaster College Black Choir in January 1971, running the group on a strict ethical code of professional practices. The rulebook is sustained by the long waiting-list of aspiring members, and Hines' self-appointed role as 'benevolent dictator'. They first made the charts under the aegis of Jimmy Jam And Terry Lewis, who had spotted the band and used them for backing vocals on their productions for Alexander O'Neal. The celebrated production duo, who had been advised to sign the choir on the advice of Janet Jackson, used Sounds Of Blackness to launch their new record label, Perspective Records, succeeding almost immediately with 'Optimistic'. Released in 1990, it single-handedly sparked off a revival in the fortunes of gospel music. The album that accompanied it subsequently won a Grammy award, as 'The Pressure' and 'Testify' also charted. Subsequent singles were also successful, and included remixes from noted dance music producers such as Sasha. The distinctive, emotive vocals from Ann Bennett-Nesby proved extremely popular in the secular arena of the club scene. Hines was pleased rather than hesitant about this exposure, insisting that their message could permeate people's consciences regardless of the environment. Sounds Of Blackness sang 'Gloryland', alongside Daryl Hall, as the official theme to the 1994 World Cup football tournament. They have also appeared on the soundtracks to the films *Posse* and *Demolition Man*, and have recorded with John Mellencamp, Elton John and Stevie Wonder. *Time For Healing* marked the 25th Anniversary of the choir, and featured cameo appearances from Brother Jack McDuff and rapper Craig Mack.

● ALBUMS: *The Evolution Of Gospel* (Perspective/A&M 1990)★★★★, *The Night Before Christmas - A Musical Fantasy* (Perspective/A&M 1992)★★★, *Africa To America* (Perspective/A&M 1994)★★★★, *Time For Healing* (A&M 1997)★★★.

SOUTH SHORE COMMISSION

This R&B funk band from Chicago, Illinois, USA, comprised Frank McCurry (vocals), Sheryl Henry (vocals), Sidney 'Pinchback' Lennear (guitar), Eugene Rogers (rhythm guitar), David Henderson (bass) and Warren Haygood (drums). The South Shore Commission played a modest role in the rising funk revolution in the 70s when many such outfits who started out as backing groups for vocalists emerged as recording groups in their own right. The unit was formed in 1960 in Washington, DC, as the Exciters. In 1965 they became the back-up band for the Five Dutones and were signed to the One-derful label in Chicago. Members of the Exciters moved to Chicago and to nearby Gary, Indiana. When the Five Dutones broke up in 1967, the Exciters became the South Shore Commission, with McCurry from the Five Dutones becoming one of the band's vocalists. The group charted locally in 1970 with 'Right On Brother' on Atlantic Records and in 1971 with 'Shadows' on Nickel. National success came when the South Shore Commission signed with New York-based Scepter Records, recording for their Wand subsidiary. Their biggest hit was 'Free Man' (number 9 R&B, number 61 pop), from 1975, and they charted twice more in the next year with 'We're On The Right Track' (number 30 R&B, number 94 pop) and 'Train Called Freedom' (number 35 R&B, number 86 pop). The latter two singles came from their only album, *South Shore Commission*, recorded in Philadelphia under producer Bunny Sigler and in Hollywood under producer Dick Griffey.

● ALBUMS: *South Shore Commission* (Wand 1975)★★★.

SOUTH SIDE MOVEMENT

A funk band from Chicago, Illinois, USA. The original members were vocalist Melvin Moore, guitarist Bobby Pointer, bassist Ronald Simmons, keyboardist Morris Beeks, drummer Willie Hayes, trumpeter Steve Hawkins, trombonist Bill McFarland and alto saxophonist Milton Johnson. The group began as the back-up band for the Chicago duo Simtec And Wylie, and when that act fell into disarray in 1972 the band took the name South Side Movement. In 1973 they were signed to the New York-based Wand label and achieved two chart singles with 'I've Been Watching You' (number 14 R&B, number 61 pop) and 'Can You Get To That' (number 56 R&B). They also recorded an album for the label, *I've Been Watching You*. The group moved to 20th Century Records in 1974 and recorded two more albums and a spate of singles, none of which charted. In 1975 the South Side Movement disbanded.

● ALBUMS: *I've Been Watching You* (Wand 1973)★★★, *Movin'* (20th Century 1974)★★, *Moving South* (20th Century 1975)★★.

SPANIELS

This vocal ensemble was formed in 1952 in Gary, Indiana, USA. The Spaniels were universally recognized as one of the great R&B vocal harmony groups of the 50s, whose magnificent body of work was not truly reflected in their moderate chart success. The group originally consisted of Roosevelt High students James 'Pookie' Hudson (lead), Ernest Warren (first tenor), Opal Courtney (baritone), Willis C. Jackson (baritone) and Gerald Gregory (bass). In 1953 the quintet enjoyed an R&B Top 10 hit with 'Baby, It's You', but the following year achieved their biggest success when 'Goodnite Sweetheart, Goodnite' reached the US pop Top 30 despite competition from an opportunistic pop-style version by the McGuire Sisters. The Spaniels' delicate doo-wop harmonies turned this ballad into one of the era's best-loved performances, with the song's emotional pull outweighing its intrinsic simplicity. The Spaniels in 1955 followed with two fine regional hits, 'Let's Make Up' and 'You Painted Pictures'. The Spaniels reorganized in 1956, and Hudson and Gregory were augmented by James Cochran (baritone), Carl Rainge (tenor) and Don Porter (second tenor). Top recordings by this group included 'You Gave Me Peace Of Mind' (1956), 'Everyone's Laughing' (number 13 R&B 1957) and 'I Lost You' (1958). Another reorganization in 1960, in which Hudson and Gregory brought in Andy McGruder, Billy Cary and Ernest Warren, yielded the group's last hit featuring the classic Spaniels sound, 'I Know' (US R&B number 23 in 1960). Hudson went solo in 1961, but formed a soul-styled Spaniels group in 1969 that brought 'Fairy Tales' to the charts in 1970.

● ALBUMS: *Goodnite, It's Time To Go* (1958)★★★, *The Spaniels* (1960)★★★, *Spaniels* (1968)★★★.

● COMPILATIONS: *Hits Of The Spaniels* (1971)★★★, *Great Googley Moo!* (Charly 1981)★★★, *16 Soulful Serenades* (1984)★★★, *Stormy Weather* (Charly 1986)★★★, *Play It Cool* (Charly 1990)★★★★, *40th Anniversary 1953-1993* (1993)★★★.

Sparrows Quartette

Influenced by the sounds of the Orioles and Ravens, the Sparrows Quartette's attempts to rekindle nostalgia for classic doo-wop was piloted by R&B aficionados Dominick 'Dom' D'Elia (lead), Sam Wood (bass) and James Brady (baritone). Dom's 11-year-old brother, Billy D'Elia (tenor), and Bob Freedman (ex-Squires; lead tenor) completed the line-up (effectively meaning the 'Quartette' was in fact a quintet). Formed in New York, USA, in 1961, the group's debut single was 'Merry Christmas Baby' on Broadcast Records in 1963. He later formed Jet Records in 1965, by which time the Sparrows' line-up had shifted, with Sal Mondrone replacing Brady, and also taking over lead duties. A single emerged, 'Deep In My Heart', but it made little headway in a declining market for traditional vocal groups. The Sparrows broke up in 1969, but re-formed two years later to record their first album (eventually released in 1974). This prompted further singles activity, first, 'I Love You So Much I Could Die', and then the agenda-setting 'We Sing For Fun'. In addition to these two a cappella treatments, they also recorded under the guise of Mel Dark And The Giants ('Darling'). Two further 'rehearsal' albums followed in 1975, as did a final single for Jet, 'The Christmas Song', but when Freedman moved to Chicago, the other members elected to discontinue the group. However, the D'Elia brothers did put together a new group in 1976, the Sharks Quintette, with members of the Heartspinners, Five Sharks and Gold Bugs. This grouping released three singles for Broadcast, but to little interest.

● ALBUMS: *Sparrows Quartette Rehearsal Session* (Jet 1974)★★★, *Sparrows Quartette Rehearsal Session Vol. II* (Jet 1975)★★★, *Sparrows Quartette Rehearsal Session Vol. III* (Jet 1975)★★★.

Specialty Records

Formed in 1946 in Los Angeles, California, USA, by Art Rupe, originally from Pittsburgh, Pennsylvania, Specialty Records gave rise to some of the most powerful early R&B and rock 'n' roll performers, particularly Little Richard. Rupe had briefly run the small-time label Juke Box Records, and with money earned there, launched Specialty. Among the label's first signings were blues singers Percy Mayfield and Joe Liggins. He also signed gospel artists including the Soul Stirrers. In 1952 Rupe expanded his artist roster beyond the west coast and signed New Orleans R&B singer Lloyd Price, who was the label's greatest success up to that time with his number 1 R&B hit 'Lawdy Miss Clawdy'. Other New Orleans acts on Specialty included Art Neville and Ernie K-Doe. In 1955, Rupe signed Little Richard (Penniman), who became the label's greatest success and one of the pioneers of early rock 'n' roll. All of Little Richard's hits, including 'Tutti Frutti', 'Good Golly Miss Molly' and 'Lucille', were on the Specialty label. Other Specialty rock 'n' roll/R&B artists included Larry Williams and Don And Dewey. The label was wound down during the 60s, but later revived in the 80s by Beverly Rupe, daughter of Art, who launched a reissue campaign making much of the classic Specialty material available once more.

● COMPILATIONS: *The Specialty Story Volume One* (1985).

Spector, Ronnie

b. Veronica Bennett, 10 August 1943, New York, USA. The distinctive lead singer in the Ronettes first embarked on a solo career in 1964 with two low-key singles credited to 'Veronica'. Her marriage to her producer, Phil Spector, effectively forestalled Ronnie's career and a three-year hiatus followed her group's 1966 offering, 'I Can Hear Music'. 'Try Some Buy Some', a then-unreleased George Harrison song, marked the recording debut of 'Ronnie Spector' in 1971. By this point her marriage was crumbling and the ensuing divorce allowed Ronnie to pursue the career her erstwhile husband struggled to deny her. She assembled a new Ronettes with Denise Edwards and Chip Fields and began recording for the Buddah label in 1973. Ronnie subsequently spent much of the 70s working in New York's clubs. During the latter part of the decade she made several appearances backed by Southside Johnny And The Asbury Dukes, while a 'comeback' single, 'Say Goodbye To Hollywood' was written by Billy Joel and produced by Bruce Springsteen and 'Miami' Steven Van Zandt. Despite such pedigree, the record failed to ignite Ronnie's career and her later work has been marred by inconsistency. Her compelling autobiography was published in 1991.

● ALBUMS: *Siren* (1980)★★★, *Unfinished Business* (Columbia 1987)★★.

● FURTHER READING: *Be My Baby*, Ronnie Spector with Vince Waldron.

SPELLBINDERS

An R&B vocal group from Jersey City, New Jersey, USA. The members were Bob Shivers, Jimmy Wright, Ben Grant, McArthur Munford and Elouise Pennington. The Spellbinders delighted audiences in the mid-60s with a series of hits that epitomized the soft-soul vocal group sound of the era. Their first and biggest national hit, 'For You' (number 23 R&B), was a sublime piece of work, written, arranged and produced by Van McCoy, as was their only album, *The Magic Of The Spellbinders*. Two other chart hits followed in 1966, namely 'Chain Reaction' (number 36 R&B), which was a mediocre Temptations sound, and 'We're Acting Like Lovers' (number 27 R&B), a delightful mid-tempo number and the group's second most impressive achievement. The Spellbinders' last single before breaking up was a 1967 remake of the Skyliners' hit, 'Since I Don't Have You'.

● ALBUMS: *The Magic Of The Spellbinders* (Columbia 1966)★★★.

SPELLMAN, BENNY

b. 11 December 1931, Pensacola, Florida, USA. Although a minor hit by chart standards, Benny Spellman's 'Lipstick Traces (On A Cigarette)' is one of the most fondly recalled New Orleans R&B hits of the early 60s and was subsequently revived by the O'Jays. Its b-side, 'Fortune Teller', impressed the young Rolling Stones enough for them to cover it. Spellman won a talent contest at college and, after a stint in the army, went professional, joining Huey Smith And The Clowns in New Orleans. In 1959, Spellman was signed to Minit Records but had little luck with his first few releases. To make ends meet he took a job as a background studio vocalist, appearing on Ernie K-Doe's 'Mother-In-Law', among others. Spellman's two-sided hit came in 1962, both songs having been penned by famed producer/writer Allen Toussaint. Benny was unable to follow it with further hits and left music in 1968. He returned to the profession in the late 80s, appearing locally in New Orleans, but prior to that made his living in the 70s as a public relations executive for Miller Beer. He never recorded an album, although the singles sessions have been compiled.

● ALBUMS: *Calling All Cars* (Bandy 1984)★★, *Fortune Teller* (Charly 1988)★★★.

SPIDERS

The members of this vocal group from New Orleans, Louisiana, USA, were lead Hayward 'Chuck' Carbo, first tenor Joe Maxon, baritone Matthew 'Mac' West, bass Oliver Howard and bass/alternate lead Leonard 'Chick' Carbo. The Spiders purveyed an original bluesy sound and added the lilting swing of their New Orleans heritage to create a unique style of 50s vocal harmony. The group began in the mid-40s singing gospel as the Zion Harmonizers. In 1953 they were still singing gospel when they were discovered by recording studio owner Cosimo Matassa. Under his encouragement they revamped themselves as a R&B group under the name Spiders. The group had three sizeable R&B hits on the charts during their first year, 1954, namely the syncopated 'I Didn't Want To Do It' (number 3 R&B), the bluesy 'You're The One' (number 8 R&B), and the swinging 'I'm Slippin' In' (number 6 R&B). Maxon and West had both left by 1955, and were replaced with new members, tenor Bill Moore and baritone Issacher Gordon. The new line-up hit the charts with 'Twenty One' (number 9 R&B) and one of their most superb records, the bouncy 'Witchcraft' (number 5 R&B). The group split in 1956, and the Carbo brothers worked to establish solo careers. Chuck Carbo was the more successful brother, recording many singles and albums including *Life's Ups And Downs* (504 1989) and *Drawers Trouble* (Rounder 1993).

● COMPILATIONS: *I Didn't Want To Do It* (Imperial 1961)★★★, *The Imperial Sessions* (Bear Family 1992)★★★.

SPINNERS (USA)

(see (Detroit) Spinners)

SPRINGFIELD, DUSTY

b. Mary Isabel Catherine Bernadette O'Brien, 16 April 1939, Hampstead, London, England. A long-standing critical favourite but sadly neglected by the mass public from the early 70s until the end of the 80s, the career of Britain's greatest white soul/pop singer has been a turbulent one. Formerly referred to as 'the White Negress', Dusty began as a member of the cloying pop trio the Lana Sisters in the 50s, and moved with her brother Tom (Dion O'Brien) and Tim Field into the Springfields, one of Britain's top pop/folk acts of the early 60s. During the Merseybeat boom, she took a bold step by going solo. Her debut in late 1963 with 'I Only Want To Be With You' (the first ever song performed on the long-running UK television programme *Top Of The Pops*) removed any doubts the previously shy convent girl may have had; this jaunty, endearing song is now a classic of 60s pop. She joined the swinging London club scene and became a familiar icon for teenage girls, with her famous beehive blonde hairstyle and her dark 'panda' eye make-up. Over the next three years Springfield was constantly in the bestselling singles chart with a string of unforgettable hits and consistently won the top female singer award in the UK, beating off stiff opposition from Lulu, Cilla Black and Sandie Shaw. During this time she campaigned unselfishly on behalf of the then little-known black American soul, R&B and Motown artists; her mature taste in music differentiated her from many of her contemporaries. Her commitment to black music carried over into her tour of South Africa in 1964, when she played in front of a mixed audience and was immediately deported.

Dusty's early albums were strong sellers, although they now appear to have been rushed works. Her pioneering choice of material by great songwriters such as Burt Bacharach, Hal David, Randy Newman and Carole King was exemplary. The orchestral arrangements by Ivor Raymonde and Johnny Franz, however, often drowned Dusty's voice, and her vocals sometimes appeared thin and strained due to insensitive production. She made superb cover versions of classics such as 'Mockingbird', 'Anyone Who Had A Heart', 'Wishin' And Hopin'', 'La Bamba', and 'Who Can I Turn To'. Her worldwide success came when her friend Vicki Wickham and Simon Napier-Bell added English words to the Italian hit 'Io Che Non Vivo (Senzate)', thereby creating 'You Don't Have To Say You Love Me'. This million-selling opus proved her sole UK chart-topper in 1966. At the end of a turbulent year she had an altercation with jazz drummer Buddy Rich, with whom she was sheduled to play at New York's prestigious Basin Street East club. The music press reported that she had pushed a pie in his face, but years later, in an interview in *Q Magazine*, Dusty revealed the true story; the often outspoken Rich was allegedly resentful at not receiving top billing and caused difficulties when she asked to rehearse her show with the (his) band. Rich was heard to respond 'you fucking broad, who do you think you fucking are, bitch?'; Dusty retaliated by punching him in the face. By the end of the following year (1967), she was becoming disillusioned with the showbusiness carousel on which she found herself trapped. She appeared out of step with the summer of love and its attendant psychedelic music. Her BBC television series attracted healthy viewing figures, but it was anathema to the sudden change in the pop scene. The comparatively progressive and prophetically titled *Where Am I Going?* attempted to redress this. Containing a jazzy, orchestrated version of Bobby Hebb's 'Sunny' and Jacques Brel's 'If You Go Away' (English lyrics by Rod McKuen), it was an artistic success but flopped commercially (or, in the words of biographer Lucy O'Brien, was 'released to stunning indifference'). The following year a similar fate awaited the excellent *Dusty ... Definitely*. On this she surpassed herself with her choice of material, from the rolling 'Ain't No Sunshine Since You've Been Gone' to the aching emotion of Randy Newman's 'I Think It's Gonna Rain Today', but her continuing good choice of songs was no longer attracting fans. In 1968, as Britain was swamped by the progressive music revolution, the uncomfortable split between what was underground and hip, and what was pop and unhip, became prominent. Dusty, well aware that she could be doomed to the variety club chicken-in-a-basket circuit in the UK, departed for Memphis, Tennessee, one of the music capitals of the world, and immediately succeeded in recording a stunning album and her finest work, *Dusty In Memphis*. The expert production team of Tom Dowd, Jerry Wexler and Arif Mardin were the first people to recognize that her natural soul voice should be placed at the fore, rather than competing with full and overpowering string arrangements. The album remains a classic and one of the finest records of the 60s. The single 'Son Of A Preacher Man' became a major hit, but the album failed in the UK and only reached a derisory number 99 in the US chart. Following this bitter blow, Dusty retreated and maintained a lower profile, although her second album for Atlantic, *A Brand New Me*, was a moderate success. Released in the UK as *From Dusty With Love*, the Thom Bell/Kenny Gamble-credited production boosted her waning popularity in her homeland, where she still resided, although she spent much of her time in the USA. *Cameo*, from 1973, exuded class and featured a superlative cover version of Van Morrison's 'Tupelo Honey', but sold little and yielded no hit singles.

Dusty had by this time disappeared from the charts, and following a veiled admission in an interview with Ray Coleman for the London *Evening Standard* in 1975 that she was bisexual, moved to Los Angeles. For the next few years she recorded sporadically, preferring to spend her time with friends such as Billie Jean King and to campaign for animal rights (she is an obsessive cat lover). Additionally, she succumbed to pills and alcohol abuse, and even attempted suicide. Following the release of the inappropriately titled *It Begins Again* some five years after her previous release, she was propelled towards a comeback, which failed, although the album did garner respectable sales. Notable tracks were the Carole Bayer Sager gem 'I'd Rather Leave While I'm In Love', and a Barry Manilow song, 'Sandra', featuring a lyric that addressed chillingly similar events to her own life. The follow-up, *Living Without Your Love*, was poorly received; it contained an indifferent version of the Miracles' 'You Really Got A Hold On Me'. 'Baby Blue' became a minor hit in 1979 but the comeback was over. Dusty went to ground again, even although one unsuccessful single in 1980, 'Your Love Still Brings Me To My Knees', remains an undiscovered nugget. In the early 80s she relocated to Toronto and resurfaced in 1982 with the energetic, disco-influenced *White Heat*. Featuring ex-Hookfoot guitarist Caleb Quaye and Nathan East (bass), it was her best album during these musically barren years, yet it failed to gain a release outside the USA. Two years later she duetted with Spencer Davis on Judy Clay and William Bell's 'Private Number', which, although an excellent choice of song, merely served to highlight Davis's limited vocal range. A further attempt to put her in the public eye was orchestrated by club owner Peter Stringfellow in 1985. He booked her at his Hippodrome and contracted her to his similarly named record label. After one single, 'Just Like Butterflies', she fluttered out of sight again. Her phoenix-like return towards the end of the 80s was due entirely to Neil Tennant and Chris Lowe of the Pet Shop Boys, who persuaded her to duet with them on their hit single 'What Have I Done To Deserve This?' in 1987. They then wrote the theme for the film *Scandal*, which Dusty took into the bestsellers; 'Nothing Has Been Proved' was an ideal song, the lyrics cleverly documenting an era that she knew only too well. She followed this with another of their compositions, 'In Private', which, although a lesser song lyrically, became a bigger hit. The subsequent album, *Reputation*, became her most successful for over 20 years. In the early 90s she moved back from America and for a time resided in the Netherlands, surrounded by her beloved cats. Having returned to Britain, in 1994 she underwent chemotherapy for breast cancer. This delayed the release and promotion of her long-awaited new album with Columbia Records. In the spring of 1995 it was announced that the cancer was in remission. The album *A Very Fine Love* arrived in the wake of the single 'Wherever Would I Be'; this Diane Warren big production ballad featured a duet with Daryl Hall. The rest of the album proved that Springfield retained a singing voice that could chill the spine and warm the heart, and with modern recording techniques she could make any song sound good. Her greatest asset, in addition to her voice, is her remarkable ability to recognize a good songwriter; her choice of material over the years has been consistently good. A diva who is able to cross over into every gender genre, adored by gays and straights, no British female singer has ever commanded such love and respect.

● ALBUMS: *A Girl Called Dusty* (Philips 1964)★★★★, *Ev'rything's Coming Up Dusty* (Philips 1965)★★★★, *Where Am I Going* (Philips 1967)★★★★, *Dusty ... Definitely* (Philips 1968)★★★★, *Dusty In Memphis* (Philips 1969)★★★★★, *A Brand New Me (From Dusty With Love)* (Philips 1970)★★★★, *See All Her Faces* (Philips 1972)★★★, *Cameo* (Philips 1973)★★★, *Dusty Sings Burt Bacharach And Carole King* (Philips 1975)★★★, *It Begins Again* (Mercury 1978)★★★, *Living Without Your Love* (Mercury 1979)★★★, *White Heat* (Casablanca 1982)★★★, *Reputation* (Parlophone 1990)★★★, *A Very Fine Love* (Columbia 1995)★★.

● COMPILATIONS: *Golden Hits* (Philips 1966)★★★★, *Stay Awhile* (Wing 1968)★★★★, *This Is Dusty Springfield* (Philips 1971)★★★★, *This Is Dusty Springfield Vol. 2: The Magic Garden* (Philips 1973)★★★★, *Greatest Hits* (Philips 1979)★★★★, *The Very Best Of Dusty Springfield* (K-Tel 1981)★★★★, *Dusty: Love Songs* (Philips 1983)★★★★, *The Silver Collection* (Philips 1988)★★★★★, *Dusty's Sounds Of The 60's* (Pickwick 1989)★★★★, *Love Songs* (Pickwick 1989)★★★★, *Dusty Springfield Songbook* (Pickwick 1990)★★★★, *Blue For You* (1993)★★★★, *Goin' Back: The Very Best Of Dusty Springfield* (Philips 1994)★★★★★, *Dusty* 4-CD box set (Phonogram 1994)★★★★, *The Legend Of Dusty Springfield* 4-CD box set (Philips 1994)★★★★, *Something Special* (Mercury 1996)★★★★.

● FURTHER READING: *Dusty*, Lucy O'Brien.

Staple Singers

This well-known US family gospel group consisted of Roebuck 'Pops' Staples (b. 28 December 1915, Winona, Mississippi, USA) and four of his children, Mavis Staples (b. 1940, Chicago, Illinois, USA), Pervis Staples (b. 1935), Cleotha Staples (b. 1934) and Yvonne Staples (b. 1939). The quintet fused an original presentation of sacred music, offsetting Mavis Staples' striking voice against her father's lighter tenor, rather than follow the accustomed 'jubilee' or 'quartet' formations, prevalent in the genre. Pops' striking guitar work, reminiscent of delta-blues, added to their inherent individuality. Singles such as 'Uncloudy Day', 'Will The Circle Be Unbroken' and 'I'm Coming Home', proved especially popular, while an original song, 'This May Be The Last Time', provided the inspiration for the Rolling Stones' hit 'The Last Time'. During the early half of the 60s, the group tried to broaden its scope. Two singles produced by Larry Williams, 'Why (Am I Treated So Bad)' and 'For What It's Worth', a Stephen Stills composition, anticipated the direction the Staples would take on signing with Stax in 1967. Here they began recording material contributed by the label's established songwriters, including Homer Banks and Bettye Crutcher, which embraced a moral focus, rather than a specifically religious one. Reduced to a quartet following the departure of Pervis, a bubbling version of Bobby Bloom's 'Heavy Makes You Happy' (1970) gave the group their first R&B hit. This new-found appeal flourished with 'Respect Yourself' (1971) and 'I'll Take You There' (1972 - a US pop number 1), both of which expressed the group's growing confidence. Their popularity was confirmed with 'If You're Ready (Come Go With Me)' (1973), 'City In The Sky' (1974), and by appearances in two films, *Wattstax* and *Soul To Soul*. The Staple Singers later moved to the Curtom label where they had an immediate success with two songs from a Curtis Mayfield-penned film soundtrack, 'Let's Do It Again' (another US pop number 1) and 'New Orleans'. These recordings were the group's last major hits although a series of minor R&B chart places between 1984 and 1985 continued the Staples' long-established ability to be both populist and inspirational.

● ALBUMS: *Uncloudy Day* (Vee Jay 1959)★★, *Swing Low* (Vee Jay 1961)★★, *Gospel Program* (Epic 1961)★★, *Hammers And Nails* (Epic 1962)★★, *Great Day* (Epic 1963)★★, *25th Day Of December* (Epic 1963)★★★, *Spirituals* (Epic 1965)★★, *Amen* (Epic 1965)★★, *Freedom Highway* (Epic 1965)★★, *Why* (Epic 1966)★★, *This Little Light* (Epic 1966)★★, *For What It's Worth* (Epic 1967)★★★, *Amen* (Epic 1967)★★★, *Staple Singers* (1968)★★★, *Pray On* (1968)★★★, *Soul Folk In Action* (Stax 1968)★★★, *We'll Get Over* (Stax 1970)★★★, *I Had A Dream* (1970)★★★, *Heavy Makes You Happy* (Stax 1971)★★★, *The Staple Swingers* (Stax 1971)★★★★, *Bealitude: Respect Yourself* (Stax 1972)★★★★, *Be What You Are* (Stax 1973)★★★, *Use What You Got* (Stax 1973)★★★, *City In The Sky* (Stax 1974)★★★, *Let's Do It Again* film soundtrack (Curtom 1975)★★★, *Pass It On* (Curtom 1976)★★★, *Family Tree* (1977)★★, *Unlock Your Mind* (1978)★★, *Hold On To Your Dream* (20th Century 1981)★★, *Turning Point* (Private 1984)★★★, *Are You Ready* (Private 1985)★★★.

● COMPILATIONS: *Tell It Like It Is* (1972)★★★, *The Best Of The Staple Singers* (Stax 1975)★★★★, *Stand By Me* (DJM 1977)★★★, *Respect Yourself: The Best Of The Staple Singers* (Stax 1988)★★★★, *Freedom Highway* (Columbia/Legacy 1991)★★★★.

Staples, Mavis

b. 1940, Chicago, Illinois, USA. The exceptional lead voice of the Staple Singers began a simultaneous solo career when the group was signed to the Stax label in 1968. Here she began recording distinctly secular material including songs by Otis Redding ('Good To Me', 'Security'), Sam Cooke ('You Send Me') and Joe Simon ('The Chokin' Kind'). The singer's gospel fervour enhanced such compositions, although her first R&B hit came with an original song, 'I Have Learned To Do Without You'. This progress was waylaid in the wake of the Staple Singers' own success with 'Heavy Makes You Happy' and her career was only resumed in 1977. 'A Piece Of The Action' was a fine collaboration with Curtis Mayfield, but later releases swamped her magnificent voice in disco and electro-pop beat. In 1987 the singer was signed to Prince's Paisley Park organization, the fruits of which appeared on *Time Waits For No One*, released two years later. Staples also made a guest appearance on Aretha Franklin's gospel set, *One Lord, One Faith, One Baptism*.

● ALBUMS: *Mavis Staples* (Volt 1969)★★, *Only For The Lonely* (Volt 1970)★★★, *A Piece Of The Action* (Curtom 1977)★★, *Time Waits For No One* (Paisley Park 1989)★★★, *The Voice* (NPG 1995)★★★, with Lucky Peterson *Spirituals & Gospel* (Verve/Gitanes 1996)★★★.

● COMPILATIONS: *Don't Change Me Now* (Stax 1988)★★★.

● FILMS: *Graffiti Bridge* (1990).

STAPLES, POPS

b. Roebuck Staples, 28 December 1915, Winona, Mississippi, USA. Despite spending most of his life (very successfully) performing gospel music, Pops Staples had a solid grounding in blues in his teenage years. Brought up on Will Dockery's Plantation outside Drew, he watched Charley Patton playing guitar on the boss's porch. He took up the guitar at 16, learning by ear and playing church songs for his father. However, at weekends, he sneaked off to chittlin' feasts to earn some money playing the blues. Married at 18, he moved his growing family to Chicago in 1935, taking menial jobs and at weekends singing with the Silver Trumpets. In 1952, he bought a cheap guitar and taught his children to sing gospel songs. Five years later, the Staple Singers went professional. Staples was 77 when he recorded his first solo album, which brought together Ry Cooder, Bonnie Raitt, Jackson Browne and Willie Mitchell. The songs ranged from Browne's title track to Cooder-produced versions of 'Down In Mississippi' and 'I Shall Not Be Moved'. *Father Father* continued in the same vein, featuring 'Jesus Is Going To Make Up (My Dying Bed)' alongside Bob Dylan's 'You Got To Serve Somebody' and Curtis Mayfield's 'People Get Ready'. Though hardly blues, Pops Staples' music represents a gentle voice of reason in a strident world.

● ALBUMS: *Peace To The Neighborhood* (PointBlank 1992)★★★, *Father Father* (PointBlank 1994)★★★, *The Kershaw Session* (Strange Fruit 1995)★★★.

STARGARD

This interracial female soul/disco trio consisted of Rochelle Runnells, Debra Anderson and Janice Williams from Los Angeles, California, USA. Runnells and Anderson had been in various groups together, including Virgin Spring, before Anderson joined Masters Children, and Runnells founded Nature's Gift. They worked together again as backing singers for Anthony Newley, and when Anderson left she was replaced by Williams. Runnells was asked by Mark Davis, right-hand man of top producer Norman Whitfield, to form a trio and she and Williams brought back Anderson (who had recorded some unsuccessful solo records on TK and Columbia). The trio, who developed an intergalactic image, made the title song from Richard Pryor's film *Which Way Is Up* an R&B number 1 and a transatlantic Top 20 hit in 1978. They returned to the R&B Top 10 later that year with the title track from *What You Waitin' For*, but it was their last real taste of success. They appeared in the ill-fated *Sgt. Pepper* film as the Diamonds and joined Warner Brothers Records in 1980. Anderson left shortly afterwards and the act continued for a while as a duo.

● ALBUMS: *Stargard* (MCA 1978)★★, *What You Waitin' For* (MCA 1978)★★, *Back 2 Back* (Warners 1981)★★.

STARLETS

A female R&B group from Chicago, Illinois, USA, the members were Liz 'Dynetta Boone' Walker, Jane Hall, Mickey McKinney and Maxine Edwards. With their strident rock 'n' roll sound, the Starlets reflected the early 60s era when African-American girl groups dominated the pop and R&B charts. Their one hit was 'Better Tell Him No' (number 24 R&B, number 38 pop, 1961), in which their mentor/composer Bernice Williams shared the lead with Edwards. The record, in retrospect, sounds harsh and unappealing, and most later listeners favoured the soul-style ballad b-side led by Walker, 'You Are The One'. Another 1961 release produced the excellent Walker-led 'My Last Cry', which received only local play in Chicago. In 1962 on a tour of east coast cities, the Starlets violated their contract by recording 'I Sold My Heart To The Junkman' for Newtown Records in Philadelphia. Label owner Harold Robinson saw in Edwards' strident lead a voice that could give tremendous drive to a song. The record was released under the name Bluebelles, and it became Patti Labelle And The Bluebelles' first hit in 1962, launching their career, even though, ironically, they did not sing on it. In 1962 the Starlets were dropped by their company, and shortly thereafter disbanded.

STARR, EDWIN

b. Charles Hatcher, 21 January 1942, Nashville, Tennessee, USA. The brother of soul singers Roger and Willie Hatcher, Edwin Starr was raised in Cleveland, where he formed the Future Tones vocal group in 1957. They recorded one single for Tress, before Starr was drafted into the US Army for three years. After completing his service, he toured for two years with the Bill Doggett Combo, and was then offered a solo contract with the Ric Tic label in 1965. His first single, 'Agent Double-O-Soul', was a US Top 30 hit and Starr exploited its popularity by appearing in a short promotional film with actor Sean Connery, best known for his role as James Bond. 'Stop Her On Sight (SOS)' repeated this success, and brought Starr a cult following in Britain, where his strident, gutsy style proved popular in specialist soul clubs. When Motown Records took over the Ric Tic catalogue in 1967, Starr was initially overlooked by the label's hierarchy. He re-emerged in 1969 with '25 Miles', a Top 10 hit that owed much to the dominant soul style of the Stax label. An album of duets with Blinky brought some critical acclaim, before Starr resumed his solo career with the strident, politically outspoken 'War', a US number 1 in

1970. Teamed with writer/producer Norman Whitfield, Starr was allowed to record material that had been earmarked for the Temptations, who covered both of his subsequent Motown hits, 'Stop The War Now' and 'Funky Music Sho Nuff Turns Me On'. Starr's own credentials as a writer had been demonstrated on 'Oh How Happy', which had become a soul standard since he first recorded it in the late 60s. He was given room to blossom on the 1974 soundtrack *Hell Up In Harlem*, which fitted into the 'blaxploitation' mould established by Curtis Mayfield and Isaac Hayes. Tantalized by this breath of artistic freedom, Starr left the confines of Motown in 1975, recording for small labels in Britain and America before striking a new commercial seam in 1979 with two major disco hits, 'Contact' and 'HAPPY Radio'. In the 80s, Starr was based in the UK, where he collaborated with the Style Council on a record in support of striking coalminers, and enjoyed a run of club hits on the Hippodrome label, most notably 'It Ain't Fair' in 1985. Between 1989 and 1991, Starr worked with Ian Levine's Motor City Records, recording a remake of '25 Miles' in a modern style and releasing *Where Is The Sound.*

● ALBUMS: *Soul Master* (Gordy 1968)★★★, *25 Miles* (Gordy 1969)★★★, with Blinky *Just We Two* (Gordy 1969)★★★, *War And Peace* (Gordy 1970)★★★, *Involved* (Gordy 1971)★★★, *Hell Up In Harlem* film soundtrack (Gordy 1974)★★★, *Free To Be Myself* (1975)★★★, *Edwin Starr* (1977)★★, *Afternoon Sunshine* (GTO 1977)★★★, *Clean* (20th Century 1978)★★, *HAPPY Radio* (20th Century 1979)★★★, *Stronger Than You Think I Am* (20th Century 1980)★★, *Where Is The Sound* (Motor City 1991)★★.

● COMPILATIONS: *The Hits of Edwin Starr* (Tamla Motown 1972)★★★, *20 Greatest Motown Hits* (Motown 1986)★★★, *Early Classics* (Spectrum 1996)★★★.

Staton, Candi

b. 1943, Hanceville, Alabama, USA. A former member of the Jewel Gospel Trio, Staton left the group, and her first husband, for a secular career. She was then discovered performing at a club by Clarence Carter, who took the singer to the Fame label. Carter wrote her debut hit, the uncompromising 'I'd Rather Be An Old Man's Sweetheart (Than A Young Man's Fool)', and helped to guide the singer's early releases. She later began pursuing a country-influenced path, especially in the wake of her successful version of Tammy Wynette's 'Stand By Your Man'. Staton and Carter were, by now, married, although this relationship subsequently ended in divorce. Staton left Fame for Warner Brothers Records in 1974 but it was two years before 'Young Hearts Run Free', an excellent pop-styled hit, consolidated this new phase. 'Nights On Broadway', written by the Bee Gees, then became a UK Top 10 single, although it unaccountably flopped in America. The singer has continued to enjoy intermittent UK success but US hits have been restricted to the R&B chart. 'You Lost The Love', a collaboration with the Force, was a popular dancefloor track and a UK Top 40 hit in 1991. In the 90s Staton recorded in the gospel field, but she made a return to the UK charts in 1997 with the successful re-release of 'Young Hearts Run Free', prompted by its inclusion on the soundtrack of the film *William Shakespeare's Romeo & Juliet* .

● ALBUMS: *I'm Just A Prisoner* (Fame 1969)★★★, *Stand By Your Man* (Fame 1971)★★★, *Candi Staton* (Fame 1972)★★★, *Candi* (Fame 1974)★★★, *Young Hearts Run Free* (Warners 1976)★★★, *Music Speaks Louder Than Words* (Warners 1977)★★, *House Of Love* (Warners 1978)★★, *Chance* (Warners 1979)★★, *Candi Staton* (Warners 1980)★★, *Suspicious Minds* (Sugarhill 1982)★★★, *Make Me An Instrument* (Myrrh 1985)★★★, *Sing A Song* (1986)★★★, *Love Lifted Me* (1988)★★★, *Stand Up And Be A Witness* (Blue Moon 1990)★★★, *It's Time* (Intersound 1995)★★★, *Cover Me* (CGI 1997)★★★.

● COMPILATIONS: shared with Bettye Swann *Tell It Like It Is* (Stateside 1986)★★★, *Nightlites* (Sequel 1992)★★★.

Stax Records

Stax Records was founded in Memphis, Tennessee, USA, by brother and sister Jim (St) Stewart (b. 1930) and Estelle (ax) Axton (b. 1918). Stewart, an aspiring fiddler, began recording local C&W artists in 1957, using a relative's garage as an improvised studio. The following year, Estelle funded the purchase of an Ampex recorder and the siblings' newly named company, Satellite, was relocated in the nearby town of Brunswick. By 1960, however, they had returned to Memphis and established themselves in a disused theatre on McLemore Avenue. Local talent was attracted to the fledgling label, and national hits for Carla Thomas and the Mar-Keys followed before the Satellite name was dropped in favour of Stax to avoid confusion with another company. These early successes were distributed by Atlantic Records, a relationship that soon proved mutually beneficial. 'Green Onions', the hypnotic instrumental by Booker T. And The MGs, was another bestseller and defined the sound that established the studio's reputation. A subsidiary outlet, Volt, secured success with Otis Redding and the Stax empire flourished with releases by Eddie Floyd, Johnnie Taylor and Rufus Thomas. However, relations between the company and Atlantic became strained and the sessions that produced Wilson Pickett's 'In The Midnight Hour' were the last recorded at Stax to bear Atlantic's imprint. Future releases bore the studio's distinctive logo (the Clicking Fingers), the most notable of which were those by Sam And Dave.

The two sides began renegotiations in 1967. The sale of Atlantic to Warner Brothers and the premature death of Otis Redding undermined Stewart's confidence, but a final twist proved irrevocable. Under the terms of the parties' original agreement, Atlantic owned every Stax master, released or unreleased, leaving the latter with a name and roster, but no back-catalogue. In 1968 Stax signed a distribution agreement with the Gulf/Western corporation, although it resulted in Estelle Axton's departure and the promotion of former disc jockey Al Bell to company vice-president. Although the immediate period was fruitful - releases by Johnnie Taylor, Booker T. Jones. and Judy Clay and William Bell were major hits - an ill-advised move into the album market proved over-ambitious. Nonetheless, Stax enjoyed considerable success with Isaac Hayes and in 1970 Stewart and Al Bell brought it back into private ownership through the financial assistance of the European classical label, Deutsche Grammophon. Within a year, Stewart relinquished control to Bell, who then secured a lucrative distribution agreement with Columbia. Despite a series of successful releases during the early 70s, including 'If Loving You Is Wrong (I Don't Want To Be Right)' (Luther Ingram) and 'Woman To Woman' (Shirley Brown), Stax grew increasingly troubled. Audits from the Internal Revenue Service and the Union Planters band revealed serious discrepancies and resulted in the indictment of several employees. In 1973, Columbia was granted an injunction preventing Stax from breaking its distribution arrangement; two years later the company was unable to meet its January payroll. Artists began seeking other outlets; Isaac Hayes sued for non-payment of royalties and despite Stewart's best efforts, Stax was closed down on 12 January 1976 on the order of the bankruptcy court judge. The feelings of the musicians at the label was summed up later when Donald 'Duck' Dunn, the label's long-standing session bassist, commented, 'I knew it was over when they signed Lena Zavaroni.' Although the bank attempted to salvage the situation, the label was sold to Fantasy Records in June the following year. Since then the new owners have judiciously repackaged the company's heritage and during the late 80s, secured the rights to all unreleased material from the Atlantic era. Three box sets released during the 90s offer an exhaustive summary of the label's output.

● COMPILATIONS: *The Stax Story Volume 1* (Stax 1975)★★★★, *The Stax Story Volume 2* (Stax 1975)★★★★, *Stax Blues Masters* (1978)★★★, *Stax Gold* (1979)★★★, *Stax Greatest Hits* (1987), *Stax Sirens And Volt Vamps* (1988)★★★, *The Complete Stax/Volt Singles, 1959-1968* 9-CD box set (Stax 1991)★★★★★, *The Complete Stax/Volt Singles 1968-1971* 9-CD box set (Stax 1993)★★★★, *The Complete Stax/Volt Soul Singles, 1972-1975* 9-CD box set (Stax 1994)★★★.

● FURTHER READING: *Soulsville USA: The Story Of Stax Records*, Rob Bowman.

STEREOS

This vocal group from Steubenville, Ohio, USA, consisted of lead Bruce Robinson, first tenor Nathaniel Hicks, second tenor Sam Profit, baritone George Otis and bass Ronnie Collins. The Stereos were typical of the early 60s transition from doo-wop to soul-singing in a style that utilized doo-wop harmonies, but was propelled by gospelized lead vocals. The genesis of the group lay in the Buckeyes, who recorded several tracks for Deluxe Records in 1956. Three members of the group - Robinson, Collins and first tenor Leroy Swearingen - joined with Profit and Otis to form the Stereos in 1959. After they made an unsuccessful record for Otis Blackwell's Gibralter label, Swearingen left and was replaced with Hicks. The group was signed to MGM's Cub subsidiary in 1961, and immediately found success with the Swearingen-penned 'I Really Love You' (number 15 R&B, number 29 pop). The Stereos were not able to successfully follow up with their two further singles on Cub, or later singles on Columbia, World Artists, and Val. The group broke up in 1965, but reassembled as a self-contained band in 1967. After two singles on Chess Records' Cadet subsidiary during 1967-68, the Stereos disbanded for good.

STEVENSON, MICKEY

b. William Stevenson. Having spent his formative years recording R&B and gospel music, Stevenson joined the nascent Tamla/Motown organization in 1959, later co-producing and arranging singles by Marv Johnson. As the company's first A&R director, he was responsible for supervising all facets of recording, assigning acts to producers and songwriters, and enlisting notable musicians such as Choker Campbell, Benny Benjamin and James Jamerson. He brought Martha Reeves to the label, where she was also employed as his secretary, and later co-wrote 'Wild One' and 'Dancing In The Streets' for her group Martha And The Vandellas. Stevenson's compositional and/or production credits included 'Beechwood 4-5789' and 'Playboy' for the Marvelettes, 'Needle In A Haystack' for the Velvelettes and 'Stubborn Kind Of Fellow' and 'Pride And Joy' for Marvin Gaye, who also recorded with Stevenson's wife, Kim Weston. Their singing partnership was sundered prematurely when she and her husband left Motown in January 1967 to join MGM Records. Although Stevenson later founded his own label, People, he was unable to recapture the considerable success he enjoyed earlier in the decade.

STEWART, BILLY

b. 24 March 1937, Washington, DC, USA, d. 17 January 1970. Introduced to music by his family's Stewart Gospel Singers, Billy embraced a more secular direction with the Rainbows, a group that also included Don Covay and Marvin Gaye. From there Stewart joined Bo Diddley's band on piano. His solo debut, 'Billy's Blues', was released on Chess in 1956, after which he worked with the Marquees. A second single, 'Billy's Heartaches' (1957), appeared on the OKeh label, but a return to Chess in the early 60s proved decisive. A succession of melodic songs, including 'I Do Love You' and 'Sitting In The Park' (both 1965), established a crafted style that blended R&B jazz and the singer's distinctive vocal delivery. These elements were prevalent in his radical interpretation of George Gershwin and DuBose Heyward's 'Summertime', a Top 10 US hit in 1966. Stewart's subsequent releases were less successful, although he remained a popular live attraction. In January 1970, while touring in North Carolina, Stewart's car plunged into the River Neuse, killing him and three of his musicians.

● ALBUMS: *I Do Love You* (Chess 1965)★★★, *Unbelievable* (Chess 1966)★★★.

● COMPILATIONS: *One More Time* (Chess/MCA 1990)★★★.

STONE CITY BAND

Kenny Hawkins, Tom McDermott, Levi Ruffin Jnr., Daniel Le Melle, Jerry Livingston, Jerry Rainer and Nat Hughes formed the Stone City Band in the USA during 1978. The following year, they were co-opted by rising funk star Rick James as his backing band. They worked with James for four years, supporting him on albums such as *Garden Of Love* and *Street Songs*. In return, James helped them record three albums in their own right, though there was little conceptual or musical difference between their work and his own. Songs such as 'Strut Your Stuff', 'Little Runaway' and 'Bad Lady' demonstrated that they had adopted James's one-dimensional view of human relations, and their hard, funk-based style was also heavily derivative of their mentor's style.

● ALBUMS: *In 'N' Out* (Gordy 1980)★★★, *The Boys Are Back* (Gordy 1981)★★, *Out From The Shadow* (Gordy 1983)★★.

STONE, HENRY

b. 3 June 1921, Bronx, New York, USA. In the 50s Henry Stone founded three blues labels, Rockin', Chart and Marlin Records, which released some of the most innovative and wonderful post-war blues music of the day. He was originally inspired by the jazz greats such as Louis Armstrong in his early teens, at which time he took up the trumpet. While stationed at military camp in Kilmer, New Brunswick, New Jersey, USA, Stone played regularly before being demobbed in 1946. He began in the music industry by selling records from the back of his car in Los Angeles, California, at the end of World War II. Employed by the Bihari Brothers' Modern group, his role as 78 rpm salesman took him across the country, mainly vending to jukebox owners. By 1952 he had established his own Crystal Recording Company and built his own studio. From this base in Florida he co-ordinated releases on two labels. The first, Rockin', was reserved for blues; the second, Glory, for spiritual and religious music. Glory's best-selling record was Rev. A. Johnson's 'God Don't Like It', though Stone's biggest discovery was Ray Charles. Charles cut four tracks at a Tampa radio station, though these were not pressed on Rockin' but leased instead to the Bihari Brothers. Many releases on both of Stone's original labels were subsequently leased to DeLuxe Records. When his original 50/50 agreement with Sydney Nathan broke down, he lost Otis Williams but kept his backing band, the Charms, and the majority of the masters from previous releases. As a result of this breakdown, Stone formed Chart Records in 1955, alongside publishing companies Pelican and Sherlyn Music. His most prestigious artists at this time included the Champions, Evergreens, Tru-Tones, Sonny Jones, Paul Tate and Sonny Thompson (whose hits included 'Juke Joint' and 'Slow Rock'). By the end of the 50s further subsidiary labels, Marlin and Glades, had been established. In 1960 Stone recorded 'Do The Mashed Potato' with James Brown - a number 8 R&B chart hit that was leased to King Records. Stone founded Alston Records in the late 60s, signing well-known artists such as Betty Wright, Timmy Thomas and Clarence Reid. Another Stone label, Glades, also had hits with Benny Latimore. With the advent of disco in 1973 Stone also guided the early career of KC And The Sunshine Band, before selling the rights to his T.K. Records empire to Maurice Levy of Roulette Records. In the 90s Ace Records began a reissue programme compiling some of the 'lost' material from Stone's pioneering Rockin', Chart and Marlin labels. Among the discoveries was underexposed material by Little Sam Davis, Eddie Hope And His Mannish Boys and Florida-based blues guitarist Willie Baker, plus rare material from Lightnin' Hopkins and John Lee Hooker.

● COMPILATIONS: *Rockin' The Blues* (Ace 1995)★★★★.

STONE, SLY

(see Sly And The Family Stone)

STRONG, BARRETT

b. 5 February 1941, Westpoint, Mississippi, USA. The cousin of two members of the R&B vocal group the Diablos, Barrett Strong launched his own singing career with Berry Gordy's fledgling Tamla label in 1959. At the end of that year, he recorded the original version of Gordy's song 'Money', a major US hit that became a rock standard after it was covered by the Beatles and the Rolling Stones. Strong also wrote Eddie Holland's US hit 'Jamie' in 1961. Later that year, he briefly joined Vee Jay Records, but he returned to the Motown stable in the early 60s to work as a writer and producer. He established a partnership with Norman Whitfield from 1966-73; together, the pair masterminded a series of hits by the Temptations, with Strong contributing the powerful lyrics to classics such as 'Cloud Nine', 'Just My Imagination' and 'Papa Was A Rolling Stone'. Strong left Motown in 1973 to resume his recording career, finding some success with 'Stand Up And Cheer For The Preacher' on Epic, and 'Is It True' on Capitol in 1975. He lacked the distinctive talent of the great soul vocalists, however, and seems destined to be remembered for his backroom work at Motown rather than his own sporadic releases.

● ALBUMS: *Stronghold* (Capitol 1975)★★★, *Live And Love* (Capitol 1976)★★, *Love Is You* (Timeless 1988)★★.

STYLISTICS

The Stylistics were formed in 1968 from the fragments of two Philadelphia groups, the Monarchs and the Percussions, by Russell Thompkins Jnr. (b. 21 March 1951, Philadelphia, Pennsylvania, USA), Airrion Love (b. 8 August 1949, Philadelphia, Pennsylvania, USA), James Smith (b. 16 June 1950, New York City, USA), Herbie Murrell (b. 27 April 1949, Lane, South Carolina, USA) and James Dunn (b. 4 February 1950, Philadelphia, Pennsylvania, USA). The quintet's debut single, 'You're A Big Girl Now' was initially issued on a local independent, but became a national hit following its acquisition by the Avco label. The Stylistics were then signed to this outlet directly and teamed with producer/composer Thom Bell. This skilful musician had already worked successfully with the Delfonics and his sculpted, sweet-soul arrangements proved ideal for his new charges. In partnership with lyricist Linda Creed, Bell fashioned a series of immaculate singles, including 'You Are Everything' (1971), 'Betcha By Golly Wow' and 'I'm Stone In Love With You' (both 1972), where Simpkins' aching voice soared against the group's sumptuous harmonies and a cool, yet inventive, accompaniment. The style reached its apogee in 1974 with 'You Make Me Feel Brand New', a number 2 single in both the USA and UK. This release marked the end of Bell's collaboration with the group, who were now pushed towards the easy listening market. With arranger Van McCoy turning sweet into saccharine, the material grew increasingly bland, while Thompkins' falsetto, once heartfelt, now seemed contrived. Although their American fortune waned, the Stylistics continued to enjoy success in Britain with 'Sing Baby Sing', 'Can't Give You Anything (But My Love)' (both 1975) and '16 Bars' (1976), while a compilation album that same year, *The Best Of The Stylistics*, became one of the UK's bestselling albums. Despite this remarkable popularity, purists labelled the group a parody of its former self. Ill health forced Dunn to retire in 1978, whereupon the remaining quartet left Avco for a brief spell with Mercury. Two years later they were signed to the TSOP/Philadelphia International stable, which resulted in some crafted recordings reminiscent of their heyday, but problems within the company undermined the group's progress. Subsequent singles for Streetwise took the Stylistics into the lower reaches of the R&B chart, but their halcyon days seemed to be over, even though they released new material in the mid-90s.

● ALBUMS: *The Stylistics* (Avco 1971)★★★, *Round 2: The Stylistics* (Avco 1972)★★★, *Rockin' Roll Baby* (Avco 1973)★★★★, *Let's Put It All Together* (Avco 1974)★★★★, *Heavy* UK title*From The Mountain* (Avco 1974)★★★, *Thank You Baby* (Avco 1975)★★★, *You Are Beautiful* (Avco 1975)★★★, *Fabulous* (H&L 1976)★★★, *Once Upon A Juke Box* (H&L 1976)★★★, *Sun And Soul* (H&L 1977)★★★, *Wonder Woman* (H&L 1978)★★★, *In Fashion* (H&L 1978)★★★, *Black Satin* (H&L 1979)★★★, *Love Spell* (1979)★★★, *Live In Japan* (1979)★★, *The Lion Sleeps Tonight* (1979)★★★, *Hurry Up This Way Again* (TSOP/Philadelphia International 1980)★★★, *Closer Than Close* (TSOP/Philadelphia International 1981)★★★, *1982* (TSOP/Philadelphia International 1982)★★★, *Some Things Never Change* (Streetwise 1985)★★, *Love Talks* (1993)★★, *Love Is Back In Style* (Marathon 1996)★★.

● COMPILATIONS: *The Best Of The Stylistics* (Avco 1975)★★★★, *Spotlight On The Stylistics* (1977)★★★, *All About Love* (Contour 1981)★★★, *Very Best Of The Stylistics* (H&L 1983)★★★★, *The Great Love Hits* (Contour 1983)★★★.

Sue Records

Former real estate entrepreneur Henry 'Juggy Murray' Jones established the Sue label in New York City on 2 January 1957. Initially situated on West 125th Street, close to the fabled Apollo Theatre, the company was well placed to sign aspiring R&B talent. Sue achieved its first hit single the following year with its seventh release, Bobby Hendricks' 'Itchy Twitchy Feeling', which reached the US Top 30. This exciting performance featured the Coasters on backing vocals and helped establish the label as one of the earliest successful black-owned companies, pre-empting Tamla/Motown's first hit by some six months. By 1960 Murray had relocated to West 54th Street, near to Bell Sound Studios where many of the label's recording sessions were undertaken. His early signings included Don Covay, but it was with Ike and Tina Turner that Juggy Murray found consistent success. Two of the duo's finest singles, 'A Fool In Love' and 'It's Gonna Work Out Fine', were released on Sue and their success allowed Murray to expand his company. Soul and R&B remained at its core, but the label also featured several jazz-based acts, including Jimmy McGriff, Bill Doggett and Hank Jacobs. Subsidiary companies were also established, including Symbol, the roster of which included Inez and Charlie Foxx, who enjoyed considerable success with 'Mockingbird' (number 2 R&B) and 'Hurt By Love'. Famed R&B songwriter Bert Berns also recorded for this outlet under the pseudonym 'Russell Byrd'. A.F.O. provided a short-lived association with a New Orleans-based collective headed by producer Harold Battiste. 'I Know' (Barbara George) and 'She Put The Hurt On Me' (Prince La La) were issued on this outlet, while the Crackerjack imprint included Derek Martin's 'Daddy Rollin' Stone', cited by George Harrison as one of his favourites of the era and later covered by the Who. A handful of Sue recordings were initially issued in Britain on Decca's London/American outlet, but in 1964 Murray struck a licensing agreement with Island's Chris Blackwell. Responsibility for the British Sue label was passed to disc jockey/producer Guy Stevens who, after 17 singles, decided to use it for product leased from other sources. Murray felt this diminished Sue's individual identity, withdrew from the arrangement and reverted to London/American for future releases. Stevens retained the Sue name, and thereafter the path of both companies was entirely different. In Britain, the label issued material by, among others, James Brown, Freddy King, B.B. King and Elmore James. It proved instrumental in introducing acts to a UK audience and many musicians, including Stevie Winwood, Steve Marriott and Eric Clapton, expressed a debt to Stevens' interest. British Sue folded in February 1967 as the Island label switched priorities from black music to white rock. The entire catalogue was deleted in 1969, but was briefly revived in 1983 with a series of commemorative EPs, *Sue Instrumentals*, *Sue Soul Brothers* and *Sue Soul Sisters*.

Juggy Murray continued to administer Sue but failed to address the changes evolving during the mid-60s. He claims to have signed Jimi Hendrix prior to the guitarist's departure for England, although no tracks were recorded. A proposed distribution agreement with Stax Records fell through, the latter company eventually opting for Atlantic Records. In 1968 Murray sold his remaining masters and publishing to United Artists. He produced several former Sue acts for their Veep and Minit subsidiaries including the Soul Sisters, Baby Washington and Tina Britt. Murray retained the rights to the Sue name, reactivating it on occasions over the ensuing years. He enjoyed a 'comeback' hit in 1969 when one-man band Wilbert Harrison re-recorded his own 'Let's Stick Together' as 'Let's Work Together'. The latter was then popularized by Canned Heat. Murray then founded another short-lived outlet, Juggernaught, before moving to Los Angeles to launch Jupiter Records. It was here he found belated success as an artist. 'Inside America', credited to Juggy Murray Jones, issued in Britain via the Contempo label, climbed to 39 in 1976. It is, however, for his pioneering

Sue label that he will be best remembered. An indispensable box set was compiled by Alan Warner in 1994.

● COMPILATIONS: *The Sue Story: Volumes One To Three* (1966)★★★, *The Sue Story* (Line 1984)★★, *The Beat Is On* (Stateside 1987)★★, *The Sue Records Story: The Sound Of Soul* 4-CD box set (EMI 1994)★★★★.

SULTANS

The Sultans trace their origins to Omaha, Nebraska, USA, gospel group the Echoes Of Joy, formed by 11-year-old Eugene McDaniels in 1946. This troupe then became the Five Echoes with the addition of brothers Willie and Gene Barnes (both on lead), James Farmer (baritone), Rosenwald Alexander (tenor) and Jimmy Mims (bass). The latter pair were soon replaced by Wesley Devereaux and Richard Beasley, respectively. Devereaux was actually the son of blues singer Wynonie Harris. Farmer's uncle owned a local record shop and the Showcase nightclub, which became the Five Echoes' semi-official home. This was 1953, at which time the group changed name to the Sultans and upped their tempo from gospel to R&B. Their first recordings took place shortly thereafter, for the Houston-based Duke Records label. Released in June, 'Good Thing Baby' was backed by a cover version of Rudy Vallee's 1932 hit 'How Deep Is The Ocean', but failed to make any impression. Johnny Otis, who had brought the Sultans to Duke, then took them on tour, before the release of their second single, 'I Cried My Heart Out'. Like 1954's 'Boppin' With The Mambo', it floundered. Dissatisfied with their label's promotion, the group found a new contract with King Records in Cincinnati, but were forced to change their name to the Admirals to break out of their existing contract. The Admirals debuted with 'Oh Yes', before a cover version of the Five Keys' 'Close Your Eyes'. It was to be their final single, though they did back other New York artists including Robert 'Bubber' Johnson and Kathy Ryan on record. The Admirals retreated to Omaha and back to their old name, the Sultans. Two singles for original home Duke Records followed, 'If I Could Tell' and 'My Love Is So High'. However, when Farmer enlisted there seemed little point in continuing the group. Willie Barnes went on to record solo for United Artists Records as Bobby Barnes. His brother, Gene (as Eugene Barnes was now called), also worked solo, finding significant early 60s success with Liberty Records ('A Hundred Pounds Of Clay' reaching number 3 in the *Billboard* charts). He also wrote a number 1 single for Roberta Flack ('Feel Like Makin' Love'). The Sultans then re-formed for a well-received appearance at Ronnie I's Collectors Group Concert Volume 3.

SUMMER, DONNA

b. Ladonna Gaines, 31 December 1948, Boston, Massachusetts, USA. Summer's 'Love To Love You Baby' made her the best-known of all 70s disco divas. Having sung with rock bands in Boston, Summer moved to Europe in 1968 and appeared in German versions of *Hair* and *Porgy And Bess*, later marrying Austrian actor Helmut Sommer, from whom she took her stage name. Summer's first records were 'Hostage' and 'Lady Of The Night' for Giorgio Moroder's Oasis label in Munich. They were local hits but it was 'Love To Love You Baby' (1975) that made her an international star. The track featured Summer's erotic sighs and moans over Moroder's hypnotic disco beats and it sold a million copies in the USA on Neil Bogart's Casablanca label. In 1977, a similar formula took 'I Feel Love' to the top of the UK chart, and 'Down Deep Inside', Summer's theme song for the film *The Deep* was a big international success. Her own film debut came the next year in *Thank God It's Friday*, in which she sang another million-seller, 'Last Dance'. This was the peak period of Summer's career as she achieved four more US number 1s in 1978-79 with a revival of Jim Webb's 'MacArthur Park', 'Hot Stuff', 'Bad Girls' and 'No More Tears (Enough Is Enough)', a duet with Barbra Streisand. The demise of disco coincided with a legal dispute between Summer and Bogart and in 1980 she signed to David Geffen's new company. Her work took on a more pronounced soul and gospel flavour, reflecting her decision to become a born-again Christian. Some of her major US hits during the early 80s were 'On The Radio', 'The Wanderer', 'She Works Hard For The Money' and 'Love Is In Control (Finger On The Trigger)' in 1982, produced by Quincy Jones. After a three-year absence from music, Summer returned in 1987 with a US and European tour and enjoyed another hit with the catchy 'Dinner With Gershwin'. Other major US and UK hits include 'This Time I Know It's For Real' and 'I Don't Wanna Get Hurt'. Her bestselling 1989 album for Warner Brothers Records was written and produced by Stock, Aitken And Waterman while Clivilles And Cole worked on *Love Is Gonna Change*. The 90s have proved only moderately successful for her.

● ALBUMS: *Love To Love You Baby* (Oasis 1975)★★★, *A Love Trilogy* (Oasis 1976)★★, *Four Seasons Of Love* (Casablanca 1976)★★, *I Remember Yesterday* (Casablanca 1977)★★★, *Once Upon A Time* (Casblanca 1977)★★★, *Live And More* (Casablanca 1978)★★, *Bad Girls* (Casablanca 1979)★★★★, *The Wanderer* (Geffen 1980)★★★★, *Donna Summer* (Geffen 1982)★★★, *She Works Hard For The Money* (Mercury 1983)★★★★, *Cats Without Claws* (Geffen 1984)★★, *All Systems Go* (Geffen 1987)★★, *Another Place And Time* (Warners 1989)★★, *Love Is Gonna Change* (Atlantic 1990)★★, *Mistaken Identity* (Atlantic 1991)★★, *This Time I Know It's For Real* (1993)★★.

● COMPILATIONS: *On The Radio - Greatest Hits, Volumes 1 And 2* (Casablanca 1979)★★★★, *Walk Away - Collector's Edition (The Best Of 1977-1980)* (Casablanca 1980)★★★, *The Best Of Donna Summer* (East West 1990)★★★★.

● FURTHER READING: *Donna Summer: An Unauthorized Biography*, James Haskins.

SUNNY AND THE SUNGLOWS

This Mexican-American group came from San Antonio, Texas, USA. The group was formed in 1959 and originally consisted of Sunny Ozuna, Jess, Oscar and Ray Villanueva, Tony Tostado, Gilbert Fernandez, and Alfred Luna. Sunny and the Sunglows (who also recorded as Sunny And The Sunliners) were one of the few Hispanic acts to succeed in the pop and soul markets, in which they sang old R&B hits with a typical Hispanic approach, laid-back and soulful. Their hits comprised a remake of Little Willie John's classic 'Talk To Me' (US R&B number 12 and pop number 11, 1963), a remake of Tony Bennett's 'Rags To Riches' (1963), and a remake of the Five Keys' 'Out Of Sight Out Of Mind' (1964). In 1965, the group scored a minor pop hit with a saxophone-dominated polka instrumental, 'Peanuts (La Cacahuata)', and much of the group's subsequent recordings were brassy polka instrumentals for the Mexican-American community.

● ALBUMS: *Talk To Me/Rags To Riches* (Tear Drop 1963)★★★, *All Night Worker* (Tear Drop 1964)★★★, *The Original Peanuts* (Sunglow 1965)★★★, *Smile Now Cry Later* (1966)★★★, *Live In Hollywood* (1966)★★, *This Is My Band* (1977)★★★.

SUPERBS

The Superbs, from California, USA, were one of the best mid-60s sweet-soul groups to meld doo-wop harmonies into the sound of soul. The members were Eleanor 'Punkin' Green' (lead), Walter White, Bobby Swain, Gordy Harmon and Ronny Cook. Green possessed a soprano lead that sounded much like a male falsetto and it was an era when falsetto-led groups were regularly on the charts. After their first record in 1964 on Lew Bedell's Dore label, 'Storybook Of Love', flopped, Harmon left to form the Whispers (the Whispers were the Superbs' labelmates and were likewise outstanding in merging doo-wop with soul). The next record, 'Baby Baby All The Time', with its relaxed lope, proved a success in 1964. Similar-sounding and equally appealing follow-ups were 'Sad Sad Day' (1964) and 'Baby's Gone Away' (1965). Around this time Swain left the group to form the Entertainers Four, who also recorded for Dore. He was replaced by Lawrence Randall. Green left in 1966 to get married and the group regrouped, but the magic was gone and by the 70s the group had broken up. Lawrence Randall formed a new Superbs group in the mid-80s to play the southern California revival circuit.

SUPERFLY

This 1972 release was one of several films starring African-American actors in a genre dubbed 'blaxploitation'. The first, and best, of these was *Shaft*, which featured a taut score by Isaac Hayes. *Superfly* featured the less fêted Jeff Alexander as its musical director, but he proved astute in enlisting former Impressions leader Curtis Mayfield to contribute several excellent compositions. Two powerful songs, 'Freddy's Dead' and the title track itself, reached the US Top 10, providing a boost to their creator's solo career. Their success helped to promote *Superfly* and gave it a prominence that the one-dimensional plot did not deserve. Ron O'Neal starred as a drug-pusher looking for the one big deal that would enable him to retire, but the ambiguous script suggested that violent New York cocaine dealers were merely behaving like noble outlaws. Indeed, black self-help groups picketed several cinemas showing the film. Mayfield himself later expressed disquiet about the theme, preferring the cautionary 'Freddy's Dead' than other, more celebratory, inclusions. The singer later wrote the scores for *Claudine* and *Short Eyes*, neither of which enjoyed the commercial approbation of *Superfly*. The film itself inspired an even more lacklustre follow-up, *Superfly TNT*.

SUPREMES

America's most successful female vocal group of all time was formed by four Detroit schoolgirls in the late 50s. Diana Ross (b. 26 March 1944, Detroit, Michigan, USA), Betty Hutton, Florence Ballard (b. 30 June 1943, Detroit, Michigan, USA, d. 22 February 1976) and Mary Wilson (b. 6 March 1944, Greenville, Mississippi, USA) named themselves the Primettes in tribute to the local male group, the Primes - who themselves found fame in the 60s as the Temptations. Having issued a solitary single on a small local label, the Primettes were signed to Berry Gordy's Motown stable, where they initially found public acceptance hard to find. For more than two years, they issued a succession of flop singles, despite the best efforts of top Motown writer/producer Smokey Robinson to find them a suitable vehicle for their unsophisticated talents. Only when Diana Ross supplanted Florence Ballard as the group's regular lead vocalist, at Gordy's suggestion, did the Supremes break into the US charts. The dynamic 'When The Lovelight Starts Shining In His Eyes', modelled on the production style of Phil Spector, was the group's first hit in 1963. The follow-up single flopped, so Gordy handed over the group to the newly formed Holland/Dozier/Holland writing and production team. They concocted the slight, but effervescent, 'Where Did Our Love Go' for the Supremes, which topped the US charts and was also a major hit in Britain. This achievement inaugurated a remarkable run of successes for the group and their producers, as their next four releases - 'Baby Love', 'Come See About Me', 'Stop! In The Name Of Love' and 'Back In My Arms Again' - all topped the US singles charts, while 'Baby Love' became the only record by an American group to reach number 1 in Britain during the beat-dominated year of 1964. All these singles were hinged around insistent, very danceable rhythms with repetitive lyrics and melodies, which placed no great strain on Ross's fragile voice. With their girl-next-door looks and endearingly unsophisticated demeanour, the Supremes became role models for young black Americans and their name was used to promote a range of merchandising, even (ironically) a brand of white bread. The rather perfunctory 'Nothing But Heartaches' broke the chart-topping sequence, which was immediately restored by the more ambitious 'I Hear A Symphony'. As Holland/Dozier/Holland moved into their prime, and Ross increased in confidence, the group's repertoire grew more mature. They recorded albums of Broadway standards, played residencies at expensive nightclubs, and were expertly groomed by Motown staff as all-round entertainers. Meanwhile, the hits kept coming, with four more US number 1 hits in the shape of 'You Can't Hurry Love', 'You Keep Me Hanging On', 'Love Is Here And Now You're Gone' and 'The Happening' - the last of which was a blatant attempt to cash in on the psychedelic movement. Behind the scenes, the group's future was in some jeopardy;

Florence Ballard had grown increasingly unhappy in the supporting role into which Berry Gordy had coerced her, and her occasionally erratic and troublesome behaviour was ultimately used as an excuse to force her out of the group. Without fanfare, Ballard was ousted in mid-1967, and replaced by Cindy Birdsong; most fans simply did not notice. At the same time, Ross's prime position in the group's hierarchy was confirmed in public, when she was given individual credit on the group's records, a move that prompted a flurry of similar demands from the lead singers of other Motown groups. 'Reflections', an eerie, gripping song that was one of Motown's most adventurous productions to date, introduced the new era. Motown's loss of Holland/Dozier/Holland slowed the group's progress in 1968, before they bounced back with two controversial slices of overt social commentary, 'Love Child' and 'I'm Livin' In Shame', the first of which was yet another US number 1. The Supremes also formed a successful recording partnership with the Temptations, exemplified by the hit single 'I'm Gonna Make You Love Me'.

During 1969, there were persistent rumours that Berry Gordy was about to launch Diana Ross on a solo career. These were confirmed at the end of the year, when the Supremes staged a farewell performance, and Ross bade goodbye to the group with the elegiac 'Someday We'll Be Together' - a US chart-topper on which, ironically, she was the only member of the Supremes to appear. Ross was replaced by Jean Terrell, sister of heavyweight boxer Ernie Terrell. The new line-up, with Terrell and Mary Wilson alternating lead vocal duties, found immediate success with 'Up The Ladder To The Roof' in early 1970, while 'Stoned Love', the group's biggest UK hit for four years, revived memories of their early successes with its rhythmic base and repetitive hook. The Supremes also tried to revive the atmosphere of their earlier recordings with the Temptations on a series of albums with the Four Tops. Gradually, their momentum was lost, and as Motown shifted its centre of activity from Detroit to California, the Supremes were left behind. Lynda Laurence replaced Cindy Birdsong in the line-up in 1972; Birdsong returned in 1974 when Laurence became pregnant. The latter move coincided with the departure of Jean Terrell, whose place was taken by Scherrie Payne (b. 14 November 1944, Detroit, Michigan, USA). With the group recording only rarely, Birdsong quit again, leaving Mary Wilson - at last established as the unchallenged leader - to recruit Susaye Greene in her place. This trio recorded the self-explanatory *Mary, Scherrie And Susaye* in 1976, before disbanding the following year. Mary Wilson attempted to assemble a new set of Supremes for recording purposes, and actually toured Britain in 1978 with Karen Rowland and Karen Jackson in the line-up. The termination of her Motown contract stymied this move, however, and since then the use of the Supremes' name has legally resided with Motown. They have chosen not to sully the memory of their most famous group by concocting an ersatz Supremes to cash in on their heritage. Jean Terrell, Scherrie Payne and Lynda Laurence won the rights to use the Supremes' name in the UK. Payne began recording disco material with producer Ian Levine in 1989, for the Nightmare and Motor City labels. Levine also signed Laurence, Wilson and ex-Supreme Susaye Greene to solo contracts and recorded Terrell, Lawrence and Greene for a remake of 'Stoned Love'. The career of Mary Wilson has also continued with a starring role in the Toronto, Canada production of the stage musical *The Beehive* in 1989 and the publication of the second volume of her autobiography in 1990. In 1988 the Supremes were inducted into the Rock And Roll Hall Of Fame.

● ALBUMS: as The Supremes: *Meet The Supremes* (Motown 1963)★★★, *Where Did Our Love Go?* (Motown 1964)★★★, *A Bit Of Liverpool* (Motown 1964)★★, *The Supremes Sing Country, Western And Pop* (Motown 1964)★, *We Remember Sam Cooke* (Motown 1965)★★★, *More Hits By The Supremes* (Motown 1965)★★★, *Merry Christmas* (Motown 1965)★★★, *The Supremes At The Copa* (Motown 1965)★★★, *I Hear A Symphony* (Motown 1966)★★★, *The Supremes A-Go-Go* (Motown 1966)★★★, *The Supremes Sing Holland, Dozier, Holland* (Motown 1967)★★★★, *The Supremes Sing Rodgers And Hart* (Motown 1967)★★, *Right On* (Motown 1970)★★★, with the Four Tops *The Magnificent Seven* (Motown 1970)★★★★, *New Ways But Love Stays* (Motown 1970)★★, *Touch* (Motown 1971)★★, with the Four Tops *The Return Of The Magnificent Seven* (Motown 1971)★★, with the Four Tops *Dynamite* (Motown 1971)★★★, *Floy Joy* (Motown 1972)★★★, *The Supremes* (Motown 1975)★★, *High Energy* (Motown 1976)★★, *Mary, Scherrie And Susaye* (Motown 1976)★★★. As Diana Ross And The Supremes: *Reflections* (Motown 1968)★★★, *Diana Ross And The Supremes Sing And Perform 'Funny Girl'* (Motown 1968)★, *Diana Ross And The Supremes Live At London's Talk Of The Town* (Motown 1968)★★, with the Temptations *Diana Ross And The Supremes Join The Temptations* (Motown 1968)★★★, *Love Child* (Motown 1968)★★★, with the Temptations *TCB* (Motown 1968)★★★, *Let The Sunshine In* (Motown 1969)★★, with the Temptations *Together* (Motown 1969)★★★, *Cream Of The Crop* (Motown 1969)★★, with the Temptations *Diana Ross And The Supremes On Broadway* (Motown 1969)★★, *Farewell* (Motown 1970)★★.

● COMPILATIONS: *Diana Ross And The Supremes Greatest Hits* (Motown 1967)★★★★, *Diana Ross And The Supremes Greatest Hits, Volume 2* (Motown 1967)★★★★, *Diana Ross And The Supremes Greatest Hits, Volume 3* (Motown 1969)★★★, *Anthology 1962-69* (Motown 1974)★★★★, *Supremes At Their Best* (Motown 1978)★★★, *20 Greatest Hits* (Motown 1986)★★★★, *25th Anniversary* (Motown 1986)★★★★, *Early Classics* (Spectrum 1996)★★★.

● FURTHER READING: *Reflections*, Johnny Bond. *Dreamgirl: My Life As A Supreme*, Mary Wilson. *Supreme Faith: Someday We'll Be Together*, Mary Wilson with Patricia Romanowski. *All That Glittered: My Life With The Supremes*, Tony Turner and Barbara Aria.

● FILMS: *Beach Ball* (1964).

SURE!, AL B.

b. 1969, New York City, New York, USA. Briefly one of the most popular voices of the New Jack Swing movement of the late 80s, Sure! represented more traditional soul values than other swingbeat singers such as Bobby Brown, concentrating on his smooth vocal stylings rather than the backing beats. Remarkably unambitious during his early years, Sure! amused himself by writing old-style soul songs with his cousin Kyle West before being persuaded to enter a national songwriting contest in 1988. Winning on a deciding vote from Quincy Jones, Sure! signed to Warner Brothers and released his debut set, *In Effect Mode*, featuring the hit singles 'Nite And Day' and 'Off On Your Own'. Production work for other artists followed before Sure! joined El DeBarge, James Ingram and Barry White on Quincy Jones's 1990 single 'The Secret Garden'. His second album concentrated on ballad work, including a duet with Diana Ross on 'No Matter What You Do'.

● ALBUMS: *In Effect Mode* (Warners 1988)★★★, *Private Times . . . And The Whole 9!* (Warners 1990)★★★.

SWALLOWS

This vocal group from Baltimore, Maryland, USA, comprised Eddie Rich (lead), Irving Turner (tenor/baritone), Earl Hurley (tenor), Herman 'Junior' Denby (second tenor/baritone), Frederick 'Money' Johnson (baritone) and Norris 'Bunky' Mack (bass). The Swallows were one of the most sophisticated of the early 50s vocal harmony groups, recording sleepy ballads much in the style of their Baltimore counterparts the Orioles, but also recording outstanding jump and bluesy tunes in the style of Charles Brown. The group was formed in 1946 and signed with King Records in 1951. Their first recordings were largely Rich-led sweet ballads, best exemplified by their first hit 'Will You Be Mine' (number 9 R&B), from 1951. The Swallows developed some notoriety for a 1952 song, the risqué 'It Ain't The Meat (It's The Motion)', an up-tempo number led by their bass Mack in the same style of the Dominoes' 'Sixty Minute Man'. Another 1952 song set a new style for the group, 'Beside You' (number 8 R&B), in which lead Denby captured perfectly the sound of the urbane blues singer Charles Brown. Much of the Swallows' subsequent material was in this style, but by 1953 it had come to sound dated next to up-and-coming groups such as the Drifters and Clovers. The Swallows left King and made one more recording, for the After Hours label in 1954, and then began to fall apart. Rich kept a group together with new members until he disbanded the Swallows in 1956. In 1958 a new Swallows group consisting of three original members - Rich, Hurley and Johnson - plus new recruits Buddy Bailey and Calvin Kollette assembled. They signed with King Records' Federal subsidiary and recorded mostly up-tempo songs. When their excellent recording of 'Itchy Twitchy Feeling' failed to compete with Bobby Hendricks' hit version, the new group disbanded.

● COMPILATIONS: *Dearest* (Charly 1991)★★★.

SWAMP DOGG

b. Jerry Williams Jnr., 12 July 1942, Portsmouth, Virginia, USA. This eccentric performer first recorded, as Little Jerry, during the 50s. His subsequent releases were as varied as the outlets on which they appeared, although Williams did achieve a minor hit in 1966 with 'Baby You're My Everything'. He later forsook a conventional direction by assuming his 'Swamp Dogg' alter ego. Although the artist is well-known for his production and/or songwriting work for Irma Thomas, Patti LaBelle, Doris Duke, Z.Z. Hill and Solomon Burke, his solo work is equally of value. His first album, *Total Destruction Of Your Mind*, has become a soul classic, incorporating the sound of early Stax recordings with the rock style of the late 60s and early 70s. The artist embraced the bayou inflections of Tony Joe White and John Fogerty, while his songs betrayed a lyrical wit and oblique perception rendering them unique. Such titles as 'Mama's Baby - Daddy's Maybe', 'Eat The Goose (Before The Goose Eats You)' and 'The Love We Got Ain't Worth Two Dead Flies' (a duet with Esther Phillips) provide a taste of this performer's vision.

● ALBUMS: *Total Destruction Of Your Mind* (Canyon 1970)★★★★, *Rat On* (Elektra 1971)★★★, *Cuffed, Collared And Tagged* (Cream 1972)★★★, *Gag A Maggot* (Stonedogg 1973)★★★, *Have You Heard This Story* (1974)★★★, *Never Too Old To Boogie* (1976)★★★, *Finally Caught Up With Myself* (MCA 1977)★★★, *An Opportunity ... Not A Bargain* (1977)★★★, *Doing A Party Tonight* (1980)★★★, *I'm Not Selling Out, I'm Buying In* (Takoma 1981)★★★.

● COMPILATIONS: *Swamp Dogg's Greatest Hits* (1976)★★★, *The Best Of* (1982)★★★★.

In addition there have been numerous collections compiled from Williams' extensive tape archive, including: *Uncut And Classified 1A* (Charly 1981)★★★, *Unmuzzled* (Charly 1983)★★★, *I Called For A Rope And They Threw Me A Rock* (Sonet 1989)★★★.

SWAN SILVERTONES

This vocal quartet was formed in 1938 in West Virginia, USA, by four coalminers, Claude Jeter (lead), Eddie Boroughas, John Myles and Leroy Watkins. The Swan in their name refers to their early sponsors, the Swan Bakery. Their first sessions were recorded for King Records in Cincinnati in 1946. At this time Henry Brossard (bass) and Soloman Womack (joint lead) joined The line-up changed frequently throughout the late 40s, with Reverend Percell Perkins, Reverend Robert Crenshaw and Roosevelt Payne all joining at some point. Paul Owens, formerly of the Nightingales and Dixie Hummingbirds, also joined the group. Although their recording career (for Specialty Records) was sparser than more celebrated gospel/R&B groups, the Silvertones continued to tour and appear on radio. William Connor of the Trumpeteers replaced Brossard in 1955, though by the time the group moved to Vee Jay Records in 1959, Louis Johnson had joined as third lead. Claude Jeter became a minister in 1963, after which the group lost much of its momentum. Various singers flitted in and out of the group, and the only remaining original member, John Miles, retired in 1978. The same year former members reunited to play a one-off concert in Chicago.

SWANN, BETTYE

b. Betty Jean Champion, 24 October 1944, Shreveport, Louisiana, USA. This superior singer first recorded during the early 60s as a member of the Fawns. A Carolyn Franklin song, 'Don't Wait Too Long', provided Swann with a solo hit in 1965, but her career was more fully launched two years later with a US R&B chart-topper, the beautiful 'Make Me Yours'. Subsequent recordings established the singer's reputation as an imaginative interpreter of country/soul. Her versions of Merle Haggard's 'Today I Started Loving You Again' (1972) and Tammy Wynette's ''Til I Get It Right' (1973) are superb. Swann continued this direction under the aegis of Millie Jackson's producer Brad Shapiro, but her last hit to date was in 1975 with 'All The Way In Or All The Way Out', which reached the lower regions of the *Billboard* R&B chart.

● ALBUMS: *Make Me Yours* (Money 1967)★★★, *The Soul View Now!* (Money 1968)★★★, *Don't You Ever Get Tired (Of Hurting Me)?* (Capitol 1969)★★★.

● COMPILATIONS: shared with Candi Staton *Tell It Like It Is* (Stateside 1986)★★★.

SWEAT, KEITH

b. Keith 'Sabu' Crier, 22 July 1961, New York, USA. A veteran of contemporary R&B, acknowledged master crooner Keith Sweat has presided over a musical style that has evolved enormously since his double-platinum debut album, *Make It Last Forever*, was released in 1987. In that time, he has never seemed out of pace with developments, incorporating new innovations such as swingbeat as they arrive, but always welding them to a traditional soul base. Part of the key to his longevity in an R&B market noted for its one-hit-wonders lies in his ability to shun the limelight between albums, whereas other artists in the same field with only a fraction of Sweat's years saturate fans with much more extensive discographies. 'My strategy is to give people just enough of me, then pull back, so they'll want to see me when I come back', he told *Billboard* magazine in 1996. By this time he had two platinum albums behind him, as well as the admiration of a sizeable contingency of the soul/R&B market. In the 90s Sweat has established his own Keia Productions management agency and constructed the Sweat Shop recording studio in his home base of Atlanta, Georgia.

● ALBUMS: *Make It Last Forever* (Vintertainment/Elektra 1987)★★★, *I'll Give All My Love To You* (Vintertainment/Elektra 1990)★★★★, *Keep It Comin'* (Elektra 1991)★★★, *Get Up On It* (Elektra 1994)★★★, *Keith Sweat* (Elektra 1996)★★★.

● COMPILATIONS: *Just A Touch* (Elektra 1997)★★★.

SWEET INSPIRATIONS

The Sweet Inspirations' career reached back to the Drinkards, a formative gospel group whose fluid line-up included Dionne Warwick and Cissy Houston. The group dropped this name on pursuing a secular path as session singers. Houston remained at the helm during several subsequent changes (Doris Troy and Judy Clay were among the former members), and the group emerged from its backroom role with a recording contract of its own. Dubbed the Sweet Inspirations by Atlantic Records producer Jerry Wexler, the line-up of Cissy Houston, Sylvia Shemwell, Myrna Smith and Estelle Brown secured a minor hit with 'Why (Am I Treated So Bad)' (1967), but it was a self-titled composition, 'Sweet Inspiration', that gave the group its best-remembered single, reaching the US Top 20 in 1968. When Cissy Houston left for a belated solo career in 1970, the remaining trio, Smith, Brown and Shemwell, joined Elvis Presley's concert retinue, and recorded a further album on their own, a good 1973 outing for Stax. After a hiatus from the recording scene, Smith and Shemwell were joined by Gloria Brown in place of Estelle Brown who had quit earlier, and a final album appeared on RSO in 1979, although Brown herself was replaced on the actual recording by Pat Terry. In 1994 Estelle Brown, Shemwell and Smith reunited for a special series of shows, including a tribute to Presley.

● ALBUMS: *The Sweet Inspirations* (Atlantic 1967)★★★, *Songs Of Faith And Inspiration* (Atlantic 1968)★★★, *What The World Needs Now Is Love* (Atlantic 1968)★★, *Sweets For My Sweet* (Atlantic 1969)★★★, *Sweet, Sweet Soul* (Atlantic 1970)★★★, *Estelle, Myrna And Sylvia* (Stax 1973)★★★, *Hot Butterfly* (RSO 1979)★★.

● COMPILATIONS: *Estelle, Myrna And Sylvia* (1991)★★★, *The Best Of The Sweet Inspirations* (Ichiban 1994)★★★.

SWEETBACK

The three members of the New York, USA-based Sweetback first worked together as backing band to soul chanteuse Sade. However, with that artist taking an extended sabbatical from the music business, Stewart Matthewman, Andrew Hale and Paul Denman decided to continue their association together as Sweetback. The project began to coalesce in 1994, shortly after Sade had completed her *Love Deluxe* world tour. Matthewman built his own studio in New York, releasing a series of 12-inch dance singles under names such as Cottonbelly and Edge Test. He also produced and co-wrote three songs for Maxwell's breakthrough debut album, *Maxwell's Urban Hang Suite*. In the interim Hale and Denman kept busy by recording music for fashion shows and clothing shops. In 1996, after months of exchanging tapes, the three recruited singers Maxwell, Bahamadia and Amel Larrieux of Groove Theory and entered the studio to record Sweetback's self-titled debut for Epic Records. With musical textures ranging from trad-soul ('You Will Rise'), to house ('Cloud People'), the album's succulent eclecticism and sophisticated musicianship won over critics from a variety of genres.

● ALBUMS: *Sweetback* (Epic 1996)★★★.

SWITCH

Bobby DeBarge (keyboards), Greg Williams (keyboards) and Jody Sims (drums) first collaborated in the Ohio-based funk band White Heat in the early 70s. After recording a self-titled album in 1975 produced by Barry White, the trio left the band, enlisting Philip Ingram (vocals), Tommy DeBarge (bass) and Eddie Fluellen (guitar) to form First Class. Jermaine Jackson helped them to secure a contract with Motown Records, and produced their first album on the label, for which they were renamed Switch. The band's dance-orientated brand of soul proved popular in clubs and discos, and they enjoyed three major hits in the late 70s, 'There'll Never Be', 'I Call Your Name' and 'Love Over And Over Again'. They were unable to break into the mainstream pop market, however, and diminishing returns for their efforts led them to leave Motown in 1982. Bobby DeBarge left the group to join other members of his family in DeBarge, before his career was cut short in the late 80s when he was convicted of cocaine trafficking. Meanwhile, Switch moved to the Total Experience label, where they had a belated UK hit with 'Keeping Secrets' in 1984.

● ALBUMS: *Switch* (Gordy 1978)★★★, *Switch II* (Gordy 1979)★★★, *Reaching For Tomorrow* (Gordy 1980)★★★, *This Is My Dream* (Gordy 1980)★★★, *Switch V* (Gordy 1981)★★, *Am I Still Your Boyfriend?* (Total Experience 1985)★★.

SWV

Standing for Sisters With Voices, these 'ghetto sisters' from Brooklyn and the Bronx, New York, USA, comprise the talents of Coko (b. Cheryl Gamble, *c.*1974), Taj (b. Tamara Johnson, *c.*1974) and Lelee (b. Leanne Lyons, *c.* 1976). Shaped by producer Teddy Riley to embody streetwise dress and attitude, the band's sound is somewhat harder than that which might be expected of 'New Jill Swingers'. On tracks such as 'Downtown', they revealed themselves as being happy to engage in intimate details about the sex wars. Their debut album also encompassed both rap and a capella, and included the hit single 'I'm So Into You', which crossed over into the *Billboard* Top 20. Nominated for a Grammy in 1995, they returned in 1996 with the equally slick *A New Beginning* and repeated the formula in 1997 with *Release Some Tension*. The latter featured more sexual innuendo recorded to perfection, but was too smooth for many fans of urban R&B.

● ALBUMS: *It's About Time* (RCA 1993)★★★, *A New Beginning* (RCA 1996)★★★, *Release Some Tension* (RCA 1997)★★.

SYLVERS

Formed in Memphis, Tennessee, USA, and originally known as the Little Angels, the Sylvers were a family act tutored by their former opera-singing mother, Shirley Sylvers. Her children, Leon Frank III, Charmaine, Olympia-Ann and James, started performing at local talent shows in Memphis, before moving to Harlem, New York - providing a more sympathetic audience for their pop R&B. Tours followed with Ray Charles and Johnny Mathis during school vacation breaks, until in the early 70s they relocated from east coast to west coast, taking up residence in Watts, Los Angeles, and calling themselves the Sylvers. By this time they had been joined by younger siblings Foster, Edmund and Ricky, and in 1972 the group, already veterans of television exposure on shows with Spike Jones, Groucho Marx and Dinah Shore, signed to Pride Records, a subsidiary of MGM Records. Their debut single, 'Fool's Paradise', reached number 13 in *Billboard*'s R&B chart. 'Wish That I Could Talk To You' repeated the success, rising three places higher (and to number 77 in *Billboard*'s pop charts). Eleven-year-old Foster, who shone through in the ensemble performances, released a solo single, 'Misdemeanour', which reached number 22 in the *Billboard* pop charts. Later, the Sylvers transferred to the main MGM label, but only one chart appearance, 'Through The Love In My Heart', preceded a more permanent move to Capitol Records. Larkin Arnold was the man behind the move, intending to link the Sylvers with producer Freddy Pearson, previously behind the Jackson Five and Tavares. The first result of this collaboration was 'Boogie Fever', which rewarded Arnold's foresight by rising to number 1 in the national charts. However, they never managed to repeat this feat, with the subsequent 'Cotton Candy' stalling at number 59. Much more successful was 'Hot Line' at number 5. Only 'High School Dance' reached the top 20, and by 1978 the Sylvers had moved over to Casablanca Records for a solitary chart excursion, 'Don't Stop, Get Off'. In 1984 there was a further switch to Geffen Records, for whom 'In One Love And Out The Other' reached number 42, but it would be their last significant success.

● ALBUMS: *The Sylvers* (Pride 1973)★★★, *The Sylvers II* (Pride 1973)★★★, *Showcase* (Capitol 1976)★★, *Something Special* (Capitol 1976)★★★, *New Horizons* (Capitol 1977)★★★, *Forever Yours* (Casablanca 1978)★★.

SYLVESTER

b. Sylvester James, 1946, Los Angeles, California, USA, d. 16 December 1988. Having moved to San Francisco in 1967, James joined the Cockettes, an androgynous theatrical group with whom he made his debut on New Year's Eve 1970. He subsequently pursed a career as 'Ruby Blue' before putting together the Hot Band with James Q. Smith (guitar), Bobby Blood (trumpet), Chris Mostert (saxophone), Kerry Hatch (bass) and Travis Fullerton (drums). The line-up later included vocalists Izora Rhodes and Martha Wash, now better known as the Weather Girls. Early recordings for the Blue Thumb label, coupled with an outrageous live show, secured James's local reputation, but his 'discovery' by former Motown producer Harvey Fuqua led to a much wider audience. In 1978 Sylvester enjoyed two massive disco hits with 'You Make Me Feel (Mighty Real)' and 'Dance (Disco Heat)', performances marked by an unswerving urgency and the singer's soaring falsetto. The artist was adopted by the city's gay community, where later releases proved especially popular. Sylvester's excellent voice and skilled arrangements bestowed a lasting quality on his work, but he died of an AIDS-related illness in 1988. Jimmy Somerville subsequently recorded a version of *Mighty Real* as a tribute to this imaginative performer's talent.

● ALBUMS: with the Hot Band *Sylvester And The Hot Band - Scratch My Flower* (1973)★★★, with the Hot Band *Bazaar* (1973)★★★, *Lights Out San Fransisco* (Blue Thumb 1973)★★★, *Sylvester* (Fantasy 1977)★★★, *Step II*

(Fantasy 1978)★★★, *Stars* (Fantasy 1979)★★★, *Living Proof* (Fantasy 1979)★★★, *Sell My Soul* (Honey 1980)★★★, *Mighty Real* (Honey 1980)★★★, *Too Hot To Sleep* (Honey 1981)★★★, *Sylvester And Griffin* (Polydor 1982)★★, *All I Need* (Megatone 1983)★★★, *Call Me* (Ecstasy 1984)★★, *M1015* (Chrysalis 1984)★★★, *Mutual Attraction* (Warners 1987)★★★.

● COMPILATIONS: *Greatest Hits* (Fantasy 1983)★★★, *Star - The Best Of Sylvester* (South Bound 1989)★★★, *The Original Hits* (1989)★★★.

Syreeta

b. Rita Wright, Pittsburgh, Philadelphia, USA. Like Martha Reeves, Syreeta joined the staff of Motown Records as a secretary rather than a recording artist. In the mid-60s she sang occasional backing vocals on Motown sessions, and in 1967 Ashford And Simpson produced her debut single, 'I Can't Give Back The Love I Feel For You', which became a cult record among British soul fans. In 1968 she met Stevie Wonder, who encouraged her to begin songwriting. She co-wrote his 1970 hit 'Signed, Sealed, Delivered (I'm Yours)', and also commenced work on the song-cycle that became *Where I'm Coming From.* The couple were married on 14 September 1970, and although they were divorced just 18 months later, they continued to work together for several years. In 1972, Wonder produced *Syreeta*, a stunning collection of soft-soul and light-funk that showcased her fluent, joyous vocals. The collaboration allowed Wonder to experiment with studio techniques that he perfected on his own later projects, and also inspired one of his earliest pronouncements of black pride on the affecting ballad 'Black Maybe'. *Stevie Wonder Presents Syreeta* in 1974 continued the pair's close musical partnership, and produced a British hit in the reggae-flavoured 'Your Kiss Is Sweet'. The couple's last joint recording, 'Harm Our Love' in 1975, was also their most commercial, and its success in the UK and USA gave Syreeta a platform on which to build. She teamed up with G.C. Cameron for a disappointing album of duets before completing a more fulfilling partnership with Billy Preston, which produced the soundtrack for the film *Fast Break*, and a US and UK Top 10 hit, the sentimental love song 'With You I'm Born Again'. Syreeta and Preston completed a further album project in 1981. Her solo recordings were less successful, and after the Jermaine Jackson-produced *The Spell* in 1983, she abandoned her career to concentrate on raising a family. In the late 80s, Syreeta recorded several tracks for Ian Levine's Motor City label, including a solo rendition of 'With You I'm Born Again' and new duets with Billy Preston.

● ALBUMS: *Syreeta* (MoWest 1972)★★★, *Stevie Wonder Presents Syreeta* (Motown 1974)★★★, *One To One* (Tamla 1977)★★★, with G.C. Cameron *Rich Love, Poor Love* (Motown 1977)★★, with Billy Preston *Fast Break* film soundtrack (Motown 1979)★★, *Syreeta* (Tamla 1980)★★★, with Preston *Billy Preston And Syreeta* (Motown 1981)★★, *Set My Love In Motion* (Tamla 1981)★★★, *The Spell* (1983)★★.

● COMPILATIONS: *Best Of Syreeta* (Motown 1981)★★★.

T-Bones (UK)

Formed in 1964, the T-Bones - Gary Farr (vocals, harmonica), Winston Whetherall (lead guitar), Andy McKechnie (rhythm guitar), Stuart Parks (bass) and Andy Steele (drums) - were one of several groups active on London's R&B circuit. They made their recording debut in November that year with an uncompromising reading of 'How Many More Years', a powerful Howlin' Wolf song later popularized by Led Zeppelin. Two further singles and an excellent EP completed the T-Bones' catalogue, but the group was unable to make a significant commercial breakthrough. Steele, who later joined the Herd, was subsequently replaced by Brian Walkeley, and by 1966 only Farr remained from the unit's original line-up. The singer continued to front the T-Bones until early 1967. This late-period version included Keith Emerson (keyboards) and Lee Jackson (bass), but their sole recorded legacy rests with 'If I Had A Ticket', on which they backed jazz trombonist Chris Barber. Emerson and Jackson were later reunited in the Nice, while Farr embarked on a solo career.

● COMPILATIONS: *London 1964-1965* (1980)★★★, *One More Chance* (1987)★★★.

T.S. Monk

This funk group was formed by New Yorker Thelonious Sphere Monk Jnr., the son of the legendary and revolutionary jazz pianist. Jazz greats Max Roach and Art Blakey started him on the road to being a drummer by giving him his first drum kit. He played in his father's group for a couple of years in the early 70s and can be heard on two of tenor man Paul Jeffrey's albums. In 1974 he recorded on Atlantic with Natural Essence, which was where he met singer Yvonne Fletcher. Together with Fletcher and his sister Boo Boo he formed the group Cycles in 1976 and played on backing sessions for hit producer Sandy Linzer. Linzer, known for his work with Odyssey, then worked with the trio and placed them (with the new name T.S. Monk) on Mirage Records. Their first single, 'Bon Bon Vie', made the R&B Top 20 and hit the UK charts, as did the follow-up 'Candidate For Love', both being taken from their US Top 100 album *House Of Music*. Despite the encouraging start, their subsequent album, *More Of The Good Life*, made a lesser impact and the act, which also included an eight-piece band, soon vanished from sight.

● ALBUMS: *House Of Music* (Mirage 1981)★★★, *More Of The Good Life* (Mirage 1982)★★★.

TAKE 6

Initially a quartet known as the Sounds Of Distinction then the Alliance, this highly rated ensemble first formed in northern Alabama, USA, in 1980. The group evolved into a six-piece a cappella gospel group of breathtaking ability. The members are Alvin Chea, Cedric Dent, David Thomas, Mervyn Warren, Mark Kibble and Claude V. McKnight. The combination of their Seventh-day Adventist beliefs and their appreciation of jazz and R&B enabled them to make inroads into both record-buying markets, winning Grammies for best Soul Gospel and best Jazz Vocal categories. Their 1990 appearance with k.d. lang in the movie *Dick Tracy* singing 'Ridin' The Rails' gave them further valuable exposure. Additionally, they have recorded with Dianne Reeves, Quincy Jones and Joe Sample. *Join The Band* marked a new direction for the group as it incorporated live musicians including Greg Phillinganes, Gerald Albright and Herbie Hancock. It also featured lead vocals from Ray Charles, Stevie Wonder and a rap from Queen Latifah. Music writer David Okamota aptly described Take 6 as 'winning over a loyal congregation of secular fans with a soothing, uplifting sound that stirs the soul without twisting the arm'.

● ALBUMS: *Take 6* (Reprise 1988)★★★, *So Much 2 Say* (Reprise 1990)★★★★, *He Is Christmas* (Reprise 1991)★★, *Join The Band* (Reprise 1994)★★★, *Brothers* (Reprise 1996)★★★.

TAMLA-MOTOWN RECORDS

(see Motown Records)

TAMS

This US group was formed in 1952 as the Four Dots, in Atlanta, Georgia, USA. Their line-up featured Joseph Pope (b. 6 November 1933, d. 16 March 1996), Charles Pope (b. 7 August 1936), Robert Lee Smith (b. 18 March 1936) and Horace Kay (b. 13 April 1934). Although such an early origin suggests longevity, it was not until 1960 that the group emerged with a single on Swan. Now dubbed the Tams (derived by their wearing of Tam O'Shanter hats on stage), they added a further member, Floyd Ashton (b. 15 August 1933), prior to signing with Bill Lowery, an Atlanta song publisher and entrepreneur. Among those already on his books were Joe South and Ray Whitley, two musicians who would work closely with the group. 'Untie Me', a South composition, was recorded at Fame and leased to Philadelphia's Arlen Records. The song became a Top 20 US R&B hit, but follow-up releases failed until 1963, when Lowery secured a new contract with ABC Paramount. The Tams' first single there, 'What Kind Of Fool (Do You Think I Am)', reached the US Top 10 and established a series of Whitley-penned successes. His compositions included 'You Lied To Your Daddy' and 'Hey Girl Don't Bother Me', ideal material for Joe Pope's ragged lead and the group's unpolished harmonies. After 1964, the group defected to Atlanta's Master Sound studio, by which time Albert Cottle (b. 1941, Washington, DC, USA) had replaced Ashton. South and Whitley continued their involvement, writing, playing on and producing various sessions, but the Tams had only one further US hit in 1968 with the bubbling 'Be Young, Be Foolish, Be Happy', which peaked on the *Billboard* R&B chart at 26 and reached the UK Top 40 in 1970. By the end of the 60s their mentors had moved elsewhere, while the Master Sound house band was breaking up. Dropped by ABC, the Tams unsuccessfully moved to 1-2-3 and Capitol Records until a chance reissue of 'Hey Girl Don't Bother Me' became a surprise UK number 1 in 1971. They were not to chart again until 16 years later when their association with the Shag, a dance craze and subsequent 80s film, offered a further lifeline to this remarkable group, giving them a UK Top 30 hit with 'There Ain't Nothing Like Shaggin''.

● ALBUMS: *Presenting The Tams* (ABC 1964)★★★, *Hey Girl Don't Bother Me* (ABC 1964)★★★★, *Time For The Tams* (ABC 1967)★★★, *A Portrait Of The Tams* (ABC 1969)★★, *Be Young, Be Foolish, Be Happy* (Stateside 1970)★★.

● COMPILATIONS: *A Little More Soul* (ABC 1968)★★★★, *The Best Of The Tams* (Capitol 1971)★★★, *The Mighty Mighty Tams* (Sounds South 1978)★★★, *Greatest Hits - Beach Party Vol. 1* (Carousel South 1981)★★★, *Atlanta Soul Connection* (Charly 1983)★★★, *Beach Music From The Tams* (Compleat 1983)★★★, *Reminiscing* (Wonder 1982)★★★, *There Ain't Nothing Like ... The Tams* (Virgin 1987)★★★.

TARHEEL SLIM

b. Alden Bunn, 24 September 1924, Bailey, North Carolina, USA, d. 21 August 1977. Tarheel Slim was a blues, gospel and doo-wop singer and guitarist who took his sobriquet from the popular nickname of North Carolina - Tarheel State. Bunn learned guitar at the age of 12 and sang in church by the age of 20. He began working with the Gospel Four following World War II and then joined the Selah Jubilee Singers, with whom he first recorded, in the late 40s. As the gospel group could not record secular music, they also worked under the names the Four Barons and the Larks, recording the R&B hits 'Eyesight To The Blind' and 'Little Side Car' for Apollo Records in 1951. Bunn recorded under his real name for Apollo and also with the group the Wheels in 1956 on Premium Records. That was followed by a partnership with his wife as the Lovers for Lamp Records in 1958. They then recorded for the Fire label as Tarheel Slim And Little Ann, a name they kept until 1962. After a spell outside the music business, Slim returned in 1970, when he recorded for Trix Records, an association that lasted until his death.

● ALBUMS: *Lock Me In Your Heart* (1989)★★★, *No Time At All* (Trix 1994)★★★.

TARVER, QUINDON

b. *c.*1982, Los Angeles, California, USA. Rising young R&B star Tarver first began performing live at the age of eight, and within five years had secured a major label recording contract with Virgin Records. Tarver, who is managed by Chris Stokes (also behind US teen phenomenons Immature, with whom Tarver has also toured), made his debut in April 1996 with 'It's You That's On My Mind', a highly stylized, commercial R&B record aimed squarely

at adolescent audiences. It was followed later in the year by Tarver's debut album, which appealed across the American teen market but was harshly treated by critics.
● ALBUMS: *Quindon* (Virgin 1996)★★.

TATE, HOWARD

b. 1943, Macon, Georgia, USA. A former member of the Gainors with Garnet Mimms, Tate also sang with Bill Doggett's band. A solo act by 1962, he (like Mimms) was guided by producer/songwriter Jerry Ragovoy. Between 1966 and 1968, Tate secured four US R&B hits including 'Ain't Nobody Home', 'Look At Granny Run, Run' (later covered by Ry Cooder) and 'Stop' (later covered by Mike Bloomfield and Al Kooper). Tate's work provided material for several acts, most notably Janis Joplin, who recorded 'Get It While You Can'. After releasing two singles on the Turntable label, 'There Are The Things That Make Me Know You're Gone' (1969) and 'My Soul's Got A Hole In It' (1970), Tate moved to Atlantic Records where he enjoyed the production assistance of former mentor Ragovoy. From there he moved on to various other labels, but sadly, with little success. Tate possessed a fabulous voice of great tone and range, and it remained a mystery why he was not more successful or prolific. He was in the class of Sam Cooke, Marvin Gaye and Johnnie Taylor, and his reissued material should be heard.
● ALBUMS: *Get It While You Can* (Verve 1967)★★★★, *Howard Tate* (Verve 1969)★★★★.
● COMPILATIONS: *Get It While You Can: The Legendary Sessions* (Mercury 1995)★★★★.

TAVARES

This US group was formed in 1964 in New Bedford, Massachusetts, USA. The line-up consisted of five brothers, Ralph, Antone 'Chubby', Feliciano 'Butch', Arthur 'Pooch' and Perry Lee 'Tiny' Tavares. Originally known as Chubby And The Turnpikes, the group assumed the family surname in 1969. Although they lacked a distinctive lead voice or a characteristic sound, the Tavares' undemanding blend of light soul and pop resulted in several commercial successes. The brothers' early run of R&B hits culminated in 1975 with 'It Only Takes A Minute', a soul chart-topper and a US pop Top 10 entry. The following year the group enjoyed their sole million-seller with 'Heaven Must Be Missing An Angel', before enjoying further success with one of their strongest songs, 'Don't Take Away The Music'. Both of these singles reached number 4 in the UK, where the Tavares enjoyed an enduring popularity. 'Whodunit' (1977) was another major release, while 'More Than A Woman' (1978), a song from that year's box-office smash, *Saturday Night Fever*, gave the group their last significant hit. Tavares continued to reach the R&B lists until 1984 (although 'Heaven Must Be Missing An Angel' and 'It Only Takes A Minute' were hits when reissued in the UK in 1986), but their safe, almost old-fashioned, style gradually fell from favour.
● ALBUMS: *Check It Out* (Capitol 1974)★★★★, *Hard Core Poetry* (Capitol 1974)★★★, *In The City* (Capitol 1975)★★★, *Sky High!* (Capitol 1976)★★★, *Love Storm* (Capitol 1977)★★★★, *Future Bound* (Capitol 1978)★★★, *Madam Butterfly* (Capitol 1979)★★★, *Supercharged* (Capitol 1980)★★★, *New Directions* (RCA 1982)★★★.
● COMPILATIONS: *The Best Of The Tavares* (Capitol 1977)★★★★.

TAYLOR, BOBBY, AND THE VANCOUVERS

Bobby Taylor (lead vocals), Tommy Chong (guitar), Wes Henderson (guitar), Robbie King (keyboards), Ted Lewis (drums) and Eddie Patterson (bass) joined forces in Vancouver, Canada, in the mid-60s. They were signed to Motown Records in 1967, supporting Gladys Knight And The Pips on a US tour. The following year, they issued their debut single, 'Does Your Mama Know About Me', an emotive ballad with a lyric that capitalized on the band's interracial line-up. The single reached the US Top 30, and was succeeded by two smaller hits, 'I Am Your Man' and 'Melinda'. After issuing a self-titled debut album, the Vancouvers split, and Tommy Chong formed the comedy double act Cheech And Chong, who achieved great popularity in the early 70s with their drug-related humour. Taylor remained with Motown as a soloist, and was responsible for alerting the company to the talents of the Jackson Five, although Diana Ross was publicly credited with the signing. He left Motown in the early 70s and recorded spasmodically for several more years, registering one minor hit in 1975 with 'Why Play Games'. In 1988 Taylor signed to Ian Levine's Motor City label and was instrumental in re-establishing contact with dozens of ex-Motown acts, many of whom are now recording again.
● ALBUMS: *Bobby Taylor And The Vancouvers* (Gordy 1968)★★★.
Solo: Bobby Taylor *Taylor Made Soul* (Gordy 1969)★★, *Find My Way Back* (Motor City 1990)★★★.

TAYLOR, FELICE

b. 29 January 1948, Richmond, California, USA. Taylor emerged from the burgeoning Los Angeles girl-group scene where she recorded with the Sweets, a trio that also featured her sisters Darlene and Norma. Signed as a solo act to the Mustang label, Taylor's three 1967 singles were each produced and co-written by Barry White. 'It May Be Winter Outside (But In My Heart It's Spring)' was an R&B hit, although the beatier 'I'm Under The Influence Of Love' unaccountably failed to chart. White later re-recorded both songs with Love Unlimited. Taylor, meanwhile, enjoyed a substantial UK hit with her third release, 'I Feel Love Comin' On'. She then moved labels to Kent, but stripped of White's imaginative arrangements, her adenoidal delivery tended to grate. Her best latter-day offering was 'All I Want To Do Is Love You'. Recorded in Britain, it was written by Derv Gordon and arranged by Eddy Grant, two former members of the Equals.

TAYLOR, 'LITTLE' JOHNNY

b. Johnny Young, 11 February 1943, Memphis, Tennessee, USA. After relocating to Los Angeles, this expressive singer joined a respected gospel group, the Mighty Clouds Of Joy, where he struck up friendships with Ted Taylor and Clay Hammond. The latter composed 'Part Time Love', an emotional blues-ballad that gave Johnny

Young, now called Little Johnny Taylor, a number 1 US R&B and national Top 20 single in 1963. The song has since become a soul standard. Despite further excellent releases, each of which were in a similar mould, it was not until 1971 that Taylor regained some of his erstwhile standing with 'Everybody Knows About My Good Thing'. Several later singles were minor hits, but Taylor did not find it easy to live up to that early success, although he nevertheless continued to perform and occasionally record.

● ALBUMS: *Part Time Love* (Galaxy 1962)★★★, *Little Johnny Taylor* (Galaxy 1963)★★★, *Everybody Knows About My Good Thing* (Ronn 1970)★★★, *Open House At My House* (Ronn 1973)★★★, with Ted Taylor *The Super Taylors* (1974)★★★, *L.J.T.* (1974)★★, *Stuck In The Mud* (Ichiban 1988)★★★, *Ugly Man* (Ichiban 1989)★★★.

● COMPILATIONS: *I Should'a Been A Preacher* (Red Lightnin' 1981)★★★, *Part-Time Love* (Charly 1981)★★★, *The Galaxy Years* (Ace 1991)★★★★.

TAYLOR, JOHNNIE

b. 5 May 1938, Crawfordsville, Arkansas, USA. Having left home at the age of 15, Taylor surfaced as a member of several gospel groups, including the Five Echoes and the Highway QCs. From there he joined the Soul Stirrers, replacing Sam Cooke on the latter's recommendation. Taylor switched to secular music in 1961; releases on Cooke's Sar and Derby labels betrayed his mentor's obvious influence. In 1965 he signed with Stax Records and had several R&B hits before 'Who's Making Love' (1968) crossed over into *Billboard*'s pop Top 5. Further releases, including 'Take Care Of Your Homework' (1969), 'I Believe In You (You Believe In Me)' and 'Cheaper To Keep Her' (both 1973), continued this success. *Wanted: One Soul Singer*, *Who's Making Love* and *Taylored In Silk* best illustrate his lengthy period at Stax. Taylor maintained his momentum on a move to Columbia. The felicitous 'Disco Lady' (1976) was the first single to be certified platinum by the RIAA, but although subsequent releases reached the R&B chart, they fared less well with the wider audience. Following a short spell with Beverley Glenn, the singer found an ideal niche on Malaco Records, a bastion for traditional southern soul. Taylor's first album there, *This Is Your Night*, reaffirmed his gritty, blues-edged approach, a feature consolidated on *Wall To Wall*, *Lover Boy* and *Crazy 'Bout You*. Taylor had one of the great voices of the era - expressive, graceful and smooth - and yet it is a mystery why he failed to reach the heights of the likes of Otis Redding, Marvin Gaye and Wilson Pickett. *Somebody's Gettin' It* compiles several Columbia recordings while Taylor's early work on Sar can be found on *The Roots Of Johnnie Taylor*. In 1996 Taylor experienced something of a revival when his Malaco album *Good Love* became a huge hit and reached the top of the *Billboard* blues chart.

● ALBUMS: *Wanted One Soul Singer* (Stax 1967)★★★★, *Who's Making Love?* (Stax 1968)★★★★, *Raw Blues* (Stax 1969)★★★★, *Looking For Johnny Taylor* (Stax 1969)★★★★, *The Johnnie Taylor Philosophy Continues* (Stax 1969)★★★, *Rare Stamps* (Stax 1970)★★★, *One Step Beyond* (Stax 1971)★★★, *Taylored In Silk* (Stax 1973)★★★, *Super Taylor* (Stax 1974)★★★, *Eargasm* (Columbia 1976)★★★, *Rated Extraordinaire* (Columbia 1977)★★, *Disco 9000* (Columbia 1977)★★, *Ever Ready* (Columbia 1978)★★, *Reflections* (RCA 1979)★★, *She's Killing Me* (1979)★★, *A New Day* (1980)★★, *Just Ain't Good Enough* (1982)★★, *Best Of The Old And The New* (Beverly Glenn 1984)★★★, *This Is Your Night* (Malaco 1984)★★★, *Wall To Wall* (Malaco 1985)★★★, *Lover Boy* (Malaco 1987)★★★, *In Control* (Malaco 1988)★★, *Crazy 'Bout You* (Malaco 1989)★★★, *Little Bluebird* (Stax 1990)★★★, *I Know It's Wrong, But I . . . Just Can't Do Right* (Malaco 1991)★★★, *Real Love* (Malaco 1993)★★★, *Good Love!* (Malaco 1996)★★★★.

● COMPILATIONS: *The Roots Of Johnnie Taylor* (Sar 1969)★★★, *Johnnie Taylor's Greatest Hits* (Stax 1970)★★★, *The Johnnie Taylor Chronicle (1968-1972)* (Stax 1978)★★★★, *The Johnnie Taylor Chronicle (1972-1974)* (Stax 1978)★★★, *20 Greatest Hits* (London 1987)★★★, *Somebody's Gettin' It* (Charly 1989)★★★, *The Best Of ... On Malaco Vol. 1* (1994)★★★.

TAYLOR, LEWIS

The first artist ever to be signed by Island Records solely on the strength of a demo tape received through the post, English R&B singer-songwriter Taylor then spent three years working on his debut album. As sessions progressed, it was immediately obvious that Taylor was not a standard soul revisionist, claiming influences as varied as Yes, Killing Joke, Tim Buckley and Miles Davis. As he stated, 'I'm very, very interested in atmospherics. I tend to conjure up an atmosphere that harks back to some experience I might have had or some other piece of music I've heard'. His background was also varied, having once played guitar in the Edgar Broughton Band. His debut solo album was originally released in a promotional pressing of 500 copies, and distributed without a press release or photograph, ensuring swathes of interest among R&B and dance music writers. The first official release was a single, 'Lucky', which incorporated a Joe Meek sample as well as strings, piano and a guitar motif. The self-titled album it accompanied was similarly eclectic, and featured Taylor playing all the instruments.

● ALBUMS: *Lewis Taylor* (Island 1996)★★★★.

TAYLOR, R. DEAN

Toronto-born R. Dean Taylor remains the most successful white artist to emerge from the Motown Records stable. The protégé of writer/producer Brian Holland, he worked on many of the mid-60s hits produced by the Holland/Dozier/Holland partnership, and later claimed to have helped to compose several songs credited to them. He began his recording career in 1965 with 'Let's Go Somewhere', but found more success with two of his compositions for the Supremes, 'Love Child' and 'I'm Living In Shame', both of which brought a new realism into the group's work. In 1967, he recorded the classic soul number 'There's A Ghost In My House', which enjoyed cult status in Britain. A year later he released the evocative 'Gotta See Jane', which also charted in the UK that summer. His most memorable single was 'Indiana Wants Me', an effect-laden melodrama that climbed high in both the UK and US charts in 1970. Despite his popularity in Britain, where a revival of 'There's A Ghost In My House' reached the Top 3 in 1974, Taylor was unable to repeat this success with his subsequent recordings, either on his own Jane label in 1973, or with Polydor Records from 1974.

● ALBUMS: *I Think Therefore I Am* (Rare Earth 1971)★★, *Indiana Wants Me* (Tamla Motown 1971)★★, *LA Sunset* (Polydor 1975)★★.

TAYLOR, TED

b. Austin Taylor, 16 February 1934, Okmulgee, Oklahoma, USA, d. 22 October 1987. Taylor was a veteran of several spiritual groups including the Mighty Clouds Of Joy and the Santa Monica Soul Seekers. This latter group then crossed over to R&B, where they followed a dual career both as the Cadets and the Jacks. Taylor embarked on a solo path in 1957 and had success with many regional hits. His most notable early singles were 'Be Ever Wonderful', for the Duke label in 1960 and 'Stay Away From My Baby', his first R&B chart hit for OKeh from 1965. Following a short spell with Atco, the singer joined Jewel/Ronn Records. He remained there until the mid-70s, although his output never achieved the recognition it deserved. After that, Taylor recorded albums for Alarm, MCA and his own Solpugdits/SPG label. Tragically, he was killed in a road accident in October 1987.

● ALBUMS: *Be Ever Wonderful* (OKeh 1963)★★★, *Blues And Soul* (OKeh 1965)★★★, *Shades Of Blue* (Ronn 1970)★★★, *You Can Dig It* (Ronn 1970)★★★, *Taylor Made* (Ronn 1971)★★★, with Little Johnny Taylor *The Super Taylors* (1974)★★★, *Ted Taylor 1976* (Alarm 1976)★★, *Keepin' My Head Above Water* (MCA 1978)★★, *Be Ever Wonderful* (SPG 1986)★★★, *Taylor Made For You* (SPG 1987)★★★.

● COMPILATIONS: *Greatest Hits* (OKeh 1966)★★★, *Keep On Walking* (Charly 1980)★★★, *Somebody's Always Trying 1958-1966* (Mr R&B 1988)★★★, *Steal Away* (1991)★★★.

TEE, RICHARD

b. 24 November 1943, New York, USA, d. 21 July 1993, New York, USA. Tee had 12 years of classical training on the piano and went to the High School of Music and Art. When he graduated, a contact secured him work as house pianist at Motown Records, which was at that time producing a string of hits. His first recording was with Marvin Gaye. In time, Tee became a staff arranger, and, as well as playing the piano, discovered the orchestral capabilities of the Hammond organ. When he returned to New York he continued to work in the studio. He described his playing thus: 'Chords and rhythm are my meat; even my solos are mostly chords. I try to be an orchestra and I feel most comfortable playing everything I can with 10 fingers.' He played on numerous records with musicians as diverse as Roland Kirk, Carly Simon, Joe Cocker and Herbie Mann. In 1976 he played in the influential funk band Stuff along with other session musicians including Eric Gale and Steve Gadd. The band recorded several well-received albums and Tee's solo career with CBS saw him marketed alongside contemporary 'smooth' jazz artists such as Bob James and Lonnie Liston Smith. Tee was one of the small core of musicians with whom Paul Simon regularly recorded and performed over the years. In 1991 Tee also played live with Paul Simon on the Rhythm Of The Saints tour. He ascribed his popularity on sessions to a willingness to keep things simple and not to restrict the leader's efforts: 'I play a constant rhythm that doesn't really change, and I try to keep it simple so that it gives others a chance to put their two cents in.'

● ALBUMS: with Stuff *Stuff* (Warners 1977)★★★, with Stuff *Live In Japan* (Warners 1979)★★★, *Strokin'* (Columbia 1979)★★★, *Natural Ingredients* (Columbia 1980)★★★, *The Bottom Line* (King 1985)★★★, *Real Time* (One Voice 1995)★★★.

TEE, WILLIE

b. Wilson Turbinton, 6 February 1944, New Orleans, Louisiana, USA. Willie Tee, although typical of the New Orleans soul sound, is best noted as a cult figure among Beach Music aficionados in the Carolinas. Tee came from a musical family and was taught piano at an early age. His father was a jazz trombonist and his brother is the famed jazz and R&B saxophonist Earl Turbinton. Tee first recorded in 1962 with a local record, 'Always Accused', on AFO. His break came when he recorded a double-sided masterpiece, 'Teasin' You'/'Walking Up A One Way Street', for the Nola label. Atlantic Records picked up the record and made 'Teasin' You' (number 12 R&B) a national hit in 1965. Later in the year Atlantic picked up 'Thank You John'/'Dedicated To You', which, although equally outstanding, never charted. Nevertheless, Beach Music dancers in the Carolinas heard these Tee songs and made them favourites on their juke-boxes. In 1969 he joined Capitol Records but his three-year stay yielded a couple of unmemorable singles and a jazz album of instrumentals. He joined United Artists in 1976, but 'Liberty Bell' and *Anticipation* were disappointments. A series of singles on his Gatur label (co-owned with Julius Gaines) gained some New Orleans radio play during the 70s. Increasingly, Tee became more involved on the production side, and produced well-received albums by the Wild Magnolias and Carl Anderson. By 1988 Tee's own projects were more jazz-orientated and he recorded an album with his brother called *Turbinton Brothers* for Rounder.

● ALBUMS: *I'm Only A Man* (Capitol 1971)★★, *Anticipation* (United Artists 1976)★★★, *Turbinton Brothers* (Rounder 1988)★★★.

TEEN QUEENS

This R&B duo of Betty and Rosie Collins came from Los Angeles, California, USA. Their entry into the recording business and signing to RPM Records in 1955 was facilitated by their older brother, Aaron Collins of the Jacks/Cadets, who recorded for the same company. The youthful amateurishness of the singing on their one hit, 'Eddie My Love' (number 2 R&B and number 14 pop), probably helped to make the record a hit in 1956. It was one of the first records specifically to direct its appeal to teenagers. It was the era of the cover record, and both the

Fontane Sisters and the Chordettes also took the song high on the pop charts, but it is the Teen Queens' version that endures. The duo could not follow up with a hit, despite recording some excellent material over the years. Moves to RCA in 1958 and Antler in 1960 did not help and the duo broke up in 1961.

● ALBUMS: *Eddie My Love* (RPM 1956)★★★, *The Teen Queens* (1963)★★★.

● COMPILATIONS: *Rock Everybody* (Ace 1986)★★★.

TEMPTATIONS

The most successful group in black music history was formed in 1961 in Detroit, Michigan, USA, by former members of two local R&B outfits. Eddie Kendricks (b. 17 December 1939, Union Springs, Alabama, USA, d. 5 October 1992, Alabama, USA) and Paul Williams (b. 2 July 1939, Birmingham, Alabama, USA, d. 17 August 1973) both sang with the Primes; Melvin Franklin (b. David English, 12 October 1942, Montgomery, Alabama, USA, d. 23 February 1995, Los Angeles, California, USA), Eldridge Bryant and Otis Williams (b. Otis Miles, 30 October 1941, Texarkana, Texas, USA) came from the Distants. Initially known as the Elgins, the quintet were renamed the Temptations by Berry Gordy when he signed them to Motown in 1961. After issuing three singles on the Motown subsidiary Miracle Records, one of them under the pseudonym of the Pirates, the group moved to the Gordy label. 'Dream Come Home' provided their first brief taste of chart status in 1962, although it was only when they were teamed with writer/producer/performer Smokey Robinson that the Temptations achieved consistent success.

The group's classic line-up was established in 1963, when Eldridge Bryant was replaced by David Ruffin (b. 18 January 1941, Meridian, Mississippi, USA, d. 1 June 1991). His gruff baritone provided the perfect counterpoint to Kendricks' wispy tenor and falsetto, a contrast that Smokey Robinson exploited to the full. Over the next two years, he fashioned a series of hits in both ballad and dance styles, carefully arranging complex vocal harmonies that hinted at the group's doo-wop heritage. 'The Way You Do The Things You Do' was the Temptations' first major hit, a stunningly simple rhythm number featuring a typically cunning series of lyrical images. 'My Girl' in 1965, the group's first US number 1, demonstrated Robinson's graceful command of the ballad idiom, and brought Ruffin's vocals to the fore for the first time (this track, featured in the movie *My Girl*, was reissued in 1992 and was once again a hit). 'It's Growing', 'Since I Lost My Baby', 'My Baby' and 'Get Ready' continued the run of successes into 1966, establishing the Temptations as the leaders of the Motown sound. 'It's Growing' brought a fresh layer of subtlety into Robinson's lyric writing, while 'Get Ready' embodied all the excitement of the Motown rhythm factory, blending an irresistible melody with a stunning vocal arrangement. Norman Whitfield succeeded Robinson as the Temptations' producer in 1966 - a role he continued to occupy for almost a decade. He introduced a new rawness into their sound, spotlighting David Ruffin as the impassioned lead vocalist, and creating a series of R&B records that rivalled the output of Stax and Atlantic for toughness and power. 'Ain't Too Proud To Beg' introduced the Whitfield approach, and while the Top 3 hit 'Beauty Is Only Skin Deep' represented a throwback to the Robinson era, 'I'm Losing You' and 'You're My Everything' confirmed the new direction. The peak of Whitfield's initial phase with the group was 'I Wish It Would Rain', a dramatic ballad that the producer heightened with the delicate use of sound effects. The record was another major hit, and gave the Temptations their sixth R&B number 1 in three years. It also marked the end of an era, when David Ruffin first requested individual credit before the group's name; when this was refused, he elected to leave for a solo career. He was replaced by ex-Contour Dennis Edwards, whose strident vocals fitted perfectly into the Temptations' harmonic blend. Whitfield chose this moment to inaugurate a new production style. Conscious of the psychedelic shift in the rock mainstream, and the inventive soul music being created by Sly And The Family Stone, he joined forces with lyricist Barrett Strong to pull Motown brutally into the modern age. The result was 'Cloud Nine', a record that reflected the increasing use of illegal drugs among young people, and shocked some listeners with its lyrical ambiguity. Whitfield created the music to match, breaking down the traditional barriers between lead and backing singers and giving each of the Temptations a recognizable role in the group. Over the next four years, Whitfield and the Temptations pioneered the concept of psychedelic soul, stretching the Motown formula to the limit, introducing a new vein of social and political comment, and utilizing many of rock's experimental production techniques to hammer home the message. 'Runaway Child, Running Wild' examined the problems of teenage rebellion; 'I Can't Get Next To You' reflected the fragmentation of personal relationships (and topped the US charts with the group's second number 1 hit); and 'Ball Of Confusion' bemoaned the disintegrating fabric of American society. These lyrical tracts were set to harsh, uncompromising rhythm tracks, seeped in wah-wah guitar and soaked in layers of harmony and counterpoint. The Temptations were greeted as representatives of the counter-culture, a trend that climaxed when they recorded Whitfield's outspoken protest against the Vietnam War, 'Stop The War Now'. The new direction alarmed Eddie Kendricks, who felt more at home on the series of collaborations with the Supremes that the group also recorded in the late 60s. He left for a solo career in 1971, after recording another US number 1, the evocative ballad 'Just My Imagination'. He was replaced first by Richard Owens, then later in 1971 by Damon Harris. This line-up recorded the 1972 number 1 'Papa Was A Rolling Stone', a production *tour de force* that remains one of Motown's finest achievements, belatedly winning the label its first Grammy award. After that, everything came to an anti-climax. Paul Williams left the group in 1971, to be replaced by another former Distant member, Richard Street; Williams shot himself in 1973, after years of depression and drug abuse. Whitfield's partnership with Strong was broken the same year, and although he continued to rework the 'Papa Was A Rolling Stone' formula, the commercial and artistic returns were smaller. The

Temptations still had hits, and 'Masterpiece', 'Let Your Hair Down' (both 1973) and 'Happy People' (1975) all topped the soul charts, but they were no longer a leading force in black music.
Whitfield left Motown in 1975; at the same time, Glenn Leonard replaced Damon Harris in the group. After struggling on for another year, the Temptations moved to Atlantic Records for two albums, which saw Louis Price taking the place of Dennis Edwards. When the Atlantic partnership brought no change of fortunes, the group returned to Motown, and to Dennis Edwards. *Power* in 1980 restored them to the charts, before Rick James engineered a brief reunion with David Ruffin and Eddie Kendricks for a tour, an album, and a hit single, 'Standing On The Top'. Ruffin and Kendricks then left to form a duo, Ron Tyson replaced Glenn Leonard, and Ali-Ollie Woodson took over the role of lead vocalist from Edwards. Woodson brought with him a song called 'Treat Her Like A Lady', which became their biggest UK hit in a decade. Subsequent releases confirmed the quality of the new line-up, although without a strong guiding hand they are unlikely to rival the achievements of the late 60s and early 70s line-ups, who represented the culmination of Motown's classic era. Franklin's death in February 1995 left Otis Williams as the sole remaining founder-member.
● ALBUMS: *Meet The Temptations* (Gordy 1964)★★★★, *The Temptations Sing Smokey* (Gordy 1965)★★★★, *The Temptin' Temptations* (Gordy 1965)★★★★, *Gettin' Ready* (Gordy 1966)★★★★, *Temptations Live!* (Gordy 1967)★★, *With A Lot O' Soul* (Gordy 1967)★★★, *The Temptations In A Mellow Mood* (Gordy 1967)★★★, *Wish It Would Rain* (Gordy 1968)★★★★, with Diana Ross And The Supremes *Diana Ross And The Supremes Join The Temptations* (Motown 1968)★★★, with Diana Ross And The Supremes *TCB* (Motown 1968)★★★, *Live At The Copa* (Gordy 1968)★★, *Cloud Nine* (Gordy 1969)★★★★, *The Temptations' Show* (Gordy 1969)★★★, *Puzzle People* (Gordy 1969)★★★, with Diana Ross And The Supremes *Together* (Motown 1969)★★★, with Diana Ross And The Supremes *On Broadway* (Motown 1969)★★, *Psychedelic Shack* (Gordy 1970)★★★★, *Live At London's Talk Of The Town* (Gordy 1970)★★★, *The Temptations Christmas Card* (Gordy 1970)★, *Sky's The Limit* (Gordy 1971)★★★, *Solid Rock* (Gordy 1972)★★★, *All Directions* (Gordy 1972)★★★, *Masterpiece* (Gordy 1973)★★★, *1990* (Gordy 1973)★★★, *A Song For You* (Gordy 1975)★★★, *House Party* (Gordy 1975)★★, *Wings Of Love* (Gordy 1976)★★, *The Temptations Do The Temptations* (Gordy 1976)★★, *Hear To Tempt You* (Atlantic 1977)★★, *Bare Back* (Atlantic 1978)★★, *Power* (Gordy 1980)★★, *Give Love At Christmas* (Gordy 1980)★, *The Temptations* (Gordy 1981)★★, with Jimmy Ruffin and Eddie Kendricks *Reunion* (Gordy 1982)★★★, *Surface Thrills* (Gordy 1983)★★, *Back To Basics* (Gordy 1984)★★★, *Truly For You* (Gordy 1984)★★, *Touch Me* (Gordy 1985)★★, *To Be Continued ...* (Gordy 1986)★★★, *Together Again* (Motown 1987)★★★, *Special* (Motown 1989)★★, *Milestone* (Motown 1991)★★.
● COMPILATIONS: *The Temptations Greatest Hits* (Gordy 1966)★★★★, *Temptations Greatest Hits, Volume 2* (Gordy 1970)★★★★, *Anthology* (Motown 1973)★★★★★, *All The Million Sellers* (Gordy 1981)★★★, *Best Of The Temptations* (Telstar 1986)★★, *25 Anniversary* (Motown 1986)★★★★, *Compact Command Performances* (Motown 1989)★★★, *Hum Along And Dance: More Of The Best 1963-1974* (Rhino 1993)★★★, *The Original Lead Singers Of The Temptations* (1993)★★★, *Emperors Of Soul* 5-CD box set (Motown 1994)★★★★, *Early Classics* (Spectrum 1996)★★★.
● VIDEOS: *Get Ready* (PMI 1988), *Temptations And The Four Tops* (Video Collection 1988), *Live In Concert* (Old Gold 1990).
● FURTHER READING: *Temptations*, Otis Williams with Patricia Romanowski.

TERRELL, TAMMI

b. Thomasina Montgomery, 29 April 1945, Philadelphia, Pennsylvania, USA, d. 16 March 1970. Tammi Terrell began recording for Scepter/Wand Records at the age of 15, before touring with the James Brown Revue for a year. In 1965, she married heavyweight boxer Ernie Terrell, the brother of future Supreme Jean Terrell. Tammi's warm, sensuous vocals won her a contract with Motown later that year, and in 1966 she enjoyed a series of R&B hits, among them a soulful rendition of 'This Old Heart Of Mine'. In 1967, she was selected to replace Kim Weston as Marvin Gaye's recording partner. This inspired teaming produced Gaye's most successful duets, and the pair issued a stream of hit singles between 1967 and 1969. 'Ain't No Mountain High Enough' and 'You're All I Need To Get By' epitomized their style, as Gaye and Terrell weaved around each other's voices, creating an aura of romance and eroticism that led to persistent rumours that they were lovers. From the beginning, their partnership was tinged with sadness, Terrell collapsing in Gaye's arms during a performance in 1967. She was diagnosed as suffering from a brain tumour, and despite a series of major operations over the next three years, her health steadily weakened. By 1969, she was unable to perform in public, and on several of the duo's final recordings, their producer, Valerie Simpson, controversially claims to have taken her place. Ironically, one of these tracks, 'The Onion Song', proved to be the most successful of the Gaye/Terrell singles in the UK. Tammi Terrell died on 16 March 1970, her burial service attracting thousands of mourners, including many of her Motown colleagues. Her death has been the subject of much speculation, centred on rumours that her brain disorders were triggered by alleged beatings administered by a member of the Motown hierarchy. These accusations were given voice in *Number One With A Bullet*, a novel by former Gaye aide Elaine Jesmer, which included a character clearly based on Terrell.
● ALBUMS: with Marvin Gaye *United* (Tamla 1967)★★★, with Gaye *You're All I Need* (Tamla 1968)★★★, with Gaye *Easy* (Tamla 1969)★★★, *Early Show* (1969)★★★, *Irresistible Tammy* (Motown 1969)★★★.
● COMPILATIONS: with Marvin Gaye *Marvin Gaye & Tammi Terrell: Greatest Hits* (Tamla 1970)★★★.

TERRY AND MONICA

Terry and Monica are former members of the vocal trio Gyrlz, who many argue were the first 'New Jill Swing' group. Managed by former Gyrlz member Tara, Terry and Monica relaunched their flagging career by signing to Epic Records and releasing the Kev Boogie-produced debut single, 'Oh Huh'. They also gained attention for 'I've Been Waiting', their contribution to the soundtrack of the John Singleton feature film *Poetic Justice*, starring Janet Jackson and 2Pac. Their 1994 debut was a palatable, energetic selection that crossed hip-hop with R&B and offered many pro-feminist messages: 'Since we represent females, we want to encourage them to help build their self-worth', they told the US press.

● ALBUMS: *Systas* (Epic 1994)★★★.

TEX, JOE

b. Joseph Arrington Jnr., 8 August 1933, Rogers, Texas, USA, d. 13 August 1982. The professional career of this popular singer began onstage at the Apollo. He won first place in a 1954 talent contest and duly secured a record contract. Releases on King, Ace and the Anna labels were derivative and disappointing, but Tex, meanwhile, honed his songwriting talent. James Brown's version of 'Baby You're Right' (1962) became a US R&B number 2, after which Tex was signed by Buddy Killen, a Nashville song publisher, who in turn established Dial as a recording outlet. Although early releases showed promise, it was not until 1965 that Tex prospered. Recorded at Fame and distributed by Atlantic, 'Hold On To What You've Got' was a US Top 5 hit. The first of several preaching singles, its homely values were maintained on 'A Woman Can Change A Man' and 'The Love You Save (May Be Your Own)'. However, Joe was equally comfortable on uptempo songs, as 'S.Y.S.L.J.F.M. (The Letter Song)' (1966) and 'Show Me' (1967) proved. Later releases were less successful and although 'Skinny Legs And All' and 'Men Are Gettin' Scarce' showed him still capable of major hits, the singer seemed unsure of his direction. A fallow period ended with 'I Gotcha' (1972), an irresistibly cheeky song, but Tex chose this moment to retire. A convert to the Muslim faith since 1966, he changed his name to Yusuf Hazziez, and toured as a spiritual lecturer. He returned to music in 1975. Two years later he enjoyed a 'comeback' hit with the irrepressible 'Ain't Gonna Bump No More (With No Big Fat Woman)'. By the 80s, however, Joe had withdrawn again from full-time performing. He devoted himself to Islam, his Texas ranch and the Houston Oilers football team. He was tempted into a Soul Clan reunion in 1981, but in August 1982 he died following a heart attack.

● ALBUMS: *Hold On* (Checker 1964)★★★, *Hold What You've Got* (Atlantic 1965)★★★, *The New Boss* (Atlantic 1965)★★★★, *The Love You Save* (Atlantic 1966)★★★, *I've Got To Do A Little Better* (Atlantic 1966)★★★★, *Live And Lively* (Atlantic 1968)★★, *Soul Country* (Atlantic 1968)★★★, *Happy Soul* (1969)★★★, *You Better Believe It* (Atlantic 1969)★★★, *Buying A Book* (Atlantic 1969)★★★, *With Strings And Things* (1970)★★★, *From The Roots Came The Rapper* (1972)★★, *I Gotcha* (Dial 1972)★★, *Joe Tex Spills The Beans* (1973)★★, *Another Man's Woman* (Powerpak 1974)★★, *Bumps And Bruises* (Epic 1977)★★, *Rub Down* (Epic 1978)★★, *He Who Is Without Funk Cast The First Stone* (Epic 1979)★★.

● COMPILATIONS: *The Best Of Joe Tex* (King 1965)★★★, *The Very Best Of Joe Tex* (Atlantic 1967)★★★★, *Greatest Hits* (Atlantic 1967)★★★★, *The Very Best Of Joe Tex - Real Country Soul ... Scarce As Hen's Teeth* (Charly 1988)★★★, *I Believe I'm Gonna Make It: The Best Of Joe Tex 1964-1972* (Rhino 1988)★★★★, *Different Strokes* (Charly 1989)★★★, *Stone Soul Country* (Charly 1989)★★★, *Ain't Gonna Bump No More* (1993)★★★, *I Gotcha (His Greatest Hits)* (1993)★★★, *Skinny Legs And All: The Classic Early Dial Sides* (Kent 1994)★★★, *You're Right Joe Tex!* (Kent 1995)★★★.

THOMAS, CARLA

b. 21 December 1942, Memphis, Tennessee, USA. The daughter of Rufus Thomas, Carla first performed with the Teen Town Singers. ''Cause I Love You', a duet with her father, was released on Satellite (later Stax) in 1960, but the following year she established herself as a solo act with 'Gee Whiz (Look At His Eyes)'. Leased to Atlantic, the song became a US Top 10 hit. 'I'll Bring It On Home To You' (1962 - an answer to Sam Cooke), 'What A Fool I've Been' (1963) and 'Let Me Be Good To You' (1965) then followed. 'B-A-B-Y', written by Isaac Hayes and David Porter, reached the US R&B Top 3, before a series of duets with Otis Redding proclaimed her 'Queen of Soul'. An excellent version of Lowell Fulson's 'Tramp' introduced the partnership. 'Knock On Wood' and 'Lovey Dovey' followed before Redding's premature death. Thomas's own career was eclipsed as Aretha Franklin assumed her regal mantle. Singles with William Bell and Johnnie Taylor failed to recapture past glories, although the singer stayed with Stax until its bankruptcy in 1975. Since that time, Thomas has not recorded, although she does tour occasionally with the Stax revival shows, and she appeared, along with her father, at the Porretta Terme Soul Festival in 1991.

● ALBUMS: *Gee Whiz* (Atlantic 1961)★★★, *Comfort Me* (Stax 1966)★★★★, *Carla* (Stax 1966)★★★★, with Otis Redding *King And Queen* (Stax 1967)★★★★, *The Queen Alone* (Stax 1967)★★★★, *Memphis Queen* (Stax 1969)★★★, *Love Means Carla Thomas* (Stax 1971)★★.

● COMPILATIONS: *The Best Of Carla Thomas* (Atlantic 1969)★★★★, *Hidden Gems* (Stax 1991)★★★, with Rufus Thomas *The Best Of - The Singles Plus! 1968-73* (Ace/Stax 1993)★★★★, *Sugar* (1994)★★★, *Gee Whiz: The Best Of Carla Thomas* (Rhino 1994)★★★★.

THOMAS, IRMA

b. Irma Lee, 18 February 1941, Ponchatoula, Louisiana, USA. The 'Soul Queen Of New Orleans' was discovered in 1958 by bandleader Tommy Ridgley. Her early records were popular locally, but an R&B hit came in 1960 with '(You Can Have My Husband But Please) Don't Mess With My Man'. The following year Thomas rejoined producer/writer Allen Toussaint, with whom she had worked on her first recordings. This reunion resulted in two of Thomas's finest singles, 'It's Raining' and 'Ruler Of

My Heart' (1962), the latter a prototype for Otis Redding's 'Pain In My Heart'. After signing with the Imperial label in 1963 she recorded 'Wish Someone Would Care' (1964), which reached the US Top 20, while the follow-up, 'Anyone Who Knows What Love Is (Will Understand)', also entered the national chart. This single is better recalled for its b-side, 'Time Is On My Side', which was successfully covered by the Rolling Stones. Thomas continued to record excellent singles without achieving due commercial success. Her final hit was a magnificent interpretation of 'Good To Me' (1968), recorded at Muscle Shoals and issued on Chess. She then moved to Canyon, Roker and Cotillion, before appearing on Swamp Dogg's short-lived Fungus label with *In Between Tears* (1973). Thomas has continued to record fine albums for Rounder Records and remains a highly popular live attraction in the 90s.

● ALBUMS: *Wish Someone Would Care* (Imperial 1964)★★★★, *Take A Look* (Imperial 1968)★★★★, *In Between Tears* (Fungus 1973)★★★, *Irma Thomas Live* (Island 1977)★★, *The Soul Queen Of New Orleans* (Maison De Soul 1978)★★★, *Safe With Me* (1979)★★★, *Hip Shakin' Mama* (Charly 1981)★★, *The New Rules* (Rounder 1986)★★, *The Way I Feel* (Rounder 1988)★★★, *'Live: Simply The Best'* (Rounder 1991)★★★★, *True Believer* (Rounder 1992)★★★, *Walk Around Heaven: New Orleans Gospel Soul* (Rounder 1994)★★, *The Story Of My Life* (Rounder 1997)★★.

● COMPILATIONS: *Irma Thomas Sings* (Bandy 1979)★★★, *Time Is On My Side* (Kent 1983)★★★★, *Down At Muscle Shoals* i (1984)★★★, *The Best Of Irma Thomas: Breakaway* (EMI America 1986)★★★, *Ruler Of Hearts* (Charly 1989)★★★, *Something Good: The Muscle Shoals Sessions* (Chess 1990)★★★, *Down At Muscle Schoals* ii (Charly 1991)★★★, *Safe With Me/Irma Thomas Live* (1991)★★, *Time Is On My Side: The Best Of Vol. 1* (Capitol 1992)★★★★, *The Soul Queen Of New Orleans* (1993)★★★, *Time Is On My Side* (Kent 1997)★★★★,*The Irma Thomas Collection* (Razor & Tie 1997)★★★★.

THOMAS, KENNY

b. *c.*1969, London, England. In the 90s Thomas established himself as one of the UK's most popular soul dance vocalists. His biggest UK hit came in 1991 with 'Thinking About Your Love' (number 4), while his debut album sold more than 600,000 copies in the UK alone. Other hit singles spawned by that debut included 'Outstanding', 'The Best Of You' and 'Tender Love', and also resulted in a Brit Award nomination for Best British Male Vocalist and Best British Newcomer. The warm, relaxed dance grooves of that debut were replicated on a second album that continued Thomas's massive commercial success. Guest musicians on this occasion included the Young Disciples, Nu Colours and the Reggae Philharmonic Orchestra. This time, the bonhomie of the original set was more restrained, with a slightly more mature lyrical vision reflecting more convincing life experiences.

● ALBUMS: *Voices* (Cooltempo 1991)★★★, *Wait For Me* (Cooltempo 1993)★★★.

THOMAS, RUFUS

b. 26 March 1917, Cayce, Mississippi, USA. A singer, dancer and entertainer, Thomas learned his trade as a member of the Rabbit's Foot Minstrels, a vaudeville-inspired touring group. By the late 40s he was performing in several Memphis nightclubs and organizing local talent shows. B.B. King, Bobby Bland and Little Junior Parker were discovered in this way. When King's career subsequently blossomed, Thomas replaced him as a disc jockey at WDIA and remained there until 1974. He also began recording and several releases appeared on Star Talent, Chess and Meteor before 'Bear Cat' became a Top 3 US R&B hit. An answer to Willie Mae Thornton's 'Hound Dog', it was released on Sun in 1953. Rufus remained a local celebrity until 1960 when he recorded with his daughter, Carla Thomas. Their duet, ''Cause I Love You', was issued on the fledgling Satellite (later Stax) label where it became a regional hit. Thomas strengthened his reputation with a series of infectious singles; 'Walking The Dog' (1963) was a US Top 10 entry, while several of his other recordings, notably 'Jump Back' and 'All Night Worker' (both in 1964), were beloved by aspiring British groups. His later success with novelty numbers – 'Do The Funky Chicken' (1970), '(Do The) Push And Pull, Part 1' (1970) and 'Do The Funky Penguin' (1971) – has obscured the merits of less brazen recordings. 'Sophisticated Sissy' (1967) and 'Memphis Train' (1968) are prime 60s R&B. Thomas stayed with Stax until its 1975 collapse, from where he moved to AVI. His releases there included *If There Were No Music* and *I Ain't Getting Older, I'm Gettin' Better*. In 1980 Thomas re-recorded several of his older songs for a self-titled collection on Gusto. In the 80s he abandoned R&B and recorded some rap with *Rappin' Rufus*, on the Ichiban label, and tackled blues with *That Woman Is Poison*, on the Alligator label. Bob Fisher's Sequel Records released a new album from Thomas in 1996. *Blues Thang* proved to be an unexpected treat from a man celebrating his 79th birthday at the time of release. He continues to perform regularly.

● ALBUMS: *Walking The Dog* (Stax 1963)★★★★, *Do The Funky Chicken* (Stax 1970)★★★★, *Doing The Push And Pull Live At PJs* (Stax 1971)★★★, *Did You Heard Me?* (Stax 1972)★★★, *Crown Prince Of Dance* (Stax 1973)★★★, *Blues In The Basement* (Artists Of America 1975)★★★, *If There Were No Music* (AVI 1977)★★★, *I Ain't Gettin' Older, I'm Gettin' Better* (AVI 1977)★★★, *Rufus Thomas* (Gusto 1980)★★, *Rappin' Rufus* (Ichiban 1986)★★, *That Woman Is Poison* (Alligator 1989)★★, *Timeless Funk* (Prestige 1992)★★, *Blues Thang* (Sequel 1996)★★★.

● COMPILATIONS: *Jump Back - A 1963-67 Retrospective* (Edsel 1984)★★★, *Can't Get Away From This Dog* (Ace/Stax 1991)★★★, *The Best Of Rufus Thomas - The Singles 1968 - 1975* (Ace/Stax 1993)★★★★.

THOMAS, TIMMY

b. 13 November 1944, Evansville, Indiana, USA. An accomplished singer, songwriter and keyboard player, Thomas first attracted attention for his work as an accompanist with jazz musicians Donald Byrd and Cannonball

Adderley. He then embarked on a spell as a session musician, most notably with the Memphis-based Goldwax label, before his solo career blossomed in 1972 with 'Why Can't We Live Together?' (US number 3/UK Top 20). His simple, Booker T. Jones-like organ style came to the fore as a hypnotic pulse punctuated an understated, but heartfelt, plea. This rhythmic song was later tastefully covered by the sophisticated British vocalist, Sade in 1984. Thomas's immediate releases continued in this vein, but he was unable to repeat that initial success. He nonetheless enjoyed a run of minor R&B hits culminating in 'Gotta Give A Little Love (Ten Years After)', a US Top 30 soul entry in 1984.

● ALBUMS: *Why Can't We Live Together* (Polydor 1972)★★★, *You're The Song I Always Wanted To Sing* (Glades 1975)★★, *The Magician* (Glades 1977)★★, *Touch To Touch* (Glades 1978)★★, *Live* (Glades 1980)★★.

Thompson, Gina

b. *c.*1974, Vineland, New Jersey, USA. A competent but somewhat uninspiring mid-90s addition to the long list of Mercury Records R&B divas, Gina Thompson made her debut with *Nobody Does It Better*. The first single to be taken from it, 'The Things That You Do', was remixed by Sean 'Puffy' Combs, and featured *de rigeur* hip-hop beats alongside rap stanzas. A 15-song collection, it was produced in New York by Rodney Jerkins, with Thompson co-writing 'several' of the tracks. Typically, Thompson first came to singing through the church, and she is still managed by the Rev. Fred Jerkins. In an attempt to distinguish Thompson in a market saturated with female R&B singers, Mercury sought to emphasize the singer's 'funkier fashion image' by placing her in fashion shoots for teen magazines - which did little to disguise the lack of originality evident in her records.

● ALBUMS: *Nobody Does It Better* (Mercury 1996)★★.

Thompson, Sonny

b. Alphonso Thompson, 22 August 1916, Centreville, Mississippi, USA, d. 11 August 1989. This long-time Chicago-based R&B bandleader and pianist first recorded boogie-woogies in 1946 for the Detroit-based Sultan label. After signing for the Miracle label in Chicago, he succeeded with 'Long Gone', which went to number 1 on the R&B chart in 1948. The gently rolling instrumental set the tone for his later hits, 'Late Freight' (R&B number 1, 1948), 'Blue Dreams' (R&B number 10, 1949) and 'Mellow Blues' (R&B number 8, 1952). His later chart records featured the vocals of his wife, Lulu Reed, notably 'I'll Drown In My Tears' and 'Let's Call It A Day', both from 1952. Thompson worked largely as a session musician during the 50s, and in 1959 succeeded Ralph Bass as an A&R director for King Records' Chicago office. After the closure of the King office in 1964, Thompson continued session work and made occasional tours of Europe.

● ALBUMS: *Moody Blues* (King 1956)★★★, *Mellow Blues For The Late Hours* (King 1959)★★★, with Freddy King, Lulu Reed *Boy, Girl, Boy* (King 1962)★★★, *Swings In Paris* (Black & Blue 1974)★★.

● COMPILATIONS: *Cat On The Keys* (Swingtime 1988)★★★, *Jam Sonny Jam* (Sequel 1996)★★★★.

Three Degrees

Protégées of producer/songwriter Richard Barrett, Fayette Pinkney, Linda Turner and Shirley Porter gained a US hit with their first single, 'Gee Baby (I'm Sorry)', in 1965. This Philadelphia-based trio, sponsored by Kenny Gamble and Leon Huff, secured further pop success the next year with 'Look In My Eyes', but struggled to sustain this momentum until 1970, when their emphatic reworking of the Chantels' standard, 'Maybe', returned them to the chart. By this point, Sheila Ferguson and Valerie Holiday had joined the line-up in place of Turner and Porter. The Three Degrees' golden period came on signing with Philadelphia International. They shared vocals with MFSB on 'TSOP', the theme song to television's successful *Soul Train* show. This US pop and R&B number 1 preceded the trio's international hits, 'Year Of Decision' and 'When Will I See You Again?' (both 1974). These glossy performances were particularly popular in the UK, where the group continued to chart, notably with the Top 10 hits 'Take Good Care Of Yourself' (1975), 'Woman In Love' and 'My Simple Heart' (both 1979). Helen Scott appeared on the 1976 album *Standing Up For Love*. Now signed to Ariola Records, the Three Degrees' releases grew increasingly bland as they emphasized the cabaret element suppressed in their early work. Fêted by royalty - Prince Charles stated they were his favourite group after booking them for his 30th birthday party - the 80s saw the group resident in the UK where they were a fixture on the variety and supper-club circuit. Ferguson entered the 90s as a solo artist (she was replaced by Victoria Wallace), heralded by the release of a remix of 'When Will I See You Again?'. As to their proud heritage as 70s hit-makers of stunning visual appearance, Valerie Holiday had this to add: 'They were wigs. You think anyone would really do that to their hair?'

● ALBUMS: *Maybe* (Roulette 1970)★★★, *Three Degrees* (Philadelphia International 1974)★★★, *International* (Philadelphia International 1975)★★★, *So Much In Love* (1975)★★, *Take Good Care Of Yourself* (Philadelphia International 1975)★★, *The Three Degrees Live* (Philadelphia International 1975)★★, *Three Degrees Live In Japan* (Columbia 1975)★★, *Standing Up For Love* (Epic 1977)★★, *The Three Degrees* (Ariola 1978)★★, *New Dimensions* (Ariola 1978)★★, *3D* (Ariola 1979)★★, *Three Degrees And Holding* (Ichiban 1989)★★, *Woman In Love* (1993)★★.

Solo: Fayette Pinkney *One Degree* (Chopper 1979)★.

● COMPILATIONS: *Golden Hour Of The Three Degrees* (Golden Hour 1979)★★, *Gold* (K-Tel 1980)★★, *Hits Hits Hits* (Hallmark 1981)★★, *20 Greatest Hits* (Epic 1984)★★★, *20 Golden Greats* (Hallmark 1984)★★★, *The Best Of The Three Degrees* (Connoisseur Collection 1990)★★, *The Complete Swan Recordings* (1992)★★, *The Roulette Years* (Sequel 1995)★★, *A Collection Of Their 20 Greatest Hits* (Columbia 1996)★★★.

3T

Comprising three brothers - Tariano Adaryll 'Taj', Taryll Arden and Tito Joe 'T.J.' Jackson - 3T are the latest additions to the extraordinary Jackson family (Michael

Jackson, Janet Jackson, Jackson Five, etc.). They are sons of original Jackson Five member Tito Jackson, who co-manages their career. The connections were heavily promoted - their aunt Janet was seen wearing their merchandise throughout 1995. They are also signed to Michael Jackson's own label, MJJ, a joint venture with Sony Records. He produced several tracks on the group's debut album, *The Brotherhood*, and sang on one of its tracks, 'Why', written by Ken 'Babyface' Edmonds. This was the second single to be taken from the album after 'Anything'. Both were typical of the smooth R&B pop of the album, which became a success in both England and the USA. The trio had actually made its debut in 1993 with the inclusion of a track, 'Didn't Mean To Hurt You', on the *Free Willy* soundtrack album.

● ALBUMS: *The Brotherhood* (MJJ/Sony 1995)★★★★.

THUNDER, JOHNNY

b. Gil Hamilton, 15 August 1941, Leesburg, Florida, USA. Adopting the name Johnny Thunder, the singer first worked with street-corner groups in the late 50s. He worked briefly as a member of the Drifters in 1959 and recorded a few singles under his real name before meeting producer Teddy Vann. They co-wrote the dance song 'Loop De Loop', which was issued on the Diamond label and reached number 4 in the US pop charts in 1963. Finding himself typecast as a performer of novelty dance records ('Ring Around The Rosey' and 'Everybody Do The Sloppy'), Thunder was unable to repeat his initial success, although he continued recording for Diamond, Calla and United Artists. He was still performing into the late 80s.

● ALBUMS: *Loop De Loop* (Diamond 1963)★★★.

TLC

This spirited, sassy female trio from Atlanta, Georgia, USA, comprises Lisa 'Left Eye' Lopes, Rozonda 'Chilli' Thomas and T-Boz (b. Tionne Watkins). They initially worked under the tutelage of manager Pebbles, enjoying immediate chart success with fresh, funky material such as 'Ain't 2 Proud 2 Beg' (US number 5), 'Baby-Baby-Baby' (number 2) and 'What About Your Friends' (number 7). They also took to adorning themselves in barrier contraceptives to advocate safe sex, before moving on to work with celebrated dance/soul producers Dallas Austin and Babyface. Primarily conducted in 'New Jill Swing' mode, their debut album addressed the joys of womanhood, with staunch advice on how to treat errant boyfriends. As with the gangsta rappers, it became evident that TLC meant every word when Lopes was jailed for burning down the mansion of Andre Rison, her Atlanta Falcons football-star boyfriend. She also trashed his cars in a drunken rage, and was later admitted to an alcohol rehabilitation clinic, becoming one of America's top news stories in the process. Luckily for TLC, her sentence was commuted to probation and probably helped rather than hindered their career. A third album repeated the group's original formula, albeit with slightly more sophisticated, less strident material. The concept behind it was described by Thomas as 'TLC's way of saying "I'm Every Woman" - you know, every woman is crazy, sexy and cool, though on some days she might be more one than the other. Certainly we're all three, though if there is a dominant side Left Eye is crazy, I'm sexy and T-Boz is the cool one.' With beats provided by Jermaine Durpri and Sean 'Puffy' Combs in addition to Austin, *CrazySexyCool* subdued some of Lopes's rapping in favour of more ensemble singing, with the hip-hop quotient maintained largely through the urban rhythms. The best example was the US number 1 'Creep', a sensuous groove embossed by lively funk flourishes. Elsewhere, a Prince cover version, 'If I Was Your Girlfriend', proved secondary to the group's own street-articulate material. 'Waterfalls' proved to be another hit single, reaching the UK Top 5 in August 1995. *CrazySexyCool* soon went quadruple platinum in America, but, nevertheless, the group was forced to file for bankruptcy in 1995 with liabilities of $3.5 million. $1.3 million of this sum was owed to Lloyd's Of London Insurance, and related to an unpaid insurance claim on the house destroyed by Lopes. Further complications arose over the group's management; LaFace Records and Pebbitone, their record label and production company, the former run by L.A. Reid and the latter by his estranged wife Perri 'Pebbles' Reid, entered a financial dispute. Perri Reid claimed that each member of TLC owed her company $566,434. She also accused LaFace and parent company Arista Records of attempting to entice TLC away from Pebbitone, and undermining the trio's obligation to return $500,000 in advances and to record at least six albums for her company. The band were able to put all this behind them when their year of success was reflected in the reward of two Grammys at the 1996 ceremony. They won Best R&B Performance By A Duo Or Group With Vocal for 'Creep' and best R&B album for *CrazySexyCool*. At the same time, their album passed 10 million copies in the USA alone, and their debut passed 4 million units in June 1996.

● ALBUMS: *Ooooooohhh ... On The TLC Tip* (LaFace/Arista 1992)★★, *TLC* (LaFace/Arista 1993)★★★★, *CrazySexyCool* (LaFace/Arista 1995)★★★★.

● VIDEOS: *Crazy Video Cool* (BMG Video 1995).

TONEY, OSCAR, JNR.

b. 26 May 1939, Selma, Alabama, USA. Oscar Toney developed his early craft singing gospel with the Sensational Melodies Of Joy. A spell with a secular group, the Searchers, preceded two solo singles for King, but several years would pass before he recorded again. Toney's debut for the Bell label, 'For Your Precious Love' (1967), revived the Jerry Butler/Impressions song, but he prefaced this impassioned reading with a spoken sermon. Further singles, including 'You Can Lead A Woman To The Altar' and 'Never Get Enough Of Your Love', failed to recapture its impact. In 1971, the singer moved outlets to Capricorn before switching to a British outlet, Contempo. Six singles and an album followed, much of which was recorded in Britain where Toney had temporarily settled. He returned to the USA in 1976, but plans to revive his career there failed.

● ALBUMS: *For Your Precious Love* (Bell 1967)★★, *I've Been Loving You Too Long* (Contempo 1974)★★.

● COMPILATIONS: *Papa Don's Preacher* (Charly 1988)★★★.

Tony Toni Toné

This R&B/hip-hop crossover band from Oakland, California, comprises brothers Dwayne (b. 14 February 1963, Oakland, California, USA; lead vocals, guitar) and Raphael Wiggins (b. 14 May 1966, Oakland, California, USA; lead vocals, bass), and their cousin Timothy Christian (b. 10 December 1965, Oakland, California, USA; drums). They arrived with 'Little Walter' in 1988, a US R&B number 1 hit, which combined the best traditions of soul with new-age rap. They were at their most successful when moving, unceremoniously, from tight, gospel-tinged harmonics to assured, laconic hip-hop, as on the ballad hit 'It Never Rains (In Southern California)'. Despite their high profile (notably as support band on Janet Jackson's 1993 US tour), they retain a sense of propriety and musical history. Christian still plays for his church when at home, while Raphael made his public debut at the age of seven playing bass with his father's semi-professional blues band. Their name (pronounced 'Tony' on each of the three occurrences) was taken from a character they invented when they went out shopping to buy vintage clothing. They have also appeared in the *House Party 2* film.

● ALBUMS: *Who?* (Wing 1988)★★★, *The Revival* (Wing/Mercury 1990)★★★, *Sons Of Soul* (Wing/Mercury 1993)★★★, *House Of Music* (Mercury 1996)★★★★.

Toscano, Eli

b. Elias P. Toscano. Toscano was of Mexican and Italian descent and lived on the west side of Chicago. He began his career in the music business operating a television repair and record shop, which he expanded into a one-stop distributorship and then a record company. He ran three important record labels, issuing blues and R&B in Chicago in the 50s. The first was Abco, on which, with co-owner Joe Brown, he issued eight releases, most notably by Arbee Stidham and Louis Myers. He then began his Cobra label, which issued more than 30 discs including classic tracks by Otis Rush, Ike Turner, Harold Burrage and Magic Sam. A subsidiary label was Artistic, whose five issues included two by Buddy Guy and another by Turner. Toscano reportedly died in a boating accident in the early 60s, but rumours continued for decades afterwards that it was a gangland slaying, reputedly over an unpaid gambling debt.

Toussaint, Allen

b. 14 January 1938, New Orleans, Louisiana, USA. This influential artist first came to prominence as the touring piano player with Shirley And Lee. The duo's producer, Dave Bartholomew, began using Toussaint on several recording sessions, including those of Smiley Lewis and, on a handful of occasions, Fats Domino. The artist's solo debut came in 1958 with his *Wild Sounds Of New Orleans* album. One of the tracks, 'Java', later became a hit single for trumpeter Al Hirt. Toussaint then joined the emergent Minit label as a producer. His first release, Jessie Hill's 'Ooh Poo Pah Doo', was a US Top 30 hit in 1960 and paved the way for similar exemplary work with Irma Thomas, Aaron Neville and Ernie K-Doe. Such artists often recorded Toussaint's songs, several of which were credited to his 'Naomi Neville' pseudonym. Toussaint's work was not restricted to one outlet and local singer Lee Dorsey recorded several 'Neville' compositions for the New York-based Fury label. Drafted into the US Army in 1963, Allen's career was temporarily sidelined, although he continued playing with the on-base band, the Stokes. On return from military service in 1965, he formed a partnership with fellow producer Marshall Sehorn. Lee Dorsey was again the lucky recipient of several exceptional songs, including 'Ride Your Pony', 'Get Out Of My Life Woman' and 'Working In The Coalmine'. Sansu, the label formed by the two entrepreneurs, was also responsible for releases by Betty Harris and the Meters, while the duo also set up their own recording studio, Sea-Saint. Toussaint's own career continued with his self-titled 1971 album, whose highlight was the excellent 'From A Whisper To A Scream'. *Life, Love And Faith* was uninspired, but 1975's *Southern Nights* was much stronger and featured the original version of 'What Do You Want The Girl To Do?', later covered by Boz Scaggs and Lowell George. Despite his inability to navigate a consistent solo path, Toussaint's gifts as a songwriter and producer were continually in demand. The Band, Dr. John and Paul Simon are only a handful of those who have called upon his talents. He remains an important figure in New Orleans' music circles.

● ALBUMS: originally released under the name of Al Tousan *Wild Sounds Of New Orleans* (1958)★★★, *Toussaint* (Wand 1971)★★★, *Life Love And Faith* (Reprise 1972)★★, *Southern Nights* (Reprise 1975)★★★★, *Motion* (Warners 1978)★★★, *With The Stokes* (Bandy 1983)★★★, *Connected* (Nyno 1996)★★★.

● COMPILATIONS: *From A Whisper To A Scream* (Kent 1985)★★★, *Mr. New Orleans* (Charly 1994)★★★.

Tower Of Power

Formed in 1967 in Oakland, California, USA, this durable group - Rufus Miller (vocals), Greg Adams (trumpet), Emilio 'Mimi' Castillo (b. Detroit, Michigan; saxophone), Steve Kupka (saxophone), Lenny Pickett (saxophone), Mic Gillette (horns), Willie Fulton (guitar), Francis Prestia (bass), Brent Byer (percussion) and David Garibaldi (drums) - was originally known as the Motowns/Motown Soul Band. One of several Bay Area outfits preferring soul to its prevalent acid-rock sound, Tower Of Power's 1969 debut album, *East Bay Grease*, followed several popular appearances at San Francisco's Fillmore auditorium. Having signed to the Warner Brothers Records label, the group's next two albums, *Bump City* and *Tower Of Power*, produced a hit single each in 'You're Still A Young Man' and 'So Very Hard To Go', but their progress was hampered by a recurring vocalist problem. Miller was replaced, firstly by Rick Stevens and then Lenny Williams (b. 1945, San Francisco, California, USA), while the rhythm section also proved unstable. Curiously, the horn section stayed intact and was much in demand for session work, a factor that doubtlessly kept the parent group intact despite dwindling commercial fortunes. 'Don't Change Horses (In The Middle Of A Stream)' (1974) was the group's last US Top 30 single, but although they switched to Columbia in 1976, the Power returned to Warners after three lacklustre albums. Still bedevilled by personnel changes, recordings under their own name are now infrequent, but the brass players remain part of the west-coast backroom circle, known for their work with, among others, Huey Lewis and Phil Collins.

● ALBUMS: *East Bay Grease* (San Fransisco 1969)★★★, *Bump City* (Warners 1971)★★★, *Tower Of Power* (Warners 1973)★★★★, *Back To Oakland* (Warners 1974)★★★★, *Urban Renewal* (Warners 1975)★★★★, *In The Slot* (Warners 1975)★★★, *Live And In Living Colour* (Warners 1976)★★★★, *Ain't Nothin' Stoppin' Us Now* (Columbia 1976)★★★, *We Came To Play!* (Columbia 1978)★★★, *Back On The Streets* (Columbia 1979)★★★, *Tower Of Power* (Sheffield Lab 1982)★★★, *Back To Oakland* (Warners 1984)★★★, *Power* (Cypress 1987)★★★, *Direct* (Sheffield Lab 1988)★★★, *Monster On A Leash* (Epic 1991)★★★, *Souled Out* (Epic 1995)★★★.

● COMPILATIONS: *What Is Hip?* (Edsel 1986)★★★★.

Townsend, Ed

b. 16 April 1929, Fayetteville, Tennessee, USA. Townsend was an R&B balladeer who placed one enduring single on the US charts, 'For Your Love', in 1958. Townsend, whose father was a minister, sang in his church choir but gained his first real performing experience while serving in the US Marine Corps in Korea, where he joined a troupe of travelling minstrels. Upon his return to civilian life, he hosted a television programme in Los Angeles and wrote songs that were recorded by Nat 'King' Cole, Etta James and others. In 1958 he signed to Capitol Records and recorded his composition 'For Your Love' (no connection with the later Yardbirds song). A lush ballad, sung in a vocal style reminiscent of Jerry Butler, it reached the US Top 20. None of Townsend's follow-up recordings for Capitol or Warner Brothers Records sold appreciably and Townsend switched over to the production and writing side of the business. Among his credits were records by the Impressions, Shirelles and Chuck Jackson, and Marvin Gaye's 'Let's Get It On'.

Toys

Three high-school friends, Barbara Harris (b. 18 August 1945, Elizabeth City, North Carolina, USA), Barbara Parritt (b. 1 October 1944, Wilmington, North Carolina, USA) and June Montiero (b. 1 July 1946, New York City, USA), formed the Toys in Jamaica, New York. The group is best recalled for their 1965 hit 'A Lover's Concerto', a Supremes-influenced performance adapted from Bach's 'Minuet In G'. 'Attack', another piece appropriated from a classical theme, also reached the US and UK charts, but further releases, 'May My Heart Be Cast To Stone' and 'Baby Toys', were only minor US pop hits. Although a 1968 single, 'Sealed With A Kiss', returned them to the US soul Top 50, the trio split up soon afterwards.

● ALBUMS: *The Toys Sing 'A Lover's Concerto' And 'Attack'* (DynoVoice 1966)★★★.

● FILMS: *It's A Bikini World* (1967).

Trammps

This Philadelphia-based group was formed by Earl Young and Jimmy Ellis, two former members of the Volcanoes, who enjoyed a local R&B hit with their 'Storm Warning' single. The duo was joined by Dennis Harris (guitar), Ron Kersey (keyboards), John Hart (organ), Stanley Wade (bass) and Michael Thompson (drums), taking their name from a jibe that 'all (they would) ever be is tramps.' Initially, the group gained its reputation updating 'standards', of which 'Zing Went The Strings Of My Heart' (1972) was a minor hit. They then followed a more individual direction on their own label, Golden Fleece, before achieving a major UK hit with the excellent 'Hold Back The Night' (1975). Two years later the Trammps completed their *tour de force*, 'Disco Inferno', which featured in the film *Saturday Night Fever*, and irrevocably linked their name to the dancefloor. By this point the line-up had undergone several changes. The group's instigators, Young and Ellis, remained at the helm, alongside Stan and Harold Wade and baritone Robert Upchurch. These changes could not, however, halt the Trammps' commercial slide when the disco bubble burst and their 80s releases made little impression on either the soul or pop charts.

● ALBUMS: *The Legendary Zing Album* (Buddah 1975)★★★, *Trammps* (Golden Fleece 1975)★★★, *Where The Happy People Go* (Atlantic 1976)★★★, *Disco Inferno* (Atlantic 1977)★★, *Trammps III* (Atlantic 1977)★★, *The Whole World's Dancing* (Atlantic 1979)★★, *Mixin' It Up* (Atlantic 1980)★★, *Slipping Out* (Atlantic 1981)★★.

● COMPILATIONS: *The Best Of The Trammps* (Atlantic 1978)★★★★.

Tresvant, Ralph

b. 16 May 1968, Boston, Massachusetts, USA. Following the success of Bel Biv DeVoe, Bobby Brown and Johnny Gill, Tresvant became the final former member of New Edition to record a solo album in 1990. Released on MCA Records and featuring moderate dance/hip-hop numbers such as 'Rated R', *Ralph Tresvant* did little to remove the impression that this artist was technically the most gifted but least inspired of the band. Even so, the album achieved platinum status and produced a number 1 US single, 'Sensitivity'. Tresvant was also the beneficiary of a song written especially for him by Michael Jackson, 'Alright Now'. A follow-up set was much more R&B-based. Though predictably seamless and well-produced, *It's Goin' Down* lacked excitement or attack.

● ALBUMS: *Ralph Tresvant* (MCA 1990)★★★, *It's Goin' Down* (MCA 1994)★★.

● FILMS: *House Party 2*.

Tribble, Thomas E., 'TNT'

b. 5 August 1921, Ferrel, Pennsylvania, USA. Tribble took up the drums upon moving to Washington, DC, in the late 30s and continued his musical studies through his army service until his demobilization in 1946, when he joined his brother Floyd's band, the Treble Clefs, and later formed his own group. In 1949, Tribble joined Frank Motley's Motley Crew, who were signed to the local DC

label as 'name' act and house band. Their session tapes were then leased or sold to other record companies, and releases appeared on Gotham and other independent labels. Tribble had records on Gotham both in his own right and as singer/drummer with the Motley Crew, as well as separate sessions recorded for RCA Victor in 1951. In 1952 he split from Motley and DC and became an exclusive Gotham artist until 1955 when he embarked upon a lengthy tour of the eastern seaboard and Cuba, recording for Miami's Chart label in 1957, Atlantic's East-West subsidiary in 1960, and the tiny Frandy label in 1961. He has managed to eke out a fairly satisfying living as a live act since the late 50s and continues to lead a rock 'n' roll and soul revival revue in Washington, DC.
● COMPILATIONS: *T.N.T. Tribble* (Krazy Kat 1987)★★★, *T.N.T. Tribble Vol. 2: Red Hot Boogie* (Krazy Kat 1988)★★★, with Frank Motley *The Best Of Washington, D.C. R 'N' B* (1991)★★★.

TROUBLE FUNK

At the forefront of Washington's early 80s go-go music scene, Trouble Funk's call-and-response vocals, and Mack Carey's mighty percussion, predicted the emergence of rap, notably on the single 'Drop The Bomb'. Trouble Funk's first album of similar title was released on the Sugarhill label, hip-hop's first home. In truth they were more accurately a development of the physical funk tradition (Parliament, etc.). Go-go was developed by Chuck Brown from drum breakdowns he would use in clubs to link Top 40 covers. Trouble Funk are still active, and ever popular in their native home of Washington, though their potential to cross over has long since dissipated.
● ALBUMS: *Drop The Bomb* (Sugarhill 1982)★★★★, *In Times Of Trouble* (DETT 1983)★★★, *Saturday Night Live From Washington, D.C.* (Island 1985)★★★, *Trouble Over Here/Trouble Over There* (Island 1987)★★.

TROY, DORIS

b. Doris Higginson, 6 January 1937, New York City, USA. The daughter of a Baptist preacher, Higginson abandoned her gospel beginnings in favour of a jazz group, the Halos. She recorded as half of Jay And Dee and soon also began making her mark as a songwriter, using her grandmother's name of Payne as a *nom de plume*. In 1960 Dee Clark recorded her song 'How About That' for Vee Jay, while Troy cut a lone single for Everest before concentrating on backing singing, with ex-Drinkard Singers Dionne and Dee Dee Warwick and their aunt Cissy Houston, behind many acts including the Drifters, Solomon Burke and Chuck Jackson. In 1963, Troy co-penned 'Just One Look', and when Juggy Murray of Sue Records 'sat on' a demo of it, she took a copy to Jerry Wexler at Atlantic Records, who promptly released it exactly as recorded and watched it become a US Top 10 hit. It was covered the following year by the Hollies, and reached the UK number 2 slot. Other releases included the equally insistent 'What'cha Gonna Do About It?', which reached the UK Top 40 in 1964, but failed to succeed in her home country. Later singles for Capitol and Calla were equally underrated. After settling in London in 1969, she recorded a self-titled album for the Beatles' label Apple, with the help of George Harrison and Eric Clapton. Troy also recorded for People and Polydor and later worked as a session singer, contributing to a number of albums including Pink Floyd's *Dark Side Of The Moon*. From the mid-80s to 1991 Troy performed in an off-Broadway musical about her life, *Mama, I Want To Sing*, and again when it opened in London in February 1995.
● ALBUMS: *Just One Look* (Atlantic 1963)★★★, *Doris Troy* (Apple 1970)★★★, *Rainbow Testament* (1972)★★, *Stretching Out* (1974)★★★, *Mama, I Want To Sing* (1986)★★★.
● COMPILATIONS: *Just One Look: The Best Of ...* (Ichiban 1994)★★★★.

TUCKER, TOMMY

b. Robert Higginbotham, 5 March 1933, Springfield, Ohio, USA, d. 22 January 1982. Renowned as an R&B performer, Tucker began his career as a jazz musician playing piano and clarinet for the Bob Woods Orchestra. He led his own group, the Dusters, recorded under the name Tee Tucker for Atco in 1961 and worked with saxophonist Roland Kirk prior to recording 'Hi-Heel Sneakers' in 1964. This simple but compulsive 12-bar blues song established the singer's reputation when it was consistently covered by other acts. This one song contained a pot-pourri of references, the bizarre 'hi-heel sneakers' and 'wig hats on her head.' The casually understated delivery of the line: 'You better wear some boxing gloves, in case some fool might want to fight', gave the song great subtle humour. Further excellent singles in a similar style, including 'Long Tall Shorty', were less successful and forced Tucker to revert to club work. He visited Britain during the 70s as part of the *Blues Legends* package and, inspired by an enthusiastic response, began recording again. This irrepressible performer, sadly, died from poisoning in 1982.
● ALBUMS: *Greatest Twist Hits (Rock And Roll Machine)* (Atlantic 1961)★★★, *Hi-Heel Sneakers & Long Tall Shorty* (Checker 1964)★★★★, *Mother Tucker* (Red Lightnin' 1974)★★★, *Rocks Is My Pillow, Cold Ground Is My Bed* (Red Lightnin' 1982)★★, *Memphis Badboy* (Zu Zazz 1987)★★★, *Tommy Tucker And His Californians* (Circle 1988)★★, *Tommy Tucker And His Orchestra* (Circle 1988)★★★.

TUNE WEAVERS

This R&B vocal ensemble came from Woburn, Massachusetts, USA, and comprised lead Margo Sylvia (b. 4 April 1936, d. 25 October 1991), her husband and bass Johnny Sylvia (b. 8 September 1935), her brother and tenor Gilbert J. Lopez (b. 4 July 1934), and her cousin and obligato Charlotte Davis (b. 12 November 1936). The group was formed in 1956 and within six months they were recording for one-time big-band leader Frank Paul. He issued on his Casa Grande label a song Margo and Lopez had written in 1952, and the result was a slice of classic rock 'n' roll balladry, 'Happy, Happy, Birthday Baby'. With Chicago-based Chess label picking up the record, it went to number 4 R&B and number 5 pop in 1957. Margo Sylvia's warm, seductive voice was utterly beguiling, and Paul put it to good use on a number of

follow-ups. Sadly, he was unable to secure another chart hit for the Tuneweavers, and the group broke up in 1961.
● ALBUMS: *Happy Happy Birthday Baby* (Official 1988)★★★.

TURBANS

This Philadelphia R&B group consisted of Al Banks (b. Andrew Banks, 26 July 1937, d. 1977; lead), Matthew Platt (tenor), Charles Williams (baritone) and Andrew 'Chet' Jones (bass). The Turbans have a place in rock 'n' roll history as proverbial one-hit-wonders for their Mambo beat classic, 'When You Dance' (US R&B number 3 and pop number 33 in 1955). It achieved a historic mystique by being one of the first rock 'n' roll tunes (as an early crossover hit) and one of the selections on Art Laboe's *Oldies But Goodies* from 1960. No other records by the Turbans ever charted, but their 'Congratulations' (1957) is a highly esteemed example of doo-wop balladry, in which Banks's falsetto voice comes to the forefront. Following their last release in 1962, the Turbans broke up.
● COMPILATIONS: *Turbans Greatest Hits* (1973)★★★, *Best Of The Turbans* (1985)★★★.

TURNER, IKE AND TINA

Ike Turner (b. 5 November 1931, Clarksdale, Mississippi, USA) and Tina Turner (b. Annie Mae Bullock, 26 November 1939, Brownsville, Tennessee, USA). The commercial rebirth of singer Tina Turner, coupled with revelations about her ex-husband's unsavoury private life, has obscured the important role Ike Turner played in the development of R&B. A former piano player with Sonny Boy Williamson and Robert Nighthawk, Turner formed his Kings Of Rhythm during the late 40s. This influential group was responsible for 'Rocket 88', a 1950 release often named as the first rock 'n' roll recording but confusingly credited to its vocalist, Jackie Brenston. Turner then became a talent scout for Modern Records where he helped develop the careers of Bobby Bland, B.B. King and Howlin' Wolf. Based in St. Louis, his Kings Of Rhythm were later augmented by a former gospel singer, Annie Mae Bullock. Originally billed as 'Little Ann', she gradually became the core of the act, particularly following her marriage to Ike in 1958. Their debut release as Ike And Tina Turner came two years later. 'A Fool In Love', a tough, uncompromising release featuring Tina's already powerful delivery, preceded several excellent singles, the most successful of which was 'It's Gonna Work Out Fine' (1961). Highlighted by Ike's wry interjections, this superior performance defined the duo's early recordings. Although their revue was one of the leading black music touring shows, the Turners were curiously unable to translate this popularity into record sales. They recorded for several labels, including Sue, Kent and Loma, but a brief spell with Philles was to prove the most controversial. Here, producer Phil Spector constructed his 'wall-of sound' around Tina's impassioned voice, but the resultant single, 'River Deep Mountain High', was an unaccountable miss in the USA, although in the UK charts it soared into the Top 3. Its failure was to have a devastating effect on Spector. Ike, unhappy at relinquishing the reins, took the duo elsewhere when further releases were less successful. A support slot on the Rolling Stones' 1969 North American tour introduced the Turners to a wider, generally white, audience. Their version of John Fogerty's 'Proud Mary' was a gold disc in 1971, while the autobiographical 'Nutbush City Limits' (1973) was also an international hit. The group continued to be a major in-concert attraction, although Tina's brazen sexuality and the show's tried formula ultimately paled. The Turners became increasingly estranged as Ike's character darkened; Tina left the group in the middle of a tour and the couple were divorced in 1976. Beset by problems, chemical or otherwise, Ike spent some 18 months in prison, a stark contrast to his ex-wife's very public profile. Since his return Turner has attempted to redress the balance of his past with little success. Other than 'Rocket 88' there is little in the Ike Turner solo catalogue to excite. An embarrasing 'I Like Ike' campaign was undertaken by the UK magazine *Juke Blues*, which failed to convince the outside world that Ike had anything to offer musically.
● ALBUMS: *The Soul Of Ike And Tina Turner* (Sue 1960)★★, *Dance With The Kings Of Rhythm* (Sue 1960)★★★, *The Sound Of Ike And Tina Turner* (1961)★★★, *Dance With Ike And Tina Turner* (Sue 1962)★★★, *Festival Of Live Performances* (Kent 1962)★★, *Dynamite* (Sue 1963)★★★★, *Don't Play Me Cheap* (Sue 1963)★★★, *It's Gonna Work Out Fine* (Sue 1963)★★★★, *Please Please Please* (Kent 1964)★★★, *The Soul Of Ike And Tina Turner* (Kent 1964)★★★, *The Ike And Tina Show Live* (Loma 1965)★★★★, *Live! The Ike And Tina Turner Show* (Warners 1965)★★★★, *River Deep - Mountain High* (London 1966)★★★★, *So Fine* (Pompeii 1968)★★★★, *In Person* (Minit 1968)★★★★, *Cussin', Cryin' And Carrying On* (Pompeii 1969)★★★, *Get It Together!* (Pompeii 1969)★★★, *A Black Man's Soul* (Pompeii 1969)★★★, *Outta Season* (Blue Thumb 1969)★★★, *In Person* (Minit 1969)★★★, *River Deep - Mountain High* (A&M/London 1969)★★★★, *The Hunter* (Blue Thumb 1969)★★★★, *Come Together* (Liberty 1970)★★★, *Workin' Together* (Liberty 1970)★★★, *Her Man, His Woman* (Capitol 1971)★★★, *Live In Paris* (Liberty 1971)★★★★, *Live At Carnegie Hall - What You Hear Is What You Get* (Liberty 1971)★★★, *'Nuff Said* (United Artists 1971)★★, *Feel Good* (United Artists 1972)★★, *Let Me Touch Your Mind* (United Artists 1973)★★, *Nutbush City Limits* (United Artists 1973)★★★★, *Strange Fruit* (1974)★★★, *Sweet Island Rhode Red* (United Artists 1974)★★, *Delilah's Power* (United Artists 1977)★★, *Airwaves* (1978)★★.
Solo: Ike Turner *Blues Roots* (United Artists 1972)★★, *Bad Dreams* (United Artists 1973)★★, *Funky Mule* (DJM 1975)★★, *I'm Tore Up* (Red Lightnin' 1978)★★, *All The Blues All The Time* (Ember 1980)★★. His early work with the Kings Of Rhythm and as a talent scout is represented on *Hey Hey* (1984)★★★, *Rockin' Blues* (1986)★★★, *Ike Turner And His Kings Of Rhythm Volumes 1 & 2* (1988)★★★, *Talent Scout Blues* (Ace 1988)★★★, *Rhythm Rockin' Blues* (Ace 1995)★★★, *Without Love I Have Nothing* (Juke Blues 1996)★★, *My Blues Country* (Mystic 1997)★★.
● COMPILATIONS: *Ike And Tina Turner's Greatest Hits* (Sue 1965)★★★, *Ike And Tina Turner's Greatest Hits*

(Warners 1969)★★★★, *Tough Enough* (Liberty 1984)★★★, *The Ike And Tina Turner Sessions* (1987)★★★, *The Best Of Ike And Tina Turner* (1987)★★★★, *Fingerpoppin' -The Warner Brothers Years* (1988)★★★, *Proud Mary: The Best Of Ike And Tina Turner* (EMI 1991)★★★★, *Live!!!* (1993)★★★.

● FURTHER READING: *I Tina*, Tina Turner with Kurt Loder.

TURNER, RUBY

b. 1958, Montego Bay, Jamaica. Ruby Turner moved to Birmingham, England, in 1967. Initially, it was her thespian talents that brought her to prominence, as she appeared in numerous plays and musicals before joining the Crescent Theatre. However, discouraged by the lack of opportunities in her chosen career, she elected to concentrate on her singing. A number of years were spent trying to attract attention in smoky pubs and clubs, until she eventually made the acquaintance of Boy George. After joining Culture Club on their world tour, she found work with UB40 and Bryan Ferry, with whom she toured and recorded. Maturing as a singer and songwriter, Turner recorded her debut single, 'Every Soul', for a small local label, before being offered a contract with Jive Records, for whom she made her debut in 1987 with *Women Hold Up Half The Sky*. Produced by Jonathan Butler, this included her four UK chart hits, 'If You're Ready (Come Go With Me)', 'I'm In Love', 'Bye Baby' and 'I'd Rather Go Blind'. This led to further collaborative projects with Billy Ocean, Womack And Womack, the Temptations, Four Tops and Jimmy Ruffin. Although neither of her subsequent albums for Jive, 1990's *Paradise* and 1991's *The Other Side*, reaped similar commercial reward in the UK, the title track of the latter album, which was used in Willy Russell's film *Dancing Through The Dark*, became a US number 1 R&B hit. In 1994 she released *Restless Moods* for a new label and toured Australia and New Zealand, where her *Best Of* compilation went to number 1. She also returned to the UK Top 40 with the single 'Stay With Me Baby'. Already an established personality, Turner furthered her celebrity reputation by presenting programmes on BBC Radio 2 and performing George Gershwin songs at the Birmingham Symphony Hall backed by a 40-piece orchestra. Before the release of her fifth album, *Guilty*, Turner also returned to a theatrical career, taking lessons part-time at the Birmingham School Of Speech And Drama and making her professional stage debut playing the part of Frankie in *Carmen Jones*. She subsequently appeared in the BBC drama series *Back Up*.

● ALBUMS: *Women Hold Up Half The Sky* (Jive 1987)★★★, *Paradise* (Jive 1990)★★, *The Other Side* (Jive 1991)★★, *Restless Moods* (M&G 1994)★★★, *Guilty* (Indigo 1996)★★★.

● COMPILATIONS: *Best Of* (Jive 1992)★★★, *BBC Live In Concert Glastonbury Festival 1986* (Windsong 1994)★★.

TURNER, TINA

b. Annie Mae Bullock, 26 November 1939, Brownsville, Tennessee, USA. A singer while in her early teens, this enduring artist was a regular performer in St. Louis's nightclubs when she was discovered by guitarist Ike Turner in 1956. She joined his group as a backing singer, but quickly became the co-star and featured vocalist, a relationship sealed two years later with their marriage. Ike And Tina Turner were a highly successful act on the R&B circuit, before expanding their audience through a controversial liaison with producer Phil Spector. They emerged as a leading pop/soul act during the late 60s/early 70s with tours in support of the Rolling Stones and hits with 'Proud Mary' (1971) and 'Nutbush City Limits' (1973). However, the relationship between husband and wife grew increasingly strained as Ike's behaviour became irrational. Tina walked out of their professional and personal relationship during a 1975 tour, incurring the wrath of concert promoters who remained unsympathetic when the singer attempted a solo act. During this time the singer appeared in Ken Russell's film of the Who's rock-opera *Tommy*, offering an outrageous portrayal of the Acid Queen; however, this acclaimed cameo failed to launch Turner's solo career. Her career was rejuvenated in 1983 when British group Heaven 17 invited her to participate in an offshoot project dubbed BEF. She contributed a suitably raucous version of the Temptations 'Ball Of Confusion' which, in turn, engendered a recording contract with Capitol Records. Turner's reading of Al Green's 'Let's Stay Together' reached the UK Top 10, while an attendant album, *Private Dancer*, hurriedly completed in its wake, spawned another major hit in 'What's Love Got To Do With It'. This melodramatic ballad topped the US chart, reached number 3 in Britain and won two Grammys as Record Of The Year and Best Pop Vocal Performance, Female. The title track, written by Mark Knopfler, was also a transatlantic hit. In 1984 Turner accepted a role in the film *Mad Max Beyond The Thunderdome*, the theme from which, 'We Don't Need Another Hero', was another international hit. The following year she duetted with Mick Jagger at the Live Aid concert and contributed to the US charity single 'We Are The World'. Turner has since enhanced her popularity worldwide through a series of punishing tours, yet her energy has remained undiminished. Although commentators have criticized her one-dimensional approach, she enjoys massive popularity. She is truly happy with her present life and talks articulately about her difficult past. The voluptuous image is kept for the stage, while a quieter Turner offstage enjoys the fruits of her considerable success. Her 1985 autobiography was filmed in 1993 as *What's Love Got To Do With It?*, which also gave its title to a bestselling album and an extensive worldwide tour. Now allegedly retired from performing, she released the title track from the James Bond movie *Goldeneye* in October 1995. The Bono/Edge composition had Turner sounding uncannily like Shirley Bassey (the vocalist on 'Goldfinger'). The Trevor Horn-produced *Wildest Dreams* was a further solid rock album, laying her strong R&B roots to rest.

● ALBUMS: *The Country Of Tina Turner* reissued in 1991 as *Goes Country* (Connoisseur 70s)★★★, *Acid Queen* (United Artists 1975)★★★, *Rough* (United Artists 1978)★★, *Love Explosion* (United Artists 1979)★★, *Private Dancer* (Capitol 1984)★★★★, *Break Every Rule*

(Capitol 1986)★★★, *Live In Europe: Tina Turner* (Capitol 1988)★★, *Foreign Affair* (Capitol 1989)★★★, *What's Love Got To Do With It* film soundtrack (Parlophone 1993)★★★, *Wildest Dreams* (Parlophone/Virgin 1996)★★★.

● COMPILATIONS: *Simply The Best* (Capitol 1991)★★★★, *Tina Turner: The Collected Recordings, 60s To 90s* (Capitol 1994)★★★★.

● VIDEOS: *Nice 'n' Rough* (EMI 1982), *Private Dancer Video EP* (PMI 1985), *Private Dancer Tour* (PMI 1985), *What You See Is What You Get* (PMI 1987), *Break Every Rule* (PMI 1987), *Rio 88* (Polygram Music Video 1988), *Foreign Affair* (PMI 1990), *Do You Want Some Action* (Channel 5 1990), *Simply The Best* (PMI 1991), *Wild Lady Of Rock* (Hendring Video 1992), *What's Love Live* (1994), *The Girl From Nutbush* (Strand 1995), *Wildest Dreams* (Feedback Fusion 1996), *Live In Amsterdam* (Castle Music Pictures 1997).

● FURTHER READING: *I, Tina*, Tina Turner with Kurt Loder. *The Tina Turner Experience*, Chris Welch.

● FILMS: *Mad Max Beyond The Thunderdome* (1984).

TURNER, TITUS

b. 11 May 1933, Atlanta, Georgia, USA, d. 13 September 1984. A US singer and songwriter, he made his first records for OKeh in 1951, but his first big success came in 1955 when Little Willie John had a Top 10 R&B hit with the Turner composition 'All Around The World'. The song was revived as 'Grits Ain't Groceries' by Little Milton in 1969. Turner made other singles for Wing and Atlantic before he gained his first hits in 1959 with a pair of 'answer' songs to bestsellers by Lloyd Price, a singer with a similar style to Turner's. 'The Return Of Stag-O-Lee' (King) was a follow-up to 'Staggerlee' while Turner's 'We Told You Not To Marry' (Glover), was a riposte to 'I'm Gonna Get Married'. In 1961, Turner had a minor pop hit with a revival of 'Sound Off', produced by Al Gallico on Jamie, but this was overshadowed by Ray Charles's success with 'Sticks And Stones', the powerful gospel blues that remains Turner's best-known composition. During the 60s, Turner discovered blues singer Tommy Tucker and worked with producer Herb Abramson. He continued to record a range of blues, soul, novelty and disco material for such companies as Josie, Atco, Philips and Mala.

● ALBUMS: *Sound Off* (Jamie 1961)★★★.

TWICE

Formed in Cleveland, Ohio, USA, in the early 90s, and comprising two pairs of identical twins, Twice are a concept act, described by their management as 'a recording act that embodies a fashion-forward sense combined with musical abilities that has gained favourable reactions from women they've performed in front of.' Signed to MCA Records' subsidiary Silas, the group's self-titled 1997 debut offered a sumptuous collection of R&B ballads, with vocal skills honed by the group members' considerable experience of church singing. Comprising Lowell and Laval Jones and Mike and Ike Owensby, the group's efforts were overseen by a star-studded cast of producers, including Mike 'Nice' Chapman, Trent Thomas and Groove Theory's Bryce Wilson. Of the record's 10 songs, Twice themselves wrote five tracks and produced two. Meanwhile, Silas selected the group's cover version of Cameo's 1979 Top 10 R&B hit, 'Sparkle', as the album's first promotional single. This was produced by Angie Stone and D'Angelo, ensuring it attracted attention among the cognoscenti of the R&B community.

● ALBUMS: *Twice* (Silas/MCA 1997)★★★.

TWO TONS O' FUN

An R&B duo from San Francisco, California, USA, consisting of Martha Walsh and Izora Rhodes. Two Tons O' Fun started out as protégées of the gay disco singer Sylvester, beginning their career singing as the background chorus, their name a reference to the substantial girth of each singer. They recorded their first two albums under the production aegis of Sylvester's producer, Harvey Fuqua, who released them on his own Honey label. In 1982 the Two Tons O' Fun moved to Columbia and changed their name to the Weather Girls, whose biggest success was the UK number 2 hit 'It's Raining Men'.

● ALBUMS: *Two Tons O' Fun* (Honey 1980)★★★, *Backatcha* (Honey 1980)★★.

● COMPILATIONS: *Megatonnage: Best Of The Two Tons* (Fantasy 1990)★★★, *Get The Feeling* (Fantasy 1993)★★★.

TYMES

Formed in Philadelphia during the 50s, George Williams, George Hilliard, Donald Banks, Albert Berry and Norman Burnett first came together in the Latineers. As the Tymes they secured a major hit with the evocative 'So Much In Love' (1962), a gorgeously simple performance that recalled the bygone doo-wop era while anticipating the sweet harmonies of 70s Philly soul. Further less successful singles then followed as the group entered a somewhat lean patch, before a version of 'People' restored them to the charts. The Tymes enjoyed international hits with two 1974 releases, 'You Little Trustmaker' and 'Ms. Grace' (a UK number 1), which pitched the group's harmonies in a modern context. Although the original line-up stayed intact for several years, Hilliard, then Berry, eventually left the group, while two later additions, Terri Gonzalez and Melanie Moore, suggested a further shake-up of their image. Such changes, however, failed to sustain the Tymes' chart career beyond 1976.

● ALBUMS: *So Much In Love* (Parkway 1963)★★★★, *The Sound Of The Wonderful Tymes* (Parkway 1963)★★★, *Somewhere* (Parkway 1964)★★, *People* (Direction 1968)★★★, *Trustmaker* (RCA 1974)★★★, *Tymes Up* (RCA 1976)★★, *Turning Point* (RCA 1976)★★, *Digging Their Roots* (RCA 1977)★★.

● COMPILATIONS: *Soul Gems* (Prestige 1990)★★★.

Ultimate Kaos

UK pop group Ultimate Kaos comprises Haydon Eshun (b. *c*.1982, England), Ryan Elliot (b. *c*.1982, England), Jomo Baxter (b. *c*.1979, England), Nicky Grant (b. *c*.1977, England) and Jayde Delpratt Spence (b. *c*.1981, England). They formed when Grant and Baxter were enrolled at the Battersea Dance Workshop in London, where they recruited the remaining members and began to hone their own style of energetic R&B and pop dance. The group's debut single, 'Some Girls', reached number 9 in the UK charts in October 1994, selling over 200,000 copies. It was followed by an album, *Kaos*, and a further hit single, 'Right Here'. Their extensive promotion of the album included tour dates as part of the Coca-Cola roadshow, while the group also signed a contract with Motown Records in the USA.

● ALBUMS: *Kaos* (Wild Card 1995)★★★.

Undisputed Truth

The Undisputed Truth were assembled by Motown producer Norman Whitfield in 1970, as a vehicle for the studio experimentation he had already begun on singles by the Temptations and Edwin Starr. Joe Harris, an ever-present member of the group, was originally teamed up with singers Billie Calvin and Brenda Evans, who had previously worked on the Four Tops' *Still Waters*. The group debuted with a stunning slice of psychedelic soul, 'Smiling Faces Sometimes', written by Whitfield with his regular lyricist, Barrett Strong. The song was an exercise in urban paranoia, widely interpreted as an oblique comment on President Richard Nixon's administration, and it allowed Whitfield room to preview new studio techniques that he hoped to use on Temptations releases. It reached the US Top 3, encouraging Whitfield to use the Undisputed Truth as a laboratory for testing his new material. The group enjoyed a small hit with Whitfield/Strong's 'Papa Was A Rolling Stone' several months before the Temptations' classic rendition reached the shops, and among their other hit songs were 'Ball Of Confusion', 'Friendship Train' and 'Just My Imagination' - all numbers that Whitfield had also recorded with other Motown acts. Whitfield continued to produce the group throughout the 70s, switching them in 1976 to his own Whitfield label, where they had a US R&B hit with 'You + Me = Love'. By this time, only Joe Harris remained of the original trio, accompanied by Tyrone Berkeley and Taka Boom, the sister of vocalist Chaka Khan. In the late 70s, their producer's attention was focused on the most successful act on his roster, Rose Royce, and the Undisputed Truth were among those who suffered from his lack of attention. The group eventually split in the early 80s after the collapse of Whitfield's label. In 1991 Joe Harris and Brenda Evans, together with ex-Brainstorm vocalist Belita Woods, recorded a new version of 'Law Of The Land' on Ian Levine's Motor City label.

● ALBUMS: *The Undisputed Truth* (Gordy 1971)★★★, *Face To Face With The Truth* (Gordy 1972)★★★, *Law Of The Land* (Gordy 1973)★★★, *Down To Earth* (1974)★★, *Cosmic Truth* (Gordy 1975)★★, *Higher Than High* (Gordy 1975)★★★, *Method To The Madness* (Whitfield 1977)★★★, *Smokin'* (Whitfield 1979)★★.

● COMPILATIONS: *The Best Of The Undisputed Truth* (Gordy 1977)★★★.

Unifics

An R&B vocal group from Washington, DC, USA, comprising members Al Johnson (b. 1948, Newport News, Virginia, USA; lead), Michel Ward (tenor), Greg Cook (tenor) and Harold Worthington (baritone). The Unifics, with their tender but intense vocals, were one of the best of the soft soul vocal groups that filled the R&B charts in the 60s. Recording in New York under the aegis of songwriter/producer Guy Draper, the group had national hits with 'Court Of Love' (number 3 R&B, number 25 pop) and the 'Beginning Of The End' (number 9 R&B, number 36 pop) in 1968. Their last chart record was in 1969. Ward and Worthington left in 1970 and were replaced by Marvin Brown and Tom Fauntleroy, but the group could not sustain itself and soon disbanded.

● ALBUMS: *Sittin' In At The Court Of Love* (Kapp 1968)★★★.

Upchurch, Phil

b. 19 July 1941, Chicago, Illinois, USA. Although this excellent guitarist later became a respected session musician, his name is synonymous with 'You Can't Sit Down', a propulsive two-part instrumental recorded with his group, the Phil Upchurch Combo. The band, with Upchurch on guitar, comprised Cornell Muldrow (organ), David Brooks (saxophone), Mac Johnson (trumpet) and Joe Hoddrick (drums). Muldrow wrote the tune and had recorded an earlier version. 'You Can't Sit Down' reached the US Top 30 in 1961 and the UK Top 40 on its reissue five years later. However, its influence was felt far beyond such placings, as the tune became a staple part of almost every budding US fraternity or bar band. Upchurch began playing in R&B backing bands, including those of the Kool Gents, the Dells, the Spaniels and for Dee Clark, who used 'You Can't Sit Down' as a theme song. He later appeared on releases by Bo Diddley, Muddy Waters, Jimmy Reed and Howlin' Wolf, and in the 70s guested on sessions for several fusion artists including Grover Washington, George Benson (*Breezin'* and *In Flight*) and the Crusaders. His own work was rather overshadowed by this workload while the artist's inventive style was marred by an anonymity resulting from his many of supporting roles. His most successful collaboration was with fellow Chicagoan, Tennyson Stephens, a keyboardist whose vocals were important to the duo's success in the R&B market in the mid-70s.

● ALBUMS: as the Phil Upchurch Combo *You Can't Sit*

Down (Boyd 1961)★★★, *You Can't Sit Down, Part Two* (United Artists 1961)★★★, *Twist The Big Hit Dances* (United Artists 1961)★★, *Feeling Blue* (Milestone 1968)★★★, *The Way I Feel* (1969)★★, *Darkness Darkness* (Blue Thumb 1972)★★★, *Lovin' Feelin'* (Blue Thumb 1973)★★★, with Tennyson Stephens *Upchurch Tennyson* (Kudu 1975)★★★, *Phil Upchurch* (1978)★★★, *Revelation* (Jam 1982)★★★, *Name Of The Game* (Jam 1983)★★★, *Companions* (Paladin 1985)★★★.

UPTOWN RECORDS

Uptown was launched in Manhattan, New York, in 1986, as a specialist black label, concentrating primarily on R&B-styled rap. The label was set up by Andre Harrell (b. *c.*1959), formerly part of Dr. Jeckyll And Mr Hyde, who had a major hit in 1981 with 'Genius Rap'. After leaving the duo he went to college to study communication and business, before joining Russell Simmons at Rush Management. It has been said that Harrell left Def Jam when he failed to persuade Simmons that they could market Heavy D as 'sexy'. Nevertheless, it was via that act that the label was established, and the 'big guy' also introduced Harrell to one of his most significant early signings, the proto-New Jill Swing act Gyrlz (Uptown having already provided a platform for Guy). Other acts on the label would include Jodeci and Mary J. Blige, becoming one of the pre-eminent dance/hip-hop labels of its age. Harrell, who also produced the movie *Strictly Business*, himself described his tastes as those of 'a lifestyle entertainment entrepreneur'.

USHER

b. Usher Raymond, *c.*1978, USA. Drawn from LaFace Records' seemingly inexhaustible wellspring of young R&B acts, Usher is one of the few who can boast of real star quality. Indeed, after the release of his self-titled debut in 1994, there seemed to be a danger that he would become better known as a face rather than a musical talent. He appeared on the *Oprah Winfrey Show* and also performed at the American Music Awards as part of the all-star recording collaboration Black Men United. However, sales of his Sean 'Puffy' Combs-produced debut were a little disappointing at just over a quarter of a million, though it did spawn the hit single 'Think Of You'. As a consequence, he took creative control over the production of a follow-up collection, *My Way*, although he did enlist Jermaine Dupri, Teddy Riley and Babyface as co-writers and co-producers. The first single to be taken from the album, 'You Make Me Wanna', was typical of the smooth ballads on offer, and went on to reach number 1 in the UK. More unusual was the experimental, hip-hop-styled 'Nice And Slow'. The album also included a remake of Midnight Star's 'Slow Jam', featuring fellow teenage R&B star Monica.

● ALBUMS: *Usher* (LaFace 1994)★★★, *My Way* (LaFace 1997)★★★.

VALENTINES

From Harlem, New York, USA, the original members of this vocal group were lead Richard Barrett, tenor Raymond Briggs, second tenor Carl Hogan, baritone Mickey Francis and bass Ronnie Bright. (Hogan was replaced by Donald Razor in 1954, who in turn was replaced by Eddie Edgehill in 1955, who, in full circle, was replaced by Hogan in 1957.) The Valentines typified the New York City doo-wop sound. The group's first record, 'Tonight Kathleen' (1954), recorded for Hy Weiss's Old Town label, established the group locally. The following year the Valentines joined George Goldner's Rama label where they achieved a string of hits. The group had success with the up-tempo 'Lily Maebelle', followed by their biggest hit, 'The Woo Woo Train' (1956). Also recorded that year was the splendid ballad 'Nature's Creation'. The Valentines made their last record in 1957. Barrett was becoming more involved in the backroom aspect of the recording industry, having discovered and brought Frankie Lymon And The Teenagers to Goldner and also begun regular production duties with the Chantels. Bright later joined the Cadillacs and was the bass player on Johnny Cymbal's 'Mr. Bassman'.

● COMPILATIONS: *The Best Of The Valentines* (Collectables 1991)★★★.

VALENTINOS

Formed in the 1950s and originally known as the Womack Brothers, the group's line-up featured Bobby Womack (b. 4 March 1944, Cleveland, Ohio, USA), Friendly Womack Jnr. (b. 1941, Cleveland, Ohio, USA), Harry Womack (b. 1946, Cleveland, Ohio, USA), Curtis Womack (b. 1943, Cleveland, Ohio, USA), Cecil Womack (b. 1941, Cleveland, Ohio, USA). They were also briefly known as the Lovers. Part of a large religious family, their father, Friendly Snr., led his own gospel group, the Voices Of Love. The Womack Brothers also sang spiritual material and were signed to singer Sam Cooke's Sar label following a Cleveland concert. They were later renamed the Valentinos. One of Bobby's songs, 'Couldn't Hear Nobody Pray', was reshaped by Cooke's manager into the secular 'Looking For A Love', a Top 10 R&B single in 1962. Another original, 'Somewhere There's A God', became 'Somewhere There's A Girl', but the Valentinos' next chart entry came in 1964 with the bubbling 'It's All Over Now'. Their own version was overshadowed by that of the Rolling Stones, and their progress was impeded further by Cooke's death. The group subsequently recorded for several labels, including Checker, although little was ever released. Disillusioned, the brothers drifted apart and

Bobby Womack began his solo career. However, the Valentinos did briefly reunite for two 70s singles, 'I Can Understand It' and 'Raise Your Hand In Anger'. The family's personal history has been remarkably complex. Cecil married and managed singer Mary Wells, but the couple were later divorced. Wells then married Curtis Womack. Cecil, meanwhile, married Sam Cooke's daughter, Linda, inaugurating the successful Womack And Womack duo. In 1986 Friendly Jnr and Curtis formed the Brothers Womack with singer Lewis Williams. The remaining brother, Harry, was stabbed to death by his wife. *Double Barrelled Soul* offers six Valentinos Sar masters alongside six by the Simms twins. *Bobby Womack And The Valentinos* divides itself between group recordings and solo material recorded for Checker.

● COMPILATIONS: one side only *Double Barrelled Soul* (1968)★★, *Bobby Womack And The Valentinos* (1984)★★.

VAN DYKE, EARL

b. 1929, Detroit, Michigan, USA, d. 18 September 1992. Van Dyke, an accomplished keyboardist, was a session player at the Motown studios from 1961-71. In 1964 he replaced Choker Campbell as leader of Tamla/Motown's studio house band. The new group, affectionately dubbed the Funk Brothers, also included James Jamerson (bass) and Benny Benjamin (drums), but was known formally as the Earl Van Dyke Six when touring in support of the label's vocal acts. For several years this unit was the bedrock of the Tamla/Motown sound, contributing to singles by the Supremes, the Temptations, the Four Tops, Marvin Gaye and Martha And The Vandellas, while their live appearances included Tamla's first, groundbreaking UK tour. However, Motown policy ensured their work remain uncredited on album sleeves and contemporary interviews. Viewed as a 'musician' rather than an 'artist', Van Dyke was obliged to use considerable persuasion to secure releases under his own name. *That Motown Sound* consisted of simple organ figures overdubbed upon the original rhythm tracks of recent hits and although subsequent recordings offered a jazz perspective, the potential of his unit was never fully exploited.

● ALBUMS: *That Motown Sound* (Motown 1965)★★★, *The Earl Of Funk* (Soul 1970)★★★.

VAN DYKES

This US group was formed in Fort Worth, Texas in 1964 when Rondalis Tandy (lead vocal) teamed with three aspiring singers, Wenzon Mosley (tenor), James Mays (bass) and Eddie Nixon (falsetto). Nixon left prior to recording 'No Man Is An Island', which was the Van Dykes' first single, and the prototype for many of their subsequent releases. This exquisite ballad featured Tandy's tight, almost claustrophobic falsetto, while a sparse instrumental section emphasized the three singers' close harmonies and their indebtedness to the Impressions. The trio folded in 1968 following Tandy's departure for California. *No Man Is An Island*, released in 1982, features previously issued material together with newly discovered masters.

● COMPILATIONS: *Tellin' It Like It Is* (Bell 1967)★★★, *No Man Is An Island* (Solid Smoke 1982)★★★.

VANDROSS, LUTHER

b. Luther Ronzoni Vandross, 20 April 1951, New York City, New York, USA. Born into a family immersed in gospel and soul singing, Vandross had already formed his own group while still at school and later worked with the musical theatre workshop Listen My Brother. This enabled him to perform at Harlem's Apollo Theatre. After a brief hiatus from the music scene in the 70s, he was invited by an old schoolfriend and workshop colleague, Carlos Alomar, to join him in the studio with David Bowie for the recording of *Young Americans*. Vandross impressed Bowie enough to be invited to arrange the vocal parts and make a substantial contribution to the backing vocals for the album. By the time Bowie's US tour was underway Vandross had also secured a position as opening act. His vocal talent was soon in demand and his session credits with Chaka Khan, Ringo Starr, Barbra Streisand and Donna Summer generated sufficient interest from the Cotillion label to sign him as part of a specially assembled vocal group, Luther. *Luther* and *This Close To You* (both 1976) flopped, partly owing to the use of a disco backing instead of allowing Vandross to express his more romantic soul style. The singer subsequently drifted back to session work, contributing outstanding performances to the work of Quincy Jones, Patti Austin, Gwen Guthrie, Chic and Sister Sledge. This work was subsidized by composing advertising jingles. His performance as guest singer with the studio group Change on the 1980 album *Glow Of Love* earned two UK Top 20 hits in 'Glow Of Love' and 'Searchin''. This led to the relaunch of a higher-profile career, this time as a solo artist with Epic/CBS Records. 'Never Too Much' earned him an R&B number 1, while the accompanying album reached the US Top 20. The single took a further eight years to reach the UK Top 20. Subsequent singles, including duets with Cheryl Lynn ('If This World Was Mine') and Dionne Warwick ('How Many Times Can We Say Goodbye'), saw him strengthen his popularity with the US R&B market and gave him two further R&B number 1 hits with 'Stop To Love' (1986) and a duet with Gregory Hines, 'There's Nothing Better Than Love' (1987). All of his recent releases have become major hits, and Vandross has now risen to become one of the finest soul singers of the 80s and 90s. He has won countless awards and his reputation as a producer has been enhanced by his work with Dionne Warwick, Diana Ross and Whitney Houston.

● ALBUMS: *Never Too Much* (Epic 1981)★★★, *Forever, For Always, For Love* (Epic 1982)★★★, *Busy Body* (Epic 1983)★★★, *The Night I Fell In Love* (Epic 1985)★★★★, *Give Me The Reason* (Epic 1986)★★★, *Any Love* (Epic 1988)★★★, *Power Of Love* (Epic 1991)★★★★, *Never Let Me Go* (Epic 1993)★★★, *Songs* (Epic 1994)★★★, *Your Secret Love* (Epic 1996)★★★.

● COMPILATIONS: *The Best Of Luther Vandross ... The Best Of Love* (Epic 1989)★★★★, *Greatest Hits 1981-1995* (Epic 1995)★★★★.

● VIDEOS: *An Evening Of Songs* (1994), *Always And Forever* (1995).

Vee Jay Records

Founded in 1953 by Vivian 'Vee' Carter (b. 1920, Tunica, Mississippi, USA, d. 12 June 1989, Gary, Indiana, USA) and James 'Jay' C. Bracken (b. 1909, Kansas City, Missouri, USA, d. 1972), this US independent record label rose from regional obscurity to a position as one of black music's leading outlets. Their initial signings included the Spaniels, who provided the company's first major success when their haunting doo-wop ballad, 'Goodnite Sweetheart, Goodnite', was a hit in the R&B and pop chart. The couple, now married, established their offices in Chicago's East 47th Street. Vivian's brother, Calvin Carter, also joined the company; this intuitive individual was responsible for attracting several important acts, including vocal groups the El Dorados and the Dells, as well as gospel artists the Staple Singers and the Swan Silvertones. Vee Jay's staff was considerably bolstered by the addition of Ewart Abner, whose business acumen did much to facilitate the label's meteoric rise. By the early 60s the Vee Jay roster included Jerry Butler, Dee Clark and Gene Chandler, each of whom enjoyed popular success, while influential blues performers Jimmy Reed and John Lee Hooker recorded their best-known material for the outlet. However, by 1963 the label was encountering financial difficulties. Vee Jay had diversified into white pop by securing the Four Seasons, and had won the rights to the Beatles' early releases when Capitol Records declined their option. When the former act had several hits, the label was unable to meet royalty payments and a protracted lawsuit ensued. Capitol then rescinded their Beatles agreement; although Vee Jay latterly retained material already licensed, the rights to future recordings were lost. This controversial period also saw Abner's departure, while the label moved its operations to Los Angeles. However, by 1965 Vee Jay was back in Chicago, with Abner reinstated in his former position. Such upheavals proved fatal. Unsettled artists moved to other outlets, and when interim manager Randy Wood sued for breach of contract, Vee Jay filed for bankruptcy. In May 1966, the company closed its offices and released its remaining employees. Arguably capable of rivalling Tamla/Motown had they overcome their internal problems, Vee Jay nonetheless holds an important place in the development of black music. Abner eventually rose to become president of Motown, while James Bracken died in 1972, the owner of a record shop. Calvin Carter died in 1986, while Vivian Carter ran a radio station in her home-town of Gary, Indiana.

Vega, Tata

b. Carmen Rose Vega, 7 October 1951, Queens, New York, USA. She made her professional musical debut in the New York cast of *Hair* in 1969. Vega subsequently joined the soul band Pollution, led by singer-songwriter Dobie Gray, before enlisting with Earthquire for their 1973 *Earthquire* album on Motown's Natural Resources subsidiary. When the group disbanded, Vega was signed to Motown as a solo artist, becoming part of a new generation of young performers who the label hoped would combat the success of leading disco artists such as Donna Summer. She enjoyed a minor soul hit in 1976 with 'Full Speed Ahead', before enjoying more substantial success in the UK with the disco-flavoured *Get It Up For Love*, and an electronic arrangement of the Diana Ross And The Supremes standard, 'You Keep Me Hanging On'. In 1979 'I Just Keep Thinking About You Baby' brought her another chart entry, and she sang joint lead vocals on Stevie Wonder's 'A Seed's A Star', one of the more commercial songs on his epic *Journey Through The Secret Life Of Plants* project. After diminishing sales in the UK and the USA, Vega was dropped by Motown in 1981. Since then she has concentrated on recording gospel material, and working as a session vocalist. She registered a US hit with Lou Rawls in 1985 with 'Learn To Love Again'. She was also the featured vocalist on four songs on Quincy Jones's 1986 film soundtrack for *The Color Purple*.

● ALBUMS: *Full Speed Ahead* (Tamla 1976)★★★, *Totally Tata* (Tamla 1977)★★★, *Try My Love* (Tamla 1979)★★★, *Givin' All My Love* (Tamla 1981)★★.

Velours

From New York, USA, the Velours - featuring the wonderfully expressive lead of Jerome Ramos, whose halting and vibrato-laden vocal style was one of the most intriguing in doo-wop - were one of the most impressive groups of the doo-wop era. Other members included Charles Moffett, John Pearson, Don Haywoode, John Cheatdom and pianist Calvin Hayes. The group first recorded for Baton, although nothing was released, but in 1957 they joined Onyx and success followed. Among their songs, 'Can I Come Over Tonight?', 'This Could Be The Night' and 'Romeo' particularly impress. After some unsuccessful singles for Studio and Gone, the Velours broke up in the early 60s. In 1965 four members of the group - Don Haywoode, Jerome Ramos, John Cheatdom and Richie Pitts regrouped. In 1967 they toured the UK and were told when they arrived that they would be appearing as the 'Fabulous Temptations'. The following year, with new member Richie Pitts, they began recording as the Fantastics with far greater success than they had ever achieved as the Velours.

Velvelettes

Two pairs of sisters, Millie and Cal Gill, and Bertha and Norma Barbee, formed the original Velvelettes line-up in 1961 at Western Michigan State University. After recording a one-off single, 'There He Goes', for IPG Records in 1963, they were signed to Motown, where they were placed in the hands of fledgling producer Norman Whitfield. This partnership spawned three classic singles, 'Needle In A Haystack', 'He Was Really Sayin' Something' and 'These Things Will Keep Me Lovin' You', that epitomized Motown's approach to the girl-group sound. A flurry of personnel changes effectively halted the Velvelettes' progress in 1965; Millie Gill and the Barbee sisters left, and were replaced briefly by Annette McMullen and two future members of Martha And The Vandellas, Sandra Tilley and Betty Kelly. This line-up also dissolved after a few months. In 1970, 'These Things Will Keep Me Loving You' became a belated UK hit, confirming the Velvelettes' cult status among British soul

fans. The original line-up regrouped in 1984 to play revival shows, and re-recorded their hits for Nightmare Records. They also recorded a disco version of 'Needle In A Haystack' for Ian Levine's label in 1987. *One Door Closes* contained half old hits and half new material, recorded in an updated Motown style.
● ALBUMS: *One Door Closes* (Motor City 1990)★★.

VELVETS

This Texas-based, 50-styled R&B vocal group was fronted by Virgil Johnson (b. 29 December 1935, Odessa, Texas, USA) and included Clarence Rigsby (d. 1978; lead tenor), Robert Thursby (tenor), William Solomon (baritone) and Mark Prince (bass). Formed by English teacher Johnson and four of his students in 1960, the group were spotted by Roy Orbison, who helped to secure them a contract with Monument. Their recording career started with a revival of 'That Lucky Old Sun'. Their follow-up, 'Tonight (Could Be The Night)', reached the US Top 40 in 1961, and was penned by Johnson. However, their next release, a Roy Orbison song called 'Laugh', became their last chart entry. The group released another six singles before returning to teaching and studying.
● COMPILATIONS: *Vibraphonic* (1993)★★★.

VIBRATIONS

Formed in Los Angeles, California, USA, in 1955 and originally known as the Jayhawks, this quartet comprised Dave Govan (b. 2 August 1940, Los Angeles, California, USA), Carl Fisher (b. 27 December 1939, Quardon, Texas, USA), James Johnson (b. 13 September 1939, Brooklyn, New York, USA) and Carver Bunkham. The Vibrations were notable for being equally proficient with smooth ballads ('Oh Cindy', 1962), and exuberant dance tunes ('Sloop Dance', 1964). Their exciting stage show made the group one of the favourites on the R&B theatre circuit. As the Jayhawks, they recorded the original version of 'Stranded In The Jungle', a novelty hit they shared with the Cadets. Ricky Owens (b. 24 April 1939, St. Louis, Missouri, USA) subsequently replaced Bunkham, and the line-up was later augmented by Don Bradley (b. 7 August 1936, St. Louis, Missouri, USA). The group became the Vibrations in 1959 and scored a hit with 'The Watusi' two years later. However, in 1961 they recorded a one-off single, the hugely successful US Top 20 hit 'Peanut Butter', under the pseudonym of the Marathons. The influential 'My Girl Sloopy' (1964) was a US Top 30 single and served as the model for 'Hang On Sloopy', a later chart-topper by the McCoys. The Vibrations enjoyed a minor R&B success every year until 1968, notably with 'Misty' (1965) and 'And I Love Her' (1966), but their commercial fortunes then faded. Richard Owens briefly joined the Temptations in 1971.
● ALBUMS: *Watusi!* (Checker 1961)★★★, *Misty* (OKeh 1964)★★★, *Shout!* (OKeh 1965)★★★, *New Vibrations* (1966)★★, *Vibrations* (1972)★★.
● COMPILATIONS: *The Vibrations Greatest Hits* (1968)★★★.

VINCENT, JOHNNY

b. John Vincent Imbragulio, 3 October 1925, Hattiesburg, Mississippi, USA. Johnny Vincent owned a successful record company operating in Jackson, Mississippi, from the 40s to the 60s. His first label was Champion, which issued an obscure disc by Arthur Crudup. Better known was the Ace label, responsible for a large number of excellent blues, R&B and rock 'n' roll by artists such as Frankie Lee Sims, Sammy Myers, Earl King and Huey 'Piano' Smith. Vincent resurrected the label in later years, but in 1997 he concluded the sale of the masters to Castle Communications for reissue on their Sequel Records label.

VINEGAR JOE

This powerful, R&B-based group was formed in 1971 at the suggestion of Island Records boss Chris Blackwell. The main core of the group comprised Elkie Brooks (b. Elaine Bookbinder, 25 February 1946, Salford, Manchester, England; vocals), Robert Palmer (b. 19 January 1949, Batley, Yorkshire, England; vocals) and Peter Gage (b. 31 August 1947, Lewisham, London, England; guitar, piano, pedal steel guitar). It evolved from the remnants of Dada (formed 1970), an ambitious 12-piece jazz-rock outfit. The three members had enjoyed limited success previously during the 60s: Brooks had recorded as a solo act, Palmer had sung with Alan Bown, while Gage was a former member of the Zephyrs and later with Geno Washington And The Ram Jam Band. The line-up additionally comprised Steve York (b. 24 April 1948, London; bass), while early members Tim Hinckley and later John Hawken were supplanted in June 1972 by Mike Deacon (b. 30 April 1945, Surrey, England; keyboards), while Bob Tait and later John Woods were replaced in January 1973 by Pete Gavin (b. 9 August 1946, Lewisham, London, England; drums). Jim Mullen was an additional guitarist from September 1972 to April 1973. Renowned for a forthright, gutsy approach, Vinegar Joe was quickly established as a popular in-concert attraction, but despite recording three solid and respectable albums, the unit was unable to capture its live appeal on record and broke up late in 1973. Palmer and Brooks then embarked on contrasting, but highly successful, individual careers.
● ALBUMS: *Vinegar Joe* (Island 1972)★★★, *Rock 'N' Roll Gypsies* (Island 1972)★★★, *Six Star General* (Island 1973)★★★.

VINX

A multi-talented American percussionist, singer and songwriter, Vinx grew up in a suburb of Kansas City and later attended the state university. He then travelled to Montreux, Switzerland, as part of the K.S.U. band, and met Taj Mahal. He found many willing employers for his session music skills in and around Los Angeles. Among his notable musical engagements have been a Grammy award-winning Ernie Watts album, live work with Rickie Lee Jones, and Herbie Hancock's 1990 *Showtime* special. Sting overheard one of Vinx's studio tracks and signed him as a solo artist through his A&M Records subsidiary,

Pangaea. *Rooms In My Fatha's House*, released in 1992, was an auspicious debut, merging samba, funk and hip-hop with the artist's highly individual rhythmic instincts. 1994's *The Storyteller* was a 15-song collection which included a collaboration with Stevie Wonder ('I Will Always Care'), an a cappella rendition of Van Morrison's 'Moondance' and vocal contributions from Omar. A breezy, upbeat record signatured with great musical skill, the songs were premiered on UK tour dates supporting Sting.

● ALBUMS: *Rooms In My Fatha's House* (Pangaea 1992)★★★, *The Storyteller* (Pangaea 1994)★★★.

Vito And The Salutations

A doo-wop vocal group from Brooklyn, New York, USA. The original members were Vito Balsamo (lead), Shelly Buchansky (first and second tenor), Lenny Citrin (baritone/bass), Randy Silverman (first tenor) and Frankie Fox (baritone/bass). The group is known for their wild, up-tempo doo-wop version of 'Unchained Melody' (number 66 pop) from 1963. The record, employing a exotic falsetto and an aggressive bass, was largely an east-coast phenomenon, which was at the time undergoing a doo-wop revival spearheaded by Italian-American groups such as Vito And The Salutations. The group's first record was 'Gloria', a perennial east-coast doo-wop favourite. Despite having been a hit previously for the Cadillacs and the Passions, 'Gloria' effectively launched the group. The English invasion in 1964 made it difficult for Vito And The Salutations to put out records in a neo-doo-wop sound, and the group broke up in 1966. Like many such groups, they experienced periodic reunions, especially during the doo-wop revival of the 70s.

● ALBUMS: *Vito And The Salutations Greatest Hits* (Kape 1973)★★★, *From Doowop To Disco* (Lifestream 1980)★★★, *An Extraordinary Group* (Madison 1990)★★★.

Vocaleers

The original members of this vocal group from Harlem, New York, USA, were Joe Duncan (lead), Herman Curtis (first tenor), William Walker (second tenor), Melvin Walton (baritone) and Teddy Williams (bass). One of the pioneering groups of the R&B era, the Vocaleers' great hit, 'Is It A Dream?' (number 4 R&B, 1953), became a part of the repertoires of a myriad of street-corner groups across the country. The group was formed in 1951 and the following year signed with Bobby Robinson's Red Robin label. Their first release was the ballad 'Be True', which established the group's sound of Duncan's plaintive lead answered by Curtis's falsetto, and earned the group local notices. Williams left the unit at this time and was replaced with Lamar Cooper. The Vocaleers made their last record in 1954, after Herman Curtis was replaced with Joe Powell; Curtis joined the Solitaires. The Vocaleers, with slightly different personnel, reunited in the late 50s, but after a few uninteresting records they disbanded for good in 1961.

● COMPILATIONS: *Is It A Dream?* (Relic 1992)★★★.

Voice Masters

An R&B vocal group from Detroit, Michigan, USA. The members were lead Ty Hunter, Lamont Dozier (b. 16 June 1941, Detroit, USA), David Ruffin (b. 18 January 1941, Meridian, Mississippi, USA, d. 1 June 1991), Walter Gaines and Crathman Spencer. The group was representative of the transitional era from doo-wop to the soul sounds of the Motown label. By the time of their formation in 1959, the Voice Masters were almost all veterans of the Detroit doo-wop scene, Hunter and Dozier having been in the Romeos and Spencer and Gaines having been in the Five Jets. The Voice Masters first recorded for the Anna label, owned by Berry Gordy's sister, Anna Gordy. Only one of their four releases for the label during 1959/60 was heard outside the confines of Detroit, 'Everything About You' (number 18 R&B) in 1960. In attempt by Anna to promote Hunter as a solo artist, the record was also released under Hunter's name alone. Hunter went on to record for Check-mate, recording the gorgeous 'Memories' in 1961 and having a hit with 'Lonely Baby (number 22 R&B) in 1962, both with backing from the Voice Masters. He moved to Chess in 1963 but was not able to sustain any success. Spencer, Gaines and Hunter all eventually became a part of the late 60s Motown group the Originals. Hunter died in 1981. Ruffin went on to join the Temptations, and later developed a solo recording career.

Volumes

This Detroit, Michigan, R&B vocal ensemble consisted of Ed Union (lead), Elijah Davis (first tenor), Larry Wright (second tenor), Joe Travillion (baritone) and Ernest Newsom (bass). Formed in 1960, the Volumes' one hit on the local Chex label, 'I Love You', reached the US R&B Top 10 and pop number 22 in 1962 and showed them to be a typical transition ensemble. Their exotic riffing harmonies, supported by Newsom's marvellous burbling bass work, harked back to the world of doo-wop, but Union's soaring and searing lead looked ahead to the emerging soul era. Despite recording a body of magnificent music over the next decade on a succession of small Detroit labels, the Volumes were never again able to achieve commercial success. The group and their lone hit remained totally forgotten until 1986, when the New Jersey-based Relic Records issued a compilation of their early 60s sides and unreleased a cappella numbers, and the world learned what an underestimated group the Volumes were.

● COMPILATIONS: *The Volumes* (Relic 1986)★★★, *I Love You* (1990)★★★.

Vontastics

The members of this vocal group from Chicago, Illinois, USA, were Bobby Newsome, Kenneth Gholar, Jose Holmes and Raymond Penn. Their soft-soul harmonized songs with a touch of gospel virtually defined the Chicago brand of soul during the 60s. The group broke into the recording scene by winning a local talent contest sponsored by radio station WVON. Their reward was a recording contract with the local St. Lawrence/Satellite label complex, and they began recording as the Vontastics, a name derived from WVON's call letters. They had hits in Chicago and Detroit with the up-tempo 'I'll Never Say Goodbye' (1965), the gentle ballad 'Peace Of Mind' (1965), the mid-tempo 'I Need You' (1965), and a cover version of the Beatles' 'Daytripper' (1966), the latter garnering some national sales. However, that marked the end of their success. Later records on Toddlin' Town, the Philadelphia-based Moonshot and Chess Records had negligible impact.

WALKER, JUNIOR, AND THE ALL STARS

b. Autry DeWalt II, 14 June 1931, Blythesville, Arkansas, USA, d. 23 November 1995. (His record label, Motown, stated that he was born in 1942.) Walker was inspired to take up the saxophone by the jump blues and R&B bands he heard in the early 50s. In his mid-teens, he formed his first instrumental group, the Jumping Jacks, adopting the stage name Junior Walker after a childhood nickname. By 1961 he had achieved a prominent local reputation, which reached the ear of label owner and former Moonglow, Harvey Fuqua. He signed Walker to his Harvey label, allowing him free rein to record a series of raw saxophone-led instrumentals with his All Stars, who comprised Walker, Willie Woods (d. 27 May 1997; guitar), Vic Thomas (organ) and James Graves (d. 1967; drums). In 1964 Walker followed Fuqua to Motown, where he perfected a blend of raunchy R&B and Detroit soul typified by his 1965 hit 'Shotgun'. With its repeated saxophone riffs and call-and-response vocals, it established Walker as the label's prime exponent of traditional R&B, a reputation that was confirmed by later hits such as 'Shake And Fingerpop' and 'Road Runner'. The latter was produced by Holland/Dozier/Holland, who also encouraged Walker to record instrumental versions of hits they had written for other Motown artists.

Walker's style became progressively more lyrical in the late 60s, a development that reached its peak on the 1969 US Top 5 hit, 'What Does It Take (To Win Your Love)?'. This also marked the pinnacle of his commercial success, as subsequent attempts to repeat the winning formula met with growing public indifference, and from 1972 onwards the All Stars recorded only sporadically. *Hot Shot* in 1976, produced by Brian Holland, marked a move towards the burgeoning disco market, which was confirmed on two further albums that year, Walker's first as a solo artist. In 1979, he was one of several Motown artists to move to Whitfield Records. Finding his career deadlocked, Walker returned to Motown in 1983, issuing *Blow The House Down*, an exercise in reclaiming lost ground. The novelty single 'Sex Pot' rekindled memories of his classic hits, although Walker's greatest commercial success in the 80s came when he guested with Foreigner and played the magnificent saxophone solo on their hit single 'Urgent'. He lost a two-year battle with cancer in November 1995.

● ALBUMS: *Shotgun* (Soul 1965)★★★★, *Soul Session* (Soul 1966)★★★★, *Road Runner* (Soul 1966)★★★★, *Live!* (Soul 1967)★★★, *Home Cookin'* (Soul 1969)★★★, *Gotta Hold On To This Feeling* (Soul 1969)★★★, *What Does It Take To Win Your Love?* (Soul 1969)★★★, *Live* (Soul 1970)★★★, *A Gasssssssss* (Soul 1970)★★★, *Rainbow Funk* (Soul 1971)★★★, *Moody Jr.* (Soul 1971)★★★, *Peace And Understanding Is Hard To Find* (Soul 1973)★★, *Hot Shot* (Soul 1976)★★, *Sax Appeal* (Soul 1976)★★★, *Whopper Bopper Show Stopper* (Soul 1976)★★, *... Smooth* (Soul 1978)★★, *Back Street Boogie* (Whitfield 1979)★★, *Blow The House Down* (Motown 1983)★★.

● COMPILATIONS: *Greatest Hits* (Soul 1969)★★★★, *Anthology* (Motown 1974)★★★★, *Junior Walker's Greatest Hits* (Motown 1982)★★★★, *Shake And Fingerpop* (Blue Moon 1989)★★★, *Compact Command Performance - 19 Greatest Hits* (Motown 1992)★★★★.

WALLACE BROTHERS

Of the fine male soul duos, the unrelated Erving Wallace and Johnny Simon were one of the earliest to record in the gospel-based southern-soul style. Raised in Atlanta, they attended the Archer High School, and are said to have had their own six-piece band in the late 50s when they were only 14 and 16 years old. Simon handled most of the vocals and doubled on saxophone, while Wallace played guitar and wrote new material. In 1963-64, the Wallace Brothers recorded the gospel-styled 'Faith'/'I'll Let Nothing Separate Us', 'Precious Words'/'You're Mine' and 'Lover's Prayer'/'Love Me Like I Love You'. Some of these tracks were cut at Rick Hall's Fame studio in Muscle Shoals where Hall had successfully recorded early black soul material such as Arthur Alexander's 'You Better Move On', and Jimmy Hughes' 'I'm Qualified'. The Brothers recorded a total of nine singles for Sims during this period, and their high quality brand of southern-soul is showcased on the rare UK Sue album *Soul Connection*, which reissued much of their best Sims material. After being away from the music scene for a time, the Wallace Brothers resurfaced in 1968/9 on Stan Lewis's Shreveport, Louisiana-based Jewel label with three more good singles, all recorded at Muscle Shoals: 'I Need Someone', a fine Dan Penn-Spooner Oldham soul-ballad, coupled with 'Airborne Shuffle'; 'My Baby's Gone' and the Clarence Carter song 'I Stayed Away Too Long'; and a rehash of Lee Diamond's 'My Mother-in-Law', backed by 'Woman, Hang Your Head In Shame'. They were all released on a 1991 Japanese P-Vine CD of Jewel material,

The Soul Clan. When the Wallace Brothers broke up, Johnny Simon joined the Naturals, who had a hit with 'I Can't Share You' for Calla in 1972.

● COMPILATIONS: *Soul Connection* (Sue 1967)★★★★, *The Soul Clan* six tracks (P-Vine 1991)★★★.

War

Veterans of the Californian west coast circuit, the core of War's line-up - Leroy 'Lonnie' Jordan (b. 21 November 1948, San Diego, California, USA; keyboards), Howard Scott (b. 15 March 1946, San Pedro, California, USA; guitar), Charles Miller (b. 2 June 1939, Olathe, Kansas, USA, d. 1980; flute, saxophone), Morris 'B.B.' Dickerson (b. 3 August 1949, Torrence, California, USA; bass) and Harold Brown (b. 17 March 1946, Long Beach, California, USA; drums) - had made several records under different names including the Creators, the Romeos and Senor Soul. In 1969, the quintet was working as Nightshift, an instrumental group, when ex-Animals lead singer Eric Burdon adopted them as his backing band. Renamed War, the ensemble was completed by Lee Oskar (b. Oskar Levetin Hansen, 24 March 1948, Copenhagen, Denmark; harmonica) and 'Papa' Dee Allen (b. 18 July 1931, Wilmington, Delaware, USA, d. 29 August 1988; percussion). Their debut, *Eric Burdon Declares War*, included the rhythmic 'Spill The Wine', but the group broke away from the UK vocalist following a second collection. War's potent fusion of funk, R&B, rock and Latin styles produced a progressive soul sound best heard on *All Day Music* and *The World Is A Ghetto*. They also enjoyed a significant success in the US singles charts with 'The Cisco Kid' (1973), 'Why Can't We Be Friends?' (1975) and 'Summer' (1976), each of which earned a gold disc, while in the UK they earned two Top 20 hits with 'Low Rider' (1976) and 'Galaxy' (1978). War's subsequent progress proved less fortunate. Despite their early promise, a move to MCA Records was largely unproductive, and the group's record sales slumped. Lee Oskar embarked on an intermittent solo career and further changes undermined their original fire and purpose. Two 1982 singles, 'You Got The Power' and 'Outlaw', suggested a renaissance, but the band was later obliged to finance its own releases. However, a 1987 remake of 'Low Rider', a previous smash hit, did reach the minor places in the R&B chart. Into the 90s the band struggle on, still performing although most of the original members have long since departed.

● ALBUMS: with Eric Burdon *Eric Burdon Declares War* (MGM 1970)★★★, with Burdon *The Black Man's Burdon* (MGM 1970)★★, *War* (United Artists 1971)★★★, *All Day Music* (United Artists 1971)★★★, *The World Is A Ghetto* (United Artists 1972)★★★★, *Deliver The Word* (United Artists 1973)★★★, *War Live!* (United Artists 1974)★★, *Why Can't We Be Friends?* (United Artists 1975)★★★★, *Galaxy* (MCA 1977)★★★, *Youngblood* (United Artists 1978)★★★, *The Music Band* (MCA 1979)★★, *The Music Band 2* (MCA 1979)★★, *The Music Band - Live* (MCA 1980)★★, *Outlaw* (RCA 1982)★★, *Life (Is So Strange)* (RCA 1983)★★, *Where There's Smoke* (Coco Plum 1984)★★, *Peace Sign* (RCA/Avenue 1994)★★.

● COMPILATIONS: *Greatest Hits* (United Artists 1976)★★★★, with Burdon *Love Is All Around* (ABC 1976)★★, *Platinum Jazz* (Blue Note 1977)★★, *The Best Of War . . . And More* (Priority 1987)★★★, *Best Of The Music Band* (MCA 1994)★★★, *Anthology 1970-1994* (Avenue/Rhino 1995)★★★★, *The Best Of War And More: Vol. 2* (Avenue/Rhino 1997)★★★.

Ward, Billy, And The Dominoes

This group was sometimes billed as the Dominoes, or Billy Ward And His Dominoes. Ward (b. 19 September 1921, Los Angeles, California, USA), a songwriter, arranger, singer and pianist, studied music as a child in Los Angeles, and at the age of 14 won a nationwide contest with his composition 'Dejection'. During a spell in the US Army in the early 40s he took up boxing, and continued with the sport when he was released. After working as a sports columnist for the *Transradio Express*, and spending some time with a New York advertising agency, Ward became a vocal coach in his own studio at Carnegie Hall, and founded the Dominoes in 1950. The vocal quintet originally consisted of Clyde McPhatter (b. Clyde Lensley McPhatter, 15 November 1932, Durham, North Carolina, USA, d. 13 June 1972), Charlie White (b. 1930, Washington, DC, USA; second tenor), Joe Lamont (baritone), Bill Brown (bass) and Ward on piano. Ward rarely sang, but, over the years, was the only constant member of the group. Important changes in personnel came in 1952 when White was replaced by James Van Loan, and Bill Brown by David McNeil; and in 1953, when Jackie Wilson (b. 9 June 1934, Detroit, Michigan, USA, d. 21 January 1984, New Jersey, USA) took over from McPhatter, who went on to found his own group, the Drifters. Ward originally formed the group as a gospel unit, and as such, they appeared on the *Arthur Godfrey Talent Show*. However, they began singing more blues numbers, and in the early 50s, made the R&B charts with 'Do Something For Me', 'Sixty Minute Man' (written by Ward and regarded by many as the prototype rock 'n' roll record, featuring a scorching lead vocal from McPhatter), 'I Am With You', 'Have Mercy Baby', 'I'd Be Satisfied', 'One Mint Julep', 'That's What You're Doing To Me', 'The Bells', 'Rags To Riches' and 'These Foolish Things'. By 1956, when *Billy Ward And The Dominoes* was released, the group's personnel consisted of Gene Mumford, Milton Merle, Milton Grayson, Cliff Owens and Ward. In the late 50s they had US Top 20 hits with 'St. Therese Of The Roses', 'Deep Purple' and 'Stardust', which sold over a million copies. Afterwards, the recorded hits dried up, but the Dominoes, regarded as one of the important, pioneering R&B vocal groups of the 50s, continued to be a popular US concert attraction throughout the 60s.

● ALBUMS: *Billy Ward And His Dominoes* (Federal 1955)★★★★, *Clyde McPhatter With Billy Ward* (Federal 1956)★★★, *24 Songs* (King 1956)★★★, *Sea Of Glass* (Liberty 1957)★★★, *Yours Forever* (Liberty 1958)★★★, *Pagan Love Song* (Liberty 1959)★★★.

● COMPILATIONS: *Billy Ward And His Dominoes With Clyde McPhatter* (King 1958)★★★★, *Billy Ward & His Dominoes Featuring Clyde McPhatter And Jackie Wilson* (King 1961)★★★★, *The Dominoes Featuring Jackie Wilson* (1977)★★★★, *Have Mercy Baby* (1985)★★★★, *14 Original Hits* (King 1988)★★★★, *21 Original Greatest Hits*

(King 1988)★★★★, *Feat* (Sing 1988)★★★, *Sixty Minute Man* (Charly 1991)★★★★.

WARD, ROBERT

b. 15 October 1938, Luthersville, Georgia, USA. Ward's rediscovery in 1990 is a rare instance of a 'legend' returning from more than a decade of obscurity with his talent undiminished. A self-taught guitarist, he formed his first band, the Brassettes, in Avon Park, Florida, in 1959 after two years' army service. Returning to Georgia, he pawned a Gibson Les Paul in order to afford the move to Dayton, Ohio, where he lived with an aunt. His next group, the Ohio Untouchables, was the quintessential R&B garage band, its celebrity owing, in large part, to Ward's use of a Magnatone amplifier with its distinctive vibrato effect. The group made a number of singles for the Detroit-based Lupine label, most famously 'Forgive Me Darling', an extended guitar showcase loosely based on Bo Diddley's 'I'm Sorry'. Producer Robert West used them to back the Falcons' 'I Found A Love', with Wilson Pickett as lead vocalist. When Pickett set out on a solo career, Ward went with him, while the other Untouchables eventually mutated into the Ohio Players. Further live and session work for the Temptations and the Undisputed Truth kept Ward out of the public eye. Following the deaths of his wife and mother in 1977, he abandoned music and returned to Dry Branch, Georgia. He was rediscovered by Black Top producer Hammond Scott after a two-year search. *Fear No Evil*, featuring re-recordings of 'Forgive Me Darling' and 'Your Love Is Real', was a resounding critical success, bringing Ward a measure of international celebrity and establishing him as a popular artist at festivals in America and Europe. *Rhythm Of The People* was slightly less focused but did introduce his wife, Roberta, who regularly appears singing gospel songs with him. *Black Bottom* was a mixture of regular blues with redolent 60s soul music, featuring Mark 'Kaz' Kazanoff (tenor and baritone saxophone), Ward Smith (tenor and baritone saxophone), Ernest Youngblood Jr. (tenor saxophone), Steve Howard (trumpet), Rick Trolsen (trombone) and Jimmy Weber (trumpet). This brass section perfectly complemented Ward's frequently thin-sounding Fender Telecaster.

● ALBUMS: *Three Shades Of Blue* (Lupine 1984)★★★, *Fear No Evil* (Black Top 1990)★★★, *Blues Cocktail Party!* (Black Top 1991)★★, *Black Top Blues-A-Rama Vol. 7* (Black Top 1993)★★★, *Rhythm Of The People* (Black Top 1993)★★★, *Black Bottom* (Black Top 1995)★★★, *Hot Stuff* (Relic 1995)★★★.

● COMPILATIONS: *Twiggs Country Soul Man* (Black Top 1997)★★★.

WARE, LEON

b. Detroit, Michigan, USA. Leon Ware was one of several Motown producers who gained their first experience of the industry in the mid-50s doo-wop group the Romeos. By the end of the decade, he had joined ABC Records, where he acted as an arranger and songwriter. He continued to work as a 'backroom boy' in the 60s, first at Motown, then at Bell Records, turning freelance at the start of the 70s. He wrote the majority of Ike And Tina Turner's *Nuff Said* in 1970, before rejoining Motown and co-writing Michael Jackson's 1972 hit 'I Wanna Be Where You Are' with T-Boy Ross, brother of Diana Ross. Ware re-emerged as a vocalist in 1973, when he was featured on Quincy Jones's *Body Heat*. With T-Boy Ross, he then began work on a romantic song-cycle, intending it to be his own solo debut. Instead, Motown boss Berry Gordy persuaded Ware to give the songs to Marvin Gaye, in return for being allowed to produce the errant superstar. The result was the delicate and tender *I Want You*, one of Gaye's most cohesive artistic achievements. This exposure enabled Ware to launch his own career with the acclaimed *Musical Massage*. Leaving Motown in 1978, he enjoyed minor US hits in 1979 and 1981 with 'What's Your Name?' and 'Baby Don't Stop Me', in the same heavily produced, lush style that he had fashioned for Gaye.

● ALBUMS: *Musical Massage* (Motown 1976)★★★★, *Inside Is Love* (Fabulous 1979)★★★, *Rockin' You Eternally* (Elektra 1981)★★★, *Leon Ware* (Elektra 1982)★★★, *Undercover Lover* (Sling Shot 1989)★★★.

WARREN, ALISTER

b. Alister Tennent, 16 January 1973, London, England. Warren's career began as a songwriter with his friend Wayne Hector in 1989. In the early 90s they were introduced to Fab 5 Freddy, who encouraged them to join forces with John and George Hammond Hagan to form the UK R&B group Rhythm And Bass. They were the first UK-based R&B group to win a major label contract, which led to two Top 40 hits, 'Roses' and 'Can't Stop The Feeling'. Their notoriety soared when they provided support to top US acts including Jodeci, Boyz II Men and Sounds Of Blackness. While work was underway for the group's debut album, *Better Late Than Never*, musical differences led to the demise of the alliance, and in 1993 Rhythm And Bass ended their recording contract. Warren and Hector decided to concentrate on writing, while the Hagans went into production work. Warren and Hector formed Aliway, securing a contract with Rondor and a showcase at the IAAAM/Best conference in 1994. Having impressed the UK showcase the duo were featured in the New York showcase, which led to work with Eddie F, Herb Middleton, Darren Whittington and the notorious Groove Theory. In late 1995 Warren returned to performing as Ali, while also writing for Ultimate Kaos and Damage, notably the UK Top 20 hits 'Forever' and 'Love II Love'. His songwriting abilities were equally efficacious in the lovers rock genre when 'Forever' was remixed at Fashion Records studios by Chris Lane for the *Pure Reggae* compilation. Alongside his writing commitments he dedicated much of 1997 to recording his debut album.

WARWICK, DEE DEE

b. 1945, New Jersey, USA. Warwick has always sung in the shadow of her older sister, Dionne Warwick, but she has created a body of work that stands up well decades later. Her first record on the Jubilee label, 'You're No Good', was superseded by the much superior production done in Chicago by Vee Jay for Betty Everett. In 1964 Warwick signed with Mercury's Blue Rock subsidiary and, with production handled by Ed Townsend, recorded a spate of finely crafted songs, notably 'We're Doing Fine' (number 28 R&B). After switching to the parent label in 1966 she reached the charts with 'I Want To Be With You' (number 9 R&B, number 41 pop), which was taken from the Broadway musical *Golden Boy*, and 'I'm Gonna Make You Love Me' (number 13 R&B, number 88 pop), which was remade the following year with much greater success in the pop market by Madelaine Bell and much later by a united Supremes/Temptations group. Warwick moved to Atco in 1970 and was produced in Miami by Dave Crawford, achieving chart success with 'She Didn't Know (She Kept On Talking)' (number 9 R&B, number 70 pop) and a remake of 'Suspicious Minds' (number 24 R&B, number 80 pop). 'Get Out Of My Life' was her last chart record in 1975.

● ALBUMS: *I Want To Be With You/I'm Gonna Make You Love Me* (Mercury 1967)★★★, *Foolish Fool* (Mercury 1969)★★, *Turning Around* (Atco 1970)★★.

WARWICK, DIONNE

b. Marie Dionne Warrick, 12 December 1940, East Orange, New Jersey, USA. One of soul music's truly sophisticated voices, Warwick first sang in Newark's New Hope Baptist Church choir. She played piano with the Drinkard Singers, a gospel group her mother managed, and studied at Connecticut's Hart School of Music. During the same period, Warwick also formed the Gospelaires with her sister, Dee Dee, and aunt Cissy Houston. Increasingly employed as backing singers, the trio's voices appeared on records by the Drifters and Garnet Mimms. Through such work Warwick came into contact with songwriters Burt Bacharach and Hal David. Her first solo single, on the Scepter label, 'Don't Make Me Over' (1963), was a fragile slice of 'uptown R&B' and set the tone for such classic collaborations as 'Anyone Who Had A Heart' and 'Walk On By'. Bacharach's sculpted, almost grandiose, compositions were the perfect setting for Warwick's light yet perfect phrasing, delicate almost to the point of vulnerability. 'You'll Never Get To Heaven (If You Break My Heart)', 'Reach Out For Me' (both 1964) and 'Are You There (With Another Girl)' (1966) epitomized the style. Although many of her singles charted, few were Top 10 hits, and the soulful edge, prevalent for the first two years, was gradually worn away. As her songwriters moved ever closer to the mainstream, so Dionne too embraced a safer, albeit classier, approach with such successes as the uplifting 'I Say A Little Prayer' (1967) and 'Do You Know The Way To San Jose?' (1968).

In 1971 Warwick abandoned both her label and mentors for Warner Brothers Records, but despite several promising releases, the relationship disintegrated. Around this time she also added an extra 'e' to the end of her name, on advice given to her by an astrologer. Her biggest hit came with the (Detroit) Spinners on the Thom Bell-produced 'Then Came You' (1974). Warwick moved to Arista Records in 1979 where her work with Barry Manilow rekindled her commercial standing. *Heartbreaker*, her collaboration with the Bee Gees, resulted in several hit singles, while a pairing with Luther Vandross on 'How Many Times Can We Say Goodbye?' was also a success. 'That's What Friends Are For' pitted Dionne with Elton John, Gladys Knight and Stevie Wonder, and became a number 1 in both the US R&B and pop charts. Duets with Jeffrey Osborne, Kashif and Howard Hewitt, of Shalamar, maintained this newly rediscovered profile in the 80s.

● ALBUMS: *Presenting Dionne Warwick* (Scepter 1963)★★★, *Anyone Who Had A Heart* (1964)★★★★, *Make Way For Dionne Warwick* (Scepter 1964)★★★★, *The Sensitive Sound Of Dionne Warwick* (Scepter 1965)★★★★, *Here I Am* (Scepter 1966)★★★★, *Dionne Warwick In Paris* (Scepter 1966)★★★, *Here Where There Is Love* (Scepter 1967)★★★, *Dionne Warwick Onstage And In The Movies* (Scepter 1967)★★★, *The Windows Of The World* (Scepter 1967)★★★, *Dionne In The Valley Of The Dolls* (Scepter 1968)★★★★, *Magic Of Believing* (1968)★★★, *Promises Promises* (Scepter 1968)★★★★, *Soulful* (Scepter 1969)★★★, *Dionne Warwick's Greatest Motion Picture Hits* (Scepter 1969)★★★, *I'll Never Fall In Love Again* (Scepter 1970)★★★, *Very Dionne* (Scepter 1970)★★, *The Dionne Warwick Story - Live* (Scepter 1971)★★, *Dionne* (Warners 1972)★★, *From Within* (Scepter 1972)★★, *Just Being Myself* (Warners 1973)★★, *Then Came You* (Warners 1975)★★★, *Track Of The Cat* (Warners 1975)★★★, with Isaac Hayes *A Man And A Woman* (HBS 1977)★, *Only Love Can Break A Heart* (Musicor 1977)★★★, *Love At First Sight* (Warners 1977)★★, *Dionne* (Arista 1979)★★★★, *No Night So Long* (Arista 1980)★★, *Hot! Live And Otherwise* (Arista 1981)★★★, *Friends In Love* (Arista 1982)★★★, *Heartbreaker* (Arista 1982)★★★, *How Many Times Can We Say Goodbye* US title *So Amazing* UK title (Arista 1983)★★★, *Finder Of Lost Loves* (Arista 1985)★★★, *Friends* (Arista 1985)★★★, *Without Your Love* (Arista 1985)★★★, *Reservations For Two* (Arista 1987)★★★, *Dionne Warwick Sings Cole Porter* (Arista 1989)★★★, *Friends Can Be Lovers* (Arista 1993)★★★, *Aquarela Do Brazil* (Arista 1995)★★★.

● COMPILATIONS: *Dionne Warwick's Golden Hits, Part 1* (Scepter 1967)★★★★, *Dionne Warwick's Golden Hits, Part 2* (Scepter 1969)★★★★, *The Dionne Warwick Collection* (Pickwick 1976)★★★, *Golden Collection* (K-Tel 1981)★★★, *20 Greatest Hits* (AFE 1981)★★★, *20 Golden Pieces* (Bulldog 1982)★★★, *The Best Of Dionne Warwick* (Warners 1983)★★★★, *Anthology* (Rhino 1985)★★★★, *Dionne Warwick Classics* (K-Tel 1986)★★★, *The Original Soul Of Dionne Warwick* (Charly 1987)★★★, *20 Greatest Hits: Dionne Warwick* (Bescol 1987)★★★, *25th Anniversary Collection* (Hallmark 1988)★★★, *The Love Songs* (Arista 1989)★★★★, *Greatest Hits 1979-1990* (Arista 1989)★★★★, *The Dionne Warwick Collection/Her All Time Greatest Hits* (Rhino 1990)★★★★, *Hidden Gems* (Rhino 1992)★★★, *The Essential Collection* (Global 1996)★★★★.

● VIDEOS: *An Evening With Dionne Warwick* (MSD 1987), *Dionne Warwick In Concert* (Video Collection 1987), *Dionne Warwick Volume 1* (Pickwick 1992), *Dionne Warwick Volume 2* (Pickwick 1992).

WASHINGTON, BABY

b. Justine Washington, 13 November 1940, Bamberg, South Carolina, USA. Washington's (aka Jeanette

Washington) tremendously moving voice, earthy but sophisticated, perfectly epitomized uptown soul. Nevertheless, unlike her southern counterparts she has never experienced great crossover recognition, although once cited by Dusty Springfield as her all-time favourite singer. Washington was raised in Harlem, singing first in a vocal group, the Hearts, in 1956 and becoming a solo artist the following year. She built a career with 16 chart entries during a decade and a half, most of them during the 60s, recording in New York first for Donald Shaw's Neptune label and then for Juggy Murray's Sue label. She established herself as a major soul singer, recording 'The Time' (US R&B Top 30) and 'The Bells' (US R&B Top 20), both in 1959, and 'Nobody Cares' (US R&B Top 20) in 1961. Moving to Sue Records in 1962, Washington hit the US national Top 40 with the sublime 'That's How Heartaches Are Made' (1963) and the US R&B Top 10 with 'Only Those In Love' (1965). Washington revived her career in the early 70s, recording in Philadelphia a duet with Don Gardner, a revival of the Marvelettes' 'Forever' (number 30 R&B), a solo release, 'I've Got To Break Away' (number 73 R&B), and a well-received album. The advent of disco in the mid-70s effectively killed her career, as it did those of many soul artists.

● ALBUMS: *That's How Heartaches Are Made* (Sue 1963)★★★★, *Only Those In Love* (Sue 1965)★★★, *With You In Mind* (Veep 1968)★★, with Don Gardner *Lay A Little Lovin' On Me* (1973)★★★, *I Wanna Dance* (1978)★★★.

● COMPILATIONS: *Great Oldies* (70s)★★★, *The One And Only* (1971)★★★, *The Best Of Baby Washington* (1987)★★★, *Only Those In Love* (1988)★★★, *That's How Heartaches Are Made* (1989)★★★, *Only Those In Love* (1989)★★★, *The Best Of ...* (1989)★★★, *The Sue Singles* (Kent 1996)★★★★.

WASHINGTON, DINAH

b. Ruth Jones, 29 August 1924, Tuscaloosa, Alabama, USA, d. 14 December 1963, Detroit, Michigan, USA. Raised in Chicago, Dinah Washington first sang in church choirs for which she also played piano. She then worked in local clubs, where she was heard by Lionel Hampton, who promptly hired her. She was with Hampton from 1943-46, recording hits with 'Evil Gal Blues', written by Leonard Feather, and 'Salty Papa Blues'. After leaving Hampton she sang R&B, again achieving record success, this time with 'Blow Top Blues' and 'I Told You Yes I Do'. In the following years Washington continued with R&B, but also sang jazz, blues, popular songs of the day, standards, and was a major voice of the burgeoning, but as yet untitled, soul movement. However, her erratic lifestyle caught up with her and she died suddenly at the age of 39. Almost from the start of her career, Washington successfully blended the sacred music of her childhood with the sometimes earthily salacious secularity of the blues. This combination was a potent brew and audiences idolized her, thus helping her towards riches rarely achieved by black artists of her generation. She thoroughly enjoyed her success, spending money indiscriminately on jewellery, cars, furs, drink, drugs and men. She married many times and had countless liaisons. Physically, she appeared to thrive on her excesses, as can be seen from her performance in the film of the 1958 Newport Jazz Festival, *Jazz On A Summer's Day*. She was settling down happily with her seventh husband when she took a lethal combination of pills, probably by accident, after having too much to drink. Washington's voice was rich and she filled everything she sang with heartfelt emotion. Even when the material was not of the highest quality, she could make the most trite of lyrics appear deeply moving. Amongst her popular successes were 'What A Diff'rence A Day Makes', her biggest hit, which reached number 8 in the USA in 1959, and 'September In The Rain', which made number 35 in the UK in 1961. Washington usually sang alone but in the late 50s she recorded some duets with her then husband, Eddie Chamblee. These records enjoyed a measure of success and were followed in 1960 with songs with Brook Benton, notably 'Baby (You Got What It Takes)' and 'A Rockin' Good Way (To Mess Around And Fall In Love)', both of which proved to be enormously popular, reaching numbers 5 and 7, respectively, in the US charts. Washington left a wealth of recorded material, ranging from *The Jazz Sides*, which feature Clark Terry, Jimmy Cleveland, Blue Mitchell and others, to albums of songs by or associated with Fats Waller and Bessie Smith. On these albums, as on almost everything she recorded, Washington lays claim to being one of the major jazz voices, and probably the most versatile of all the singers to have worked in jazz.

● ALBUMS: *Dinah Washington Songs* 10-inch album (Mercury 1950)★★★, *Dynamic Dinah* 10-inch album (Mercury 1951)★★★, *Blazing Ballads* 10-inch album (Mercury 1952)★★★, 10-inch album *After Hours With Miss D* (EmArcy 1954)★★★, *Dinah Jams* (EmArcy 1954)★★★, *For Those In Love* (EmArcy 1955)★★★, *Dinah* (EmArcy 1956)★★★, *In The Land Of Hi Fi* (EmArcy 1956)★★★★, *The Swingin' Miss D* (EmArcy 1956)★★★, *Dinah Washington Sings Fats Waller* (EmArcy 1957)★★★, *Music For A First Love* (Mercury 1957)★★★, *Music For Late Hours* (Mercury 1957)★★★★, *The Best In Blues* (Mercury 1958)★★★, *Dinah Washington Sings Bessie Smith* (EmArcy 1958)★★★, *Newport '58* (EmArcy 1958)★★★★, *The Queen* (Mercury 1959)★★★, *What A Difference A Day Makes!* (Mercury 1959)★★★, *Unforgettable* (Mercury 1960)★★★, *I Concentrate On You* (Mercury 1961)★★★, *For Lonely Lovers* (Mercury 1961)★★★★, *September In The Rain* (Mercury 1961)★★★★, *Tears And Laughter* (Mercury 1962)★★★, *Dinah '62* (Roulette 1962)★★★★, *In Love* (Roulette 1962)★★★, *Drinking Again* (Roulette 1962)★★★, *I Wanna Be Loved* (Mercury 1962)★★★★, *Back To The Blues* (Roulette 1963)★★★, *Dinah '63* (Roulette 1963)★★★.

● COMPILATIONS: with the Quincy Jones Orchestra *This Is My Story, Volume One* (Mercury 1963)★★★★, *This Is My Story, Volume Two* (Mercury 1963)★★★★, *In Tribute* (Roulette 1963)★★★, *The Good Old Days* (Mercury 1963)★★, with Sarah Vaughan, Joe Williams *We Three* (1964)★★★, *Stranger On Earth* (Roulette 1964)★★★, *The Best Of Dinah Washington* (Roulette 1965)★★★, *The Queen And Quincy* (Mercury 1965)★★★,

The Original Queen Of Soul (Mercury 1969)★★★, *The Jazz Sides* (EmArcy 1976)★★★, with Brook Benton coupled with a Sarah Vaughan and Billy Eckstine collection *The Two Of Us* (Mercury 1978)★★★, *Spotlight On Dinah Washington* (1980)★★★★, *A Slick Chick (On The Mellow Side)* (EmArcy 1983)★★★★, *The Best Of Dinah Washington* (Mercury 1987)★★★★, *The Complete Dinah Washington Vols. 1-14 (1943-55)* (Mercury 1990)★★★★, *Best Of Dinah Washington* (Roulette 1992)★★★★, *Mellow Mama* recorded 1945 (Delmark 1992)★★★★, *The Dinah Washington Story* (Mercury 1993)★★★★, *First Issue: The Dinah Washington Story, The Original Recordings* 1943-61 recordings (Mercury 1993)★★★★, *Blue Gardenia* (EmArcy/Verve 1995)★★★.

● FURTHER READING: *Queen Of The Blues: A Biography Of Dinah Washington*, James Haskins.

WASHINGTON, ELLA

b. Miami, Florida, USA. Washington was a deep-soul southern singer, thoroughly steeped in gospel music, who made a minor impact during the soul era of the late 60s. She made her first recordings in Miami in 1965 for the local Octavia label, but no hits resulted. In 1967 she signed with John Richbourg's Sound Stage 7, based in Nashville. Most of Washington's singles were recorded in Muscle Shoals, Alabama, where the session musicians had a feel for soul, and the happy result was Washington's evocative reading of the Harlan Howard ballad 'He Called Me Baby' (number 18 R&B, number 77 pop) in 1969. Lesser hits followed - a remake of the 1961 Joyce Davis classic, 'Stop Giving Your Man Away' (number 38 R&B) from 1969, and 'Trying To Make You Love Me' (number 53 R&B) from 1970. Two of her finest ballad singles, 'I Want To Walk Through This World With You' (1969) and 'Doing The Best I Can' (1969), failed to find an audience. In 1973, with the market for southern soul diminishing rapidly, Washington left the R&B field to sing gospel music.

● ALBUMS: *Ella Washington* (Sound Stage 7 1969)★★★.

● COMPILATIONS: *Nobody But Me* (Charly 1987)★★★.

WASHINGTON, GENO (AND THE RAM JAM BAND)

Born in Indiana, USA, Washington was in the US Air Force, stationed in East Anglia, England, when he initiated his singing career by climbing onstage to join a local band for an impromptu performance. On leaving the services, he remained in Britain and headed for London, where he fronted the Ram Jam Band, which comprised Pete Gage (guitar), Lionel Kingham (tenor saxophone), Buddy Beadle (baritone saxophone), Jeff Wright (organ), John Roberts (bass) and Herb Prestige (drums). The group adopted a fast-paced, almost frantic style that pitched one soul favourite after another, deliberately leaving the audience with little time to breathe, or to question the ensemble's lack of subtlety. Although none of Washington's singles reached the UK Top 30, his fervent in-concert popularity ensured that the first two albums charted, both reaching the UK Top 10. The formula was repeated on later collections, but by 1968 the mixture was growing ever more anachronistic as progressions elsewhere in music left the Ram Jam Band behind. Peter Gage went on to join Vinegar Joe. They disbanded by the end of the decade and Washington's several comebacks notwithstanding, the group remained fixed to a particular mid-60s era. Although immortalized in the 1980 UK number 1 hit 'Geno', by Dexys Midnight Runners, Washington was more of a footnote than innovator. He continues to record sporadically, and performs the occasional London club date and tour. Part of his current act incorporates, with audience participation, Washington's musical talents with hypnotism. In the mid-90s he had seemingly reinvented himself as a blues singer.

● ALBUMS: with the Ram Jam Band *Hand Clappin' - Foot Stompin' - Funky Butt - Live!* (Piccadilly 1966)★★★, *Hipsters, Flipsters, Finger Poppin' Daddies* (Piccadilly 1967)★★, *Shake A Tail Feather* (Piccadilly 1968)★★, *Running Wild - Live* (Pye 1969)★★, *Up Tight* (1969)★★. Solo: Geno Washington *Geno's Back* (1976)★★, *Live* (1976)★★, *That's Why Hollywood Loves Me* (DJM 1979)★★, *Put Out The Cat* (Teldec 1981)★★, *Live Sideways* (Ammunition 1986)★★, *Take That Job And Stuff It* (Konnexion 1987)★★, *Loose Lips* (Uncensored 1995)★★, *What's In The Pot?* (Sound FX 1997)★★★.

WASHINGTON, GROVER, JNR.

b. 11 November 1943, Buffalo, New York, USA. Growing up in a musical family, Washington was playing tenor saxophone before he was a teenager. He studied formally and also paid his dues gigging locally on tenor and other instruments in the early 60s. After military service in the late 60s he returned to his career, recording a succession of albums under the aegis of producer Creed Taylor that effectively crossed over into the new market for jazz fusion. By the mid-70s, Washington's popular success had begun to direct the course of his music-making and he moved further away from jazz. Commercially, this brought continuing successes, among them 'The Two Of Us', with vocals by Bill Withers, which reached number 2 in the US pop charts in 1981, and the popular album *The Best Is Yet To Come* with Patti Labelle. Over the years, Washington has earned five gold albums. *Winelight* sold over a million copies, achieving platinum status, and gained two Grammy awards. Washington's playing displays great technical mastery and early in his career his often blues-derived saxophone styling sometimes gave his playing greater depths than the quality of the material warranted. The fact that much of his recorded output proved to be popular in the setting of discos tended to smooth out his playing as the years passed, depleting the characteristics that had attracted so much attention at the start of his career. By the late 80s Washington was still enjoying a degree of popular success, although not at the same high level as a few years before. He has continued to record for Columbia Records into the 90s.

● ALBUMS: *Inner City Blues* (Kudu 1971)★★, *All The King's Horses* (Kudu 1972)★★, *Soul Box* (Kudu 1973)★★, *Mister Magic* (Kudu 1975)★★★, *Feels So Good* (Kudu 1975)★★★, *A Secret Place* (Kudu 1976)★★★, *Live At The Bijou* (Kudu 1977)★★★, with Locksmith *Reed Seed* (Motown 1978)★★, *Paradise* (Elektra 1979)★★★★, *Skylarkin'* (Motown 1980)★★★, *Winelight* (Elektra 1980)★★★★, *Come Morning* (Elektra 1981)★★★, *The*

Best Is Yet To Come (Elektra 1982)★★★, *Inside Moves* (Elektra 1984)★★★, *Playboy Jazz Festival* (Elektra 1984)★★★, *Strawberry Moon* (Columbia 1987)★★, *Then And Now* (Columbia 1988)★★, *Time Out Of Mind* (Columbia 1989)★★, *Next Exit* (Columbia 1992)★★, *All My Tomorrows* (Columbia 1994)★★★, *Soulful Strut* (Columbia 1996)★★★.
● COMPILATIONS: *Baddest* (Motown 1980)★★★, *Anthology* (Motown 1981)★★★, *Greatest Performances* (Motown 1983)★★★, *At His Best* (Motown 1985)★★★, *Anthology* (Elektra 1985)★★★.

WATLEY, JODY

b. 30 January 1959, Chicago, Illinois, USA. Formerly one third of Shalamar between 1977 and 1984, a hugely successful group of the disco era, Watley's first professional experience had come as a dancer on the television show *Soul Train*. After Shalamar disbanded she made the progression to solo artist, working in a contemporary soul/urban R&B vein. Her self-titled debut album, released in 1987, became a million-seller and included three US Top 10 hits - 'Looking For A New Love', 'Don't You Want Me' and 'Some Kind Of Lover'. It brought her a Grammy award for best new artist of 1987. The subsequent *Larger Than Life* achieved gold status, and included the US number 2 hit 'Real Love', as well as further hits 'Everything' and 'Friends', a collaboration with Eric B And Rakim and Whodini. 'Precious Love' (1990) was remixed by Soul II Soul's Simon Law and 'I'm The One You Need' by David Morales and Drizabone as part of the remix project *You Wanna Dance With Me?*. Though not replicating the scale of earlier successes, the release of *Affairs Of The Heart* and *Intimacy* consolidated her position as one of the most energetic and able contemporary soul singers, readily adaptable to changes in R&B such as the 'swing' and hip-hop movements. She moved to Avitone Records in 1995 for *Affection*.
● ALBUMS: *Jody Watley* (MCA 1987)★★★, *Larger Than Life* (MCA 1989)★★★, *You Wanna Dance With Me?* (MCA 1989)★★, *Affairs Of The Heart* (MCA 1991)★★★, *Intimacy* (MCA 1994)★★★, *Affection* (Avitone 1995)★★★.

WATSON, JOHNNY 'GUITAR'

b. 3 February 1935, Houston, Texas, USA, d. 17 May 1996, Yokohama, Japan. Before Watson made a name for himself in the 70s playing funk R&B, he had a long career stretching back to the early 50s. His father played piano, which also became Johnny's first instrument. On seeing Clarence 'Gatemouth' Brown perform, he convinced himself that he had to play guitar. He inherited a guitar from his grandfather, a sanctified preacher, on the condition that he did not play the blues on it - 'that was the first thing I played', Watson later said. In the early 50s his family moved to Los Angeles, where he started playing piano in the Chuck Higgins band and was billed as 'Young John Watson'. Switching to guitar, he was signed to Federal and recorded 'Space Guitar', an instrumental far ahead of its time in the use of reverberation and feedback. He also played 'Motorhead Baby' with an enthusiasm that was to become his trademark. He recorded the same track for Federal with the Amos Milburn band in tow. Watson became in demand as a guitarist and in the late 50s toured and recorded with the Olympics, Don And Dewey and Little Richard. Johnny 'Guitar' Watson was from the same mould of flamboyance that motivated another of Little Richard's guitarists, Jimi Hendrix. Watson later stated: 'I used to play the guitar standing on my hands, I had a 150 foot cord and I could get on top of the auditorium - those things Jimi Hendrix was doing, I *started* that shit!'. Moving to the Modern label in 1955, he had immediate success with a bluesy ballad, 'Those Lonely, Lonely Nights' (US R&B Top 10), but failed to follow up on the label. In 1957 the novelty tune 'Gangster Of Love' (later adopted by Steve Miller) gave him a minor hit on the west coast. A partnership with Larry Williams was particularly successful and in 1965 they toured England and recorded an album for Decca. Watson did not return to the charts until 1962, when on the King label he hit with 'Cuttin' In' (US R&B number 6), which was recorded with string accompaniment. The following year he recorded *I Cried For You*, a 'cocktail-lounge' album with hip renditions of 'Polkadots And Moonbeams' and 'Witchcraft'. The Beatles invasion signified hard times for the inventors of rock 'n' roll. Watson recorded two soulful funk albums for the Fantasy label (*Listen* and *I Don't Want To Be Alone, Stranger*) with keyboardist Andre Lewis (who later toured with Frank Zappa). As if to repay his enthusiasm for Watson's guitar playing, which Zappa had often admitted to admiring, Watson was recruited for Zappa's *One Size Fits All* in 1975. In 1976 Watson released *Ain't That A Bitch* on DJM Records, a brilliant marriage of 50s rockin' R&B, Hollywood schmaltz and futuristic funk. Watson produced, played bass, keyboards and drums on the album, which went gold; a further six albums appeared on DJM to the same formula. In 1981 he left the label for A&M Records, but the production diluted Watson's unique sound and the record was a failure. One positive side effect was a characteristic solo on Herb Alpert's *Beyond*. Watson retired to lick his wounds, emerging with *Strike On Computers* at the end of the 80s and an appearance at London's Town & Country Club in 1987. In the 90s his music was sampled by Snoop Doggy Dogg and Dr Dre, and the album *Bow Wow* made the US charts. Watson died of a heart attack while performing at the Yokohama Blues Cafe on 17 May 1996.
● ALBUMS: *Gangster Of Love* (King 1958)★★★★, *Johnny Guitar Watson* (King 1963)★★★, *The Blues Soul Of Johnny Guitar Watson* (Chess 1964)★★★★, *Bad* (Chess 1966)★★★★, with Larry Williams *Two For The Price Of One* (OKeh 1967)★★★★, *Johnny Watson Plays Fats Waller In The Fats Bag* (OKeh 1968)★★★, *Listen* (Fantasy 1974)★★★, *I Don't Want To Be Alone, Stranger* (Fantasy 1975)★★★, *Captured Live* (1976)★★★, *Ain't That A Bitch* (DJM 1976)★★★, *A Real Mother For Ya* (DJM 1977)★★, *Funk Beyond The Call Of Duty* (DJM 1977)★★, *Gangster Of Love* (DJM 1977)★★★, with the Watsonian Institute *Master Funk* (1978)★★, *Giant* (DJM 1978)★★, with Papa John Creach *Inphasion* (DJM 1978)★★, with the Watsonian Institute *Extra Disco Perception* (1979)★★, *What The Hell Is This?* (DJM 1979)★★, *Love Jones* (DJM 1980)★★, *Johnny 'Guitar' Watson And The Family Clone*

(DJM 1981)★★, *That's What Time It Is* (A&M 1981)★★, *Strike On Computers* (Valley Vue 1984)★★, *Bow Wow* (M-Head 1994)★★.

● COMPILATIONS: *The Very Best Of Johnny 'Guitar' Watson* (DJM 1981)★★★★, *I Heard That!* (Chess 1985)★★★★, *Hit The Highway* (Ace 1985)★★★★, *Gettin' Down With Johnny 'Guitar' Watson* (Chess 1987)★★★, *Three Hours Past Midnight* (Flair 1991)★★★, *Gangster Of Love* (Charly 1991)★★★★★, *Listen/I Don't Want To Be Alone, Stranger* (Ace 1992)★★★, *Gangster Of Love: The Best Of Johnny 'Guitar' Watson* (Castle 1995)★★★★, *Hot Just Like TNT* (Ace 1996)★★★★.

WATTS 103RD STREET RHYTHM BAND

Originally conceived as an instrumental group, Bernard Blackman (guitar), Raymond Jackson (trombone), John Rayford (b. 1943; tenor saxophone), Melvin Dunlap (bass) and James Gadson (drums), were still known by their former name, the Soul Runners, when a 1967 release, 'Grits And Cornbread', reached the US R&B Top 30. Having changed their name in deference to the Watts district of Los Angeles, they enjoyed further success with 'Spreadin Honey' the same year. The group also backed comedian Bill Cosby, whose influence helped to secure a contract with Warner Brothers Records. The new signings then acquired a featured vocalist, Charles Wright (b. 1942, Clarksdale, Mississippi, USA), and following two 1969 singles, 'Do Your Thing' and 'Till You Get Enough', the band's name was changed to Charles Wright And The Watts 103rd Street Band. Subsequent singles 'Express Yourself' (1970) and 'Your Love (Means Everything To Me)' (1971) both reached the soul Top 10, but their unstable personnel constantly undermined the group's potential. Wright later left the group for a solo career.

● ALBUMS: *Cornbread And Grits* (Keymen 1967)★★★, *Together* (Warners 1968)★★, *In The Jungle, Babe* (Warners 1969)★★; as Charles Wright And The Watts 103rd Street Band *Express Yourself* (Warners 1970)★★★, *You're So Beautiful* (Warners 1971)★★.

WATTSTAX

During the 60s, the Memphis-based Stax label established itself as a leading outlet for southern soul music. Otis Redding, Sam And Dave, Rufus Thomas and Booker T. And The MGs were among the successful acts of its early, halcyon era. By 1973 the company had severed its ties with Atlantic Records, opting instead for a liaison with the Gulf-Western group, whose ties with the Paramount Film Studio gave rise to this feature film. The black ghetto of Watts, a suburb of Los Angeles, had been the site of several riots and had come to symbolize aspects of the civil rights struggle. Nevertheless, crippling poverty remained, inspiring Stax to stage and film a concert there, celebrating the area's communal aspects while criticizing social policies. Interviews and documentary-styled footage brought home the scandalous slum conditions while the sometimes emotional music offered a sense of hope. The entire contemporary Stax roster made contributions, including established stars Isaac Hayes, Eddie Floyd, Rufus Thomas, Carla Thomas, the Bar Kays and Johnnie Taylor. The label's new generation of acts - Luther Ingram, Mel And Tim, Frederick Knight and the Dramatics - was set beside veterans Albert King and Little Milton, celebrating the achievements Stax, although white-owned, had made. Compered by Richard Prior, punctuated by a speech by the Reverend Jesse Jackson and commemorated further by a double-album set, *Wattstax* glistens with justified pride. It also captures several leading soul acts at the height of their popularity.

WEATHER GIRLS

Izora Rhodes and Martha Wash met in the San Francisco-based gospel group, NOW (News Of The World) prior to joining the backing group of rising disco star Sylvester. Dubbed 'Two Tons O' Fun' in deference to their rotund stature, the duo recorded for the Fantasy Records label before securing a measure of infamy for their tongue-in-cheek release, 'It's Raining Men'. First released in the USA in 1982, the single achieved a greater success in the UK where it later peaked at number 2 in 1984 after re-entering the chart. Subsequent releases lacked the undeniable charm of their major hit, but admirably showcased the Weather Girls' powerful voices. In th 90s Wash has provided distinctive lead vocals for several dance acts, including Black Box ('Everybody Everybody'), C+C Music Factory ('Gonna Make You Sweat') and Todd Terry (*Ready For A New Day*).

● ALBUMS: *Success* (Columbia 1983)★★★, *Big Girls Don't Cry* (Columbia 1985)★★★, *Weather Girls* (Columbia 1988)★★★.

WELCH, LENNY

b. 15 May 1938, Asbury Park, New Jersey, USA. Treading the same path as Johnny Mathis, Welch built his career singing pop tunes with a hint of R&B flavour and a succinct sweetness in the voice. He began singing professionally in 1958, and signed with Archie Bleyer's Cadence label in 1960. His first record was a remake of an old Jerry Vale hit, 'You Don't Know Me', and it went to number 45 on the pop chart in 1960, shaping the course of his career. In 1963 Welch's remake of the 40s-era big-band standard 'Since I Fell For You' became his biggest hit (US pop number 4). He followed with another revival of a standard, 'Ebb Tide' (US pop Top 30 and R&B Top 10 in 1964). The b-side, 'Congratulations Baby', was a splendid doo-wop song and revealed his R&B origins. Welch signed with Kapp in 1965 where his musical direction was increasingly directed towards an MOR style, notably with 'Two Different Worlds' (1965). His last pop chart record was a minor hit revival of 'A Sunday Kind Of Love' (1972), but Welch lingered on the R&B charts until 1974.

● ALBUMS: *Since I Fell For You* (Cadence 1963)★★★, *Two Different Worlds* (Kapp 1965)★★, *Rags To Riches* (Kapp 1966)★★, *Lenny* (Kapp 1967)★★.

WELLS, BRANDI

b. Philadelphia, USA. Wells, a Philadelphia-born funk singer, first appeared professionally in the group Twilight while still at school. In 1972 she left to join Major Harris's backing singers Brown Sugar. A year later she formed Breeze, who backed acts such as Billy Paul, Fat Larry and Philly Cream, as well as recording in their own right on the WMOT label. Breeze then evolved into Slick who had a UK Top 20 hit 'Space Bass' in 1979 and then hit with 'Sexy Cream' shortly afterwards. Wells joined WMOT as a soloist in 1981 and with an all-star line-up of musicians that included Thom Bell, Dexter Wansell and Michael Pedicin Jnr., recorded her debut *Watch Out*. She made the US R&B charts with 'When It's Love' in 1981 and the album's title track became her biggest hit, making the R&B Top 40 and the bottom of the UK charts. Other releases failed to keep her name in the public eye.

● ALBUMS: *Watch Out* (Virgin 1982)★★★.

WELLS, JEAN

b. 1 August 1942, West Palm Beach, Florida, USA, and raised in Belgrade, Florida. Wells began singing in gospel groups as a child, and established herself as a secular singer in the early 60s performing in clubs in Philadelphia. She made her recording debut in 1959, followed by several other singles, but it was not until she was discovered by producer Clyde Otis that her career took off. He arranged for her to be signed to the New York-based Calla Records in 1967 and she immediately had success with the splendid 'After Loving You' (number 31 R&B). Two other excellent records followed that year, 'I Feel Good' (number 33 R&B) and 'Have A Little Mercy' (number 25 R&B). Her last chart record was in 1968, and later attempts at recording with other companies were unsuccessful commercially and perhaps artistically, never equalling the thrilling intensity of her Calla singles.

● ALBUMS: *World! Here Comes Jean Wells* (Sonet 1969)★★★, *Number One* (Sunshine 1981)★★★.

WELLS, MARY

b. 13 May 1943, Detroit, Michigan, USA, d. 26 July 1992. At the age of 17, Mary Wells composed 'Bye Bye Baby', a song that she offered to R&B star Jackie Wilson. His producer, Berry Gordy, was sufficiently impressed to offer her a contract with the newly formed Motown label, and Wells' rendition of her song became one of the company's first Top 50 hits in 1960. Gordy entrusted her career to Smokey Robinson, who masterminded all her subsequent Motown releases. Robinson composed a remarkable series of clever, witty soul songs, full of puns and unexpected twists, and set to irresistible melody lines. Wells responded with the fluency of a natural vocalist and the results were Motown's most mature and adventurous records of the early 60s. 'The One Who Really Loves You' set the pattern as a Top 10 hit in 1962, while 'You Beat Me To The Punch' and 'Two Lovers' matched that success and offered two of Robinson's more subtle lyrics. 'What's Easy For Two Is So Hard For One' was Wells' answer to the predominant New York girl-group sound, and another Top 30 hit in 1964. The pinnacle of the Robinson/Wells partnership, however, was 'My Guy', a US number 1 and UK Top 5 contender in 1964. Sophisticated and assured, it introduced the Motown sound to a worldwide audience, and marked out Wells as America's most promising soul vocalist. At the same time, Berry Gordy encouraged her to record an album of duets with Motown's top male star, Marvin Gaye, from which 'Once Upon A Time' was pulled as another major hit single. Just as Wells' career reached its peak, she chose to leave Motown, tempted by an offer from 20th Century Fox that included the promise of film work. Without the guidance of Smokey Robinson, she was unable to recapture her hit form, and she left the label the following year. In 1966, she married Cecil Womack of the Valentinos, and moved to Atco Records, where she had three further minor hits with 'Dear Lover', 'Such A Sweet Thing' and 'The Doctor'. This marked the end of her chart career; subsequent sessions for a variety of US labels proved less than successful, and after a long period without a contract she was reduced to re-recording her Motown hits for Allegiance in the early 80s. Despite being diagnosed as having throat cancer she continued touring during the late 80s. Wells signed to Ian Levine's Motor City label in 1987 and released *Keeping My Mind On Love* in 1990. She lost her battle against her illness on 26 July 1992.

● ALBUMS: *Bye Bye Baby, I Don't Want To Take A Chance* (Motown 1961)★★★, *The One Who Really Loves You* (Motown 1962)★★★, *Two Lovers And Other Great Hits* (Motown 1963)★★★, *Recorded Live On Stage* (Motown 1963)★★★, *Second Time Around* (Motown 1963)★★★, with Marvin Gaye *Together* (Motown 1964)★★★, *Mary Wells Sings My Guy* (Motown 1964)★★★, *Mary Wells* (20th Century 1965)★★★, *Mary Wells Sings Love Songs To The Beatles* (20th Century 1965)★★★, *Vintage Stock* (Motown 1966)★★★, *The Two Sides Of Mary Wells* (Atco 1966)★★★, *Ooh!* (Movietone 1966)★★★, *Servin' Up Some Soul* (Jubilee 1968)★★, *In And Out Of Love* (1981)★★, *Keeping My Mind On Love* (Motor City 1990)★★.

● COMPILATIONS: *Greatest Hits* (Motown 1964)★★★, *The Old, New And Best Of Mary Wells* (Allegiance 1984)★★★, *Compact Command Performances* (Motown 1986)★★★, *The Best Of* (1993)★★★, *The Complete Jubilee Sessions* (Sequel 1993)★★★, *Ain't It The Truth: The Best Of 1964-82* (1993)★★★, *Looking Back 1961-64* (1993)★★★, *My Guy* (Charly 1994)★★★, *Dear Lover - the Atco Years* (1994)★★★, *Early Classics* (Spectrum 1996)★★★, *Never, Never Leave Me: The 20th Century Sides* (Ichiban 1997)★★★.

● FILMS: *Catalina Caper* (1967).

WESLEY, FRED

Although Wesley joined the James Brown revue in 1968, in keeping with several of the soul star's accompanists, this accomplished trombonist left and rejoined on several occasions. In 1970, Brown pushed Wesley to the forefront of a new, crisper JBs, who made their recording debut the following year with 'Hot Pants'. The ensemble also began releasing spin-off singles, the earliest of which were written, arranged and produced by their mentor. The unit was soon dubbed Fred Wesley And The JBs. Their most successful single, 'Doin' It To Death', topped the R&B chart in 1973, and several more excellent, hard-funk releases followed. However, the core of the group, including Wesley, Bootsy Collins and Maceo Parker (of Maceo And The King's Men), later defected to George Clinton's rival Parliament/Funkadelic organization. A new group, Fred Wesley And The Horny Horns, maintained a dance-based direction, but their leader later embarked on a solo career before returning to the James Brown fold. In 1990 Wesley toured the UK supporting the re-formed Meters.

● ALBUMS: as the JBs *Food For Thought* (1972)★★★; as Fred Wesley And The JBs *Doing It To Death* (1973)★★★, *Exorcist* (1974)★★★, *Damn Right I Am Somebody* (1974)★★★; as Fred And The New JBs *Breakin' Bread* (1974)★★, *A Blow For Me, A Toot To You* (Atlantic 1977)★★★; as Fred Wesley *To Someone* (Hi-Note 1990)★★★, *New Friends* (Antilles/New Directions 1991)★★★, *Comme Ci Comme Ca* (1991)★★, *Swing & Be Funky* (1993)★★★, *Amalgamate* (1995)★★★.

Weston, Kim

b. Agatha Natalie Weston, 20 December 1939, Detroit, Michigan, USA. Kim Weston received her musical education with the Wright Specials gospel group, an influence that survived throughout her subsequent career. Torn between pursuing music or acting, she was persuaded to join the Motown label in the early 60s by Johnny Thornton, the cousin of two of the label's top producers, Eddie and Brian Holland. After a minor hit with 'Love Me All The Way' in 1963, Weston joined Marvin Gaye's soul revue, forming a partnership that was captured on record in 1964 and again in 1967. In the interim, Weston was produced by Holland/Dozier/Holland on a series of classic dance records that highlighted her versatile, gospel-tinged vocals. 'Take Me In Your Arms' was a substantial soul hit in 1965, followed the next year by the equally fluent 'Helpless'. In 1967, she and Gaye recorded 'It Takes Two', one of the finest of Motown's love duets. That same year, Weston married Motown producer Mickey Stevenson, who encouraged her to join him in a new venture at MGM Records. The move proved a commercial disappointment, and later releases on People and Pride failed to restore Weston to the charts. In the 70s, she devoted much time to community projects and art groups, besides finding time to record an album of jazz standards with the Hastings Street Jazz Experience. More recently, she was one of several Motown artists to re-record her hits on Ian Levine's Nightmare label. In 1987 she became the first ex-Motown artist to work with producer Ian Levine, who proceeded to sign virtually every Motown act over the next three years. Weston teamed up with Marvin Gaye's brother Frankie for a remake of 'It Takes Two' in 1989. She has so far released two new albums, which mix new material with fresh versions of 60s Motown hits.

● ALBUMS: with Marvin Gaye *Take Two* (Tamla 1966)★★★, *For The First Time* (MGM 1967)★★★, *This Is America* (MGM 1968)★★★, *Kim Kim Kim* (Volt 1970)★★, *Investigate* (Motor City 1990)★★, *Talking Loud* (Motor City 1992)★★.

● COMPILATIONS: *Greatest Hits And Rare Classics* (1991)★★★, *The Very Best* (Essential Gold 1996)★★★.

Wexler, Jerry

b. 10 January 1917, New York City, USA. A high school graduate at the age of 15, Wexler completed a degree in journalism following his spell in the US Army. Having initially worked at BMI, writing biographies of contemporary stars, he joined the staff of *Billboard* magazine, but left, having refused to compile a dossier on the Weavers during the height of the McCarthy era. In 1952 Wexler was invited to run the publishing arm of Atlantic Records, but demurred, only joining the company as a partner and shareholder the following year when an opportunity in record promotion arose. He entered production with LaVern Baker's 'Soul On Fire', which he co-wrote with Ertegun and Jesse Stone. Weeks later he produced the Drifters' single 'Money Honey', one of the biggest R&B hits of 1953, and was instrumental in insisting on the high quality that marked Atlantic's subsequent releases, notably those of Ray Charles. This was reinforced by Herb Abramson and Ahmet Ertegun. The following decade he produced several hits for Solomon Burke and became a pivotal figure in the company's distribution and recording agreement with Stax Records. The arrangement breathed new life into Atlantic, giving it access to southern soul artists and musicians. Wexler brought Aretha Franklin to the label, and their collaborations, including 'I Never Loved A Man (The Way I Love You)' and 'Respect', resulted in some of the era's finest recordings, which in turn won him industry awards as best producer in 1967 and 1968. He retained an interest in 'roots' music through work with Delaney And Bonnie, Dr. John and Jesse Davis. However, Wexler gradually distanced his commitment to Atlantic following its absorption into the WEA Records group, and resigned in 1975. He undertook 'outside' production, notably with Bob Dylan (*Slow Train Coming*) and Dire Straits (*Communique*), and remains one of the most respected professionals of post-war music.

● FURTHER READING: *Rhythm And The Blues: A Life In American Music*, Jerry Wexler with David Ritz. *Making Tracks*, Charlie Gillett.

Whatnauts

This soulful vocal trio from Baltimore, USA, consisted of Billy Herndon (lead), Garrett Jones (tenor) and Gerard 'Chunky' Pinkney (baritone). The trio first came to national prominence in 1970 when their socially conscious single 'Message From A Black Man', on A&I Records, made the R&B Top 20. They then joined Sylvia Robinson's Stang label and recorded some of the most underrated R&B vocal group records of the early 70s, including 'Please Make The Love Go Away' in 1970 and their biggest US success, 'I'll Erase Away The Pain', a year later. The group also recorded with other Stang artists including Linda Jones and the Moments. It was 'Girls' that teamed them with the Moments, and gave them a UK number 3 hit in 1975. The group also had limited success with releases on GSF in 1973 and Harlem International in 1982.

Wheeler, Caron

b. *c*.1962, England, but raised in Jamaica. Her father a bass player, her mother a singer with a Jamaican drama company, Wheeler's interest in music began at the age of 12, singing lovers' rock with female reggae trio Brown Sugar, who had four number 1 singles in the specialist charts by the time she was 16. She moved on to form backing trio Afrodiziak, whose vocals were utlilized live or on sessions with artists including the Jam (other backing duties for Elvis Costello, Phil Collins, Neneh Cherry and Aswad followed, and she earned a gold record for her liaison with Erasure in 1988). However, she became frustrated with the record business and effectively retired that year, taking a job in a library. The break refuelled her creative instincts, and when she returned as part of Soul II Soul in 1990, it produced her greatest success. Though never part of the group proper, she won a Grammy for Best Vocal Performance on 'Back To Life', one of the two platinum singles on which she sang (the other being 'Keep On Movin'') . She subsequently embarked on her solo career by signing with Orange Tree Productions, eventually securing a contract with RCA. Her distinctive voice was soon utilized not only for the blend of pop, soul and hip-hop that diffused the music of her former employers, but also for blasting the white domination of the UK record industry. Her feeling of alienation was evident in the title track of her debut album: 'Many moons ago, We were told the streets were paved with gold, So our people came by air and sea, To earn a money they could keep, Then fly back home, Sadly this never came to be, When we learned that we had just been invited, To clean up after the war'. Afterwards, her frustration with Britain saw her move to the USA for a second collection. This diverse set included a collaboration with Jam and Lewis on 'I Adore You', the production of former Soul II Soul man Jazzie B. on 'Wonder', and a cover version of Jimi Hendrix's 'And The Wind Cries Mary'.

● ALBUMS: *UK Blak* (RCA 1990)★★★, *Blue (Is The Colour Of Pain)* (RCA 1991)★★★, *Beach Of The War Goddess* (1993)★★★.

WHISPERS

Formed in the Watts area of Los Angeles, California, USA, in 1964, soul group the Whispers were originally comprised of Nicholas Caldwell (b. 5 April 1944, Loma Linda, California, USA), twin brothers Wallace and Walter Scott (b. 23 September 1943, Fort Worth, Texas, USA), Marcus Hutson (b. 8 January 1943, St. Louis, Missouri, USA) and Gordy Harmon. The group recorded its first single, 'It Only Hurts For Awhile', for Dore Records but it was not until 1969 that they reached the R&B charts with 'Time Will Come', on the Soul Clock label. Their first Top 10 soul record, 'Seems Like I Gotta Do Wrong', followed in 1970 and the group switched to Janus Records for the next four years, during which time Leaveil Degree (b. 31 July, 1948, New Orleans, Louisiana, USA) replaced Harmon in 1971. In 1975 the group switched labels again, to Soul Train, and enjoyed such hits as 'One For The Money' and 'Make It With You', a remake of the Bread pop hit. The Soul Train label evolved into Solar Records in 1978, where the Whispers stayed for 10 years, reaching their commercial peak. Emphasizing lush arrangements and sweet vocal harmonies, the group earned hits with the US number 1 R&B single 'And The Beat Goes On', which also reached number 2 in the UK pop chart. The group continued their success in the US R&B charts with six Top 10 hits with 'Lady' (1980), 'It's A Love Thing' (1981, also a UK Top 10), 'In The Raw', 'Tonight' (1983), 'Keep On Lovin' Me', 'Contagious', and another US R&B number 1, 'Rock Steady', in 1987. Maintaining the same line-up, the group signed to Capitol Records in 1990, releasing *More Of The Night*.

● ALBUMS: *Planet Of Life* (Soul Clock 1969)★★★, *The Whispers Love Story* (Janus 1972)★★★, *One For The Money* (Soul Train 1976)★★★, *Open Up Your Love* (Soul Train 1977)★★★, *Headlights* (Solar 1978)★★★, *Whisper In Your Ear* (Solar 1979)★★★, *The Whispers* (Solar 1980)★★★, *Imagination* (Solar 1981)★★★, *This Kind Of Lovin'* (Solar 1981)★★★, *Love Is Where You Find It* (Solar 1982)★★★, *Love For Love* (Solar 1983)★★★, *So Good* (Solar 1984)★★★, *Just Gets Better With Time* (Solar 1987)★★★, *More Of The Night* (Capitol 1990)★★★.

● COMPILATIONS: *The Best Of The Whispers* (Solar 1982)★★★★, *Love Thing* (Spectrum 1995)★★★, *Greatest Hits* (Capitol 1997)★★★★.

WHITE, BARRY

b. 12 September 1944, Galveston, Texas, USA. Raised in Los Angeles, White immersed himself in the local music fraternity while still very young, playing piano on Jesse Belvin's hit 'Goodnight My Love', at the age of 11. White made several records during the early 60s, under his own name, as 'Barry Lee', and as a member of the Upfronts, the Atlantics and the Majestics. However, he found a greater success as a backroom figure, guiding the careers of, among others, Felice Taylor and Viola Wills. In 1969 White put together Love Unlimited, a female vocal trio made up of Diana Taylor, Glodean James (his future wife) and her sister Linda. He also founded the Love Unlimited Orchestra, a 40-piece ensemble to accompany himself and the singing trio, for which he conducted, composed and arranged. Love Unlimited's success in 1972 with 'Walkin' In The Rain With The One I Love', featuring White's gravelly, passion-soaked voice on the telephone, rejuvenated Barry's own career, during which he enjoyed major US hits with 'I'm Gonna Love You Just A Little More Baby', 'Never, Never Gonna Give Ya Up' (both 1973), 'Can't Get Enough Of Your Love, Babe' and 'You're The First, The Last, My Everything' (both 1974) all of which proved just as popular in the UK. With these, the artist established a well-wrought formula where catchy pop/soul melodies were fused to sweeping arrangements and the singer's husky growl. The style quickly verged on self-parody as the sexual content of the lyrics grew more explicit, but although his pop hits lessened towards the end of the 70s, he remained the idolatrized subject of live performances. The singer's had a major hit in 1978 with Billy Joel's 'Just The Way You Are'. He later undertook several recordings with Glodean White before returning to the UK Top 20 in 1987 with 'Sho' You Right'. The subject of critical approbation, particularly with reference to his large frame, White's achievements during the peak of his career, in securing gold and platinum discs for worldwide sales, should not be underestimated. Lisa Stansfield has often voiced her approval of White's work and in 1992, she and White re-recorded a version of Stansfield's hit 'All Around The World'.

● ALBUMS: *I've Got So Much To Give* (20th Century

1973)★★★, *Stone Gon'* (20th Century 1973)★★★, *Can't Get Enough* (20th Century 1974)★★★, *Just Another Way To Say I Love You* (20th Century 1975)★★★, *Let The Music Play* (20th Century 1976)★★★, *Is This Whatcha Wont?* (20th Century 1976)★★★, *Barry White Sings For Someone You Love* (20th Century 1977)★★★, *Barry White The Man* (20th Century 1978)★★★, *The Message Is Love* (Unlimited Gold 1979)★★★, *I Love To Sing The Songs I Sing* (20th Century 1979)★★, *Barry White's Sheet Music* (Unlimited Gold 1980)★★, *The Best Of Our Love* (Unlimited Gold 1981)★★, with Glodean James *Barry And Glodean* (Unlimited Gold 1981)★★★, *Beware!* (1981)★★, *Change* (Unlimited Gold 1982)★★, *Dedicated* (Unlimited Gold 1983)★★, *The Right Night And Barry White* (A&M 1987)★★, *The Man Is Back!* (A&M 1990)★★, *Put Me In Your Mix* (A&M 1991)★★★, *The Icon Is Love* (A&M 1994)★★.

● COMPILATIONS: *Barry White's Greatest Hits* (20th Century 1975)★★★★, *Barry White's Greatest Hits Vol. 2* (20th Century 1977)★★★, *Heart And Soul* (K-Tel 1985)★★, *Satin & Soul* (Connoisseur 1987)★★★, *The Collection* (Polydor 1988)★★★★, *Satin & Soul Vol. 2* (Connoisseur 1990)★★, *Just For You* (1993)★★★.

WHITFIELD, BARRENCE

Often hailed as the new Little Richard, and championed by the UK disc jockey Andy Kershaw, US rocker Barrence Whitfield (b. Barry White, East Orange, New Jersey, USA) emerged with his Savages in the mid-80s and looked set to make a commotion with his wild, primal rock 'n' roll. His first two album releases admirably captured the atmosphere of their live concerts. After the release of the mini-album *Call Of The Wild* in 1987, Whitfield's momentum was unbalanced when his record distributors went out of business. He released two albums on the French label New Rose, before experimenting with country music on two releases with singer-songwriter Tom Russell. He returned to his old backing band for 1995's *Ritual Of The Savages*.

● ALBUMS: *Barrence Whitfield And The Savages* (Mamou 1984)★★★, *Dig Yourself* (Rounder 1985)★★★, *Call Of The Wild* mini-album (Demon/Rounder1987)★★★, *Ow! Ow! Ow!* (Rounder 1987)★★★, with Jonathan Richman *Jonathan Richman & Barence Whitfield* (Rounder 1988)★★, *Live Emulsified* (Rounder 1989)★★, *Let's Lose It* (New Rose 1990)★★★, *Savage Tracks* (New Rose 1992)★★, with Tom Russell *Hillbilly Voodoo* (Round Tower 1993)★★★, with Russell *Cowboy Mambo* (Round Tower 1994)★★★, *Ritual Of The Savages* (Ocean 1995)★★★.

WIGGINS, SPENCER

Seven singles and an album, *Soul City USA*, for Quinton Claunch's Memphis-based Goldwax label in the late 60s gave Wiggins his place in soul-music history, with his deep-soul, 'churchy' style, similar to that of Solomon Burke, except that Wiggins seemed capable of even greater vocal power and range, and a telling occasional falsetto. As well as Wiggins, the Goldwax roster in that era boasted O.V. Wright (for his first single), James Carr, the Ovations, Willie Walker and Percy Milem. Perhaps his best-known track was the Dan Penn/Spooner Oldham ballad 'Uptight Good Woman', taken at an almost funerial pace. Some of Wiggins' other Goldwax recordings were equally emotive, notably 'That's How Much I Love You', 'The Power Of A Woman', 'Take Me (Just As I Am)', and an excellent cover version of Aretha Franklin's first ever hit for Atlantic, 'I Never Loved A Man' (suitably retitled 'I Never Loved A Woman' by Wiggins). Both versions were recorded at Fame studios, Muscle Shoals, and Wiggins' recording was enhanced by the guitarwork of Duane Allman. In the early 70s Wiggins moved briefly to Rick Hall's Fame label itself, first cutting 'Love Me Tonight', and then re-recording Etta James's original version of the deep ballad 'I'd Rather Go Blind', which had also been cut at Fame back in 1967. Nothing more was heard of Wiggins until he resurfaced in the mid-70s, along with other Memphis-based soul artists such as Ollie Nightingale and Barbara And The Browns, on the XL/Sounds of Memphis labels, where his few sides were produced by Earl Cage and Dan Greer. As with his Goldwax material, it was left largely to the Japanese Vivid Sound label to reissue this product, and it remains rare and expensive. The Goldwax company survives, and is expected to include original Wiggins tracks on their future US compilations.

● ALBUMS: *Soul City USA* (Goldwax 1968)★★★.

● COMPILATIONS: *Bell's Cellar Of Soul Volume 2* one track (1968), *Bell's Cellar Of Soul Volume 3* one track (1969), *Goldwax Collection Volume 2* five tracks (1978) *Goldwax Collection* four tracks (1986), *Soul Sounds Of Memphis* five tracks (1991).

WILLIAMS, ANDRE

b. 1936, Chicago, Illinois, USA. As a recording artist Williams was noted for his sly, streetwise songs in which he basically spoke (with a rhythmic feel) the lyrics rather than sang them. He built a parallel career as a producer of the first doo-wop vocal groups and soul acts. Like many African-American artists, Williams began his career in the church, singing in the Cobbs Baptist Church choir in the 40s. He began singing in vocal groups in the early 50s, forming the Cavaliers. He later moved to Detroit and formed the Five Dollars, who recorded for the Fortune label. Williams soon disengaged himself to establish a solo career on Fortune, making his biggest impact with two jokey records, 'Jail Bait' and 'Bacon Fat' (number 9 R&B), in 1957. By the early 60s Williams was back in Chicago working as a producer for various labels. He produced Alvin Cash for the One-derful label complex, Joyce Kennedy for Blue Rock, and JoAnn Garrett for Checker and Duo. Meanwhile, he recorded some solo tracks for Checker, obtaining a modest chart entry with 'Cadillac Jack' (number 46 R&B) in 1968. He also recorded some singles for Avin in Detroit. In the early 70s Williams went to Texas to produce for Duke Records, but after the label was sold to ABC in 1974 he left. Williams continued to work as an artist manager and independent producer into the early 90s.

● ALBUMS: *Fat Back And Corn Liquor* (St. George 1996)★★★.

● COMPILATIONS: *Jail Bait* (Fortune 1984)★★★.

WILLIAMS, BILLY

b. 28 December 1910, Waco, Texas, USA, d. 17 October 1972. Williams formed the very successful gospel group the Charioteers in the early 30s while studying theology at Wilberforce College, Ohio. The group had regular radio spots in Cincinnati and New York and worked with Bing Crosby on the west coast. In the 40s they had seven hits of their own and also charted with Frank Sinatra. In 1949 Williams left and formed the Billy Williams Quartet with Eugene Dixon (bass), Claude Riddick (baritone) and John Ball (tenor). The group were often seen on television, including over 160 appearances on Sid Caesar's *Your Show Of Shows*. They recorded with little impact for Mercury and MGM Records before joining Coral in 1954, and after a few unsuccessful cover versions of R&B hits, the group achieved nine US chart entries. The biggest of these was a revival of Fats Waller's 'I'm Gonna Sit Right Down And Right Myself A Letter', a US Top 3 and UK Top 30 hit in 1957. The jazzy R&B artist sadly lost his voice, due to diabetes, in the early 60s. He moved to Chicago where he became a social worker, employed on a model cities project and helping alcoholics until his death in 1972.

WILLIAMS, DENIECE

b. Deniece Chandler, 3 June 1951, Gary, Indiana, USA. Williams is a gospel/soul singer whose successes span the 70s and 80s. As a child she sang in a gospel choir and made her first recordings in the late 60s for the Chicago-based Toddlin' Town label. After training as a nurse, she was hired by Stevie Wonder to join his Wonderlove vocal backing group. She contributed to four of his albums before leaving Wonder to pursue a solo career. Produced by Maurice White of Earth, Wind And Fire, her first album included the UK hits 'That's What Friends Are For' and the number 1 'Free' which was revived in 1990 by British group BEF for their *Music Of Quality & Distinction Vol II* album of cover versions. In 1978, Williams joined Johnny Mathis for the immensely popular ballad 'Too Much Too Little Too Late' This was followed by an album of duets by the couple, *That's What Friends Are For*. Returning to a solo career, Williams moved to Maurice White's own label, ARC, but her next two albums made little impact. However, a revival of the 1965 song 'It's Gonna Take A Miracle', produced by Thom Bell, returned her to the US Top 10 in 1982. This was a prelude to the release of Williams' most well-known song, 'Let's Hear It For The Boy'. Originally made for the soundtrack of the 1984 film *Footloose*, it was issued as a single the following year and headed the US charts. Later records had no pop success although Williams remained popular with the R&B audience and in 1988 she made her first gospel album for Sparrow. Williams is a prolific songwriter and her compositions have been recorded by Merry Clayton, the Emotions, the Whispers, Frankie Valli and others.

● ALBUMS: *This Is Niecy* (Columbia 1976)★★★★, *Songbird* (Columbia 1977)★★★, with Johnny Mathis *That's What Friends Are For* (Columbia 1978)★★★, *When Love Comes Calling* (ARC 1979)★★★, *My Melody* (ARC 1981)★★★★, *Niecy* (ARC 1982)★★★★, *I'm So Proud* (Columbia 1983)★★★, *Let's Hear It For The Boy* (Columbia 1984)★★★, *Hot On The Trail* (Columbia 1986)★★★, *Water Under The Bridge* (Columbia 1987), *So Glad I Know* (Sparrow 1988)★★★, *As Good As It Gets* (Columbia 1989)★★★.

● FILMS: *Footloose* (1984).

WILLIAMS, JOHNNY

b. 15 January 1942, Tyler, Texas, USA, d. December 1986. Williams was one of many R&B singers that had a greater impact in the clubs than on record. In Chicago - where he settled in 1956 - he was acclaimed for his full-bodied, deep-soul style, yet his legacy on record is small. He began his career in gospel, singing with the Royal Jubilees. Williams first recorded in 1966, when he achieved a minor local hit with 'My Baby's Good' for Chess Records. It was not a great record but two of his best, 'The Breaking Point', recorded for Twinight Records in 1967, and 'I Made A Mistake', recorded for Carl Davis's Bashie label in 1969, inexplicably failed to find an audience. In 1972, he finally reached the national charts with 'Slow Motion (Part 1)' (number 12 R&B, number 78 pop), which was recorded in Philadelphia for Gamble And Huff's Philadelphia International Records label. Unable to repeat this achievement, he went back to working the Chicago clubs. He had some local success with a single on the Babylon label, 'You're Something Kinda Mellow', in 1974. His death in December 1986 went unnoticed by the music world.

WILLIAMS, LARRY

b. 10 May 1935, New Orleans, Louisiana, USA, d. 2 January 1980, Los Angeles, California, USA. Williams recorded a handful of raucous rock 'n' roll songs for Specialty Records that later influenced, among others, John Lennon. Williams learned to play the piano while in New Orleans, and moved to Oakland, California, with his family while in his teens. There he joined a group called the Lemon Drops. In 1954, while visiting his old hometown of New Orleans, he met and was hired as a pianist by Lloyd Price, who recorded for Specialty. Price introduced Williams to producer Robert 'Bumps' Blackwell. At that time Speciality head Art Rupe signed Williams. His first record was a cover of Price's 'Just Because', which reached number 11 on the R&B chart for Williams and number 3 for Price. Backed by fellow Specialty artist Little Richard's band, Williams recorded his own 'Short Fat Fannie', which reached number 1 in the R&B chart and number 5 in the pop chart during 1957. To follow up his song about a fat girl, Williams next recorded one about a skinny girl, 'Bony Moronie', which was almost as big a hit. Williams had one final chart single for Specialty the following year, 'Dizzy, Miss Lizzy', which reached number 69 (it was later covered by the Beatles, with Lennon singing - they also covered 'Slow Down' and 'Bad Boy', while Lennon later recorded 'Bony Moronie' and 'Just Because', providing Williams with a steady royalties income until his death). A number of singles and an album were issued by Specialty up to 1959, none of which were hits. In that year, he was arrested for selling drugs and sent to jail, causing Specialty to drop him and his career to fade. He recorded later for Chess Records, Mercury Records and for Island Records and Decca Records in the mid-60s, by which time he was working with Johnny 'Guitar' Watson. In 1966 Williams became a producer for OKeh Records and recorded an album with Watson for that label. He was virtually inactive between 1967 and 1979, at which point he recorded a funk album for Fantasy Records. In January 1980, Williams was found in his Los Angeles home with a gunshot wound in the head, judged to be self-inflicted, although it was rumoured that Williams was murdered owing to his involvement with drugs and, reportedly, prostitution.

● ALBUMS: *Here's Larry Williams* (Specialty 1959)★★★★, *Larry Williams* (Chess 1961)★★★, *Live* (1965)★★★, *The Larry Williams Show* (1965)★★★, with Johnny 'Guitar' Watson *Two For The Price Of One* (OKeh 1967)★★★★, *That Larry Williams* (Fantasy 1979)★★.

● COMPILATIONS: *Greatest Hits* (OKeh 1967)★★★★, *Dizzy Miss Lizzy* (Ace 1985)★★★, *Unreleased Larry Williams* (Specialty 1986)★★★, *Hocus Pocus* (Specialty 1986)★★★, *Alacazam* (Ace 1987)★★★, *Slow Down* (Specialty 1987)★★★, *The Best Of Larry Williams* (Ace 1988)★★★★, *Bad Boy* (Specialty 1989)★★★★, *Fabulous Larry Williams* (Ace 1991)★★★.

WILLIAMS, LEE 'SHOT'

b. Henry Lee Williams, 21 May 1938, Tchula, Mississippi, USA. For most of his career, Williams has been a journeyman singer on the chitlin circuit, eschewing identification with the blues scene until recently. He grew up with his cousins, Little Smokey Smothers and Otis 'Big Smokey' Smothers. When his mother died in the mid-50s, he was adopted by the family of singer Arlean Brown. After spending time in Detroit, he moved to Chicago in 1958 and worked in a bakery until the pressure of gigging every night led to a full-time singing career. He made his first single, 'Hello Baby', for Foxy in 1961. Two years later, he signed to Federal and released three singles, including 'You're Welcome To The Club', later covered by Little Milton. Other records emerged during the 60s on labels such as Palos, Gamma, Shama and Sussex. During much of that time, he toured the south with Earl Hooker's band. In the 70s, he indulged a talent for cooking by opening Lee's Diner on Chicago's West Side. Early in the 80s, he moved to Memphis, where in 1991 he recorded *I Like Your Style* at Otis Clay's studio. The following year, *Shot Of Rhythm And Blues* was recorded for the Japanese Soul Trax label. In 1993, he sang on four tracks on Little Smokey Smothers' *Bossman*, which led to a contract with Black Magic and *Cold Shot*.

● ALBUMS: *I Like Your Style* (4 Way 1991)★★★, *Shot Of Rhythm And Blues* (Soul Trax 1992)★★★, *Cold Shot* (Black Magic 1995)★★★, *Hot Shot* (Ecko 1996)★★★.

● COMPILATIONS: *Cause I Love You* (Ichiban 1996)★★★.

WILLIAMS, MAURICE, AND THE ZODIACS

This R&B vocal group from Lancaster, South Carolina, USA, was led by Maurice Williams (pianist/songwriter). The hit record 'Stay', which went to number 3 R&B and number 1 pop in 1960, immortalized the Zodiacs as a one-hit-wonder group (in the UK, 'Stay' went to number 14 in 1961). Williams, however, had a long history before and after the hit, forming his first group, the Gladiolas, in 1955. Besides Williams (b. 26 April 1938, Lancaster, South Carolina, USA), the group consisted of Earl Gainey (tenor), William Massey (tenor/baritone), Willie Jones (baritone), and Norman Wade (bass). Their one hit for the Nashville-based Excello label was 'Little Darlin'', which went to number 11 R&B and number 41 pop in 1957. The record was covered with greater success by the Canadian group the Diamonds. In 1960 Williams formed the Zodiacs, consisting of Wiley Bennett (tenor), Henry Gaston (tenor), Charles Thomas (baritone), Albert Hill (double bass) and Little Willie Morrow (drums). After the unforgettable 'Stay', the group honoured themselves with many outstanding compositions, most notably 'I Remember' (number 86 pop in 1961), 'Come Along' (number 83 pop in 1961) and 'May I' (1966), but nothing close to a hit materialized. The latter song was re-recorded in 1969 by Bill Deal And The Rhondels who had a Top 40 national hit with it. The most frequently remade Williams song was 'Stay', which the Hollies in the UK (1963), the Four Seasons (1964) and Jackson Browne (1978) all placed on the charts. Its timeless lyric of teenage lust and angst has been passed through the decades: 'Well your mama don't mind, well your papa don't mind', leading to the punchline, 'Oh won't you stay, just a little bit longer'. During the 70s and 80s Williams sustained a career with a new group of Zodiacs, playing their classic catalogue to the Beach Music club circuit in the Carolinas.

● ALBUMS: *Stay* (Herald 1961)★★★★, *At The Beach* (early 60s)★★★ *Maurice Williams And The Zodiacs* (Herald 1988)★★★.

● COMPILATIONS: *The Best Of Maurice Williams & the Zodiacs* (Collectables 1982)★★★★, *Little Darlin'* (1991)★★★.

WILLIAMS, OTIS, AND THE CHARMS

This US R&B vocal group came from Cincinnati, Ohio, and was formed in 1953. Like the Jacks/Cadets for Modern records in Los Angeles, the Charms for King served as the 'house group' who were available to cover the latest hits. Similarly, the group had some of their hits covered, such as 'Hearts Of Stone' by the Fontane Sisters, 'Two Hearts' by Pat Boone and 'Ivory Tower' by Cathy Carr. They first recorded for the Miami-based Rockin' label in 1953, but later in the year, the Cincinnati-based King purchased Rockin' and also the Charms' contract. Their membership at the time of the Charms' joining King was Otis Williams (b. 2 June 1936, Cincinnati, Ohio, USA; lead), Rolland Bradley (tenor), Donald Peak (tenor), Joe Penn (tenor/baritone) and Richard Parker (bass). The group had a zestful approach that made them a rock 'n' roll act, and they first had success with a Jewels cover version, 'Hearts Of Stone' (US R&B number 1 and pop number 15 in 1954), a Five Keys cover version 'Ling Ting Tong' (US R&B number 5 and pop number 26 in 1955), and an original, 'Two Hearts' (US R&B number 8 in 1955). Williams lost the Charms in 1955, but carried on with a new group, appropriately called 'New Group', which included besides Williams, Rollie Willis (tenor), Larry Graves (baritone) and Chuck Barksdale (bass, later to join the Dells). This group took the name 'Charms' in 1956, and soon replaced Graves and Barksdale with Matt Williams and Winfred Gregory, respectively, and added Lonnie Carter (tenor). This group hit with two more cover versions - 'Ivory Tower' (US R&B number 5 and pop number 11 in 1956) and 'United' (US R&B number 5 in 1957), the group's last hit. After the Charms broke up in the early 60s, Otis Williams went on to pursue a solo career in C&W music and even recorded a surprisingly good album in that genre.

● ALBUMS: *Their All Time Hits* (Deluxe 1957)★★★, *This Is Otis Williams And The Charms* (King 1959)★★★, as Otis Williams And the Midnight Cowboys *Otis Williams And the Midnight Cowboys* (Stop 1971)★★★.

● COMPILATIONS: *Otis Williams And His Charms Sing Their All-Time Hits* (King/Gusto 1978)★★★, *16 Original Greatest Hits* (King 1988)★★★.

Williams, Vanessa

b. 18 March 1963, Tarrytown, New York, USA. Williams grew up in a household surrounded by musical influences from Broadway shows, before she attended Syracuse University to major in musical theatre. A mother of three and an actress as well as a singer, she has come a long way since becoming embroiled in a minor scandal over her appearance in *Penthouse* magazine (after becoming the first black woman to win the Miss USA pageant). Four years later Williams began to pursue a recording contract, and found a sympathetic ear in Ed Eckstine at Wing Records (a Mercury Records subsidiary). Her husband, Ramon Hervey, took over her management. Nevertheless, Williams' talents have been inadequately displayed over the course of her albums. Her musical career began in 1989 with *The Right Stuff*, which provided a number 8 single in 'Dreamin'', a song recognized by ASCAP as one of the most frequently played singles of 1989 (it also featured other hits in 'He's Got The Look' and 'Darling I'). It brought her the NAACP Image Award, which she won once again for the massive-selling ballad 'Save The Best For Last'. The album that accompanied the single, *The Comfort Zone*, achieved double platinum status. However, there was more invention and ambition displayed on a third collection, *The Sweetest Days*, delayed for three years while she gave birth to her third child, Devin, and moved back to New York from Los Angeles. This featured vocals that were pleasant rather than striking, hovering over gentle jazz, soul or Latin arrangements. The stronger material, such as the warm, sensuous 'Higher Ground', was deprived of its potential stature by disappointments such as 'Moonlight Over Paris', or the joyless Sting cover version, 'Sister Moon' (with Toots Thielemans on harmonica). Sting also produced, alongside other big names including Babyface and Roy Ayers. Wendy Waldman, Jon Lind, Phil Galdston and producer Keith Thomas, the team responsible for 'Save The Best For Last', wrote the title track. The album was released while Williams was also the toast of Broadway for her role in *Kiss Of The Spiderwoman*. She has also appeared widely on film and television, including the Emmy Award-winning *Motown Returns To The Apollo*, *The Boy Who Loved Christmas* and *Stompin' At The Savoy*. Earlier she had starred alongside Richard Pryor and Gene Wilder in *Another You* and Micky Rourke and Don Johnson in *Harley Davidson And The Marlboro Man*. She has also hosted her own contemporary R&B television show, *The Soul Of VH-1*. In January 1996 Williams sang the national anthem at Super Bowl XXX in Phoenix, Arizona.

● ALBUMS: *The Right Stuff* (Wing 1989)★★★, *The Comfort Zone* (Wing 1992)★★★★, *The Sweetest Days* (Wing 1995)★★, *Star Bright* (Mercury 1996)★★.

Willis, Bruce

b. 19 March 1955, Germany. Before beginning his acting career in the mid-70s, Willis played saxophone in the R&B band Loose Goose. His musical ambitions were quickly overshadowed by his growing success as an actor, which included starring roles in the highly popular US television series *Moonlighting*, and later, a succession of films, including the *Die Hard* series and *Pulp Fiction*. In 1987, Willis conceived and starred in the television special *The Return Of Bruno*, a biography (or 'rockumentary') of a fictional rock star in which many real-life musicians testified to his influence on their careers. For the soundtrack, Willis revamped several classic soul songs, achieving a surprise 1987 hit with the Staple Singers' 'Respect Yourself', and following up with the Drifters' 'Under The Boardwalk', on which he was supported by the Temptations. He married actress Demi Moore in November 1987, and has since gone on to become one of Hollywood's highest-grossing actors.

● ALBUMS: *The Return Of Bruno* (Motown 1987)★★, *If It Don't Kill You It Just Makes You Stronger* (Motown 1989)★.

Willis, Chuck

b. 31 January 1928, Atlanta, Georgia, USA, d. 10 April 1958. R&B singer Willis made his recording debut in 1951. The following year he reached number 2 in the black music charts with 'My Story', the first of several hits the artist enjoyed while signed to the renowned OKeh label. In 1956 Willis had his first hit for Atlantic Records when 'It's Too Late' reached the US R&B Top 3, and the following year he topped the same chart with the compulsive 'C.C. Rider'. In April 1958, the singer succumbed to peritonitis, in the wake of which his posthumous single, 'What Am I Living For', sold in excess of one million copies. The ironically titled b-side, 'I'm Gonna Hang Up My Rock 'N' Roll Shoes', also reached the R&B Top 10, and despite his brief life and career, Willis remained an influential stylist in the development of R&B. He composed many of his best-known recordings, and cover versions by acts as disparate as Derek And The Dominos, the Animals, Buddy Holly, Jerry Lee Lewis, the Band, Ted Taylor and Otis Redding are a tribute to their longevity.

● ALBUMS: *Chuck Willis Wails The Blues* (Epic 1958)★★★, *The King Of The Stroll* (Atlantic 1958)★★★.

● COMPILATIONS: *Tribute To Chuck Willis* (Epic 1960)★★★, *I Remember Chuck Willis* (Atlantic 1963)★★★, *His Greatest Recordings* (Atlantic 1971)★★★,

Chuck Willis - My Story (Official 1980)★★★, *Keep A Drivin'* (Charly 1984)★★★, *Be Good Or Be Gone* (Edsel 1986)★★★.

WILLOWS

A New York doo-wop group formed in 1953 as the Five Willows, this quintet is best remembered for the uptempo rocker 'Church Bells May Ring', a song that still enjoys airplay on US nostalgia-orientated radio stations. The group consisted of Tony Middleton, brothers Ralph and Joe Martin, Richie Davis and John Steele. Relying on bass singer Steele's vocal acrobatics to give them an identity, they were signed to small labels Allen and Pee-Dee before recording one single for Herald, and finally, their hit for Melba. The shuffle 'Church Bells May Ring' was released in early 1956 and the chimes on the track were played by a then unknown Neil Sedaka. The Willows continued to record for such labels as Club, Eldorado, Gone and Heidi, and the group finally retired in 1965. They recorded no albums, but their one hit, which peaked at number 62 pop and number 11 on the R&B charts, is featured on numerous anthologies.

WILLS, VIOLA

b. Los Angeles, California, USA. This soul-songstress only entered the music business after having her sixth child. She was discovered by Barry White, who initially used her as a session vocalist, and in 1965 signed her to Bronco Records where he was A&R head. A handful of singles for the label failed to find success, as did a release on A Bem Soul in 1969. The next break came when she replaced Claudia Lennear on tour with Joe Cocker, which brought her to Europe and led to her recording in the UK for Goodear in 1974. In 1977 Wills joined Arista Records and in 1979 she recorded for Ariola/Hansa. It was there that she enjoyed her biggest hit with a disco revival of Patience And Prudence's 1957 hit, 'Gonna Get Along Without You Now', which made the UK Top 10. She became one of the most successful exponents of Hi-NRG music with other club successes such as 'If You Could Read My Mind' and 'Up On The Roof'. She returned to the UK Top 40 in 1986 with the double a-side 'Both Sides Now'/'Dare To Dream', which she produced for the Wide Angle label. This much recorded singer has also appeared on many labels since 1979, including Island Records in 1987.

● ALBUMS: *Soft Centres* (Goodear 1974)★★★, *Without You* (Ariola 1979)★★★.

WILMER X

Comprising Nils Hellberg (guitar, vocals, songwriting), Jalle Lorenseeon (harmonica), Pelle Ossler (guitar), 'Sticky Bomb' (drums), Thomas Holst (bass) and Mats Bengtsson (keyboards), European R&B/pop band Wilmer X formed in Malmo, Sweden, in the early 90s. Immediately Hellberg focused on the southern states of the USA for his principal inspiration, as his band perfected a smooth, accessible mix of blues and R&B. Having won three domestic Grammys, the group released its first English language album in 1994. The most distinctive feature of that year's self-titled release was the harmonica playing of Lorenseeon. Though Hellberg's lyrics did not translate to English as comfortably as they might have done, the group drew on the universality of R&B as a musical language with commendable tenacity.

● ALBUMS: *Mambo Fever* (MNW 1991)★★★, *Pontiac Till Himmelen* (MNW 1993)★★★, *Wilmer X* (MNW 1994)★★★.

WILSON, AL

b. 19 June 1939, Meridian, Mississippi, USA. Wilson was a former member of the Jewels, and also the Rollers, a San Bernardino-based quartet who had a hit in 1961 with 'The Continental Walk'. He was later signed as a solo act to Soul City, a short-lived label owned by singer Johnny Rivers. 'Do What You Gotta Do' and 'The Snake' reached the R&B chart in 1968, but it was not until the mid-70s that Wilson achieved a more consistent success. 'Show And Tell' (1973) was a US number 1 single while 'I've Got A Feeling (We'll Be Seeing Each Other Again)' reached number 3 in the R&B lists. Wilson's later releases were less fortunate and his last chart appearance was in 1979 with 'Count The Days'.

● ALBUMS: *Searching For The Dolphins* (Soul City 1968)★★★, *Weighing In* (1973)★★★, *Show And Tell* (Rocky Road 1973)★★★, *La La Peace Song* (Rocky Road 1974)★★★, *I've Got A Feeling* (Playboy 1976)★★, *Count The Days* (RCA 1979)★★.

WILSON, JACKIE

b. 9 June 1934, Detroit, Michigan, USA, d. 21 January 1984, New Jersey, USA. When parental pressure thwarted his boxing ambitions, Wilson took to singing in small local clubs. He sang with the Thrillers (a predecessor group to the Royals) and recorded some solo tracks for Dizzy Gillespie's Dee Gee label as Sonny Wilson, before replacing Clyde McPhatter in Billy Ward And The Dominoes. Wilson joined this notable group in 1953, but embarked on a solo career four years later with Brunswick Records. His first single for that label was the exuberant 'Reet Petite', a comparative failure in the USA where it crept to a lowly pop position and missed the R&B lists altogether. In the UK, however, it soared to number 6, thereby establishing Wilson in the minds of the British pop-purchasing audience. 'Reet Petite' had been written by Berry Gordy and Tyran Carlo (Roquel 'Billy' Davis), who went on to compose several of Wilson's subsequent releases, including the hits 'Lonely Teardrops' (1958), 'That's Why (I Love You So)' (1959) and 'I'll Be Satisfied' (1959).

In 1960, Wilson enjoyed two R&B number 1 hits with 'Doggin' Around' and 'A Woman, A Lover, A Friend'. His musical direction then grew increasingly erratic, veering from mainstream to pseudo-opera. There were still obvious highlights such as 'Baby Workout' (1963), 'Squeeze Her Please Her' (1964), 'No Pity (In The Naked City)' (1965), but all too often his wonderfully fluid voice was wasted on cursory, quickly dated material. The artist's live appearances, however, remained both exciting and dramatic, capable of inspiring the ecstasy his sometimes facile recordings belied. Wilson's career was rejuvenated in 1966. Abandoning his New York recording base, he moved to Chicago, where he worked with producer Carl Davis. He offered a more consistent empathy and 'Whispers (Gettin' Louder)' (1966), '(Your Love Keeps Lifting Me) Higher And Higher' (1967) and the sublime 'I Get The Sweetest Feeling' (1968) stand among his finest recordings. However, it did not last; 'This Love Is Real (I Can Feel Those Vibrations)' (1970) proved to be Wilson's last Top 10 R&B entry, by which time his work was influenced by trends rather than setting them. In September 1975, while touring with the Dick Clark revue, Wilson suffered a near-fatal heart attack onstage at New Jersey's Latin Casino. He struck his head on falling and the resulting brain damage left him comatose. He remained hospitalized until his death on 21 January 1984.

Wilson's career remains a puzzle; he never did join Berry Gordy's Motown empire, despite their early collaboration and friendship. Instead, the singer's legacy was flawed - dazzling in places, disappointing in others. Immortalized in the Van Morrison song 'Jackie Wilson Said', which was also a UK Top 5 hit for Dexys Midnight Runners in 1982, his name has remained in the public's eye. Fate provided a final twist in 1987, when an imaginative video (which some claimed belittled the singer's memory), using plasticine animation, propelled 'Reet Petite' to number 1 in the UK charts. He was inducted into the Rock And Roll Hall Of Fame the same year.

● ALBUMS: *He's So Fine* (Brunswick 1958)★★★, *Lonely Teardrops* (Brunswick 1959)★★★★, *Doggin' Around* (Brunswick 1959)★★★, *So Much* (Brunswick 1960)★★★, *Night* (Brunswick 1960)★★★, *Jackie Wilson Sings The Blues* (Brunswick 1960)★★★★, *A Woman A Lover A Friend* (Brunswick 1961)★★★★, *Try A Little Tenderness* (Brunswick 1961)★★★, *You Ain't Heard Nothing Yet* (Brunswick 1961)★★★, *By Special Request* (Brunswick 1961)★★★, *Body And Soul* (Brunswick 1962)★★★, *Jackie Wilson At The Copa* (Brunswick 1962)★★★, *Jackie Wilson Sings The World's Greatest Melodies* (Brunswick 1962)★★★, *Baby Workout* (Brunswick 1963)★★★★, *Merry Christmas* (Brunswick 1963)★★, with Linda Hopkins *Shake A Hand* (Brunswick 1963)★★, *Somethin' Else* (Brunswick 1964)★★★★, *Soul Time* (Brunswick 1965)★★★★, *Spotlight On Jackie Wilson* (Brunswick 1965)★★★, *Soul Galore* (Brunswick 1966)★★★, *Whispers* (Brunswick 1967)★★★, *Higher And Higher* (Brunswick 1967)★★★★, with Count Basie *Manufacturers Of Soul* (Brunswick 1968)★★★, with Basie *Too Much* (1968)★★★, *I Get The Sweetest Feeling* (Brunswick 1968)★★★★, *Do Your Thing* (Brunswick 1970)★★★, *This Love Is Real* (Brunswick 1970)★★★, *You Got Me Walking* (Brunswick 1971)★★, *Beautiful Day* (Brunswick 1973)★★, *Nowstalgia* (Brunswick 1974)★★, *Nobody But You* (Brunswick 1976)★★.

● COMPILATIONS: *My Golden Favourites* (Brunswick 1960)★★★, *My Golden Favourites - Volume 2* (Brunswick 1964)★★★, *Jackie Wilson's Greatest Hits* (Brunswick 1969)★★★, *It's All Part Of Love* (Brunswick 1969)★★★, *Jackie Wilson: S.R.O.* (1982)★★★, *Classic Jackie Wilson* (Skratch 1984)★★★, *Reet Petite* (Ace 1985)★★★★, *The Soul Years* (Kent 1985)★★★★, *The Soul Years Volume 2* (Kent 1986)★★★, *Higher And Higher* i (Kent 1986)★★★, *Through The Years* (Rhino 1987)★★★, *The Very Best Of Jackie Wilson* (Ace 1987)★★★, *Mr Excitement!* 3-CD box set (Rhino 1992)★★★★, *Higher And Higher* ii (1993)★★★, *The Dynamic Jackie Wilson* (1993)★★★★, *The Chicago Years Vol. 1* (1993)★★★★, *Original Hits* (1993)★★★★, *The Jackie Wilson Hit Story Vol. 1* (1993)★★★★, *The Jackie Wilson Hit Story Vol. 2* (1993)★★★, *The Very Best Of ...* (Rhino 1994)★★★★, *A Portrait Of ...* (Essential Gold/Pickwick 1995)★★★★, *Higher And Higher* (Rhino 1995)★★★★.

● FURTHER READING: *Lonely Teardrops: The Jackie Wilson Story*, Tony Douglas.

● FILMS: *Go Johnny Go* (1958).

WILSON, MARY

b. 6 March 1944, Greenville, Mississippi, USA. Raised by her aunt and uncle in Detroit, Wilson began singing in her local church choir as a teenager. There she met Florence Ballard, with whom she formed an R&B vocal group called the Primettes, and subsequently the Supremes. Wilson remained a backing vocalist with the group from their inception in 1960 until 1977, becoming the senior member after the departure of Diana Ross in 1969, and taking occasional lead vocals from 1974 onwards. At that time, she renegotiated the Supremes' recording contract, so that she owned 50 per cent of the group's name, though Motown Records maintained a veto over its use. After the Supremes disbanded in 1977, Wilson filed a legal suit against Motown that was settled out of court. She then assembled a fresh line-up of the group for a UK tour in 1978, before beginning a solo recording career in 1979. After the Hal Davis-produced *Mary Wilson* proved a commercial failure, Motown rejected her 1980 demos, and she was left without a recording contract. She continued to tour throughout the 80s as 'Mary Wilson of the Supremes', appearing in the 1983 film *Tiger Town* and contributing to the soundtrack album. In 1986, she published a controversial autobiography, in which she attacked both Diana Ross and Motown boss Berry Gordy. In 1989 she starred in the stage production of *The Beehive* in Toronto and in 1990 published the second volume of her memoirs.

● ALBUMS: *Mary Wilson* (Motown 1979)★★.

● FURTHER READING: *Dreamgirl: My Life As A Supreme*, Mary Wilson. *Supreme Faith: Someday We'll Be Together*, Mary Wilson and Patricia Romanowski.

● FILMS: *Tiger Town* (1983).

WINANS

Contemporary Christian music group the Winans are four brothers, Marvin, Carvin, Ronald and Michael Winans, from Detroit, Michigan, USA. The family has additionally produced two well-known solo/duo gospel performers, Bebe and CeCe Winans. Having sung in gospel choirs all their lives, the brothers began their professional career in the 80s. Staying close to their gospel roots but always maintaining a distinctive, jazzy sound, their reputation saw them work and perform with leading artists including Vanessa Bell Armstrong, Anita Baker and Michael McDonald, the latter pair both appearing on their 1987 album *Decisions*. Their two QWest albums of the early 90s, *Return* and *All Out*, saw them attempt to convert their popularity into mainstream R&B success. Even this, however, was motivated by moral concerns: 'The whole purpose was to win over young people who might have been on the verge of going into a life of crime or going off track,' Ronald Winans told *Billboard* magazine in 1995. Drawn from *Return*, 'It's Time' peaked at number 5 on the US R&B charts in 1990 and was produced by Teddy Riley, who also rapped on the single. In consequence, *Return* reached number 12 on the R&B album charts and was certified a gold record. However, *All Out* was less successful, and by 1995 and *Heart And Soul*, the Winans had returned to their trademark gospel sound. As well as 11 other original songs it included a re-make of 'The Question Is', a popular stage favourite originally featured on their 1981 debut album, *Introducing The Winans*. The original version been produced by gospel legend Andrae Crouch, with his nephew, Keith Crouch, playing drums. The guests on *Heart And Soul* included R&B star R. Kelly, as well as previous collaborators Riley, McDonald and Baker.

● ALBUMS: *Introducing The Winans* (QWest 1981)★★★★, *Let My People Go* (QWest 1985)★★★, *Decisions* (QWest 1987)★★★, *Tomorrow* (Light 1988)★★★, *Live At Carnegie Hall* (QWest 1989)★★★, *Return* (QWest 1990)★★★★, *All Out* (QWest 1993)★★★, *Heart And Soul* (QWest 1995)★★★.
Solo: CeCe Winans *Alone In His Presence* (Sparrow 1995)★★★.

Winans, Mario

b. USA. One of the younger members of the extensively recorded Winans musical family, in the mid-90s, after over a decade of work in gospel music, Mario moved into contemporary R&B. He produced R. Kelly's multi-platinum self-titled album of 1996, and followed this with his own effort, *Story Of My Heart*. He made his reasons clear: 'There's a gospel audience, but much more people buy R&B and pop than gospel, and for my songs to be heard, I knew it had to be done.' Apparently, the switch caused friction with his parents, Vicky and Marvin Winans, but they withdrew their objections on the condition that Winans' new R&B material did not contain anything 'offensive'. Winans began as a gospel producer at the age of 14, and has maintained his commitment to the church. As he told *Billboard* magazine in 1997, 'I know in my heart it's not bad to write a love song, because the best example of love is God.' *Story Of My Heart* was preceded by a single, 'Don't Know', which included a guest appearance from Mase, a rapper from Sean 'Puffy' Combs' Bad Boy Entertainment stable.

● ALBUMS: *Story Of My Heart* (Motown 1997)★★★.

Winbush, Angela

Beginning as half of the successful duo René & Angela, Winbush has gone on to have a successful solo career in the 90s soul arena. *Angela Winbush*, recorded from November 1992 through to April 1993, saw her gain full creative control with new label Elektra Records and produce her best work. Premiered by the Chuck Booker-written 'Treat U Rite', this dance-orientated rhythmic track was not typical of the album's more traditional R&B concerns. A better example was her duet with husband Ronald Isley (Isley Brothers) on the Philly-styled 'Baby Hold On', complete with a Thom Bell string arrangement (it also included brother-in-law Ernie Isley on sitar). Winbush had already completed an album with the Isley Brothers, *Smooth Sailin'*, for Warner Brothers in 1987. Another track, 'Sensitive Heart', was co-written with her new family members, and Winbush also wrote material especially for the Isley Brothers, who shared her new label. However, the album's stand-out track was the ballad 'I'm The Kind Of Woman'.

● ALBUMS: *Sharp* (Mercury 1987)★★★, *The Real Thing* (Mercury 1989)★★★, *Baby Hold On* (Mercury 1990)★★★, *Angela Winbush* (Elektra 1994)★★★★.

Windsong

This R&B vocal group, despite a history reaching back more than 20 years, remain condemned to obscurity by dint of their lack of recording opportunities. Henry Richard 'Dickie' Harmon (lead and tenor), Anthony Giusto (tenor), Jordan Montanaro (baritone) and Clinton 'Jaki' Davis (bass) formed the group as teenagers in Hackensack, New Jersey, USA. They soon found a regular source of employment at school hops and talent shows, originally operating under the title Bachelors. Although Harmon and Davis recorded with both the Connotations and Notations, the quartet itself never managed to find time to enter the studio (Harmon would also work with Strut on their solitary album for Brunswick Records). They changed their name to Windsong in 1971 when they recruited local female singer Jackie Bland (rendering the Bachelors a suddenly inappropriate name). This formation appeared at a United In Group Harmony Association show shortly thereafter, and this finally led to a recording date in 1981 when Ronnie Italiano brought the group to Clifton Records. Their only release, an EP featuring 'Young Wings Can Fly', 'Lucky Old Sun', 'Imagination' and 'Canadian Sunset', emerged following the sessions. Windsong broke up shortly thereafter, with Harmon reappearing in the Del-Vikings.

Winstons

An R&B band from Washington, DC, USA. The members were Richard Spencer (lead vocals, tenor saxophone), Ray Maritano (vocals, alto saxophone), Quincy Mattison (vocals, lead guitar), Phil Tolotta (second lead, organ), Sonny Peckrol (vocals, bass guitar), and G.C. Coleman (vocals, drums). The Winstons, like many black self-contained bands during the soul years, created records that sounded like a stand-up vocal group. Spencer, Mattison and Coleman had all previously worked in Otis Redding's band. The three later joined Peckrol, Tolotta and Maritano to form a backing band for the Chicago-based Impressions. They then decided to play on their own under the name Winstons. Their one hit, 'Color Him Father', written by Spencer, featured moving and heartfelt lyrics about being brought up by a wonderful father. The public was enchanted by this delightful song, making it an enormous hit; it sold a million copies, and went to number 1 R&B and number 7 pop in 1969. The Winstons, however, were a proverbial one-hit-wonder. Their follow-up, 'Love Of The Common People', lacked the magic of their big hit, and only reached number 54 on the pop chart, a position owed solely to the reflected glory of 'Color Him Father'.

● ALBUMS: *Color Him Father* (Metromedia 1969)★★★

Winwood, Steve

b. 12 May 1948, Birmingham, England. Steve and his older brother Muff Winwood were born into a family with parents who encouraged musical evenings at their home. Steve was playing guitar with Muff and their father in the Ron Atkinson Band at the age of eight, soon after he mastered drums and piano. The multi-talented Winwood first achieved 'star' status as a member of the pioneering 60s R&B band the Spencer Davis Group. His strident voice and full-sounding Hammond Organ helped to create one of the mid-60s' most distinctive pop sounds. The group had a successful run of major hits in the UK and USA until their musical horizons became too limited for the musically ambitious Winwood. In 1965, Winwood had previously recorded the UK turntable soul hit 'Incense' under the name of the Anglos, written by Stevie Anglo; this gave fuel to rumours of his imminent departure. It was not until 1967 that he left and went on to form Traffic, a seminal band in the development of progressive popular music. The short-lived 'supergroup' Blind Faith briefly interrupted Traffic's flow. Throughout this time his talents were sought as a session musician and he became the unofficial in-house keyboard player for Island Records. During 1972 he was seriously ill with peritonitis and this contributed to the sporadic activity of Traffic. When Traffic slowly ground to a halt in 1974, Winwood maintained a low profile rather than pursuing a solo career; he subsequently became a musicians' musician, contributing keyboards and backing vocals to many fine albums, including John Martyn's *One World*, Sandy Denny's *Rendezvous*, George Harrison's *Dark Horse* and Toots And The Maytals' *Reggae Got Soul*. His session work reads like a who's who: Jimi Hendrix, Joe Cocker, Leon Russell, Howlin' Wolf, Sutherland Brothers, Muddy Waters, Eric Clapton, Alvin Lee, Marianne Faithfull and many others. In 1976 he performed with Stomu Yamash'ta and Klaus Schulze, resulting in *Go* and *Go 2*. He also appeared on stage with the Fania All Stars playing percussion and guitar. The eagerly anticipated self-titled solo album did not appear until 1977, and was respectfully, rather than enthusiastically, welcomed. It displayed a relaxed Winwood, performing only six numbers and using first-class musicians such as Willy Weeks and Andy Newmark. Following its release, Winwood retreated to his 50-acre Oxfordshire farm and shunned interviews. He became preoccupied with the rural life, and took up clay pigeon shooting, dog training and horse-riding. It appeared to outsiders that his musical activity had all but ceased.

During the last week of 1980 the majestic *Arc Of A Diver* was released on an unsuspecting public. With his former songwriting partner Jim Capaldi now living in Brazil, Winwood had been working on lyrics supplied to him by Vivian Stanshall, George Fleming and Will Jennings. The album was an unqualified and unexpected triumph, particularly in the USA where it went platinum. The stirring single 'While You See A Chance' saw him back in the charts. He followed with the hastily constructed (by Winwood standards) *Talking Back To The Night*, which became another success. Winwood, however, was not altogether happy with the record and seriously contemplated retiring to become a record producer. His brother, Muff, wisely dissuaded him. Winwood began to be seen more frequently, now looking groomed and well preserved. Island Records were able to reap rewards by projecting him towards a younger market. His European tour in 1983 was a revelation; a super-fit Steve, looking 20 years younger, bounced on stage wearing a portable keyboard and ripped into Junior Walker's 'Roadrunner'. Almost giving the impression that the 17-year-old 'Stevie' from the Spencer Davis Group had returned, he performed his entire catalogue with energy and confidence. It was hard to believe that this was the same man who for years had hidden shyly behind banks of amplifiers and keyboards with Traffic. Two years later, while working in New York on his forthcoming album, his life further improved when he met his future wife Eugenia, following a long and unhappy first marriage. His obvious elation spilled over into *Back In The High Life* (1986). Most of the tracks were co-written with Will Jennings and it became his most commercially successful record to date. The album spawned three hits, including the superb disco/soul hit 'Higher Love', which reached number 1 in the USA. In 1987 his long association with Chris Blackwell and Island Records ended amidst press reports that his new contract with Virgin Records guaranteed him $13 million. The reclusive 'Midland maniac' had become one of the hottest properties in the music business, while the world eagerly awaited the next album to see whether the star was worth his transfer fee.

The single 'Roll With It' preceded the album of the same name. Both were enormous successes, providing a double chart-topping achievement in the USA. The album completed a full circle. Winwood returned with 60s-inspired soul/pop, and his co-writer once again was the talented Will Jennings, although older aficionados were delighted to see one track written with Jim Capaldi. In 1990, Winwood was involved in a music publishing dispute in which it was alleged that the melody of 'Roll With It' had been plagiarized from 'Roadrunner'. That year *Refugees Of The Heart* became his least successful album, although it contained another major US hit single with the Winwood/Capaldi composition 'One And Only Man'. Following the less than spectacular performance of that album, rumours began to circulate that Traffic would be reborn; this was confirmed in early 1994. *Far From Home* sounded more like a Winwood solo album than any Traffic project, but those who loved any conglomeration that had Winwood involved were not disappointed. Later that year, he participated on Davey Spillane's album *A Place Among The Stones*, singing 'Forever Frozen', and sang the theme song 'Reach For The Light' from the animated movie *Balto*.

● ALBUMS: *Steve Winwood* (Island 1977)★★★★, *Arc Of A Diver* (Island 1980)★★★★, *Talking Back To The Night* (Island 1983)★★★, *Back In The High Life* (Island

1986)★★★★, *Roll With It* (Virgin 1988)★★★, *Refugees Of The Heart* (Virgin 1990)★★★, *Junction 7* (Virgin 1997)★★.

● COMPILATIONS: *Chronicles* (Island 1987)★★★★, *The Finer Things* 4-CD box set (Island 1995)★★★★.

● FURTHER READING: *Back In The High Life: A Biography Of Steve Winwood*, Alan Clayson. *Keep On Running: The Steve Winwood Story*, Chris Welch.

WITHERS, BILL

b. 4 July 1938, Slab Fork, West Virginia, USA. Having moved to California in 1967 after nine years in the US Navy, Withers began hawking his original songs around several west coast companies. He was eventually signed to Sussex Records in 1971 and secured an immediate hit with his debut single, 'Ain't No Sunshine'. Produced by Booker T. Jones, with Stephen Stills among the guest musicians, this sparse but compulsive performance was a million-seller, a feat emulated in 1972 by two more excellent releases, 'Lean On Me' and 'Use Me'. Withers' light, folksy/soul continued to achieve further success with 'Make Love To Your Mind' (1975), the sublime 'Lovely Day' (1977 - a single revamped by a remix in 1988) and 'Just The Two Of Us' (1981), an exhilarating duet with saxophonist Grover Washington Jnr. that earned the two artists a Grammy award in 1982 for the Best R&B performance. 'Lovely Day' re-entered the UK pop charts in 1988 as a result of its use in a British television commercial, reaching the Top 5. A professional rather than charismatic performer, Withers remains a skilled songwriter.

● ALBUMS: *Just As I Am* (Sussex 1971)★★★★, *Still Bill* (Sussex 1972)★★★★, *Bill Withers Live At Carnegie Hall* (Sussex 1973)★★, *+'Justments* (Sussex 1974)★★★, *Making Music* (Columbia 1975)★★★, *Naked And Warm* (Columbia 1976)★★★, *Menagerie* (Columbia 1977)★★★, *'Bout Love* (Columbia 1979)★★★, *Watching You Watching Me* (Columbia 1985)★★★, *Still Bill* (1993)★★★.

● COMPILATIONS: *The Best Of Bill Withers* (Sussex 1975)★★★★, *Bill Withers' Greatest Hits* (Columbia 1981)★★★, *Lean On Me: The Best Of...* (Columbia/Legacy 1995)★★★.

WOMACK AND WOMACK

One of modern soul's most successful duos, comprising husband-and-wife team Cecil Womack (b. 1947, Cleveland, Ohio, USA) and Linda Cooke Womack (b. 1953). Cecil was the youngest of the Womack Brothers, who later evolved into the Valentinos. With them he signed to Sam Cooke's Star label, but Cooke's subsequent death left them homeless, and after a brief liaison with Chess Records, Bobby Womack left the group to go solo. Cecil later married singer Mary Wells, whom he managed until the couple separated. Linda, the daughter of Sam Cooke, had begun a songwriting career in 1964 at the age of 11, composing 'I Need A Woman'. She would also provide 'I'm In Love' for Wilson Pickett and 'A Woman's Gotta Have It' for James Taylor, but later forged a professional and personal partnership with Cecil. As she recalls: 'My father had the deepest regard for all the Womack brothers. He had talked about how talented Cecil was since I was four years old ... We didn't actually meet until I was eight'. Together they worked extensively as a writing team for Philadelphia International, numbering the O'Jays and Patti Labelle among their clients. The couple achieved a notable success with 'Love TKO', a soul hit in 1980 for Teddy Pendergrass. This melodic ballad also provided the Womacks with their first US chart entry (and was also covered by Blondie), since which time the duo's fortunes have prospered both in the USA and UK with several excellent singles, including the club favourite 'Love Wars' (1984), and 'Teardrops' (1988), the latter reaching the UK Top 3. They also continued to write for other artists, contributing 'Hurting Inside' and 'Sexy' to Ruby Turner. In the early 90s the couple journeyed to Nigeria, where they discovered ancestral ties to the Zekkariyas tribe. They consequently adopted the names Zeriiya (Linda) and Zekkariyas (Cecil), in a nod to the Afrocentricity movement.

● ALBUMS: *The Composers/Love Wars* (Elektra 1983)★★★, *Radio M.U.S.I.C. Man* (Elektra 1985)★★★, *Starbright* (Manhattan/EMI 1986)★★★, *Conscience* (Island 1988)★★, *Family Spirit* (Arista 1991)★★, *Transformed Into The House Of Zekkariyas* (1993)★★.

WOMACK, BOBBY

b. 4 March 1944, Cleveland, Ohio, USA. A founder-member of the Valentinos, this accomplished musician also worked as a guitarist in Sam Cooke's touring band. He scandalized the music fraternity by marrying Barbara Campbell, Cooke's widow, barely three months after the ill-fated singer's death. Womack's early solo singles, 'Nothing You Can Do' and the superb 'I Found A True Love', were all but shunned and, with the Valentinos now in disarray, he reverted to session work. Womack became a fixture at Chips Moman's American Recording Studio, but although he appeared on many recordings, this period is best recalled for his work with Wilson Pickett. 'I'm In Love' and 'I'm A Midnight Mover' are two of the 17 Womack songs that particular artist would record. Womack, meanwhile, resurrected his solo career with singles on Keymen and Atlantic Records. Signing with Minit, he began a string of R&B hits, including 'It's Gonna Rain', 'How I Miss You Baby' (both 1969) and 'More Than I Can Stand' (1970). His authoritative early album, *The Womack Live*, then introduced the freer, more personal direction he would undertake in the 70s. The final catalyst for change was *There's A Riot Going On*, Sly Stone's 1971 collection on which Womack played guitar. Its influence was most clearly heard on 'Communication', the title track to Womack's first album for United Artists Records. Part of a prolific period, the follow-up album, *Understanding*, was equally strong, and both yielded impressive singles, which achieved high positions in the R&B charts. 'That's The Way I Feel About Cha' (number 2), 'Woman's Gotta Have It' (number 1) and 'Harry Hippie' (number 8) confirmed his new-found status. Successive albums, *Facts Of Life*, *Looking For A Love Again* and *I Don't Know What The World Is Coming To*, consolidated the accustomed mixture of original songs, slow raps and cover versions. *BW Goes C&W* (1976), a self-explanatory experiment, closed his United Artists contract, but subsequent work for CBS Records and Arista was undistinguished. In 1981 Womack signed with Beverly Glen, a small Los Angeles independent, where he recorded *The Poet*. This powerful set re-established his career, while a single, 'If You Think You're Lonely Now', reached number 3 on the R&B chart. *The Poet II* in 1984 featured three duets with Patti LaBelle, one of which, 'Love Has Finally Come At Last', was another hit single. Womack moved to MCA Records in 1985, debuting with *So Many Rivers*. A long-standing friendship with the Rolling Stones was emphasized that year when he sang back-up on their version of 'Harlem Shuffle'. Womack's more recent work proclaims him as 'the last soul singer'. An expressive, emotional singer, his best work stands among black music's finest moments.

● ALBUMS: *Fly Me To The Moon* (Minit 1968)★★★, *My Prescription* (Minit 1969)★★★, *The Womack Live* (Liberty 1970)★★★, *Communication* (United Artists 1971)★★★, *Understanding* (United Artists 1972)★★★, *Across 110th Street* film soundtrack (United Artists 1972)★★, *Facts Of Life* (United Artists 1973)★★★, *Looking For A Love Again* (United Artists 1974)★★, *I Don't Know What The World Is Coming To* (United Artists 1975)★★★, *Safety Zone* (United Artists 1976)★★★, *BW Goes C&W* (United Artists 1976)★★, *Home Is Where The Heart Is* (Columbia 1976)★★, *Pieces* (Columbia 1977)★★, *Roads Of Life* (Arista 1979)★★, *The Poet* (Beverly Glen 1981)★★★, *The Poet II* (Beverly Glen 1984)★★, *Someday We'll All Be Free* (Beverly Glen 1985)★★, *So Many Rivers* (MCA 1985)★★, *Womagic* (MCA 1986)★★, *The Last Soul Man* (MCA 1987)★★.

● COMPILATIONS: *Bobby Womack's Greatest Hits* (United Artists 1974)★★★★, *Somebody Special* (Liberty 1984)★★★, *Check It Out* (Stateside 1986)★★★, *Womack Winners 1968-75* (Charly 1989)★★★, *Midnight Mover: The Bobby Womack Collection* (1993)★★★★, *The Poet Trilogy* 3-CD set (1994)★★★, *I Feel A Groove Comin' On* (Charly 1995)★★★, *The Soul Of Bobby Womack: Stop On By* (EMI 1997)★★★.

● VIDEOS: *Soul Seduction Supreme* (Castle Music Pictures 1991).

WONDER, STEVIE

b. Steveland Judkins, 13 May 1950, Saginaw, Michigan, USA. Born Judkins, Wonder now prefers to be known as Steveland Morris after his mother's married name. Placed in an incubator immediately after his birth, baby Steveland was given too much oxygen, causing him to suffer permanent blindness. Despite this handicap, he began to learn the piano at the age of seven, and had also mastered drums and harmonica by the age of nine. After his family moved to Detroit in 1954, Steveland joined a church choir, the gospel influence on his music balanced by the R&B of Ray Charles and Sam Cooke he heard on his transistor radio. In 1961, he was discovered by Ronnie White of the Miracles, who arranged an audition at Motown Records. Berry Gordy immediately signed Steveland to the label, renaming him Little Stevie Wonder (the 'Little' was dropped in 1964). Wonder was placed in the care of writer/producer Clarence Paul, who supervised his early recordings. These accentuated his prodigal talents as a multi-instrumentalist, but did not indicate a clear musical direction. In 1963, however, the release of the ebullient live recording 'Fingertips (Part 2)' established his commercial success, and Motown quickly marketed him on a series of albums as 'the 12-year-old genius' in an attempt to link him with the popularity of 'the genius', Ray Charles. Attempts to repeat the success of 'Fingertips' proved abortive, and Wonder's career was placed on hold during 1964 while his voice was breaking. He re-emerged in 1965 with a sound that was much closer to the Motown mainstream, achieving a worldwide hit with the dance-orientated 'Uptight (Everything's Alright)', which he co-wrote with Henry Cosby and Sylvia Moy. This began a run of US Top 40 hits that continued unbroken (apart from seasonal Christmas releases) for over six years. From 1965-70, Stevie Wonder was marketed like the other major Motown stars, recording material that was chosen for him by the label's executives, and issuing albums that mixed conventional soul compositions with pop standards. His strong humanitarian principles were allowed expression on his version of Bob Dylan's 'Blowin' In The Wind' and Ron Miller's 'A Place In The Sun' in 1966. He co-wrote almost all of his singles from 1967 onwards, and also began to collaborate on releases by other Motown artists, most notably co-writing Smokey Robinson And The Miracles' hit 'The Tears Of A Clown', and writing and producing the (Detroit) Spinners' 'It's A Shame'. His contract with Motown expired in 1971; rather than re-signing immediately, as the label expected, Wonder financed the recording of two albums of his own material, playing almost all the instruments himself, and experimenting for the first time with more ambitious musical forms. He pioneered the use of the synthesizer in black music, and also broadened his lyrical concerns to embrace racial problems and spiritual questions. Wonder then used these recordings as a lever to persuade Motown to offer a more open contract, which gave him total artistic control over his music, plus the opportunity to hold the rights to the music publishing with his own company, Black Bull Music. He celebrated the signing of the contract with the release of the solo recordings *Where I'm Coming From* and *Music Of My Mind*, which, despite lukewarm critical reaction, quickly established him at the forefront of black music.

Talking Book in 1972 combined the artistic advances of recent albums with major commercial success, producing glorious hit singles in the poly-rhythmic funk of 'Superstition', and the crafted ballad 'You Are The Sunshine Of My Life'. Wonder married fellow Motown artist Syreeta on 14 September 1970; he premiered many of his new production techniques on *Syreeta* (1972) and *Stevie Wonder Presents Syreeta* (1974), for which he also wrote most of the material. *Innervisions* (1973) consolidated the growth and success of *Talking Book*, bringing further hit singles with the socially aware 'Living For The City' and 'Higher Ground'. Later that year, Wonder was seriously injured in a car accident; his subsequent work was tinged with a strong awareness of mortality, fired by his spiritual beliefs. The release of *Fulfillingness' First Finale* in 1974 epitomized this more austere approach. The double album *Songs In The Key Of Life* (1976) was widely greeted as his most ambitious and satisfying work to date. It demonstrated a mastery and variety of musical forms and instruments, offering a joyous tribute to Duke Ellington on 'Sir Duke', and heralding a pantheon of major black figures on 'Black Man'. This confirmed Wonder's status as one of the most admired musicians and songwriters in contemporary music. Surprisingly, after this enormous success, no new recordings surfaced for over three years, as Wonder concentrated on perfecting the soundtrack music to the documentary film *The Secret Life Of Plants*. This primarily instrumental double album was greeted with disappointing reviews and sales. Wonder quickly delivered the highly successful *Hotter Than July* in 1980, which included a tribute song to the late Dr. Martin Luther King, 'Happy Birthday', and a notable essay in reggae form in 'Masterblaster (Jamming)'. The failure of his film project brought an air of caution into Wonder's work, and delays and postponements became a consistent factor in his recording process. After compiling the retrospective double album *Stevie Wonder's Original Musiquarium I* in 1982, which included four new recordings alongside the cream of his post-1971 work, Wonder scheduled an album entitled *People Move Human Play* in 1983. This never appeared; instead, he composed the soundtrack music for the film *The Woman In Red*, which included his biggest-selling single to date, the sentimental ballad 'I Just Called To Say I Loved You'. The album on which he had been working since 1980 eventually appeared in 1985 as *In Square Circle*. Like his next project, *Characters*, in 1987, it heralded a return to the accessible, melodic music of the previous decade. The unadventurous nature of both projects, and the heavy expectations engendered by the delay in their release, led to a disappointing reception from critics and public alike. However, he was inducted into the Rock And Roll Hall Of Fame in 1989.

Wonder's status as an elder statesman of black music, and as a champion of black rights, was boosted by his campaign in the early 80s to have the birthday of Dr. Martin Luther King celebrated as a national holiday in the USA. This request was granted by President Reagan, and the first Martin Luther King Day was celebrated on 15 January 1986 with a concert at which Wonder topped the bill. Besides his own recordings, Wonder has been generous in offering his services as a writer, producer, singer and musician to other performers. His most public collaborations included work with Paul McCartney, which produced a cloying but enormous hit, 'Ebony And Ivory', Gary Byrd, Michael Jackson and the Eurythmics, and on the benefit records by USA For Africa and Dionne Warwick & Friends. *Conversation Peace* in 1995 was an average album with no outstanding songs, but highlighted the fact that the public's expectations of Wonder are different to those of most other artists. He could release ten indifferent, poor, weak or spectacular records over the next 20 years and nothing would change the fixed perception of him and of the body of outstanding music he has produced since 1963.

● ALBUMS: *Tribute To Uncle Ray* (Tamla 1962)★★★, *The Jazz Soul Of Little Stevie* (Tamla 1962)★★★, *The 12-Year-Old Genius Recorded Live* (Tamla 1963)★★★, *With A Song In My Heart* (Tamla 1963)★★, *Stevie At The Beach* (Tamla 1964)★★, *Up-Tight (Everything's Alright)* (Tamla 1966)★★★, *Down To Earth* (Tamla 1966)★★★, *I Was Made To Love Her* (Tamla 1967)★★★★, *Someday At Christmas* (Tamla 1967)★★, *For Once In My Life* (Tamla 1968)★★★★, *My Cherie Amour* (Tamla 1969)★★★★, *Stevie Wonder Live* (Tamla 1970)★★, *Stevie Wonder Live At The Talk Of The Town* (Tamla 1970)★★★, *Signed, Sealed And Delivered* (Tamla 1970)★★★★, *Where I'm Coming From* (Tamla 1971)★★★, *Music Of My Mind* (Tamla 1972)★★★, *Talking Book* (Tamla 1972)★★★★★, *Innervisions* (Tamla 1973)★★★★★, *Fulfillingness' First Finale* (Tamla 1974)★★★, *Songs In The Key Of Life* (Tamla 1976)★★★★, *Stevie Wonder's Journey Through The Secret Life Of Plants* (Tamla 1979)★★, *Hotter Than July* (Tamla 1980)★★★, *The Woman In Red* film soundtrack (Motown 1984)★★, *In Square Circle* (Tamla 1985)★★, *Characters* (Motown 1987)★★, *Music From The Movie Jungle Fever* film soundtrack (Motown 1991)★★★, *Conversation Peace* (Motown 1995)★★, *Natural Wonder* (Motown 1995)★★.

● COMPILATIONS: *Greatest Hits* (Tamla 1968)★★★★, *Stevie Wonder's Greatest Hits, Volume Two* (Tamla 1971)★★★★, *Anthology* aka *Looking Back* 1962-71 recordings (Motown 1977)★★★★, *Stevie Wonder's Original Musiquarium I* (Tamla 1982)★★★, *Song Review* (Motown 1996)★★★.

● FURTHER READING: *Stevie Wonder*, Sam Hasegawa. *The Story Of Stevie Wonder*, Jim Haskins. *Stevie Wonder*, Ray Fox-Cumming. *Stevie Wonder*, Constanze Elsner. *The Picture Life Of Stevie Wonder*, Audrey Edwards. *Stevie Wonder*, C. Dragonwagon. *Stevie Wonder*, Beth P. Wilson. *The Stevie Wonder Scrapbook*, Jim Haskins with Kathleen Benson. *Stevie Wonder*, Rick Taylor.

● FILMS: *Bikini Beach* (1964).

WOOD, BRENTON

b. Alfred Jesse Smith, 26 July 1941, Shreveport, Louisiana, USA. Smith was a veteran of several vocal groups, including the Dootones, the Quotations and Little Freddie And The Rockets, before assuming the name Brenton Wood in deference to his home district in Los Angeles. As a solo act he enjoyed fame with 'The Oogum Boogum Song' (1967), a nonsense novelty record. The follow-up, 'Gimme Little Sign' (although not a novelty), was in a similar style, but its more lasting appeal was confirmed when the single reached the UK and US Top 10. Further releases, 'Baby You Got It' (1967) and 'Some Got It, Some Don't' (1968), diluted the pattern and were less successful. Wood later recorded a duet with Shirley Goodman, before making a belated return to the US R&B chart in 1977 with 'Come Softly To Me'.

● ALBUMS: *Gimme Little Sign* (Liberty 1967)★★★, *The Oogum Boogum Man* (Double Shot 1967)★★★, *Baby You Got It* (1967)★★★.

● COMPILATIONS: *Brenton Wood's 18 Best* (1991)★★★.

WRAY, LINK

b. 1930, Fort Bragg, North Carolina, USA. Guitarist Wray formed his first group in 1942, but his musical ambitions were thwarted by his induction into the US Army. He subsequently formed the Wraymen with Shorty Horton (bass) and Doug Wray (drums), and enjoyed a million-seller in 1958 with 'Rumble', a pioneering instrumental on which the artist's frenzied style and distorted tone invoked a gang-fight. The single incurred bans both on technical grounds and on account of its subject matter, but is now recognized as one of pop's most innovative releases, and includes the Who's Pete Townshend as a vociferous proponent. Wray achieved another gold disc for 'Rawhide' (1959), but ensuing releases, including 'Jack The Ripper' (1960), 'The Sweeper' (1963) and 'Batman Theme' (1965), failed to match this success. He continued to record, using a home-made three-track studio built in a converted chicken shack, and a 1971 album, *Link Wray*, was the subject of critical acclaim. It drew heavily on the artist's country roots - he is part-Shawnee Indian - yet was still imbued with the primitive atmosphere of his early work. Renewed interest in Wray resulted in several archive releases, while contemporary recordings, although of interest, failed to match the promise of his initial 'rediscovery' collection. In the late 70s the guitarist forged a fruitful partnership with new-wave rockabilly singer Robert Gordon, before resurrecting a solo career the following decade. Wray's primeval sound is echoed in the work of the Cramps and many other more contemporary groups. He is particularly respected in the UK where his influence on 'trash' guitar groups, notably the Stingrays and Milkshakes, has been considerable. In 1997 he made a new album with UK's prime R&B/Rock 'n' Roll reissue label Ace Records, having been previously associated with their Chiswick label. 'Rumble On The Docks' is vintage Link Wray and worth the price of the CD alone.

● ALBUMS: *Link Wray And The Raymen* (Epic 1959)★★★★, *Jack The Ripper* (Swan 1963)★★★, *Great Guitar Hits* (Vermillion 1963)★★★, *Link Wray Sings And Plays Guitar* (Vermillion 1964)★★★, *Yesterday And Today* (Record Factory 1969)★★★, *Link Wray* (Polydor 1971)★★★, *Be What You Want To Be* (Polydor 1973)★★★, *The Link Wray Rumble* (Polydor 1974)★★★, *Interstate 10* (Virgin 1975)★★★, *Stuck In Gear* (Virgin 1976)★★★, with Robert Gordon *Robert Gordon With Link Wray* (Private Stock 1977)★★★, with Gordon *Fresh Fish Special* (Private Stock 1978)★★★, *Bullshot* (Charisma 1979)★★★, *Live At The Paradiso* (Magnum Force 1980)★★★, *Live In '85* (Big Beat 1986)★★★, *Indian Child* (Creation 1993)★★★, *Shadowman* (Ace 1997)★★★.

● COMPILATIONS: *There's Good Rockin' Tonight* (Union Pacific 1971)★★★, *Beans And Fatback* (Virgin 1973)★★★, *Rockin' And Handclappin'* (Epic 1973)★★★, *Rock 'N' Roll Rumble* (Charly 1974)★★★★, *Early Recordings* reissue of*Jack The Ripper* (Chiswick 1978)★★★★, *Link Wray: Good Rocking' Tonight* (Chiswick 1983)★★★★, *Link Wray And The Raymen* (Edsel 1985)★★★★, *Growlin' Guitar* (Ace 1987)★★★, *Mr. Guitar* (Norton 1995)★★★.

● VIDEOS: *Link Wray: The Rumble Man* (Visionary 1996).

Wreckx-N-Effect

With their Teddy Riley-produced single of the same name in 1988, USA-based Wreckx-N-Effect announced the arrival of New Jack Swing. The group comprised Aquil Davidson, Markell Riley (brother of Teddy) and Brandon Mitchell (who was shot dead in 1990). The intervening period has not been especially kind in terms of commercial fortunes, with others capitalizing on their style. However, they did enjoy a hit in 1992 with 'Rump Shaker' for MCA. They were joined for a rap by Apache Indian on their 1994 single 'Wreckz Shop'.

● ALBUMS: *Hard Or Smooth* (MCA 1992)★★★.

Wright, Betty

b. 21 December 1953, Miami, Florida, USA. A former member of her family gospel group, the Echoes Of Joy, Wright's first recordings were as a backing singer. She later embarked on a solo career and had a minor hit with 'Girls Can't Do What The Guys Do' in 1968. 'Clean Up Woman' (1972), a US R&B number 2/pop number 6 hit, established a punchier, less passive style that later releases, 'Baby Sitter' (1972) and 'Let Me Be Your Lovemaker' (1973), consolidated. Although 'Shoorah Shoorah' and 'Where Is The Love?' reached the UK Top 30 in 1975, the singer was unable to sustain a wider success. Wright nonetheless continued recording into the 80s and has also forged a career as a US television talk show hostess.

● ALBUMS: *My First Time Around* (1968)★★★, *I Love The Way You Love* (Alston 1972)★★★, *Hard To Stop* (Alston 1973)★★★, *Danger: High Voltage* (Alston 1975)★★★, *Explosion* (Alston 1976)★★★, *This Time For Real* (Alston 1977)★★, *Betty Wright Live* (Alston 1978)★★★, *Betty Wright* (TK 1978)★★, *Betty Travellin' In The Wright Circle* (TK 1979)★★, *Betty Wright* (Epic 1981)★★, *Wright Back At You* (Epic 1983)★★, *Sevens* (First String 1986)★★, *Mother Wit* (Ms B 1988)★★, *4U2 Njoy* (Ms B 1989)★★.

● COMPILATIONS: *Golden Classics* (Collectables 1988)★★★, *Betty Wright Live* (1991)★★★, *The Best Of ... The T.K. Years* (Sequel 1994)★★★★.

● VIDEOS: *Betty Wright Live* (PMI 1992).

Wright, Billy

b. 21 May 1932, Atlanta, Georgia, USA, d. 28 October 1991, Atlanta, Georgia, USA. A promising gospel singer as a child, Wright would often sneak into Atlanta's famous 81 Theater to watch the secular shows and eventually turned to performing the blues. His soulful voice came to the attention of Savoy Records, who secured a US R&B Top 5 hit with his debut record 'Blues For My Baby' in 1949. Other less successful releases followed, but Wright's strength was in his live performances, earning him the nickname 'Prince Of The Blues'. After his Savoy tenure, Wright recorded for Peacock in 1955 and then passed on the baton to his devoted admirers Little Richard, James Brown and Otis Redding. In the late 50s he made his final recordings for Bobby Robinson's Fire Records and tiny local labels, Carrollton and Chris, before settling down in Atlanta, where he continued to perform and introduce acts as a compere until his death in 1991.

● ALBUMS: *Stacked Deck* (Route 66 1980)★★★, with Little Richard *Hey Baby, Don't You Want A Man Like Me?* (Ace 1987)★★★, *Goin' Down Slow* (Savoy 1995)★★★.

WRIGHT, O.V.

b. Overton Vertis Wright, 9 October 1939, Memphis, Tennessee, USA, d. 16 November 1980. One of deep soul's most impressive stylists, O.V. Wright's first recordings were in the gospel tradition and it was while a member of the Harmony Echoes that he became acquainted with Roosevelt Jamison. This aspiring songwriter penned the singer's secular debut, 'That's How Strong My Love Is', an impassioned ballad later covered by Otis Redding and the Rolling Stones. Wright's plaintive delivery excelled on slow material, as two imploring R&B hits, 'You're Gonna Make Me Cry' (1965) and 'Eight Men, Four Women' (1967), testified. Wright's next single, 'Heartaches-Heartaches' (1967), confirmed a working relationship with producer Willie Mitchell, but despite excellent collaborations in 'Ace Of Spades' (1970), 'A Nickel And A Nail' (1971) and 'I'd Rather Be (Blind, Crippled And Crazy)' (1973), the singer was unable to reach a wider audience. Imprisoned for narcotics offences during the mid-70s, he re-emerged on Hi Records in 1975, but intense recordings here, including 'Rhymes' (1976) and 'I Feel Love Growin'' (1978), met a similar fate. Hard living and a continuing drug problem weakened his health and in 1980, O.V. Wright died from a heart attack. For many he remains one of southern soul's most authoritative and individual artists.

● ALBUMS: *If It's Only For Tonight* (Back Beat 1965)★★★, *8 Men And 4 Women* (Back Beat 1967)★★★, *Nucleus Of Soul* (Back Beat 1968)★★★, *A Nickel And A Nail And Ace Of Spades* (Back Beat 1971)★★★, *Memphis Unlimited* (Back Beat 1973)★★, *Into Something I Can't Shake Loose* (Hi 1977)★★, *The Wright Stuff* (Hi 1977)★★★, *The Bottom Line* (Hi 1978)★★★, *O.V. Wright Live* (Hi 1979)★★, *We're Still Together* (Hi 1979)★★★.

● COMPILATIONS: *Gone For Good* (Charly 1984)★★★, *Here's Another Thing* (Charly 1989)★★★, *That's How Strong My Love Is* (Hi 1991)★★★, *The Soul Of O.V. Wright* (1993)★★★.

WYCOFF, MICHAEL

b. 1956, Torrance, California, USA. This classy and soulful singer worked as a pianist and backing vocalist for Natalie Cole, D.J. Rogers and Phoebe Snow in the 70s. He also did much session work and can be heard on Stevie Wonder's chart-topping *Songs In The Key Of Life*. Wycoff's first solo album was the self-composed, jazz-orientated *Come To My World* in 1981. It was critically acclaimed but sold relatively few copies, as did the follow-up, *Love Conquers All*. He made the decision that *On The Line* would be a less serious, more commercial and danceable album. It contained his biggest hit to date, '(Do You Really Love Me) Tell Me Love', which gave him his first US R&B Top 40 single and a UK chart entry. Wycoff, who has been compared favourably with acts such as Stevie Wonder, Peabo Bryson and Donny Hathaway, is arguably 'too classy' ever to be commercially successful. He moved to the independent Valley Vue label in 1984.

● ALBUMS: *Come To My World* (RCA 1981)★★★, *Love Conquers All* (RCA 1982)★★★, *On The Line* (RCA 1983)★★★.

WYNN, 'BIG' JIM

b. 21 June 1912, El Paso, Texas, USA, d. 1976, Los Angeles, California, USA. After moving to Los Angeles as a child, Wynn began his musical tuition on clarinet before switching to tenor sax and playing professionally with the band of Charlie Echols. In 1936, Wynn had his own band and soon linked up with the young 'T-Bone' Walker; this association would last until the end of the famous blues musician's life, with the Wynn band regularly touring and recording with him. The Wynn band's own recording career lasted through R&B's golden years, when records were released on 4 Star/Gilt Edge (1945 - including his biggest hit, 'Ee-Bobaliba', which was lucratively covered in various guises by the likes of Helen Humes and Lionel Hampton), Modern (1946), Specialty and Supreme (1948), Mercury and Recorded In Hollywood (1951) and Million (1954). By the late 40s, Wynn increasingly eschewed his tenor in place of a beefy baritone saxophone, and its deep honking, coupled with his own histrionic stage act, was the role model for the next generation of west coast R&B saxophonists. A respected session musician from the late 50s into the 70s, Wynn often played with the bands of his good friends 'T-Bone' Walker and Johnny Otis.

● COMPILATIONS: *Blow Wynn Blow* (Whiskey 1985)★★★.

XAVIER

This eight-piece funk group featured Ernest 'Xavier' Smith (lead guitar, bass, lead vocals), Ayanna Little (lead vocals), Tim Williams (drums), Ralph Hunt Jnr. (bass), Jeffrey Mitchell (guitar), Lyburn Downing (percussion), Emonie Branch and Chuck Hughes (vocals). Smith started in the mid-60s as bass player with the Coasters. Between 1969 and 1973 he joined Wilson Pickett's backing band, the Midnight Movers, and later worked with Isaac Hayes and the Temptations. In the late 70s he moved to Hartford, Connecticut, where he transformed local group the Shades Of Directions into Xavier and LUV (Life's Universal Vibration). The group joined Liberty, shortened their name and released their first single, 'Work That Sucker To Death'. This dance record with a positive message also featured George Clinton and

Smith's old friend Bootsy Collins. The record went into the R&B Top 10 and reached the UK charts in 1982. Their follow-up, 'Do It To The Max', also reached the R&B chart and their album *Point Of Pleasure* narrowly missed the Top 100, yet despite this encouraging start the group did not chart again.

● ALBUMS: *Point Of Pleasure* (Liberty 1982)★★★.

Xscape

An initially rather laboured attempt at emulating the 'swingbeat' success of SWV and their ilk, this four-piece was assembled in Atlanta, Georgia, USA, by writer/producer Jermaine Dupri, who was previously the force behind Kriss Kross's chart success. However, there was an important difference - while groups such as TLC (another group overseen by Dupri) had been closely identified with provocative sexuality, Xscape had roots in the gospel tradition and eschewed such salacious themes. Xscape comprises sisters LaTocha 'Juicy' Scott (b. *c*.1973, USA), Tamika 'Meatball' Scott (b. *c*.1975, USA), Kandi Burruss (b. *c*.1976, USA) and Tameka 'Tiny' Cottle (b. *c*.1975, USA). The intention was to offer a 'female Jodeci', and they certainly achieved commercial recognition with their 'Just Kickin' It' debut single, which made number 2 on the *Billboard* Hot 100. A subsequent album, *Hummin' Comin' At Cha'*, also achieved mainstream success alongside a second single, 'Who's That Man', which was included on the soundtrack to the film *The Mask*. The group's second album, *Off The Hook*, also charted in the Top 3 of the US R&B Albums chart and went platinum. It featured more expansive song arrangements, including electric guitar and acoustic piano.

● ALBUMS: *Hummin' Comin' At Cha'* (Columbia 1994)★★, *Off The Hook* (Columbia 1995)★★★.

Yarbrough And Peoples

The duo of Calvin Yarbrough and Alisa Peoples was one of the most popular R&B pairings of the 80s, placing five singles in the R&B Top 10. The married couple had known each other since childhood, when they shared the same piano teacher in the Dallas, Texas, USA area and sang together in their church choir. They lost track of each other during their college days and Yarbrough joined the R&B group Grand Theft. He was discovered by members of the Gap Band, who offered him work as a backing singer, after which Yarbrough returned to his own group. Peoples soon joined him onstage and they were taken on as a duo by the Gap band's manager and producer. Yarbrough And Peoples recorded their debut album for Mercury Records in 1980, which yielded the number 1 R&B single 'Don't Stop The Music', which later reached the pop Top 20. Yarbrough and Peoples switched over to the Total Experience label in 1982 and continued their winning streak for four more years with the singles 'Heartbeats' (number 10 R&B in 1983), 'Don't Waste Your Time' (number 1 R&B in 1984), 'Guilty' (number 2 R&B in 1986) and 'I Wouldn't Lie' (number 6 R&B in 1986).

● ALBUMS: *The Two Of Us* (Mercury 1980)★★★, *Heartbeats* (Total Experience 1983)★★★, *Be A Winner* (Total Experience 1984)★★★.

Young & Co

This funky sextet revolved around a nucleus of brothers Billy, Mike and Kenneth Young from West Virginia, USA. After moving to East Orange, New Jersey, in 1970 they formed the Young Movement with Buddy 'Hank' Hankerson, an ex-member of Aurra (bass, keyboards, guitar) and Dave Reyes (drums). The group changed their name to Flashflood in 1974 and recorded with Slave and Aurra. When vocalist and sole distaff member Jackie Thomas joined in 1979 they first recorded as Young & Co. Among the first three tracks they demoed was 'I Like What You're Doing', which helped to secure a contract with Brunswick Records. When released, this single reputedly sold over 250,000 in the USA alone, yet never made the R&B or pop chart there. It did, however, reach the UK Top 20 in 1980 when picked up by the newly formed Excalibur label. The group later recorded for Sounds Of London and Atlantic Records but never again tasted success.

Young Hearts

An R&B vocal group from Los Angeles, California, USA, the original members were Ronald Preyer, Charles Ingersoll, Earl Carter and James Moore. The Young Hearts were typical of the falsetto-led, stand-up vocal groups that populated the R&B scene of the late 60s and early 70s. Their impact was purely on the R&B charts, gaining moderate hits with 'I've Got Love For My Baby' (number 19 R&B) in 1968 for the Minit subsidiary of Imperial Records, and 'Wake Up And Start Standing' (number 48 R&B) in 1974 for 20th Century. A stay at ABC in 1977 produced an album and several singles that did nothing, and the group subsequently disappeared.

● ALBUMS: *Sweet Soul Shakin'* (Minit 1968)★★★, *A Taste Of The Younghearts* (20th Century 1974)★★, *All About Love* (ABC 1977)★★.

Young Rascals

This expressive act, one of America's finest pop/soul ensembles, made its debut in a New Jersey club, the Choo Choo, in February 1965. Felix Cavaliere (b. 29 November 1943, Pelham, New York City, USA; organ, vocals), Eddie Brigati (b. 22 October 1946, New York City, USA; vocals, percussion) and Dino Danelli (b. 23 July

1945, New York City, USA; drums) were each established musicians on the city's R&B circuit, serving time in several popular attractions, including Joey Dee And The Starlighters. It was here that the trio encountered Gene Cornish (b. 14 May 1946, Ottawa, Canada; vocals, guitar), who became the fourth member of a breakaway group, initially dubbed Felix And The Escorts, but later known as the Young Rascals. The quartet enjoyed a minor hit with 'I Ain't Gonna Eat Out My Heart Anymore' before securing a US number 1 with the energetic 'Good Lovin''. Despite a somewhat encumbering early image - knickerbockers and choirboy shirts - the group's soulful performances endeared them to critics and peers, earning them a 'group's group' sobriquet. Now established as one of the east coast's most influential attractions, spawning a host of imitators from the Vagrants to Vanilla Fudge, the Young Rascals secured their biggest hit with 'Groovin''. This melancholic performance became an international hit, signalling a lighter, more introspective approach, and although Brigati was featured on the haunting 'How Can I Be Sure', a US Top 5 entry, Cavaliere gradually became the group's focal point. In 1968 the group dropped its 'Young' prefix and enjoyed a third US number 1 with 'People Got To Be Free'. An announcement that every Rascals live appearance must also include a black act emphasized the group's commitment to civil rights, but effectively banned them from southern states. The quartet later began exploring jazz-based compositions, and although remaining respected, lost much of their commercial momentum. Brigati and Cornish left the group in 1971, and although newcomers Buzzy Feiten (guitar), Ann Sutton (vocals) and Robert Popwell (drums) contributed to final albums, *Peaceful World* and *The Island Of Real*, the Rascals were clearly losing momentum and broke up the following year. Felix Cavaliere then enjoyed a moderately successful solo career while Danelli and Cornish formed Bulldog and Fotomaker. The three musicians were reunited in 1988 for an extensive US tour. They were inducted into the Rock And Roll Hall Of Fame in 1997.

● ALBUMS: as the Young Rascals *The Young Rascals* (Atlantic 1966)★★★, *Collections* (Atlantic 1966)★★★, *Groovin'* (Atlantic 1967)★★★★; as the Rascals *Once Upon A Dream* (Atlantic 1968)★★★, *Freedom Suite* (Atlantic 1969)★★★, *See* (Atlantic 1969)★★, *Search And Nearness* (Atlantic 1971)★★, *Peaceful World* (Columbia 1971)★★, *The Island Of Real* (Columbia 1972)★★.

● COMPILATIONS: *Timepeace - The Rascals' Greatest Hits* (Atlantic 1968)★★★★, *Star Collection* (1973)★★★, *Searching For Ecstasy - The Rest Of The Rascals 1969-1972* (1988)★★★★, *The Rascals Anthology (1965-1972)* (Rhino 1992)★★★★.

Young, Tommie

A southern-soul singer about whom little biographical detail exists, Young's voice was compared to that of Aretha Franklin in the early 70s, although she has a rare vocal quality of her own. In the early 70s, she recorded six singles and one album for Bobby Patterson's Soul Power label out of Shreveport, Louisiana, distributed by Stan Lewis's local Jewel/Paula/Ronn group. The most impressive tracks were 'Do You Still Feel The Same Way', 'She Don't Have To See You', 'You Can't Have Your Cake And Eat It Too', 'You Brought It All On Yourself', 'Everybody's Got A Little Devil In Their Soul', and a cover version of O.V. Wright's 'That's How Strong My Love Is'. UK Contempo issued two Young singles in 1972/3, plus two of the same sides on their 1975 album *Soul Deep Volume 1*. In 1983, a Japanese P-Vine album of Young's Soul Power output included three previously unissued tracks, and UK Charly released a total of seven Young sides on their 80s compilations *Southern Soul Belles* and *Soul Jewels Volume 2*. After her Soul Power days, nothing more was heard of Young until she sang on the 1978 MCA soundtrack album *A Woman Called Moses*. The film told the story of Harriet Ross Tubman, who founded an underground railway that helped southern slaves to freedom. The score was chiefly composed by Van McCoy. Since then, Tommie Young seems to have faded from the soul music scene, although she resurfaced with a gospel CD in 1993, spelling her first name Tommye, and also appending West to her surname as a result of her marriage to Calvin R. West Jnr.

● ALBUMS: *Do You Still Feel The Same Way* (Soul Power 1973)★★★, *A Woman Called Moses* film soundtrack (MCA 1978)★★, *Just Call Me Tommye* (Command 1993)★★★.

● COMPILATIONS: *Soul Deep Volume 1* two tracks (Contempo 1975)★★, *Southern Soul Belles* three tracks only (Charly 1982)★★, *Do You Still Feel The Same Way/Take Time To Know Him* (P Vine 1983)★★★, *Soul Jewels Volume 2* four tracks only (Charly 1989)★★, *Grits & Grooves* two tracks only(1992)★★.

Young, Val

Young was discovered in the late 70s by George Clinton, who incorporated her into the Brides Of Funkenstein, one of the many acts in his Funkadelic stable. After performing on the US hit 'Disco To Go', Young joined the Gap Band, where she was featured on the funk classic 'Oops Upside Your Head'. She recorded five albums with the group before being spotted by another black music notable, Rick James. Impressed as much by her striking physical appearance as by her musical talents, James promoted her as the 'black Marilyn Monroe'. He also produced her 1985 hit 'Seduction', a blatant attempt to capitalize on her erotic image. 'If You Should Ever Be Lonely' was a successful follow-up in 1986, before Young left James's stable to forge a solo career on Amherst Records.

● ALBUMS: *Seduction* (Motown 1985)★★.

Young-Holt Unlimited

This US group was formed in Chicago in 1965 as the Young-Holt Trio with Eldee Young (b. 7 January 1936, Chicago, Illinois, USA; bass), Isaac 'Redd' Holt (b. 16 May 1932, Rosedale, Mississippi, USA; drums) and Don Walker (piano). Young and Holt both studied at Chicago's American Conservatory Of Music. They later joined the Ramsey Lewis Trio and were featured on two of the group's best-known singles, 'The In Crowd' and 'Hang On Sloopy' (both 1965). The bassist and drummer then broke away to pursue their own direction - although their debut hit on Brunswick Records, 'Wack Wack' (1967), was as undemanding as Lewis's. In 1968 pianist Walker was replaced by Ken Chancey. Soon, Chancey had left and the act was reconstituted as the Young-Holt Unlimited. Under that name, the act enjoyed a hit in 1968 with the million-selling 'Soulful Strut'. This instrumental was, in fact, the backing track to a Barbara Acklin single, 'Am I The Same Girl?', but with Floyd Morris's piano part replacing the vocal line. Ironically, neither Young nor Holt was on the record, as the instrumental was by the Brunswick studio band. Despite that, Young-Holt Unlimited continued to make technically precise, but rather sterile, records before the group's two mainstays decided to rejoin Ramsey Lewis in 1983.

● ALBUMS: *Wack Wack* (Brunswick 1967)★★, *Young-Holt Unlimited Onstage* (Brunswick 1967)★, *The Beat Goes On* (Brunswick 1967)★★, *Funky But!* (Brunswick 1968)★★★, *Soulful Strut* (Brunswick 1968)★★★★, *Just A Melody* (Brunswick 1969)★★, *Young-Holt Unlimited Plays 'Superfly'* (Paula 1973)★★.

● COMPILATIONS: *Wack Wack* (Kent 1986)★★★.

YURO, TIMI

b. Rosemarie Yuro, 4 August 1940, Chicago, Illinois, USA. Yuro moved to Los Angeles as a child, and by the late 50s was singing in her mother's Italian restaurant. She was signed to Liberty by the head of the company, Al Bennett, and recorded her most famous track, 'Hurt', in 1961. Produced by Clyde Otis, who had supervised many of Dinah Washington's hits, the dramatic ballad was a revival of Roy Hamilton's 1954 R&B hit. Yuro's searing white soul rendering entered the Top 10 in 1961 and inspired numerous artists to cover the song, notably Elvis Presley, whose version was a Top 30 hit in 1976. The follow-ups 'I Apologise' and 'Smile' made less impact, but in 1962, 'What's A Matter Baby?' reached the Top 20. Yuro had minor hits with 'Make The World Go Away' (a greater success the following year for Eddy Arnold) and the country song 'Gotta Travel On'. Her Liberty albums contained a mix of standard ballads such as Mitchell Parish and Hoagy Carmichael's 'Stardust' and soul songs ('Hallelujah I Love Him So'), but mid-60s records for Mercury found Yuro veering towards a more mainstream cabaret repertoire. There were later records for Playboy (1975), and in 1981 a reissued 'Hurt' was a big hit in the Netherlands. This led to a new recording contract with Polydor. During the late 80s Yuro recorded an album of songs by Willie Nelson, but soon afterwards her performing career was curtailed by serious illness.

● ALBUMS: *Hurt* (Liberty 1961)★★★★, *Let Me Call You Sweetheart* (Liberty 1962)★★★, *Soul* (Liberty 1962)★★★, *What's A Matter Baby?* (Liberty 1963)★★★, *Make The World Go Away* (Liberty 1963)★★★, *Amazing* (1964)★★★, *All Alone Am I* (1981)★★, *Today* (1982)★★.

● COMPILATIONS: *Very Best Of Timi Yuro* (Liberty 1980)★★★, *Very Original And Greatest Hits* (EMI Holland 1983)★★★, *The Sensational Voice Of* (Mercury 1984)★★★, *Hurt* (Charly 1986)★★★★, *18 Greatest Hits* (K-Tel 1988)★★★, *18 Unforgettable Ballads* (Mainline 1990)★★, *The Lost Voice Of Soul* (RPM 1993)★★★.

ZHANÉ

This east coast R&B/dance duo consists of Renee Neufville (b. 1970, Brooklyn, New York, USA) and Jean Norris (b. 1970, Moorestown, New Jersey, USA), who started singing together while studying at Philadelphia Temple University, and were discovered at a talent show by DJ Jazzy Jeff And The Fresh Prince. They went on to contribute backing vocals to the latter's 1991 single 'Ring My Bell', before linking with another prominent rapper, Queen Latifah, as part of her Flavor Unit collective. Their debut, 'Hey Mr DJ', was first featured on the compilation album *Roll Wit Tha Flava*, before subsequent release as a single saw it reach the Top 5 in the USA. Like Latifah, they signed with Motown, enjoying further success with the follow-up single 'Groove Thang'. Both hits were produced in association with DJ Kay Gee of Naughty By Nature fame, and prefaced a similarly successful debut album, the title of which offered instruction as to the pronounciation of Zhané's name. As to their musical bent: 'Our music is R&B with a jazzy attitude and hip hop flavour'.

● ALBUMS: *Pronounced Jah-Nay* (Illtown/Motown 1994)★★★, *Saturday Night* (Illtown/Motown 1997)★★★★.

INDEX

C

F

G

J

K

L

M

N

O

P

Q

R

S

T

U

V

W

X

Y

Z